BANKRUPTCY AND INSOLVENCY LAW IN CANADA

Cases, Materials, and Problems

Stephanie Ben-Ishai & Thomas G.W. Telfer,

EDITORS

BANKRUPTCY AND INSOLVENCY LAW IN CANADA

Stephanie Ben-Ishai & Thomas G.W. Telfer,

Contributors

Stephanie Ben-Ishai   Chapters 1 and 7
of Osgoode Hall Law School

Thomas G.W. Telfer   Chapters 1 and 11
of the Faculty of Law, Western University

Jassmine Girgis   Chapters 5, 10, 13, 14, 15, and 17
of the Faculty of Law, University of Calgary

Anna Lund   Chapters 8, 16, and 18
of the Faculty of Law, University of Alberta

Alfonso Nocilla   Chapters 3, 4, and 9
of the Faculty of Law, Western University

Virginia Torrie   Chapters 2, 6, and 12
of the Faculty of Law, University of Manitoba

Bankruptcy and Insolvency Law in Canada: Cases. Materials, and Problems
© Irwin Law, 2019

Published in 2019 by
Irwin Law Inc
Suite 206, 14 Duncan Street
Toronto, ON   M5H 3G8
www.irwinlaw.com

ISBN: 978-1-55221-517-3 e-book ISBN: 978-1-55221-518-0

Cataloguing in Publication available from Library and Archives Canada

Canadä   Ontario
              Ontario Media Development
              Corporation
              Société de développement
              de l'industrie des médias
              de l'Ontario

Printed and bound in Canada.
1 2 3 4 5   23 22 21 20 19

Summary Table of Contents

Detailed Table of Contents

Preface

Bankruptcy and Insolvency Law in Canada: Cases, Materials, and Problems represents a new approach for a law school casebook. The work is accompanied by a separate teacher's manual (*Bankruptcy and Insolvency Law in Canada: Teaching Materials*) that contains full answers to the problems at the end of each chapter in the casebook. In addition, a companion graphic manual (*Bankruptcy and Insolvency Law in Canada: A Visual Guide*) has been published to assist readers with bankruptcy and insolvency law's underlying concepts. The casebook comprises eighteen chapters from six different Canadian law professors; covers the *Bankruptcy and Insolvency Act* (*BIA*) and the *Companies' Creditors Arrangement Act* (*CCAA*) and related provincial statutes; and includes recent developments in both personal and corporate insolvency law.

Five recent Supreme Court of Canada decisions are contained in the volume: *407 ETR Concession Co v Canada (Superintendent of Bankruptcy)*, 2015 SCC 52 and *Alberta (Attorney General) v Moloney*, 2015 SCC 51 (dealing with the discharge and federalism); *Saskatchewan (Attorney General) v Lemare Lake Logging Ltd*, 2015 SCC 53 (receiverships and federalism); *Wilson v Alharayeri*, 2017 SCC 39 (director liability and the oppression remedy); and *Orphan Well Association v Grant Thornton Ltd*, 2019 SCC 5 (environmental liabilities).

In addition, there have been significant developments from the provincial appellate courts. We have included three recent appellate decisions on personal insolvency: *Charles v Hernandez Becerra*, 2016 SKCA 163 (dealing with exempt property); *Conforti (Re)*, 2015 ONCA 268 (surplus income); *Canada (Attorney General) v Collins*, 2013 NLCA 17 (student loans and the discharge). Five leading appellate cases on the *CCAA* have also been incorporated into the casebook: *8640025 Canada Inc (Re)*, 2018 BCCA 93 (dealing with the monitor); *US Steel Canada Inc (Re)*, 2016 ONCA 662 (equitable subordination); *Pacer Construction Holdings Corporation v Pacer Promec Energy Corporation*, 2018 ABCA 113 (claims); *8640025 Canada Inc (Re)*, 2018 BCCA 93 (sales); *Callidus Capital Corporation v 9354-9186 Québec Inc (Bluberi Gaming Technologies Inc)*, 2019 QCCA 171 (approval of plan).

On 8 April 2019 the federal government introduced Bill C-97, *An Act to implement certain provisions of the budget tabled in Parliament on March 19, 2019 and other measures*. At the time of writing, Bill C-97 has passed the House of Commons and is awaiting third reading in the Senate, making it likely that the bill will become law. Bill C-97 includes proposed amendments to both the *BIA* and the *CCAA*. If Bill C-97 becomes law, it will institute a new provision requiring all parties in a proceeding under either statute to act in good faith. The *BIA* amendments will also allow courts to inquire into certain payments made to *inter alia* directors or offices of a corporation in the year preceding insolvency and impose liability on directors of corporations in respect of those payments. The *CCAA* amendments will limit relief under initial orders to that which is "reasonably necessary" to the continued operations of the debtor and limit the time period of the initial stay of proceedings to ten days. Furthermore, the *CCAA* amendments will allow courts to issue orders compelling certain persons to disclose any aspect of their economic interests in the debtor. Readers should be aware that the book went to press before Bill C-97 became law and that the bill is not covered in the casebook.

We divided up the work on the casebook as follows: Stephanie Ben-Ishai and Thomas Telfer assumed the role of editors of the casebook. Contributors authored the following chapters:

Professor Stephanie Ben-Ishai was responsible for: Chapter 1, "Introduction, Historical Perspectives, and Bankruptcy Theory" (with Professor Telfer) and Chapter 7, "*BIA* Claims." **Professor Thomas GW Telfer** was responsible for Chapter 1, "Introduction, Historical Perspectives, and Bankruptcy Theory" (with Professor Ben-Ishai) and Chapter 11, "Consumer Bankruptcy." **Professor Girgis** contributed Chapter 5, "Reviewable Transactions"; Chapter 10, "Corporate Liability During Insolvency"; Chapter 13, "Business Operations in a *CCAA* Proceeding"; Chapter 14, "Claims in a *CCAA* Proceeding"; Chapter 15, "*CCAA* Plans and Approval"; and Chapter 17, "Receiverships." **Professor Lund** was responsible for Chapter 8, "Priority Creditors"; Chapter 16, "Proposals Under the *BIA*"; and Chapter 18, "Cross-Border Insolvencies." **Professor Nocilla** contributed Chapter 3, "Bankruptcy: Commencement and Consequences"; Chapter 4, "Property"; and Chapter 9, "Priorities and Distribution." **Professor Torrie** was responsible for Chapter 2, "Constitutional Aspects and the Judicial and Administrative Structure of the Bankruptcy System"; Chapter 6, "Executory Contracts"; and Chapter 12, "*CCAA* Overview."

We would like to extend our thanks to Lesley Steeve, who acted as the managing editor at Irwin Law, and to everyone else at Irwin Law for their assistance in bringing this project to completion.

We would also like to thank JD students David Pak (Osgoode Hall), Steven Huryn (Western University), Amanda Van Waes (University of Ottawa), and LLM student Oluwabukola Fadahunsi (Western University) for their timely, detailed, and thoughtful assistance in the editing of this casebook.

Thank you to the Canadian Association of Insolvency and Restructuring Professionals (CAIRP) for its support in publishing this textbook. CAIRP's funding and permissions to reprint content from CAIRP publications has helped deliver a textbook we are truly proud of and one we believe will be a highly valued resource for students, lawyers, and trustees studying insolvency law.

CAIRP is the national not-for-profit organization that represents approximately 1,000 insolvency and restructuring professionals across Canada who have earned the professional designation Chartered Insolvency and Restructuring Professional (CIRP), as well as over 500 articling, life, and corporate associates. Through an MOU with the Office of the Superintendent of Bankruptcy, CAIRP develops and delivers the CIRP Qualification Program that leads to the OSB practice license, Licensed Insolvency Trustee (LIT). Over 90 percent of LITs licensed under Canada's *BIA* are members of CAIRP.

Canada Day, 2019

Stephanie Ben-Ishai
Thomas GW Telfer
Jassmine Girgis
Anna Lund
Alfonso Nocilla
Virginia Torrie

Rebuilding Success · Rétablir le succès

PART I

Introduction

CHAPTER 1

Introduction, Historical Perspectives, and Bankruptcy Theory

I. INTRODUCTION

Sears, Payless, Target, Toys "R" Us, and Nortel are just a few of the recent corporate bankruptcies that have drawn national and international attention. The loss of more than CAD$190 million of investor funds and the bankruptcy proceedings in the cryptocurrency exchange Quadriga CX raise a new challenge for the bankruptcy system. Large-scale disasters like the Lac-Mégantic train disaster in Canada with its mass tort claims, and the constant media attention paid to the debt problems felt by millennial students and the elderly also keep bankruptcy in the media on a near daily basis. Globally, we see what happens when there is no way to offer a country bankruptcy relief as we watch in horror as Venezuelan citizens struggle to stay alive in the face of draconian austerity measures.

The way that a country chooses to deal with the debts of its citizens (corporate and individual) tells a deep and complex story about the underlying values in that society. We learn about what constitutes a "fresh start," who we give second chances to, which voices and interests are valued and which institutions are entrusted to make these decisions.

In order to understand and unpack the interests that frame a particular system we first need to understand this system and how it operates on the ground. This is the task we set out to help you accomplish in this casebook.

A. Scope of Casebook

This casebook sets out to provide clear, accessible, and elucidating textual commentary on the law, modern and illustrative cases, and plenty of realistic problems to challenge students to do what lawyers actually do — address and solve clients' problems.

A particularly helpful aspect of this book generally will be that it describes the law both on the books and in action. The empirical, historical, and practical work that the authors have done on both the consumer and the business side is usefully reflected in this book.

Each chapter includes problems to be taken up in class and an illustrated guide is available in conjunction for students. Our goal is for this book to serve as a "course in a box" for both professors and students.

Chapter 2 sets out the key constitutional aspects and structures that are unique in Canada's bifurcated bankruptcy system. Next, Chapter 3 explains the process for initiating a bankruptcy and the consequences. In Chapter 4, we define the contours of what counts as "property" for the purpose of the bankruptcy estate. This leads into our discussion in Chapter 5 of the types of pre-bankruptcy transactions that can be challenged in order to bring more property back into the estate. Chapter 6 considers the treatment of executory contracts or contracts where both parties still have actions to perform in a bankruptcy proceeding.

Chapter 7 explains how creditors can make claims in a bankruptcy and Chapter 8 deals with the claims of secured creditors, who are often referred to as "strangers to the bankruptcy." Chapter 9 sets out the ranking of creditors and the manner for distribution of proceeds in a bankruptcy. Chapter 10 deals with one particular issue that often arises in a corporate bankruptcy—liability of corporate directors.

Chapter 11 could in itself be the basis of a complete course and it provides a detailed examination of consumer bankruptcy issues.

Chapters 12 through to 15 take us through commercial reorganizations under the *Companies' Creditors Arrangement Act*, RSC 1985, c C-36 (*CCAA*). Chapters 16 deals with the *Bankruptcy and Insolvency Act*, RSC 1985, c B-3 (*BIA*) corporate and consumer proposals. Chapter 17 examines the law of receiverships. Chapter 18, the concluding chapter, addresses international insolvency issues.

B. Bankruptcy Terminology

Under the *BIA*, the terms "bankruptcy" and "bankrupt"[1] are confined to straight liquidation proceedings under Part III of the Act and a "bankrupt" is the subject of a "bankruptcy order." All other proceedings under the *BIA* are known as insolvency proceedings (hence the title of the Act, the *Bankruptcy and Insolvency Act*) or are identified by the part and division of the *BIA* under which the proceedings are brought.[2] The subject of these proceedings is referred to as a "debtor." Importantly, however, unlike the British *Insolvency Act 1986*, c 45, the *BIA* draws no distinction between corporate and personal or individual bankruptcies. All liquidation bankruptcies are basically governed by the same rules. The term "reorganization" is not actually used in the *BIA* or the *CCAA* to describe non-liquidation proceedings designed to enable an insolvent business to stay alive or to enable an insolvent individual to avoid the stigma of bankruptcy by reaching an agreement with the debtor's creditors to pay off all or part of the indebtedness over a period of years. Instead, *BIA*, Part III, Division 1 and *BIA*, Part III, Division 2, speak of commercial and consumer proposals, respectively; the object of proceedings under the *CCAA* is referred to as an "arrangement." However, "reorganization" (or, increasingly commonly, "restructuring") are the non-technical terms frequently used to describe proceedings under *BIA*, Part III, Division 1, and the *CCAA*, and they are used in the same sense in this casebook.

The US *Bankruptcy Code*[3] draws no terminological distinction between straight bankruptcy and reorganizational proceedings. All are referred to as "bankruptcy" or "case" proceedings,[4] and particular bankruptcy proceedings are usually identified by the Code chapter under which they are brought—for example, Chapter 7 for straight liquidations, Chapter 11

---

1   "Bankrupt" is defined in *BIA*, s 2. The expression is of Italian origin, *banke rota* or *bancarupta*, and was used in the Italian city states in the Middle Ages to describe the breaking of the bench of a merchant who had defaulted on his debts: see the Tassé Report, extracted below in this chapter.

2   To avoid needless repetition and unless otherwise indicated, references in notes in the casebook to bankruptcy proceedings cover all types of bankruptcy and insolvency proceedings under the *BIA* and the *CCAA*.

3   11 USC §101.

4   American terminology has also been picked up by Canadian media and it is common for news reports to refer to a Canadian company seeking "bankruptcy protection" under the *CCAA* even though the *CCAA* is quite independent of the *BIA*. What is meant is that a stay of proceedings is in effect precluding creditors from suing or invoking remedies against the debtor company while the company is preparing a plan of reorganization to put before its creditors or is preparing to sell its assets.

for commercial reorganizations, and Chapter 13 for wage-earner debt adjustments. More-over, chapters 1, 3, and 5 apply to all case proceedings under the Code unless otherwise provided. The Code also eschews use of the word "bankrupt"; instead, persons who are the subject of case proceedings under any chapter of the Code are referred to as "debtors."[5]

In England and Wales (Scotland has its own insolvency legislation) the term "bankruptcy" is restricted to liquidation proceedings involving the assets of *individual* debtors; "winding up" or "winding-up order" is the expression used to describe the liquidation of insolvent companies, although under the *Insolvency Act 1986*, many of the substantive rules are the same for both individual and company insolvencies.[6]

Unhappily, common law jurisdictions also differ in their terminology in reporting sta-tistical results. The Canadian statistics published by Industry Canada distinguish between personal insolvencies and business insolvencies. "Insolvencies" cover bankruptcy and reorganizational proceedings under the *BIA* (but not proceedings under the *CCAA*). Busi-ness insolvencies cover the insolvencies of corporations, partnerships, and individuals where, in the case of individuals, 50 percent or more of the indebtedness is of business ori-gin.[7] Personal insolvencies cover business and consumer insolvencies, whereas consumer insolvencies are restricted to personal, non-business insolvencies. Consumer insolvencies are subdivided into consumer bankruptcy proceedings and consumer proposals under *BIA* III.2.[8] The other common law jurisdictions—for example, England and Australia—use dif-ferent terminology in reporting personal insolvencies; hence considerable care must be used in comparing their statistics with Canada's.

---

5   Query: Should Canada follow suit and avoid the use of the pejorative term "bankrupt"? See Industry Canada, *Corporate, Insolvency and Competition Policy: Statutory Review of the* Bankruptcy and Insolvency Act *and the* Companies' Creditors Arrangement Act (Ottawa: Industry Canada, 2014) [*Corporate, Insol-vency and Competition Policy*]: "Some stakeholders have expressed concern that the term 'bankruptcy' in the title of the legislation and for 'trustee in bankruptcy' may create an unintended social stigma that may prevent some Canadians from seeking much needed professional assistance to obtain debt relief. As a result, these debtors may suffer greater economic and social consequences than would otherwise be the case. It has been suggested that the term 'bankruptcy' be removed from use."

6   The reason for the distinction is historical, but the distinction continues to enjoy popular support in England. The Canadian *Winding-Up and Restructuring Act*, RSC 1985, c W-11 (*WURA*), first adopted in 1882, was copied from British legislation after the federal Parliament repealed the *Insolvent Act of 1875* in 1880. See Section III of this chapter. The *WURA* is now little used except in cases where its use is mandatory for designated incorporated entities such as banks and insurance companies. See Bruce Welling & Thomas Telfer, "The Winding-Up and Restructuring Act: Realigning Insolvency Law's Orphan to the Modern Law Reform Process" (2008) 24 *Banking & Finance Law Review* 235.

7   This is the definition of business used by the Office of the Superintendent of Bankruptcy. See Office of the Superintendent of Bankruptcy Canada, *Insolvency Statistics in Canada—2018 (Glossary)* (Ottawa: OSB, 2019), online: www.ic.gc.ca/eic/site/bsf-osb.nsf/eng/br04044.html.

8   There is also a small number of orderly payment of debts (OPD) proceedings under Part X of the *BIA*, but these are statistically insignificant and are often overlooked. In 2007, there were only 596 OPD orders for all of Canada compared to 101,293 consumer insolvencies.

II. EVOLUTION OF BANKRUPTCY LAW

Canada, Study Committee on Bankruptcy and Insolvency Legislation, *Report of the Study Committee on Bankruptcy and Insolvency Legislation* (Ottawa: Information Canada, 1970) (Chair: Roger Tassé), ss 1.1–1.3 (footnotes omitted) [Tassé Report]

An Expanding Concept: The long history of bankruptcy has been one of an expanding concept. From the harsh and merciless treatment of debtors, the law, through many stages, has come to recognize that, while there may be fraudulent debtors from whom society must be protected, an honest bankrupt is not a contradiction of terms. Upon this cornerstone has been built the modern law of bankruptcy.

In primitive societies, the debtor's lot was hard. There was no exception to the rule that he must pay his debts in full. If he could not pay with his property, he paid with his person.

The Code of Hammurabi: Written more than 4000 years ago, the Code of Hammurabi, King of Babylon, contained several actions concerning the relations between debtors and creditors. According to this Code, the creditor was entitled to levy a "distress" or "pledge," called a *nipûtum*, if the debt was not paid when it became due. It was not necessary for the creditor to first obtain judgment, but he was penalized if he wrongfully levied a distress. While oxen of the plough and grain were exempted from seizure, the debtor's wife, a child or a slave could be brought as *nipûtum* to the creditor's house. There they were put to work until the debt was satisfied. In addition to the *nipûtum*, the Code considered the case where the debtor voluntarily surrendered a dependant into bondage by selling him, with or without right of redemption, to a merchant or to the creditor himself. The position of the dependant in the house of his new master seems to be similar to that of the *nipûtum*, but, in the case of a wife or child, the servitude came to an end after three years service. Finally, if the debt of the creditor was not satisfied one way or another, there seems little doubt that the debtor could be adjudicated to him as a bond-servant.

The Law of Ancient Greece: By the end of the 7th Century, BC, in Athens, the new class of mercantile capitalists virtually owned the entire peasant class with mortgages on nearly every small holding in Attica. The peasants could not resist foreclosures on their lands and on their persons, which often were included in their pledges. The poor were in a state of bondage to the rich, both themselves, their wives, and their children. The political situation was critical. In order to avert a revolution, Solon cancelled all existing mortgages and debts, released debtors from bondage and made illegal those contracts in which a person's liberty was pledged.

The Roman Law: When, in the middle of the 5th Century, BC, Rome decided to codify its laws, it sent three commissioners to Greece to study the laws of Solon. The code that resulted is known as the *Law of the Twelve Tables*. Contrary to the spirit of the reform of Solon, the Roman jurists maintained the execution against the person. After the fulfillment of certain formalities, the unpaid creditor had the power to seize the debtor himself. This seizure, called *manus injectio*, gave the creditor authority to bring the debtor to his home and keep him in chains for sixty days. During this period, the debtor, still the owner of his property and a Roman citizen, could try to settle his debts with his creditor. To allow for the possibility of a ransom being paid, the creditor was required to take him three times to the market place giving notice of the amount of the debt each time. Finally, if at the end of sixty days, the creditor was not fully paid, he could, it would seem, put the debtor to death or sell him into foreign slavery. According to certain modern writers, the creditors could even divide between them the body of the debtor. If this was so, there is no proof that such an inhuman treatment was ever applied. It must also be noted that the *paterfamilias* could, as was the case under the *Hammurabi Code*, in order to avoid his slavery, raise money by leasing out the services of the members of his family. In Roman law, this is known as *mancipium*. During the centuries that followed the promulgation of the *Law of the Twelve Tables*, the severity of the *manus injectio* was progressively reduced. By the end of the Republic, the unpaid creditor could still imprison the debtor or make the debtor work for him in satisfaction of the debt but he could no longer put him to death or sell him into slavery....

This was the rule under Roman law until the end of the Republic, when the *Edict of the Praetor* alleviated the harshness of the old quiritarian law. About that time, one praetor developed a method of execution against property known as *venditio bonorum*. This fundamental reform, for the first time, established a link between the assets and the liabilities of a person. Moreover, this was in the nature of a procedure for the collective execution against the property of an insolvent or recalcitrant debtor. To quote W.W. Buckland, "It is in effect the Roman equivalent of bankruptcy proceedings."

Thus, by the end of the Republic, Roman law recognized two methods of execution, one against the person and the other against property. The debtor could, however, by the time of Augustus, avoid execution against his person by making a *cessio bonorum*, that is to say, by surrendering to his creditors everything he owned. About three centuries later, the *cessio bonorum* was not available to debtors who had squandered their property or concealed it from their creditors. According to an imperial ordinance of the year 379, this procedure was only allowed when the insolvency of the debtor was due to an act of God. Under Justinian, the use of the *cessio bonorum* had become so widespread that the *Corpus Juris* scarcely mentions imprisonment for debt.

The Italian Cities: As trade and the use of credit developed, the ordinary law of debtor and creditor became inadequate to cope with the problem of the insolvent trader. Towards the end of the Mediaeval [sic] Ages, the Italian cities attempted to deal with this problem and new concepts, such as the "act of bankruptcy" were developed by legal writers of the time. It is from the Italian *bancarupta* that the word "bankrupt" is derived. It may be literally translated as "bank broken" or "bench broken." The allusion is said to be the custom of breaking the table of a defaulting tradesman....

The English Law: In England, one of the first insolvency statutes was enacted in 1351. In an attempt to promote commercial integrity, it provided that, if any merchant of the Company of Lombard Merchants acknowledged himself bound in a debt, the Company should answer for it. Apparently, this was by reason of the fact that some of these merchants had, in the past, left the country without paying their debts.

At Common Law, a creditor has to resort to a very expensive, lengthy and cumbersome procedure to obtain an attachment of his debtor's property. Execution cannot [sic] be obtained against a debtor's entire estate but only against the property described in the writ. If there was a plurality of creditors, they took the property of the debtor in the order of their attachments. The race was to the swift. The rule was "first come, first served."

The first Bankruptcy Statutes provided a summary method for the collective execution of all of the debtor's property, both movable and immovable. They stressed the rights of creditors. The only concern shown in respect of the debtor was that he should surrender all of his property and that no fraud on his part should go undetected and unpunished. Under the first of these statutes [*Bankruptcy Act of 1542*], the property was liquidated and distributed "to every of the said creditors a portion, rate and rate alike, according to the quantity of their debts." The preamble of this statute stated: "where divers and sundry persons craftily obtaining into their own hands great substance of other Mens [*sic*] Goods, do suddenly flee to Parts unknown, or keep their Houses not minding to pay or restore to any [*sic*] their Creditors, their Debts and Duties, but at their own Wills and Pleasures Consume the Substance obtained by credit of other Men for their own Pleasure and delicate Living against all Reason, Equity and good Conscience."

Although the English *Bankruptcy Act* of 1542 was directed against any debtor who attempted to defeat his creditors by fraudulent means, the Act of 1571 restricted bankruptcy to those who were engaged in trade. This distinction was to be maintained for almost 300 years. A debtor who was not in trade and who could not pay his debts was imprisoned until some person paid them for him.

The first English Act showing concern for the rehabilitation of the debtor was enacted in 1705 in the reign of Anne. A debtor who was a merchant could get a discharge of all his debts owing at the time of his bankruptcy provided he surrendered all of this property and conformed to the other provisions of the statute. However, the legislator remained very much aware of the continuing problem of the fraudulent debtor. So, while being given new privileges, the debtor had to be free from fraud and submit himself to the control of the Court. Evidence of the concern of the legislator that debtors might abuse the privileges given to them was the severity of the penalty for a debtor who did not strictly comply with the law. The penalty, in the past, had been to stand in the pillory or have an ear cut off. The new penalty was hanging. This penalty applied, for example, if the bankrupt failed to surrender himself to the court, committed perjury on his examination or fraudulently concealed his assets.

In the middle of the 18th Century, Sir William Blackstone, commenting on the Law of England, had this to say about bankruptcy:

> The Laws of England, more wisely, have steered in the middle between both extremes: providing at once against the inhumanity of the creditor, who is not suffered to confine an honest bankrupt after his effects are delivered up; and at the same time taking care that all his just debts shall be paid; so far as the effects will extend. But still they are cautious of encouraging prodigality and extravagance by this indulgence to debtors; and therefore they allow the benefit of the laws of bankruptcy to none but actual traders; since that set of men are, generally speaking, the only persons liable to accidental losses, and to an inability of paying their debts, without any fault of their own. If persons in other situations of life run in debt without the power of payment, they must take the consequences of their own indiscretion, even though they may meet with sudden accidents that may reduce their fortunes: for the law holds it to be an unjustifiable practice, for any person but a tradesman to encumber himself with debts of any considerable value. If a gentleman, or one in a liberal profession, at a time of contracting his debts, has a sufficient fund to pay them, the delay of payment is a species of dishonesty, and a temporary injustice to his creditor: and if, at such time, he has no sufficient fund, the dishonesty and the injustice is the greater. He cannot therefore, murmur, if he suffers the punishment which he has voluntarily drawn upon himself. But in mercantile transactions, the case is far otherwise. Trade cannot be carried on without mutual credit on both sides: the contracting of debts is therefore here not only justifiable, but necessary. And if by accidental calamities, as by the loss of a ship in a tempest, the failure of brother traders, or by the non-payment of

persons out of trade, a merchant or tradesman becomes incapable of discharging his own debts, it is his misfortune and not his fault. To the misfortunes, therefore, of debtors, the law had given a compassionate remedy, but denied it to their faults: since at the same time that it provides for the security of commerce, by enacting that every considerable trader may be declared a bankrupt, for the benefit of his creditors as well as himself, it has also to discourage extravagance, declared that no one shall be capable of being made a bankrupt, but only a trader, nor capable of receiving the full benefit of the statutes, but only an industrious trader. . . .

In the early part of the 19th Century, a number of statutes were passed for the relief of insolvent debtors who were not engaged in trade and therefore could not be made bankrupt. Originally, the insolvency acts provided only for the release from imprisonment of the debtor. He was not released of his debts and remained liable for their repayment. Later legislation provided for the discharge of persons who were imprisoned for their debts if they surrendered all of their goods for the benefit of their creditors. In 1812, the laws relating to insolvency were administered by a court of record known as the Court for the Relief of Insolvent Debtors. By the *Bankruptcy Act* of 1861, which made persons other than traders subject to bankruptcy law, this Court was abolished and its jurisdiction transferred to the Court of Bankruptcy. In 1869, by the *Bankruptcy Repeal and Insolvent Court Act*, all insolvency statutes theretofore existing were extinguished. Imprisonment for debt was abolished altogether, except in the case of a dishonest person who could pay his debts but refused to do so. The legal distinction between bankruptcy and insolvency was thus all but eliminated.

In the history of bankruptcy, there is much experimentation concerning who should liquidate and supervise an estate. In 1831, for example, the English legislation provided for the joint administration by official assignees and assignees chosen by the creditors. In 1869, the system of administration, at the insistence of the trading community, reverted to a system of creditor liquidation. The creditors chose the trustee who was supervised by a committee of inspectors also chosen by the creditors. Abuses soon arose, however, particularly in regard to the solicitation of proxies, which often permitted a minority of creditors to control and manipulate the administration of an estate in their interests to the prejudice of the majority of creditors.

It was recognized in England that the system of creditor control over the administration of a bankruptcy estate, as provided by the 1869 Act, had failed. The English *Bankruptcy Act of 1883* devised a new system of joint official and creditor control. Although minor amendments have been made to this Act, the system of administration, that it created, has not changed in any material respect. When Joseph Chamberlain, the then President of the Board of Trade, spoke on the second reading of the Bill for the 1883 Act, he explained the philosophy of his new legislation as follows:

> He, (Joseph Chamberlain), asked the House to keep in mind two main, and, at the same time, distinct objects of any good Bankruptcy Law. Those were, firstly, in the honest administration of bankrupt estates, with a view to the fair and speedy distribution of the assets among the creditors, whose property they were; and, in the second place their object should be, following the idea that prevention was better than cure, to do something to improve the general tone of commercial morality, to promote honest trading, and to lessen the number of failures. In other words, Parliament had to endeavour, as far as possible, to protect the salvage, and also to diminish the number of wrecks.

His next point was that, with regard to those two most important objects, there was only one way by which they could be secured and that was by securing an independent and impartial examination into the circumstances of each case; and that was the cardinal principle of this Bill. . . . What happened when a bankruptcy took place which might easily cause misery to thousands of people and bring ruin on many homes? It was treated as if it were entirely a matter of private concern, and allowed to become a scramble between the debtor and his advisers—who were often his confederates—on the one hand, and the creditors on the other. Meanwhile, the great public interests at stake in all these questions were entirely and absolutely ignored, as there was nobody to represent them, and the practice which was followed in the case of other calamities was, in this case, entirely absent. In the case of accidents by sea and by land—railway accidents, for instance—it was incumbent upon a Government Department to institute an inquiry. There were inquiries in the case of accidents in mines, and of boiler explosions, and sad as those disasters were, they did not, in the majority of cases, cause so much misery as a bad bankruptcy, which brought ruin to many families by carrying off the fruits of their labour and industry. . . .

Now, it would be seen that the provision which he had described (a description of duties and responsibilities of the official receiver, the office of which was first created by this Bill) constituted a system which he thought they might fairly call a system of official inquiry, and which went on all fours with a similar system in the matters of accident to which he had referred. He did not think that without some such limited officialism as this any satisfactory inquiry was even possible. No investigation could be worth anything unless it was conducted by an independent and impartial officer. . . .

THE CANADIAN LEGISLATION SINCE CONFEDERATION

Principal Milestones: In the hundred years since Confederation, the following Statutes constitute the important milestones of bankruptcy and insolvency legislation:

1869: *The Insolvent Act of 1869*, 32 & 33 Vic, SC 1869, c 16

1875: *The Insolvent Act of 1875*, 38 Vic, SC 1875, c 16

1880: *An Act to repeal the Acts Respecting Insolvency now in force in Canada*, 43 Vic, SC 1880, c 1

1882: *An Act respecting Insolvent Banks, Insurance Companies, Loan Companies, Building Societies and Trading Corporations*, 45 Vic, SC 1882, c 23 (for insolvent companies)

1889: *The Winding Up Amendment Act, 1889*, 52 Vic., SC 1889, c 32 (extended to solvent companies)

1919: *The Bankruptcy Act*, 9 & 10 Geo V, SC 1919, c 36

1923: *The Bankruptcy Act Amendment Act, 1923*, 13 & 14 Geo V, SC 1923, c 31 (companies prohibited from making proposals without previously being adjudged bankrupt; office of custodian created; office of official receivers created)

1932: *The Bankruptcy Act Amendment Act, 1932*, 22 & 23 Geo V, SC 1932, c 39 (office of Superintendent created)

1933: *The Companies' Creditors Arrangement Act, 1933*, 23 & 24 Geo V, SC 1932-33, c 36

1934: *The Farmers' Creditors Arrangement Act, 1934*, 24 & 25 Geo V, SC 1934, c 53

1943: *The Farmers' Creditors Arrangement Act, 1943*, 7 Geo VI, SC 1943, c 26

1949: *Bankruptcy Act, 1949*, 13 Geo VI, SC 1949 (2nd Session), c 7

1953: *An Act to Amend the Companies' Creditors Arrangement Act, 1933,* 1-2 El II, SC 1952–
53, c 3 (act restricted to arrangement including an arrangement between a company and its bondholders)
1966: *An Act to Amend the Bankruptcy Act,* 14-15 El II, SC 1966-67, c 32

Thomas GW Telfer, *Ruin and Redemption: The Struggle for a Canadian Bankruptcy Law 1867–1919* (Toronto: University of Toronto Press, Osgoode Society for Canadian Legal History, 2014) (footnotes omitted)

Modern bankruptcy scholarship has long moved past the question of "whether bankruptcy law should exist at all" and has now focused on "how much it should do." But in late nineteenth and early twentieth century Canada, the central question was whether there should be a bankruptcy law at all. During this time, Canadian bankruptcy legislation was not widely accepted as a means to distribute assets to creditors or as a way to discharge debts. Both of these central goals of bankruptcy law proved to be controversial....

The *Insolvent Act of 1869* ... marked only a tentative beginning for a bankruptcy regime. First, Parliament designed the law as a temporary four-year measure. However, Parliament extended the law twice, in 1873 and again in 1874. Second, the year the Act came into force Parliament debated its repeal. This was followed by two further attempts to remove the legislation from the statute books in 1871 and 1872. These repeal efforts, although unsuccessful, were significant given that the law would have expired on its own terms.

The law that Parliament was seeking to overturn was not broad in its scope but even a narrowly drafted bankruptcy law proved objectionable. Rather, the legislation did not make the discharge available to all debtors. The legislation only applied to traders who traditionally were defined by the courts as a person "seeking to gain his living by buying or selling." Non-traders such as labourers or farmers were excluded from the scope of the legislation and debate over whether to broaden the bill's scope to encompass them threatened its very success. Parliament could only agree on a law that retained the trader rule. In addition, the Act did not define "trader," leaving the courts to work their way through the confused state of English jurisprudence.

Debtors, who qualified as traders, gained access to the legislation by one of two means. Creditors could force a debtor into bankruptcy on proof that the debtor had engaged in one of the listed acts of bankruptcy.... The legislation also permitted debtors to file for bankruptcy.... By adopting a voluntary procedure in 1869, Parliament moved beyond what was acceptable to society.... The high rate of voluntary proceedings contributed to the growing sense that bankruptcy law was a pro-debtor measure. Assignments became unpopular as debtors used the ability to threaten assignment "as a lever to secure extension of time". Creditors who sought to collect on debts "were continually met by a threat to assign if they ventured to press their legal remedies." Small traders often made a voluntary assignment in bankruptcy without consulting their creditors.

The *Insolvent Act of 1875* ... replaced the *Insolvent Act of 1869.* There was a consensus that the Act of 1869 had not gone far enough to protect creditors who required further means of discovering and punishing fraud.... Although the 1869 legislation had contained many provisions favourable to creditors, the "object of the [1875] bill was to give the creditors greater control of the estate." Parliament's decision to abolish voluntary assignments was the most significant policy change.... In 1875, the creation of a single compulsory system represented a sharp return to the creditor-oriented regimes of the past. The abolition of voluntary assignments appeased those who sought repeal of all bankruptcy laws.

Parliament debated further repeal bills in 1877, 1878, 1879, and again in 1880. . . . Momentum and support in favour of repeal could not be stopped and in 1880 the House of Commons passed a repeal bill with little debate. In the Senate, Macdonald's government finally conceded and decided to allow the *Insolvent Act of 1875* to be repealed. The Senate approved repeal by an almost 3-1 margin on 11 March 1880, and the repeal bill received Royal Assent on 1 April 1880. The idea of bankruptcy and insolvency law as an essential national power had been tested and lost. The rather quick demise of national bankruptcy statutes over the course of just over a decade raises important questions of why the legislation did not fit well with late nineteenth century conceptions of credit and debt.

[© Osgoode Society for Canadian Legal History 2014.
Reprinted with permission of the publisher]

Canada, Study Committee on Bankruptcy and Insolvency Legislation, *Report of the Study Committee on Bankruptcy and Insolvency Legislation* (Ottawa: Information Canada, 1970) (Chair: Roger Tassé), ss 1.1–1.3 (footnotes omitted) [Tassé Report]

By a coincidence that appears not to be accidental, the *Bill to Repeal the Insolvency Acts* was read for the third time on March 4, 1880, while on March 5, 1880, assent was given, in Ontario, to "An *Act to Abolish Priorities of and Amongst Execution Creditors.*" In the discussion in the House of Commons, it was said that the Ontario Bill, which was similar to the law prevailing in Quebec, would provide for the just and equitable distribution of estates and the hope was expressed that other provinces would enact similar legislation.

The Winding-Up Act: It was soon found that, without an *Insolvency Act*, there was no convenient way to wind up insolvent companies. Boards of Trade, in most of the large cities, passed resolutions requesting new legislation. In 1882, the *Insolvent Banks, Insurance Companies and Trading Corporations Act*, later to be known as the *Winding-Up Act*, was enacted.

In some countries, such as England and Australia, the *Bankruptcy Act* applies only to individuals and there is other legislation for the liquidation of insolvent companies. With the existence of the *Winding-Up Act*, this dichotomy could have developed in Canada. However, when the *Bankruptcy Act* of 1919 was enacted, it applied to both individuals and corporations. From 1919 until 1966, there were, in effect, two separate Acts in competition with each other relating to the insolvency of limited liability companies. These two Acts differ in substance and technique. In bankruptcy, for example, the property of the bankrupt vests in the trustee; under the *Winding-Up Act*, title to the property of the company remains in the company, but its control and management are taken from the directors and placed in the liquidator. The *Bankruptcy Act* binds the Crown, while the *Winding-up Act* does not. Under the *Bankruptcy Act*, an act of bankruptcy must be proved to obtain a receiving order, while, under the *Winding-Up Act*, a winding-up order may be obtained if the debtor is insolvent or deemed to be insolvent. Neither banks, insurance companies nor railway companies may be liquidated under the *Bankruptcy Act*, but they may be wound up under the *Winding-Up Act*. The *Bankruptcy Act* is characterized by an administration, for the most part, controlled by creditors, while, under the *Winding-Up Act*, the administration is controlled by the court. This duality is restricted by the amendments to the *Bankruptcy Act* in 1966 [see now *BIA*, s 213], which provide in effect that the *Bankruptcy Act* should take precedence over the *Winding-Up Act*. Thus, now, where a petition for a receiving order or an assignment is filed under the

Bankruptcy Act, in respect of a corporation, the *Winding-Up Act* does not extend or apply to that corporation.

The Period from 1880 to 1919: During the thirty-nine years when there was no federal bankruptcy or insolvency legislation relating to individuals, the only relief available to insolvent individuals was through provincial legislation. There were, in Quebec, articles 763-780 of *The Code of Civil Procedure* and, in the other provinces, the Assignment and Preferences Acts. The first of these Acts was an *Act Respecting Assignments for the Benefit of Creditors* passed by the Ontario Legislature in 1885, some five years after enacting what is now *The Creditors' Relief Act*.

Under provincial legislation, an insolvent debtor makes an assignment of his property to an authorized trustee licensed by the province. The authorized trustee is then required to liquidate the estate under the supervision of inspectors. For this, he is paid a fee from the debtor's estate. What characterizes provincial legislation, and since 1919, distinguishes it from the *Bankruptcy Act* is that a creditor cannot force a debtor to make an assignment; once an assignment is made, there is no provision in the legislation permitting a debtor to make a composition with his creditors and a debtor does not receive a release of his debts or a discharge.

The 1919 Bankruptcy Act: By 1917, there was considerable agitation across the country in support of the enactment of a national *Bankruptcy Act*. A committee of the Canadian Bar Association was created to draft such an act. This, in turn, disturbed some businessmen and authorized trustees licensed by the provinces. They felt that an act drafted by lawyers would provide for some form of court controlled administration instead of the provincial system of creditor control whereby estates were liquidated by the authorized trustees under the supervision of inspectors. One of the largest firms of authorized trustees, the Canadian Credit Men's Trust Association, retained Mr. H.P. Grundy, KC of Winnipeg, and instructed him to draft a Bill based upon creditor control and retaining the essential features of the provincial Assignments and Preferences Acts.

The Bill, based upon Mr. Grundy's draft, was first introduced in the House of Commons on March 27, 1918 as a war measure. On the motion for first reading, it was said:

> *Mr. Jacobs*: . . . I think that I can claim for this Bill that it is essentially a war measure at this particular time. We must be prepared when the war comes to a close, to be able to handle the situation which is bound to arise in this country as a result of the long continued struggle and of the readjustments which must be made. . . . By this measure it is proposed that the courts shall carefully scrutinize the business dealings and the business relations of traders, and shall make a distinction — shall separate the sheep from the goats. When the court is of the opinion that a debtor has been obliged to assign through misfortune, he shall be given the necessary relief. If, on the other hand, it should be found in scrutinizing his affairs, that he wrecked his own business wilfully, then, of course, he should receive no relief whatever.

The Bill, later referred to a special committee and then reintroduced in the House of Commons during the following session, was enacted in 1919.

The Office of the Custodian Created in 1923: It had been hoped that the system of administration established by the 1919 Act and based upon the practice prevailing under the provincial Assignments Acts would prevent the occurring of the abuses that had helped to discredit the old Insolvency Acts. It was soon found, however, that most of the business under the new Act was not going to the experienced organizations of trustees that had efficiently handled most of the business under the provincial Assignments Acts. The work of a trustee attracted many unqualified and inexperienced persons, and, as there was then not enough business, this resulted in many trustees openly soliciting business and often lead [sic] to collusive and inefficient administration of estates.

In an attempt to rectify the abuses surrounding the appointment of trustees, particularly in voluntary assignments where the debtor was nominating his own trustee, the office of custodian was created in 1923. In many respects, the custodian fulfilled several of the functions of the official receiver in England until the first meeting of the creditors. The custodian was in effect the first trustee in every estate. He had to take possession of the property of the debtor and was responsible for its safekeeping until the appointment of the trustee at the first meeting of creditors. In practice, it soon developed that the custodian was invariably appointed trustee. As a result, the office of the custodian served no useful purpose and was ultimately abolished in 1949.

The Office of Superintendent of Bankruptcy created in 1932: The lack of safeguards surrounding the appointment of trustees encouraged the activities of dishonest trustees. There were scandals involving inefficient and collusive liquidations by incompetent and untrustworthy trustees. The supervision of trustees by creditors was ineffectual and the demand grew for some form of government supervision.

At the Annual Meeting of the Canadian Credit Men's Trust Association Ltd., in 1927, attention was called to the office of "Accountant of Court" created under the *Bankruptcy Act* of Scotland. The Accountant, who was appointed by the court on the recommendation of the Crown, had the responsibility to examine the charges and conduct of trustees and inspectors in every proceeding.

In 1929, the late Lewis Duncan, QC, an acknowledged bankruptcy specialist, after comparing the English, French and United States systems, suggested that there was a need in Canada for an adequately staffed bankruptcy department with offices at strategic centres.

In 1932, the office of the Superintendent was created. It was contemplated that the Superintendent would provide an independent, impartial and official supervision of trustees administering estates under the *Bankruptcy Act*. Except for the increased investigatory powers given to it in 1966, the office of the Superintendent has remained unaltered and compares with that of the Inspector General in Bankruptcy established in England in 1883.

The 1949 Bankruptcy Act: The present Canadian *Bankruptcy Act* was enacted in 1949. The intention of the new Act was said to be "to clarify and simplify the legislation." The following extract from Hansard, when the Bill was first introduced in the Senate, explains the history of the Bill and the principal changes:

> *Hon. J. Gordon Fogo:* Honourable senators, it has sometimes been said that legislation in Canada is passed hastily and that those interested and the public in general are not given an opportunity to study its provisions. I do not think that can be said of this Bill F, which appears to have had a rather checkered career. This, I believe, is the fourth time that the bill has been introduced in this honourable House. It was first brought down in the year 1946, in a somewhat different form from the present measure, and was laid over for study for a period during which representations concerning it were made. Subsequently, in 1948, it came up again in a revised form. And, as most honourable senators will remember, it was introduced for a third time at the first session of this year, but unfortunately,

owing to early dissolution, consideration of it was not completed. The present bill, I am informed, with very few exceptions, is practically identical with the bill that was before the Senate last session. . . . The bill provides a more orderly arrangement of subjects and the language in many sections of the Act has been simplified. One or two of the more notable changes should be mentioned. The bill reinstates a provision which was in the *Bankruptcy Act* of 1919. During the period from 1919 to 1923 the Act contained a provision whereby an insolvent person could make a proposal to his creditors without making an assignment or having a receiving order made against him, and thereby suffering the stigma of bankruptcy. The bill now provides that an insolvent person may make such a proposal without going through the procedure of bankruptcy.

A further change which has been generally accepted as an improvement is a code for the administration of small estates in an economical and inexpensive manner. This section of the bill covers estates with assets of $500 or less, and provides a simplified procedure for their administration.

One other notable innovation of this bill is found in sections 127 to 129, which deal with the discharge of bankrupts. Under the existing legislation it has been necessary for a bankrupt, after the administration was completed, to apply to get his discharge. For various reasons, whether because the debtor did not know he was entitled to do this, or for other reasons, it was not customary for bankrupts to apply to their discharge. Following legislation in other countries—I think in the United States, and perhaps in Australia—this bill incorporates what might be regarded as an automatic application for discharge, because the occurring of the bankruptcy through assignment or receiving order in the first instance is also treated as an application for discharge. The debtor of course has to satisfy the court that he qualifies before he gets his discharge, and the conditions are laid down.

To move on quickly and in a very summary way: there are other miscellaneous provisions which might be mentioned. The new bill vests a greater measure of control in the creditors and inspectors. The powers of the superintendent have been made more explicit. . . . The remuneration of trustees has been increased; that is, the maximum remuneration has been enlarged from 5 to 7 1/2 per cent. . . . The office of the custodian is eliminated. . . .

The 1966 Amendment: During the fifties and early sixties, there was an increasing number of complaints about fraudulent bankruptcies. The complaint was also made that the investigatory machinery was not adequate to cope with the problem. As a result, the *Bankruptcy Act* was amended in 1966 so as to give the Superintendent wider powers of investigation. He may now investigate offences under any Act of Parliament, whether they have occurred before or after bankruptcy.

Many other significant amendments were made in 1966. One relates to non-arms' length transactions, and enables trustees better to deal with the transactions entered into by a debtor to the prejudice of his creditors. Part X of the *Bankruptcy Act* was also enacted. It provides for a system of orderly payment of debts under the supervision of the courts, but it is effective only in provinces where the Lieutenant Governor in Council has requested the Governor in Council to proclaim it in force.

The Companies' Creditors Arrangement Act: Prior to 1914, when most of Canada's financing was done in England, the practice, in issuing securities, was to follow English precedents. As a consequence, almost all trust deeds during this period contained clauses permitting a majority of debenture holders to vary the terms of a trust deed. Sometime later, in the twenties, when financing in the United States became more common, such provisions were no longer included in a great many trust deeds as they were not at that time usual in the United States. When the depression came, many companies needed to be reorganized. Often, to the embarrassment of the directors, it was found that the trust deeds did not contain provisions permitting reorganization by agreement. As a result, without the existence of enabling legislation, there was no way by which such companies could be reorganized. . . .

The Companies' Creditors Arrangement Act worked well and gave general satisfaction to investors and to companies with secured indebtedness who wished to make arrangements with their creditors. There were, however, abuses of the Act by insolvent companies that used it, instead of the *Bankruptcy Act*, to make arrangements with their unsecured creditors. The *Companies' Creditors Arrangement Act* was never intended for this purpose, as it did not provide an appropriate procedure to give sufficient protection to unsecured creditors against false or misleading statements by the company concerning its affairs, thereby inducing them to accept proposals not in their best interests.

"Debenture holders" did not, however, have to rely solely on this Act for protection. The investing public had other facilities available. Most debentures gave the indenture trustee wide powers to intervene in the affairs of the debtor upon certain conditions. Institutional investors and underwriters that have large blocks of debentures on their hands or in their portfolios would, as a rule, also intervene in order to prevent any serious abuse. . . .

In 1953, the *Companies' Creditors Arrangement Act* was amended, as originally suggested by the Dominion Mortgage and Investments Association, so as to restrict its application to a debtor company that had an outstanding debenture issue and wished to make a proposal with the debenture holders.

[The report continues to point out that the *CCAA* was seldom used after 1953 because of its restricted application and the fact that trust indentures usually contained their own machinery for the contractual reorganization of financially troubled companies.]

Conclusion: At the end of this brief description of how the bankruptcy and insolvency system developed in Canada, there are a number of comments that come to mind.

Although, at the outset, the legislation was almost entirely borrowed from England, in the course of time, amendments were made to the original legislation to better adapt it to Canadian conditions and special statutes were passed to meet particular problems. Little attempt was made, however, to integrate new legislation with the existing legislation or to make a single comprehensive Act. The result has been a multiplicity of statutes and systems which often lead to inequity and inefficiency.

With the multiplicity of systems, the debtor and the creditor sometimes have the choice of the system under which to proceed and, under certain circumstances, they can fare better under one system than another. A creditor, for example, may be better protected or may have a higher priority for a dividend under one system than another. Similarly, the penalty provisions applicable to debtors may vary.

Many corporations may be liquidated under either the *Winding-Up Act* or the *Bankruptcy Act*. There are transactions that may be set aside as fraudulent preferences under one of these Acts, which could not be set aside, as such, under the other. However, since the 1966 amendments to the *Bankruptcy Act*, the *Winding-Up Act* does not apply to a corporation, where a petition is filed under the *Bankruptcy Act*. While the opportunity of a debtor or creditor to elect to take proceedings under the *Winding-Up Act*, and thus forestall proceedings under the *Bankruptcy Act*, has been reduced, inequities are still possible. The majority of creditors, for example, may wish to take proceedings under the *Winding-Up Act* to reach a creditor who has received a preference that may be set aside as fraudulent under the *Winding-Up Act*, but not under the *Bankruptcy Act*. The creditor who is alleged to have obtained a fraudulent preference, or a creditor friendly to him, may effectively block the proceedings under the *Winding-Up Act* by making a petition under the *Bankruptcy Act*.

There are situations, however, where no choice is given to the debtor or the creditors as to which statute may be used. A number of statutes apply in whole or in part, for example, to particular debtors, such as banks, insurance companies and railways. This situation may also lead to inequity as both debtors and creditors, under the particular statutes, may, without good reason, fare differently than those who come within the provisions of other statutes.

Moreover, in spite of the multiplicity of systems and statutes, there are a number of debtors whose affairs cannot be liquidated under existing federal legislation. The non-trading corporations, for example, would be in that category. It is not clear, either, whether any of this legislation applies to the winding-up, by reason of their insolvency, of some corporations, such as provincial trust companies and certain building societies.

Finally, the existing legislation may also be criticized for being, to a considerable degree, either rudimentary or out-dated. Much of it was designed when social and commercial conditions were very much different than what they are today. In other cases, legislation designed to meet a particular emergency survived long after the emergency had passed and the conditions changed. The procedure for the liquidation of insolvent railways is a good example of rudimentary legislation. Under present conditions, as a practical matter, special legislation would probably be required to effectively liquidate a railway company by reason of its insolvency, as existing legislation is silent in respect to many matters of importance. The *Farmers' Creditors Arrangement Act* is an example of special legislation inspired by a national emergency that has been long out of date, but which has never been repealed, brought up to date or incorporated into the principal statute.[9]

* * * * *

Historical update
Following the publication of the Tassé Report, the federal government introduced Bill C-60 in 1975. This was a complete revision of the *Bankruptcy Act (BA)* and adopted most of the Task Force's recommendations. The bill was strongly criticized on technical and policy grounds by various bankruptcy constituencies in hearings before the Senate Banking and Commerce Committee and was withdrawn by the government for further review. A revised bill, Bill C-12, was introduced in 1980 but it, and three other bills introduced over the next four years, never emerged from the committee stage in the House of Commons. See further, Jacob S Ziegel, "The Travails of Bill C-12" (1982-83) 8 *Canadian Business Law Journal* 374.

In 1984, the newly elected Mulroney government abandoned further attempts to enact a revised act and opted instead for incremental changes to the *BA*. To this end, the federal government established an advisory committee (the Colter Committee) composed of insolvency practitioners and trustees to recommend those changes that were deemed to be most urgent. The committee reported in 1986.

---

9   The Act has now been repealed.

The committee's recommendations were largely adopted in Bill C-22, first introduced in the summer of 1991. The bill nearly came to grief over Part I of the bill, which would have enacted a separate *Wage Claim Payment Act*. The Bill was given parliamentary approval in 1992 (SC 1992, c 27), but only after the government had dropped Part I entirely. The most important changes contained in the 1992 amendments were the following:

1) A totally revised Part III, Division I, dealing with the reorganization of insolvent business debtors (although, technically speaking, not restricted to business debtors), and a new Division II aimed at the composition of consumer debts.
2) A new Part XI requiring secured creditors to give ten days' notice to the debtor before seeking to repossess the collateral where the collateral comprises all or substantially all of the debtor's assets or all or substantially all of the debtor's inventory or accounts receivable, and subjecting privately appointed or court appointed receivers and receiver-managers to judicial supervision.
3) The substantial recasting of section 136 (which deals with the ranking of creditors for the purpose of distributing the net assets of the estate) and the elimination of preferred creditor status for Crown claims.
4) The recognition of deemed trusts, established pursuant to federal and provincial tax legislation, of monies collected and deductions made by a taxpayer on behalf of the Crown (*BIA*, s 67(3)).
5) Introduction of registration requirements for Crown lien claims as a condition of their recognition in bankruptcy (*BIA*, ss 86–87).
6) Creation of an unpaid seller's right to recover the goods on the buyer's bankruptcy and, in the case of unpaid farmers, fishermen, and aquaculturists, to claim a charge on the debtor's inventory for the unpaid amounts.
7) Automatic discharge of first-time individual bankrupts nine months after the bankruptcy order unless the discharge is opposed (*BIA*, ss 168.1–172).
8) Mandatory system of credit counselling of bankrupts as precondition to discharge from bankruptcy (*BIA*, s 157).

The 1992 Act (s 92) required Parliament to review the *BIA* three years after the amendments came into effect. To prepare for this event, Industry Canada established a Bankruptcy and Insolvency Act Advisory Committee (BIAC) in 1993 to consider what further amendments should be recommended. The BIAC in turn established a series of working groups to study the various parts of the Act. The most important groups were those dealing with arrangements and proposals, preferences and priorities, consumer bankruptcies, and international insolvencies. The working group recommendations were then reviewed by the BIAC and, if approved, were incorporated in the BIAC's report to the federal government. The federal government accepted most of the BIAC's recommendations and they were enshrined in Bill C-109 and, later, Bill C-5, amending the *BIA* and *CCAA*, and were enacted in 1997 as SC 1997, c 12. See further RG Marantz & RH Chartrand, "Bankruptcy and Insolvency Law Reform Continues: The 1996–1997 Amendments" (1997–98) 13 *Banking and Finance Law Review* 107, and JS Ziegel, "Canadian Bankruptcy Reform, Bill C-109, and Troubling Asymmetries" (1996) 27 *Canadian Business Law Journal* 108.

Some of the important changes made to the *BIA* and the *CCAA* were the following:

- Protection against environmental liability was extended to receivers, interim receivers, and trustees under proposals.
- The 1992 provisions involving lessors' claims for leases repudiated by a debtor making a commercial proposal were relaxed to make them more flexible and to afford lessors better protection against unreasonable disclaimers.

- The commercial proposal and *CCAA* provisions were enlarged to permit corporate debtors to include in the proposal the compromising of claims against directors in their capacities as directors that arose before the proposal was made.
- New provisions were added to the *BIA* and *CCAA* governing the recognition of foreign insolvencies and authorizing Canadian courts to provide assistance to foreign insolvency administrators.
- A new Part XII was added dealing with the insolvency of securities firms and the handling of claims against such firms.
- Various amendments, favourable and unfavourable to debtors, were added to the consumer bankruptcy provisions. The single most important amendment was the recasting of section 68 to make it mandatory for individual bankrupts to remit the bankrupt's surplus income to the trustee until the date of the bankrupt's discharge, the surplus income being determined by directives issued by the Office of the Superintendent of Bankruptcy. For further discussion of the surplus income payment requirements, see Chapter 13 of this text.
- Important amendments to the *CCAA* included the following features: the Act was restricted to corporate debtors and their affiliates having a minimum indebtedness of $5 million; the requirements for an outstanding issue of debentures or bonds and a trust deed as preconditions of the Act's applicability were dropped; the court's initial *ex parte* order is only effective for thirty days and a new hearing must be held thereafter; and the court is required to appoint a monitor to protect creditor interests and report to the court at required intervals pending the debtor's preparation of a plan and its being voted on.

The 1997 amendments envisaged a third phase of amendments to the *BIA* and further possible amendments to the *CCAA*. They also required the federal government to submit a report to Parliament on the operation of the *BIA* and the *CCAA* within five years of the proclamation of the 1997 amendments. In preparation for this event, Industry Canada commissioned many research reports on specific issues.[10]

The superintendent of bankruptcy also established a Personal Insolvency Task Force (PITF) in 2000 to advise him on desirable amendments to the personal insolvency provisions in the *BIA*. The PITF's report was published in late 2002[11] and contains many recommendations of varying importance. Some of the more radical recommendations provoked strong dissents within the task force.[12] The Insolvency Institute of Canada, an influential body of senior insolvency practitioners across Canada, also conducted its own series of studies on many aspects of the operation of the *CCAA* and presented its recommendations to the minister of industry in March 2002.[13]

Industry Canada published its own statutorily required report in late 2002.[14] The report discussed many of the issues relevant to further amendments to Canada's insolvency legislation.

---

10 Many of the research papers are available in electronic form on Innovation, Science and Economic Development Canada's website: www.ic.gc.ca.
11 See Personal Insolvency Task Force, Canada, *Final Report* (Ottawa: Office of the Superintendent of Bankruptcy, 2002) [PITF Report].
12 See, *inter alia*, annex 3 and Chapter 2(V) of the PITF Report, *ibid.*
13 See Insolvency Institute of Canada/Canadian Association of Insolvency and Restructuring Professionals Joint Task Force on Business Insolvency Law Reform, *Report* (2002) [unpublished], online: www.insolvency.ca/en/iicresources/resources/JTF_Report_ReformProposals_2002.pdf.
14 Industry Canada, Market Framework Policy Branch, Policy Sector, *Report on the Operation and Administration of the Bankruptcy and Insolvency Act and the Companies' Creditors Arrangement Act* (Ottawa: Industry Canada, 2002), online: http://publications.gc.ca/site/eng/237359/publication.html.

Disappointingly, the report avoided putting forward the department's own solutions, but somehow seemed to expect the Senate Banking, Trade and Commerce Committee (Senate Committee) to do this job for the government. The Senate Committee conducted public hearings in the spring of 2003 and published its substantial report in November of that year.[15] The report was largely based on the recommendations in the submissions of the Insolvency Institute of Canada and Canadian Association of Insolvency and Restructuring Professionals and the recommendations in the PITF Report. The federal government issued no report indicating its own position in the light of these developments. Instead, and rather earlier than expected, the federal government introduced Bill C-55 in the House of Commons in June 2005. This massive 140-page bill involved the most extensive amendments to Canada's insolvency legislation since 1949. The most important changes involved the following areas:

- the introduction of a *Wage Earner Protection Program Act* (*WEPPA*), guaranteeing payment of unpaid wages of employees of a bankrupt employer out of the federal Consolidated Revenue Fund up to a maximum of $3,000 per worker;
- new and revised treatment of executory contracts in straight bankruptcies and commercial proposals;
- revision of provisions involving fraudulent and below-value pre-bankruptcy transactions;
- protection of collective bargaining agreements from interference by the courts;
- conferment of superpriority security status against debtor's assets for unpaid wages up to prescribed amounts and for shortfalls in contributory employer-employee pension plans;
- extension of automatic discharge entitlement for first-time insolvent individuals from nine months to twenty-one months;
- substitution of UNCITRAL Model Law Crossborder Insolvency provisions for Part XIII of the *BIA*;
- major expansion of the skeletal *CCAA* provisions to cover most of the gaps in the statutory framework previously bridged by court orders made under the judicially crafted "inherent jurisdiction" doctrine;
- replication in *CCAA* (but often not verbatim) of *BIA* provisions, as amended, dealing with executory contracts and assignment of contracts and with the treatment of cross-border insolvencies.

Bill C-55 attracted much criticism from professional groups, not so much on grounds of principle, but because of defects in craftsmanship. One of the most comprehensive critiques of Bill C-55 — covering policy as well as drafting issues — was presented to the Industry Committee of the House of Commons in November 2005 by a group of academics.[16] Among the concerns expressed by the academics were the following:

- the unnecessary duplication of provisions in the revised *BIA* and the *CCAA* and inconsistencies between the *BIA* and the *CCAA* covering identical topics;
- the failure to integrate the *CCAA* as part of the *BIA*;

---

15   Standing Senate Committee on Banking, Trade and Commerce, *Debtors and Creditors Sharing the Burden: A Review of the* Bankruptcy and Insolvency Act *and the* Companies' Creditors Arrangement Act (Ottawa: Senate, November 2003) (Chair: Hon Richard H Kroft).

16   Jacob Ziegal et al, *Submissions on Bill C-55, 2005: The Wage Earner Protection Program Act and Amendments to the* Bankruptcy and Insolvency Act *and the* Companies' Creditors Arrangement Act (November 2005), online: www.law.utoronto.ca/documents/Ziegel/submission_c55.pdf.

- the need for a complete overhaul and modernization of the *BIA*, including the *BIA* regulations, forms and policy statements adopted under the *BIA*;
- objections to the extension of the automatic discharge period for first-time bankrupts with surplus income from nine months to twenty-one months;
- the need for more studies of the impact of the rapid expansion of consumer credit on the number of consumer insolvencies and the adequacy and fairness of the existing provisions and proposed amendments to the *BIA*.

The Industry Committee of the House of Commons began hearings on Bill C-55 in October 2005, but was obliged to discontinue (after hearing from only a few witnesses) because Parliament was dissolved on 25 November 2005 in anticipation of forthcoming elections. Before the dissolution of Parliament, the government prevailed on the Senate to approve Bill C-55, without the bill receiving the scrutiny of the Senate's Banking, Trade and Commerce Committee. To secure the Senate's consent, the Martin government gave an undertaking that it would not proclaim Bill C-55, after its enactment, without giving the Senate Committee an opportunity to study the bill in detail. Despite the government's assurance to the Senate, the net result of these events was that the 140-page Bill C-55 (now SC 2005, c 47) was approved by both Houses of Parliament without scrutiny or serious debate in either House.

The Senate Committee did not in fact study SC 2005, c 47, in 2007 after Parliament was reconvened following the defeat of the Martin government and the installation of the Harper administration. Rather, the Harper government announced its intention to introduce changes to SC 2005, c 47, and did so in the form of a Motion to Amend SC 2005, c 47, which was introduced in the House of Commons in December 2006. The motion was opposed by members of Parliament from Quebec and Saskatchewan representing vested interests in those provinces and the amendments were not adopted.[17] Department of Industry officials spent the next few months negotiating with the opponents of the RRSP amendments in SC 2005, c 47, and ended up essentially capitulating to their demands.

In June 2007, the Harper government introduced Bill C-62, a ninety-page bill amending SC 2005, c 47. Bill C-62 died on the Order Paper and was reintroduced in the next Session as Bill C-12. The Bill was approved by the House without debate and without being referred to committee for study. In a remarkable replay of the November 2005 events, government ministers appeared before the Senate Banking, Trade and Commerce Committee in December 2007 and persuaded the committee to approve the bill without prior study. The ministers justified the request on the ground that the government was anxious to proclaim SC 2005, c 47, and Bill C-12 (once it was enacted) so that the government could proceed with adoption of the regulations necessary to implement *WEPPA*. The Senate Committee reluctantly agreed to the government's request, so that, for the second time, a major bankruptcy amendment bill was approved by Parliament without serious debate or scrutiny in either House.

There was one modest glimmer of hope. The Senate reserved the right to hold hearings on SC 2005, c 47, and on what had now become SC 2007, c 36. The Senate Banking, Trade and Commerce Committee actually began hearings in February 2008. Because of other commitments, the Committee was not able to complete its hearings in the spring of 2008 and

---

17 The opposition was to the amendments in s 67 of SC 2005, c 47, involving the exempt status of Registered Retirement Savings Plans (RRSPs). The amendments imposed a ceiling on the size of a plan that could be exempted from the trustee's reach after the RRSP holder became bankrupt. The critics were concerned that these restrictions would make RRSPs less attractive as an investment vehicle and affect their sales by insurance companies and other financial intermediaries. For further discussion of the issues, see PITF Report, above note 11 at 17–23 and Chapter 11 of this text.

before Parliament adjourned for the summer. On 7 July 2008, the *WEPPA* (which was part of SC 2005, c 47) was proclaimed into force. SC 2005, c 47, and SC 2007, c 36, were proclaimed into force on 18 September 2009 by SI 2009-68 (Canada Gazette Part II, 19 Aug 2009).

In 2014, the government began its consultation process with a view to enacting further amendments to the *BIA* and the *CCAA*.[18] The government has not adopted any of the 2014 recommendations. In 2018, the government announced consultation on *Enhancing Retirement Security for Canadians*. According to the consultation document, "company insolvencies have raised concerns about the security of pension, wage and benefit entitlements for workers and retirees."[19]

III. MODERN BANKRUPTCY OBJECTIVES

In common law jurisdictions, it is now well established that bankruptcy law serves three principal functions: (1) to solve the "collective action problem" discouraging creditors from collaborating outside bankruptcy and to provide a mechanism in bankruptcy legislation for the orderly liquidation of a bankrupt's estate and distribution of the proceeds among the creditors; (2) to enable basically viable enterprises to reorganize themselves to allow them to stay in business; and (3) to enable overextended debtors to make a "fresh start" by surrendering their non-exempt assets and obtaining a discharge for the balance of their debts. The following extracts from the book by Prof Thomas Jackson and the articles by Senator Elizabeth Warren and Prof Douglas Baird address the first two questions. The fresh-start policy for individual bankrupts is examined below in Chapter 11. The interaction of reorganization policies and actual reorganization rules is explored in some detail in chapters 12 to 16.

Thomas H Jackson, *The Logic and Limits of Bankruptcy Law* (Cambridge, MA: Harvard University Press, 1986) at 7–27 (footnotes omitted)

1.   The Role of Bankruptcy Law and Collective Action in Debt Collection

Bankruptcy law and policy have been subject to long-standing debate. This debate is not so much about whether bankruptcy law should exist at all but about how much it should do. All agree that it serves as a collective debt-collection device. Whether, when firms are involved, it should do more is the crux of the dispute. I plan to start by establishing in this chapter what accepted wisdom has already acknowledged — that bankruptcy's system of collectivized debt collection is, in principle, beneficial. Most of this book will then be concerned with exploring how that benefit can be realized and, as importantly, how viewing bankruptcy as a collectivized debt-collection device imposes limits on what else bankruptcy can do well. It is in the latter area that the most conflict arises. It exists because bankruptcy analysts have failed to follow through on the first principles of establishing a collectivized debt-collection system. To show why bankruptcy's principal role limits what other functions it can usefully perform is the objective of this book. Toward that end we shall first examine why bankruptcy law *should* be doing what everyone takes as a given.

---

18   See *Corporate, Insolvency and Competition Policy*, above note 5.

19   Innovation, Science and Economic Development Canada, Enhancing Retirement Security for Canadians: Consultation Document (Ottawa: 2018), online: https://www.ic.gc.ca/eic/site/116.nsf/eng/00001.html.

Bankruptcy law is a response to credit. The essence of credit economies is people and firms—that can be called *debtors*—borrowing money. The reasons for this are varied. In the case of individuals credit may serve as a device to smooth out consumption patterns by means of borrowing against future income. In the case of corporations and other firms it may be a part of a specialization of financing and investment decisions. And just as the reasons for borrowing are varied, so, too, are the methods. The prototype creditor may be a bank or other financial institution that lends money, but that is only one of many ways in which credit is extended. An installment seller extends credit. So does a worker who receives a paycheck on the first of December for work performed in November. The government, in its role as tax collector, also extends credit to the extent that taxes accrue over a year and are due at the end. Similarly, a tort victim who is injured today and must await payment until the end of a lawsuit extends credit of sorts, although involuntarily and (probably) unhappily. Finally, credit is not extended just by "creditors." First-round purchasers of common and preferred stock of a corporation are also lending money to the debtor. Their repayment rights are distinct (they are the residual claimants), but it is proper to view them, too, as having defined rights to call on the assets of the debtor for payment.

Whatever the reasons for lending and whatever its form, the terms on which consensual credit is extended depend to a substantial extent on the likelihood of voluntary repayment and on the means for coercing repayment. We are not concerned here with the means for getting paid when the debtor is solvent—when it has enough assets to satisfy all its obligations in full—but is simply mean-spirited or is genuinely disputing whether it has a duty of payment (as the debtor might be with our putative tort victim or with a supplier who the debtor believes sold it defective goods). The legal remedies for coercing payment when the debtor is solvent concern the rights of a creditor to use the power of the state in pursuit of its claim. This is a question of debtor-creditor law and one to which bankruptcy law historically has had nothing to add, directly at least.

Bankruptcy law can be thought of as growing out of a distinct aspect of debtor-creditor relations: the effect of the debtor's obligation to repay Creditor A on its remaining creditors. This question takes on particular bite only when the debtor does not have enough to repay everyone in full. Even then, however, a developed system exists for paying creditors without bankruptcy. The relevant question is whether that existing system of creditor remedies has any shortcomings that might be ameliorated by an ancillary system known as bankruptcy law.

To explore that question, it is useful to start with the familiar. Creditor remedies outside of bankruptcy (as well as outside other formal, non-bankruptcy collective systems) can be accurately described as a species of "grab law," represented by the key characteristic of first-come, first-served. The creditor first staking a claim to particular assets of the debtor generally is entitled to be paid first out of those assets. It is like buying tickets for a popular rock event or opera: the people first in line get the best seats; those at the end of the line may get nothing at all.

When the issue is credit, the ways that one can stake a place in line are varied. Some involve "voluntary" actions of the debtor: the debtor can simply pay a creditor off or give the creditor a security interest in certain assets that the creditor "perfects" in the prescribed manner (usually by giving the requisite public notice of its claim). In other cases a creditor's place in line is established notwithstanding the lack of the debtor's consent: the creditor can, following involvement of a court, get an "execution lien" or "garnishment" on the assets of the debtor. Or, sometimes, a place in line may simply be given to a particular claimant by governmental fiat, in the form of a "statutory lien" or similar device.

Although the *methods* for establishing a place in line are varied, the fundamental ordering principle is the same. Creditors are paid according to their place in line for particular assets. With a few exceptions, moreover, one's place in line is fixed by the time when one acquires an interest in the assets and takes the appropriate steps to publicize it. A solvent debtor is like a show for which sufficient tickets are available to accommodate all prospective patrons and all seats are considered equally good. In that event one's place in line is largely a matter of indifference. But when there is not enough to go around to satisfy all claimants in full, this method of ordering will define winners and losers based principally on the time when one gets in line.

The question at the core of bankruptcy law is whether a *better* ordering system can be devised that would be worth the inevitable costs associated with implementing a new system. In the case of tickets to a popular rock event or opera, where there must be winners and losers, and putting aside price adjustments, there may be no better way to allocate available seats than on a first-come, first-served basis. In the world of credit, however, there are powerful reasons to think that there *is* a superior way to allocate the assets of an insolvent debtor than first-come, first-served.

The basic problem that bankruptcy law is designed to handle, both as a normative matter and as a positive matter, is that the system of individual creditor remedies may be bad for the creditors *as a group* when there are not enough assets to go around. Because creditors have conflicting rights, there is a tendency in their debt-collection efforts to make a bad situation worse. Bankruptcy law responds to this problem. Debt-collection by means of individual creditor remedies produces a variant of a widespread problem. One way to characterize the problem is as a multiparty game—a type of "prisoner's dilemma." As such, it has elements of what game theorists would describe as an *end period* game, where basic problems of cooperation are generally expected to lead to undesirable outcomes for the group of players as a whole. Another way of considering it is as a species of what is called a *common pool* problem, which is well known to lawyers in other fields, such as oil and gas.

This role of bankruptcy law is largely unquestioned. But because this role carries limits on what *else* bankruptcy law can do, it is worth considering the basics of the problem so that we understand its essential features before examining whether and why credit may present that problem. The vehicle will be a typical, albeit simple, common pool example. Imagine that you own a lake. There are fish in the lake. You are the only one who has the right to fish in that lake, and no one constrains your decision as to how much fishing to do. You have it in your power to catch all the fish this year and sell them for, say, $100,000. If you did that, however, there would be no fish in the lake next year. It might be better for you—you might maximize your total return from fishing—if you caught and sold some fish this year but left other fish in the lake so that they could multiply and you would have fish in subsequent years. Assume that, by taking this approach, you could earn (adjusting for inflation) $50,000 each year. Having this outcome is like having a perpetual annuity paying $50,000 a year. It has a present value of perhaps $500,000. Since (obviously, I hope) when all other things are equal, $500,000 is better than $100,000, you, as sole owner, would limit your fishing this year unless some other factor influenced you.

But what if you are not the only one who can fish in this lake? What if a hundred people can do so? The optimal solution has not changed: it would be preferable to leave some fish in the lake to multiply because doing so has a present value of $500,000. But in this case, unlike that where you have to control only yourself, an obstacle exists in achieving that result. If there are a hundred fishermen, you cannot be sure, by limiting *your* fishing, that there will be any more fish next year, unless you can also control the others. You may, then, have an incentive to catch as many fish as you can today because maximizing your take this year (catching, on average, $1,000 worth of fish) is better for you than holding off (catching, say, only $500 worth of fish this year) while others scramble and deplete the stock entirely. If you hold off, your aggregate return is only $500, since nothing will be left for next year or the year after. But that sort of reasoning by each of the hundred fishermen will mean that the stock of fish will be gone by the end of the first season. The fishermen will split $100,000 this year, but there will be no fish — and no money — in future years. Self-interest results in their splitting $100,000, not $500,000.

What is required is some rule that will make all hundred fishermen act as a sole owner would. That is where bankruptcy law enters the picture in a world not of fish but of credit. The grab rules of nonbankruptcy law and their allocation of assets on the basis of first-come, first-served create an incentive on the part of the individual creditors, when they sense that a debtor may have more liabilities than assets, to get in line today (by, for example, getting a sheriff to execute on the debtor's equipment), because if they do not, they run the risk of getting nothing. This decision by numerous individual creditors, however, may be the wrong decision for the creditors as a group. Even though the debtor is insolvent, they might be better off if they held the assets together. Bankruptcy provides a way to make these diverse individuals act as one, by imposing a *collective* and *compulsory* proceeding on them. Unlike a typical common pool solution, however, the compulsory solution of bankruptcy law does not apply in all places at all times. Instead, it runs parallel with a system of individual debt-collection rules and is available to supplant them when and if needed.

This is the historically recognized purpose of bankruptcy law and perhaps is none too controversial in itself. Because more controversial limits on bankruptcy policy derive from it, however, less allegorical and more precise analysis is necessary. Exactly *how* does bankruptcy law make creditors as a group better off? To find the answer to that question, consider a simple hypothetical example involving credit, not fish. Debtor has a small printing business. Potential creditors estimate that there is a 20 percent chance that Debtor (who is virtuous and will not misbehave) will become insolvent through bad luck, general economic downturn, or whatever. (By insolvency, I mean a condition whereby Debtor will not have enough assets to satisfy his creditors.) At the point of insolvency — I shall make this very simple — the business is expected to be worth $50,000 if sold piecemeal. Creditors also know that each of them will have to spend $1,000 in pursuit of their individual collection efforts should Debtor become insolvent and fail to repay them. Under these circumstances Debtor borrows $25,000 from each of four creditors, Creditors 1 through 4. Because these creditors know that there is this 20 percent chance, they can account for it — and the associated collection costs — in the interest rate they charge Debtor. Assume that each party can watch out for its own interest, and let us see whether, as in the example of fishing, there are reasons to think that these people would favor a set of restrictions on their own behaviour (apart from paternalism or other similar considerations).

Given that these creditors can watch out for their own interests, the question to be addressed is *how* these creditors should go about protecting themselves. If the creditors have to protect themselves by means of a costly and inefficient system, Debtor is going to have to pay more to obtain credit. Thus, when we consider them all together — Creditors

1 through 4 *and* Debtor—the relevant question is: would the availability of a bankruptcy system reduce the costs of credit?

This requires us to try to identify what bankruptcy's advantages might plausibly be. Identification of abstract advantages is not, however, the end of the issue. One must also compare those possible advantages with the costs of having a bankruptcy system. Determining whether a bankruptcy system would reduce the cost of credit requires a net assessment of charges.

But first the case for bankruptcy's advantages. The common pool example of fish in a lake suggests that one of the advantages to a collective system is a larger aggregate pie. Does that advantage exist in the case of credit? When dealing with businesses, the answer, at least some of the time, would seem to be "yes." The use of individual creditor remedies may lead to a piecemeal dismantling of a debtor's business by the untimely removal of necessary operating assets. To the extent that a non-piecemeal collective process (whether in the form of a liquidation or reorganization) is likely to increase the aggregate value of the pool of assets, its substitution for individual remedies would be advantageous to the creditors as a group. This is derived from a commonplace notion: that a collection of assets is sometimes more valuable together than the same assets would be if spread to the winds. It is often referred to as the surplus of a going-concern value over a liquidation value.

Thus, the most obvious reason for a collective system of creditor collection is to make sure that creditors, in pursuing their individual remedies, do not actually decrease the aggregate value of the assets that will be used to repay them. In our example this situation would occur when a printing press, for example, could be sold to a third party for $20,000, leaving $30,000 of other assets, but the business as a unit could generate sufficient cash so as to have a value of more than $50,000. As such it is directly analogous to the case of the fish in the lake. Even in cases in which the assets should be sold and the business dismembered, the aggregate value of the assets may be increased by keeping groups of those assets together (the printing press with its custom dies, for example) to be sold as discrete units.

This advantage, however, is not the only one to be derived from a collective system for creditors. Consider what the creditors would get if there were no bankruptcy system (putting aside the ultimate collection costs). Without a collective system all of the creditors in our example know that in the case of Debtor's insolvency the first two creditors to get to (and through) the courthouse (or to Debtor, to persuade Debtor to pay voluntarily), will get $25,000, leaving nothing for the third and fourth. And unless the creditors think that one of them is systematically faster (or friendlier with Debtor), this leaves them with a 50 percent chance of gaining $25,000, and a 50 percent chance of getting nothing. A collective system, however, would ensure that they would each get $12,500.

Would the creditors agree in advance to a system that, in the event of Debtor's insolvency, guaranteed them $12,500, in lieu of a system that gave them a 50 percent chance of $25,000—payment in full—and a 50 percent chance of nothing? Resolution of this question really turns on whether the creditors are better off with the one than the other. There are two reasons to think that they are, even without looking to the question of a going-concern surplus and without considering the costs of an individual collection system. First of all, if these creditors are risk averse, assurance of receiving $12,500 is better than a 50 percent chance of $25,000 and a 50 percent chance of nothing. Even if they can diversify the risk—by lending money to many people—it is probably preferable to eliminate it in the first place. This, then, represents a net advantage to having a collective proceeding.

One other possible advantage of a collective proceeding should also be noted: there may be costs to the individualized approach to collecting (in addition to the $1,000 collection costs). For example, since each creditor knows that it must "beat out" the others if it wants to be paid in full, it will spend time monitoring Debtor and the other creditors — perhaps frequently checking the courthouse records — to make sure that it will be no worse than second in the race (and therefore still be paid in full). Although some of these activities may be beneficial, many may not be; they will simply be costs of racing against other creditors, and they will cancel each other out. It is like running on a treadmill: you expend a lot of energy but get nowhere. If every creditor is doing this, each one *still* does not know if there is more than a fifty-fifty chance that it will get paid in full. But in one sense, unless the creditors can negotiate a deal with each other, the creditors have no choice. Each creditor has to spend this money just to stay in the race because if it does not, it is a virtual certainty that the others will beat it to the payment punch. Of course, a creditor could decide that it did not want to stay in the race, and just charge Debtor at the time of lending the money for coming in last should Debtor become insolvent. Debtor is not likely, however, to agree to pay a creditor that extra charge for having a lower priority provision, because, once paid that extra amount, the creditor may have an incentive to take steps to remain in the race and make money that way. For that reason it may be hard for a creditor to opt out of the race and get compensated for doing so.

These various costs to using an individual system of creditor remedies suggest that there are, indeed, occasions when a collective system of debt-collection law might be preferable. Bankruptcy provides that system. The single most fruitful way to think about bankruptcy is to see it as ameliorating a common pool problem created by a system of individual creditor remedies. Bankruptcy provides a way to override the creditors' pursuit of their own remedies and to make them work together.

This approach immediately suggests several features of bankruptcy law. First, such a law must usurp individual creditor remedies in order to make the claimants act in an altruistic and cooperative way. Thus, the proceeding is inherently *collective*. Moreover, this system works only if all the creditors are bound to it. To allow a debtor to contract with a creditor to avoid participating in the bankruptcy proceeding would destroy the advantages of a collective system. So the proceeding must be *compulsory* as well. But unlike common pool solutions in oil and gas or fishing, it is not the exclusive system for dividing up assets. It, instead, supplants an existing system of individual creditor remedies, and as we shall see, it is this feature that makes crucial an awareness of its limitations.

Note that the presence of a bankruptcy system does not mandate its use whenever there is a common pool problem. Bankruptcy law stipulates a minimum set of entitlements for claimants. That, in turn, permits them to "bargain in the shadow of the law" and to implement a consensual collective proceeding outside of the bankruptcy process. Because use of the bankruptcy process has costs of its own . . . , if creditors can consensually gain the sorts of advantages of acting collectively that bankruptcy brings, they could avoid those costs. Accordingly, one would expect that consensual deals among creditors outside the bankruptcy process would often be attempted first. The formal bankruptcy process would presumably be used only when individual advantage-taking in the setting of multiparty negotiations made a consensual deal too costly to strike — which may, however, occur frequently as the number of creditors increases. . . .

It is possible that the rules specifying when a bankruptcy petition may be filed prevent the commencement of a collective proceeding until it is too late to save the debtor's assets from the self-interested actions of various creditors. Another possibility, however, is that the collective proceeding will begin too soon. Forcing all the creditors to refrain from individual actions (many of which have the effect of monitoring the debtor and preventing it from misbehaving) brings its own costs. Thus, to say that bankruptcy is designed to solve a common pool problem is not to tell us how to design the rules that do that well. These concerns do not, however, undermine the basic insight of what bankruptcy law is all about.

Like all justifications, moreover, this one is subject to a number of qualifications. To say that a common pool problem exists is not to say that individual behavior is entirely self-interested or that legal rules can solve all collective action problems. We often observe people behaving in a cooperative fashion over time even if it appears contrary to their short-run interest. In the credit world, for example, creditors do not always rush to seize a debtor's assets whenever it seems to be in financial trouble. Yet despite this qualification the underlying point remains: sometimes people behave in a self-interested way and would be better off as a group if required to work together. The tragedy of the Texas oil fields in the first half of this century is a notable example of how self-interest led to the depletion of oil that otherwise could have been enjoyed by the group of oil field owners. Creditor relations almost certainly are another area where this essential truth has validity, especially given the fact that creditors may have fewer incentives to cooperate when a debtor is failing than they do when there are greater prospects of repeat dealings with a debtor.

Nor can we be confident that the bankruptcy rules themselves do not create problems. They do, and we will examine later how they should be dealt with. Because these complications play out against a backdrop of basic bankruptcy principles, however, it is preferable for now to make two simplifying assumptions. The first assumption is that insolvency occurs without warning. By this assumption, we eliminate consideration of strategic behavior that is likely to exist when some creditors sense the imminent likelihood of bankruptcy's collective proceeding and attempt to avoid it. ... The second assumption is that bankruptcy proceedings take no time. By this assumption, we can set aside problems that occur through the passage of time and the fact that this passage of time affects various claimants in different ways. We can also set aside the complications that result from a debtor's need to encourage people to deal with it while in bankruptcy and the fact that some of these people may wear both prepetition and postpetition hats. ...

Although imposing these two assumptions is, of course, somewhat unrealistic, doing so clarifies several key features of bankruptcy law. We can later extend our examination by making the inquiry somewhat more realistic. For now, however, it is sufficient to ask whether there is in fact a common pool problem that cannot be solved by creditors contracting among themselves. If the number of creditors is sufficiently small and sufficiently determinate, it may be possible for them to negotiate a solution at the time of insolvency that would avoid many, if not most, of the costs of an individual remedies system, even if they were not bargaining in the shadow of the law. But in cases in which there are large numbers of creditors or the creditors are not immediately known at a particular time (perhaps because they hold contingent or nonmanifested claims), the ability of the creditors to solve the problem of an individual remedies system by an actual agreement may be lost. Bankruptcy provides the desired result by making available a collective system after insolvency has occurred. It is the implications of that view of bankruptcy law that we can now begin to explore.

2. Determining Liabilities and the Basic Role of Nonbankruptcy Law

Bankruptcy provides a collective forum for sorting out the rights of "owners" (creditors and others with rights against a debtor's assets) and can be justified because it provides protection against the destructive effects of an individual remedies system when there are not enough assets to go around. This makes the basic process one of determining *who* gets *what*, in *what order*. *Who* is fundamentally a question of claims, or what shall often be referred to as *liabilities*. *What* is fundamentally a question of property of the estate, or what shall often be referred to as *assets*. At one level there is nothing magical about these basic building blocks. A liability is something that makes you less valuable — that you would pay to get rid of. An asset is something that makes you more valuable — that someone would pay you for.

In looking at all of this, it is helpful to think of bankruptcy as follows. What bankruptcy should be doing, in the abstract, is asking how much someone would pay for the assets of a debtor, assuming they could be sold free of liabilities. The resulting money is then taken and distributed to the holders of the liabilities according to their nonbankruptcy entitlements. Essentially, [the following discussion] simply [fleshes] out this idea against the basic role of bankruptcy law. .... The question [to be] addressed ... is exactly what this means in considering how claimants should be treated in bankruptcy. The basic answer involves seeing the bankruptcy process as protecting, at a minimum, the relative *value* of particular nonbankruptcy entitlements instead of the rights themselves. This is the subject of determining liabilities in bankruptcy and involves the question of how to divide the assets. The question of ... assets is integrally related to the question of liabilities.

The Destructive Effect of Changes of Relative Entitlements in Bankruptcy

Bankruptcy's basic procedures are designed to ameliorate a common pool problem. The key to effective implementation of this goal is to trigger bankruptcy when, and only when, it is in the interests of the creditors as a group. Consider what this means. Insolvency may be an occasion to collectivize what hitherto had been an individual remedies system. It does not, however, justify the implementation of a different set of relative entitlements, unless doing so is necessary as a part of the move from the individual remedies system. It is not just that the need for a collective proceeding does not go hand in hand with new entitlements. It is that the establishment of new entitlements in bankruptcy conflicts with the collectivization goal. Such changes create incentives for particular holders of rights in assets to resort to bankruptcy in order to gain for themselves the advantages of those changes, even when a bankruptcy proceeding would not be in the collective interest of the investor group. These incentives are predictable and counterproductive because they reintroduce the fundamental problem that bankruptcy law is designed to solve: individual self-interest undermining the interests of the group. These changes are better made *generally* instead of in bankruptcy only.

The problem of changing relative entitlements in bankruptcy not only underlies this book's normative view of bankruptcy law but also forms the basis of the bankruptcy system that has been enacted. The Supreme Court made this point in a case that is as important for recognizing it as the actual issue decided is unimportant. The case, *Butner v. United States* [440 US 48], decided in 1979, involved a secured creditor's claim to rents that accrued on the property serving as collateral after the filing of the bankruptcy petition relative to the claims of the unsecured creditors generally. Under relevant state law, as the Supreme Court described it, the debtor was entitled to the rents as long as it remained in possession or until a state court, on request, ordered the rents to be paid over to the secured creditor. In bankruptcy the unsecured creditors of an insolvent debtor can be viewed as the new equity owners of the debtor and hence entitled to what the debtor was entitled to outside of bankruptcy. This gave rise to the conflict between the secured creditor and the trustee, as representative of the unsecured creditors. The issue that the Supreme Court considered in *Butner* was: What should the source of law be (state or federal) in deciding how the secured creditor may realize on the post-bankruptcy rents? The Court saw the source of law as nonbankruptcy and observed that "the federal bankruptcy court should take whatever steps are necessary to ensure that the [secured creditor] is afforded in federal bankruptcy court the same protections he would have under state law if no bankruptcy had ensued." It justified this result as follows:

> Property interests are created and defined by state law. Unless some federal interest requires a different result, there is no reason why such interests should be analyzed differently simply because an interested party is involved in a bankruptcy proceeding. Uniform treatment of property interests by both state and federal courts within a State serves to reduce uncertainty, to discourage forum shopping, and to prevent a party from receiving "a windfall merely by reason of the happenstance of bankruptcy."

In the notion of forum shopping the Supreme Court expressed the fundamental point.

Yet to say that *Butner* denounced changing relative entitlements only in bankruptcy does not end the matter. It is important to understand *why* such rule changes cut against bankruptcy's recognized goal. This requires the separation of two issues that arise when a debtor is in bankruptcy: first, it is necessary to decide what to do with the debtor's assets, and, second, it is necessary to decide who gets them. The principal proposition I wish to establish here is that only by treating the answer to the second question as a nonbankruptcy issue can it be kept from unfavorably altering the answer to the first. To put this another way, in its role as a collective debt-collection device, bankruptcy law should not create rights. Instead, it should act to ensure that the rights that exist are vindicated to the extent possible. Only in this way can bankruptcy law minimize the conversion costs of transferring an insolvent debtor's assets to its creditors.

This point is easiest to demonstrate by examining a case where there is no occasion to use bankruptcy as a response to a common pool problem—where only one person has rights to the debtor's assets. Such a person, the sole owner of the assets, would have no creditors. Irrespective of any thought of bankruptcy, this sole owner would continually re-evaluate his use of the assets. If he were manufacturing buggy whips, at every moment (in theory at least) he would reassess whether this was the best use for those assets. If it was, he would continue; but if it was not, he would stop and either use the assets for some other purpose or sell them, piecemeal or as a unit, to others. This decision would be his alone. And he presumably would make it after determining which action would bring him the most from the assets.

This is, of course, an oversimplification. No person has *full* ownership of assets in the sense that he has absolutely unfettered control over their use. I do not have the right to sell cocaine even if I could make a great deal of money doing so. Similarly, a person making buggy whips may be subject to regulations governing the types of materials he can use, the minimum wages he must pay, or the environmental controls he must observe. These regulations will constrain his decisions and may lead him to choose a different use than he would choose in their absence.

This qualification, however, does not fundamentally undercut the basic point that given an existing array of legal rules, a sole owner would presumably decide to use the assets in the way that would bring him the most. He has, by definition, no need to use bankruptcy to ameliorate a common pool problem because a common pool exists only when there is more than one person with rights. He, accordingly, would be utterly indifferent to bankruptcy policy, unless the debtor's use of it benefited him (by permitting the debtor, for example, to escape an undesirable nonbankruptcy charge). If a charge were placed on assets only in bankruptcy law (such as that a debtor could not go out of business without first protecting employees), this owner would remain free to ignore it by going out of business without using bankruptcy. He would only be obligated to take account of such a charge if it were imposed by nonbankruptcy law.

When rights to assets are spread among a number of people, however, as they almost always are, things change. It then becomes necessary to decide not only how best to deploy the assets but also how to split up the returns from those assets. Because of the diversity of the owners, the deployment question creates a common pool problem. Bankruptcy law exists to solve that problem. But the lessons from the common pool show that the answer to the distributional question should not affect the determination of how to deploy the assets. As a group these diverse owners—bondholders, tort victims, trade creditors, shareholders, and others—would want to follow the same course as a sole owner. It is in the interest of the owners as a *group*, in other words, to keep the distributional question from spilling over into the deployment question.

Bankruptcy law is best approached by separating these two questions—the question of how the process can maximize the value of a given pool of assets and the question of how the law should allocate entitlements to whatever pool exists—and limiting bankruptcy law to the first. This distinction makes clear the relationship between bankruptcy rules and nonbankruptcy rules and provides a principle of bankruptcy policy capable of identifying which nonbankruptcy rules may need to be supplanted.

Because there is perhaps no point in bankruptcy policy that is more easily misunderstood, it is worth proceeding carefully. Let us consider one of the most common views of what bankruptcy law should do. This view is that bankruptcy law exists, in part, to help firms stay in business because of an increased social value and/or the jobs that are saved. In one guise this simply restates the common pool problem—that diverse owners, if unconstrained, will pull apart assets that would be worth more to the group of owners if kept together. Usually, however, the notion of keeping firms in business seems to be meant as an independent policy. For that policy to have independent force, it must mean that, irrespective of the wishes of the owners, a firm's assets should be kept in their current form because somebody—society or workers—is better off.

Incorporating such a policy in a bankruptcy statute, however, would be to mix apples and oranges, if one accepts the view (as everyone seems to) that bankruptcy law also exists as a response to a common pool problem. The question is really one of defining substantive rights. If the group in question—society, or workers, or whatever—deserves such rights, it is counterproductive to locate them only in a bankruptcy statute. Under existing nonbankruptcy law, for example, workers have no substantive entitlements to keep assets in their current form; they are not owners with substantive rights against the assets. For that reason the owners are free to close the business without considering the interests of the workers if doing so brings the owners more money. The fact that those owners have a common pool problem and need to use a collective proceeding to ameliorate it is not a reason to suddenly give a new group—workers—rights that they would not otherwise have and that could be ignored if the bankruptcy process was avoided. The decision whether they should have such rights should not be bankruptcy-specific. It addresses a distributional question as well as a deployment question.

Another way to put this is to note the distinction between saying that something is a problem that Congress should address and saying that something is a problem that Congress should address through bankruptcy law. The first is a federalism question, the second a collective debt-collection question. Whether giving workers substantive rights with regard to how assets are used is desirable, just as whether secured creditors should come ahead of unsecured creditors, is a question of underlying entitlements. Although protecting the victims of economic misfortune who have not been given rights against assets may be an important social and legal question, it is not a question specific to bankruptcy law. However the question is answered, a bankruptcy statute would still be necessary, because answering these substantive questions one way instead of the other does not eliminate the common pool problem. Because the issues of who should have entitlements and how to address a common pool problem are distinct, they should be kept separate in the legal response.

Nor is this simply an academic point. Bankruptcy law cannot both give new groups rights and continue effectively to solve a common pool problem. Treating both as bankruptcy questions interferes with bankruptcy's historic function as a superior debt-collection system against insolvent debtors. Fashioning a distinct bankruptcy rule — such as one that gives workers rights they do not hold under nonbankruptcy law — creates incentives for the group advantaged by the distinct bankruptcy rule to use the bankruptcy process even though it is not in the interest of the owners as a group. The consequences can be seen frequently: many cases are begun where the reason for filing for bankruptcy quite clearly is nothing more than the fact that the entity bringing the case is advantaged because of a bankruptcy rule change. Bankruptcy proceedings inevitably carry costs of their own. When bankruptcy is activated for a rule change that benefits one particular class, the net effect may be harmful to the owners as a group. It is this problem that makes such rule changes undesirable as a matter of bankruptcy law.

Even though a nonbankruptcy rule may suffer from infirmities such as unfairness or inefficiency, if the nonbankruptcy rule does not undermine the advantages of a collective proceeding relative to the individual remedies that exist given those entitlements, imposing a different bankruptcy rule is a second-best and perhaps a counterproductive solution. At bottom, bankruptcy is justified in overriding nonbankruptcy rights *because* those rights interfere with the group advantages associated with creditors acting in concert. If the non-bankruptcy rule — for example, a rule permitting owners to close down a business without considering the plight of workers — is thought undesirable for reasons other than its interference with a collective proceeding, the proper approach for Congress would be to face that issue squarely and to overturn the rule in general, not just to undermine or reverse it in bankruptcy. The latter course is undesirable because, as *Butner* recognized, it creates incentives for strategic "shopping" between the nonbankruptcy and bankruptcy forums.

[THE LOGIC AND LIMITS OF BANKRUPTCY LAW by Thomas H. Jackson, Cambridge, Mass.: Harvard University Press, copyright © 1986 by the President and Fellows of Harvard College.]

Elizabeth Warren, "Bankruptcy Policy" (1987) 54 *University of Chicago Law Review* 775–801 (footnotes omitted)

Bankruptcy is a booming business — in practice and in theory. From headlines about LTV's 10,000-page filing to feature stories about bankrupt consumers (usually Joe-and-

Ethel-whose-names-have-been-changed-to-protect-their-privacy), bankruptcy has become an increasingly popular news item in the past few years. Both organized labor and the consumer credit industry made concerted efforts to put bankruptcy issues before the public in their recent pushes to amend the new Bankruptcy Code. Lawyers have been drawn to the bright lights. Firms that did not have a single bankruptcy practitioner five years ago now field large bankruptcy sections. Bankruptcy seminars have been sellouts. And—perhaps the most reliable indicator of increased attention and activity—bankruptcy jokes have begun to make the rounds.

As bankruptcy has flourished in the popular press and in law practice, it enjoys what may be looked back on as a golden age in academe. Law review articles on bankruptcy abound, and enrollments in bankruptcy and related commercial law classes are reported to be on the rise across the country. Uncertainty about how the new Bankruptcy Code will be interpreted and dramatic shifts in the strategic use of bankruptcy have prompted reporters to call law professors for in-depth interviews or quotable statements for the evening news. Rumor has it that requests for expert help are on the increase and consultation fees are up for more than a few academics specializing in bankruptcy. All in all, it's not a bad time to know something about bankruptcy.

In the midst of this attention and noise and clamor, however, there is a quiet but persistent question: what function does bankruptcy serve? After the statutory arguments have been exhausted and the cases have been explored, most academic discussions of bankruptcy can be distilled to this question. Currently, the policies endorsed to support bankruptcy pronouncements are wide-ranging and, at the extremes, very much in opposition. Despite the critical importance of different policy presumptions, the policy elements underlying most discourses are asserted only obliquely, and they are rarely challenged directly.

Professor Douglas Baird and I have undertaken to debate in writing the basis of bankruptcy policy. We offer this paired set of essays in the spirit of the old "Point-Counterpoint" segment of television's "Sixty Minutes." While we cannot promise the dripping invective and snarling satire that made that old feature so delightful, we can try to push forward the debate by making direct challenges and responses. In the belief that a good fight is far more interesting than a host of polite compliments and careful hedgings, Professor Baird and I undertake an aggressive and irreverent debate.

In order to join issue more clearly and to narrow the focus of the debate somewhat, Professor Baird and I have agreed to debate the basis of bankruptcy policy in the context of business bankruptcies. While we both believe that the principles we discuss have significance in a consumer setting as well, we recognize that additional issues should be a part of a discussion about consumer bankruptcy policy and that those issues would make the discussion even more complex.

Professor Baird and I hold very different views of the purpose bankruptcy law serves. I see bankruptcy as an attempt to reckon with a debtor's multiple defaults and to distribute the consequences among a number of different actors. Bankruptcy encompasses a number of competing—and sometimes conflicting—values in this distribution. As I see it, no one value dominates, so that bankruptcy policy becomes a composite of factors that bear on a better answer to the question, "How shall the losses be distributed?"

By contrast, Baird has developed a coherent, unified view of bankruptcy that revolves around a single economic construct. According to Baird, the only goal of bankruptcy is to enhance the collection efforts of creditors with state-defined property rights. He explains that all bankruptcy laws are to be tested by a single measure: whether they enhance or diminish the creditors' collective benefits. With that construct, Baird purports to answer a host of wide-ranging questions and translate his policy into specific statutory recommendations.

As Baird and I begin this debate, I am acutely aware that we disagree not only about what bankruptcy policy should be, but also about how that policy should be derived. Baird begins with hypothetical behavior and ends with firmly fixed answers. I begin with a historical observation about legal structures, I surmise the concerns of the drafters, and I end only with tentative conclusions and more complex questions. Baird presumes that there can be a simple answer to explain all of bankruptcy, and that the relationship between statutory law and modification of the behavior of debtors and creditors is known and can be predicted in new circumstances. I see bankruptcy as a more complex and ultimately less confined process than does Baird.

In this paper I discuss our differing views, explaining first the central policy justification of bankruptcy as I see it. In the second section, I contrast my conception of bankruptcy with Baird's view, and I take up his application of theory to the difficult problem of undersecured creditors. In the spirit of forthright debate, I try to expose my ideas enough to provide a target for Baird, and I take direct and specific aim at his work.

I.   THE CENTRAL POLICY JUSTIFICATION OF BANKRUPTCY: COPING WITH DEFAULT IN AN INTEGRATED SYSTEM

Discussing the debtor-creditor system is much like focusing a camera. Different elements of the system are always in view, but depending on where the focus is directed, different features of the system take on greater importance. I want to begin the discussion of bankruptcy by looking briefly at the role the debtor-creditor system plays in a much broader pattern of promise enforcement.

A. Default and Contract Enforcement

The debtor-creditor system is itself part of a larger, integrated order of public enforcement of promises between individuals. An analysis of promise enforcement should begin with contract law—the laws enforcing private promises—and come full circle with bankruptcy law—the laws sanctioning default on private promises. Each element of this system balances against the other.

The enforcement scheme in debtor-creditor law acknowledges values different from those central to contract law. Idiosyncratic factors involved in the changed circumstances of debtors in extreme financial distress become important. Debtors may not be able to meet their obligations for a host of different reasons. Their stupidity, greed, misfortune, bad judgment, or inadequate foresight may leave them unable to pay. They may not be able to pay over the short term or the long term. They may be victims of their own mistakes or of unforeseeable circumstances. Contract law need not take account of the values relevant to sanctioning debtor default, because these values are accounted for in the debtor-creditor collection scheme. Without the refined and balanced system of debtor-creditor law—which includes a well-developed concept of bankruptcy—contract law itself would look very different, and its enforcement would be considerably more constrained.

The definition of an enforceable contract allows some leeway to consider social concerns. Contract principles such as impossibility, mutual mistake, and more recently, duress and unconscionability undercut any naive view of "strict" enforcement. But for the point of this paper, it is sufficient to note that once an agreement has been struck, the subsequent inability of a party to pay or the high cost of payment is rarely an overt feature of contract doctrine. Relatively strict enforceability of contract can prevail precisely because the debtor-creditor system instills a measure of temperance, an ability to respond to changed circumstances, a notion that enforcement should not offend deeply held social norms.

Default—or nonpayment—of debt has long been an essential feature of a system of promise enforcement. Centuries before bankruptcy law became an integrated part of the collection scheme, default existed. Biblical jubilees, medieval English debtor sanctuaries, and poorhouses are evidence of society's past attempts to balance rightful demands for payment with some possibility of escape. When organized forgiveness has been unavailing, debtors have devised their own nonpayment plans. Debtors have been known to flee the jurisdiction, to threaten their creditors, or—as an extreme measure—to die. Even today, with corporate debtors and risk-spreading creditors, a significant feature of the debt collection system is the possibility of escape from payment through a variety of maneuvers, both legal and extralegal. Anyone who ever extends credit faces the possibility that repayment will not be forthcoming. Interest is structured, among other things, to pay the creditor for assuming the risk of nonpayment.

B. Default and the Collection System

The current debt collection system has two primary responses to a debtor's default: state collection law and federal bankruptcy law. When discussing the two collection schemes, it is important to bear in mind that property and contract rights are not synonymous with collection rights. Bankruptcy is only a collection scheme; it necessarily depends on other legal rules for the determination of substantive rights underlying bankruptcy claims. Whether a contract is enforceable, a tort has been committed, or an owner has clear title to a piece of land are issues of substantive state or federal law. Similarly, state collection law is different from the underlying substantive law. State collection law presupposes the enforceability of an underlying claim (as does bankruptcy) and focuses on the rights of a creditor to extract the payment owed (as does bankruptcy). State collection law is about judgments, statutory liens, voluntary security interests, exemptions, garnishment, prejudgment remedies, and so on. The state system and the bankruptcy system are both only collection systems.

Although this distinction between substantive rights and collection rules might seem obvious, it is important to the policy debate, which often centers on the degree to which bankruptcy law should "rely" on underlying state law. The answer depends on which underlying state law is under discussion. The real issue is not whether bankruptcy law—or state collection law, for that matter—relies on state law for the definition of substantive rights. The issue is whether the state collection and distribution scheme presumptively should be the federal scheme. That bankruptcy builds on state substantive law does not require it to build on state collection law.

It would, of course, be possible to create a single, fully integrated debt collection scheme rather than the separate state and federal schemes now in effect. But even a unified scheme would have to consider two prototypes of default: first, the single default where only one creditor complains about repayment and the remaining creditors are evidently (even if only temporarily) content with their repayment prospects; and second, the debtor's widespread default and collapse in which every creditor's prospects for repayment are sharply diminished. These two kinds of default involve some overlapping issues about appropriate collection rights, and a factual continuum from a single default to complete collapse better describes the world that includes the two extremes. Nonetheless, the policy issues involved in the two exemplary circumstances differ importantly, and they must be addressed separately whether they are part of one collection system or two.

The current debt collection system treats these issues in different fora: state collection laws cope with a wide spectrum of limited defaults, while the bankruptcy scheme concentrates on default in the context of the debtor's imminent collapse. The state collection scheme occasionally deals with complete collapse, but overall it is rationalized in order to serve a wide variety of collection needs. The federal bankruptcy scheme, by contrast, reckons with a much more limited factual context, and with very different legal devices such as discharge of debt and distribution of unavoidable losses. The different factual contexts change the focus of the policymaking decisions of state collection law and bankruptcy. . . .

D. Default and Bankruptcy

By contrast with state law, which sees only one default, bankruptcy begins with a presumption of default on every obligation the debtor owes. Although some debtors are able to repay all their debts in bankruptcy, the statutory scheme presumes that some creditors will not enjoy repayment in full. Bankruptcy law aims first to conserve and divide an estate that cannot meet all its obligations, and second to terminate the rights of unpaid creditors. Unlike state law, which considers innumerable circumstances of default, bankruptcy law is sharply focused on the consequences of a debtor's imminent collapse.

The difference from state collection law is fundamental. Bankruptcy disputes do not share the debtor-versus-creditor orientation of state collection law. In bankruptcy, with an inadequate pie to divide and the looming discharge of unpaid debts, the disputes center on who is entitled to shares of the debtor's assets and how these shares are to be divided. Distribution among creditors is not incidental to other concerns; it is the center of the bankruptcy scheme. Accordingly, bankruptcy disputes are better characterized as creditor-versus-creditor, with competing creditors struggling to push the losses of default onto others. The Bankruptcy Code reflects this orientation: a significant part of its distributional scheme is oriented toward establishing priorities among creditors.

The battle between secured and unsecured creditors has commanded much interest, but the Bankruptcy Code tackles a wide variety of other distributional issues as well. Some rights are destroyed in bankruptcy, and some are preserved. Priority distributions reorder the competing interests of employees, taxing authorities, fishermen, and farmers. Landlords and business partners receive special treatment. Parties to executory contracts hold an identified place in the bankruptcy pecking order. The beneficiaries of state statutory liens find their rights reordered in bankruptcy. Ordinary course creditors and creditors making contemporaneous exchanges discover that their positions differ from other unsecured creditors. Creditors lending to consumers are distinguished from creditors lending to businesses. Banks with setoff rights are treated differently from banks not in a setoff position. This list is suggestive rather than definitive, but it serves to show that the Bankruptcy Code is concerned with making hard choices about which creditors belong where in a financial hierarchy. These are choices about distribution and redistribution, and they are not controlled by state law.

The distributional design of the Code is even more thorough than the straight-forward state law's rank-ordering of easily identified creditors such as fishermen and farmers. The bankruptcy system goes so far as to anticipate the consequences of default on a host of potential creditors, including, for example, future tort claimants who have not yet discovered their injuries or their legal rights and a government agency that might uncover toxic wastes and demand that a debtor clean them up. Bankruptcy law recognizes these rights even though they may not be mature under state law at the time of the bankruptcy filing. In the state law system, these creditors would simply wait until they discovered the injuries and then would sue one at a time for the appropriate remedy. They would take their debtors—tortfeasors or toxic polluters—as they found them when their claims matured, whether the debtors were fat with profits or stripped to a hollow shell after earlier creditors had concluded other disputes.

But because bankruptcy recognizes that the pre-bankrupt debtor will not survive to be sued another day, its distributional scheme necessarily focuses on how to deal with future claimants. Several alternatives are possible. Bankruptcy's distributional scheme could leave future claimants to bear their losses in full, refusing to compensate them at all and effectively barring their future claims. If, instead, their rights to compensation continue notwithstanding the bankruptcy, the distributional consequences of bankruptcy will depend on whether the debtor succeeds or fails in any reorganization attempt. Still a third distributional scheme is created if the future claimants are participants in a distribution plan and provisions are made for their eventual—if limited—recovery.

The Bankruptcy Code clearly rejects the alternative of leaving future claimants uncompensated. It defines "claim" broadly to pull future creditors into the debtor's distribution plan and to require participation by anticipated claimants. The Code does not specifically address how to establish funds to pay future claimants and determine appropriate payout priorities, and as a result, the courts must take on the difficult task of devising workable plans. Nonetheless, it is clear that dealing with the effects of default on future claimants was intended to be a significant feature of bankruptcy's distributional scheme.

The Bankruptcy Code accomplishes other distributional ends less directly. By providing for impairment of state law collection rights in a court-supervised reorganization, Chapter 11 of the Bankruptcy Code gives bankrupt businesses another opportunity to succeed. The opportunity may not often result in genuine success, but the reports of Toys-R-Us, Wickes, Continental Airlines, Evans Home Products, and a host of other bankruptcy success stories serve as a reminder that at least some Chapter 11 reorganizations conserve and maximize the wealth of the debtor's estate for the benefit of all claimants—an important objective of bankruptcy.

But the revival of an otherwise failing business also serves the distributional interests of many who are not technically "creditors" but who have an interest in a business's continued existence. Older employees who could not have retrained for other jobs, customers who would have to resort to less attractive, alternative suppliers of goods and services, suppliers who would have lost current customers, nearby property owners who would have suffered declining property values, and states or municipalities that would have faced shrinking tax bases benefit from the reorganization's success. By giving the debtor business an opportunity to reorganize, the bankruptcy scheme acknowledges the losses of those who have depended on the business and redistributes some of the risk of loss from the default. Even if dissolution is inevitable, the bankruptcy process allows for delay, which in turn gives time for all those relying on a business to accommodate the coming change....

E. Distributive Rationales in Bankruptcy

By definition, the distributional issues arising in bankruptcy involve costs to some and benefits to others. Enforcing the state law collection rights of secured creditors often comes at the cost of defeating the state law collection rights of unsecured creditors whose claims are discharged without payment. A priority payment to one unsecured creditor necessarily leaves less for the remaining creditors. The debtor's estate—and thus its creditors—profits from assigning a favorable lease, but this costs the landlord whose lease specifically provided for no assignments. The benefits reaped by the employees or suppliers relying on the continuation of a business are purchased at the expense of every creditor who gives up valuable state collection rights as part of the plan to allow the debtor business a second chance at success.

It might be reasonable to ask about the legitimacy of forcing losses on those with lawful expectations of repayment. The difficulty with this question, however, is that it posits that bankruptcy is the "cause" of the cost. Bankruptcy is not the cause of the cost— it is merely the distributor of the cost. The cost of default is occasioned by the debtor's inability to repay.

Without a bankruptcy system, someone would still bear the costs of default. Perhaps, under the state law collection system, those costs would be borne entirely by unsecured creditors or employees or suppliers or landlords or creditors with loans secured by inventory that is difficult to monitor. But speculation on what would happen at state law is nothing more than the substitution of a different distributional scheme—one created indirectly by focus on the collection of a single debt rather than one created deliberately with an overriding attention to widespread default.

Even if there were no legal scheme to distribute the costs of default, the losses would be distributed by some method. The distribution of losses might be determined by creditor speed (who first backs up to the warehouse with big trucks) or strength (who can carry away the most while others look on) or by debtor favoritism (who gets the first call when the debtor decides to give up). Indeed, outside bankruptcy, it is not clear as an empirical matter whether losses are distributed according to the state law scheme or according to creditor strength, debtor favoritism, or some other factor. But the point is that the costs must be distributed in some manner. Bankruptcy is simply a federal scheme designed to distribute the costs among those at risk. . . .

II. BAIRD'S APPROACH: COLLECTIVISM ALONE

Professor Baird's view of the bankruptcy world is much neater than mine. He explains that there is a single justification for bankruptcy: enhancing the collective return to the creditors. He also explains that there is only one interest to be protected: the interest of those "who, outside of bankruptcy, have property rights in the assets of the firm filing a petition." Baird has rejected the notion that any values other than collectivism may be important in fashioning bankruptcy policy. As the following passage indicates, he at times recognizes the questions that lead eventually to a complex, multifactored analysis:

> Consider the "rehabilitation" goal of a Chapter 11 proceeding. No one, to our knowledge, argues that keeping a firm intact is always a good thing. Yet as soon as one concedes that a reorganization may not always be desirable, one is faced with the problem of understanding and articulating why reorganizations are favored in the first place and how much should be given up to facilitate them.

Yet Baird evidently sees the questions he poses as either unanswerable or too silly to answer, for, having identified them, he says no more. He simply observes:

> The economy of an entire town can be disrupted when a large factory closes. Many employees may be put out of work. The failure of one firm may lead to the failure of those who supplied it with raw materials and those who acquired its finished products. Some believe that preventing such consequences is worth the costs of trying to keep the firm running and justifies placing burdens on a firm's secured creditors. We think that this view is, as a matter of bankruptcy policy, fundamentally wrong.

Without further discussion, Baird concludes that such attempts are "beyond the competence of a bankruptcy court."

Baird makes a point he can defeat by making it too big. Because bankruptcy will not always save a company, and because sometimes the cost of saving the company is too high, this must never be a goal of any bankruptcy policy. Baird refuses to acknowledge the possibility that bankruptcy might give a corporation a limited opportunity to succeed—an opportunity that balances the cost of trying to the creditors against the likelihood of eventual success. He acknowledges neither the potential benefit of a second chance nor the possibility that bankruptcy policy might aim toward a broad balance between the competing interests of the debtor, the creditors, and the many others who may be injured by the debtor's collapse.

Baird also considers the role of other distributional issues in bankruptcy and concludes that they should play none. He explains, for example, that the question of whether secured creditors should be paid ahead of anyone else "is not one peculiar to bankruptcy law" and then does little more than assert that the arguments for or against favoring the payment rights of secured creditors

> would apply with equal force to any group given favored treatment under nonbankruptcy law. The desirability of secured credit—or other nonbankruptcy property rights—is ultimately not a bankruptcy question and attempting to transform it into one creates incentives that are perverse and counterproductive.

Thus, the distributional issues involved in determining the creditors' legal pecking order are, according to Baird, the same whether the debtor is in default on a single obligation or in a state of complete collapse.

Having dispensed with any other policy considerations, Baird is ready to turn to his single justification for bankruptcy: enhancing the collective return for creditors who have identified property rights. Here Baird purports to use only careful logic to answer some of the most intractable bankruptcy problems, all the while avoiding any discussion of the distributional consequences of his work. The difficulty with Baird's approach is that collectivism alone won't get him where he is going. He necessarily uses—even if he does not discuss—distributional principles. Moreover, Baird endorses the wholesale use of the state law distributional scheme, but he does not defend the distributional rationale of that scheme, nor does he address the possibility that the state scheme was designed to resolve questions significantly different from those to which he applies it.

Baird is engaged in a game of pulling rabbits from other hats. He may actually have a distributional principle to defend; he could argue that state law better distributes risks between secured and unsecured creditors than does current bankruptcy law. We could debate that conclusion, but even that debate would accept the premise that bankruptcy is designed to resolve difficult distributional choices. Instead, Baird purports to avoid distributional concerns—and the attendant normative and empirical issues—by discussing only the "neutral" principle of collectivism. I believe Baird only diverts the debate from the central issues.

A. Collectivism: The Test That Isn't

Collectivism provides a useful way to examine some bankruptcy problems. Baird shows how the need for collectivism can explain why the bankruptcy system substitutes a single, lower-cost action for expensive, multiple individual actions. His analogy between state collection law and the wild car races of "It's a Mad, Mad, Mad, Mad World" makes a delightful story that helps explain a very important function of bankruptcy: bankruptcy calls a halt to the superaggressive, wasteful, and potentially damaging creditor activity permitted by state law.

My dispute with Baird centers instead upon his attempts to use collectivism not only to explain significant features of the bankruptcy system, but also to justify the entire system and to provide answers to specific, complex questions. Baird sees collectivism as something of an intellectual yardstick, a tool that he can use to determine whether a particular bankruptcy proposal is good or bad—solely by measuring whether it promotes or impairs collectivism. Yet Baird ultimately uses collectivism, once a useful theme in a more complex bankruptcy system, to obscure a very different analysis.

Baird chooses to test his collectivist principle in an *American Mariner* situation where he wrestles with the very difficult question of how to determine appropriate rights for the undersecured creditor during a pending bankruptcy proceeding. Baird observes that creditors often have interests hostile to each other in the resolution of a bankruptcy case. The secured creditor is often interested in immediate liquidation, repossession, and repayment from the sale of the repossessed collateral. By contrast, the unsecured creditors—who are likely to receive little or nothing in a liquidation—are interested in allowing the company to retain the collateral and to make one more try at reorganization. Secured creditors claim that unsecured creditors are trying to deny them access to their collateral and to risk its eventual loss, while unsecured creditors claim that secured creditors are destroying the reorganization before it can begin. Baird resolves this impasse with the measuring stick of collectivism: collectivist goals will be met only if the bankruptcy estate (effectively, in Baird's example, the debtor and the unsecured creditors) bears the interest costs of using the secured creditor's collateral during the period of the reorganization and repayment plan. According to Baird, only if all secured creditors—including the undersecured—receive post-petition interest will collectivism be served.

[Permission requested.]

Douglas G Baird, "Loss Distribution, Forum Shopping, and Bankruptcy: A Reply to Warren" (1987) 54 *University of Chicago Law Review* 815 at 816–22 and 828–31 (footnotes and page references omitted)

[This response to] Warren's attack on the theory of bankruptcy that I have developed with Thomas Jackson goes to methodology. Jackson and I claim that we can isolate bankruptcy issues (such as whether the trustee should be able to void preferences) from the question of how losses should be borne in the event that a firm fails (such as whether secured creditors should be paid before tort victims). Warren insists that we cannot do this. The issue, it must be noted, is not *how* losses from a firm failure should be distributed, but whether this question (however hard it may be to answer) is a question of the law generally (as Jackson and I would argue) or one peculiar to bankruptcy law (as Warren would argue).

Even though Warren and I usually end up in the same place, our debate is important. The way in which Jackson and I think about bankruptcy law is so different from the approach of traditional scholars like Warren that we may reach different conclusions about new issues that confront both Congress and the courts. In the first part of my response to Warren, I briefly review the major features of her view of bankruptcy policy and explain why I find it wanting. In the subsequent parts, I try to show what drives my own view of bankruptcy policy.

I. THE TRADITIONAL VIEW OF BANKRUPTCY POLICY

Warren admits that her own view of bankruptcy policy is "dirty, complex, elastic, [and] interconnected" But like most traditional views of bankruptcy policy, it rests on a number of fairly simple propositions: (1) bankruptcy law has a special role to play in determining how losses from a business failure should be borne; (2) creditors as well as others may sometimes be required to give up some of their ultimate rights to the assets of the firm so that the firm will have a better chance of surviving; (3) entrusting a bankruptcy judge with equitable discretion is a useful and unobjectionable way to balance the conflicting and competing interests of the parties; and (4) creditors in bankruptcy have no cause to complain when they lose some rights they had outside of bankruptcy, because bankruptcy is an entirely new game that deals with different kinds of problems. These propositions sound innocuous enough, but none of them can withstand close scrutiny, and adhering to them invites analysis that is unfocused and misguided.

Warren asserts that the law must distribute losses that flow from a business failure and that distributing such losses should be the central concern of bankruptcy law. The second observation, however, does not follow from the first. As long as many firms close or fail outside of bankruptcy, treating the question of how to distribute the losses that flow from a business failure as a bankruptcy question ignores much of the problem and creates perverse incentives. Warren argues, for example, that bankruptcy law should favor those who are least able to bear the costs of a business failure. For this reason, she argues, employees rightly enjoy their limited priority under existing bankruptcy law. Warren, however, needs to explain why those who are least able to bear these costs should nevertheless bear them when the firm closes or fails outside of bankruptcy. (Warren cannot be arguing that the costs should be distributed the same way regardless of whether a bankruptcy petition is filed, because when losses are distributed the same way inside of bankruptcy as outside, distribution of losses is not a *bankruptcy* problem.)

Warren's argument for protecting workers only when the firm is in bankruptcy (and not when a firm closes without defaulting to its creditors or when the creditors work out their differences with the firm without filing a bankruptcy petition) is hard to understand:

> Bankruptcy does not, of course, offer complete protection to all those who might be affected by the outcome of a bankruptcy dispute.... [T]he *debtor* is always free to redeploy the firm's assets.... Chapter 11 offers only limited protection against the *creditors'* making the decision to dissolve the business [emphasis in original].

Warren seems to derive what bankruptcy law ought to be from what it is, but one cannot derive the normative from the positive. Moreover, it seems odd to argue, as a matter of policy, that existing management should be able to close a plant and throw workers out, but that those who lent money to the management and who come into control of the firm only because the firm failed to meet its obligations to them should not. From the perspective of the workers who are tossed out, the loss is the same in both cases.

Even if one argues that creditors should bear greater legal obligations to workers than should shareholders, it will not do to advocate giving workers a special priority in bankruptcy but not elsewhere. In a world in which workers enjoy a special priority only in bankruptcy, creditors will strive to resolve their differences outside of bankruptcy. To argue that there should be differences between the obligations of the debtor and those of the creditors is not the same as arguing that there should be differences between obligations in and out of bankruptcy.

Warren thinks that the benefits of bankruptcy justify additional burdens on creditors. But the issue is not whether the burdens on creditors in bankruptcy are just, but whether the burdens should exist only in bankruptcy. Creditors enjoy the benefits of the non-bankruptcy debt collection system as well. Why should they not have to take the rights of workers into account when they use that system? More to the point, taxing creditors differently depending on which enforcement mechanism they use invites troublesome forum shopping. But Warren does not take the problem of forum shopping seriously. In Warren's world, workers are protected from the costs of a business failure only when their employer and its creditors choose to enter bankruptcy. Why the rights of workers should turn on the decision of those who have every incentive to ignore them is baffling.

Warren seems to inhabit the middle ground between the position that Jackson and I have developed (that *bankruptcy* policy is limited only to the problems associated with multiple default) and the opposite position (that bankruptcy policy and the problem of distributing losses from firm failures and closings are one and the same). Warren must believe that there is a special set of concerns when a firm fails and at the same time defaults to multiple creditors, for Warren's conception of bankruptcy, like mine, does not extend to cases in which a firm fails or closes without defaulting to multiple creditors. (Indeed, such a conception of bankruptcy would be so foreign that it would be hard to call it bankruptcy.) Warren, however, never explains the link that she and many others see between multiple default and firm failure; she never explains why the presence of a dispute among creditors requires a special set of rules governing the distribution of losses from the closing or failure of a firm.

Warren and others seem to think that a glance at history and situation sense make the link self-evident. Jackson and I, however, have made two points that should give pause to those who find it hard to put aside the lay intuition that a firm that fails is a firm that "goes bankrupt." First, we raise the problem of forum shopping, which I have already mentioned and to which I shall return. Even if bankruptcy's gatekeeping rules were much better than they are, those who want a special legal regime governing loss distribution when a firm fails or closes at the same time it defaults to creditors must expect to see in bankruptcy many cases that do not belong there, and many cases outside bankruptcy that belong in bankruptcy.

The second point is deeper. To argue that a special set of distributional concerns arises when a debtor defaults to many creditors at the same time it fails or closes is to assume a link exists between who has rights to the assets of a firm and how those assets are used. Such links are hard to show and harder to justify, as a large body of literature has shown. Traditional bankruptcy scholars are alone in the academy in their belief that the financing decisions of a firm and its investment decisions are inseparable. Whether a firm continues to manufacture a particular product or even stays in business is an issue utterly distinct from the question of who owns the firm's assets. Thus, in a world in which all assertions of ownership rights are stayed (as they are in bankruptcy), how much a particular owner gets should have *nothing* to do with how a firm's assets are used or whether it stays in business. To assert, as Warren does, that a creditor may need to sacrifice some of its ownership interest so that the firm might survive takes issue with most of what has been written about corporate finance over the last three decades. Warren argues that the legislative history of the Bankruptcy Code shows that some legislators embraced the idea that limiting the rights of creditors may increase a firm's chances of reorganizing successfully. I could dispute whether that is a fair reading of the legislative history, but this is quite beside the point. Limiting the rights of creditors either affects a firm's chance of surviving or it does not. The truth of the proposition is completely independent of what Congress may or may not have thought; the proposition must stand or fall on its own. If Warren wants to rely on it, she should at least acknowledge the body of authority that goes the other way.

Warren relies throughout on the bankruptcy judge to ensure that everything comes out right in the end. But judicial discretion is no panacea, even in a court of equity. Warren puts too much faith in the ability of bankruptcy judges to control the conflicting incentives of the various parties. Controlling a party who has an incentive to misbehave is inherently difficult, and alternatives such as eliminating the incentive entirely are sometimes available. As between eliminating a bad incentive and asking a bankruptcy judge to police misbehavior, Jackson and I favor the former. Allowing someone to gamble with someone else's money is always a bad idea, even when a conscientious judge is looking over the gambler's shoulder. Jackson and I have no objection to judicial discretion per se. The art of judging inevitably requires an intelligent weighing of competing interests. But we live in an imperfect world. Judges, like the rest of us, are prone to error. The advantages and disadvantages of judicial discretion under any set of conditions must be weighed against the alternatives. Our argument is simply that Warren and other traditional scholars are too willing to accept the steady hand of a fair judge when other ways of keeping the parties in line may be preferable.

The last theme that Warren dwells upon arises from her observation that the rights of secured creditors change for better as well as worse when a bankruptcy petition is filed. Tracking down assets may be easier when a bankruptcy petition is filed and a trustee is appointed. From this, Warren draws the conclusion that the secured creditor has nothing to complain about. A creditor who claims both the benefits of bankruptcy procedures and the benefits of substantive rights under nonbankruptcy law is trying to have it both ways.

This strand to Warren's argument, however, is defective in two respects. First, it assumes that Jackson and I would neglect the procedural difficulties that creditors would have under state law in calculating the value of their rights. But we have consistently taken the opposite view. We would insist, for example, that for purposes of adequate protection, the value of the secured creditor's rights should be measured as of the time it would have been able to repossess and sell the collateral under state law. Second, Warren confuses the question of whether an inquiry is difficult and inexact with whether it should be undertaken at all. Jackson and I have argued that powerful reasons exist for ensuring that rights in and outside of bankruptcy remain constant. To assert that maintaining parity is difficult may be an argument for settling on an approximation and being content with rough justice, but it is not an argument against parity. The difficulty of keeping rights constant inside and outside of bankruptcy should not mean that anything goes. . . .

All that Jackson and I require is that the differences in the two avenues follow from the reasons for having the two avenues in the first place. We have no objection to differences in multiple avenues of enforcement. We object only to *unnecessary* differences.

Warren agrees that a tension will exist in bankruptcy between senior and junior creditors; but she argues that there are many ways of overcoming these tensions, including, for example, denying recognition to secured creditors in bankruptcy altogether. There are, of course, many ways of ensuring that fights between creditors in bankruptcy do not destroy the value of the firm as a whole, including relying (as Warren would) on the steady hand of a fair bankruptcy judge. But each way is different, and one must have a method for choosing among them. Jackson and I have argued that we should adopt the alternative that minimizes forum shopping. Warren misses that point when she claims that giving all creditors equal status in bankruptcy is the logical extension of our position. Allowing priorities outside of bankruptcy but not inside is an open invitation to forum shopping and would exacerbate all the problems Jackson and I want to minimize. Treating secured and unsecured creditors alike in bankruptcy while recognizing priority rights elsewhere makes no more sense than making the rights of workers turn on the city in which the litigation is brought. . . .

IV. "REHABILITATION," NONCOGNIZABLE INJURIES, AND BANKRUPTCY POLICY

Warren suggests that bankruptcy law should be designed to keep businesses from closing even when those with legally cognizable interests in the business want it to close. She does not, however, explain why special rules in bankruptcy are necessary to achieve this goal. One could, for example, have a federal statute that prevented any business from ceasing operations without making a showing in court that the business was unprofitable, destined to fail, or whatever. One cannot say that bankruptcy is necessary to protect those without legally cognizable interests without first answering the question of why these individuals cannot be given such interests. Similarly, one should not assert that bankruptcy law is necessary to prevent the owners of firms from taking actions that injure third parties without explaining why some other kind of legal rule cannot prevent these injuries without encouraging forum shopping.

The law by omission or commission affects who bears the losses from a failed business, but one must explain why placing the solution in bankruptcy law is the preferred course of action. Business "failure" is not necessarily connected with default. Moreover, default itself is not necessarily connected with bankruptcy. Any time resources are shifted from one use to another, or from one place to another, there are likely to be spillover effects — both positive and negative. If I run a business that makes widgets, I might decide tomorrow to get out of that business and invest my money elsewhere. I can make that decision even if the business is not insolvent. I can make that decision even if the business is not in default. Indeed, I can make that decision even if the business has no creditors at all. The rust belt is littered with firms that have closed or moved elsewhere, not because these businesses did not have enough to pay off creditors, but because they had better opportunities elsewhere. Such a decision has exactly the same effect on workers and customers and nearby property owners as does the decision to close up shop of an insolvent business after default to numerous creditors and a bankruptcy petition is filed. Warren nowhere explains what it is about default in bankruptcy against those with legally cognizable injuries that suddenly makes the injuries of others relevant. If Warren thinks bankruptcy proceedings are appropriate whenever a firm fails or closes and such dislocations happen, she must contemplate court intervention so dramatically different from current bankruptcy proceedings that using the word "bankruptcy" to describe it is inappropriate.

As I noted earlier, one should not link default and bankruptcy. Default is not necessarily connected with a collective action problem. Indeed, it is because default does not *always* raise a collective problem that there are two avenues of enforcement: the existence of bankruptcy's avenue of enforcement springs from the collective action problem. When Warren focuses on *default*, she does not tell us why default policies should exist only in bankruptcy. To discuss bankruptcy policy, one must discuss default in connection with the existence of more than one procedure for vindicating the legal rights that arise from the default. Linking—without explanation—default to only one of several different avenues of enforcement threatens to undermine whatever justifications exist for having multiple avenues of enforcement in the first instance.

In thinking about bankruptcy policy as applied to corporations and other business entities, one must be careful not to confuse them with flesh-and-blood persons. Warren is rhetorically most effective when she alludes to poorhouses, sanctuaries, and escapes to foreign jurisdictions in discussing the problem of insolvent debtors, but none of this has much to do with the bankruptcy of a corporation. Legal disputes in corporate bankruptcies frequently are between financial institutions and sophisticated investors. The bankruptcy of a corporation does not necessarily mean that anyone will starve. Warren can argue that we should have a special concern for those who are not professionals, but she must show both that this concern is a bankruptcy concern and that it should affect all bankruptcy disputes—even those between professionals. As a positive matter, Warren is wrong to think that existing bankruptcy law cares about the rights of noncreditors. A bankruptcy judge takes these into account only when there is a dispute between those with legally cognizable claims. Contrary to Warren's assertion, creditors are as free to close a firm down as are its managers, inside of bankruptcy and out, as long as the creditors present a united front.

The problem of retiree health benefits provides a good test for Warren's claim that only bankruptcy law is primarily concerned with priorities when there is not enough to go around. A firm promises health benefits to its workers when they retire. If the firm files a Chapter 7 petition, the retirees probably have only unsecured claims against the firm. Section 507 gives them no special priority. Under existing law, the retirees will receive only a few cents on the dollar for their health claims. If a legislator asked Warren about the problem, what would she say? Would Warren advocate bringing retiree health benefits within the scope of section 507? Would she raise the $2,000 cap? Would she insist on empirical data? Would she want to leave the rights of retirees to a bankruptcy judge and have the judge balance the worth of these rights against other interests?

[Permission requested.]

Practice Questions

Question 1
As you make your way through the materials in the casebook, consider the extent to which the Jackson and Baird belief that bankruptcy's only legitimate function (using bankruptcy

in the broader American sense) is to resolve the collective-action problem existing outside bankruptcy, and that other goals must be eschewed, is reflected in the Canadian system. In particular, they say that pre-bankruptcy rights should not be changed in bankruptcy because this distorts bankruptcy's goals. Is this the case in the Canadian system?

CHAPTER 2

Constitutional Aspects and the Judicial and Administrative Structure of the Bankruptcy System

I. CONSTITUTIONAL ASPECTS

A. Introduction

Section 91(21) of the *Constitution Act, 1867* vests "exclusive" power in the federal government to enact laws in relation to "bankruptcy and insolvency." Despite the clarity of those words, the constitutional jurisprudence interpreting them contains inconsistencies and contradictions which remain difficult to reconcile in their totality. In large part, this can be attributed to the fact that conceptions of bankruptcy and insolvency have changed over time. Modern views are much evolved from nineteenth-century ideas. Over time, the growth and development of the Canadian economy and the changing function of debt in society have seen the bankruptcy and insolvency law power applied in new contexts, in pursuit of new objectives. The history of bankruptcy and insolvency in Canada is very much that of an "expanding concept," as described by Roger Tassé.[1] This expansion has benefited from judicial imprimatur, as no federal bankruptcy or insolvency statute has ever been declared ultra vires. It also represents part of a broader trend toward greater federalism following the Great Depression and World War II.

The expansion of bankruptcy and insolvency legislation has led to new areas of overlap, and sometimes conflict, most often vis-à-vis the provincial governments' jurisdiction under section 92(13) "property and civil rights." Since 2015, the Supreme Court of Canada has considered five cases relating to bankruptcy and insolvency law, four of which represented a contest between sections 91(21) and 92(13). In two instances, this conflict was resolved in favour of the federal power, while in two cases no conflict was found to exist. Today, constitutional discussions are among the hottest topics in the bankruptcy and insolvency field.

At earlier points in Canada's history, the lack of a federal bankruptcy law, or the deficiencies of bankruptcy legislation, prompted the Provinces to enact legislation dealing with overindebtedness. One such statute came under constitutional scrutiny in the *Ontario (Attorney General) v Canada (Attorney General) [1894]* case, and was ultimately upheld as valid provincial legislation. In 1960, a similar voluntary debt repayment statute was declared ultra vires, prompting Parliament to enact essentially the same voluntary debt repayment program as part of federal bankruptcy law. These two cases — decided just over sixty-five years apart — offer contrasting approaches to determining the constitutionality of provincial regimes relating to overindebtedness. They illustrate one of the unresolved contradictions in the constitutional caselaw on bankruptcy and insolvency.

---

1   Canada, Study Committee on Bankruptcy and Insolvency Legislation, *Report of the Study Committee on Bankruptcy and Insolvency Legislation* (Ottawa: Information Canada, 1970) at 5 (Chair: Roger Tassé) [Tassé Report].

Part I of this chapter reproduces extracts from some of the leading cases that illustrate the scope of the federal power and the validity of provincial laws addressing insolvency issues. The key issues are: (1) the meaning of "bankruptcy and insolvency" in section 91(21) of the Constitution; (2) restrictions on federal legislation adopted under the bankruptcy and insolvency power and on administrative powers delegated under bankruptcy legislation on courts, trustees, and other officials; (3) circumstances under which the courts will uphold insolvency-type legislation adopted by the provinces; and (4) conflicts where provincial remedial legislation may encroach on the federal bankruptcy and insolvency authority. The closing section of this Part considers the influence of the Superintendent of Bankruptcy as a party in constitutional cases concerning the bankruptcy and insolvency power. The Office of the Superintendent is discussed further in Part II of this chapter, which provides an overview of the structure of the bankruptcy system under the *Bankruptcy and Insolvency Act*, RSC 1985, c B-3 (*BIA*).

Ontario (Attorney General) v Canada (Attorney General), [1894] UKPC 13, [1894] AC 189

THE LORD CHANCELLOR: This appeal is presented by the Attorney-General of Ontario against a decision of the Court of Appeal of that province.

The decision complained of was an answer given to a question referred to that Court by the Lieutenant-Governor of the province in pursuance of an Order in Council.

The question was as follows:

> Had the Legislature of Ontario jurisdiction to enact the 9th section of the Revised Statutes of Ontario, c. 124, and entitled "An Act respecting Assignments and Preferences by Insolvent Persons"?

The majority of the Court answered this question in the negative; but one of the judges who formed the majority only concurred with his brethren because he thought the case was governed by a previous decision of the same Court; had he considered the matter *res integra* he would have decided the other way. The Court was thus equally divided in opinion.

It is not contested that the enactment, the validity of which is in question, is within the legislative powers conferred on the provincial legislature by sect. 92 of the *British North America Act, 1867*, which enables that legislature to make laws in relation to property and civil rights in the province unless it is withdrawn from their legislative competency by the provisions of the 91st section of that Act which confers upon the Dominion Parliament the exclusive power of legislation with reference to bankruptcy and insolvency.

The point to be determined, therefore, is the meaning of those words in sect. 91 of the *British North America Act, 1867*, and whether they render the enactment impeached *ultra vires* of the provincial legislature. That enactment is sect. 9 of the Revised Statutes of Ontario of 1887, c. 124, entitled "An Act respecting Assignment and Preferences by Insolvent Persons." The section is as follows:

> An assignment for the general benefit of creditors under this Act shall take precedence of all judgments and of all executions not completely executed by payment, subject to the lien, if any, of an execution creditor for his costs, where there is but one execution in the sheriff's hands, or to the lien, if any, of the creditor for his costs, who has the first execution in the sheriff's hands.

In order to understand the effect of this enactment it is necessary to have recourse to other sections of the Act to see what is meant by the words "an assignment for the general benefit of creditors under this Act."

The first section enacts that if any person in insolvent circumstances, or knowing himself to be on the eve of insolvency, voluntarily confesses judgment, or gives a warrant of attorney to confess judgment, with intent to defeat or delay his creditors, or to give any creditor a preference over his other creditors, every such confession or warrant of attorney shall be void as against the creditors of the party giving it.

The 2nd section avoids as against the other creditors any gift or assignment of goods or other property made by a person at a time when he is in insolvent circumstances, or knows that he is on the eve of insolvency, with intent to defeat, delay, or prejudice his creditors or give any of them a preference.

Then follows sect. 3, which is important:

Its 1st sub-section provides that nothing in the preceding section shall apply to an assignment made to the sheriff of a county in which the debtor resides or carries on business, or to any assignee resident within the province with the consent of his creditors as thereinafter provided for the purpose of paying, rateably and proportionately, and without preference or priority all the creditors of the debtor their just debts.

The 2nd sub-section enacts that every assignment for the general benefit of creditors which is not void under sect. 2 but is not made to the sheriff nor to any other person with the prescribed consent of the creditors shall be void as against a subsequent assignment which is in conformity with the Act, and shall be subject in other respects to the provisions of the Act, until and unless a subsequent assignment is executed in accordance therewith.

The 5th sub-section states the nature of the consent of the creditors which is requisite for assignment in the first instance to some person other than the sheriff.

These are the only sections to which it is necessary to refer in order to explain the meaning of sect. 9.

Before discussing the effect of the enactments to which attention has been called, it will be convenient to glance at the course of legislation in relation to this and cognate matters both in the province and in the Dominion. The enactment's of the 1st and 2nd sections of the Act of 1887 are to be found in substance in sects. 18 and 19 of the Act of the Province of Canada passed in 1858 for the better prevention of fraud. There is a proviso to the latter section which excepts from its operation any assignment made for the purpose of paying all the creditors of the debtor rateably without preference. These provisions were repeated in the Revised Statutes of Ontario, 1877, c. 118. A slight amendment was made by the Act of 1884, and it was as thus amended that they were re-enacted in 1887. At the time when the statute of 1858 was passed there was no bankruptcy law in force in the Province of Canada. In the year 1864 an Act respecting insolvency was enacted. It applied in Lower Canada to traders only; in Upper Canada to all persons whether traders or non-traders. It provided that a debtor should be deemed insolvent and his estate should become subject to compulsory liquidation if he committed certain acts similar to those which had for a long period been made acts of bankruptcy in this country. Among these acts were the assignment or the procuring of his property to be seized in execution with intent to defeat or delay his creditors, and also a general assignment of his property for the benefit of his creditors otherwise than in manner provided by the statute. A person who was unable to meet his engagements might avoid compulsory liquidation by making an assignment of his estate in the manner provided by that Act; but unless he made such an assignment within the time limited the liquidation became compulsory.

This Act was in operation at the time when the *British North America Act* came into force.

In 1869 the Dominion Parliament passed an *Insolvency Act* which proceeded on much the same lines as the Provincial Act of 1864, but applied to traders only. This Act was repealed by a new *Insolvency Act of 1875*, which, after being twice amended, was, together with the Amending Acts, repealed in 1880.

In 1887, the same year in which the Act under consideration was passed, the provincial legislature abolished priority amongst creditors by an execution in the High Court and county courts, and provided for the distribution of any moneys levied on an execution rateably amongst all execution creditors, and all other creditors who within a month delivered to the sheriff writs and certificates obtained in the manner provided for by that Act.

Their Lordships proceed now to consider the nature of the enactment said to be *ultra vires*. It postpones judgments and executions not completely executed by payment to an assignment for the benefit of creditors under the Act. Now there can be no doubt that the effect to be given to judgments and executions and the manner and extent to which they may be made available for the recovery of debts are *prima facie* within the legislative powers of the provincial parliament. Executions are a part of the machinery by which debts are recovered, and are subject to regulation by that parliament. A creditor has no inherent right to have his debt satisfied by means of a levy by the sheriff, or to any priority in respect of such levy. The execution is a mere creature of the law which may determine and regulate the rights to which it gives rise. The Act of 1887 which abolished priority as amongst execution creditors provided a simple means by which every creditor might obtain a share in the distribution of moneys levied under an execution by any particular creditor. The other Act of the same year, containing the section which is impeached, goes a step further, and gives to all creditors under an assignment for their general benefit a right to a rateable share of the assets of the debtor, including those which have been seized in execution.

But it is argued that inasmuch as this assignment contemplates the insolvency of the debtor, and would only be made if he were insolvent, such a provision purports to deal with insolvency, and therefore is a matter exclusively within the jurisdiction of the Dominion Parliament. Now it is to be observed that an assignment for the general benefit of creditors has long been known to the jurisprudence of this country and also of Canada, and has its force and effect at common law quite independently of any system of bankruptcy or insolvency, or any legislation relating thereto. So far from being regarded as an essential part of the bankruptcy law, such an assignment was made an act of bankruptcy on which an adjudication might be founded, and by the law of the Province of Canada which prevailed at the time when the *Dominion Act* was passed, it was one of the grounds for an adjudication of insolvency.

It is to be observed that the word "bankruptcy" was apparently not used in Canadian legislation, but the insolvency law of the Province of Canada was precisely analogous to what was known in England as the bankruptcy law.

Moreover, the operation of an assignment for the benefit of creditors was precisely the same, whether the assignor was or was not in fact insolvent. It was open to any debtor who might deem his solvency doubtful, and who desired in that case that his creditors should be equitably dealt with, to make an assignment for their benefit. The validity of the assignment and its effect would in no way depend on the insolvency of the assignor, and their Lordships think it clear that the 9th section would equally apply whether the assignor was or was not insolvent. Stress was laid on the fact that the enactment relates only to an assignment under the Act containing the section, and that the Act prescribes that the sheriff of the county is to be the assignee unless a majority of the creditors consent to some other assignee being named. This does not appear to their Lordships to be material. If the enactment would have been *intra vires*, supposing sect. 9 had applied to all assignments without these restrictions, it seems difficult to contend that it became *ultra vires* by reason of them. Moreover, it is to be observed that by sub-sect. 2 of sect. 3, assignments for the benefit of creditors not made to the sheriff or to other persons with the prescribed consent, although they are rendered void as against assignments so made, are nevertheless, unless and until so avoided, to be "subject in other respects to the provisions" of the Act.

At the time when the *British North America Act* was passed bankruptcy and insolvency legislation existed, and was based on very similar provisions both in Great Britain and the Province of Canada. Attention has already been drawn to the Canadian Act.

The English Act then in force was that of 1861. That Act applied to traders and non-traders alike. Prior to that date the operation of the Bankruptcy Acts had been confined to traders. The statutes relating to insolvent debtors, other than traders, had been designed to provide for their release from custody on their making an assignment of the whole of their estate for the benefit of their creditors.

It is not necessary to refer in detail to the provisions of the Act of 1861. It is enough to say that it provided for a legal adjudication in bankruptcy with the consequence that the bankrupt was divested of all his property and its distribution amongst his creditors was provided for.

It is not necessary in their Lordships' opinion, nor would it be expedient to attempt to define, what is covered by the words "bankruptcy" and "insolvency" in sect. 91 of the *British North America Act*. But it will be seen that it is a feature common to all the systems of bankruptcy and insolvency to which reference has been made, that the enactments are designed to secure that in the case of an insolvent person his assets shall be rateably distributed amongst his creditors whether he is willing that they shall be so distributed or not. Although provision may be made for a voluntary assignment as an alternative, it is only as an alternative. In reply to a question put by their Lordships the learned counsel for the respondent were unable to point to any scheme of bankruptcy or insolvency legislation which did not involve some power of compulsion by process of law to secure to the creditors the distribution amongst them of the insolvent debtor's estate.

In their Lordships' opinion these considerations must be borne in mind when interpreting the words "bankruptcy" and "insolvency" in the *British North America Act*. It appears to their Lordships that such provisions as are found in the enactment in question, relating as they do to assignments purely voluntary, do not infringe on the exclusive legislative power conferred upon the Dominion Parliament. They would observe that a system of bankruptcy legislation may frequently require various ancillary provisions for the purpose of preventing the scheme of the Act from being defeated. It may be necessary for this purpose to deal with the effect of executions and other matters which would otherwise be within the legislative competence of the provincial legislature. Their Lordships do not doubt that it would be open to the Dominion Parliament to deal with such matters as part of a bankruptcy law, and the provincial legislature would doubtless be then precluded from interfering with this legislation inasmuch as such interference would affect the bankruptcy law of the Dominion Parliament. But it does not follow that such subjects, as might properly be treated as ancillary to such a law and therefore within the powers of the Dominion Parliament, are excluded from the legislative authority of the provincial legislature when there is no bankruptcy or insolvency legislation of the Dominion Parliament in existence.

Their Lordships will therefore humbly advise Her Majesty that the decision of the Court of Appeal ought to be reversed, and that the question ought to be answered in the affirmative.

Decision of Ontario Court of Appeal reversed.

Discussion

Section 2 of the *BIA* defines bankruptcy as "the state of being bankrupt or the fact of becoming bankrupt" and an insolvent person as:

> a person who is not bankrupt and who resides, carries on business or has property in Canada, whose liabilities to creditors provable as claims under this Act amount to one thousand dollars, and
>
> (a) who is for any reason unable to meet his obligations as they generally become due,
> (b) who has ceased paying his current obligations in the ordinary course of business as they generally become due, or
> (c) the aggregate of whose property is not, at a fair valuation, sufficient, or, if disposed of at a fairly conducted sale under legal process, would not be sufficient to enable payment of all his obligations, due and accruing due.

The definition of insolvency describes a period that is prior to bankruptcy, but where the debtor is financially distressed such as to come within the parameters of the legislation.

The *Companies' Creditors Arrangement Act*, RSC 1985, c C-36 (*CCAA*) does not contain a definition for insolvency, and for many years the courts simply referred to the *BIA* definition. However, in *Re Stelco Inc* (2004), 48 CBR (4th) 299 (Ont Sup Ct J) (*Re Stelco*), leave to appeal to CA refused [2004] OJ No 1903, Farley J of the Ontario Superior Court held that "insolvent" should be given an expanded meaning under the *CCAA* in order to give effect to the rehabilitative goal of the *Act* (at para 23). The Court concluded that it would defeat the purpose of the *CCAA* to limit or prevent an application until the financial difficulties of the applicant are so advanced that the applicant would not have sufficient financial resources to successfully complete its restructuring. Under this approach, a court should determine whether there is a reasonably foreseeable expectation at the time of filing that there is a looming liquidity condition or crisis that will result in the applicant running out of money to pay its debts as they generally become due in the future without the benefit of the stay and ancillary protection. How far forward the court should look will vary according to the complexity of and time required to complete a restructuring. Justice Farley did not consider the constitutional aspects of his contextual and functional approach and whether section 91(21) admits of this degree of flexibility. *Re Stelco* is extracted in Chapter 12. Justice Farley's reasoning has subsequently been adopted in numerous *CCAA* judgments. See *ATB Financial v Metcalfe & Mansfield Alternative Investments II Corp* (2008), 42 CBR (5th) 90 (Ont Sup Ct J) and *Re Priszm Income Fund*, 2011 ONSC 2061.

As far as US law is concerned, under the US *Bankruptcy Code*,[2] a debtor can file a petition for relief under a chapter of the Code — for example, chapter 7 or chapter 11 — without having to prove that the debtor is insolvent, because US courts have given a very elastic meaning to "bankruptcy" and to Congressional power under art 1, §8 of the Constitution to adopt bankruptcy legislation. US courts do not treat the word "bankruptcy" as a term of art and the US Supreme Court has consistently refused to restrict Congressional powers to the type of bankruptcy legislation extant in England in 1776. In an oft cited passage, the US Supreme Court,

---

2   11 USC §101.

while noting that "[t]he subject of bankruptcies is incapable of final definition," also defined "bankruptcy" as the "subject of the relations between an insolvent or nonpaying or fraudulent debtor and his creditors, extending to his and their relief."[3] Tabb states the position still more broadly and claims that "[t]oday virtually any law that addresses the relationship between creditors and a financially distressed debtor, and readjusts the respective rights of those parties, falls within the 'subject of bankruptcies.'"[4]

Validity of Orderly Payment of Debts Act, 1959 (Alta), [1960] SCR 571

KERWIN CJC (for himself and Taschereau, Fauteux, Abbott, Judson and Ritchie JJ): Under the provisions of *The Constitutional Questions Act*, RSA 1955, c. 55, the Lieutenant-Governor in Council of the Province of Alberta referred to the Appellate Division of the Supreme Court of the Province [(1959), 20 DLR (2d) 503] the following question for hearing and consideration:

> Is The *Orderly Payment of Debts Act*, being Chapter 61 of the Statutes of Alberta, 1959, *intra vires* the Legislature of Alberta, either in whole or in part, and if so, in what part or parts, and to what extent? . . .

Mr. Steer [counsel on behalf of the creditors] contended that the subject matter of the Act dealt with bankruptcy and insolvency and was therefore within the sole competence of the legislative authority of the Parliament of Canada under Head 21 of s. 91 of the *British North America Act*. He also contended it was *ultra vires* because it encroached upon the following heads of s. 91 of that Act: [the court cited ss. 91(15), 91(18), and 91(19), and continued]:

> 15. Banking, incorporation of Banks and the issue of Paper Money.
> 18. Bills of Exchange and Promissory Notes.
> 19. Interest.

and because it gives to the clerk of a District Court the powers of a judge contrary to the provisions of s. 96 of the *British North America Act*.

I agree with the Appellate Division that the Act is *ultra vires* on the ground that in pith and substance it is bankruptcy and insolvency legislation and that it is therefore unnecessary to consider the other grounds of attack.

Section 3 of *The Orderly Payment of Debts Act* provides:

> 3. (1) This Act applies only
> (a) to a judgment for the payment of money where the amount of the judgment does not exceed one thousand dollars,
> (b) to a judgment for the payment of money in excess of one thousand dollars if the creditor consents to come under this Act, and
> (c) to a claim for money, demand for debt, account, covenant or otherwise, not in excess of one thousand dollars.
>
> (2) This Act does not apply to a debt due, owing or payable to the Crown or a municipality or relating to the public revenue or one that may be levied and collected in the form of taxes or, unless the creditor consents to come under this Act,

---

3 *Continental Illinois National Bank & Trust Co of Chicago v Chicago, Rock Island & Pacific Ry Co*, 294 US 648 at 668–69 (1935).

4 Charles Jordan Tabb, *The Law of Bankruptcy* (New York: Foundation Press, 1997) at 46.

(a) to a claim for wages that may be heard before, or a judgment therefor by, a magistrate under *The Masters and Servants Act*,

(b) to a claim for lien or a judgment thereon under *The Mechanics Lien Act*, or

(c) to a claim for a lien under *The Garagemen's Lien Act*.

(3) This Act does not apply to debts incurred by a trader or merchant in the usual course of his business.

Provision is then made whereby a debtor may apply to the clerk of the District Court of the judicial district in which he resides for a consolidation order, showing by affidavit all his creditors together with the amount he owes to each one, his income from all sources and, if he is married, the amount of the income of his wife, the number of persons dependent upon him, the amount payable for board or lodging or rent or as payment on home property and whether any of his creditors' claims are secured, and if so, the nature and particulars of the security held by each. The clerk is to settle an amount proposed to be paid by the debtor into court periodically or otherwise on account of the claims of his creditors and provide for hearing objections by the latter. After such a hearing, if necessary, a consolidation order is to be made, which order is a judgment of the Court in favour of each creditor, and provision is made for a review by the Court of any such order.

Sections 12, 13 and 14 are important and read as follows:

12. The court may, in deciding any matter brought before it, impose such terms on a debtor with respect to the custody of his property or any disposition thereof or of the proceeds thereof as it deems proper to protect the registered creditors and may give such directions for the purpose as the circumstances require.

13. Upon the making of a consolidation order no process shall be issued in any court against the debtor at the instance of a registered creditor or a creditor to whom this Act applies

(a) except as permitted by this Act or the regulations, or

(b) except by leave of the court.

14. (1) The clerk may at any time require of, and take from, the debtor an assignment to himself as clerk of the court of any moneys due, owing or payable or to become due, owing or payable to the debtor or earned or to be earned by the debtor.

(2) Unless otherwise agreed upon the clerk shall forthwith notify the person owing or about to owe the moneys of the assignment and all moneys collected thereon shall be applied to the credit of the claims against the debtor under the consolidation order.

(3) The clerk may issue a writ of execution in respect of a consolidation order and cause it to be filed with the sheriff of a judicial district and at any land titles office.

While the Act applies only to claims or judgments which do not exceed one thousand dollars, unless in the case of a judgment for the payment of money in excess of one thousand dollars the creditor consents to come under the Act, I can read these provisions in no other way than showing that they refer to a debtor who is unable to pay his debts as they mature. Why else is authority given [to] the Court to impose terms with respect to the custody of his property or any disposition thereof or of the proceeds thereof as it deems proper to protect the registered creditors (s. 12)? And why else may no process be issued in any court against the debtor at the instance of a registered creditor or a creditor to whom the Act applies, except as stated (s. 13)? Section 14 authorizing the clerk to require an assignment to him by the debtor of any monies due, owing or payable or to become due, owing or payable to the debtor, or earned or to be earned by the debtor is surely consonant only with the position of an insolvent debtor. In fact a debtor under the Act is ceasing to meet his liabilities generally as they become due and therefore falls within s. 20(1)(j) of the *Bankruptcy Act*, RSC 1952, c. 14.

In *Attorney-General for British Columbia v Attorney General for Canada et al* [18 CBR 217], Lord Thankerton speaking for the Judicial Committee states at p. 402:

> In a general sense, insolvency means inability to meet one's debts or obligations; in a tech-
> nical sense, it means the condition or standard of inability to meet debts or obligations,
> upon the occurrence of which the statutory law enables a creditor to intervene, with the
> assistance of a Court, to stop individual action by creditors and to secure administration
> of the debtor's assets in the general interest of creditors; the law also generally allows the
> debtor to apply for the same administration. The justification for such proceeding by a
> creditor generally consists in an act of bankruptcy by the debtor, the conditions of which
> are defined and prescribed by the statute law.

This was said in an appeal affirming the decision of the majority of this Court in the *Reference as to the Validity of The Farmers' Creditors Arrangement Act of the Dominion*, as amended [[1936] SCR 384].

In *Canadian Bankers' Association v Attorney General of Saskatchewan* [[1956] SCR 31], this Court held that *The Moratorium Act of Saskatchewan* was *ultra vires* as being in rela-
tion to insolvency. There the decision of the Judicial Committee in *Abitibi Power and Paper Company v The Montreal Trust Company* [25 CBR 6] was relied upon, but, for the reasons given by Mr. Justice Locke, it was held that it had no application. As was pointed out, the Judicial Committee in the 1943 case held that the purpose of the impugned legislation was to stay proceedings in the action brought under the mortgage granted by the Abitibi Company until the interested parties should have an opportunity of considering such plan for the re-organization of the company as might be submitted by a Royal Commission appointed for that purpose. For the same reason that decision is inapplicable here. The older decision of the Privy Council in *Attorney General for Ontario v The Attorney General of Canada* [[1894] AC 189], dealing with *The Ontario Assignments and Preference Act*, is quite distinguishable, although in my view it is doubtful whether in view of later pronouncements of the Judicial Committee it would at this date be decided in the same sense, even in the absence of Dominion legislation upon the subject of bankruptcy and insolvency.

The Act in question is not legislation for the recovery of debts. It has no analogy to prov-
incial bulk sales legislation because there the object is to make sure that when a person sells his stock of goods, wares, merchandise and chattels, ordinarily the subject of trade and commerce, the creditors will not be placed in any difficulty because of the disappearance of the proceeds of the sale. It is unnecessary to express any opinion as to the validity of s. 156 of *The Division Courts Act of Ontario*, RSO 1950, apparently introduced for the first time in 1950 by c. 16 of the statutes of that year, which provides for a consolidation order.

The debtor under *The Orderly Payment of Debts Act* is not in the same position as the appellant in *L'Union St Jacques de Montréal v Bélisle* [(1874) LR 6 PC 31], and the appellant can gain no comfort from *Ladore v Bennett* [21 CBR 1], because there it was held that the *City of Windsor (Amalgamation) Act, 1935* and Amendment were in pith and substance Acts passed in relation to "municipal institutions in the Province" and did not encroach upon the exclusive legislative power of the Dominion Parliament in relation to bankruptcy and insolvency, interest, or private rights outside the Province. This was a decision of the Judicial Committee affirming that of the Court of Appeal for Ontario [[1938] OR 324], which latter, in the meantime, had been applied by the Court of Appeal for British Columbia in

Day v Corporation of the City of Vancouver, McGavin and McMullen [(1938), 4 DLR 345]. The legislation in question in each of these cases was quite different from the effort by Alberta in *Board of Trustees of the Lethbridge Northern Irrigation District v IOF* [[1940] 2 DLR 273].

The appeal should be dismissed.

LOCKE J [for himself and Martland J]: ... While the [Alberta] Act does not require that the debtor who applies must be insolvent in the sense that he is unable to pay his debts as they become due, it must, in my opinion, be so construed since it is quite impossible to believe that it was intended that the provisions of the Act might be resorted to by persons who were able to pay their way but do not feel inclined to do so. In my opinion, this is a clear invasion of the legislative field of insolvency and is, accordingly, beyond the powers of the legislature.

There have been bankruptcy laws in England since 1542 dealing with the estates of insolvent persons, and the terms of statutes in force in England prior to 1867 may be looked at as an aid in deciding what subject matters were generally regarded as included in these terms.

The *Bankruptcy Consolidation Act of 1849*, 12-13 Vict., c. 106, which consolidated the law relating to bankrupts, contained in ss. 201 to 223 provisions by which a trader unable to meet his engagements with his creditors might petition the court to approve a composition or scheme of arrangement for the payment of his debts and declared the manner in which such a proposal might be submitted to the creditors and, if approved, to the court for its approval.

The manner in which disputes between the official assignee and the creditors as to the carrying out of a deed of composition or arrangement were to be settled was further dealt with in 1861 in s. 136 of an *Act to amend the law relating to bankruptcy and insolvency in England*, 24-25 Vict., c. 134.

Compositions and schemes of arrangement have thus for more than 100 years past been treated as subject matters falling within the scope of the statutes relating to bankruptcy and insolvency. The provisions dealing with this subject at the present day in England are to be found in the *Bankruptcy Act* of 1914 as amended (see *Williams on Bankruptcy*, 17th ed., p. 92). When the *Bankruptcy Act* was enacted in Canada in 1919 it contained in s. 13 provisions whereby an insolvent debtor who wished to make a proposal to his creditors for a composition in satisfaction of his debts or an extension of time for payment thereof or a scheme of arrangement of his affairs might, either before or after the making of a receiving order against him or the making of an authorized assignment by him, require in writing an authorized trustee to convene a meeting of his creditors for the consideration of such proposal and provisions whereby the scheme, if approved, might become binding upon the parties concerned. Similar provisions for dealing with such a proposal, a term which is defined to include a proposal for a composition, an extension of time, or for a scheme of arrangement, are contained in the *Bankruptcy Act* as it is today....

Some support for the validity of this legislation is sought in the judgment of the Judicial Committee in *Attorney General of Ontario v Attorney General of Canada* [[1894] AC 189]. The question in that appeal was as to whether s. 9 of c. 124, RSO 1887, was within the powers of the legislature. The Act was entitled "An Act respecting assignments and preferences by insolvent persons." A majority of the members of the Court of Appeal who considered the question had found the section to be *ultra vires*. In an earlier case, *Clarkson v Ontario Bank* [(1890), 15 OAR 166], Haggarty CJO and Osler JA had held the Act as a whole to be *ultra vires* as legislation relating to bankruptcy and insolvency, while Burton and Patterson JJA considered it to be *intra vires* as being in relation to property and civil rights in the province.

Prior to the passing of that statute the *Insolvency Act of 1875* (c. 16) had been repealed by Parliament by c. 1 of the Statutes of 1880 and there was no *Bankruptcy or Insolvency Act* of the Dominion.

The judgment allowing the appeal was delivered by Herschell LC. The Act, the first two sections of which dealt with fraudulent preferences by insolvents or those knowing themselves to be on the eve of insolvency, permitted a debtor-solvent or otherwise—to make an assignment of his exigible assets to a sheriff for the purpose of realization and distribution pro rata among his creditors. Section 9 provided that such an assignment should take precedence of all judgments and all executions not completely executed by payment. There were no provisions permitting proposals for a composition or extension of time for payment of debts. It was said that the effect to be given to judgments and executions and the manner and the extent to which they might be enforced was *prima facie* within the legislative powers of the legislature and that the validity of the assignment and the application of s. 9 did not depend on whether the assignor was or was not insolvent. Such an assignment, their Lordships said, did not infringe on the exclusive legislative power of Parliament under head 21. The concluding portion of the judgment reads (pp. 200–201):

> Their Lordships do not doubt that it would be open to the Dominion Parliament to deal with such matters as part of a bankruptcy law, and the provincial legislature would doubtless be then precluded from interfering with this legislation inasmuch as such interference would affect the bankruptcy law of the Dominion Parliament. But it does not follow that such subjects, as might properly be treated as ancillary to such a law and therefore within the powers of the Dominion Parliament, are excluded from the legislative authority of the provincial legislature when there is no bankruptcy or insolvency legislation of the Dominion Parliament in existence.

As Parliament has dealt with the matter, the concluding portion of this judgment would be fatal to the appellant's contention, even if the subject of bankruptcy and insolvency were one in relation to which the province might legislate in the absence of legislation by the Dominion. But the language of s. 91 is that the exclusive legislative power of the Parliament of Canada extends to all matters in relation to, *inter alia*, bankruptcy and insolvency, and the provinces are excluded from that field. As Lord Watson said in *Union Colliery v Bryden* [[1899] AC 580, at 588]:

> The abstinence of the Dominion Parliament from Legislating to the full limit of its power could not have the effect of transferring to any provincial legislature the legislative power which had been assigned to the Dominion by s. 91 of the Act of 1867.

Neither *Ladore v Bennett* [21 CBR 1] nor *Abitibi Power and Paper Co v Montreal Trust Co* [25 CBR 6], affect the question, in my opinion. In the former case the legislation, while it affected the rights of persons who had claims against insolvent municipalities, was found to be in pith and substance in relation to municipal institutions in the province and, as such, was intra vires the legislature under s. 92(8). In the latter case the purpose of the impugned legislation was to stay proceedings in an action brought under a mortgage until the interested parties should have an opportunity of considering a plan for the reorganization of the company, and the true nature of the legislation was held to be to regulate property and civil rights within the province.

[Justice Cartwright delivered a concurring judgment for himself and Maitland J.]

Appeal dismissed.

Discussion

Following the Supreme Court's decision in *Validity of Orderly Payment of Debts Act*, the federal government amended the *Bankruptcy Act* in 1965 and added a new Part X reproducing the essential features in the Alberta *Orderly Payment of Debts Act*. Part X applies only to those provinces that have elected to adopt it; only six provinces elected to do so. Québec has its own consolidation provisions, popularly known as the *Lacombe Law*, which were adopted even earlier than the Alberta provisions and have never been challenged constitutionally. See now Québec *Code of Civil Procedure*, book VIII, arts 664–70. The number of consolidation orders under Part X dropped off sharply following adoption of the 1992 amendments of the *BIA* and introduction of the consumer proposal provisions in *BIA* Part III.2. As will be explained in Chapter 17, consumer proposals are much more attractive to insolvent debtors than Part X, because consumer proposals are designed to provide relief from at least part of the consumer's indebtedness, whereas an Orderly Payment Order only gives the debtor more time to discharge the indebtedness.

Robinson v Countrywide Factors Ltd, [1978] 1 SCR 753 [*Robinson*]

LASKIN CJC (for himself, Martland, Dickson, and de Grandpré JJ) (dissenting): There are two issues in this appeal which is here by leave of this Court. The first is whether a certain transaction and, in particular, a certain debenture, granted on a debtor's stock-in-trade in pursuance of the transaction between the debtor and the respondent creditor, was a fraudulent preference that was impeachable under ss. 3 and 4 of *The Fraudulent Preferences Act*, RSS 1965, c. 397; and the second is whether, if it was so impeachable, those provisions of the provincial Act were *ultra vires* as an invasion of exclusive federal power in relation to bankruptcy and insolvency or, alternatively, were inoperative in the face of the preference provisions of the *Bankruptcy Act*, RSC 1970, c. B-3.

The appellant is trustee in bankruptcy of Kozan Furniture (Yorkton) Ltd. pursuant to a receiving order of November 19, 1968. On November 19, 1966, Kozan entered into a transaction with a pressing creditor, the respondent, whereby it sold certain stock-in-trade to a third person (payment being made to the respondent which reduced Kozan's indebtedness accordingly) and also agreed to give the respondent a debenture on its stock-in-trade for its remaining indebtedness. The debenture was executed on or about March 20, 1967, and duly registered. After the receiving order against Kozan was made, proceedings were taken by the appellant trustee in bankruptcy to set aside the transaction of November 19, 1966, as constituting a fraudulent preference under the provincial *Fraudulent Preferences Act* and to recover the money paid to the respondent and to annul the debenture.

MacPherson J found that Kozan was insolvent at the time of the transaction of November 19, 1966, that there was a concurrent intention of Kozan and the respondent to give and receive a preference, and that, consequently, both the payment made to the respondent and the debenture constituted fraudulent preferences under the provincial statute and were hence impeachable. On appeal, this judgment was set aside on the view of the majority of the Saskatchewan Court of Appeal that the appellant had failed to prove that Kozan was insolvent on November 19, 1966. The trial judge was not called upon to deal with any constitutional issue, and the majority of the Court of Appeal did not have to do so in view of its finding on insolvency. Hall JA who dissented supported the trial judge's finding of insolvency, and in a one sentence assertion, in reliance upon *Re Panfab Corp Ltd*, he rejected the contention that *The Fraudulent Preferences Act* was *ultra vires*.

I would not interfere with the findings of the judge of first instance that Kozan was insolvent at the material time and that Kozan intended to give and the respondent intended to receive a preference. This is the view of my brother Spence who, in exhaustive reasons, also concluded that *The Fraudulent Preferences Act* as a whole was not *ultra vires* nor was either s. 3 or s. 4 inoperative in the face of the *Bankruptcy Act*. I have a different opinion on the constitutional issue in this case, as appears from what now follows. That issue does not invite this Court to pronounce on the validity of provincial legislation dealing with fraudulent conveyances or with fraudulent transactions in general. Thus, to take as an example the *Fraudulent Conveyances Act*, RSO 1970, c. 182, nothing said in these reasons is to be taken as impugning the validity of that or similar enactments. They do not, *ex facie*, depend on proof of insolvency or on bankruptcy. In so far as any of the case law, some of it canvassed by my brother Spence, relates to such legislation and carries it into a consideration of the validity of provincial preference legislation which depends, as do ss. 3 and 4 of the Saskatchewan *Fraudulent Preferences Act*, on a condition of insolvency, I find it inapt for the determination of the constitutional question in this appeal.

Sections 3 and 4 aforesaid are in the following terms: ...

Sections 8, 9, 10 and 11, to which each of the foregoing provisions is subject, do not affect the constitutional issue, being concerned with *bona fide* sales or payments to innocent purchasers, to valid sales for consideration and to protection of security given up by a creditor. The present cases does not involve ss. 8 to 11 [*sic*].

I approach the question of validity on principle and on authority. So far as principle is concerned, the starting point is in relevant words of the *British North America Act*, namely s. 91(21), "bankruptcy and insolvency," as they relate to s. 92(13), "property and civil rights in the Province." The elucidation of the meaning and scope of s. 91(21), as of the meaning and scope of any other heads of legislative power, can hardly ever be a purely abstract exercise, even where an attempt is made at neutral definition; but I see no reason why judicial pronouncements, especially at the appellate level where they are those of the Court, should not be considered as throwing light upon the integrity of the head of power in the scheme of the *British North America Act* as a whole.

Four things stand out. First, s. 91(21) is an exclusive federal power; second, it is a power confided to the Parliament of Canada notwithstanding anything else in the Act; third, it is a power, like the criminal law power, whose ambit, did not and does not lie frozen under conceptions held of bankruptcy and insolvency in 1867: see the *Farmers' Creditors Arrangement Act* reference, *Attorney-General for British Columbia v Attorney General for Canada*, at pp. 402–403; and, fourth, the term "insolvency" in s. 91(21) has as much an independent operation in the reservation of an exclusive area of legislative competence to the Parliament of Canada as the term "bankruptcy"; see *Canadian Bankers Association v Attorney-General of Saskatchewan*, per Rand J, at p. 46.

The view taken by the Privy Council and by this Court as to the meaning of "insolvency," as well after as before the abolition of Privy Council appeals, has been a uniform one. Lord Thankerton, speaking for the Privy Council in the *Farmers' Creditors Arrangement Act* reference, *supra*, at p. 402, expressed it as follows:

> In a general sense, insolvency means inability to meet one's debts or obligations; in a technical sense, it means the condition or standard of inability to meet debts or obligations, upon the occurrence of which the statutory law enables a creditor to intervene with the assistance of a Court, to stop individual action by creditors and to secure administration

of the debtor's assets in the general interest of creditors; the law also generally allows the debtor to apply for the same administration.

This definition was referred to with approval in the majority judgment of the Supreme Court of Canada delivered by Kerwin CJC in *Reference re Validity of the Orderly Payment of Debts Act, 1959 (Alta)*, at p. 576. Earlier in *Reference re Alberta Debt Adjustment Act*, at p. 40, Duff CJC speaking for all but one of the members of the Court took as an additional ground for invalidating the challenged provincial legislation in that case that the powers of the provincial statutory tribunal set up under that legislation would normally "come into operation when a state of insolvency exists"; and he continued: "It is not too much to say that it is for the purpose of dealing with the affairs of debtors who are pressed and unable to pay their debts as they fall due that these powers and duties are created." If it is for Parliament alone to deal with insolvency, indeed to define it where it chooses to do so and to leave it otherwise to judicial definition, there can be no argument about unlawful invasion of provincial power in relation to property and civil rights. A limitation upon such power necessarily inheres in the federal catalogue of powers in s. 91, and it was recognized as early as 1880 in *Cushing v Dupuy*, at p. 415, in respect of the federal bankruptcy and insolvency power.

I refer to two other propositions before turning to what I consider to be the relevant cases. First, there is the well-recognized proposition that federal abstinence from legislation in relation to an exclusive head of legislative power does not leave that legislative area open to provincial action: see *Union Colliery Co v Bryden*, at p. 588. The principle of our Constitution as it relates to legislative power is not one of simple concurrency of authority subject only to a variable doctrine of paramountcy. Exclusiveness is central to the scheme of distribution, save as to a specified number of concurrent powers, such as those in s. 95. It is only under the umbrella of the doctrine of exclusiveness that the relative scope of federal and provincial authority is assessed, the assessment being carried forward to determine whether there is preclusion or supercession where both federal and provincial legislation are in competition. This brings me to the second point. I take the same view here that was taken by Duff CJC in the *Alberta Debt Adjustment Act* reference and I adopt his words at p. 40, namely that although the motives of a provincial Legislature may be laudable ones, it is precluded from seeking to realize its object by entering into a field not open to it.

Attorney-General of Ontario v Attorney-General for Canada, generally known as the *Voluntary Assignments* case, stands as the general support for provincial legislation that is challenged in the present case. It concerned only one section, s. 9, of the *Ontario Assignments and Preferences Act*, RSO 1887, c. 124, first enacted in 1885 by 1885 (Can), c. 26. That section was as follows:

An assignment for the general benefit of creditors under this Act shall take precedence of all judgments and of all executions not completely executed by payment, subject to the lien, if any, of an execution creditor for his costs, where there is but one execution in the sheriff's hands, or to the lien, if any, of the creditor for his costs, who has the first execution in the sheriff's hands.

This Act replaced the earlier pre-Confederation legislation found in CSUC 1859, c. 6, under the title *The Indigent Debtors Act*, which was continued in the post-Confederation legislation of Ontario as *An Act respecting The Fraudulent Preference of Creditors by persons in insolvent circumstances*, and included in RSO 1877, c. 118. What is significant in this earlier legislation is that (as set out in s. 2 of RSO 1877, c. 118) it dealt with "any person being at the time in insolvent circumstances or unable to pay his debts in full, or know-ing himself to be on the eve of insolvency." The substituted Act of 1885 continued the reference to insolvency in respect of preferences, but it also introduced new provisions respecting assignments for the benefit of creditors and these provisions, as was noted in the *Voluntary Assignments* case, were not predicated on insolvency and, indeed, were to a large degree separated from the preference provisions of the Act, as is reflected in s. 3 of RSO 1887, c. 124.

Certainly, as the Privy Council noted, the challenged provision, s. 9, had to be taken in the context of the entire Act. There is no doubt, as well, that the issue of validity was recognized as arising at a time when there was no federal bankruptcy or insolvency legislation in force, the only such legislation, the *Insolvency Act* of 1875 having been repealed in 1880 by 1880 (Can.), c. 1. The majority of the Ontario Court of Appeal, to which the question of the validity of s. 9 had been referred, found that it was *ultra vires* as invading exclusive federal power in relation to bankruptcy and insolvency; see *Re Assign-ments and Preferences Act, Section 9*. The reversal of this judgment by the Privy Council was accompanied by an acknowledgement of the broad scope of federal power under s. 91(21) when affirmatively exercised but it was held that this power was not invaded by an enactment relating to an assignment that was purely voluntary.

The explanation for this result is found in two passages of the Privy Council's rea-sons. First, "it is to be observed that an assignment for the general benefit of creditors has long been known to the jurisprudence of this country and also of Canada, and has its force and effect at common law quite independently of any system of bankruptcy or insolvency, or any legislation relating thereto" (at p. 198). Second, "the operation of an assignment for the benefit of creditors was precisely the same, whether the assignor was or was not insolvent. ... The validity of the assignment and its effect would in no way depend on the insolvency of the assignor, and their Lordships think it clear that the 9th section would equally apply whether the assignor was or was not insolvent" (at p. 199). What is evident, therefore, from that case is that, unlike the situation here, the operation of the provincial enactment did not depend on insolvency and the Privy Council was willing to treat s. 9 as having an object that was independent of it. This may even be a supportable view today, albeit there is a range of existing federal legislation dealing with bankruptcy and insolvency. I should note, however, that the majority judgment of this Court in *Reference re the Validity of the Orderly Payment of Debts Act, 1959 (Alta)*, at pp. 576–577, Kerwin CJC referring to the *Voluntary Assignments* reference, said "it is doubtful whether in view of later pronouncements of the Judicial Committee it would at this date be decided in the same sense, even in the absence of Dominion legislation upon the subject of bankruptcy and insolvency."

The later pronouncements of the Privy Council include its judgment in the *Alberta Debt Adjustment Act* reference, as well as in the *Farmers' Creditors Arrangement Act* ref-erence, *supra*. Equally important is the judgment of this Court in *Canadian Bankers Association v Attorney-General of Saskatchewan*, dealing with the validity of provincial moratorium legislation. It was in line with the decision in the *Alberta Debt Adjustment Act* reference in finding an invasion of federal power in relation to bankruptcy and insol-vency. I think it enough, for present purposes, to refer to what Locke J, speaking for the majority of the Court, said, at p. 42:

> Power to declare a moratorium for the relief of the residents of a Province generally in
> some great emergency, such as existed in 1914 and in the days of the lengthy depression

in the thirties is one thing, but power to intervene between insolvent debtors and their creditors irrespective of the reasons which have rendered the debtor unable to meet his liabilities is something entirely different.

Although judgments of the Privy Council and of this Court (and I add to those already cited *Royal Bank of Canada v Larue*) have recognized the broad power of Parliament to embrace in its legislation in relation to bankruptcy or insolvency provisions which might otherwise fall within provincial competence, I know of no case in those Courts, other than *Ladore v Bennett*, where provincial legislation has been sustained, either in the absence of or in the face of federal legislation, when such provincial legislation depends for its operation only upon insolvency. *Ladore v Bennett* can best be explained as involving municipal reorganization and hence as being concerned with the amalgamation and financial restructuring of units of local government for which the provincial Legislature has a direct responsibility, albeit some of the municipalities involved in the legislatively-directed reorganization were insolvent. It is, indeed, a special case of a piece of special legislation enacted in pursuance of the power conferred by s. 92(8) of the *British North America Act*, and I do not regard it as offering any lead to continuing legislation relating to private debtors and their creditors.

It is plain to me that if provincial legislation avowedly directed to insolvency, and to transactions between debtor and creditor consummated in a situation of insolvency, can be sustained as validly enacted, unless overborne by competent federal legislation, there is a serious breach of the principle of exclusiveness which embraces insolvency under s. 91(21). This Court so held in a series of cases where the encroachment on the federal bankruptcy and insolvency power was less obvious than that exhibited here. I refer, of course, to the *Alberta Debt Adjustment Act* reference, *supra*, to the *Canadian Bankers' Association* case, *supra*, and to the *Orderly Payment of Debts Act 1959 (Alta)* reference, *supra*. It would be a curious reversal of the proposition, enunciated in *Madden v Nelson and Fort Sheppard Railway Co*, namely, that you cannot do indirectly what you cannot do directly, to hold that the Province can do directly what it cannot do indirectly.

The case put forward by the appellant and by the intervening Provinces which supported him goes even farther. It is contended that notwithstanding the existence of federal bankruptcy legislation dealing with preferences, the challenged provincial legislation can still operate in respect of a particular preference which is given outside of the time limits within which the federal control operates, so long at least as the provincial provision is not more stringent.

I do not follow this line of reasoning, especially on the submission of greater or lesser stringency. The relevant federal provision is s. 73 of the *Bankruptcy Act* [see now section 95] which reads as follows: ...

This provision cannot be taken in isolation. The *Bankruptcy Act* is a code on the subject of bankruptcy and insolvency, defining what is an act of bankruptcy, who is an insolvent person, prescribing what are vulnerable settlements as well as what are vulnerable preferences, declaring what is comprised in a bankrupt's estate, providing for priorities in distribution and for rateable distribution. It provides also, as in the present s. 31(1), for the making of an assignment by an insolvent person for the benefit of creditors as well as providing by s. 24(1)(a) that it is an act of bankruptcy to make an assignment for the benefit of creditors whether the assignment is or is not authorized by the *Bankruptcy Act*. In short, apart from the question whether provincial legislation predicated on insolvency is *ipso facto* invalid, I see no room for any assertion that such provincial legislation can continue to have operative effect in the face of the scope of the *Bankruptcy Act* embracing both bankruptcy and insolvency in its provisions.

It is worth a reminder that there is no common law of bankruptcy and insolvency, and hence it cannot be said that there was an existing common law course of decision which was being embraced by provincial legislation. The common law did not distinguish the fraudulent from the insolvent debtor; it was through legislation that such a distinction was made. If a provincial Legislature wishes to proscribe fraudulent transactions, it is compelled by the *British North America Act* to ensure that its legislation dealing with such transactions does not focus on insolvency....

I wish now to address myself to an issue which, I think, has influenced the approach by single judges to the constitutional question in this case, and wrongly so. That issue is the undesirability of interfering with what appeared to be a practical way of reaching as many alleged preferences in fraud of creditors as possible, to use provincial legislation where federal legislation did not reach far enough, and to use provincial insolvency legislation if nothing else was available. Hence, the approach by way of construction, albeit a dip into a constitutional area was inevitable, avoiding a direct constitutional confrontation. There are cases even in this Court and on this very subject which have proceeded on a straight construction basis to examine whether operative effect can be given to provincial legislation in the face of a federal enactment. Two examples are *Traders Finance Corp Ltd v Levesque*, and *Produits de Caoutchouc Marquis Inc v Trottier*. I do not regard either of these cases as requiring a decision on constitutional grounds. The *Traders Finance* case concerned a largely procedural matter, namely, whether the failure of a trustee in bankruptcy to impeach a preference illegal under the *Bankruptcy Act*, precluded a suit by a creditor to that end. The *Trottier* case dealt with the effect of the *Bankruptcy Act* on the extent of a landlord's claim to rank as a preferred creditor....

I conclude, therefore, as follows. Provincial legislation which purports to provide for impeachment of preferences to creditors given by a person who is then insolvent, where insolvency is the *sine qua non* of impeachability, is invalid as a direct invasion of exclusive federal power in relation to bankruptcy and insolvency. Hence, ss. 3 and 4 of Saskatchewan *Fraudulent Preferences Act* are *ultra vires*. Moreover, in so far as these sections prescribe an impeachment period which enables a creditor to set aside a preference made beyond the period fixed by the *Bankruptcy Act*, and hence not impeachable under that Act, it interferes with the operation of the *Bankruptcy Act* and is, indeed, repugnant to it. It must be remembered that where, as in the present case, there has been a receiving order, the intrusion of provincial legislation relating to transactions entered into by an insolvent, must interfere with the rateable distribution of the bankrupt's property according to the scheme of distribution prescribed by the *Bankruptcy Act*. Whether that scheme is faulty in the view of a Court is immaterial; the correction must come from the responsible Legislature. No more under bankruptcy and insolvency law than under the criminal law can a Province make unlawful what is lawful under valid federal legislation, nor make lawful what is unlawful under valid federal legislation....

SPENCE J (for the majority): ... I have dealt with what, in my view, are the main cases upon the subject in Canada. Upon considering them *all*, as well as the decision of the Judicial Committee in *AG of Ontario v AG for Canada*, *supra*, I have come to the conclusion that the better view is to confine the effect of what is now s. 73 of the *Bankruptcy Act* to providing for the invalidity of transactions within its exact scope. To that extent, the Parliament of Canada, by valid legislation upon "bankruptcy" and "insolvency," has covered the field but has refrained from completely covering the whole field of transactions avoided by provincial legislation. I am of the opinion that the enactment in 1949 of the provisions now found in s. 50(6) of the *Bankruptcy Act* is a plain indication that Parliament recognized that provisions in provincial statutes dealing with preferential transactions were still valid provincial enactments in reference to "property" and "civil rights" and were valuable aids to trustees in bankruptcy in attacking the validity of such transactions and should be available to the said trustees in bankruptcy.

I am assisted in coming to this conclusion by the view which I believe was behind the Lord Chancellor's reasons in *AG of Ontario v AG for Canada, supra*, that the words "bankruptcy" and "insolvency" in s. 91, para. 21, of the *British North America Act* were aimed at legislative schemes which had the purpose of governing the distribution of a debtor's property amongst his creditors. There may well be, and there are, provisions in such legislative schemes, i.e., the *Bankruptcy Act*, dealing with "property" and "civil rights." Such provisions are properly ancillary to the bankruptcy and insolvency legislation, and to the extent to which they do overcome existing valid provincial legislation and bar future provincial legislation *contra* thereto but do not purport to extend beyond that point to invalidate other valid provincial legislation upon "property" and "civil rights." ...

BEETZ J: I have had the advantage of reading the opinions of the Chief Justice and of Mr. Justice Spence. I agree with Mr. Justice Spence. To his reasons for judgment I would however like to add some of my own.

The power to repress fraud by avoiding fraudulent conveyances and preferences is an indisputable part of provincial jurisdiction over property and civil rights. The risk of fraud is increased when a debtor finds himself in a situation of impending or actual insolvency and, in my view, provincial laws can, without undergoing a change in nature, focus upon that situation as upon a proper occasion to attain their object. Given their purpose, they do not cease to be laws in relation to property and civil rights simply because they are timely and effective or because Parliament could enact similar laws in relation to bankruptcy and insolvency.

Insolvency has been defined by Lord Thankerton in the *Farmers' Creditors Arrangement Act* reference, *Attorney-General for British Columbia v Attorney-General for Canada*, at p. 402:

> In a general sense, insolvency means inability to meet one's debts or obligations; in a technical sense, it means the condition or standard of inability to meet debts or obligations, upon the occurrence of which the statutory law enables a creditor to intervene, with the assistance of a Court, to stop individual action by creditors and to secure administration of the debtor's assets in the general interest of creditors; the law also generally allows the debtor to apply for the same administration.

The primary meaning of "insolvency" in s. 91.21 of the Constitution is insolvency in the technical sense, not in the general sense. This Lord Thankerton made just a few lines after the passage quoted above: with respect to the jurisdiction of Parliament under s. 91.21, he referred to "... the statutory conditions of insolvency which enabled a creditor or the debtor to invoke the aid of the bankruptcy laws. ..."

There is no common law of bankruptcy and insolvency in the technical sense, but the disruptions resulting from insolvency in the general sense had of necessity to be taken into account by general legal systems such as the common law and the civil law. Insolvency lies at the core of those parts of the common law and of the civil law which relate to such matters as mortgage, pledge, pawning, suretyship and the securing of debts generally which are implicitly or explicitly predicated on the risk of insolvency and which produce their full effect when the risk has been converted into reality; so it is with the rules which determine the rank of privileges and hypothecs or which ordain that an insolvent or bankrupt debtor shall lose the benefit of the term (art. 1092 of the Québec *Civil Code*). Some of the most fundamental principles of the civil law are expressed in arts. 1980, 1981 and 1982 of the Québec *Civil Code*:

> Art. 1980. Whoever incurs a personal obligation, renders liable for its fulfilment all his property, moveable and immoveable, present and future, except such property as is specially declared to be exempt from seizure.

> Art. 1981. The property of a debtor is the common pledge of his creditors, and where they claim together they share its price rateably, unless there are amongst them legal causes of preference.

> Art. 1982. The legal causes of preference are privileges and hypothecs.

Although not expressly referred to, insolvency forms the web of these articles; there would be little need for them, particularly the last two, were it not for insolvency. But I cannot be persuaded that they are not laws relating to property and civil rights.

When the exclusive power to make laws in relation to bankruptcy and insolvency was bestowed upon Parliament, it was not intended to remove from the general legal systems which regulated property and civil rights a cardinal concept essential to the coherence of those systems. The main purpose was to give to Parliament exclusive jurisdiction over the establishment by statute of a particular system regulating the distribution of a debtor's assets. However, given the nature of general legal systems, the primary jurisdiction of Parliament cannot easily be exercised together with its incidental powers without some degree of overlap in which case federal law prevails. On the other hand, provincial jurisdiction over property and civil rights should not be measured by the ultimate reach of federal power over bankruptcy and insolvency any more than provincial competence in relation to the administration of justice can be determined by every conceivable and potential use of the criminal law power. This, I believe, is the general import of the *Voluntary Assignments* case, *Attorney-General of Ontario v Attorney-General for Canada*. The Judicial Committee declared that the validity of the provision it had to consider and of the assignments made under the authority of that provision did not depend on the insolvency of the assignor: an assignment was also open "to any debtor who might deem his insolvency doubtful. ...." All that one can say is that legislation of the type considered in the *Voluntary Assignments* case presents little interest for prosperous persons; it is of concern chiefly to debtors in strained circumstances whose solvency is, at best, uncertain. It should be noted that the impugned voluntary assignments enactment did not only deal with assignments: it also provided that an assignment for the general benefit of creditors should take *precedence* of all judgments and of all executions not completely executed by payment.

I am reinforced in those views by a consideration of the *Civil Code of Lower Canada, 1866*, in light of *An Act Respecting Insolvency, 1864* (Can), c. 17. Both were enacted at a time when Confederation was being discussed. The French title of *The Insolvent Act of 1864*, was "*l'Acte concernant la faillité, 1864*," the word "faillite" being the one now currently used to translate the word "bankruptcy." In spite of its English title, the Act was in fact a bankruptcy act. It applied to all persons in Upper Canada and to traders only in

Lower Canada and it contained detailed provisions relating to fraudulent conveyances and preferences. Nevertheless, the *Civil Code* comprised a section of nine articles (arts. 1032 to 1040 incl.), entitled "Of the Avoidance of Contracts and Payments made in Fraud of Creditors," applicable to traders and to non-traders alike except where *The Insolvent Act* was to prevail. The legislative history of those articles was set forth by Mr. Justice Pigeon in *Gingras v General Motors Products of Canada Ltd.* Some have been amended. It will suffice to quote a few of them as they then read:

> 1034. A gratuitous contract is deemed to be made with intent to defraud, if the debtor be insolvent at the time of making it.

> 1035. An onerous contract made by an insolvent debtor with a person who knows him to be insolvent is deemed to be made with intent to defraud.

> 1036. Every payment by an insolvent debtor to a creditor knowing his insolvency, is deemed to be made with intent to defraud, and the creditor may be compelled to restore the amount or thing received or the value thereof, for the benefit of the creditors according to their respective rights.

> 1037. Further provisions concerning the presumption of fraud and the nullity of acts done in contemplation of insolvency are contained in *The Insolvent Act of 1864.*

Article 17.23 of the Code defines "bankruptcy" ("faillite") as meaning "the condition of a trader who has discontinued his payments"; insolvency was left undefined, the word being clearly used by the Code in the general sense. Even though articles 1034, 1035 and 1036 are predicated on insolvency, the Commissioners appointed for codifying the laws of Lower Canada in civil matters would have been astonished had they been told that those articles formed no part of the civil law: except perhaps for art. 1036 which appears to be an improvement of relatively modern origin (although it was not considered new law), such provisions were derived from a division of Roman law called Paulian law and, from time immemorial, had constituted a pivot of the civil law system. Other provisions of the Code are of the same nature and also depend on insolvency, such as art. 803 (revocation of a gift made by an insolvent debtor), and art. 2023 (hypothec consented to by an insolvent debtor). Other provisions still, although not expressly predicated on insolvency are related to insolvency and to the protection of creditors, for instance, art. 655 (the creditors of an heir who renounces a succession to their prejudice can have the renunciation rescinded and accept the succession in his stead).

The constitutional validity of such provisions is not in issue: they antedate Confederation and were continued by s. 129 of the Constitution. The only issue which could arise with respect to them is whether they are in conflict with federal law. But the content and integrity of the *Civil Code* are indicative of the extent of provincial jurisdiction over property and civil rights: *Citizens Insurance Company of Canada v Parsons*, at pp. 110 and 111. The fact that there existed a statutory scheme of bankruptcy and insolvency to which the Code explicitly referred as to a distinct and specific body of law, without curtailing for that reason its own normal ambit, illustrates how the respective domains of property and civil rights and of bankruptcy and insolvency were viewed during the very period when the federal union was being discussed; it also reveals how it was intended that the distribution of powers should operate with respect to those domains.

In the *Alberta Debt Adjustment Act* reference, in *Canadian Bankers Association v Attorney-General of Saskatchewan*, and in *Reference re Validity of the Orderly Payment of Debts*

Act, 1959 (Alta), the various provincial laws found *ultra vires* were predicated upon insolvency. But they went further and set up elaborate statutory schemes involving one or more of the following features: the denial of creditors' access to courts or the restriction of their right to enforce their claims, the establishment of administrative boards, mediation, composition, arrangements, moratoriums, consolidation orders, staying of proceedings and the relief of debtors from liability to pay their debts. No such features are to be found in the presently impugned Saskatchewan statute where all that is at stake is the avoidance of fraudulent acts for the better enforcement of civil obligations. Some doubt was expressed in the *Orderly Payment of Debts Act*, (1959) (Alta) reference at pp. 576 and 577 as to whether the *Voluntary Assignments* case would have been decided in the same way at a later date even in the absence of federal legislation on the subject of bankruptcy and insolvency. But even if this doubt was not expressed in an obiter dictum, I would regard it as questioning not the general principles enunciated in the *Voluntary Assignments* case, but their application in that particular instance. Accordingly, I do not think that those previous decisions of the Judicial Committee and of this Court preclude my abiding by my conclusions: laws provincial in their purpose, object and nature as those under attack cannot be rendered *ultra vires* because of virtual federal paramountcy: they can only become inoperative in case of actual repugnancy with valid federal laws.

On this latter point, I believe the test of repugnancy to be applied in this case should not differ from the one which was admitted in *Provincial Secretary of Prince Edward Island v Egan; O'Grady v Sparling*, and *Ross v The Registrar of Motor Vehicles et al.*: provincial law gives way to federal law in case of operational conflict. Even if the test be one of conflict of legislative policies entailing no operational inconsistency and depending solely "upon the intention of the paramount Legislature" as was said by Dixon J, in a passage of *Ex p. McLean*, at p. 483, quoted by Mr. Justice Pigeon in the *Ross* case (at p. 15), I am of the view that s. 50, subs. (6) of the *Bankruptcy Act* provides a clear indication that Parliament, far from intending to depart from the rule of operational conflict, did in fact aim at the highest possible degree of legal integration of federal and provincial laws: attacks upon transactions within the three-month period provided by s. 73 of the *Bankruptcy Act* constitute a minimum but the trustee in bankruptcy is entitled to avail himself of all other rights and remedies provided by provincial law "as supplementary to and in addition to the rights and remedies provided by" the *Bankruptcy Act*.

Appeal allowed.

Discussion

Generally speaking, the provinces have retained the fraudulent transfer and preferential payment provisions discussed by the Supreme Court in *Robinson*. With a view to reducing the overlap between the federal and provincial provisions and the complexity of litigation arising from the duplication, a group of law teachers making submissions in 2003 on bankruptcy law reform to the Senate Banking, Trade and Commerce Committee recommended adoption of a provision in the *BIA* staying any provincial action where proceedings to set aside pre-bankruptcy transactions were initiated after the debtor's bankruptcy. The recommendation was not accepted and no such provision appears in the 2009 *BIA* amendments. However, these amendments did substantially revise the earlier provisions. For the details, see Chapter 5.

Sam Lévy & Associés Inc v Azco Mining Inc, 2001 SCC 92, [2001] 3 SCR 978 [*Azco Mining*]

BINNIE J (for the Court):

[1] The long arm of the Québec Superior Court sitting in Bankruptcy reached out to the appellant in Vancouver, British Columbia, in respect of a claim for shares and warrants and other debts allegedly due to the bankrupt which the trustee in bankruptcy values in excess of $4.5 million. The appellant protested that the dispute, which involves the financing of an African gold mine, has nothing to do with Québec. It argues that the claim of the respondent trustee in bankruptcy is an ordinary civil claim that rests entirely on agreements that are to be interpreted according to the laws of British Columbia. For this and other reasons of convenience and efficiency, the appellant says, the claim ought to proceed in British Columbia. The bankruptcy court and the Québec Court of Appeal rejected these submissions and, in my view, the further appeal to this Court ought also to be dismissed....

III. RELEVANT STATUTORY PROVISIONS

[16] *Bankruptcy and Insolvency Act*, RSC 1985, c. B-3

2. (1) In this Act
"locality of a debtor" means the principal place
(a) where the debtor has carried on business during the year immediately preceding his bankruptcy,
(b) where the debtor has resided during the year immediately preceding his bankruptcy, or
(c) in cases not coming within paragraph (a) or (b), where the greater portion of the property of the debtor is situated;

30. (1) The trustee may, with the permission of the inspectors, do all or any of the following things: ...
(d) bring, institute or defend any action or other legal proceeding relating to the property of the bankrupt;

43. (5) The petition shall be filed in the court having jurisdiction in the judicial district of the locality of the debtor.

72. (1) The provisions of this Act shall not be deemed to abrogate or supersede the substantive provisions of any other law or statute relating to property and civil rights that are not in conflict with this Act, and the trustee is entitled to avail himself of all rights and remedies provided by that law or statute as supplementary to and in addition to the rights and remedies provided by this Act.

183. (1) The following courts are invested with such jurisdiction at law and in equity as will enable them to exercise original, auxiliary and ancillary jurisdiction in bankruptcy and in other proceedings authorized by this Act during their respective terms, as they are now, or may be hereafter, held, and in vacation and in chambers: ...
(b) in the Province of Québec, the Superior Court;
(c) in the Provinces of Nova Scotia and British Columbia, the Supreme Court;

187. (7) The court, on satisfactory proof that the affairs of the bankrupt can be more economically administered within another bankruptcy district or division, or for other sufficient cause, may by order transfer any proceedings under this Act that are pending before it to another bankruptcy district or division.

188. (1) An order made by the court under this Act shall be enforced in the courts having jurisdiction in bankruptcy elsewhere in Canada in the same manner in all respects as if the order had been made by the court hereby required to enforce it.

(2) All courts and the officers of all courts shall severally act in aid of and be auxiliary to each other in all matters of bankruptcy, and an order of one court seeking aid, with a request to another court, shall be deemed sufficient to enable the latter court to exercise, in regard to the matters directed by the order, such jurisdiction as either the court that made the request or the court to which the request is made could exercise in regard to similar matters within its jurisdiction.

Bankruptcy and Insolvency General Rules, CRC, c. 368 (am. SOR/98-240)

3. In cases not provided for in the Act or these Rules, the courts shall apply, within their respective jurisdictions, their ordinary procedure to the extent that that procedure is not inconsistent with the Act or these Rules.

Civil Code of Québec, SQ 1991, c. 64

3135. Even though a Québec authority has jurisdiction to hear a dispute, it may exceptionally and on an application by a party, decline jurisdiction if it considers that the authorities of another country are in a better position to decide. . . .

3148. In personal actions of a patrimonial nature, a Québec authority has jurisdiction where

. . .

(5) the defendant submits to its jurisdiction.

However, a Québec authority has no jurisdiction where the parties, by agreement, have chosen to submit all existing or future disputes between themselves relating to a specified legal relationship to a foreign authority or to an arbitrator, unless the defendant submits to the jurisdiction of the Québec authority.

IV. ANALYSIS

[17] Parliament has conferred on the bankruptcy court the capacity and authority to exercise "original, auxiliary and ancillary jurisdiction in bankruptcy and in other proceedings authorized by this Act" (s. 183(1)). On the face of it, the intent of this provision is to confer on the bankruptcy court powers and duties co-extensive with Parliament's jurisdiction over "Bankruptcy" under s. 91(21) of the *Constitution Act, 1867* except insofar as that jurisdiction has been limited or specifically assigned elsewhere by Parliament itself.

[18] While the appellant's motion simply asked that the dispute be transferred to the Vancouver Division of the Supreme Court of British Columbia sitting in Bankruptcy (thereby appearing to concede that the dispute is properly dealt with as a bankruptcy matter), its motion also contended that the trustee's claims are "exclusively contractual" (para. 6) and that the "Superior Court of the Bankruptcy Division of Hull does not have jurisdiction to hear this contractual claim against Azco" (para. 20). Moreover, much of its oral argument suggested that the dispute ought to be tried in the ordinary civil courts. In addition the appellant takes the position that Québec is not the convenient forum to deal with this dispute, and that the Québec Superior Court sitting in Bankruptcy lacks a sufficiently long arm to require Azco to take its witnesses east to litigate. The proper forum, it says, is British Columbia because there is no substantial connection at all between this case and the Province of Québec. . . .

2. Did the Bankruptcy Court Thereby Acquire Jurisdiction to Deal with Matters Affecting the Bankrupt Estate Arising in British Columbia?

[25] The Act establishes a nationwide scheme for the adjudication of bankruptcy claims. As Rinfret J pointed out in *Boily v McNulty*, [1928] SCR 182, at p. 186: "This is a federal statute that concerns the whole country, and it considers territory from that point of view." The national implementation of bankruptcy decisions rendered by a court within a particular province is achieved through the cooperative network of superior courts of the provinces and territories under s. 188: *In re Mount Royal Lumber & Flooring Co* (1926), 8 CBR 240 (Que CA), per Rivard JA, at p. 246, "The *Bankruptcy Act* is federal and the orders of the Québec Superior Court sitting as a bankruptcy court under that Act are enforceable in Ontario ..." See also: *Associated Freezers of Canada Inc (Trustee of) v Retail, Wholesale Canada, Local 1015* (1996), 39 CBR (3d) 311 (NSCA), at p. 314, and *Kansa General International Insurance Co (Liquidation de)*, [1998] RJQ 1380 (CA), at p. 1389.

[26] The trustees will often (and perhaps increasingly) have to deal with debtors and creditors residing in different parts of the country. They cannot do that efficiently, to borrow the phrase of Idington J in *Stewart v LePage* (1916), 53 SCR 337, at p. 345, "if everyone is to be at liberty to interfere and pursue his own notions of his rights of litigation." *Stewart* dealt with the winding up of a federally incorporated trust company in British Columbia. As a result of the winding up, a client in Prince Edward Island instituted a proceeding in the superior court of that province for a declaration that certain moneys held by the bankrupt trust company were held in trust and that the bankrupt trust company should be removed as trustee. This Court held that the dispute, despite its strong connection to Prince Edward Island, could not be brought before the court of that province without leave of the Supreme Court of British Columbia. Anglin J commented at p. 349:

> No doubt some inconvenience will be involved in such exceptional cases as this where the winding-up of the company is conducted in a province of the Dominion far distant from that in which persons interested as creditors or claimants may reside. But Parliament probably thought it necessary in the interest of prudent and economical winding-up that the court charged with that duty should have control not only of the assets and property found in the hands or possession of the company in liquidation, but also of all litigation in which it might be involved. The great balance of convenience is probably in favour of such single control though it may work hardship in some few cases.

[27] *Stewart* was, as stated, a winding-up case, but the legislative policy in favour of "single control" applies as well to bankruptcy. There is the same public interest in the expeditious, efficient and economical clean-up of the aftermath of a financial collapse. Section 188(1) ensures that orders made by a bankruptcy court sitting in one province can and will be enforced across the country.

[28] I have concluded that the jurisdiction of the Québec Superior Court sitting in Bankruptcy was properly invoked by the petitioning creditors in this case but counsel for the appellant company says that his client, with its office in British Columbia, is not within its reach. The argument, in part, is that whatever the power of Parliament to confer national jurisdiction on a provincial superior court, that court is nevertheless provincially constituted, and for service of process its long arm statute must be complied with. The factual record does not show precisely how service of the trustee's petition was effected on the appellant, but if the appellant had any concerns regarding the proprieties

of service of the petition to initiate proceedings against it, such concerns were waived when Azco did not raise them in its motion brought in Hull. A good deal of time was occupied on the appeal with arguments about how a Québec court could acquire in personam jurisdiction over a corporation resident in British Columbia, and whether the Québec rules for service *ex juris* applied. The argument that the Québec Superior Court sitting in Bankruptcy cannot exercise *in personam* jurisdiction over creditors in another province under the Act is rejected for the reasons of national jurisdiction already mentioned. Any objections regarding service of process are answered by the fact that Azco not only appeared in Québec but invoked the jurisdiction of the Québec Superior Court sitting in Bankruptcy to transfer the proceedings pursuant to s. 187(7) of the Act to the bankruptcy court sitting in Vancouver. Any remaining issue with respect to in personam jurisdiction was thereby waived.

[29] Azco did not, of course, waive its objection to jurisdiction over the subject matter of this particular dispute. That was a major point in its motion. I turn now to that issue.

3. Are Contract Claims Nevertheless Excluded from Federal Bankruptcy Jurisdiction?

[30] The appellant's motion, as stated, argued that the trustee's claims against it are "exclusively contractual in nature" (para. 6) and that "[t]he Superior Court of the Bankruptcy Division of Hull does not have jurisdiction to hear this contractual claim against Azco" (para. 20). The theory underlying these contentions seems to be that contract claims relate to "Property and Civil Rights" within the meaning of s. 92(13) of the *Constitution Act, 1867* and on that account lie outside the jurisdiction of the bankruptcy court. At para. 42 of its factum, for example, the appellant argues:

> Contrary to what the Court of Appeal affirms, the trustee's claim is therefore purely contractual in nature, under the civil law. It is not a remedy specifically provided for under the *BIA* such as the application to have preferential payments declared void (see sections 91 to 100 *BIA*). The mere fact that the plaintiff is a trustee does not alter the nature of the claim and does not turn it into a bankruptcy dispute.

[31] Most bankruptcy issues, of course, present a property and civil rights aspect. It is true, however, that some of the decided cases which deny jurisdiction to the bankruptcy court do so on grounds that have a constitutional flavour, e.g., *In re Morris Lofsky* (1947), 28 CBR 164 (Ont CA), per Roach JA, at p. 167; *Sigurdson v Fidelity Ins Co* (1980), 35 CBR (NS) 75 (BCCA), at p. 102; *Re Holley* (1986), 54 OR (2d) 225 (Ont CA); *In re Ireland* (1962), 5 CBR (NS) 91 (Que Sup Ct), per Bernier J, at p. 94, and *Falvo Enterprises Ltd v Price Waterhouse Ltd* (1981), 34 OR (2d) 336 (Ont HCJ).

[32] It is therefore necessary to come to an understanding of what is included in the subject matter of "bankruptcy" within the meaning of s. 91(21) of the *Constitution Act, 1867*.

[33] In *In re The Moratorium Act* (Sask), [1956] SCR 31, it was stated by Rand J, at p. 46, that:

> Bankruptcy is a well understood procedure by which an insolvent debtor's property is coercively brought under a judicial administration in the interests primarily of the creditors.

[34] The core concept of coercive administration appeared early in our bankruptcy jurisprudence. In *Union St Jacques de Montréal v Bélisle* (1874), LR 6 PC 31, Lord Selborne LC, speaking at p. 36 of general laws governing bankruptcy and insolvency, said: "The words describe in their known legal sense provisions made by law for the administration

of the estates of persons who may become bankrupt or insolvent, according to rules and definitions prescribed by law, including of course the conditions in which that law is to be brought into operation, the manner in which it is to be brought into operation, and the effect of its operation."

[35] More helpful still was Lord Selborne's description of bankruptcy in the context of the English Act in *Ellis v Silber* (1872), LR 8 Ch. App. 83, at p. 86:

> That which is to be done in bankruptcy is the administration in bankruptcy. The debtor and the creditors, as the parties to the administration in bankruptcy, are subject to that jurisdiction. The trustees or assignees, as the persons intrusted with that administration, are subject to that jurisdiction. The assets which come to their hands and the mode of administering them are subject to that jurisdiction; and there may be, and I believe are, some special classes of transactions which, under special clauses of the Acts of Parliament, may be specially dealt with as regards third parties. But the general proposition, that whenever the assignees or trustees in bankruptcy or the trustees under such deeds as these have a demand at law or in equity as against a stranger to the bankruptcy, then that demand is to be prosecuted in the Court of Bankruptcy, appears to me to be a proposition entirely without the warrant of anything in the Acts of Parliament, and wholly unsupported by any trace or vestige whatever of authority.

[36] Despite the fact that England is a unitary state without the constitutional limitations imposed by our division of powers, the courts in Canada have generally hewn ever since 1874 to the basic dividing line between disputes related to the administration of the bankrupt estate and disputes with "strangers to the bankruptcy." The principle is that if the dispute relates to a matter that is outside even a generous interpretation of the administration of the bankruptcy, or the remedy is not one contemplated by the Act, the trustee must seek relief in the ordinary civil courts. Thus in the Québec case of *Re Ireland*, supra, the trustee brought proceedings to determine who had the right to proceeds of insurance policies taken out by the trustee on properties of the bankrupt estate. Bernier J concluded that the Québec Superior Court sitting in Bankruptcy lacked jurisdiction over the subject matter of the dispute. The controversy raised purely civil law questions and nothing in the Act conferred on the bankruptcy court a special jurisdiction to entertain these matters. Similar arguments prevailed in *Cry-O-Beef Ltd/Cri-O-Boeuf Ltée (Trustee of) v Caisse Populaire de Black-Lake* (1987), 66 CBR (NS) 19 (Que CA); *In re Martin* (1953), 33 CBR 163 (Ont SC), at p. 169; *In re Reynolds* (1928), 10 CBR 127 (Ont SC), at p. 131; *Re Galaxy Interiors Ltd* (1971), 15 CBR (NS) 143 (Ont SC); *Mancini (Trustee of) v Falconi* (1987), 65 CBR (NS) 246 (Ont SC), and *In re Morris Lofsky*, supra, at p. 169.

[37] The Québec Court of Appeal has perhaps led the argument for a more expansive interpretation of what disputes properly come under the bankruptcy umbrella and can therefore properly be litigated in the bankruptcy court: *Geoffrion v Barnett*, [1970] CA 273; *Arctic Gardens inc (Syndic de)*, [1990] RJQ 6 (CA); *Excavations Sanoduc inc c Morency*, [1991] RDJ 423 (CA). See also the dissenting judgment of LeBel JA, as he then was, in *Cry-O-Beef Ltd/Cri-O-Boeuf Ltée*, supra, and *In re Atlas Lumber Co v Grier and Sons Ltd* (1922), 3 CBR 226 (Que Sup Ct); but the push is not confined to Québec: *In re Maple Leaf Fruit Co* (1949), 30 CBR 23 (NSCA); *Re Westam Development Ltd* (1967), 10 CBR (NS) 61 (BCCA), at p. 65; *Re MB Greer & Co* (1953), 33 CBR 69 (Ont SC), at p. 70; *Re MP Industrial Mills Ltd* (1972), 17 CBR 226 (Man QB).

[38] It seems to me that the decided cases recognize that the word "Bankruptcy" in s. 91(21) of the *Constitution Act, 1867* must be given a broad scope if it is to accomplish its

purpose. Anything less would unnecessarily complicate and undermine the economical and expeditious winding up of the bankrupt's affairs. Creation of a national jurisdiction in bankruptcy would be of little utility if its exercise were continually frustrated by a pinched and narrow construction of the constitutional head of power. The broad scope of authority conferred on Parliament has been passed along to the bankruptcy court in s. 183(1) of the Act, which confers a correspondingly broad jurisdiction.

[39] There are limits, of course. If the trustee's claim is in relation to a stranger to the bankruptcy, i.e. "persons or matters outside of [the] Act" (*Re Reynolds*, supra, at p. 129) or lacks the "complexion of a matter in bankruptcy" (*Re Morris Lofsky*, supra, at p. 169) it should be brought in the ordinary civil courts and not the bankruptcy court. However, claims for specific property may clearly be advanced in the bankruptcy courts (*Re Galaxy Interiors*, supra, and *Sigurdson*, supra), as can claims for relief specifically granted by the Act (*Re Ireland*, supra, and *Re Atlas Lumber Co*, supra). That said, it is sometimes difficult to discern the particular "golden thread" running through the cases. L.W. Houlden and L.B. Morawetz observe:

> There has been a great deal of litigation on this issue, and the cases are not always easy to reconcile. The difficulty flows from the division of constitutional powers in Canada, bankruptcy and insolvency being a federal power, and property and civil rights and the administration of justice being provincial powers.

> *Bankruptcy and Insolvency Law of Canada* (3rd ed. (looseleaf)), at I§4.

[40] The short answer to the "property and civil rights" argument, however, is that the appellant poses the wrong question. The issue is whether the contractual dispute between it and the respondent trustee properly relates to the bankruptcy. If so, the fact it also has a property and civil rights aspect does not in any way impair the bankruptcy court's jurisdiction.

[Justice Binnie went on to hold that the contract claim in dispute before the court fell within the Bankruptcy Court's jurisdiction. He also dismissed the appellant's argument that the Québec bankruptcy court had misdirected itself in refusing the appellant's request under *BIA*, section 187(7), to transfer the action to a bankruptcy court in British Columbia. Section 187(7) provides that the court, "on satisfactory proof that the affairs of the bankrupt can be more economically administered within another bankruptcy district or division, or for other sufficient cause, may by order transfer any proceedings under this Act that are pending before it to another bankruptcy district or division." The appellant argued that the action should be tried in British Columbia because (1) Azco Mining Co was incorporated under BC law; (2) the contract between the parties provided that it was to be governed by BC law; and (3) the contract also contained a choice of forum clause in favour of the BC courts. Justice Binnie held that great deference should be shown to the decision of the bankruptcy court in dealing with section 187(7) applications and that, in any event, the Québec bankruptcy court had ample grounds for concluding that no particular hardship would be inflicted on the appellant in allowing the litigation to proceed in Québec. Justice Binnie also indicated that bankruptcy courts should pay great deference to a choice of forum clause, but were not absolutely bound by the parties' choice. In any event, in his opinion, there was no choice of forum clause in the contract between the parties.]

Appeal dismissed.

Discussion

Justice Binnie accepts the proposition that there are clear advantages to all actions by the trustee being brought in the same court as the one in which the bankruptcy is being administered, but he does not spell out what the advantages are. Most bankruptcies, commercial or consumer, generate little litigation for a number of reasons. The trustee usually has no funds with which to initiate expensive litigation, though in some cases the trustee may be able to persuade a lawyer to accept a retainer on a contingency fee basis. If the trustee is in doubt about a claim or needs other guidance from the court, the trustee can make a summary application under *BIA*, section 34(1). So far as parties with a claim against the estate are concerned, unless they are trying to recover specific assets in the trustee's hands, for example, because the other party claims to hold a security interest in them, or to obtain a declaration about the status of particular funds, it may not be worth their while to bring the action if a favourable judgment will only result in their being treated as unsecured creditors of the estate for the amount awarded. Unsecured creditors typically only recover five cents on the dollar on the liquidation of the estate and often not even that. Recall, too, that in many actions before the bankruptcy courts, the courts will be applying non-bankruptcy law, pursuant to *BIA*, section 72(1), to resolve the dispute because there are no applicable bankruptcy provisions that provide an answer. In these cases, entitling the trustee to sue in the bankruptcy court where the insolvency was filed gives the trustee a clear logistical advantage if, as Azco Mining argued in the present case, the applicable law and most of the relevant evidence is linked to another province.

BIA, section 187(7), was obviously designed to address this type of situation. It is also a familiar one in non-bankruptcy situations where the litigating parties are in different jurisdictions and the defendant argues that, although the court in which the action was brought has jurisdiction under the applicable jurisdictional rules, the court should yield its jurisdiction to another court on *forum non conveniens* grounds. The *forum non conveniens* doctrine is of relatively recent origin in Canadian law; it was first officially embraced by the Supreme Court of Canada in *Amchen Products Inc v British Columbia Workers' Compensation Board*, [1993] 1 SCR 897. (A corresponding decision based on the Québec Civil Code is *Spar Aerospace v American Mobile Satellite*, 2002 SCC 78.) A leading Ontario Court of Appeal decision spelling out in great detail the many factors a court should consider in determining a *forum non conveniens* application is *Muscutt v Courcelles* (2002), 60 OR (3d) 20 (CA) (*Muscutt*). The Supreme Court of Canada reframed the test from *Muscutt*—the "real and substantial connection test"—in *Van Breda v Village Resorts Ltd*, 2012 SCC 17 (*Van Breda*). The test required two steps: (1) a court must determine whether there are one or more presumptive connecting factors present to assume jurisdiction using the jurisdiction *simpliciter* test; and (2), only if the jurisdiction is objected to by a party raising a *forum non conveniens* argument, then that party must show that there is another jurisdiction that is "clearly more appropriate" to hear the matter (*Van Breda* at para 108). This approach was recently affirmed by the Supreme Court of Canada in *Haaretz.com v Goldhar*, 2018 SCC 28. Justice Binnie, in *Azco Mining* (decided in 2001, when the *Muscutt* test had not yet been adapted by the Supreme Court of Canada in *Van Breda*), does not refer to this line of cases. Do you think that the courts sitting in bankruptcy will develop a different or more forum-biased *forum non conveniens* doctrine from the one embraced in non-bankruptcy cases? Would such an interpretation be desirable?

In *Re Essar Steel Algoma Inc et al*, 2016 ONSC 595 (*Re Essar Steel*) and in *Nortel Networks Corp*, 2015 ONSC 1354 (*Nortel*), the Ontario Supreme Court determined that the principles from *Sam Lévy* (also known as *Re River Eagle International Ltd*, 2001 SCC 92) also apply to *CCAA* proceedings, as "[t]he central nature of insolvency and the resolution of issues caused by insolvency are common to both *BIA* and *CCAA* proceedings and so too should the underlying principles" (*Re Essar Steel* at para 30, *Nortel* at para 24).

Janis P Sarra, "Of Paramount Importance: Interpreting the Landscape of Insolvency and Environmental Law" in Janis P Sarra, ed, *Annual Review of Insolvency Law 2012* (Toronto: Carswell, 2013) 453 at 453–508 (footnotes omitted)

Sections 91 and 92 of the *Constitution Act, 1867* distribute legislative authority between the provinces and the federal government. When validly enacted federal and provincial laws collide, courts have developed a framework of constitutional doctrines to address the effects, one such tool being the doctrine of federal paramountcy. The doctrine has generally been interpreted to mean that where there are two validly enacted statutes and there is a conflict, the provincial law is rendered inoperative only to the extent of the inconsistency. In the context of environmental legislation and insolvency proceedings, the courts have considered and applied both the "operational conflict" and the "frustration of federal purpose" tests. . . .

Both federal insolvency legislation and provincial environmental protection legislation engage and advance a public interest, although insolvency law is also principally a law regulating the conduct of private parties, including commercial parties, when a business or individual encounters financial distress. The Supreme Court of Canada has signalled a number of important principles in the interpretation of overlap between federal and provincial law, and these principles, when considered together, offer important guideposts to the issues. . . .

However, these principles by themselves may not be sufficient to help the courts resolve the issues that come up when insolvency law and environmental law intersect. While the operational conflict aspects of the paramountcy doctrine are well-settled law, establishing a high threshold before they are engaged, there has been considerable lack of clarity or consistency in the application of the frustration of purpose part of the doctrine. Given the broad purpose of the *CCAA*, there is some risk that courts will conclude that many environmental protection provisions are rendered inoperative, given that uneven interpretation. The issues regarding environmental protection law are also complex because the environment is not an express subject matter of legislation under the *Constitution Act, 1867*; rather, the Supreme Court of Canada has observed that it is a diffuse subject that cuts across many different areas of constitutional responsibility, some federal and some provincial. The Supreme Court has observed that broad wording is unavoidable in environmental protection legislation because of the breadth and complexity of the subject; and it is important not to frustrate the legislature in its attempt to protect the public against the dangers flowing from pollution. Equally, the Supreme Court has observed that the *CCAA* offers flexibility and considerable judicial discretion, making it responsive to complex reorganizations. Arguably, there is need for further development of interpretive principles when that flexibility and discretion are used in determining the applicability of the frustration of purpose part of the paramountcy doctrine. . . .

The Supreme Court of Canada has held that the courts should facilitate co-operation between federal and provincial laws where overlap exists, if this cooperation can be done within the rules laid down by the Constitution. The Supreme Court has held that where a federal statute can be interpreted so as not to interfere with a provincial statute, such an interpretation is to be applied in preference to another applicable construction that would bring about a conflict in the two statutes. Incidental effects on a federal law will not disturb the constitutionality of an otherwise valid provincial law. Provincial laws should not be rendered inoperative just because they touch on a matter in an area in which the federal government has legislated [*Robinson v Countrywide Factors*, [1977] 2 SCR 753]. . . .

As a corporation approaches insolvency, it is less likely to have assets available to meet requirements for environmental monitoring, much less remediation of contaminated sites. In part, environmental concerns arise during insolvency proceedings because the corporation did not adequately deal with environmental risks when it was solvent. The optimal approach to corporate environmental responsibility is to engage in good preventive strategies, including prevention and maintenance systems, monitoring, reporting and remediation programs, with strong accountability mechanisms for corporate directors and officers. Problems can arise when corporations have failed to implement effective systems, or have failed to maintain them as the corporation approaches insolvency. As the corporation becomes financially distressed, remedying environmental harm drops down the list of tasks to accomplish, as corporate officers struggle to meet ongoing operating expenses and debt repayment obligations. At the point of insolvency, the failure to address problems at an earlier time may have substantially increased the cost of complying with environmental obligations; and the status of environmental issues then becomes a critical issue for creditors in determining whether to enforce their claims through liquidation or to allow the corporation a chance to negotiate a workout that could potentially increase the longer term value of the corporation.

At the heart of some of the insolvency disputes is not only the claims on the value of the assets of the company, but the personal liability faced by officers, which they are seeking to compromise in a *CCAA* plan. Many environmental protection statutes in Canada impose personal liability on those persons who have charge, management or control of the corporation's activities or property. Many environmental statutes specify that if the corporation commits an offence, any director that authorizes, permits or acquiesces in the offence commits the same offence. Directors can face fines, and in the case of serious conduct, imprisonment. The trend in Canada has been to strengthen statutory provisions that impose consequences on directors for environmental harms. In most cases, these statutes also provide a defence of due diligence, which the directors and officers must establish on the civil standard of balance of probabilities. It is at the point of insolvency that corporate directors and officers face a greater potential of personal liability for their activities as the directing minds of the corporation because there may not be sufficient assets in the corporation to indemnify their good faith but erring conduct. . . .

These issues drive some of the paramountcy disputes under the *CCAA*. However, the *CCAA* does not preclude the provinces from exercising their extensive powers to regulate and control environmental protection; and where the *CCAA* can be interpreted so as not to interfere with a provincial statute, such an interpretation is to be applied in preference to another construction that would bring about a conflict in the two statutes. . . .

Where dual compliance with federal and provincial legislation is possible, but compliance with the provincial legislation is incompatible with the purpose of federal legislation, paramountcy can be invoked. While the operational conflict aspects of the paramountcy doctrine are well-settled law, the frustration of purpose part of the doctrine has had uneven and sometimes unclear treatment in the lower courts, creating some risk that provincial statutory provisions may be rendered inoperative where there is an overreaching interpretation of this aspect of the doctrine.... The Supreme Court of Canada has observed that paramountcy looks at the way in which federal and provincial power are exercised. It held that there is an operational conflict where dual compliance with the laws is not possible; and where it would be possible to comply with both statutes, the Court has found that there was no operational conflict [*Multiple Access v McCutcheon*, [1982] 2 SCR 161]....

The Supreme Court of Canada in *Re AbitibiBowater Inc* held that regulatory bodies may become involved in reorganization proceedings when they order the debtor to comply with statutory rules. As a matter of principle, reorganization does not amount to a licence to disregard rules. Yet there are circumstances in which valid and enforceable orders will be subject to an arrangement under the *CCAA*. One such circumstance is where a regulatory body makes an environmental order that explicitly asserts a monetary claim. The Supreme Court held that not all orders issued by regulatory bodies are monetary in nature and thus provable claims in an insolvency proceeding, but some may be, even if the amounts involved are not quantified at the outset of the proceedings. In the environmental context, the *CCAA* court must determine whether there are sufficient facts indicating the existence of an environmental duty that will ripen into a financial liability owed to the regulatory body that issued the order. Environmental claims do not have a higher priority than is provided for in the *CCAA* and considering substance over form prevents a regulatory body from artificially creating a priority higher than the one conferred on the claim by federal legislation. To exempt orders that are in fact monetary claims from the *CCAA* proceedings would amount to conferring on provinces a priority higher than the one provided for in the *CCAA*. If the order is not framed in monetary terms, the *CCAA* court must determine, in light of the factual matrix and the applicable statutory framework, whether it is a claim that will be subject to the claims process. There are three requirements that orders must meet in order to be considered claims that may be subject to the insolvency process. First, there must be a debt, a liability or an obligation to a creditor. In this case, the first criterion was met because the Province had identified itself as a creditor by resorting to environmental protection enforcement mechanisms. Second, the debt, liability or obligation must be incurred as of a specific time. This requirement was also met since the environmental damage had occurred before the time of the *CCAA* proceedings. The creditor's claim will be exempt from the single proceeding requirement if the debtor's corresponding obligation has not arisen as of the time limit for inclusion in the insolvency process; for example, to a debtor's statutory obligations relating to polluting activities that continue after the reorganization, because in such cases, the damage continues to be sustained after the reorganization has been completed. Third, it must be possible to attach a monetary value to the debt, liability or obligation. The present case turned on this third requirement, and the question was whether orders that are not expressed in monetary terms can be translated into such terms. The criterion used by courts to determine whether a contingent claim will be included in the insolvency process is whether the event that has not yet occurred is too remote or speculative. In the context of an environmental protection order, there must be sufficient indications that the regulatory body that triggered the enforcement mechanism will ultimately perform remediation work and assert a monetary claim to have its costs reimbursed; if there is sufficient certainty, the court will conclude that the order can be subject to the insolvency process. The Court observed that if activities at issue are ongoing, the *CCAA* court may well conclude that the order cannot be included in the insolvency process because the activities and resulting damages will continue after the reorganization is completed and hence exceed the time limit for a claim. If, on the other hand, the regulatory body, having no realistic alternative but to perform the remediation work itself, simply delays framing the order as a claim in order to improve its position in relation to other creditors, the *CCAA* court may conclude that this course of action is inconsistent with the insolvency scheme and decide that the order has to be subject to the claims process. Similarly, if the property is not under the debtor's control and the debtor does not, and realistically will not, have the means to perform the remediation work, the *CCAA* court may conclude that it is sufficiently certain that the regulatory body will have to perform the work. Certain indicators can guide the *CCAA* court in this assessment, including whether the activities are ongoing, whether the debtor is in control of the property, and whether the debtor has the means to comply with the order. The court may also consider the effect that requiring the debtor to comply with the order would have on the insolvency process. In this case, the *CCAA* court's assessment of the facts, particularly its finding that the orders were the first step towards performance of the remediation work by the Province, led to the conclusion that it was sufficiently certain that the Province would perform remediation work and therefore fall within the definition of a creditor with a monetary claim. The Court held that subjecting such orders to the claims process does not extinguish the debtor's environmental obligations; it merely ensures that the creditor's claim will be paid in accordance with insolvency legislation. Full compliance with orders that are found to be monetary in nature would shift the costs of remediation to third-party creditors, and replace the polluter-pay principle with a "third-party-pay" principle. The Court held that subjecting the orders to the insolvency process does not amount to issuing a licence to pollute, since insolvency proceedings do not concern the debtor's future conduct; a debtor that is reorganized must comply with all environmental regulations going forward in the same way as any other person. Moreover, to subject environmental protection orders to the claims process is not to invite corporations to restructure in order to rid themselves of their environmental liabilities. Processing creditors' claims against an insolvent debtor in an equitable and orderly manner is at the heart of insolvency legislation. Federal legislation governing the characterization of an order as a monetary claim is valid; and the Court held that because the provisions relate directly to Parliament's jurisdiction, the ancillary powers doctrine was not relevant to the case. It also held that the interjurisdictional immunity doctrine was not applicable, because a finding that a claim of an environmental creditor is monetary in nature does not interfere in any way with the creditor's activities; its claim is simply subjected to the insolvency process. Parliament recognized that regulatory bodies sometimes have to perform remediation work, when one does so, its claim with respect to remediation costs is subject to the insolvency process, but the claim is secured by a charge on the contaminated real property and certain other related property and benefits from a priority under s. 11.8(8) of the *CCAA*. Thus, Parliament struck a balance between the public's interest in enforcing environmental regulations and the interest of third-party creditors in being treated equitably [*Newfoundland and Labrador v AbitibiBowater Inc*, 2012 SCC 67 (*AbitibiBowater*)]. . . .

The purpose of Canadian environmental statutes is to prevent and remedy environmental contamination or harm. Environmental protection statutes are generally referred to as "public welfare" legislation, aimed at preventing potentially adverse effects through the enforcement of minimum standards of care and conduct of corporations and their directors and officers. They prohibit discharge of contaminants that have adverse effects and require remediation of contaminated sites, prompt reporting and clean-up of spills, and proper disposal of waste from corporate activities. The potential liability varies depending on the type and severity of the conduct giving rise to the environmental condition or damage....

The purposes of both the *CCAA* and provincial environmental protection legislation are remedial, and both advance important public interests. To differing degrees, they also affect private rights. The issue in respect of the frustration of purpose part of the paramountcy doctrine is whether compliance with a statutory obligation or regulatory directive frustrates the very purpose of the *CCAA*, to facilitate the process of negotiation with respect to approval of a plan of arrangement and/or compromise for the benefit of multiple stakeholders. In many cases, compliance with the provincial legislation will not frustrate or displace that facilitative purpose of the federal statute. That question is quite a distinct one from the court's exercise of its authority regarding aspects of the restructuring negotiations or ordering a stay on the particular facts in a *CCAA* proceeding, a distinction that is important, but not always made in the judgments....

The broad purpose ascribed to the *CCAA*, while extremely important, may result in abuse of the frustration of purpose part of the paramountcy doctrine. The purpose of the *CCAA* is furthered by private party negotiations. It lets a debtor claim that it is going to liquidate rather than reorganize if environmental compliance is "too expensive". Such an argument leaves the court to try and decide how much expense equals frustration of the purpose in each case, which is an inappropriate application of the frustration of purpose test. The alternative, throwing the costs to the "deep pockets" of provincial governments, will be tempting for parties, since it is less risky to the ultimate success of the federal "purpose" of facilitating a restructuring, also an inappropriate approach to the doctrine.

[Reprinted by permission of the publisher.]

Discussion

In addition to *AbitibiBowater*, the Supreme Court of Canada recently ruled on two other aspects of the intersection between federal and provincial law: (1) obligations under family law when one of the spouses becomes bankrupt in *Schreyer v Schreyer*, 2011 SCC 35; and (2) the relationship between provincial pension law and federal insolvency law, in *Sun Indalex Finance, LLC v United Steelworkers*, 2013 SCC 6 (*Indalex*). Both cases raise important social and economic issues in terms of the priorities under insolvency and bankruptcy legislation and their relationship with, and effect on, provincial remedial legislation. *Schreyer v Schreyer* is discussed in Chapter 7, Section I, "Introduction." *Indalex* is extracted in Chapter 13, "Carrying on Business During *CCAA* Proceedings," Section III, "Governance," and Chapter 14, "Claims," Section IV.E, "Priorities: Deemed Trusts." Please note that the Ontario Court of Appeal recently distinguished *Indalex* from the case before it in *Grant Forest Products Inc v Toronto-Dominion Bank*, 2015 ONCA 570 (*Grant Forest*), due to factual differences, including that fact that the *BIA* was not implicated in the proceedings in *Indalex* (as *Indalex* pertained solely to a *CCAA* proceeding) but were implicated in the proceedings from the beginning in *Grant Forest*.

In the context of bankruptcy discharge, there have also been two recent judgments in which the Supreme Court of Canada has struck down attempts by a provincial licensing authority of other highway regulatory authority to collect debts under provincial legislation after bankruptcy discharge: see *407 ETR Concession Company Limited v Canada (Superintendent of Bankruptcy)*, 2015 SCC 52 (*407 ETR*) (extracted below) and *Alberta (Attorney General) v Moloney*, 2015 SCC 51, discussed below and extracted in Chapter 11, Individual Bankruptcies and Consumer Issues.

In *Orphan Well Association v Grant Thornton Ltd*, 2017 ABCA 124 (the *Redwater* case), the Alberta Court of Appeal considered whether the insolvent company's environmental remediation obligations required by the provincial industry regulatory body trenched on the federal government's bankruptcy powers. The issue was whether the environmental obligations were provable claims. If the obligations were determined to be provable claims, the debtor could disclaim certain assets and disregard its environmental obligations. The Court considered arguments regarding general policy considerations, the overall fairness or reasonableness of the outcome, and the impact that the trial court's decision would have on environmental regulation, but ultimately determined Parliament would have made these considerations when drafting the *BIA* and the bankruptcy court could not make these exceptions itself. Relying on the test from *AbitibiBowater*, the court found that the environmental obligations were provable claims and that there was an operational conflict between those obligations and the priority of environmental claims under the *BIA*. The obligations were therefore unenforceable by the regulator. This decision was appealed to the Supreme Court of Canada.

In the interim between the Court of Appeal and Supreme Court decisions, creditors in Alberta rushed in bankruptcies based on the appellate decision, which resulted in debtor companies disclaiming $110 million in liabilities.[5] These liabilities have become the responsibility of the regulator and thus of the public. Author Sarah Hawco noted in a 2017 article, "A number of critics of the decisions have insinuated that there has been abuse of the insolvency system by the receivers, the secured lenders, and the debtor companies," but came to the conclusion that any loopholes would need to be closed by Parliament and not by the Courts.[6]

To the surprise of many insolvency practitioners and commentators, the majority of the Supreme Court of Canada (2019 SCC 5) overturned the Alberta Court of Appeal decision. The Majority ruled that there was no conflict between the provincial regulatory regime and federal bankruptcy and insolvency law, and that the *BIA* provision relied upon (s 14.06(4)) does not empower a trustee to walk away from the environmental liabilities of the estate it is administering. Chief Justice Wagner for the majority wrote: "Bankruptcy is not a licence to ignore rules, and insolvency professionals are bound by and must comply with valid provincial laws during bankruptcy" (at para 160). This decision is notable among the Supreme Court's recent bankruptcy decisions for upholding provincial jurisdiction by adopting a restrained interpretation of section 91(21) and so avoiding a federal-provincial conflict which would have triggered the paramountcy rule.

407 ETR Concession Co v Canada (Superintendent of Bankruptcy), 2015 SCC 52, [2015] 3 SCR 397

Gascon J (Abella, Rothstein, Cromwell, Moldaver, Karakatsanis and Wagner JJ concurring)

I.   INTRODUCTION

[1] Like its companion case, *Alberta (Attorney General) v Moloney*, 2015 SCC 51, this appeal concerns an alleged conflict between overlapping federal and provincial laws. The question at issue is whether Ontario's *Highway 407 Act*, 1998, S.O. 1998, c. 28 ("407

---

5   Fenner Stewart, "Interjurisdictional Immunity, Federal Paramountcy, Co-operative Federalism, and the Disinterested Regulator: Exploring the Elements of Canadian Energy Federalism in the Grant Thornton Case" (2018) 33:2 *Banking and Finance Law Review* at 227–64.

6   Sarah Hawco, "Redwater. Why Are We Still Talking About This Issue?" in Janis P Sarra & Barbara Romaine, eds, *Annual Review of Insolvency Law 2017* (Toronto: Carswell, 2018), art 7.

Act"), which sets out a debt enforcement mechanism in favour of the private owner and operator of an open-access toll highway, conflicts with the federal *Bankruptcy and Insolvency Act*, R.S.C. 1985, c. B-3 ("*BIA*"), which provides that a discharged bankrupt is released from all provable claims.

[2] For the reasons that follow, I find that, like in the companion appeal, the provincial law conflicts with the *BIA*. As a result, it offends the doctrine of federal paramountcy and is inoperative to the extent of the conflict.

II. FACTS

[3] Highway 407 is an open-access private highway. The highway was privatized in 1999 and has since been operated by 407 ETR Concession Company Limited ("ETR"). The *407 Act* governs the operation of Highway 407. While Highway 407 is a toll highway, its use is unrestricted. ETR cannot prevent anyone from accessing the highway. There is an electronic system that reads licence plates at the points of entry onto and exit from the highway. Alternatively, highway users can lease a toll device, which is affixed to the vehicle and is read instead of the licence plates. This electronic system records all trips made on the highway. The toll amount is then calculated. A corresponding invoice is delivered to the person in whose name the licence plates for the vehicle are issued, or if there is a toll device, to the lessee of the device.

[4] The *407 Act* defines ETR as the "owner" (s. 1) and empowers ETR to establish, collect and enforce the payment of tolls, administration fees and interest. This process begins with ETR delivering an invoice setting out the amount due. The amount becomes payable on the day the invoice is mailed, delivered by hand or sent by any other prescribed method: s. 15(1). If a person fails to pay the toll debt within 35 days, ETR may send that person a notice of failure to pay: s. 16(1). If the debt is not paid within 90 days of the debtor receiving that notice, s. 22(1) allows ETR to notify the Registrar of Motor Vehicles ("Registrar")....

[5] Upon receipt of this notice, the Registrar must ("shall") refuse to issue or renew the debtor's vehicle permit. As a result, the debtor is incapable of having a vehicle registered in his or her name. The Registrar has no discretion in that regard ...

[6] This provision is effective until the Registrar receives notice that the debt and related fees and interest have been paid....

[7] Matthew David Moore drove two cars, each registered under his name: a 1993 Pontiac and a 2002 Mercedes-Benz. Between August 1998 and March 2007, he had used Highway 407 1,973 times. As a result, he had accumulated a toll debt of $34,977.06. In March 2005, and then later in December 2006, ETR notified the Registrar of Mr. Moore's failure to pay the toll debt relating to his numerous trips on Highway 407, using both the Mercedes-Benz and the Pontiac. When the registration of the former vehicle expired, the Registrar refused to renew Mr. Moore's licence plates. Mr. Moore nonetheless continued to drive his Mercedes-Benz on Highway 407 for 18 months, without valid licence plates, contravening s. 51 of the *Highway Traffic Act*, R.S.O. 1990, c. H.8.

[8] On November 10, 2007, Mr. Moore made an assignment in bankruptcy. His Statement of Affairs listed ETR as an unsecured creditor. Although ETR was notified of Mr. Moore's assignment, it did not file a proof of claim and chose not to participate in the bankruptcy proceeding. On February 1, 2011, Mr. Moore obtained a discharge from bankruptcy, conditional on the payment of an amount of $1,210. As a result of paying that amount, he obtained an absolute discharge on June 21, 2011.

[9] Subsequently, Mr. Moore moved before the Registrar in Bankruptcy for an order that ETR's claim had been discharged in bankruptcy and that the Ministry of Transportation was compelled to issue him a permit upon payment of the usual fees. The order was granted but was later set aside before the matter was heard *de novo* in the Superior Court. At the hearing before the Superior Court, Mr. Moore contended that ETR could not use s. 22(4) of the *407 Act* to collect and enforce the toll debt because it had been discharged pursuant to s. 178 of the *BIA*. He claimed that s. 22(4) conflicted with s. 178 and offended the doctrine of federal paramountcy such that the federal bankruptcy provision should prevail over the *407 Act*. He sought an order that his debt had been released by his discharge and an order compelling the Ministry of Transportation to issue his vehicle permits.

III. JUDICIAL HISTORY

A. Ontario Superior Court of Justice, 2011 ONSC 6310, 30 M.V.R. (6th) 137 (Ont Sup Ct J)

[In the lower court, Newbould J found no conflict between the *407 Act* and the *BIA*.]

B. Ontario Court of Appeal, 2013 ONCA 769, 118 O.R. (3d) 161 (Ont CA)

[12] Having settled his dispute with ETR, Mr. Moore did not appeal the order. The Superintendent of Bankruptcy, concerned with the impact of the Superior Court's order on the bankruptcy system, filed an appeal. He argued that s. 22(4) of the *407 Act* conflicted with the operation of s. 178(2) of the *BIA* and that it frustrated the purposes of bankruptcy

[The Court of Appeal unanimously determined that there was no operational conflict, but that s 22(4) frustrated the rehabilitative purpose of the *BIA* since the denial of a vehicle permit can have a significant detrimental impact on the debtor and was therefore inoperative to the extent that it denies a debtor a fresh start. ETA was ordered to issue a vehicle permit to the Mr. Moore once he paid the applicable licensing fees.]

IV. ISSUE

[15] The Chief Justice formulated the following constitutional question:

> Is s. 22(4) of the *Highway 407 Act, 1998*, S.O, 1998, c. 28, constitutionally inoperative under the doctrine of federal legislative paramountcy, having regard to the *Bankruptcy and Insolvency Act*, R.S.C. 1985, c. B-3?

V. ANALYSIS

[16] ... there is no dispute here concerning the independent validity of the provincial and federal laws. Section 22 of the *407 Act* and s. 178 of the *BIA* were validly enacted by their respective governments. The only question before the Court is whether their concurrent operation results in a conflict. Building on my comments in the companion appeal, I need only examine s. 22(4) of the *407 Act* and ascertain its true meaning and substantive effect in the context of bankruptcy before applying the doctrine of paramountcy.

A. The 407 Act

[17] There is no question that the *407 Act* creates, in substance, a debt enforcement scheme. This was the legislative purpose identified by the motions judge and the Court of Appeal....

[21] I consequently agree with the Court of Appeal that the purpose and the effect of s. 22(4) of the *407 Act* are to allow a creditor, ETR, to enforce the collection of toll debts, which in the context of this appeal constitutes a claim provable in bankruptcy. The remaining issue is whether this enforcement scheme conflicts with s. 178(2) of the *BIA*.

B. Operational Conflict

[22] In the companion appeal, I describe what I consider to be a proper application of the operational conflict branch of the paramountcy test: Is it possible to apply the provincial law while complying with the federal law? Here, the Court of Appeal held that there was no operational conflict. In its view, the debtor was not required to pay the toll debt and could forego his right to a vehicle permit (para. 86), while ETR could comply with both laws by declining to pursue its remedy under s. 22 of the *407 Act* (para. 90). Although the Court of Appeal acknowledged that, with respect to the collection of a debt from a discharged bankrupt, the *BIA* said "no", while the *407 Act* said "yes" (para. 91), it nonetheless concluded that, on a strict reading of the test, there was no operational conflict....

[24] In my view, the respondent is correct on this issue of operational conflict. Pursuant to s. 178(2) of the *BIA*, creditors cease to be able to enforce their provable claims upon the bankrupt's discharge: *Schreyer v Schreyer*, 2011 SCC 35, [2011] 2 S.C.R. 605, at para. 21. As I indicate in the companion appeal, it is undisputed that a discharge under s. 178 of the *BIA* releases a debtor, thus preventing creditors from enforcing claims that are provable in bankruptcy. They are deemed to give up their right to enforce those claims. This includes both civil and administrative enforcement. In this case, ETR, the creditor, is faced with a clear prohibition under s. 178(2) of the *BIA*. It cannot enforce its provable claim, which has been released by an order of discharge. Since the debt collection mechanism put in place by s. 22(4) provides the creditor with an administrative enforcement scheme, it is impossible for ETR to use that remedy while also complying with s. 178(2) ... Indeed, ETR's toll debt is not listed as an exemption under s. 178(1), and the resulting financial liability of the debtor cannot survive his or her discharge. As a result, the *407 Act* says "yes" to the enforcement of a provable claim, while s. 178(2) of the *BIA* says "no", such that the operation of the provincial law makes it impossible to comply with the federal law.

[25] In other words, while the provincial scheme has the effect of maintaining the debtor's liability beyond his or her discharge, the federal law expressly releases him or her from that same liability. Both laws cannot "apply concurrently" ... or "operate side by side without conflict" ... a debtor cannot be found liable under the provincial law after having been released from that same liability under the federal law .... I respectfully disagree with my colleague that this conflict is "indirect" or concerns something that is merely "implicitly" prohibited by s. 178(2) of the *BIA* ... or that I am resorting to a broad interpretation of s. 178(2) in order to find that an operational conflict exists (para. 36). Under the federal law, the debt is not enforceable; under the provincial law, it is. The inconsistency is clear and definite. One law allows what the other precisely prohibits.

[26] In that regard, unlike my colleague, I do not believe that the language of s. 22(1) provides a possibility for there to be no operational conflict (para. 39). Once the Registrar is notified by ETR, as was the case on the facts on this appeal, s. 22(4) uses mandatory language ("shall"), such that the Registrar has no choice but to refuse to validate the debtor's vehicle permits. From that point in time, the Registrar is left with no discretion to terminate the enforcement process after, for instance, the debtor's discharge in bankruptcy. The Registrar is only required to reinstate the debtor's permits once notified

that the debt is paid: ss. 22(6) and 22(7). To suggest that dual compliance with both laws remains possible if ETR declines to pursue its remedy under s. 22 of the *407 Act* would be to turn a blind eye to the factual reality of this case, on the basis of which it was argued. In addition, as I explain in the companion appeal, to suggest that an operational conflict can be avoided in circumstances in which the provincial law does not operate leads, with respect, to a circular reasoning that removes a key condition for consideration of either of the two branches of the paramountcy doctrine, that is, the existence of two valid laws that operate side by side. Nor, as in the companion appeal, is it in my view valid to suggest that, to negate the operational conflict that exists here, the debtor can renounce his right under the *BIA* by paying the released debt or by accepting the debt collection mechanism of the *407 Act* and foregoing his right to a vehicle permit. If that were the case, the situation would no longer be one of a possibility of dual compliance with both laws. Rather, it would be one of "single" compliance with one of the laws, and renunciation of the operation of the other law by one of the actors involved. When the two laws operate side by side, ETR cannot comply with both at the same time, and the provincial law denies the debtor the benefit of the federal law.

[27] I therefore conclude that the operation of s. 22(4) to enforce a debt that was discharged in bankruptcy is in conflict with s. 178(2) of the *BIA*. Section 178 is a complete code in that it sets out which debts are released on the bankrupt's discharge and which debts survive the bankruptcy. Through s. 22(4), the province creates a new class of exempt debts that is not listed in s. 178(1). This operational conflict offends the doctrine of federal paramountcy.

C. Frustration of Federal Purpose

(a) Financial Rehabilitation

[28] That said, I consider that the operation of s. 22(4) also frustrates Parliament's purpose of providing discharged bankrupts with the ability to financially rehabilitate themselves. In the companion appeal, I explain this purpose of the *BIA* and its close relationship with the language of s. 178(2), which is aimed precisely at providing the bankrupt with a fresh start. While the intent of s. 178(2) is that the debtor will no longer be encumbered by the burden of pre-bankruptcy indebtedness, s. 22(4) allows ETR to continue burdening the discharged bankrupt until full payment of the debt, as if the discharge in bankruptcy had never occurred.

[29] When making his assignment in bankruptcy, Mr. Moore was indebted to ETR in the amount of $34,977.06. This was in November 2007. At the time of the hearing in the Superior Court, that is, in October 2011, the debt had more than doubled to $88,767.83. As time passes, the burden of ETR's debt gets heavier as interest accrues. In early 2011, the interest alone amounted to almost $1,400 per month. This is a crushing financial liability. Yet the more Mr. Moore delays payment of the toll debt, the more unlikely it is that he will ever be able to pay it and recover his vehicle registration privileges.

[30] If s. 22(4) is allowed to operate despite the debtor's bankruptcy and subsequent absolute discharge, this effectively creates an ever-increasing financial burden on the debtor. This burden attaches to the debtor despite a discharge in bankruptcy, even though the debtor will most likely never be able to pay ETR's debt in full. The debtor will be forever burdened by a pre-bankruptcy financial liability. This is contrary to Parliament's intention to give discharged bankrupts a fair opportunity to rehabilitate financially, freeing them from past indebtedness.

[31] ETR was notified of Mr. Moore's bankruptcy. It chose not to participate in the proceeding. It did not file a proof of claim, nor did it oppose Mr. Moore's discharge. In order to enforce its provable claim, ETR was required to take part, like any creditor, in the bankruptcy process. Had Parliament wished to exempt ETR's toll debt from that process, as well as from the consequences of a discharge, it would have done so expressly in s. 178(1) of the *BIA*. It did not. Therefore, I conclude that s. 22(4), if allowed to operate with respect to toll debts that are discharged in bankruptcy, frustrates the financial rehabilitation purpose of bankruptcy pursuant to s. 178(2). . . .

VI. DISPOSITION

[33] In my view, s. 22(4) of the *407 Act* is inoperative to the extent that it conflicts with s. 178(2) of the *BIA*. The provision cannot be used by ETR to enforce an otherwise discharged provable claim contrary to s. 178(2) of the *BIA*. In any event, the operation of s. 22(4) frustrates the financial rehabilitation purpose of s. 178(2). I would dismiss the appeal with costs . . .

Appeal dismissed

[Justice Côté and McLachlin CJC concurring in separate reasons.]

Discussion Related to Section 91(21) of *The Constitution Act, 1867*

In *Weddell (Trustee of) v Institute of Chartered Accountants of Alberta*, 2016 ABQB 248, the corporate trustee in a bankruptcy applied to the court for a declaration that the *Regulated Accounting Profession Act*, RSA 2000, c R-12 (*RAPA*) had no application to the bankruptcy proceedings of *Weddell* in that the Institute of Chartered Accountants of Alberta could not interfere with the bankruptcy trustee by exercising its investigatory powers under *RAPA*. The corporate trustee argued that the *BIA* and its regulations "constitute a complete code designed to provide for the administration of bankruptcies and proposals by a trustee in accordance with the *BIA* without interference, except with leave of the Court."[7] The trustee further argued that the doctrines of interjurisdictional immunity and federal paramountcy should be applied so that Part 5 of *RAPA* be read down as not applying to the *BIA* Administration Actions. The Court found that any entrenchment of *RAPA* on the *BIA* was not serious enough to invoke the doctrine of interjurisdictional immunity. In finding that the two pieces of legislation did not conflict operationally and *RAPA* did not frustrate the purpose of the *BIA* (and thus the doctrine of paramountcy was not to be applied), KG Neilson J wrote at paragraph 101:

> Clearly, in the Canadian federal system, there will be interplay or overlap between provincial and federal legislation. The Supreme Court has made it clear that courts should favour an interpretation of such legislation which does not result in incompatibility. In my view, the *BIA* is not in any way intended to be a complete code to address any and all matters which may arise in relation to a particular bankruptcy or insolvency. The *BIA* itself contemplates that provincial legislation continues to apply. The above noted decisions make it clear that it is entirely possible for both federal legislation (the *BIA*) and provincial legislation (those statutes dealing with the regulation of professional bodies) to be applied to the investigation and discipline of trustees who are also members of other professional bodies. Rather than frustrating the provisions of the *BIA* as respects

---

7   *Weddell (Trustee of) v Institute of Chartered Accountants of Alberta*, 2016 ABQB 248 at para 47.

the conduct of trustees, the provisions in provincial legislation such as RAPA may be interpreted so as to complement the provisions in the *BIA*.

This is a fairly recent lower court decision and therefore is not very authoritative, however, it offers a contrasting approach to interpreting the scope of the *BIA*. Please note that the Alberta Court of Appeal affirmed the Queen's Bench decision when the decision was appealed on other grounds (*AC Waring & Associates Inc v Institute of Chartered Accountants of Alberta*, 2017 ABCA 152).

Anna Lund, "Lousy Dentists, Bad Drivers, and Abandoned Oil Wells: A New Approach to Reconciling Provincial Regulatory Regimes with Federal Insolvency Law" (2017) 80:1 *Saskatchewan Law Review* 157

Insolvency law conflicts with provincial regulatory regimes in a number of different areas, ranging from securities regulation to occupational health and safety to rodent control. This summary of case law focuses on the conflict between insolvency law and environmental regulations, and insolvency law and individual licensing regimes. These are two areas on which the Supreme Court of Canada has opined in recent years, and where recent case law strikes a different balance between provincial and federal powers than earlier precedents.

The decisions discussed in this section grapple with the question of when a regulatory obligation becomes a provable claim. The concept of a provable claim is central to insolvency law. Once insolvency proceedings commence, a regulator with a provable claim is stayed from enforcing it. The debtor can compromise or release the provable claim in the insolvency proceedings. Conversely, a nonprovable obligation is not stayed, compromised, or released by insolvency proceedings. A regulator to whom a non-provable obligation is owed can continue to enforce it notwithstanding the insolvency proceedings. It is crucial to determine whether or not a regulatory obligation is a provable claim, because it informs whether a regulator will be able to demand compliance with the obligation during and following insolvency proceedings. . . .

These cases serve as an important reminder that insolvency law clashes with provincial regulatory regimes in a range of contexts. The licence denial cases are divorced from the (sometimes) antagonistic debate around environmental protection and economic development. It can be useful to consider the conflict between regulatory and insolvency law in a less fraught area.

The 2015 cases of *Moloney* and *407 ETR* concerned individuals who owed debts as a result of driving. One had caused a motor vehicle accident while driving without insurance. The other made regular use of a toll highway but did not pay the toll. In the provinces where the individuals resided, the provincial legislation authorized the motor vehicle regulator to deny individuals their driver's licences, or other authorizations needed to drive, unless they were making efforts to repay the debts. In both cases, the individuals made assignments into bankruptcy and received discharges. Notwithstanding the bankruptcies, the provincial regulators continued the suspensions of the individuals' driver's licences.

In *Moloney*, the Court applied the *AbitibiBowater* test and succinctly determined that the debts were provable claims. The regulator had exercised its enforcement power, the debt arose before the bankruptcy, and it was "clearly monetary in nature." This point was conceded by the regulator in *407 ETR*.

In both cases, the Court characterized the suspension of the driver's licence as a debt enforcement measure that had the effect of compelling a debtor to either pay the debt or forgo driving. The suspension provisions conflicted with the bankruptcy stay—the *BIA* bars claimants from taking steps to enforce provable claims. Because of this conflict, the provincial legislation was rendered inoperative under the doctrine of paramountcy and the regulator could not maintain the suspension once the debtor discharged the debt in bankruptcy.

III. EVALUATING THE CURRENT APPROACH: FOUR CRITIQUES

Critics of the *AbitibiBowater* test contend that it foments uncertainty and creates perverse incentives. This section summarizes these criticisms and adds two additional criticisms. First, the test fails to directly engage the key question of how to balance competing regulatory and insolvency interests in an intellectually honest and open way. Second, the test does not adequately respect the division of powers between federal and provincial governments....

1. The Limits of the Bankruptcy and Insolvency Power

A regulator could argue that there is a constitutional limit on the degree to which insolvency law can interfere with regulatory obligations. The federal government passed the *BIA* and the *CCAA* pursuant to its "bankruptcy and insolvency" power. A regulator could argue that the definition of a provable claim is invalid to the extent it includes regulatory obligations, because such a definition extends beyond the scope of the federal bankruptcy and insolvency power, and into the classes of subjects over which the provincial governments have exclusive jurisdiction. Courts will deem a law to be invalid if it is passed by one government with respect to a matter that falls under the classes of subjects that the *Constitution Act, 1867* assigns to the other level of government. Alternatively, the regulator could argue that the definition of provable claim should be interpreted narrowly. Courts will prefer an interpretation of a law that results in it being characterized as constitutional over one that results in it being deemed unconstitutional. Where a law could be read broadly or narrowly, and the broad construction of the law appears to extend to matters outside of the enacting government's jurisdiction, the court will "read down" the law "so as to keep it within the permissible scope of [the enacting legislative body's] power."

A regulator contesting the validity of the definition of provable claim, or seeking to have it read down, would need to define the scope of the bankruptcy and insolvency power and explain how this definition of the federal power limits the degree to which insolvency legislation can interfere with provincial regulatory obligations. A regulator mounting such a constitutional challenge faces a significant hurdle. There is no agreed upon definition of the bankruptcy and insolvency power. Courts and scholars have attempted to articulate one. For instance, in a concurring opinion in the 1955 Supreme Court decision of *Canadian Bankers' Association v Attorney-General of Saskatchewan*, Justice Rand offered the following definitions of bankruptcy and insolvency:

> Bankruptcy is a well understood procedure by which an insolvent debtor's property is coercively brought under a judicial administration in the interests primarily of the creditors. To this proceeding not only a personal stigma may attach but restrictions on freedom in future business activity may result. The relief to the debtor consists in the cancellation

of debts which, otherwise, might effectually prevent him from rehabilitating himself economically and socially.

Insolvency, on the other hand, seems to be a broader term that contemplates measures of dealing with the property of debtors unable to pay their debts in other modes or
arrangements as well. There is the composition and the voluntary assignment, devices
which, in appropriate circumstances, may avoid technical bankruptcy without too great
prejudice to creditors and hardship to debtors.

A regulator might point out that these definitions contemplate interfering with
financial claims, not regulatory obligations, to suggest that interfering with the latter
falls beyond the scope of the bankruptcy and insolvency power. But the definition is not
static; bankruptcy and insolvency are evolving concepts. In dissenting reasons in the
1978 Supreme Court case of *Robinson v Countrywide Factors Ltd*, Chief Justice Laskin
noted that bankruptcy and insolvency "is a power . . . whose ambit, did not and does not
lie frozen under conceptions held of bankruptcy and insolvency in 1867." Arguably, the
conceptions of bankruptcy and insolvency have expanded to include a greater focus on
rehabilitation that extends well beyond the release of debtors' financial claims. Many
legislative provisions allow for additional forms of relief. For example, a court can stay
and compromise financial claims against third parties, in addition to those against the
debtor. Likewise, insolvency legislation authorizes courts to stay non-monetary regulatory claims against a debtor when it is not contrary to the public interest. The terms
"bankruptcy" and "insolvency" might mean something quite different nowadays than
they did in 1867 or 1955. The federal government's powers to enact legislation that stays
and compromises a broad range of obligations may have likewise expanded.

On the other hand, if the bankruptcy and insolvency power is defined too broadly, it
could render the division of powers contemplated in the *Constitution Act, 1867* meaningless by giving the federal government carte blanche to interfere with provincial heads
of power including property, civil rights, and non-renewable natural resources. If the
division of powers means anything, there must be a constitutional limit to the types of
obligations that can be stayed, compromised, or released by insolvency legislation. . . .

IV. A BETTER TEST FOR PROVABLE CLAIMS

The clash between provincial regulatory obligations and federal insolvency law implicates the division of powers. Neither level of government, acting alone, can be entrusted
with policing the division of powers—this role falls to the courts. Certainty is valued in
insolvency law, and courts may be inclined to develop a bright line rule to resolve the
regulatory-insolvency clash. However, a principled standard can better respond to the
criticisms levied in the previous section. This section starts by outlining and critiquing
one permutation of a bright line rule. Next, it articulates a principled standard for determining when regulatory obligations become provable claims. The section explains how
the test would be implemented and then illustrates as much by applying the standard to
resolve three recent disputes.

A. A Bright Line Rule

Courts have sought to avoid the uncertainty of the *AbitibiBowater* test—and before it
the *Northern Badger* test—by adopting a bright line rule. Justice Morawetz, in the first
instance decisions in *Nortel* and *Northstar*, held that a regulatory claim should be provable if the claim relates to past, as opposed to ongoing, operations of the company and

requires the debtor "to react or respond to a step taken by the [regulator] and in doing so, incur a financial obligation." Morawetz J was concerned that imposing such an expense on the debtor would result in funds being "directed away from creditors participating in the insolvency proceedings." In *Redwater*, Chief Justice Wittmann made a similar point. He opined that the abandonment orders must be provable claims, because otherwise the trustee and receiver would be required to expend funds to abandon the wells, resulting in reduced recovery for the other creditors. This bright line rule would result in a broad swath of regulatory obligations being treated as provable claims.

A bright line rule does not strike the right balance when it deems any regulatory obligation a provable claim if the obligation relates to a past operation and would require the debtor or insolvency professional to incur an expense. Such broad-based relief gives the debtor too much leeway to disregard the general law, putting important public interests at risk. It creates too much of a moral hazard. The insolvency system risks eroding public support if it allows debtors to use insolvency proceedings as a "car wash" to avoid regulatory obligations.

Faced with such a wide-reaching approach to defining regulatory obligations as provable claims, regulators may take preventative measures to compel compliance. These measures may impose additional costs on debtors and impede economic activity. For instance, environmental regulators may require companies to post significant security before undertaking potentially polluting activities. The affected regulator responded to the *Redwater* decision by increasing the solvency threshold a licencee must meet before the regulator will approve a transfer of licences. This change is expected to restrict economic activity in Alberta's oil and gas industry. Regulators of individual licences (e.g., driving or professional) may impose harsher measures—such as the complete revocation of a licence—if they are concerned that less harsh sanctions may be avoided using insolvency proceedings. Regulators would not be prone to such stifling reactions if courts adopted a narrower view of which regulatory obligations are provable claims.

B. A Principled Standard

Writing about the clash of insolvency law on the one hand, and environmental or pension law on the other, Justice Romaine of the Alberta Court of Queen's Bench opined that "[t]here are no bright-line answers to these balancing issues." This observation applies broadly to the clash between provincial regulatory obligations and federal insolvency law. Instead of seeking a bright line rule, courts need to develop a principled standard for determining when regulatory obligations should be treated as provable claims and when they should not. This standard should require the courts to engage with the key question of balancing the competing public interests advanced by insolvency legislation and regulatory regimes, and do more to safeguard provincial governments' constitutional powers.

The idea of a court considering the public interest to resolve the conflict between provincial regulatory and federal insolvency law is already contemplated by federal insolvency legislation. In insolvency proceedings, a regulator is automatically stopped from pursuing monetary claims against a debtor. In a Division I Proposal or *CCAA* proceedings, the debtor can apply to have this stay extended to cover a regulator's non-monetary claims if it can show that such an order is necessary for a viable restructuring and would not otherwise be contrary to the public interest. This test recognizes that interfering with a regulator's powers may not be justified in some cases because of the concomitant risk to important public interests like health, safety, and the environment.

The *AbitibiBowater* test could be modified to include public interests as a key consideration when determining whether or not a regulatory obligation should be treated as a provable claim. In *AbitibiBowater*, the Supreme Court articulated a three-part test for determining whether or not a regulatory obligation is a provable claim. The Court's analysis, in that case, focused on the third part of the test, that is, whether or not it is possible to attach a monetary value to the claim. Most courts applying *AbitibiBowater* have adopted a similar focus on the third part. Very little has been said about the first part of the test, that is, whether or not there is a debt, liability, or obligation owed to a creditor. In *AbitibiBowater*, the Supreme Court indicated that this part was satisfied as soon as the regulator has "exercised its enforcement power against a debtor." This interpretation of the first part of the test sets a very low bar that is easily surpassed.

And yet, another interpretation of the first part of the *AbitibiBowater* test is possible. The first part of the *AbitibiBowater* test borrows language from the Northern Badger case, which distinguished between debts owed to the Crown and duties owed to the public. A court could read this distinction back into the first part of the *AbitibiBowater* test, and consider the importance of the public interests protected by the regulatory obligation when deciding whether the debtor owes a debt, liability or obligation to a creditor. I propose that the court should then weigh the public interest protected by the regulatory obligation (i.e. health, safety, or the environment) against the impact of compliance on the viability of the insolvency proceedings, and the public interests advanced by the insolvency proceedings.

Under the reformulated test, the second and third parts of the *AbitibiBowater* test would still be relevant to the analysis, but courts would place less emphasis on them than they currently do. An obligation would not be provable if it "has not arisen as of the time limit for inclusion in the insolvency process." Usually this means the obligation must have arisen prior to the commencement of insolvency proceedings, but there are exceptions which allow for the inclusion of environmental remediation obligations that arise later. Where a regulatory obligation has been turned into a debt, it would be subjected to the scheme of distribution set out in the insolvency proceedings. To hold otherwise would create too much scope for litigation over the competing public values underlying different Crown debts. However, where the obligation remains unliquidated, the court's focus would shift from determining the likelihood of the obligation being monetized to weighing the competing public interests.

The first benefit of this test is that it would refocus the discussion onto relevant considerations. As compared to the *AbitibiBowater* test, this approach would invite the court to make the decision about what gets stayed, compromised, or discharged in insolvency proceedings with respect to the relevant competing policies as opposed to seemingly arbitrary details, such as whether or not a piece of property is jointly owned, or whether the legislation provides a mechanism to liquidate an obligation. The test would also remove some of the perverse incentives created by the current test. Debtors could not be certain whether their regulatory obligations will be deemed provable and therefore would have little incentive to purposefully avoid complying with them. Regulators would not delay enforcing obligations. Instead, if a regulator thought an obligation should not be impacted by the insolvency, it would have to articulate what public interest was at stake and why it outweighed the benefits derived from facilitating a successful restructuring or liquidation.

This reformulated test also better reflects the division of power between federal and provincial governments. The *AbitibiBowater* test allows the federal government to interfere with any regulatory power if it is sufficiently certain that the regulator will liquidate the obligation and enforce it against the debtor company. The Canadian legal system is extremely adept at monetizing obligations, and so the scope for federal intrusion into provincial regulatory regimes could be very large. The federal insolvency power trumps, regardless of the importance, or lack thereof, the public interest protected by provincial regulations. The reformulated test would require a court to consider provincially protected public interests, instead of automatically preferring public interests advanced by federal insolvency legislation. The jurisdiction of provincial legislatures should be safeguarded when public interests protected by provincial regulatory regimes outweigh the benefits of successful insolvency proceedings.

The reformulated test is not a bright line rule, but rather a flexible standard. It will create some uncertainty. This uncertainty can be (partially) dispelled by articulating the types of factors a court should consider ...

[The author then discusses the types of facts a court should consider, including: (1) ongoing and past operations; (2) financial means; (3) imminence of harm; (4) control of regulated property; (5) party expectations; and (6) efforts to comply.]

[Reprinted by permission of the publisher.]

Saskatchewan (Attorney General) v Lemare Lake Logging Ltd, 2015 SCC 53, [2015] 3 SCR 419

Abella, Gascon JJ (Cromwell, Moldaver, Karakatsanis and Wagner JJ concurring):

[1] Prior to 2005, receivership proceedings involving assets in more than one province were complicated by the simultaneous appointment of different receivers in different jurisdictions. Because of the inefficiency resulting from this multiplicity of proceedings, the federal government amended its bankruptcy legislation to permit their consolidation through the appointment of a national receiver. This appeal involves a constitutional challenge to provincial farm legislation on the grounds that it conflicts with this national receivership regime. For the reasons that follow, we see no such conflict.

[2] Lemare Lake Logging Ltd., a secured creditor, brought an application pursuant to s. 243(1) of the *Bankruptcy and Insolvency Act*, R.S.C. 1985, c. B-3 (*BIA*), for the appointment of a receiver over substantially all of the assets except livestock of its debtor, 3L Cattle Company Ltd, a "farmer" within the meaning of *The Saskatchewan Farm Security Act*, S.S. 1988–89, c. S-17.1 (*SFSA*). 3L Cattle contested the appointment and argued that Lemare Lake had to comply with Part II of the *SFSA* before seeking the appointment of a receiver under s. 243(1).

[3] Part II of the *SFSA* provides that, before starting an action with respect to farm land, a creditor must serve a "notice of intention", engage in mandatory mediation, and prove that the debtor has no reasonable possibility of meeting its obligations or is not making a sincere and reasonable effort to meet its obligations. This includes an action for a receivership order pursuant to s. 243(1) of the *BIA*.

[4] Lemare Lake argued that the doctrine of paramountcy rendered certain provisions of the *SFSA* constitutionally inoperative where an application is made to appoint a receiver pursuant to s. 243(1) of the *BIA*.

[5] Lemare Lake and 3L Cattle were incorporated by David Dutcyvich in the 1980s. As a result of disagreements beginning in January 2010 between Mr. Dutcyvich and his two sons, the businesses were restructured, with Mr. Dutcyvich retaining the sole interest in 3L Cattle, and his two sons retaining the sole interest in Lemare Lake.

[6] In connection with the restructuring, 3L Cattle assumed the primary obligation to repay a loan of $10 million to Concentra Financial Services Association. Lemare Lake,

however, remained contingently liable for the debt. By written agreement dated December 21, 2010, 3L Cattle indemnified Lemare Lake from any liability in respect of the Concentra loan.

[7] To secure the payment and performance of its obligations to Lemare Lake, 3L Cattle gave Lemare Lake a mortgage dated January 21, 2011 in respect of its interest in 120 parcels of land in Saskatchewan, and a security interest in all non-inventory goods and equipment of 3L Cattle, including machinery, fixtures and tools, by means of a security agreement dated January 19, 2011.

[8] When 3L Cattle failed to repay the Concentra loan when it became due on January 29, 2013, Concentra sought repayment from both 3L Cattle and Lemare Lake. In turn, Lemare Lake, which was experiencing its own financial problems and had secured a protection order under the *Companies' Creditors Arrangement Act*, R.S.C. 1985, c. C-36, attempted to realize on its security over 3L Cattle's assets. It accordingly applied to the Saskatchewan Court of Queen's Bench for the appointment of a national receiver pursuant to s. 243(1) of the *BIA* over substantially all of the assets of 3L Cattle, except livestock.

[9] 3L Cattle argued that because it was a "farmer" within the meaning of the *SFSA*, Lemare Lake had to comply with Part II of the *SFSA* before applying for the appointment of a national receiver. Part II requires, in part, that before commencing an action with respect to farm land, a person must submit a notice of intention, await the expiry of a 150-day notice period, and engage in a mandatory review and mediation process.

[10] The chambers judge found that the provisions in Part II of the *SFSA* did not conflict with s. 243(1) of the *BIA* and dismissed Lemare Lake's application. She found no operational conflict between the federal and provincial legislation, because a secured creditor can comply with both the federal and provincial legislation by obtaining a court order under the *SFSA* permitting it to commence an action before applying for the appointment of a receiver under s. 243(1) of the *BIA*. Nor did she find any conflict in purpose. In her view, the purpose of s. 243(1) was to allow for the appointment of a national receiver, a purpose that was not frustrated by compliance with Part II of the *SFSA*. This means that a secured creditor must comply with the provisions of Part II of the *SFSA* before making an application pursuant to s. 243(1) of the *BIA*, which Lemare Lake had failed to do. The chambers judge's alternative view was that even if she had found Part II of the *SFSA* to be inoperative, she would not have appointed a receiver.

[The Court of Appeal dismissed Lemare Lake's appeal, agreeing with the chambers judge that a receiver should not be appointed and that there was no operational conflict. However, it found that Part II of the *SFSA* frustrated the purpose of s 243 of the *BIA*—to authorize the appointment of national receivers and to ensure that such receivers be able to act effectively in insolvency—and is inoperative in circumstances where an application is made to appoint a receiver pursuant to s 243(1) of the *BIA*.]

[13] The Attorney General for Saskatchewan was granted leave to appeal to this Court. Subsequent to the decision of the Court of Appeal, however, Lemare Lake and 3L Cattle settled their dispute. The Court appointed former counsel for Lemare Lake as *amicus curiae* to respond to the submissions of the Attorney General. *Amicus* was content to have the matter heard by this Court despite its mootness. In our view, the ongoing importance of resolving this issue in Saskatchewan supports our deciding this appeal ... Moreover, it is worth noting that this is an appeal from the reasons, not the disposition, of the Court of Appeal, which is fully authorized by s. 40 of the *Supreme*

Court Act, R.S.C. 1985, c. S-26 ... Neither the Attorney General of Canada nor the Superintendent of Bankruptcy intervened.

[14] Before this Court, the submissions were focussed on whether ss. 9 to 22 in Part II of the *SFSA* are constitutionally inoperative when an application is made to appoint a national receiver under s. 243(1) of the *BIA* by reason of the doctrine of paramountcy. For the following reasons, we agree with the chambers judge that there is no conflict, and therefore that ss. 9 to 22 of the *SFSA* are not constitutionally inoperable....

[24] The litigation in this case proceeded on the assumption that s. 243 of the *BIA* and Part II of the *SFSA* were validly enacted. Section 243 of the *BIA* falls within Parliament's exclusive power to enact laws in relation to bankruptcy and insolvency, while Part II of the *SFSA* falls within Saskatchewan's power to enact laws in relation to property and civil rights: *Constitution Act, 1867*, ss. 91(21) and 92(13).

[25] The parties essentially accepted the conclusion of the chambers judge and the Court of Appeal about the absence of operational conflict because it is possible to comply with both statutes by obtaining an order under the *SFSA* before seeking the appointment of a receiver under s. 243 of the *BIA*. The creditor can comply with both laws by observing the longer periods required by provincial law. In that regard, the federal law is permissive and the provincial law, more restrictive. This has been regularly considered not to constitute an operational conflict ... The issue before this Court therefore centres on whether the Court of Appeal was right to conclude that the provincial legislation frustrates the purpose of the federal legislation.

[26] To prove that provincial legislation frustrates the purpose of a federal enactment, the party relying on the doctrine "must first establish the purpose of the relevant federal statute, and then prove that the provincial legislation is incompatible with this purpose" ... The burden a party faces in successfully invoking paramountcy is accordingly a high one; provincial legislation restricting the scope of permissive federal legislation is insufficient on its own ...

[27] And, as previously noted, paramountcy must be applied with restraint. In the absence of "very clear" statutory language to the contrary, courts should not presume that Parliament intended to "occupy the field" and render inoperative provincial legislation in relation to the subject ...

[28] It is in light of the above principles that we turn to the federal and provincial provisions at issue.

[29] Section 243(1) is found in Part XI of the *BIA*, dealing with secured creditors and receivers. It authorizes a court, upon the application of a secured creditor, to appoint a receiver where such appointment is "just or convenient." ...

[30] In s. 243, courts are given the authority to appoint a receiver with the power to act nationally, thereby eliminating the need to apply to courts in multiple jurisdictions for the appointment of a receiver.

[31] Under s. 244(1), a secured creditor who intends to enforce a security on all or substantially all of the inventory, accounts receivable or other property of an insolvent debtor that was acquired for, or used in relation to, a business carried on by the insolvent person, is generally required to send a notice of that intention to the insolvent person. Section 243(1.1) states that, where notice is to be sent under s. 244(1), the appointment of a national receiver cannot be made before the expiry of 10 days after the day on which the secured creditor sends the notice....

[32] The national receivership regime does not oust a secured creditor's power to have a receiver appointed privately, or by court order under provincial law or any other

federal law. Where, however, that receiver takes possession or control of all or substantially all of the inventory, accounts receivable or other property of the insolvent debtor or bankrupt, he or she is a "receiver" for purposes of Part XI of the *BIA* and must comply with the provisions in that part: see s. 243(2).

[33] The provincial scheme at issue, the *SFSA*, was enacted in 1988, with roots in legislation governing Saskatchewan farm land dating back several decades: see Donald H. Layh, *A Legacy of Protection: The Saskatchewan Farm Security Act: History, Commentary & Case Law* (2009), at pp. 54–57.

[34] Part II of the *SFSA* is entitled "Farm Land Security". Its purpose is "to afford protection to farmers against loss of their farm land." . . .

[Part II of the *SFSA* prohibits commencement of any "action" with respect to farm land, including the appointment of a receiver. There is an exception for mortgagees under section 11 but unless an order under section 11 is given, any action commenced is a nullity. Mortgagees must serve a notice of intention on the farmer and the Farm Land Security Board and wait 150 days before applying under section 11. Prior to the expiry of the 150 days, the mortgagee and the farmer must partake in mediation and the board will prepare a report as part of the section 11 application. If mediation is unsuccessful and the 150 days passes, the mortgage can apply for leave to commence an action. "The Court will dismiss the application is it is satisfied that it is not 'just and equitable' according to the purpose and spirit of the *SFSA* to make the order" (para 37).]

[38] As a result of the concurrent operation of s. 243(1) of the *BIA* and Part II of the *SFSA*, a secured creditor wishing to enforce its security interest against farm land must wait 150 days, rather than the 10 days imposed under federal law. The creditor must also comply with the various additional requirements of the *SFSA*, such as the statutory presumptions described above. That interference with s. 243(1), however, does not, in and of itself, constitute a conflict. A conflict will only arise if such interference frustrates the purpose of the federal regime. This requires inquiring into the purpose of s. 243(1). . . .

[45] . . .What the evidence shows instead is a simple and narrow purpose: the establishment of a regime allowing for the appointment of a national receiver, thereby eliminating the need to apply for the appointment of a receiver in multiple jurisdictions. . . .

[49] Any uncertainty about whether s. 243 was meant to displace provincial legislation like the *SFSA* is further mitigated by s. 72(1) of the *BIA*, which states:

> 72. (1) The provisions of this Act shall not be deemed to abrogate or supersede the substantive provisions of any other law or statute relating to property and civil rights that are not in conflict with this Act, and the trustee is entitled to avail himself of all rights and remedies provided by that law or statute as supplementary to and in addition to the rights and remedies provided by this Act.

This too demonstrates that Parliament has explicitly recognized the continued operation of provincial law in the bankruptcy and insolvency context, except to the extent that it is inconsistent with the *BIA*. . . .

Conclusion

[73] *Amicus* has, with respect, been unable to satisfy his burden to prove that ss. 9 to 22 of the *SFSA* conflict with the purpose of s. 243 of the *BIA*. Parliament's purpose of providing bankruptcy courts with the power to appoint a national receiver is not frustrated

by the procedural and substantive conditions set out in the provincial legislation. While these conditions require a secured creditor to seek leave before bringing an application for the appointment of a receiver under s. 243 — a process which takes at least 150 days and imposes other procedural and substantive requirements — they do not hinder the purpose of allowing for the appointment of a national receiver. The purpose of permissive federal legislation is not frustrated simply because provincial legislation restricts the scope of that permission. . . .

[74] The Court of Appeal's conclusion that Part II of the *SFSA* is constitutionally inoperative where an application is made to appoint a receiver pursuant to s. 243(1) of the *BIA*, is accordingly set aside. In view of the agreement of the parties, there will be no further order with respect to costs.

[In dissenting reasons, Côté J would have found that timeliness was a purpose of a national receivership appointment. Accordingly, she would have found a frustration of federal purpose and declared Part II of the *Saskatchewan Farm Security Act* inoperative to the extent of its conflict with the federal receivership regime.]

Appeal allowed.

Discussion

As noted by the Court at paragraph 13 of this decision, this case was appealed to the Supreme Court of Canada by the attorney general for Saskatchewan despite the fact that the parties had settled their dispute. Former counsel for the creditor was appointed as amicus curiae to respond to the submissions of the attorney general. The Government of Saskatchewan's choice to appeal this decision demonstrates the importance of the constitutional question to the province. Why do you think the resolution of this question was so important to Saskatchewan?

This dispute arose as an inter-family dispute. The father established the creditor corporation in 1984 and brought his two sons into the business. The father also established the debtor corporation. For reasons that are unclear, the family could no longer continue doing business together. They restructured their affairs by 2011 so that the father was the shareholder and director of the debtor corporation and the sons were the directors of the creditor corporation and the trustees of the shareholder of the creditor corporation. How do you think these circumstances affected the behaviour of the creditor in realizing its security interest?

Recall the Tassé Report excerpted in Chapter 1. In this report, the authors described bankruptcy as an "expanding concept."[8] This expansion of bankruptcy and insolvency law now provides for prioritization of claims and secured creditor remedies. As discussed in Chapter 8, secured creditors enjoy a historically privileged position in the priority of claims, meaning that secured creditors generally can collect the entirety of their claim from the debtor before an unsecured creditor is paid at all. In the excerpt below, Professor Virginia Torrie discusses the implications of the Supreme Court's *Lemare Lake Logging* decision in terms of how recognizing efficiency and timeliness as federal purposes could undermine provincial jurisdiction. She argues that the Court's decision is likely to result in greater centralization of receivership law, expanding the protection of secured creditor rights and sacrificing provincial autonomy in policy decisions.

---

8   Tassé Report, above note 1.

Virginia Torrie, "Should Paramountcy Protect Secured Creditor Rights? Saskatchewan v Lemare Lake Logging in Historical Context" (2017) 22:3 *Review of Constitutional Studies* **403 at 413–16 and 421 (footnotes omitted)**

Lemare Lake illustrates that one's understanding of the purpose of a federal provision or statute significantly influences one's determination of a paramountcy issue in the field of bankruptcy and insolvency law. While the trial court and the Majority of the SCC found a narrow purpose and no frustration, the SKCA and Justice Côté found a broader purpose and frustration. Yet, neither the courts nor the parties questioned whether federal bankruptcy and insolvency law should apply to receiverships in the first place....

Although it upheld the *SFSA*, the Majority's decision in *Lemare Lake* does not go much further in safeguarding provincial jurisdiction. Their reasoning implies that "timeliness" is an acceptable purpose of federal receivership provisions. To secured creditors and their representatives, which are likely to be dissatisfied with the SCC's decision, this reads like a blueprint for law reform when Parliament conducts its next review of bankruptcy and insolvency legislation. The Majority decision in *Lemare Lake* implies that if Parliament amends the *BIA* to make it clear that the receivership provisions are intended to facilitate timely receivership proceedings, the *SFSA* receivership regime will frustrate this federal purpose. The likely result of such a conflict is that the *SFSA* will be inoperable to the extent that it conflicts with the *BIA* receivership regime.

It is hard to reconcile the SCC's tacit acceptance of timeliness and efficiency concerns as potentially valid purposes of a federal receivership regime with the Court's express circumspection of these same principles when it comes to other federal legislation that overlaps with section 92(13). For example, in the *Securities Reference* the Court found that the main thrust of the federal legislation went beyond Parliament's legislative jurisdiction under section 91(2) "trade and commerce". The court acknowledged that there might be room for federal regulation of the securities market which was "qualitatively different from what the provinces can do." But the court went on to say that the policy concerns raised by the federal government did not "justify a wholesale takeover of the regulation of the securities industry which is the ultimate consequence of the proposed federal legislation."

Applying this reasoning to the constitutional issue in the *Lemare Lake* case, federally appointed receivers enjoy a national appointment, enabling them to operate in multiple provinces and territories, which is something that the provinces cannot do. However, there is no condition in the Act which limits the applicability of *BIA* receiverships to cases where a receiver needs to operate in multiple jurisdictions (e.g. because the debtor's assets are located in two or more provinces). In other words, a secured creditor can apply for a *BIA* receiver, instead of a provincially appointed receiver, even if there is no jurisdictional reason for seeking a federal appointment. This is different from the "cooperative approach" proposed by the SCC in the *Securities Reference* which would permit "a scheme that recognizes the essentially provincial nature of securities regulation [or receivership] while allowing Parliament to deal with genuinely national concerns..."

On the other hand, integrating timeliness and efficiency as policy objectives of receivership regimes is within provincial jurisdiction under section 92(13). In this regard, the federal receivership provisions are not qualitatively different from what the provinces can do; they are qualitatively different from what two provinces—Saskatchewan and Manitoba—are doing. This reflects a difference in policy, not legislative ability, between the provinces and federal government.

In the extreme, timeliness and efficiency can amount to arguments against federalism and in favour of a single law-making body. This is at odds with the modern paradigm's view of "interplay and ... overlap" as the "ultimate in harmony" in a federal state. Thus, the principle of federalism requires that federal policy objectives that are inherently geared toward greater centralization, such as timeliness and efficiency, be weighed carefully against the importance of giving effect to the broader scheme of the Division of Legislative Powers in general, and provincial heads of power in particular. ...

The combination of piecemeal reforms and changing ideas about bankruptcy and insolvency has tended to lend implicit vires to any exercise of Parliamentary jurisdiction under section 91(21). This helps to explain why receivership, an area of longstanding and exclusive provincial jurisdiction, was added to federal bankruptcy and insolvency law without any constitutional controversy. We need to avoid the tendency to let "pith and substance" drop out of constitutional analyses. The potential for federal dominance inherent in the constitution necessitates scrutiny of new exercises of Parliamentary jurisdiction, including under section 91(21). Greater centralization may be necessary to a certain extent in order to give effect to modern ideas about bankruptcy and insolvency, but we should be mindful that it is likely to be a one-way street in favour of more federal jurisdiction. Thus, it must be balanced with the need to preserve real and meaningful jurisdiction for the provinces under section 92, and give effect to the Division of Legislative Powers as a whole. ...

The constitutional case law bears out a pattern of expanding interpretations of bankruptcy and insolvency, facilitated in part by little substantive discussion of what bankruptcy and insolvency law actually means. Instead, tacit ideas about bankruptcy and insolvency have often "carried the day", demonstrating their malleability when discussed in the abstract, even though the extent to which they have changed attests to how embedded in social context they also are. Thus, the most significant impact of the *Lemare Lake* case is unlikely to be the ratio of the Majority's decision, but rather the open door it leaves for greater centralization of law-making under section 91(21).

The forum of law-making is not neutral to policy development in the area of insolvency law. Greater centralization of receivership law is likely to benefit secured creditors, both because creditors are an organized interest group in insolvency law-making (unlike most debtors), and because federal politicians and political parties tend to be less concerned with debtor interests and regional constituencies (e.g. Prairie farmers) than their provincial counterparts. Furthermore, "timeliness" and "efficiency" are not neutral policy objectives in the area of receivership law. They are inherently geared toward advancing the interests of secured creditors over those of debtors, just as they inherently promote greater exercises of federal jurisdiction. The potential for more centralization of bankruptcy and insolvency law is compounded by the SCC's tendency to decide jurisdictional disputes through the doctrine of federal paramountcy. If "timeliness" and "efficiency" are accepted as purposes of federal bankruptcy and insolvency law, then much provincial legislation seems likely to conflict with these objectives. Efficiency and timeliness alone provide insufficient reasons to undermine provincial jurisdiction and autonomy over policy choices. In this sense, paramountcy should not protect secured creditor rights.

[Reprinted by permission of the publisher.]

Discussion

A number of insolvency professionals criticized the *Lemare Lake* decision as impractical for imposing unjustifiable constraints on national receivers, adding time and cost to debt enforcement proceedings, and generally creating uncertainty in the law. See Michael W Milani, "Corralling the Ability to Appoint National Receivers: A Commentary on 3l Cattle Company" (2015) 4 *Journal of the Insolvency Institute of Canada* 6; Christian Lachance & Hugo Babos-Marchand, "The 'Impractical Effect' of *Lemare Lake Logging Ltd.* in the Enforcement of Security in Quebec" (2016) 28.3 *Commercial Insolvency Reporter* 25; Jonathan Milani, "Frustrating the Purpose of the Receivership Remedy: Federal Paramountcy in *Saskatchewan (Attorney General) v. Lemare Lake Logging Ltd.*" (2017) 80 *Saskatchewan Law Review* 254; Jeffrey M Lee, "The Glorious Uncertainty of the Law': Taking and Enforcing Security in Saskatchewan" in Janis P Sarra & Barbara Romaine, eds, *Annual Review of Insolvency Law 2017* (Toronto: Carswell, 2018) at 983.

Prior to the Supreme Court of Canada's decision, Michael W Milani warned that if the case was decided in favour of Saskatchewan "other provincial legislation may be brandished by debtors seeking to avoid the appointment of a receiver under section 243(1) of the *BIA*."[9] There is a point to made that the outcome of this decision does not unequivocally advance commercial interests. However, there are a couple important qualifications to be borne in mind about the impact of this decision in practice.

First, the jurisdiction preserved for the provinces by the *Lemare Lake* case represent fairly narrow exceptions to the ability to appoint a national receiver under the *BIA*. Only Saskatchewan (*Saskatchewan Farm Security Act*, SS 1988–89, c S-17.1) and Manitoba (*Family Farm Protection Act*, SM 1986–87, c 6) have farm protection statutes which impose delays on the enforcement efforts of national receivers, and these statutes only apply in respect of farm property. The *Lemare Lake* decision does not constrain national receivers that enforce security interests in any other instance. Although more provinces could potentially enact similar legislation, it is also possible that Saskatchewan and Manitoba might repeal their farm protection legislation. Thus, the question of jurisdiction is separate from the question of policy and whether or not a province chooses to enact a law relating to receiverships.

Second, there is sometimes a tendency in commercial law circles to regard the division of legislative powers as an inconvenience to streamlined commercial practice. So it is worth remembering that in division of powers questions such as that posed by the *Lemare Lake* case, commercial practice is subordinate to the Canadian constitution. Although commercial parties may rely on federal legislation and the doctrine of federal paramountcy in pursuit of economic efficiency, the advancement of commercial interests in itself is not the purpose of the Canadian constitution. Federalist systems represent a principled, political choice to distribute legislative powers—leading inevitably to duplication and overlap—instead of pursuing a more efficient, unitary approach to lawmaking. In this light, the use of federal legislation to override provincial jurisdiction in pursuit economic efficiency could even be seen as a subversion of the distributive principle on which federalism is based. See Richard E Simeon, "Criteria for Choice in Federal Systems" (1982–1983) 8 *Queen's Law Journal* 131.

The three 2015 Supreme Court of Canada decisions regarding the bankruptcy and insolvency law power and the 2019 *Redwater* case offer an interesting vantage on the role and influence of the Superintendent of Bankruptcy. The Superintendent was directly involved in two of the four cases: in *407 ETR Concession Co v Canada (Superintendent of Bankruptcy* it was

---

9   Michael W Milani, "Corralling the Ability to Appoint National Receivers: A Commentary on 3L Cattle Company" (2015) 4 *Journal of the Insolvency Institute of Canada* 6.

the respondent, and in *Alberta (Attorney General) v Moloney* it was an intervener. In both cases the Superintendent made submissions in support of a broad interpretation of the federal bankruptcy and insolvency law power, and the court rendered concurring decisions broadly consistent with this view. In *Saskatchewan (AG) v Lemare Lake Logging Ltd*, however the court was split (6-1) and the majority afforded comparatively less weight to the federal bankruptcy and insolvency law power. In the *Redwater* case the Supreme Court was similarly split (5-2) with the majority reading the bankruptcy legislation so as not to conflict with provincial environmental regulations. These observations are noteworthy when considering the role that the Superintendent plays as an advocate for the Canadian bankruptcy and insolvency system and a source of expert information in bankruptcy and insolvency cases.

The influence of the Superintendent in Canadian constitutional cases contrasts with the US experience, where there is no major administrative agency charged with overseeing the bankruptcy system. American law professor Ronald J Mann argues that the lack of an administrative agency has hindered the development of a coherent bankruptcy system and left the US Supreme Court poorly informed about the importance of a robust bankruptcy system. Professor Mann observes that this contributed to a theme in judicial decision-making in the US Supreme Court where the judges tend to adopt narrow interpretations of the federal bankruptcy power. The relatively less weight afforded to the bankruptcy and insolvency power by the Supreme Court of Canada in *Lemare Lake* and *Redwater* seem broadly in line with Professor Mann's thesis. See Ronald J Mann, *Bankruptcy and the U.S. Supreme Court* (New York: Cambridge University Press, 2017); Virginia Torrie, *Book Review: Ronald J Mann, Bankruptcy and the U.S. Supreme Court* (New York: Cambridge University Press, 2017) (2018) 34:1 *Business & Finance Law Review* 109. On the origins of the Canadian Superintendent of Bankruptcy, see Thomas GW Telfer, "The New Bankruptcy 'Detective Agency'?: The Origins of the Superintendent of Bankruptcy in Great Depression Canada" [unpublished].

Notes and Questions

1) The Supreme Court of Canada recently released a decision about allowing a cooperative approach to securities regulation in *Reference re Pan-Canadian Securities Regulation*, 2018 SCC 48. The Court acknowledged that most matters related to securities regulation fall under provincial jurisdiction but matters of a genuine national concern, such as the prevention and management of systemic risk in Canadian capital markets, may fall under federal jurisdiction. In this case, the federal government and the governments of six provinces and territories set out an agreement for a cooperative system of regulating the securities industry. The Court considered whether this agreement was valid from the perspective of cooperative federalism. Cooperative federalism dictates that, where possible, courts should favour a harmonious reading of statutes enacted by the federal and provincial governments which allows for them to operate concurrently. This interpretative aid "discourages courts from interfering with cooperative regulatory schemes so long as they are not incompatible with the boundaries dictated by the *Constitution Act, 1867*."[10] The Court noted that the aspect of the scheme that fell under federal purview would not displace provincial and territorial securities legislation, distinguishing this scheme from the scheme under review (and found to be ultra vires) in the *Securities Reference*. This scheme "was instead designed to complement these statutes by addressing economic objectives that are considered to be national in character" (para 96). The Court determined that the federal aspect of the scheme was not ultra vires Parliament's power

---

10 *Reference re Pan-Canadian Securities Regulation*, 2018 SCC 48 at para 18.

over trade and commerce under section 91(2) of the *Constitution Act, 1867*. Could such an approach be adopted into the context of the federal-provincial interface over debtor-creditor law?

2) In *Callidus Capital Corp v Canada*, 2018 SCC 47, the Crown claimed that Callidus Capital Corp (CCC) owed a large sum in unremitted GST and HST by the operation of the deemed trust mechanism in section 222 of the *Excise Tax Act*, as CCC had realized a security interest in the assets of the debtor prior to bankruptcy and prior to notice of the deemed trust. The Court considered the following question at paragraph 2: "Does the bankruptcy of a tax debtor and subsection 222(1.1) of the *Excise Tax Act*, RSC 1986, c E-15, as amended (the "ETA") render the deemed trust under section 222 of the ETA ineffective as against a secured creditor who received, prior to bankruptcy, proceeds from the assets of the tax debtor that were deemed to be held in trust for the Plaintiff."

   The Supreme Court of Canada adopted the dissenting opinion of the Federal Court of Appeal and allowed the appeal in favour of Callidus Capital Corp. By considering the interplay of the two statutes, the Court determined that the bankruptcy of the debtor essentially rendered the amount payable to CCC to nil, meaning there was no subject matter in the deemed trust owed to the Crown. The Court noted that Parliament intended to eliminate deemed trusts in bankruptcy so as not to allow the government's claims to take priority over those of secured creditors.

3) In *Alberta (Attorney General) v Moloney*, 2015 SCC 51, the companion case to *407 ETR Concession Co v Canada (Superintendent of Bankruptcy)*, the Court considered whether Alberta's *Traffic Safety Act* (*TSA*) conflicted with the *BIA*. The debtor had gotten into a car accident while uninsured. The province of Alberta compensated the other driver and sought to recover this sum from the debtor. The debtor made an assignment into bankruptcy and therefore was discharged from paying this sum. However, Alberta then suspended the debtor's license and vehicle permits for lack of payment.

   The Court found that Alberta's post-discharge enforcement of the discharged debt through the suspensions of the license and permits violated the "fresh start" purpose of the *BIA* and also conflicted operationally. It determined that the *TSA* and the *BIA* conflicted and applied the doctrine of paramountcy. The *TSA* was therefore determined to be inoperative to the extent of the conflict with the *BIA*.

II. THE STRUCTURE OF THE BANKRUPTCY SYSTEM

A. Introduction

The following text provides a brief outline of some of the principal features of the *BIA* and the role played by the principal actors in the *BIA*'s judicial and administrative structure, drawing in part on Lloyd Houlden, Geoffrey Morawetz, & Janis Sarra, *The 2014 Annotated Bankruptcy and Insolvency Act* (Toronto: Carswell, 2014), and, for historical materials, on the Tassé Report, extracted in Chapter 1.[11] A more detailed account is provided in subsequent chapters. The account here is essentially descriptive, but readers should not be misled. Many of the features here involve important normative and policy decisions, and what may appear on

---

11 Above note 1.

the surface to be a simple and straightforward proposition, on closer examination hides a myriad of challenges, particularly as the nature of credit is constantly evolving.

Bankruptcy involves the liquidation of the debtor's assets. For a business, liquidation means the end of the company in most cases and the legal form of incorporated business or partnership is wound up on liquidation. For an individual, bankruptcy means a fresh start. Many assets are liquidated, but the debtor is permitted to keep specific assets and the outcome of the bankruptcy process is a fresh start, free from the crushing burden of debts. The difference is significant for the means by which liquidation of a debtor's property may be initiated under the *BIA*. First, the debtor may voluntarily enter bankruptcy by making an assignment of their property (*BIA*, s 49). Most cases of individual bankruptcy and some business bankruptcies are initiated by voluntary application. Second, a debtor may be forced into bankruptcy by the application of one or more creditors (*BIA*, s 43(1)). A debtor who has filed a commercial or consumer proposal under the *BIA* may also be forced into bankruptcy if the creditors do not give their approval of the proposal or if the court either does not ratify or annuls the proposal (*BIA*, ss 50, 50.4(8), 57, 62(2), 63(6), 66.3, & 66.31).

B. Application by Creditor

A creditor may make an application for a bankruptcy order if the debts owing to the applicant creditor amount to $1000 and the debtor has committed an "act of bankruptcy," a defined term (*BIA*, s 43(1)). A debtor commits an act of bankruptcy if the debtor:

1) makes an assignment of the debtor's property or any part thereof;
2) makes a fraudulent gift, delivery, or transfer of the debtor's property or any part thereof;
3) makes any transfer of the debtor's property or any part thereof or creates any change on it that under the *BIA* would be void as a fraudulent preference;
4) with intent to defeat or delay creditors, departs or remains out of Canada;
5) permits any execution or other process issued against the debtor under which any of the debtor's property is seized, levied on, or taken in execution to remain unsatisfied;
6) exhibits to any meeting of creditors any statement of the debtor's assets and liabilities that shows insolvency or the debtor's inability to pay the debtor's debts;
7) assigns, removes, secretes, or disposes of or attempts or is about to do so with intent to defraud, defeat, or delay creditors;
8) gives notice to any of the debtor's creditors that the debtor has suspended or is about to suspend payment of debts;
9) defaults in any proposal; and
10) ceases to meet liabilities generally as they become due.

The application for bankruptcy is filed with the registrar in bankruptcy or, in some provinces, with a master of the superior court who can issue a bankruptcy order. In some instances where the application is contested, it may be brought before a superior court judge.

The phrase "date of initial bankruptcy event" is used throughout the Act to establish the effective date of bankruptcy in certain transactions. By section 2, the "date of the initial bankruptcy event," in respect of a person, means the earliest of the days on which any one of the following is commenced:

1) an assignment by or in respect of the person;
2) a proposal by or in respect of the person;
3) a notice of intention by the person;

4) the first application for a bankruptcy order against the person in the context of proposal proceedings;

5) the application in respect of which a bankruptcy order is made, other than one referred to in point 4; or

6) proceedings under the *Companies' Creditors Arrangement Act*, RSC 1985, c C-36 (*CCAA*).

C. Interim Receiver

The court may, if it is shown to be necessary for the protection of the estate of a debtor, at any time after the filing of the application for a bankruptcy order, appoint a licensed trustee as interim receiver of the property of the debtor (*BIA*, s 46). For a court to exercise its discretion to appoint an interim receiver for the period between the filing of an application for a bankruptcy order and the making of the bankruptcy order, the applicant creditor must establish through evidence that, on a balance of probabilities, the applicant creditor is likely to succeed in obtaining a bankruptcy order and there is an immediate need for protection of the debtor's estate due to the grave danger that assets will disappear or the estate is otherwise in jeopardy (*BIA*, s 46(1)).

D. Assignment by Debtor

Before filing an assignment for an individual, a trustee must first make an assessment of the debtor. Under the assessment procedure, the trustee must conduct a financial appraisal of the debtor and review the statutory and non-statutory options open to the debtor. The trustee may delegate the assessment duties to a person who has registered with the designated assistant superintendent. The assessment procedure is contained in directive no 6R3 of the superintendent of bankruptcy, "Assessment of an Individual Debtor." An assessment certificate must be filed at the time of filing the assignment with the official receiver. Mandatory e-filing of all new summary administrations and ordinary administrations became effective in 2007.[12] In practice, the trustee is chosen by the debtor before the assignment is filed. The trustee, before accepting the appointment, must be satisfied that the proceeds from the realization of the estate will be at least sufficient to secure the payment of the trustee's fee. In "no asset cases," cash deposits or third-party guarantees are usually required by the trustee. The trustee, having accepted the appointment and been approved by creditors, cannot withdraw from serving except with permission of the court.

E. Summary Administration

If the realizable assets of the debtor, after deducting claims of secured creditors, will not exceed $15,000, the provisions of the *BIA* relating to summary administration apply where the debtor is an individual, not a corporation.[13] The majority of individual bankruptcies fall within these provisions. Prior to filing a summary administration assignment, the trustee must make an assessment of the debtor, which includes a financial appraisal and review of the statutory and non-statutory options open to the debtor. The trustee prepares the assignment, and the words "Summary Administration" must appear in the title of the proceedings

---

12   See Office of the Superintendent of Bankruptcy Canada, "For Licensed Insolvency Trustees: Directive No 9R3" (15 December 2006), online: https://www.ic.gc.ca/eic/site/bsf-osb.nsf/eng/br01664.html.

13   *BIA*, ss 49(6) and 155; *Bankruptcy and Insolvency General Rules*, CRC, c 368, s 130.

on all forms. Unlike ordinary administration bankruptcies, a joint assignment may be filed where the debts of the individuals making the assignment are substantially the same and the trustee is of the opinion that a joint assignment is in the best interests of the debtors and the creditors. In a joint file, only one statement of receipts and disbursements is required. The trustee prepares the preliminary statement of affairs, which the debtor signs and swears or affirms is accurate (s 49(2); form 78 or 79). The trustee then prepares the certificate of the official receiver and, unless directed by the official receiver, no security will be required (*BIA*, s 155(b)) and then the documents are filed with the official receiver.

F. Surplus Income

Since the 1997 *BIA* amendments, bankrupt individuals have also been obliged to pay over to the trustee their surplus income up to the time of their discharge from bankruptcy. The size of the surplus income depends on the bankrupt's family status and income and is determined by the court, receiving guidance from directives issued by the superintendent of bankruptcy. For details, see Chapter 11 in this text.

G. Official Receivers

Each province of Canada is a bankruptcy district, and some provinces are divided into bankruptcy divisions; for each division, one or more official receivers may be appointed by the governor in council. The principal duties of the official receivers are to accept and file assignments; to examine all debtors as to their conduct, the causes of their bankruptcy, and the disposition of their property; and to preside over or nominate someone else to preside over the first meeting of creditors.

H. Creditors' Meeting

The appointment of the trustee by a bankruptcy order or an assignment is effective only until the creditors have an opportunity to meet. The appointment must be affirmed at the first meeting of creditors or a substitute trustee must be appointed. The purpose of the first meeting of creditors is to consider the affairs of the bankrupt, to affirm the appointment of the trustee or substitute another, to appoint up to five inspectors, and to give such directions to the trustee as the creditors may see fit with reference to the administration of the bankrupt estate (*BIA*, s 102(5), 116(1)). Meetings of creditors other than the first meeting are rare, usually called only when the trustee and inspectors are faced with some extraordinary problem. The trustee must call a meeting when directed to do so by the court, requested in writing by a majority of inspectors, or requested by 25 percent of the creditors holding 25 percent in value of the proved claims (*BIA*, s 103(1)).

I. Inspectors

As a rule, the first meeting of inspectors takes place at the conclusion of the first meeting of creditors. The inspectors discuss with the trustee how the estate is to be administered. All of the trustee's major decisions relating to the liquidation of the debtor's property must be authorized by the inspectors. Inspectors stand in a fiduciary relation to the general body of creditors and must perform their duties impartially and in the interests of the creditors who appoint them. From time to time, inspectors must verify the bank balance of the estate, examine the trustee's accounts, inquire into the adequacy of the security filed by the trustee, and approve the trustee's final statement of receipts and disbursements, dividend sheet, and disposition of unrealized property (*BIA*, s 120(3)).

J. The Trustee

Only a trustee licensed by the superintendent of bankruptcy can be appointed an estate trustee. Most trustees are accountants by training and must pass a series of qualifying examinations before they are eligible to be appointed trustees. There are about 1,000 trustees at the present time, most of them members of the Canadian Association of Insolvency and Restructuring Practitioners (CAIRP), a professional association. The trustee is an officer of the court and subject to its direction. The trustee's responsibility is to collect and liquidate the assets of the debtor and to distribute the proceeds to the creditors. The trustee is required to go beyond mere appearances in identifying and taking possession of the property of the bankrupt. Certain transactions entered into within varying suspect periods may be examined and avoided or reviewed under the *BIA* or the applicable provincial legislation.

K. Preferences and Transfers at Undervalue

Sections 95 and 96 of the *BIA* create a complete framework for challenging transactions that may diminish the value of the insolvent debtor's estate, reducing the amount of money available for distribution to the creditors. These types of transactions are called "preferences" and "transfers at undervalue." A preference occurs when an insolvent debtor pays one or more creditors at the expense of other creditors. A transfer at undervalue is a disposition of property or provision of services for which no consideration is received by the debtor or for which the consideration received is conspicuously less than the fair market value of the consideration given by the debtor. The framework is aimed at ensuring fairness and predictability when dealing with these types of transactions in the insolvency system.

Effective 2009, settlements and reviewable transactions were replaced with a single cause of action, "transfer at undervalue." The court determines as a question of fact whether the transfer was at undervalue and whether the parties were at arm's length or non-arm's length. People who are related to each other are deemed not to deal at arm's length unless there is evidence to the contrary. If the court finds that the transaction was a transfer at undervalue and that the other party was at arm's length, the court may grant judgment for the difference between the actual consideration and the fair market value if the transfer took place within one year before the date of the initial bankruptcy event and the debtor was insolvent at the time of the transfer and intended to defeat the interests of creditors. If the court finds that the transaction was a transfer at undervalue and that the other party was not at arm's length, the court may grant judgment for the difference between the actual consideration and the fair market value if the transfer took place within one year before the date of the initial bankruptcy event or within one to five years before the date of the initial bankruptcy event if the debtor was insolvent at the time of the transfer or intended to defeat the interests of creditors.

If the preference was made to a non-arm's length creditor within one year, no proof of intention is required; rather, the test is an effects-based one. For transfers at undervalue within one year before the date of the initial bankruptcy event between non-arm's length parties, the trustee has to demonstrate intent to defraud, defeat, or delay a creditor. The trustee can look back up to five years where parties are not dealing at arm's length and the transaction may be declared void where intention to defraud, defeat, or delay creditors can be established or where the debtor was insolvent at the time of the transfer (*BIA*, s 96).

In terms of preferences, the Act specifies that a transfer of property made, provision of services made, a charge on property made, a payment made, an obligation incurred, or a judicial proceeding taken or suffered by an insolvent person in favour of a creditor who is dealing at arm's length with the insolvent person, or a person in trust for that creditor with a view to giving that creditor a preference over another creditor is void as against the trustee or, in Quebec, may not be set up against the trustee if it is made during the period beginning on the day that is three months before the date of the initial bankruptcy event and ending on the date of the bankruptcy. For creditors not dealing at arm's length with the insolvent person or a person in trust for that creditor, the period is twelve months (*BIA*, s 95). See Chapter 5 in this text for a fuller account.

L. The Role of the Creditors

An underlying principle of the *BIA* is that the creditors have oversight of the administration of an estate in bankruptcy. The theory of creditor control is that, because the assets of the bankrupt are liquidated for the benefit of creditors, creditors are in the best position to look after their own interests. Creditors appoint the trustee and may substitute one trustee for another, within the limits of the system requiring trustees to be licensed. In the administration of the estate, the trustee must consider the directions of the creditors, so long as they are not contrary to the Act. Not only is the trustee bound by these instructions in order for the trustee's actions to be valid but, to avoid being subject to personal liability, the trustee generally requires specific authorization for all that the trustee does. In addition, the trustee is required to report to the creditors, at their request, concerning administration of the estate.

M. Claims in the Bankruptcy Process

All creditors to whom the bankrupt is indebted as of the date of the bankruptcy may prove a claim against the estate of the bankrupt. The trustee may disallow the claim or allow it, in whole or in part, subject to an appeal to the court. Where a secured creditor realizes is security, the creditor may prove for the balance due, after deducting the net amount realized. Instead of realizing its security, the secured creditor may surrender its security and prove its claim. The trustee may redeem the security at the value assessed by the creditor or, if the secured creditor takes no action, the trustee may redeem the security by paying the debt; see, further, Chapter 7 in this text.

N. Distribution of Property

The trustee is required to pay dividends in the course of realizing the property as funds become available, subject to the retention of such sums as may be necessary for the costs of administration. Certain claims are paid in priority to others. After payment of the costs of administration, these claims must be paid in full before a dividend may be paid to the ordinary creditors. The creditors who have priority include those to whom are owed:

- wages and salaries for services rendered within six months prior to bankruptcy, to the extent the claims are not satisfied by the sections 81.3 and 81.4 liens for unpaid wages and salaries;

- municipal taxes for a two-year period, if they are not secured by the preferential lien on real property, provided they do not exceed the value of the property against which the taxes are imposed;
- arrears of rent for a period of three months prior to bankruptcy and accelerated rent for three months, if permitted by the lease, provided the total amount does not exceed the realization from the property on the premises under the lease.

O. Limits on the Bankrupt's Ability to Conduct Business

During the period after filing an assignment in bankruptcy and prior to discharge from bankruptcy, there are restrictions on the bankrupt's activities. The bankrupt may not:

- engage in trade or business without disclosing to all persons with whom they enter into a business transaction that they are an undischarged bankrupt;
- obtain credit for a purpose, other than the supply of necessaries for self and family, to the extent of five hundred dollars or more, without disclosing that they are an undischarged bankrupt; and
- be a director of a limited liability corporation.

P. The Bankruptcy Discharge

The *BIA* entitles first-time bankrupts to an automatic discharge nine months after the bankruptcy order unless the discharge is opposed by the trustee, superintendent of bankruptcy, or a creditor. In practice, 90 percent of first-time bankruptcies are unopposed. A second-time bankrupt is eligible for an automatic discharge twenty-four months after the date of bankruptcy unless an opposition to the discharge has been filed or the bankrupt has been required to make payments under section 68 (*BIA*, s 168.1). If the bankrupt has been required to make payments under section 68, a second-time bankrupt is eligible for an automatic discharge thirty-six months after the date of bankruptcy unless an opposition has been filed before the automatic discharge takes effect. An order of discharge does not release the bankrupt from:

1) any fine, penalty, restitution order, or other order similar in nature to a fine, penalty, or restitution order imposed by a court in respect of an offence or any debt arising out of recognizance or bail;
2) any award of damages by a court in civil proceedings in respect of bodily harm intentionally inflicted, sexual assault, or wrongful death arising therefrom;
3) any debt or liability for alimony or alimentary pension;
4) any debt or liability arising under a judicial decision establishing affiliation or respecting support or maintenance, or under an agreement for maintenance and support of a spouse, former spouse, former common law partner, or child living apart from the bankrupt;
5) any debt or liability arising out of fraud, embezzlement, misappropriation, or defalcation while acting in a fiduciary capacity;
6) any debt or liability resulting from obtaining property or services by false pretences or fraudulent misrepresentation, other than a debt or liability that arises from an equity claim;
7) liability for the dividend that a creditor would have been entitled to receive on any provable claim not disclosed to the trustee, unless the creditor had notice or knowledge of the bankruptcy and failed to take reasonable action to prove its claim; or

8) any debt or obligation in respect of a loan made under the *Canada Student Loans Act*, the *Canada Student Financial Assistance Act*, or any enactment of a province that provides for loans or guarantees of loans to students where the date of bankruptcy of the bankrupt occurred before the date on which the bankrupt ceased to be a full- or part-time student, as the case may be, under the applicable Act or enactment, or within seven years after the date on which the bankrupt ceased to be a full- or part-time student (*BIA*, s 178(1)).

Q. Discharge of Trustee

Where a trustee has completed the administration of the estate, the trustee is required to apply for discharge. The court may grant the trustee a discharge if the trustee has accounted to the satisfaction of the inspectors and the court for all property that came under the trustee's control. The discharge has the effect of releasing the trustee from all liability in respect of any act done or default made in the administration of the property of the bankrupt and from all liability in relation to conduct as a trustee.

R. Bankruptcy Offences

In order to ensure their full cooperation in the administration of estates, the *BIA* imposes on bankrupts many duties with penalties for their non-performance—for example, bankrupts are obliged to make discovery of and deliver their property to the trustee, to prepare a statement of their affairs, to attend the first meeting of creditors, and to examine the correctness of all proofs of claim. The Act also provides that the doing of certain things by the bankrupt, such as a fraudulent disposition of property or the making of a false entry in a statement, constitutes an offence.

S. The Superintendent of Bankruptcy

Official oversight of the bankruptcy process is exercised by the superintendent of bankruptcy. The superintendent heads the Office of the Superintendent of Bankruptcy (OSB), which is an executive agency of the federal government. The OSB must investigate allegation that offences have been committed under the *BIA* where it appears that they would not otherwise be investigated. It also supervises the administration of all estates to which the Act applies. The superintendent of bankruptcy may intervene as a party in any matter or proceeding in court. Every application for a bankruptcy order is served on the superintendent. The superintendent also examines every statement of receipts and disbursements and the final dividend sheet prepared by the trustee when the administration of an estate is completed. The superintendent's comments on these documents are considered by the court when the trustee's accounts are passed. The superintendent is also responsible for the granting of licenses to trustees in bankruptcy. An important power also vested in the superintendent is the power to issue directives to facilitate the carrying out of the purposes and provisions of the *BIA* and the general rules adopted under the Act. Directives are not statutory instruments (*BIA*, s 5(6)) and are therefore not subject to parliamentary scrutiny. Nevertheless, directives are widely used by the superintendent and play an important role in the administration of the *BIA*.

III. CONCLUSION

As the extracts and commentary in this chapter demonstrate, bankruptcy and insolvency law is highly codified in Canada, offering a measure of certainty and predictability to debtors and creditors when either an individual or a company becomes insolvent. However, where federal legislation intersects with important social, environmental, or economic legislation enacted at the provincial level, courts face the challenge of interpreting both types of legislation in a manner that will advance their respective socially important objectives within the framework of Canadian federalism.

Practice Questions

Question 1
In Canadian bankruptcy law, there is the principle of a single forum for all bankruptcy matters; the court will not divide a matter with one aspect being argued in bankruptcy court and another aspect being argued in another court. The *BIA* gives bankruptcy powers to superior courts in each province and these provincial justices will exercise federal powers when sitting as bankruptcy judges. What are the advantages of the single forum principle for bankruptcy? Are there any disadvantages of a single forum for bankruptcy?

Question 2
Does *Robinson v Countrywide Factors Ltd* essentially allow the provinces to fill in the gaps of the *BIA*? What do you think will happen if the *BIA* is amended to no longer have those gaps?

Question 3
In your view, which of the following two options provides a better interpretation of the ratio of the *Ontario (Attorney General) v Canada (Attorney General)*, also known as the *Voluntary Assignments* case? Provide support for your answer.

a) Legislation does not meet the section 91(21) threshold requirements unless it covers involuntary bankruptcies as well as voluntary assignments; or,
b) Legislation cannot be characterized as insolvency or bankruptcy legislation unless the insolvency or acts of bankruptcy by the debtor are a precondition of the statute's applicability.

Question 4
Can you reconcile the Privy Council's decision in the *Voluntary Assignments* with the Supreme Court's decision in *Validity of Orderly Payment of Debts Act, 1959 (Alta)*? Or was Kerwin CJC correct in suggesting in the latter case that *Voluntary Assignments* would be decided differently today?

Question 5
Does Binnie J's decision in *Azco Mining* provide that there are limits to the jurisdiction that Parliament can confer on the federal bankruptcy courts, or, more accurately, on federal powers conferred on provincial Superior Court judges under *BIA*, Part VII? What are the limits, if any?

Question 6
As a matter of policy, do you think that the *BIA* should provide that class actions against a bankrupt or a reorganizing debtor can only be continued under the supervision of the bankruptcy court? Should the bankruptcy court approve the establishment of a trust fund for the

settlement of class action claims, relieving the debtor of the obligation to make further payments? Provide policy support for your answer.

Question 7
Do you think the federal government and the courts have achieved the appropriate balance between insolvency and bankruptcy legislation and environmental protection legislation in terms of recognizing the division of powers and practical implementation of law? Is the Supreme Court's decision in *Orphan Well Association v Grant Thornton Ltd*, 2019 SCC 5, a positive step toward better balancing the interests of commercial parties and private individuals with the interests of Canadians more broadly?

Question 8
Do you agree with the decision of the Supreme Court of Canada in *407 ETR* that the suspension of a driver's permit can constitute a severe deprivation with serious repercussions on financial rehabilitation and therefore frustrates the fresh start principle of the *BIA*? Why or why not?

Question 9
As stated previously, the *BIA* does not bind secured creditors and much of the process for and rights of secured creditors are dealt with under provincial legislation. Should secured creditors be dealt with under federal legislation? Why or why not?

Question 10
Recall that the Tassé Report[14] described bankruptcy and insolvency law in Canada as "expanding concepts" and that the courts have never held a federal bankruptcy or insolvency statute to be ultra vires. The Courts have found provincial statutes to conflict operationally with the *BIA* and applied the doctrine of paramountcy several times. Do you think that Parliament should be able to expand their power by legislating further into provincial powers or should the courts stop the federal government from expanding bankruptcy and insolvency concepts any further? Why?

---

14   Above note 1.

PART II

Bankruptcy

CHAPTER 3

Bankruptcy: Commencement and Consequences

Bankruptcy proceedings can be initiated in three ways: (1) voluntarily by the debtor; (2) involuntarily by application of one or more of the debtor's creditors; and (3) through a deemed assignment. Each of these processes is discussed below in parts I, II, and III, respectively.

Section 71 of the *Bankruptcy and Insolvency Act*, RSC 1985, c B-3 (*BIA*) provides that upon a bankruptcy order being made or an assignment being filed, all of the bankrupt's property "immediately pass[es] to and vest[s] in the trustee named in the bankruptcy order or assignment." This is discussed later in Part IV.

I. VOLUNTARY BANKRUPTCY: ASSIGNMENT BY A DEBTOR

A. Who May Make an Assignment?

Section 49(1) provides that "an insolvent person or, if deceased, the executor or administrator of their estate or the liquidator of the succession, with the leave of the court" may make an assignment of "all of the insolvent person's property for the general benefit of the insolvent person's creditors."

Section 2 defines a "person" as including the following entities:

- partnerships;
- unincorporated associations;
- corporations;
- cooperative societies or organizations;
- the successors of a partnership, association, corporation, society or an organization; and
- the heirs, executors, liquidators of the succession, administrators or other legal representatives of a person.

In addition, section 2 defines an "insolvent person" as a person who is not bankrupt and who resides, carries on business, or has property in Canada, whose liabilities to creditors provable as claims amount to $1,000, and:

(a) who is for any reason unable to meet his obligations as they generally become due,

(b) who has ceased paying his current obligations in the ordinary course of business as they generally become due, or

(c) the aggregate of whose property is not, at a fair valuation, sufficient, or, if disposed of at a fairly conducted sale under legal process, would not be sufficient to enable payment of all his obligations, due and accruing due.

B. Filing Requirements and Appointment of Trustee

Section 49(2) provides that the assignment must be accompanied by a sworn statement listing the debtor's property along with the names and addresses of all creditors and the amounts of their respective claims. According to section 49(3), the assignment and the sworn statement must be delivered to the official receiver in the debtor's locality. Section 2 defines the "locality of the debtor" as the principal place where the debtor has: (a) resided, or (b) carried on business during the year immediately preceding the initial bankruptcy event, or, where neither (a) nor (b) apply, where the greater portion of the debtor's property is situated. The date of the "initial bankruptcy event," under section 2, is defined as follows:

> *date of the initial bankruptcy event*, in respect of a person, means the earliest of the day on which any one of the following is made, filed or commenced, as the case may be:
>
> (a) an assignment by or in respect of the person,
> (b) a proposal by or in respect of the person,
> (c) a notice of intention by the person,
> (d) the first application for a bankruptcy order against the person, in any case
>> (i) referred to in paragraph 50.4(8)(a) or 57(a) or subsection 61(2), or
>> (ii) in which a notice of intention to make a proposal has been filed under section 50.4 or a proposal has been filed under section 62 in respect of the person and the person files an assignment before the court has approved the proposal,
> (e) the application in respect of which a bankruptcy order is made, in the case of an application other than one referred to in paragraph (d), or
> (f) proceedings under the *Companies' Creditors Arrangement Act*;

Section 49(3) provides that the official receiver "shall refuse" to file the assignment unless it is in the prescribed form and accompanied by the sworn statement required by section 49(2). However, the official receiver is required to accept an assignment if all of the filing requirements are met.[1]

Section 49(4) provides that if the official receiver files the assignment, he shall appoint a licensed trustee selected "by reference to the wishes of the most interested creditors if ascertainable at the time." Section 49(5) states that if the official receiver is unable to find a trustee willing to act, they must cancel the assignment after giving the bankrupt five days' notice. The following excerpt from *Bad Boy Mobile Homes Ltd (Re)* (1976), 66 DLR (3d) 324 (BCSC), demonstrates that the effective date and time of the assignment is the time that the official receiver actually files it:

> In my opinion the words "the making of ... an assignment for the benefit of creditors" fix a point in time with reference to which conflicting claims to property are to be determined under s. 16 of The Bills of Sale Act. It would, in my view, be unreasonable to conclude that the Legislature intended that that point in time be determined by the bare execution of a document of assignment, an act which, in itself, has no legal effect. The narrow construction for which counsel for the trustee contends could give rise to absurd situations. Counsel for C.A.C. gave me this example. A person executes an assignment

---

1   See also *Ferme CGR enr, senc (Syndic de)*, 2010 QCCS 2 at para 13, aff'd 2010 QCCA 719: "Selon le paragraphe 49(3) de *LA LOI*, le *SÉQUESTRE OFFICIEL* ne peut refuser la production d'une cession de biens que si elle n'est pas présentée dans la forme prescrite au paragraphe 49(2) de *LA LOI*."

for the benefit of creditors, then changes his mind and puts it away and nothing more is heard of it for six months. Then the document is discovered; on what I have called the narrow construction the executed document could be used to make void, as against a trustee, a chattel mortgage in respect of which a lawful seizure had been made at any time within the six-month period. Likewise, if an assignment document were executed and placed in the post and there followed a strike of postal workers and the envelope was not delivered for a month or so, the same situation might occur. It is a well-known rule of construction that, where two interpretations are open, the one which produces an absurd or unjust result should be rejected. For these reasons I hold that the words I am considering, properly construed, mean making a complete and effective assignment.

Having held that the word "assignment" used in s. 16 should be construed as meaning a complete and effective assignment, not the document by which an assignment is made, it remains to consider whether the Bankruptcy Act provides that the bare execution of an assignment is sufficient to effect a complete transaction of assignment. This question presents no difficulty, because the Bankruptcy Act specifically provides that an assignment is inoperative until filed with an official receiver. Section 31(3) [now section 49(3)] reads:

> (3) The assignment shall be offered to the official receiver in the locality of the debtor, and it is inoperative until filed with such official receiver, who shall refuse to file the assignment unless it is in the prescribed form or to the like effect and accompanied by the sworn statement required by subsection (2).

Under *BIA*, section 49(6), and *Bankruptcy and Insolvency General Rules*, CRC, chapter 368, section 130, if the official receiver determines that the realizable assets of a bankrupt who is not a corporation will not exceed $15,000 after deducting the secured creditors' claims, the summary administration provisions of the Act shall apply under sections 155, 156, 156.1, and 157.

C. Annulment of Assignments

Section 181(1) provides that the court may annul an assignment if, in the opinion of the court, the assignment ought not to have been filed. Under section 181(2), if the court annuls an assignment, all sales and other dispositions of property, and all payments duly made and acts done by the court or by the trustee or anyone acting under the trustee's authority remain valid, but all other property of the bankrupt shall revert to the bankrupt or vest in such other person as the court may appoint. Section 182(1) provides that the annulment order shall be dated on the day on which it is made, but shall not be issued or delivered until the time allowed for an appeal has expired, and if an appeal is made, until the appeal is decided.

In general, an assignment will only be annulled if the court determines that the assignment constituted an abuse of process, or that the debtor committed a fraud against his creditors or he was not, in fact, insolvent at the time of filing. In *Re Wale* (1996), 45 CBR (3d) 15 (Ont Ct J (Gen Div)) (*Re Wale*), for example, the bankrupt's former spouse sought an order annulling his assignment on the basis that the filing was an abuse of the bankruptcy court's process that was merely intended to defeat her claims in a family law trial. Wale claimed that he had no such intention and that he was an "insolvent person" within the meaning of the Act, and was therefore entitled to make the assignment. With respect to the question of whether Wale was insolvent, the court stated the following:

[17] An annulment will be granted only where it is shown either the debtor was not an insolvent person when he made the assignment or where it is shown that the debtor abused the process of the court or committed a fraud on his creditors....

[22] Mr. Wale had ceased paying his current obligations in the ordinary course of business as they generally became due. The cheques he wrote in payment of some of his trade creditors were returned NSF and he has not replaced them. Perhaps better organization of his affairs or the use of money he held as cash and put to personal use would have permitted payment of some or all of the trade creditors. However, unlike ss. (a) which requires the debtor to show an inability to meet obligations, ss. (b) requires only that the debtor "has ceased paying his current obligations in the ordinary course of business...." Unlike ss.(a) there is no requirement in ss. (b) for the debtor to show and thus no need to investigate his inability to make payments. If he has ceased paying current obligations, which he had, he meets the criteria of this sub-section. I must assume the reference by parliament to a debtor's "inability" in ss. (a) and not in ss. (b) is intentional and the easier test in the business oriented subsection, i.e. ss. (b), was imposed for a specific reason.

[23] Mr. Wale qualifies as an insolvent person, if only marginally so, and was therefore entitled to make an assignment in bankruptcy, unless in doing so he abused the process of the court or committed a fraud on his creditors.

Although Wale was an "insolvent person" within the meaning of the Act, the court nonetheless annulled the assignment pursuant section 181 on the basis that the assignment was an abuse of the bankruptcy process. In reaching this decision, the court pointed to the following facts that "overwhelmingly demonstrate[d]" bad faith by Wale and supported the court's conclusion, at para 28, that Wale had made the assignment in order to remove assets from the reach of the court and his former spouse:

- Wale "barely" met the definition of an insolvent person and "could easily have worked his way through his less than formidable financial problems";
- Wale was on good terms with his major secured creditor, Scotiabank, which had agreed to reduce his payments owing to it until the family trial was resolved;
- His mortgage to National Trust was current and he was making three times the required payments in the year prior to his bankruptcy assignment;
- His trade debts amounted to only $5,700 and he made no attempt to reduce or postpone any of those debts;
- He made the assignment on the day of the family law trial, which the court determined was "not coincidental, nor motivated by a desire to assist the Court";
- He sold his assets and pocketed the cash shortly prior to the assignment, contrary to a court order; and
- He displayed bad faith through his "visceral antipathy toward his former wife", particularly by leaving a mobile sign at the matrimonial home, after removing all of the furnishings and contents, which stated "Joyce Wale Your Kids Lost Their Home God Bless You. Closed Sorry."[2]

---

2   *Re Wale*, at para 7.

The result in *Re Wale* can be contrasted with *Re Dahl* (1985), 57 CBR (NS) 296 (AB QB), in which the debtor made an assignment in bankruptcy that benefitted the debtor but was nonetheless legitimate. In *Re Dahl*, the plaintiff brought an action against Dahl, an individual bankrupt, as well as the trustee and several other parties, without leave of the court. The plaintiff sought a stay of the bankruptcy and a declaration that the bankruptcy was a nullity so that the plaintiff could pursue his action. The plaintiff did not seek an annulment of the assignment pursuant to section 181. Instead, the plaintiff pointed to the fact that the bankruptcy had the effect of terminating a shareholders agreement between Dahl and him, potentially to Dahl's benefit, as the basis for staying the bankruptcy proceedings:

> [14] The crux of the dispute between Kalau and Dahl revolves over a shareholder agreement between them dated 1st December 1982. In brief, that agreement provided that upon the death of one of the parties the survivor would purchase the shares of the deceased in Spade Construction Ltd., a company whose shares were held in equal number by Kalau and Dahl. Under the agreement insurance in the sum of $1,000,000 was placed on each party and the policies assigned to James B. McCashin as a party to the agreement as trustee. The agreement provided that the proceeds of the life insurance on a deceased be used for the purchase of the shares of the deceased by the survivor with any surplus of insurance moneys going to the survivor.

> [15] The agreement provided a method for fixing the price to be paid for the shares. Clause 9 of the agreement gave the right to each shareholder on termination of the agreement to purchase from the trustee the policy of insurance on his own life. Clause 10 of the agreement in subcl. (b) provided:

>> Except for the rights and duties provided for in clause 9 hereof, this agreement shall cease and determine on the occurrence of any of the following events namely ...
>> (b) Bankruptcy or receivership of either or both of the Shareholders.

The court ruled, firstly, that the plaintiff's statement of claim was a nullity and should be set aside because the plaintiff issued it without leave of the court, as currently stated under *BIA*, section 215. Secondly, the court ruled that the plaintiff had leave to bring a motion for annulment, as that was the proper process for challenging the validity of Dahl's assignment. In making this ruling, however, the court made it clear that the assignment should not be annulled simply because it provided some benefit to Dahl:

> [31] ... In the case at bar the fact that the assignment may have the effect of terminating the shareholders' agreement, thus giving one or other of the shareholders an economic advantage, and even though the debtor sought that advantage, would not appear to be of sufficient ground for annulling the bankruptcy.

> [32] The validity of the assignment, therefore, would depend entirely on the debtor satisfying the requirements of the Bankruptcy Act as long as there is no abuse of the process of the court. If I am correct in this, an interested person wishing to have the bankruptcy annulled would adduce evidence to show that the debtor was not an insolvent person when he made his assignment, or alternatively, there is some other ground recognized by the court that satisfies the court that the assignment ought not to have been filed.

In short, an assignment in bankruptcy will not be annulled on the basis that it improves the debtor's situation; rather, the party seeking the annulment order must satisfy the court that the filing requirements were not met or that there was an abuse of process.

II. INVOLUNTARY BANKRUPTCY: APPLICATION BY A CREDITOR

A. Requirements for a Bankruptcy Order

Section 43(1) provides that one or more creditors may file an application for a bankruptcy order against a debtor if the application alleges that (a) the debts owing amount to at least $1,000, and (b) the debtor has committed an "act of bankruptcy" within six months preceding the filing. Under section 2, a "debtor" includes "an insolvent person and any person who, at the time an act of bankruptcy was committed by him, resided or carried on business in Canada and, where the context requires, includes a bankrupt." The application must be accompanied by an affidavit of the applicant and must be filed in a court of competent jurisdiction in the judicial district of the locality of the debtor (see *BIA*, ss 43(3) and 43(5)).

Unlike an assignment, which is merely reviewed by the official receiver so as to confirm that it satisfies the filing requirements, an application for a bankruptcy order must be heard before a court sitting in bankruptcy. Section 43(6) provides that the court "shall require proof of the facts alleged in the application ... and, if satisfied with the proof, may make a bankruptcy order." Section 43(7) states that the court must dismiss the application if it is not satisfied with the proof of the facts alleged in the application, if the debtor satisfies the court that the debtor is able to pay its debts, or if for some other sufficient cause the bankruptcy order should not be made. Alternatively, if the debtor denies the facts alleged in the application at the hearing, the court may stay the proceedings "on any terms that it may see fit to impose ... and for any period of time that may be required for trial of the issue relating to the disputed facts" (see *BIA*, ss 43(10) & (11)).

Section 43(7) provides that a bankruptcy order will not be made against a debtor who is able, but unwilling, to pay its debts. The court "shall dismiss" the application for a bankruptcy order if the debtor satisfies the court that it is able to pay its debts as demonstrated from the following excerpt from *Moody v Ashton* (1997), 47 CBR (3d) 91 (Sask CA):

> After determining that Mr. Ashton owed the Moodys more than $275,000, the learned bankruptcy judge made two other findings critical to this appeal. He found that Mr. Ashton had committed an act of bankruptcy by ceasing to meet his liabilities generally as they became due. But later in the judgment he also found Mr. Ashton was able to repay this amount. He said:

>> [T]he evidence establishes that Ashton is a wealthy individual who is quite capable of paying his debts, but has simply chosen not do so. He earned over $1.4 million in his last four years as a professional hockey player in the NHL. He has the means to pay his debts and should be required to do so.

> He then directed that a receiving order should issue.

>> In our opinion, these last two findings cannot stand together. If Mr. Ashton was able to pay his debts, s. 43(7) of the *Bankruptcy and Insolvency Act*, R.S.C. 1985, c. B-3 prevented the bankruptcy judge from issuing the receiving order. Section 43(7) provides:

>>> 43(7) *Where the court* is not satisfied with the proof of the facts alleged in the petition or of the service of the petition, or *is satisfied by the debtor that he is able to pay his debts,* or that for other sufficient cause no order ought to be made, *it shall dismiss the petition.* (Emphasis added.)

> We see no reason to give these words any meaning other than the one they would ordinarily bear. They are clear on their face. Once a bankruptcy court finds that a debtor is able to pay his or her debts, it "shall dismiss the petition."

In short, the Act is designed to facilitate the orderly payments of debts by insolvent debtors only. Where a debtor is able but unwilling to pay its debts, the appropriate remedy for a creditor is to enforce its rights under provincial law.

As noted above, one of the requirements for granting a bankruptcy order is that the debtor must have committed an "act of bankruptcy" within the six months preceding the filing of the application. Section 42(1) defines an act of bankruptcy as follows:

42 (1) A debtor commits an act of bankruptcy in each of the following cases:

(a) if in Canada or elsewhere he makes an assignment of his property to a trustee for the benefit of his creditors generally, whether it is an assignment authorized by this Act or not;

(b) if in Canada or elsewhere the debtor makes a fraudulent gift, delivery or transfer of the debtor's property or of any part of it;

(c) if in Canada or elsewhere the debtor makes any transfer of the debtor's property or any part of it, or creates any charge on it, that would under this Act be void or, in the Province of Quebec, null as a fraudulent preference;

(d) if, with intent to defeat or delay his creditors, he departs out of Canada, or, being out of Canada, remains out of Canada, or departs from his dwelling-house or otherwise absents himself;

(e) if the debtor permits any execution or other process issued against the debtor under which any of the debtor's property is seized, levied on or taken in execution to remain unsatisfied until within five days after the time fixed by the executing officer for the sale of the property or for fifteen days after the seizure, levy or taking in execution, or if any of the debtor's property has been sold by the executing officer, or if the execution or other process has been held by the executing officer for a period of fifteen days after written demand for payment without seizure, levy or taking in execution or satisfaction by payment, or if it is returned endorsed to the effect that the executing officer can find no property on which to levy or to seize or take, but if interpleader or opposition proceedings have been instituted with respect to the property seized, the time elapsing between the date at which the proceedings were instituted and the date at which the proceedings are finally disposed of, settled or abandoned shall not be taken into account in calculating the period of fifteen days;

(f) if he exhibits to any meeting of his creditors any statement of his assets and liabilities that shows that he is insolvent, or presents or causes to be presented to any such meeting a written admission of his inability to pay his debts;

(g) if he assigns, removes, secretes or disposes of or attempts or is about to assign, remove, secrete or dispose of any of his property with intent to defraud, defeat or delay his creditors or any of them;

(h) if he gives notice to any of his creditors that he has suspended or that he is about to suspend payment of his debts;

(i) if he defaults in any proposal made under this Act; and

(j) if he ceases to meet his liabilities generally as they become due.

As it is usually difficult to prove many of the foregoing acts of bankruptcy, creditors most commonly rely on section 42(1)(j). Accordingly, an important question in the case law is under what circumstances a court will conclude that a debtor has "ceased to meet his liabilities generally as they become due." In general, a debtor's default on one or more payments to a single creditor will not constitute a failure by the debtor to pay his debts generally as they become due. This is not to say that a single creditor cannot avail itself of the remedies under the Act, provided that it can demonstrate that the debtor has also defaulted on debts owing to other creditors. The foregoing was demonstrated in Re Mastronardi (In Bankruptcy) (2000), 21 CBR (4th) 107 (Ont CA) (Mastronardi):

> [36] The fact that the petitioning creditor desires, as he candidly admitted when he was cross-examined on his Affidavit of Verification in support of the petition, to collect on the debt owing to him, is not an impermissible or disqualifying feature. Virtually every creditor who initiates a bankruptcy petition would have this as an objective. On this point I agree with Catzman J. who said in Re Four Twenty-Seven Investments Limited; Re 495487 Ontario Limited (1985), 55 C.B.R. (N.S.) 183 at 188 (Ont. S.C.), aff'd (1985), 58 C.B.R. (N.S.) 266 (Ont. C.A.):
>
>> I also reject the debtor's submission based upon the alleged improper or ulterior motive of the petitioning creditor. It is not an abuse of process or an improper purpose to commence a petition for the collection of a debt. It is not improper to petition to gain remedies not available outside of bankruptcy, including a thoroughgoing investigation of the bankrupt's affairs. Indeed, on the evidence, I consider this to be a prototypal case where the full arsenal of investigatory mechanisms and remedies available to a trustee in bankruptcy would be useful, appropriate and desirable.
>
> [37] I agree with that passage and regard it as equally applicable to the present appeal. Mastronardi owes substantial debts to several creditors, he has made several suspicious transfers of assets and he has not demonstrated any intention or inclination to pay even a penny of the debts he owes. In these circumstances, the petition for a receiving order brought by John Brabander, as administrator of his son's estate, complies with the requirements of the BIA and a receiving order would be "useful, appropriate and desirable."

Similarly, there is nothing intrinsically improper with a secured creditor petitioning a debtor into bankruptcy for the purpose of improving the secured creditor's position vis-à-vis other creditors of the bankrupt. In Bank of Montreal v Scott Road Enterprises Ltd (1989), 57 DLR (4th) 623 (BCCA) (Scott Road), the British Columbia Court of Appeal was asked to dismiss a secured creditor's application for a bankruptcy order on the basis that the application was intended to defeat the claims of other creditors under the section 136 scheme of distribution. The Court of Appeal held that the bankruptcy order should be made:

> Were it not for one matter to which I have not yet referred, I would conclude that the facts and circumstances to which I have referred constitute "sufficient cause" why no order ought to be made, and that the petition ought to have been dismissed on that ground. That matter is a decision of the Supreme Court of Canada released since the granting of the petition in this case. On 26th May 1988 the court gave judgment in FBDB v Que (Comm de la santé et de la sécurité du travail) [1988] 1 S.C.R. 1061, 68 C.B.R. (N.S.) 209, 50 D.L.R. (4th) 577, 14 Q.A.C. 140, 84 N.R. 308. In that case, the contest was between a trustee for bondholders and the Workers' Compensation Commission. The Court of Appeal of Quebec had distinguished Rainville, supra, and Deloitte, Haskins, supra, and had granted priority to the commission. The Supreme Court held that it erred in doing so. The specific facts and issues of the case need not concern us—the decision does

not directly touch the issue which has arisen here. But, in giving judgment for the court, Lamer J. made an obiter statement which is clearly in point. At p. 1072 he said:

Conclusion

I therefore consider that the claims of the parties to the case must be ranked in the order determined by the *Bankruptcy Act*. As the federal Parliament has exclusive jurisdiction to set priorities in a bankruptcy matter, the scheme of distribution in s. 107 of the *Bankruptcy Act* must be applied here. As respondent's claim was covered by s. 107(1)(h) of the Act, respondent is a preferred creditor whose claim must be ranked after that of appellant, whether or not the trustee realized on his security outside the bankruptcy proceeding. Once the bankruptcy has occurred, the federal statute applies to all creditors of the debtor.

It is true that such a solution may encourage secured creditors to bring about the bankruptcy of their debtor in order to improve their title. On the other hand, this solution has obvious advantages. As soon as the bankruptcy occurs the *Bankruptcy Act* will be applied: the mere fact that a creditor is mentioned in s. 107 of the Act suffices for such creditor to be ranked as a preferred creditor and in the position indicated in that provision. As provincial statutes cannot affect the priorities created by the federal statute, consistency in the order of priority in bankruptcy situations is ensured from one province to another.

It is the last paragraph which is relevant to the issue raised here. This is a case in which the secured creditor brought about the bankruptcy of its debtor solely in order to improve its title. The paragraph represents a considered dictum of the court in relation to a question, essentially one of policy, as to the effect to be given to a federal statute. It is a dictum which, in my view, we are bound to follow and to apply by holding that such a circumstance is not sufficient cause to refuse to grant the receiving order. If the present state of the law is unsatisfactory, it is for Parliament to remedy it.

It is important to distinguish here between a creditor petitioning a debtor into bankruptcy for a legitimate purpose, such as debt collection or improving the creditor's priority vis-à-vis other creditors, and an improper purpose. In *Re Laserworks Computer Services Inc* (1997), 46 CBR (3d) 226 (NSSC), (1997) 48 CBR (3d) 8 (NSSC), aff'd 1998 NSCA 42, a creditor that operated a business that was in competition with the debtor sought to put the debtor into bankruptcy for the purpose of eliminating its competitor. The court held that this was an improper purpose and an abuse of the bankruptcy process:

It has long been held that the court will not grant a petition in bankruptcy where the petition is filed for an improper purpose: *Re E De La Hooke* (1934), 15 C.B.R. 485 (Ont.S.C.), *Re Pappy's Good Eats Limited* (1985), 56 C.B.R. (N.S.) 304 (Ont.S.C.), *Dimples Diapers Inc v Paperboard Industries Corporation* (1992), 15 C.B.R. (3d) 204 (Ont.G.D.), *Re Shepard* (1996), 40 C.B.R. (3d) 145 (Man.Q.B.).

In Hooke the petitioner obtained an assignment of a judgment against the debtor for the sole purpose of filing a petition in bankruptcy and of removing the debtor as a business competitor. In that case, as is the situation in this case, there was no evidence that the debtor had any business dealings with the party seeking to place the debtor in bankruptcy. The petition was dismissed. ...

While this case does not involve a bankruptcy petition, it does involve the placing of Laserworks into bankruptcy. In my view, it would be wrong to allow Datarite to do in the proposal process what it could not do by petition. Datarite's intention was to place Laserworks in bankruptcy. The motive was to remove a competitor. That motive reveals an improper purpose. The court will not allow to be done by the back door what may not be done by the front.

While *Mastronardi* and *Scott Road* illustrate the circumstances in which a single creditor will be able to invoke the bankruptcy process in order to improve its own position, the general rule is that the Act is intended to be a collective remedy for creditors as a whole. In *Re Holmes and Sinclair* (1975), 9 OR (2d) 240 (Ont SC) (*Re Holmes*), for example, the court dismissed an application for a bankruptcy order because the applicant creditor failed to discharge its onus of proving that the debtor had defaulted on payments to other creditors:

> Resort to the statutory machinery of the Bankruptcy Act, rather than to the remedies to enforce a debt or claim in the ordinary Courts, is intended by Parliament to be for the benefit of the creditors of a debtor as a class, and the act of bankruptcy described in s. 24(1)(j) is in my judgment, an act that singles out the conduct of the debtor in relation to the class, rather than to the individual (as is the case under s. 24(1)(e)). It is for this reason that the Court must be satisfied that there is sufficient evidence from which an inference of fact can fairly be drawn that creditors generally are not being paid. This requires as a minimum some evidence that liabilities other than those incurred towards the petitioning creditor, have ceased to be met. The Court ought not to be asked to draw inferences with respect to the class on the basis of one creditor's experience where evidence of the debtor's conduct towards other members of the class could, with reasonable diligence, be discovered and produced. The Court's intuition is no substitute for the diligence of the petitioning creditor.

At the same time, the court in *Re Holmes* recognized that in certain special circumstances, a court may grant a bankruptcy order even though the debtor has only defaulted on payments to a single creditor. In *Valente v Courey*, 2004 CanLII 8018 (ON CA) (*Valente*) the Ontario Court of Appeal reiterated the general rule from *Re Holmes* and summarized the three categories of special circumstances as follows:

> [8] It is now well-settled in the case law that the failure to pay a single creditor can constitute an act of bankruptcy under s. 42(1)(j) when there are special circumstances, which have been recognized in three categories: (a) where repeated demands for payment have been made within the six-month period; (b) where the debt is significantly large and there is fraud or suspicious circumstances in the way the debtor has handled its assets which require that the processes of the *BIA* be set in motion; and (c) prior to the filing of the petition, the debtor has admitted its inability to pay creditors generally without identifying the creditors: *Re Holmes* (1976) 9 O.R. (2d) 240 (Sup. Ct.); see also Houlden and Morawetz, *The 2004 Annotated Bankruptcy and Insolvency Act* (Toronto: Carswell, 2003) at 147 D10(3).

The Court of Appeal in *Valente* identified several factors for courts to consider when determining whether special circumstances exist:

> [16] Before the court can be satisfied that the failure to pay one judgment debt is tantamount to failing to meet liabilities generally as they become due, the court must examine and consider all of the circumstances including:
> -- the size of the judgment—a small unpaid judgment is less likely to indicate an act of bankruptcy than a very large one;
> -- how long the judgment has been outstanding—there may be reasons why a recently obtained judgment has not been paid as yet, including a potential appeal, the need to

arrange for the marshalling of funds, the intent to make arrangements for payment over time or in the case of a default judgment, knowledge of the judgment;

-- if a judgment has been outstanding for a long time, it may be that the debtor believes that the creditor is willing to wait for payment, and is paying his or her other debts as they fall due;

-- whether the judgment creditor has conducted a judgment debtor examination and the results of that examination; if the judgment creditor can collect without invoking the mechanism of the bankruptcy process, a petition ought not to be granted;

-- what steps the judgment creditor has taken to determine whether the debtor has other creditors and the results of those inquiries.

[17] In this case, the bankruptcy court judge appeared to conclude that the one judgment automatically constituted special circumstances and an act of bankruptcy, without considering whether, in all of the circumstances, the petitioning creditor had proved that the debtor was not meeting his liabilities generally as they fell due.

More recently, in *Re Levesque*, 2016 ONCA 393, 36 CBR (6th) 217, the Ontario Court of Appeal upheld a lower court decision dismissing an application for a bankruptcy order where the applicant creditor failed to demonstrate that special circumstances existed:

[11] The application judge was not satisfied that special circumstances had been proven. While she acknowledged that the debt was significant, she found there was no evidence of fraud or suspicious circumstances. And while she considered the respondent's view of the value of the corporate assets to approach the "grandiose", she also found that the debt had only been outstanding a relatively short time, the appellant appeared to have taken no steps to collect on a general security interest in its favour, and the appellant had not given any evidence on what steps it had taken to collect from the corporate judgment debtor. She concluded that the appellant had failed to provide the necessary evidence to invoke the bankruptcy process.

[12] These factual findings were reasonably open to the application judge on the evidence before her. She did not err in considering that other steps to enforce the judgment could have been taken by the appellant.

[13] We note that the application was dismissed without prejudice to a new application being made in future on further and better evidence.

As noted earlier, the second part of the act of bankruptcy requirement in section 43(1)(b) is that the act of bankruptcy was committed "within the six months preceding the filing of the application." In *Malmstrom v Platt* (2001), 53 OR (3d) 502 (CA), the Ontario Court of Appeal held that demands for payment of multiple judgment debts owing to different creditors were not necessary in order to establish that the debtor committed an act of bankruptcy within the six months preceding the application. In that case, the bankruptcy judge held that the judgment creditors were not required to demand payment within the six-month period preceding the application, and that the judgments made against the debtor more than six months prior to the application satisfied section 43(1)(b). The Court of Appeal upheld the bankruptcy judge's decision:

[8] The theory behind the six-month period appears to be that a petitioning creditor should not be permitted to rely upon stale-dated debts which have not been pursued in order to establish current acts of bankruptcy. However, it has been accepted that even in situations where a debt has become due more than six months before the date of the

petition, a demand for payment made within the six-month period revives the original debt. Such a demand makes the debts current and failure to act on such a demand can serve as a current act of bankruptcy. As noted by Henry J in *Re Harrop of Milton Inc* (1979), 29 C.B.R. (N.S.) 289 (Ont. Bktcy.) at p.293:

> As I understand those judgments, they interpret the [Bankruptcy Act, R.S.C. 1970, c. B-3] as meaning that, where the act of bankruptcy occurred prior to the six-month period and thereafter nothing was done by creditors with respect to the debts in default for a period of six months or more, the act of bankruptcy ceases to be current and cannot found a receiving order. But in my opinion that does not apply where the debtor has received continued demands for payment since the initial defaults and has not paid. This is the case here....

[9] In this case, there is some evidence of a demand for payment being made within the six-month period, but leaving that aside for the moment, it is still important to consider the bald question of whether it is necessary to make a demand where the debt is reduced to a judgment of the court pronounced outside the six-month period. In my opinion, this question has not been dealt with satisfactorily in Canada.

[10] It was the view of the bankruptcy judge that court judgments did not require a demand from the judgment creditor within six months of the petition in bankruptcy. As he put it in his reasons of February 7, 2000:

> ... As I discussed before, court judgments and orders are sufficient in themselves. They're the ultimate demand. There is no necessity to keep on demanding on a periodic basis as to the payment under those directions of the Court.

[11] I agree with the position taken by the bankruptcy judge.

The Court of Appeal, in para 18, further stated that there was no need for a judgment creditor to apply for a bankruptcy order immediately after the judgment is issued or to make repeated demands for payment after filing the application because "a judgment is a continuing demand for payment by the judgment creditor just as the failure to satisfy the judgment is a continuing refusal by the judgment debtor."

B. Appointment of Trustee and Interim Receiver

Section 43(9) provides that on a bankruptcy order being made, the court shall appoint a trustee for the bankrupt's property, "having regard, as far as the court considers just, to the wishes of the creditors." In certain cases, before a bankruptcy order is made, section 46(1) authorizes the court to appoint an interim receiver to take immediate possession of all or part of the debtor's property if such an appointment is "shown to be necessary for the protection of the estate of a debtor." The role and duties of receivers are discussed in further detail in Chapter 17.

III. DEEMED ASSIGNMENTS

The commercial and consumer proposal provisions of the Act deem a debtor to have made an assignment in bankruptcy in certain circumstances. In general, these deemed assignments occur upon the failure of a commercial or consumer proposal. The following are the relevant provisions:

1) Section 50(12.1): where the court deems the creditors to have refused a proposal.
2) Sections 50.4(8) and (11): respectively, where the insolvent debtor or trustee miss certain filing deadlines, or where the court on application by the trustee terminates the period for making a proposal.
3) Section 57: where the creditors refuse a proposal.
4) Section 61(2): where the court refuses to approve a proposal.
5) Section 63(4): where the court annuls a proposal at the request of the trustee or a creditor.

Commercial and consumer proposals are discussed in Chapter 16. The consequences of a deemed assignment are the same as for a voluntary assignment and a bankruptcy order: the debtor becomes a bankrupt and its assets vest in the trustee in bankruptcy.

IV. CONSEQUENCES OF BANKRUPTCY: APPOINTMENT OF TRUSTEE, VESTING OF BANKRUPT'S PROPERTY, AND STAY OF PROCEEDINGS

As noted earlier, section 43(9) provides that on a bankruptcy order being made, the court shall appoint a trustee over the bankrupt's property. Similarly, section 49(4) of the Act provides that when the official receiver files an assignment, the official receiver must appoint a trustee. Both of these provisions reflect the fact that upon bankruptcy, the bankrupt loses all ability to deal with their property, which vests immediately in the trustee pursuant to section 71:

> On a bankruptcy order being made or an assignment being filed with an official receiver, a bankrupt ceases to have any capacity to dispose of or otherwise deal with their property, which shall, subject to this Act and to the rights of secured creditors, immediately pass to and vest in the trustee named in the bankruptcy order or assignment, and in any case of change of trustee the property shall pass from trustee to trustee without any assignment or transfer.

What constitutes the "property" of the bankruptcy estate is discussed further in Chapter 4. Importantly, section 71 provides that the vesting of the bankrupt's property in the trustee is "subject . . . to the rights of secured creditors." Chapter 8 discusses the role and rights of secured creditors in further detail.

In addition to the creation of the bankruptcy estate and the appointment of the trustee, the other major outcome of a bankruptcy order or assignment is the imposition of an automatic stay of proceedings on all claims against the bankrupt and their property. Specifically, section 69.3(1) of the Act provides that:

> Subject to subsections (1.1) and (2) and sections 69.4 and 69.5, on the bankruptcy of any debtor, no creditor has any remedy against the debtor or the debtor's property, or shall commence or continue any action, execution or other proceedings, for the recovery of a claim provable in bankruptcy.

The foregoing language sets out several exceptions to the stay of proceedings with reference to other provisions of the Act, as follows:

1) Section 69.3(1.1) provides that the stay of proceedings ceases on the day that the trustee is discharged from their duties.

2) Section 69.3(2) provides that secured creditors may enforce their rights to the bankrupt's property notwithstanding the stay, unless the court orders otherwise. This is discussed further in chapters 4 and 8.

3) Section 69.4 provides that a creditor or any other person who is affected by the stay may apply to the court to lift the stay in respect of that person, provided that the court is satisfied that the applicant is "likely to be materially prejudiced" by the stay or that "it is equitable on other grounds" to lift the stay.

   In practice, this is a difficult hurdle for an applicant creditor to overcome. In *Ma v Toronto-Dominion Bank* (2001), 24 CBR (4th) 68 (Ont CA) the Ontario Court of Appeal, at para 3, stated that the onus is on the applicant to establish that there are "sound reasons" for lifting the stay. Although this requirement for establishing "sound reasons" does not require the applicant to show that it has a *prima facie* case, the Court of Appeal stated that "if it were apparent that the proposed action had little prospect of success, it would be difficult to find that there were sound reasons for lifting the stay." See also *Global Royalties Limited v Brook*, 2016 ONCA 50 at para 35, 33 CBR (6th) 1.

   Schreyer v Schreyer, 2011 SCC 35, provides an example of circumstances in which courts may agree to lift the bankruptcy stay in order to permit a claimant to pursue an action against the bankrupt. In that case, a non-bankrupt spouse sought to bring a claim for certain property of the bankrupt spouse which was exempt from the bankruptcy estate. The Supreme Court of Canada, at para 32, stated that the non-bankrupt spouse should apply to lift the bankruptcy stay pursuant to section 69.4:

   > In such circumstances, the appropriate remedy for a creditor like the appellant would be to apply to the bankruptcy judge under s. 69.4 *BIA* for leave to pursue a claim against the exempt property. Since this property is beyond the reach of the ordinary creditors, lifting the stay of proceedings cannot prejudice the estate assets available for distribution. In keeping with the wording of s. 69.4(*b*) *BIA*, this is why it would be "equitable on other grounds" to make such an order. This procedure would also accord with the policy objective of bankruptcy law of maximizing, under the *BIA*, returns to the family unit as a whole rather than focussing on the needs of the bankrupt: see, on this point, *Hildebrand v Hildebrand* (1999), 13 C.B.R. (4th) 226 (Man. Master), at para. 16; and, generally, on Parliament's concern for the support of families, *Marzetti v Marzetti*, [1994] 2 S.C.R. 765 (S.C.C.), at pp. 800–01.

4) Lastly, section 69.5 provides that the stay does not apply in respect of the operation of any provincial legislation designed to collect amounts owing by the bankrupt in respect of income tax source deductions and Canada Pension Plan contributions in any manner similar to section 224(1.2) of the *Income Tax Act*.

Aside from the foregoing exceptions, the automatic bankruptcy stay is very broad. In *Vachon v Canada (Employment & Immigration Commission)*, [1985] 2 SCR 417, the Supreme Court of Canada stated that the word "remedy" in what is now section 69.3(1) covers all attempts at recovery:

> [17] Appellant in my view properly relied upon the English version of s. 49(1) of the *Bankruptcy Act*, where the word "recours" is rendered by the word "remedy", giving to it and the words "autres procédures" ("other proceedings") a very broad meaning which covers any kind of attempt at recovery, judicial or extra-judicial. *Black's Law Dictionary* (5th ed. 1979) defines "remedy":

> The means by which a right is enforced or the violation of a right is prevented, redressed, or compensated.

and below:

> Remedy means any remedial right to which an aggrieved party is entitled with or without resort to a tribunal.

> [18] *Jowitt's Dictionary of English Law* (2nd ed 1977), vol. 2, gives an almost identical definition:

> the means by which the violation of a right is prevented, redressed, or compensated. Remedies are of four kinds: (1) by act of the party injured ... ; (2) by operation of law ... ; (3) by agreement between the parties ... ; (4) by judicial remedy, *e.g.*, action or suit. The last are called judicial remedies, as opposed to the first three classes, which are extrajudicial.

> [19] The courts have also interpreted the stay of proceedings imposed by s. 49(1) of the *Bankruptcy Act* very broadly.

The Supreme Court of Canada went on to explain that Parliament clearly intended for the bankruptcy stay to apply to all forms of proceedings outside of the Act in order to further the objectives of the bankruptcy regime:

> [26] The *Bankruptcy Act* governs bankruptcy in all its aspects. It is therefore understandable that the legislator wished to suspend all proceedings, administrative or judicial, so that all the objectives of the Act could be attained.

> [27] Accordingly, I consider that s. 49(1) of the *Bankruptcy Act* is sufficiently broad to include recovery by retention from subsequent benefits, such as the recovery at issue here.

In particular, the broad stay is intended to further the Act's goal of ensuring an orderly and fair distribution of the bankrupt's property to its creditors. The Supreme Court of Canada articulated this purpose more fully in *R v Fitzgibbon*, [1990] 1 SCR 1005 at 10–11 as follows:

> It is to be observed that the section prohibits the granting of any "remedy against" or "recovery of" any claim against the debtor or his property without leave of the court in bankruptcy. The aim of the section is to provide a means of maintaining control over the distribution of the assets and property of the bankrupt. In doing so, it reflects one of the primary purposes of the *Bankruptcy Act*, namely, to provide for the orderly and fair distribution of the bankrupt's property among his or her creditors on a pari passu basis: see Duncan and Honsberger, *Bankruptcy in Canada* (3rd ed. 1961), at p. 4. The object of the section is to avoid a multiplicity of proceedings and to prevent any single unsecured creditor from obtaining a priority over any other unsecured creditors by bringing an action and executing a judgment against the debtor. This is accomplished by providing that no remedy or action may be taken against a bankrupt without leave of the court in bankruptcy, and then only upon such terms as that court may impose.

In the absence of the stay, some creditors would be able to gain an unfair advantage by enforcing their claims ahead of other creditors and thereby depleting the bankruptcy estate. An important caveat however, is that generally this stay only applies to unsecured creditors. As will be discussed further in chapters 4 and 8, in most cases secured creditors remain free to enforce their rights to the bankrupt's property notwithstanding the bankruptcy.

Practice Questions

Question 1

Do the court's statements in *Re Dahl* regarding the requirements for annulling an assignment make sense in light of *Re Wale*? Why or why not?

Question 2

Michael has three creditors: Mary, Gabe, and Nancy. Michael has defaulted on several payments to Mary. He may default soon on payments owing to each Gabe and Nancy, but so far, he has been current in his payments to them. Mary has brought an application for a bankruptcy order against Michael. If the order is granted, it will have the effect of improving Mary's priority ranking relative to both Gabe and Nancy because Mary is a secured creditor, while they are not. There is some evidence that Michael is able to pay Mary but has chosen not to pay her, for unclear reasons. Assume that the total amount of all of Michael's debts exceeds $1,000. Is the court likely to grant the bankruptcy order? Why or why not?

Question 3

Assume that the court has granted Mary's application and Michael is now bankrupt. You represent a plaintiff who is considering whether to seek an order lifting the stay so that it can pursue a personal injury claim against Michael. Your client would like to know its chances of success on the motion to lift the stay—how would you advise them?

CHAPTER 4

Property

Section 71 of the *Bankruptcy and Insolvency Act*, RSC 1985, c B-3 (*BIA*) provides that upon bankruptcy, the bankrupt immediately loses all capacity to deal with or dispose of its property, which vests in the trustee and forms the bankruptcy estate, "subject to the rights of secured creditors." Part I of this chapter discusses the meaning of "property" under the Act and the various types of exempt property—that is, types of property that do not form part of the bankruptcy estate. Part II discusses the rights of secured creditors with respect to the property of the bankrupt. Lastly, Part III examines set-off, a rule which permits parties with reciprocal obligations to "net out" their positions.

I. WHAT CONSTITUTES THE BANKRUPTCY ESTATE?

A. Definition of "Property"

Section 2 of the Act defines property as follows:

> *property* means any type of property, whether situated in Canada or elsewhere, and includes money, goods, things in action, land and every description of property, whether real or personal, legal or equitable, as well as obligations, easements and every description of estate, interest and profit, present or future, vested or contingent, in, arising out of or incident to property.

In general, courts have interpreted this definition broadly. In *Saulnier v Royal Bank of Canada*, 2008 SCC 58 (*Saulnier*), the Supreme Court of Canada held (at paras 23–24) that a commercial fishing licence was property of the bankruptcy estate, even though (1) the federal minister of fisheries had "absolute discretion" over granting, transferring, and terminating the licence, and (2) a simple licence typically would not be considered property at common law. In reaching this decision, the Supreme Court stated that the definition of "property" under the Act must be interpreted broadly with regard to the overall purpose of the Act:

> [17] In determining the scope of the definition of "property" in a statutory context, it is necessary to have regard to the overall purpose of the *BIA*, which is to regulate the orderly administration of the bankrupt's affairs, keeping a balance between the rights of creditors and the desirability of giving the bankrupt a clean break: *Husky Oil Operations Ltd v Minister of National Revenue*, [1995] 3 S.C.R. 453, at para. 7. The exemption of designated property from distribution among creditors under s. 67(1) is to allow the bankrupt to continue a living pending discharge and, when discharged, to make a fresh start. Those exemptions do not, it seems to me, bear much similarity to the proposed

"exempting" of a valuable asset such as a commercial fishing licence. If Saulnier had "sold" his licences prior to discharge the cash proceeds would, it seems, be after-acquired property that would be divided amongst his creditors under s. 67(1)(c) of the *BIA*.

Although the fishing licence alone would not be considered property under the Act, the licence coupled with the licence holder's proprietary interest in the fish caught met the definition:

> [22] The fishery is a public resource. The fishing licence permits the holder to partici-pate for a limited time in its exploitation. The fish, once caught, become the property of the holder. Accordingly, the fishing licence is more than a "mere licence" to do that which is otherwise illegal. It is a licence coupled with a proprietary interest in the harvest from the fishing effort contingent, of course, on first catching it.

In these regards, it is important to emphasize that the mere fact that the fishing licence had commercial value did not make the licence "property" within the meaning of the Act:

> [42] The criticism of [the commercial realities] approach is that many things that have commercial value do not constitute property, while the value of some property may be minimal. There is no necessary connection between proprietary status and commercial value. See generally T. G. W. Telfer, "Statutory Licences and the Search for Property: the End of the Imbroglio?" (2007), 45 Can. Bus. L.J.224, at p. 238. I agree with the Court of Appeal that "commercial realities" cannot legitimate wishful thinking about the notion of "property" in the BIA and the PPSA, although commercial realities provide an appro-priate context in which to interpret the statutory provisions. The BIA and the PPSA are, after all, largely commercial statutes which should be interpreted in a way best suited to enable them to accomplish their respective commercial purposes.

The Supreme Court further stated (in para 44) that the definition of property in section 2 was "very wide" and that "Parliament unambiguously signalled an intention to sweep up a variety of assets of the bankrupt not normally considered property at common law." Accordingly, it was appropriate to treat the fishing licence as property that vested in the trustee upon the licence holder's bankruptcy:

> [46] I prefer to look at the substance of what was conferred, namely a licence to partici-pate in the fishery coupled with a proprietary interest in the fish caught according to its terms and subject to the Minister's regulation. As noted earlier, the *BIA* is intended to fulfill certain objectives in the event of a bankruptcy which require, in general, that non-exempt assets be made available to creditors. The s. 2 definition of property should be construed accordingly to include a s. 7(1) fishing licence.
>
> [47] It is true that the proprietary interest in the fish is contingent on the fish first being caught, but the existence of that contingency is contemplated in the *BIA* defin-ition and is no more fatal to the proprietary status for *BIA* purposes than is the case with the equivalent contingency arising under a *profit à prendre*, which is undeniably a property interest.
>
> [48] Counsel for the Attorney General of Canada was greatly concerned that a hold-ing that the fishing licence is property in the hands of the holder even for limited statu-tory purposes might be raised in future litigation to fetter the Minister's discretion, but I do not think this concern is well founded. The licence is a creature of the regulatory system. Section 7(1) of the *Fisheries Act* speaks of the Minister's "absolute discretion." The Minister gives and the Minister (when acting properly within his jurisdiction under

s. 9 of the Act) can take away, according to the exigencies of his or her management of the fisheries. The statute defines the nature of the holder's interest, and this interest is not expanded by our decision that a fishing licence qualifies for inclusion as "property" for certain statutory purposes.

[49] It follows that in my view the trustee was entitled to require the appellant Saulnier to execute the appropriate documentation to obtain a transfer of the fishing licences to the third party purchaser.

[50] It may well be that in the course of a bankruptcy the fishing licence will expire, or has already expired. If so, the trustee will have the same right as the original holder of an expired licence to go to the Minister to seek its replacement, and has the same recourse (or the lack of it) if the request is rejected. The bankrupt can transfer no greater rights than he possesses. The trustee simply steps into the shoes of the appellant Saulnier and takes the licence "warts and all."

The Act's broad definition of property is subject to several important qualifications. As noted in para 43 of *Saulnier*, licences generally are not property within the meaning of the Act unless they can be linked to some proprietary interest. In addition, even though section 2 of the *BIA* explicitly refers to "things in action," causes of action that are personal in nature to the bankrupt do not fall within the definition of property. In *Re Holley* (1986), 54 OR (2d) 225 (CA), for example, Holley made an assignment in bankruptcy and subsequently sued her former employer for wrongful dismissal while Holley was still an undischarged bankrupt. Holley's claim contained several heads of damages, including damages for mental distress and punitive damages. The lower court held that the action was property of the bankruptcy estate that vested in the trustee, and that Holley had no status to bring the action. On appeal, the Ontario Court of Appeal overturned the lower court's decision. The Court of Appeal held that the determination of whether Holley's claim was property of the estate depended on the nature of the damages awarded, if any, which could only be determined at trial:

> There is a further difficulty in the path of the bankruptcy court assuming jurisdiction in the matter. Although the only cause of action asserted is that of wrongful dismissal, the appellant has asserted several heads of damages. The respondents in their statement of defence denied that the appellant suffered any damages. The nature of the damages, if any, suffered by the appellant, can only be determined after a trial, with all the attendant pre-trial proceedings available to the parties under the rules of court. The appellant's statement of claim clearly claims damages for mental distress and punitive damages, both of which are personal in nature. The amount claimed under these headings is in excess of the amount which appears to be claimed for damages for salary in lieu of reasonable notice. As may be seen from authorities previously cited, it is possible that the appellant will recover damages solely or principally for mental distress and anxiety. In my view it is only after the nature of the damages, if any, to which the appellant claims to be entitled, has been ascertained, that the court can properly determine whether the cause of action is vested wholly or in part in the appellant or the trustee in bankruptcy. I agree with the opinion expressed by Southey J in *Cherry v Ivey*, supra, that such question should be determined at trial, although Southey J did not have to consider in that case any proceedings launched in bankruptcy court.

The Ontario Court of Appeal based its decision on a well-established line of cases holding that damages awarded to an individual bankrupt for personal injuries or mental anguish belong to the bankrupt and not to the estate:

The appellant submitted that the bankruptcy court judge erred in finding that the cause of action referred to in the appellant's action was property which vested in the trustee. *Re Hollister*, 30 O.W.N. 328, (1926), 7 C.B.R. 629 was concerned with an action in which the trustee in bankruptcy applied for payment to it of moneys awarded to the debtor, an undischarged bankrupt for personal injuries sustained in an automobile accident. Fisher J said at pp., pp. 630–31, 7 C.B.R.:

> The law is well settled that the *Bankruptcy Act* never intended to increase the assets of an insolvent for division amongst his creditors, by monies recovered in an action for personal injuries, as these monies are awarded as damages to the debtor for his pain, suffering and loss of comfort of life . . .

and further:

> Causes of action arising from bodily or mental suffering, such as actions for assault, seduction, criminal conversation, and damages for personal injuries, remain in the bankrupt.

. . . In *Cherry v Ivey et al*, 37 O.R. (2d) 361, the defendants moved for an order staying the action until the plaintiff, a bankrupt, was discharged from bankruptcy. The plaintiff's action was for damages for malicious prosecution and for slander. He alleged that the acts of the defendants had irreparably impaired his business activities and had caused him embarrassment, anxiety, emotional trauma, mental distress and physical upset. The defendants took the position that the causes of action were essentially claims of action interfering with the plaintiff's business and were therefore property within the definition thereof in the *Bankruptcy Act* and accordingly, only the trustee in bankruptcy could prosecute the actions. Southey J said at pp. 363:

> In the case at bar, the causes of action are malicious prosecution and slander, both of which are essentially claims for outrage at the wrongs done to an individual. In my view, such causes of action do not vest in the trustee, simply because the outrage involved the plaintiff in his business. No case was cited to me in which a court has held that an action should be stayed because some of the damages claimed relate to the business of the plaintiff where the cause of action is otherwise clearly a personal one.

He then dismissed the application of the defendants. It should be noted that the defendants had not yet pleaded.

The types of property that will form part of the estate are further clarified in section 67(1), which supplements the definition in section 2 as follows:

Property of bankrupt
67 (1) The property of a bankrupt divisible among his creditors shall not comprise
(a)   property held by the bankrupt in trust for any other person;
(b)   any property that as against the bankrupt is exempt from execution or seizure under any laws applicable in the province within which the property is situated and within which the bankrupt resides;
(b.1) goods and services tax credit payments that are made in prescribed circumstances to the bankrupt and that are not property referred to in paragraph (a) or (b);
(b.2) prescribed payments relating to the essential needs of an individual that are made in prescribed circumstances to the bankrupt and that are not property referred to in paragraph (a) or (b); or

(b.3) without restricting the generality of paragraph (b), property in a registered retirement savings plan or a registered retirement income fund, as those expressions are defined in the *Income Tax Act*, or in any prescribed plan, other than property contributed to any such plan or fund in the 12 months before the date of bankruptcy,

but it shall comprise

(c) all property wherever situated of the bankrupt at the date of the bankruptcy or that may be acquired by or devolve on the bankrupt before their discharge, including any refund owing to the bankrupt under the *Income Tax Act* in respect of the calendar year — or the fiscal year of the bankrupt if it is different from the calendar year — in which the bankrupt became a bankrupt, except the portion that

  (i) is not subject to the operation of this Act, or

  (ii) in the case of a bankrupt who is the judgment debtor named in a garnishee summons served on Her Majesty under the *Family Orders and Agreements Enforcement Assistance Act*, is garnishable money that is payable to the bankrupt and is to be paid under the garnishee summons, and

(d) such powers in or over or in respect of the property as might have been exercised by the bankrupt for his own benefit.

Part I.B immediately below discusses the treatment of after-acquired property of the bankrupt, which is covered by sections 67(1)(c) and section 68. The balance of Part I discusses the different types of exempt property.

B. After-Acquired Property

Section 2 provides that the property of the bankrupt includes all "present or future, vested or contingent" property. Section 67(1)(c) further provides that the property of the bankrupt includes all property on the date of bankruptcy or that the bankrupt acquired after the date of bankruptcy and before the date of discharge, that is, after-acquired property. The general rule is that where such after-acquired property is a claim or an award for damages, it vests immediately in the trustee. In general, the undischarged bankrupt has no status to bring claims — as with all of the other property forming part of the estate, only the trustee has the capacity to deal with a claim or an award of damages. This general rule was affirmed in *Vetro v Canadian National Exhibition Association*, 2014 ONSC 4324, aff'd 2015 ONCA 87:

> [18] Section 71 of the *Bankruptcy and Insolvency Act* expressly provides that upon a bankruptcy order being made or an assignment being filed with an official receiver, a bankrupt ceases to have any capacity to dispose of or otherwise deal with his or her property, which immediately passes to and vests in the trustee named in the bankruptcy order or assignment.
>
> [19] The definition of "property" under s. 2 of the *Bankruptcy and Insolvency Act* is extremely broad and covers property of every kind whatsoever, including assets in relation to which the bankrupt has contractual or contingent rights, such as the licence agreements in the present case.
>
> [20] Under the scheme of the *Bankruptcy and Insolvency Act*, it is not simply the property of the bankrupt owned at the date of bankruptcy which passes to the trustee; any property acquired by the bankrupt prior to his discharge also vests in the trustee.
>
> [21] As the Supreme Court of Canada held in *Wallace v United Grain Growers Ltd*, per Iacobucci J for the Court:

The clear wording of the statute indicates that, upon assignment into bankruptcy, the bankrupt relinquishes his ability to deal with both existing and after-acquired property, all of which vests in the trustee in bankruptcy. As property has been defined under the Act to include things in action, it appears that an undischarged bankrupt has no capacity to maintain an action for breach of contract.

[22] An action commenced by an undischarged bankrupt in relation to property that vests in the trustee is a nullity. If a bankrupt brings an action relating to property that vests in the trustee, the action should be struck as an abuse of process of the court.

[23] It is undisputed that the plaintiff in the present case was bankrupt at the time of the licence renewals with the defendant and that he is not yet discharged from bankruptcy. At the time that he became bankrupt, all of the plaintiff's property vested with his trustee in bankruptcy.

There are a number of exceptions to this general rule. Firstly, as discussed earlier, the Ontario Court of Appeal held in *Re Holley* that, where the after-acquired property is a claim or an award of damages that is personal in nature, it belongs to the bankrupt and does not vest in the trustee. The Supreme Court of Canada reaffirmed this exception in *Wallace v United Grain Growers Ltd*, [1997] 3 SCR 701 (*Wallace*):

[38] The parties agreed that the claim for mental distress, loss of reputation and punitive damages is one that is personal in nature. Such a cause of action does not become the property of the trustee in bankruptcy and thus may be pursued by Wallace in his own right: *Re Holley* (1986), 59 C.B.R. (N.S.) 17 (Ont. C.A.).

Secondly, section 68 exempts from the after-acquired property of the estate all income earned or received by the bankrupt after the date of bankruptcy and before the discharge, up to such maximum amounts as the trustee may determine to be "surplus income" of the bankrupt:

Directives re surplus income
68 (1) The Superintendent shall, by directive, establish in respect of the provinces or one or more bankruptcy districts or parts of bankruptcy districts, the standards for determining the surplus income of an individual bankrupt and the amount that a bankrupt who has surplus income is required to pay to the estate of the bankrupt.

Definitions
(2) The following definitions apply in this section.

surplus income means the portion of a bankrupt individual's total income that exceeds that which is necessary to enable the bankrupt individual to maintain a reasonable standard of living, having regard to the applicable standards established under subsection (1). (*revenu excédentaire*)

total income
(a) includes, despite paragraphs 67(1)(b) and (b.3), a bankrupt's revenues of whatever nature or from whatever source that are earned or received by the bankrupt between the date of the bankruptcy and the date of the bankrupt's discharge, including those received as damages for wrongful dismissal, received as a pay equity settlement or received under an Act of Parliament, or of the legislature of a province, that relates to workers' compensation; but

(b) does not include any amounts received by the bankrupt between the date of the bankruptcy and the date of the bankrupt's discharge, as a gift, a legacy or an inheritance or as any other windfall. (*revenu total*)

In other words, section 68 carves out an additional exception to the general rule that after-acquired property of the bankrupt belongs to the estate. The trustee is only entitled to the portion of the bankrupt's personal income that constitutes "surplus income," if any. Under section 68(3), the trustee is responsible for determining whether the bankrupt has surplus income within the meaning of section 68. Furthermore, under section 68(4) the trustee shall fix any amounts that the bankrupt is required to pay to the estate, and inform the official receiver and any creditors who request such information. See also *Conforti (Re)*, 2015 ONCA 268 at paras 24–25. In *Wallace*, the Supreme Court explained the section 68 exception as follows (note that section 68 was amended after *Wallace* and the Supreme Court's below reference to "salary, wages, or other remuneration" was replaced with "total income"):

> [58] The wording of the Act is clear. An undischarged bankrupt has no capacity to deal with his or her property and no distinction is made with respect to whether that property was acquired before or after the assignment in bankruptcy. I must therefore respectfully reject the Court of Appeal's holding that a bankrupt has the capacity to bring an action for breach of contract concerning after-acquired property unless the trustee intervenes. In my view, the bankrupt generally will not be able to deal with his or her property outside the circumstances described in s. 99(1).
>
> [59] Nevertheless, this is not sufficient to determine that Wallace's claim is a nullity because s. 68(1) of the Act carves out an additional exception to this general rule where the property in question can be characterized as "salary, wages or other remuneration." Unlike the Court of Appeal, I believe an undischarged bankrupt can maintain an action against a former employer for damages in lieu of reasonable notice, not because of the timing of the acquisition of such property but rather, because of the nature of the property in question.

The amendments to section 68 after *Wallace* did not alter this rule. In *Re Landry* (2000), 50 OR (3d) 1 (CA), the trustee sought a declaration that an arbitral award of damages for unjust dismissal in favour of the bankrupt vested in the trustee. The Court of Appeal at para 17 reasoned that, insofar as the damages for unjust dismissal related to lost wages, they "can be equated to actual wages." Accordingly, the award did not vest automatically in the trustee because section 68 exempts all personal earnings of the bankrupt that are not "surplus income." The Court of Appeal stated that the post-*Wallace* amendments to section 68, if anything, had widened the exemption for personal income of the bankrupt:

> [27] The current s. 68 in the *BIA* differs from the former version in a number of respects. The full text is appended to these reasons for ease of reference. First, the section does not refer to "salary, wages or other remuneration" but to "total income." "[T]otal income" is defined for the purpose of s. 68 as including, "*notwithstanding s. 67(1)(b)* and (b.1), all revenues of a bankrupt of whatever nature or source." The section still allows the trustee to apply to the court for a determination of the amount that a bankrupt is required to pay to the estate of the bankrupt out of her total income but an elaborate procedure must be followed before such an application is made. . . .
>
> [30] In my view, the reasoning in *Marzetti* and *Wallace* that led to the conclusion that s. 68 was a complete code with respect to wages applies equally to this new section.

The current provision applies to the "total income" of the bankrupt and, as such, is even wider than the earlier reference to "salary, wages and other remuneration"; the provision expressly excludes the application of s. 67(1)(b); its purpose is no different than that described in *Marzetti* (except that applications to the court now appear to be limited to those cases where the issue cannot be otherwise resolved); and the jurisprudential principles reviewed by the Supreme Court in *Marzetti* are equally relevant.

[31] I therefore conclude that s. 67 is superseded by the provisions of the current s. 68 in so far as the "total income" of the bankrupt is concerned. It follows that, as in *Wallace*, Landry's claim against her former employer and any consequent award relating to lost wages do not automatically vest in the trustee under ss. 67 and 71. Resort can only be had to s. 68 for payment of any portion thereof to the estate of the bankrupt.

It followed that the trustee would need to apply to the bankruptcy court for a determination of the amount of the arbitral award for lost wages that constituted surplus income, if any, once the arbitral proceedings had concluded. Any such surplus income would then vest in the trustee and be divisible among the creditors. The Court of Appeal in paras 42, 43, and 46 therefore ordered that any amounts awarded by the arbitrator to the bankrupt as compensation for lost wages would be paid into the bankruptcy court pending the determination of the amount of any surplus income. Surplus income is discussed further in Chapter 11.

C. Trusts

As noted earlier, section 67(1)(a) provides that the property of the bankrupt divisible among its creditors shall not comprise property held by the bankrupt in trust for others. Technically, such property still passes into the possession of the trustee, but the trustee is not entitled to distribute it among the creditors. The Supreme Court of Canada explained this rule as follows in *Royal Bank of Canada v North American Life Assurance Co*, [1996] 1 SCR 325:

[48] Unlike provisions of the Act such as ss. 71(2), 91 or 68, s. 67(1) tells us nothing about the property-passing stage of bankruptcy. Instead, it relates to the estate-administration stage by defining which property in the estate is available to satisfy the claims of creditors. It effectively constitutes a direction to the trustee regarding the disposition of property. Thus, property which is divisible among creditors is defined very broadly in s. 67(1) as:

(c) all property wherever situated of the bankrupt at the date of his bankruptcy or that may be acquired by or devolve on him before his discharge, and

(d) such powers in or over or in respect of the property as might have been exercised by the bankrupt for his own benefit.

However, the trustee is barred from dividing two categories of property among creditors: property held by the bankrupt in trust for another person (s. 67(1)(a)), and property rendered exempt from execution or seizure under provincial legislation (s. 67(1)(b)). *While such property becomes part of the bankrupt's estate in the possession of the trustee, the trustee may not exercise his or her estate distribution powers over it by reason of s. 67.* [Emphasis added.]

What qualifies as trust property for the purposes of the exemption in section 67(1)(a)? A trust is a legal device in which legal and beneficial ownership of an asset is separated between a trustee, who takes possession of the asset, and a beneficiary, who holds beneficial title to the asset. In general, a trust is created in one of three ways: (1) when a settlor transfers property to a trustee for a beneficiary; (2) when a court imposes a constructive trust or resulting trust; and (3) when a trust is deemed to exist in certain circumstances by statute. Each of these cases is discussed immediately below.

The most common type of trust is created when a settlor transfers property to a trustee to hold in trust for a beneficiary, also known as an express trust. When this occurs, trust law sets out various requirements for determining whether a valid trust was created. A fundamental requirement is that the settlor must have clearly intended to create the trust. In *Re Ontario Worldair Limited* (1983), 45 CBR (NS) 116 (Ont Sup Ct J), aff'd (1983), 48 CBR (NS) 112 (Ont CA) a charter airline, Worldair, set up a bank account for the maintenance of a Boeing 707 which it was subleasing from Air Belgium. Although the sublease stipulated that Worldair would open the bank account in trust for maintaining the engines of the 707, Worldair's instructions to the bank did not refer to a trust. Worldair merely instructed the bank to make interest payments to Worldair while forwarding reports on account activity to Air Belgium. The court held (at 8–10) that the evidence was insufficient to establish that Worldair intended to create a trust:

> In my opinion, the evidence here does not disclose an intention to create a trust. It was submitted that the property was under the control of the bankrupt which was consistent with its position as trustee; that the absence of any power in Air Belgium to seize the funds or to appoint a receiver indicated that it already had a proprietary interest in the moneys; and that the existence of the account provided a significant benefit to Air Belgium. The absence of any designation of Air Belgium as beneficiary of the fund or the fact that the income from the account went to the bankrupt, it was submitted, did not necessarily mean that the funds were not trust property. It was pointed out that even though the bankrupt was in serious financial difficulties, moneys in the account were not withdrawn, which it was said showed a recognition by the bankrupt that the funds did not belong to it. Notwithstanding all such submissions, the overriding circumstance seems to me to be that there is nothing in the letters to the bank which indicates an intention to create a trust and that the provisions in the sublease do not indicate that the funds in the account are to be beneficially owned by or available to Air Belgium. It is plain that the funds were owned by and were to be available to the bankrupt to enable it to perform its obligations under art. 7. If default occurred, there are extensive remedies available to Air Belgium in art. 16 but they do not appear to include a resort to the moneys in the bank account. In all circumstances, I am bound to conclude that the moneys in the account were not impressed with a trust for the benefit of Air Belgium.
>
> In my opinion, the moneys in the bank account are not trust funds for the benefit of Air Belgium and to the extent not claimed by Price Waterhouse Limited under the debentures are available for division amongst the ordinary creditors of the bankrupt.

Where no express trust is found to exist, the court may impose a constructive trust, usually as a remedy for unjust enrichment or fiduciary breach. In *Baltman v Melnitzer* (1996), 43 CBR (3d) 33 (Ont Gen Div), Melnitzer had purchased various pieces of artwork several years prior to his bankruptcy. His wife at the relevant times, Baltman, claimed ownership of some of the artwork based on a personal arrangement between them. At the same time, Melnitzer's main banker and secured creditor, the Royal Bank, asked the court to impose a constructive trust in the Royal Bank's favour as a remedy for unjust enrichment—in short, Melnitzer had obtained various loans from the Royal Bank based on fraudulent misrepresentations and forgeries. Coopers & Lybrand and the National Bank, in turn, asked the court to declare that the artwork was part of the bankruptcy estate divisible among the unsecured creditors. The court held (at 9 and 11) that the Royal Bank failed to establish that Melnitzer had been unjustly enriched because, even though he was clearly enriched and the bank suffered a corresponding deprivation, the bank failed to prove the absence of a juristic reason for the deprivation:

> However, I conclude, here, as I did in *Royal Bank v Harowitz, supra,* that the Bank's claim must founder and fail on the shoals created by the third element of the unjust enrichment cause of action—the absence of a juristic reason—as well as at the remedial stage where the Bank seeks the imposition of constructive trust.
>
> In his now-famous dictum in *Rathwell, supra,* at p. 459, Dickson J described the third element of the formula somewhat delphically:
>
> > ... for the principle to succeed, the facts must display an enrichment, a corresponding deprivation, *and the absence of any juristic reason—such as a contract or disposition of law—for the enrichment.* (Emphasis added.)
>
> ... The plain fact of the matter is that the contract went into effect and stayed in effect for almost two years down to early August, 1991, when Mr. Melnitzer's fraudulent schemes were opened to the light of day.
>
> One should note the following facts about the course of the contract dealings. The Bank entered the contract with its eyes open even though, as I found in the *Harowitz* case, *supra,* the Bank was negligent in doing its due diligence leading up to the grant of the credit line to Mr. Melnitzer. The loan commitment was made subject to apparently stringent terms demanded by the Bank, including the hypothecation of $1.5 million in cash by Mr. Melnitzer in an interest-bearing account along with a full-loan guarantee by Melfan Investments, the hypothecation of Melfan Investments shares and other collateral undertakings and guarantees by Mr. Melnitzer personally.
>
> There were no defaults under the credit line down through 1990 and well into 1991. In the interim, Mr. Melnitzer made several draws on the line and the Bank was earning up to $38,000 per month in interest at good rates.

Citing the Supreme Court of Canada's decision in *Lac Minerals Ltd v International Corona Resources Ltd,* [1989] 2 SCR 574, the court went on to say (at 14–16) that even if the bank had proven that Melnitzer was unjustly enriched, it would be inappropriate to impose a constructive trust in these circumstances:

> On the facts of this case, I do not believe it would be appropriate to award a constructive trust. The factors which I identify telling against its application are these:
>
> (1) the relationship between Mr. Melnitzer and the Bank was a purely commercial and contractual relationship;
> (2) while the Bank took certain security interests as it saw fit, such as the $1.5 million deposit account, none of the property at issue—the artwork—was secured by the Bank;
> (3) the availability to the Bank of its normal contractual remedies;
> (4) the availability to the Bank of its claims as a creditor in the bankruptcy;
> (5) the fact that the Bank is asserting a constructive trust only as a result of its own negligence, lack of investigation and breach of its own internal credit-granting rules incidental to the issuance of a credit line to Mr. Melnitzer;
> (6) the fact that an otherwise unsecured creditor is seeking, in effect, to "jump the queue" over other unsecured creditors in the bankruptcy;

This is not a case, like *LAC Minerals, supra,* where one party effectively stole a property from another party by taking advantage of confidential information. Also, it is not a case where one party has obtained all the fruits of a property on the back of another as in *Rathwell, supra,* or *Sorochan, supra.* Rather, this is a case where a large and sophisticated commercial enterprise entered a loan contract with a person it was anxiously and almost desperately courting and chose to dictate the terms and conditions of the arrangement. Now, having been burned by the contract, the Bank is attempting to re-write that contract and, after the fact, obtain new security at the expense of other creditors who were also victims of the same fraudster. Equity, in my view, should not come to the aid of that single creditor at the expense of the other equally victimized creditors.

The court further found that Melnitzer and Baltman had purchased most of their artwork using funds from their joint account with CIBC, into which account Baltman had deposited all of her personal earnings. The court concluded that Baltman was the absolute owner of several pieces of artwork which Melnitzer and she had agreed belonged solely to her, and one-half owner of the balance of the artwork, with the other half interest vesting in the trustee in bankruptcy for the benefit of Melnitzer's unsecured creditors.

In certain circumstances, a court may also imply a resulting trust, in which the trustee is deemed to be holding the transferred property in trust for the settlor. The Supreme Court of Canada defined resulting trusts as follows in *Pecore v Pecore,* 2007 SCC 17:

> [20] A resulting trust arises when title to property is in one party's name, but that party, because he or she is a fiduciary or gave no value for the property, is under an obligation to return it to the original title owner: see D.W.M. Waters, M.R. Gillen and L.D. Smith, eds., *Waters' Law of Trusts in Canada* (3rd ed. 2005), at p. 362. While the trustee almost always has the legal title, in exceptional circumstances it is also possible that the trustee has equitable title: see *Waters' Law of Trusts,* at p. 365, noting the case of *Carter v Carter* (1969), 70 W.W.R. 237 (B.C. S.C.).

A resulting trust arises, for example, where an express trust has failed; the trustee is then implied to be holding the property in trust for the settlor. The Supreme Court in *Pecore* (at para 24) would state as a general rule, gratuitous transfers give rise to a rebuttable presumption of a resulting trust "because equity presumes bargains, not gifts." However, the Supreme Court acknowledged the exception to this rule in cases where the nature of the relationship between the transferor and transferee gives rise to a presumption of "advancement" instead:

> [28] Historically, the presumption of advancement has been applied in two situations. The first is where the transferor is a husband and the transferee is his wife: *Hyman v Hyman,* [1934] 4 D.L.R. 532 (S.C.C.), at p. 538. The second is where the transferor is a father and the transferee is his child, which is at issue in this appeal.
>
> [29] One of the earliest documented cases where a judge applied the presumption of advancement is the 17th century decision in *Grey (Lord) v Grey (Lady)* (1677), [1677] Rep. Temp. Finch, 23 E.R. 185 338 (H.C. Ch.):
>
>> ...the Law will never imply a *Trust,* because the natural Consideration of Blood, and the *Obligation which lies on the Father in Conscience* to provide for his Son, are predominant, and must over-rule all manner of Implications. [Emphasis added; at 187]
>
> [30] As stated in *Grey,* the traditional rationale behind the presumption of advancement between father and child is that a father has an obligation to provide for his sons.

See also *Oosterhoff on Trusts,* at p. 575. The presumption also rests on the assumption that parents so commonly intend to make gifts to their children that the law should presume as much: *ibid.,* at pp. 581 and 598. . . .

[33] . . . As women now have both the means as well as obligations to support their children, they are no less likely to intend to make gifts to their children than fathers. The presumption of advancement should thus apply equally to fathers and mothers.

The Supreme Court (at para 36) went on to say that the presumption of advancement should not apply with respect to gratuitous transfers between parents and their independent adult children because the parental support obligation does not apply to adult children. In fact, as it is common for ageing parents to transfer their assets into joint accounts with their adult children, there should be a rebuttable presumption that the adult child is holding the property in trust for the parent.

Another type of resulting trust is known as the Quistclose trust, based on the English case of *Barclays Bank Ltd v Quistclose Investments Ltd,* [1968] UKHL 4 (Eng). In that case, Quistclose loaned money to a related company, Rolls Razor Ltd, for the express purpose of Rolls paying a dividend to its shareholders. At the same time, Rolls owed money to Barclays. Quistclose transferred the money into Rolls' bank account with Barclays, but before Rolls could pay the dividend, it went into liquidation. Barclays sought to take the funds in the account as partial repayment of its loans to Rolls. However, the House of Lords held that Rolls was holding the funds in trust for payment of the dividends, and since the purpose of the trust failed when Rolls failed to pay the dividends, Rolls was holding the funds in trust for Quistclose. Courts in Canada have recognized Quistclose trusts in a number of cases — the key requirements are that the lender and borrower clearly intended to create a trust for a specific purpose and that the third party that received the money had notice of same. See *Del Grande v McCleery* (1998), 5 CBR (4th) 36 (Ont Ct J (Gen Div)), aff'd (2000), 127 OAC 394 (CA); *Gignac, Sutts v National Bank of Canada* (1987), 5 CBR (4th) 44 (Ont Sup Ct), aff'd 1989 CarswellOnt 1860 (CA).

A third type of trust, known as a statutory and/or deemed trust, arises by operation of statute. Deemed trusts are discussed in Chapter 9.

D. Property Exempt Under Provincial Law

Section 67(1)(b) exempts from the bankruptcy estate all property that is exempt from execution or seizure under laws applicable in the province where the bankrupt resides and the property is situated. The effect of this provision is to exempt all property of the bankrupt that, at the time of bankruptcy, is situated in the province where the bankrupt resides and is exempt under that province's Execution Act or such other applicable provincial or federal legislation. The Supreme Court of Canada explained the purpose of this provision in *Vachon v Canada (Employment & Immigration Commission),* [1985] 2 SCR 417 at 14:

> As Estey J. wrote, in giving the unanimous judgment of this court in *Industrial Acceptance Corp v Lalonde,* [1952] 2 S.C.R. 109, at p 120:
>
>> The purpose and object of the *Bankruptcy Act* is to equitably distribute the assets of the debtor and to permit of his rehabilitation as a citizen, unfettered by past debts.
>
> The rehabilitation of the bankrupt is not the result only of his discharge. It begins when he is put into bankruptcy with measures designed to give him the minimum needed for subsistence.

The specific types of property and the dollar values of the exemptions vary in each province, but in general, the exemptions are limited to the types of property and amounts required to give effect to the foregoing objectives. Exempt property in a bankruptcy is considered in more detail in Chapter 11.

E. The Intersection Between Bankruptcy and Family Law

When a marriage breaks down, the former spouses may claim ownership of assets to which the other holds legal title. The resolution of such disputes turns primarily on provincial matrimonial property laws. When one of the spouses becomes bankrupt, the trustee will take possession of all of the bankrupt's property subject to the usual exceptions. If the bankrupt holds title to any property claimed by the non-bankrupt spouse, then the non-bankrupt spouse will have a personal claim in the bankruptcy which will rank as an unsecured claim. Thus, if the property is disposed of, the non-bankrupt spouse will share in the net proceeds from the disposition on a *pro rata* basis with the other unsecured creditors. This rule is encapsulated in the below excerpt from *Fischel v Fischel* (1991), 6 CBR (3d) 154 (NBQB) (*Fischel*):

> This is a motion for an interim order pursuant to s. 42(7) of the Marital Property Act restraining Price Waterhouse Limited from taking possession and disposing of certain properties.
>
> The motion also seeks an order granting Mr. Fischel possession of these properties until the final determination of his application under the Act.
>
> In brief, the background is as follows.
>
> Gordon R. Fischel and Marlene Z. Fischel were married in June 1964, and there is no evidence that they have separated or that the marriage has broken down.
>
> During the marriage they acquired certain properties including a house in Moncton, New Brunswick; a cottage in Cap-Brûlé, New Brunswick; a condominium in Florida; a car, and other personal property.
>
> Mr. Fischel was at all material times a non-titled spouse in connection with those properties.
>
> On June 15, 1990, Marlene Z. Fischel was declared bankrupt and Price Waterhouse appointed as her trustee in bankruptcy.
>
> In a decision rendered on February 26, 1991, pursuant to the *Bankruptcy Act* and formalized by an order dated April 10, 1991, I authorized the trustee in bankruptcy to take possession and dispose of the properties subject to the provisions of the *Marital Property Act*.
>
> In disposing of the present motion I adopt the reasoning of the Court in *Re Mauro*, 32 R.F.L. (2d) 362, which, as I understand it, supports the proposition that in circumstances such as this one, the non-titled spouse is not entitled to possession. Accordingly, it is my view that the interests of Mr. Fischel, pending the hearing of his application under the *Marital Property Act*, will be preserved if the net proceeds from the sale of the properties are kept in trust until the final determination of that application.
>
> My conclusion is that any interest that Gordon R. Fischel may have in the property which the trustee has been authorized to seize and sell only entitles him to a share of the net proceeds of the sale and does not affect the trustee's right to possession and disposition.

There are a few circumstances in which the non-owning spouse will be able to assert a proprietary right to the property, and thereby remove the property from the other spouse's bankruptcy estate. Firstly, as the court alluded to in *Fischel*, provincial law will alter the ownership rights of the parties in the disputed property where, for example, the spouses have divorced or there is evidence that they have separated. See *Re Radovini* (1981), 37 CBR (NS) 264 (SC). Alternatively, the non-owning spouse can assert a proprietary interest in the disputed property where a court has previously ordered that the property be transferred to the non-owning spouse pursuant to provincial family law. Importantly, however, matrimonial property legislation in most provinces does not grant the non-owning spouse a proprietary interest in the disputed assets until a court actually orders that the assets be transferred to the non-owning spouse. This was affirmed in *Maroukis v Maroukis*, [1984] 2 SCR 137 at 4–5:

> The judgment of the Court of Appeal is now reported at 24 R.F.L. (2nd) 113. Wilson JA (as she then was), with whom Brooke and Thorson JJA concurred on this issue, disagreed with the trial judge and said, at p. 117:
>
> > I must respectfully disagree with the effect Luchak J has given to s. 4(1) of the *Family Law Reform Act*. I do not think the subsection confers rights in property in the absence of an order of the court. I think the subsection simply sets out the circumstances in which the court may make an order for equal division of the family assets. I appreciate that the subsection uses the words 'is entitled to', which seem to suggest a statutory right, but the opening words of the subsection 'Subject to subsection 4', which empowers the court to make an unequal division, make it clear that subs. (1) does not confer the right to an equal division, but merely states that, prima facie, the court should order an equal division, but not if equality would be inequitable having regard to the items listed in paras. (*a*) to (*f*) of subs. (4). I believe, therefore, that until Luchak J made his order of 10th October 1979 the matrimonial home continued to be held in joint tenancy and that the executions against the husband filed prior to that date attached to his interest in it. The learned judge accordingly had no jurisdiction to vest the property in the wife free and clear of those executions.
>
> I am in complete agreement with this statement and adopt it in concluding that the full estate in the matrimonial home vested in the appellant wife only on the making of the order by Luchak J on October 10, 1979.

In short, if the order transferring the property to the non-owning spouse is not made before the owning spouse's bankruptcy, then the disputed property vests in the trustee. British Columbia is an exception to this rule, as matrimonial property legislation there provides that each spouse receives a half-interest in all family assets, effective as against a trustee in bankruptcy, upon the occurrence of a triggering event. As with a court order transferring the property to a non-owning spouse, however, these statutory provisions are only effective if the triggering event occurs before the date of the bankruptcy. See *Biedler v Biedler*, [1983] BCJ No 815 (SC).

Lastly, the non-owning spouse may be able to recover the disputed property through one of the means discussed earlier, namely, by obtaining a court order lifting the bankruptcy stay or declaring a constructive trust over the disputed property. The process for lifting the stay is discussed in Chapter 3; the relevant provision is section 69.4 of the Act. In any case, the non-owning spouse will need to overcome significant legal hurdles to convince the court that it is appropriate to remove the property from the estate, as the effect would be to deprive the other unsecured creditors of the value of the disputed property. For a recent example of a court lifting the stay for a non-bankrupt spouse to pursue a family law claim, see *Fiorito v Wiggins*, 2017 ONCA 765.

On the other hand, there will be circumstances in which a bankrupt spouse has a claim for certain property to which the non-bankrupt spouse holds legal title. In such cases, the bankrupt spouse's claim will vest in the trustee like all other non-exempt property of the bankrupt. The Alberta Court of Appeal articulated this rule in *Tinant v Tinant*, 2003 ABCA 211:

> [11] There are good reasons why the capacity to act is vested in the trustee. First, the assets of the bankrupt are in the control of the trustee. If the proceeding is unsuccessful it is likely that there will be a costs consequence. A costs order against the bankrupt will generally be meaningless. Further if any of the property of the bankrupt is available to satisfy the costs award then it is likely that the property should have been turned over to the trustee. Also, if the bankrupt has legitimate means to raise costs, those means would generally be better spent on contribution to his or her creditors.
>
> [12] Second, one of the purposes of cost awards is to ensure that parties will carefully consider whether there is any merit to a proceeding. When a party is bankrupt that careful consideration is easily set aside as the party is insulated from costs consequences as he or she has already lost all his or her assets to the trustee. Also the party against whom costs consequences have some meaning, the trustee, has already assessed the risks and has determined that the potential benefits of the proceeding are outweighed by the risks of a costs award. . . .
>
> [19] There is no good reason why matrimonial property should enjoy a different status than does other property. In fact there is a good reason why it should not. It is not unusual for bankrupts to attempt to place their property beyond the reach of their creditors and the trustee. One possible way of achieving this objective would be to have one's spouse commence a matrimonial property application and then agree to a generous order. If such orders do not relate to property, then neither the trustee or any creditor would have a say in the matter.

The trustee's right to bring the claim is contingent upon the occurrence of a triggering event giving rise to the claim, such as a separation or divorce. Where there has been a triggering event, the claim vests in the trustee upon bankruptcy and the bankrupt has no standing to pursue it: see *Blowes v Blowes* (1993), 16 OR (3d) 318 (CA). That said, if the bankrupt has a claim for a constructive trust over the property, the trustee can pursue that claim even in the absence of a triggering event: see *Kopr v Kopr*, 2006 ABQB 405.

Lastly, as noted earlier, section 67(1)(c)(ii) exempts from the bankruptcy estate any money payable to the bankrupt that is subject to a garnishee summons under the *Family Orders and Agreements Enforcement Assistance Act*, RSC 1985, c 4 (2nd Supp). A garnishee summons under this statute instructs the federal government to redirect any monies payable by it to the bankrupt into a separate account for the benefit of the garnishor. The purpose is to ensure that any such federal monies will not go to the bankrupt or its creditors but to satisfy the support order — that is, an order for maintenance, alimony, or other family financial support — in the garnishor's favour.

F. Bona Fide Purchasers

Upon bankruptcy, the bankrupt loses all capacity to deal with their property, which vests in the trustee pursuant to section 71. Generally, where a bankrupt purports to sell property to another person, the sale will be void and the purchaser will have a right of action for breach of contract against the bankrupt, which claim survives the bankruptcy discharge. This is discussed further in Chapter 7.

Notwithstanding the general rule set out above, section 75 of the Act protects bona fide purchasers of real property by providing that a sale is valid even if the property is part of the bankruptcy estate. The key requirements for the sale to be valid are that the bankruptcy was not registered in the provincial land registry system and the terms of the sale comply with the laws of the province in which the property is situated:

Law of province to apply in favour of purchaser for value
75 Despite anything in this Act, a deed, transfer, agreement for sale, mortgage, charge or hypothec made to or in favour of a bona fide purchaser, mortgagee or hypothecary creditor for adequate valuable consideration and covering any real property or immovable affected by a bankruptcy order or an assignment under this Act is valid and effectual according to the tenor of the deed, transfer, agreement for sale, mortgage, charge or hypothec and according to the laws of the province in which the property is situated as fully and effectually and to all intents and purposes as if no bankruptcy order or assignment had been made under this Act, unless the bankruptcy order or assignment, or notice of the order or assignment, or caution, has been registered against the property in the proper office prior to the registration of the deed, transfer, agreement for sale, mortgage, charge or hypothec in accordance with the laws of the province in which the property is situated.

These provisions permit third parties to rely on the information contained in the provincial land registry system when deciding whether to purchase real property. In order to foreclose such a result, the trustee is required to register the bankruptcy against the real property, which the trustee is entitled to do pursuant to section 74. The effect of registration is to make the trustee the registered owner of the property.

Section 99 creates a second exception to the general rule that the bankrupt cannot dispose of property after the date of bankruptcy. Specifically, section 99 provides that all transactions between the bankrupt and any person dealing with the bankrupt in good faith and for value in respect of after-acquired property are valid against the estate and the trustee, unless the trustee intervenes prior to the completion of the sale. The manner in which section 99 operates to protect a good faith purchaser can be summarized from the following excerpt from *Re Dhaliwal*, 2010 ONSC 793:

[49] The effect of s. 99(1) is not to vest after-acquired property in the Bankrupt until the Trustee in bankruptcy intervenes; rather, under the subsection after-acquired property vests immediately in the Trustee in bankruptcy. The Bankrupt has, however, a right of possession and a right of disposal of the property until the Trustee intervenes. See commentary at s. F-239, Houlden and Morawetz and Sarra.

[50] For a transaction to be protected by s. 99(1), it must satisfy the following five criteria:

The transaction must be:
(a) between an undischarged bankrupt and a third party;
(b) in respect of after acquired property;
(c) in good faith;
(d) for value;
(e) completed before the intervention of the Trustee.

Houlden and Morawetz and Sarra, s. F-240. Further, the good faith required by s. 99(1) refers only to the conduct of a person dealing with the undischarged bankrupt. If the person dealt in good faith, the fact that the bankrupt was not dealing in good faith is immaterial: *Re Hord* (1945), 27 C.B.R. 175. Further, even if the person acquiring after acquired property from a bankrupt knows of the bankruptcy, the person acquiring the property is protected so long as the person is acting in good faith and gives value: *Re Hord, supra.*

G. Other Types of Sales

Although the Act protects bona fide purchasers who purchase real property or after-acquired property from the bankrupt, it should be noted that there are no such protections for parties who agreed to purchase goods from the bankrupt prior to the date of bankruptcy. Where a seller agrees to sell goods to a purchaser in the future and the seller becomes bankrupt before the sale can be completed, the purchaser's remedies depend upon the nature of the goods. Section 18(1) of the *Sale of Goods Act*, RSO 1990 c S.1 (*SGA*) provides that title to goods that are "specific or ascertained" will pass to the purchaser "at such time as the parties to the contract intend it to be transferred"; usually, the parties' intentions with respect to the timing of the transfer will be reflected in the agreement of purchase and sale. Accordingly, if all of the conditions for the sale of specific goods have been fulfilled, the purchaser can bring an action against the trustee for specific performance pursuant to section 50 of the *SGA*. Note that Chapter 6 discusses the powers of the trustee to disclaim (terminate) unprofitable contracts entered into by the bankrupt prior to the date of bankruptcy.

Importantly, however, section 17 of the *SGA* provides that "[w]here there is a contract for the sale of unascertained goods, no property in the goods is transferred to the buyer until the goods are ascertained." In other words, if the goods are comprised of some, but not all, of a larger bulk of widgets and have not yet been identified, or they form part of a crop that has not yet been harvested, then title to the goods cannot pass to the purchaser until the goods are ascertained. Consequently, the purchaser will be unable to rely on section 50 of the *SGA* and its remedy will be to prove a claim in the bankruptcy that will rank alongside the claims of other unsecured creditors.

H. Leases, Intellectual Property Licenses, and Other Interests

The definition of property in the *BIA* is sufficiently broad to include interests such as leases of real property, liens and intellectual property licenses. Thus, section 30(1)(k) empowers the trustee to retain, assign, surrender, disclaim or, in Quebec, resiliate any lease or other temporary interest or right in any property of the bankrupt. That said, special protections exist in the Act for lessors as well as for both licensors and licensees of intellectual property. The relevant provisions of the Act depend upon the property in question—for example, section 83 provides that where an author's manuscripts or copyrights were assigned to a person who later becomes bankrupt, the property reverts to the author or their heirs. These issues are discussed in Chapter 6.

II. SECURED CREDITORS

Technically, all property of the bankrupt that is subject to a valid security interest does not become part of the estate upon bankruptcy, and the secured creditors remain free to enforce their interests notwithstanding the bankruptcy stay. As noted earlier, section 71 of the Act provides that all property vests in the trustee upon bankruptcy "subject ... to the rights of secured creditors." Section 69.3(2) provides that the stay of proceedings does not prevent a secured creditor from realizing or otherwise dealing with its security. Likewise, the priority scheme of distribution in section 136 sets out a ranking of creditors that is "[s]ubject to the rights of secured creditors." Note in section 127, however, that where a secured creditor realizes upon its security and a balance remains owing to the creditor, that balance is not secured; in order to collect, the creditor must file a proof of claim for the balance, which claim will rank as unsecured. In short, secured creditors can be said to stand outside of the bankruptcy process, unless they elect to surrender their security interest and to prove their whole claim as an unsecured creditor pursuant to section 127(2).

Chapter 8 deals with the rights of secured creditors in greater detail. For present purposes, note that there are a few exceptions to the rule that secured creditors can continue to enforce their security interests in bankruptcy. The first exception is that an unperfected security interest in collateral is ineffective as against the trustee in bankruptcy. This exception is set out in the *Personal Property Security Act* (*PPSA*) of each province. Section 20 of Ontario's *Personal Property Security Act*, RSO 1990, c P.10, for example, provides that an unperfected security interest in collateral is both ineffective against the trustee and subordinate to the interest of any person who has either a perfected security in the same collateral, a lien given by statute or law, or priority granted by any other legislation. Pursuant to section 23 of Ontario's *PPSA*, a security interest is perfected when it is registered in the provincial personal property security registry. More specifically, section 45(1) of Ontario's *PPSA* provides that a financing statement must be registered. Section 1(1) of Ontario's *PPSA* defines "financing statement" as "the information required for a financing statement presented in a required format." Registration must occur prior to the date of bankruptcy in order for the security interest to be effective in bankruptcy.

In *Re Giffen*, [1998] 1 SCR 91, a lessor leased a motor vehicle to the BC Telephone Company, which in turn leased the car to its employee, Giffen. Neither the lessor nor the company registered the financing statement in the BC personal property security registry. When Giffen became bankrupt, the lessor seized the vehicle and sold it with the trustee's consent. The trustee then sought a court order awarding the proceeds to the trustee, citing the relevant section of BC's *Personal Property Security Act*, SBC 1989, c 36 [now RSBC 1996, c 359] which provided that the unperfected security interest was ineffective against the trustee. The bankruptcy court held that the trustee was entitled to the proceeds because the PPSA explicitly rendered the lessor's security interest ineffective against the trustee. The BC Court of Appeal overturned the lower court's decision, reasoning that the car belonged to the lessor and that the *PPSA* could not have the effect of transferring title to the bankrupt or the trustee. The Supreme Court of Canada reversed the Court of Appeal's decision and restored the lower court's order:

> [26] The Court of Appeal did not recognize that the provincial legislature, in enacting the *PPSA*, has set aside the traditional concepts of title and ownership to a certain extent. T.M. Buckwold and R.C.C. Cuming, in their article "The *Personal Property Security Act* and the *Bankruptcy and Insolvency Act*, Two Solitudes or Complementary Systems?" (1997), 12 Banking & Finance L. Rev. 467, at pp. 469–70, underline the fact that provincial legislatures, in enacting personal property security regimes, have redefined traditional concepts of rights in property:
>
>> Simply put, the property rights of persons subject to provincial legislation are what the legislature determines them to be. While a statutory definition of rights may incorporate common law concepts in whole or in part, it is open to the legislature to redefine or revise those concepts as may be required to meet the objectives of the legislation. This was done

in the provincial *PPSAs*, which implement a new conceptual approach to the definition and assertion of rights in and to personal property falling within their scope. The priority and realization provisions of the Acts revolve around the central statutory concept of "security interest." *The rights of parties to a transaction that creates a security interest are explicitly not dependent upon either the form of the transaction or upon traditional questions of title. Rather they are defined by the Act itself.* [Emphasis added.]

[27] In *International Harvester, supra*, the Saskatchewan Court of Appeal recognized that the regime put in place to regulate competing interests in personal property does not turn on title to the collateral (at p. 204):

> There is nothing in the language of the section [s. 20 of the Saskatchewan *PPSA* which is the equivalent of s. 20 of the British Columbia *PPSA*], or its relationship with other sections, or indeed in the overall scheme of the Act to suggest, for example, that an unperfected security interest, because it is rooted in and attached to the title of particular goods in the possession of a debtor, should be treated as superior to the more generally derived and broadly attached interest which an execution creditor comes to have in a debtor's goods. Indeed, the very opposite is suggested not only by the language of the section, but by the overall thrust of the Act.

[28] The Court of Appeal in the present appeal did not look past the traditional concepts of title and ownership. But this dispute cannot be resolved through the determination of who has title to the car because the dispute is one of priority to the car and not ownership in it. It is in this context that the *PPSA* must be given its intended effect and it is to this question that I now wish to turn.

The Supreme Court of Canada held that when the car was delivered to the bankrupt, the lessor had a valid security interest in the car that it could assert against the lessee and any third party claiming a right to the car. However, the lessor failed to register that security interest, "leaving it vulnerable to the claims of third parties who obtain an interest in the car through the lessee including, trustees in bankruptcy": see para 32. The bankrupt's right to use and possess the car constituted property within the broad definition of the *BIA*, and as such, the car vested in the trustee on bankruptcy pursuant to *BIA*, section 71. This conclusion was supported by the Supreme Court (in para 36) where they noted that section 12(2) of BC's *PPSA*, gives a lessee a proprietary interest in goods when the lessee obtains possession of them in accordance with the lease. Although the lessor continued to have a proprietary interest in the car, as well, the effect of section 20 of the *PPSA* was to render that interest ineffective as against the trustee, such that the trustee's interest in bankruptcy was actually greater than Giffen's interest prior to the bankruptcy. In this sense, section 20 of the *PPSA* modifies both the basic property law principle of *nemo dat* and the bankruptcy law principle that the trustee cannot obtain a greater interest in property than the interest held by the bankrupt: see paras 50–52. In short, the lessor should have perfected its interest by registration, thereby giving public notice of its interest and preserving its priority interest in the car in the event of bankruptcy.

What if the car in *Re Giffen* had been exempt property under provincial law? As noted earlier, section 67(1)(b) of the *BIA* exempts from the bankruptcy estate all property that is exempt from execution or seizure under laws applicable in the province where the bankrupt resides and the property is situated. In Ontario, for example, section 2(1) of the *Execution Act*, RSO 1990, c E.24 exempts from seizure up to one motor vehicle belonging to the debtor with a value not exceeding the amount prescribed by the regulations, which is currently $6,600: see O Reg 657/05, s 1(1). In *Re Fields* (2002), 59 OR (3d) 611 (Sup Ct J), aff'd (2004), 71 OR (3d) 11 (CA), a lessor leased a motor vehicle to a lessee but did not register its security interest. The lessee later became bankrupt. The parties agreed that the vehicle was worth at least $11,000, which was in excess of the prescribed maximum amount to qualify for an exemption under the *Execution Act* at that time, namely, $5,000. The lessor nonetheless sought a court order declaring that the trustee in bankruptcy had no interest in the proceeds from the sale of the vehicle over and above the $5,000 prescribed maximum. The court dismissed the lessor's application:

> [52] In my view, s. 2(b) is clear in its language. In order for a motor vehicle to be exempt, it must have a value not exceeding $5,000.00. No other meaning can be given to these words. Thus the vehicle in question does not qualify for an exemption as it has an admitted value of at least $11,000.00.
>
> [53] I am supported in this interpretation by sections 3(1) and (2) of the *Ontario Execution Act*. Section 3(1) provides, in essence, that where an exemption is claimed for a chattel referred to in paragraph 3 of s. 2 that has a sale value in excess of the prescribed amount ... the chattel is subject to seizure and sale, and the prescribed amount shall be paid to the debtor out of the proceeds of sale. Section 3(1) refers to "sale value" and only refers to paragraph 3 of s. 2. Thus there is a clear statement in the legislation that only when dealing with tools and instruments and other chattels ordinarily used by the debtor in the debtor's business profession or calling (other than farming) that the debtor would get the first $10,000.00 if the property was sold. Had the Legislature so intended, it could have made s. 3(1) applicable to paragraph 6 of s. 2.
>
> [54] Section 3(2) applies only to paragraph 4 of s. 2. A farmer may, in lieu of the chattels referred to, receive the proceeds of sale thereof up to the prescribed amount. Again, had the Legislature intended, it could have made s. 3(2) applicable to paragraph 6 of s. 2. Thus while s. 3 of the *Execution Act* specifically provides a scheme of selection and distribution in the event that the value of certain assets exceed the exemption amount, this section was not made applicable to paragraph 6 of s. 2, to motor vehicles. This supports the interpretation that the exemption in paragraph 6 was only intended to apply to vehicles under $5,000.00.
>
> [55] Counsel for the DCFS argued that this Court should apply s. 3 of the *Execution Act* to paragraph 6 by analogy. In my view that argument flies in the face of the maxim of statutory interpretation, *expressio unius est exclusio alterius*. He also argued that most vehicles would not fall within this nominal exemption amount. However, the Ontario legislature, in passing the subject provision in 2001, must have been presumed to know this fact and did not see fit to subject motor vehicles to s. 3. It is also to be noted that the Legislature chose the value of $5,000.00 for motor vehicles while at the same time increasing the values with respect to other paragraphs in s. 2.

In the result, the vehicle vested in the trustee and the trustee was entitled to retain the full amount of the proceeds from the sale of the vehicle for distribution to the bankrupt's creditors.

III. SET-OFF

Set-off, also known as compensation or netting, is a rule which permits parties with reciprocal claims to "net out" their positions. Section 97(3) of the *BIA* provides that set-off is applicable to "all claims made against the estate of the bankrupt and also to all actions instituted by the trustee for the recovery of debts due to the bankrupt" except insofar as the claim for set-off is affected by the provisions of the Act respecting frauds or fraudulent preferences. This provision covers the two forms of set-off that are available outside of bankruptcy, namely, legal and equitable. Legal set-off can only be exercised where the claims being set-off are liquidated and mutual cross-obligations, whereas equitable set-off can be exercised wherever a court determines that it would be unfair or inequitable not to permit set-off. The below excerpt from *Coopers & Lybrand Ltd v Lumberland Building Materials Ltd* (1983), 150 DLR (3d) 411, 49 BCLR 239 at 4–6 (SC), explains and applies the requirements for both types of set-off:

Section 75 of the *Bankruptcy Act* clearly allows a set-off and I must here determine whether at law one is permitted on the facts here.

There are two kinds of set-off: legal/statutory and equitable set-off. Legal set-off originated in England by statute, s. XIII of cap. XXII of 2 Geo. 2 (1729), amended and made effective "for ever" by s. IV of cap. XXIV of 8 Geo. 2 (1735), and carried forward into the law of British Columbia in 1858 by the predecessor of the present s. 2 of the *Law and Equity Act*. Equitable set-off has its origins in equity and does not rest on the statute of 1729. It followed and even extended the law, the courts of equity holding that certain cases were within the equity of the statute, although not within their actual words.

In the *Tuckerr Industries Inc* case (B.C.C.A. June 16th, 1983), Vancouver Registry No. CA820748) Lambert JA, speaking for the court, held that statutory set-off is available only if two conditions are fulfilled, i.e. (1) both obligations must be debts; and (2) both debts must be mutual cross obligations, and both conditions must be fulfilled at the same time.

The first requirement is that both the plaintiff's and the defendant's claims be for a debt which can be ascertained with certainty at the time of pleading. (See *Royal Trust Co v Holden* (1915) 8 W.W.R. 500.). Here the defendant owes the plaintiff the sum of $11,613.40 for goods purchased. This is a liquidated amount and can be ascertained at the time of pleading. On the other hand the defendant claims entitlement from the plaintiff its share of the advertisement costs and the amount of rebate available to the defendant. These are also ascertainable with certainty at the time of pleading and then amounted to $6,681.40. The rebate programme (quoted supra) provides that value earned rebates are based and paid on the plateau achieved by year end in accordance with the schedule. After the date of bankruptcy, July 19th, 1982, the plaintiff could no longer sell any goods to the defendant. Prior to that, between January 1st, 1982 and July 19th, 1982, the defendant had purchased goods in an amount entitling it to a rebate in the amount it seeks to set off. Clearly then, on July 19th, 1982 the debt owed by the plaintiff to the defendant was a liquidated sum which is ascertainable.

The second condition as stated in the *Tuckerr Industries* case is that there must be cross-obligations.

A set-off is available only between the same parties and in the same right as the claim. A right of set-off cannot be maintained against a plaintiff suing to enforce his demand or against an assignee when the demand which it is sought to set off arises upon an independent contract and is not due at the date of the suit, for in that case it has not become a "debt" so as to be subject to the statute. The right of set-off depends on the existence of the debt due to the defendant and thus the fact of its debtor being a bankrupt does not prevent the set-off arising. The time that both obligations must exist in a bankruptcy situation is at the time of the bankruptcy, i.e. the assignment in bankruptcy or the pronouncement of a receiving order.

Here on July 19th, 1982 there were mutual and cross obligations between the parties. On that date the defendant owed the plaintiff the amount of goods purchased and the plaintiff owed the defendant the costs of advertisements and the rebate. Even though the latter amounts were not "due" at that time, that does not defeat the defendant's right of set-off. In the *Anderson's Case* (1886), L.R. 3 Eq. 337, the court held that if a company goes into liquidation, debts which accrued before the winding-up may be set off against one another.

The court concluded (at 7–8) that the defendant was entitled to a legal set-off and, failing that, equitable set-off as well:

Even if I am wrong in that conclusion, I find that the defendant is entitled to the right of equitable set-off. In the *Tuckerr Industries* case (supra) the Court of Appeal said that equitable set-off can apply where the cross-obligations are not debts, or where mutuality is lost or never existed. It may also arise where the cross-obligations arise from the same contract, though mutuality has been lost, or where the cross-obligations are closely related, or where the parties have agreed that a right to set-off may be asserted between them, or where a court of equity would otherwise have permitted a set-off.

In *Aboussafy v Abacus Cities Ltd* 39 C.B.R. (N.S.) 1 the court held that with equitable set-off, even though unliquidated amounts could be set off against liquidated amounts and there is no need of mutuality, nonetheless the claim by the defendant has to be related to the claim by the plaintiff against the defendant.

In addition, in equitable set-off cases the party seeking the benefit of it has to show some equitable ground for being protected against his adversary's demand. In *Rawson v Samuel* (1841) 41 E.R. 451 cited in the *Abacus* case at page 7, the court said that the mere existence of cross-demands is not sufficient. In *Equitable Remedies* by Spry, 2nd ed., the learned author stated at pp. 170–71:

"What generally must be established is such a relationship between the respective claims of the parties that the claim of the defendant has been brought about by, or has been contributed to by, or is otherwise so bound up with, the rights which are relied upon by the plaintiff that it would be unconscionable that he should proceed without allowing a set-off. Thus if conduct of the plaintiff is such as to induce the defendant to incur an obligation in favour of the plaintiff, and that conduct itself is fraudulent, negligent or otherwise wrongful so as to give a cause of action to the defendant, the plaintiff will nor ordinarily be permitted to proceed until he has made good the material claims of the defendant."

In the circumstances here I conclude that the relationship between the parties is one in which it would be inequitable not to allow the defendant to set off its claims. The rebate programme was offered to induce the defendant to purchase more goods. The defendant had fulfilled all the stipulations and qualified for the rebate programme, thus it is equitable that it be allowed to set off the rebate and the advertisement costs against the debt it owes to the plaintiff.

An order granting set-off interferes with the scheme of distribution under section 136 of the Act and represents an exception to the general rule that bankruptcy law should seek to maximize the value of the estate for the benefit of the creditors as a whole. As the party seeking set-off would otherwise have had an unsecured claim in the bankruptcy, set-off effectively permits that party to elevate its claim ahead of the claims of other unsecured creditors. Accordingly, courts will be reluctant to grant equitable set-off unless there is a clear justification to do so, that is, unless it is clear from the facts of the case that denying set-off would be unfair or inequitable: see *Canada Trustco Mortgage Co v Sugarman* (1999), 179 DLR (4th) 548 (Ont CA).

Practice Questions

Adam is an undischarged bankrupt. Roughly ten years prior to the date of bankruptcy, Adam and his wife Anna purchased a sizeable collection of antiques and rare books at an estate auction, which they decided to keep in their home for their personal enjoyment. In the months leading up to his bankruptcy assignment, and after becoming bankrupt, Adam sold many of these antiques and rare books to friends, family, and third parties, some of whom had knowledge of his bankruptcy. He also gave some of the books to his daughter.

Recently, Anna decided to leave the marital home to stay with her brother in northern Ontario. It is unclear for how long she intends to be away from home, but she left her daughter and many of her clothes and belongings in the marital home with Adam. She did, however, take several of the rare books with her. Adam did not object, as Anna and he had previously agreed that the books belonged solely to her. However, he now regrets doing so, as he misses the books and wants them back.

Based on the foregoing facts, answer the following questions:

Question 1
The trustee in bankruptcy is attempting to gather up all of Adam's property for the benefit of Adam's creditors. Can the trustee recover any of the books?

Question 2
Adam thinks that the marriage may be breaking down and wants the books back from Anna. Can he apply for a court order declaring that the books belong to him?

Question 3
One of Adam's creditors has an unregistered general security agreement in all of Adam's property. The creditor now seeks to enforce its interest against the trustee in order to claim any books that the trustee is able to recover. Will the creditor be successful?

Assume that all of the parties are located in the province of Ontario.

Reviewable Transactions

I. INTRODUCTION

This chapter deals with the trustee's powers to claw assets back into the bankrupt's estate. These are assets the bankrupt may have disposed of in pre-bankruptcy transactions. These transactions fall into two categories: preferring certain creditors over others and conveying assets to keep them out of the reach of creditors. The *Bankruptcy and Insolvency Act*, RSC 1985, c B-3 (*BIA*) preference provision, section 95, catches the first category, and the provincial assignments and preferences laws supplement it. The second category is caught by the *BIA* provisions relevant to gifts and transfers at undervalue, section 96 (transfers at undervalue) and section 101 (dividends and redemptions of shares), which are supplemented by the provincial fraudulent conveyance laws.

The trustee can use any or all these provisions to overturn pre-bankruptcy transactions. In some cases, the provincial laws are the exclusive or predominant basis for challenging a pre-bankruptcy transaction; in other cases, there is substantial overlap between the *BIA* and the provincial provisions. Where there is no overlap, section 72 of the *BIA* appears to envisage continued application of provincial law. This is supported constitutionally by the provincial jurisdiction over property and civil rights.[1]

In *Robinson v Countrywide Factors Ltd*, [1978] 1 SCR 753, the Supreme Court, over a strong dissent by Laskin CJ, upheld the constitutional validity of the provincial fraudulent preference laws. The key passage from the judgment of Spence J (for the majority) reads as follows:

> I have dealt with what, in my view, are the main cases upon the subject in Canada. Upon considering them all, as well as the decision of the Judicial Committee in *AG of Ontario v AG for Canada*, [[1893] AC 189], I have come to the conclusion that the better view is to confine the effect of what is now s. 73 of the Bankruptcy Act [now s 95] to providing for the invalidity of transactions within its exact scope. To that extent, the Parliament of Canada, by valid legislation upon "bankruptcy" and "insolvency," has covered the field but has refrained from completely covering the whole field of transactions avoided by provincial legislation. I am of the opinion that the enactment in 1949 of the provisions now found in s. 50(6) [now s 72(1)] of the Bankruptcy Act is a plain indication that Parliament recognized that provisions in provincial statutes dealing with preferential transactions were still valid provincial enactments in reference to "property" and "civil rights" and were valuable aids to trustees in bankruptcy in attacking the validity of such transactions and should be available to the said trustees in bankruptcy.

---

1   *Constitution Act, 1867 (UK)*, 30 & 31 Vict, c 3, s 92(13).

The practical implication of the decision is that a trustee may rely on either the *BIA* anti-preference provisions or the provincial laws, or both, depending on which system of law is more favourable to the trustee in the particular case.

These topics are discussed under the following four headings: (1) the provincial fraudulent conveyance laws; (2) the *BIA* transfers at undervalue provision; (3) the *BIA* preference provisions; and (4) the provincial preference provisions.

II. THE PROVINCIAL FRAUDULENT CONVEYANCE LAWS

A. Introduction

The origins of the fraudulent conveyance laws lie in the *Statute of Elizabeth*.[2] The *Statute of Elizabeth* was received into Canadian provincial law at the time of settlement and it still applies in most parts of Canada on that basis. Four provinces (British Columbia, Manitoba, Newfoundland and Labrador, and Ontario) have enacted fraudulent conveyances laws codifying the *Statute of Elizabeth*. It is not settled whether the *Statute of Elizabeth* still applies in these provinces,[3] but the question may not matter much because the provincial fraudulent conveyance statutes are, in substance, the same as the *Statute of Elizabeth* (see further below). The provincial assignments and fraudulent preferences laws (in force in all provinces except Manitoba, Newfoundland and Labrador, and the Northwest Territories), which apply primarily to fraudulent preferences (discussed below), also contain fraudulent conveyance provisions, but these apply only if the debtor is insolvent or near insolvency at the date of the transaction. Neither the *Statute of Elizabeth* nor the fraudulent conveyances laws are limited in this way.

The *Statute of Elizabeth* prohibits a conveyance of property by A to B if it is made for the purpose of defeating A's creditors. A creditor can sue to have the conveyance set aside. There are two main kinds of cases: (1) where A transfers an asset to B by way of gift; and (2) where A transfers an asset to B at an undervalue.

There is an evidentiary presumption that applies in case (1), arising from *Freeman v Pope*, [1870] 6 WLUK 24 (Eng). The "rule in *Freeman v Pope*" says that, in case (1), the courts will presume A's intention to defeat creditors if A was insolvent at the date of the transaction or the transaction caused A to become insolvent. This rule is a substantial evidentiary concession in favour of a creditor who is attempting to have the transaction set aside. A can rebut the presumption by showing that they had an honest purpose while making the transaction. Case (2) is different; there is no presumption of A's intention that arises in case (2). In case (2), the courts require actual proof of A's intention to defeat creditors. They also read the statute as requiring proof of B's collusion in A's illegal purpose. Requiring proof of A's intention and B's collusion places a significant evidentiary burden on the parties, and it is for that reason that the courts look to "badges of fraud" in case (2): if the transaction displays one or more of the badges of fraud that have been developed in caselaw, an inference will arise as to A's illegal purpose unless A provides an innocent explanation. The badges of fraud include the transaction being carried out in secret or in great haste, A and B being related to one another, there is litigation pending against A, or the consideration is grossly inadequate. See *FL Receivables Trust 2002-A (Administrator of) v Cobrand Foods Ltd*, 2007 ONCA 425. The next case, *Profile United Industries Ltd v Coopers & Lybrand*, deals with case (2), where the

---

2   The *Statute of Fraudulent Conveyances 1571* (UK), 13 Eliz I, c 5.

3   See *Royal Bank of Canada v North American Life Assurance Co*, [1996] 1 SCR 325 at para 63.

presumption in *Freeman v Pope* does not arise. The court found two categories of badges of fraud to support the shared intention between the parties to defeat the creditor.

These laws are not specifically bankruptcy laws. Neither the *Statute of Elizabeth* nor the provincial fraudulent conveyance statutes are limited to eve-of-bankruptcy transactions. The policy behind the provincial fraudulent conveyance laws is the prevention of debtor dishonesty. It is the equivalent of theft for A, having made a promise of payment to C, to deprive herself of the capacity for performance by transferring her assets to B. Theft is theft whether it occurs inside or outside bankruptcy. Outside bankruptcy, the provincial fraudulent conveyance laws give judgment creditors a weapon to attack fraudulent transfers. Inside bankruptcy, the weapon passes to A's trustee to exercise on behalf of all unsecured creditors. The corresponding provision in *BIA*, section 96, applies only inside bankruptcy, but this is not because the policy is different. It is simply because the *BIA* is a bankruptcy statute. If A makes a gift to B when A is insolvent or near insolvency, the transfer is still voidable under the *Statute of Elizabeth* and the provincial fraudulent conveyance laws. It is important to be clear about the reason why. The reason is not that bankruptcy policy dictates this outcome. It is that, in the circumstances, the courts presume A's intention to defeat creditors. In other words, the policy is still to prevent dishonesty.

Profile United Industries Ltd v Coopers & Lybrand (1987), 64 CBR (NS) 242 (NBCA)

STRATTON CJNB: This appeal raises two questions: whether a payment made by one related company to another was a "settlement" within the meaning of s. 69 of the *Bankruptcy Act* [now *BIA*, s 91], RSC 1970, c. B-3; and whether the payment was made in contravention of the *Statute of Elizabeth* (*Fraudulent Conveyances Act*), 1571, 13 Eliz. I, c. 5.

In 1980 the appellant, Profile United Industries Limited ("Profile"), Associated Freezers of Canada Limited ("Freezers") and Associated Fisheries of Canada Limited ("Fisheries"), were associated companies, all controlled by one Joseph Yvon Robichaud.

Fisheries operated a fish processing plant at Shippegan, New Brunswick. On February 29, 1980, Fisheries sold its fish-processing business to Connors Bros. Ltd. for $3,650,000.00. After the payment of several encumbrances Fisheries' solicitors paid the balance of the sale price in the amount of $578,308.06 to Profile. Profile then proceeded to liquidate Fisheries' remaining assets, collect its receivables and pay its outstanding accounts. Among Fisheries' outstanding accounts was one due Profile of $150,570.04, one due Metrocan Leasing Ltd. of $220,149.79 and one due Excel Packaging Ltd. of $220,071.23. Profile off-set against the sums it received its own account with Fisheries while Freezers assumed payment of the Metrocan account.

When the sale by Fisheries to Connors Bros. took place, Excel Packaging Ltd. had commenced legal action in the courts of Quebec to collect its account with Fisheries. In that litigation Fisheries had counterclaimed against Excel for substantially the same amount as was claimed against it. But the counterclaim was unsuccessful and Excel was awarded judgment against Fisheries for the full amount of its account. On July 23, 1981, Excel registered its judgments against Fisheries in New Brunswick. The registered judgment was for $238,638.92. On December 11, 1981, Excel petitioned for a receiving order against Fisheries. On January 8, 1982, a receiving order was made and Coopers & Lybrand Limited was appointed Trustee of the Estate of Fisheries.

The Trustee commenced the present action against Profile claiming that the sum of $578,308.06 that was paid to it by Fisheries' solicitors was paid at a time when Fisheries was unable to pay its debts without these funds, that it was paid with intent to defraud the creditors of Fisheries, and in particular Excel, and that such payment contravened the *Statute of Elizabeth* and was therefore void and should be set aside. At the trial of the action a judge of the Court of Queen's Bench made the following findings:

1) When the payment of $578,308.06 was made to Profile, Fisheries was insolvent;
2) The payment made to Profile was not an ordinary business transaction but one which prevented Fisheries from paying its debts in a fair and equitable manner;
3) The sum of $578,308.06 was paid to Profile so that it could control the payment of Fisheries' accounts and thus exclude Excel;
4) The assumption by Freezers of Fisheries' account with Metrocan Leasing Limited in the amount of $220,149.79 reduced the Trustee's claim by this amount;
5) As the Trustee did not contest the set-off by Profile of its own account with Fisheries in the sum of $150,570.04 the Trustee's claim was reduced by this amount;
6) The payment made to Profile was a "settlement" within the meaning of s. 69(1) of the *Bankruptcy Act* and therefore void as against the Trustee;
7) Additionally the Trustee was entitled to succeed on the basis of the *Statute of Elizabeth*; and
8) The Trustee was entitled to judgment against Profile for $263,945.20 together with interest at the rate of 10% per annum from October 31, 1983 and to costs of $11,875.00.

Profile has appealed the decision at trial contending that the learned trial judge erred in law in two respects: (1) in finding that the payment to Profile was a "settlement" within the meaning of s. 69 of the *Bankruptcy Act*, and (2) in finding that the payment to Profile was in contravention of the *Statute of Elizabeth*. The Trustee has cross-appealed submitting that the trial judge erred in giving credits to Profile in respect of Profile's own account of $150,507.04 and the account of Metrocan Leasing Ltd. in the amount of $220,149.79....

Profile contends that the payment of $578,308.06 to it by Fisheries' solicitors did not contravene the *Statute of Elizabeth* because, it argues, the statute does not prohibit a debtor from preferring one creditor to another. Indeed, Profile further submits that even though a debtor may know that a judgment is pending against him or that what is at issue is a substantial portion of the proceeds of sale of the debtor's principal asset yet the statute is not necessarily offended when all creditors save one are paid. There is support for this submission in 17 Halsbury (3rd ed), para. 1267, where it is stated:

> Unlike the bankruptcy laws, the statute does not prohibit a debtor preferring one creditor to another, and therefore a conveyance executed in favour of one or some only of the creditors of the grantor may be bona fide and valid, notwithstanding that the grantor knows at the time that execution is about to be issued against him, or that he is insolvent, and even though the conveyance comprises the whole of the grantor's property. Such an alienation will, however, be avoided if it is a mere cloak to secure a benefit to the grantor, and the fact that one creditor obtains an advantage will not of itself prevent a transaction from being avoided.

It has been said that the *Statute of Elizabeth* was merely declaratory of what was previously the common law of the land. The purpose of its enactment is described in *Kerr on Fraud and Mistake*, 7th ed. (1952), at p. 298, as follows:

> The statute 13 Eliz. c. 5, was made for the protection of creditors. It provided, in effect, that all conveyances and dispositions of property real or personal, made with the intention of

delaying, hindering, or defrauding creditors, should be null and void as against them, their heirs, etc., and assigns. It also provided that nothing therein contained should extend to any estate or interest made on good consideration and bona fide to any person not having, at the time, any notice of such fraud.

The question whether the *Statute of Elizabeth* was in effect in Nova Scotia and the relationship between that enactment and the *Assignments and Preferences Act* was widely canvassed by Mr. Justice Hallett of the Nova Scotia Supreme Court in *Bank of Montreal v Crowell et al* (1980), 109 DLR (3d) 442. In that decision Hallett J concluded that it had been decided many years ago that the law set forth in the *Statute of Elizabeth* was applicable and necessary in that province and therefore in force. In this respect I would observe that there are as well decisions by New Brunswick courts that have adopted the statute as the law of this province: see, for example, *Bank of Montreal v Vandine and Taylor*, (1952), 33 M.P.R. 368 (C.A.). Hallett J also states the following conclusion to which I too would respectfully subscribe (p. 449):

> In my opinion, the *Assignments and Preferences Act*, although it deals with the same subject-matter as the Statute of Elizabeth (fraudulent conveyances), does not repeal the Statute of Elizabeth by implication. The Statute of Elizabeth enables an attack on conveyances made by solvent persons while the *Assignments and Preferences Act* deals with insolvent persons and the matter of preferences which are not subject to attack under the Statute of Elizabeth. The two Acts are not inconsistent or repugnant. I am satisfied that effect can be given to both statutes at the same time and there is therefore no repeal by implication: *Craies on Statute Law*, 7th ed. (1971), p. 366; *Bank of Montreal v Reis et al*, [1925] 3 D.L.R. 125, [1925] 2 W.W.R. 169.

I would observe that the *Assignments and Preferences Act*, R.S.N.B. 1973, c. A-16 was not raised as an issue either at the trial of this action or on the hearing of the appeal.

It is to be noted that the *Statute of Elizabeth* makes a distinction between voluntary conveyances and *bona fide* transfers for consideration. Section 6 of the Statute provides that the Statute does not extend to any conveyance made upon good consideration and "bona fide lawfully conveyed" to any person not having notice or knowledge of the fraud or collusion against the creditors. The applicable rule is stated in 17 Halsbury (3rd ed.) at para. 1261, as follows:

> "For creditors to be in a position to impeach an alienation of property by their debtor they must prove, in addition to fraudulent intent on the part of the grantor, either that the alienation was not made for valuable consideration or upon good consideration, or that the grantee was privy to the fraud. Otherwise the grantee will be entitled to the protection given by the provision, even where a creditor is in fact defeated by the grant."

The decision in *Bank of Montreal v Vandine and Taylor* cited previously involved a conveyance that was made for valuable consideration. In the judgment of Harrison J in that case it was stated at p. 373:

> "Two questions have to be determined under the *Statute of Elizabeth* — (1) Whether the conveyance in question was made by the debtor with the intent "to delay, hinder or defraud" his creditors; and (2) If there was such intent, whether the party buying such property participated in such fraudulent intent."

When a transaction is entered into for good and valuable consideration the burden of proving that it was made in fraud of creditors is upon those who seek to set the transaction aside. Although it is recognized that there can be no hard and fast rule as to what constitutes a fraudulent transaction, since the decision in *Twyne's Case* (1602), 3 Rep. 806, the existence of certain unexplained circumstances have sometimes been looked upon as "badges of fraud" so as to take the case out of the protection afforded to a *bona fide* purchaser. Two of the categories mentioned that have some relevance to the present case are the generality of the transfer, i.e., the inclusion therein of substantially all of the debtors' property, and the transfer of assets *pendente lite*. But overall what must be determined in each case as a question of fact is whether a concurrent intent on the part of the parties to defraud a creditor has been established by a preponderance of evidence.

In the instant case it was established that Fisheries sold its only substantial revenue producing asset, i.e., its fish-processing plant, and diverted the net sale proceeds to Profile in an effort to avoid payment to Excel which had sued it. While it is true that Profile undertook to collect Fisheries' receivables and to pay its outstanding accounts it is also true that Profile, Fisheries and Freezers were associated companies, all controlled by Mr. Robichaud. And as the trial judge took pains to point out, although he was present at the trial, Mr. Robichaud did not testify. In all of the circumstances, the trial judge categorized the diversion of Fisheries' funds to Profile as an unusual business transaction and one which prevented Fisheries from paying its debts in a fair and equitable manner at a time when it was insolvent. More importantly, he also found that Profile shared Fisheries' desire to exclude Excel from the payment of debts. As he put it:

> "The balance of the purchase price was paid to a related company, Profile, so that it could choose which of [Fisheries] debts to liquidate. It might be natural that the management of Profile would not want to pay the Excel account which was thought to have caused [Fisheries] downfall."

The learned trial judge therefore concluded that the trustee was entitled to succeed on the basis of the *Statute of Elizabeth* because, he said, as a result of the impugned transaction there were no funds left for Excel "as Profile chose to pay other creditors instead." In my opinion, the trial judge's conclusion is substantiated by the evidence. I would respectfully agree with him that there was present here a shared intention on the part of Fisheries and Profile to delay, hinder or defraud Excel, a potential judgment creditor. Adopting the language of Halsbury, the diversion of Fisheries' funds to Profile "was a mere cloak to secure a benefit" to Fisheries and under the *Statute of Elizabeth* it was void.

Appeal allowed in part.

Optical Recording Laboratories v Digital Recording Corp (1990), 1 OR (3d) 131 (CA)

GRIFFITHS JA (for the Court): On the petition of the respondent creditor, Granger J, by judgment dated August 27, 1989 [now reported 69 OR (2d) 628, 75 CBR (NS) 216 (SC Bkcy)], adjudged the appellant debtor bankrupt and issued a receiving order against it finding that the appellant had committed acts of bankruptcy contrary to ss. 42(1)(b) and 42(1)(g) of the *Bankruptcy Act*, RSC 1985, c. B-3 (as amended). The appellant appeals from the receiving order, contending that the trial judge erred in finding the particular acts of bankruptcy. The respondent cross-appeals, contending that the trial judge erred in failing to go further and find that the appellant had committed, in addition, an act of bankruptcy under s. 42(1)(c) of the Act by creating a fraudulent preference.

The Facts

The facts are set out at length in the reasons of the learned trial judge. The following is a summary of those facts pertinent to this appeal.

The appellant, Optical Recording Laboratories Inc. ("Laboratories"), had a sister company, Optical Recording Corporation ("O.R.C."). Mr. G. John Adamson owned all of the common shares of John Adamson Associates Limited which controlled Laboratories and O.R.C. Adamson was the directing mind of both Laboratories and O.R.C.

On March 28, 1985 the respondent, Digital Recording Corporation Inc. ("Digital"), sold a complete experimental facility known as a Document Storage Development System ("DSDS") to Laboratories for $21,500,000 of which $2,730,000 was paid in cash and the balance of $18,770,000 was secured by a promissory note made by Laboratories in favour of Digital. The promissory note provided that instalment payments on account of principal and interest would not commence until March 28, 1990 unless there was a default on the part of Laboratories in which case the whole of the principal amount outstanding together with accrued interest thereon would be due and payable immediately. Default under the note would include the following:

1. If Laboratories failed to pay any instalment payment within five days of the due date; or
2. If Laboratories became bankrupt or involved in an insolvency proceeding; or
3. If Laboratories defaulted on any obligation of $100,000 or more which gave the holder of such obligation the right to accelerate payment thereof.

Pursuant to the agreement of March 28, 1985, Laboratories received from Digital the "hard assets," that is, the technology and hardware necessary to undertake research and to develop new products with the DSDS. At the same time as the sale to Laboratories, there was a separate transaction wherein Digital assigned to O.R.C. the patent rights to the technology involved in the DSDS. Under this separate arrangement, O.R.C. was to pay to Digital a certain percentage of royalties received.

On August 31, 1987, Mr. Eli Jacobs (principal shareholder of Digital), Laboratories and O.R.C. entered into a credit arrangement whereby Jacobs was to provide Laboratories and O.R.C. with a line of credit up to $500,000 (US). Laboratories and O.R.C. were jointly and severally liable under this agreement and were, pursuant to the agreement, required to pay monthly interest payments on the principal amount owing.

By January 1988, Laboratories and O.R.C. were indebted to Jacobs under the credit arrangement in the amount of $650,000 (US). On February 12, 1988, Jacobs served Laboratories and O.R.C. with a notice of default under the credit agreement and instituted an action in New York State to recover the amount owing. Jacobs, on behalf of Digital, also took the position that this default under the credit agreement constituted an event of default under the promissory note in that Laboratories had defaulted on an obligation of $100,000 or more. On March 8, 1988, Digital instituted proceedings in the Supreme Court of Ontario against Laboratories for $18,770,000 plus accrued interest owing on the note.

On April 12, 1988, the action brought by Jacobs in New York State was settled and the amount owing under the credit agreement was satisfied when ORC paid approximately $761,000 (US) or $960,000 (Cdn.) directly to Jacobs. Laboratories purported to treat this payment by O.R.C. as a loan to it by O.R.C. On May 13, 1988, Laboratories executed a general security agreement in favour of O.R.C. purporting to secure the $761,000 US.

On June 30, 1988, Laboratories entered into an asset sale agreement with O.R.C. pursuant to which Laboratories purported to sell all its assets to O.R.C. except the DSDS and a term deposit held in trust for Revenue Canada, for $1,922,000. The terms of the sale were $200,000 cash, assumption of $360,000 of Laboratories' debt and satisfaction of the $1,362,000 of debt owing by Laboratories to O.R.C.

On July 1, 1988, Laboratories terminated all its employees, who were immediately rehired by O.R.C. Laboratories' research business was then carried on by O.R.C. on premises formerly occupied by Laboratories, using the same employees and facilities to carry on the business previously pursued by Laboratories.

On August 8, 1988, Digital petitioned Laboratories for a receiving order. The trial judge granted the order, holding that Laboratories had committed acts of bankruptcy contrary to what are now ss. 42(1)(b) and 42(1)(g) of the *Bankruptcy Act*. Those subsections read:

> 42 (1) A debtor commits an act of bankruptcy in each of the following cases:
>
> ...
>
> (b) if in Canada or elsewhere he makes a fraudulent conveyance, gift, delivery or transfer of his property or of any part thereof;
>
> ...
>
> (g) if he assigns, removes, secretes or disposes of or attempts or is about to assign, remove, secrete or dispose of any of his property with intent to defraud, defeat or delay his creditors or any of them. ...

The learned trial judge declined to make a finding that Laboratories had committed an act of bankruptcy pursuant to s. 42(1)(c) which reads:

> (c) if in Canada or elsewhere he makes any conveyance or transfer of his property or any part thereof, or creates any charge thereon, that would under this Act be void as a fraudulent preference.

The Findings of the Trial Judge

The findings of the trial judge may be summarized as follows:

1. That Digital was a creditor of Laboratories within the meaning of s. 2 of the *Bankruptcy Act*, that is, Digital was a person having a claim "preferred, secured or unsecured, provable as a claim" under the Act.

2. That the issue of whether the entire sum owing under the promissory note was due must await the trial of the Supreme Court action in Ontario brought by Digital against Laboratories and in which Laboratories denied liability under the promissory note and counterclaimed for damages. The trial judge ruled that, until the issue of what was due under the promissory note was settled in the Supreme Court action, he was not prepared to find that Laboratories had committed a fraudulent preference within the meaning of s. 42(1)(c) of the *Bankruptcy Act* since proof of the insolvency of Laboratories at the time of the transfer is an essential requisite under s. 95 of the Act. For the same reasons, the trial judge was not prepared to find that Laboratories had committed an act of bankruptcy within the meaning of s. 42(1)(j) of the *Bankruptcy Act*, that is, had ceased to meet its liabilities generally as they became due.

3. The general security agreement dated May 13, 1988 and the asset sale agreement dated June 30, 1988 were both fraudulent and constituted acts of bankruptcy within ss. 42(1)(b) and (g) of the *Bankruptcy Act*.

4. The trial judge found on the evidence that Adamson clearly intended in both instances to protect the assets of Laboratories from "attack by Digital". He concluded that

the "timing of the actions" by Laboratories corroborated the expressed intent of Adamson to protect the assets of Laboratories and defeat Digital, the major creditor.

5. With respect to the asset sale agreement of June 30, 1988, the trial judge found that the alleged consideration for this transaction, wherein Laboratories purported to sell not only its hard assets but also its potential ability to generate income from the DSDS, was totally inadequate and that this alleged consideration did not "in any manner breathe legitimacy into the agreement".

6. The trial judge found that, by hiring the former employees and taking over Laboratories' former premises, O.R.C. would continue to use the DSDS and research developed by Laboratories. The trial judge said that he was "convinced beyond any doubt that the transfer was fraudulent and an act of bankruptcy within s. 42(1)(b)" of the *Bankruptcy Act*.

Attack on the Findings of the Trial Judge

On this appeal, counsel for Laboratories submitted that the trial judge erred in concluding on the evidence that the two transactions constituted fraudulent conveyances. It is submitted that the general security agreement of May 13, 1988 and the asset sale agreement of June 30, 1988 were each entered into for *bona fide* business purposes and for good consideration.

In arriving at his conclusions, the trial judge made findings of fact that, in my view, were open to him to make on the evidence and an appellate court should not interfere with those findings. The trial judge expressly rejected the position of Laboratories that all of its actions were legitimate business actions and were not fraudulent within the meaning of the *Bankruptcy Act*. The trial judge found, on the testimony of John Adamson, the directing mind of both Laboratories and O.R.C., that his object in both transactions under attack was to ensure that if the principal sum on the promissory note was due, the income-producing assets developed by Laboratories would be protected from attack by Digital. He found, in effect, that the timing of the transactions and the lack of "good and valuable consideration" raised general suspicion as to the *bona fides* of the transactions. The question of whether both transactions were entered into with an intent to defraud creditors is one of fact, to be decided in the particular circumstances of the case. Here, the trial judge concluded in effect that the actions of Laboratories were intended to denude it of all its revenue-producing assets, so that the principal creditor, Digital, could not be repaid. This conclusion was justified on the evidence. The first ground of appeal must fail.

Whether the "Conveyances" Constitute Fraudulent Conveyances in Law

Counsel for Laboratories submitted as a central ground of appeal that the trial judge erred in law in making a finding under the *Bankruptcy Act* that the two transactions in question constituted fraudulent conveyances. Counsel submitted that a fraudulent conveyance within the meaning of s. 42(1)(b) of the *Bankruptcy Act* and a fraudulent preference within the meaning of s. 42(1)(c) are mutually exclusive categories. Counsel argued that a fraudulent conveyance is a conveyance to a person who is not a creditor of the transferor. A fraudulent preference, it was submitted, by contrast is a conveyance to a person who is a creditor. O.R.C. was a creditor to some extent at the material time and therefore, it was argued, the conveyance to that company would not qualify as a fraudulent conveyance but should only be considered as a possible "fraudulent preference" within the meaning of s. 42(1)(c).

Counsel for Laboratories submits that in order for a conveyance to be considered a fraudulent preference under s. 95 of the *Bankruptcy Act*, the party challenging the conveyance must prove at the outset that the transferor, Laboratories, was insolvent at the time the conveyance was made. It is submitted that Digital failed to satisfy the trial judge that Laboratories was insolvent at the date of the conveyances and, therefore, the transactions would not constitute fraudulent preferences under the Act.

The only authority that counsel for Laboratories cited in support of the proposition that ss. 42(1)(b) and (g) of the *Bankruptcy Act* apply only where the transfer or conveyances are made to a third party that is not a creditor, was the following statement contained in the report of the Ontario Law Reform Commission on the *Enforcement of Judgement Debts and Related Matters* (Toronto, 1983), Part IV:

> "Conceptually, and for the purposes of this chapter, a distinction may be drawn between a fraudulent conveyance and a fraudulent or unjust preference. A fraudulent conveyance is a transfer by the debtor of his property to a third party other than a creditor, whereas a fraudulent preference is a payment by the debtor to one or more, but not all, of his creditors, the transferee or transferees being preferred thereby. While the language of the *Fraudulent Conveyances Act* would seem to comprehend both fraudulent conveyances and fraudulent preferences, the orthodox view is that the Act is restricted to the voiding of fraudulent conveyances."

No case authority was cited for the above proposition. In my view, the distinction drawn by the authors of the Law Reform Commission report between fraudulent conveyances and fraudulent preferences was drawn solely for the purpose of the discussion that followed in the ensuing chapter.

Although the *Bankruptcy Act* is the governing federal legislation, it has long been recognized that creditors are entitled to make use of the rights and remedies provided under provincial legislation to the extent that such legislation is not in conflict with the *Bankruptcy Act*: see *Re Panfab Corp Ltd*, [1971] 2 O.R. 202 at p. 207 per Houlden J.

The two provincial statutes that operate concurrently in the area of fraudulent transfers are the *Fraudulent Conveyances Act*, RSO 1980, c. 176 and the *Assignments and Preferences Act*, RSO 1980, c. 33.

There is no definition of "fraudulent conveyance" in the *Bankruptcy Act*. Under the *Fraudulent Conveyances Act*, a debtor makes a "fraudulent conveyance" if he makes a "conveyance" of property "with intent to *defeat, hinder, delay or defraud* creditors or others of their just and lawful actions" (s. 2) (emphasis added). By s. 1(a), the term "conveyance" includes a "charge" on the debtor's property and, accordingly, the general security agreement of May 13, 1988 executed by Laboratories in favour of O.R.C. would qualify as a "conveyance."

The provisions of the *Fraudulent Conveyances Act* defining a fraudulent conveyance in no way limit such transaction to conveyances to third parties other than creditors. In my view, there is no rational reason to read into the legislative definition such a restrictive interpretation. The legislation, being remedial, should be given a liberal construction.

The author Dunlop, in his textbook *Creditor-Debtor Law in Canada* (1981), at p. 513, states the purpose of fraudulent conveyance legislation as follows:

> "The purpose of the *Statute of Elizabeth* and of the Canadian Acts based on it, as interpreted by the courts, is to strike down all conveyances of property made with the intention of delaying, hindering or defrauding creditors and others except for conveyances made for good consideration and bona fide to persons not having notice of such fraud. *The legislation is couched in very general terms and should be interpreted liberally.* Lord Mansfield concluded

that the common law had always been strongly against fraud in every shape and that the Statute of Elizabeth *"cannot receive too liberal a construction, or be too much extended in suppression of fraud." Relying on this policy, the courts have interpreted the statute to include any kind of alienation of property made with the requisite intent, the form of the transaction being immaterial.* Similarly the legislation has been held to invalidate a conveyance of any kind of exigible or attachable property of the debtor, so long as it is of some real value." (Emphasis added.)

In my view, in determining whether a conveyance is fraudulent under s. 42(1)(b) or (c) of the *Bankruptcy Act*, it is irrelevant whether the transfer was made to a creditor. Instead, what is germane to such an inquiry is the genuineness of the conveyance. To this end, s. 3 of the *Fraudulent Conveyances Act* precludes the impeachment of a conveyance "upon good consideration and *bona fide* to a person not having at the time of the conveyance to him notice or knowledge of the intent set forth" in s. 2 (i.e., to defeat, hinder, delay or defraud creditors). If the argument of Laboratories were correct, debtors could avoid a finding of fraudulent conveyance under the *Fraudulent Conveyances Act*, even though they conveyed assets intending to defeat, hinder or delay their creditors, so long as the recipient of the conveyance was a creditor for any amount, no matter how nominal. In my view, if such a limitation were intended, then it would surely have been expressly stipulated in the legislation.

This second ground fails and, accordingly, the appeal must be dismissed.

The Cross-Appeal

In the cross-appeal, counsel for Digital submits that the learned trial judge erred in failing to find that the sale under the asset sale agreement of June 30, 1988 from Laboratories to O.R.C. was a transfer of property between a debtor and a creditor made within three months of the date of the petition for the receiving order. Counsel argues it was therefore void as a fraudulent preference under s. 95 of the *Bankruptcy Act* because (a) Laboratories was insolvent at the time of the transfer; (b) the transferee, O.R.C., was a creditor; and (c) the transfer had the effect of giving that creditor a preference over other creditors such as Digital.

There is no question that conditions (b) and (c) are satisfied in the light of the findings of the trial judge. As the trial judge said:

> "If the sum of $18,770,000 plus accrued interest was due when O.R.L. (Laboratories) entered into the asset sale agreement, such agreement would have been a transfer by an insolvent company providing a creditor with a preference and therefore deemed fraudulent and void, as made within three months of the bankruptcy."

However, the trial judge declined to make a finding that the sum of $18,770,000 was owing on the promissory note at the material time and that Laboratories was therefore insolvent. He directed his mind to s. 42(1)(j) of the *Bankruptcy Act* which provides:

> 42 (1) A debtor commits an act of bankruptcy in each of the following cases:
> . . .
> (j)   if he ceases to meet his liabilities generally as they become due.

The trial judge held that the issue of whether or not the sum of $18,770,000 was a liability that had become due must await the outcome of the Supreme Court action brought by Digital against Laboratories for recovery of that sum under the note. In that respect, he said:

"That action, however, is for a determination as to whether or not the actions of O.R.L. (Laboratories) constituted a default under the promissory note and thereby rendered the total amount owing, not whether Digital has a claim against O.R.L. The unliquidated amount of damages O.R.L. alleges are due to it under the counterclaim cannot be set off against Digital's claim and do not affect Digital's status as creditor. Accordingly Digital has status to bring this petition."

Counsel for Digital submits that the trial judge erred in limiting his consideration to the issue of whether Laboratories was insolvent in the sense that it had ceased to meet its liabilities generally as they became due as at May 13, 1988 under s. 42(1)(j) of the *Bankruptcy Act*. Counsel submits that the 1987 and 1988 financial statements filed at trial demonstrate that Laboratories had approximately $400,000 of assets at the time and liabilities in excess of several million dollars made up substantially of the debt owing to Digital. It was submitted that the trial judge should have directed his attention to the definition of "insolvent person" as defined by s. 2 "insolvent person" (c) of the Act as follows:

"insolvent person" means a person who is not bankrupt and who resides or carries on business in Canada, whose liabilities to creditors provable as claims under this Act amount to one thousand dollars, and

. . .

(c) the aggregate of whose property is not, at a fair valuation, sufficient, or, if disposed of at a fairly conducted sale under legal process, would not be sufficient to enable payment of all his obligations, due and accruing due.

In my respectful view, the learned trial judge erred in failing to make a finding of insolvency within the meaning of the definition in s. 2 (c). At the material time of the petition, the financial statements filed in the proceedings clearly established that the liabilities of Laboratories far exceeded its assets. In its evidence at trial, Adamson admitted that the obligation of $18,770,000 plus interest *was owing* but disputed whether it was due. In the Supreme Court action brought in Ontario, the counterclaim of Laboratories was for a sum of approximately $200,000 damages. Whatever success Laboratories might enjoy in the pending Supreme Court action, it seems to me improbable that its liabilities on the promissory note, which are now in excess of $23,000,000, would be reduced to a point where its assets at any fair valuation would be sufficient to meet those liabilities. It must not be overlooked, as well, that the trial judge earlier found that Laboratories was a "creditor" of Digital and this finding could only be supported on the basis that money was owing to Digital under the promissory note.

Accordingly, I would allow the cross-appeal and vary the judgment below to include a finding that the appellant committed an act of bankruptcy as well, contrary to s. 42(1) (c) of the *Bankruptcy Act* by making a conveyance of its property and creating a charge thereon that would, under the *Bankruptcy Act*, be void as a fraudulent preference. . . .

Appeal dismissed with costs; cross-appeal allowed.

III. THE *BIA* TRANSFERS AT UNDERVALUE PROVISION

Fraudulent conveyances in the *BIA* are governed by section 96, dealing with gifts and transfers at undervalue, and section 101, dealing with dividends and redemptions of shares. There were amendments made to the *BIA* in 2009, prior to which the relevant *BIA* provisions were section 91 (settlements), section 100 (reviewable transactions), and section 101 (dividends and redemptions of shares). The 2009 amendments repealed sections 91 and 100 and replaced them with a new section 96 but they did not affect section 101. The language in section 96 is similar to the old section 91, so caselaw interpreting section 91 remains relevant under the new provision. In *Indarsingh, Re*, 2015 ABQB 158 at paras 3–4, the court described the provisions as follows:

> [3] [Section 96, a] general and very powerful remedy was part of the 2009 amendments to the Act. It replaced the sections dealing with settlements and reviewable transactions. The Court's permission is required and the remedy remains discretionary. (Section 96(1) says "may" and see: *People's Department Stores Inc. (Trustee of) v. Wise* [2004] 3 SCR 461, at p. 498, para. 81, which deals with old section 100). The new section allows the trustee, with the court's permission, not only to ignore an undervalue transfer and claim the property transferred for the benefit of the estate, it also allows the trustee to claim the difference from the transferee or a person who is privy. Section 96(2) creates a classic self-contained presumption in favour of the trustee's opinion of value.

> [4] An undervalue transfer is not the end of the story. A transfer that is conspicuously less than fair market value starts the process but the court's ability to deal with the transaction is a function of the elements of time, relationship, insolvency or an intent to defraud, defeat or delay. In a manner of speaking, proof of an undervalue transfer gets you to the door but it doesn't get you through it.

"Transfer at undervalue," under section 2, is defined to mean "a disposition of property or provision of services for which no consideration is received by the debtor or for which the consideration received by the debtor is conspicuously less than the fair market value of the consideration given by the debtor." The application of section 96 turns on whether the transaction is arm's-length or non-arm's-length. Its elements can be summarized as follows:

1) The provision applies to both arm's-length and non-arm's-length transactions.
2) In the case of an arm's-length transaction, the review period is one year before the date of the initial bankruptcy event; in the case of a non-arm's length transaction, the review period is five years.
3) In the case of an arm's-length transaction, the trustee must prove (a) that the debtor was insolvent at the time of the transaction or the transaction rendered the debtor insolvent; *and* (b) that the debtor intended to defeat the interests of creditors.
4) In the case of a non-arm's-length transaction occurring within one year before the date of the initial bankruptcy event, the trustee must prove *neither* that (a) the debtor was insolvent at the time of the transaction or the transaction rendered the debtor insolvent; *nor* (b) that the debtor intended to defeat the interests of creditors. This means the trustee need only prove that the transaction occurred.
5) In the case of a non-arm's length transaction occurring between two and five years before the date of the initial bankruptcy event, the trustee must prove that (a) the debtor was insolvent at the time of the transaction or was rendered insolvent by the transaction; *or* (b) the debtor intended to defeat the interests of creditors.
6) The trustee has a choice of remedies, either to avoid the transfer or sue the counterparty for the value shortfall.

Under section 4(5), a presumption arises, that persons who are related to each other are deemed not to deal with each other at arm's length while so related and that, in the context of sections 95(1)(b) and 96(1)(b), this presumption is a rebuttable one. Section 4(2) defines "related persons" to include, among other things, persons who are related by blood or marriage, while a person who has direct or indirect control of a corporation is a related person vis-à-vis the corporation. Persons do not have to be related to be found not at arm's length; *BIA*, section 4(4), provides that it is a question of fact whether persons not related to one another were at a particular time dealing with each other at arm's length. The "arm's-length" concept derives from the *Income Tax Act*, RSC 1985, c 1 (*ITA*). In *Piikani Energy Corporation (Re)*, 2013 ABCA 293, it was held that cases on the meaning of "arm's-length transaction" in the *ITA* context are relevant also in the *BIA* context. The court said (at paras 28–30):

> [28] In *McClarty v R*, 2008 SCC 26, Rothstein J discussed the term "not dealing at arm's length" in s 69, *ITA*. Justice Rothstein explained that the general concern in non-arm's length transactions is that "there is no assurance that the transaction 'will reflect ordinary commercial dealing between parties acting in their separate interests'": at para 43, citing *Swiss Bank Corp v Minister of National Revenue*, [1974] SCR 1144 at 1152. Thus, the *ITA* provisions dealing with non-arm's length parties are "intended to preclude artificial transactions from conferring tax benefits on one or more of the parties": at para 43.
>
> [29] While Rothstein J held that a court must consider all the relevant circumstances to determine if the parties in a transaction are at arm's length, he also noted that the Canada Revenue Agency Income Tax Interpretation Bulletin IT-419R2 "Meaning of Arm's Length" (June 8, 2004) contains the following "useful criteria that have been developed and accepted by the courts": (i) was there a common mind which directs the bargaining for both parties to a transaction; (ii) were the parties to a transaction acting in concert without separate interests; and (iii) was there *de facto* control: *Swiss Bank Corp* at para 62.
>
> [30] We are of the view that the above mentioned factors provide helpful guidance and apply in the *BIA* context to determine whether, as a question of fact, two parties dealt with each other at arm's length ... courts should approach their task of characterizing a relationship between a creditor and a bankrupt in light of these principles.

One of the criticisms of the current provisions is the concurrent application of the provincial fraudulent conveyance laws with the *BIA* provisions. There would be a case for leaving fraudulent conveyances law entirely to the provinces. Alternatively, fraudulent conveyances provisions could be brought into the *BIA* for administrative convenience. The current structure, however, allows the trustee to fall back on provincial laws where the *BIA* provisions do not apply or are less advantageous, which creates uncertainty in this area and is administratively inconvenient.

For a critical analysis of *BIA*, section 96, see Anthony Duggan and Thomas GW Telfer, "Gifts and Transfers at Undervalue" in Stephanie Ben-Ishai and Anthony Duggan, eds, *Canadian Bankruptcy and Insolvency Law: Bill C-55, Statute c. 47 and Beyond* (Toronto: LexisNexis, 2007) 175 at 190–98.

A. *BIA*, Section 96: Three Important Parts

First, section 96 refers to a "conspicuous disparity" between the fair market value of the property or services and the amount given or received for it. The courts have not articulated a bright line test as to what will constitute a conspicuous disparity, but the disparity must be noticeable enough to attract attention. In *Peoples Department Stores Inc (Trustee of) v Wise* (below), the court found that a disparity of just over 6 percent between the fair market value and the consideration received was not conspicuous. Second, section 96 uses permissive language, suggesting that the court can take a contextual approach to the provisions, and providing it with discretion to grant relief, even if the conditions in the provision have been satisfied. The court also has discretion to grant relief that extends beyond the factors specifically enumerated in the provision itself. These factors are considered below, in *Mercado*. Finally, section 96 makes remedies available against the immediate parties as well as a party who is privy to the transfer. Given that the purpose of the provision is to nullify transactions that removed value from the estate, persons who are "privy" to a transaction has been interpreted to mean those who benefit directly or indirectly from the transaction, and who are not simply aware of it or participating in it.

Mercado Capital Corporation v Qureshi, 2017 ONSC 5572, 63 CBR (6th) 190

Hainey J:

Background

[1] The applicant, Mercado Capital Corporation, seeks a declaration that what it characterizes as a notional gift of 50% of the equity in property located at 55 Davina Circle, Aurora, ("Davina") by Faisal Iqbal Qureshi ("Faisal"), a bankrupt, to his spouse, Hafsa Faisal Qureshi ("Hafsa"), is a transfer at undervalue and is therefore void pursuant to s. 96(1)(b)(i) of the *Bankruptcy and Insolvency Act*, R.S.C. 1985, c. B-3 ("*BIA*")....

[The following facts are from the Agreed Statement of Facts, which was attached as Appendix 1 to the judgment:]

The Applicant MERCADO CAPITAL CORPORATION and the Respondent HAFSA FAISAL QURESHI agree to the following facts for the purpose of the hearing of this Application:

1. The Respondent Hafsa Faisal Qureshi ("*Mrs. Qureshi*") is the spouse of Faisal Iqbal Qureshi ("*Mr. Qureshi*"). They were married on December 28, 2001, They have three children together.
2. Mr. Qureshi is the sole owner of a business corporation named Client360 Group Inc. ("Client360").
3. Mrs. Qureshi has no ownership interest in Client360.
4. Throughout their marriage, Mrs. Qureshi has never assisted Mr. Qureshi with any of his business activities.
5. Throughout their marriage, Mrs. Qureshi has not been employed outside the home. Mrs. Qureshi obtained her MBA but did not work outside the house especially after Mr. and Mrs. Qureshi's eldest child became sick with autism and epilepsy.
6. Mr. and Mrs. Qureshi resided together at Mr. Qureshi's parents' house from the date of their marriage until 2011.
7. At some point prior to July 25, 2011, Mr. Qureshi borrowed the sum of $50,000.00 from Mrs. Qureshi's parents. Mr. Qureshi offered to repay the loan prior to purchasing the Selwyn Road property (as defined in paragraph 8). Mrs. Qureshi's parents declined his offer and said he could use the money for the purchase of Selwyn Road.
8. Mr. Qureshi purchased a house municipally known as 278 Selwyn Road ("*Selwyn Road*") in Richmond Hill on July 25, 2011. Only Mr. Qureshi held registered title to the Selwyn Road property.
9. Mr. Qureshi and Mrs. Qureshi resided at the Selwyn Road property together as husband and wife. This was a matrimonial home.
10. Mrs. Qureshi was responsible for raising the children and the performance of all household responsibilities.

11. Mr. Qureshi mortgaged the Selwyn Road property to Bay Point Financial Services Inc. ("*Bay Point*") on May 28, 2014 in exchange for a loan of $250,000.00 (the "*Second Mortgage*") which was fully advanced pursuant to his direction.

12. Mr. Qureshi swore (incorrectly) in an affidavit delivered to Bay Point in connection with the advance of the Second Mortgage and Mr. Qureshi made an incorrect statement of fact on the face of this $250,000 Second Mortgage instrument to the effect the Selwyn Road property was not a matrimonial home on May 28, 2014, which was absolutely incorrect. Selwyn Road was the Qureshi's matrimonial home from its purchase in July of 2011 until June 30, 2015.

13. Mr. Qureshi sold Selwyn Road on June 30, 2015. The net proceeds resulting from the sale, after encumbrances and expenses had been paid, was $372,177.02 (the "*Selwyn Road Net Sale Proceeds*").

14. On February 18, 2015, Mrs. Qureshi entered into an Agreement of Purchase and Sale (the "*APS*") on behalf of herself and Mr. Qureshi with a builder for the purchase of a new home municipally described as 55 Davina Circle ("*Davina Circle*") in Aurora.

15. The APS set out that two refundable deposits (the "*Deposits*") aggregating $256,250.00 were payable during the first 60 days after the execution of the APS.

16. Mr. Qureshi arranged to have the Deposits paid to the vendor.

17. Mr. Qureshi directed Client360 to pay the Deposits.

18. Client360 directly or indirectly paid the Deposits.

19. The actual amount of Deposits paid was $256,240.00.

20. Mr. and Mrs. Qureshi completed the transaction set out in the APS on June 30, 2015 when they took title to Davina Circle. They took tide to Davina Circle as joint tenants.

21. On closing, the vendor of Davina Circle credited Mr. and Mrs. Qureshi with the Deposits in the amount of $256,240.00.

22. The Selwyn Road Net Sale Proceeds in the amount of $372,177.02 were used to partially pay the purchase price of Davina Circle on June 30, 2015.

23. Mr. and Mrs. Qureshi mortgaged Davina Road and used the borrowed loan proceeds of $1,902,081.04 to partially pay the purchase price of Davina Circle.

24. Just prior to closing, Mr. Qureshi needed the additional sum of $89,654.80 (the "*Shortfall*") in order to complete the purchase.

25. On June 29, 2015, Mrs. Qureshi's parents provided Client360 with two bank drafts, one in the amount of $60,000 in Canadian funds and the other in the amount of $30,000 in US dollars (in order to assist Mr. and Mrs. Qureshi with their purchase of Davina Circle). The Canadian dollar draft ($60,000) was deposited into Client360's Canadian dollar current account and the US dollar draft ($30,000) was deposited into Client360's US dollar bank account

26. On or about June 30, 2015, Mr. Qureshi provided his real estate lawyer with a bank draft drawn on Client360's Canadian dollar current account in the amount of $89,654.80. This amount was used by Mr. and Mrs. Qureshi to cover the Shortfall.

27. The amount of funds used to purchase Davina Circle less the mortgage proceeds was $718,071.82.

28. Bank of Montreal commenced a lawsuit against Mr. Qureshi, Client360 and Mrs. Qureshi (among others) on September 11, 2015 alleging that Mr. Qureshi and Client360 had committed fraud against it ...

30. Mercado Capital Corporation commenced a lawsuit against Mr. Qureshi and Client360 (and others) on March 18, 2016 alleging that Mr. Qureshi and Client360 had committed fraud against it

31. Mercado Capital Corporation sought a Mareva injunction against Mr. Qureshi which Mr. Qureshi consented to.

32. Polaris Leasing Ltd. commenced a lawsuit against Mr. Qureshi and Client360 (and others) on April 14, 2016 alleging that Mr. Qureshi and Client360 had committed fraud against it

33. Mr. Qureshi departed from Canada in March or April of 2016....

35. Mr. and Mrs. Qureshi became separated in March or April of 2016.

36. The date of Mr. Qureshi's initial bankruptcy event was June 2, 2016, when Mercado Capital Corporation had a Bankruptcy Application issued against Mr. Qureshi

37. Mr. Qureshi was adjudged a bankrupt on July 5, 2016.

38. Pollard & Associates Inc. was appointed by the court to act as the trustee for Mr. Qureshi's estate.

39. Pollard & Associates Inc. has admitted the sum of $4,129,284.89 of unsecured debt owed by Mr. Qureshi's estate as at January 24, 2017.

40. Pollard & Associates Inc. has admitted Mercado Capital Corporation's claim of $1,131,133.59.

41. Mrs. Qureshi and Mr. Qureshi's trustee sold the Davina Circle property on November 28, 2016 for a sale price of $2,838,000.00.

42. The net sale proceeds from the sale of Davina Circle was $696,815.74. The sum of $348,407.87 was paid to Mr. Qureshi's estate.

43. The sum of $323,407.87 is being held by the trustee to the credit of the successful party in this Application pursuant to the 2016 Order of Mr. Justice Newbould....

45. Mr. Qureshi was arrested at the airport upon his return to Canada in February of 2017 and charged with multiple counts of fraud over $5,000.00....

Issue

[14] The issue that I must determine is whether Hafsa is entitled to 50% of the net proceeds from the sale of Davina or whether she is disentitled to receive this amount because it constitutes a transfer from Faisal to her at undervalue and is therefore void pursuant to s. 96(1)(b)(i) of the *BIA*.

Positions of the Parties

[15] The applicant submits that because Faisal was the sole wage earner in the family and Hafsa was a "stay at home" mother earning no income, Faisal "notionally" gifted one-half of the purchase price of Davina to her in order to enable her to acquire a one-half interest in their new home.

[16] The applicant further submits that Faisal's "gift" to Hafsa had a fair market value of $359,035 and that Hafsa did not provide Faisal with any consideration for this gift. Accordingly, the gift to Hafsa, which occurred on June 30, 2015, less than one year before Faisal's initial bankruptcy event on June 2, 2016, is a transfer at undervalue pursuant to s. 96(1)(b)(i) of the *BIA*. It is therefore void as against the applicant.

[17] Hafsa submits that there was no transfer or gift from Faisal to her when they purchased Davina and took title as joint tenants. She submits that even if there was, Hafsa's domestic services and childcare and her parents' direct financial contribution toward the purchase price of Selwyn and Davina constitute sufficient consideration to support the transfer to her of one-half of the equity in Davina, which was their matrimonial home.

Analysis

[18] Section 96(1)(b) of the *BIA* provides as follows:

Transfer at undervalue

96. (1) On application by the trustee, a court may declare that a transfer at undervalue is void as against, or, in Quebec, may not be set up against, the trustee — or order that a party to the transfer or any other person who is privy to the transfer, or all of those persons, pay to the estate the difference between the value of the consideration received by the debtor and the value of the consideration given by the debtor — if . . .

(b) the party was not dealing at arm's length with the debtor and

    (i) the transfer occurred during the period that begins on the day that is one year before the date of the initial bankruptcy event and ends on the date of the bankruptcy; or

    (ii) the transfer occurred during the period that begins on the day that is five years before the date of the initial bankruptcy event and ends on the day before the day on which the period referred to in subparagraph (i) begins and

        (A) the debtor was insolvent at the time of the transfer or was rendered insolvent by it, or

        (B) the debtor intended to defraud, defeat or delay a creditor.

[19] The applicant submits in its factum that "this application fits squarely within the confines of the ratio" of the decision of Myers J in *Re Lee*, 2017 ONSC 388 at para. 16 as follows:

> Section 96 imposes a strict test to remedy non-arm's length transfers among family members. While the statute allows relief using the word "may", in my view, on proof of the requisite facts, relief should be granted at the amount calculated in accordance with the statute, in all but the most exceptional circumstances. This is especially so in the case of a non-arm's length transaction that is attacked within one year... In my view, judgment should be nearly automatic in such case.

[20] I disagree that the decision in *Re Lee* applies to this case. There is much to distinguish this case from the case of *Re Lee*. In *Re Lee*, the bankrupt and his spouse were joint tenants of the property in question and severed their joint tenancy by the bankrupt transferring his one-half interest in the property to his spouse for nominal consideration. This left the bankrupt with no interest on title to the property within one year of the initial bankruptcy event. In my view this clearly constituted a deliberate attempt by the bankrupt to defeat his creditors. In this case there is no evidentiary basis for concluding that Faisal was attempting to defeat his creditors when Davina was purchased and held by Hafsa and him as joint tenants. This is a significant difference from the facts in *Re Lee*.

[21] I agree with Myers J's conclusion in *Re Lee* on the facts of that case. However, I have concluded that his decision does not apply in this case because of the significant differences in the underlying facts.

[22] In *Re Lee*, Myers J acknowledged the discretionary nature of the relief provided for under s. 96 which provides that the court "may" declare a transfer at undervalue void. There is no jurisprudence concerning when it is appropriate to exercise the court's discretion not to declare a transfer at undervalue void under s. 96 of the *BIA*. It is, therefore, helpful to review the jurisprudence that considered the section of the *BIA* that s. 96 replaced when amendments were made to the *BIA* in 2009.

[23] Section 96 of the *BIA* replaced the reviewable transaction provision contained in the former s. 100 of the *BIA*. This previous section also gave the court discretion by providing that a court "may" give judgment to the trustee for the difference in the value of the consideration in a reviewable transaction.

[24] The relevant provisions of the previous s. 100 provided as follows:

Examination of consideration in a reviewable transaction

100 (1) Where a bankrupt sold, purchased, leased, hired, supplied or received property or services in a reviewable transaction within the period beginning on the day that is one year before the date of the initial bankruptcy event and ending on the date of the bankruptcy, both dates included, the court may, on the application of the trustee, inquire into whether the bankrupt gave or received, as the case may be, fair market value in consideration for the property or services concerned in the transaction.

Judgment for difference

(2) Where the court in proceedings under this section finds that the consideration given or received by the bankrupt in the reviewable transaction was conspicuously greater or less than the fair market value of the property or services concerned in the transaction, the court may give judgment to the trustee against the other party to the transaction, against any other person being privy to the transaction with the bankrupt or against all those persons for the difference between the actual consideration given or received by the bankrupt and the fair market value, as determined by the court, of the property or services concerned in the transaction. (Emphasis added)

[25] The Ontario Court of Appeal in *Standard Trust Co Ltd v Standard Trust Co* (1995), 26 O.R. (3d) 1 (Ont. C.A.) held that granting the remedy under the former s. 100 (2) of the *BIA* was discretionary having regard to factors such as the good faith of the parties, the intention with which the transaction took place and whether fair value was given and received by the parties.

[26] The Supreme Court of Canada in *Peoples Department Stores Inc (Trustee of) v Wise*, 2004 SCC 68, endorsed the view of the Ontario Court of Appeal in *Standard Trust Co* and held that "equitable principles guide the exercise of discretion".

[27] Major and Deschamps JJ concluded as follows at paras. 81 and 82 of the Supreme Court's decision in *Peoples Department Stores*:

81. The word "may" is found in both ss. 100(1) and 100(2) of the *BIA* with respect to the jurisdiction of the court. In *Standard Trustco Ltd (Trustee of) v Standard Trust Co* (1995), 26 O.R. (3d) 1 (Ont. C.A.), a majority of the Ontario Court of Appeal held that, even if the necessary preconditions are present, the exercise of jurisdiction under s. 100(1) to inquire into the transaction, and under s. 100(2) to grant judgment, is discretionary. Equitable principles guide the exercise of discretion. We agree.

82. Referring to s. 100(2) of the *BIA*, in *Standard Trustco, supra*, at p. 23, Weiler JA explained that:

When a contextual approach is adopted it is apparent that although the conditions of the section have been satisfied the court is not obliged to grant judgment. The court has a residual discretion to exercise. The contextual approach indicates that the good faith of the parties, the intention with which the transaction took place, and whether fair value was given and received in the transaction are important considerations as to whether that discretion should be exercised.

We agree with Weiler JA and adopt her position; ...

[28] In light of this jurisprudence, which I have concluded applies to the exercise of my discretion under s. 96 of the *BIA*, it is not necessary for me to decide whether Hafsa's

50% interest in the equity of Davina resulted from a transfer at undervalue contrary to s. 96(1)(b)(i) of the *BIA*. Even if it did, which I doubt, I would exercise my equitable discretion not to declare her 50% interest in Davina void.

[29] I have arrived at this conclusion by taking a contextual approach to the evidence. I find that Faisal and Hafsa were acting in good faith and intended that their joint tenancy in Davina represented the fact that it was their matrimonial home in which they each believed that they held a 50% interest. I find that there was no intention on the part of Faisal to defeat his creditors by taking title to Davina as a joint tenant with Hafsa. In adopting an equitable approach to the exercise of my discretion I have relied upon the following factors in deciding not to declare Hafsa's 50% interest in Davina void:

- Faisal's and Hafsa's good faith;
- The fact that Faisal did not take joint title in Davina to defeat his creditors;
- Hafsa's substantial non-monetary contribution to the family by her hard work managing the household and caring for their children, particularly in light of their special needs child;
- Hafsa's parents' contributions to the purchase price of both of their matrimonial homes;
- Hafsa's and Faisal's honest belief that Hafsa was entitled to a 50% interest in Davina because it was their matrimonial home;
- The fact that Hafsa and her children have no other guaranteed form of financial support and that Davina was her only asset which she needs to carry on an independent life with her children; and
- The fact that the Agreement of Purchase and Sale for Davina was signed by Hafsa in February 2015, well before the one year period preceding Faisal's initial bankruptcy event.

Conclusion

[30] For all of these reasons the application is dismissed.

[31] The Trustee is hereby ordered to deliver to Hafsa her share of the net proceeds from the sale of Davina within 15 days. . . .

Application dismissed.

Discussion

The decision was appealed (2018 ONCA 711) and the appeal was dismissed. The Court of Appeal commented on whether there was a "transfer at undervalue," the effective date of the impugned disposition of property and proof of intent to delay, defraud, or defeat a creditor. The following is an excerpt from the appeal decision:

(1) Issue 1: Was there a transfer at undervalue?

[22] Transfer at undervalue is defined in s. 2 of the *BIA* to mean:

> [A] disposition of property or provision of services for which no consideration is received by the debtor or for which the consideration received by the debtor is conspicuously less than the fair market value of the consideration given by the debtor[.]

[23] Mrs. Qureshi submits that, besides the cash contributions made by her parents which were for her benefit, she made a non-financial contribution to the purchase of both homes by running the household and looking after the children, allowing Mr. Qureshi to work and earn income. She asks that that contribution be given legal recognition in determining whether there was any disposition of property at all when Davina was purchased, or in calculating the value of her contribution.

[24] This submission is consistent with the evidence that was accepted by the application judge: Mr. and Mrs. Qureshi both believed that each had an equal interest in their matrimonial homes, even though the Selwyn home was registered in Mr. Qureshi's name alone, and the funds used to purchase both homes came from Mr. Qureshi's business and from Mrs. Qureshi's parents. Mrs. Qureshi's direct contribution was in running the home and raising the children. . . .

[27] It is not necessary for this court to decide whether the Selwyn property was impressed with Mrs. Qureshi's beneficial interest. The issue does not need to be decided because even if — as the appellant submits — there was a transfer at undervalue, the effective date of the impugned transaction was more than a year before the bankruptcy event and the appellant failed to prove that Mr. Qureshi was insolvent or intended to defraud, defeat or delay a creditor on the day of disposition.

(2) Issue 2: What is the effective date of the impugned disposition of property?
[28] Mrs. Qureshi entered into the agreement of purchase and sale for the purchase of Davina on behalf of herself and Mr. Qureshi on February 18, 2015. The transaction closed on June 30, 2015, when the property was registered in the names of Mr. and Mrs. Qureshi as joint tenants.

[29] The initial bankruptcy event occurred on June 2, 2016, when the appellant creditor brought a bankruptcy application against Mr. Qureshi. If the closing of the Davina purchase and the joint registration on title is the impugned disposition of property, then it occurred within one year of the initial bankruptcy event and is captured by s. 96(1)(b)(i). If, however, the date of the agreement of purchase and sale constitutes the disposition of property, then s. 96(1)(b)(ii) applies.

[30] This court settled the above legal issue in *Buchanan v Oliver Plumbing & Heating Ltd*, [1959] O.R. 238 (C.A.). There, the court adopted Jessel M.R.'s definition of the relationship between a vendor and purchaser of land who have entered into a valid contract for sale, as set out in *Lysaght v Edwards* (1876), 2 Ch. D. 499, at pp. 505–6:

> It appears to me that the effect of a contract for sale has been settled for more than two centuries; certainly it was completely settled before the time of Lord Hardwicke, who speaks of the settled doctrine of the Court as to it. What is that doctrine? It is that the moment you have a valid contract for sale the vendor becomes in equity a trustee for the purchaser of the estate sold, and the beneficial ownership passes to the purchaser, the vendor having a right to the purchase-money, a charge or lien on the estate for the security of that purchase-money, and a right to retain possession of the estate until the purchase-money is paid, in the absence of express contract as to the time of delivering possession.

[31] As long as a contract for the sale of land is carried out or is specifically performable, "the completion relates back to the contract": *Buchanan*, citing *Rayner v Preston* (1881), 18 Ch. D. 1, at p. 13. Even if the purchaser pays the sale price upon closing, the purchaser becomes the beneficial owner of the property as soon as the contract is formed.

[32] Further, in *Russo Corp v Deborah Essery*, 2016 ONSC 321, Pattillo J held that the word "transfer" in the context of s. 96 does not refer to the act of registering an interest in property on title. In that case, the alleged transfer at undervalue was a husband's conveyance of a half-interest in a property to his wife. Pattillo J held that the date of transfer for s. 96 purposes was the date the document executing the transfer was signed, rather than the date wife's title was registered on the property. In coming to this conclusion, Pattillo J observed at paras. 37–38:

> The wording of Section 96 speaks of "transfer". It does not contain the words "register" or "registration". Black's Law Dictionary, 10th ed., defines "transfer" as "any mode of disposing of or parting with an asset or an interest in an asset". By contrast, "registration" is something completely different. It is the act of registering something, in the case of a transfer of land, in the land titles or registry office. In that regard, s. 20 of the *BIA*, which deals with the trustee's divestiture of property, refers to registration of a quit claim or renunciation in land titles or registry.
>
> It is also important to note that s. 96 does not deal just with land. It deals with a disposition of property in general and provision of services.

[33] Because Mr. and Mrs. Qureshi carried out the terms of the agreement of purchase and sale for Davina, Mrs. Qureshi acquired her beneficial interest in Davina upon signing that agreement, making February 18, 2015 the effective date of the impugned disposition of property, not the date of registration. I note as well that while the balance of the funds for the purchase was paid on the date of registration, the March and May 2015 deposits by Mr. Queshi for the purchase of Davina—which form part of the transfer impugned by Mercado—were also made more than one year before the date of the initial bankruptcy event.

(3) Issue 3: Did the appellant creditor prove that the bankrupt was insolvent or intended to defraud, defeat, or delay a creditor on the date of the disposition to the respondent?

[34] Since the beneficial ownership of Davina passed to Mrs. Qureshi on February 18, 2015, more than one year before the initial bankruptcy event, but within five years of that event, s. 96(1)(b)(ii) applies. The transaction may be declared void if the appellant creditor proves that Mr. Qureshi was insolvent on that date or that he intended to defraud a creditor in making the disposition of property. Mercado, as a creditor authorized by the court to bring this proceeding in the trustee's stead, bears the burden of establishing one of the above requirements in order to impugn the transfer at undervalue. . . .

[35] Mr. Qureshi was insolvent when he was petitioned into bankruptcy on June 2, 2016. He swore in his statement of affairs of July 28, 2016 that he had not made any significant financial changes in the one year prior to that date. From that, the appellant argues that there was no evidence that he was also not insolvent when he made the Davina deposits in March and May 2016.

[36] This submission is misconceived: the onus is on the appellant to prove all of the factors in the subsection in order to be entitled to the order under s. 96. While it is certainly possible that Mr. Qureshi was already insolvent in February 2015, there is no evidence on the record that proves that fact on a balance of probabilities. The record is silent on his financial status on that date and at that time. . . .

[40] Because the appellant has not proved the elements required to satisfy s. 96(1)(b)(ii), there is no basis for the court to void the purchase of Davina in joint names and in particular, to void the impugned disposition to Mrs. Qureshi.

* * * * *

Peoples Department Stores Inc (Trustee of) v Wise, 2004 SCC 68, [2004] 3 SCR 461

[The facts are set out in a second extract from the case that appears in Chapter 10, Section III. Peoples's trustee sued the Wise brothers, alleging breach of their duties as directors to Peoples's creditors under section 122(1) of the *Canada Business Corporation Act*. This aspect of the case is addressed in Chapter 10. In the alternative, the trustee claimed that the Wise brothers were privy to transactions in which Peoples's assets had been transferred to Wise for conspicuously less than fair market value within the meaning of *BIA*, section 100. The following extract deals with this aspect of the case.]

Major and Deschamps JJ: . . .

[79] The trustee also claimed against the Wise brothers under s. 100 of the *BIA*. . . .

[80] The provision has two principal elements. First, subs. (1) requires the transaction to have been conducted within the year preceding the date of bankruptcy. Second, subs. (2) requires that the consideration given or received by the bankrupt be "conspicuously greater or less" than the fair market value of the property concerned.

[81] The word "may" is found in both ss. 100(1) and 100(2) of the *BIA* with respect to the jurisdiction of the court. In *Standard Trustco Ltd (Trustee of) v Standard Trust Co* (1995), 26 O.R. (3d) 1, a majority of the Ontario Court of Appeal held that, even if the necessary preconditions are present, the exercise of jurisdiction under s. 100(1) to inquire into the transaction, and under s. 100(2) to grant judgment, is discretionary. Equitable principles guide the exercise of discretion. We agree.

[82] Referring to s. 100(2) of the *BIA*, in *Standard Trustco, supra*, at p. 23, Weiler JA explained that:

> "When a contextual approach is adopted it is apparent that although the conditions of the section have been satisfied the court is not obliged to grant judgment. The court has a residual discretion to exercise. The contextual approach indicates that the good faith of the parties, the intention with which the transaction took place, and whether fair value was given and received in the transaction are important considerations as to whether that discretion should be exercised."

We agree with Weiler JA and adopt her position; however, this appeal does not turn on the discretion to ultimately impose liability. In our view, the Court of Appeal did not interfere with the trial judge's exercise of discretion in reviewing the facts and finding a palpable and overriding error.

[83] Within the year preceding the date of bankruptcy, Peoples had transferred inventory to Wise for which the trustee claimed Peoples had not received fair market value in consideration. The relevant transactions involved, for the most part, transfers completed in anticipation of the busy holiday season. Given the non-arm's length relationship between Wise and its wholly-owned subsidiary Peoples, there is no question that these inventory transfers could have constituted reviewable transactions.

[84] We share the view of the Court of Appeal that it is not only the final transfers that should be considered. In fairness, the inventory transactions should be considered over the entire period from February to December 1994, which was the period when the new policy was in effect.

[85] In *Skalbania (Trustee of) v Wedgewood Village Estates Ltd* (1989), 37 B.C.L.R. (2d) 88 (C.A.), the test for determining whether the difference in consideration is "conspicuously greater or less" was held to be not whether it is conspicuous to the parties at the time of the transaction, but whether it is conspicuous to the court having regard to all the relevant factors. This is a sound approach. In that case, a difference of $1.18 million between fair market value and the consideration received by the bankrupt was seen as conspicuous, where the fair market value was $6.6 million, leaving a discrepancy of more than 17 percent. While there is no particular percentage that definitively sets the threshold for a conspicuous difference, the percentage difference is a factor.

[86] As for the factors that would be relevant to this determination, the court might consider, *inter alia*: evidence of the margin of error in valuing the types of assets in question; any appraisals made of the assets in question and evidence of the parties' honestly held beliefs regarding the value of the assets in question; and other circumstances adduced in evidence by the parties to explain the difference between the consideration received and fair market value: see L.W. Houlden and G.B. Morawetz, *Bankruptcy and Insolvency Law of Canada* (3rd ed. (loose-leaf)), vol. 2, at p. 4-114.1.

[87] Over the lifespan of the new policy, Peoples transferred to Wise inventory valued at $71.54 million. As of the date of bankruptcy, it had received $59.50 million in property or money from Wise. As explained earlier, the trial judge adjusted the outstanding difference down to a balance of $4.44 million after taking into account, *inter alia*, the reallocation of general and administrative expenses, and adjustments necessitated by imported inventory transferred from Wise to Peoples. Neither party disputed these figures before this Court. We agree with the Court of Appeal's observation that these findings directly conflict with the trial judge's assertion that Peoples had received no consideration for the inventory transfers on the basis that the outstanding accounts were "neither collected nor collectible" from Wise. Like Pelletier JA, we conclude that the trial judge's finding in this regard was a palpable and overriding error, and we adopt the view of the Court of Appeal.

[88] We are not satisfied that, with regard to all the circumstances of this case, a disparity of slightly more than 6 percent between fair market value and the consideration received constitutes a "conspicuous" difference within the meaning of s. 100(2) of the *BIA*. Accordingly, we hold that the trustee's claim under the *BIA* also fails.

[89] In addition to permitting the court to give judgment against the other party to the transaction, s. 100(2) of the *BIA* also permits it to give judgment against someone who was not a party but was "privy" to the transaction. Given our finding that the consideration for the impugned transactions was not "conspicuously less" than fair market value, there is no need to consider whether the Wise brothers would have been "privy" to the transaction for the purpose of holding them liable under s. 100(2). Nonetheless, the disagreement between the trial judge and the Court of Appeal on the interpretation of "privy" in s. 100(2) of the *BIA* warrants the following observations.

[90] The trial judge in this appeal had little difficulty finding that the Wise brothers were privy to the transaction within the meaning of s. 100(2). Pelletier JA, however, preferred a narrow construction in finding that the Wise brothers were not privy to the transactions. He held, at para. 136, that:

> "[TRANSLATION] ... the legislator wanted to provide for the case in which a person other than the co-contracting party of the bankrupt actually received all or part of the benefit resulting from the lack of equality between the respective considerations."

To support this direct benefit requirement, Pelletier JA also referred to the French version which uses the term *ayant intérêt*. While he conceded that the respondent brothers received an indirect benefit from the inventory transfers as shareholders of Wise, Pelletier JA found this too remote to be considered "privy" to the transactions (paras. 140–41).

[91] The primary purpose of s. 100 of the *BIA* is to reverse the effects of a transaction that stripped value from the estate of a bankrupt person. It makes sense to adopt a more inclusive understanding of the word "privy" to prevent someone who might receive indirect benefits to the detriment of a bankrupt's unsatisfied creditors from frustrating the provision's remedial purpose. The word "privy" should be given a broad reading to

include those who benefit directly or indirectly from and have knowledge of a transaction occurring for less than fair market value. In our opinion, this rationale is particularly apt when those who benefit are the controlling minds behind the transaction.

[92] A finding that a person was "privy" to a reviewable transaction does not of course necessarily mean that the court will exercise its discretion to make a remedial order against that person. For liability to be imposed, it must be established that the transaction occurred: (a) within the past year; (b) for consideration conspicuously greater or less than fair market value; (c) with the person's knowledge; and (d) in a way that directly or indirectly benefited the person. In addition, after having considered the context and all the above factors, the judge must conclude that the case is a proper one for holding the person liable. In light of these conditions and of the discretion exercised by the judge, we find that a broad reading of "privy" is appropriate.

IV. THE *BIA* PREFERENCE PROVISIONS

A. What Is a Preference?

Broadly speaking, a preference is a payment of money or transfer of property made by a debtor to a creditor on the eve of the debtor's bankruptcy that is for a larger amount than the creditor would recover in a bankruptcy distribution. Like a fraudulent conveyance, the purpose of a fraudulent preference transaction is to defeat creditors. However, not all preference payments are fraudulent. Rather, a preference payment becomes fraudulent depending on its timing. Payments made on the eve of the debtor's bankruptcy are fraudulent because they are an attempt to avoid the bankruptcy scheme: the recipient creditor is receiving more than it would in a distribution under bankruptcy laws. As articulated in *Re Norris*, 1996 ABCA 357 at 7: "[i]t is called fraudulent because it prejudices other creditors who will receive proportionately less, or nothing at all, and upsets the fundamental scheme of the Act for equal sharing among creditors." If the debtor is not insolvent, however, payments made to creditors do not run afoul preference laws, and a debtor is free to pay any of its creditor in any order it wishes. Here are three simple examples that would be addressed by *BIA*, section 95:

1) Fred has five unsecured creditors, A, B, C, D, and Wilma. A, B, C, and D are all trade creditors. Wilma is Fred's wife. Each of the five debts is for $100. Fred's total assets are $200. He pays Wilma her $100 and a week later goes into bankruptcy. If Fred had not paid Wilma, there would have been $200 for distribution among A, B, C, D, and Wilma. The basic bankruptcy distribution rule is pro rata, so that each would have recovered $40. Fred's payment to Wilma means there is now only $100 for distribution among A, B, C, and D. They each get $25 on a pro rata basis, but Wilma has $100.

2) Fred is the director and controlling shareholder of Flintstone Enterprises Limited (FEL). FEL has five unsecured creditors, A, B, C, D, and Rubble Bank. A, B, C, and D are all trade creditors; Rubble Bank is FEL's general lender. FEL owes all five creditors $100 each. Fred has given a personal guarantee in support of FEL's debt to Rubble Bank. FEL's total assets are $200. Fred causes FEL to pay Rubble Bank its $100. A week later, FEL goes into bankruptcy. The effect on A, B, C, and D of the payment to Rubble is the same as in example (1).

3) Fred runs a retail store specializing in the sale of dinosaur parts. He has five unsecured creditors, A, B, C, D, and Barney. He owes them each $100. His total assets are $200. Barney is Fred's main inventory supplier. Barney threatens to cancel further deliveries

until Fred pays him. Fred pays Barney because he needs the inventory to stay in business. Unfortunately, the business fails anyway, and, two weeks later, Fred goes into bankruptcy.

B. Section 95: Arm's-Length v Non-Arm's-Length Transactions

Section 95 pivots on whether the transaction in issue is arm's-length or non-arm's-length (as to which, see Part III, above). In the case of an arm's-length transaction, the trustee must prove the debtor's intention to prefer, subject to the rebuttable presumption that the debtor intended to prefer the creditor. However, in the case of a non-arm's-length transaction, the trustee only needs to prove that the transaction has the effect of giving the creditor a preference. In other words, in the case of a non-arm's-length transaction, if the transaction has the effect of giving the creditor a preference, there is, so to speak, an irrebuttable presumption that the debtor intended to prefer the creditor.

Example (3), above, illustrates the practical implications of this reform. The transaction between Fred and Barney clearly has the effect of giving Barney a preference. Therefore, if Fred and Barney are at arm's length, there is a presumption that Fred intended to prefer Barney, but Barney can rebut the presumption by leading evidence of the kind described above. However, if Fred and Barney are not at arm's length, Barney does not have a leg to stand on. What is the justification for discriminating in this way between arm's-length and non-arm's-length transactions? A possible explanation is that, if the parties are not at arm's length, the debtor is more likely to have intended a preference. However, this consideration supports at most a rebuttable presumption, leaving the creditor the ability to prove that, despite the parties' relationship, the transaction was an innocent one. In the United States, the debtor's intention to prefer is irrelevant, as its provisions are based on an effects-based test; if the trustee can show that the transaction has the effect of giving the creditor a preference, then, subject to various "safe-harbour provisions," they can recover the payment.[4] The current *BIA* provisions could be seen as a step toward the US position, but, if that is the case, it is arguable that we should not be retaining the requirement for proof of intention.

The concern about an across-the-board effects-based test is that an effects-based test would make it too easy for the trustee to set payments aside. This concern is shared by stakeholders, most notably the Insolvency Institute of Canada. In other words, the concern is with finality of transactions: if creditors cannot be certain of keeping the debtor's repayments, this increases the risks of lending, which consequently may affect the cost and availability of credit. On the other hand, if the overriding concern is really with the finality of transactions, then it needs to be asked whether the preference provisions should be repealed altogether: see Schwartz, "A Normative Theory of Business Bankruptcy," below.

C. Doctrine of Pressure

As mentioned above, if the arm's-length transaction had the effect of giving a preference, the section will presume the debtor's intention to prefer in the absence of proof to the contrary, and it goes on to specify that evidence of pressure was not admissible to support the transaction. The purpose of the presumption is to reduce the burden on the trustee and make it easier for the trustee to win cases. Why is evidence of pressure not admissible? The purpose is to shore up the presumption. Before the pressure exception was enacted, the preferred

---

4   US *Bankruptcy Code*, 11 USC § 547.

creditor only had to show that it had given the debtor some sort of ultimatum. If that could be shown, there was a fair chance the court would find that the debtor's motive was not to prefer the creditor, but simply to get the creditor off their back. The purpose of the statutory pressure exception was to foreclose this line of argument: the statute prevents courts from viewing creditor pressure on the debtor as a way to negate the debtor's intention to prefer that creditor. However, things have not gone as planned. The courts have reintroduced the doctrine of pressure by the back door. They have done this by inventing a so-called diligent-creditor defence. The thinking is that a creditor should not be penalized just because its collection methods are more efficient than its competitors. Unfortunately, there is no easy way of telling on which side of the line a creditor's conduct will fall. For instance, in example (3), above, some courts might say that Barney's threat to cancel further deliveries is just Barney being diligent and so he can rely on the threat to rebut the presumption. Other courts might say it is pressure and so the evidence is inadmissible.

Another tack Barney might take is to argue that Fred's motivation was not to prefer Barney, but simply to make sure Barney would keep supplying him so that he could stay in business: see *Hapco Farms* and *St Anne Nackawic*, both extracted below. This line of cases reveals two competing policy considerations. The first is the importance of facilitating transactions that may improve the return to creditors in the debtor's bankruptcy (as in *St Anne Nackawic*) or, better still, help the debtor trade out of its difficulties and avoid bankruptcy altogether. The second is the importance of preventing one creditor from obtaining an advantage over the others.

D. Why Do We Need Anti-Preference Laws? Three Competing Rationales

There are three competing versions of the need for anti-preference laws: debtor deterrence, creditor deterrence, and equal sharing. The debtor deterrence rationale can be traced back to Lord Coke's statement in *The Case of Bankrupts* (1584), 76 ER 441 at 473 (KB) (Eng): "[T]here ought to be an equal distribution ... ; [for] if, after the debtor becomes bankrupt, he may prefer a [creditor] and defeat and defraud many other poor men of their true debts, it would be unequal and unconscionable, and a defect in the law." In other words, the debtor should not play favourites among creditors in defiance of the bankruptcy laws: paying out friends, relatives, and business connections ahead of other creditors is wrong because, given the debtor's looming bankruptcy, it deprives "other poor men of their true debts." Another way of making the same point is to say that debtors may not set themselves up as the lawgivers in a bankruptcy distribution. This is how Lord Mansfield expressed the idea in *Alderson v Temple*, [1768] 1 WLUK 25, two hundred or so years later.

The creditor-deterrence rationale derives from Thomas Jackson, *The Logic and Limits of Bankruptcy Law* (Cambridge, MA: Harvard University Press, 1986), ch 6. The basic idea is that we do not want creditors jumping the queue on the eve of the debtor's bankruptcy because this might cause a scramble for payment, leaving only the "tag ends and remnants" of the debtor's assets for distribution in the bankruptcy proceedings. In other words, preferential payments are inconsistent with the basic purpose of the bankruptcy laws. A related consideration is that if preferences were allowed, every creditor would want to monitor every other creditor as well as the debtors themselves to make sure they were not left behind in any eve-of-bankruptcy collection race. The preference laws avoid these monitoring costs.

According to the equal-sharing rationale, the purpose of the preference provisions is to make sure that all creditors are treated equally in bankruptcy. Statements like this should not be taken literally, however, given the large number of exceptions to the *pari passu* principle. In real life, creditors are not treated equally in bankruptcy. For example, secured creditors get paid ahead of unsecured creditors, and some classes of unsecured creditor are entitled to priority payment ahead of others—for example, employees and lessors.

A better statement of the equal-sharing rationale might be to say that creditors should share in accordance with the overall scheme of distribution the bankruptcy laws provide for. The key feature of the equal-sharing rationale is that it focuses on the outcome of the bankruptcy distribution, not on the debtor's supposed fraud in giving the preference or on the creditor's supposed fraud in receiving it. For a fuller discussion of the policies underlying the preference laws, see Anthony Duggan and Thomas Telfer, "Voidable Preferences," in Stephanie Ben-Ishai and Anthony Duggan, eds, *Canadian Bankruptcy and Insolvency Law: Bill C-55, Statute c. 47 and Beyond* (Toronto: LexisNexis, 2007), ch 6.

The choice between these competing explanations is important, because it affects the shape of the legislation and, therefore, case outcomes. For example, if we conceive of preferential transactions as fraudulent conduct on the debtor's part, it makes sense to limit the preference provisions by requiring proof of the debtor's intention to prefer. On the other hand, if we view preferences as strategic behaviour on the creditor's part, the more appropriate response is to limit the provisions by requiring proof of the creditor's state of mind (as pre-1978 US bankruptcy law did). Yet again, if our primary objective is to achieve some sort of equality between creditors in the bankruptcy distribution, the debtor's state of mind and the creditor's state of mind are both irrelevant and a strict liability rule should apply. Which of these three objectives does section 95 most closely reflect? What is the policy underlying section 95? The preference provision in §547 of the US *Bankruptcy Code* imposes a strict liability rule. Does this reflect a commitment to the equal-sharing rationale? The preference provisions in the provincial assignments and preferences statutes, which apply in tandem with *BIA*, section 95 (see Section V), require proof of *concurrent* intention: see *Benallack*, below. Can this limitation be justified in terms of any of the theories discussed above?

In example (1), above, it seems Fred intended to give Wilma a preference and, similarly, Wilma was likely conscious of receiving one. On this footing, Fred's payment to Wilma would be a preferential one under any of the preference-law models identified above. In example (2), it seems that Fred intended to prefer Rubble Bank, but it is at least possible that Rubble Bank was unaware of the payment's preferential effect. On this footing, the payment is a potentially preferential one under *BIA*, section 95, as well as post-1978 US bankruptcy law, but not under the provincial laws or pre-1978 United States bankruptcy law. In example (3), Fred's immediate reason for paying Barney may have been to guarantee future supplies rather than to prefer Barney (but see *Hapco*, below). On this footing, the payment may be a preference under section 95 if Fred and Barney are not at arm's length, and it may or may not be a preference under §547 of the US *Bankruptcy Code*, depending on whether it falls within the "ordinary-course-of-business" safe harbour in section 547(c)(2).

Alan Schwartz, "A Normative Theory of Business Bankruptcy" (2005) 91 *Virginia Law Rev* **1199, at 1224–30 (footnotes omitted)**

> The preference sections of the Code ... create incentives for the trustee to redistribute wealth from some creditors—those that received preferences—to other creditors—those that did not. These redistributions ... come at positive cost, and thus reduce the net value of the bankrupt estate. The Code permits the trustee to recover payments to a creditor made in the ninety days before bankruptcy unless (a) the creditor made a contemporaneous transfer to the debtor; or (b) the payment was made in the ordinary course of the debtor's business. Payments in the former category do not reduce the value

of the firm because cash out is replaced with cash or goods in. The exception for payments in category (b) has a similar justification. Shipments in the ordinary course, over time, will offset payments in the ordinary course; the typical transaction sequence thus will not deplete the firm's value. The trustee's power otherwise to avoid preferences can be partly restricted by private agreement. A firm may contract out of the law by issuing security. An eve-of-bankruptcy payment to a secured creditor is not a preference: The creditor has a property right in the firm's assets, and it is entitled to realize that right in whatever way the security agreement permits.

There are two traditional justifications for preventing distressed firms from preferring some general creditors over others: the prohibition is *ex post* efficient, and the prohibition treats all general creditors equally. This part shows the following: (a) the preference law is *ex post* inefficient; (b) a mandatory rule prohibiting the payment of preferences is *ex ante* inefficient; rather, the preference law should be a default; and (c) the pursuit of *ex post* equality among general creditors is without justification.

The *ex post* efficiency case for prohibiting preferences is thought to follow from the justification for bankruptcy law itself. A firm's survival prospects may be fatally worsened by last minute depletions of its capital. Some such firms may be only financially distressed, however, and so should be continued. Prohibiting preferences thus advances the goal of saving viable firms.

A distressed firm would pay preferences, in the traditional theory, either because it may yield to creditor pressure or because the firm's principals may be in league with powerful creditors. The former reason is unpersuasive because creditors cannot force a distressed firm to pay preferences. To be sure, in the absence of a bankruptcy filing, creditors will attach property pursuant to judicial orders. The debtor, however, need not make voluntary payments. Creditors can threaten attachment in order to force the debtor to pay, but the debtor can respond by credibly threatening to file, which would stay all attachments. Thus, if the preference law were repealed, distressed firms would pay preferences because they wanted to, not because they had to.

The question when a distressed firm would want to prefer some creditors has never been seriously explored. If no preference law existed, a distressed firm would pay preferences only if it expected to be liquidated. To see why, recall that the pro rata bankruptcy distribution rule requires each general creditor to receive a sum that equals the firm's ratio of total value to total debt times the creditor's unpaid debt. A distressed firm that pays one creditor more than this must pay at least one other creditor less. When would a distressed firm default in this asymmetric way? Consider first a firm that believes its continuation value to exceed its liquidation value (that is, that it is liquidity-constrained but only financially distressed). The firm could either file for bankruptcy or attempt to settle privately with its creditors. Suppose that the firm preferred to settle. To prefer a creditor is to pay it more than its pro rata bankruptcy share. Nonpreferred creditors, however, would reject a work-out offer that offered them less than their pro rata bankruptcy payoffs. Instead, these creditors would bring suit and attempt to attach the distressed firm's assets. These efforts would cause the firm to file. From the firm's point of view, then, the goals of settling privately and paying preferences are inconsistent. Rather, a firm that wants to settle privately would offer each creditor its pro rata share plus a portion of the cost savings from avoiding bankruptcy. In other words, the pro rata rule precludes a firm interested in survival from paying today what are defined as preferences. Consequently, a separate prohibition against preferences does not materially increase a financially distressed firm's commitment to the pro rata rule.

Now consider a firm that believes its liquidation value to exceed its continuation value. This debtor, in its capacity as a firm, is indifferent as to how its assets are divided because the firm will disappear with certainty. It has no incentive to adhere to any rule of distribution. The firm's principals, in their individual capacities, however, may not be indifferent as to whom the firm pays. Rather, the principals may cause the firm to pay particular creditors either to ensure good will for the principals, in consequence of a personal relationship, or to avoid liability exposure if a principal has guaranteed the firm's debt. The trustee's power to recover preferences thus is exercised *only on behalf of the general creditors of economically failing firms*. Redistributing the assets of a failed firm among its general creditors amounts to redecorating the Titanic's salon. Because redecoration is costly, enforcing the preference prohibition diminishes the value of the bankrupt estate. The preference law is actually *ex post* inefficient.

Turning to *ex ante* efficiency, ... legal rules which reduce the value of distressed firms raise interest rates. Thus, parties would wish to avoid the rules if possible. This reasoning implies that the parties' current ability to contract out of the preference law by giving security should be expanded. It is a more difficult question whether the default rule should permit distressed firms to pay whomever they choose, so that firms would have to contract into the preference law, or whether current law should be the default, so that firms would have to contract out. It is worth stressing, however, that the question regarding what the default should be is the ground on which preference law should be discussed. Bankruptcy reasons cannot justify the Code's current mandatory rule.

A preliminary consideration of the default question should begin with a possible strategy of creditors who are unsure, *ex ante*, whether the debtor, if economically distressed, would later prefer anyone. The equilibrium strategy is to charge interest rates that assume preferences will be paid. The interest rate increases from this "assume the worst" strategy could exceed the interest rate reductions that repeal of the preference law would produce. Hence, if repealing the preference law altogether would materially increase uncertainty, current law should be the default because parties would commonly prefer it.

Any increase in uncertainty, however, is unlikely to be of this magnitude. A creditor with the power to exact a preference often will be the firm's main bank. Primary bank lenders commonly require borrowers to keep their accounts with the bank, and the bank will set off the borrower's debt to it against the bank account. Because set-offs are not considered preferences under the Code, current creditors must price the bank's ability to get them. Creditors today thus face the uncertainty of material asymmetric defaults. In addition, which creditors will likely receive preferences seems predictable. This reasoning suggests that the better default would permit the firm to pay whomever it chooses.

Turning from efficiency to equity, the pro rata rule gives each creditor the same proportional payoff. Making the preference law a default sometimes would subvert this *ex post* equality result. That bankruptcy law should pursue equality of any type, however, is a position whose correctness is incorrectly assumed. Principles of equality are principles of entitlement. Thus, in conditions of scarcity, each actor who has an equal entitlement is entitled to an equal share. An actor can have such an entitlement either instrumentally (respecting the entitlement would advance an independent goal) or intrinsically (equality in the context at issue is a good in and of itself). Making the pro rata rule mandatory, it has been shown here, is inefficient, and no other non-equality goal has been identified that a mandatory preference law would advance. Business bankruptcy also is an inappropriate arena in which to pursue intrinsic equality claims. For example, the equal welfare doctrine holds that the disadvantaged are entitled to more pleasure because they have the capacity to experience more pleasure. Such reasoning would be misplaced if applied to business firms. There is, therefore, no good reason, in the business bankruptcy context, to temper the pursuit of efficiency with equality considerations. And to summarize the argument of this section, although the current preference law is mandatory as regards monetary payments, it should be a default that would permit insolvent firms to make irreversible payments to creditors at any time preceding the filing of a bankruptcy petition.

[Reprint permission requested.]

E. Rebutting the Presumption: How Creditors Can Keep Preferential Payments

Upon the presumption arising to show that the debtor did intend to prefer that creditor over others, the onus shifts to the creditor to try to rebut it. Although the statute is silent about ways in which the presumption can be rebutted, there are a number of categories that emerge from caselaw to show when courts will find that, on the balance of probabilities, the dominant intent of the debtor was not to prefer the creditor. The "dominant intent" test can be traced back to Houlden J's statement in *Re Van der Leik* (1970), 14 CBR (NS) 229 (Ont SC) at para 9. The dominant intent of the debtor is to be determined objectively, by considering the circumstances of the debtor, and not "the debtor's personal ruminations."[5]

Determining the nature of the requisite intent needed to rebut the presumption has generated much caselaw, and from that, several categories have been articulated (for general commentary, see Roderick J Wood, *Bankruptcy & Insolvency Law*, 2d ed (Toronto: Irwin Law Inc, 2015) at 211–14). Caselaw shows that the presumption is typically rebutted if the preference payment occurs for one of the following reasons. First, if the preference payment is made in the ordinary course of business, the presumption will be rebutted and the payment will not be set aside. This is a factual question and the context of the business relationship, the type of business and the industry standard can be considered.[6] This exception is primarily applicable to a commercial enterprise, but an individual debtor can also use it to rebut the presumption. The courts have found individuals' desire to free themselves from financial pressures to be analogous to a business paying creditors in the ordinary course in order to maintain its operations.[7]

In *Deloitte & Touche*, the presumption was not rebutted when a bankrupt, who was habitually late in making payments, made payments to two creditors in the three months preceding its bankruptcy. The bankrupt had been unable to pay its other creditors at the time the preference payments were made and had been overdue in paying many of its creditors, thereby preventing it from being able to carry on business in the ordinary course. Conversely, in *Robitaille*, the presumption was rebutted because the late payment to the creditor was in the ordinary course of the business relationship between the debtor and creditor, and was also standard in the industry (para 5).

Second, if the preference payment is made as a requirement to stay in business, the presumption can be rebutted. An example of the foregoing was seen in *Davis v Ducan Industries Ltd* (1983), 45 CBR (NS) 290, where the debtor's preference payment allowed the debtor to

---

5 *St Anne-Nackawic Pulp Co (Trustee of) v Logistec Stevedoring (Atlantic) Inc*, 2005 NBCA 55 at para 6 [*St Anne-Nackawic*].

6 *Robitaille v American Biltrite (Canada)*, [1985] 1 SCR 290 [*Robitaille*]; *Deloitte & Touche Inc v White Veal Meat Packers Ltd* (2000), 16 CBR (4th) 74 [*Deloitte & Touche*]; *St Anne-Nackawic, ibid* at para 8.

7 *Andrews (Trustee of) v Minister of National Revenue*, 2011 MBQB 50 at para 46.

finish refurbishing vehicles that obtained a much higher sale price than they would have had they been sold unfinished. The court concluded that the debtor's dominant purpose was to stay in business and maximize recovery for its creditors, thereby rebutting the presumption. In *Re Spectrum Interiors (Guelph) Ltd* (1979), 29 CBR (NS) 218, the debtor's preference payment, which was a return of merchandise to the creditor, simply reduced the debtor's debt, and allowed it to continue dealing with that creditor only on a COD basis. The presumption was not rebutted in this case, as the judge found the creditor had not assisted the debtor to stay in business, but only to continue purchasing from that creditor. Similarly, in *Leon Friedman & associés Inc v Creations KTM Inc* (1983), 51 CBR (NS) 123 (Que SC), the debtor's return of the merchandise to the creditor was not in the ordinary course of business nor had it benefited the debtor or the other creditors, thereby failing to rebut the presumption.

Hudson v Benallack, [1976] 2 SCR 168

DICKSON J:

I

This appeal raises a question of statutory construction which, one should think, would not cause difficulty, but which has indeed given rise to an abundance of conflicting legal opinion and a thoroughly obfuscated state of the law. The question is whether the words "with a view to giving such creditor a preference" contained in s. 73(1) of the *Bankruptcy Act*, RSC 1970, c. B-3, require only an intention on the part of the insolvent debtor to prefer or a concurrent intent on the part of both debtor and creditor. Sections 73 and 74 of the Act [*BIA*, s 95] read as follows: ...

Any conveyance or transfer of property or payment made by an insolvent person in favour of any creditor with a view to giving such creditor a preference over other creditors is deemed fraudulent and void as against the trustee in bankruptcy if the insolvent person becomes bankrupt within three months thereafter or within twelve months where the insolvent person and the preferred creditor are related persons.

II

In the present case the transaction impugned is the assignment on March 1, 1972, by G.S. & D. Construction Ltd. to the respondents, John Alexander Benallack and Lillian M. Benallack, of the assignor's interest, as purchaser, in an agreement for sale of certain lands in the City of Calgary. The consideration for the assignment was stated to be $15,250. At the time the assignor company was indebted to the assignees in the amount of $15,000 with interest and this indebtedness was used to offset the purchase price of the assignor's interest in the agreement of sale. All of the issued shares of G.S. & D. Construction Ltd. were owned by George Bayard Benallack and Shirley Edna May Benallack, the son and daughter-in-law respectively of the respondents. G.S. & D. Construction Ltd. made an assignment in bankruptcy on June 27, 1972, within the 12-month period mentioned in s. 74 of the Act, and the appellant Hudson was named as trustee. The learned Chambers Judge, Cullen J., made a number of findings, of which the following are of moment:

1. On March 1, 1972, the date of the assignment, the bankrupt company was an insolvent person within the meaning of the *Bankruptcy Act*;
2. The bankrupt and the respondents were related persons within the meaning of the Act and s. 74 applied;

3. The respondents received a preference over other creditors as a result of the assignment;
4. The bankrupt intended to give the respondents a preference over its other creditors.

Cullen J held against the need for concurrent intent and declared the assignment to be void as against the trustee in bankruptcy. The Appellate Division of the Supreme Court of Alberta reversed . . .

III

On the question whether proof of concurrent intent on the part of the debtor and creditor must be shown before the transaction can be set aside, there is, as I have indicated, a wide divergence of opinion. There are many decisions in which it has been held that concurrent intent must be proved; others in which it has been held that the Court is concerned only with the intent of the debtor; and still others in which the point has been left unresolved.

IV

Although the Courts of the country appear divided, more or less evenly, on the need for a concurrent intent before invalidating a transaction, the textbook writers and commentators do not evidence such divergence of opinion. The editors of Duncan & Honsberger, *Bankruptcy in Canada*, 3rd ed., p. 485, point out that s. 64 (now s. 73) makes no reference to the view of the creditor and that the cases in England and in the other Dominions on corresponding sections in *Bankruptcy Acts* contain no references to the view of the creditor, the view of the debtor alone being considered. The editors of Houlden & Morawetz, *Bankruptcy Law of Canada*, Cumulative Supplement, 1974, at p. 83, say:

> "In view of the plain meaning of Sec. 73, the concurrent intent of both debtor and creditor is not necessary to show a fraudulent preference. The intention of the debtor alone is to be considered."

[A]nd in Bradford & Greenberg's *Canadian Bankruptcy Act*, 3rd ed., p. 163, the authors cite "an intention on the part of the debtor to prefer" as one of the two circumstances constituting a fraudulent preference. See also 2 C.E.D. (Ont. 3rd) 15-334: "The intention of the debtor alone is to be considered" and *Comment* in (1958–59), 37 C.B.R. 153, and *Notes on Section 64 of the Bankruptcy Act* by Professor Réginald Savoie in (1967), 9 C.B.R. (N.S.) 1.

V

If this Court is free to decide the issue of concurrent intent untrammelled by earlier decisions, there would seem to be at least three reasons why we should not engraft upon s. 73 of the *Bankruptcy Act* an additional concept, that of concurrent intent: first, the policy of the *Bankruptcy Act*; second, the history of the Act; third, the language of s. 73.

The object of the bankruptcy law is to ensure the division of the property of the debtor rateably among all his creditors in the event of his bankruptcy. Section 112 of the Act provides that, subject to the Act, all claims proved in the bankruptcy shall be paid *pari passu*. The Act is intended to put all creditors upon an equal footing. Generally, until a debtor is insolvent or has an act of bankruptcy in contemplation, he is quite free to deal with his property as he wills and he may prefer one creditor over another but, upon becoming insolvent, he can no longer do any act out of the ordinary course of business which has the effect of preferring a particular creditor over other creditors.

If one creditor receives a preference over other creditors as a result of the debtor acting intentionally and in fraud of the law, this defeats the equality of the bankruptcy laws.

The cognizance of the creditor or its absence should be irrelevant. One can sympathize with the rationale of concurrent intent, which is the desire to protect an innocent creditor who accepts payment of a debt in good faith, but it is hard to reconcile this point of view with the language of the statute, with the history of bankruptcy legislation, and with the right of other innocent creditors to equal protection....

VII

I come now to consider the decision of this Court in *Benallack v Bank of British North America*. The case has stood on the books for seventy years. Many judges have considered it controlling on the question of concurrent purpose as applied to s. 73(1) of the *Bankruptcy Act*. I approach the case, therefore, with the respect to which those considerations entitle it, but I must at once observe that the case was decided in 1905, some fourteen years before the enactment of the Canadian *Bankruptcy Act* in 1919. It concerned a Yukon Ordinance having to do with preferential assignments, c. 38 of the Consolidated Ordinances of the Yukon Territory 1902. To permit comparison with s. 73(1) of the *Bankruptcy Act*, I will give the Ordinance in its entirety:

> *An Ordinance Respecting Preferential Assignments.*
> 1. Every gift, conveyance, assignment or transfer, delivery over or payment of goods, chattels or effects or of bonds, bills, notes, securities or of shares, dividends, premiums or bonus in any bank, company or corporation made by any person at any time when he is in insolvent circumstances or is unable to pay his debts in full or knows that he is on the eve of insolvency with intent to defeat or delay or prejudice his creditors or to give to any one or more of them a preference over his other creditors or over any one or more of them or which has such effect shall as against them be utterly void.
> 2. Every such gift, conveyance, assignment, transfer, delivery over or payment whether made owing to pressure or partly owing to pressure or not, which has the effect of defeating, delaying or prejudicing creditors or giving one or more of them a preference shall as against the other creditors of such debtor be utterly void.
> 3. Nothing in this Ordinance shall apply to any deed of assignment made and executed by a debtor for the purpose of paying and satisfying rateably and proportionately and without preference or priority all the creditors of such debtor their just debts or any *bona fide* sale of goods or payment made in the ordinary course of trade or calling, to innocent purchasers or parties."

The wording of the Ordinance differs from that of s. 73(1) of the *Bankruptcy Act*; in particular s. 3 introduces concepts of *bona fides* and "innocent purchasers or parties" not found in s. 73(1).

The action in the 1905 *Benallack* case was brought to set aside several instruments, consisting of a chattel mortgage, land transfer and book debt assignments, in favour of a bank, as being void against creditors under the Ordinance. The bank was ignorant of the true financial condition of the debtor. Idington J, who delivered the unanimous judgment of a five-man Court, after referring to the cases of *Stephens v McArthur*, and *Gibbons v McDonald*, said:

> "And if a fraudulent preference to whom is the having such a purpose to be attributed?
> Is it enough to shew that the assignor may have had such an intent?

Must not the assignee as well as the assignor be a party to the fraudulent intent?

Such would seem to be the result of a long line of decisions upon which the commercial world has had a right to act for a long time past. And though there may not have been any express decision on the point upon this legislation in this Court the late Chief Justice, Sir William Ritchie, in *Gibbons v. McDonald*, at page 589 indicates that in his view there must be a concurrence of intent on the one side to give and on the other to accept a preference over other creditors.

Counsel for the appellants properly conceded that the evidence here did not show knowledge on the part of the bank such as would enable us to find this concurrence of purpose.

Until the legislature obliterates the element of intent in such legislation and clearly declares that, quite independently of intent, the preferential result or effect of the transaction impeached is to govern, it will be exceedingly difficult to arrive at any other conclusion in cases of this kind. The results that might flow from such legislation ought not to be brought about without such purpose being most clearly expressed by the legislature."

The case is unsatisfactory, if I may, with respect, say so, in that none of the "long line of decisions" upon which Idington J relies is identified and no reasons are given for concluding that the intent to which the Ordinance refers must be entertained by the creditor as well as the debtor. In the later case of *Salter & Arnold, Ltd v Dominion Bank, supra,* as I have already mentioned, Duff J observed that whatever else may be said about the intention to give a preference envisaged by s. 31 (now s. 73) "it must be an intention entertained by the debtor." These words have been interpreted by some judges to mean that the intention with which one is concerned is only that of the debtor. I think, however, that we must give effect to the words of Duff J "whatever else may be said about it." What Duff J intended, in my opinion, was merely to leave the matter open, just as Cartwright J, as he then was, did in the penultimate paragraph of his judgment in *Velensky v Canadian Credit Men's Trust Association Limited* (reported in 38 C.B.R. 162 as *In re Bernard Motors Ltd*). The paragraph in question, for some reason, was not printed in the report of the case in the Supreme Court Reports but is contained in the 38 Canadian Bankruptcy Reports, p. 167 and reads:

> "Before parting with the matter, I wish to observe that Bridges J suggests a doubt as to whether if he were untrammelled by authority he would hold that, on the true construction of s. 64, to render void a preference in fact it is necessary that there be an intention on the part of the creditor to be preferred as well as an intention on the part of the debtor to prefer. In *In re Blenkarn Planer Ltd* (1958), 37 C.B.R. 147, 26 W.W.R. 168, 14 D.L.R. (2d) 719, 1958 Can. Abr. 55, Ruttan J examines a number of decisions and expresses the opinion that the view of the debtor alone has to be considered. I mention this for the purpose of making it clear that in the case before us this point does not require decision and I express no opinion upon it."

I have concluded that a finding of concurrent intent is not necessary in order to set aside a payment as a fraudulent preference under s. 73 of the *Bankruptcy Act.* I do not believe that the decision of this Court in *Benallack v Bank of British North America* is authoritative in interpreting s. 73 of the *Bankruptcy Act.* However similar may be the wording, I do not think that a phrase in a provincial or territorial Ordinance of three paragraphs dealing with preferential assignments and having a particular legislative history and jurisprudence should govern the language of a federal Act of some 213 sections dealing with bankruptcy and having an entirely different legislative history and jurisprudence.

One must recall that fraudulent preference statutes and fraudulent conveyance statutes outside of the bankruptcy laws have generally contained a section exempting from the application of the statute any assignment or payment or *bona fide* sale of goods made in the ordinary course of trade to innocent purchasers. Such saving provisions are contained in our provincial fraudulent preference statutes and in each of the cases relied on in the 1905 *Benallack* judgment a similar statute was under consideration. These statutes required consideration of the knowledge or *bona fides* of the creditor. Under the law relating to bankruptcy the rule has been different, as the English authorities cited earlier in these reasons will confirm.

I am further of the view that s. 3 of the Yukon Ordinance plays the same role in the interpretation of the Ordinance as the proviso to s. 92 of the English Act of 1869 played in *Butcher v Stead*, requiring consideration of the knowledge and intent and privity of the creditor; but there is no counterpart of s. 3 of the Ordinance to be found in s. 73(1) of the *Bankruptcy Act*. Section 75(1) of the Act, which protects certain transactions, is the only section in which the *bona fides* of the creditor emerges. Section 75(1) is very limited in scope. It is expressly made "Subject to the foregoing provisions of this Act ... with respect to the avoidance of certain settlements and preferences ... " and only comes into operation when s. 73(1) does not apply. Section 75(1) in express terms calls for double intent whereas s. 73(1) does not.

Our duty is to construe the language of s. 73 of the *Bankruptcy Act* within the ambit and policy of that Act; if we go to the words of the statute we find that what is to be considered as fraudulent and void is:

> "Every conveyance ... of property" (i.e., the assignment in favour of respondents) "... made by any insolvent person" (i.e., G.S. & D. Construction Ltd.) "in favour of any creditor" (i.e. the respondents) "... with a view to giving such creditor a preference ... "

It seems to me plain from the quoted words that the view, the only view, with which s. 73(1) of the Act is concerned is that of the insolvent person making the conveyance and we should not be diverted to any other conclusion by reliance upon a case in which a different statute in different language was construed. Whether or not a conveyance or payment is a fraudulent preference depends entirely on the intention of the debtor. The trial judge has found against the respondents on this point. ...

Appeal allowed.

Canadawide Fruit Wholesalers Inc, Re (1998), 80 ACWS (3d) 261, 1998 CarswellQue 412 (CA)

MAILHOT JA: This is an appeal from a judgment of the Honourable Daniel H. Tingley (Superior Court, Bankruptcy & Insolvency Division, District of Montreal, November 9, 1994), dismissing the trustee's petition to annul as preferential two payments made by the debtor company (Canadawide) to respondent (Hapco).

Applicable law

Section 95(1) of the *Bankruptcy and Insolvency Act* concerning fraudulent preferences provides that every payment made by any insolvent person in favour of any creditor with a view to giving that creditor a preference over the other creditors shall, if the person making it becomes bankrupt within three months after the date of making it, be deemed fraudulent and void as against the trustee in the bankruptcy.

Subsection (2) provides that where any payment mentioned in subsection (1) has the effect of giving any creditor a preference over other creditors, or over any one or more of them, it shall be presumed, in the absence of evidence to the contrary, to have been made with a view to giving the creditor a preference over other creditors.

In other words, if, in the three-month period prior to the bankruptcy of his debtor, one creditor is paid over other creditors, that payment is presumed to be preferential. The onus is on the creditor to prove he was not paid by preference, but in the ordinary course of his debtor's business. If the creditor fails to satisfy the Court that the payment was made in the ordinary course of his debtor's business, the payment is considered fraudulent (a legal or constructive fraud) and void as against the trustee.

In my opinion, this principle was not correctly applied in the first instance.

Facts

Canadawide is a wholesaler of fruits and vegetables. As a result of financial problems, its bank appointed a consultant to supervise its affairs in November of 1992. All accounts payable, including the disputed payments to Hapco, were approved by the consultant.

Hapco is an American wholesaler and exporter of fruits and vegetables. Canadawide began buying from Hapco in early 1993. It placed only three orders with Hapco in February and March 1993. The last two orders are at issue in these proceedings.

Hapco delivered a first shipment of fruit to Canadawide on February 19, 1993, for a price of slightly over US$14,000.00. Canadawide made out a cheque on April 6, 1993. A second shipment of fruit was made to Canadawide on March 15, 1993, for over US$20,000.00.

The cheque for the first shipment was not honoured by Canadawide's bank, due to insufficient funds. Hapco discovered this fact only after Canadawide had received the second shipment. One of Hapco's representatives called Canadawide to ask for a replacement cheque. Canadawide's representative, Mr. Katsabanis, explained to the Hapco representative that his company was in financial difficulty. Canadawide was however willing to issue a replacement cheque, but on the condition that Hapco would undertake to supply Canadawide with additional products in the future. According to Katsabanis' uncontradicted testimony, Hapco made such an undertaking. Katsabanis authorized the issuance of the replacement cheque, which was subsequently approved by the bank consultant. The cheque for the second shipment dated May 19, 1993 was cleared by Canadawide's bank on May 31, 1993. The replacement cheque for the first shipment dated June 1, 1993 was cleared by the bank on June 9, 1993.

Thereafter Canadawide called Hapco several times to request quotes on produce. Mr. Katsabanis testified that the quotes he received were above market prices or he was told that the requested product was not available. No orders were received from Hapco after the second shipment.

Canadawide's financial situation did not improve over time. The company filed a Notice of Intention to make a Proposal on August 30, 1993. At that time, the company carried a debt load of some 13 million dollars and was running a deficit of approximately 11 million dollars.

Since the payments to Hapco were made in the three months prior to the filing of the notice of intention, the trustee asked the Court to declare them void and to order Hapco to remit the sum of CDN$42,792.74, with interest and costs, under s. 95 of the *Bankruptcy Act*.

The trial judge concluded that Canadawide was insolvent when it made the two payments. The effect of these payments was to give Hapco a preference in fact over other ordinary creditors, i.e. those who had not undertaken to continue doing business with

Canadawide. But the judge found that these payments did not constitute fraudulent preferences, because they were not made with a view of giving Hapco a preference over other creditors.

The payments to Hapco were made pursuant to a policy intended to keep Canadawide in business, wrote the judge. Canadawide had decided in April 1993, undoubtedly in concert with its bank, to pay only the claims of those of its creditors who were prepared to continue trading with it, so as to permit it to continue its operations.

His specific words are as follows:

> "The most probable effect of this payment policy was that a creditor could expect to be paid on a cash basis for all future deliveries or services. Hapco was paid in the pursuit of this policy which was intended, not to prefer, but to encourage all creditors to continue to trade with the debtor company.
>
> The Court concludes that the trustee has not established an intention on the part of the debtor company to give Hapco a preference over its other creditors. It dealt with Hapco in the same way it intended to deal with all its other creditors who undertook to continue trading with it. By doing so, it hoped to stay in business."

The judge then stated that had the trustee succeeded in proving an intention to prefer, he would have considered Hapco had rebutted the presumption established by subsection 95(2), because the payments were made in the normal course of Canadawide's business, given the context at the time.

Discussion

Houlden and Morawetz comment s. 95 of the Bankruptcy Act as follows:

> "Under s. 95 the trustee is required to prove: (1) that the conveyance, transfer, payment, etc., took place within three months or one year of bankruptcy; (2) that the debtor was an insolvent person at the date of the alleged preference; and (3) that at the date when the conveyance, transfer, payment, etc., was made, it gave the creditor a preference in fact over other creditors [...] . When the trustee has proved these three essentials, s. 95(2) provides that the conveyance, transfer, payment, etc., is presumed to have been made with a view to giving the creditor a preference over other creditors [...]."

In the instant case, the three conditions mentioned above are met. It is undisputed that the payments occurred in the three months prior to the notice of proposal and that Canadawide was insolvent when it made these payments. The payments gave also Hapco a preference in fact over other creditors, simply because Hapco was paid, while other creditors, who also had debts outstanding, were not.

In my respectful opinion, the trial judge erred at law when he required the trustee to first establish the debtor's intention to prefer for subsection 95(2) to apply. I also find, as a matter of law, that the trustee had no more to do than simply prove a preference in fact. In this case the evidence quite obviously demonstrates that Hapco was paid, while other creditors were not.

Since the trustee has established the necessary conditions for the prima facie presumption of subsection 95(2) to apply, the onus should properly have rested on Hapco to prove, by balance of probabilities, that the payments were not fraudulent, because they were not made with a view to prefer.

There are a number of ways to achieve this. The authors Houlden and Morawetz list thirteen examples (see F§98). The trial judge seems to have considered two, i.e. that the payments were intended to keep the company in business and that they were made in the ordinary course of business.

The trial judge held that Canadawide had adopted a policy of paying only the claims of its creditors who were prepared to continue trading with it, so as to continue its operations. These payments were made in the pursuit of this policy and were intended to keep Canadawide in business.

The trustee argues before us that Hapco knew of Canadawide's insolvency at the time the payments were made because of the NSF cheque and because Mr. Katsabanis had explained the financial difficulties to Hapco. The trustee submits Hapco then deceptively offered to supply further goods if the invoices were paid, but had actually no intention of doing so, adding that such trade practices should not be sanctioned by the Court, because it allows a creditor to make a promise it does not intend to fulfil in order to escape the principle of equal distribution among creditors.

Mr. Katsabanis testified that Canadawide payed Hapco to obtain more goods, so as to stay in business. That was no doubt his reason for paying. But to do so, Canadawide had no choice but to prefer Hapco over its other suppliers with debts outstanding. The first judge ruled that the probable effect of the payment policy was that creditors could expect to be paid on a cash basis for future deliveries. I agree. If Hapco had indeed been paid cash on delivery, the presumption would have been rebutted. It could have been easily argued that the deliveries were necessary to carry on business. However, there were no orders pending with Hapco at the time of payment. Mr. Katsabanis' expectations were founded on the hope that Hapco would fulfil future orders. I find his hope unreasonable, given that he had just told Hapco of Canadawide's financial difficulties and that it was too tempting for Hapco, which was not a major supplier of Canadawide and which did not depend on its business, far from it, to say whatever it had to in order to secure immediate payment. In short, Mr. Katsabanis' expectation that this payment would help Canadawide stay in business was unreasonable.

The judge also held that the payments were not made outside the normal course of Canadawide's business, given the circumstances. The trustee answers that Canadawide's "ordinary course of business" must be judged objectively, not subjectively. A company experiencing financial difficulty, running under the supervision of a consultant appointed by its bank, systematically preferring certain creditors over others and delaying payment is not operating in the ordinary course of its business. It would be a bad precedent, claims the trustee, for the Court to conclude that an extraordinary course of business carried out by an insolvent debtor, making desperate moves to avoid bankruptcy, is an ordinary course of business for the purposes of the *Bankruptcy Act*. Creditors who were preferred, due to this extraordinary means of carrying on business, should not be able to justify the payments in question by the argument that they were made in the ordinary course of business.

I agree with the trustee. I see nothing "ordinary" about Canadawide's operations at the time the payments were made. The trial judge focuses on the fact that the payment terms of 45 days for the first invoice and of 65 days for the second were not abnormal under the circumstances. I find these considerations irrelevant given the more general context, namely that Canadawide had implemented a policy of paying only certain creditors under certain conditions.

Appeal allowed.

Logistec Stevedoring (Atlantic) Inc v AC Poirier & Associates Inc, **2005 NBCA 55, 255 DLR (4th) 137**

JT ROBERTSON JA:

[1] We are asked to decide whether the application judge erred in holding that a $500,000 payment made by an insolvent debtor to one of its creditors qualifies as a fraudulent preference within the meaning of s. 95 of the *Bankruptcy and Insolvency Act*, RSC 1985, c. B-3 (*BIA*). In my respectful view, the application judge erred. Specifically, he failed to ask whether the impugned payment was made with the "dominant intent" of preferring one creditor over the others. When that test is applied to the facts of the present case, it is evident that the debtor harboured no such intent. Admittedly, the creditor in receipt of the payment received a "preference in fact," but that is not a sufficient basis for declaring the payment a fraudulent preference. As will be explained, s. 95 has no application in circumstances where the insolvent debtor is effecting a payment with a view to generating income to be applied against the debts of both secured and unsecured creditors. This remains true even if it were unrealistic to expect that the unsecured creditors would share in the income generated.

[2] The essential facts are as follows. Until September 15, 2004, St. Anne Nackawic Pulp Company Ltd. had been operating a pulp mill in Nackawic, New Brunswick. That corporation is a wholly owned subsidiary of St. Anne Industries Ltd. St. Anne Industries is also the primary secured creditor of St. Anne Pulp under a registered general security agreement, the validity of which is being challenged in other proceedings. Finally, St. Anne Industries is a wholly owned subsidiary of Parsons & Whittemore Inc. of New York. On September 15, 2004, St. Anne Pulp made a voluntary assignment in bankruptcy. A trustee was appointed on that date, but later replaced by the respondent, A.C. Poirier & Associates Inc. Prior to the bankruptcy, it was customary for St. Anne Pulp to transport its pulp to Saint John where it was stored in a dockside warehouse belonging to the appellant, Logistec Stevedoring (Atlantic) Inc. Logistec was also responsible for loading of pulp onto ships and trucks. On September 14, 2004, one day prior to the filing for bankruptcy, Logistec was informed by St. Anne Pulp that it would be ceasing operations but that it wanted to ensure that the 10,800 tonnes of pulp, being presently stored in Logistec's warehouse, would be released and loaded onto two ships that were to arrive in Saint John on or about September 18, 2004. As well, one shipment was to be effected by truck. In response, Logistec asserted that it possessed a warehouseman's lien on the goods and refused to release and load any pulp unless it received prior payment, in full, with respect to past due accounts. Logistec informed St. Anne Pulp that it was owed $562,574.72 plus amounts not yet posted to the account. Initially, Logistec demanded payment from anyone other than St. Anne Pulp in order to avoid the possibility of someone alleging the payment was a fraudulent preference. Eventually, Parsons & Whittemore agreed to indemnify Logistec in the event the payment from St. Anne Pulp to Logistec was successfully challenged. The impugned payment was made on September 14, 2004. The next day St. Anne Pulp made a voluntary assignment in bankruptcy. On the same date, St. Anne Industries appointed a receiver under the terms of its security agreement. On September 16, 2004, Logistec determined that a further $232,945.91 would be needed to settle the account. The receiver paid this amount with funds drawn on St. Anne Pulp's bank account, over which St. Anne Industries had taken security. As of September 27, 2004, all the pulp in the warehouse had been shipped.

[3] On December 10, 2004, the respondent trustee filed an application for a declaration that the $562,574.72 payment was fraudulent and void under s. 95 of the *BIA*.

Correlatively, the trustee sought judgment for that amount. On December 21, 2004, the application was heard. On the same date the application judge granted the relief requested. His decision is now reported at [2004] N.B.J. No. 477 (Q.B.) (QL). The reasons for judgment address two issues. The first was whether the application proceedings should be converted into an action. On this issue, the application judge ruled in favour of the trustee. Although Logistec pursued this issue on appeal, there is no need to convert this matter into an action. The only factual matter which the parties failed to resolve concerns the extent to which the $500,000 payment related to work already performed, as opposed to work to be performed. However, that factual determination is only relevant if the payment in question were declared a fraudulent preference, in which case part of the payment may have been valid. As I find that the payment in question does not constitute a fraudulent preference, there is no need to dwell on the first issue. As to the second issue, I turn to s. 95. . . .

[4] The law is settled with respect to the interpretation and application of s. 95 of the *BIA*. In order for a payment to a creditor to qualify as a fraudulent preference three conditions precedent must be met: (1) the payment must have been made within three months of bankruptcy; (2) the debtor must have been insolvent at the date of the payment; and (3) as a result of the payment the creditor must have in fact received a preference over other creditors (see *Re Van der Liek* (1970), 14 C.B.R. (N.S.) 229 (Ont. H.C.J.).

[5] Once the three conditions precedent have been met, a presumption arises that the payment was made "with a view to giving that creditor a preference over the other creditors." However, it is a rebuttable presumption. In that regard, the courts have interpreted the above-quoted phrase as placing an onus on the creditor to establish that the debtor's dominant intent was not to prefer that creditor. The genesis of the dominant intent test is invariably traced to the following passage in *Re Van der Liek*, at pages 231–32:

> "When the trustee has proved these three essentials, he need proceed no further and the onus is then on the creditor to satisfy the court, if he can, that there was no intent on the part of the debtor to give a preference. If the creditor can show on the balance of probabilities that the dominant intent of the debtor was not to prefer the creditor but was some other purpose, then the application will be dismissed, but if the creditor fails to meet the onus, then the trustee succeeds."

[6] Certain factors may or may not be relevant to the task of ascertaining the debtor's dominant intent. Based on the Supreme Court's decision in *Hudson v Benallack*, [1976] 2 S.C.R. 168, it is settled law that the creditor's knowledge of the debtor's insolvency at the time of the payment is an irrelevant consideration. On the other hand, it is relevant that the corporate debtor knew of its insolvency at the date of the payment. If the debtor is related to the creditor the payment will be scrutinized with greater care and suspicion. However, it is no defence to an allegation of fraudulent preference that the creditor exerted pressure on the insolvent debtor to secure the payment. According to s. 95(2), pressure is no longer a ground for upholding a transaction which is otherwise preferential within the meaning of s. 95(1). Finally, as the dominant intent test is an objective one, we need not be concerned with the subjective intent of the insolvent debtor at the time of the payment. The requisite intent will be drawn from all of the relevant circumstances, as opposed to the debtor's personal ruminations. See generally Lloyd W. Houlden & Geoffrey B. Morawetz, *Bankruptcy & Insolvency Law of Canada*, looseleaf (Toronto: Carswell, 1992) at 4–66 to 4–67, 4–79.

[7] Returning to the facts of the present case, the parties agree that conditions precedent (1) and (2) have been met. However, Logistec argues that it was not the beneficiary of a preference in fact and, therefore, s. 95 has no application. A concise and accurate statement of the law as to the relationship between the concept of preference in fact and dominant intent is found in *Re Norris* (1996), 193 A.R. 15 at para. 16 (C.A.):

> "In considering this section, it is well to keep in mind the distinction between preference in fact and fraudulent preference as that latter is defined in the Act. There can be no doubt in this case that Revenue Canada received a preference in fact from the payment of tax made by this debtor on November 25, 1992. Its debt was paid where the debts owing to other ordinary creditors were not. What would render that preference in fact a fraudulent one under s. 95 is the accompanying intent of the insolvent debtor who in the face of imminent bankruptcy is moved to prefer or favour, before losing control over his assets, a particular creditor over others who will have to wait for and accept as full payment their rateable share on distribution by the Trustee in the ensuing bankruptcy. It is called fraudulent because it prejudices other creditors who will receive proportionately less, or nothing at all, and upsets the fundamental scheme of the Act for equal sharing among creditors. That accompanying intent to favour one creditor over another is what makes a preference in fact a fraudulent preference and is referred to in the cases as the "dominant intent." ...

[8] In my view, Logistec's argument would have been persuasive had the impugned payment related solely to work or services to be performed in regard to the pulp that was being stored in Logistec's warehouse at the time of the payment. In other words, had the entire $500,000 payment related to the storage and shipping of the 10,800 tonnes of pulp in Logistec's warehouse, Logistec's argument would have been well founded. The situation would be no different had Logistec sold St. Anne Pulp a piece of machinery within the three months preceding the bankruptcy and St. Anne Pulp paid in cash. Such a payment would not qualify as a preference, but rather as a purchase and sale made in the ordinary course of business. However, counsel for Logistec conceded that part of the $500,000 was to be applied against amounts already owing for work undertaken in the past. In these circumstances, Logistec did receive a preference in fact when contrasted with St. Anne Pulp's other creditors who were also awaiting payment of their outstanding accounts. That said, the mere establishment of a preference in fact does not lead to the conclusion that the payment qualifies as a fraudulent preference within the meaning of s. 95 of the *BIA*. What we are left with is a rebuttable presumption that the payment in question so qualifies.

[9] Logistec bore the onus of establishing that St. Anne Pulp's dominant intent was not to prefer Logistec over the other creditors. Alternatively stated, the onus was on Logistec to establish that St. Anne Pulp's dominant intent was to achieve a purpose other than to prefer Logistec. Regrettably, the application judge did not address that issue. For this reason, this court must draw the necessary inference from the primary findings of fact, as found by the application judge. Those facts are not in dispute.

[10] St. Anne Pulp's dominant intent may be formulated in at least one of four ways. First, it can be argued that it intended to bestow a preference on Logistec over the other creditors. This is the position of the trustee in bankruptcy. Second, it can be argued that St. Anne Pulp made the payment in order to honour its contractual obligations to its customers who had purchased the pulp and, hence, to ensure that the goods were duly shipped. This is the position of Logistec. The third and fourth characterizations flow from the second. Third, it can be argued that St. Anne Pulp's dominant intent was to

generate income in the form of accounts receivable. Moneys collected would be applied against amounts owing to creditors and in the order of priority established at law. Fourth, it can be argued that St. Anne Pulp's dominant intent was to maximize St. Anne Industries' recovery on its secured debt. This characterization is a logical extension of the reality that, as the primary secured creditor, St. Anne Industries is entitled to the proceeds arising from the sale of inventory in priority to the unsecured creditors. If it can be fairly said that St. Anne Pulp's dominant intent falls within either the second, third or fourth formulations, it is my view that the payment in question does not qualify as a fraudulent preference under s. 95 of the *BIA*. I so find. My formal reasoning is as follows.

[11] At common law and even after passage of the *Statute of Elizabeth* in 1570 (fraudulent conveyances) there was no impediment against an insolvent debtor preferring one creditor over another. The question of why a debtor would prefer one creditor over another goes to the question of the debtor's underlying motive, which text writers point out is irrelevant to the issue of dominant intent. Admittedly, it is easy to blur the legal distinctions often drawn between motive, intent, purpose or object. Be that as it may, one cannot help but ask why a debtor would prefer one creditor over another. In some cases the answer is self-evident. The common law allowed an insolvent debtor to engage in selective generosity by paying first those he liked most. Thus, payment to a creditor who is a family member or friend is more apt than not to qualify as a fraudulent preference within the meaning of s. 95 of the *BIA*: see *Craig (Trustee of) v Devlin Estate* (1989), 63 Man. R (2d) 122 (C.A.). Ironically, there is also a reported case in which the debtor allegedly made the payment to a non-related creditor (Revenue Canada) in order to prefer a creditor who was a close but distant relative: see *Norris (Re)*. But even if there is no close relationship between the debtor and the preferred creditor, the payment may be caught by s. 95. For example, where the payment is made to a creditor with respect to an indebtedness that had been guaranteed by the debtor's spouse, the payment has been held to be a fraudulent preference: see *Royal Bank of Canada v Roofmart Ontario Ltd* (1990), 74 O.R. (2d) 633 (C.A.) and also *Re Royal City Chrysler Plymouth Limited* (1998), 38 O.R. (3d) 380 (C.A.).

[12] As a general observation, it is evident that the cases in which the creditor has been unable to rebut the presumption arising under s. 95 of the *BIA* generally involve two factual patterns. First, the insolvent debtor and the creditor in receipt of the payment are somehow related (e.g., family members). Second, the payment to an arm's length creditor has the subsidiary effect of conferring an unjustified benefit or advantage on the insolvent debtor or a family member. While these factual patterns are not exhaustive, it is clear that the facts of the present case do not support a finding that St. Anne Pulp's dominant intent was to prefer Logistec over the other creditors. But that is not the end of the matter. It is still necessary to isolate, by inference, St. Anne Pulp's dominant intent. In my view, its ultimate goal was to generate income from its accounts receivable, the proceeds of which would be applied first against the debt owing to St. Anne Industries, the primary secured creditor. In brief, St. Anne Pulp's dominant intent was to maximize the amount that the receiver would recover on behalf of St. Anne Industries from the sale of the existing inventory. Does this inference support the allegation of fraudulent preference under s. 95 of the *BIA*? In my view, it does not for two reasons. First, s. 95 speaks of fraudulent preference in terms of the creditor who received the payment. In this case, it was Logistec who received the payment, not St. Anne Industries. Second, and more importantly, St. Anne Industries cannot be accused of obtaining a fraudulent preference when as a matter of law it is entitled to a preference as a secured

creditor of St. Anne Pulp. It is St. Anne Industries that has priority over the unsecured creditors by virtue of its security agreement. St. Anne Industries is to be paid first. If the income generated resulted in a surplus that surplus would be shared pro-rata amongst the unsecured creditors. The fact that St. Anne Pulp made the impugned payment to Logistec with a view to generating income which would be applied first against the debt owing to the secured creditor, St. Anne Industries, and then against amounts owing to the unsecured creditors, cannot be regarded as a valid basis on which to declare the payment to Logistec a fraudulent preference.

[13] My understanding of the law is that in circumstances where an insolvent debtor pays one creditor at the expense of another for purposes of carrying on business, the payment will more likely than not be deemed not to constitute a fraudulent preference within the meaning of s. 95 of the *BIA*. I need only refer to two cases in support of this proposition. In *Davis v Ducan Industries Ltd.* (1983), 45 C.B.R. (N.S.) 290 (Alta. QB) the bankrupt was a manufacturer of recreational vehicles. The creditor who received the questionable payment was a supplier of parts that the debtor used in its business. The supplier refused to continue to do business with the debtor unless payments were made towards its large outstanding account. Less than three months before the bankruptcy, the debtor made payments to the supplier. Once the debtor became bankrupt, another creditor challenged this transaction as a fraudulent preference. The court found that the dominant intent of the bankrupt in making the payments to the supplier was to secure supplies to continue to run its business and not to give the creditor a preference. Similarly, in *Econ Consulting Ltd (Trustee of) v Deloitte, Haskins & Sells* (1985), 31 Man. R (2d) 313 (C.A.) the bankrupt made a payment of $10,000 to accountants in respect of an outstanding account sixteen days prior to making an assignment in bankruptcy. The debtor's income tax returns were due and the accountants required the payment before they would prepare income tax returns for the debtor. The Court of Appeal cited this finding of the application judge with approval:

> "I am satisfied that Econ made this payment not to give a preference to Deloitte but to get what it needed and required, i.e. its income tax returns prepared. I think that Deloitte would not have received payment if it had not been necessary for Econ to do so in order to persuade Deloitte to do the work that had to be done."

[14] Under Canadian law, if a creditor refuses to perform an act for an insolvent debtor, such as delivering goods or preparing income tax returns, unless its existing account is paid in full or in part, and the account is so paid in order to have the act performed, the transaction will not be deemed a fraudulent preference. This is because the debtor made the payment, not for purposes of preferring the creditor, but rather to obtain the performance of an act which is consistent with what is expected of someone who is acting in the ordinary course of business: see Houlden & Morawetz at 4–79 to 4–80.

[15] I admit that in the present case St. Anne Pulp did not make the payment for purposes of carrying on its pulp business in the long term. The impugned payment was made one day prior to St. Anne Pulp's voluntary assignment in bankruptcy. In the interim, however, it was entitled to carry on business albeit for a day. The truth of the matter is that St. Anne Pulp was acting in the best interests of all concerned when it made the payment to Logistec. Let me explain.

[16] It would have been irresponsible for either St. Anne Pulp, the trustee or the privately appointed receiver to allow the inventory of pulp to sit in Logistec's warehouse. St. Anne Pulp had entered into binding contracts for the sale of this product. The goods had to be shipped, otherwise St. Anne Pulp would have been in breach of its contractual

obligations and liable for any consequential damages. When completed, those contracts generated income for St. Anne Pulp. The net amount invoiced on the three contracts in question was $1.3 million (U.S.), $2.3 million (U.S.) and $300,000 (Cdn.). Together, the shipment of the pulp generated more than $4.6 million (Cdn.) in accounts receivable. That amount is net of the $800,000 paid to Logistec to ensure the shipment of the pulp ($562,574.72 + $232,945.91 = $795,520.63). In effect, for every $1 paid to Logistec, St. Anne Pulp generated at least $5 in accounts receivable. In addition, by fulfilling the pulp contracts, future pulp sales might not otherwise be jeopardized if the trustee or the receiver decided to operate St. Anne Pulp pending a disposition of the mill.

[17] What the trustee fails to appreciate is that although a debtor is insolvent, it is entitled to carry on in the ordinary course of business even if only for a day, so long as it is acting in a commercially reasonable manner and, therefore, in the best interests of all concerned. As well, the trustee appears to be proceeding on the mistaken assumption that prior to the voluntary assignment in bankruptcy any moneys held in St. Anne Pulp's bank account could be used only for purposes of effecting a settlement of all debts on a pro-rata basis. The reality is that if anyone possessed a priority with respect to moneys in St. Anne Pulp's bank account, it was St. Anne Industries under its general security agreement. That security extended not only to St. Anne Pulp's accounts receivable and inventory, but also to all moneys held on St. Anne Pulp's account. It is out of that bank account that the receiver paid Logistec $232,000 in order to secure shipment of the pulp. Had St. Anne Pulp not made the payment to Logistec on September 14, 2004, here is what would have happened. On the following day, the newly appointed receiver would have seized the moneys held in St. Anne Pulp's bank account. From that account the receiver would have paid the full amount owing to Logistec, for both past and present work. As it happens, the fact that a substantial payment was made one day prior to the bankruptcy is of no moment. Finally, I should point out that the payment to Logistec will work to the benefit of the unsecured creditors in the event St. Anne Industries' security agreement is successfully challenged and declared invalid. The income generated by that payment ($5 for every $1 paid to Logistec) would become available to all unsecured creditors.

[18] At first blush the "optics" of this case cast a long shadow over the actions of St. Anne Pulp, St. Anne Industries and, ultimately, Parsons & Whittemore. It is understandable that Logistec was adamant that it receive an indemnity from Parsons & Whittemore with respect to the possibility the payment in question would be successfully challenged as a fraudulent preference under s. 95 of the *BIA*. The fact that the payment was made one day prior to the voluntary assignment in bankruptcy, and that both Logistec and St. Anne Pulp were aware of the latter's insolvency, threw suspicion over the transaction. However, when properly viewed, the transaction made good commercial sense. There is no doubt that St. Anne Industries was the true beneficiary of St. Anne Pulp's payment to Logistec. But no one can complain of the preferential treatment being accorded that secured creditor. The preference arises as a matter of the security contract and is sanctioned by both the common law and the *BIA*.

V. THE PROVINCIAL PREFERENCE PROVISIONS

The provincial preference provisions are different in a number of material respects from *BIA* section 95. There has been criticism about having these provisions at both the federal and the provincial level, particularly given the differences between them. (Recall that there is no constitutional issue involved: see Chapter 2.) Here is what the Standing Senate Committee on Banking, Trade and Commerce has said:

> [T]here should be a uniform system nationwide for the examination of fraudulent and reviewable transactions in situations of insolvency. At present, there is a lack of fairness, uniformity and predictability by virtue of both federal and provincial/territorial legislation addressing fraudulent and reviewable transactions. We feel that a national standard is needed for reviewable transactions that diminish the value of the insolvent debtor's estate and thereby reduce the value of creditors' realizable claims. Provincial/territorial legislation would continue to exist for transactions not occurring in the context of insolvency. A national system for review of such transactions would provide the fairness and predictability that we want in our insolvency system.[8]

One cost of retaining the provincial preference provisions is the threat to national uniform laws inside bankruptcy. This point should not be understated. Canadian bankruptcy and insolvency law is by and large a federal responsibility and this reflects a commitment to the value of national uniformity. As the above-quoted passage implies, the continued concurrent operation of provincial laws is inconsistent with having federal bankruptcy laws in the first place. Uniformity is not the only issue. Another potential cost of retaining the provincial laws is that the concurrent operation of federal and provincial laws creates the potential for confusion at the policy level — for example, where provincial laws allow a trustee in bankruptcy to circumvent limitations on the scope of the federal preference provisions. It also adds to the complexity of the law because it requires parties, their legal advisers, and the courts to negotiate two layers of provisions instead of just one.

Below is an excerpt from a report recommending reform of fraudulent preference law.

Tamara M Buckwold, *Reform of Fraudulent Conveyances and Fraudulent Preferences Law, Part II: Preferential Transfers* **(Report prepared for the Uniform Law Conference of Canada, Civil Law Section, August 2008), paras 4 and 7–18 (footnotes omitted)**

> Provincial preferential transfer legislation is a product of the introduction of creditors' relief legislation during the late 19th century as part of a package of legislation designed to fill the void created by the absence of federal bankruptcy law. Although elements of the provincial package were repealed when the federal government re-entered the field with the *Bankruptcy Act* of 1919, the creditors' relief and companion preferences legislation generally continued in effect....
>
> [P]ayments and the provision of security resulting in satisfaction of a debt owed to one creditor in circumstances in which others of equal rank will be unsatisfied or receive a proportionately smaller amount are regulated in most provinces by provincial legislation and, where bankruptcy or restructuring proceedings have been commenced under federal legislation, by provisions of the *Bankruptcy and Insolvency Act*. Because secured creditors are able to recover through resort to their collateral the concern in both contexts is the equal satisfaction of unsecured debts through enforcement against the debtor's unencumbered assets.

---

8 Standing Senate Committee on Banking, Trade and Commerce, *Debtors and Creditors Sharing the Burden: A Review of the* Bankruptcy and Insolvency Act *and the* Companies' Creditors Arrangement Act (Ottawa: Senate, November 2003) at 122 (Chair: Hon Richard H Kroft).

Provincial preferences legislation differs in name and in various points of detail as among jurisdictions and the interpretational overlay added by the judiciary is far from uniform. What follows below is therefore of necessity only an outline of regularly appearing provisions and principles.

Transactions Regulated by the Statute

The language defining the scope of the Alberta *Fraudulent Preferences Act* is representative of the provincial statutes generally. It provides that "every gift, conveyance, assignment, transfer, delivery over or payment of ... any property, real or personal" made in the circumstances prescribed is "void as against the creditor or creditors injured, delayed, prejudiced or postponed." However, qualifying provisions substantially limit the scope of the legislation by exempting the various transactions described further below from challenge, most notably payments of money to a creditor. Therefore the word "payment" used in relation to the operation of the provincial statutes should be understood to refer to a payment through the transfer of property other than money and to include the transfer of an interest in property by way of security for antecedent debt. A transfer of value through the provision of services or the assumption of an obligation is not subject to challenge.

Only transfers to a "creditor" can be challenged. The statutes provide an expanded definition under which "creditor" includes a surety and the endorser of a promissory note or bill of exchange who may become a creditor on fulfillment of their legal obligations, as well as a *cestui que trust* "or other person to whom liability is equitable only."

Requirement of Insolvency

A transfer to a creditor may only be avoided if made by a person who is insolvent or who knows him or herself to be on the eve of insolvency. As indicated above, the assumption is that a payment made by a solvent debtor cannot be a preference because he or she is by definition financially able to satisfy all creditors in full. Whether or not this is in fact so may depend upon the definition of insolvency applied and whether the value of exempt property is taken into account in the determination. The state of insolvency is not defined in the statute and courts have taken various approaches. However to quote a leading author, "[w]hat must be established is incapacity to pay one's debts."

Debtor's Intention

A preferential transfer may be avoided only if it is established that the debtor *intended* to give the recipient creditor a preference. The requirement of intention to prefer has been part of Canadian preferences law since its inception and, as the discussion below indicates, its suitability as the factor determining the legal vulnerability of a preferential payment is the most significant issue in reform of this area of law.

What is required to establish the requisite intention to prefer varies depending the period of time that has elapsed between the date of the challenged transaction and the commencement of proceedings to set it aside. If the challenge is mounted within a prescribed period the debtor is presumed to have intended to prefer the creditor to whom the payment was made if it had the effect of giving that creditor a preference over others, provided the debtor was insolvent or knowingly on the eve of insolvency at the date of the transaction. If action is commenced outside the prescribed time period, the plaintiff must bring evidence establishing an actual intention to prefer.

Proof of Intention Outside the Prescribed Time Period

Proof that the debtor knows they are insolvent when a creditor is paid may be accepted as proof of an intention to prefer, since the necessary consequence of the payment is that the recipient creditor is advantaged relative to those who cannot be satisfied. However, there is little doubt that any such inference is rebuttable, since the courts will not find an intention to prefer when it is established that the debtor acted pursuant to another dominant motive. Thus a debtor who responds to a creditor's pressure to pay will likely not be regarded as having acted with the requisite intention to prefer, on the view that the payment is not truly voluntary. Similarly a preferential payment made by a debtor in the genuine hope of staying in business may not be subject to avoidance. The difficulty of proving the debtor's intention to prefer along with uncertainty over what will be accepted by the courts as an exculpatory motive and the evidence required to establish it has severely limited the ability of creditors to successfully use the provincial statutes to set aside a payment that has preferential effect.

Proof of Intention within the Presumptive Time Period
In most provinces the presumption of intention to prefer arising from the preferential effect of a payment operates when it is challenged through the commencement of litigation within 60 days of the date the payment was made, though in Alberta the period is a full year. In Ontario the presumption is *"prima facie,"* so it may be rebutted by evidence proving a contrary motive, though not on the basis of pressure exerted by the benefiting creditor. In the western provinces the presumption is explicitly irrebuttable. In jurisdictions in which the statutory language is ambiguous, the presumption will likely be regarded as rebuttable.

Intention of Preferred Creditor
Under the terms of the statute, the state of mind of a creditor receiving a preferential payment is irrelevant. Nevertheless, the courts have protected creditors by refusing to set aside a transfer if the recipient did not in some fashion participate in or at least know of the debtor's intention to confer a preference. Judicial proclivity to impose a dual intention requirement varies as among jurisdictions, and one province has explicitly abolished it as a relevant consideration. This inconsistency in judicial approach is exacerbated by uncertainty over the degree of creditor participation required to warrant avoidance of a transfer.

Standing to Challenge a Transfer or Payment
Since a preferential transfer is void as against "the creditor or creditors injured, delayed, prejudiced or postponed," only a person who is a creditor at the time it occurs has standing to challenge a transfer under the statute. The expanded definition noted under heading a. above applies in this context, but the weight of authority indicates that the holder of an unliquidated or contingent claim is not otherwise a creditor. Although a secured creditor is a "creditor" in the strict sense, such a creditor is ordinarily not adversely affected by a preferential payment and will not have standing under the statute, except to the extent the debt is unsecured.

Protected Transactions
The law of all jurisdictions in some way shelters preferential transfers that are regarded as legitimate or that for reasons of commercial stability should not be disrupted, regardless of the intention of the debtor in making them. The statutes differ slightly in their definition of transactions that are above challenge, and the terms by which the exceptions are defined are generally far from clear. However, the range of such transactions includes, along with payments of money noted earlier, those listed below, cast in language sprinkled liberally throughout with references to "bona fides" and good faith:

- Transactions involving an exchange in which the money paid or property transferred bears a "fair and reasonable relative value to the consideration for it," in the form of:
  › A sale or payment made in the ordinary course of business to an "innocent party."
  › A conveyance or delivery of property in exchange for a reciprocal sale or delivery of goods or other property or a money payment.
  › A transfer by way of security for a present advance of money.
  › A payment given to a creditor who has in good faith given up a security, unless the value of the security is restored.
  › The provision of one form of security in substitution for another.
  › A security given for pre-existing debt that induces a further advance intended to enable the debtor to carry on business and satisfy creditors in full.
  › An assignment made for the purpose of paying creditors rateably.

[Permission requested.]

Practice Questions

Question 1
Trevor Mortenson is insolvent. He owes $45,000 to Visa, $20,000 to the government for his student loans, and $5,000 to his lessor for rent. Trevor owns a stamp collection worth $35,000. He sold the stamp collection to a hobby shop for $33,000 on Tuesday and assigned himself into bankruptcy the day after, on Wednesday. The $33,000 is sitting in Trevor's bank account, untouched. Is this a fraudulent conveyance?

Question 2
Briana Whitaker, who lives in Alberta, is insolvent. She has unsecured debts and liabilities in the amount of $75,000. She also owns a car free and clear worth $5,000. On 2 September 2018, Briana gave her car to her brother as a birthday gift and on 3 September 2018, tired of her creditors harassing her, assigned herself into bankruptcy. Can Briana's creditors reach the car? See BIA, ss 1, 67(1)(b) and 96(1)(b); Alberta's Civil Enforcement Act, RSA 2000, C c-15, s 88; and Alberta's Civil Enforcement Regulation, AR 276/1995, s 37.

Question 3
Assume exactly the situation in Question 2 but instead of an individual debtor, we have a corporate debtor, and the conveyance occurred on 4 September, one day after the assignment in bankruptcy, to the brother of the sole shareholder. Would any part of your answer change? How?

Question 4
Debtor lives in Alberta. He is on the verge of bankruptcy. His main asset is a share portfolio valued at $40,000. Debtor and his family live in a rented apartment. Debtor sells the shares and uses the sale proceeds to buy a mobile home. Debtor and his family move out of their rented apartment and into the mobile home. Three months later, Debtor makes an assignment into bankruptcy. Can the trustee claim the mobile home? (Note that the Civil Enforcement Act, RSA 1994, s 171, exempts from execution or seizure a debtor's principal place of residence to the value of $40,000, which includes a mobile home if actually lived in.)

Question 5
Shoes Ltd makes shoes. It has a warehouse full of leather soles and machines for manufacturing shoes, but its shoe sales have been declining ever since one shipment containing

faulty shoes resulted in a number of injuries to the shoe purchasers. On 1 August, the main supplier of leather soles, Leather Inc, called Shoes Ltd to discuss its outstanding unsecured account of $75,000. Leather Inc told Shoes Ltd that if Shoes Ltd wished to continue ordering leather soles from Leather Inc, it would have to make a payment of at least $10,000, and thereafter, all transactions between the two companies would be on a cash-only delivery basis. At the time of the call, there were no orders pending with Shoes Ltd. Shoes Ltd immediately transferred $10,000 to Leather Inc. The following day, Shoes Ltd assigned itself into bankruptcy. The unsecured creditors each received 10 percent of their debt in the bankruptcy. Did Leather Inc receive a preference?

Question 6
Assume the same scenario as in Question 5 but instead of a cash payment, Shoes Ltd returned merchandise to Leather Inc. Is that a voidable preference?

Question 7
Layla Contractors is having financial difficulty. The economy took a turn and its main contracting job has stalled. Costs have risen and the machines it is leasing sit unused at the site. One of its creditors, Cranes Inc, is owed $30,000, and has one crane at the site under an unsecured sale agreement. Once Cranes Inc found out about Layla Contractors' financial difficulty, it got Layla Contractors to convert the unsecured agreement to a secured one by taking a security interest in Layla Contractors' own excavator. The next day, Layla Contractors assigned itself into bankruptcy. Is this a voidable preference?

Question 8
Layla Contractors has a revolving line of credit with TD Bank, for $250,000. It opened this line of credit ten years ago. The terms of the agreement allow Layla Contractors to take any amount of money from its line of credit and require it to deposit all payments from its builders directly into the line of credit. Layla Contractors strictly adhered to the agreement for eight years. Over the last two years, however, as the economy took a downturn, Layla Contractors was habitually late in making payments to its line of credit because its own creditors were late in paying. On 1 September, Layla Contractors received two payments, for $30,000 and $45,000. It paid them directly into its line of credit that same day. At that time, it was unable to pay its other creditors. On 1 October, Layla Contractors assigned itself into bankruptcy. Can the trustee get at those two payments?

Question 9
Oilwell Drilling Inc owes $2 million to Royal Bank, secured by its principal asset, a rig valued at $1.5 million. Under its security agreement, it pays $40,000 to the Royal Bank on the first of every month. It has continued paying this debt without fail despite its financial difficulties and despite being unable to pay its other creditors. On 2 October, it assigned itself into bankruptcy. Can the trustee reverse the payments made to Royal Bank within the voidable preference period?

Question 10
Oilwell Drill Inc stopped making its insurance payments on the rig, contrary to its security agreement with the Royal Bank. After a fire in its warehouse on 25 September, the rig was completely destroyed. On 1 October, Oilwell Drill Inc paid its usual $40,000 to the Royal Bank, just as it always had. On 2 October, it assigned itself into bankruptcy. Can the trustee reverse the payments made to Royal Bank within the voidable preference period?

Question 11

ABC Grocers is a family-owned corner store. ABC Grocers has been insolvent for four months because a Safeway opened up right across the street, diverting most of ABC Grocers's clientele. Brady and Jamie, the owners, paid themselves $50,000 on 1 February, for an unsecured loan they had made to the store. On 28 February, Priddis Dodge repossessed the car registered to ABC Grocers. ABC Grocers owed $40,000 to Larry Stern, a contractor who had remodeled the store. Larry came in to demand payment. ABC Grocers paid him by signing over its large refrigerators, which are worth $80,000, on 1 March. They also made a series of small payments from February 1 to 10, totaling $10,000, to family members who had lent them money on an unsecured basis so they could open up a corner store. Unfortunately, by making these payments, ABC Grocers has been unable to make any other payments on loans, specifically to Small Loans Inc, one of its creditors that also happens to be your client. ABC Grocers assigned itself into bankruptcy on 1 April. Small Loans Inc has come to see you. What do you advise?

CHAPTER 6

Executory Contracts

I. INTRODUCTION

This chapter deals with the treatment of a special kind of contract—an executory contract—in *Bankruptcy and Insolvency Act*, RSC 1985, c B-3 (*BIA*) bankruptcies. Executory contracts are contracts where both parties have only partly performed their obligations under the contract at the date of bankruptcy. Recall that the broad definition of "property" for the purposes of defining the bankrupt estate includes contractual rights held by the bankrupt, and that these rights vest in the bankruptcy trustee. Where the debtor has fully performed a contract, the contract is considered an "asset" of the bankruptcy estate and the trustee can therefore demand performance by the counterparty. Where the debtor has not performed the contract, but the counterparty has fully carried out its obligations under the contract, the trustee can refuse to perform the contract. In that case, the counterparty can claim as a creditor in the debtor's bankruptcy and the contract would be considered a "liability" of the bankrupt estate. In a case where both parties have only partly performed their contractual obligations, however, the situation is more complex. The partly performed contract is not simply an "asset" or "liability" of the bankrupt estate. This is where the law governing executory contracts comes into play.

Generally speaking, a trustee has three options in terms of how to deal with an executory contract in bankruptcy. The trustee can "disclaim" the contract, essentially putting the debtor in breach of the contract and relieving the counterparty of further performance. Alternatively, the trustee can "affirm" the contract, opting to continue performance of the contract and requiring the counterparty to do the same. Lastly, the trustee can "assign" the contract, by finding another party to assume the role of the bankrupt vis-à-vis performing the contract. The trustee's decision of which option to elect is guided by the goal of maximizing the value of the bankrupt estate for the benefit of creditors.

Historically there was relatively little legislative guidance on the treatment of executory contracts in bankruptcy or insolvency, with the exception of commercial realty leases. The 2009 amendments to the *BIA* added three new provisions—sections 65.11, 84.1, and 84.2—which now provide statutory guidance on disclaimer, affirmation, and assignment of executory contracts in general, including commercial realty leases. However, the *BIA* still does not provide a comprehensive scheme for the treatment of executory contracts in bankruptcy. Of the new provisions, section 65.11 is limited to proposals and does not apply in bankruptcies. Section 84.1 does not apply in individual bankruptcy proceedings unless the individual is carrying on a business, and section 84.2 does not apply in corporate bankruptcy proceedings. Therefore it is still necessary to rely on common law principles and provincial legislation depending on the type of executory contract and what the trustee elects to do with respect to the executory contract. Most notably, the treatment of commercial realty leases is largely determined by the application of provincial law (except in Quebec and Newfoundland and Labrador), which is incorporated into the *BIA* by an express provision (s 146). For other kinds of executory contracts, the court must look to common law principles to resolve matters on which the *BIA* is silent. For an analysis of the reforms, see Anthony Duggan, "Partly Performed Contracts," in Stephanie Ben-Ishai and Anthony Duggan, eds, *Canadian Bankruptcy and Insolvency Law: Bill C-55, Statute c. 47 and Beyond* (Toronto: LexisNexis, 2007), ch 2.

In 2018, Parliament enacted amendments relating to the treatment of intellectual property licences in insolvency proceedings as part of the Government of Canada's new national intellectual property strategy. These amendments are not yet in force. When the amendments come into force, they will clarify and simplify the treatment of intellectual property licences in *BIA* and *Companies' Creditors Arrangement Act*, RSC 1985, c C-36 (*CCAA*) proceedings.

This chapter discusses the law relating to Disclaimer, Affirmation, and Assignment of executory contracts in *BIA* bankruptcies. It also discusses some of the special issues that arise in the context of intellectual property licences. For a discussion of the treatment of executory contracts in *CCAA* and *BIA* proposal proceedings, see chapters 13 and 16.

II. DISCLAIMER

A. Introduction

In bankruptcy, the trustee and the debtor are different legal persons. Therefore the trustee is not automatically bound by the debtor's contracts, and the trustee must affirm a contract if they want to obtain the benefit of the contract for the estate. The flip-side is that, by affirming the contract, the trustee assumes responsibility for performing the debtor's side of the bargain and non-performance will give the contract counterparty a damages claim against the estate which is payable in full as a post-filing administrative expense. The trustee may avoid this liability by disclaiming the contract. Disclaimer puts the debtor in breach of contract, giving the counterparty a damages claim against the estate. However, as discussed further below, the counterparty's claim is a provable claim within the meaning of *BIA*, section 121(1); the result is that the counterparty will typically not be paid in full, but will receive only a *pro rata* share of its entitlement. The flip-side of disclaimer is that it relieves the counterparty of its performance obligations and so the estate does not obtain the benefit of the contract. In summary, the trustee's decision to affirm or disclaim a contract requires an assessment of whether the benefits to the estate of performing the contract outweigh the costs of performance.

It follows from these principles that the trustee must elect within a reasonable time whether to affirm a contract, and if they fail to make an election one way or the other, they are deemed to have disclaimed the contract: see *Re Thomson Knitting Co* (1924), 5 CBR 189 (Ont SC), aff'd (1925), 5 CBR 489 (Ont CA) and *New Skeena Forest Products Inc v Don Hull & Sons Contracting Ltd*, 2005 BCCA 154, both extracted below.

BIA, section 121(1), provides as follows:

> All debts and liabilities, present or future, to which the bankrupt is subject on the date on which the bankrupt becomes bankrupt *or to which the bankrupt may become subject before the bankrupt's discharge by reason of any obligation incurred before the day on which the bankrupt becomes bankrupt* shall be deemed to be claims provable in proceedings under this Act [emphasis added].

Duncan explains the meaning of the italicized words as follows:

The class of claims covered by [these words] includes cases of contract where the trustee either disclaims or ceases to perform the contract. In such cases, the creditor may prove against the estate for the damages occasioned by the breach of the contract, and this is his only remedy.[1]

B. Lessor and Tenant Agreements

BIA, section 30(1)(k), provides that the trustee may, with the permission of the inspectors, elect to retain or to assign or disclaim any lease of any property of the bankrupt. This provision is supplemented by *BIA*, section 146, which incorporates by reference the provisions in provincial lessor and tenant statutes relating to the disclaimer, affirmation, and assignment of commercial tenancy agreements. Sections 38 and 39 of the *Commercial Tenancies Act*, RSO 1990, c L.7, reproduced below, are reasonably representative. Section 39(1) gives a trustee the right by notice in writing to surrender or disclaim a lease. This more or less restates the common-law position. But assume the trustee makes no election either to disclaim or affirm the lease: at common law, the default rule is that the trustee is deemed to have disclaimed. Does the statute, by requiring notice in writing of disclaimer, displace the common-law default rule?

BIA, section 136(1)(f), limits the amount of the lessor's claim following disclaimer of a lease: it gives the lessor a claim for three months' arrears of rent and three months' accelerated rent. In *Re Vrablik* (1993), 17 CBR (3d) 152 (Ont Ct J (Gen Div)) (*Re Vrablik*), extracted below, the court held that the claim for three months' accelerated rent was in substitution for loss of bargain damages. In other words, lessors cannot claim loss of bargain damages on top of the claim that section 136(1)(f) gives them.

The lessor's claim under section 136(1)(f) is a preferred claim. This means the trustee must pay the lessor's claim in full ahead of the ordinary unsecured creditors. On the other hand, section 136(1) is "subject to the rights of secured creditors." This means the lessor's preferred claim ranks behind the right of a secured creditor to enforce its security interest. The preferred claim is for three months' arrears of rent and three months' accelerated rent. Assume the tenant is more than three months in arrears of rent. Can the lessor file a proof of claim for the balance? The answer is yes: section 136(3) provides that creditors whose rights are restricted by section 136(1) are entitled to rank as unsecured creditors for any balance of claim due to them. Consequently, the lessor ranks as a preferred creditor for three months' arrears of rent and an ordinary unsecured creditor for any arrears of rent beyond three months.

The preferred claim, under section 136(1)f, shall not exceed the "realization from the property on the premises under lease." The reference is to the value of the tenant's goods. The *Commercial Tenancies Act* gives a commercial lessor a right of distress for non-payment of rent. This means that, outside bankruptcy, the lessor can seize the tenant's goods and sell them, using the sale proceeds to pay off the rent. *BIA*, section 70(1), takes away the lessor's right of distress when the tenant becomes bankrupt. The section 136(1)(f) preferred claim is meant to compensate the lessor for loss of the right of distress, hence the limitation. Assume the value of the tenant's goods is less than the three months' arrears of rent. Can the lessor claim the difference? The answer is yes: again, section 136(3) applies.

---

1   Lewis Duncan, *The Law and Practice of Bankruptcy in Canada* (Toronto: The Carswell Company Limited, 1922) at 428–29. See Roderick J Wood & David J Bryan, "Creeping Statutory Obsolescence in Bankruptcy Law" (2014) 3 *Journal of the Insolvency Institute of Canada* 3.

The closing words of section 136(1)(f) say that any payment on account of accelerated rent shall be credited against the amount payable by the trustee for occupation rent. Section 38(2) of the *Commercial Tenancies Act* gives the trustee three months to elect between affirming or disclaiming the lease. The trustee is liable for occupation rent during that period. The lessor cannot claim both occupation rent and accelerated rent from the trustee. On the relationship between the lessor's claims for accelerated rent and occupation rent, see *Dancole Investments Ltd v House of Tools Company (Trustee of)*, 2011 ABCA 145, noted below.

Commercial Tenancies Act, RSO 1990, c L.7, ss 38 & 39

38 (1) In case of an assignment for the general benefit of creditors, or an order being made for the winding up of an incorporated company, or where a receiving order in bankruptcy or authorized assignment has been made by or against a tenant, the preferential lien of the landlord for rent is restricted to the arrears of rent due during the period of three months next preceding, and for three months following the execution of the assignment, and from thence so long as the assignee retains possession of the premises, but any payment to be made to the landlord in respect of accelerated rent shall be credited against the amount payable by the person who is assignee, liquidator or trustee for the period of the person's occupation. RSO 1990, c L.7, s 38(1).

(2) Despite any provision, stipulation or agreement in any lease or agreement or the legal effect thereof, in case of an assignment for the general benefit of creditors, or an order being made for the winding up of an incorporated company, or where a receiving order in bankruptcy or authorized assignment has been made by or against a tenant, the person who is assignee, liquidator or trustee may at any time within three months thereafter for the purposes of the trust estate and before the person has given notice of intention to surrender possession or disclaim, by notice in writing elect to retain the leased premises for the whole or any portion of the unexpired term and any renewal thereof, upon the terms of the lease and subject to the payment of the rent as provided by the lease or agreement, and the person may, upon payment to the landlord of all arrears of rent, assign the lease with rights of renewal, if any, to any person who will covenant to observe and perform its terms and agree to conduct upon the demised premises a trade or business which is not reasonably of a more objectionable or hazardous nature than that which was thereon conducted by the debtor, and who on application of the assignee, liquidator or trustee, is approved by a judge of the Ontario Court (General Division) as a person fit and proper to be put in possession of the leased premises. RSO 1990, c L.7, s 38(2), 2006, c 19, Sched. C, s 1(1).

39 (1) The person who is assignee, liquidator or trustee has the further right, at any time before so electing, by notice in writing to the landlord, to surrender possession or disclaim any such lease, and the person's entry into possession of the leased premises and their occupation by the person, while required for the purposes of the trust estate, shall not be deemed to be evidence of an intention on the person's part to elect to retain possession under section 38. RSO 1990, c L.7, s 39(1).

(2) Where the assignor, or person or firm against whom a receiving order has been made in bankruptcy, or a winding up order has been made, being a lessee, has, before the making of the assignment or such order demised any premises by way of underlease, approved or consented to in writing by the landlord, and the assignee, liquidator or trustee surrenders, disclaims or elects to assign the lease, the under-lessee, if

the under-lessee so elects in writing within three months of such assignment or order, stands in the same position with the landlord as though the under-lessee were a direct lessee from the landlord but subject, except as to rental payable, to the same liabilities and obligations as the assignor, bankrupt or insolvent company was subject to under the lease at the date of the assignment or order, but the under-lessee shall in such event be required to covenant to pay to the landlord a rental not less than that payable by the under-lessee to the debtor, and if such last mentioned rental was greater than that payable by the debtor to the said landlord, the under-lessee shall be required to covenant to pay to the landlord the like greater rental. RSO 1990, c L.7, s 39(2).

(3) In the event of any dispute arising under this section or section 38, the dispute shall be disposed of by a judge of the Superior Court of Justice upon an application. RSO 1990, c L.7, s 39(3); 2006, c 19, Sched. C, s 1(1).

Re Vrablik (1993), 17 CBR (3d) 152 (Ont Ct J (Gen Div))

MALONEY J: This is a motion brought by the Trustee in this bankruptcy for:

1. An Order of the Court determining whether the contingent claim of Donald Raymond Stasiuk, Kathryn Marta Stasiuk, Andrew Findlay Coffey, Roberta Joan Coffey and 705514 Ontario Limited is a provable claim;
2. If the contingent claim is a provable claim then, an Order of the Court valuing the claim;

The reason for the bringing of the motion is that the above-named landlords of the bankrupt tenant are claiming damages in lieu of payments which would otherwise be due under the portion of the lease as yet unexpired at the time of the assignment in bankruptcy made by the tenant on November 16th, 1989.

On June 10, 1988 Melanie Vrablik (the "Tenant") entered into a commercial lease with Donald Raymond Stasiuk, Kathryn Marta Stasiuk, Andrew Findlay Coffey, Roberta Joan Coffey and 705514 Ontario Limited (hereinafter referred to as the "Landlord") as the lessor. The tenant had hoped to establish a fitness and exercise salon. The leased premises were known municipally as 104 North Syndicate Avenue in the City of Thunder Bay. The term of the lease was from July 1, 1988 to June 30, 1993. The monthly rental under the lease was $1,606.67. The tenant was responsible for the payment of municipal taxes, hydro, water and maintenance costs as set out in the lease. On November 16, 1989 the Tenant filed an assignment in bankruptcy (Bankruptcy No. 027144), the Trustee in Bankruptcy of the Estate of Melanie Vrablik being Ignit Stetsko (the "Trustee"). The landlord filed Proof of Claim dated December 11, 1989 in the amount of $99,412.59. A portion of this claim was a preferred claim, being the arrears of rent for a period of three months immediately preceding the bankruptcy of the tenant and the accelerated rent for a period of three months following the bankruptcy of the tenant. The Proof of Claim dated December 11, 1989 disclosed a sum of $13,886.09 as the preferred claim. A revised Proof of Claim dated November 22, 1991 filed by the Landlord reduced that sum to $8,167.41. The Proof of Claim dated December 11, 1989 also disclosed that the landlord has advanced a contingent and unliquidated claim in the amount of $85,526.50 based on the damages the landlord alleges it has sustained as a result of the tenant's default under the lease. The revised Proof of Claim dated November 22, 1991 outlines the landlord's unliquidated claim as follows:

(1)	rent from February 16, 1990 to August 1, 1991 at $1,606.67	$28,116.72
(2)	1989 taxes	$2,949.81
(3)	1990 taxes	$4,685.94
(4)	1991 taxes to August 1, 1991	$3,043.64
(5)	maintenance in 1990	$1,121.95
(6)	maintenance in 1991	$839.08
(7)	shortfall on re-letting August 1, 1991 to June 30, 1993	$5,623.44
		$46,380.58

In summary, the Revised Proof of Claim dated November 22, 1991 lists the landlord's preferred claim at $8,167.41 and the unliquidated claim at $46,380.58. Section 38 of the *Landlord and Tenant Act*, RSO 1990, c. L.7 ("*Landlord Tenant Act*") gives a landlord a preferential lien for the arrears of rent due during the period of three months preceding the assignment in bankruptcy and for three months following the execution of the assignment of bankruptcy:

> 38 (1) In case of an assignment for the general benefit of creditors, or an order being made for the winding up of an incorporated company, or where a receiving order in bankruptcy or authorized assignment has been made by or against a tenant, the preferential lien of the landlord for rent is restricted to the arrears of rent due during the period of three months next preceding, and for three months following the execution of the assignment, and from thence so long as the assignee retains possession of the premises, but any payment to be made to the landlord in respect of accelerated rent shall be credited against the amount payable by the person who is assignee, liquidator or trustee for the period of the person's occupation.

Section 136 of the *Bankruptcy Act*, RSC 1985, c. B-3 ("*Bankruptcy Act*") lays out a scheme of distribution of priorities subject to the rights of secured creditors. It is interesting to note that the preferential lien granted to a landlord in s. 38 of the Ontario *Landlord and Tenant Act*, reflects exactly the lien granted by s. 136(1) of the *Bankruptcy Act* and Parliament in its wisdom has ranked this priority sixth behind various other security interests:

> 136 (1) Subject to the rights of secured creditors, the proceeds realized from the property of a bankrupt shall be applied in priority of payment as follows ...
>
> (f) the landlord for arrears of rent for a period of three months immediately preceding the bankruptcy and accelerated rent for a period not exceeding three months following the bankruptcy if entitled thereto under the lease, but the total amount so payable shall not exceed the realization from the property on the premises under lease, and any payment made on account of accelerated rent shall be credited against the amount payable by the trustee for occupation rent;

The preference provided by the *Bankruptcy Act*, *supra*, is only to the extent of the availability of property of the bankrupt on the premises at the time of the bankruptcy and is subject to the rights of other secured creditors having a higher priority under the *Bankruptcy Act*. The law is quite explicit in designating the Landlord as a preferred creditor compensating him for his vacant premises and in substitution of his right to distrain. This motion is brought on the basis of the combined strength of s. 121 of the *Bankruptcy Act* and Rule 94 of the *Bankruptcy Rules* which state that when an unliquidated claim is made, the Trustee in Bankruptcy must apply to the Court to determine whether or not the claim is provable, and if provable to have the claim valued. Counsel have all agreed that the central issue is whether or not the contingent, unliquidated claim is provable.

Upon making an Assignment in Bankruptcy or Receiving Order, all of the obligations and rights of the tenant in the lease vest in the Trustee in Bankruptcy as per s. 71(2) of the *Bankruptcy Act*:

> 71 (2) On a receiving order being made or an assignment being filed with an official receiver, a bankrupt ceases to have any capacity to dispose of or otherwise deal with his property, which shall, subject to this Act and to the rights of secured creditors, forthwith pass to and vest in the trustee named in the receiving order or assignment, and in any case of change of trustee the property shall pass from trustee to trustee without any conveyance, assignment or transfer.

The Trustee in Bankruptcy has the right for a period of up to three months from the date of bankruptcy in which to elect whether to retain, assign, surrender or disclaim the lease as per s. 38(2) of the *Landlord Tenant Act* [see *supra*].

The Trustee in this case decided to disclaim and surrendered the lease in question to the landlord on December 11, 1989. Upon this action on the part of the Trustee, all rights and obligations of the Trustee under the lease are terminated as of the effective date of the disclaimer or surrender.

Counsel for the landlord in this matter argues that the landlord possesses a valid claim against the tenant or Trustee for amounts falling due *after* the date of the surrender or disclaimer of the lease. He relies upon the 1971 Supreme Court of Canada decision in *Highway Properties Ltd v Kelly, Douglas & Co*, [1971] SCR 562, 17 DLR (3d) 710 ("*Highway Properties*") for this proposition. In that case, a major tenant in a shopping centre repudiated an unexpired lease. The landlord resumed possession of the premises and gave notice to the defaulting tenant that it would be held liable for damages suffered by the landlord as a result of the admittedly wrongful repudiation. In deciding whether or not to allow the damages, Laskin J, as he then was, considered the various options open to a landlord when faced with a repudiation of a lease:

1. The landlord may refuse to accept the repudiation of the lease by the tenant. Nothing is done to alter the landlord-tenant relationship. The landlord simply insists on the performance of the terms of the lease and sues for rent or damages as they accrue on the basis that the lease remains in force.

2. The landlord may elect to terminate the lease and retake possession of the premises. In this case, the landlord may sue for rent accrued due, or for damages to the date of termination for previous breaches of the covenant. The landlord may not sue for prospective damages because it is a principle of common law that once the lease is terminated, all obligations under the lease cease to exist.

3. The landlord may advise the tenant that he refuses to accept the repudiation of the lease but that he proposes to re-enter the premises and, unless otherwise directed by tenant, relet the property *on the tenant's behalf* and hold the original tenant liable for any deficiency in rental for the balance of the lease term.

Noting the increasing intermingling of property law with contract law in the area of leasehold estates in land, Laskin J recognized the common law principle that a lease of land for a term of years, under which possession is taken, creates an estate in land. In many situations legislation or a strict literal reading of contractual terms have superseded the common law, for example, the provision of payment of rent in advance, and the provision of re-entry for non-payment of rent or for breaches of other covenants by the tenant. For some reason the courts had stopped short in refusing to apply to lease-hold estates in land the contractual doctrine of anticipatory breach and its accompanying principle governing relief upon repudiation of contract. On p. 716 he continues after noting that this doctrine has been applied without question to contracts for the sale of land:

> I think it is equally open to consider its application to a contractual lease, although the lease is partly executed. Its anticipatory feature lies, of course, in the fact that instalments of rent are payable for future periods, and repudiation of the lease raises the question whether an immediate remedy covering the loss of such rent and of other advantages extending over the unexpired term of the lease may be pursued notwithstanding that the estate in the land may have been terminated.

In allowing a new, fourth alternative—the right of the landlord to sue for prospective damages—Laskin J overruled *Goldhar v Universal Sections & Mouldings Ltd* (1963), 36 DLR (2d) 450 (Ont CA) ("*Goldhar*"). *Goldhar* formulated the doctrine of surrender such that once a lease is terminated, there can be no claim for prospective damages because that claim may only be founded on rights accruing to the tenant under the lease when still alive. Laskin J did not think it fair that, once an election to terminate the lease had been communicated through repudiation, all covenants and potential claims for relief in damages are terminated. At p. 731 he made this observation:

> It is no longer sensible to pretend that a commercial lease, such as the one before this Court, is simply a conveyance and not also a contract. It is equally untenable to persist in denying resort to the full armoury of remedies ordinarily available to redress repudiation of covenants, merely because the covenants may be associated with an estate in land.

Counsel for the Landlord has urged that the analysis and decision in *Highway Properties* be adopted in the present case. This would be a grave error in that the present case involves a bankruptcy, which is quite different from an outright repudiation of contract. A bankruptcy is a final and irreversible situation. In fact the Legislature has foreseen the present situation in that it has very distinctly created a comprehensive scheme for administering the leasehold interests of bankrupt tenants. It is not a coincidence that s. 38 of the *Landlord Tenant Act* reflects almost verbatim s. 136(1)(f) of the federal *Bankruptcy Act*. Section 136(1)(f) outlines the priority of a landlord for arrears and accelerated rent as against other secured and unsecured creditors. When it comes to the rights of the landlord and tenant with regards to the repudiation of the lease contract because of the bankruptcy, s. 146 of the *Bankruptcy Act* refers the parties back to the wording of the appropriate sections of the *Landlord Tenant Act* and not to the common law as counsel for the Trustee has stated:

> 146. Subject to priority of ranking as provided by section 136 and subject to subsection 73(4) [*right to distrain for arrears of rent*], the rights of landlords shall be determined according to the laws of the province in which the leased premises are situated. [insert added]

It has been argued that the "laws of the province" referred to in s. 146 are the common law as well as the statute law and that in this situation the common law right to sue for prospective damages as outlined in *Highway Properties* should be adopted in this case. Despite this argument, the "laws of the province in which the leased premises are situated" are, of course, sections 38 and 39 of the *Landlord Tenant Act*. As stated above, the combined effect of the *Bankruptcy Act* and the *Landlord Tenant Act* provides a comprehensive scheme for the administration of the leasehold interest of bankrupt tenants, *Re Limestone Electrical & Supply Co*, [1955] OR 291 (Ont CA).

Quite often Trustees in Bankruptcy elect under s. 38(2) to assign the lease with the approval of the Ontario Court (General Division). This is the kinder option for the landlord but it is only possible if an assignor can be found and approved by the Court. In an effort to promote fairness in commercial dealings, Trustees in Bankruptcy have been held personally liable for occupation rent during the time of disposal of the bankrupt's assets where there has been no clear agreement waiving such rights between the landlord and the Trustee, *Sasso v D & A MacLeod Co* (1991), 3 OR (3d) 472 (Ont Ct Gen Div); *Re Auto Experts Ltd* (1921), 3 CBR 591 (Ont CA). Nonetheless, where the Trustee legally disclaims the lease as per s. 39(1) of the *Landlord Tenant Act*, the effect of such a surrender is the same as if the lease had been surrendered with the consent of the lessor: *Re Mussens Ltd* (1933), 14 CBR 479 (Ont SC) at p. 482; *Cummer-Yonge Investments Ltd v Fagot* (1965), 2 OR 152 (Ont HC), affirmed (1965) 2 OR 157 (Ont CA); *Clarkson, Gordon Inc (Trustee) v Glenview Corporation and Bank of Montreal* (1988), 67 CBR (NS) 204 (Ont HC). Any cause of action under the lease that arises against a tenant prior to bankruptcy remains a liability of the tenant and is accordingly, a responsibility of the Trustee as per s. 38(1) of the *Landlord Tenant Act*. However, a claim for rent after bankruptcy is restricted to the statutory three months next following the execution of assignment in bankruptcy or for so long as the Trustee elects to retain possession of the property. This is the law of this province. The landlord's claim for damages is therefore not provable in this bankruptcy and the Trustee's motion is hereby determined accordingly, and I am relieved of the necessity of assessing quantum.

Motion determined.

Discussion

In addition to *Re Vrablik*, there are a few other noteworthy cases which are instructive in terms of how the courts have interpreted the interface between federal bankruptcy law and provincial law relating to lessors' claims. In *Re Gingras automobile Ltée*, [1962] SCR 676, the lessor claimed three months' arrears of rent and $1,398.22 for the cost of repairs the lessor was entitled to recover under the terms of the lease. The trustee allowed the first claim but disallowed the second. The lessor relied on the provisions of the (old) *Quebec Civil Code* (CC), giving him a privilege for both claims, and on CC 1994 ranking a lessor's claim is seventh among the claims of competing creditors. The Supreme Court held (1) that *Bankruptcy Act* (BA) section 95(1)(f) (now *BIA*, s 136(1)(f)), exclusively determines the lessor's priority; (2) that section 105 of the BA (now *BIA*, s 146) relates only to the validity of the lessor's claim and not to its priority; (3) that a lessor is not a secured creditor for the purposes of section 2 of the Act; and (4) even if the lessor's *privilège* could be so construed, section 95(1)(f) (now s 136(1)(f)), inferentially denies it that status.

Because whether a valid contract exists is usually a question of common law, the issue of the legal status of a contract under common law can be a factor when dealing with executory contracts in bankruptcy. In *Re TNG Acquisition Inc*, 2011 ONCA 535, the court dealt with a question of whether there had been repudiation or rescission of a lease contract prior to the debtor's bankruptcy. The court found that there had been an effort to repudiate the lease, but the repudiation was not accepted by the counterparty. As a result, the contract was still in force at the date of the debtor's bankruptcy, and therefore the bankruptcy trustee was able to successfully disclaim the lease.

The issue in *Re TNG Acquisition Inc* came about when the debtor-tenant sent the lessor a notice repudiating the lease. The lessor never responded to the repudiation. The debtor subsequently became bankrupt and the landlord submitted a proof of claim for unpaid rent over the entire term of the lease. The trustee thereupon disclaimed the lease and disallowed the bulk of the lessor's claim. The lessor brought proceedings to have the disallowance set aside. The trial judge dismissed the lessor's motion and the Court of Appeal upheld his decision. The decision turned on what it means to repudiate a contract. Repudiation is different from rescission:

> Rescission is a remedy available to an innocent party when the other party has made a false or misleading representation. It allows the innocent party to treat the contract as void ab initio. In contrast, repudiation occurs by words or conduct that show an intention not to be bound by the contract. The consequences of repudiation depend on the election made by the innocent party. The innocent party can elect to treat the contract as remaining in full force and … effect. In that case, both parties have the right to sue for damages for past or future breaches. Alternatively, the innocent party can elect to accept the repudiation and the contract is terminated. Each party is then discharged from future obligations. (at para 25)

In the present case, the lessor failed to elect one way or the other. The court held that since the lessor had not accepted the repudiation, the lease was still in force at the date of the debtor's bankruptcy and the trustee was entitled to disclaim it. The effect of the disclaimer was to limit the lessor's claim to the amount provided for by *BIA*, section 136.

Another issue that has confronted the courts is how to interpret the provisions of the *BIA* providing that amounts paid as occupation rent should be set off against a lessor's preferred claim for accelerated rent. Section 136(1)(f) of the *BIA* provides that payments of occupation rent made by or payable *by the trustee* are to be set off against a lessor's preferred claim for accelerated rent. In *Dancole Investments Ltd v House of Tools Company (Trustee of)*, 2011 ABCA 145 (*Dancole*), the court considered the issue of whether occupation rent paid by *a receiver* to the lessor should be considered "payable by the trustee" pursuant to *BIA*, section 136(1)(f).

In *Dancole*, the debtor made an assignment in bankruptcy and a secured creditor subsequently obtained the appointment of an interim receiver. Pursuant to an agreement between the debtor and the receiver, the receiver occupied the leased premises for more than two months and paid rent to the lessor, and thereafter delivered up the premises to the lessor. The trustee in bankruptcy never took possession of the leased premises and indicated that they had no interest in the premises. The Alberta Court of Appeal held that section 136(1)(f) should not be interpreted to apply to occupation rent paid by a receiver:

> [30] The *BIA* and the *Landlord's Rights on Bankruptcy Act* represent a balancing of the rights of the landlord against the rights of the other creditors. Under the statutory scheme, the landlord's right to claim for the value of the balance of the lease is cut off at the three-month point following termination of the lease, as is the related power of the landlord to distrain on goods found on the premises: *Landlord's Rights on Bankruptcy Act*, ss 3(b) and 4. That limits the claim that the landlord might make as an unsecured creditor, and truncates its claim against the goods found on the premises. The quid pro quo is that the landlord is given a preferred claim for three months of accelerated rent. The preferred status of this three month claim is intended to compensate the landlord for the loss of the value of the lease past the three-month point, and is separate and apart from any compensation the landlord may be entitled to for actual occupation of the

premises. The express proviso that credit must nevertheless be given for occupation rent payable by the trustee is simply a further refinement of the balancing of rights between the landlord and the other creditors of the estate.

[31] Conceptually, the argument is that [the landlord] is achieving a "double recovery" that should not be allowed, or that [the landlord] must essentially "mitigate its losses" by accounting for the rent received from the Receiver. This argument fails to recognize that the landlord is recovering for two different bundles of rights, and there is no "double recovery" for any one loss. The landlord is not required to establish that it actually sustained a loss to establish its entitlement to accelerated rent as a preferred claim under s. 136(1)(f). It need only establish that it was entitled to accelerated rent under the lease. It is therefore not inconsistent for the legislature to recognize the right of the landlord to claim both accelerated rent and occupation rent.

In 2016, a similar issue concerning the interpretation of section 136(1)(f) vis-à-vis occupation rent paid by receivers came before the Ontario Superior Court of Justice. In *Re Danier Leather Inc*, 2016 ONSC 6077, the court determined that the occupation rent paid to the lessor by the Receiver was appropriately deducted from the accelerated rent payable by the Trustee under section 136(1)(f). The court distinguished *Re Danier Leather Inc* from *Dancole* due to the determination that the Receiver in *Re Danier Leather Inc* was acting as an agent for the Trustee in entering the Occupation Agreement with the lessor. To reconcile the differing conclusions of the courts, the court in *Re Danier Leather Inc* wrote:

[35] Dancole cannot stand as authority that in no case can rent paid by a receiver not be rent "payable by the trustee" under section 136(1) of the *BIA*. It depends on the facts. A trustee who disclaimed any interest in the property and told the receiver to make its own deal with the landlord could not say that the rent paid by the receiver to the landlord was rent payable by the trustee. A trustee with the right of occupancy that exercised that right by authorizing a receiver to occupy the leased premises on its behalf is in a far different position as it would then be liable for occupation rent. That is the situation in this case under the Occupancy Agreement.

Therefore, *Re Danier Leather* adds a nuance to the court's decision in *Dancole*. *Re Danier Leather* stands for the proposition that rent paid by a receiver can be considered rent "payable by the trustee" in certain circumstances.

C. Other Contracts

New Skeena Forest Products Inc v Don Hull & Sons Contracting Ltd, 2005 BCCA 154, 251 DLR (4th) 328

BRAIDWOOD JA:

[21] Although it is not necessary for me to decide for the purposes of this case, in light of the Intervenor's submissions on the confusion in the law regarding the power of trustees to disclaim contracts, and with a view to clarifying the matter, I make these observations.

[22] There is no provision in the *Bankruptcy & Insolvency Act*, RSC 1985, c. B-3 that gives a trustee power to disclaim contracts. The Act only addresses those powers that may be exercised with permission of inspectors. Thus, under s. 30(1)(k) of the *Bankruptcy & Insolvency Act* the trustee may disclaim a "lease of, or other temporary interest in, any property of the bankrupt."

[23] The power to disclaim contracts has been included in statutes in other common-law jurisdictions. Notably, s. 23 of the English *Bankruptcy Act, 1869* (32 & 33 Vict.), c. 71 first gave trustees the power to disclaim contracts of the bankrupt. The modern English statute, *Insolvency Act 1986* (UK), 1986, c. 45, s. 315 confers the same right upon a trustee. Similarly, in both Australia (*Bankruptcy Act 1966*, (Cth.), s. 133) and the United States (11 USC §365) there is a statutory power for trustees to disclaim contracts.

[24] However, the power of trustees to disclaim contracts has its roots in the English law where there was a common-law power in assignees (who took control of debtor property prior to use of trusteeships in bankruptcy) to disclaim contracts. There is a weight of authority supporting the existence of such a power prior to the enactment of the 1869 Act.

[25] In his 1922 text, Lewis Duncan, in *The Law and Practice of Bankruptcy in Canada* (Toronto: Carswell, 1922) at 304–5, cites several venerable English cases for the proposition that:

> There is no section in the Canadian *Act* corresponding with section 54 of the English *Act* [earlier s. 23] which gives the trustee the right to disclaim onerous contracts or property. The law under *The* [Canadian] *Bankruptcy Act* will be the same as the law in England before the Act of 1869 was passed, with the exception that section 44 of the *Bankruptcy Act* gives a right of proof against the estate of the debtor with respect to contracts entered into before the date of the receiving order or authorized assignment. The law under the *Bankruptcy Act* would seem to be that a trustee may at his option perform the contract into which the bankrupt has entered or he may abandon it.

[26] In *In re Sneezum ex parte Davis* (1876), 3 Ch. D 463 (CA) at 472, James LJ said that at common law, prior to the passing of the *1869 Act*, assignees in bankruptcy had the option of deciding whether or not to carry on with performance of an executory contract.

[27] To similar effect, in *Gibson v Carruthers* (1841), 8 M & W 321 at 326–27, a case in which the assignees wished to assume a contract under which the defendant, who had contracted with the bankrupt, had agreed to deliver 2000 quarters of linseed to a charter ship, Gurney B said:

> ... it is clear that assignees of a bankrupt are entitled to the benefit of all contracts entered into by the bankrupt and which are in fieri at the time of the bankruptcy. They may elect to adopt or reject such contracts, according as they are likely to be beneficial or onerous to the estate.

[28] In Canada, the Ontario Supreme Court Appellate Division in *Re Thomson Knitting Company*, [1925] 2 DLR 1007 (Ont. SC (AD)) recognized such a power; see also *Denison v Smith* (1878), 43 UCR 503 (QB); *Stead Lumber Co v Lewis* (1958), 37 CBR 24, 13 DLR (2d) 34 at 43 (Nfld. SC); *Re Salok Hotel Co* (1967), 11 CBR (NS) 95, 66 DLR (2d) 5 at 8 (Man. QB).

[29] In more recent times, L.W. Houlden & G.B. Morowetz in their text *Bankruptcy and Insolvency Law of Canada*, 3d ed, looseleaf (Toronto: Thomson Carswell, 2004) at F§45.2 state quite unequivocally that a trustee may disclaim a contract entered into by the bankrupt. Similarly, in a case comment on *Potato Distributors Inc v Eastern Trust Co* (1955), 35 CBR 161 at 166 (PEICA), L.W. Houlden writes:

> It is well established law that a trustee may elect to carry on with a contract entered into prior to bankruptcy, provided he pays up arrears and is ready to perform the contract. The trustee could also, if he saw fit, elect not to go on with the contract in which event the vendor would have the right to prove a claim for damages.

[30] I observe that several Canadian commentators have recently opined that in the absence of an express statutory power, trustees in Canada may not disclaim executory contracts, specifically licences: see Piero Ianuzzi, "Bankruptcy and the Trustee's Power to Disclaim Intellectual Property and Technology Licencing Agreements: Preventing the Chilling Effect of Licensor Bankruptcy in Canada" (2001) 18 CIPR 367; Gabor F.S. Takach and Ellen Hayes, "Case Comment," *Re Erin Features #1 Ltd* (1993) 15 CBR (3d) 66 (BCSC).; Mario J. Forte and Amanda C. Chester, "Licences and the Effects of Bankruptcy and Insolvency Law on the Licensee" (2001) 13 Comm. Insol. R 25. However, the position taken by the authors of these articles departs from the traditional understanding of the law in this area.

[31] In view of the position in the English authorities pre-dating the English Act of 1869, there is a common-law power in trustees to disclaim executory contracts. This power has been relied on for many years by trustees, and in the absence of a clear statutory provision overriding the common law, in my view trustees should have this power to assist them fulfill the duties of their office.

[32] I observe that recently, in its 2002 *Report on the Operation of the Administration of the Bankruptcy and Insolvency Act and the Companies' Creditors Arrangements Act,* Industry Canada's Marketplace Framework Policy Branch considered the extent to which insolvency law should intervene in private contracts to ensure fair distribution or maximize value during an insolvency. The Report notes there is not universal support for the enactment of a detailed statutory provision like the American one. In a 2001 report on business insolvency law reform, the Insolvency Institute of Canada and the Canadian Association of Insolvency & Restructuring Professionals proposed the enactment of more detailed rules for both powers of trustees to disclaim executory contracts .... Ultimately, it may therefore be preferable for the legislature to move to include a power in the statute, but until that time, in my view, trustees enjoy the power protected by the common law.

Re Thomson Knitting Co, (1924), 5 CBR 189 (Ont SC), aff'd (1925), 5 CBR 489 (Ont CA)

FISHER J: The debtor company was incorporated under *The Ontario Companies Act,* RSO, 1914, ch. 178, and carried on business at Bowmanville as wholesale and retail manufacturers of hosiery and designers and dealers in textile products.

Bever & Wolf carried on business in Bradford, England.

In October, 1922, the debtor company ordered from the creditors 5,000 pounds of artificial silk wool, of which 3,240 pounds were delivered. On December 29, 1922, the debtor company ordered 10,000 pounds and only 307 pounds were delivered. On January 5, 1923, the debtor company ordered 10,000 pounds; no delivery was made under this order. On January 13, 1923, the debtor company ordered 2,500 pounds and only 379 pounds were delivered. The wool was to be delivered in instalments.

Exhibits (1) (2) (3) (4) (5) and (6) show the contracts entered into and the correspondence in connection therewith.

Slater & Company were the Toronto agents of the creditors, and it was through these agents that all the orders were obtained.

On September 23, 1923, the debtor company made an authorized assignment and the creditors filed with the trustee the usual declaration proving their claim. The trustee admitted the claim, excepting as to any amount the creditors were claiming damages for, because of the insolvent company's failure to take delivery of the goods as ordered.

The facts and terms of the contracts are not in dispute. The goods were to be paid for, net 60 days from date of invoice.

One of the conditions in all the contracts reads:

> If any payment is in arrear, either under this or any other contract, deliveries may be suspended or contract cancelled at our option.

The purchasers confirmed all the contracts in these words:

> To Bever & Wolf: We have received your contract dated ... and we hereby accept and confirm.
>
> Yours Truly,
>
> (Sgd.) Thomson Knitting Co. Ltd.

The creditors now claim £675-16-5, as damages by reason of the insolvent company's failure to take delivery.

Counsel for both parties agreed that if it was found the creditors were entitled to any damages for breach of contract, they would agree on the *quantum* of damages.

Slater was the only witness called on behalf of the creditors, and he swore that the only reason deliveries were not made was because the insolvent company was unable to make payments for the goods already sold and delivered and for the goods they subsequently requisitioned under their contracts. All the correspondence, excepting that referred to in Exs. (1) (2) (3) (4) (5) and (6), was put in as Ex. (7).

From the correspondence it appears the purchasers were endeavouring, through Slater & Company, to obtain deliveries, and Slater communicated with the vendors. The correspondence indicates the purchasers were always hard-pressed for money. Slater & Company at one time were satisfied the company was in a position to pay and so communicated to the vendors. Slater & Company went even so far as to become personally responsible for a portion of some of the deliveries. They also obtained the personal guarantee of the directors of the debtor company and forwarded it to the vendors; Slater & Company agreeing to be personally responsible, and the guarantee, relieved the situation somewhat, but the vendors were not satisfied with the guarantee and so stated in the correspondence, because there was too much money owing.

It is only necessary to refer to a few of the letters to show the readiness on the part of the vendors to deliver and the desire on the part of the purchasers to obtain delivery and the inability on their part to pay. ....

The learned counsel for the trustee does not attack the contracts but contends that as the contracts called for delivery at certain stated periods, if there is any liability, it is at the time a delivery was to be made; that failure by the purchasers to pay does not relieve the vendors from the necessity of delivering, and that, whilst the vendors, on failure to pay, could have cancelled the contracts, not having done so there can now be no claim for damages; that the vendors cannot say "we will refuse delivery" and then claim damages for failure to pay; that the vendors having elected to retain the goods cannot now come into competition, on a claim for damages, with those creditors who had sold and delivered goods to the purchaser and were unpaid when they became insolvent, and that in any event, even if there was a failure to pay, it was the duty of the vendors, if they wished to hold the purchasers liable in damages for breach of contract, to have tendered the goods.

The learned counsel for the vendors contends that as they had not cancelled the contracts, and as they had kept in stock goods for the purpose of fulfilling the contracts when the purchasers called for deliveries, they are entitled to damages for breach of the contracts as of the date of its cancellation.

The questions for determination are: Are these creditors entitled to any damages; and if so, at what time is the damage to be ascertained?

The trustee's contention that the vendors' refusal to make deliveries operated as a rescission of the contracts is not borne out by the facts, as the correspondence clearly indicates there never was any intimation by the purchasers they would and could not pay, but on the contrary the purchasers were repeatedly calling for deliveries, making occasional payments and promising to pay, and as I have stated there was always readiness on the part of the vendors to deliver if payments were made. All the circumstances point to an intention on the part of both vendors and purchasers to have the contract continued. There was only a suspension of deliveries, and I hold the contract was not cancelled, and on these findings *Morgan v Bain* (1874), LR 10 CP 15, 44 LJCP 47, 31 LT 616, 23 WR 239, relied on by counsel for the trustee, has no application.

A vendor is entitled to consider his contract cancelled on the insolvency of the purchaser if the trustee within a reasonable time after his appointment fails to notify the vendor he intends to adopt the contract, and a reasonable time, in my opinion, would be after the first meeting of creditors, as there is no one, until that meeting is called, authorized to act for the debtor. If a trustee remains silent a vendor is entitled to assume the contract is at an end.

The trustee in this case did not notify the vendors he intended to carry out the contract, and I therefore hold, if the vendors can prove any damages, they will be measured as of the date of the first meeting of creditors.

The law is well settled that a contract for the purchase of goods is not cancelled merely on account of the purchaser becoming bankrupt; see *Boorman v Nash* (1829), 9 B & C 145, 7 LJKB 150; *Griffiths v Perry* (1859) 1 E & E 680, 28 LJQB 204, 5 Jur. (NS) 1076. It seems to me the terms of the contracts must govern. The vendors expressly provided, if payments were in arrear for two separate and distinct contingencies, namely, at their option (1) suspension of deliveries and (2) cancellation of their contracts. They could adopt either. The purchasers made their first default under the contracts on or about January 14, 1924, and according to the correspondence, at the solicitation of the purchasers, several deliveries were subsequently made and payments on account received from time to time. The vendors did not know the purchasers were going into insolvency, and they had a right to believe they might be able to pay for the goods purchased, and in order that they could make deliveries instead of cancelling the contracts kept them alive. The purchasers at any time up to the insolvency, if they could have provided for payment of the money, the contracts not having been cancelled, could have compelled the vendors to deliver all the goods covered by the contracts. But the evidence in this case is that the purchasers did not want the contracts cancelled, on the contrary they wanted them continued.

This is not a case where there was only one default by the purchasers (they were always in default) but rather that of a case where the sellers were ready and willing to deliver and were anxious for the buyers to take delivery. There was no object in the vendors tendering the goods, as default had already been made, and the correspondence shows the purchasers could not pay. In such circumstances the vendors were not bound to tender deliveries. See *Ex parte Chalmers; In re Edwards* (1873), LR 8 Ch. 289, 42 LJ Bk. 37, 28 LT 325, 21 WR 349, and at p. 291, Mellish LJ, said:

> The first question that arises is, what are the rights of the seller of goods when the purchaser becomes insolvent before the contract for sale has been completely performed.
> I am of opinion that the result of the authorities is this—that in such a case the seller,

> notwithstanding he may have agreed to allow credit for the goods, is not bound to deliver any more goods under the contract until the price of the goods not yet delivered is tendered to him; and that, if a debt is due to him for goods already delivered, he is entitled to refuse to deliver any more till he is paid the debt due for those already delivered as well as the price of those still to be delivered.

And at p. 293:

> I am, therefore, of opinion that, in the present case, when the insolvency of the purchaser had been declared the vendor was not bound to deliver any more goods until the price of the goods delivered in November, as well as those which were to be delivered in December, had been tendered to him.

... There must be a finding that these contracts were outstanding and uncancelled at the date of the debtor company's bankruptcy; and, as the trustee refused to take them over and accept delivery of the goods, there will be judgment in favor of the creditors, and the damages, if any, will be measured as of the date of the first meeting of creditors.

Judgment for creditors.

Creditel of Canada Ltd v Terrace Corp, 1983 ABCA 258, 50 CBR (NS) 87

BELZIL JA: The appellants appeal a judgment against them for $11,991 and costs.

The plaintiff's action in its final form as amended at trial alleged a debt owing by the appellant to Formex Ltd. The debt is alleged to have been assigned by Formex Ltd. to Formex Location Rental Inc., and by the latter to the present respondent, Creditel of Canada Ltd., on October 1, 1980. The assignment from Formex Location to Creditel filed as an exhibit at trial was an assignment of an account or debt receivable. Notwithstanding that the action was pleaded in debt, the judgment awarded was for damages for breach of contract, without amendment of the pleading to fit the evidence. This discrepancy between the award of damages and the pleading in debt was raised before us but apparently not before the trial judge. ...

The assignment from Formex Ltd. to Location Formex Rental Inc. was not filed as an exhibit. It appears from the evidence of Norbert Dubois, an officer of both corporations, that Location Formex Rental Inc. was entirely owned by Formex Ltd., that Formex Ltd. went into bankruptcy on February 23, 1978, and that Formex Location Rental Inc. bought all the assets of Formex Ltd. on September 19, 1979, presumably from a trustee in bankruptcy, although that is not indicated in evidence.

The debt sued for is alleged to be due under an agreement for the fabrication and sale by Formex Ltd. to the appellants of three metal forms for the moulding of pre-cast concrete construction panels for a building being undertaken by the appellants in Edmonton. The trial judge found, correctly on the evidence, that there was one contract for the three forms. That contract is evidenced by quotation from Formex Ltd. submitted to and accepted by the appellants for fabrication of the units as per the appellants' design.

The first two units required modification of the design at extra cost. Responsibility for the additional cost was settled amicably by the parties and the two first units so modified were delivered and likewise specified by the appellants, over and above the modifications made to the first two units. Formex Ltd. sent a quotation to the appellants covering those extra modifications and requested approval of the extra costs by issuance of a supplementary purchase order. The appellants did not formally respond to this request, although it is indicated in evidence that there were telephone consultations between the parties. On February 13, 1978, Formex Ltd. sent a telegram to the appellants reaffirming its quotation for the modified third unit and again requesting a purchase order to cover. On February 27, 1978, Formex Ltd. sent a follow-up telegram to the appellants advising that work on the unit was being delayed pending advice from the appellants. The appellants did not respond because in the meantime they had received information from an employee of Formex Ltd. that Formex Ltd. was in bankruptcy. The trial judge found that the action of Formex Ltd. in delaying completion of the work on the third unit did not amount to a breach disentitling it to payment for work already done on the unit. He attributed fault to the appellants for having failed to supply a purchase order as requested. He awarded judgment to the value of the work done by Formex Ltd. on the third unit.

While the learned trial judge did not specifically qualify the award as one in damages, it obviously must have been so intended. It could not be for the contract debt since the contract remained uncompleted. It could only succeed in damages or *quantum meruit* and then only if the appellants had repudiated the contract by failing to furnish a new purchase order in acceptance of the quotation of Formex Ltd.

The learned trial judge did not take into account the effect on the contract of the bankruptcy of Formex Ltd. That effect is stated concisely as follows in *Re Thomson Knitting Co Ltd*, 56 OLR 625 at 631:

> While the bankruptcy did not of itself constitute a breach of the contract, it did not on the other hand cast any further burden upon the vendors. But it had this effect: it entitled the vendors to treat the contract as broken if the trustee did not, within a reasonable time, approbate the contract and call for its completion.

In *Emden and Watson's Building Contracts and Practice*, 6th Edition, the proposition is stated as follows at p. 220:

> *Rights which Pass to Trustee*—Ordinarily the benefits and rights under contracts which would pass as part of the bankrupt's personal estate to his personal representatives if he had died, pass to the trustee as part of the bankrupt's property, subject to the trustee's right to disclaim unprofitable contracts ...

> *Election to Perform or Disclaim*—As regards those contracts which the trustee can perform, he has an election and may disclaim them, in which cases the persons who have contracted with the bankrupt may prove in the bankruptcy for damages to the value of any injury sustained by them, or the trustee may insist on the contract being performed, and in such case must perform the bankrupt's part of the contract, as and when the bankrupt should have done so himself.

There is no evidence to show that an election to perform was ever made by the trustee in bankruptcy, and certainly no evidence that such an election was ever communicated to the appellants. The issue was never addressed at trial. In these circumstances, the appellants could not be found in breach of the contract for their failure to issue a purchase order to the bankrupt vendor after learning of the bankruptcy. No case was made out by the plaintiff to support an award either in damages or in debt.

Appeal allowed.

* * * * *

D. Technology Licences

The most common approach to the distribution of software technology is for the owner of the technology to copyright the software and license its use to others. A licence agreement is a form of permission by the licensor (A) for the licensee (B) to use some property belonging to A for a specified purpose: *Re T Eaton Co* (1999), 14 CBR (4th) 288 at para 12 (Ont Sup Ct J), Farley J. The licence may be exclusive or non-exclusive. A software licence agreement is a promise by A to B that A will not enforce its copyright in the software for the duration of the licence. The consideration is usually in the form of royalties payable by B to A while the agreement continues. The agreement may be a software-distribution licence agreement or a software end-use licence agreement. In the case of a software-distribution licence agreement, B will need the rights to: (1) copy the software, and (2) distribute copies to the public by way of sale, lease, and so on. The agreement gives B these rights. In the case of an end-use licence agreement, B will need the right to use the software free of legal restrictions that might otherwise apply. The agreement gives B this right: see J Dianne Brinson, "Software Distribution Agreements and Bankruptcy: The Licensor's Perspective" (1989) 64 *Washington Law Review* 497 at 501–10.

The business uses of software have increased dramatically in recent times. Online businesses depend almost entirely on software, but software is important for brick-and-mortar enterprises as well. Many business organizations rely on software to carry out key operations, such as the processing of customer orders, payrolls, and warehouse movements: see Michael Geist, "When Dot-coms Die: The E-commerce Challenge to Canada's Bankruptcy Law" (2002) 37 *Canadian Business Law Journal* 34. In these cases, A (the software producer or distributor) contracts with B (the end user) to develop and supply the software. A will often also contract to supply B with support services such as training, maintenance, update facilities, and the like. The contract is likely to be in the form of a licence giving B end-user rights to the software together with associated benefits. If A (the licensor) becomes bankrupt, A's trustee may want to terminate the agreement because: (1) they do not want to have to provide the support services; or (2) they want to resell the licence rights or the underlying intellectual property to a third party. Loss of the right to use the software may devastate B's business. The risk of this outcome may discourage B from contracting with A in the first place. In other words, it may inhibit the development and supply of software systems and limit the commercial uses to which software systems are put.

In *Lubrizol Enterprises v Richmond Metal Finishers Inc*, 756 F 2d 1043 (4th Cir 1985), the court held that a technology licence was an executory contract to which §365 of the US *Bankruptcy Code* applied. This meant that A's trustee was entitled to reject (disclaim) the contract subject to the court's approval. The court approved the trustee's election. The effect of the rejection was to cancel the licence. A software licence is probably also an executory contact to which Code §365 applies. The decision had a potentially chilling effect on the development and exploitation of intellectual property. In 1988, Congress enacted §365(n) to reverse the outcome. Code §365(n) gives B two options: (1) to treat the contract as terminated if A's rejection would constitute a breach outside bankruptcy; or (2) to retain its rights under the agreement, including the right to enforce any exclusivity provision, subject to a continued obligation to make the royalty payments. If B chooses option (1), they have a claim against A's estate for any loss caused by the rejection. If B chooses option (2), they can continue to use the technology for the duration of the term, but they have no right to compel specific performance of other aspects of the agreement (for example, A's obligation to provide training or maintenance, or update facilities). In other words, §365(n) allows B to enforce A's negative obligations under the agreement, but not the positive obligations. In this respect, the provision attempts to strike a balance between B's individual interest in having the agreement enforced and the collective interests of A's creditors in having it set aside.

In Canada, *BIA*, section 65.11, which was enacted as part of the 2009 amendments, provides for the disclaimer of contracts in *BIA* commercial proposal proceedings, and *CCAA*, section 32(6), is a parallel provision applicable in *CCAA* proceedings. Both provisions make a specific exception for intellectual property licences as follows:

> [I]f the debtor has granted a right to use intellectual property to a party to an agreement, the disclaimer or resiliation does not affect the party's right to use the intellectual property—including the party's right to enforce an exclusive use—during the term of the agreement, including any period for which the party extends the agreement as of right, as long as the party continues to perform its obligations under the agreement in relation to the use of the intellectual property.

In 2018, Parliament added further protection for intellectual property licences in *BIA* and *CCAA* proceedings as part of the Government of Canada's new national intellectual property strategy. These amendments have received Royal Asset and will come into force on dates to be set by Order in Council [*Budget Implementation Act*, SC 2018 c 27, ss 265–72 (not yet in force)]. In the context of commercial proposals, the amendments add a new subsection (9) to section 65.13, which provides that the rights of intellectual property licencees are maintained notwithstanding the trustee's sale or disposition of the debtor's property under section 65.13(7). "Sale or disposition" of the debtor's property appears to encompass the assignment of the agreement. In order to maintain their rights, intellectual property licencees must continue to perform their obligations under the licencing agreement in relation to the intellectual property.

The amendments also add a new section, 72.1, to the *BIA*, which applies to intellectual property licences in bankruptcies. This new section essentially extends the same protections provided in the context of *BIA* proposals to intellectual property licencees in bankruptcies. Subsection 72.1(1) provides that the rights of intellectual property licencees are maintained notwithstanding the trustee's sale of the debtor's property. Subsection 72.1(2) provides that disclaimer or resiliation of an agreement by the trustee does not affect the licencee's right to use intellectual property provided that the licencee continues to perform its obligations under the agreement in relation to the intellectual property. Further amendments extend the same protections in the context of *BIA* receiverships and *CCAA* proceedings.

These provisions loosely corresponds with § 365(n) of the *Bankruptcy Code*, 11 USC, in the United States. When they come into force, the new provisions will restrain breach by the licensor of a negative covenant in a licensing agreement. (The negative covenant is A's express or implied promise not to assert its ownership rights against B for the duration of the agreement.) This will bring insolvency law in line with earlier suggestions that insolvent licensors should not be able to refuse to honour the licence: see Wendy A Adams and Gabor GS Takach, "Insecure Transactions: Deficiencies in the Treatment of Technology Licences in Commercial Transactions Involving Secured Debt or Bankruptcy" (2000), 33 *Canadian Business Law Journal* 321 at 356–61; Duggan, "Partly Performed Contracts," above, at 26–27.

On the other hand, prior to the 2018 amendments coming into force, the trustee remains free to assign the technology to which the licence relates and, in the absence of agreement, the assignee may not be bound by the licence: *Royal Bank of Canada v Body Blue Inc* (2008), 42 CBR (5th) 125 (Ont Sup Ct J) (*Body Blue*). In *Body Blue*, the debtor, Body Blue, held the intellectual property rights to certain technology. The debtor granted Herbal Care an exclusive licence to use the technology in the manufacture and sale of products. The debtor later went into receivership and the receiver sold certain assets, including the technology, to a third-party purchaser. The sale was effected by court order (the Approval and Vesting Order), dated 17 May 2006. Herbal Care claimed that the licence was unaffected by the Approval and Vesting Order. Justice Morawetz disagreed, holding that, under the terms of the Approval and Vesting Order, the purchaser acquired the technology free and clear of any claim by Herbal Care. The main ground of the decision was that, although Herbal Care was aware of the vesting order, it took no steps to appeal during the time allowed. However, the case could be read as suggesting that a licence is not property in the sense of an entitlement that runs with the underlying asset and thus, even if Herbal Care had appealed the vesting order in time, it still might not have been successful. The Supreme Court's decision in *Saulnier v Royal Bank of Canada*, 2008 SCC 58 lends some support to this suggestion (note Binnie J's repeated statements that a licence is not property at common law). The reasoning in *Body Blue* would presumably have been the same if the debtor had gone into bankruptcy and the trustee had sold the assets in question.

The principles applied by the court in *Body Blue* were confirmed and elaborated on by the Saskatchewan Court of Queen's Bench in 2016. In *Golden Opportunities Fund Inc v Phenomenome Discoveries Inc*, 2016 SKQB 306, the Receiver purported to sell the debtor company's assets to another company, Med-Life. Med-Life did not seek an assignment of a licensing agreement to which the debtor company was the licensee. The Receiver sought an order approving its activities and the licensor objected, asserting that it had a proprietary interest in the assets in question and that the order approving the Receiver's activities would extinguish the licensor's proprietary rights. The court found that the licensor's interest was contractual — not proprietary — and that the Receiver of the debtor company was entitled to sell the assets of the debtor free and clear of any claim of the licensor. While the licensor could not stop the sale of the debtor's assets that would effectively extinguish its interest, the licensor could pursue a claim for damages against the proceeds of the sale of the debtor's assets. It is interesting to note that counsel for the licensor argued that the principles from *Body Blue* were no longer good law due to the 2009 amendments to section 65.11(7) of the *BIA*, which counsel argued now prohibited a receiver from disclaiming an agreement pertaining to intellectual property. The court noted that that section 65.11(7) has no bearing on court-appointed receiverships and that this particular section relates to proposals in bankruptcy. While the court confirmed that the principles from *Body Blue* continue to apply in the context of court-appointed receiverships, the court left the door open as to whether the principles would not apply in the context of bankruptcy and *CCAA* proceedings. The coming into force of the 2018 amendments will clarify and simplify the treatment of intellectual property licences in *BIA* and *CCAA* proceedings.

There are strong policy reasons for preventing an intellectual property licensor from disclaiming the licence. As indicated above, loss of the licence may have a devastating effect on the licensee's business to the extent of possibly triggering the licensee's own insolvency. A related concern is that permitting disclaimer of the licence in insolvency proceedings increases the up-front risk to licensees and it may have a chilling effect on the licensing of intellectual property across the board. These are the main considerations underlying § 365(n) of the US *Bankruptcy Code* and amendments made to the *BIA* and *CCAA*.

The foregoing discussion addresses the status of the licence in the *licensor's* bankruptcy. Assume A grants B a patent licence and B becomes bankrupt while the licence is still current. Can B's trustee disclaim the licence?

Armadale Properties Ltd v 700 King St (1997) Ltd, (2001), 25 CBR (4th) 198 (Ont Sup Ct J) [*Armadale*]

LAX J: This motion is brought by Deloitte & Touche Inc. in its capacity as Construction Lien Trustee and in its capacity as Trustee in Bankruptcy. It raises the issue whether the Trustee should perform an agreement for the purchase and sale of land where the estate will receive no benefit from the transaction. The facts are unique.

700 King Street (1997) Ltd. was incorporated to convert 700 King Street West to mixed residential and commercial condominium use. Richard Crenian was its sole officer and director. He was also president and a 50% owner of Peregrine Hunter, a real estate developer and the project manager for 700 King. Armadale Properties Limited was a principal investor and 50% owner of the King Street project.

On February 9, 2001, Armadale obtained an order appointing Deloitte & Touche Inc. as Trustee and Receiver and Manager of 700 King and of 140085 Ontario Limited, a company which held title to the remaining real property assets of 700 King. On February 19, 2001, 700 King was assigned into bankruptcy and Deloitte & Touche Inc. was also appointed Trustee in Bankruptcy.

Yotam Goldschlager was directly or indirectly a purchaser of three residential units and one commercial unit at 700 King. The residential units were purchased for members of his family. The commercial unit, Unit 8, was purchased for his business. With respect to each of these purchases, Goldschlager dealt exclusively with Crenian, who had apparent and actual authority to enter into the agreements of purchase and sale on behalf of 700 King. This motion concerns the purchase of Unit 8.

On March 20, 1999, Goldschlager, through a numbered company as purchaser, entered into an Agreement of Purchase and Sale with Peregrine Homes Ltd. and 700 King as vendors. The purchase price provided in the Agreement of Purchase and Sale was $185,000 and by Amending Agreement dated January 5, 2000 was increased to $206,082. The uncontradicted evidence of Goldschlager is that initially, he was only prepared to pay $185,000 for Unit 8 and Crenian was only willing to sell it to him at that price if he paid a deposit of $100,000. Goldschlager agreed to this. Goldschlager's company provided cheques for $100,000 in May 1999, $22,557.74 in June 2000 (in accordance with the Amending Agreement) and $85,000 (the balance of the purchase price) in December 2000, with the result that the entire purchase price was paid by way of deposit. At the request of Crenian, the cheques were made payable to Peregrine Homes Ltd. In July 2000, Goldschlager moved his business from its former premises to Unit 8 and spent about $80,000 in improvements and moving costs.

The residential units closed on January 5, 2001. The transfer date for Unit 8 was scheduled for January 15, 2001 and postponed to February 7, 2001, but did not take place. The Receivership and Bankruptcy followed shortly after.

After its appointment, the Trustee proceeded to close sales of the residential and commercial units that had been sold. When it reviewed the files for Unit 8, it became apparent that all of the purchase monies for this unit had been paid by way of deposit to Peregrine Homes Limited, which was a personal company of Crenian, and had never been received by 700 King. There are no further funds to be delivered to the Construction Lien Trustee or to the Trustee in Bankruptcy upon the closing of the transaction. There is therefore no benefit to the creditors of the bankrupt in completing the transaction. The Trustee now applies for the advice and direction of the court.

The Trustee advances two arguments. First, it submits that the manner of payment is an essential term of a contract and that payment to one of two joint vendors in the absence of a written direction relieves the other contracting party from performing. Second, it submits that as the Trustee and the court must protect the assets of the estate for the benefit of the creditors, where the estate will receive no benefit, the court should direct the Trustee to disclaim the contract. In any event, as Trustee in Bankruptcy, it can only convey the bankrupt's interest, which is subject to mortgage and lien claims. Goldschlager would not accept this title. Although its powers as Construction Lien Trustee permit it to convey clear title, it questions whether it would be appropriate for the Trustee to use its lien powers in this way.

In my opinion, these arguments are both answered in the circumstances of this case and the Trustee should be directed to use its lien powers to convey clear title to Gold-schlager in accordance with the Agreement of Purchase and Sale and consistent with the Statement of Adjustments that was prepared in anticipation of the scheduled closing.

As to the Trustee's first argument, I was provided with no case that stands for this proposition, but assuming this is sound law, it cannot apply in this case. The Trustee concedes that Crenian had actual authority to enter into the Agreement of Purchase and Sale and to direct the manner in which the funds were to be paid. This is precisely what occurred. Crenian determined that the funds should be paid to Peregrine Homes Ltd. and Goldschlager complied with this direction. It makes no difference that there is no written direction for payment. Crenian did not pay the funds to 700 King, but this cannot affect the performance obligations of 700 King under the contract.

As to the second argument, the circumstances under which a trustee can disclaim a contract entered into by a bankrupt prior to its bankruptcy have long been the subject of uncertainty: *Re Triangle Lumber and Supply Co Ltd* (1978), 21 OR (2d) 221; *Re Erin Features 91 Ltd* (1991), 8 CBR (3d) 205 (BCSC). Assuming a trustee has this right, section 75 of the *Bankruptcy and Insolvency Act*, RSC 1985, c. B-3 prevents the Trustee from disclaiming this contract. As was noted by Saunders J in *Re Triangle, supra*:

> A reading of s. 53 [now s 75] would appear to dispose of the problem. An agreement for sale in favour of a bona fide purchaser or mortgagee for valuable consideration is valid and effectual as if no receiving order had been made. It would therefore appear that the Trustee is bound by the agreement and may not disclaim it.

In the event that I am wrong and section 75 does not apply, I would not allow the Trustee to disclaim this contract. It is clear that a trustee can only succeed to the rights of a bankrupt and has no higher or greater interest. A trustee cannot terminate property rights that have passed under the contract prior to the bankruptcy: *Re Triangle, supra; Re Erin Features 91, supra.* The equitable interest under this contract passed prior to the bankruptcy and Goldschlager could have enforced the transfer of title by way of specific performance. In my opinion, the property was validly conveyed and all that remained was the delivery of a deed.

I was referred to the decision in *Re Bakermaster Foods Limited* (1985), 56 CBR (NS) 314 as contrary authority. In that case, if the Trustee had closed the transaction, there would have been a substantial deficit, which could only be made up from the funds in the estate to the prejudice of the unsecured creditors. The Trustee was directed not to close the transaction. In my view, these were exceptional circumstances, which have no application here.

The Trustee submitted that Goldschlager was the author of his own misfortune in providing the entire purchase monies as deposit and it is therefore he and not the credit-ors of 700 King who should bear this loss. In my view, if there is culpability, it does not rest with Goldschlager. He had no relationship with Crenian except as a purchaser of real estate. He has offered an explanation for providing the deposit he did. Although Peregrine Homes Ltd. had no beneficial interest in Unit 8, it was the bankrupt that gave Crenian apparent authority to act as he did. Prior to the bankruptcy, 700 King could not assert as against Goldschlager that Crenian lacked the authority to direct payment of the funds to Peregrine Homes Ltd. As the Trustee stands in the shoes of the bankrupt, it cannot now complain of the very loss to the estate that the bankrupt brought about.

Finally, the Trustee is an officer of the court and must act fairly to all parties with an interest in the estate. It would be dishonourable for the Trustee to disclaim this contract. I therefore find that the Trustee is bound by the contract in the same manner and to the same extent as the bankrupt was at the time of the bankruptcy and has no power to disclaim the contract. The Trustee is directed to complete the transaction in its capacity as Construction Lien Trustee. It may discharge the caution registered on title by 1333203 Ontario Limited. The Trustee and the numbered company should have their costs out of the estate. I fix the costs of the numbered company at $2500.

Order accordingly.

Discussion

Note that the trustee in *Armadale* wanted to disclaim the contract because Goldschlager had already paid the whole of the purchase price. Therefore, there was no benefit to the creditors in completing the contract. By disclaiming the contract, the trustee was attempting to keep both the unit and Goldschlager's money, leaving Goldschlager in return with only a right to prove in the bankruptcy for the amount of his payment.

Think about whether you agree with Lax J's decision in *Armadale*. There are two competing principles involved, and the judge's decision represents a trade off between these two principles. The first principle is that the trustee in bankruptcy gets no larger property rights than the debtor had. The second principle is that unsecured creditors are entitled to share pro rata in the bankruptcy distribution. The first principle suggests that, in a case like *Armadale*, the purchaser should still be allowed to sue for specific performance even though the vendor is bankrupt. The second principle suggests that the purchaser should not have a right of specific performance in bankruptcy, because that gives them an advantage over the other unsecured creditors: in effect, their claim is satisfied in full, leaving less in the estate for everyone else.

Justice Lax's decision in *Armadale* is consistent with the first principle, but inconsistent with the second one. Section 365(i) of the US *Bankruptcy Code* allows a purchaser of real estate to sue for specific performance, but only if they have gone into possession of the land. If they have not gone into possession, the Code reduces their claim to damages and they rank for payment equally with the other unsecured creditors. One reason for the different rules is that a purchaser in possession is likely to have spent money on the property (for improvements, and so on), and the specific performance remedy protects their reliance interest.

In a situation in which the lessor (rather than the tenant) becomes bankrupt, *Armadale* suggests that the bankruptcy trustee cannot disclaim the lease. Just as in the case of a bankrupt tenant, the trustee in bankruptcy for a bankrupt lessor may wish to disclaim the lease in order to maximize the value of the bankrupt estate. For instance, it is possible that by disclaiming the lease the lessor can let the property to someone else at a higher price. Or the lessor may be able to sell the property at a higher price if it is untenanted. The court's decision in *Armadale* indicates that the trustee's right of disclaimer in the case of the lessor's bankruptcy cannot override established property rights. The US *Bankruptcy Code* also disallows rejection in a case like this. On the other hand, it does allow rejection of a lessor and tenant agreement if the debtor is the tenant. Likewise, Canada, *BIA*, section 65.11 (disclaimer in commercial proposals) and *CCAA*, section 32 (disclaimer in *CCAA* proceedings) specifically exclude "a lease of real property ... if the debtor is the lessor."

There are at least two reasons for allowing rejection (disclaimer) when the debtor is the tenant, but not when it is the lessor. First, outside bankruptcy, the debtor could not dispossess a tenant so long as the tenant paid the rent and observed the other terms of the lease. The trustee's rights against the tenant should be no larger than the debtor's rights outside bankruptcy because, otherwise, the debtor's creditors will have an incentive to use the bankruptcy laws opportunistically as a means of avoiding the lease. The second reason is that the tenant is likely to have spent money either on the property itself or otherwise in reliance on the lease and disallowing disclaimer protects the tenant's reliance interest. Failure to protect the tenant's reliance interest would increase the upfront risk to prospective tenants and presumably lower both the demand for rental properties and the rent tenants are willing to pay. Furthermore, dispossession might trigger the tenant's own financial crisis, putting in train a whole new set of bankruptcy proceedings, and this would be too high a price to pay for facilitating the debtor's own proceedings.

III. AFFIRMATION

A. Introduction

Affirmation is the other side of the coin from disclaimer. Disclaimer is Trustee's decision not to proceed with performance of a contract debtor negotiated before becoming bankrupt. Affirmation is Trustee's decision to adopt the contract. As *Re Thomson Knitting Co* indicates, disclaimer does not require a positive election on Trustee's part; the default rule, subject to any statutory provision to the contrary, is that if Trustee fails to make an election they will be deemed to have disclaimed the contract. On the other hand, affirmation does require a positive choice. The reason is that Debtor and Trustee are separate persons and Trustee does not automatically become party to Debtor's pre-bankruptcy contracts. Assume Trustee affirms a contract, but subsequently fails to perform, so that Counterparty has a claim for damages. Counterparty's claim lies against the estate and is payable, as an administrative expense, in priority to the unsecured creditors: *BIA*, sections 31(4) and 32 and *Re North American Steamships Ltd*, 2007 BCSC 267, extracted below. This priority can be rationalized as a form of *quid pro quo* to Counterparty for forcing it to accept performance from Trustee.

B. Lessor and Tenant Agreements

Provincial lessor and tenant statutes give the trustee of a bankrupt tenant the right to affirm a commercial tenancy agreement. In Ontario, the governing provision is *Commercial Tenancies Act*, section 38(2), extracted above, which provides that, despite any provision in the lease agreement to the contrary, the trustee may, within three months after the debtor goes into bankruptcy and by notice in writing to the lessor, elect to retain the leased premises. The trustee must pay rent as provided for in the lease and these payments come out of the estate.

In *Re Limestone Electrical & Supply Co Ltd*, [1955] OR 291(CA), Laidlaw JA described the operation of the affirmation part of the provision as follows:

The procedure and requisites for the acquisition and exercise of the rights created by the subsection, and as prescribed therein, are these:

1. The right to retain the leased premises for the period of three months described above does not depend upon any condition or stipulation, but is unqualified and unconditional.
2. In order to acquire the right to retain the leased premises for any period after the expiration of the three months described above, it is essential to comply with the following statutory requirements:
    (a) that the assignee, liquidator or trustee elect by notice in writing to retain the leased premises for the whole or any portion of the unexpired term and any renewal thereof, upon the terms of the lease and subject to the payment of the rent as provided therein;
    (b) that such notice be given by the assignee, liquidator or trustee within the period of three months;
    (c) that the notice be given before the assignee, liquidator or trustee has given notice of intention to surrender possession or disclaim."

C. Other Contracts

There is no express provision for the affirmation of contracts other than lessor and tenant agreements. Instead, the trustee's rights depend on the general principles outlined in parts II(A) and III(A), above.

Professionally drafted agreements commonly provide that a party's bankruptcy or insolvency entitles the other party to cancel or amend the agreement, demand the return of goods (in the case of chattel leases or bailments), and claim damages that may be in a liquidated amount. Such provisions are known as *ipso facto* clauses. Prior to the 2009 amendments, the status of *ipso facto* clauses in bankruptcy was uncertain. The question turned partly on whether the counterparty's right of cancellation fell within the terms of the stay in *BIA*, section 69.3, and partly also on the fraud on the bankruptcy law principle, discussed below.

BIA, section 84.2, which was enacted as part of the 2009 amendments, provides in part that no person may terminate or amend a contract with a bankrupt individual by reason only of the individual's bankruptcy. This provision does not expressly give the trustee power to affirm contracts, but it assumes such a power because there would be no point in prohibiting *ipso facto* clauses unless the trustee, but for such a clause, had the option of keeping the contract on foot.

Section 84.2 only applies where the bankrupt debtor is an individual. The reform was enacted with the fresh start policy specifically in mind:

> [T]he intention of the reform is to ensure that agreements in good standing be respected by all parties. Therefore, the individual bankrupt, who is attempting to obtain his or her "fresh start", will not be unreasonably evicted from their home, denied basic and essential services or denied other benefits to which they would otherwise be entitled.[2]

The fresh start policy underlies the bankruptcy discharge. As a general rule, corporations are not entitled to a discharge, as seen in *BIA*, section 169(4), and this is why section 84.2 is limited to individuals. But there is another reason for prohibiting *ipso facto* clauses which

---

2   Innovation, Science and Economic Development Canada, Bill C-55 Clause-by-Clause Analysis (30 September 2011), online: https://www.ic.gc.ca/eic/site/cilp-pdci.nsf/eng/h_cl00790.html.

Industry Canada's explanation overlooks. Where the debtor is in business, the trustee may need to carry on the business for a time, typically so that it can be sold on a going concern basis. *BIA*, section 30(1)(c) specifically recognizes this need by providing that the trustee may carry on the business of the bankrupt "so far as may be necessary for the beneficial administration of the estate." However, to carry on the debtor's business, the trustee must have power to continue existing contracts, as well as entering into new ones and *ipso facto* clauses, if valid, may interfere with the trustee's functions. This consideration applies whether the debtor is an individual or a corporation and it suggests that the limitation of section 84.2 to individual bankruptcies may be misconceived. There are parallel provisions in *BIA*, section 65.1 (relating to *BIA* proposals), and *CCAA*, section 34 (relating to *CCAA* proceedings), and both these provisions apply where the debtor is a corporation. Nevertheless, as *BIA*, section 84.2, is presently drafted, it has no bearing on the status of *ipso facto* clauses in corporate bankruptcy proceedings and the pre-2009 law continues to govern.

However, the so-called fraud on the bankruptcy law principle may apply. The idea underlying the fraud on the bankruptcy law principle is that parties should not be allowed to use contractual provisions as a means of avoiding the bankruptcy laws. The fraud on the bankruptcy law principle has two applications: (1) to contractual provisions which have the effect of diverting assets from the bankruptcy estate; and (2) to contractual provisions which interfere with the statutory scheme of distribution among creditors. In England, the courts now treat these two applications as being the subject of different rules, known respectively as the anti-deprivation rule and the *pari passu* rule: see *Belmont Park Investments Pty Ltd v BNY Corporate Trustee Services Ltd*, [2011] UKSC 38 (*Belmont Park Investments*). Canadian courts have not yet taken this step, though they do recognize the two applications of the principle. The leading Canadian case on the principle's anti-deprivation application is *CIBC v Bramalea Inc* (1995), 33 OR (3d) 692 (Ont Ct J (Gen Div)) (*Bramalea*) where it was held that a contractual provision triggered only in the event of bankruptcy or insolvency that would deprive creditors of value otherwise available to them, and effectively divert the value to an unsecured creditor, is void. The majority in *Capital Steel Inc v Chandos Construction Ltd*, 2019 ABCA 32, leave to appeal allowd (*Capital Steel*), affirmed this view. *Aircell Communications Inc (Trustee of) v Bell Mobility Cellular Inc*, 2013 ONCA 95, suggests that the anti-deprivation component of the fraud on the bankruptcy law principle may, in appropriate circumstances, apply to *ipso facto* clauses and that it may be relevant in cases where *BIA*, section 84.2, does not apply.

In England, it has been held that the common law anti-deprivation rule requires proof of a deliberate intention to avoid the insolvency laws and that where the parties acted in good faith and the transaction serves a legitimate commercial purpose, the rule does not apply: see *Belmont Park Investments*. This is in contrast to the position in Canada, where the courts have held that proof of dishonesty or impropriety is not required: *Bramalea* at para 8; *Capital Steel* at para 52. *BIA*, section 84.2, likewise applies regardless of the parties' intentions. Other points of comparison between *BIA*, section 84.2, and the common law principle are as follows: (1) the common law principle applies only to contractual provisions which are triggered by a party's insolvency, whereas, in its application to leases and services provided by public utilities, *BIA*, section 84.2, also applies where the triggering event is the non-payment of rent or utility bills; (2) *BIA*, section 84.2, does not apply to derivatives contracts, see *Eligible Financial Contract General Rules (Bankruptcy and Insolvency Act)*, SOR/2007-256 s 2, whereas the common law principle is not so limited; and (3) a court may declare *BIA*, section 84.2, to be inapplicable if it would cause significant financial hardship to the contract counterparty, but the common law principle cannot be displaced in this way. For a fuller account, see Roderick J Wood, "Direct

Payment Clauses and the Fraud Upon the Bankruptcy Law Principle: *Greenview (Municipal District No. 16) v. Bank of Nova Scotia*" (2014) 51 *Alberta Law Review* 171. See Chapter 9, Part I, below, for discussion of the *pari passu* component of the fraud on the bankruptcy law principle.

Potato Distributors Inc v Eastern Trust Company (1955), 35 CBR 161 (PEI CA)

TWEEDY J: This is an appeal from a judgment of my Lord the Chief Justice, upon an application by Potato Distributors Incorporated for an order declaring a certain contract to be frustrated and void by reason of bankruptcy of the debtor, or in the alternative, for an order that the trustee in bankruptcy disclaim the said contract as onerous.

The learned Chief Justice refused the application and as to the alternative order sought he held it clearly could not be considered upon the application before him as the above appellant was only a contractor and not a creditor at that time.

Since then, however, Russell Hammill and Russell Ching, two creditors of the debtor, have been added as intervenants. Some objection was made to this procedure, but for the purpose of this appeal it was agreed that the appeal be considered as properly before the Court and that the appeal should be heard and determined upon its merits.

The contract in question is dated April 9, 1955, and is between the debtor of the one part and the appellant of the other part and is for sale and delivery by the debtor to the appellant in each of the years, 1955, 1956, and 1957, of 25,000 bags of certified Number One Canada A Grade Sebago Seed Potatoes and also 1,750 bags of certified Number One Canada A Grade Small Sebago Seed Potatoes, ship's tackle at Summerside, Charlotte-town or Souris in Prince Edward Island.

The date of delivery of said potatoes in each of the said three years was to be during the months of November and December, and the price agreed to be paid by the purchaser appellant to the debtor was $1.75 United States funds per 100 pound bag.

On August 25, 1955, a receiving order was made against the debtor and the respondent was appointed trustee in bankruptcy. No potatoes have been delivered under the contract.

The grounds of appeal are as follows:

1. From the very nature of bankruptcy, performance of a three year contract by the trustee is inapt.
2. More especially is this so where, as in the present case, performance of the contract involves gambling on the potato market.
3. *The Bankruptcy Act* does not contemplate carrying on the business of the bankrupt by the trustees where that business is of a highly speculative nature.
4. Carrying on business by the trustee must be confined to such business as will promote a reasonably speedy winding up of the estate.
5. The undertaking given by the trustee in the present case would be worthless in certain circumstances, and His Lordship therefore erred in refusing the appellant's application upon such an undertaking.

The argument was devoted mainly to s. 10(1)(c) of *The Bankruptcy Act*, 1949, 2nd Sess. (Can.), c. 7 [now *BIA*, s 30(1)], which reads as follows:

> The trustee may, with the permission of the inspectors, do all or any of the following things: ...
>
> (c) carry on the business of the bankrupt, so far as may be necessary for the beneficial administration of the estate.

It was contended by the appellant that the completion of the contract by the trustee is the carrying on of the business of the debtor; business that is not necessary for the beneficial administration of the estate.

Our *Bankruptcy Act* was no doubt modelled after and largely copied from the English Act, 1914, c. 59. An examination of the English cases therefore will be of some assistance in the consideration of this case.

The original *Bankruptcy Act* was enacted by the Dominion Parliament in the Session of 1919 (9-10 Geo. V, c. 36) and was to become operative by Royal Proclamation. A proclamation was issued on December 31, 1919, bringing the Act into force on July 1, 1920.

Various amendments were passed and these were consolidated and revised and the new *Bankruptcy Act* was contained in RSC 1927, c. 11.

What is now s. 10(1)(c) already quoted, was s. 43(1)(b) in RSC 1927, c. 11, and was s. 20(1)(b) of *The Bankruptcy Act*, 1919 and amendments thereto with this variation:

Section 43(1)(b) of RSC 1927, c. 11 reads as follows:

> 43. The trustee may, with the permission in writing of the inspectors, do all or any of the following things: ...
>
> (b) carry on the business of the debtor, so far as may be necessary for the beneficial winding-up of the same.

From a perusal of the English cases, it would appear that this section of the English *Bankruptcy Act* reads exactly the same way.

However, our *Bankruptcy Act*, 1949, in s. 10 does not require the permission of the inspectors to be in writing; refers to the "debtor" as a "bankrupt" in s. 10(1)(c) and states that the business should be carried on "so far as may be necessary for the beneficial administration of the estate," not "so far as may be necessary for the beneficial winding-up of the business of the debtor."

It is contended by the appellant that "administration" and "winding-up" are the same thing. I realize that the words are used interchangeably in the English cases. Also that Morawetz's 3rd edition of *Bradford & Greenberg's Canadian Bankruptcy Act* at p. 43 states that "Para. (c) corresponds to former para. (b)." I cannot help feeling, however, that there is a difference in meaning in the words of the two sections. One of the dictionary meanings of "administration" is "The management and disposal of the estate of a deceased person."

The dictionary meaning of "wind-up" is to close, conclude, finish.

A very common use of the word administration is in connection with the administration of estates of deceased persons. In that use it does not mean that contracts of the deceased be frustrated or voided or that the administrator should disclaim contracts of the deceased as being onerous.

Neither do I think that Parliament intended this to be the case when it deliberately changed the wording of the section as used in the English Act, *The Bankruptcy Act*, 1919 and *The Bankruptcy Act*, 1927.

However, it is not necessary for the disposition of this appeal that I should determine this point although I must confess it is fascinating and very interesting.

[To deal] now with the main question whether or not by carrying out this contract the trustee is carrying on business not necessary for the beneficial administration of the estate.

I was much impressed with the argument and the cases cited. I am quite prepared to admit too that the pith and substance of this section is whether or not the carrying on of the bankrupt business is necessary for the beneficial administration of the estate. See

In re Wreck Recovery and Salvage Company (1880), 15 Ch D 353, per Jessel MR at p. 360: "Now the word 'necessary' means that it must not be merely beneficial but something more. . . . Then it must be for the 'beneficial winding-up' of the business of the company, therefore it must be with a view to the winding-up of the company, not with a view to its continuance."

I am also in agreement with the quotation from the judgment of Macdonald J in *In re Sechart Fisheries Limited* (1929), 10 CBR 565 at 569, [1929] 2 WWR 413, 41 BCR 323, [1929] 4 DLR 536, 3 Can Abr 442, where he states: ". . . in my opinion it is the duty of a trustee to speedily realize the assets, and divide the proceeds among the creditors."

In re Delisle (Colonial Construction Co), Bonnier and Fels, 23 CBR 333, [1942] Que SC 72, Abr Con 285, and *In re Grobstein and Capra* (1929), 11 CBR 250, 3 Can Abr 443, were cited by the appellant as cases showing where it was proper that the business of the bankrupt debtor should be carried on for a time.

The leading English case of *Clark v Smith*, [1940] 1 KB 126, [1939] 4 All ER 59, while it is very interesting and illuminating, yet is not of much assistance in the present case.

After carefully considering all the above cases and the other cases cited, I cannot reach the conclusion that the trustee in this case is carrying on business of the bankrupt that is not necessary for the beneficial administration of the estate.

The potato business of the bankrupt was only one branch of many other lines of business carried on by it. Among others mentioned were plumbing, feed business, hardware business and many others.

All the trustee is trying to do by carrying out this contract is to endeavour to mitigate the liabilities as much as possible and not try to make a profit.

As so often pointed out, *The Bankruptcy Act* was passed for two main objects: 1. To secure the creditors the best result, i.e., an economical administration, and 2. To enable an honest bankrupt to obtain a discharge and to make a fresh start.

The Bankruptcy Act was passed primarily for the purpose of securing to creditors the wreckage of bankrupt estates, and extricating from an intolerable situation the unfortunate trader who, through no fault of his own, finds himself weighed down with financial burdens which he cannot discharge: Per Barry, CJKBD, in *In re Holdengraber; Ex parte Royal Brand Clothing Co* (1927), 8 CBR 411 at 413, 3 Can Abr 662.

> "In the performance of his duties a trustee . . . should have regard to the fact that his principal duty is to realize the assets of the debtor . . . and distribute such assets *pari passu* amongst the unsecured creditors after having satisfied all preferred creditors. . . . The trustee cannot carry on the business for the purpose of making a profit for the debtor or with a view of saving the business for him, but only for the purpose of beneficially winding-up the business in the interest of the general body of creditors:" Per Maclennan J, in *In re Gareau; Ex parte Joseph Bros* (1922), 3 CBR 76, 3 Can Abr 486.

Here the inspectors instructed the trustee to carry out the contract under consideration.

The whole scope of *The Bankruptcy Act* indicates that in the administration of the estate of a debtor the governing authority shall be the inspectors and not the Court. If, however, they act fraudulently or in bad faith and not for the benefit of the estate, the Court may interfere, but otherwise the policy of the Act is to leave the matter entirely in their hands: *In re JL Jacobs & Co* (1941), 22 CBR 208, Abr Con 323.

It is not as though the trustee were entering upon some new project. Here he is trying to do the best possible, guided by the views of his inspectors for the creditors as a body and not for any one group.

I am of the opinion, therefore, that the learned Chief Justice was right in refusing to grant an order declaring the contract to be frustrated and void subject to the express undertaking given by the trustee that no distribution of assets would be made among the creditors until after the date of the completion of the three-year contract with the appellant, and that the assets of the bankrupt in the hands of the trustee would be answerable to the appellant for any damages arising from a breach of the contract.

Appeal dismissed.

[Justice MacGuigan delivered a short concurring judgment.]

Re North American Steamships Ltd, 2007 BCSC 267, 2007 CarswellBC 414

Tysoe J:

Introduction

[1] The Trustee in Bankruptcy (the "Trustee") of North America Steamships Ltd. (the "Bankrupt") applies for two declarations in connection with the necessity and effect of the Trustee affirming two freight forward swap agreements between the Bankrupt and AWB Geneva S.A. ("Geneva") and one freight forward swap agreement between the Bankrupt and Pioneer Metal Logistics, B.V.I. ("Pioneer").

[2] On January 10, 2007, I granted an *ex parte* Order declaring that the reasonable time for affirmation by the Trustee of these freight forward swap agreements (the "Geneva/Pioneer Swap Agreements" or the "Swap Agreements") would not expire until five business days after a decision by the court of an application set for hearing with respect to the liability of the Trustee in the event it affirmed the Geneva/Pioneer Swap Agreements. The Trustee subsequently made a separate application for a declaration that it is not required to affirm the Swap Agreements. I heard these two applications concurrently.

Background

[3] The Bankrupt began carrying on a ship brokering business in 1993 or 1994. Its focus shifted after a few years to the ship chartering business. In 2004, the Bankrupt acted as agent for another company in dealing with a swap agreement in the shipping industry. It became involved in swap agreements on its own account in 2005.

[4] In simple terms, a swap agreement in the shipping industry is considered to be a derivative product that does not actually involve shipping physical products. It can be used as a hedge by parties involved in shipping products to protect themselves against fluctuation in shipping rates or, as was the case with the Bankrupt, it can be a form of trading in futures. It was referred to in the submissions before me as a form of gambling.

[5] A representative of the Trustee described the main elements of the swap agreements entered into by the Bankrupt as follows in his affidavit:

(a) the [swap agreement] is entered into between two parties — a Buyer and a Seller;

(b) the parties agree on a route;

(c) the parties agree on a day, month and year of settlement;

(d) the parties agree on the contract quantity (ie. number of days, although I believe that it must be a minimum of 3 months);

(e) the parties agree on a Contract Rate and Settlement Rate. The Settlement Rate is established by an independent Index or Baltic Exchange (the "Exchange");

(f) essentially, the Buyer is wagering that the Settlement Rate on the Exchange will be higher than the Contract Rate at a future time. Conversely, the Seller is wagering that the Settlement Rate on the Exchange will be lower than the Contract Rate at a future time;

(g) settlement is made by the parties in cash within five days following the end of each calendar month; and

(h) the transactions under the [swap agreements] are derivative products only—i.e. there are no physical shipping transactions involved.

[6] The Bankrupt became insolvent as a result of losses of approximately $13 million under swap agreements covering all or parts of 2006. During the course of 2006, the Bankrupt entered into approximately 20 swap agreements for the 2007 year. Most of the 2007 agreements are anticipated to result in losses. The Trustee estimates that the total losses under the 2006 and 2007 swap agreements will be approximately $55 million. As at the time of the hearing of the *ex parte* application, the Trustee had collected approximately $3.5 million and had additional receivables.

[7] While the Bankrupt was largely unsuccessful with respect to the swap agreements it entered into during the past two years, the likely outcome of the Geneva/Pioneer Swap Agreements is positive. The Bankrupt is the buyer under each of the Swap Agreements, and the contract period for each of them expires on December 31, 2007 (two of them had contract periods of one year and the third had a contract period of one-half year). The contract rates under the Swap Agreements range from US $13,700 a day to US $17,500 a day, while the current settlement rate is approximately US $36,000 a day. If the settlement rate were to stay at US $36,000 for the entire year, the Trustee estimates that the payments due to the Bankrupt under the Swap Agreements would amount to US $18.3 million. The concern of the Trustee is that there is a possibility that the settlement rate could fall below the contract rates and that monies could be owing to Geneva and Pioneer under the Swap Agreements.

[8] Each of the Geneva/Pioneer Swap Agreements incorporated by reference the 1992 ISDA Master Agreement (Multicurrency—Cross Border) (without Schedule) (the "Master Agreement"). This is a detailed agreement developed by the International Swap Dealers Association. One of the provisions of the Master Agreement is that if one of the parties goes bankrupt, the other party may terminate the swap agreement, in which case the payments due under the agreement are determined by a market quotation of the average settlement rate for the year. The quoted rate for 2007 is US $31,625, which would mean that Geneva and Pioneer would have to pay the Bankrupt an amount somewhat less than the US $18.3 million figure mentioned above if they were to elect to terminate the Swap Agreements at the present time.

Issues

[9] The issues raised by the Trustee's applications are as follows:

(a) is it necessary for the Trustee to affirm the Geneva/Pioneer Swap Agreements in order to take the benefit of them?

(b) if the Trustee does affirm the Geneva/Pioneer Swap Agreements, will the Trustee be personally liable in respect of the obligations of the buyer under the Swap Agreements or will the liability of the Trustee be limited to the assets in the bankruptcy estate?

Discussion

(a) Necessity to Affirm

[10] The requirement for a trustee in bankruptcy to affirm a contract entered into by the bankrupt stems from the decision in *Re Thomson Knitting Co Ltd* (1925), 5 CBR 489

(Ont SC (AD)). In that case, the bankrupt had entered into a contract for the purchase of goods from the vendor. At issue was whether the vendor qualified as a creditor of the bankrupt in respect of damages for breach of contract. In holding that the vendor was a creditor, the Court said the following at p. 490:

> While the bankruptcy did not of itself constitute a breach of the contract, it did not on the other hand cast any further burden upon the vendors. But it had this effect: it entitled the vendors to treat the contract as broken if the trustee did not, within a reasonable time, approbate the contract and call for its completion. Nor was it necessary for the vendors first to tender the goods to the trustee: *Ex parte Stapleton; In re Nathan* (1879), 10 Ch. D 586, 40 LT 14, 27 WR 327. And the trustee could not insist upon delivery of the balance of the goods except upon full payment, not only of the prices of the goods so delivered, but also of all the arrears. In other words, the trustee cannot call for completion of the contract by the vendors without full performance on his part of all the purchasers' obligations there-under: *William Hamilton Mfg Co v Hamilton Steel and Iron Co* (1911), 23 OLR 270.

[11] The Appellate Division of the Ontario Supreme Court did not explain why the trustee should be required to approbate the contract and call for its completion. In my view, such a requirement is reasonable and makes commercial sense. If a party to a contract becomes bankrupt, a question arises as to whether the obligations of that party under the contract will be performed. The bankrupt itself is no longer in a position to perform the obligations and one could consider the contract to be frustrated unless someone else standing in the place of the bankrupt (i.e., the trustee in bankruptcy) is prepared to perform the obligations. It is not reasonable for the other party to be bound to perform its obligations under the contract after the date of bankruptcy without know-ing how the obligations of the bankrupt will be treated if they are not performed. If the other party performs its obligations, it is entitled to know that it will not simply become an unsecured creditor of the bankrupt if the obligations of the bankrupt under the con-tract are not performed. Thus, if the trustee in bankruptcy wants to benefit from the contract, it is incumbent on it to affirm the contract and thereby assure the other party that it will not be treated as an unsecured creditor of the bankrupt in respect of the obli-gations it performs after the date of bankruptcy.

[12] A similar point arose in *Potato Distributors Inc v Eastern Trust Company* (1955), 35 CBR 161 (PEICA), where a party to a contract with the bankrupt applied for an order declaring the contract to be frustrated and void by reason of the bankruptcy. The Prince Edward Island Court of Appeal said the following at p. 166 in holding that the contract was not frustrated:

> I am of the opinion, therefore, that the learned Chief Justice was right in refusing to grant an order declaring the contract to be frustrated and void subject to the express undertak-ing given by the trustee that no distribution of assets would be made among the creditors until after the date of the completion of the three-year contract with the appellant, and that the assets of the bankrupt in the hands of the trustee would be answerable to the appellant for any damages arising from a breach of the contract.

In that case, the trustee had not explicitly approbated or affirmed the contract but the undertaking given by the trustee had the same effect. The trustee was undertaking that the bankruptcy estate would stand behind the obligations of the bankrupt under the agreement in priority to the claims of the bankrupt's unsecured creditors.

[13] In the present case, counsel for the Trustee submits that these authorities do not apply in the present circumstances because the Geneva/Pioneer Swap Agreements contain provisions allowing Geneva and Pioneer to terminate the Swap Agreements as a result of the bankruptcy of the Bankrupt. In other words, the contracting parties turned their minds to the possibility of one of them becoming bankrupt and provided a remedy for the protection of the non-bankrupt party. With respect, I do not accept this submission.

[14] While Geneva and Pioneer have the option of terminating the Swap Agreements as a result of the bankruptcy, they are entitled to know whether the Trustee is prepared to commit the assets in the bankruptcy estate towards the obligations of the Bankrupt under the Swap Agreements if they do not choose the termination option. In my view, nothing turns on whether the bankruptcy of one of the contracting parties does constitute a breach of the contract or otherwise entitles the other party to terminate the contract.

[15] There is potentially an important difference between the termination of the contract in accordance with its provisions and the contract coming to an end due to frustration of the contract. In the present case, there is a significant difference between the two alternatives. If Geneva and Pioneer were to terminate the Swap Agreements in accordance with their provisions at the present time, they would have to make a significant payment to the Trustee. On the other hand, if the Swap Agreements are frustrated, they are entitled to treat them at an end without making any further payment.

[16] Another way of looking at the point is to consider the right of the trustee in bankruptcy to disclaim a contract entered into by the bankrupt, in which case the other party to the contract may claim as an unsecured creditor of the bankrupt in respect of the damages suffered by it. The BC Court of Appeal recently had occasion to consider the right of trustees in bankruptcy to disclaim contracts in the decision of *New Skeena Forest Products Inc v Don Hull & Sons Contracting Ltd*, 2005 BCCA 154. The Court said the following at para 29:

> In more recent times, L.W. Houlden & G.B. Morawetz in their text *Bankruptcy and Insolvency Law of Canada*, 3d ed, looseleaf (Toronto: Thomson Carswell, 2004) at F§45.2 state quite unequivocally that a trustee may disclaim a contract entered into by the bankrupt. Similarly, in a case comment on *Potato Distributors Inc v Eastern Trust Co* (1955), 35 CBR 161 at 166 (PEICA), L.W. Houlden writes:
>
> > It is well established law that a trustee may elect to carry on with a contract entered into prior to bankruptcy, provided he pays up arrears and is ready to perform the contract. The trustee could also, if he saw fit, elect not to go on with the contract in which event the vendor would have the right to prove a claim for damages.

In his case comment, L.W. Houlden cited the *Thomson Knitting* decision immediately following the passage quoted above.

[17] A trustee in bankruptcy has two alternatives with respect to contracts entered into by the bankrupt. The trustee can either affirm or disclaim the contract. Support for this proposition is found in *Saan Stores Ltd v United Steelworkers of America, Local 596 (Retail Wholesale Canada, Canadian Service Section Division)* (1999), 172 DLR (4th) 134 (NSCA) at p. 151:

> As a general rule, with respect to contracts that a trustee can perform, the trustee may, within a reasonable time, elect to either adopt the contracts or to disclaim them (*Re Thomson*

Knitting Company (1925), 2 DLR 1007 (Ont SC); Houlden, L.W. and C.H. Morawetz, *Bankruptcy and Insolvency Law of Canada*, 3rd ed. (Toronto: Carswell, 1993) paragraph F45.2).

[18] The trustee cannot choose to do nothing. It must elect between the two alternatives because the other contracting party is entitled to know whether it will be a creditor of the bankrupt or a creditor of the bankruptcy estate (or the trustee personally) with respect to any unfulfilled obligations on the part of the bankrupt. The other contracting party is entitled to know which alternative the trustee is choosing irrespective of whether it is entitled to terminate the contract as a result of the bankruptcy.

[19] Counsel for the Trustee made submissions to the effect that the obligation to affirm a contract of a bankrupt only applies when the contract is executory in nature and that a contract is not executory in nature when the only obligation remaining is payment. In my view, the requirement of affirmation should apply if there is a prospect that obligations on the part of the bankrupt under the contract may have to be performed prior to the end of the contract. Such a prospect exists in this case and, indeed, it is the existence of this prospect that has caused the Trustee to make these applications.

(b) Personal Liability of the Trustee

[20] The history of personal liability of trustees in bankruptcies was reviewed in the decision of *Transalta Utilities Corporation v Hudson* (1982), 44 CBR (NS) 97 (Alta QB). Registrar Funduk concluded after his review that until 1949 a trustee was *prima facie* personally liable for debts incurred in operating the business of the bankrupt and that the trustee was required to rebut this presumption if he wished to establish that the debt was incurred on behalf of the bankruptcy estate. This was changed in 1949 with the enactment of what is now s. 31(4) of the *Bankruptcy and Insolvency Act*, RSC 1985, c. B-3, as amended, which reads as follows:

> All debts incurred and credit received in carrying on the business of a bankrupt are deemed to be debts incurred and credit received by the estate of the bankrupt.

Registrar Funduk concluded, correctly in my view, that liability in respect of post-bankruptcy liabilities now lies *prima facie* with the bankruptcy estate and that the onus is on the creditor to show that the liability rests with the trustee personally.

[21] This is consistent with the following passage from the decision of the Ontario Court of Appeal in *Re St Marys Paper Inc* (1994), 26 CBR (3d) 273 at p. 288:

> Nor do we see any impediment to that conclusion in the *BIA*. Section 31(4) of the *BIA* deems all debts incurred in carrying on the business of a bankrupt to be incurred by the estate of the bankrupt. This presumption is not irrefutable, nor is it incompatible with the personal liability of the trustee, in appropriate circumstances. In a section entitled "Trustee Protecting Himself Against Liability for Debts and Liabilities Incurred in Carrying on the Business of the Bankrupt," Houlden and Morawetz state, in *Bankruptcy and Insolvency Law of Canada*, 3rd ed., Vol. 1 (Toronto: Carswell, 1992) at pp. 103–04:
>
> > Notwithstanding s. 31(4), there are still situations where a trustee may be personally liable for obligations incurred in carrying on the debtor's business. Thus, if a trustee enters into a contract to act as agent for a secured creditor in realizing its security and in doing so carries on the business of the bankrupt, s. 31(4) is no protection to the trustee. In these circumstances, the trustee is personally liable to account to the secured creditor for the proceeds of the realization and if he fails to do so, judgment will be given against him personally for the amount owing: *Re*

PE Lapierre Inc; Bank of Nova Scotia v Gagnon (1970), 16 CBR (NS) 43 (Que SC). Again, if a supplier will not supply goods unless the trustee pledges his personal credit and the trustee accepts the goods on that basis, the trustee will, notwithstanding s. 31(4), be personally liable to the supplier: *Transalta Utilities Corp v Hudson* (1982), 44 CBR (NS) 97, 22 Alta LR (2d) 139, 40 AR 134 (MC).

[22] This result is also consistent with the reasoning in the decision of *Potato Distributors Inc* which I quoted above. The decision was made after 1949, and the court held that there was sufficient affirmation if the trustee in bankruptcy undertook that the assets in the bankruptcy estate would be answerable for any damages arising from a breach of the contract. It was not necessary for the affirmation to have been done by the trustee in his personal capacity.

[23] It has been suggested that, as s. 31(4) refers to "debts" and not "liabilities," the provision may not reverse the presumption against personal liability of trustees in bankruptcy in respect of liabilities which are not debts (see *Glick v Jordan* (1967), 11 CBR (NS) 70 (Ont SC (HCJ)), where a plaintiff was suing a trustee in bankruptcy in his personal capacity for the tort of negligence). As I am satisfied that any amounts which the buyer may have to pay under the Geneva/Pioneer Swap Agreements to Geneva and Pioneer would constitute "debts" in the ordinary sense of the word, I need not consider whether "debts" should be given a broader meaning.

[24] Counsel for Geneva and Pioneer submits that I do not have the jurisdiction to immunize the Trustee against personal liability. I agree with this proposition but I am able to make a declaration with respect to the circumstances in which the Trustee will not be personally liable according to law. While the court is usually reluctant to make prospective declarations, s. 34(1) of the *Bankruptcy and Insolvency Act* specifically contemplates that trustees in bankruptcy may apply to the court for directions in relation to any matter affecting the administration of the bankruptcy estate.

[25] As there is only a rebuttable presumption against personal liability on the part of trustees in bankruptcy, I cannot make the unequivocal declaration which the Trustee seeks. However, I am able to make a declaration of a general nature.

Conclusion

[26] I declare as follows:

(a) it is necessary for the Trustee to affirm the Geneva/Pioneer Swap Agreements in order to take the benefit of them; and

(b) the affirmation of the Geneva/Pioneer Swap Agreements by the Trustee will not itself make the Trustee personally liable in respect of the obligations of the buyer under the Swap Agreements as long as the Trustee affirms the Swap Agreements on behalf of the bankruptcy estate and not in its personal capacity.

IV. ASSIGNMENT

Does a trustee in bankruptcy have the right to assign a pre-bankruptcy contract between Counterparty and Debtor regardless of Counterparty's wishes? Does it make any difference if there is a provision in the contract prohibiting assignments? The provincial lessor and tenant laws discussed in Part II(B), above, provide for the assignment of commercial tenancy agreements in bankruptcy and these rules apply in bankruptcy proceedings by virtue of *BIA*, section 146. The governing provision in Ontario is *Commercial Tenancies Act*, section 38(2), extracted above. Section 38(2) overrides any anti-assignment clause in the lease and it relieves the trustee from post-assignment liability for non-payment of rent and other breaches. However, it also enacts safeguards for the lessor's protection. The requirements for a valid assignment are that: (1) the trustee must pay all arrears of rent; (2) the assignee must covenant to observe and perform all the terms of the lease and agree to conduct on the premises "a trade or business which is not reasonably of a more objectionable or hazardous nature than that which was thereon conducted by the debtor"; and (3) the court must approve the assignee as a fit and proper person.

Prior to the 2009 amendments, there was no statutory right of assignment for contracts other than commercial tenancy agreements. A new *BIA* section, 84.1, was enacted as part off the 2009 amendments and this provision creates a statutory right of assignment for all contracts entered into before the bankruptcy date, except eligible financial contracts and collective agreements. Section 84.1 provides that the court must approve a proposed assignment and the factors it has to consider include: (1) whether the assignee is able to perform the obligations; and (2) whether it is "appropriate" to assign the contract to the assignee. It is unclear whether section 84.1 applies to commercial lessor and tenant agreements or whether the provincial laws continue to govern. In practical terms, the question may not matter because section 84.1 is in substance the same as the provincial provisions.

Ford Motor Company of Canada v Welcome Ford Sales Ltd, 2011 ABCA 158, 44 Alta LR (5th) 81 [*Ford*]

THE COURT (Ritter, Martin, and Bielby JJA): . . .

[2] This was an appeal from a decision granting permission to a bankruptcy trustee to sell an auto dealership agreement to a third party over the objections of the other party to the agreement, an auto manufacturer, pursuant to the provisions of the relatively new s. 84.1 of the *Bankruptcy and Insolvency Act*, R.S.C. 1985, c. B-3 ("*BIA*").

[3] Welcome Ford, owned by Royale Smith ("Smith"), operated a franchise dealership with the Appellant, Ford Motor Company of Canada, Limited ("Ford") in Fort Saskatchewan, Alberta pursuant to the terms of a written dealership agreement. The dealership ceased operations on January 13, 2010 after Ford Credit Canada Ltd. ("Ford Credit"), while conducting a physical audit on its premises, discovered a large defalcation apparently made by a senior employee of the dealership. The following day, the chambers judge, acting as de facto case manager, appointed Myers Norris Penny ("MNP") the Receiver of Welcome Ford on the application of Ford Credit.

[4] Ford Credit tendered evidence in support of that application showing that over $3.7 million to which it was entitled had been misappropriated. At that time, Welcome Ford owed Ford Credit approximately $7.7 million and owed the Bank of Montreal ("BMO") approximately $2.7 million. Ford Credit had priority in relation to the vehicle inventory, while BMO had a priority claim to all other assets. As a result, Ford Credit seized and removed all vehicles over which it had security. It is an unsecured creditor for any shortfall on its debt remaining after the sale of those vehicles.

[5] The order appointing the Receiver stayed all rights and remedies against Welcome Ford; in particular, it ordered that no agreements then in place, including the dealership agreement, be terminated without consent of the court. Ford advised as early as January 29, 2010 that it would not consent to the assignment/sale of the dealership agreement to any party. However, on March 23, 2010, the chambers judge granted an order authorizing MNP to market the dealership while adjourning Ford Credit's application to lift the stay so as to be able to terminate the dealership agreement ("the March order").

[6] On May 19, 2010, BMO obtained an order placing Welcome Ford into bankruptcy with MNP as trustee, which had the effect of making the administration subject to the *BIA*, including s. 84.1 of that statute.

[7] MNP marketed the dealership to existing Ford dealers only, receiving offers to purchase from the ultimate purchaser and two others. Ford maintained its refusal to consent to a sale, even to one of its own dealers, notwithstanding that the offer made by the ultimate purchaser, the highest bidder, would have produced sufficient funds to retire the debt to BMO in its entirely and produce a further $570,000 (before professional fees) to be distributed among the unsecured creditors. In comparison, liquidation of the assets without sale of the dealership agreement was expected to produce a far smaller sum, one which would leave more than $1 million of the debt to BMO unpaid and produce nothing for any other creditor.

[8] On December 10, 2010, the chambers judge approved MNP's application to assign the rights and obligations of Welcome Ford under the dealership agreement to the ultimate purchaser pursuant to s. 84.1 of the *BIA*. At the same time, he dismissed Ford's application for a declaration that the dealership agreement could not be assigned without its consent and to lift the stay ("the December orders"). This appeal was then brought against each of the March and December orders.

[9] The *BIA* was amended on December 15, 2009 by the addition of s. 84.1, which allows a court, upon being satisfied that certain prerequisites are met, to grant an order assigning the rights and obligations of the bankrupt under any agreement to a purchaser, even without the consent of the counter-party to the agreement.

[10] The Respondents argued that the dealership agreement was properly assignable to the ultimate purchaser under this section, even absent Ford's consent. Ford argued that the dealership agreement had been terminated as a result of a fundamental breach occurring before the granting of the receivership order such that there was nothing left to assign to the ultimate purchaser. It, alternatively, argued that the dealership agreement is not assignable by reason of its nature and, as such, the issues of whether the ultimate purchaser is able to perform the obligations under it and whether it is appropriate to assign it are irrelevant.

[11] The issues raised on appeal are:

(A) Has the dealership agreement terminated because of fundamental breach?
(B) How is s. 84.1 of the *BIA* to be interpreted?
   (i)   Is s. 84.1(3) to be interpreted without reference to s. 84.1(4)?
   (ii) Are the rights and obligations imposed by the dealership agreement not assignable by reason of their nature because:
        (a) the estate will not benefit from the assignment?; or
        (b) they are personal in nature?
   (iii) Should the dealership agreement not be assigned because of the capacity of the proposed assignee or because it is inappropriate to assign Welcome Ford's rights and obligations under s. 84.1(4)? ...

(A) Has the dealership agreement terminated because of fundamental breach?

... [28] The standard of review in relation to the chambers judge's findings of fact and application of facts to the law are subject to deference absent clear and palpable error. The application of deference is amplified when, as noted above, the judge is a case management judge whose decision is part of a series of decisions. His decision that no fundamental breach of the dealership agreement had occurred was reasonable and is entitled to our deference. Indeed, had we been required to consider the issue of correctness, we would have concluded his decision to be correct. The ultimate purchaser will be able to perform the dealers obligations under the agreement such that its commercial purpose will be effected. Ford will receive the benefit the parties intended it to receive when that agreement was created.

(B) How is s. 84.1 of the *BIA* to be interpreted?

[29] The position at common law was always that if one party breached a condition (and not a mere warranty) in a contract, the other party to that contract had an election, either to treat the contract as continuing and insist on future performance, or to accept the repudiation and bring the contract to an end. In the latter case certain obligations survived the termination depending upon the construction of the contract.

[30] The effect of s. 84.1 of the *BIA* is to override the common law unilateral right of the innocent party to the contract to accept the repudiation and end the contract. It has been designed to preserve the value of the estate as a whole, even if the contractual rights of some creditors, such as Ford in this case, are compromised. Therefore, even if Ford otherwise had the right to terminate the dealership agreement for breach of condition, and its assignment clause was not one which survived the termination, s. 84.1 nonetheless allows the trustee to apply to the Court for permission to assign the contract so long as the provisions of the statute are met.

[31] Ford argues that the provisions of s. 84.1 which are prerequisite to granting permission to assign have not been met....

[33] The Appellant did not argue, nor did the chambers judge find, that s. 84.1 expressly excludes auto dealership agreements from its operation. Indeed, the word "agreement" found in that section is wide enough to cover this type of agreement. The chambers judge correctly concluded, therefore, that he had jurisdiction under s. 84.1 to order the assignment (sale) in the proper circumstances.

[34] Ford argued, rather, that those proper circumstances did not exist, as discussed below.

(i) Is s. 84.1(3) to be interpreted without reference to s. 84.1(4)?

[35] Ford argued that whether the rights and obligations of an agreement are assignable "by reason of their nature" pursuant to s. 84.1(3) must be decided before, and independently of, any consideration under s. 84.1(4) as to whether the proposed assignee is capable of performing the obligations and it is appropriate to assign the rights and obligations. If so, it is irrelevant that the ultimate purchaser is an otherwise approved dealer and a proven performer. The issue of whether the nature of the agreement precludes its assignment would thus have to be resolved independently of any consideration of whether the agreement's commercial purpose would be achieved in the hands of the proposed assignee.

[36] This interpretation is not supported by the literal words found in s. 84.1 which do not make a determination under s. 84.1(3) an independent precondition to a determination under s. 84.1(4). Legislative intent may be taken into account as an aide to interpretation only in the case of ambiguity in the words of the statute. Even if such an ambiguity existed here, and one is not apparent, Parliament's intent does not support Ford's interpretation. The chambers judge concluded that s. 84.1 should be interpreted in light of Parliament's intention that the provision be used to protect and enhance the

assets of the estate of a bankrupt by permitting the sale/assignment of existing agreements to third parties for value: see Houlden, Morawetz and Sarra, *Bankruptcy and Insolvency Law of Canada*, 4th ed., looseleaf (Toronto: Carswell, 2009) vol. 2 at 3-499. He purported to interpret s. 84.1 in the context of its role as remedial legislation.

[37] Prior to the coming into force of s. 84.1 in 2009, a trustee in bankruptcy could not assign (sell) a contract to a third party where the counter-party to that contract opposed the assignment. As a result, a bankrupt estate was vulnerable to losing the benefit of a valuable contract to the detriment of the estate and often to the detriment of third parties.

[38] The estate of a bankrupt may include various forms of property. Sometimes the most valuable property in an estate will be the contractual rights possessed by the bankrupt as of the date of bankruptcy. Those rights may be embodied in, for example, a franchise agreement, a purchase agreement, a license agreement, a lease, a supply agreement or an auto dealership agreement.

[39] The clear intent of Parliament in enacting s. 84.1 of the *BIA* was to address this vulnerability; it made a policy decision that a court ought to have the discretion to authorize a trustee to assign (sell) the rights and obligations of a bankrupt under such an agreement notwithstanding the objections of the counter-party.

[40] A statutory provision analogous to s. 84.1 is that of s. 8(2) of the *Landlord's Rights on Bankruptcy Act*, R.S.A. 2000, c. L-5. It provides that, notwithstanding the legal effect of a provision in a lease purporting to terminate the lease upon the tenant becoming bankrupt, the trustee in bankruptcy may elect to retain the leased premises for some or all of the unexpired term of the lease. The trustee may then, upon payment of all overdue rent, assign the lease to a capable third party upon securing an order to that effect from the Court of Queen's Bench. The purpose of the legislation is to enable the trustee to maximize realization without putting the landlord in any worse position that it would have been under the lease before the bankruptcy: see *Bank of Montreal v Phoenix Rotary Equipment Ltd*, 2007 ABQB 86 at para. 51, 72 Alta. L.R. (4th) 321.

[41] Similarly, s. 84.1 of the *BIA* allows a court to approve the assignment (sale) of any agreement to obtain maximum benefit for creditors upon payment of any monetary breaches and upon concluding that the rights and remedies of the counter-party will be preserved.

[42] Ford suggested the contrary, offering an extract from the Briefing Book placed before Parliament when it considered this amendment. The Briefing Book gives as a reason for the enactment of the language "not assignable by reason of its nature" (then subsection 3(d)) that it "is intended to provide flexibility to the court to review each agreement in light of the circumstances to determine whether or not it would be appropriate to allow the assignment". It further states, "[s]ubsection (4) provides the courts with legislative guidance as to when an agreement may be assigned. The guidance is limited to enable the court to exercise its discretion to address individual fact situations". These stated purposes are not, however, mutually exclusive.

[43] Rather, to the extent that legislative intent is at all relevant, it is as described by the chambers judge as well as Justice Romaine of the Alberta Court of Queen's Bench in *Alberta Health Services v Networc Health Inc*, 2010 ABQB 373 at para. 20, 28 Alta. L.R. (5th) 118:

> The *BIA* is remedial legislation. It is clear that it should be given "such fair, large and liberal construction and interpretation as best ensures the attainment of its objects":

Interpretation Act, R.S.C., 1985, c. I-21 at section 12. In *Mercure v. A. Marquette & Fils Inc.*, [1977] 1 S.C.R. 547 at 556, the Supreme Court commented:

> Before going on to another point it is perhaps not inappropriate to recall that the Bankruptcy Act, while not business legislation in the strict sense, clearly has its origins in the business world. Interpretation of it must take these origins into account. It concerns relations among businessmen, and to interpret it using an overly narrow, legalistic approach is to misinterpret it.

[44] Ford has suggested no business reason to support its interpretation of s. 84.1(3) and (4). There is no apparent reason as to why appropriateness of the assignment or the capability of the proposed assignee would not be relevant to determining whether the rights and obligations are assignable by their nature. Rather, the opposite would appear to be true.

[45] Therefore, I conclude that s. 84.1(3) is to be interpreted upon considering, among other things, the capacity of the proposed assignee and whether it is appropriate to assign the rights and obligations as set out in s. 84.1(4).

(ii)(a) Are the rights and obligations established by the dealership agreement not assignable by reason of their nature because the estate will not benefit from the assignment?

[46] Ford argued that a court should not exercise its discretion under s. 84.1 to override the Appellant's clear contractual rights to withhold consent to the sale of the dealership in the absence of very clear evidence that the bankrupt estate will benefit: see *Teragol Investments Ltd v Hurricane Hydrocarbons Ltd*, 2005 ABQB 324 at para. 11, 382 A.R. 383; *Kelly v Watson* (1921), 61 S.C.R. 482 at 490, [1921] 1 W.W.R. 958. However, unlike the Courts in these two cases, the chambers judge here was not asked to re-write or make the parties' contract by implying missing terms in the existing contract. All other rights and obligations under the assigned dealership agreement were to remain unchanged but for the change in the identity of the dealer from Welcome Ford to the ultimate purchaser.

[47] Ford suggested that the chambers judge lacked clear evidence that the proposed assignment would benefit the estate. However, he described the supporting evidence at para. 52 of the December decision, which he found in the addendum to MNP's fourth report. Concluding that an assignment of the dealership agreement would benefit the creditors and enhance the value of the estate, the addendum confirmed that an *en bloc* sale of the assets of Welcome Ford which included the dealership agreement would result in full satisfaction of its indebtedness to BMO, would not prejudice Ford Credit's recovery on its secured collateral, and might make funds available for the unsecured creditors. Ford submitted that this evidence is nonetheless inadequate, criticizing MNP's method of marketing the land on which the dealership was located and the fact that the proposed sale would not, as a certainty, assure any recovery for the unsecured creditors.

[48] This criticism falls far short of being persuasive given that the alternative, termination of the dealership agreement, would not generate sufficient funds to satisfy even the secured creditors. The chambers judge's conclusion that the proposed assignment (sale) would benefit the estate is therefore reasonable and deserving of deference.

(ii)(b) Are the rights and obligations established by the dealership agreement not assignable by reason of their nature because they are personal?

[49] The dealership agreement expressly provides, among other things, that:

(a) Ford reserves the sole discretion to determine, from time to time, the numbers, locations and sizes of its franchised dealers;

(b) The dealership agreement is personal in nature and Ford expressly reserves the right to execute dealership agreements with individuals and others specifically selected and approved by it;

(c) Ford has the right to approve or decline to approve any transfer or change in voting control of a dealer based on the character, automotive experience, management, capital and other qualifications of the acquirer of the voting control, or the equity or beneficial interest, or the dealership business or its principal assets;

(d) Ford acknowledges a responsibility to ensure that dealers are owned and operated by qualified individuals of good reputation who are able to meet the requirements of the dealership agreement and the challenges of the marketplace;

(e) The dealership agreement may be terminated upon the happening of a number of events, including any transfer or attempted transfer by the dealer of any interest, right, privilege or obligation under the dealership agreement, or transfer by operation of law or otherwise of the principal assets of the dealer without the consent of Ford which "shall not be unreasonably withheld"; and

(f) Where there is a change in voting control of the principal owners of the dealership or a transfer of the dealership business or its principal capital assets, Ford's written approval is required; in declining any such approval (not to be unreasonably withheld), Ford has the right to consider the character, automotive experience, management capital and other qualifications of the proposed acquirer.

[50] Ford argued that these provisions characterize the dealership agreement as "personal" to the parties who executed it, and therefore non-assignable notwithstanding the express provision permitting assignment with Ford's permission. The chambers judge concluded otherwise. The dealership agreement was not a "personal contract" which by its "nature" could not usefully be performed by another. Instead, he described it as "a rather standard commercial franchise which could be performed by virtually any business person and entity with some capital and experience in automotive retailing" (para. 73). As such, it did not fall within the s. 84.1(3) exception.

[51] The dealership agreement is the same type of agreement as that found to be distinguishable from an employment or "personal service arrangement" by the Ontario Superior Court of Justice in *Struik v Dixie Lee Food Systems Ltd*, 2006 CarswellOnt 4932 at para. 69.

[52] Parties to a contract cannot insulate it from the effect of s. 84.1 simply by including a clause describing it as creating "personal" obligations where the contract is, in fact, a commercial one which could be performed by many others than the contracting parties.

[53] Ford correctly pointed out that s. 84.1(3) does not speak of a personal contract as being the only type of contract which contains rights and obligations that are not assignable by their nature. It argued that the above terms of the dealership agreement evidence that it is not assignable by reason of its nature even if it is not a personal contract.

[54] However, those express provisions—including those which describe it as personal in nature as well as Ford's reservation of the right to execute dealership agreements with those specifically selected and approved by it—are not sufficient to attract the application of s. 84.1(3) if other circumstances suggest the contrary. Otherwise, s. 84.1(4) would have no meaning, if a simple contractual provision to the effect that it was not "by reason of its nature" capable of unilateral assignment would be enough to make that so.

[55] Ford accepted that the test to be applied to determine if the dealership agreement contains rights and obligations which by their nature are not assignable is that set out in *Black Hawk Mining Inc v Manitoba (Provincial Assessor)*, 2002 MBCA 51 at paras. 79, 81–82, [2002] 7 W.W.R. 104. At para. 82 of *Black Hawk Mining*, the Manitoba Court of Appeal cited *Maloney v Campbell* (1897), 28 S.C.R. 228 at 233 as follows:

> Agreements are said to be personal in this sense when they are based on confidences, or considerations applicable to special personal characteristics, and so cannot be usefully performed to or by another.

[56] Ford argued that it requires its dealers to have special personal characteristics, including specific requirements of knowledge, capital and experience. It led evidence that the value of a dealership is based primarily on the ability of the person operating it. However, the test for "non-assignability" found in *Black Hawk Mining* is not that it is important to Ford who would be performing the rights and obligations of Welcome Ford in the future, but rather whether those rights and obligations cannot be performed by the proposed assignee.

[57] In any event, the evidence did not support the argument that it was important to Ford to have Smith and no other act as the Welcome Ford dealer. The chambers judge relied upon the fact that there was no evidence Ford had made any inquiry in respect of Smith, the owner of Welcome Ford, before signing the original dealership agreement or its most recent renewal in 2007, even to the extent of a credit check or confirmation as to his or the dealership's financial status from their bankers. Indeed, Ford did not know that Smith had relocated to the Dominican Republic well before the receivership order was granted; there was no evidence that it monitored him or stayed in regular contact with him throughout the period he controlled Welcome Ford.

[58] Ford responded that it had no ability to review the qualifications of dealers when the 2007 renewal was signed; it was the dealers alone who had the obligation of signing onto the new form or continuing with the extant form of agreement. However, Ford was presumably responsible for the drafting of the original dealership agreement signed by Smith. If it failed to provide for ongoing proof of financial and other stability, that is an indicator that Ford did not consider those factors to be important.

[59] The gist of the dealership agreement is that Ford agreed to provide automobiles to Welcome Ford, who in turn agreed to purchase and pay for them, and thereafter to promote their sale and provide after-market service. The operation of this agreement unfolded in a commercial manner. The evidence did not disclose anything which Smith alone could or did provide. The conclusions of the chambers judge that nothing in the agreement rendered it unassignable, either because it was said to be "personal" or not to be assigned without Ford's consent, are reasonable and should be accorded deference.

(iii) Should the dealership agreement not be assigned because of the capacity of the proposed assignee or because it is inappropriate to assign Welcome Ford's rights and obligations under s. 84.1(4)?

[60] Section 84.1(4) of the *BIA* directs a judge, in determining if an order approving an assignment (sale) is to be made, to consider whether the party to whom the rights and obligations are proposed to be assigned can perform those obligations in the same manner as the original dealer. If not, court approval of the assignment should be withheld.

[61] Ford argued the chambers judge did not have sufficient evidence to be able to conclude that the principal of the ultimate purchaser, the proposed assignee, would

be able to perform the dealership obligations in the same fashion as had Smith. Notwithstanding the fact that principal was already successfully operating another Ford dealership in the area, Ford argued there was no evidence before the chambers judge as to i) the financial capability of its principal (even though he was proposing to make the purchase without the need of financing), ii) a business plan for operating multiple dealerships, or iii) his ability to satisfy Ford's criteria for owning and operating multiple dealerships.

[62] Presumably some, if not all, of this evidence would have been internally available to Ford, yet it led no evidence to show any disability on the part of the ultimate purchaser. The chambers judge expressly relied on unchallenged affidavit evidence from another local Ford dealer to the effect that the proposed assignee had an excellent track record in terms of operating a profitable Ford dealership and had received many national awards from Ford over the years; the quality of its business premises met Ford's standards, unlike those which Ford had permitted Welcome Ford to operate. From this, the chambers judge inferred that the proposed assignee had both the capital and relevant experience in automotive retailing to enable him to operate the Welcome Ford dealership.

[63] Ford went on to argue that the "good faith" obligation imposed on the parties under the dealership agreement takes into account the particular dealer. It is akin to the duty of good faith found in an employment contract: see *Transamerica Life Canada Inc v ING Canada Inc* (2003), 68 O.R. (3d) 457 at para. 46 (Ont. C.A.). This means Ford would have a right of action for damages where a dealer breached the duty of fair dealing in the performance or enforcement of the dealership agreement: see Frank Zaid, *Canadian Franchise Guide*, looseleaf (Toronto: Thomson Reuters, 1992) at 2-142Z.36.

[64] An assignment to any third party could conceivably increase the risk of that party not honouring its good faith obligation. However, the dealership agreement will be assigned only upon the court finding the appropriate prerequisite capability, with the resulting reduction in risk that the new dealer will be less honest than the old. Indeed, in this situation where the former dealership encountered a significant problem with employee misappropriation, these risks will likely be well reduced by the proposed assignment to an existing Ford dealer who presumably operates its other dealerships under a similar "good faith" obligation.

[65] Section 84.1(4) of the *BIA* also directs a judge, in determining if an order approving an assignment (sale) should be made, to consider whether it is appropriate to assign the rights and obligations under the agreement.

[66] The chambers judge assumed, for the purposes of his decision, that "the consent of Ford Motor to the proposed assignee is required", and that the unreasonable failure to provide that consent is a consideration in determining that it is appropriate to nonetheless assign (sell) the agreement. There is nothing in s. 84.1 which expressly requires that the consent of the contracting party be canvassed as a prerequisite to the application for approval of an assignment of an agreement. The chambers judge did not find that such canvassing was required; he simply assumed it was for the purpose of his analysis. There is no reason to interpret the section as containing such an implicit prerequisite. Rather, an unreasonable withholding of consent is simply one factor to consider in determining whether it is otherwise appropriate to assign the agreement pursuant to s. 84.1(4).

[67] The chambers judge found that Ford would never consent to the assignment of this dealership agreement because it would not consent to the assignment of any dealership agreement where a dealership had ceased operation. In withholding consent, Ford

had not taken into account the merits of the proposed assignee. The chambers judge therefore concluded that Ford had unreasonably withheld its consent.

[68] Ford argued that a wider investigation needed to be undertaken when determining the appropriateness of assigning the dealership agreement than simply one of its refusal to consent. This investigation would canvass the terms of the agreement, the departing dealer's misconduct, the Receiver's failure to continue to operate the dealership pending approval of the proposed sale, Ford's standard criteria when considering a request to assign a dealership agreement outside of an insolvency context, and the results of an analysis it had done subsequent to the closure of Welcome Ford which concluded that future direct representation of the Ford brand was not warranted in the Fort Saskatchewan area.

[69] While the chambers judge described his investigation into these issues as "limited", he did consider factors in addition to Ford's unreasonable refusal to consent. Those other factors were the uncontradicted evidence that the ultimate purchaser was up to the job, his conclusion that the proposed assignment would substantially cure the breaches which Ford argued were fundamental, and that all of Ford's rights and remedies under the dealership agreement would be preserved against the proposed assignee. There was no obligation upon the chambers judge to expressly address each additional factor which Ford argued should bear on his determination. His approval of the assignment conveys the results of his assessment of those arguments.

[70] Ford argued that the chambers judge should not have considered its failure to consent to any assignment as a factor at all; to do so would amount to a limitation on access to justice in a new area in which it wished to test the effects of s. 84.1 of the *BIA*. Even if that is so today, it does not counteract the other reasons given by the chambers judge for concluding that it was appropriate to approve the assignment.

[71] In summary, the chambers judge concluded the dealership agreement was assignable by reason of its nature based on an assessment of evidence showing the proposed assignee would be able to discharge the dealer's obligations thereunder and upon concluding that it was appropriate to assign the agreement based on evidence that Ford unreasonably withheld its consent, that the effect of earlier breaches of the agreement would be remedied through its assignment, and that Ford's rights and remedies under the agreement would carry on unchanged. That decision was reasonable; deference should be accorded to it.

Appeal dismissed.

Discussion

The *Ford* case gives rise to a question as to whether the court can approve an assignment under section 84.1, overriding objections of the counterparty based on faulty business judgment. For example, if the proposed assignee in the *Ford* case really was "up to the job" and the counterparty's other interests were adequately protected, the counterparty's objection to the assignment was irrational. Alternatively, section 84.1 could be interpreted to mean that the court can approve an assignment, even if it harms the counterparty, provided that the cost to the counterparty is less than the benefit to the debtor's estate.

Cases decided before the 2009 amendments suggest that the latter interpretation may be the correct one. In *Re Playdium Entertainment Corp* (2001), 31 CBR (4th) 302 (Ont Ct J), it was held that the court in *CCAA* proceedings had power, as part of its broad statutory discretion, to approve the assignment of a contract and that there were four main factors to consider:

(1) whether the debtor had made a sufficient effort to obtain the best price for the contract; (2) *the competing interests of the counterparty and the debtor's other stake-holders*; (3) the efficacy and integrity of the process by which the offers were obtained; and (4) whether there has been any unfairness in the working out of the process (at paras 26–28, citing *Canadian Red Cross Society, Re* (1998), 5 CBR (4th) 299 (Ont Ct J (Gen Div)) (emphasis added)). In *Re Nexient Learning Inc* (2009), 62 CBR (5th) 248 (Ont Sup Ct J) the court, having approved this four-part test, went on to say that the requested relief must not adversely affect the counterparty's rights "*beyond what is absolutely required to further the reorganization process*" and that such interference must "not *entail an inappropriate imposition upon the [counterparty] or an inappropriate loss of claims of the [counterparty]*" (at para 59) (emphasis added). Although these are *CCAA* cases, the courts are likely to take them into account when interpreting *BIA*, section 84.1.

In light of the similarity between *BIA*, section 84.1, and the provincial laws governing the assignment of lessor and tenant agreements, as well as the fact that there is limited caselaw under *BIA*, section 84.1, to date, looking to the cases applying the provincial provisions can provide some guidance on the application of *BIA*, section 84.1. One such case is *Darrigo Consolidated Holdings Ltd v Norfinch Construction (Toronto) Ltd* (1987), 63 CBR (NS) 216 (Ont SC). In this case, the debtor carried on a retail business at two stores in Toronto, which it held on lease. The trustee wanted to sell the debtor's business on a going concern basis and this involved being able to assign the leases to the new owner. The lessors objected to the proposed assignments on the ground that the assignee was a newly formed company with no business history and so its financial credentials were uncertain. Alternatively, they argued that if the court approved the assignment, it should require the assignee to provide security for the rent. The court disagreed. On the one hand, it expressed concern that if the assignment was disallowed, the trustee's efforts to sell the business on a going concern basis might fail. On the other hand, the court concluded that there was no real basis for the lessor's fears about not being paid. And, as for ordering that the assignee should provide security for the rent, the court held that this would put the lessors in a better position than they were before the debtor became bankrupt.

In *Micro Cooking Centres (Can) Inc (Trustee of) v Cambridge Leaseholds Ltd* (1988), 68 CBR (NS) 60 (Ont SC), the debtor leased retail premises in two shopping centre developments where it sold microwave ovens and cooking appliances. The trustee wanted to assign the leases to a company that planned to sell frozen yoghurt and fruit juices. Both leases contained a "user covenant," which stated that the premises were only to be used as a retail store for the sale of microwave ovens and kitchenware. The lessor objected on the ground that the shopping centre depended on a pre-arranged business mix and the assignee's proposed business was inconsistent with the mix. The trustee argued that the assignee had agreed "to conduct upon the demised premises a trade or business which is not reasonably of a more objectionable or hazardous nature than that which was thereon conducted by the debtor," as required by section 38(2), and therefore the court should approve the application. The court rejected the application on the ground that the assignee was not a fit and proper person to be put in possession of the leased premises: "to confer a right on the assignee to ignore the user clause in the lease would be to emasculate the terms of the lease by sweeping aside, what in the context of a shopping mall, is a fundamental term." Note that the court could have found for the lessors on the alternative ground that under section 38(2), the proposed assignee must agree to observe the terms of the lease and these would include the user covenant. Under *BIA*, section 84.1, the case would presumably turn on whether it was "appropriate" to assign the premises to the assignee.

Practice Questions

Question 1

Lemoney Lemonade Inc (LL Inc) leases space in a strip mall in Fergus, Ontario for its boutique lemonade store for $1,000 per month. There is a worldwide lemon shortage that forces LL Inc to raise its prices. With the higher prices, demand for lemonade decreases and business slows down. As a result, LL Inc is unable to pay its lemon suppliers. On 1 March, LL Inc files for bankruptcy under the *BIA*. On the date of the bankruptcy, LL Inc is two months in arrears on its lease to the lessor. Under the terms of the lease, the lessor is entitled to three months accelerated rent. The trustee causes LL Inc to occupy the premises for one month. Then, on 1 April, the trustee causes LL Inc to vacate the premises and provides the lessor with notice that it is disclaiming the lease under sections 30(1)(k) and 146 of the *BIA* and sections 38 and 39 of the *Commercial Tenancies Act*, RSO 1990, c L.7. How will the law apply to the lessor's claims for: (1) rental arrears; (2) accelerated rent; (3) rent payments for occupation of premises during bankruptcy; and, (4) other future payments due under the lease?

Question 2

Davinder has a cellphone contract with a telecommunications company that lasts for one more year. He uses his cellphone for personal matters. Davinder becomes bankrupt. What options does the bankruptcy trustee have regarding the cell phone contract? What are the consequences for the telecommunication company's claim for each option? What is the main consideration for the trustee in determining which option to take?

Question 3

Muhammad opened a video rental store in 1990. He never incorporated the store. Business was going great until technology started to change in the early 2000s and his customers stopped renting videos from brick-and-mortar stores. Muhammad was able to keep his store open while most of his competitors closed their doors. In trying to keep his business going, Muhammad put most of his money into the business and fell behind on his monthly personal bills. Unfortunately, Muhammad's effort to save his store was not successful, and he is not able to make his store profitable again. Muhammad files for bankruptcy. On the date of his bankruptcy, Muhammad has not paid his personal hydro bill for six months. A few weeks later, the company that supplies his electricity threatens to stop supplying Muhammad with electricity until he pays his bill in full. Is the hydro company allowed to do this? Which sections of the *BIA* apply?

Question 4

Rebecca leases a commercial space in London, Ontario to a local artist. The local artist uses the space as an art studio and a gallery in which to showcase and sell her work. The lease between Rebecca and the local artist states that the lease cannot be assigned without express permission from Rebecca. This provision is extremely important to Rebecca, as she enjoys supporting local businesses. The local artist becomes bankrupt. There are three years left on the lease. As soon as the bankruptcy trustee is appointed, he writes to Rebecca to let her know that he intends to assign the lease to a franchisee of a large US art corporation. Rebecca writes back to the bankruptcy trustee to tell him that she refuses to give permission for the bankruptcy trustee to assign the lease. Can Rebecca do this?

Question 5

Toboggans, Toboggans, Toboggans Ltd (TTT Ltd) operates a business manufacturing toboggans. TTT Ltd leases a factory from a lessor in Windsor, Ontario. This past winter, there was not very much snow in Ontario and sales suffered. TTT Ltd becomes bankrupt. A trustee is appointed. The trustee finds another business willing to take on the lease of the factory space. What requirements must be followed for the lease to be validly assigned? Please cite the relevant caselaw and sections from the *BIA* and the *Commercial Tenancies Act*.

CHAPTER 7

BIA Claims

I. INTRODUCTION

To be entitled to participate in the debtor's bankruptcy, a creditor must have a "provable" claim (*Bankruptcy and Insolvency Act*, RSC, 1985, c B-3, s 2(1), "creditor" [*BIA*]). The amount of the creditor's claim is relevant to determining the size of the dividend it will receive from the bankrupt's estate. For example, assume there are enough assets in the estate to pay unsecured creditors 5 cents on the dollar. If the creditor's claim is for $200, it will receive $10. If, however, its claim is for $500, it will receive $25. The amount of a creditor's claim also matters because it determines the number of votes it can cast in a creditor's meeting (*BIA*, s 115). Similarly, in the context of commercial proposals undertaken under the *BIA*, the amount of a creditor's claim determines its voting power in a class meeting to approve a proposal (*BIA*, s 54(1)). Section 54(1) of the *BIA* further provides that a proposal is accepted if all classes of unsecured creditors vote in favour by a majority in number and two thirds in value: see further, Chapter 16. The *Companies' Creditors Arrangement Act*, RSC 1985, c C-36 (*CCAA*), section 6, enacts a similar rule for *CCAA* plans: see Chapter 15.

This chapter addresses two issues:

1) What is a provable claim?
2) What are the rules for valuing claims?

A. Provable Claims

BIA, section 121(1), provides:

> All debts and liabilities, present or future, to which the bankrupt is subject on the day on which the bankrupt becomes bankrupt or to which the bankrupt may become subject before the bankrupt's discharge by reason of any obligation incurred before the day on which the bankrupt becomes bankrupt shall be deemed to be claims provable in proceedings under this Act.

This definition covers present debts (debts owed to the creditor on the date of the debtor's bankruptcy); future debts (debts that are owing, but not payable on the date of the bankruptcy); contingent debts (debts subject to a condition that has not been fulfilled); and unliquidated claims (claims for an amount that is undetermined at the date of the bankruptcy). However, the definition is limited to pre-bankruptcy claims and, as a general rule, debts and liabilities incurred after the date of bankruptcy are not provable claims (*Re Sanderson* (1978), 21 OR (2d) 539 (Ont CA)). One exception is post-filing claims for environmental clean-up costs (*BIA*, s 14.06(8)). Another exception arises in the context of executory contracts: if a contract is disclaimed in a bankruptcy, the other party to the contract has a provable claim for damages, even though it arises post-filing (see Chapter 6, Section II). It is important to note that before a contract is disclaimed, the counterparty does not have a provable claim, since the trustee may choose to affirm the contract.

Section 124(1) provides that every creditor must prove their claim, and a creditor who does not prove their claim is not entitled to share in any distribution. Section 178(2) provides that, as a general rule, an order of discharge releases the debtor from all claims provable in the bankruptcy. This includes provable claims from creditors where no proof of claim was filed pursuant to section 124(1). The threat of receiving nothing from the bankrupt's estate gives a creditor with a provable claim a strong incentive to file a proof of claim. If, however, the claim is not a provable claim, the creditor cannot file a proof of claim under section 124(1), and its claim will not be released when the debtor is discharged. The consequences of failing to lodge a proof of claim in restructuring proceedings are roughly comparable: see chapters 14 and 16.

B. Valuation of Claims

A contingent claim or an unliquidated claim will be an unprovable claim if it is too difficult to value. This follows from sections 121(2) and 135(1.1) read in combination. Section 121(2) states that the classification of a contingent or unliquidated claim is provable, and the value of that claim will be made in compliance with section 135. Section 135(1.1) provides that the trustee shall determine whether any contingent or unliquidated claim is a provable claim, and if it is a provable claim, it will be valued by the trustee. If a creditor disputes the trustee's decision about the claim, it has thirty days to appeal to the court (*BIA*, s 135(4)).

The scheme is driven by two competing policy considerations: (1) debtor rehabilitation; and (2) the need for finality of bankruptcy proceedings. In the case of an individual debtor, one of the objects of the bankruptcy laws is to wipe the slate clean so the debtor can make a fresh start. This means that "provable claim" should be defined as widely as possible so the debtor is not left with outstanding liabilities after the discharge. The discharge provisions only apply to individuals. Where the debtor is a company, the fresh start policy is to be found in the restructuring laws (*BIA*, Part III, Div 1, and the *CCAA*). A *BIA* proposal, if accepted by creditors, releases the debtor from provable claims except for payments the debtor agrees to make under the proposal. The same is true for restructuring plans organized under the *CCAA*. Again, in the restructuring context, it makes sense in terms of the fresh start policy to define "provable claim" as widely as possible.

The opposing element is the need for finality of bankruptcy proceedings. Unliquidated and contingent claims are by definition uncertain. The only sure way to resolve the uncertainty in the case of an unliquidated claim is to wait and see what the court hearing the claim decides. Similarly, the only sure way to resolve the uncertainty in the case of a contingent claim is to wait and see whether the contingency materializes. The difficulty with the wait and see option is that it may take years to determine if the claim will arise, and it would be undesirable to hold up bankruptcy or restructuring proceedings indefinitely. The main solutions are to estimate the present value of the claim and admit it to proof on that basis or, alternatively, if the estimation is too difficult, determine that the claim is not a provable claim. The first option is consistent with the rehabilitation goal of the bankruptcy laws, but it means doing rough and ready justice so far as the value of the creditor's claim is concerned. The second option is consistent with the need for finality in bankruptcy proceedings, but it is inconsistent with the fresh start policy.

The Supreme Court of Canada was recently called upon to address these competing policy considerations in the context of family law proceedings in a Manitoba case. In *Schreyer v Schreyer*, 2011 SCC 35 (*Schreyer*), the Supreme Court of Canada held that if an equalization claim is liquidated before the date of bankruptcy, the claim is undisputedly provable. On the other hand, if the claim was still unliquidated as of the date of bankruptcy, the court must decide whether it is capable of valuation under section 135 of the *BIA*, taking into account any provincial equalization schemes (*Schreyer*, at para 27; see also *Bukvik v Bukvik* (2007), 86 OR (3d) 297 (Sup Ct J)), excerpted in Part II, below). Specifically, at what point does the province's equalization scheme give rise to a right of payment, and how certain is the amount of the payment? In *Schreyer*, a right to payment existed from the time of separation of the spouses, which pre-dated the bankruptcy (*Schreyer*, at para 27). This left only the issue of quantification, where the court could rely on the clear formula in Manitoba's family law legislation, leaving little scope for judicial discretion. Accordingly, the claim arose prior to bankruptcy and was provable.

In many estates, these issues create no problems, particularly because there is often not enough left in the estate to make it worthwhile for unsecured creditors to press their claims. As noted, problems arise where the claim is unliquidated or contingent in character. The cases extracted in Part II illustrate some of these problems in the context of *BIA* proceedings, as well as the innovative approach taken by American courts in resolving deadlocks.

II. ILLUSTRATIVE CASES

Ontario New Home Warranty Program v Jiordan Homes Ltd (1999), 43 OR (3d) 756 (Ont Ct J (Gen Div))

FERGUSON J:

The Facts
The defendant is a former shareholder in Jiordan which was in the business of building houses.

The sequence of events is this:

July 14, 1989—the defendant signed a guarantee in which he agreed to indemnify the plaintiff if it had to make good any obligations of Jiordan

July 17, 1989—Jiordan agreed to indemnify the plaintiff if it had to make good any obligations of Jiordan under an agreement of purchase and sale

August 14, 1991—Jiordan agreed to sell a house to Ramos with a closing date of March 30, 1992

November 14, 1991—the defendant filed an assignment in bankruptcy

March 30, 1992—the sale of the house did not close

October 29, 1992—the defendant was discharged from bankruptcy

October 30, 1992—Ramos made a claim against the plaintiff for the return of the deposit it had paid Jiordan under the sale agreement

January 22, 1993—the plaintiff paid Ramos compensation of $8,000 pursuant to s. 14 of the *Ontario New Home Warranties Plan Act*, RSO 1990, c. O.31.

The plaintiff is claiming the $8,000 from the defendant under his personal guarantee.

There are two issues: first, did the bankruptcy terminate the guarantee? Second, if not, is the claim barred because of the defendant's bankruptcy?

Counsel advise me there are no cases on point.

I shall consider the two issues in reverse order.

Is the Claim Barred by Section 69 [now s 69.3] of the Bankruptcy Act?

Section [69.3(1)] of the *Bankruptcy and Insolvency Act*, RSC 1985, c. B-3, as amended, states that a creditor has no remedy against an insolvent for a claim provable in bankruptcy.

Section 121(1) states:

> 121(1) All debts and liabilities, present or future, to which the bankrupt is subject at the date of the bankruptcy or to which he may become subject before his discharge by reason of any obligation incurred before the date of the bankruptcy shall be deemed to be claims provable in proceedings under this Act.

Subsection (2) provides that the court shall on application by the trustee determine whether any contingent claim is a provable claim. No such application was made.

It appears to me that when the defendant went bankrupt, the claim by the plaintiff against the defendant was a future liability to which the defendant might theoretically become subject before his discharge by reason of an obligation incurred before the date of the bankruptcy. The obligation was the indemnity agreement.

The theoretical risk was this: before the defendant's discharge, Jiordan had failed to close the sale, and if it did not repay the deposits, Ramos might claim the amount from the plaintiff, and the plaintiff might pay and claim the amount from the defendant. However, s. 121(1) makes the claim a provable claim only if the defendant "is subject" to a liability before his discharge; that is, it is a provable claim only if the defendant actually becomes liable before his discharge. While the section includes liabilities which may become due at a future time after discharge, it appears to me that it does not include liabilities which do not arise until after discharge.

Here, the defendant did not become subject to a liability until the plaintiff made the payment for which it claims indemnity and that payment was made after discharge.

Consequently, I conclude that the claim in this action was not a provable claim in the defendant's bankruptcy and this action is not barred by s. [69.3(1)] of the *Bankruptcy and Insolvency Act*, as amended.

Did the Bankruptcy Terminate the Guarantee?

There appears to be no provision in the Act which governs this issue.

It may seem anomalous that where a person's wealth is erased by bankruptcy, and that wealth is the reason why he was asked for and gave a guarantee, that he should continue to be liable on the guarantee after bankruptcy for claims which were not provable in bankruptcy and therefore not erased by it. However, I can see no indication in the Act that the guarantee should somehow evaporate in the bankruptcy. If the bankrupt were a party to other kinds of contracts which imposed obligations on him then these would not evaporate because of the bankruptcy.

I conclude that the guarantee here survives the bankruptcy and that the Act does not bar this action.

Motion granted.

Bukvic v Bukvic (2007), 86 OR (3d) 297 (Sup Ct J)

DJ GORDON J: ...

[79] The *Divorce Act* and *Family Law Act* have long been considered to create a debtor–creditor relationship when one spouse is obliged to make payment, either as to property or for support, to the other spouse.

[80] Prior to the amendments to the *BIA*, support recipients were not considered creditors in insolvency matters. In *Burrows, Re*, [1996] OJ No. 2825 (Ont. Gen. Div. [Commercial List]), the bankrupt support payor sought to have his support arrears declared provable such that enforcement would be stayed. Feldman J, as she then was, in finding the arrears were not provable, set out the common law position on support in the bankruptcy context, saying, at para. 7:

> In my view the Director's position is correct. Although the genesis of the rule is correctly articulated by the debtor, that is, because support payments can always be varied they cannot be quantified for proof in bankruptcy, it has become accepted law that maintenance and support payments including all arrears, whether court-ordered or made by agreement between the parties do not amount to a claim provable in bankruptcy.

[81] The rationale for the common law, as I understand it, was:
a) support claims were too uncertain; and,
b) the support debt would continue to exist post-bankruptcy and the support recipient was free to enforce the obligation on non-excluded property during bankruptcy.

The common law was seen as a hindrance to support recipients and, thus, legislative amendment was deemed necessary.

[82] The 1997 amendments to the *BIA* included what is now section 121(4). Support obligations were recognized as a provable claim where:
a) there is a debt or liability of the bankrupt to pay support;
b) such support is payable pursuant to an order or agreement made before the bankruptcy date;
c) the spouses are separated; and,
d) periodic support or lump sum amounts are provided in the order or agreement.

[83] In the case at bar, the wife meets this threshold test. The support order granted 23 February 2006 obligated the husband to pay periodic support, thus creating a liability.

[84] There were no support arrears on the bankruptcy date. Section 121(1), however, speaks of "all debts and *liabilities*, present or *future* ...." Future support obligations are an obvious liability. Section 121(2) refers to "contingent and unliquidated claims" and section 121(3) addresses "debts payable at a future time," all of which are provable claims if such are capable of calculation.

[85] There appears to be some disagreement as to the interpretation of section 121 with respect to support.

[86] As noted previously, Mr. Klotz is of the view section 121(4) only applies to support arrears arising before the bankruptcy date. Other commentators offer a similar interpretation. For example, Ronald E. Pizzo, in his paper "*Support Claims in Bankruptcy and Related Enforcement Issues*" 1999, 16 National Insolvency Review at p. 21 said:

> The new amendments affect only pre-bankruptcy arrears which arose while the spouses were living separate and apart. All other support obligations, including ongoing periodic

support obligations and arrears arising after the date of bankruptcy, have not been affected by the new amendments. These claims are not provable in bankruptcy.

[87] Section 121(4) makes no mention of "support arrears" and, in my view, the above interpretation is incorrect. It would appear these commentators may be relying on the initial draft amendments as contained in Bill C-109. Bill C-109, which expired on the order paper, would have restricted provable support amounts to those assigned priority under section 136(1)(d.1). Bill C-5, as passed by Parliament, deleted such a restriction from section 121(4). It is logical to conclude Parliament thus intended to allow all support, "present or future," to be a provable claim. Support arrears accruing in the year prior and any lump sum payments in arrears are then left as priority claims under section 136(1)(d.1).

[88] Tamara M. Buckwold, in her book review "*Bankruptcy, Insolvency and Family Law,* 2nd ed., by Robert A. Klotz (Toronto, Carswell, 2001)," (2002) 37 Can. Bus. LJ 469, at pp. 471–2, provides this comment:

> In the same chapter, Klotz expresses in unqualified terms, and without supporting authority, the proposition that the provability of support arrears (and the special priority attaching to them under *BIA* s. 136) is limited to arrears accrued up to, but not after, the date of bankruptcy. This appears to represent a misreading of *BIA* s. 121. Subsection (4), specifically addressing the provability of support claims, might have been worded more clearly. However, it must be read in conjunction with subsection (1), which stipulates that provable claims include "liabilities, present or future ... to which the bankrupt may become subject before the bankrupt's discharge by reason of any obligation incurred before the date on which the bankrupt becomes bankrupt." This must mean that support obligations payable after the date of bankruptcy but before the bankrupt payor's discharge are to be included in the provable claim, provided that they arise under a pre-bankruptcy agreement or order. This point, which may be significant in some circumstances, reappears at several other junctures in the book.

[89] Prof. Buckwold, in my view, provides the correct interpretation of section 121 as found in the present legislation.

[90] Accordingly, I conclude the wife has a provable claim although it does not have priority. Clearly, the bankrupt's obligation for future support arose by virtue of the court order prior to the bankruptcy date. The wife is, therefore, an unsecured creditor of the bankrupt estate.

[91] Mr. Snider relied on Misener J's decision in *Burson v Burson* (1990), 29 RFL (3d) 454 (Ont. Gen. Div.) where, at para. 24, he said:

> Whatever might have been the effect of any of the provisions of the *Family Law Reform Act,* none of the provisions of the *Family Law Act, 1986* grant to one spouse a legal or beneficial interest in any property of the other spouse at any stage. At the highest, the *Family Law Act, 1986* statutorily created a creditor–debtor relationship between the spouses upon permanent separation, with the calculation of the amount of the debt to be made by a formula that requires the valuation of their respective properties. There are, of course, provisions that empower the court to order the transfer of the property of one spouse to the other, either for the satisfaction of the debt or as security for the debt, but these provisions are remedial only, and discretionary at that. Absent the actual making of such an order pursuant to them, those sections cannot possibly be construed so as to grant, on their face, property rights.

[92] This passage has been cited with approval on several occasions. For example, in *Gaudet (Litigation Guardian of) v Young Estate* (1995), 11 RFL (4th) 284 (Ont. Gen. Div.), LaForme J, at para. 16, concluded:

> I am of the view that the more recent cases of *Burson* and *Nevare Holdings Ltd* more properly reflect the law than does *Beck*. These recent cases are consistent with the view, which I share, that a spouse should not have priority over business creditors. Spouses should only share in the profits of a marriage generated during the relationship. As a result, Patricia Young's interest arising out of the continuing preservation order and her right to equalization, does not grant her priority over third party creditors of the estate.

[93] *Burson* and *Gaudet*, although decided prior to the 1997 amendments to the *BIA*, dealt with property issues, specifically equalization of net family property. Accordingly, these decisions are distinguishable and ought not be relied upon in connection with support issues.

[94] Sections 178(1)(b) and (c), *BIA*, provide that a discharge order does not release the bankrupt from support obligations. As well, pursuant to section 69.41, support enforcement proceedings are not stayed by an assignment in bankruptcy. Accordingly, in the vast majority of cases, support recipients will pursue their claim personally against the support payor, particularly by garnishment of wages.

[95] When the bankrupt has left the jurisdiction and abandoned his family, as here, there is no reasonable likelihood of the support recipient receiving future support. In those circumstances, she may wish, and must be allowed, to prove her claim as against the bankrupt estate.

[96] The practical difficulty, in most cases, will be in quantifying the future support obligation. As noted by Professor Buckwold above, section 121(1) includes provable support claims "... payable after the date of bankruptcy but before the bankrupt payor's discharge." The discharge date for most first-time bankrupts, pursuant to section 168.1, automatically occurs nine months after the bankruptcy date.

[97] In this case, however, the husband will not be seeking a discharge and, in my view, he is also ineligible for such relief. The husband has not participated in mandatory counselling pursuant to section 157.1(3), a prerequisite for discharge. He has fled the jurisdiction in circumstances which make it unlikely he will return. It appears, as I have found, the husband left with the money accumulated from financial institutions which may be a bankruptcy offence under section 198.

[98] Accordingly, the wife's claim is not restricted to nine months but, rather, includes the whole of the husband's future support obligation. This claim is capable of validation as such has already been calculated and converted into a lump sum amount as provided in my order granted 20 December 2006. The amount required from the bankrupt support payor is $389,666. This amount, therefore, is the provable claim of the wife against the bankrupt estate of the husband pursuant to section 121(1).

[99] From a policy perspective, it would be an obvious injustice if support creditors were not treated as creditors under the *BIA*. This proposition is amply supported by the comments in *Marzetti* and *Backman* previously mentioned. At the very least, all unsecured creditors, including support recipients, must be treated equally. Just as unconscionable as was the conduct of the husband in abandoning his family obligations, so too would be the action of a commercial creditor in attempting to assert absolute priority over a support recipient and thus subjecting her to a state of poverty.

[100] There is, in my view, a strong argument, from a policy perspective, for absolute priority in favour of provable spousal and child support claims, liability for such which occurs prior to the bankruptcy date. Priority, however, is restricted to the circumstances described in section 136(1)(d.1). Accordingly, it would not be proper for the court to declare a higher priority. Such is a function of Parliament. ...

[101] For the above reasons, an order shall issue on the following terms: ...

b) declaring Visnja Bukvic to be an unsecured creditor of the bankrupt estate with a provable claim in the amount of $389,666 ...

Order accordingly.

Bittner v Borne Chemical Company, Inc, 691 F (2d) 134 (3rd Cir 1982) *[Bittner]*

GIBBONS Cir J:

Stockholders of The Rolfite Company appeal from the judgment of the district court, affirming the decision of the bankruptcy court to assign a zero value to their claims in the reorganization proceedings of Borne Chemical Company, Inc. (Borne) under Chapter 11 of the Bankruptcy Code (Code), 11 USC §§1–151326 (Supp. IV 1981). Since the bankruptcy court neither abused its discretionary authority to estimate the value of the claims pursuant to 11 USC §502(c)(1) nor relied on clearly erroneous findings of fact, we affirm.

I.

Prior to filing its voluntary petition under Chapter 11 of the Code, Borne commenced a state court action against Rolfite for the alleged pirating of trade secrets and proprietary information from Borne. The Rolfite Company filed a counterclaim, alleging, *inter alia*, that Borne had tortiously interfered with a proposed merger between Rolfite and the Quaker Chemical Corporation (Quaker) by unilaterally terminating a contract to manufacture Rolfite products and by bringing its suit. Sometime after Borne filed its Chapter 11 petition, the Rolfite stockholders sought relief from the automatic stay so that the state court proceedings might be continued. Borne then filed a motion to disallow temporarily the Rolfite claims until they were finally liquidated in the state court. The bankruptcy court lifted the automatic stay but also granted Borne's motion to disallow temporarily the claims, extending the time within which such claims could be filed and allowed if they should be eventually liquidated.

Upon denial of their motion to stay the hearing on confirmation of Borne's reorganization plan, the Rolfite stockholders appealed to the district court, which vacated the temporary disallowance order and directed the bankruptcy court to hold an estimation hearing. The parties agreed to establish guidelines for the submission of evidence at the hearing, and, in accordance with this agreement, the bankruptcy court relied on the parties' choice of relevant pleadings and other documents related to the state court litigation, and on briefs and oral argument. After weighing the evidence, the court assigned a zero value to the Rolfite claims and reinstated its earlier order to disallow temporarily the claims until such time as they might be liquidated in the state court, in effect requiring a waiver of discharge of the Rolfite claims from Borne. Upon appeal, the district court affirmed.

II.

Section 502(c) of the Code provides:

> There shall be estimated for purposes of allowance under this section—
> (1) any contingent or unliquidated claim, fixing or liquidation of which, as the case may
>   be, would unduly delay the closing of the case. ...

The Code, the Rules of Bankruptcy Procedure, 11 USC App. (1977), and the Suggested Interim Bankruptcy Rules, 11 US CA (1982), are silent as to the manner in which contingent or unliquidated claims are to be estimated. Despite the lack of express direction on the matter, we are persuaded that Congress intended the procedure to be undertaken initially by the bankruptcy judges, using whatever method is best suited to the particular contingencies at issue. The principal consideration must be an accommodation to the underlying purposes of the Code. It is conceivable that in rare and unusual cases arbitration or even a jury trial on all or some of the issues may be necessary to obtain a reasonably accurate evaluation of the claims. See 3 *Collier on Bankruptcy* ¶502.03 (15th ed. 1981). Such methods, however, usually will run counter to the efficient administration of the bankrupt's estate and where there is sufficient evidence on which to base a reasonable estimate of the claim, the bankruptcy judge should determine the value. In so doing, the court is bound by the legal rules which may govern the ultimate value of the claim. For example, when the claim is based on an alleged breach of contract, the court must estimate its worth in accordance with accepted contract law. See, e.g., 3 *Collier on Bankruptcy* ¶57.15[3.2] (14th ed. 1977). However, there are no other limitations on the court's authority to evaluate the claim save those general principles which should inform all decisions made pursuant to the Code.

In reviewing the method by which a bankruptcy court has ascertained the value of a claim under section 502(c)(1), an appellate court may only reverse if the bankruptcy court has abused its discretion. ...

According to the Rolfite stockholders, the estimate which section 502(c)(1) requires is the present value of the probability that appellants will be successful in their state court action. Thus, if the bankruptcy court should determine as of this date that the Rolfite stockholders' case is not supported by a preponderance or 51% of the evidence but merely by 40%, they apparently would be entitled to have 40% of their claims allowed during the reorganization proceedings, subject to modification if and when the claims are liquidated in state court. The Rolfite stockholders contend that instead of estimating their claims in this manner, the bankruptcy court assessed the ultimate merits and, believing that they could not establish their case by a preponderance of the evidence, valued the claims at zero.

We note first that the bankruptcy court did not explicitly draw the distinction that the Rolfite stockholders make. Assuming however that the bankruptcy court did estimate their claims according to their ultimate merits rather than the present value of the probability that they would succeed in their state court action, we cannot find that such a valuation method is an abuse of the discretion conferred by section 502(c)(1).

The validity of this estimation must be determined in light of the policy underlying reorganization proceedings. In Chapter 11 of the Code, Congress addressed the complex issues which are raised when a corporation faces mounting financial problems.

> The modern corporation is a complex and multi-faceted entity. Most corporations do not have a significant market share of the lines of business in which they compete. The success,

and even the survival, of a corporation in contemporary markets depends on three elements: First, the ability to attract and hold skilled management; second, the ability to obtain credit; and third, the corporation's ability to project to the public an image of vitality. . . .

One cannot overemphasize the advantages of speed and simplicity to both creditors and debtors. Chapter XI allows a debtor to negotiate a plan outside of court and, having reached a settlement with a majority in number and amount of each class of creditors, permits the debtor to bind all unsecured creditors to the terms of the arrangement. From the perspective of creditors, early confirmation of a plan of arrangement: first, generally reduces administrative expenses which have priority over the claims of unsecured creditors; second, permits creditors to receive prompt distributions on their claims with respect to which interest does not accrue after the filing date; and third, increases the ultimate recovery on creditor claims by minimizing the adverse effect on the business which often accompanies efforts to operate an enterprise under the protection of the *Bankruptcy Act.*

124 Cong. Rec. H 11101-H 11102 (daily ed. Sept. 28, 1978) (statement of Rep. D. Edwards of California, floor manager for bankruptcy legislation in the House of Representatives). Thus, in order to realize the goals of Chapter 11, a reorganization must be accomplished quickly and efficiently.

If the bankruptcy court estimated the value of the Rolfite stockholders' claims according to the ultimate merits of their state court action, such a valuation method is not inconsistent with the principles which imbue Chapter 11. Those claims are contingent and unliquidated. According to the bankruptcy court's findings of fact, the Rolfite stockholders' chances of ultimately succeeding in the state court action are uncertain at best. Yet, if the court had valued the Rolfite stockholders' claims according to the present probability of success, the Rolfite stockholders might well have acquired a significant, if not controlling, voice in the reorganization proceedings. The interests of those creditors with liquidated claims would have been subject to the Rolfite interests, despite the fact that the state court might ultimately decide against those interests after the reorganization. The bankruptcy court may well have decided that such a situation would at best unduly complicate the reorganization proceedings and at worst undermine Borne's attempts to rehabilitate its business and preserve its assets for the benefit of its creditors and employees. By valuing the ultimate merits of the Rolfite stockholders' claims at zero, and temporarily disallowing them until the final resolution of the state action, the bankruptcy court avoided the possibility of a protracted and inequitable reorganization proceeding while ensuring that Borne will be responsible to pay a dividend on the claims in the event that the state court decides in the Rolfite stockholders' favor. Such a solution is consistent with the Chapter 11 concerns of speed and simplicity but does not deprive the Rolfite stockholders of the right to recover on their contingent claims against Borne.

III.

The Rolfite stockholders further contend that, regardless of the method which the bankruptcy court used to value their claims, the court based its estimation on incorrect findings of fact. Rule 810 of the Rules of Bankruptcy Procedure permits an appellate court to overturn a bankruptcy referee's findings of fact only when they are clearly erroneous. . . . A bankruptcy court may not, however, mask its interpretation of the law as findings of fact. In determining the legal merits of a case on which claims such as those of the Rolfite stockholders are based, the bankruptcy court should be guided by the applicable state law. The determination of such law is of course subject to plenary review. . . .

The Rolfite stockholders argue that in assessing the merits of its state court action for the purpose of evaluating their claims against Borne, the bankruptcy court erred both in finding the facts and in applying the law. In reviewing the record according to the standards we have just described, we cannot agree. ...

The court's ultimate finding of fact—that the Rolfite stockholders' claims in the reorganization proceeding were worth zero—must also be upheld since it too is not clearly erroneous. The subsidiary findings of the court plainly indicated that the Rolfite counter-claim in the state action lacked legal merit. Faced with only the remote possibility that the state court would find otherwise, the bankruptcy court correctly valued the claims at zero. On the basis of the court's subsidiary findings, such an estimation was consistent both with the claims' present value and with the court's assessment of the ultimate merits.

District Court judgment affirmed.

In re Chavez, 381 BR 582 (Bankr EDNY 2008)

CARLA E CRAIG Chief US Bktcy J:

This matter comes before the Court on the motion ("Motion") of the debtor, Marco Antonio Chavez (the "debtor" or "Mr. Chavez") to estimate proof of claim No. 6 under 11 USC §502(c) at one dollar, representing nominal damages to *pro se* claimant Carla Duncan (the "claimant" or "Ms. Duncan"). For the reasons set forth below, Ms. Duncan's claim, which arose from her wrongful eviction by the debtor from her apartment, is estimated at $28,916.04 representing compensatory and punitive damages, including $4,416.04, representing prejudgment interest at the rate of 9% per annum provided by CPLR §§5001(b). ...

Legal Standard

The debtor's motion to estimate the Claim is governed by §502(c) of the *Bankruptcy Code*, which provides:

(c) There shall be estimated for purpose of allowance under this section—
    (1) any contingent or unliquidated claim, the fixing or liquidation of which, as the case may be, would unduly delay the administration of the case;

11 USC §502(c).

Bankruptcy courts are required to estimate claims "[t]o achieve reorganization, and/or distributions on claims, without awaiting the results of legal proceedings." *In re Adelphia Business Solutions, Inc*, 341 BR 415, 423 (Bankr. SDNY 2003) (citation omitted); "[W]hen the liquidation of a claim is premised on litigation pending in a non-bankruptcy court, and the final outcome of the matter is not forthcoming, the bankruptcy court should estimate the claim." *In re Lionel LLC*, Case No. 04-17324, 2007 WL 2261539, at 2, 2007 Bankr. LEXIS 2652, at *7 (SDNY August 3, 2007) (citation omitted).

Ms. Duncan's action for damages has already continued for several years in the Civil Court, only to be transferred to the Supreme Court for further litigation. It is clearly within this Court's authority to estimate Ms. Duncan's claim to avoid further delay in the administration of the debtor's bankruptcy case.

"Neither the Bankruptcy Code nor the Federal Rules of Bankruptcy Procedure provide any procedures or guidelines for estimation." *DeGeorge Financial Corp v Novak (In re DeGeorge Financial Corp)*, Case No. 3:01CV0009(CFD), 2002 WL 31096716, at 10, 2002 US Dist. LEXIS 17621, at 34 (D.Conn. July 15, 2002). Courts addressing the issue have held that bankruptcy judges may use "whatever method is best suited to the particular contingencies at issue." *Id.* (quoting *Bittner v Borne Chemical Co,* 691 F.2d 134, 135 (3d Cir. 1982)). "The methods used by courts have run the gamut from summary trials to full-blown evidentiary hearings to a mere review of pleadings [and] briefs." *Id.* at 10, 2002 US Dist. LEXIS 17621 at 35 (citations omitted). In exercising this broad discretion, the "[c]ourt must apply 'the legal rules which govern the ultimate value of the claim,' which ordinarily requires the application of state law." *In re Enron Corp,* Case No. 01-16304, 2006 WL 544463, at 4, 2006 Bankr. LEXIS 4294, at 10 (SDNY January 17, 2006) (quoting *In re Brints Cotton Marketing, Inc,* 737 F.2d 1338, 1341 (5th Cir. 1984)). "In general, the truncated trial process that can be developed under 502(c) has been found to be consistent with the dictates of due process of law." *Lionel,* 2007 WL 2261539, at 5, 2007 Bankr. LEXIS 2652, at 16–17 (citations omitted).

Wrongful Eviction

The debtor testified that he locked Ms. Duncan out of the Apartment because he believed that she had voluntarily moved out. The Court finds that the debtor's account lacks credibility for many reasons.

For one thing, the debtor failed even once to mention, let alone to explain, the flood and resulting water damage in the Apartment, although Ms. Duncan introduced numerous photographs into evidence showing that it had occurred. (Claimant's Exhibits 2-A, 2-K, 2-M, 2-N and 25.) Ms. Duncan also introduced Officer Boyette's testimony that the kitchen was dismantled, and the cabinets removed, and introduced additional photographs showing that closet doors were broken and removed from their hinges. The condition of the Apartment described by Mr. Boyette and shown in the photographs is consistent with the explanation offered by Ms. Duncan for the debtor's actions—that he locked her out because he knew that he had rented her an illegal basement apartment and that the authorities were investigating this as a result of her complaint, and he wanted to get rid of the evidence that the basement was being used as an apartment. (Tr. 2, 14:5-6; 38:1-3; Claimant's Exhibits 3-A, 3-F.)

The debtor's omission of any mention of the flood and damage to the Apartment from his testimony adds credibility to Ms. Duncan's version of events. The debtor's failure to offer any alternative explanation why the Apartment was flooded and the kitchen cabinetry and appliances removed is difficult to understand and undermines the credibility of his testimony. (Tr. 2, 14:5-6; 38:2.) In fact, the debtor's entire story lacked credibility. His testimony was peppered with omissions, obvious falsehoods, and inconsistencies. The debtor's only supporting evidence was provided by his brother, Enrique Chavez, whose testimony was equally lacking in credibility.

For example, the debtor and his brother testified that they resided in the Apartment with Ms. Duncan and her daughter, and that Ms. Duncan and her daughter were guests and were never asked to pay any rent in exchange for living there. (Tr. 2, 29:11-13; 24:12-13; 93:2-8.) This distinction is not relevant to Ms. Duncan's claim for wrongful eviction; even the landlord of a squatter may not resort to self-help "[w]hen a landlord gives permission, whether implicit or express, to occupy his property." *Walls v Giuliani,* 916 F.Supp. 214, 218 (EDNY 1996). Apparently, however, the debtor believes that Ms. Duncan's status as a rent-paying tenant is relevant to whether it was legal for the Apartment to be used by her as a dwelling. Mr. Chavez states in his Declaration dated July 16, 2006, submitted in connection with the Debtor's Objection to Proof of Claim Number Six, that "[t]he basement does not contain a legal apartment or dwelling space, so it could not be rented to her, but it was habitable. I never requested any money from Ms. Duncan because of her relationship with my brother." (Declaration dated 7/10/06, ¶2.) The fact that the debtor concocted this patently incredible story of a communal living arrangement in the Apartment adds credibility to Ms. Duncan's explanation of events: there would be no reason for the debtor to fabricate such a story unless he was concerned about liability for renting an illegal basement apartment...

Officer Boyette's testimony directly contradicted the debtor's, and was unbiased, credible and uncontroverted. Officer Boyette's testimony further undermined the debtor's credibility, and added to the credibility of Ms. Duncan's version of events. Based on Ms. Duncan's and Officer Boyette's testimony, and based on the lack of credibility of the testimony offered by the debtor, this Court finds that the debtor locked Ms. Duncan out of the Apartment and removed and disposed of her property.

Damages

"One who enters upon lands by permission of the owner without any term being prescribed or without reservation of rent is a tenant at will and, as such, is entitled to one month's notice to quit." *Fisher v Queens Park Realty Corp*, 41 AD 2d 547, 549, 339 NYS 2d 642, 645 (2d Dept. 1973); see also *Walls v Giuliani*, 916 F.Supp. at 219 (A landlord may terminate a tenancy at will only by delivering written notice of at least 30 days demanding the tenant leave the premises). The debtor did not employ lawful process for evicting Ms. Duncan from the Apartment. The debtor had no right to lock Ms. Duncan out of the Apartment or to remove her possessions, and is therefore liable for any resulting damages.

Compensatory Damages

"The measure of compensatory damages for wrongful eviction is the value of the unexpired term of the lease over and above the rent the lessee must pay under its terms, together with any actual damages flowing directly from the wrongful eviction." *Long Isl Airports Limousine Serv Corp v Northwest Airlines*, 124 AD 2d 711, 713, 508 NYS 2d 223, 225 (2d Dept. 1986). Damages measured by the value of the unexpired term of the lease would be inapplicable here, as Ms. Duncan was a tenant at will. However, Ms. Duncan may recover the value of her personal property lost, stolen or discarded during the course of the wrongful eviction.

The value of Ms. Duncan's personal property need not be determined to an exact certainty. "Receipts are not required to establish the value of [Ms. Duncan's] property; actual monetary loss, value of the property to the owner, [and] reasonable value ... are all admissible to prove damages." *Foxworth v Tjutjulis*, 4 Misc. 3d 133A, 791 NYS 2d 869, 2007 NY Misc. LEXIS 1061, 2004 WL 1574703 (NY Misc. 2d Dept. 2004) (some testimonial or other evidence is required to establish the items lost and their estimated value); *N Main Bagel Corp v Duncan*, 37 AD 3d 785, 787, 831 NYS 2d 239, 242 (NY App. Div. 2d Dept. 2007) (holding that the Supreme Court erred in not granting the tenants the value of personal property lost in the unlawful eviction based on a lack of documentation showing exact prices paid, because there was credible testimony that the items were actually purchased and of their estimated values, and no evidence was offered by the landlord to the contrary.)

Ms. Duncan testified that she valued the items lost from the Apartment at $25,000, because that is the upper limit of damages available in Civil Court. (Tr. 2, 186: 11-12.) That is obviously not an appropriate method of valuing the items she lost. Though she testified generally that she lost food, clothes, toys, and household goods (Tr. 2, 166), Ms.

Duncan was unable to provide testimony identifying with any specificity the items she lost and their approximate value. (Tr. 2, 183-196.)

Ms. Duncan did, however, specifically identify the value of several items of property she lost as a result of the debtor's actions; she testified that she lost $5,000 in cash which she kept in the Apartment (Tr. 2, 167:15), as well as a blender, for which she paid $200, and a microwave, for which she paid $300 (Tr. 2, 189:3-4.) Ms. Duncan's testimony on these points was credible. Ms. Duncan testified that she did not have a bank account because she was a traveling surgical technician and had recently gone through an acrimonious divorce. (Tr. 2, 173:25; 174:1-3.) She stated that she would cash her pay checks weekly, and keep the money in the only closet in the Apartment that had a lock. (Tr. 2, 167:15-18; 174:6-8.) She further testified that she did not think that the debtor necessarily stole the $5,000 she had in her closet at the time she was locked out, but that he possibly threw it out along with the rest of her belongings. (Tr. 2, 167:23-25; 168:1-4.) In either event, the funds were lost as a result of the wrongful eviction, and the debtor is liable.

It is clear from Ms. Duncan's testimony as well as Officer Boyette's that Ms. Duncan lost other household goods, and although Ms. Duncan was unable to provide testimony concerning the value of those items, this Court assigns a value of $1,000 for estimation purposes to the other items of property lost by Ms. Duncan as a result of the debtor's actions. Ms. Duncan's claim for property damage is therefore estimated at $6,500.

Treble Damages

Section 853 of the *New York Real Property Actions and Proceedings Law* ("RPAPL") provides in pertinent part:

> If a person is disseized, ejected, or put out of real property in a forcible or unlawful manner, or after he has been put out, is held and kept out by force or by putting him in fear of personal violence or by unlawful means, he is entitled to recover treble damages in an action therefor against the wrong-doer.

RPAPL §853.

"Damages for the removal, destruction or discarding of property in the course of an unlawful eviction are included under §853." *H & P Research, Inc v Liza Realty Corp*, 943 F.Supp. 328, 330 (SDNY 1996). The record supports the conclusion that the debtor put Ms. Duncan out of the Apartment in an unlawful manner. Ms. Duncan is therefore entitled to treble damages, for a compensatory award of $19,500.

Punitive Damages

"An award for treble damages pursuant to RPAPL §853 does not preclude an additional award of punitive damages." *H & P Research, Inc*, 943 F.Supp. at 330. Punitive damages is a common-law remedy which is "only available in the extreme cases where the [landlord] is shown to have been motivated by actual malice or to have acted in such a reckless, wanton or criminal manner so as to indicate a conscious disregard of the rights of others." *Lyke v Anderson*, 147 AD 2d 18, 31, 541 NYS 2d 817, 825-826 (2d Dept. 1989). The record supports a finding that the debtor acted with a complete disregard for Ms. Duncan's property, for her safety and that of her daughter, and for her legal rights. *Suffolk Sports Center v Belli Construction Corp*, 212 AD 2d 241, 248, 628 NYS 2d 952, 956 (2d Dept. 1995) (Punitive damages are appropriate when denying such damages "[c]ould be interpreted as tacit permission for a landlord to engage in threats and intimidation ... conversely, the sanctioning of punitive damages will serve the public good by acting as [a] deterrent to similar actions in the future.") In this case, the record, including the debtor's patently incredible account of his living arrangements with Ms. Duncan, and his failure to offer any credible explanation of the circumstances under which he locked her out of the Apartment, or any account at all of the flooding of the Apartment and destruction of the kitchen, supports the conclusion that he acted in an attempt to force her out in order to cover up the fact that he had rented her an illegal apartment. As noted by the court in *Pleasant East Associates v Cabrera*:

> This case cries out for the imposition of punitive damages. Such a remedy should serve to deter the petitioner from repeating such conduct and serve as a warning to others.

125 Misc. 2d 877, 883-884, 480 NYS 2d 693 (NY City Civ. Ct. 1984) (citations omitted).

The measure of punitive damages must be proportionate to the amount of compensatory damages and to the nature of the landlord's conduct. In *Suffolk Sports Center*, 212 AD 2d at 248, 628 NYS 2d 952, the court set aside the amount awarded for punitive damages, stating that although punitive damages were appropriate where a landlord "embarked upon a calculated effort to vitiate the landlord–tenant relationship between it and [its tenant]," the $300,000 awarded should be reduced to $60,000, which the court found to be proportionate to the $99,364.45 compensatory damages awarded. *Id.* This Court finds an award of $4,000 in estimated punitive damages satisfies the purpose and public policy set forth above in light of the debtor's conduct and that such an award is proportionate to the $6,500 awarded in estimated compensatory damages.

Emotional Distress

The emotional distress suffered by Ms. Duncan as a result of the trauma of losing her home and her belongings may be compensable damage. "The principle of awarding damages for emotional distress is not unknown in New York and the application of such principle to a case where a tenant is unceremoniously evicted from [her] home is entirely in accord with analogous decisions and 'civilized public policy.'" *Williams v Llorente*, 115 Misc. 2d 171, 173, 454 NYS 2d 930, 932 (NY App. Term 1982) (citations omitted) (quoting *Stiles v Donovan*, 100 Misc. 2d 1048, 1050, 420 NYS 2d 453, 455 (Civ. Ct. NY Cty. 1979)) (awarding $250 for emotional distress finding sufficient testimony given by the tenant regarding the emotional impact of being unlawfully locked out of his apartment and having his belongings removed.); *Lopez v City of NY*, 78 Misc. 2d 575, 577, 357 NYS 2d 659, 661 (Civ. Ct. NY Cty. 1974) (awarding $500 to the tenant for emotional distress where the landlord unlawfully and forcibly evicted the tenant and, destroyed and discarded his belongings.); *Bianchi v Hood*, 128 AD 2d 1007, 1008, 513 NYS 2d 541, 542 (3d Dept. 1987) (awarding $1,000 for pain and suffering and mental distress based on the testimony of the tenant and her father, who verified the tenant's emotional distress and the aggravation to an ankle injury as a result of the "flagrant, unlawful interference by [the landlord] with [her] right to enjoy and possess her leased premises.") The record here supports an estimated award of $1,000 in damages for emotional distress. Ms. Duncan testified to the mental anguish she suffered because of the debtor's actions, as well as to her diagnosis of bipolar disorder and depression and the exacerbation of these problems as a result of the debtor's actions. (Tr. 2, 196:10-12; 203:1-3.)

Prejudgment Interest

Ms. Duncan is entitled to recover prejudgment interest because of the debtor's interference with her "possession or enjoyment of property." NYCPLR §§5001(a); see *also N Main Bagel*, 37 AD 3d 785 at 787, 831 NYS 2d 239 ("Prejudgment interest should be awarded on the plaintiff's recovery, from ... the date of the wrongful eviction"). "Such interest is to be calculated at the simple rate of 9% per annum." *H & P Research, Inc*, 943 FSupp. at 332. Therefore, Ms. Duncan's estimated award shall be increased by $4,416.04, representing 9% interest or $6.04 per diem, from May 8, 2004 through May 9, 2006, the date this bankruptcy case was commenced.

Conclusion

For the reasons stated in this opinion, this Court holds that proof of claim No. 6, filed by Ms. Duncan, is estimated in the amount of $28,916.04, representing compensatory, treble and punitive damages, including prejudgment interest of 9% per annum from May 8, 2004 through May 9, 2006. A separate order will be issued herewith.

Order accordingly.

Newfoundland and Labrador v AbitibiBowater Inc, 2012 SCC 67, [2012] 3 SCR 443 [Abitibi]

DESCHAMPS J:

[1] The question in this appeal is whether orders issued by a regulatory body with respect to environmental remediation work can be treated as monetary claims under the *Companies' Creditors Arrangement Act*, R.S.C. 1985, c. C-36 ("*CCAA*").

[2] Regulatory bodies may become involved in reorganization proceedings when they order the debtor to comply with statutory rules. As a matter of principle, reorganization does not amount to a licence to disregard rules. Yet there are circumstances in which valid and enforceable orders will be subject to an arrangement under the *CCAA*. One such circumstance is where a regulatory body makes an environmental order that explicitly asserts a monetary claim.

[3] In other circumstances, it is less clear whether an order can be treated as a monetary claim. The appellant and a number of interveners posit that an order issued by an environmental body is not a claim under the *CCAA* if the order does not require the debtor to make a payment. I agree that not all orders issued by regulatory bodies are monetary in nature and thus provable claims in an insolvency proceeding, but some may be, even if the amounts involved are not quantified at the outset of the proceeding. In the environmental context, the *CCAA* court must determine whether there are sufficient facts indicating the existence of an environmental duty that will ripen into a financial liability owed to the regulatory body that issued the order. In such a case, the relevant question is not simply whether the body has formally exercised its power to claim a debt. A *CCAA* court does not assess claims—or orders—on the basis of form alone. If the order is not framed in monetary terms, the court must determine, in light of the factual matrix and the applicable statutory framework, whether it is a claim that will be subject to the claims process.

[4] The case at bar concerns contamination that occurred, prior to the *CCAA* proceedings, on property that is largely no longer under the debtor's possession and control. The *CCAA* court found on the facts of this case that the orders issued by Her Majesty the Queen in right of the Province of Newfoundland and Labrador ("Province") were simply a first step towards remediating the contaminated property and asserting a claim for the resulting costs. In the words of the *CCAA* court, "the intended, practical and realistic effect of the EPA Orders was to establish a basis for the Province to recover amounts of money to be eventually used for the remediation of the properties in question" (2010 QCCS 1261, 68 C.B.R. (5th) 1, at para. 211). As a result, the *CCAA* court found that the

orders were clearly monetary in nature. I see no error of law and no reason to interfere with this finding of fact. I would dismiss the appeal with costs.

I. Facts and Procedural History

[5] For over 100 years, AbitibiBowater Inc. and its affiliated or predecessor companies (together, "Abitibi") were involved in industrial activity in Newfoundland and Labrador. In 2008, Abitibi announced the closure of a mill that was its last operation in that province.

[6] Within two weeks of the announcement, the Province passed the *Abitibi-Consolidated Rights and Assets Act*, S.N.L. 2008, c. A-1.01 ("*Abitibi Act*"), which immediately transferred most of Abitibi's property in Newfoundland and Labrador to the Province and denied Abitibi any legal remedy for this expropriation.

[7] The closure of its mill in Newfoundland and Labrador was one of many decisions Abitibi made in a period of general financial distress affecting its activities both in the United States and in Canada. It filed for insolvency protection in the United States on April 16, 2009. It also sought a stay of proceedings under the *CCAA* in the Superior Court of Quebec, as its Canadian head office was located in Montréal. The *CCAA* stay was ordered on April 17, 2009.

[8] In the same month, Abitibi also filed a notice of intent to submit a claim to arbitration under NAFTA (the *North American Free Trade Agreement Between the Government of Canada, the Government of the United Mexican States and the Government of the United States of America*, Can. T.S. 1994 No. 2) for losses resulting from the *Abitibi Act*, which, according to Abitibi, exceeded $300 million.

[9] On November 12, 2009, the Province's Minister of Environment and Conservation ("Minister") issued five orders (the "*EPA* Orders") under s. 99 of the *Environmental Protection Act*, S.N.L. 2002, c. E-14.2 ("*EPA*"). The *EPA* Orders required Abitibi to submit remediation action plans to the Minister for five industrial sites, three of which had been expropriated, and to complete the approved remediation actions. The *CCAA* judge estimated the cost of implementing these plans to be from "the mid-to-high eight figures" to "several times higher" (para. 81).

[10] On the day it issued the *EPA* Orders, the Province brought a motion for a declaration that a claims procedure order issued under the *CCAA* in relation to Abitibi's proposed reorganization did not bar the Province from enforcing the *EPA* Orders. The Province argued—and still argues—that non-monetary statutory obligations are not "claims" under the *CCAA* and hence cannot be stayed and be subject to a claims procedure order. It further submits that Parliament lacks the constitutional competence under its power to make laws in relation to bankruptcy and insolvency to stay orders that are validly made in the exercise of a provincial power.

[11] Abitibi contested the motion and sought a declaration that the *EPA* Orders were stayed and that they were subject to the claims procedure order. It argued that the *EPA* Orders were monetary in nature and hence fell within the definition of the word "claim" in the claims procedure order.

[12] Gascon J of the Quebec Superior Court, sitting as a *CCAA* court, dismissed the Province's motion. He found that he had the authority to characterize the orders as "claims" if the underlying regulatory obligations "remain[ed], in a particular fact pattern, truly financial and monetary in nature" (para. 148). He declared that the *EPA* Orders were stayed by the initial stay order and were not subject to the exception found in that

order. He also declared that the filing by the Province of any claim based on the *EPA* Orders was subject to the claims procedure order, and reserved to the Province the right to request an extension of time to assert a claim under the claims procedure order and to Abitibi the right to contest such a request.

[13] In the Court of Appeal, Chamberland JA denied the Province leave to appeal (2010 QCCA 965, 68 C.B.R. (5th) 57). In his view, the appeal had no reasonable chance of success, because Gascon J had found as a fact that the *EPA* Orders were financial or monetary in nature. Chamberland JA also found that no constitutional issue arose, given that the Superior Court judge had merely characterized the orders in the context of the restructuring process; the judgment did not "'immunise' Abitibi from compliance with the *EPA* Orders" (para. 33). Finally, he noted that Gascon J had reserved the Province's right to request an extension of time to file a claim in the *CCAA* process. . . .

IV. Claims Under the *CCAA*

[20] Several provisions of the *CCAA* have been amended since Abitibi filed for insolvency protection. Except where otherwise indicated, the provisions I refer to are those that were in force when the stay was ordered.

[21] One of the central features of the *CCAA* scheme is the single proceeding model, which ensures that most claims against a debtor are entertained in a single forum. Under this model, the court can stay the enforcement of most claims against the debtor's assets in order to maintain the status quo during negotiations with the creditors. When such negotiations are successful, the creditors typically accept less than the full amounts of their claims. Claims have not necessarily accrued or been liquidated at the outset of the insolvency proceeding, and they sometimes have to be assessed in order to determine the monetary value that will be subject to compromise.

[22] Section 12 of the *CCAA* establishes the basic rules for ascertaining whether an order is a claim that may be subjected to the insolvency process:

> 12. (1) [Definition of "claim"] For the purposes of this Act, "claim" means any indebtedness, liability or obligation of any kind that, if unsecured, would be a debt provable in bankruptcy within the meaning of the *Bankruptcy and Insolvency Act*. . . .

[26] These provisions highlight three requirements that are relevant to the case at bar. First, there must be a debt, a liability or an obligation to a *creditor*. Second, the debt, liability or obligation must be incurred *before the debtor becomes bankrupt*. Third, it must be possible to attach a *monetary value* to the debt, liability or obligation. I will examine each of these requirements in turn.

[27] The *BIA*'s definition of a provable claim, which is incorporated by reference into the *CCAA*, requires the identification of a creditor. Environmental statutes generally provide for the creation of regulatory bodies that are empowered to enforce the obligations the statutes impose. Most environmental regulatory bodies can be creditors in respect of monetary or non-monetary obligations imposed by the relevant statutes. At this first stage of determining whether the regulatory body is a creditor, the question whether the obligation can be translated into monetary terms is not yet relevant. This issue will be broached later. The only determination that has to be made at this point is whether the regulatory body has exercised its enforcement power against a debtor. When it does so, it identifies itself as a creditor, and the requirement of this stage of the analysis is satisfied.

[28] The enquiry into the second requirement is based on s. 121(1) of the *BIA*, which imposes a time limit on claims. A claim must be founded on an obligation that was "incurred before the day on which the bankrupt becomes bankrupt". Because the date when environmental damage occurs is often difficult to ascertain, s. 11.8(9) of the *CCAA* provides more temporal flexibility for environmental claims:

> 11.8 ...
>
> (9) A claim against a debtor company for costs of remedying any environmental condition or environmental damage affecting real property of the company shall be a claim under this Act, <u>whether the condition arose or the damage occurred before or after the date on which proceedings under this Act were commenced</u>.

[29] The creditor's claim will be exempt from the single proceeding requirement if the debtor's corresponding obligation has not arisen as of the time limit for inclusion in the insolvency process. This could apply, for example, to a debtor's statutory obligations relating to polluting activities that continue after the reorganization, because in such cases, the damage continues to be sustained after the reorganization has been completed.

[30] With respect to the third requirement, that it be possible to attach a monetary value to the obligation, the question is whether orders that are not expressed in monetary terms can be translated into such terms. I note that when a regulatory body claims an amount that is owed at the relevant date, that is, when it frames its order in monetary terms, the court does not need to make this determination, because what is being claimed is an "indebtedness" and therefore clearly falls within the meaning of "claim" as defined in s. 12(1) of the *CCAA*.

[31] However, orders, which are used to address various types of environmental challenges, may come in many forms, including stop, control, preventative, and clean-up orders (D. Saxe, "Trustees' and Receivers' Environmental Liability Update" (1998), 49 C.B.R. (3d) 138, at p. 141). When considering an order that is not framed in monetary terms, courts must look at its substance and apply the rules for the assessment of claims.

[32] Parliament recognized that regulatory bodies sometimes have to perform remediation work (see House of Commons, *Evidence of the Standing Committee on Industry*, No. 16, 2nd Sess., 35th Parl., June 11, 1996). When one does so, its claim with respect to remediation costs is subject to the insolvency process, but the claim is secured by a charge on the contaminated real property and certain other related property and benefits from a priority (s. 11.8(8) *CCAA*). Thus, Parliament struck a balance between the public's interest in enforcing environmental regulations and the interest of third-party creditors in being treated equitably.

[33] If Parliament had intended that the debtor always satisfy all remediation costs, it would have granted the Crown a priority with respect to the totality of the debtor's assets. In light of the legislative history and the purpose of the reorganization process, the fact that the Crown's priority under s. 11.8(8) of the *CCAA* is limited to the contaminated property and certain related property leads me to conclude that to exempt environmental orders would be inconsistent with the insolvency legislation. As deferential as courts may be to regulatory bodies' actions, they must apply the general rules.

[34] Unlike in proceedings governed by the common law or the civil law, a claim may be asserted in insolvency proceedings even if it is contingent on an event that has not yet occurred (for the common law, see *Canada v McLarty*, 2008 SCC 26, [2008] 2 S.C.R. 79, at paras. 17–18; for the civil law, see arts. 1497, 1508 and 1513 of the *Civil Code of Québec*, S.Q. 1991, c. 64). Thus, the broad definition of "claim" in the *BIA* includes contingent

and future claims that would be unenforceable at common law or in the civil law. As for unliquidated claims, a *CCAA* court has the same power to assess their amounts as would a court hearing a case in a common law or civil law context.

[35] The reason the *BIA* and the *CCAA* include a broad range of claims is to ensure fairness between creditors and finality in the insolvency proceeding for the debtor. In a corporate liquidation process, it is more equitable to allow as many creditors as possible to participate in the process and share in the liquidation proceeds. This makes it possible to include creditors whose claims have not yet matured when the corporate debtor files for bankruptcy, and thus avert a situation in which they would be faced with an inactive debtor that cannot satisfy a judgment. The rationale is slightly different in the context of a corporate proposal or reorganization. In such cases, the broad approach serves not only to ensure fairness between creditors, but also to allow the debtor to make as fresh a start as possible after a proposal or an arrangement is approved.

[36] The criterion used by courts to determine whether a contingent claim will be included in the insolvency process is whether the event that has not yet occurred is too remote or speculative (*Confederation Treasury Services Ltd (Bankrupt), Re* (1997), 96 O.A.C. 75). In the context of an environmental order, this means that there must be sufficient indications that the regulatory body that triggered the enforcement mechanism will ultimately perform remediation work and assert a monetary claim to have its costs reimbursed. If there is sufficient certainty in this regard, the court will conclude that the order can be subjected to the insolvency process.

[37] The exercise by the *CCAA* court of its jurisdiction to determine whether an order is a provable claim entails a certain scrutiny of the regulatory body's actions. This scrutiny is in some ways similar to judicial review. There is a distinction, however, and it lies in the object of the assessment that the *CCAA* court must make. The *CCAA* court does not review the regulatory body's exercise of discretion. Rather, it inquires into whether the facts indicate that the conditions for inclusion in the claims process are met. For example, if activities at issue are ongoing, the *CCAA* court may well conclude that the order cannot be included in the insolvency process because the activities and resulting damages will continue after the reorganization is completed and hence exceed the time limit for a claim. If, on the other hand, the regulatory body, having no realistic alternative but to perform the remediation work itself, simply delays framing the order as a claim in order to improve its position in relation to other creditors, the *CCAA* court may conclude that this course of action is inconsistent with the insolvency scheme and decide that the order has to be subject to the claims process. Similarly, if the property is not under the debtor's control and the debtor does not, and realistically will not, have the means to perform the remediation work, the *CCAA* court may conclude that it is sufficiently certain that the regulatory body will have to perform the work.

[38] Certain indicators can thus be identified from the text and the context of the provisions to guide the *CCAA* court in determining whether an order is a provable claim, including whether the activities are ongoing, whether the debtor is in control of the property, and whether the debtor has the means to comply with the order. The *CCAA* court may also consider the effect that requiring the debtor to comply with the order would have on the insolvency process. Since the appropriate analysis is grounded in the facts of each case, these indicators need not all apply, and others may also be relevant.

[39] Having highlighted three requirements for finding a claim to be provable in a *CCAA* process that need to be considered in the case at bar, I must now discuss certain policy arguments raised by the Province and some of the interveners.

[40] These parties argue that treating a regulatory order as a claim in an insolvency proceeding extinguishes the debtor's environmental obligations, thereby undermining the polluter-pay principle discussed by this Court in *Imperial Oil Ltd v Quebec (Minister of the Environment)*, 2003 SCC 58, [2003] 2 S.C.R. 624, at para. 24. This objection demonstrates a misunderstanding of the nature of insolvency proceedings. Subjecting an order to the claims process does not extinguish the debtor's environmental obligations any more than subjecting any creditor's claim to that process extinguishes the debtor's obligation to pay its debts. It merely ensures that the creditor's claim will be paid in accordance with insolvency legislation. Moreover, full compliance with orders that are found to be monetary in nature would shift the costs of remediation to third-party creditors, including involuntary creditors, such as those whose claims lie in tort or in the law of extra-contractual liability. In the insolvency context, the Province's position would result not only in a super-priority, but in the acceptance of a "third-party-pay" principle in place of the polluter-pay principle.

[41] Nor does subjecting the orders to the insolvency process amount to issuing a licence to pollute, since insolvency proceedings do not concern the debtor's future conduct. A debtor that is reorganized must comply with all environmental regulations going forward in the same way as any other person. To quote the colourful analogy of two American scholars, "Debtors in bankruptcy have—and should have—no greater license to pollute in violation of a statute than they have to sell cocaine in violation of a statute" (D. G. Baird and T. H. Jackson, "Comment: *Kovacs* and Toxic Wastes in Bankruptcy" (1984), 36 *Stan. L. Rev.* 1199, at p. 1200).

[42] Furthermore, corporations may engage in activities that carry risks. No matter what risks are at issue, reorganization made necessary by insolvency is hardly ever a deliberate choice. When the risks materialize, the dire costs are borne by almost all stakeholders. To subject orders to the claims process is not to invite corporations to restructure in order to rid themselves of their environmental liabilities.

[43] And the power to determine whether an order is a provable claim does not mean that the court will necessarily conclude that the order before it will be subject to the *CCAA* process. In fact, the *CCAA* court in the case at bar recognized that orders relating to the environment may or may not be considered provable claims. It stayed only those orders that were monetary in nature.

[44] The Province also argues that courts have in the past held that environmental orders cannot be interpreted as claims when the regulatory body has not yet exercised its power to assert a claim framed in monetary terms. The Province relies in particular on *Panamericana de Bienes y Servicios SA v Northern Badger Oil & Gas Ltd* (1991), 81 Alta. L.R. (2d) 45 (C.A.), and its progeny. In *Panamericana*, the Alberta Court of Appeal held that a receiver was personally liable for work under a remediation order and that the order was not a claim in insolvency proceedings. The court found that the duty to undertake remediation work is owed to the public at large until the regulator exercises its power to assert a monetary claim.

[45] The first answer to the Province's argument is that courts have never shied away from putting substance ahead of form. They can determine whether the order is in substance monetary.

[46] The second answer is that the provisions relating to the assessment of claims, particularly those governing contingent claims, contemplate instances in which the quantum is not yet established when the claims are filed. Whether, in the regulatory context, an obligation always entails the existence of a correlative right has been discussed

by a number of scholars. Various theories of rights have been put forward (see W. N. Hohfeld, *Fundamental Legal Conceptions as Applied in Judicial Reasoning* (new ed. 2001); D. N. MacCormick, "Rights in Legislation", in P. M. S. Hacker and J. Raz, eds., *Law, Morality, and Society: Essays in Honour of H. L. A. Hart* (1977), 189). However, because the Province issued the orders in this case, it would be recognized as a creditor in respect of a right no matter which of these theories was applied. As interesting as the discussion may be, therefore, I do not need to consider which theory should prevail. The real question is not to whom the obligation is owed, as this question is answered by the statute, which determines who can require that it be discharged. Rather, the question is whether it is sufficiently certain that the regulatory body will perform the remediation work and, as a result, have a monetary claim.

[47] The third answer to the Province's argument is that insolvency legislation has evolved considerably over the two decades since *Panamericana*. At the time of *Panamericana*, none of the provisions relating to environmental liabilities were in force. Indeed, some of those provisions were enacted very soon after, and seemingly in response to, that case. In 1992, Parliament shielded trustees from the very liability imposed on the receiver in *Panamericana* (*An Act to amend the Bankruptcy Act and to amend the Income Tax Act in consequence thereof*, S.C. 1992, c. 27, s. 9, amending s. 14 of the *BIA*). The 1997 amendments provided additional protection to trustees and monitors (*An Act to amend the Bankruptcy and Insolvency Act, the Companies' Creditors Arrangement Act and the Income Tax Act*, S.C. 1997, c. 12). The 2007 amendments made it clear that a *CCAA* court has the power to determine that a regulatory order may be a claim and also provided criteria for staying regulatory orders (s. 65, amending the *CCAA* to include the current version of s. 11.1). The purpose of these amendments was to balance the creditor's need for fairness against the debtor's need to make a fresh start.

[48] Whether the regulatory body has a contingent claim is a determination that must be grounded in the facts of each case. Generally, a regulatory body has discretion under environmental legislation to decide how best to ensure that regulatory obligations are met. Although the court should take care to avoid interfering with that discretion, the action of a regulatory body is nevertheless subject to scrutiny in insolvency proceedings.

V. Application

[49] I now turn to the application of the principles discussed above to the case at bar. This case does not turn on whether the Province is the creditor of an obligation or whether damage had occurred as of the relevant date. Those requirements are easily satisfied, since the Province had identified itself as a creditor by resorting to EPA enforcement mechanisms and since the damage had occurred before the time of the *CCAA* proceedings. Rather, the issue centres on the third requirement: that the orders meet the criterion for admission as a pecuniary claim. The claim was contingent to the extent that the Province had not yet formally exercised its power to ask for the payment of money. The question is whether it was sufficiently certain that the orders would eventually result in a monetary claim. To the *CCAA* judge, there was no doubt that the answer was yes.

[50] The Province's exercise of its legislative powers in enacting the *Abitibi Act* created a unique set of facts that led to the orders being issued. The seizure of Abitibi's assets by the Province, the cancellation of all outstanding water and hydroelectric contracts between Abitibi and the Province, the cancellation of pending legal proceedings by Abitibi in which it sought the reimbursement of several hundreds of thousands of

dollars, and the denial of any compensation for the seized assets and of legal redress are inescapable background facts in the judge's review of the *EPA* Orders.

[51] The *CCAA* judge did not elaborate on whether it was sufficiently certain that the Minister would perform the remediation work and therefore make a monetary claim. However, most of his findings clearly rest on a positive answer to this question. For example, his finding that "[i]n all likelihood, the pith and substance of the EPA Orders is an attempt by the Province to lay the groundwork for monetary claims against Abitibi, to be used most probably as an offset in connection with Abitibi's own NAFTA claims for compensation" (para. 178), is necessarily based on the premise that the Province would most likely perform the remediation work. Indeed, since monetary claims must, both at common law and in civil law, be mutual for set-off or compensation to operate, the Province had to have incurred costs in doing the work in order to have a claim that could be set off against Abitibi's claims.

[52] That the judge relied on an implicit finding that the Province would most likely perform the work and make a claim to offset its costs is also shown by the confirmation he found in the declaration by the Premier that the Province was attempting to assess the cost of doing remediation work Abitibi had allegedly left undone and that in the Province's assessment, "at this point in time, there would not be a net payment to Abitibi" (para. 181).

[53] The *CCAA* judge's reasons not only rest on an implicit finding that the Province would most likely perform the work, but refer explicitly to facts that support this finding. To reach his conclusion that the *EPA* Orders were monetary in nature, the *CCAA* judge relied on the fact that Abitibi's operations were funded through debtor-in-possession financing and its access to funds was limited to ongoing operations. Given that the *EPA* Orders targeted sites that were, for the most part, no longer in Abitibi's possession, this meant that Abitibi had no means to perform the remediation work during the reorganization process.

[54] In addition, because Abitibi lacked funds and no longer controlled the properties, the timetable set by the Province in the *EPA* Orders suggested that the Province never truly intended that Abitibi was to perform the remediation work required by the orders. The timetable was also unrealistic. For example, the orders were issued on November 12, 2009 and set a deadline of January 15, 2010 to perform a particular act, but the evidence revealed that compliance with this requirement would have taken close to a year.

[55] Furthermore, the judge relied on the fact that Abitibi was not simply designated a "person responsible" under the *EPA*, but was intentionally targeted by the Province. The finding that the Province had targeted Abitibi was drawn not only from the timing of the *EPA* Orders, but also from the fact that Abitibi was the only person designated in them, whereas others also appeared to be responsible—in some cases, primarily responsible—for the contamination. For example, Abitibi was ordered to do remediation work on a site it had surrendered more than 50 years before the orders were issued; the expert report upon which the orders were based made no distinction between Abitibi's activities on the property, on which its source of power had been horse power, and subsequent activities by others who had used fuel-powered vehicles there. In the judge's opinion, this finding of fact went to the Province's intent to establish a basis for performing the work itself and asserting a claim against Abitibi.

[56] These reasons—and others—led the *CCAA* judge to conclude that the Province had not expected Abitibi to perform the remediation work and that the "intended, practical and realistic effect of the EPA Orders was to establish a basis for the Province to recover amounts of money to be eventually used for the remediation of the properties

in question" (para. 211). He found that the Province appeared to have in fact taken some steps to liquidate the claims arising out of the *EPA* Orders.

[57] In the end, the judge found that there was definitely a claim that "might" be filed, and that it was not left to "the subjective choice of the creditor to hold the claim in its pocket for tactical reasons" (para. 227). In his words, the situation did not involve a "detached regulator or public enforcer issuing [an] order for the public good" (para. 175), and it was "the hat of a creditor that best fi[t] the Province, not that of a disinterested regulator" (para. 176).

[58] In sum, although the analytical framework used by Gascon J was driven by the facts of the case, he reviewed all the legal principles and facts that needed to be considered in order to make the determination in the case at bar. He did at times rely on indicators that are unique and that do not appear in the analytical framework I propose above, but he did so because of the exceptional facts of this case. Yet, had he formulated the question in the same way as I have, his conclusion, based on his objective findings of fact, would have been the same. Earmarking money may be a strong indicator that a province will perform remediation work, and actually commencing the work is the first step towards the creation of a debt, but these are not the only considerations that can lead to a finding that a creditor has a monetary claim. The *CCAA* judge's assessment of the facts, particularly his finding that the *EPA* Orders were the first step towards performance of the remediation work by the Province, leads to no conclusion other than that it was sufficiently certain that the Province would perform remediation work and therefore fall within the definition of a creditor with a monetary claim.

VI. Conclusion

[59] In sum, I agree with the Chief Justice that, as a general proposition, an environmental order issued by a regulatory body can be treated as a contingent claim, and that such a claim can be included in the claims process if it is sufficiently certain that the regulatory body will make a monetary claim against the debtor. Our difference of views lies mainly in the applicable threshold for including contingent claims and in our understanding of the *CCAA* judge's findings of fact.

[60] With respect to the law, the Chief Justice would craft a standard specific to the context of environmental orders by requiring a "likelihood approaching certainty" that the regulatory body will perform the remediation work. She finds that this threshold is justified because "remediation may cost a great deal of money" (para. 86). I acknowledge that remediating pollution is often costly, but I am of the view that Parliament has borne this consideration in mind in enacting provisions specific to environmental claims. Moreover, I recall that in this case, the Premier announced that the remediation work would be performed at no net cost to the Province. It was clear to him that the *Abitibi Act* would make it possible to offset all the related costs.

[61] Thus, I prefer to take the approach generally taken for all contingent claims. In my view, the *CCAA* court is entitled to take all relevant facts into consideration in making the relevant determination. Under this approach, the contingency to be assessed in a case such as this is whether it is sufficiently certain that the regulatory body will perform remediation work and be in a position to assert a monetary claim.

[62] Finally, the Chief Justice would review the *CCAA* court's findings of fact. I would instead defer to them. On those findings, applying any legal standard, be it the one proposed by the Chief Justice or the one I propose, the Province's claim is monetary

in nature and its motion for a declaration exempting the *EPA* Orders from the claims procedure order was properly dismissed.

[63] For these reasons, I would dismiss the appeal with costs.

Appeal dismissed.

Nortel Networks Corporation (Re), 2013 ONCA 599, 6 CBR (6th) 159

JURIANSZ JA:

A. OVERVIEW

[1] The *CCAA* judge, whose decision is the subject of this appeal, aptly described the issues as arising "from the untidy intersection" of the *Companies' Creditors Arrangement Act*, R.S.C. 1985, c. C-36, ("*CCAA*") and the powers of the provincial Minister of the Environment ("MOE") "to make orders with respect to the remediation of real property in Ontario."

[2] After the usual order staying proceedings (the "Initial Order") was granted to the insolvent respondents, Nortel Networks Corporation, Nortel Networks Limited, Nortel Networks Global Corporation, Nortel Networks International Corporation and Nortel Networks Technology Corporation (collectively, "Nortel" or the "respondents"), the MOE issued orders pursuant to the *Environmental Protection Act*, R.S.O. 1990, c. E-19, ("*EPA*") requiring Nortel Networks Limited to remediate environmental contamination remaining on properties it once or currently owned.

[3] In his order dated March 9, 2012, the *CCAA* judge declared that the MOE's remediation orders were subject to the stay granted by the Initial Order. Ancillary to that declaration, he granted certain other relief. He declared that all proceedings against the respondents or the Former Directors and Officers before the Ontario Environmental Review Tribunal in relation to the EPA orders were subject to the stay of proceedings; he authorized the respondents to cease performing remediation of property; he declared that any claims in relation to current or future remediation requirements imposed by orders under the EPA against the respondents or the Former Directors and Officers were subject to the insolvency claims process; and he authorized the respondents to repudiate all contractual obligations to carry out remediation at the properties.

[4] The MOE appeals.

[5] For the reasons that follow, I would allow the appeal.

B. FACTS

[6] Nortel is engaged in a liquidating insolvency and has no operations. The sites where Nortel and its predecessors once conducted manufacturing operations were largely disposed of in the late 1990s. At that time Nortel identified environmental impacts that arose from its past operations at Brampton, Brockville, Kingston, Belleville, and London (the "Impacted Sites") and was conducting remediation at those sites on a voluntary or contractual basis.

[7] On January 14, 2009, Nortel filed for protection under the *CCAA*. At that time, Nortel maintained only a partial interest in the London site. It had disposed of its interests in the other Impacted Sites. As well, the MOE had not issued any remediation orders against Nortel. Nortel says that it spent some $28.5 million on remediation of the sites before filing under the *CCAA*. After Nortel's *CCAA* filing, the MOE issued remediation

orders (the "MOE Orders") that Nortel estimates would require further expenditures of approximately $18 million.

[8] Nortel brought a motion before the *CCAA* judge seeking an order declaring that the relief the MOE Orders sought was financial and monetary in nature; that the Initial Order stayed the MOE Orders; and an order staying all related proceedings before the Ontario Environmental Review Tribunal. Nortel also sought authorization and direction that it cease performing remediation at the Impacted Sites and a declaration that any claims in relation to current or future remediation by the MOE or any other person against Nortel were stayed and had to be dealt with according to the *CCAA* claims procedure. In addition, Nortel sought an order repudiating or disclaiming any contractual obligations to carry out remediation at the Impacted Sites; and finally, advice and direction with respect to the London site where Nortel maintained a partial interest in the property.

[9] On March 9, 2012, the *CCAA* judge determined that, where operations had ceased on a particular property and a company could only comply with the EPA or MOE Orders by expending funds, the environmental liabilities involved amount to financial obligations to pay. Therefore, they were subject to the Initial Order and had to be addressed as claims in the *CCAA* process.

[10] On June 22, 2012, the MOE was granted leave to appeal the *CCAA* judge's order.

[11] While the MOE's appeal was pending, the Supreme Court released its decision in *Newfoundland and Labrador v AbitibiBowater Inc*, 2012 SCC 67 , [2012] 3 S.C.R. 443, on December 7, 2012. On March 28, 2013, the parties were given leave to file "fresh" factums and fresh evidence.

[12] The parties dispute the interpretation of the Supreme Court's decision, and how it should be applied to the case under appeal.

C. SUPREME COURT'S DECISION IN ABITIBIBOWATER

[13] AbitibiBowater Inc. ("Abitibi") had carried on industrial activities in the Province of Newfoundland and Labrador for over 100 years. In 2009, Abitibi sought protection under the *CCAA*.

[14] Subsequently, the Minister of Environment and Conservation of Newfoundland and Labrador issued five ministerial orders against Abitibi under the province's environmental legislation. These orders required Abitibi to remediate several sites, most of which had been expropriated by the province. The province also brought a motion for a declaration that the *CCAA* claims process did not bar the province from enforcing the orders. The province argued, among other things, that the remediation orders were regulatory orders, not "claims" under the *CCAA*, and therefore they could not be stayed or subjected to compromise in the *CCAA* restructuring process.

[15] The Supreme Court decided that a *CCAA* court could determine whether an environmental order that is not framed in monetary terms is in fact a "provable claim". Justice Deschamps, writing for the majority, held that "[a] finding that a claim of an environmental creditor is monetary in nature does not interfere in any way with the creditor's activities. Its claim is simply subjected to the insolvency process" (at para. 18). The *CCAA* court should consider the substance of an order rather than its form: "[i]f the Province's actions indicate that, in substance, it is asserting a provable claim within the meaning of federal legislation, then that claim can be subjected to the insolvency process" (at para. 19).

[16] The *CCAA*, informed by the *Bankruptcy and Insolvency Act*, R.S.C. 1985, c. B-3 ("*BIA*"), establishes three requirements for establishing a provable claim. First, there

must be a debt, liability or obligation to a creditor. This requirement is satisfied simply by the regulatory body exercising its enforcement power against a debtor: at paras. 26–27.

[17] Second, a claim must be founded on an obligation that falls within the time limit for claims. Section 11.8(9) of the *CCAA* provides temporal flexibility for environmental claims by providing that

> [a] claim against a debtor company for costs of remedying any environmental condition or environmental damage affecting real property of the company shall be a claim under this Act, whether the condition arose or the damage occurred before or after the date on which proceedings under this Act were commenced.

However, statutory environmental obligations relating to polluting activities that continue after the reorganization will not satisfy the time limits: at paras. 28–29.

[18] Both the first and second requirements were easily satisfied in the Abitibi case.

[19] The third requirement is "that it be possible to attach a monetary value to the obligation"; that is, "the question is whether orders that are not expressed in monetary terms can be translated into such terms" (at para. 30). A court must look at the substance of the order not its form and apply its usual approach in dealing with future or contingent claims.

[20] The usual test courts use to decide if a contingent claim will be included in insolvency proceedings is whether it is "too remote or speculative": at para. 36, citing *Confederation Treasury Services Ltd (Re)* (1997) 96 O.A.C. 75, leave to appeal to S.C.C. refused, [1997] S.C.C.A. No. 229. This means that there must be "sufficient indications" that the regulatory body that made the remediation order "will ultimately perform remediation work" itself, thus entitling it to seek reimbursement by means of a monetary claim: *AbitibiBowater*, at para 36.

[21] Accordingly, Deschamps J concluded that the *CCAA* court must assess whether "it is sufficiently certain that the regulatory body will perform the remediation work and, as a result, have a monetary claim" (at para. 46).

[22] The *CCAA* judge's discretion will govern the assessment, but several considerations may be relevant, depending on the circumstances of the case. Justice Deschamps identified four potential factors: "whether the [polluting] activities are ongoing, whether the debtor is in control of the property..., whether the debtor has the means to comply with the order," and "the effect that requiring the debtor to comply with the order would have on the insolvency process" (at para. 38).

[23] In the circumstances of *AbitibiBowater*, Deschamps J acknowledged that the *CCAA* judge had not addressed whether it was "sufficiently certain" that the Province would remediate the property and seek reimbursement, but she concluded that his reasons rested on the implicit finding that the Province would do so (at para. 51). The *CCAA* judge explicitly referred to the facts that supported this finding, at paras. 53–55:

- Abitibi was not in a position to carry out the remediation because it was no longer in possession of most of the sites;
- Abitibi's operations were funded through debtor-in-possession financing and its access to funds would limited to ongoing operations;
- the timetable set by the Province in the remediation orders suggested that the Province never truly expected Abitibi to perform the remediation work;
- and the surrounding facts suggested that the Province had intentionally targeted Abitibi.

[24] On this reasoning, Deschamps J, writing for the majority, deferred to the CCAA judge's implicit conclusion it was sufficiently certain that the Province would perform the remediation work. Therefore, the Province fell within the definition of a creditor with a monetary claim.

[25] McLachlin CJ and LeBel J dissented.

D. THE RESPONDENTS' EFFORT TO DISTINGUISH ABITIBIBOWATER

[26] The respondents submit that it is an oversimplification of the AbitibiBowater decision to read it as requiring all future courts to examine environmental remediation orders "through the exclusive and binary test" of determining whether it is sufficiently certain that the province would perform the remediation and claim reimbursement. The respondents suggest that in AbitibiBowater the court used this language because it was particularly apt for the circumstances in the case. They claim that a careful reading of the reasons makes evident that the test the court established is less specific.

[27] The respondents point to the more general language in Deschamps J's reasons. They highlight the various factors that Deschamps J indicated could be relevant depending on the circumstances of each case to determine whether remediation orders will be subject to a CCAA stay: at para. 38. They argue that as long as the order requires an expenditure of funds its nature is monetary. In setting out the three basic requirements to determine whether an environmental order is a "claim", Deschamps J said with respect to the third requirement, "that it be possible to attach a monetary value to the obligation, the question is whether orders that are not expressed in monetary terms can be translated into such terms" (at para. 30).

[28] Instead, the respondents posit that in *AbitibiBowater*, the Supreme Court set out the policy approach to be followed in determining whether nonmonetary orders can be translated into monetary terms. This approach, as Deschamps J emphasized, concerns: the importance of the single proceeding model of insolvency in Canada; the necessity of examining the substance, not only the form, of an environmental remediation order; the balance struck by Parliament between enforcement of environmental regulation and the interests of insolvency stakeholders; and the need to have regard to the interests of third-party creditors.

[29] Turning to this case, the respondents submit that it was sufficiently certain that compliance with the orders would require the expenditure of a minimum of $18 million. Whether the money is paid to the MOE as reimbursement for the costs of performing the remediation, or paid to third parties retained to perform the remediation should make no difference. The environmental problems at the impacted sites were long-standing; the soil had been contaminated decades earlier. In fact, the Brockville site was already contaminated when Nortel bought it. Historical environmental problems, the respondents argue, should be distinguished from current ones, where the debtor is polluting at the time.

[30] Finally, the respondents stress that the CCAA court should be mindful of the impact on the debtor and the stakeholders and avoid giving the MOE a super-priority it would not have under the BIA. Under the BIA there is no debtor-in-possession, only a trustee, and the trustee could abandon the contaminated property. In a liquidating reorganization there was no good reason why the MOE should do better under the CCAA than under the BIA.

E. ANALYSIS

[31] I cannot accept the respondents' proposed interpretation of *Abitibi Bowater*. In determining whether a regulatory order is a provable claim, a CCAA court must apply the general rules that apply to future or contingent claims. As I read it, the Supreme Court's decision is clear: ongoing environmental remediation obligations may be reduced to monetary claims that can be compromised in CCAA proceedings only where the province has performed the remediation work and advances a claim for reimbursement, or where the obligation may be considered a contingent or future claim because it is "sufficiently certain" that the province will do the work and then seek reimbursement.

[32] The respondents' approach is not only inconsistent with *Abitibi Bowater*, it is too broad. It would result in virtually all regulatory environmental orders being found to be provable claims. As Deschamps J observed, a company may engage in activities that carry risks. When those risks materialize, the costs are borne by those who hold a stake in the company. A risk that results in an environmental obligation becomes subject to the insolvency process only when it is in substance monetary and is in substance a provable claim.

[33] Parliament has struck a balance between the interests of the stakeholders and that of the public in designing the CCAA process. Parliament, in s. 11.8(8) of the CCAA, granted the MOE's claims with respect to remediation costs the security of a charge on the contaminated property. And Parliament, in s. 11.1(3), made it clear that a CCAA court has the discretion to stay regulatory orders on specified criteria. . . .

G. IS IT SUFFICIENTLY CERTAIN THE MOE WILL UNDERTAKE THE REMEDIATION?

[39] Considering the matter afresh, I would conclude that it is not sufficiently certain that the MOE will perform the remediations ordered. The MOE orders respecting in the Belleville, Brockville and Kingston sites are directed to Nortel together with other current and former owners of the properties. In fact with respect to the Kingston site, the other current and former owners named in the orders are jointly and severally liable with Nortel to carry out the activities required by the orders. Under s. 18 of the EPA, the MOE clearly has the power to make orders against subsequent (or past) owners for anything it ordered Nortel to do.

[40] In *Abitibi Bowater*, the province had expropriated most of the properties and remained the owner. It would seem reasonable to expect that the MOE would enforce the orders against other parties instead of undertaking the remediation itself. Indeed, the CCAA judge observed that subsequent purchasers of the properties may have unsecured contractual claims against Nortel.

[41] Matters at the London site are not so clear. Evidently, in 1997 and 1998 Nortel subdivided and sold three parts of the London site to others, but retained the fourth part. The MOE order respecting the London site is directed to Nortel and the three entities who own the other parts and imposes joint responsibilities as well as some individual responsibilities on them. After the insolvency there will be no going-forward entity. Evidently Nortel's retained portion of the land is worth less than the cost of remediating it and it seems probable that the retained portion will eventually be abandoned. There is no one to carry out Nortel's responsibilities under the MOE Order. As a result, I consider it "sufficiently certain" that MOE will ultimately undertake Nortel's obligations under the order, and may seek to claim the security provided by s. 11.8(8).

H. CONCLUSION

[42] I would conclude that the MOE Orders in relation to the Impacted Sites other than the retained portion of the London property have not been established to be provable claims that must be included in the insolvency process.

[43] In paragraph 2 of his order, the CCAA judge declared that the MOE's remediation orders "are subject to the stay of proceedings granted in the initial order ... and stayed thereunder". This declaration cannot stand. Paragraph 15 of the initial order contains the caveat that "nothing in this Order shall ... (ii) exempt the [respondents] from compliance with statutory or regulatory provisions relating to health, safety or the environment". The conclusion that the remediation orders are regulatory rather than provable claims brings them within the ambit of this caveat.

[44] The CCAA judge himself acknowledged, at para. 104 that "if the Minister is solely acting in its regulatory capacity, it can do so unimpeded by the Stay. This is the effect of s. 11.1(2) of the CCAA." Section 11.1(2) provides:

> (2) Subject to subsection (3), no order made under section 11.02 affects a regulatory body's investigation in respect of the debtor company or an action, suit or proceeding that is taken in respect of the company by or before the regulatory body, other than the enforcement of a payment ordered by the regulatory body or the court.

[45] I would therefore allow the appeal and modify the *CCAA* judge's declaration that the MOE Orders are stayed by the Initial Order so that it applies only to the retained London lands. ...

Appeal allowed.

Discussion

The question of how environmental clean-up costs should be valued in bankruptcy continues to be the subject of litigation. In *Orphan Well Association v Grant Thornton Ltd*, 2019 SCC 5, excerpted below, the Supreme Court was asked to adjudicate the costs of plugging and capping abandoned oil wells. Applying the test in *Abitibi*, a majority of the Supreme Court held that insolvent oil and gas companies are required to pay the costs associated with environmental clean up, even though they do not meet the definition of a provable claim. The Court also clarified that *Abitibi* does not stand for the proposition that a regulator is always a creditor when exercising its enforcement powers against a debtor. It remains to be seen how future cases will address *Abitibi* in light of this new decision.

Orphan Well Association v Grant Thornton Ltd, 2019 SCC 5, 430 DLR (4th) 1

WAGNER CJ: ...

[119] The resolution of this issue turns on the proper application of the *Abitibi* test for determining whether a particular regulatory obligation amounts to a claim provable in bankruptcy. To reiterate:

> First, there must be a debt, a liability or an obligation to a *creditor*. Second, the debt, liability or obligation must be incurred *before the debtor becomes bankrupt*. Third, it must be possible to attach a *monetary value* to the debt, liability or obligation. [Emphasis in original; para. 26.]

[120] There is no dispute that in this appeal, the second part of the test is met. Accordingly, I will discuss only the first and the third parts of the test.

[121] In this Court, the Regulator, supported by various interveners, raised two concerns about how the *Abitibi* test has been applied, both by the courts below and in general. The first concern is that the "creditor" step of the *Abitibi* test has been interpreted too broadly in cases such as the instant appeal and *Nortel Networks Corp, Re*, 2013 ONCA 599, 368 D.L.R. (4th) 122 ("*Nortel* CA"), and that, in effect, this step of the test has become so pro forma as to be practically meaningless. The second concern has to do with the application of the "monetary value" step of the *Abitibi* test by the chambers judge and Slatter JA This step is generally called the "sufficient certainty" step, based on the guidance provided in *Abitibi*. The argument here is that the courts below went beyond the test established in *Abitibi* by focusing on whether Redwater's regulatory obligations were "intrinsically financial". Under *Abitibi*, the sufficient certainty analysis should have focused on whether the Regulator would ultimately perform the environmental work and assert a monetary claim for reimbursement.

[122] In my view, both concerns raised by the Regulator have merit. As I will demonstrate, *Abitibi* should not be taken as standing for the proposition that a regulator is always a creditor when it exercises its statutory enforcement powers against a debtor. On a proper understanding of the "creditor" step, it is clear that the Regulator acted in the public interest and for the public good in issuing the Abandonment Orders and enforcing the LMR requirements and that it is, therefore, not a creditor of Redwater. It is the public, not the Regulator or the General Revenue Fund, that is the beneficiary of those environmental obligations; the province does not stand to gain financially from them. Although this conclusion is sufficient to resolve this aspect of the appeal, for the sake of completeness, I will also demonstrate that the chambers judge erred in finding that, on these facts, there is sufficient certainty that the Regulator will ultimately perform the environmental work and assert a claim for reimbursement. To conclude, I will briefly comment on why the *effects* of the end-of-life obligations do not conflict with the priority scheme in the *BIA*.

(1) The Regulator Is Not a Creditor of Redwater

[123] The Regulator and the supporting interveners are not the first to raise issues with the "creditor" step of the *Abitibi* test. In the six years since *Abitibi* was decided, concerns about the "creditor" step and the fact that, as it is commonly understood, it will seemingly be satisfied in all—or nearly all—cases have also been expressed by academic commentators, such as A. J. Lund, "Lousy Dentists, Bad Drivers, and Abandoned Oil Wells: A New Approach to Reconciling Provincial Regulatory Regimes with Federal Insolvency Law", (2017) 80 *Sask. L. Rev.* 157, at p. 178, and Stewart. This Court has not had an opportunity to comment on *Abitibi* since it was decided. However, the interpretation of the "creditor" step adopted by lower courts, including the majority of the Court of Appeal in this case, has focused on certain comments found at para. 27 of *Abitibi*, and the "creditor" step has accordingly been found to be satisfied whenever a regulator exercises its enforcement powers against a debtor (see, for example, C.A. reasons, at para. 60; *Nortel* CA, at para. 16).

[124] GTL submits that these lower courts have correctly interpreted and applied the "creditor" step. It further submits that, because of *Abitibi*, the 1991 Alberta Court of Appeal decision in *Northern Badger* is of no assistance in analyzing the creditor issue. Conversely, the Regulator forcefully argues that *Abitibi* must be understood in the

context of its own unique facts and that it did not overrule *Northern Badger.* Relying on *Northern Badger,* the Regulator argues that a regulator exercising a power to enforce a public duty is not a creditor of the individual or corporation subject to that duty. Like Martin JA, I agree with the Regulator on this point. If, as GTL urges and the majority of the Court of Appeal concluded, the "creditor" step is satisfied whenever a regulator exercises its enforcement powers against a debtor, then it is hard to imagine a situation in which the "creditor" step would not be satisfied by the actions of an environmental regulator. Stewart was correct to suppose that "[s]urely, the Court did not intend this result" (p. 189). For the "creditor" step to "have meaning, there must be situations where the other two steps could be met but the order [or obligation] is still not a provable claim because the regulator is not a creditor of the bankrupt" (Attorney General of Ontario's factum, at para. 39).

[125] Before further explaining my conclusion on this point, I must address a preliminary issue: the fact that the Regulator conceded in the courts below that it was a creditor. It is well established that concessions of law are not binding on this Court: see *Ocean Port Hotel Ltd v British Columbia (General Manager, Liquor Control and Licensing Branch),* 2001 SCC 52, [2001] 2 S.C.R. 781, at para. 44; *M v H,* [1999] 2 S.C.R. 3, at para. 45; *R v Sappier,* 2006 SCC 54, [2006] 2 S.C.R. 686, at para. 62. As noted by L'Heureux-Dubé J., in dissent, but not on this point, in *R v Elshaw,* [1991] 3 S.C.R. 24, at para. 48, "the fact that an issue is conceded below means nothing in and of itself". Although concessions by the parties are often relied upon, it is ultimately for this Court to determine points of law. For several reasons, no fairness concerns are raised by disregarding the Regulator's concession in this case.

[126] First, in a letter to GTL dated May 14, 2015, the Regulator advanced the position that it was "not a creditor of [Redwater]", but, rather, had a "statutory mandate to regulate the oil and gas industry in Alberta" (GTL's Record, vol. 1, at p. 78). I note that this was the initial communication between the Regulator and GTL, only two days after the latter's appointment as receiver of Redwater's property. Second, the issue of whether the Regulator is a creditor was discussed in the parties' factums. Third, during oral arguments before this Court, the Regulator was questioned about its concession. Counsel made the undisputed point that higher courts are not bound by such concessions and took the position that, on the correct interpretation of *Abitibi,* the Regulator was not a creditor. Fourth, when the Regulator's status as a creditor was raised as an issue before this Court, opposing counsel did not argue that they would have adduced further evidence on the issue had it been raised in the courts below. Finally, a proper understanding of the "creditor" step of the *Abitibi* test is of fundamental importance to the proper functioning of the national bankruptcy scheme and of provincial environmental schemes throughout Canada. I conclude that this case is one in which it is appropriate to disregard the Regulator's concession in the courts below.

[127] Returning to the analysis, I note that the unique factual matrix of *Abitibi* must be kept in mind. In that case, Newfoundland and Labrador expropriated most of Abitibi-Bowater's property in the province without compensation. Subsequently, AbitibiBowater was granted a stay under the *CCAA.* It then filed a notice of intent to submit a claim to arbitration under the *North American Free Trade Agreement between the Government of Canada, the Government of the United Mexican States and the Government of the United States of America,* Can. T.S. 1994 No. 2 ("NAFTA"), for losses resulting from the expropriation. In response, Newfoundland's Minister of Environment and Conservation ordered AbitibiBowater to remediate five sites pursuant to the *Environmental Protection*

Act, S.N.L. 2002, c. E-14.2. Three of the five sites had been expropriated by Newfoundland and Labrador. The evidence led to the conclusion that "the Province never truly intended that Abitibi was to perform the remediation work", but instead sought a claim that could be used as an offset in connection with AbitibiBowater's NAFTA claim (*Abitibi*, at para. 54). In other words, the Province sought a financial benefit from the remediation orders.

[128] In this appeal, it is not disputed that, in seeking to enforce Redwater's end-of-life obligations, the Regulator is acting in a *bona fide* regulatory capacity and does not stand to benefit financially. The Regulator's ultimate goal is to have the environmental work actually performed, for the benefit of third-party landowners and the public at large. There is no colourable attempt by the Regulator to recover a debt, nor is there an ulterior motive on its part, as there was in *Abitibi*. The distinction between the facts of this appeal and those of *Abitibi* becomes even clearer when one examines the comprehensive reasons of the chambers judge in *Abitibi*. The crux of the findings of Gascon J (as he then was) is found at paras. 173–76:

> ... the Province stands as the direct beneficiary, from a monetary standpoint, of Abitibi's compliance with the EPA Orders. In other words, the execution in nature of the EPA Orders would result in a definite credit to the Province's own "balance sheet". Abitibi's liability in that regard is an asset for the Province itself.
>
> With all due respect, this is not regulatory in nature; it is rather purely financial in reality. This is, in fact, closer to a debtor-creditor relationship than anything else.
>
> This is quite far from the situation of the detached regulator or public enforcer issuing order for the public good. Here, the Province itself derives the direct pecuniary benefit from the required compliance of Abitibi to the EPA Orders. The Province stands to directly gain in the outcome. None of the cases submitted by the Province bear any similarity to the fact pattern in the present proceedings.
>
> From this perspective, it is the hat of a creditor that best fits the Province, not that of a disinterested regulator

(*AbitibiBowater Inc., Re*, 2010 QCCS 1261, 68 C.B.R. (5th) 1)

[129] This Court recognized in *Abitibi* that the Province "easily satisfied" the creditor requirement (para 49). It was therefore not necessary to consider at any length how the "creditor" step should be understood or how it would apply in other factual situations. However, even at para. 27 of *Abitibi*, the paragraph relied on by the majority of the Court of Appeal, Deschamps J made a point of noting that "[m]ost environmental regulatory bodies *can be* creditors in respect of monetary or non-monetary obligations imposed by the relevant statutes" (emphasis added). The interpretation of the "creditor" step adopted by the majority of the Court of Appeal and urged upon this Court by GTL leaves no room for a regulator that enforces obligations not to be a creditor, though this possibility was clearly contemplated by para. 27 of *Abitibi*. As noted above, GTL's interpretation leaves the "creditor" step with no independent work to perform.

[130] *Northern Badger* established that a regulator enforcing a public duty by way of non-monetary order is not a creditor. I reject the claim in the dissenting reasons that *Northern Badger* should be interpreted differently. First, I note that whether the Regulator has a contingent claim is relevant to the sufficient certainty test, which presupposes that the Regulator is a creditor. I cannot accept the proposition in the dissenting reasons that *Northern Badger* was concerned with what would become the third prong of the *Abitibi* test. In *Northern Badger*, Laycraft CJA accepted that abandonment was a liability

and identified the issue as "whether that liability is to the Board so that it is the Board which is the creditor" (para. 32). Second, the underlying scenario here with regards to Redwater's end-of-life obligations is exactly the same as in *Northern Badger*—a regulator is ordering an entity to comply with its legal obligations in furtherance of the public good. This reasoning from *Northern Badger* was subsequently adopted in cases such as *Strathcona (County) v Fantasy Construction Ltd (Trustee of)*, 2005 ABQB 794, 261 D.L.R. (4th) 221, at paras. 23–25, and *Lamford Forest Products Ltd (Re)* (1991), 86 D.L.R (4th) 534.

[131] I cannot agree with the suggestion by the majority of the Court of Appeal in this case that *Northern Badger* "is of limited assistance" in the application of the *Abitibi* test (para. 63). Rather, I agree with Martin JA that *Abitibi* did not overturn the reasoning in *Northern Badger*, but instead "emphasized the need to consider the substance of provincial regulation in assessing whether it creates a claim provable in bankruptcy" (para. 164). As Martin JA noted, even following *Abitibi*, the law continues to be that "public obligations are not provable claims that can be counted or compromised in the bankruptcy" (para. 174). *Abitibi* clarified the scope of *Northern Badger* by confirming that a regulator's environmental claims will be provable claims under certain circumstances. It does not stand for the proposition that a regulator exercising its enforcement powers is always a creditor. The reasoning in *Northern Badger* was simply not applicable on the facts of *Abitibi*, given the actions of the Province as outlined above.

[132] In *Abitibi*, Deschamps J noted that insolvency legislation had evolved in the years since *Northern Badger*. That legislative evolution did not, however, change the meaning to be ascribed to the term "creditor". In this regard, I agree with the conclusion in *Strathcona County v Fantasy Construction Ltd (Trustee of)*, 2005 ABQB 559, 256 D.L.R. (4th) 536, that the amendments to the *BIA* dealing with environmental matters in the years following *Northern Badger* cannot be interpreted as having overturned the reasoning in that case. As should be clear from the earlier discussion of s. 14.06, the amendments to the *BIA* do not speak to when a regulator enforcing an environmental claim is a creditor.

[133] The conclusion that the reasoning in *Northern Badger* continues to be relevant since *Abitibi* and the amendments to insolvency legislation also finds support in the writings of academic commentators. Stewart's position is that, while *Abitibi* discussed *Northern Badger*, it did not overturn it. He urges this Court to clarify that there remains "a distinction between a regulatory body that is a creditor because it is enforcing a debt, and a regulatory body that is not a creditor because it is enforcing the law" (p. 221). Similarly, Lund argues that a court should "consider the importance of the public interests protected by the regulatory obligation when deciding whether the debtor owes a debt, liability or obligation to a creditor" (p. 178).

[134] For the foregoing reasons, *Abitibi* cannot be understood as having changed the law as summarized by Laycraft CJA I adopt his comments at para. 33 of *Northern Badger*:

> The statutory provisions requiring the abandonment of oil and gas wells are part of the general law of Alberta, binding every citizen of the province. All who become licensees of oil and gas wells are bound by them. Similar statutory obligations bind citizens in many other areas of modern life ... But the obligation of the citizen is not to the peace officer, or public authority which enforces the law. The duty is owed as a public duty by all the citizens of the community to their fellow citizens. When the citizen subject to the order complies, the result is not the recovery of money by the peace officer or public authority, or of a judgment for money, nor is that the object of the whole process. Rather, it is simply

the enforcement of the general law. The enforcing authority does not become a "creditor" of the citizen on whom the duty is imposed.

[135] Based on the analysis in *Northern Badger*, it is clear that the Regulator is not a creditor of the Redwater estate. The end-of-life obligations the Regulator seeks to enforce against Redwater are public duties. Neither the Regulator nor the Government of Alberta stands to benefit financially from the enforcement of these obligations. These public duties are owed, not to a creditor, but, rather, to fellow citizens, and are therefore outside the scope of "provable claims". I do not intend to suggest, however, that a regulator will be a creditor only where it acts exactly as the province did in *Abitibi*. There may very well be situations in which a regulator's actions fall somewhere between those in *Abitibi* and those in the instant case. Notably, unlike some previous cases, the Regulator has performed no environmental work itself. I leave such situations to be addressed in future cases in which there are full factual records. Here, it is clear that the Regulator is seeking to enforce Redwater's public duties, whether by issuing the Abandonment Orders or by maintaining the LMR requirements. The Regulator is not a creditor within the meaning of the *Abitibi* test.

[136] I reject the suggestion that the foregoing analysis somehow overrules the first prong of the *Abitibi* test. The facts in *Abitibi* were not comparable to the facts of this appeal. Although this Court discussed *Northern Badger* in *Abitibi*, it merely referenced the subsequent amendments to the *BIA*, and did not overturn the earlier decision. The Court was clear that the ultimate outcome "must be grounded in the facts of each case" (para. 48). The dissenting reasons claim that, given the foregoing analysis, it will be nearly impossible to find that regulators are ever creditors. *Abitibi* itself shows this not to be the case. Furthermore, as I have said, there may well be cases that fall between *Abitibi* and the present case. However, if *Abitibi* is read as requiring only a determination of whether the regulator has exercised an enforcement power, it will in fact be impossible for a regulator *not* to be a creditor. The dissenting reasons do not seriously deny this, merely suggesting that regulators can publish guidelines or issue licences. The Regulator does both, yet, under the approach taken in the dissenting reasons, it is powerless to take any practical steps in the public interest regarding its guidelines or licences without qualifying as a creditor. As I have explained, *Abitibi* clearly contemplates a place for regulators who are not creditors.

[137] Strictly speaking, this is sufficient to dispose of this aspect of the appeal. However, additional guidance on the sufficient certainty analysis may prove helpful in future cases. Accordingly, I turn now to a discussion of the "sufficient certainty" step and of the reasons why the Abandonment Orders and the LMR conditions both fail on this step of the *Abitibi* test.

(2) There Is No Sufficient Certainty that the Regulator Will Perform the Environmental Work and Advance a Claim for Reimbursement

[138] The "sufficient certainty" test articulated in paras. 30 and 36 in Abitibi essentially does no more than reorganize and restate the requirements of the relevant provisions of the BIA. Section 121(2) provides that contingent claims may be provable claims. In other words, contingent debts or liabilities owed by a bankrupt to a creditor may be, but are not necessarily, provable claims. Section 135(1.1) provides for the valuation of such a claim. A contingent claim must be capable of valuation under s. 135(1.1) — it cannot be too remote or speculative—in order to be a provable claim under s. 121(2).

[139] Before the third step of the Abitibi test can even be reached, a regulator must already have been shown to be a creditor. I have concluded that, on the facts of this case, the Regulator is not a creditor of Redwater. However, for the purpose of explaining how I differ from the chambers judge on the "sufficient certainty" analysis, I will proceed as if the Regulator were, in fact, a creditor of Redwater in respect of the Abandonment Orders and LMR requirements. These end-of-life obligations do not directly require Redwater to make a payment to the Regulator. Rather, they are obligations requiring Redwater to do something. As discussed in Abitibi, if the Regulator were in fact a creditor, end-of-life obligations would be its contingent claims.

[140] What a court must determine is whether there are sufficient facts indicating the existence of an environmental duty that will ripen into a financial liability owed to a regulator. In determining whether a non-monetary regulatory obligation of a bankrupt is too remote or too speculative to be included in the bankruptcy proceeding, the court must apply the general rules that apply to future or contingent claims. It must be sufficiently certain that the contingency will come to pass—in other words, that the regulator will enforce the obligation by performing the environmental work and seeking reimbursement.

[141] I will now discuss the Abandonment Orders and the LMR requirements in turn and demonstrate how they fail to satisfy the "sufficient certainty" step of the Abitibi test.

(a) The Abandonment Orders

[142] The Regulator has issued orders under the *OGCA* and the *Pipeline Act* requiring Redwater to abandon the Renounced Assets. Even if the Regulator were a creditor of Redwater, the Abandonment Orders would still have to be capable of valuation in order to be included in the bankruptcy process. In my view, it is not established either by the chambers judge's factual findings or by the evidence that it is sufficiently certain that the Regulator will perform the abandonments and advance a claim for reimbursement. The claim is too remote and speculative to be included in the bankruptcy process.

[143] The chambers judge acknowledged that it was "unclear" whether the Regulator would perform the abandonments itself or would deem the wells subject to the Abandonment Orders to be orphans (para. 173). He stated that, in the latter case, the OWA would probably carry out the abandonments, although it was not clear when they would be completed. Indeed, the chambers judge acknowledged that, given the OWA's resources, it could take as long as 10 years for it to get around to performing the required environmental work on the Redwater property. He nonetheless concluded that—even though the "sufficient certainty" step was not satisfied in a "technical sense"—the situation met what had been intended in *Abitibi*. That conclusion was at least partly based on his finding that the Abandonment Orders were "intrinsically financial" (para. 173).

[144] In my view, the chambers judge did not make a finding of fact that the Regulator would carry out the abandonments *itself*. As noted, he acknowledged that it was "unclear" whether the Regulator would perform the abandonments. This can hardly be deemed a finding of fact deserving of deference. In my view, considered as a whole, the evidence in this case leads to the conclusion that the Regulator will not abandon the Renounced Assets itself.

[145] The Regulator is not in the business of performing abandonments. It has no statutory duty to do so. Abandonment is instead an obligation of the licensee. The evidence of the Regulator's affiant was that the Regulator very rarely abandons properties on behalf of licensees and virtually never does so where the licensee is in receivership or

bankruptcy. The affiant stated that the Regulator had no intention of abandoning Red-water's licensed assets. As noted by the chambers judge, it is true that, in its letter to GTL dated July 15, 2015, the Regulator threatened to perform the abandonments itself, but the Regulator subsequently took no steps to follow up on that threat. Even if this letter should be accorded any weight, the contradiction between it and the Regulator's subsequent affidavits at the very least makes it difficult to say with anything approaching sufficient certainty that the Regulator intends to carry out the abandonments. These facts distinguish this case from *Abitibi*, in which the restructuring judge's findings were based on the premise that the province would most likely perform the remediation work itself.

[146] Below, I will explain why the OWA's involvement is insufficient to satisfy the "sufficient certainty" test. First, I note that any reliance the chambers judge placed on the intrinsically financial nature of the Abandonment Orders was an error. In this regard, I am in complete agreement with Martin J.A. Considering whether an order is intrinsically financial is an erroneous interpretation of the third step of the *Abitibi* test. It is too broad and would result in a provable claim being found even where the existence of a monetary claim in bankruptcy is merely speculative. Thus, in *Nortel* CA, Juriansz JA rightly rejected the argument that the *Abitibi* test did not require a determination that the regulator would perform the environmental work and claim reimbursement, and that it was sufficient for there to be an environmental order requiring an expenditure of funds by the bankrupt estate. He held the following, at paras. 31–32:

> As I read it, the Supreme Court's decision is clear: ongoing environmental remediation obligations may be reduced to monetary claims that can be compromised in *CCAA* proceedings only where the province has performed the remediation work and advances a claim for reimbursement, or where the obligation may be considered a contingent or future claim because it is "sufficiently certain" that the province will do the work and then seek reimbursement.
>
> The respondents' approach is not only inconsistent with *Abitibi Bowater Inc, Re*, it is too broad. It would result in virtually all regulatory environmental orders being found to be provable claims. As Deschamps J observed, a company may engage in activities that carry risks. When those risks materialize, the costs are borne by those who hold a stake in the company. A risk that results in an environmental obligation becomes subject to the insolvency process only when it is in substance monetary and is in substance a provable claim.

[147] As the chambers judge correctly acknowledged, the fact that the Regulator would not conduct the abandonments itself does not mean that it would wash its hands of the Renounced Assets. Rather, if necessary, it would designate them as orphans pursuant to the *OGCA* and leave them for the OWA. I am not suggesting that a regulator can strategically avoid the "sufficient certainty" test simply by delegating environmental work to an arm's length organization. I would not decide, as the Regulator urges, that the *Abitibi* test *always* requires that the environmental work be performed by the regulator itself. However, the OWA's true nature must be emphasized. There are strong grounds to conclude that, given the particular features of this regulatory context, the OWA is not the regulator.

[148] The creation of the OWA was not an attempt by the Regulator to avoid the *BIA* order of priorities in bankruptcy. It is a non-profit organization with its own mandate and independent board of directors, and it operates as a financially independent entity pursuant to legally delegated authority. Although the OWA's board includes a representative of the Regulator and a representative of Alberta Environment and Parks, its independence is not in question. The OWA's 2014-2015 annual report indicates that five

out of six voting directors represent industry. The OWA uses a risk assessment tool to prioritize when and how it will perform environmental work on the many hundreds of orphans in Alberta. There is no suggestion that the Regulator has any say in the order in which the OWA chooses to perform environmental work. The 2014-2015 annual report also states that, since 1992, 87 percent of the money collected and invested to fund OWA activities has been provided by industry via the orphan levy. The Regulator, at para. 99 of its factum, hints obliquely that additional provincial or federal funding may be forthcoming in the future, but even if it materializes, it will be almost entirely in the form of loans. I cannot accept the suggestion in the dissenting reasons that the Regulator and the OWA are "inextricably intertwined" (para. 273).

[149] Even assuming that the OWA's abandonment of Redwater's licensed assets could satisfy the "sufficient certainty" test, I agree with Martin J.A. that it is difficult to conclude that there is sufficient certainty that the OWA will in fact perform the abandonments. I also agree with her view that there is no certainty that a claim for reimbursement will be advanced should the OWA ultimately abandon the assets.

[150] The dissenting reasons suggest that the facts of this appeal are more akin to those of *Northstar Aerospace Inc, Re*, 2013 ONCA 600, 8 C.B.R. (6th) 154, than to those of *Nortel CA*, arguing that the "sufficient certainty" test is satisfied because, as in *Northstar*, there is no purchaser to take on Redwater's assets and the debtor itself is insolvent, so only the OWA can perform the work. In my view, *Northstar* is easily distinguishable. In that case, the bankrupt had been voluntarily carrying out remediation prior to its bankruptcy. After it made its assignment into bankruptcy, the Ministry of the Environment ("MOE") took over the remediation activities itself, purporting to do so on a without prejudice basis. Jurianz JA found that the fact that the MOE had already undertaken remediation activities made it sufficiently certain that it would do so. As I will now demonstrate, the facts here are very different.

[151] At the beginning of this litigation, the OWA estimated that it would take 10 to 12 years to get through the backlog of orphans. By 2015, that backlog was increasing rapidly, and it may well have continued to increase at the same or an even greater speed in the intervening years, as submitted by the Regulator. If anything, this suggests the possibility of an even larger backlog. There is no indication that the Renounced Assets would have a particularly high priority in the backlog. Even if the potential additional funding materializes, the Regulator submits that it will be a generation or more before the OWA can address its existing inventory of orphans.

[152] The dissenting reasons rely on the chambers judge's conclusion that the OWA would "probably" perform the abandonments eventually, while downplaying the fact that he also concluded that this would not "necessarily [occur] within a definite timeframe" (paras. 261 and 278, citing the chambers judge's reasons, at para. 173). Given the most conservative timeline—the 10 years discussed by the chambers judge—it is difficult to predict anything occurring with sufficient certainty. Much could change within the next decade, both in terms of government policy and in terms of the willingness of those in the Alberta oil and gas industry to discharge environmental liabilities. This is not at all the same situation as in *Northstar*, in which the MOE had already commenced environmental work.

[153] Perhaps more to the point, this lengthy timeline means that, should it ultimately perform the work, the OWA will not advance a claim for reimbursement. Advancement of a claim is an element of the test that is just as essential as performance of the work. The OWA itself has no ability to seek reimbursement of its costs from licensees and, although

the costs of abandonment carried out by a person authorized by the Regulator constitute a debt payable to the Regulator under s. 30(5) of the *OGCA*, no evidence has been adduced that the Regulator has exercised its power to recover such costs in comparable cases. There is a good reason for this: the reality is that, by the time the OWA got around to abandoning any of Redwater's wells, the estate would be finalized and GTL long since discharged. In sum, the chambers judge erred in failing to consider whether the OWA can be treated as the regulator and in failing to appreciate that, even if it can, it is not sufficiently certain that the OWA will in fact perform the abandonments and advance a claim for reimbursement.

[154] Accordingly, even if the Regulator had acted as a creditor in issuing the Abandonment Orders, it cannot be said with sufficient certainty that it would perform the abandonments and advance a claim for reimbursement....

(3) Conclusion on the *Abitibi* test

[159] Accordingly, the end-of-life obligations binding on GTL are not claims provable in the Redwater bankruptcy, so they do not conflict with the general priority scheme in the *BIA*. This is not a mere matter of form, but of substance. Requiring Redwater to pay for abandonment before distributing value to creditors does not disrupt the priority scheme of the *BIA*. In crafting the priority scheme set out in the *BIA*, Parliament intended to permit regulators to place a first charge on real property of a bankrupt affected by an environmental condition or damage in order to fund remediation (see s. 14.06(7)). Thus, the *BIA* explicitly contemplates that environmental regulators will extract value from the bankrupt's real property if that property is affected by an environmental condition or damage. Although the nature of property ownership in the Alberta oil and gas industry meant that s. 14.06(7) was unavailable to the Regulator, the Abandonment Orders and the LMR replicate s. 14.06(7)'s effect in this case. Furthermore, it is important to note that Redwater's only substantial assets were affected by an environmental condition or damage. Accordingly, the Abandonment Orders and LMR requirements did not seek to force Redwater to fulfill end-of-life obligations with assets unrelated to the environmental condition or damage. In other words, recognizing that the Abandonment Orders and LMR requirements are not provable claims in this case does not interfere with the aims of the *BIA*—rather, it facilitates them.

[160] Bankruptcy is not a licence to ignore rules, and insolvency professionals are bound by and must comply with valid provincial laws during bankruptcy. They must, for example, comply with non-monetary obligations that are binding on the bankrupt estate, that cannot be reduced to provable claims, and the effects of which do not conflict with the *BIA*, notwithstanding the consequences this may have for the bankrupt's secured creditors. The Abandonment Orders and the LMR requirements are based on valid provincial laws of general application—exactly the kind of valid provincial laws upon which the *BIA* is built. As noted in *Moloney*, the *BIA* is clear that "the ownership of certain assets and the existence of particular liabilities depend upon provincial law" (para. 40). End-of-life obligations are imposed by valid provincial laws which define the contours of the bankrupt estate available for distribution.

[161] Finally, as noted earlier, the *BIA*'s general purpose of facilitating financial rehabilitation is not relevant for a corporation such as Redwater. Corporations with insufficient assets to satisfy their creditors will never be discharged from bankruptcy because they cannot satisfy all their creditors' claims in full (*BIA*, s. 169(4)). Thus, no conflict with this purpose is caused by the conclusion that the end-of-life obligations binding Redwater are not provable claims.

IV. CONCLUSION

[162] There is no conflict between Alberta's regulatory regime and the *BIA* requiring portions of the former to be rendered inoperative in the context of bankruptcy. Although GTL remains fully protected from personal liability by federal law, it cannot walk away from the environmental liabilities of the bankrupt estate by invoking s. 14.06(4). On a proper application of the *Abitibi* test, the Redwater estate must comply with ongoing environmental obligations that are not claims provable in bankruptcy.

III. THE RULE AGAINST DOUBLE PROOF

The cases excerpted in Part II focus on the proof and valuation of unliquidated and contingent claims. The so-called rule against double proof also concerns the proof and valuation of claims, but is a separate and different issue. The rule against double proof states that there cannot be two proofs of claim filed for the same debt, even if there are separate contracts relating to the debt. Insolvency practitioners often refer to the problem that the rule against double proof addresses as "double-dipping."

Re Olympia & York Developments Ltd (1998), 4 CBR (4th) 189 (Ont Ct J (Gen Div))

BLAIR J:

Overview
[1] The issues on this appeal turn on what is known as the rule against double proof in bankruptcy matters.

[2] Olympia & York Developments Limited ("OYDL") and Olympia & York Resources Credit Corporation ("OYRCC") are bankrupt corporations. OYRCC is a wholly owned subsidiary of OYDL created for the single purpose of receiving the sum of US $2.5 billion by way of what was termed a "Jumbo Loan" from a syndicate of lenders known as the "A&G Lenders". Immediately upon receipt, the monies were advanced by OYRCC to OYDL, which gave back a Promissory Note and entered into a Repayment Agreement with OYRCC. OYDL also guaranteed the OYRCC indebtedness to the A&G Lenders.

[3] It is admitted that the A&G Lenders comprise substantially all of the creditors of OYRCC. In fact, they are the only creditors who have filed proofs of claim in the OYRCC bankruptcy. All of the inspectors in that bankruptcy are representatives of the A&G Lenders.

[4] Deloitte & Touche, the trustee in bankruptcy for OYRCC, has filed a proof of claim in the OYDL bankruptcy for the principal amount of the loan—which remained outstanding in full at the time of the insolvency proceedings—together with interest. At the same time, the A&G Lenders have also filed a proof of claim in the OYDL bankruptcy, based upon the OYDL guarantee of the OYRCC indebtedness, together with interest.

[5] OYDL's Trustee disallowed the claims on the ground that they constitute a double proof of claim against the estate for the same debt. It was, and is, prepared to acknowledge one claim, by either OYRCC or the A&G Lenders. The amount the Trustee is prepared to acknowledge is the sum of $1,759,108,979 (Cdn), representing the outstanding principal on the Jumbo Loan less the sum of $1,281,281,018 (Cdn) recovered by the A&G Lenders on security pledged to it to guarantee the Jumbo Loan by certain OYRCC subsidiaries.

[6] Both the A&G Lenders and the Trustee in Bankruptcy of OYRCC appealed the disallowances to the Registrar in Bankruptcy. On May 21, 1998, Registrar Ferron allowed

the appeals, Re Olympia and York Developments Ltd, [1998] O.J. No. 2114. OYDL's Trustee now appeals from the decision of Registrar Ferron, and seeks,

(a) an Order setting aside the decision of the Registrar;
(b) an Order that the claims of the A&G Lenders and of OYRCC against the estate of OYDL ("the Claims") constitute a double proof against the estate;
(c) a declaration that the A&G Lenders and OYRCC may rank for payment of one dividend out of the estate of OYDL based on a claim in the sum of $1,759,108,979 (Cdn); and,
(d) costs.

Background

[7] In December 1988, OYDL and the A&G Lenders began negotiations in respect of what was to become the $2.5 billion (U.S.) loan facility. A commitment letter from Credit Lyonnais to OYDL, dated December 1988, set out the initially proposed terms. The borrower for purposes of the loan facility was to be a wholly owned subsidiary of OYDL and OYDL was to guarantee the Loan. The proposal was that the Loan Agreement and other documents would contain covenants and other provisions "as are usual in Olympia & York loan agreements". The commitment letter concluded by saying that Credit Lyonnais was "very pleased to have this opportunity to provide this facility to Olympia & York and [looked] forward to the continuation of [their] mutually beneficial relations".

[8] The negotiations eventually ripened into the Jumbo Loan transaction — or, more accurately, series of transactions. Except for US $500 million which was remitted directly to OYDL by one of the lenders upon the direction of OYRCC, the funds were advanced by the A&G Lenders to OYRCC. OYRCC, in turn and on the same day, "onloaned" the monies to OYDL. At the end of the day, OYDL had a loan facility of US $2.5 billion.

[9] In exchange, OYDL (a) gave its guarantee of the OYRCC indebtedness to the A&G Lenders (the "OYDL Guarantee") not just as guarantor but also as principal debtor, (b) agreed to maintain a current value net worth of at least US $2.5 billion throughout the life of the facility, (c) executed a Promissory Note in the principal amount of US $2.5 billion in favour of OYRCC, and (d) entered into a Repayment Agreement in that regard with OYRCC. Apart from the OYDL Guarantee, the central underlying security which the A&G Lenders received from the Jumbo Loan consisted of a pledge of the shares that OYDL held (indirectly through subsidiaries) in Abitibi Price Inc. ("Abitibi") and in Gulf Canada Resources Limited ("Gulf"). . . .

The Rule Against Double Proof

[23] The rule against double proof in bankruptcy matters prohibits two proofs of claim in the same estate for the same debt. That the two claims may be based on separate contracts is of no matter, provided they are in respect of the same debt. Sir G Mellish LJ put the concept very succinctly in *Re Oriental Commercial Bank; Ex parte European Bank* (1871), 7 L.R. Ch. App. 99, where he stated (at pp. 103–104):

> [T]he true principle is, that there is only to be one dividend in respect of what is in substance the same debt, although there may be two separate contracts. (Emphasis added)

[24] See also, *Barclays Bank Ltd v TOSG Trust Fund Ltd*, [1984] 1 All E.R. 628 (C.A.), at pp. 636–637, affirmed on different grounds [1984] 1 All E.R. 1060 (H.L.); Houlden & Morawetz, *Bankruptcy and Insolvency Law of Canada* 3rd ed., at paragraph G-40; *Re Melton; Milk v. Towers* [1918] 1 Ch 37, at p. 47.

[25] There is a reason for this rule. It was developed to ensure the pari passu distribution of the assets of the bankrupt on a pro rata basis amongst the unsecured creditors—the central tenet of bankruptcy legislation. In the words of Oliver LJ in Barclays Bank, supra, at p. 653:

> p. 653 ... The purpose of the rule is, of course, to ensure pari passu distribution of the assets comprised in the estate of an insolvent in pro rata discharge of his liabilities. The payment of more than one dividend in respect of what is in substance the same debt would give the relevant proving creditors a share of the available assets larger than the share properly attributable to the debt in question.

[26] The Parties do not disagree as to the foregoing statement of the rule against double proof, or as to the rationale underlying it. They simply disagree as to its application in the circumstances of this case.

The Authorities

[27] Whether or not a "double proof" has been lodged with respect to what is in substance the same debt is a matter to be determined on the facts of each individual case. From my understanding of the authorities, the underlying principles which should frame this analysis in group corporate insolvency situations may be summarized as follows. First, where the interests of different creditors of the various corporate entities come into play, the courts should be careful to respect the axiom regarding separate corporate existence enunciated by the House of Lords in *Salomon v Salomon* [1897] A.C. 22. At the same time, however, the courts should strive to give effect to the ethic of pari passu distribution and to the fundamental underlying principle of justice as between all creditors. Balancing these sometimes competing principles calls for a consideration of the true nature of the transaction, and the relationship between, and the presumed common intention of the parties. Finally, in seeking a just solution in novel situations the court may engage in an analysis which, while not ignoring the separate corporate being of the members of the corporate group, nonetheless transcends the mere legal fact of that existence. See in particular, as to the foregoing summary, *Ford & Carter Ltd v Midland Bank Ltd* (1979) 129 NLJ 543, per Lord Wilberforce at p. 544; *Polly Peck, supra,* at pp. 444–445; and *Barclays Bank, supra,* per Kerr L.J., at pp. 645 and 647–648, and per Oliver L.J. at pp. 636 and 640.

[28] In insolvency cases—as in, for example, tax cases—the court will not allow technicalities to obscure the essence of the transaction. This includes, in my opinion, not being either too dazzled or too immobilized by intricate corporate footwork which is designed to accomplish legitimate business and tax purposes, but which may not be as directly dispositive in resolving insolvency cases. This point was emphasized by Oliver L.J. in *Barclays Bank* at pp. 640 and 636:

> p.640 This argument is perfectly intelligible, and indeed almost unanswerable if one regards the payment of those customers who were paid to TOSG as an entirely separate transaction isolated from any other arrangement made with the agency, but to my mind it ignores the reality. *If one is to look for analogies, it is, I think, essential first to analyse what the total effect of the arrangements was and the reasoning behind them.* All the cases stress that in relation to the rule against double proofs it is the substance and not the form that is to be regarded (see eg *Re Melton, Milk v Towers* [1918] 1 Ch 37, at 60, [1916–17] All ER Rep 672 at 683, *Re Oriental Commercial Bank* (1871) LR 7 Ch App 99). (emphasis added)

p.636 I accept the submission of counsel for TOSG and the agency that the rule ought more properly to be styled the rule against double dividends, *for its object is to absolve the liquidator from paying out two dividends on what is essentially the same debt* ... (emphasis added)

Second, it is, I think, a fallacy to argue ... that, because overlapping liabilities result from separate and independent contracts with the debtor, that, by itself, is determinative of whether the rule can apply. <u>The tests is in my judgment a much broader one which transcends a close jurisprudential analysis of the persons by and to whom the duties are owed</u>. It is simply whether the two competing claims are, in *substance*, claims for payment of the same debt twice over. (Italics in original; underlining added)

Application of the Rule in the Circumstances of this Case

[29] To adopt the language of Oliver LJ, then, what is "the total effect of the arrangements ... and the reasoning behind them" in the circumstances of this case? In my view, a careful reading of all of the documentation including in particular, the Repayment Agreement, supports the conclusion that the "loan" from the A&G Lenders to OYRCC and the "on-loaning" of the same funds from OYRCC to OYDL are in substance the same debt....

The Registrar's Decision and the "Genuine Debtor-Creditor", "Separate Corporate Existence", and "Group Enterprise" Issues

[35] Registrar Ferron concluded that there existed a genuine debtor-creditor relationship between OYDL and OYRCC and that there was nothing in the circumstances which would allow him to disregard the separate corporate existence of OYRCC. In my view, these conclusions are simply mirror images of each other. Registrar Ferron said:

> If one acceded to the position taken by the trustee of OYDL and concluded that OYRCC's loan to its parent company was of no significance, the transaction involving the loan from the A&G Lenders would have to be seen as something of a sham and that [the] A&G Lenders were misled in loaning funds to OYRCC which until this point no one denied. [OYRCC] had a corporate existence separate and distinct from its parent including the capacity to borrow and loan funds.

[36] While the latter observation is accurate, it is not conclusive; and, in my respectful view, the learned Registrar erred in law in deciding that once he found the existence of a separate corporate entity and a debtor-creditor relationship between parent and subsidiary, the same-debt-in-substance test could not be met. The case law illustrates that the existence of separate and distinct claims or liabilities is not determinative of the double proof issue. The crucial question is whether or not the separate and distinct claims relate in substance to the same debt. For the reasons that I have outlined, I am satisfied that they do....

[46] Registrar Ferron considered this test for determining whether the rule against double proof had been contravened, and concluded that the test was not met on the facts of this case. He said:

> If OYDL were to pay the A&G Lenders under the guarantee this could not affect the loan due to OYRCC under its note. Similarly, if OYDL were to pay OYRCC and thus discharge the Promissory Note, the obligation under the guarantee would still exist and be enforceable. One payment would not discharge both claimants' debts against OYDL and accordingly, on the test suggested by Oliver, LJ the rule is not offended.

[47] I respectfully disagree. The Registrar's conclusion flows from a misunderstanding of the constating documents which frame the Jumbo Loan deal. Suppose, for example, that OYDL remained solvent, but that OYRCC had become insolvent and unable to pay the A&G Lenders. One payment by OYDL to the A&G Lenders would satisfy its liability on the OYDL Guarantee, and would eliminate the liability as between the A&G Lenders and OYRCC. There would accordingly be no further payments to be made by OYRCC under the Term Loan Agreements; and, since OYDL's obligation under the Note is to pay interest on the principal at the times provided in the Term Loan Agreements, and under the Repayment Agreement is "to make payments of principal under the Note to [OYRCC] *under the Term Loan Agreements*", OYDL could have no more liability to OYRCC under the Promissory Note. Thus, one payment would discharge both debts, having regard to the total contractual framework of the arrangement. . . .

III. CONCLUSION

Accordingly,

a) the order of the Registrar is set aside;

b) an order is granted directing that claims of A&G Lenders and of OYRCC against the estate of OYDL constitute a double proof against the estate;

c) a declaration is granted that the A&G Lenders and OYRCC may rank for payment of one dividend out of the estate of OYDL based on a claim in the sum of $1,759,108,979.00 (Cdn.); and,

d) the Appellant is entitled to its costs of the appeal and of the proceeding before the Registrar.

Appeal allowed.

Practice Questions

Question One
Christopher operates Christopher's Chemicals as a sole proprietorship. The company, and Christopher, were assigned into bankruptcy on 1 January 2020 after a number of key customers went out of business. At the date of bankruptcy, Christopher's Chemicals has a number of outstanding accounts and obligations for the trustee to assess. Sally's Supplies is owed $15,000 on invoices due before 1 January, with another $2,000 due on 1 February 2020. The trustee in bankruptcy has disclaimed the continuing contract with Sally's Supplies. Christopher is also concerned about a personal guarantee he extended to the bank for another of his businesses, Christopher's Cleaning, several years ago. The company is now experiencing financial difficulties but has not yet defaulted. In February 2020, Christopher borrowed $500 from Henry to buy groceries. In March 2020, Christopher's Chemicals accidentally spilled toxic chemicals onto neighbouring protected lands, damaging the sensitive ecosystem. The province's environmental protection agency estimates their clean up efforts will cost at least $25,000. Applying what you've learned about provable claims, assess what, if any, claim Christopher's creditors will have. Under what circumstances will Christopher's creditors not receive a distribution?

Question Two
Sarah is currently in bankruptcy. To help her pay for groceries, her friend Sanjit lent her $500. Unfortunately, Sarah is unable to pay Sanjit, and he wants his money back. Can Sanjit

approach Sarah's trustee with a provable claim? Under what circumstances would Sanjit be successful in receiving his money back as a provable claim?

Question Three
Albert runs a general store in a small town. One of his customers, who owes the store $1,000, has assigned themselves into bankruptcy. What steps can Albert take to ensure that he can get money from the bankrupt customer's estate?

Question Four
The court in *Bittner* could have valued Rolfite's claim by assigning a present probability to its likelihood of success in the state court. Why did the court reject this approach?

CHAPTER 8

Priority Creditors

I. INTRODUCTION

Canadian insolvency law has long been respectful of secured creditors' rights and this continues to be the case. For example, the *Bankruptcy and Insolvency Act*, RSC 1985, c B-3 (*BIA*), section 71 provides that the debtor's property vests in the trustee subject to the rights of secured creditors, and *BIA*, section 69.3(2) provides that a secured creditor is not subject to the automatic bankruptcy stay of proceedings.

There are two explanations for the favourable treatment of secured creditors in Canadian insolvency law. The first is political: in England and Canada, banks and other financial intermediaries have historically played and continue to play an influential role in the shaping of bankruptcy rules: see Anna Lund, "Engaging Canadians in Commercial Law Reform: Insights and Lessons from the 2014 Industry Canada Consultation on Insolvency Legislation" (2016) 58 *Canadian Business Law Journal* 123. The second reason is conceptual and economic. Anglo-Canadian common law permits a creditor to secure a business debt with all of the debtor's present and after-acquired property. This liberal tradition is continued in the personal property security legislation now in force in all the common law provinces and territories. In Quebec, *sûreté mobilières* were also greatly liberalized in the new Civil Code of 1994: Anthony Duggan and Jacob Ziegel, *Secured Transactions in Personal Property*, 5th ed (Toronto: Emond Montgomery, 2009), ch 1. Obviously, secured creditors are anxious to ensure that bankruptcy law recognizes their pre-bankruptcy claims, because it is on the debtor's insolvency that secured creditors most often find it necessary to enforce their security. The *BIA* allows secured creditors to enforce their claims after the debtor's bankruptcy. The first part of this chapter describes how the *BIA* regulates the exercise of secured creditor's rights.

This solicitous attitude vanishes when the claimant is the Crown and the proprietary right that secures the obligation is created by statute rather than through a consensual agreement between the parties. The Crown often occupies the position of a creditor in insolvency proceedings. This may result from the debtor's failure to pay an obligation owing to the Crown, such as a workers' compensation assessment levied on an employer, or to remit amounts collected by the debtor from third parties on behalf of the Crown, such as when a debtor collects and remits sales tax from its customers. Federal and provincial governments have attempted to use two techniques to confer an elevated priority status on their claims. First, they have enacted statutes that give the Crown a proprietary right in the debtor's property, akin to a secured creditor. The statute usually creates a statutory lien or charge on the debtor's assets. Sometimes the statute also provides a priority rule that gives the statutory lien or charge priority over a prior-in-time secured creditor. Second, the Crown has created statutory deemed trusts in its favour. The legislation deems that the debtor's property is held in trust for the Crown, even if the common law requirements of a trust are lacking. The legislation sometimes also includes a priority rule that gives the statutory deemed trust priority over a prior secured creditor. The Crown's ability to rely on such devices to claim a secured status was originally curtailed by the judiciary, and then by amendments to the *BIA* in 1992. The second part of this chapter describes how Crown-secured claims and statutory trusts are treated in bankruptcy.

II. SECURED CREDITORS' CLAIMS

A. Introduction

One of the fundamental principles of Canadian bankruptcy law is that only the property of the bankrupt is made available to satisfy the claims of the bankrupt's creditors. A trustee in bankruptcy therefore has no right to confiscate the property of a third party, notwithstanding that it may be in the possession or control of the bankrupt. This principle applies even if the third party has only a limited proprietary right in the property, as opposed to full ownership of it. This explains the treatment of secured creditors in bankruptcy. Secured creditors have limited proprietary rights in the debtor's property, and they can enforce these rights against the debtor's property if the debtor defaults on its obligations to the secured creditors. What amounts to a default may be set out in legislation or contract. For example, section 1(1) of the *Personal Property Security Act*, RSO 1990, c P-10 (*PPSA*) defines default as a failure to make a payment or otherwise perform an obligation when due. A security agreement may require a debtor to insure its property, and failure to carry adequate insurance could be an act of default.

The proprietary rights of a secured creditor are largely unaffected by the bankruptcy of the debtor. Upon default, the secured creditor may enforce the security interest through seizure and sale of the property or through foreclosure of the security interest. A secured creditor thereby withdraws the asset from the bankrupt estate. If there is a surplus after the secured creditor and any subordinate interests are satisfied, it must be paid over to the trustee in bankruptcy. If there is a deficiency (the proceeds from the sale of the collateral are insufficient to satisfy the obligation secured), the secured creditor may prove for it as an ordinary unsecured creditor in the bankruptcy of the debtor. The trustee in bankruptcy has only a limited ability to interfere with the right of a secured creditor to enforce its security.

There is an exception to the principle that the rights of a secured creditor are largely unaffected by a bankruptcy. Under provincial law, secured creditors may need to comply with certain registration or perfection requirements in order for a security interest to have priority over a trustee in bankruptcy. Provincial personal property security legislation provides that an unperfected security interest is subordinate to a trustee in bankruptcy: see for example *PPSA*, section 20(1)(b). The Supreme Court of Canada in *Re Giffen*, [1998] 1 SCR 91 (excerpted in Chapter 4, Part II) upheld the constitutionality of these provisions. Provincial statutes governing real property do not contain equivalent provisions that subordinate an unregistered interest in land to a trustee in bankruptcy. A secured creditor is therefore able to enforce its security in real property against the trustee in bankruptcy despite its failure to register its interest in a land title or land registration system: *Citifinancial Canada East Corp v Morrow Estate (Trustee of)*, 2006 NBQB 132; *Re Canadian Engineering & Contracting Co* (1994), 28 CBR (3d) 136 (Ont Ct J (Gen Div)).

B. Definition of Secured Creditor

Secured creditor is defined in section 2 of the *BIA* to include "a person holding a mortgage, hypothec, pledge, charge or lien on or against the property of the debtor or any part of that property as security for a debt due or accruing due to the person from the debtor or a person whose claim is based on, or secured by, a negotiable instrument held as collateral security and on which the debtor is only indirectly or secondarily liable" as well as some specific commercial relationships contemplated in Quebec's *Civil Code.*

This definition predates the adoption of personal property security legislation in the provinces. The provincial personal property security laws use a substantive test to define "security interest," and consequently a number of commercial relationships that were not previously characterized as security agreements now qualify as security agreements under provincial personal property security law. For example, in a conditional sales contract the vendor retains title until the purchaser pays the purchase price of the goods in full. Personal property security laws treat the conditional sales contract as though it were a security agreement, where title has passed to the purchaser and the vendor retains a security interest in the goods: Ronald Cuming, Roderick Wood, and Catherine Walsh, *Personal Property Security Law,* 2d ed (Toronto: Irwin Law, 2012) at 12.

The fact that definition of secured creditor in the *BIA* predates and differs from the definition in personal property security legislation raises an important question: does the *BIA* definition cover security interests that are not enumerated in the definition, but qualify as security interests under provincial law—for example, conditional sales contracts?

In *R v Ford Credit Canada Limited,* excerpted below, the court assumed that the *BIA* definition includes conditional sales contracts. We believe the court was right, not because the inclusion of conditional sales is implicit in the enumeration of security interests in the definition, but because serious practical difficulties would otherwise arise in applying the *BIA* provisions governing the enforcement of security interests. The same reasoning would apply to finance leases that in substance secure payment of an obligation. This question, however, is not clear-cut because there is a line of Canadian authorities that interpret a similar definition of "secured creditor" contained in the *Income Tax Act,* RSC 1985, c 1 (5th Supp) (*ITA*) as not encompassing a conditional sales contract or a finance lease that in substance secures payment of an obligation. This issue will be revisited later in this chapter and in Chapter 9.

Personal property security law also deems a number of commercial relationships to be security interests for the purposes of registration and priorities, but not in relation to the enforcement remedies. Examples of these deemed security interests include an outright sale of accounts or chattel paper and a lease for a term of more than one year. These transactions do not fall within the definition of a secured creditor in the federal insolvency statutes since they do not constitute "a mortgage, hypothec, pledge, charge or lien," and nor do they secure a "debt due or accruing due" from the debtor. A lessor under a non-security lease who wishes to recover the leased goods must invoke the procedure set out in *BIA* section 81(1); see discussion below.

A second question about the scope of the *BIA*'s definition of "secured creditor" is whether it includes non-consensual security interests arising by operation of law and not by agreement? The answer to this second question is clearly "yes," although there is surprisingly little authority that states this explicitly. The reasons for this construction are that the definition of secured creditor is not confined to consensual claims as it expressly covers liens, and the term "charge" is wide enough to encompass non-consensual security interests created by statute. A repairer who has a common-law possessory lien therefore qualifies as a secured creditor, as would a person who is entitled to claim a statutory lien on goods pursuant to legislation such as the *Repair and Storage Liens Act,* RSO 1990, c R.25 or the *Garage Keepers' Lien Act,* RSA 2000, c G-2.

A landlord's distress for unpaid rent originally qualified as a secured claim, because it gave the landlord an interest akin to a lien on the goods. However, in 1949, the *Bankruptcy Act* was changed. A landlord's right to distrain for unpaid rent was taken away and the landlord was instead afforded the status of a preferred claimant. Any property that had been seized under a distress for rent had to be turned over to the trustee, unless the process had been fully completed by payment to the landlord before the occurrence of the bankruptcy: *BIA*, sections 73(4) and 136(1)(f). The courts held that these changes indicated that Parliament intended that landlords were no longer to be treated as secured creditors in bankruptcy proceedings: *Re Radioland Ltd* (1957), 36 CBR 158 (Sask CA); *Re Gingras Automobile Ltée*, [1962] SCR 676.

Although provincial judgment enforcement law may provide that a writ or other judgment enforcement process creates a lien or charge on the property or confers upon it the same priority as a secured creditor, this will not give the creditor the status of a secured creditor in a bankruptcy: *Re Sklar* (1958), 37 CBR 187 (Sask CA), *Toronto Dominion Bank v Phillips*, 2014 ONCA 613. Section 70(1) of the *BIA* provides that a bankruptcy order or assignment takes precedence over all judgment enforcement proceedings except those that have been completely executed by payment to the creditor: *Canadian Credit Men's Trust Assn v Beaver Trucking Ltd*, [1959] SCR 311 (SCC).

Saskatchewan adopted a new judgment enforcement law in 2010, which purports to give the insolvency trustee the benefit of a judgment creditor's charge: see *The Enforcement of Money Judgments Act*, SS 2010, c E-9.22, section 26 (*EMJA*) and a comparable provision in *Land Titles Act, 2000*, SS 2010, c L-5.1, section 173.3(9) (*LTA*). Tamara Buckwold explains:

> As a general rule, a security interest registered after a judgment is registered will be subordinate to the enforcement charge. However, the enforcement rights of judgment creditors under provincial law are suspended if the debtor becomes bankrupt. Without a countervailing rule, an enforcement charge that has priority over a security interest under the EMJA or the LTA may therefore be subordinated to the security interest if bankruptcy intervenes and provincial judgment enforcement law ceases to operate. A perfected security interest is enforceable against the debtor's property notwithstanding bankruptcy and will accordingly have priority over the rights of unsecured creditors exercised through the trustee in bankruptcy. The EMJA and LTA provisions prevent this from occurring.[1]

Although statutory liens and charges in favour of the Crown qualify as secured claims and give the Crown the status of a secured creditor, the Crown's ability to assert such claims in a bankruptcy has been restricted by sections 86–87 of the *BIA*. Although statutory deemed trusts have essentially the same function as statutory liens and charges, they are afforded different treatment under the *BIA*. Crown security interests and deemed trusts are both discussed in greater detail below in Part III.

C. Enforcement of Security Interests

BIA section 69.3 establishes the basic principle that the general stay of proceedings consequent on the debtor's bankruptcy does not apply to secured claims unless a court imposes a stay at the trustee's request. Even then the stay can only be of limited duration and is rarely granted in practice. However, there is an unresolved conflict in the case law regarding whether a secured creditor may engage in self-help in repossessing the collateral or whether

---

1   "The Reform of Judgment Enforcement Law in Canada: An Overview and Comparison of Models for Reform" (2017) 80 *Saskatchewan Law Review* 71 at 96. Buckwold notes that the constitutionality of these provisions remains untested.

it must file a proof of claim and comply with the requirements in *BIA*, section 81: see *R v Ford Credit Canada Limited*, below.

Assuming that the secured creditor has seized and/or realized the collateral after the debtor's bankruptcy, *BIA*, sections 127–34, then come into play to determine the trustee's and secured creditor's rights. If there is a deficiency in the amount owing to the secured creditor after the collateral has been realized, section 127 allows the secured party to file a proof of claim for the balance. However, in the case of an individual debtor, any unpaid balance will be discharged upon the debtor's discharge from bankruptcy under section 168.1 or 172. (For discussion of consumer discharges from bankruptcy, see Chapter 11.) The trustee's rights vis-à-vis a secured creditor are outlined in the case of *R v Ford Credit Canada Limited*.

R v Ford Credit Canada Limited (1990), 78 CBR (NS) 266 (Ont SC) [*Ford*]

[The debtors, a married couple, bought a vehicle with financing from Ford Credit Canada Limited (Ford). The debtors subsequently filed for bankruptcy. Ford filed a proof of claim with the trustee and indicated that its claim was secured against the vehicle. The trustee requested that Ford provide better evidence of its security interest and warned it not to seize the vehicle. Ford disregarded the trustee's warning and seized the vehicle.

The trustee was of the view that Ford should not have seized the vehicle and had a charge laid against Ford under s 174 [now s 203] of the *BIA*. This provision makes it an offence for a party, who has claimed a proprietary interest under s 59 [now s 81] of the *BIA*, to remove the property unless either the trustee consents to its removal or more than thirty days have elapsed since the party has submitted its claim. In the excerpt below, the court considers whether this offence provision applied to secured creditors, like Ford, or only to parties who claimed to be the rightful owners of property in the debtor's possession. The court determined that the offence provision did not apply to secured creditors and therefore, Ford could not be guilty of the offence. In doing so, it drew a distinction between security interests and proprietary interests, such as "where a person leaves his suit with the drycleaner and the drycleaner goes bankrupt." A party with a proprietary interest has to follow the procedure set out in s 81 of the *BIA* and secured creditors' rights are modified by sections 79 and 127–34.]

AUSTIN J:

[28] Section 59(1) [now s 81(1)] ... deals with the situation "where a person claims any property, or interest therein, in the possession of the bankrupt." It is clear that s 59 is intended to deal with a bailment situation, eg, where a person leaves his suit with the drycleaner and the drycleaner goes bankrupt. Whether it applies to more than bailments need not be decided here. Section 59 sets out a code or procedure to be followed in those circumstances. The claimant must file a proof of claim. The trustee may allow it or dispute it. If disputed, the claimant may appeal. If he does not, he is deemed to have abandoned the property. The onus of establishing a claim is on the claimant. Section 59 provides the only method of determining such a claim.

[29] It is clear that the procedure to be followed where a security claim only is made is quite different. In the event of a dispute, the trustee's recourse is not to give notice of disallowance but to apply to the court for directions: *Household Finance v Davis*. Section 59 does not provide an exclusive procedure for this situation: *Re Leblanc*.

[30] This difference in procedure raises the question whether Parliament intended s 59 to have any application at all where a security interest only is claimed. Having

regard to the language of s 49(2) [now s 69.3(1), the stay provision] and of s 59, it would appear that Parliament did not.

[31] On its face, s 49(2) indicates that s 59 does *not* apply. Section 49(2) says that with certain exceptions, a secured creditor may deal with his security as if this section had not been passed. "This section" refers to s 49(1). The "certain exceptions" are set out in ss 57 [now s 79] and 98 to 105 [now ss 127–134]. They are commented on below, but none of those sections has any application in the present circumstances. Section 59 is not even mentioned in s 49(2). On a plain reading of s 49(2), therefore, it is not subject to s 59. Since s 174 is only applicable to the property or property interest referred to in s 59, it would appear that s 174 is not applicable to security.

[32] Section 57 [now s 79] deals with property of the bankrupt held by another as a pledge, pawn or other security. In such a case, the trustee may inspect the property and redeem it. On receipt of notice from the trustee, the holder is not to realize the security until the trustee has had an opportunity to inspect, and if he so wishes, to redeem. That section has no application here as the property was in the possession of Mrs. Szucsko at the time of the bankruptcy.

[33] Sections 98 to 105 are under the heading "Proof by Secured Creditors." Section 98(1) [now s 127(1)] says that where a secured creditor realizes his security, he may prove (as an ordinary creditor) for the balance of the debt.

[34] Section 98(2) [now s 127(2)] provides that where the creditor surrenders his security to the trustee, he may file a proof of claim for the whole amount of his claim. Clearly s 98 has no application to the present circumstances.

[35] Section 99 [now s 128] provides that where a secured creditor neither realizes nor surrenders his security, he shall, if the trustee so demands, value the security. If he does this, he is entitled to share in the bankruptcy only to the extent that his claim exceeds the stated value of the security. The trustee, for his part, may accept the creditor's valuation and may redeem the security if he so wishes.

[36] Section 100 [now s 129] deals with the situation where the secured creditor has failed to value his security or the trustee is not satisfied with the creditor's valuation. In either of these events, the trustee may require that the security be put up for sale.

[37] Section 101 [now s 130] empowers the creditor to require the trustee to elect whether he is going to redeem or require a sale. This was what Ford purported to do on February 8, 1988. No response from the trustee is revealed in the evidence.

[38] Sections 102 and 103 [now ss 131 and 132] deal with amending the valuation of the security.

[39] Section 104 [now s 133] provides that if a secured creditor does not comply with ss 98 to 103, he shall be excluded from any dividend.

[40] Section 105 [now s 134] provides that subject to s 101 [now s 130], a creditor shall not receive more than 100 cents on the dollar, plus interest.

Appeal dismissed.

As a result of the court's decision in *Ford*, trustees would appear to be in a stronger position vis-à-vis proprietary claimants (for example, bailors of goods left with the bankrupt for storage or dry cleaning) than toward secured creditors, as the former must file a proof of claim and either get the trustees consent or wait thirty days before removing the goods, whereas secured creditors need not file any paperwork with the trustee and can remove the goods immediately.

In addition to *BIA*, sections 127–34, which apply only in bankruptcy proceedings, section 244 of the *BIA* limits the ability of a secured creditor to enforce its security. The secured creditor must give the debtor a ten-day notice before enforcing a security on all or substantially all the inventory, accounts receivable, or other property of the debtor. This limitation applies outside the bankruptcy context as well, and frequently arises when a secured creditor appoints a receiver. It is discussed in Chapter 17.

D. Approaches to Secured Creditors in Other Jurisdictions

The *BIA* supports secured creditors' claims at almost every stage. Is this sound policy? See Ronald Cuming, "Canadian Bankruptcy Law: A Secured Creditors Heaven" (1994) 24 *Canadian Business Law Journal* 17; compare Jacob Ziegel, "The New Personal Property Security Regimes: Have We Gone Too Far?" (1990) 28 *Alberta Law Review* 739. The pervasive use of secured credit can mean that there is little or no value available for unsecured creditors in a bankruptcy. Other jurisdictions have adopted less deferential approaches to the rights of secured creditors.

In the United States, section 362(a) of the *Bankruptcy Code* makes it clear that the automatic stay triggered on the filing of a bankruptcy petition (and Chapter 11 filing) also applies to the enforcement of security interests, although a court may grant relief in some circumstances. The American theory of the automatic stay appears to be that secured creditors, as well as other creditors, will be better off if the trustee is allowed to deal with all the assets of the estate. The Canadian theory, on the other hand (embodied in section 69.3(2)), adopts the view that the secured creditor's bargain (which includes the right to foreclose and sell the collateral on default or other prescribed events) should be respected in bankruptcy as well as outside bankruptcy.

In the United Kingdom, the *Insolvency Act, 1986* was amended to provide that a prescribed percentage of a company's assets must be made available for distribution to the ordinary unsecured creditors. In Canada, the trend has been to create a statutory charge in favour of certain types of claimants who are considered to be particularly vulnerable in terms of their reliance on the debt owed to them and their inability to adjust by restricting credit or charging a higher interest rate. See Chapter 9.

III. CROWN CLAIMS

A. Introduction

Federal and provincial legislatures use a wide variety of measures to secure priority for Crown claims over other creditors, both inside and outside bankruptcy. At common law, Crown debts were afforded priority over competing creditors as part of the Crown prerogative. This rule was justified on the basis that the English sovereign was superior to their subjects—a sentiment captured in the phrase *detur digniori* or "let it given to the worthier": Anne Hardy, *Crown Priority in Insolvency* (Toronto: Carswell, 1986) at 2. This justification no longer attracts support, and arguments in favour of granting the Crown preferential treatment in insolvency have evolved to engage with contemporary notions of fairness and efficiency. However, the justifications for according priority to government claims (which are often tax claims) have been hotly contested, as the following excerpt indicates:

Barbara K Morgan, "Should the Sovereign Be Paid First—A Comparative International Analysis of the Priority for Tax Claims in Bankruptcy" (2000) 74 *American Bankruptcy Law Journal* **461 at 463–68**

Traditionally, there have been several justifications for the priority for tax claims. First, unlike the claims of private commercial creditors, tax claims are for the benefit of the entire community. The priority protects the revenue base for the common good, and avoids shifting the burden of the debtor's unpaid taxes to other taxpayers.

Second, unlike private creditors, taxing authorities are involuntary creditors, unable to choose their debtor or obtain security for debt before extending credit. The priority compensates for this disadvantage, giving the taxing authorities an opportunity to assess the amounts due and mobilize their collection remedies.

Third, with regard to taxes for which the debtor acts as the government's tax collector—such as sales tax, value added tax, or employee withholding tax—the argument is made that, if no priority or trust is imposed, the moneys collected by the debtor will increase the estate for the benefit of unsecured creditors. In these circumstances, the tax priority operates to prevent a windfall to general unsecured creditors who have no fair claim to the collected funds.

Fourth, some argue that if the taxing authorities are not reasonably secure they will be discouraged from negotiating payment terms with debtors, thus forcing premature and possibly unnecessary business failures. . . .

As new forms of taxation have been created and tax rates have increased, tax claims have consumed more and more of an insolvent debtor's estate, leading to questions about the tax priority. Critics of the priority reject the community interest argument, contending that the debt owed to the government is unlikely to be significant in terms of total government receipts, whereas the loss to private creditors may cause substantial hardship and precipitate additional insolvencies. Moreover, to the extent private creditors receive a higher return on their claims, part of the loss to the taxing authorities can be recouped through additional taxes paid by those creditors. And, of course, a loss of priority does not prevent the taxing authorities from sharing in an insolvent estate pro rata with general unsecured creditors.

Critics of the priority similarly reject the involuntary creditor argument, on the ground that the government has other enhancements of its ability to collect debts, offsetting its involuntary position, that are not shared by private creditors, including (1) the imposition of penalties and relatively high interest rates, (2) third party liability, and (3) collection procedures such as statutory lien and levy. Furthermore, there is no general rule that involuntary creditors should receive priority—several other categories of involuntary creditors are not entitled to any kind of priority.

Critics also argue that abolishing priority for tax claims will provide a greater incentive to the taxing authorities to collect taxes in a commercially reasonable manner, by removing reliance on an artificial ability to be paid ahead of other creditors. These critics . . . argue instead that any incentive to delay collection is counterproductive. According to this view, delaying collection compromises the uniform enforcement of the tax laws and constitutes a state subsidy, which undermines the disciplinary force of an effective insolvency law. Particularly in situations where the debtor is acting as tax collector, the taxing authorities have better information available about the debtor's financial condition than general business creditors. The debtor is required to submit periodic returns in connection with payroll, value added taxes, sales taxes, and taxes withheld from employee wages, and the authorities receiving these returns are likely to know without delay when there is a delinquency. Allowing tax debts to accumulate under those circumstances can unfairly disadvantage other unsecured creditors who go on trading with the debtor not knowing that there is a tax delinquency.

[Reprinted by permission of the publisher.]

Prior to 1992, the *BIA* ranked Crown claims as preferred claims under section 136. Although one of the fundamental principles of bankruptcy law is the equal treatment of creditors, section 136 sets out a number of different claims that are entitled to be paid before ordinary unsecured creditors. (Preferred claims under section 136 are covered in more detail in Chapter 9.) All preferred claims in section 136 rank behind secured claims. Federal and provincial governments long felt that they deserved to be treated better and rather than waiting for Parliament to revise the *BIA*, the federal and provincial governments adopted two key tactics to improve their chances of recovering from insolvent debtors: using statutes to create deemed trusts in the debtor's assets, and using statutes to create deemed security interests in the debtor's assets. When undertaken by provincial governments, such tactics raise constitutional issues about the interface of the *BIA* with provincial laws regarding property and civil rights: these issues are explored below in Part B. Amendments to the *BIA* passed in 1992 removed the preference given to Crown claims and circumscribed the effectiveness of Crown-deemed trusts and security interests. Once a debtor has become bankrupt, the effectiveness of Crown-deemed trusts and security interests may depend on these 1992 amendments to the *BIA*, the statute under which the Crown interest arises, and the particular facts of the case. The rules governing Crown security interests are discussed below in Part C and those applicable to deemed trusts are canvassed in Part D.

B. Constitutional Context

The provincial and federal Crowns' efforts to enhance their recovery in bankruptcy have led to fierce (and ongoing) litigation. In a quartet of cases decided in the 1980's, consensual secured creditors took the position that provincial governments were trying to circumvent the ranking prescribed in *BIA*, section 136(1), and that these efforts were unconstitutional. The Supreme Court of Canada agreed with the secured creditors and decided that provincial legislation could not be used to bypass the section 136(1) ranking by converting Crown claims into lien claims. In the last of the four cases, *British Columbia v Henfrey Samson Belair Ltd*, [1989] 2 SCR 24, the Court also held that a deemed trust created under the BC *Social Service Tax Act* in respect of sales tax collected by the bankrupt, but not remitted to the province, did not qualify as a trust under section 67(1) of the pre-1992 *BIA*, and therefore was not effective in bankruptcy. In 1995, the Supreme Court of Canada added a fifth decision, discussed below.

Husky Oil Operations Ltd v Minister of National Revenue, [1995] 3 SCR 453 [*Husky Oil*]

GONTHIER J: ...

(ii) The Principles and Philosophy Embodied in the Quartet
[29] What principles should be distilled from the quartet? The intervener Attorney General for Saskatchewan suggested that there are two possible interpretations of these decisions: what it called a broader "bottom line" approach which posits that "any time provincial law affects the final result of a bankruptcy, the province is improperly attempting to alter the priorities of distribution"; and a narrower "jump the queue" approach to

the effect that "the province cannot attempt to alter the position of a person within the scheme of distribution created by Parliament, vis-à-vis the other creditors who are claiming from the bankrupt's estate."

[30] My colleague Iacobucci J properly rejects the broader "bottom line" approach since, as he indicates, such an approach "risks nullifying the broad array of provincial legislation underpinning the *Bankruptcy Act*" (at para 142). It is trite to observe that the *Bankruptcy Act* is contingent on the provincial law of property for its operation. The Act is superimposed on those provincial schemes when a debtor declares bankruptcy. As a result, provincial law necessarily affects the "bottom line," but this is contemplated by the *Bankruptcy Act* itself. Indeed, it is no exaggeration to say that there is no "bottom line" without provincial law. The "bottom line" approach is therefore not the appropriate characterization of the quartet.

[31] However, even rejecting the simplistic "bottom line" approach, I do not agree that the quartet stands for the sole proposition that the provinces cannot "jump the queue." In my opinion, the quartet embodies a consistent and general philosophy as to the purposes of the federal system of bankruptcy and its relation to provincial property arrangements. That philosophy cannot be captured in the pithy but limited proposition that the provinces cannot "jump the queue."

[32] The quartet is better stated, in my view, as standing for a number of related propositions which are themselves part of a consistent philosophy. In their lucid and thorough study of the quartet, "The Conflict Between Canadian Provincial Personal Property Security Acts and the Federal Bankruptcy Act: The War is Over" (1992), 71 Can Bar Rev 77, at pp 78–79, Andrew J Roman and M Jasmine Sweatman state that the quartet stands for the following four propositions:

(1) provinces cannot create priorities between creditors or change the scheme of distribution on bankruptcy under s 136(1) of the *Bankruptcy Act*;

(2) while provincial legislation may validly affect priorities in a non-bankruptcy situation, once bankruptcy has occurred section 136(1) of the *Bankruptcy Act* determines the status and priority of the claims specifically dealt with in that section;

(3) if the provinces could create their own priorities or affect priorities under the *Bankruptcy Act* this would invite a different scheme of distribution on bankruptcy from province to province, an unacceptable situation; and

(4) the definition of terms such as "secured creditor," if defined under the *Bankruptcy Act*, must be interpreted in bankruptcy cases as defined by the federal Parliament, not the provincial legislatures. Provinces cannot affect how such terms are defined for purposes of the *Bankruptcy Act*.

[33] See also for concurrence with Roman and Sweatman's general conclusions drawn from the quartet, Jacob S Ziegel, "Personal Property Security and Bankruptcy: There is no War! — A Reply to Roman and Sweatman" (1993), 72 Can Bar Rev 44, at p 45.

[34] My colleague Iacobucci J states at para 141 that the quartet "stands for the position that only those provincial laws which *directly* improve the priority of a claim upon the actual property of the bankrupt over that accorded by the *Bankruptcy Act* are inoperative" (emphasis added). This statement falls within Roman and Sweatman's proposition 1. However, as my summary of those cases has hopefully indicated, the quartet is clearly not limited to provincial "laws which directly improve the priority of a claim." To quote Roman and Sweatman, *supra*, at p 78:

... the reasoning in [the quartet] is not limited to trusts, nor to situations of colourable legislation attempting to give an artificial preference to government. Rather, these rulings are broad enough to encompass any potential area of conflict between provincial power to legislate in the area of property and civil rights, and exclusive federal jurisdiction over bankruptcy and insolvency.

In a similar vein these authors add at p 81:

The Supreme Court of Canada's quartet of decisions, although dealing with provincial statutory trusts which affected priorities in bankruptcy, has progressively and finally provided a definite ruling on the relationship between priorities under the *Bankruptcy Act* and *any* other provincial statute which directly or indirectly affects priorities. [Emphasis in original.]

Importantly, they conclude at p 105:

The law, in our opinion, is settled by these four judgments of the Supreme Court of Canada. In all four cases the issues were not whether the provinces could directly and blatantly attempt to alter the scheme of interests of secured and other creditors under what is now section 136(1) of the *Bankruptcy Act*. Rather, the issue was whether a province could indirectly influence priorities under the *Bankruptcy Act*. Even in this weaker version of influence, the Supreme Court of Canada has held that the provinces could not.

And in so concluding, they are also quick to caution at p 106:

It is also incorrect to state that in all four cases the provinces attempted to redistribute or change priorities by explicitly elevating one of the lower ranked claims to a higher rank. As seen from an examination of the dissenting judgments in *Deloitte Haskins* and *Henfrey*, the provinces were not attempting specifically to target the bankruptcy situation but, rather, to create a general priority.

[35] As a result, the "jump the queue" or "directly improve bankruptcy priorities" approach captures only part of the reasoning of the quartet. As Roman and Sweatman noted, in the *Deloitte Haskins* and *Henfrey Samson* cases, for example, the provinces were not directly or intentionally attempting to influence bankruptcy priorities. Rather, the provinces enacted laws of general application which sought to create a general priority not necessarily targeted to bankruptcy, but which had the effect of altering bankruptcy priorities. This Court nevertheless ruled that such provincial laws were inapplicable in the event of bankruptcy.

[36] I underline that the "effect" which Roman and Sweatman speak of is the effect on bankruptcy priorities (Roman and Sweatman, *supra*, at pp 81–105). Consequently, clear conflict, that is an inconsistent or mutually exclusive result, which in this case entails a reordering of federal priorities, is necessary in order to declare a provincial law to be inapplicable in bankruptcy.

[37] I also think it is important to emphasize the importance of Roman and Sweatman's proposition 3. While I agree with my colleague Iacobucci J that complete standardization of the distribution of property in bankruptcies is not possible across Canada having regard to the diversity of provincial laws relating to property and civil rights, yet the value of a national bankruptcy system is confirmed by the placing of bankruptcy under exclusive federal jurisdiction. As Professor Hogg has explained (*supra*, at pp 25-1 and 25-2):

... debtors may move from one province to another, and may have property and creditors in more than one province. A national body of law is required to ensure that all of a debtor's property is available to satisfy his debts, that all creditors are fairly treated, and that all are bound by any arrangements for the settlement of the debtor's debts. Indeed, without these assurances, lenders would be reluctant to extend credit to persons who could evade their obligations simply by removing themselves or their assets across a provincial boundary.

Furthermore, as my overview of the quartet hopefully indicated, the goal of maintaining a nationally homogeneous system of bankruptcy priorities has properly been a constant concern of this Court. Were the situation otherwise, "Canada [would] have a balkanized bankruptcy regime which [would] diminish the significance of the exclusivity of federal jurisdiction over bankruptcy and insolvency. ... Otherwise there could be a different scheme in every jurisdiction; ten different bankruptcy regimes would make ordinary commercial affairs extremely complex, unwieldy and costly, not only for Canadians but also for our international trading partners" (Roman and Sweatman, *supra*, at pp 80, 104). This is a prospect which this Court has been acutely mindful of in the past, and its vigilance has ensured the continuing vitality of our nation's bankruptcy legislation. In my view, its past vigilance commends itself to the present and, barring an amendment to s 91(21) of the *Constitution Act, 1867*, also to the future.

[38] In this regard, I agree with Iacobucci J, at para 147, that a bankruptcy priority is a category, and also that provincial law may result in the content of such categories being different from province to province. However, provincial law does not and cannot define the content of bankruptcy priorities or categories without limitation. Indeed, crucial limitation is imposed by the order of priorities in the *Bankruptcy Act* itself. Thus, while individual provinces can define and rank categories such as "secured creditor" and "trust" as they each have their own purposes, those provincial laws which enter into conflict with the provisions of the *Bankruptcy Act* are simply without application in bankruptcy. Such, indeed, was this Court's unequivocal holding in *Re Bourgault*, *Deloitte Haskins*, and *FBDB* with respect to "secured creditors" and in *Henfrey Samson* with respect to "trusts."

[39] Finally, I would observe that while in agreement with the above four propositions as embodying the reasoning of the quartet, in my view the list would be more complete with the addition of a fifth and sixth, as follows:

(5) in determining the relationship between provincial legislation and the *Bankruptcy Act*, the form of the provincial interest created must not be allowed to triumph over its substance. The provinces are not entitled to do indirectly what they are prohibited from doing directly;

(6) there need not be any provincial intention to intrude into the exclusive federal sphere of bankruptcy and to conflict with the order of priorities of the *Bankruptcy Act* in order to render the provincial law inapplicable. It is sufficient that the effect of provincial legislation is to do so.

Appeal dismissed.

The status of Crown claims in bankruptcy was fundamentally altered in the 1992 amendments to the *BIA*. Section 136(1)(h) and (j) were modified so that Crown claims and Workers' Compensation Board claims that arose after 30 November 1992 were no longer afforded the status of a preferred claim in a bankruptcy. This means that the quintet of SCC decisions that culminated in *Husky Oil*, above, were no longer necessary to resolve the pre-1992 conflict between *BIA*, section 136 and the provincial legislation. Crown claims are now dealt with by

[handwritten margin note: conflicts between unpaid employees are resolved in favour of]

BIA, section 67(2) and (3) (dealing with statutory deemed trusts) and by *BIA*, sections 86–87 (dealing with statutory liens, charges, and security interests).

The analysis in *Husky Oil* is relevant in connection with provincial statutes that create deemed trusts, liens, charges, or security interests in favour of persons other than the Crown. For example, provincial employment standards legislation creates statutory deemed trusts, liens, charges, or security interests in respect of unpaid employees. Although the *BIA*, section 81.3 now provides for a security in favour of unpaid employees to the extent of $2,000, the amount covered by the provincial devices are often higher. For example, the Alberta *Employment Standards Code*, RSA 2000, c E-9, section 109 creates a statutory security interest to secure unpaid wages to a maximum of $7,500. These statutory security interests are fully operative outside of bankruptcy, but are rendered ineffective in a bankruptcy because unpaid employees are afforded a preferred claimant status for their unpaid wages under section 136(1)(d) and the resulting conflict between the provincial and federal legislation is resolved in favour of the *BIA*. The constitutional principles set out in *Husky Oil* have also been used by courts to resolve other conflicts between provincial legislation and the *BIA*, such as in the case of *Alberta (Attorney General) v Moloney*, 2015 SCC 51.

C. Deemed Security Interests

[handwritten margin note: Statute may give the Crown a charge / lien]

A statute may give the Crown a lien, charge, or security interest over assets of the debtor to secure payment of the Crown claim. For example, Alberta's *Environmental Protection and Enhancement Act*, RSA 2000, c E-12, section 216 stipulates that if the Crown incurs costs to contain or remediate pollution it is granted a charge for the costs incurred which attaches to the land where the work was carried out.

Outside of a bankruptcy, the priority of the Crown interest vis-à-vis a third-party's interest may be governed by the statute that creates it. There are all sorts of possible approaches. For example, the statute may provide that the Crown's claim has priority over both earlier and later interests: for example, the *Workers' Compensation Act*, RSA 2000, s 129(3). In some cases, the Crown's claim is made subordinate to a purchase money security interest: for example, the *Workers Compensation Act*, CCSM c W200, s 104(3). If the statute says nothing about priorities, the courts will give priority on the basis of the first interest to come into existence: see *Royal Bank of Canada v Sparrow Electric Corp*, [1997] 1 SCR 411. *[handwritten margin note: first in time, better claim]*

In 1992, the *BIA* was amended to add provisions dealing specifically with Crown security interests, sections 86–87. These provisions direct that all Crown secured claims will be treated as unsecured claims in bankruptcy, unless the security interest falls into one of the following categories: *[handwritten margin note: Crown gets priority if it is a SI operating as an SI]*

- If the security interest is "of a kind that can be obtained by persons other than" the Crown: *BIA*, section 86(2)(a). For example, if the Crown loans money to a debtor and takes a consensual mortgage over the debtor's property to secure the loan, this security interest is akin to the consensual mortgage that a bank might take. The Crown mortgage would be treated as a valid security interest in an ensuing bankruptcy. *[handwritten margin note: reg]*
- If the security interest is of a kind that is only available to the Crown, but has been "registered under a prescribed system of registration": *BIA*, ss 86(2)(b) and 87. Note that under *BIA*, section 87(1), the Crown security must be registered before the date of the initial bankruptcy event. This term is defined in *BIA*, section 2. In the case of an involuntary bankruptcy, it is the date that the application for a bankruptcy order is filed and not the date of the bankruptcy order.

- If the Crown's interest arises pursuant to the statutory garnishment remedy provided for under specified provisions of the *ITA*, *Canada Pension Plan*, *Employment Insurance Act* or provincial equivalents, *BIA*, s 86(3). These statutory garnishment remedies are discussed in greater detail below.

Section 223 of the *ITA* provides an example of the second type of security interest contemplated in sections 86–87. Under section 223(2), the minister may certify an amount that is payable to the Crown by a debtor. Under section 223(3) this can be registered in the Federal Court and when so registered it has the same effect as if it were a judgment. Sections 223(5) and (6) provide that a writ issued by the court in respect of this deemed judgment can be registered in the provincial land and personal property registries in the same manner as a writ or other judgment enforcement process of a judgment creditor, and has the same binding effect or creates the same lien or charge as a writ. These provisions merely give the minister the same status as an ordinary judgment enforcement creditor. However, *ITA*, section 223(11.1) goes on to provide that if the minister's certification is registered in accordance with *BIA*, section 87 it is deemed "to be a claim that is secured by a security and that, subject to subsection 87(2) of that Act, ranks as a secured claim under that Act." This is very different from the treatment afforded to an ordinary judgment enforcement creditor. All of the provinces permit registration of a writ or other judgment enforcement process in the land registration systems. Many, but not all, of the provinces permit registration of writs in the personal property registry system: see Ronald Cuming, Catherine Walsh, and Roderick Wood, *Personal Property Security Law*, 2d ed (Toronto: Irwin Law, 2012) at 500–3. Registration of a writ or other judgment enforcement process will give the judgment enforcement creditor the same basic priority as a secured creditor in competitions with other claimants, but upon a bankruptcy the judgment creditor's claim is nevertheless regarded as an unsecured claim. Under *BIA*, section 70(1), the bankruptcy order or assignment takes precedence over all judgment enforcement process that has not been completely executed by payment to the creditor. Unlike the Crown, an ordinary judgment enforcement creditor is therefore not afforded the status of a secured creditor in the bankruptcy.

A consensual secured party can protect its priority through prospective registration of its interest in a registry, meaning the priority attached to future advances will be determined based on the secured party's initial registration. The Crown cannot protect the secured status of its non-consensual claims through prospective registration. The Crown's security interest is subordinate to prior perfected security interests and is only valid in respect of amounts owing at the time of registration, plus any interest accruing on such amounts: *BIA*, ss 86(2)(b), 87. The effect of these provisions was considered in the case of *Re Gillford Furniture Mart Ltd.*

Re Gillford Furniture Mart Ltd, (1995) 36 CBR (3d) 157 (BCCA)

[The debtor owed the Provincial Crown money arising under provincial sales tax legislation. The debtor had collected the sales tax from clients and failed to remit it to the Crown. The Crown had registered a lien in the provincial Personal Property Registry in respect of an amount of $26,000. Subsequent to that registration and before the debtor made an assignment into bankruptcy, the debtor collected and failed to remit an additional $4,300 in sales tax and the Crown incurred costs of approximately $15,000 hiring a bailiff to collect from the debtor. The Crown claimed that it was a secured creditor for all three amounts, the initial $26,000 debt, the additional $4,300 debt and the $15,000 in realization costs. The trustee ruled that the Provincial Crown should only be treated as a secured creditor with respect to the initial $26,000 debt. The British Columbia Court of Appeal affirmed the trustee's interpretation.]

2nd lien was't perfected

[13] It is acknowledged the lien in question falls within the description in s 87(1) as a "security provided for the sole or principal purpose of securing a claim of Her Majesty in right of ... a province." It is also acknowledged that registration of lien in respect of the second amount claimed, that is to say, under the second writ of seizure and sale, was not perfected before the bankruptcy of the debtor: see s 87(1)(b) of the *Act* [*BIA*].

[14] I will refer to other sections of the *Act* when I come to Mr. Butler's principal argument.

[15] He says on behalf of the Province that the chambers judge erred in his analysis of all relevant statutory provisions. He contends, not that the costs of execution are themselves a secured claim, but, rather, that the security created by provincial law extends to the net amount owing. And, he says, as the province is entitled to realize under valid provincial legislation net of costs so must the notional realization here be net of costs.

[16] He contends that realization net of costs is expressly authorized by valid provincial legislation and that the *Act* recognizes provincial legislation determines this result. As a first step, he referred us to s 54 of the *Court Order Enforcement Act*, RSBC 1979, c 75, which provides:

> 54. The sheriff or other officer shall pay over to the execution creditor the money recovered, or a part of it as is sufficient to discharge the amount by the writ of execution directed to be levied; and if, after satisfaction of the amount directed to be levied, together with sheriff's fees, poundage and expenses, any surplus remains in the hands of the sheriff or other officer, it shall be paid to the execution debtor.

There is no doubt this entitles the sheriff to deduct from the amount realized his costs. Mr. Butler says the same result must follow in the case at bar by virtue of s 127 of the *Act* ...

[17] I think it clear s 127 reflects a basic premise of the *Act*, namely, the right of a secured creditor to realize on his security. ...

[18] This now brings me to the primary issue here, the construction of s 86 and s 87 of the *Act* in light of Mr. Butler's contentions with respect to the effect of provincial legislation.

[19] I think the plain meaning of subs. (1) of s 86 is clear: claims on behalf of the Crown in Right of either Canada or a Province rank as unsecured claims subject to subsections (2) and (3). Mr. Butler does not question the right of Parliament to enact s 86. In my view the exceptions in subsections (2) and (3) are to be construed consistently with the scope of s 86.

[20] We are not concerned with the exceptions provided in subsection (2)(a) of s 86; the security in question is not available to persons other than Her Majesty and its sole purpose is to create what I would call "after the fact" security.

[21] Clause (b) of subsection (2) of s 86 is relevant. The words "to the extent" which are found at the beginning of clause (b) imply the exception is qualified, something less than a complete reversal of the unsecured ranking provided in s 86(1).

[22] The extent to which that ranking is to be varied is as follows: the words at the end of clause (b) — "if the security is registered in accordance with that subsection" — is a condition precedent, the requirements of which are to be found in subsection (1) of s 87. We go then to s 87(1) and from that it is clear the registration in question must occur before the act of bankruptcy. That is sufficient, of course, to rule out the second writ of seizure and sale.

[23] Then, going to subsection (2) of s 87 I refer to clause (b), which provides that the registration is valid "only" in respect of amounts owing to Her Majesty at the time of that

registration. The emphatic "only" is exclusionary of other amounts. This is made clear by the clause that follows which permits the addition of interest accrued subsequent to the time of registration. No other addition to the sum owing at the time of registration is recognized.

[24] Turning to the Act as a whole I am not persuaded s 127 requires us to read s 86 or s 87 in a strained fashion as would be the case if we recognized the bailiff's costs which arise subsequent to registration are to be an exception to the general provision. Sections 86 and 87 deal with a particular problem and I see no reason why the general should govern the particular. I do not think s 127 opens the door to a construction that flies in the face of the plain wording of s 86 and s 87. . . .

[26] I do not consider the result is either absurd or in conflict with the general scheme of the *Act*. If Parliament meant to provide for subsequent additions to the principal debt other than interest it could have done so. As it now stands, the effect is that only security to the extent to which public notice has been given is recognized.

Appeal dismissed.

More recent cases have considered what amounts to registration of a security interest in a "prescribed system of registration." The *Bankruptcy and Insolvency General Rules*, CRC c 368, section 111, defines this term:

[A] system of registration of securities that is available to Her Majesty in right of Canada or a province and to any other creditor holding a security, and is open to the public for inspection or for the making of searches.

Whether or not a provincial registry amounts to a "prescribed system of registration" will depend on a court's interpretation of the applicable provincial legislation.

In the 2010 case of *Re Tom Woodford*, 2010 NLTD(G) 118, the court held that the Crown was not a secured creditor despite having registered a memorial—issued under the *Excise Tax Act*, RSC 1985, c E-15 (*ETA*)—in the provincial judgment enforcement registry. Newfoundland's judgment enforcement registry allows judgment creditors to bind a debtor's personal and real property by registering their judgment in one registry. Secured creditors do not register their interests in the judgment enforcement registry, and on this basis the court held that it did not amount to a prescribed system of registration.

In the 2018 case of *Re Meredith*, 2018 NSSC 153 (*Re Meredith*), the court held that the Crown had satisfied the registration requirements of section 87 when it registered an *ITA* certificate in the judgment roll established under the provincial *Land Registration Act*, SNS 2000, c 6. The court held that this amounted to registration in a prescribed system of registration, even though other secured creditors could not register their security interests in the judgment roll, but rather had to register against specific pieces of land. The court seems to have justified the different outcome in *Re Meredith* on the basis that the Nova Scotia judgment roll was part of the land titles registry, in which other creditors could register security interests, and therefore fit within the definition contemplated in *Bankruptcy and Insolvency General Rules*, section 111, even if the Crown did not register its interest in the same manner as a consensual secured creditor.

Section 86(3) provides an exception in respect of the statutory garnishment remedy (also referred to as a "requirement to pay") created by section 224(1.2) of the *ITA*, and comparable provisions in the *Canadian Pension Plan, Employment Insurance Act*, and their provincial equivalents. This gives the Canadian Revenue Agency (CRA) the right to intercept debts that are owed by third parties to the debtor. The *ITA* provides that this remedy has priority over a prior secured creditor who has a security interest in the debtor's accounts. The CRA there-fore does not need to register in respect of its *ITA* garnishment remedy, it is not subject to the *BIA*, section 87(2)(a), subordination to prior perfected security interests, and the remedy can be enforced by the CRA following the bankruptcy.

The *ETA* also contains a statutory garnishment remedy. Section 317(3) provides that upon giving notice to the person who owes money to the debtor of the requirement to pay, "the amount of those moneys that is so required to be paid to the Receiver General shall, despite any security interest in those moneys, become the property of Her Majesty in right of Canada to the extent of that liability as assessed by the Minister." *BIA*, section 86(3), does not exempt the *ETA* statutory garnishment remedy from being rendered an unsecured claim.

Courts have been called upon to resolve priorities where the CRA has issued an *ETA* requirement to pay on a person that owes an obligation to the debtor, but the debtor goes bankrupt before any of the funds are paid. *BIA* section 70(1) provides that bankruptcy pro-ceedings take precedence "over all judicial or other attachments, garnishments, executions or other process against the property of a bankrupt, except those that have been completely executed by payment to the creditor." In *Toronto Dominion Bank v Canada*, 2010 FCA 174, aff'd 2012 SCC 1, the Court held that under *ETA*, section 317(3), the debt that is being gar-nished becomes the property of the minister of revenue as soon as the person is notified of the requirement to pay. The Crown therefore became the owner of the moneys required to be paid before the bankruptcy occurred, and those moneys therefore did not constitute part of the tax debtor's property that would be dealt with in the *BIA* proceedings. However, if at the time of the bankruptcy proceedings the minister has not sent a requirement to pay to a per-son who owes money to the tax debtor, the minister cannot thereafter invoke the statutory garnishment remedy under the *ETA* to recover GST (although it can invoke the *ITA* statutory garnishment remedy in respect of an income tax debt).

Note that the statutory garnishment remedy under the *ETA* is different from the ordin-ary garnishment remedies of judgment enforcement creditors. The service of an ordinary garnishee summons on a garnishee (the person who owes an obligation to the judgment enforcement debtor) does not give the garnishor ownership of the debt. The process is completed and the garnishor acquires an interest in the funds only upon the payment of the funds to the garnishor. As a result, the incomplete garnishment is ineffective and the money must instead be paid to the trustee in bankruptcy.

D. Deemed Trusts

When a debtor holds property in trust for a third party, that property is not divisible amongst the debtor's creditors, because the debtor merely holds bare legal title to the property and the third party holds the beneficial title: *BIA*, s 67(1)(a). A trust can arise at common law, but only if three certainties are satisfied: the certainty of intent (the settlor meant to set up a trust), of object (the beneficiary of the trust is identifiable), and of subject (the property subject to the trust is identifiable, meaning either that it has been kept separate or can be identified using tracing principles; see *The Guarantee Company of North America v Royal Bank of Canada*, 2019 ONCA 9 at paras 86–90).

The federal and provincial Crowns have sought to give their claims priority in bankruptcy by using statutes to set up trusts in their favour. These statutes direct that the debtor's property is held in trust for the Crown. The statute may expressly or by implication limit the trust to the case where the subject property remains separate and identifiable in the debtor's hands. Alternatively, it may assert a trust even if certainty of subject is lacking, or in other words, if the property subject to the trust has not been kept separate from other property and is not identifiable using the doctrines of tracing. Deemed trust provisions are commonly used in situations where the debtor is collecting or withholding money from a third party and remitting it to the government. For example, a debtor may collect sales tax on a sale made to a client, or it may withhold income tax from an employee's paycheque. Deemed trusts arise under the *ETA*; the *ITA*; the *Employment Insurance Act*, SC 1996, c 23; the *Canada Pension Plan*, RSC 1985, c C-8; and provincial workers' compensation statutes.

If the statute creates a deemed trust over the debtor's property, it may set out priority rules to apply where a third party claims a competing interest. Alternatively, the statute may say nothing about priorities. If the statute says nothing, a court is likely to say the holder of an earlier in time competing interest has priority over the Crown's trust claim on the ground that, in the absence of a clear indication of the legislature's intention to the contrary, a statute should not be construed in a manner that could deprive third parties of their pre-existing property rights.

BIA, section 67(2), provides that deemed trusts in favour of the Crown will generally not be valid in bankruptcy, but there are two exceptions to this rule:

- If it would be valid trust notwithstanding the statute, or in other words, the three certainties (intent, object, and subject) are present, or
- If it arises under one of the provisions specifically contemplated in *BIA*, section 67(3), which includes deemed trusts arising for source deductions under the *ITA*, the *Canada Pension Plan*, the *Employment Insurance Act*, and equivalent provincial legislation.

A note of caution is warranted here. In its recent *The Guarantee Company of North America v Royal Bank of Canada*, 2019 ONCA 9 at para 72, the Ontario Court of Appeal made the following comment: "Properly interpreted, s. 67(2) thus excludes deemed statutory trusts in favour of the Crown that would otherwise qualify as trusts under the *Henfrey* principles from protection under s 67(1)(a)." This comment, offered in *obiter*, would mark a departure from the accepted interpretation of section 67(2), as summarized in the first bullet point, above, and Roderick Wood's text, *Bankruptcy and Insolvency Law*, 2d ed (Toronto: Irwin Law, 2015) at 113. Wood indicates that section 67(2) codified the decision in *Henfrey* as it applies to deemed trusts in favour of the Crown. We believe that the Ontario Court of Appeal was mistaken when it made this comment, as adopting such an interpretation would render the italicized portion of the statutory provision, reproduced below, devoid of any meaning:

> Subject to subsection (3), notwithstanding any provision in federal or provincial legislation that has the effect of deeming property to be held in trust for Her Majesty, property of a bankrupt shall not be regarded as held in trust for Her Majesty for the purpose of paragraph (1)(a) *unless it would be so regarded in the absence of that statutory provision.*

One of the most significant deemed trusts that remains valid in bankruptcy is the claim of the CRA arising under section 227(4.1) of the *ITA*, which arises when an employer deducts income tax from an employees' paycheque, but fails to remit it to the CRA. The scope of this deemed trust is wide and it has been described as providing the CRA with a "superpriority" (see, for example, *Attorney General of Canada v Nortip Development Corporation*, 2019 NLCA 34 at paras 7 and 54). What is the nature of the so-called superpriority and what is the rationale for protecting this Crown claim in this manner? In *First Vancouver Finance v Canada (Minister of National Revenue)*, 2002 SCC 49, Iacobucci J offered the following justification for the deemed trust arising under the *ITA*:

[22] The collection of source deductions has been recognized as "at the heart" of income tax collection in Canada: see *Pembina on the Red Development Corp v Triman Industries Ltd* (1991), 85 DLR (4th) 29 (Man CA), at p 51, per Lyon JA (dissenting), quoted with approval by Gonthier J (dissenting on another issue) in *Royal Bank of Canada v Sparrow Electric Corp*, [1997] 1 SCR 411, at para 36. Because of the importance of collecting source deductions, the legislation in question gives the Minister the vehicle of the deemed trust to recover employee tax deductions which employers fail to remit to the Minister.

[23] It has also been noted that, in contrast to a tax debtor's bank which is familiar with the tax debtor's business and finances, the Minister does not have the same level of knowledge of the tax debtor or its creditors, and cannot structure its affairs with the tax debtor accordingly. Thus, as an "involuntary creditor," the Minister must rely on its ability to collect source deductions under the *ITA*: *Pembina on the Red Development, supra*, at pp 33–34, per Scott CJM, approved by Cory J in *Alberta (Treasury Branches), supra*, at paras. 16–18. For the above reasons, under the terms of the *ITA*, the Minister has been given special priority over other creditors to collect unremitted taxes.

Secured creditors have long objected to the Crown's attempt to override consensual security interests. Ziegel notes that secured creditors object to the "unfairness and destabilizing effect of superpriority liens that undermine security agreements made in good faith by a secured creditor before the taxpayer was in default in its statutory obligations or, at any rate, where the secured creditor was not privy to the default and had done nothing to encourage it" (Jacob S Ziegel, "Conditional Sales and Superpriority Crown Claims Under the *ITA* s 227" (2003) 38 *Canadian Bankruptcy Reports* (4th) 161). In the face of the existence of the deemed trust, secured creditors have sought to convince the courts to give a narrow interpretation to the provisions. In some instances, secured creditors have been successful. However, as Ziegel notes, such victories "are usually short-lived because the federal government has often reacted quickly to reverse an unfavourable judicial construction by amending the *ITA*" (at 161).

The original statutory deemed trust did not contain any provisions that dealt with the priority of the deemed trust as against secured creditors. The Supreme Court of Canada in *Royal Bank of Canada v Sparrow Electric Corp*, [1997] 1 SCR 411 (*Sparrow*) held that in the absence of any legislative provision, priorities would be ordered on the basis of the first interest that came into existence. Parliament subsequently amended the *ITA* by adding language that gives the deemed trust priority over competing secured creditors. The *Sparrow* decision and the consequent 1998 amendments to the *ITA* were discussed by the Supreme Court of Canada in *First Vancouver Finance v Canada (Minister of National Revenue)*, below.

First Vancouver Finance v Canada (Minister of National Revenue), 2002 SCC 49, [2002] 2 SCR 720 [*First Vancouver*]

IACOBUCCI J (for the Court):

[24] This Court had occasion to interpret the deemed trust provisions in *Sparrow Electric, supra*. At that time, the relevant provisions were ss 227(4) and 227(5) of the *ITA* which read as follows:

> 227 (4) Every person who deducts or withholds any amount under this Act shall be deemed to hold the amount so deducted or withheld in trust for Her Majesty.
>
> (5) Notwithstanding any provision of the *Bankruptcy Act*, in the event of any liquidation, assignment, receivership or bankruptcy of or by a person, an amount equal to any amount

(a) deemed by subsection (4) to be held in trust for Her Majesty, or . . .

shall be deemed to be separate from and form no part of the estate in liquidation, assignment, receivership or bankruptcy, whether or not that amount has in fact been kept separate and apart from the person's own moneys or from the assets of the estate.

[25] In *Sparrow Electric*, both Royal Bank and the Minister claimed an interest in the proceeds of inventory of the tax debtor. In characterizing the nature of the deemed trust provisions, Gonthier J (dissenting, but not on this issue) stated at para 34 that, even if collateral was subject to a fixed charge at the time of a triggering event such as bankruptcy or liquidation, the deemed trust operated to attach the Minister's interest to such collateral as long as it was not subject to the fixed charge at the time the source deductions were made:

Thus, s 227(5) [now 227(4.1)] alternatively permits Her Majesty's interest to attach retroactively to the disputed collateral if the competing security interest has attached *after* the deductions giving rise to Her Majesty's claim in fact occurred. Conceptually, the s 227(5) deemed trust allows Her Majesty's claim to go back in time and attach its outstanding s 227(4) interest to the collateral before that collateral became subject to a fixed charge. [Emphasis in original.]

Royal Bank's interest was characterized as a fixed and specific charge over the inventory of the tax debtor. This had the effect of making the bank the legal owner of inventory as it came into possession of the tax debtor, subject to the debtor's equitable right of redemption. The majority of the Court concluded that, since the inventory was subject to the bank's security interest before the deductions giving rise to the deemed trust occurred, the bank's interest attached to the inventory in priority to Her Majesty's interest under the deemed trust.

[26] However, in reaching this conclusion, the majority of the Court noted at para 112 that Parliament was free to grant absolute priority to the deemed trust by adopting the appropriate language:

Finally, I wish to emphasize that it is open to Parliament to step in and assign absolute priority to the deemed trust. A clear illustration of how this might be done is afforded by s 224(1.2) *ITA*, which vests certain moneys in the Crown "notwithstanding any security interest in those moneys" and provides that they "shall be paid to the Receiver General in priority to any such security interest." All that is needed to effect the desired result is clear language of that kind.

[27] In response to *Sparrow Electric*, the deemed trust provisions were amended in 1998 (retroactively to 1994) to their current form. Most notably, the words "notwithstanding any security interest . . . in the amount so deducted, or withheld" were added to s 227(4). As well, s 227(4.1) (formerly s 227(5)) expanded the scope of the deemed trust to include "property held by any secured creditor . . . that but for a security interest . . . would be property of the person." Section 227(4.1) was also amended to remove reference to the triggering events of liquidation, bankruptcy, etc, instead deeming property of the tax debtor and of secured creditors to be held in trust "at any time an amount deemed by subsection (4) to be held by a person in trust for Her Majesty is not paid to Her Majesty in the manner and at the time provided under this Act." Finally, s 227(4.1) now explicitly deems the trust to operate "from the time the amount was deducted or withheld."

[28] It is apparent from these changes that the intent of Parliament when drafting ss 227(4) and 227(4.1) was to grant priority to the deemed trust in respect of property that is also subject to a security interest regardless of when the security interest arose in relation to the time the source deductions were made or when the deemed trust takes effect. This is clear from the use of the words "notwithstanding any security interest" in both ss 227(4) and 227(4.1). In other words, Parliament has reacted to the interpretation of the deemed trust provisions in *Sparrow Electric*, and has amended the provisions to grant priority to the deemed trust in situations where the Minister and secured creditors of a tax debtor both claim an interest in the tax debtor's property.

[29] As noted above, Parliament has also amended the deemed trust provisions in regard to the timing of the trust. Reference to events triggering operation of the deemed trust such as liquidation or bankruptcy have been removed. Section 227(4.1) now states that the deemed trust begins to operate "*at any time* [source deductions are] not paid to Her Majesty in the manner and at the time provided under this Act" [emphasis added]. Thus, the deemed trust is now triggered at the moment a default in remitting source deductions occurs. Further, pursuant to s 227(4.1)(a), the trust is deemed to be in effect "from the time the amount was deducted or withheld." Thus, while a default in remitting source deductions triggers the operation of the trust, the trust is deemed to have been in existence retroactively to the time the source deductions were made. It is evident from these changes that Parliament has made a concerted effort to broaden and strengthen the deemed trust in order to facilitate the collection efforts of the Minister.

Appeal dismissed.

In *First Vancouver*, the Court considered whether after-acquired property (that is, property that came into the tax debtor's hands after the deemed trust arose) was subject to the trust. In addition, the Court also considered whether the sale of trust property releases property from the trust. The Court held (at para 4) that the "trust arises the moment the tax debtor fails to remit source deductions by the specified due date, but is deemed to have been in existence from the moment the deductions were made. . . . [Therefore,] at any given point in time, whatever property then belonging to the tax debtor is subject to the deemed trust." The Court also held that property that is sold is released from the trust. However, the proceeds of the sale are "captured by the trust."

The *ITA* deemed trust is subject to the right of an unpaid supplier to repossess goods (s 81.1) and the special rights of farmers, fishermen, and aquaculturalists (s 81.2). These provisions are discussed in Chapter 9.

Section 227(4.2) of the *ITA* excludes certain limited prescribed security interests and thus provides further limited exceptions to the deemed trust. Section 2201 of the *Income Tax Regulations*, CRC c 945, says that a mortgage on land or a building that was voluntarily given and "registered pursuant to the appropriate land registration system before the time the amount is deemed to be held in trust by the person" is a prescribed security interest. Such a specified security interest will take priority over the deemed trust.

Section 222(1) of the *ETA* creates a deemed statutory trust in respect of unremitted GST. In language and structure it is similar to *ITA* section 227(4.1). It is imposed on all the property of the debtor as well as any property held by a secured creditor and has priority over all security interests. However, the *ETA* deemed trust does not fall within the exception in *BIA*, section 67(3), and therefore does not apply to a debtor's assets after a bankruptcy unless a trust can be established in the absence of the statutory provision.

Prior to bankruptcy, the *ETA* deemed trust applies to the debtor's assets, even if they have been transferred to a secured creditor. Natasha DiCicco and Daniel Richer explain the scope of the *ETA* deemed trust, as it applies to property in the hands of a secured creditor, in "A Cautionary Tale: Now You See It—Now You Don't" (2017) 33 *Banking & Finance Law Review* 103:

> Subsection 222(3) of the *ETA* extends the trust to apply to property of the tax debtor (which would include proceeds of such property) held by a secured creditor. Subsection 222(3) provides that (i) such property is deemed to be held by the secured creditor in trust for the Crown, (ii) the property is beneficially owned by the Crown despite any security interest the secured creditor may have in the property and (iii) "the proceeds of such property shall be paid to the Receiver General in priority to all security interests."

Until recently, there was some question about whether this deemed trust continued to apply to assets held by the secured creditor even after the tax debtor had declared bankruptcy. In the case of *Callidus Capital Corp v Canada*, 2018 SCC 47, the Court considered whether the CRA had a right of recovery against a secured creditor, who had received property from the tax debtor prior to the debtor's bankruptcy. In a ruling delivered from the bench, the Court held that the tax debtor's bankruptcy extinguished the *ETA* deemed trust that would otherwise extend to assets held by a secured creditor. A secured creditor will therefore have a strong incentive to invoke bankruptcy proceedings where significant amounts of GST are payable.

E. Definition of Secured Creditor in the *ITA*

Secured creditors have sought to convince the courts to take a narrow interpretation of the deemed trust. They have succeeded on at least one account: by convincing the courts to adopt a restrictive definition of "security interest," as that term is used in the *ITA*. A series of decisions, including *Canada (Deputy Attorney General) v Schwab Construction Ltd*, 2002 SKCA 6, below, have concluded that when the term "security interest" is used in the *ITA*, it does not include title retention devices such as financing leases or conditional sales contracts.[2] As a result, the Crown's deemed trust takes priority over secured creditors, but not over these other interests that fall outside the *ITA* definition of "security interest."

Canada (Deputy Attorney General) v Schwab Construction Ltd, 2002 SKCA 6, 231 Sask R 278

LANE JA (for the Court):

[1] The Federal Government ("Crown"), as represented by the Minister of Customs and Revenue, appeals a decision out of Queen's Bench chambers dismissing its application to have a receiver appointed for the purpose of collecting and disposing of the assets of the bankrupt, Schwab Construction Ltd ("Schwab" or "bankrupt"). The Crown contended that all of the equipment of the bankrupt is property beneficially owned by the Crown in priority to the interests of the respondents by virtue of ss 227(4) and (4.1) of the *Income Tax Act* [RSC 1985, c 1, 5th Supp] ("the Act") the so-called superpriority provisions.

[2] The application also involved the Saskatoon Credit Union, the Kenaston Credit Union, and Joe Gourley Construction Ltd as secured creditors of the bankrupt, however

---

2   Roderick Wood, "The Definition of Secured Creditor in Insolvency Law" (2010) 25 *Business & Finance Law Review* 341 at 350–51.

on appeal the credit unions did not defend their interests and the Crown abandoned its appeal of that portion of the order pertaining to the construction company.

[3] The respondents' position below and on appeal is they do not have secured interests as defined in s 224 of the *Income Tax Act* as leases do not come within such definition.

[4] The facts are more completely set out in the judgment below but a brief summary is as follows: the bankrupt did not submit the required payroll source deductions for income tax, Canada pension, and employment insurance totalling over $350,000 including interest and penalties. The Crown claimed the sum of approximately $272,000 as the amount it claimed to be held in trust as property beneficially owned by the Crown pursuant to the provisions of ss 227(4) and (4.1) of the Act. The Crown claimed each of the respondents was a secured creditor of the bankrupt having supplied to, or financed the acquisition of, equipment held by the bankrupt and that each held a security interest in the equipment.

[5] All agreements in issue were described as "leases," with the title to the equipment being reserved and not passing until the financing institution was fully paid, the exception being a Mack truck financed by the Canadian Western Bank (CWB) which was to be returned to the vendor after 30 months. Save for that piece of equipment the bankrupt had the option to purchase at the end of the lease, the equipment financed by the CWB for $100 per lease agreement. In the cases of Ford and GMAC, there was a buy back option with a residual price of an estimated depreciated value at the end of the lease. The details of the agreements are set out in the decision of the chambers judge.

[6] The following are the relevant provisions of the Act:

224(1.3) "secured creditor" means a person who has a security interest in the property of another person or who acts for or on behalf of that person with respect to the security interest and includes a trustee appointed under a trust deed relating to a security interest, a receiver or receiver-manager appointed by a secured creditor or by a court on the application of a secured creditor, a sequestrator or any other person performing a similar function;

"security interest" means any interest in property that secures payment or performance of an obligation and includes an interest created by or arising out of a debenture, mortgage, lien, pledge, charge, deemed or actual trust, assignment or encumbrance of any kind whatever, however or whenever arising, created, deemed to arise or otherwise provided for.

[The Court also set out in full provisions from section 227(4), and 227(4.1).]

[7] The Crown took the position the equipment, in all cases, was the property of the bankrupt because of all of the "incidents" of ownership supported only a finding the equipment was owned by Schwab. In the Canadian Western Bank agreement the appellant says the master lease agreement was, in effect, a money purchase plan and not a lease because there was only a nominal sum required to be paid by the bankrupt to obtain title after all obligations were met.

[8] The Crown argued the definition of "security interest" is broad enough to include "leases" of the nature of those in question. The Crown contended it was entitled to a priority over all of the property and did not argue it was entitled to only a priority over any equity or property interest, if any, the bankrupt may have had in any of the equipment. Further, the Crown argued the agreements in issue are agreements "to secure the payment or performance of an obligation."

[9] I am of the view the chambers judge was correct. The equipment covered by the lease was not the property of the bankrupt and the leases were not "a security interest"

within the meeting of s 224(1.3) of the Act. As the chambers judge stated, "[t]o decide otherwise would allow the applicant (the Crown) to claim as part of its deemed trust property not owned by the bankrupt but owned by an innocent third party who had just agreed to allow the bankrupt to use its property for a certain price pursuant to the terms of a lease agreement." She correctly found that finding the Crown had a priority interest would offend the principle as set out in *Royal Bank of Canada v Sparrow Electric Corporation*, [[1997] 1 SCR 411] by Gonthier J:

> This provision does not permit Her Majesty to attach Her beneficial interest to property which, at the time of liquidation, assignment, receivership or bankruptcy, in law belongs to a party other than the tax debtor. Section 227(4) and (5) are manifestly directed towards the property of the tax debtor, and it would be contrary to well-established authority to stretch the interpretation of section 227(5) to permit the expropriation of the property of third parties who are not specifically mentioned in the statute. [At para 39.]

I might add he went on to refer to the presumption against expropriation of property where he quoted Twaddle JA in *Re Pembina on the Red Development Corp Ltd v Triman Industries Ltd* [(1991), 85 DLR (4th) 29 (Man CA)]: "It is a long-established principle of law that, in the absence of clear language contrary, a tax on one person cannot be collected out of property belonging to another." [at p 46]

[10] The appeal must therefore be dismissed with costs on double Column V.

Appeal dismissed.

In *DaimlerChrysler Financial Services (Debis) Canada Inc v Mega Pets Ltd*, 2002 BCCA 242, the court also considered the definition of "security interest" under the *ITA*. The Court held that the interest under a conditional sales agreement does not create a security interest as defined under the *ITA*. Ziegel argues that Newbury JA in *DaimlerChrysler* was too quick to reject the relevance of the British Columbia *PPSA* as an aid in construing section 224(1.3). Further, he argues that the wording of section 224(1.3) illustrates that Parliament intended "security interest" to have the same meaning as under provincial personal property security acts.[3]

The exclusion of financing leases and conditional sales agreements from the definition of security interest in the *ITA* has the potential to create a circular priority problem. Suppose that SP1 is granted a security interest in all of the debtor's present and after-acquired personal property, and SP1 properly registers a financing statement in the personal property registry. SP2 sells a piece of equipment to the debtor under a conditional sales agreement under which the seller reserves title to the goods until the full purchase price is paid. SP2 neglects to register with the result that SP2 is unable to claim the priority over SP1 that would otherwise be available to it (SP2 has a purchase money security interest and is given priority over an earlier security interest, but only if SP2 perfects its security interest within a certain time). The debtor fails to remit source deductions, with the result that a statutory deemed trust arises by virtue of *ITA*, section 227(4.1). A circularity arises: SP1 has priority over SP2; SP2 has priority over the Crown; and the Crown has priority over SP1. This problem would be avoided if the deemed trust were given priority over all types of security interests, including title retention devices. The ranking would be: (1) Crown; (2) SP1; (3) SP2. For guidance on resolving circular priority problems see Roderick J Wood, "Circular Priorities in Secured Transactions Law" (2010) 47:4 *Alberta Law Review* 823.

---

3   Jacob Ziegel, "Conditional Sales and Superpriority Crown Claims Under the ITA s 227" (2003) 38 *Canadian Bankruptcy Reports* (4th) 161.

Section 2 of the *BIA* defines a secured creditor as "a person holding a mortgage, hypothec, pledge, charge or lien on or against the property of the debtor or any part of that property as security for a debt due or accruing due to the person from the debtor." Compare this definition with the definition of "secured creditor" under *ITA*, section 244(1.3). If the interest of a lessor under a finance lease or the interest of a seller under a conditional sales agreement does not constitute a mortgage, lien, pledge, or charge for the purposes of the *ITA* definition, one might expect that it also would not constitute a mortgage, lien, pledge, or charge for the purposes of the *BIA* definition: see Roderick J Wood, "The Definition of Secured Creditor in Insolvency Law" (2010), 25 *Business & Finance Law Review* 341 for a discussion of this problem. The easiest solution would be to amend the *BIA* definition to ensure that all security interests that secure payment or performance of an obligation are covered, including leases and conditional sales agreements.

F. Statutory Trusts in Favour of Third Parties

BIA, section 67(2), provides that property of a bankrupt shall not be regarded as held in trust for the purposes of section 67(1)(a) unless it would be so regarded in the absence of a statutory provision. This provision governs when a statutory deemed trust is created in favour of the Crown. However, sometimes a statutory deemed trust is conferred on a person other than the Crown — for example, the Ontario *Pension Benefits Act*, RSO 1990, c P.8 contains the following provisions:

> 57(3) An employer who is required to pay contributions to a pension fund shall be deemed to hold in trust for the beneficiaries of the pension plan an amount of money equal to the employer contributions due and not paid into the pension fund.
>
> (4) Where a pension plan is wound up in whole or in part, an employer who is required to pay contributions to the pension fund shall be deemed to hold in trust for the beneficiaries of the pension plan an amount of money equal to employer contributions accrued to the date of the wind up but not yet due under the plan or regulations.
>
> (5) The administrator of the pension plan has a lien and charge on the assets of the employer in an amount equal to the amounts deemed to be held in trust under this section.

The validity of these trusts turns on how one interprets the 1989 Supreme Court of Canada decision in *British Columbia v Henfrey Samson Belair Ltd*, [1989] 2 SCR 24 (*Henfrey*). In *Henfrey*, one of the quintet of constitutional cases referenced above, the Supreme Court of Canada was asked to decide whether the debtor's assets were held in trust for the Provincial Crown. The debtor had collected provincial sales tax and failed to remit it to the Crown. The Court determined that the Crown's trust was ineffective notwithstanding the statute because the tax proceeds were no longer identifiable:

> [45] I turn next to s 18 of the *Social Service Tax Act* and the nature of the legal interests created by it. At the moment of collection the trust property is identifiable and the trust meets the requirements for a trust under the principles of trust law. The difficulty in this, as in most cases, is that the trust property soon ceases to be identifiable. The tax money is mingled with other money in the hands of the merchant and converted to other property so that it cannot be traced. At this point it is no longer a trust under general principles of law. In an attempt to meet this problem, s 18(1)(b) states that tax collected shall be deemed to be held separate from and form no part of the collector's money, assets

or estate. But, as the presence of the deeming provision tacitly acknowledges, the reality is that after conversion the statutory trust bears little resemblance to a true trust. There is no property which can be regarded as being impressed with a trust. Because of this, s 18(2) goes on to provide that the unpaid tax forms a lien and charge on the entire assets of the collector, an interest in the nature of a secured debt.

The Supreme Court of Canada held that Provincial Crown's trust was not a valid trust, because it lacked certainty of subject, and therefore should be treated as an unsecured claim. This case was decided before the 1992 amendments to the *BIA*, and so the Crown was able to take advantage of a preference under section 136. If decided today, *BIA*, section 67(2), would invalidate the Provincial Crown's trust claim, and due to the removal of the Crown's preference from section 136, the Provincial Crown would be left with an ordinary, unsecured claim. An important question is how the ratio of this case should be applied to statutory trusts created in favour of third parties.

There is both a narrow and a broad interpretation of the *Henfrey* decision. The narrow view is that the decision must be restricted to cases where a province is attempting to use a statutory deemed trust to elevate a claim that is designated as a preferred claim under the *BIA*. On this view, *Henfrey* would not apply in respect of a statutory deemed trust that is created in favour of a third party; the claimant could therefore assert the trust in the bankruptcy. The broad view is that the Court in *Henfrey* intended to establish the general proposition that, in order to fall within *BIA*, section 67(1)(a), every trust must satisfy the requirements of a trust under principles of trust law. The Ontario Court of Appeal adopted this broad view in *Re Ivaco Inc* (2006), 83 OR (3d) 108 (Ont CA) and *The Guarantee Company of North America v Royal Bank of Canada*, 2019 ONCA 9, holding that a statutory deemed trust in respect of a third party will qualify as a trust under section 67(1)(a) of the *BIA* "only if it also meets the three attributes — the three certainties — of a common law trust." The Alberta Court of Appeal has affirmed this approach in *Bassano Growers Ltd v Price Waterhouse Ltd*, 1998 ABCA 198 at para 12, and more recently in *Iona Contractors Ltd v Guarantee Company of North America*, 2015 ABCA 240 at para 35:

> This is not to say that a trust that meets the requirements of the general law, and therefore qualifies as a trust under s 67(1)(a) of the *BIA*, may not have its genesis in a deemed or statutory trust. It must, however, satisfy the essential requirements of a valid trust under the general law in order to do so.

G. Priority Flips and Regime Shopping

The current rules regarding Crown claims may lead creditors to use insolvency proceedings strategically in two different ways. A creditor may trigger insolvency proceedings if the result of doing so is that the creditor's priority, relative to other creditors, is improved. This phenomenon is called a "priority flip" or "inversion of priorities." A creditor may also select one insolvency regime over another if the rules in one regime are more favourable to the creditor. This phenomenon is called regime shopping.

A secured creditor, who is subordinate to a Crown claim under provincial or non-bankruptcy federal law, may be able to produce a priority flip by invoking the *BIA*.[4] In other words,

---

4   Tamara Buckwold & Rod Wood, "Priorities" in Stephanie Ben-Ishai & Anthony Duggan, eds, *Canadian Bankruptcy and Insolvency Law: Bill C-55, Statute c 47 and Beyond* (Markham, ON: LexisNexis Canada, 2007).

the *BIA* provisions governing Crown claims in bankruptcy improve the position of other creditors relative to the Crown when the debtor becomes bankrupt.

The Court confirmed that secured creditors can invoke bankruptcy proceedings solely for strategic reasons in *Bank of Montreal v Scott Road Enterprises Ltd* (1989), 57 DLR (4th) 623 (BCCA), reproduced in Chapter 3, and more recently in *Grant Forest Products Inc v Toronto-Dominion Bank*, 2015 ONCA 570 at para 118.

Consider the change in priorities that is caused by the occurrence of bankruptcy in the following scenario. A business debtor located in Alberta grants a security interest in all of its present and after-acquired personal property to a bank. The bank properly registers a financing statement under the *PPSA*. The debtor fails to pay an assessment under the Alberta *Workers' Compensation Act*, RSA 2000, c W-15. Section 129 of that Act provides that an assessment "creates a fixed, specific and continuing charge in favour of the Board" and has "priority over all writs, judgments, debts, liens, charges, security interests ... whether crystallized or otherwise perfected or not and whenever created or to be created." Outside of bankruptcy, the assessment does not need to be registered and has priority over the bank's security interest. Upon bankruptcy, the outcome is significantly different. If the Board did not register its assessment in the *PPSA* before the date of the initial bankruptcy event, it is relegated to the status of an ordinary unsecured claimant. And even if it does register in time, it is subordinate to the bank's security interest by virtue of *BIA*, section 87(2)(a).

Rules that improve creditor A's entitlements relative to creditor B's inside bankruptcy are contrary to good bankruptcy policy. The reason is that they create an incentive for A to put the debtor into bankruptcy in order to obtain a priority advantage over B. The danger is that the debtor may end up in bankruptcy prematurely. While this may be in A's individual interest, it would not be in the interest of the creditors as a group. Bankruptcy is likely to result in the dismantling of the debtor's business. The interest of the creditors as a group lies in maximizing the returns from realization of the debtor's assets. The debtor's business may be worth more if it continues to operate.

Professor Wood in *Bankruptcy and Insolvency Law*, 2d ed, (Toronto: Irwin Law, 2015) at 140–43, identifies four different situations where an inversion of priorities can arise. The first occurs where a creditor is given a preferred creditor status under the *BIA*. The second situation is in respect of Crown claims that are secured by a lien or charge. These are fully effective outside bankruptcy, and they are often given a superpriority over prior security interests. However, in bankruptcy they are effective only if registered and, even if this is done, they are rendered subordinate to a prior security. See the discussion of Crown claims under the 1992 reforms above. The third situation involves statutory deemed trusts. Section 67(2) provides that a deemed trust in favour of the Crown is ineffective unless it would constitute a valid trust in the absence of the statutory provisions. The fourth situation arises when a secured creditor is subordinate to a writ or judgment held by an ordinary unsecured creditor. For example, a writ creditor may have registered a writ of execution against the debtor's land prior to the granting of a mortgage to a lender. Under non-bankruptcy law, the writ has priority over the mortgage. However, by invoking bankruptcy, the secured creditor will cause the writ creditor to lose this priority.[5]

Unlike some of the other priority rules of the *BIA* that apply to both bankruptcies and receiverships (for example, *BIA*, sections 14.06(7) and 81.1), sections 86 to 87 apply only in bankruptcy proceedings. As a consequence, secured creditors will continue to have a strong

---

5   *Westcoast Savings Credit Union v McElroy* (1981), 39 CBR (NS) 52 (BCSC); *James Hunter & Associates Inc v Citifinancial Inc* (2007), 40 CBR (5th) 149 (Ont Sup Ct).

incentive to put a debtor into bankruptcy if there are Crown claims that are afforded priority by statute over the claim of the secured creditor.

Professors Buckwold and Wood, referenced above at footnote 4, argue that the current state of the law produces the possibility of regime shopping under which a creditor has a strong incentive to invoke the insolvency regime—bankruptcy, restructuring, or receivership—that gives it the best priority ranking. Courts have permitted the restructuring regimes to be used to effect a going-concern sale of the business. Thus, all three insolvency regimes can be used to effect a liquidation, yet the priorities that govern are often markedly different. In particular, Crown claims that are afforded a secured status and statutory deemed trusts are effective outside bankruptcy, but are limited by sections 86–87 and BIA, section 67(2), when bankruptcy proceedings are commenced. In *Re Ted Leroy Trucking [Century Services] Ltd*, 2010 SCC 60 at para 47, Deschamps J commented that these differences in priorities can give rise to a "strange asymmetry" that "can only encourage statute shopping by secured creditors in cases such as this one where the debtor's assets cannot satisfy both the secured creditors' and the Crown's claims." She commented that "[g]iving a key player in any insolvency such skewed incentives ... can only undermine that statute's remedial objectives and risk inviting the very social ills that it was enacted to avert."

Practice Questions

Donuts-A-Plenty, a local donut shop, is having financial difficulties. A numbered company (the "Debtor") operates the shop. Janice, the sole director and president of the Debtor, has attempted to keep the shop afloat, a task that became significantly more difficult when the HSBC Bank of Canada froze the Debtor's operating line of credit. Janice paid for the shop's continued operations using three sources of funds:

- income tax that the Debtor had deducted from the employees' paycheques, but not yet remitted to the CRA;
- goods and services tax (GST) that the Debtor had collected from customers, but not yet remitted to the CRA; and,
- funds the Debtor had earmarked to pay its employees. The Debtor's employees are paid monthly, but the Debtor will not be in a position to pay any of the employees at the end of this month.

Question 1

You are approached by the HSBC Bank of Canada. It is owed $150,000 and has a properly registered security interest against all of the Debtor's present and after-acquired personal property. It is considering applying for a bankruptcy order against the Debtor.

a) Will the HSBC Bank of Canada's priority position improve vis-à-vis the other creditors if a court grants a bankruptcy order against the Debtor?

b) Does your answer to (a) change if you are provided with the following information? The CRA registered a memorial for the amount of collected but unremitted GST at the personal property registry. The memorial was registered after the HSBC Bank of Canada's security agreement, but before any steps were taken to get a bankruptcy order against the Debtor.

c) Does your answer to (a) change if you are provided with the following information? The Debtor is set to be paid a large sum of money as the result of settling a trademark infringement lawsuit with a competing donut shop. The CRA has issued requirements to pay to the competing donut shop under both the *ITA* and the *ETA*.

Question 2

The Debtor purchased a donut-making machine (the "Equipment") from a company called Russell Hendrix Foodservice Equipment on the following terms:

- The total cost of the equipment is $10,000.
- The Debtor will make monthly payments of $500.
- Russell Hendrix will remain the owner of the Equipment until the Debtor has paid $10,000.

Russell Hendrix properly registered its security interest in the Equipment at the provincial personal property security registry. Russell Hendrix's purchase money security interest has priority over the HSBC Bank of Canada's general security interest. As of today's date, the Debtor has paid $3,000 to Russell Hendrix, leaving an unpaid balance of $7,000.

a) If a bankruptcy order is granted against the Debtor, who will have priority to the Equipment as between Russell Hendrix, the HSBC Bank of Canada, and the CRA with its claim for deducted but unremitted income tax?

b) Assume that a bankruptcy order is granted against the debtor. Does Russell Hendrix need to file a proof of its claim with the trustee?

c) Russell Hendrix has served a section 130 notice on the insolvency trustee with respect to the equipment. The trustee believes that the equipment is worth $9,000. What should the trustee do?

CHAPTER 9

Priorities and Distribution

One of the key purposes of the bankruptcy regime is to ensure the orderly distribution of the proceeds from the realization of the bankrupt's assets among its creditors. This chapter examines the scheme of distribution and the various classes of claims established by the *Bankruptcy and Insolvency Act*, RSC 1985, c B-3 (*BIA*). Part I below discusses the basic concept of the *pari passu* ranking of creditors for distribution purposes. Parts II discusses the priority ranking of creditors established by section 136 of the *BIA* and the various types of postponed claims. Part III discusses certain special claims upon which the *BIA* confers superpriority status.

I. PAYMENT OF DIVIDENDS AND THE *PARI PASSU* PRINCIPLE

A. Requirement to Pay Dividends; Secured vs Unsecured Creditors

A dividend is a creditor's share in the proceeds from the realization of the bankrupt's assets. Section 148(1) provides that the trustee in bankruptcy is required to declare and distribute dividends among the unsecured creditors "subject to the retention of such sums as may be necessary for the costs of administration or otherwise." Notably, this requirement makes no mention of any requirement to pay dividends in respect of secured claims, because technically secured creditors stand outside of the bankruptcy process. As discussed in Chapter 4, section 71 provides that assets that are subject to valid security interests do not vest in the trustee upon bankruptcy and do not form part of the bankruptcy estate. Section 69.3(2), meanwhile, provides that secured creditors are entitled to realize upon their security interests in the same way as they would outside of bankruptcy, notwithstanding the bankruptcy stay of proceedings. To the extent that secured creditors are unable to achieve a full recovery from realizing upon their collateral, they are permitted to prove the balance owing to them as an unsecured claim in the bankruptcy pursuant to section 127. The process and rules by which creditors can prove their claims so that they can participate in the distribution of the proceeds of the estate are discussed in Chapter 7.

B. The *Pari Passu* Principle

Subject to the *BIA*, the unsecured creditors of the bankrupt rank *pari passu* for distribution purposes. That is, they rank equally and each is entitled to receive a rateable (i.e. proportionate) share of the proceeds from the realization of the bankrupt's assets. This rule is reflected in section 141, which provides that "[s]ubject to this Act, all claims proved in a bankruptcy shall be paid rateably." Crucially, however, the *BIA* varies this general rule significantly by carving out exceptions and establishing various classes of preferred and special claims. In the absence of such exceptions, these claims would rank as ordinary unsecured claims. In practice, therefore, unsecured creditors do not truly rank *pari passu*. The priority ranking of claims is discussed in further detail below in Part II.

In addition to the preferred status that section 136 accords to certain types of claims, there are circumstances in which courts will permit certain ordinary unsecured creditors to collect ahead of others. For example, if the bankrupt is a contractor who failed to complete a job, the party that hired the bankrupt is entitled to perform the work and deduct the costs of the work from any outstanding amounts that it owes to the bankrupt. Importantly, however, pre-bankruptcy contractual terms giving a party discretion to pay amounts owing to the bankrupt directly to creditors of the bankrupt are ineffective in bankruptcy, as demonstrated in the following excerpt from *Iona Contractors Ltd v Guarantee Company of North America*, 2015 ABCA 240:

> [15] There is nothing objectionable about a provision in a contract allowing the owner to complete work that was not performed by a bankrupt contractor, and to deduct the amount from what was otherwise owing to the contractor. Section 97(3) of the *Bankruptcy and Insolvency Act* allows such set-offs. After a bankruptcy, however, no such clause is effective to the extent that it gives a discretion to the owner to pay creditors of the bankrupt contractor otherwise than as authorized in the *Bankruptcy and Insolvency Act*: *AN Bail Co v Gingras*, [1982] 2 SCR 475 at pp. 485–7. It is at this stage of the analysis that it is relevant that the owner has no "obligation" to pay the subcontractors, but only the "right" or "discretion" under clause 6.3.3(d). After bankruptcy, that discretion cannot be exercised in such a way that it disturbs the priorities in the *Bankruptcy and Insolvency Act*.

In *AN Bail Co v Gingras*, [1982] 2 SCR 475, Bail, a construction company, had subcontracted the bankrupt, Maçonnerie Montmorency Inc, to perform masonry work in a construction project. Upon Montmorency's bankruptcy, Bail still owed $27,116.28 to Montmorency. At the same time, Montmorency owed money to a third party supplier of construction materials. Bail therefore paid the supplier the $27,116.28 instead of paying Montmorency. The Supreme Court of Canada, at 486–87, held that Bail was not entitled to pay the supplier and was obliged to pay Montmorency's trustee:

> The payment made by appellant to Tuyaux Vibrés Inc. remains a payment made on behalf of the bankrupt company, which as of the date of the bankruptcy can make no further payments (*Bankruptcy Act*, s. 50(5)).
>
> From the date of the bankruptcy also, the debt of Maçonnerie Montmorency Inc. against appellant passed into the hands of the trustee as part of the property of the bankrupt company, and only the trustee can obtain payment of it (*Bankruptcy Act*, ss. 47, 50).
>
> It would be to disregard the *Bankruptcy Act* and deprive it of all meaning if the debtor of a bankrupt, instead of paying the trustee, were authorized, by contract or some other means, to pay one or other of the creditors of the bankrupt as he saw fit.
>
> I adopt the conclusion of Montgomery JA, speaking for the Court of Appeal:
>
> > The above clause of the general conditions may be perfectly valid and effective where there is no question of bankruptcy. I cannot, however, agree with Appellant that it can supplant the provisions of the Bankruptcy Act and entitle one unsecured creditor to be paid by preference, which would almost necessarily operate to the detriment of the other unsecured creditors. I regard this as contrary to the policy of the Bankruptcy Act.

Under s. 112 of the *Bankruptcy Act*, "Subject to this Act, all claims proved in the bankruptcy shall be paid *pari passu*."

Tuyaux Vibrés Inc. was not a preferred creditor or a secured creditor, and had no claim to assert against appellant or against Defence Construction (1951) Ltd., which were under no obligation toward it: it therefore had to submit its claim to the trustee and be paid *pari passu* with the other claims proven in the bankruptcy.

One might query whether, instead of suing appellant, the trustee could not have claimed from Tuyaux Vibrés Inc. the monies paid to it, or whether appellant can now recover them. The Court is not required to answer these questions in this appeal. As it is, the payment made to Tuyaux Vibrés Inc. by appellant did not release the latter from its obligation to the trustee.

Pre-bankruptcy contractual terms imposing monetary penalties upon a debtor's insolvency have also been held by courts as ineffective within the context of bankruptcy. This was observed in the recent case of *Capital Steel Inc v Chandos Construction Ltd*, 2019 ABCA 32, leave to appeal allowed (*Capital Steel*). In *Capital Steel*, the majority of the Alberta Court of Appeal voided a contractual penalty imposed upon a subcontractor when it became insolvent. The rationale was that such a penalty would defeat the *pari passu* principle through diverting monetary assets away from the bankrupt's estate, thereby depriving other creditors of value.

The *pari passu* principle is the subject of some controversy in bankruptcy scholarship because every bankruptcy regime creates various types of preferred claims. Accordingly, some commentators have questioned whether the principle has any real meaning in modern bankruptcy systems. The following excerpt, from Rizwaan Jameel Mokal, "Priority as Pathology: The *Pari Passu* Myth" (2001) 60:3 *Cambridge Law Journal* 581 at 587–88, provides an example of this belief:

> So the claims of creditors able to assert set-off, utility companies, post-liquidation creditors, pre-liquidation creditors with post-insolvency leverage, nineteen different types of preferential claims, and claims of deferred creditors, all fall outside the purview of the *pari passu* principle. And even these "deviations" from the "normal rule," while patently substantial, might in fact be "something of a minor qualification" to the "equality" norm. There are numerous other types of creditor not affected by it. Under certain circumstances, this includes claims held by accountants, solicitors, stockbrokers, factors and bankers, all of whom might be able to benefit from common law liens which arise by operation of law. Statute gives the unpaid seller a lien on the goods sold, and rights of stoppage in transit....
>
> Even more significant is the fact that, in an overwhelming majority of formal insolvency proceedings, *nothing* is distributed to general unsecured creditors (the only category of claimant truly subject to the *pari passu* rule). It is estimated that there are zero returns to them in 88% of administrative receiverships, 75% of creditors' voluntary liquidations, and 78% of compulsory liquidations. On average, they receive 7% of what they are owed.

Other commentators, meanwhile, have suggested that the *pari passu* principle has simply been eroded as a result of political responses to pressures from different special interest groups, as seen in the following excerpt from Jose Garrido, "The Distributional Question in Insolvency: Comparative Aspects" (1995) 4:1 *International Insolvency Review* 25 at 34:

> As priorities are granted by legislation, every pressure group tries to influence parliaments in order to reach a better treatment for their credits. The development of legislation is the consequence of the political struggle among social groups, leading to a race

for the top in the creditors' graduation. The legislative power has sought to satisfy the demands for protection of very different categories of creditors: the legislature feels free to grant a preferential status, because new priorities do not suppress previous ones. Superimposition has become the rule in the field of priorities: legislation superimposes new preferential credits on old ones, so that old preferential credits are not eliminated, but displaced to a lower position in the graduation.

Notwithstanding the foregoing critiques, courts in Canada continue to refer to the "general rule ... that creditors are to rank equally"; see below in Part II the excerpts from *Husky Oil Operations Ltd v Minister of National Revenue*, [1995] 3 SCR 453 (*Husky Oil*) at para 9.

II. PRIORITY RANKING AND POSTPONED CLAIMS

A. Section 136

Section 136 of the *BIA* sets out the main priority ranking in the bankruptcy scheme of distribution, while subsequent sections deal with various types of postponed claims. Together, these sections establish different classes of creditors based upon the types of claims that they hold. Aside from secured creditors, who stand outside of the process, there are three basic types of creditors, ranked in the following order:

1) Preferred creditors;
2) Ordinary unsecured creditors; and
3) Postponed creditors.

sections 81.3 81.4

Section 136 provides as follows:

Priority of claims

136 (1) Subject to the rights of secured creditors, the proceeds realized from the property of a bankrupt shall be applied in priority of payment as follows:

(a) in the case of a deceased bankrupt, the reasonable funeral and testamentary expenses incurred by the legal representative or, in the Province of Quebec, the successors or heirs of the deceased bankrupt; *deceased bankrupt*

(b) the costs of administration, in the following order,
  (i) the expenses and fees of any person acting under a direction made under paragraph 14.03(1)(a),
  (ii) the expenses and fees of the trustee, and
  (iii) legal costs;

(c) the levy payable under section 147;

(d) the amount of any wages, salaries, commissions, compensation or disbursements referred to in sections 81.3 and 81.4 that was not paid;

(d.01) the amount equal to the difference a secured creditor would have received but for the operation of sections 81.3 and 81.4 and the amount actually received by the secured creditor;

(d.02) the amount equal to the difference a secured creditor would have received but for the operation of sections 81.5 and 81.6 and the amount actually received by the secured creditor;

(d.1) claims in respect of debts or liabilities referred to in paragraph 178(1)(b) or (c), if provable by virtue of subsection 121(4), for periodic amounts accrued in the year before the date of the bankruptcy that are payable, plus any lump sum amount that is payable;

(e) municipal taxes assessed or levied against the bankrupt, within the two years immediately preceding the bankruptcy, that do not constitute a secured claim against the real property or immovables of the bankrupt, but not exceeding the value of the interest or, in the Province of Quebec, the value of the right of the bankrupt in the property in respect of which the taxes were imposed as declared by the trustee;

(f) the lessor for arrears of rent for a period of three months immediately preceding the bankruptcy and accelerated rent for a period not exceeding three months following the bankruptcy if entitled to accelerated rent under the lease, but the total amount so payable shall not exceed the realization from the property on the premises under lease, and any payment made on account of accelerated rent shall be credited against the amount payable by the trustee for occupation rent;

(g) the fees and costs referred to in subsection 70(2) but only to the extent of the realization from the property exigible thereunder;

(h) in the case of a bankrupt who became bankrupt before the prescribed date, all indebtedness of the bankrupt under any Act respecting workers' compensation, under any Act respecting unemployment insurance or under any provision of the *Income Tax Act* creating an obligation to pay to Her Majesty amounts that have been deducted or withheld, rateably;

(i) claims resulting from injuries to employees of the bankrupt in respect of which the provisions of any Act respecting workers' compensation do not apply, but only to the extent of moneys received from persons guaranteeing the bankrupt against damages resulting from those injuries; and

(j) in the case of a bankrupt who became bankrupt before the prescribed date, claims of the Crown not mentioned in paragraphs (a) to (i), in right of Canada or any province, rateably notwithstanding any statutory preference to the contrary.

As noted earlier, creditors will only be paid if there are sufficient proceeds from the realization of the bankrupt's property. Chapter 4 discusses which types of assets vest in the trustee. In particular, secured assets and any proceeds from their realization do not form part of the bankruptcy estate and are not available for distribution to the unsecured creditors, which is why section 136(1) provides that the priority ranking is "[s]ubject to the rights of secured creditors." In addition, before any creditor can receive a dividend, that creditor must first prove its claim in the bankruptcy. The process and rules for proving claims are set out in Chapter 7.

The Supreme Court of Canada explained the *BIA*'s distribution scheme as follows in *Husky Oil* at paras 7–9:

[7] At the outset, it is useful to remember that our bankruptcy system serves two distinct goals. The first is to ensure the equitable distribution of a bankrupt debtor's assets among the estate's creditors *inter se*. As one commentator has noted (Aleck Dadson, "Comment" (1986), 64 *Can. Bar Rev.* 755, at p. 755):

[b]ankruptcy serves this goal by replacing a regime of individual action with a regime of collective action. While the pre-bankruptcy regime of individual action allows creditors to pursue their separate and competing claims to the debtor's assets, bankruptcy's regime of collective action sorts out those diverse claims and deals with the debtor's assets in a way

which brings benefits to creditors as a group (reduced costs, increased recovery).... The collectivization of insolvency proceedings can only be achieved by denying to creditors the use of pre-bankruptcy remedies.

See also Peter W. Hogg, *Constitutional Law of Canada* (3rd ed. 1992) (supplemented), at p. 25–3. The second goal of the bankruptcy system is the financial rehabilitation of insolvent individuals (Dadson, *supra*, at p. 755). This goal is furthered through the opportunity for an insolvent individual's discharge from outstanding debts. *[rehabilitation of the insolvent]*

[8] It has long been accepted that the first goal of ensuring an equitable distribution of a debtor's assets is to be pursued in accordance with the federal system of bankruptcy priorities. In the seminal case of *Royal Bank of Canada v Larue*, [1928] A.C. 187, affirming [1926] S.C.R. 218, Viscount Cave L.C. confirmed that the exclusive federal power over bankruptcy and insolvency in s. 91 (21) of the *Constitution Act, 1867* enables Parliament to provide for the ranking of creditors in bankruptcy....

[9] The power to determine priorities of distribution of the bankrupt's assets thus confirmed, Parliament has created an equitable distribution wherein the general rule is that creditors are to rank equally, with claims provable in bankruptcy being paid rateably (*Bankruptcy Act*, s. 141). The rule of creditor equality is subject to ten classes of debt which are accorded priority in a stated order, the so-called list of "preferred" creditors (s. 136). Included in these classes of exceptions is "all indebtedness of the bankrupt under any Workmen's Compensation Act" in s. 136(1)(*h*), ranked eighth in the list. Lastly, the entire scheme of distribution is "[s]ubject to the rights of secured creditors" (s. 136) which, as Professor Hogg has noted, "enables secured creditors to realize their security as if there were no bankruptcy" (Hogg, *supra*, at p. 25–9).

More recently, in *Alberta (Attorney General) v Moloney*, 2015 SCC 51, the Supreme Court of Canada, at para 33, reaffirmed the "general rule" that "all creditors rank equally and share rateably in the bankrupt's assets." Within the same paragraph, the Supreme Court also commented that the equitable distribution of assets is the underlying purpose of bankruptcy's collective proceeding model, which avoids inefficiencies and "maximizes global recovery for all creditors." However, the Supreme Court also recognized that there are notable exceptions to the general rule as seen in the following excerpt from *Moloney*:

> [35] Yet there are exceptions to the principle of equitable distribution. Section 136 of the *[descriptive]* *BIA* provides that some creditors will be paid in priority. These creditors are referred to as "preferred creditors." There are also creditors that are paid only after all ordinary creditors have been satisfied: ss. 137(1), 139 and 140.1 of the *BIA*. Furthermore, the automatic stay of proceedings does not prevent secured creditors from realizing their security interest: s. 69.3(2) of the *BIA*; *Husky Oil*, at para. 9. A court may also grant leave permitting a creditor to begin separate proceedings and enforce a claim: s. 69.4 of the *BIA*. These exceptions reflect the policy choices made by Parliament in furthering this purpose of bankruptcy.

Query whether these statements make sense in light of the critiques of the *pari passu* rule discussed above in Part I.

postponed claims mean they haven't been able to rank into a dividend

B. Postponed Claims

Sections 137 through 140.1 postpone certain types of claims, meaning that creditors holding those claims are not entitled to receive a dividend until all of other creditors have been satisfied. Specifically, the following sections postpone the following types of claims:

postpones non-arm's length transactions

postpones silent partners

postpones officer wages

- Section 137 postpones the claims of creditors who entered into a non-arm's-length transaction with the bankrupt at any time before the bankruptcy, unless the transaction was a proper one in the opinion of the trustee or the court.
- Section 139 postpones the claims of silent partners. A silent partner is someone who advances money to a borrower engaged or about to be engaged in trade or business under a contract granting the lender a share of the profits, or a rate of interest varying with the profits of the business.
- Where the bankrupt is a corporation, section 140 postpones the claims of officers and directors of the bankrupt for wages, salary, commission, or compensation, which claims would otherwise receive priority under section 136(1)(d).
- Section 140.1 postpones all "equity claims," that is, claims in respect of "equity interests." These are defined as follows in section 2:

> *equity claim* means a claim that is in respect of an equity interest, including a claim for, among others,
> (a) a dividend or similar payment,
> (b) a return of capital,
> (c) a redemption or retraction obligation,
> (d) a monetary loss resulting from the ownership, purchase or sale of an equity interest or from the rescission, or, in Quebec, the annulment, of a purchase or sale of an equity interest, or
> (e) contribution or indemnity in respect of a claim referred to in any of paragraphs (a) to (d); (réclamation relative à des capitaux propres)

> *equity interest* means
> (a) in the case of a corporation other than an income trust, a share in the corporation — or a warrant or option or another right to acquire a share in the corporation — other than one that is derived from a convertible debt, and
> (b) in the case of an income trust, a unit in the income trust — or a warrant or option or another right to acquire a unit in the income trust — other than one that is derived from a convertible debt; (intérêt relatif à des capitaux propres).

What is the rationale for postponing the foregoing types of claims? In the case of creditors that entered into non-arm's-length transactions with the bankrupt, section 137 merely reflects the general rule under the BIA that non-arm's-length transactions are reviewable and, if improper, will be disallowed. Chapter 5 discusses reviewable transactions in greater detail. As for the postponement of claims of silent partners, section 139 codifies a very old rule to the effect that persons who make capital contributions to a business and share in the benefits thereof should not be permitted to characterize their contributions as loans in order to enhance their chances of recovery in bankruptcy. This rule is demonstrated in the following excerpt from *Sukloff v AH Rushforth & Co*, [1964] SCR 459:

equity interest

> Laidlaw JA, speaking on behalf of the Court of Appeal in this case, expressed the view that the moneys advanced by the appellant were not intended to be a mere loan of money, but rather that they were a contribution to the capital of a business enterprise in which the appellant had a personal and business interest, and in this regard he replied upon the decision of Romer J in *In Re Meade; Ex parte Humber v Palmer*, [1951] Ch. 774 in which the Court of Appeal in England followed the case of *In Re Beale; Ex parte Corbridge* (1876), 4 Ch. D. 246. *In Re Meade; Ex parte Humber v Palmer* was a case in which a woman who was living with the debtor Meade as his wife, entered into a riding academy business

with him and furnished him with the money to buy the riding academy and much of the equipment. The intention was that the two persons concerned should live together on the property and operate the business together living on the proceeds thereof. Laidlaw JA cites this case ([1962] O.R. at 693) as authority for the proposition that:

> Where a person has authorized the employment of his assets in a business he cannot prove in competition with the creditors of the business in respect of the assets so authorized to be employed.

In my opinion, the key to the decision in the Meade case appears to be furnished by the following comment on the appellant's argument which occurs towards the end of Mr. Justice Romer's judgment where he says (p. 783):

> The truth of the matter is that the whole foundation of Mr. Davies' argument is undermined by the realization that the moneys which the appellant advanced did not constitute, and were never intended to constitute, a loan at all. They represented her contribution to the capital of a business enterprise in which she plainly had an interest herself; and in my judgment she is no more entitled, as against the ordinary creditors of the business, to prove in respect of her contribution than the proprietor is entitled to prove in respect of his.

In Halsbury's Laws of England, 3rd. ed., vol. 2, p. 495, the cases of Meade and Beale are cited as authority for the proposition that:

> If a person advances money to another not by way of loan but as a contribution to the capital of a business carried on for their joint benefit, the person who has made the advance, even though he is not a partner in the business and has received no share of the profits as such, is debarred from proving in the bankruptcy of the recipient of the money in competition with the creditors of the business.

For similar reasons, where a court determines that a claim which the claimant seeks to characterize as a debt is so closely connected to an underlying equity claim, section 140.1 will postpone that claim: see *Dexior Financial Inc, Re*, 2011 BCSC 348. In *Re Blue Range Resource Corp*, 2000 ABQB 4, the Alberta Court of Queen's Bench explained the rationale for postponing equity claims as follows:

> [33] Another policy reason which supports subordinating the Big Bear claim is a recognition that creditors conduct business with corporations on the assumption that they will be given priority over shareholders in the event of an insolvency. This assumption was referred to by Laskin, J in *Central Capital (supra)*, in legal textbooks (Hadden, Forbes and Simmonds, Canadian Business Organizations Law Toronto: Butterworths, 1984 at 310, 311), and has been explicitly recognized in American case law. The court in *Matter of Stirling Homex Corp.*, 579 F.2d 206 (U.S. 2nd Cir. N.Y. 1978) at page 211 referred to this assumption as follows:
>
> > Defrauded stockholder claimants in the purchase of stock are presumed to have been bargaining for equity type profits and assumed equity type risks. Conventional creditors are presumed to have dealt with the corporation with the reasonable expectation that they would have a senior position against its assets, to that of alleged stockholder claims based on fraud.
>
> [34] The identification of risk-taking assumed by shareholders and creditors is not only relevant in a general sense, but can be illustrated by the behaviour of Big Bear in this

particular case. In the evidence put before me, Big Bear's president described how, in the course of Big Bear's hostile takeover of Blue Range, it sought access to Blue Range's books and records for information, but had its requests denied. Nevertheless, Big Bear decided to pursue the takeover in the absence of information it knew would have been prudent to obtain. Should the creditors be required to share the result of that type of risk-taking with Big Bear? The creditors are already suffering the results of misrepresentation, if it occurred, in the inability of Blue Range to make full payment on its trade obligations.

Section 140, meanwhile, postpones the wage claims of officers and directors based on the longstanding rule that they are not to be treated like regular employees of the bankrupt. For an illustrative example see *Eastern Ontario Milk Products Co, Re*, [1923] 1 DLR 591 (ON SC).

C. Equitable Subordination

There is no express statutory provision in the *BIA* that empowers a bankruptcy court to subordinate claims beyond the types of claims that are specifically postponed pursuant to sections 137 through 140.1. Importantly, however, section 183 invests bankruptcy courts "with such jurisdiction at law and in equity as will enable them to exercise original, auxiliary and ancillary jurisdiction in bankruptcy and in other proceedings authorized by [the] Act." The Supreme Court of Canada has stated that section 183 is intended to confer broad jurisdiction on the bankruptcy court, as seen in the following excerpt from *Eagle River International Ltd, Re*, 2001 SCC 92 (*Eagle River*):

> [38] It seems to me that the decided cases recognize that the word "Bankruptcy" in s. 91(21) of the *Constitution Act, 1867* must be given a broad scope if it is to accomplish its purpose. Anything less would unnecessarily complicate and undermine the economical and expeditious winding up of the bankrupt's affairs. Creation of a national jurisdiction in bankruptcy would be of little utility if its exercise were continually frustrated by a pinched and narrow construction of the constitutional head of power. The broad scope of authority conferred on Parliament has been passed along to the bankruptcy court in s. 183(1) of the Act, which confers a correspondingly broad jurisdiction.

Notably, *Eagle River* did not focus on the interpretation of "equity" within the meaning of section 183. However, bankruptcy courts in Canada have exercised their equitable jurisdiction in various circumstances, for example to rectify contracts (see *Re Middleton* (1977), 24 CBR (NS) 66 (SC)), issue injunctions (see *Interclaim Holdings Ltd v Down*, 1999 ABCA 329)), and order specific performance (see *Re Western Canada Pulpwood & Lumber Co* (1929), 11 CBR 28 (MBCKB), aff'd (1929), 11 CBR 125 (MBCA)). It is unclear whether the bankruptcy court's equitable jurisdiction is sufficiently robust to ground the exercise of equitable subordination: see the discussion below of *US Steel Canada Inc (Re)*, 2016 ONCA 662.

In the United States, the *Bankruptcy Code*[1] empowers courts to subordinate all or part of a claim for distribution purposes where the court determines that it is equitable to do so. The US doctrine of equitable subordination has been summarized as follows:

> The ruling [in *Pepper v Litton*] began a long debate over the meaning of these highly abstract concepts, and indeed one author suggests that it is impossible to extract from the decision a basic rule that can be followed consistently. Nine years later, the [US] Supreme Court in *Comstock v. Group of Institutional Investors* [335 US 211 (1948)] divided

---

1   11 USC §101.

5-4 on the scope of the doctrine.... It was not until 1977 that a framework emerged to provide some consistency to the principles of equitable subordination.

In 1977, the Fifth Circuit in *Re Mobile Steel* [563 F 2d 692 (1977)] distilled the principles from the earlier case law and developed a three-part test for equitable subordination.... Before exercising the power of equitable subordination, a court must be satisfied that:

(i) The claimant must have engaged in some type of inequitable conduct; (ii) The misconduct must have resulted in injury to the creditors of the bankrupt or conferred an unfair advantage on the claimant; (iii) Equitable subordination of the claim must not be inconsistent with the provisions of the Bankruptcy Act.

The *Mobile Steel* three-part test quickly became the new framework by which courts analyzed equitable subordination. The following year, Congress gave statutory recognition to the power of equitable subordination. In enacting the provision, Congress purposely left the wording vague, thus allowing the courts the freedom to continue to develop and define the scope of the doctrine. Section 510(c) of the Bankruptcy Code provides that after notice and a hearing, the court may,

(1) under the principles of equitable subordination, subordinate for purposes of distribution all or part of an allowed claim to all or part of another claim or all or part of an allowed interest to all or part of another allowed interest; (2) or order that any lien securing such a subordinated claim be transferred to the estate.

The principles developed by the courts, including the *Mobile Steel* test, continue to provide the only guidelines on the meaning of the doctrine. The United States Supreme Court in the 1996 decision of *United States v Noland* [517 US 535] endorsed the *Mobile Steel* three-part test.[2] *Canada declined to apply equitable*

In *Canada Deposit Insurance Corp v Canadian Commercial Bank*, [1992] 3 SCR 558 at 60, the Supreme Court of Canada considered the US doctrine of equitable subordination, but declined to apply it:

As I understand it, in the United States there are three requirements for a successful claim of equitable subordination: (1) the claimant must have engaged in some type of inequitable conduct; (2) the misconduct must have resulted in injury to the creditors of the bankrupt or conferred an unfair advantage on the claimant; and (3) equitable subordination of the claim must not be inconsistent with the provisions of the bankruptcy statute. See *In re Mobile Steel Co.*, 563 F.2d 692 (5th Cir. 1977), at p. 700; *In re Multiponics Inc.*, 622 F.2d 709 (5th Cir. 1980); A. DeNatale and P.B. Abram, "The Doctrine of Equitable Subordination as Applied to Nonmanagement Creditors" (1985), 40 Bus. Law. 417, at p. 423; and L. J. Crozier, "Equitable Subordination of Claims in Canadian Bankruptcy Law" (1992), 7 C.B.R. (3d) 40, at pp. 41–42. Even if this Court were to accept that a comparable doctrine to equitable subordination should exist in Canadian law, I do not view the facts of this case as giving rise to the "inequitable conduct" and ensuing "detriment" necessary to trigger its application.

As noted in the above passage, the Supreme Court declined to answer the question of whether the US doctrine of equitable subordination could be applied in Canada. The Supreme Court (at 63–64) concluded that "[e]ven if equitable subordination is available under Canadian law,

---

2   Thomas Telfer "Transplanting Equitable Subordination: The New Free-Wheeling Equitable Discretion in Canadian Insolvency Law?" (2001) 36 *Canadian Business Law Journal* 36 at 41–43.

a question which I leave open for another day, the facts of this case do not call for an intervention with the *pari passu* ranking of the respondents in the name of equity." More recently, the Ontario Court of Appeal in *US Steel Canada Inc (Re)*, 2016 ONCA 662 (*US Steel*), held that *CCAA* (*Companies' Creditors Arrangement Act*, RSC 1985, c C-36) courts had no authority to apply equitable subordination:

> [101] I would not grant the relief sought because, applying the principles of statutory interpretation, nowhere in the words of the *CCAA* is there authority, express or implied, to apply the doctrine of equitable subordination. Nor does it fall within the scheme of the statute, which focuses on the implementation of a plan of arrangement or compromise. The *CCAA* does not legislate a scheme of priorities or distribution, because these are to be worked out in each plan of compromise or arrangement. The subordination of "equity claims" is directed towards a specific group, shareholders, or those with similar claims. It also has a specific function, consistent with the purpose of the *CCAA*: to facilitate the arrangement or compromise without shareholders' involvement.
>
> [102] The success of the *CCAA* in fulfilling its statutory purpose has been in large measure due to the ability of judges to fashion creative solutions, for which there is no express authority, through the exercise of their jurisdiction under s. 11. As Blair JA noted in *Metcalfe and Mansfield*, however, the court's powers are not limitless. They are shaped by the purpose and scheme of the *CCAA*. The appellant has not identified how equitable subordination would further the remedial purpose of the *CCAA*.

Although the Supreme Court of Canada granted leave to appeal the Ontario Court of Appeal's decision, the appeal was withdrawn before the Supreme Court heard the case. Accordingly, there has been no final word yet as to the applicability of the doctrine of equitable subordination in Canada. In *US Steel*, the Ontario Court of Appeal appeared to suggest *in obiter* that the result may have been different if the proceedings had been brought under the *BIA* rather than the *CCAA*:

> [104] There is no provision in the *CCAA* equivalent to s. 183 of the *BIA* or §105(a) of the U.S. *Bankruptcy Code*. Section 183 invests the bankruptcy court with "such jurisdiction at law and in equity" as will enable it to exercise its bankruptcy jurisdiction. This is significant, because if equitable subordination is to become a part of Canadian law, it would appear that the *BIA* gives the bankruptcy court explicit jurisdiction as a court of equity to ground such a remedy and a legislative purpose that is more relevant to the potential reordering of priorities.

Is the foregoing a correct interpretation of the bankruptcy court's equitable powers under section 183?

III. SPECIAL CLAIMS

In addition to the priority ranking set out in section 136, certain types of special claims receive priority for distribution purposes. These special claims are discussed below.

A. Unpaid Suppliers

Section 81.1 provides that if a supplier has sold and delivered goods for use in the purchaser's business but the purchaser has not fully paid for the goods, the supplier is entitled to repossess the goods at its own expense provided that the following conditions are met:

A. Unpaid Suppliers, Sells and delivered goods repossess → notice of
for use in the biz, Supplying not entirely claim not
the goods at its own expenses provided (1) w.r.t. demand

(a) the supplier presents a written demand for repossession to the purchaser, trustee or receiver, in the prescribed form and containing the details of the transaction, within a period of 15 days after the day on which the purchaser became bankrupt or became a person who is subject to a receivership; *— written demand within 15 days*

(b) the goods were delivered within 30 days before the day on which the purchaser became bankrupt or became a person who is subject to a receivership; *— 30 days before bankruptcy*

(c) at the time when the demand referred to in paragraph (a) is presented, the goods

    (i) are in the possession of the purchaser, trustee or receiver, *— possession*

    (ii) are identifiable as the goods delivered by the supplier and not fully paid for, *— identifiable + not fully paid for*

    (iii) are in the same state as they were on delivery, *— same state*

    (iv) have not been resold at arms' length, and *— not resold*

    (v) are not subject to any agreement for sale at arms' length; and *— not subject to an agreement*

(d) the purchaser, trustee or receiver does not, forthwith after the demand referred to in paragraph (a) is presented, pay to the supplier the entire balance owing.

In determining whether there has been a sale of the goods—an essential requirement in order to trigger the unpaid supplier's right under section 81.1—courts will generally look to the provincial sale of goods legislation. Where the unpaid supplier has retained title and property in the goods, no sale has occurred. Importantly, section 81.1(5) provides that the unpaid supplier's right to repossess the goods expires after fifteen days unless an extension is granted by the trustee, the receiver, or the court.

In *Royal Bank of Canada v Stereo People of Canada Ltd*, 44 CBR (3d) 213 (CA), at 4–6, the Alberta Court of Appeal stated that the purpose of Section 81.1 was to provide relief to recent unpaid suppliers of goods to the bankrupt while protecting innocent third-party purchasers:

> We agree with the chambers judge's interpretation of s.81.1(1). That interpretation follows from the clear wording of the section. Section 81.1 does not require that complete identification information be supplied with the demand, only that the details of the transaction be provided. Subsection (c) refers to goods which are *identifiable* as delivered to the supplier and not fully paid for. It does not require that complete identification be supplied with the demand, even though the directions in Form 63.1 encourage identification information and the supply of supporting documents. In sum, the claim form is the notice of claim, not the proof of claim. *— notice of claim not proof of claim*
>
> Clearly, the supplier must make a *bona fide* effort to provide as soon as possible details of the transaction including information relating to the identification of the goods claimed in the demand. Under the scheme of the Act, the claim must be made quickly, in some cases in a matter of hours. It is not reasonable to require that complete verification be provided with the claim. Identification may only be possible on the physical inspection of the goods. Much may depend on the type of goods, and the inventory records and organizational methods of the bankrupt. We recognize, as did Parliament, that the timing of the demand is critical to the supplier's demand, and of necessity the demand may have to be made without lengthy consideration as to the description of the goods or the means of identification of the goods. Provided that a *bona fide* effort is made to provide details of the transaction and the goods claimed in the demand, the trustee may supplement that information with such other information as the trustee considers necessary.
>
> Nor do we see any reason to limit the supplier to goods supplied within the period of thirty days from the date on which identification information satisfactory to the trustee

was provided to the trustee. As we have said, it may not be possible to predict what information the trustee will require to identify the goods.

The intention of Parliament in enacting this section is clear. Parliament intended to grant to suppliers who have recently delivered goods, limited relief from the inequities imposed upon them in the earlier legislation. These inequities include the complete loss of all unpaid goods shipped by the supplier to the bankrupt, leaving the suppliers subject to the risk that a debtor will order goods just prior to bankruptcy to improve his position in the bankruptcy. As pointed out by Farley J in *Re Rizzo Shoes (1989) Ltd* (1995), 29 C.B.R. (3d) 270 at 272:

> It appears that the repossession section was included in the 1992 amendment of the *BIA* to protect 'recent' unsecured creditors, especially in those situations where the bankrupt has "bulked up" with inventory to liquidate so as to generate funds to pay third parties.

The protection accorded to suppliers is strictly limited to goods recently supplied which have not been paid for, which have not been resold, and which are in the same state as they were on delivery. Parliament ensured that rights of innocent third parties who obtained an interest in the goods subsequent to delivery would not be affected. We see no inequity to the secured creditor who is not given recourse against inventory, the cost of which has not been paid by the bankrupt.

Section 81.2(1) provides that unpaid farmers, fishermen, and aquaculturists have a security interest in respect of the unpaid amount against the bankrupt's inventory, except any inventory that is subject to a claim under section 81.1, where the farmer, fisherman, or aquaculturists has sold and delivered their products to the bankrupt for use in its business within fifteen days preceding the bankruptcy. This first charge is in addition to the rights of normal unpaid suppliers under section 81.1, which farmers, fishermen, and aquaculturists can also claim pursuant to section 81.2(4).

B. Wage Claims

Section 81.3(1) creates a superpriority claim, up to a maximum of $2,000, for employee compensation in respect of services rendered up to six months prior to the date of the initial bankruptcy event. Section 81.3(9) defines "compensation" as including vacation pay but not termination or severance. In addition, section 81.3(3) creates a superpriority claim for disbursements incurred by travelling salespersons during the same six-month period, up to a maximum of $1,000. In both cases, the charge is secured against the bankrupt's "current assets" on the date of the bankruptcy; this term is defined in section 2 as "cash, cash equivalents—including negotiable instruments and demand deposits—inventory or accounts receivable, or the proceeds from any dealing with those assets." Any unpaid balance from the foregoing amounts is a preferred claim under section 136(1)(d), ranking after expenses, the costs of administration of the bankruptcy, and the Superintendent of Bankruptcy's levy. Section 81.4 extends the same protections to unpaid employees in receiverships.

There are a number of exceptions to the superpriority charge created under section 81.3. Firstly, section 81.3(4) provides that the superpriority ranking for remuneration and disbursements is subject to the claims of unpaid suppliers under sections 81.1 and 81.2 as well as to any amounts deemed to be held in trust by the bankrupt pursuant to section 67(3). Secondly, section 81.3(6) provides that no officer or director of the bankrupt is entitled to a superpriority claim. Thirdly, section 81.3(7) provides that any person who was not dealing at arm's length with the bankrupt is not entitled to a superpriority claim under section 81.3 unless, in the trustee's opinion, "it is reasonable to conclude that they would have entered into a substantially similar transaction if they had been dealing with each other at arm's length."

In addition to the foregoing protections contained in the Act, the enactment in 2005 of the *Wage Earner Protection Program Act*, SC 2005, c 47 (*WEPPA*) established an insurance scheme to protect unpaid employees of employers that are bankrupt or in receivership. Under section 7 of *WEPPA*, eligible wages are covered up to a maximum of an amount equal to seven times the maximum weekly insurable earnings under the *Employment Insurance Act*, SC 1996, c 23. Note that the definition of "eligible wages" in section 2 of *WEPPA* excludes wages earned, and termination and severance pay that relate to, the period that is more than six months prior to the date of the bankruptcy or receivership appointment. Section 6 of *WEPPA* excludes from these protections individuals who are officers and directors of the bankrupt, who held a controlling interest in the bankrupt, or who occupied a managerial position or was not dealing at arm's length with the bankrupt.

C. Pension Fund Contributions

Section 81.5 confers superpriority status on claims for unremitted pension contributions that are outstanding as of the date of bankruptcy. Section 81.5(2) provides that this security interest ranks above every other claim, right, charge, or security against the bankrupt's assets except for those arising under sections 81.1 and 81.2 (unpaid suppliers), amounts referred to in Section 67(3) that have been deemed to be held in trust (source deductions for income tax, employment insurance, and Canada Pension Plan), and securities under sections 81.3 and 81.4 (wage claims). Section 81.6 confers the same superpriority on pension claims in receiverships. The superpriority charge created by sections 81.5 and 81.6 is broader than the charge for wage claims under sections 81.3 and 81.4 because it has no monetary limit and covers all assets of the bankrupt, not simply current assets.

It is important to note that sections 81.5 and 81.6 do not confer priorities for pension deficits generally or for amounts other than those that were deducted from employees' remuneration for payment to a pension plan: see *ITB Marine Group Ltd v Northern Transportation Company Limited*, 2017 BCSC 2007 at paras 54–68. In other words, the superpriority covers only normal pension payments, not special payments. In *Bloom Lake, gpl (Arrangement relatif à)*, 2015 QCCS 3064, the Quebec Superior Court held that federal pension claims under the *Pension Benefits Standards Act*, 1985, RSC 1985, c 32 (2nd Supp), were protected only to the extent set out in sections 81.5 and 81.6 of the *BIA* and sections 6(6) and 37 of the *CCAA*:

> [77] The Court therefore adopts the following reasoning to resolve the conflict in the present case:
>
>> Given that the pension provisions of the *BIA* and *CCAA* came into force much later than s. 8 of the *PBSA*, normal interpretation would require that the later legislation be deemed to be remedial in nature. Likewise, since those provisions of the *BIA* and *CCAA* are the more specific provisions, normal interpretation would take them to have precedence over the general. Finally, the limited scope of the protection given to pension claims in the *BIA* and the *CCAA* would, by application of the doctrine of implied exclusion, suggest that Parliament did not intend there to be any additional protection. In enacting *BIA* subs. 60(1.5) and 65.13(8) and ss. 81.5 and 81.6 and *CCAA* subs. 6(6) and 37(6), while not amending subs. 8(2) of the *PBSA* (by adding explicit priority language or by removing the insolvency trigger), *Parliament demonstrated the intent that pension claims would have*

protection in insolvency and restructurings only to the limited extent set out in the BIA and the CCAA. [Emphasis added]

D. Environmental Claims

Section 14.06(7) creates a superpriority for claims by the Crown or a province against the debtor in a bankruptcy, proposal, or receivership for costs of remedying any environmental damage affecting real property, secured against the real property and any contiguous real property that is related to the activity that caused the damage. This security interest is enforceable in accordance with the law of the jurisdiction in which the real property is located in the same way as a mortgage, hypothec or other security on real property, and it ranks above any other claim, right, charge, or security against the property "despite any other provision of this Act or anything in any other federal or provincial law." This interest is limited only by section 14.06(6), which provides that if the costs of remedying the environmental damage exceed the value of the property, those costs rank as an unsecured claim. Section 14.06(8) further provides that a claim for environmental damage is a provable claim in bankruptcy, regardless of whether the damage occurred before or after the date of bankruptcy or the date that a proposal was filed.

In *Canadian Imperial Bank of Commerce v Isobord Enterprises Inc*, 2002 MBQB 127, the Manitoba Court of Queen's Bench held that in order for a provincial government to obtain the superpriority conferred by section 14.06(7)(b), the government must take all steps required by the provincial environmental legislation that creates the claim:

[17] If Manitoba Conservation has a valid claim against the sale proceeds by virtue of s. 24(9) of *The Environment Act*, that claim would rank above the claim of the secured lenders by virtue of s. 14.06(7)(b) of the *BIA*. However, it has failed to satisfy me it has such a claim.

[18] Pursuant to s. 24(9) of *The Environment Act*, costs incurred by the Government of Manitoba for any action taken or caused to be taken by the director or a person acting on instructions of the director in accordance with ss. 24(5) or (6) of the Act become a debt due to the Government. However, the steps taken by Manitoba Conservation following Isobord's non-compliance with Order D1-042 were not in accordance with the requirements of ss. 24(5) and (6).

[19] Subsequent to Isobord's failure to comply with the order, Manitoba Conservation did not apply for an order authorizing an environment officer to enter the affected area and take such steps as might be necessary to resolve the situation as it was required to do by s. 24(5). It simply went ahead and contracted directly with Poulin Exterminators on April 18, 2001 to develop and implement a rodent control program. There was no emergency situation which required it to act without first obtaining judicial approval that might have justified its actions under s. 24(6) of *The Environment Act*.

[20] Given the absence of judicial approval, the steps taken by Manitoba Conservation were not in accordance with ss. 24(5) and (6) and, as a result, it did not acquire a claim against Isobord under s. 24(9) of *The Environment Act*.

Notwithstanding the superpriority claim created by section 14.06(7), section 14.06(4) provides that the trustee in bankruptcy is not personally liable for failure to comply with environmental remediation orders, nor for any costs that are or would be incurred by any person in carrying out such orders if the trustee: (1) abandons, disposes of, or otherwise releases its interest in the real property; (2) contests the order; or (3) applies for a stay of the order pursuant to section 14.06(4)(b)(ii) so that the trustee can assess the economic viability of complying with the order.

In *Orphan Well Association v Grant Thornton Ltd*, 2019 SCC 5, the Supreme Court of Canada held that section 14.06(4) is concerned with the personal liability of the trustee and not the bankruptcy estate. Accordingly, the trustee's ability under section 14.06(4) to disclaim real property that is subject or becomes subject to a valid provincial remediation order does not relieve the bankruptcy estate from the obligation to comply with the order:

> [78] I have concluded that s. 14.06(4) is concerned with the personal liability of trustees, and not with the liability of the bankrupt estate. I emphasize here the well-established principle that, "[w]hen a federal statute can be properly interpreted so as not to interfere with a provincial statute, such an interpretation is to be applied in preference to another applicable construction which would bring about a conflict between the two statutes" (*Canadian Western Bank*, at para. 75).
>
> [79] Section 14.06(4) says nothing about the "bankrupt estate" avoiding the applicability of valid provincial law. In drafting s. 14.06(4), Parliament could easily have referred to the liability of the bankrupt estate. Parliament chose instead to refer simply to the personal liability of a trustee. Notably, s. 14.06(7) and s. 14.06(8) both refer to a "debtor in a bankruptcy." Parliament's choice in this regard cannot be ignored. I agree with Martin JA that there is no basis on which to read the words "the trustee is not personally liable" in s. 14.06(4) as encompassing the liability of the bankrupt estate. As noted by Martin JA, it is apparent from the express language chosen by Parliament that s. 14.06(4) was motivated by and aimed at concerns about the protection of trustees, not the protection of the full value of the estate for creditors. Nothing in the wording of s. 14.06(4) suggests that it was intended to extend to estate liability.
>
> [80] The Hansard evidence leads to the same conclusion. J. Hains, Director, Corporate Law Policy Directorate, Department of Industry Canada, noted the following during the 1996 debates preceding the enactment of s. 14.06(4) in 1997:

> > The aim is to provide a better definition of the liability of insolvency professionals and practitioners in order to encourage them to accept mandates where there may be problems related to the environment. It is hoped that this will reduce the number of abandoned sites both for the benefit of the environment and the safeguard of businesses and jobs.

> > (Standing Committee on Industry, *Evidence*, No. 16, 2nd Sess., 35th Parl., June 11, 1996, at 15:49–15:55, as cited in C.A. reasons, at para. 197)

> Several months later, Mr. Hains stated:

> > What Parliament tried to do in 1992 was to provide a relief to insolvency practitioners ... because they were at risk when they accepted a mandate to liquidate an insolvent business. Under environmental laws, therefore, they could have been subject to personal liability to clean up the environment. I am speaking of personal liability here, meaning "out of their own pockets."

> > (*Proceedings of the Standing Committee on Banking, Trade and Commerce*, No. 13, 2nd Sess., 35th Parl., November 4, 1996, at p. 15)

> Mr. Hains proceeded to explain how the 1997 amendments were intended to improve on the 1992 reforms to the *BIA* that had included the original version of s. 14.06(2) (as

discussed further below), but he gave no indication that the focus had somehow shifted away from a trustee's "personal liability."

[81] Prior to the enactment of the 1997 amendments, G. Marantz, Legal Advisor to the Department of Industry Canada, noted that they were intended to "provide the trustee with protection from being chased with deep-pocket liability" (Standing Committee on Industry, *Evidence*, No. 21, 2nd Sess., 35th Parl., September 25, 1996, at 17:15, as cited in C.A. reasons, at para. 198). I agree with the Regulator that the legislative debates give no hint of any intention by Parliament to immunize bankrupt estates from environmental liabilities. The notion that s. 14.06(4) was aimed at encouraging trustees in bankruptcy to accept mandates, and not at limiting estate liability, is further supported by the fact that the provision was inserted under the general heading "Appointment and Substitution of Trustees."

[82] Furthermore, in drafting s. 14.06(4), Parliament chose to use exactly the same concept it had used earlier in s. 14.06(2): by their express wording, where either provision applies, a trustee is not "personally liable." This cannot have been an oversight given that s. 14.06(4) was added to the *BIA* some five years after the enactment of s. 14.06(2). Since both provisions deal expressly with the protection of trustees from being "personally liable," it is very difficult to accept that they could be concerned with different kinds of liability. By their wording, s. 14.06(2) and s. 14.06(4) are clearly both concerned with the same concept. Indeed, if one interprets s. 14.06(4) as extending to estate liability, then there is no principled reason not to interpret s. 14.06(2) in the same way. However, it is undisputed that this was not Parliament's intention in enacting s. 14.06(2).

[83] Similarly, Parliament has also chosen to use the same concept found in both s. 14.06(4) and s. 14.06(2) in a third part of the 14.06 scheme, namely s. 14.06(1.2). This provision states that a trustee carrying on the business of a debtor or continuing the employment of a debtor's employees is not "personally liable" in respect of certain enumerated liabilities, including as a successor employer. Although this provision is not directly raised in this litigation, by its own terms, it clearly does not and cannot refer to the liability of the bankrupt estate. Again, it is difficult to conceive of how Parliament could have specified that a trustee is not "personally liable," using the ordinary, grammatical sense of that phrase, in both s. 14.06(1.2) and s. 14.06(2), but then intended the phrase to be read in a completely different and illogical manner in s. 14.06(4). All three provisions refer to the personal liability of a trustee, and all three must be interpreted consistently. Indeed, I note that the concept of a trustee being "not personally liable" is also used consistently in other parts of the *BIA* unrelated to the s. 14.06 scheme—see, for example, s. 80 and s. 197(3).

[84] This interpretation of s. 14.06(4) is also bolstered by the French wording of s. 14.06. The French versions of both s. 14.06(2) and s. 14.06(4) refer to a trustee's protection from personal liability "*ès qualités.*" This French expression is defined by *Le Grand Robert de la langue française* (2nd ed. 2001) dictionary as referring to someone acting "à cause d'un titre, d'une fonction particulière," which, in English, would mean acting by virtue of a title or specific role. The *Robert & Collins* dictionary translates "*ès qualités*" as in "one's official capacity" (online). In using this expression in s. 14.06(4), Parliament is therefore stating that, where "disclaimer" properly occurs, a trustee, is not personally liable, in its capacity as trustee, for orders to remedy any environmental condition or damage affecting the "disclaimed" property. These provisions are clearly not concerned with the concept of estate liability. The French versions of s. 14.06(2) and s. 14.06(4) thus utilize identical language to describe the limitation of liability they offer trustees. It is almost impossible

to conceive of Parliament using identical language in two such closely related provisions and yet intending different meanings. Accordingly, a trustee is not personally liable in its official capacity as representative of the bankrupt estate where it invokes s. 14.06(4).

[85] Prior to this litigation, the case law on s. 14.06 was somewhat scarce. However, this Court has considered the s. 14.06 scheme once before, in *GMAC Commercial Credit Corp— Canada v TCT Logistics Inc*, 2006 SCC 35, [2006] 2 S.C.R. 123. In that case, comments made by both the majority and the dissenting judge support my conclusion that s. 14.06(4) is concerned only with the personal liability of trustees. Abella J, writing for the majority, explained that "where Parliament has intended to confer immunity on trustees or receivers from certain claims, it has done so explicitly" (para. 67). As examples of this principle, she referred to 14.06(1.2) and, most notably for our purposes, to s. 14.06(4), which she described as follows: "trustee immune in certain circumstances from environmental liabilities" (para. 67). In her dissent, Deschamps J explained that a "trustee is not personally bound by the bankrupt's obligations." She noted that trustees are protected by the provisions that confer immunity upon them, including s. 14.06 (1.2), (2) and (4).

[86] Although the dissenting reasons focus on the source of the "disclaimer" power in s. 14.06(4), nothing in this case turns on either the source of the "disclaimer" power or on whether GTL successfully "disclaimed" the Renounced Assets. I would note that, while the dissenting reasons rely on a purported common law power of "disclaimer," the Court has been referred to no cases—and the dissenting reasons have cited none—demonstrating the existence of a common law power allowing trustees to "disclaim" *real property*. In any case, regardless of the source of the "disclaimer" power, nothing in s. 14.06(4) suggests that, where a trustee does "disclaim" real property, the result is that it is simply free to walk away from the environmental orders applicable to it. Quite the contrary—the provision is clear that, where an environmental order has been made, the result of an act of "disclaimer" is the cessation of personal liability. No effect of "disclaimer" on the liability of the bankrupt estate is specified. Had Parliament intended to empower trustees to walk away entirely from assets subject to environmental liabilities, it could easily have said so.

In the result, the Supreme Court overturned the orders of the trial judge and the Alberta Court of Appeal and ordered that the proceeds from the sale of the bankrupt's assets be used to pay for the bankrupt's ongoing environmental obligations. Although the trustee was not personally liable for the costs of the bankrupt's environmental obligations, the Supreme Court stated, at para 160, that "[b]ankruptcy is not a license to ignore rules, and insolvency professionals are bound by and must comply with valid provincial laws during bankruptcy." Consequently, the environmental claims of the Alberta Energy Regulator ranked ahead of the secured creditors' claims in the bankruptcy.

Practice Questions

Acme Canning Company made an assignment in bankruptcy and a trustee was appointed on 3 January 2019. Various employees remain unpaid; some, including the officers and directors of Acme, are owed wages for work performed as far back as March 2018.

In the months leading up to its bankruptcy filing, Acme had fallen behind on its payments to Frank's Greenhouses Inc, which had been supplying hothouse tomatoes for Acme's canning business. Acme also owes money to other trade creditors.

Lastly, an industrial waste spill at one of Acme's canneries in Stratford has caused significant damage to the surrounding property (all of which belongs to Acme) and the Ontario

Ministry of the Environment has ordered Acme to carry out environmental remediation of the lands. Acme's bank owns first and second mortgages on the lands.

Question 1
Can the unpaid employees and pensioners collect from Acme? How much?

Question 2
What should Acme's trade creditors do?

Question 3
Is Acme or its trustee required to perform the environmental remediation or pay the costs thereof? Assume that the Ministry of the Environment has taken all steps required by validly enacted provincial law.

Question 4
In what order will each of the foregoing creditors collect?

ORDER
UE
TC
MoE

MOE for secured creditors 1st
against real property
US → ranked 2-1
UE Employee

CHAPTER 10

Corporate Liability During Insolvency

I. INTRODUCTION

When a corporation is insolvent, should directors take some responsibility for its debts? Should the directors incur personal liability either to the debtor company or directly to the creditors themselves, most notably for the actions they took during the time the corporation was financially distressed? The starting point for these issues is always the basic company law principle that the corporation is a separate legal entity and is therefore distinct from its members. This starting point, however, does not exist in a legal vacuum, since, practically, the company is a legal fiction and directors and officers are the agents, the ones who exercise the will of the company. Directors control the company's affairs and they know about the company's finances. This has led to numerous legislative provisions that allow directors to be held personally liable for some of the debts of the corporation. Part II of this chapter considers a range of Canadian statutes which impose that liability on directors (see, for example, Janis Sarra and Ronald Davis, *Director and Officer Liability in Corporate Insolvency: A Comprehensive Guide to Rights and Obligations*, 2d ed (Markham: LexisNexis, 2010) at 1–2). Director liability arises for unpaid wages under federal and provincial corporation statutes, as well as under employment standards legislation. Similarly, directors face the prospect of personal liability for unpaid remittances by the corporation of income tax.

When a debtor corporation is in financial distress and the directors engage in conduct that is detrimental to creditors, the directors can be subject to sanctions. See Part III of this chapter for this issue. Under corporate law, directors owe a fiduciary duty to the corporation, to act in the best interests of the corporation. Creditors in Canada have been attempting to expand this duty for years, arguing that the duty should encompass creditors when the corporation is insolvent or in the vicinity of insolvency, as creditors become the residual owners of the corporation at that time. Canada, England, Australia, New Zealand, and the United States have all considered this question, in varying forms. Part III examines how the Supreme Court of Canada addressed that question, as well as what it said about other remedies creditors can use in these circumstances, in *Peoples Department Stores Inc (Trustee of) v Wise (Peoples Department Stores)*. The chapter includes a study of the Canadian oppression remedy and a comparative examination of wrongful or reckless trading statutes found in other jurisdictions. While the parameters of the topic of director liability are wide, this chapter focuses on specific instances of director liability in the context of bankruptcy and insolvency.

II. DIRECTORS' PERSONAL LIABILITY FOR CORPORATE DEBTS

A. Federal Liability Under the *Canada Business Corporations Act*

Under the *Canada Business Corporations Act*, RSC 1985, c C-44 (*CBCA*), directors are held liable for unpaid employee wages. Section 119 holds directors jointly and severally liable to employees of the corporation for the debts not exceeding six months wages payable to each employee for the services performed for the corporation while they were directors. Directors also have a due diligence defence, as in, they will not be liable if they exercised the care, diligence, and skill that a reasonably prudent person would have exercised in comparable circumstances (*CBCA*, s 123(4)).

As noted by L'Heureux-Dubé J in *Barrette v Crabtree Estate*, [1993] 1 SCR 1027 (*Barrette*), below, the remedy against directors for unpaid wages can be traced back to the nineteenth century. Eric Tucker, in "Shareholder and Director Liability for Unpaid Workers' Wages in Canada: From Condition of Granting Limited Liability to Exceptional Remedy" (2008) 26 *Law & History Review* 57 at 58–59 (footnotes omitted), describes the history as follows:

> The recurring demand for wage protection arises from the near universal practice of paying workers in arrears—that is, after they have provided service. As a result, workers become their employers' creditors and bear some risk that they will not be paid. It is clearly unacceptable, however, for workers not to be remunerated for the service they provided: non-payment of wages is a breach of employers' most fundamental contractual obligation to workers. It is a cause of hardship to workers and their dependent family members who, without the cushion of significant savings or accumulations of property, rely on wages to meet their basic needs. . . .
>
> [I]n parts of Canada and the United States the demand for wage protection did not arise to confront a preexisting corporate law, but was present in the process of its creation, needing to be accommodated in the first general incorporation statutes. Numerous Canadian and American legislatures responded to this demand by making shareholder and later director liability for unpaid workers' wages a condition of granting widespread access to the privilege of forming limited liability corporations. Yet within a short time, judicial decision making inverted this understanding of the conditionality of limited liability. It reconstructed limited liability as a basic norm of capitalist legality rather than as an exceptional privilege. In so doing, the courts also transformed the protection of workers' wages from a normative and legal condition of granting corporate investors and managers the privilege of limited liability into an exceptional privilege granted by the state in derogation of the norm of limited liability. Then, on the basis of this inversion, judges narrowly interpreted the scope of director liability for unpaid workers' wages both in relation to who and what was protected.

Employees are a particularly vulnerable group in a bankruptcy, since "[u]nlike other creditors, employees are likely the last to know that a firm is failing. Employees are not able to diversify their credit risk and are unable to switch employers at the first sign of trouble" (Thomas Telfer, "Justice Rand's Commercial Law Legacy: Contracts and Bankruptcy Policies" (2010) 34 *Manitoba Law Journal* 243 at 257). To that end, as L'Heureux-Dubé J notes in *Barrette*, the "primary purpose of the remedy . . . is to protect employees in the event of bankruptcy or insolvency of the corporation" (para 26). Other courts have expressed similar sentiments. The British Columbia Court of Appeal in *Canadian-Automatic Data Processing Services Ltd v Bentley*, 2004 BCCA 408 at para 57, offered the same rationale for director liability in the British Columbia *Employment Standards Act*, RSBC 1996, c 113:

The obligation of corporate directors and officers under the *Employment Standards Act* is a statutory exception to the general rule that the separate legal personality of a corporation insulates principals of the company from liability for its debts. The justification for this exception is the particular vulnerability of employees compared to other creditors.

The provision is typically used when the corporation is experiencing financial difficulty.

On the other hand, the provisions that impose personal liability on directors have typically been seen as an exception to the principle of limited liability. This is likely a misapprehension of the principle of limited liability, but it has not prevented courts from consequently interpreting these types of provisions narrowly. Limited liability is one of the bedrocks of corporate law and courts are jumpy at interfering with it. In *Archibald, Re*, [2000] BCESTD No 134 at para 16, the court maintained,

> [O]ur Court of Appeal and the Supreme Court of Canada have both recognized that the imposition of a personal unpaid wage liability on corporate officers and directors is an extraordinary exception to the general principle that directors and officers are not personally liable for corporate debts. Accordingly, while the *Act* as a whole is to be interpreted in a broad and generous fashion, the provisions imposing a personal liability on corporate directors and officers should be narrowly construed.

In fact, however, the principle of limited liability applies to shareholders in the course of acting as shareholders (*CBCA*, s 45). With regard to directors, it does not apply to provide blanket immunity to them in the course of carrying out their duties to the corporation, but it does apply to exclude them from liability from actions involving breach of the corporation's contracts. Hence, if directors are to be held personally liable for these types of contracts, an explicit provision is necessary. Therefore, section 119 is required if directors are to be held liable for employee wages.

Interpreting these provisions narrowly does not only arise from fear of violating the principle of limited liability; it also arises from other factors. Fear of causing a chilling effect on directors is a significant consideration. Directors may resign once they know a corporation is struggling, fearing personal liability for its debts. The chill can also discourage qualified people from accepting directorships. For general commentary see Bryan Haynes, "Directors' Liability for Termination Pay: Barrette v. Crabtree Estate" (1994) 23:2 *Canadian Business Law Journal* 283; Shafik Bhalloo and Devin Lucas, "Section 96 of the Employment Standards Act: Balancing Competing Interests" (2014) 72 *Advocate* 855.

Barrette v Crabtree Estate, [1993] 1 SCR 1027

L'HEUREUX-DUBÉ J:

[1] This appeal concerns the interpretation of s. 114(1) of the *Canada Business Corporations Act*, SC 1974-75-76, c. 33 ("*C.B.C.A.*") (now s. 119(1) of the *Canada Business Corporations Act*, RSC, 1985, c. C-44). Specifically, the question is whether, under that provision, the directors of a corporation against which employees have obtained a judgment, can be held personally liable for sums of money awarded by a court as pay in lieu of notice of dismissal. . . .

I. Facts

[2] On May 17, 1985 Wabasso Inc. (hereinafter "the corporation") closed its plant at Trois-Rivières after experiencing serious financial difficulties. The appellants, 29 former

managerial employees, were laid off. There being no agreement as to the amount to be paid by the corporation to its managerial employees in lieu of notice of dismissal, the appellants brought an action in the Quebec Superior Court. By judgment dated December 14, 1987, JE 88-416, Laroche J ordered the corporation to pay the appellants $300,358.66 as pay in lieu of notice of dismissal, in addition to the indemnity provided for in art. 1078.1 *C.C.L.C.*

[3] That decision was not appealed.

[4] On January 27, 1988, after the corporation became insolvent, the appellants brought an action in the Court of Quebec pursuant to s. 114(1) *C.B.C.A.* seeking a personal order against the directors of the corporation (the respondents). By judgment dated May 25, 1989 Judge Gagnon allowed the appellants' action and ordered the respondents jointly and severally to pay the appellants the sum of $300,358.66 as well as the additional indemnity provided for in art. 1078.1 *C.C.L.C.*

[5] On April 15, 1991 the Quebec Court of Appeal allowed the respondents' appeal. . . .

[11] The Court of Appeal therefore concluded, unlike the Court of Quebec judge, that the sums awarded by the Superior Court did not fall within the scope of s. 114 *C.B.C.A.*

III. Issue

[12] The only issue in this Court is whether the sums awarded by the Superior Court as pay in lieu of notice of dismissal were "debts . . . for services performed for the corporation" within the meaning of that expression in s. 114(1) *C.B.C.A.* . . .

IV. Analysis

[14] According to the appellants, the rules of statutory interpretation generally give a broad meaning to the word "debts" in s. 114(1) *C.B.C.A.* Thus, by reason of the remedial nature of that provision, a broad and liberal interpretation should be adopted so as to include the amounts awarded by the Superior Court as pay in lieu of notice. The respondents, on the other hand, point out that s. 114(1) *C.B.C.A.* imposes a liability on them that goes beyond what the law ordinarily prescribes, being an exception to the general rule that directors are not liable for a company's debts. The respondents accordingly submit that, given the exceptional nature of directors' personal liability, s. 114(1) *C.B.C.A.* requires instead a strict interpretation. . . .

(B) Origin and Background of Section 114(1) *C.B.C.A.*

(1) New York Legislation
[16] The remedy provided for in s. 114(1) *C.B.C.A.* is based on a New York State law dating from 1848. That statute, *An Act to authorise the formation of corporations for manufacturing, mining, mechanical or chemical purposes, NY Laws 1848*, c. 40, s. 18, provided that shareholders of companies covered by the law "shall be jointly and severally individually liable for all debts that may be due and owing to all their laborers, servants and apprentices, for services performed for such corporation." . . .

(2) Canadian Legislation
[22] Unlike its American precursor, the federal provision at issue here places the liability for certain debts of the corporation to its employees on the shoulders of the directors, rather than on those of the shareholders. Its original wording goes back to the first general legislation dealing with the incorporation of federal companies. Section 49 of the *Canada Joint Stock Companies Letters Patent Act*, 1869, SC 1869, c. 13, read as follows:

"49. The Directors of the Company shall be jointly and severally liable to the laborers, servants and apprentices thereof, for all debts, not exceeding one year's wages, due for services performed for the Company whilst they are such Directors respectively; but no Director shall be liable to an action therefor, unless the Company has been sued therefor within one year after the debt became due, nor yet unless such Director is sued therefor within one year from the time when he ceased to be such Director, nor yet before an execution against the Company has been returned unsatisfied in whole or in part; and the amount due on such execution shall be the amount recoverable with costs against the Directors."

[23] By specifying that the sums paid by one director could be recovered from other directors, the federal statute avoided reproducing one of the flaws inherent in the American provision. Similarly, by placing this liability on the shoulders of directors rather than shareholders, the federal provision avoided the problem of the potential liability of shareholders with small holdings who had no part in the administration of the company. On the other hand, unlike its New York counterpart, the Canadian provision never formulated a specific definition of the amounts covered by the remedy. . . .

[25] Accordingly, the issue in this case is whether, in the absence of a specific definition of the nature of the debts Parliament had in mind, s. 114(1) *C.B.C.A.* applies to amounts awarded by a court as pay in lieu of notice. Parliament places the liability imposed by s. 114(1) *C.B.C.A.* on the shoulders of directors, on the one hand, for the benefit of a particular category of creditors, on the other. While clarifying the context of the remedy, both the case law and the doctrine indicate that these two facets are inseparable from its purpose.

(C) Purpose and Context of the Remedy

[26] The primary purpose of the remedy provided for in s. 114(1) *C.B.C.A.* is to protect employees in the event of bankruptcy or insolvency of the corporation. This protection is part of a range of legislative measures which go far beyond the bounds of company law:

> [TRANSLATION] "According to traditional wisdom, Parliament always was or should have been concerned with protecting employees affected by bankruptcy or insolvency.
>
> This concern to provide protection can take various forms. It can be demonstrated by giving priority to a wage claim against the debtor's assets or against immovable property the value of which was increased by the employee's work, up to the amount of the value added. It can also take the form of providing a preferred claim in the debtor's bankruptcy or in the liquidation of the company.
>
> *In addition to these measures ... the protection of employees can take the form of a remedy against third parties, primarily* the bank which has taken possession of the debtor's assets under s. 178(6) of the *Bank Act*, the beneficiary of an assignment of inventory and *the directors of an insolvent company*." [Emphasis added.]

> (A. Bohémier and A.-M. Poliquin, "Réflexion sur la protection des salariés dans le cadre de la faillite ou de l'insolvabilité" (1988), 48 R du B 75, at p. 81.)

[27] This overview of the general context indicates that the recourse provided for in s. 114(1) *C.B.C.A.* is distinguishable because it is brought against third parties, the directors. The observations of Hall J in *Fee v Turner* (1904), 13 Que. KB 435, clearly summarize the rationale underlying the remedy itself (at p. 446):

"For lack of any other reason it occurs to me that what must have been had in view, was to protect to a limited extent those who were employed by such companies in positions which do not enable them to judge with any special intelligence what is the company's real financial position. The directors have personally this knowledge or should have it, and if, aware of the company's embarrassed affairs, and specially of the danger of a speedy collapse and insolvency, they continue to utilize the services of employees who have no means of securing this knowledge and who give their time and labour upon their sole reliance, often, on the good faith and respectability of the company's directors, it is not inequitable that such directors should be personally liable, within reasonable limits, for arrears of wages, thus given to their service."

[28] Scholarly commentary has endorsed these observations concerning the purpose of the protection inherent in such measures. Thus, distinguishing employees from the corporation's other creditors, Professor Marie-Louis Beaulieu dismisses as follows the argument that directors' liability is penal in nature:

> [TRANSLATION] "And why would this penalty involve requiring them to pay the employees rather than the company's other creditors?
>
> It will perhaps be said that such creditors deserve special consideration by the law: that is very true; and it is more logical to say that Parliament wished to protect the worker and nothing more, to give him a remedial action, a guarantee of payment, in view of his often difficult situation. As he has nothing to do with administration, he should not suffer the consequences of a disaster; he does not speculate, he will be paid for what his work is worth, whatever the company's profits."

("De la responsabilité des directeurs de compagnies pour le salaire des employés" (1930–31), 9 R du D 218 and 483, at p. 220.)

[29] Iacobucci, Pilkington and Prichard similarly justify the protection at issue here by the special vulnerability of employees as compared with other creditors of the corporation:

> This liability is an intrusion on the principle of corporate personality and limited liability, but it can be justified on the grounds that directors who authorize or acquiesce in the continued employment of workers when the corporation is not in a position to pay them should not be able to shift the loss onto the shoulders of the employees. Other creditors who supply goods and services to a failing corporation are not entitled to this kind of preference, but neither are they as dependent on the corporation as employees, nor as vulnerable.

(*Canadian Business Corporations* (1977), at p. 327.) . . .

[31] Section 114(1) *C.B.C.A.* is located within a specific legal framework. In terms of the general principles governing company law, the provision is exceptional in at least three respects. First, the rule departs from the fundamental principle that a corporation's legal personality remains distinct from that of its members. In so doing, s. 114(1) *C.B.C.A.* creates an exception to the more general principle that no one is responsible for the debts of another. Further, unlike other statutory rules which may impose personal liability on directors, s. 114(1) *C.B.C.A.* does not contain an exculpatory clause as such:

> Contrary to the liability resulting from the inappropriate declaration of dividends, inappropriate financial assistance to shareholders and other statutorily created liability of directors, the statutes do not contain any exculpatory availabilities with respect to unpaid

wages: the mere fact of having been a director at the time that the services were rendered by the employee renders the directors jointly and severally liable, provided the various statutory procedural requirements are fulfilled by the employee.

The only possible exculpation, therefore, is proof by the director that he was *not* a director at the time the liability was incurred, that he was not sued within the proper pre-scriptive or statute of limitations period, or that the employee did not fulfil the relevant statutory pre-conditions which give rise to the director's liability. [Emphasis in original.]

(Yoine Goldstein, "Bankruptcy As it Affects Third Parties: Some Aspects," in Meredith Memorial Lectures 1985, *Bankruptcy— Present Problems and Future Perspectives* (1986), 198, at p. 212.)

[32] Finally, the provision in question imposes on directors a positive obligation. This distinguishes it from most statutory rules, which prohibit directors from engaging in certain acts or transactions. As Marc Chabot points out:

[TRANSLATION] In general, the statutory liability of directors involves the prohibition of certain actions. Liability is then associated with a decision which they took at some point on their own initiative. The obligation imposed on them is to avoid certain decisions in certain circumstances. The liability of directors for unpaid wages is perhaps the only case where a positive obligation is imposed on them: they must ensure that wages are paid in the event of bankruptcy or insolvency.

(*La protection des salaires en cas de faillite ou d'insolvabilité* (1985), at p. 91.)

[33] It is against this background that the present appeal must be considered. While its purpose is to ensure that certain sums, including wages, are paid to employees in the event the corporation becomes bankrupt or insolvent, s. 114(1) *C.B.C.A.* constitutes a major exception to the fundamental principles of company law applicable to directors' liability. As we have seen, it also overrides the more general principle that no one is liable for the debts of another.

[34] In this regard, there are two important parameters in connection with the employee's remedy. First, the directors' maximum liability is set at six months' wages. This parameter provides a ceiling which, while establishing a quantitative limit to the liability of the directors, does not in so doing determine the nature of the amounts covered by the action. The nature of the sums which Parliament had in mind must be considered instead from a second angle: regardless of quantum, the amounts claimed must be "debts ... for services performed for the corporation." I therefore cannot subscribe to the appellants' arguments that the first question to be answered is whether the job loss compensation falls within the broad concept of "wages." In the context of s. 114(1) *C.B.C.A.*, the word "wages" refers solely to the quantum of the directors' liability and cannot in itself guide the Court in disposing of the present case.

[35] The parameter which is at the heart of the appeal is therefore not the concept of "wages," but the expression "debts ... for services performed for the corporation." In thus limiting the debts covered by the remedy, Parliament indicated that directors will not be personally liable for all debts assumed by the corporation to its employees. As Beauregard JA pointed out in *Schwartz v Scott*, [[1985] CA 713], at pp. 716–17:

[TRANSLATION] The purpose of this provision is not to make directors liable for all the debts which a corporation may at its option assume more or less retroactively to its employees for past services.

[36] In order to determine whether the amounts awarded as job loss compensation are "debts ... for services performed for the corporation," the nature of pay in lieu of notice of dismissal must therefore be examined in light of this criterion....

[Justice L'Heureux-Dubé noted that where there is an employment contract for an indefinite term, either of the parties may terminate the contract at any time by giving the other party reasonable notice.]

[40] In light of the foregoing, it seems necessary to mention two separate errors made by the lower courts. These relate, first, to the characterization of the amounts awarded by the Superior Court, and second, to the requirements of s. 114(1) C.B.C.A.

[41] After stressing that the notice of dismissal was mandatory and necessary, the trial judge concluded (at p. 12):

> [TRANSLATION] *The notice period is therefore not comparable to damages since its purpose is to minimize the impact of the job loss by allowing the employee to make reasonable advance provision for the effects of dismissal. Reasonable notice of dismissal is therefore an integral part of the employment contract* for an indefinite term, as was the case with the plaintiffs. Accordingly, this debt is associated with the performance of services for the corporation. [Emphasis added.]

[42] With respect, the outcome of the appeal cannot depend simply on whether or not the obligation to give reasonable notice is part of the contract for an indefinite term. First, since the employer's failure to give reasonable notice is a contractual fault, the penalty for that failure must necessarily take the form of contractual damages. Second, as I noted earlier, the purpose of s. 114(1) C.B.C.A. is not to cover all debts assumed by the corporation to its employees. This point cannot be disregarded. Accordingly, the fact that the employer has an obligation under a contract of employment cannot in itself be conclusive for purposes of an action brought by the employee.

[43] On the other hand, the fact that an obligation imposed on the employer is not expressed in specific monetary terms under the law or in the employment contract cannot be a bar to a remedy under s. 114(1) C.B.C.A. By concluding that this provision applied only to a debt [TRANSLATION] "the amount of which is known because the rates are specified in the employment contract (individual or collective, as the case may be) or by law" (p. 1196), the Court of Appeal added a condition that is not found in the wording of the provision. Section 114(1) C.B.C.A. establishes a quantitative limit on the amounts for which directors will be personally liable, and that is a sum equivalent to six months' wages. Directors are therefore in a position to know in advance the maximum amount of their potential liability in the event the company becomes bankrupt or insolvent. For the purposes of the present appeal, it does not seem necessary to dispose of the controversy that may arise as to the interpretation of the word "debts" taken in isolation. I am thus prepared to assume, without deciding, that the amounts payable in lieu of notice of dismissal are "debts" within the meaning of s. 114(1) C.B.C.A. However, the appellants' appeal must fail on another ground.

[44] The term "debts" cannot be dissociated from the context in which it is used. According to the language used by Parliament, the debts must result from "services performed for the corporation." An amount payable in lieu of notice does not flow from services performed for the corporation, but rather from the damage arising from non-performance of a contractual obligation to give sufficient notice. The wrongful breach of the employment relationship by the employer is the cause and basis for the amounts awarded by the Superior Court as pay in lieu of notice. It is primarily for this

reason that the Ontario Court of Appeal has excluded this type of compensation from the scope of s. 114(1) *C.B.C.A.* (see *Mesheau v Campbell*, [(1982), 141 DLR (3d) 155 (Ont CA)], at p. 157, and *Mills-Hughes v Raynor* (1988), 47 D.L.R. (4th) 381, at pp. 386–87). In the absence of additional legislative indicia, the performance of services by the employee remains the cornerstone of the directors' personal liability for debts assumed by the corporation. On the pretext of a broad interpretation, this Court cannot add to the text of the provision words which it does not contain. Taking account of the context in which s. 114(1) *C.B.C.A.* was enacted and the nature of the specific liability which departs from what the law ordinarily prescribes, it seems to me that only one conclusion logically follows. . . .

(E) Conclusion

[49] As with the examination of context surrounding the remedy provided for in s. 114(1) *C.B.CA.*, reference to comparative law makes it clear that the ambiguity of the provision in question should not be resolved by a mechanical application of a given rule of construction. Although the purpose of this provision is to ensure that certain sums are paid to employees in the event that the corporation becomes bankrupt or insolvent, the rule it states cannot be separated from either the legal context or the language in which Parliament has chosen to state the rule. In such circumstances, amounts awarded by a court for damages the basis of which is located, as here, in the non-performance of a contractual obligation and the wrongful breach of a contract of employment by the employer are not "debts . . . for services performed for the corporation" for which the corporation's directors can thus be personally liable.

[50] However much sympathy one may feel for the appellants, who have here been deprived of certain benefits resulting from the contract of employment with their employer, that does not give a court of law the authority to confer on them rights which Parliament did not intend them to have. In the absence of the provision here at issue, the employees would have suffered the same fate as any creditor dealing with an insolvent debtor, in this case the bankrupt employer. The Act provides a remedy, giving them recourse against the directors of the corporation, but it has limited that remedy both in quantity and in duration. Only Parliament is in a position, if it so wishes, to extend these benefits after weighing the consequences of so doing. This, in the final analysis, remains a political choice and cannot be the function of the courts.

Appeal dismissed.

* * * * *

B. Provincial Liability

Directors face liability for unpaid wages under provincial corporations law and/or employment standards legislation. See, for example, *Employment Standards Code*, RSA 2000, c E-9, s 112; *Business Corporations Act*, RSA 2000, c B-9, s 119; *Employment Standards Act, 2000*, SO 2000, c 41, s 81; *Ontario Business Corporations Act*, RSO 1990, c B.16, s 131(1) (*OBCA*); *Employment Standards Act*, RSBC 1996, c 113, ss 87, 96.

In *Canadian-Automatic Data Processing Services Ltd v CEEI Safety & Security Inc* (2004), 246 DLR (4th) 400 at paras 17–21, the Ontario Court of Appeal set out the framework of section 131 of the *OBCA*:

Broadly speaking, s. 131 of the *OBCA* is in the nature of employee protection legislation. The primary purpose of legislation of that nature, which is found in the corporate legislation of the federal government and that of most provinces, is to protect employees in the event of bankruptcy or insolvency of their corporate employers. . . .

Therefore, as with corporate statutes in most other Canadian jurisdictions, s. 131 sets out a legislative framework that enables employees to pursue claims for unpaid wages, not exceeding six months' wages, against the directors of corporate employers. Although s. 131(1) speaks of directors being liable to employees for certain debts payable to a corporation's employees while the directors hold office, the directors are not primarily liable for these debts. The preconditions to a director's liability in s. 131(2) and (3) make it clear that the primary liability for debts to the employees rests with the corporation. . . .

Two conclusions follow from the foregoing discussion. First, without s. 131 of the *OBCA*, an employee would have no remedy against the director of a corporation that has failed to pay his or her wages. Second, a director's liability to an employee for unpaid wages is secondary to that of his or her corporate employer.

. . . [T]he liability of directors under s. 131 of the *OBCA* to pay unpaid wages arises only when such wages are in fact unpaid. This liability arises only when the corporation has defaulted on its primary contractual obligation as an employer to pay its employees' wages.

[In the case below, the court finds that employees' unpaid out-of-pocket expenses constitute a debt of the corporation owed to employees for services they performed for the corporation within the meaning of section 131 of the *OBCA*.]

Proulx v Sahelian Goldfields Inc (2001), 55 OR (3d) 775 (CA)

The judgment of the court was delivered by

BORINS JA:

[1] The only issue in this appeal is the liability of the directors of a corporation to its employees "for all debts not exceeding six months' wages that become due and payable while they are directors for services performed for the corporation" under s. 131(1) of the *Ontario Business Corporations Act*, R.S.O. 1990, c. B.16 ("*OBCA*"). On the employees' motion for partial summary judgment pursuant to rule 20 of the Rules of Civil Procedure, Spence J. held that the directors were liable to reimburse the employees for expenses they incurred on behalf of the corporation in carrying out their contracts of employment with the corporation, which had ceased to operate. The directors have appealed, contending that the Motion Judge erred in his interpretation of s. 131(1) of the *OBCA*. For the reasons that follow, I would dismiss the appeal . . . .

Background

[3] The respondents were hired by Sahelian Goldfields Inc. ("Sahelian") to provide their services at the corporation's mine in West Africa. Typical of the provisions for the remuneration of the employees are those contained in the contract between the respondent Roy and Sahelian:

4. Remuneration

a. You shall be paid an annual salary for your services of Cdn. $10,000 per month. No additional salary shall be payable to you and any vacation pay payable to you shall be included in, and not in addition to, your annual salary. Your annual salary shall be payable on the first day of each month, less any deductions or withholdings required by applicable law.

b.   We shall provide you with the following benefits:
    (i)   return airfare for yourself when you are required to work in Burkina Faso; and
    (ii) life and foreign worker's compensation insurance, together with health and international SOS coverage with Telfer International or such other insurer as we may deem appropriate from time to time; and

c.   We shall provide you with food and lodgings while working overseas for the Company.

7. Expenses—You may be required to travel to various destinations in North America, Europe, and Africa in furtherance of our business. You shall be reimbursed for all reasonable travel and out-of-pocket expenses incurred by you in connection with carrying out these duties. You shall supply us with originals of all invoices or statements for all expenses for which you seek reimbursement. The Company shall also pay for all the costs associated with running your office.

[4] The employees worked for the corporation until it failed and was unable to pay their salaries, their vacation pay, and the expenses they had incurred in carrying out their employment duties, such as air fare and food and lodging while at the mine site. The appellants were directors of Sahelian during all relevant times.

[5] Consequently, the employees commenced an action against Sahelian and its directors to recover unpaid wages, vacation pay, and expenses that they had incurred while performing their employment contracts. Their claim against the directors is based on s. 131(1) of the *OBCA* which provides as follows:

> 131. (1) The directors of a corporation are jointly and severally liable to the employees of the corporation *for all debts not exceeding six months' wages that become payable while they are directors for services performed for the corporation* and for the vacation pay accrued while they are directors for not more than twelve months under the Employment Standards Act, and the regulations thereunder, or under any collective agreement made by the corporation. [Emphasis added.]

[6] Thereafter, the employees moved for partial summary judgment against the directors for a total of $83,527.47 for vacation pay and a total of $60,556.86 for unpaid expenses. Before the Motion Judge, the directors contested their liability for unpaid expenses on the ground that expenses do not constitute wages within the meaning of s. 131(1) of the *OBCA*. The Motion Judge rejected the directors' contention and awarded the employees the amounts claimed for vacation pay and unpaid expenses. . . .

[8] The directors' appeal is limited to the employees' claim for unpaid expenses.

Analysis

[9] Before this Court the directors maintained their contention that they were not liable to pay the employees' unpaid expenses on the ground that the expenses do not constitute wages within the meaning of s. 131(1) of the Act. They focused on the clause "all debts not exceeding six months' wages … for services performed for the corporation," and submitted that as expenses do not constitute wages, they incurred no liability under s. 131(1). As neither debts nor wages are defined in the *OBCA*, they provided a number of definitions of these terms from dictionaries and other legislation which they contended supported their position. In addition, they relied on the decision of the Supreme Court of Canada in *Barrette v Crabtree Estate* (1993), 101 D.L.R. (4th) 66 (S.C.C.). As I will

explain, on the view that I hold of the proper interpretation of s. 131(1) there is no need to determine whether expenses fall within the meaning of wages. This is because expenses which an employee incurs in the course of providing services for a corporation constitute a debt of the corporation for which its directors are liable.

[10] As I will explain, the directors have misconstrued the language of s. 131(1) of the *OBCA*. The issue is not whether the employees' claim for the unpaid expenses constitutes a claim for wages. Rather, the issue is whether their claim for unpaid expenses constitutes a debt for services which they performed for the corporation. Thus, on the facts of this appeal there is no need to determine whether "wages" can include expenses incurred by an employee on behalf of his or her employer.

[11] As Arnup JA pointed out in *Zavitz v Brock* (1974), 3 O.R. (2d) 583 (CA) at 588, the first legislation protecting employees of a corporation whose wages were unpaid, and imposing a limited liability on its directors to pay the wages, was s. 52 of the Ontario *Joint Stock Companies Letters Patent Act*, 1874 (Ont.), c. 35. As such, it is an exception to the principle that normally directors are not liable for the debts of a corporation absent an express statutory provision imposing such liability on them. Significantly, the clause "all debts ... due for services performed for the company" in s. 52 of the 1874 legislation is virtually identical to the clause "all debts ... for services performed for the corporation" in s. 131(1) of the *OBCA*.

[12] A provision similar, but not identical to s. 131(1) of the *OBCA*, imposing liability on directors of federally incorporated corporations for unpaid wages of employees is contained in s. 119 of the *Canada Business Corporations Act*, R.S.C. 1985, c. C-44 ("*CBCA*"). Section 119(1) of the *CBCA* contains language similar to that of s. 131(1) of the *OBCA*, imposing liability for "all debts ... payable to each employee for services performed for the corporation." Both provisions limit the amount of a director's liability to six months' wages. For more than a century, these provisions have been the subject of judicial scrutiny.

[13] In *Zavitz* this Court interpreted s. 73(1) of the *Corporations Act*, R.S.O. 1960, c. 71 which, although somewhat different from s. 131(1) of the *OBCA*, contained the clause "all debts due ... for services performed for the company." From the reasons of Arnup JA it is clear that liability imposed by s. 131(1) is not limited to the unpaid wages of an employee. At p. 590 he stated:

> Some further limited assistance is gained from the fact that the right of a person in the prescribed class to sue is a right to claim "for all debts due ... for services performed for the company, not exceeding six months' wages, and for the vacation pay ..."

[14] In *Mesheau v Campbell* (1982), 39 O.R. (2d) 702 (C.A.) this court interpreted s. 114(1) of the *Canadian Business Corporation Act*, 1975 (Can.), c. 33, which is identical to s. 119(1) of the *CBCA*. At p. 704 Weatherstone JA interpreted s. 114(1) as follows:

> The history of the section and its manifest purpose make it perfectly clear that the words "all debts" are modified by the phrase "for services performed for the corporation" and are subject to the quantitative limit of six months' wages payable to each such employee.

This interpretation was applied in *Mills-Hughes v Raynor* (1988), 47 D.L.R. (4th) 381 (Ont. C.A.).

[15] As I have stated, the appellants relied on the decision of the Supreme Court of Canada in *Barrette* in support of their submission they are not liable for payment of the respondents' expenses. In my view, this reliance is misplaced as the reasons of

L'Heureux-Dubé J. in *Barrette* confirm the interpretation which this Court has placed on s. 131(1) of the *OBCA* and s. 119(1) of the *CBCA* in the cases to which I have referred.

[16] In *Barrette*, as in *Mesheau*, the Supreme Court was required to interpret s. 114(1) of the 1975 Federal Act. The reasons of L'Heureux-Dubé J are instructive ...

[18] At p. 81 L'Heureux-Dubé J stated the following as the two critical factors in defining the remedy provided by the legislation:

> Section 114(1) C.B.C.A. establishes a quantitative limit on the amounts for which directors will be personally liable, and that is a sum equivalent to six months' wages. Directors are therefore in a position to know in advance the maximum amount of their potential liability in the event the company becomes bankrupt or insolvent. ...
>
> In the absence of additional legislative indicia, the performance of services by the employee remains the cornerstone of the director's personal liability for debts assumed by the corporation.

At p. 82 she concluded that "the only bench-mark provided by the wording of s. 114(1) *CBCA* is the performance by the employee of services for the corporation."

[19] In summary, it is clear from the above authorities that under s. 131(1) of the *OBCA* and s. 119(1) of the *CBCA* directors are not liable for all debts owed by a corporation to its employees. Rather, liability will be imposed only where the debts are for "services performed for the corporation." The maximum amount for which a director may be held liable is an amount equivalent to six months wages payable to each employee. Although not relevant to this appeal, I would note that under the *OBCA*, unlike the *CBCA*, a director has an additional liability for up to twelve months vacation pay of each employee.

[20] Based on the foregoing analysis of s. 131(1) it was unnecessary for the Motion Judge to decide whether the employees' unpaid expenses were "properly to be regarded as wages." All that had to be decided was whether the expenses they incurred constituted a debt owed to them for services that they had performed for the corporation. On the uncontested evidence of the employees there is no doubt that the expenses which the employees claimed resulted from the performance of their individual employment contracts with the corporation and were included within the provisions for remuneration contained in the contracts. The expenses constitute a debt of the corporation owing to the employees for services which they had performed for the corporation within the meaning of s. 131(1) of the *OBCA* which the directors are required to pay. Although my analysis differs somewhat from that of the Motion Judge, I am satisfied that he reached the correct result.

Appeal dismissed.

C. Other Legislation to Protect Unpaid Employees

Business corporation statutes and labour standards acts are not the only legislation protecting employees against the prospect of unpaid wages. The *Bank Act*, SC 1991, c 46, ss 210 and 797, subordinates a bank's security interest to the claims of unpaid employees. Under section 427(7) of the *Bank Act*, if the employer becomes bankrupt, "claims for wages, salaries or other remuneration owing in respect of the period of three months immediately preceding the making of the order or assignment, to employees ... have priority over the rights of the bank in a security given to the bank under this section."

See also section 40 of the Ontario *Employment Standards Act, 2000*, SO 2000, c 41, which provides that "[e]very employer shall be deemed to hold vacation pay accruing due to an employee in trust for the employee whether or not the employer has kept the amount for it separate and apart." (Note that section 40(2) of the *Employment Standards Act, 2000* provides that an amount equal to vacation pay becomes a lien and charge on the assets of the employer.) This provision interacts with section 30(7) of the Ontario *Personal Property Security Act*, RSO 1990, c P.10 (*PPSA*). Under section 30(7) of the *PPSA*, "[a] security interest in an account or inventory and its proceeds is subordinate to the interest of a person who is the beneficiary of a deemed trust arising under the *Employment Standards Act*." (Section 30(7) of the *PPSA* also subordinates the interest of a person who is the beneficiary of a deemed trust arising under section 57 of the *Pension Benefits Act*, RSO 1990, c P.8). This deemed trust is upheld under personal property security legislation, as section 30(7) of the Ontario *PPSA* also provides that "a security interest in an account or inventory is subordinate to the interest who is the beneficiary of a deemed trust arising under the Pension Benefits Act." For the status of a *Pension Benefits Act* deemed trust in *CCAA* (*Companies' Creditors Arrangement Act*, RSC 1985, c C-36) proceedings see *Sun Indalex Finance LLC v United Steelworkers*, 2013 SCC 6, discussed in Chapter 13.

Directors also face personal liability under the *Income Tax Act*, RSC 1985, c 1 (5th Supp). Section 153(1) of the *Income Tax Act* imposes a duty on corporations to withhold taxes and other source deductions from an employee's salary. Where the corporation fails to remit such amounts, section 227.1(1) imposes liability on directors for unremitted source deductions. Directors have a section 227.1(3) due diligence defence and will not be liable if they can establish that they "exercised the degree of care, diligence and skill to prevent the failure that a reasonably prudent person would have exercised in comparable circumstances." The Supreme Court of Canada in *Peoples Department Stores* at para 63 concluded that the standard of care of a director should be determined on an objective basis. In *Soper v Canada* (1997), 149 DLR (4th) 297 (FCA), the Federal Court of Appeal explained the rationale for section 227.1 of the *Income Tax Act* as follows:

> Prior to the coming into force of section 227.1 of the Act, the Department of National Revenue faced two related but distinct problems. The first was the non-payment of corporate taxes per se and the second was the non-remittance of taxes that were to be withheld at source on behalf of a third party (e.g. employees). The 1981 recession exacerbated both of these problems. As companies experienced difficult financial times, corporations and directors actively and knowingly sought to avoid the payment of taxes in a variety of ways. For example, some companies allowed themselves to be stripped of their assets by a related entity, and left with an uncollectible I.O.U., with the result that the Crown's claim for unpaid corporate taxes could not be satisfied. Yet other corporations that were short of capital "sold" their unused investment tax credits or scientific research deductions with little concern for whether the company would subsequently be able to fulfil its obligations under the Act. Non-remittance of taxes withheld on behalf of a third party was likewise not uncommon during the recession. Faced with a choice between remitting such amounts to the Crown or drawing on such amounts to pay key creditors whose goods or services were necessary to the continued operation of the business, corporate directors often followed the latter course. Such patent abuse and mismanagement on the part of directors constituted the "mischief" at which section 227.1 was directed.

Directors also face personal liability under section 323 of the *Excise Tax Act*, RSC 1985, c E-15 for failure to remit GST. Section 323(3) also contains a due diligence defence. The

Canada Pension Plan, RSC 1985, c C-8, s 21.1(2) and the *Employment Insurance Act*, SC 1996, c 23, s 83 impose liability on directors for failure to remit the specified amounts. Beyond the above-mentioned statutes, director liability may arise in relation to pensions, environmental obligations, securities law, and criminal law (see Janis Sarra and Ronald Davis, *Director and Officer Liability in Corporate Insolvency: A Comprehensive Guide to Rights and Obligations*, 2d ed (Markham: LexisNexis, 2010)). For a detailed discussion of the provincial statutes, see Sarra & Davis, at 129–174 and Natasha MacParland and Dina Milivojevic, "Director and Officer Issues in Insolvency: 2002–2012" in Janis Sarra, ed, *Annual Review of Insolvency Law 2012* (Toronto: Thomson Carswell, 2013) 37.

D. Bankruptcy Legislation

The *Bankruptcy and Insolvency Act*, RSC 1985, c B-3 (*BIA*) creates a number of bankruptcy offences for directors under section 198. If a corporation commits an offence under section 204, a director who "directed, authorized, assented to, acquiesced in or participated in the commission of the offence" is a party to the offence and is liable to conviction whether or not the corporation has been prosecuted or convicted.

Under *CCAA*, section 5.1, "[a] compromise or arrangement made in respect of a debtor company may include in its terms a provision for the compromise of claims against directors of the company that arose before the commencement of the proceedings under [the *CCAA*]." The compromise of claims against the directors must relate to the "obligations of the company where the directors are by law liable in their capacity as directors for the payment of such obligations." Such compromises of claims against directors are not available where the claim (1) relates to contractual rights of one or more creditors; or (2) where the claim is based on allegations of misrepresentations made by directors to creditors or of wrongful or oppressive conduct by directors. The court has the power under section 5.1(3) to declare that "a claim against directors shall not be compromised if it is satisfied that the compromise would not be fair and reasonable in the circumstances." A similar provision is found in section 50(13) of the *BIA*. The provisions were added in 1997. The Ontario Court of Appeal, in *Metcalfe & Mansfield Alternative Investments II Corp, (Re)*, 2008 ONCA 587 concluded (at para 99):

> The rationale behind these amendments was to encourage directors of an insolvent company to remain in office during a restructuring, rather than resign. The assumption was that by remaining in office the directors would provide some stability while the affairs of the company were being reorganized.

E. Director Protection

Director and officer liability (D&O) insurance may be available to meet some of the claims against directors. Once the company has commenced proceedings under the *CCAA*, a debtor company may make application for an order that all or part of the company's property is subject to a charge in favour of any director or officer to indemnify the director or officer against obligations and liabilities incurred as a director or officer of the company after the commencement of proceedings. The charge will not be available where the debtor company can obtain adequate indemnification insurance for directors and officers at a reasonable charge. Such a charge will not apply to a liability that was incurred as a result of the director's or officer's gross negligence or wilful misconduct. Because the court may order that the charge take priority over other secured claims, the application for the charge must be on notice to secured creditors likely to be affected by the charge.

The concern about the potential adverse incentive effects of directors' personal liability was articulated by the Standing Senate Committee on Banking, Trade and Commerce, *Debtors and Creditors Sharing the Burden: A Review of the* Bankruptcy and Insolvency Act *and the* Companies' Creditors Arrangement Act (Ottawa: Senate, November 2003) (Chair: Hon Richard H Kroft) at 118–20:

> Federal and provincial/territorial statutes expose corporate directors to personal liability for a range of corporate debts, including unpaid wages and taxes. While due diligence and/or good faith reliance defences are available in most cases, directors are subject to absolute liability for some debts, and no defence is possible. Even in the former instances, however, there is some risk.
>
> This liability may dissuade highly competent individuals from becoming corporate directors, and from remaining with the organization during periods of financial difficulty. From this perspective, reduced exposure to personal liability might encourage desirable individuals to accept positions as directors. A high level of personal liability, however, might be supported on the basis that it should lead to highly responsible behaviour by directors in order to reduce their risks....
>
> Our 1996 report *Corporate Governance* recommended incorporating provisions covering directors' liability for wages into the *BIA*, with a due diligence defence. Furthermore, in our 1997 report on Bill C-5, we recommended legislating, in the *BIA*, a generally applicable due diligence defence against personal liability for directors. We continue to support this change, and believe that it is, in essence, a question of fairness and of responsibility. We also hope that such a change might have the desirable effect of increasing the number of competent individuals who wish to serve as directors, since in our June 2003 report *Navigating Through "The Perfect Storm": Safeguards to Restore Investor Confidence* we identified the concern of some about the limited pool of directors in Canada. For this reason, the Committee recommends that: The *Bankruptcy and Insolvency Act* be amended to include a generally applicable due diligence defence against personal liability for directors.

Another reform possibility, known as the exoneration or safe-harbour model, would release directors from specific liabilities that arise within a specific time prior to the commencement of the *BIA* or *CCAA* proceedings. Janis Sarra and Ron Davis suggest that an exoneration model or the creation of a safe-harbour period will remove an important protection for one of the most vulnerable groups in insolvency: employees.

III. SANCTIONS FOR DIRECTOR AND OFFICER CONDUCT DETRIMENTAL TO CREDITORS

A. Directors' Duties and the Interests of Creditors: The Evolution of the Duty

Under the *CBCA*, section 122, and provincial business corporations' legislation, directors have a duty to act "honestly and in good faith with a view to the best interests of the corporation." Directors owe this fiduciary duty to the corporation, not to its stakeholders. Creditors in Canada have been attempting to expand this duty for years, arguing that creditors should be the recipients of this duty when the corporation is insolvent or in the vicinity of insolvency, as they effectively become the owners of the corporation during that time. Other countries have recognized that this duty should be expanded to include creditors, as explained below. The argument was put to the Supreme Court of Canada in the *Peoples Department Stores*, excerpted below, and it was denied, with the Supreme Court finding that the fiduciary duty to the corporation does not change, even when the corporation is insolvent. The Supreme Court also found that any honest and good faith attempt to redress the corporation's financial problems will, "if *unsuccessful … not* qualify as a breach of the statutory fiduciary duty" (para 46, [emphasis added]) and concluded that "[t]he directors' fiduciary duty does not change when a corporation is in the nebulous 'vicinity of insolvency'" (para 46). That phrase has not been defined; moreover, it is incapable of definition and has no legal meaning. Christopher Nicholls, "Liability of Corporate Officers and Directors to Third Parties" (2001) 35 *Canadian Business Law Journal* 1 at 34–35 explains as follows:

> There are several ways of formulating the rationale upon which a director's or officer's duty to a corporation's creditors might be said to be based, at least when a firm is in the vicinity of insolvency … [I]t appears sensible to mandate some duty on the part of the directors to consider the interests of creditors when a corporation is on the verge of insolvency. After all, at that point in a corporation's life only the creditors have a non-trivial economic interest in the corporation. Yet this argument does bring to mind a variation of Zeno's paradox. Before a company becomes insolvent, there must be an earlier moment when it is almost insolvent. Before that moment, there must be still an earlier point in time when the firm is *almost* almost insolvent. And so on. Since the obligations of the firm in insolvency will be to preserve the assets of the corporation, surely such an obligation should also exist the instant before insolvency. Yet, if the obligation arises the instant before insolvency, why, then, not the instant before that? And the instant before that? And so on, back, presumably, to the moment of original incorporation. Perhaps directors *should* owe a duty to creditors from the moment of incorporation, but the supporters of the "vicinity of insolvency" approach do not necessarily argue that such a duty would be necessary or desirable.
>
> A weakness of the "vicinity of insolvency" approach revealed by this paradox is that it tends to minimize the significance of the shift of duties that occurs upon an insolvency. Consider the case of an individual debtor who becomes bankrupt or insolvent. Although we properly forbid all types of fraudulent conveyances or preferences occurring within some period of time prior to such an insolvency, we do not typically forbid an individual to continue a high risk career while approaching insolvency, or even from switching careers from one of low financial risk to one of high financial risk. Similarly, in the case of corporate debtors, while fraudulent conveyances and preferences ought rightly to be prevented, it is not as clear that significant constraints should be placed on (non-fraudulent) business activities undertaken prior to insolvency, notwithstanding that they might involve an assumption of greater risk.

Many aspects of the *Peoples Department Stores* decision have been criticized by legal scholars. See, for example, "Symposium on Supreme Court's Judgment in the Peoples Department Stores Case" (2005) 41 *Canadian Business Law Journal* 167–246. See also Janis Sarra, "Canada's Supreme Court Rules No Fiduciary Obligation Towards Creditors on Insolvency—Peoples Department Stores v. Wise" (2006) 15:1 *International Insolvency Review* 1; Robert Flannigan, "Reshaping the Duties of Directors" (2005) 84 *Canadian Business Review* 365. Another issue in *Peoples Department Stores* was the application of *BIA*, section 100 (the reviewable transactions provision). This aspect is discussed in Chapter 5.

Jacob Ziegel, "Creditors as Corporate Stakeholders: The Quiet Revolution—An Anglo Canadian Perspective" (1993) 43:3 *University of Toronto Law Journal* **511 at 517–18 (footnotes omitted)**

The time-honoured formula for describing directors' duties in British and Canadian company law is that directors must act "honestly and in good faith with a view to the best interests of the corporation." [*CBCA*, s 122(1)(a); *OBCA*, s 134(1)(a)] For more than a century "best interests of the corporation" has been held to mean the interests of shareholders. Creditors were wholly excluded, even when they were bondholders, unless the legislation gave them a specific status in the corporation's decisional machinery. The result was that the directors had no accountability to the company's creditors even where the creditors' stake in the company's fortunes were much larger than the shareholders' stake, as typically is true in many highly leveraged modern businesses.

The directors owed them no fiduciary duties and no prudential rules of care and skill. The directors were completely free to ignore creditors' welfare, subject only to specific prohibitions in the corporate legislation and subject to such restraining rules as were imposed by general tort and contract rules. Even when corporate rules were clearly designed for the protection of creditors—as with respect to rules governing the maintenance of shared capital and the prohibition of financial assistance for the purchase of the company's securities—the creditors had no standing to attack violations; only the shareholders, by bringing a derivative action (an unlikely event), and the company's liquidator on the voluntary or involuntary winding up of the company could do so.

This passive view of creditors' rights changed radically from 1976 onwards, starting with Mason J's judgment in the High Court of Australia in *Walker v Wimborne* [(1976), 50 ALJR 446, at 449], as Australian, New Zealand, and British trial and appellate courts rendered judgments emphasizing that the best interests of the company were not restricted to shareholder interests but included creditors' interests as well. Indeed, we have been told, creditors' interests are pre-eminent if the company is insolvent or close to insolvency at the time of the impugned action or if the proposed action will jeopardize the company's solvency. In several of the cases judgments were actually rendered against directors for breaching this new-found duty to creditors.

Andrew Keay & Hao Zhang, "Incomplete Contracts, Contingent Fiduciaries, and a Director's Duty to Creditors" (2008) 32 *Melbourne University Law Review* **141 at 141–48 (footnotes omitted)**

It is now almost accepted without question, in the courts of a number of common law jurisdictions including Australia and the United Kingdom, that directors of a firm owe a fiduciary duty to their company to consider the interests of creditors ahead of the interests of shareholders when the firm is actually insolvent. But over the years, there has also been a gradual acknowledgement by courts in various jurisdictions that directors owe a fiduciary duty to the company to consider the interests of the company's creditors as well as its shareholders when the firm is short of actual insolvency but near to, or in danger of, it. In the case of *Credit Lyonnais Bank Nederland NV v Pathe Communications Corporation* [1991 WL 277613 (Del. Ch.)] (*"Credit Lyonnais"*), Chancellor Allen of the Delaware Chancery Court ruled that "[a]t least when a corporation is operating in the vicinity of insolvency, a board of directors is not merely the agent of the residue risk bearers [shareholders], but owes its duty to the corporate enterprise [including creditors]."

The Anglo-Australian jurisprudence on this subject can be traced back to the well-known dictum of Mason J of the High Court of Australia in the case of *Walker v Wimborne* [(1976), 50 ALJR 446] (*"Walker"*) in 1976. His Honour said [at 449]:

In this respect it should be emphasized that the directors of a company in discharging their duty to the company must take account of the interest of its shareholders and its creditors. Any failure by the directors to take into account the interests of creditors will have adverse consequences for the company as well as for them.

Later, in something of a controversial judgment, Lord Templeman in the House of Lords' decision in *Winkworth v Edward Baron Development Co Ltd* [[1987] 1 All ER 114] (*"Winkworth"*) said [at 118]:

A duty is owed by the directors to the company and to the creditors of the company to ensure that the affairs of the company are properly administered and that its property is not dissipated or exploited for the benefit of the directors themselves to the prejudice of the creditors.

All three judges recognised that when a company is in financial difficulty, some element of obligation is owed to creditors by directors at some point. . . .

The reason given for the shift to consider creditor interests either along with, or in substitution for, shareholder interests is the gradual realisation that if the company is insolvent, in the vicinity of insolvency or embarking on a venture which it cannot sustain without relying totally on creditor funds, "the interests of the company are in reality the interests of existing creditors alone." At this time, the shareholders are no longer the owners of the residual value of the firm as they have been usurped by the creditors, whose rights are transformed into equity-like rights. Thus, the directors are effectively playing with the creditors' money, which means that the creditors may instead be seen as the major stakeholders in the company. . . .

Perhaps the most severe damage that has been done in relation to the concept of a direct duty has been in Australia and Canada, where the highest courts in both jurisdictions have rejected a direct duty. For the first time since *Walker*, the Australian High Court had an opportunity to consider the issue in *Spies v The Queen* [(2000) 201 CLR 603] (*"Spies"*). However, the case did not turn on whether directors owed a responsibility to creditors and what the Court had to say on the topic only constituted dicta at best. The Court denied, clearly, that directors owe an independent duty to creditors. The same result occurred in *Peoples Department Stores Inc. (Trustee of) v Wise* (*"Peoples Department Stores"*) [see extract below].

[Reprinted by permission of the publisher.]

Peoples Department Stores Inc (Trustee of) v Wise, 2004 SCC 68, [2004] 3 SCR 461

MAJOR and DESCHAMPS JJ:

I. Introduction

[1] The principal question raised by this appeal is whether directors of a corporation owe a fiduciary duty to the corporation's creditors comparable to the statutory duty owed to the corporation. For the reasons that follow, we conclude that directors owe a duty of care to creditors, but that duty does not rise to a fiduciary duty. We agree with the disposition of the Quebec Court of Appeal. The appeal is therefore dismissed.

[2] As a result of the demise in the mid-1990s of two major retail chains in eastern Canada, Wise Stores Inc. ("Wise") and its wholly-owned subsidiary, Peoples Department Stores Inc. ("Peoples"), the indebtedness of a number of Peoples' creditors went

unsatisfied. In the wake of the failure of the two chains, Caron Bélanger Ernst & Young Inc., Peoples' trustee in bankruptcy (the "trustee"), brought an action against the directors of Peoples. To address the trustee's claims, the extent of the duties imposed by s. 122(1) of the *Canada Business Corporations Act*, RSC 1985, c. C-44 ("*CBCA*"), upon directors with respect to creditors must be determined ....

[3] In our view, it has not been established that the directors of Peoples violated either the fiduciary duty or the duty of care imposed by s. 122(1) of the *CBCA*. ...

II. Background

[Wise Stores Inc (Wise) operated clothing stores mainly in urban Quebec. Wise was controlled by the three Wise brothers. Peoples Department Stores Inc (Peoples) operated stores in rural areas from Ontario to Newfoundland and Labrador. Peoples experienced financial difficulties posting annual losses of $10 million. In 1992, Wise acquired Peoples from Marks & Spencer Canada Inc for a purchase price of $27 million. The agreement provided that $5 million was payable at the closing of the transaction, while the balance of the transaction was payable in installments over an eight-year period. The initial $5 million payment was financed by TD Bank. The Supreme Court described the sale as a "fully leveraged buyout." The agreement prohibited Wise from merging with Peoples prior to the complete payment of the purchase price. The agreement also precluded Peoples from providing financial assistance to Wise. However, in 1993, as a result of a corporate reorganization, Peoples became a subsidiary directly owned and controlled by Wise. The three Wise brothers became Peoples' only directors.

After the amalgamation, Wise sought to consolidate the operations of Wise and Peoples to maximize profits. Wise gradually merged operations and head office services with Peoples. By 1993, there was a consolidation of administration, advertising, and purchasing departments of Peoples and Wise. However, the expected benefits of the consolidation of operations did not arise. The merger of shipping, receiving, and storage activities created a number of difficulties, often leading to the misdirection of inventory to the wrong store. This resulted in incorrect inventory records for each company. In October 1993, the Wise brothers, in response to the numerous problems, approved a new domestic joint inventory procurement system that had been recommended by the vice president of Wise. The new system integrated the inventory management for Wise and Peoples as if the two entities comprised a single company operating 125 stores. Under the new system, Wise would make all purchases from overseas suppliers. Peoples assumed responsibility for all purchases of North American inventory for the two companies. Peoples in turn charged Wise for any inventory transferred to Wise. The new policy exposed Peoples to substantial debt, particularly when Wise did not pay Peoples for the inventory. Approximately 82 percent of the total inventory of the two companies was purchased from North American suppliers. The directors were aware of the new policy but it was never established in writing or approved by a formal board meeting or resolution. In January 1995, Wise and Peoples were declared bankrupt.]

[25] Following the bankruptcy, Peoples' trustee filed a petition against the Wise brothers. In the petition, the trustee claimed that they had favoured the interests of Wise over Peoples to the detriment of Peoples' creditors, in breach of their duties as directors under s. 122(1) of the *CBCA*. ...

[27] The trial judge, Greenberg J, relying on decisions from the United Kingdom, Australia and New Zealand, held that the fiduciary duty and the duty of care under

s. 122(1) of the *CBCA* extend to a company's creditors when a company is insolvent or in the vicinity of insolvency. Greenberg J found that the implementation, by the Wise brothers qua directors of Peoples, of a corporate policy that affected both companies, had occurred while the corporation was in the vicinity of insolvency and was detrimental to the interests of the creditors of Peoples. The Wise brothers were therefore found liable and the trustee was awarded $4.44 million in damages. . . .

[28] The Quebec Court of Appeal . . . allowed the appeals by Chubb and the Wise brothers. The Court of Appeal expressed reluctance to follow Greenberg J in equating the interests of creditors with the best interests of the corporation when the corporation was insolvent or in the vicinity of insolvency, stating that an innovation in the law such as this is a policy matter more appropriately dealt with by Parliament than the courts. . . .

III. Analysis

. . .

[30] . . . This case came before our Court on the issue of whether directors owe a duty to creditors. The creditors did not bring a derivative action or an oppression remedy application under the *CBCA*. Instead, the trustee, representing the interests of the creditors, sued the directors for an alleged breach of the duties imposed by s. 122(1) of the *CBCA*. The standing of the trustee to sue was not questioned. . . .

[32] Subsection 122(1) of the *CBCA* establishes two distinct duties to be discharged by directors and officers in managing, or supervising the management of, the corporation:

122 (1) Every director and officer of a corporation in exercising their powers and discharging their duties shall

(a) act honestly and in good faith with a view to the best interests of the corporation; and

(b) exercise the care, diligence and skill that a reasonably prudent person would exercise in comparable circumstances.

The first duty has been referred to in this case as the "fiduciary duty." It is better described as the "duty of loyalty." We will use the expression "statutory fiduciary duty" for purposes of clarity when referring to the duty under the *CBCA*. This duty requires directors and officers to act honestly and in good faith with a view to the best interests of the corporation. The second duty is commonly referred to as the "duty of care." Generally speaking, it imposes a legal obligation upon directors and officers to be diligent in supervising and managing the corporation's affairs.

[33] The trial judge did not apply or consider separately the two duties imposed on directors by s. 122(1). As the Court of Appeal observed, the trial judge appears to have confused the two duties. They are, in fact, distinct and are designed to secure different ends. For that reason, they will be addressed separately in these reasons.

A. The Statutory Fiduciary Duty: Section 122(1)(a) of the *CBCA*

[34] Considerable power over the deployment and management of financial, human, and material resources is vested in the directors and officers of corporations. For the directors of *CBCA* corporations, this power originates in s. 102 of the Act. For officers, this power comes from the powers delegated to them by the directors. In deciding to invest in, lend to or otherwise deal with a corporation, shareholders and creditors transfer control over their assets to the corporation, and hence to the directors and officers, in the expectation that the directors and officers will use the corporation's resources to make reasonable business decisions that are to the corporation's advantage.

[35] The statutory fiduciary duty requires directors and officers to act honestly and in good faith *vis-à-vis* the corporation. They must respect the trust and confidence that have been reposed in them to manage the assets of the corporation in pursuit of the realization of the objects of the corporation. They must avoid conflicts of interest with the corporation. They must avoid abusing their position to gain personal benefit. They must maintain the confidentiality of information they acquire by virtue of their position. Directors and officers must serve the corporation selflessly, honestly and loyally: see K.P. McGuinness, *The Law and Practice of Canadian Business Corporations* (1999), at p. 715. . . .

[37] The issue to be considered here is the "specific substance" of the fiduciary duty based on the relationship of directors to corporations under the *CBCA*.

[38] It is settled law that the fiduciary duty owed by directors and officers imposes strict obligations: see *Canadian Aero Service Ltd v O'Malley* (1973), [1974] SCR 592 (SCC), at pp. 609–10, *per* Laskin J (as he then was), where it was decided that directors and officers may even have to account to the corporation for profits they make that do not come at the corporation's expense. . . .

[39] However, it is not required that directors and officers in all cases avoid personal gain as a direct or indirect result of their honest and good faith supervision or management of the corporation. In many cases the interests of directors and officers will innocently and genuinely coincide with those of the corporation. If directors and officers are also shareholders, as is often the case, their lot will automatically improve as the corporation's financial condition improves. Another example is the compensation that directors and officers usually draw from the corporations they serve. This benefit, though paid by the corporation, does not, if reasonable, ordinarily place them in breach of their fiduciary duty. Therefore, all the circumstances may be scrutinized to determine whether the directors and officers have acted honestly and in good faith with a view to the best interests of the corporation.

[40] In our opinion, the trial judge's determination that there was no fraud or dishonesty in the Wise brothers' attempts to solve the mounting inventory problems of Peoples and Wise stands in the way of a finding that they breached their fiduciary duty. . . .

[41] As explained above, there is no doubt that both Peoples and Wise were struggling with a serious inventory management problem. The Wise brothers considered the problem and implemented a policy they hoped would solve it. In the absence of evidence of a personal interest or improper purpose in the new policy, and in light of the evidence of a desire to make both Wise and Peoples "better" corporations, we find that the directors did not breach their fiduciary duty under s. 122(1)(a) of the *CBCA*. See *820099 Ontario Inc v Harold E Ballard Ltd* (1991), 3 BLR (2d) 123 (Ont. Gen. Div.) (aff'd. (1991), 3 BLR (2d) 113 (Ont. Div. Ct.)), in which Farley J, at p. 171, correctly observes that in resolving a conflict between majority and minority shareholders, it is safe for directors and officers to act to make the corporation a "better corporation."

[42] This appeal does not relate to the non-statutory duty directors owe to shareholders. It is concerned only with the statutory duties owed under the *CBCA*. Insofar as the statutory fiduciary duty is concerned, it is clear that the phrase the "best interests of the corporation" should be read not simply as the "best interests of the shareholders." From an economic perspective, the "best interests of the corporation" means the maximization of the value of the corporation: see E.M. Iacobucci, "Directors' Duties in Insolvency: Clarifying What Is at Stake" (2003), 39(3) *Can. Bus. LJ* 398, at pp. 400–1. However, the courts have long recognized that various other factors may be relevant in determining

what directors should consider in soundly managing with a view to the best interests of the corporation. For example, in *Teck Corp v Millar* (1972), 33 D.L.R. (3d) 288 (B.C.S.C.), Berger J stated, at p. 314:

> A classical theory that once was unchallengeable must yield to the facts of modern life. In fact, of course, it has. If today the directors of a company were to consider the interests of its employees no one would argue that in doing so they were not acting *bona fide* in the interests of the company itself. Similarly, if the directors were to consider the consequences to the community of any policy that the company intended to pursue, and were deflected in their commitment to that policy as a result, it could not be said that they had not considered bona fide the interests of the shareholders.
>
> I appreciate that it would be a breach of their duty for directors to disregard entirely the interests of a company's shareholders in order to confer a benefit on its employees: *Parke v. Daily News Ltd.*, [1962] Ch. 927. But if they observe a decent respect for other interests lying beyond those of the company's shareholders in the strict sense, that will not, in my view, leave directors open to the charge that they have failed in their fiduciary duty to the company.

The case of *Re Olympia & York Enterprises Ltd and Hiram Walker Resources Ltd* (1986), 59 O.R. (2d) 254 (Div. Ct.), approved, at p. 271, the decision in *Teck, supra.* We accept as an accurate statement of law that in determining whether they are acting with a view to the best interests of the corporation it may be legitimate, given all the circumstances of a given case, for the board of directors to consider, inter alia, the interests of shareholders, employees, suppliers, creditors, consumers, governments and the environment.

[43] The various shifts in interests that naturally occur as a corporation's fortunes rise and fall do not, however, affect the content of the fiduciary duty under s. 122(1)(a) of the *CBCA*. At all times, directors and officers owe their fiduciary obligation to the corporation. The interests of the corporation are not to be confused with the interests of the creditors or those of any other stakeholders.

[44] The interests of shareholders, those of the creditors and those of the corporation may and will be consistent with each other if the corporation is profitable and well capitalized and has strong prospects. However, this can change if the corporation starts to struggle financially. The residual rights of the shareholders will generally become worthless if a corporation is declared bankrupt. Upon bankruptcy, the directors of the corporation transfer control to a trustee, who administers the corporation's assets for the benefit of creditors.

[45] Short of bankruptcy, as the corporation approaches what has been described as the "vicinity of insolvency," the residual claims of shareholders will be nearly exhausted. While shareholders might well prefer that the directors pursue high-risk alternatives with a high potential payoff to maximize the shareholders' expected residual claim, creditors in the same circumstances might prefer that the directors steer a safer course so as to maximize the value of their claims against the assets of the corporation.

[46] The directors' fiduciary duty does not change when a corporation is in the nebulous "vicinity of insolvency." That phrase has not been defined; moreover, it is incapable of definition and has no legal meaning. What it is obviously intended to convey is a deterioration in the corporation's financial stability. In assessing the actions of directors it is evident that any honest and good faith attempt to redress the corporation's financial problems will, if successful, both retain value for shareholders and improve the position of creditors. If unsuccessful, it will not qualify as a breach of the statutory fiduciary duty.

[47] For a discussion of the shifting interests and incentives of shareholders and creditors, see W.D. Gray, "*Peoples v Wise* and *Dylex*: Identifying Stakeholder Interests upon or near Corporate Insolvency—Stasis or Pragmatism?" (2003), 39 *Can. Bus. L.J.* 242, at p. 257; E.M. Iacobucci & K.E. Davis, "Reconciling Derivative Claims and the Oppression Remedy" (2000), 12 *S.C.L.R.* (2d) 87, at p. 114. In resolving these competing interests, it is incumbent upon the directors to act honestly and in good faith with a view to the best interests of the corporation. In using their skills for the benefit of the corporation when it is in troubled waters financially, the directors must be careful to attempt to act in its best interests by creating a "better" corporation, and not to favour the interests of any one group of stakeholders. If the stakeholders cannot avail themselves of the statutory fiduciary duty (the duty of loyalty, *supra*) to sue the directors for failing to take care of their interests, they have other means at their disposal.

[48] The Canadian legal landscape with respect to stakeholders is unique. Creditors are only one set of stakeholders, but their interests are protected in a number of ways .... The oppression remedy of s. 241(2)(c) of the *CBCA* and the similar provisions of provincial legislation regarding corporations grant the broadest rights to creditors of any common law jurisdiction: see D. Thomson, "Directors, Creditors and Insolvency: A Fiduciary Duty or a Duty Not to Oppress?" (2000), 58(1) *U.T. Fac. L. Rev.* 31, at p. 48. One commentator describes the oppression remedy as "the broadest, most comprehensive and most open-ended shareholder remedy in the common law world": S.M. Beck, "Minority Shareholders' Rights in the 1980s" in *Corporate Law in the 80s* (1982), 311, at p. 312. While Beck was concerned with shareholder remedies, his observation applies equally to those of creditors.

[49] The fact that creditors' interests increase in relevancy as a corporation's finances deteriorate is apt to be relevant to, *inter alia*, the exercise of discretion by a court in granting standing to a party as a "complainant" under s. 238(d) of the *CBCA* as a "proper person" to bring a derivative action in the name of the corporation under ss. 239 and 240 of the *CBCA*, or to bring an oppression remedy claim under s. 241 of the *CBCA*.

[50] Section 241(2)(c) authorizes a court to grant a remedy if

> (c) the powers of the directors of the corporation or any of its affiliates are or have been exercised in a manner that is oppressive or unfairly prejudicial to or that unfairly disregards the interests of any security holder, creditor, director or officer ....

A person applying for the oppression remedy must, in the court's opinion, fall within the definition of "complainant" found in s. 238 of the *CBCA*: ...

> (d) any other person who, in the discretion of a court, is a proper person to make an application under this Part.

Creditors, who are not security holders within the meaning of para. (a), may therefore apply for the oppression remedy under para. (d) by asking a court to exercise its discretion and grant them status as a "complainant."

[51] Section 241 of the *CBCA* provides a possible mechanism for creditors to protect their interests from the prejudicial conduct of directors. In our view, the availability of such a broad oppression remedy undermines any perceived need to extend the fiduciary duty imposed on directors by s. 122(1)(a) of the *CBCA* to include creditors....

[53] In light of the availability both of the oppression remedy and of an action based on the duty of care, which will be discussed below, stakeholders have viable remedies at their disposal. There is no need to read the interests of creditors into the duty set out in

s. 122(1)(a) of the *CBCA*. Moreover, in the circumstances of this case, the Wise brothers did not breach the statutory fiduciary duty owed to the corporation.

B. The Statutory Duty of Care: Section 122(1)(b) of the *CBCA*

. . .

[57] ... Indeed, unlike the statement of the fiduciary duty in s. 122(1)(a) of the *CBCA*, which specifies that directors and officers must act with a view to the best interests of the corporation, the statement of the duty of care in s. 122(1)(b) of the *CBCA* does not specifically refer to an identifiable party as the beneficiary of the duty. Instead, it provides that "[e]very director and officer of a corporation in exercising his powers and discharging his duties shall ... exercise the care, diligence and skill that a reasonably prudent person would exercise in comparable circumstances." Thus, the identity of the beneficiary of the duty of care is much more open-ended, and it appears obvious that it must include creditors. ...

[59] That directors must satisfy a duty of care is a long-standing principle of the common law, although the duty of care has been reinforced by statute to become more demanding. Among the earliest English cases establishing the duty of care were *Dovey v Cory*, [1901] A.C. 477 (H.L.); *Brazilian Rubber Plantation & Estates Ltd, Re*, [1911] 1 Ch. 425 (C.A.); and *City Equitable Fire Insurance Co, Re* (1924), [1925] 1 Ch. 407 (C.A.). In substance, these cases held that the standard of care was a reasonably relaxed, subjective standard. The common law required directors to avoid being grossly negligent with respect to the affairs of the corporation and judged them according to their own personal skills, knowledge, abilities and capacities. See McGuinness, *supra*, at p. 776: "Given the history of case law in this area, and the prevailing standards of competence displayed in commerce generally, it is quite clear that directors were not expected at common law to have any particular business skill or judgment." ...

[63] The standard of care embodied in s. 122(1)(b) of the *CBCA* was described by Robertson JA of the Federal Court of Appeal in *Soper v Canada* (1997), [1998] 1 F.C. 124 (at para. 41, as being "objective subjective." Although that case concerned the interpretation of a provision of the *Income Tax Act*, it is relevant here because the language of the provision establishing the standard of care was identical to that of s. 122(1)(b) of the *CBCA*. With respect, we feel that Robertson JA's characterization of the standard as an "objective subjective" one could lead to confusion. We prefer to describe it as an objective standard. To say that the standard is objective makes it clear that the factual aspects of the circumstances surrounding the actions of the director or officer are important in the case of the s. 122(1)(b) duty of care, as opposed to the subjective motivation of the director or officer, which is the central focus of the statutory fiduciary duty of s. 122(1)(a) of the *CBCA*.

[64] The contextual approach dictated by s. 122(1)(b) of the *CBCA* not only emphasizes the primary facts but also permits prevailing socio-economic conditions to be taken into consideration. The emergence of stricter standards puts pressure on corporations to improve the quality of board decisions. The establishment of good corporate governance rules should be a shield that protects directors from allegations that they have breached their duty of care. However, even with good corporate governance rules, directors' decisions can still be open to criticism from outsiders. Canadian courts, like their counterparts in the United States, the United Kingdom, Australia and New Zealand, have tended to take an approach with respect to the enforcement of the duty of care that respects the fact that directors and officers often have business expertise that courts

do not. Many decisions made in the course of business, although ultimately unsuccessful, are reasonable and defensible at the time they are made. Business decisions must sometimes be made, with high stakes and under considerable time pressure, in circumstances in which detailed information is not available. It might be tempting for some to see unsuccessful business decisions as unreasonable or imprudent in light of information that becomes available *ex post facto*. Because of this risk of hindsight bias, Canadian courts have developed a rule of deference to business decisions called the "business judgment rule," adopting the American name for the rule.

[65] In *Maple Leaf Foods Inc v Schneider Corp* (1998), 42 O.R. (3d) 177, Weiler JA stated, at p. 192:

> The law as it has evolved in Ontario and Delaware has the common requirements that the court must be satisfied that the directors have acted reasonably and fairly. The court looks to see that the directors made a reasonable decision not a perfect decision. Provided the decision taken is within a range of reasonableness, the court ought not to substitute its opinion for that of the board even though subsequent events may have cast doubt on the board's determination. As long as the directors have selected one of several reasonable alternatives, deference is accorded to the board's decision. This formulation of deference to the decision of the Board is known as the "business judgment rule." The fact that alternative transactions were rejected by the directors is irrelevant unless it can be shown that a particular alternative was definitely available and clearly more beneficial to the company than the chosen transaction [reference omitted]. [Underlining added; italics in original]

[66] In order for a plaintiff to succeed in challenging a business decision he or she has to establish that the directors acted (i) in breach of the duty of care and (ii) in a way that caused injury to the plaintiff: W.T. Allen, J.B. Jacobs, and L.E. Strine, Jr., "Function Over Form: A Reassessment of Standards of Review in Delaware Corporation Law" (2001), 26 *Del. J. Corp. L* 859, at p. 892.

[67] Directors and officers will not be held to be in breach of the duty of care under s. 122(1)(b) of the *CBCA* if they act prudently and on a reasonably informed basis. The decisions they make must be reasonable business decisions in light of all the circumstances about which the directors or officers knew or ought to have known. In determining whether directors have acted in a manner that breached the duty of care, it is worth repeating that perfection is not demanded. Courts are ill-suited and should be reluctant to second-guess the application of business expertise to the considerations that are involved in corporate decision making, but they are capable, on the facts of any case, of determining whether an appropriate degree of prudence and diligence was brought to bear in reaching what is claimed to be a reasonable business decision at the time it was made.

[68] The trustee alleges that the Wise brothers breached their duty of care under s. 122(1)(b) of the *CBCA* by implementing the new procurement policy to the detriment of Peoples' creditors. After considering all the evidence, we agree with the Court of Appeal that the implementation of the new policy was a reasonable business decision that was made with a view to rectifying a serious and urgent business problem in circumstances in which no solution may have been possible. The trial judge's conclusion that the new policy led inexorably to Peoples' failure and bankruptcy was factually incorrect and constituted a palpable and overriding error.

[69] In fact, as noted by Pelletier JA, there were many factors other than the new policy that contributed more directly to Peoples' bankruptcy. Peoples had lost $10 million annually while being operated by M & S. Wise, which was only marginally profitable

and solvent with annual sales of $100 million (versus $160 million for Peoples), had hoped to improve the performance of its new acquisition. Given that the transaction was a fully leveraged buyout, for Wise and Peoples to succeed, Peoples' performance needed to improve dramatically. Unfortunately for both Wise and Peoples, the retail market in eastern Canada had become very competitive in the early 1990s, and this trend continued with the arrival of Wal-Mart in 1994. . . .

[70] The Wise brothers treated the implementation of the new policy as a decision made in the ordinary course of business and, while no formal agreement evidenced the arrangement, a monthly record was made of the inventory transfers. Although this may appear to be a loose business practice, by the autumn of 1993, Wise had already consolidated several aspects of the operations of the two companies. Legally they were two separate entities. However, the financial fate of the two companies had become intertwined. In these circumstances, there was little or no economic incentive for the Wise brothers to jeopardize the interests of Peoples in favour of the interests of Wise. In fact, given the tax losses that Peoples had carried forward, the companies had every incentive to keep Peoples profitable in order to reduce their combined tax liabilities.

[71] Arguably, the Wise brothers could have been more precise in pursuing a resolution to the intractable inventory management problems, having regard to all the troublesome circumstances involved at the time the new policy was implemented. But we, like the Court of Appeal, are not satisfied that the adoption of the new policy breached the duty of care under s. 122(1)(b) of the *CBCA*. The directors cannot be held liable for a breach of their duty of care in respect of the creditors of Peoples. . . .

Appeal dismissed.

BAE-Newplan Group Limited v Dalton, 2012 NLCA 21, 321 Nfld & PEIR 152

WELSH JA:

[1] BAE-Newplan filed a statement of claim naming, among others, the directors of three companies as defendants. On applications by the directors, the Trial Division judge struck out portions of the statement of claim as against some of the defendant directors on the basis that the pleadings do not disclose a reasonable cause of action. The issues raised in the appeal and cross-appeals relate to whether the defendant directors are proper parties against whom BAE-Newplan may have a claim for monies owing as a result of work done pursuant to a contract with one of the companies. The possible liability of directors at common law and under the *Corporations Act* is considered in the context of striking portions of a statement of claim as against a defendant and removing a defendant who is not a proper party . . . .

BACKGROUND

[2] Newfoundland and Labrador Refining Corporation ("NLRC") contracted with BAE-Newplan for engineering services in relation to an oil refinery development project. Between June 2007 and February 2008, BAE-Newplan invoiced NLRC for services provided under the contract, and was paid on a monthly basis an amount totaling approximately $14,500,000. However, the company alleges that a balance of approximately $20,600,000 remains unpaid for work done during latter months when NLRC ceased making the required monthly payments. In June 2008, NLRC was petitioned into bankruptcy and, therefore, is not named as a defendant in these proceedings.

[3] The statement of claim sets out claims by BAE-Newplan against two companies, Altius Minerals Corporation and Altius Resources Inc. (first and second defendants), as well as Brian Dalton (third defendant), and the directors, including Brian Dalton, of NLRC and the two Altius companies (fourth, fifth and sixth defendants). The Altius companies and their directors are sued based on their relationship to NLRC. The applications on appeal to this Court relate only to the fourth, fifth and sixth defendants, that is, the directors of the three companies.

[4] NLRC was established as "a development-stage equity investment company to assess the feasibility of building an oil refinery in Placentia Bay, Newfoundland and Labrador" (decision of the applications judge, 2010 NLTD(G) 133, 301 Nfld. & P.E.I.R. 214, at paragraph 2). Altius Minerals Corporation is the parent company of, and holds all the voting shares in, Altius Resources Inc. which, in turn, is a significant, but minority shareholder in NLRC. The Altius companies, as a single entity, along with three European entrepreneurs provided equity financing for the project and are shareholders in NLRC. In October 2007, the three European entrepreneurs ceased providing funding. As a result, NLRC encountered some difficulty in meeting its financial obligations. However, there was other money available to NLRC from a share offering and an anticipated loan. In December 2007, "Altius Minerals took $30,092,865.00 of the November 2007 share offering proceeds and advanced it to NLRC as debt financing, to be used by NLRC to make a milestone payment to IJK Consortium to secure the heavy walled vessels fabrication contract" (paragraph 81 of the statement of claim). In addition, "[t]hroughout the latter part of 2007, Dalton, Altius Minerals, Altius Resources and NLRC had been negotiating with a US finance company specializing in construction project component financing, with a view to securing specific asset backed bridge finance funding to secure the IJK contract until such time as the capital finance funding for the project construction was in place" (paragraph 83 of the statement of claim). The bridge financing was not expected to be in place until at least February 2008. BAE-Newplan claims that monies that should have been used to pay for its contract were misdirected to the IJK contract, and that it should have been advised when the European entrepreneurs ceased providing funding.

[5] The claims against the directors set out in the statement of claim are based on allegations of oppression, breach of duty of care, negligent misrepresentation and deceit. Prior to filing statements of defence, the directors of NLRC and the Altius companies brought applications to be removed as parties pursuant to rule 7.04, or, in the alternative, to have the statement of claim struck out as against them under rule 14.24 on the basis that the pleadings do not disclose a reasonable cause of action ....

The Appeal

Statement of Claim — Context for the Analysis

[18] The applications judge summarized the foundation on which BAE-Newplan proceeded:

> [49] ... The basis of these allegations from my reading of [BAE-Newplan's] pleadings appears to be focused as follows:
>
> 1) That the directors of NLRC and the Altius companies represented to [BAE-Newplan] that NLRC was able to make its payment obligations based upon committed pre-development funding from the equity investment partners;

2) That the directors of NLRC and the Altius companies remained silent and did not inform [BAE-Newplan] when the European investors decided to no longer provide pre-development investment funding to NLRC in December 2007, meaning NLRC was insolvent at that time, while at the same time authorizing further work at an accelerated level by [BAE-Newplan]; and

3) That the directors of NLRC and the Altius companies improperly and without notice to [BAE-Newplan] diverted funds, raised for the purpose of meeting pre-development costs incurred by NLRC, to the vessel development contract.

[50] Specifically with regard to the directors of NLRC and the Altius companies, the Second Amended Statement of Claim indicates as follows:

1) At paragraph 47: That they represented to [BAE-Newplan], directly or indirectly, by words and conduct, that NLRC was able to meet its financial obligations for pre-development work on the project through committed incremental equity financing from the equity investment partners;

2) At various paragraphs: That Brian Dalton, the Project Director and/or Roland Butler, represented various things to [BAE-Newplan] on behalf of each of the Defendants, including the directors of NLRC and the Altius companies and that the directors authorized, condoned and approved of these representations;

3) At paragraph 54: That each of the directors knew or ought to have known that the representations were made to induce [BAE-Newplan] to perform its services pursuant to its contract with NLRC;

4) At paragraph 80: That each of the directors of the Altius companies decided that Altius Minerals and Altius Resources would no longer provide pre-development financing by December, 2007 and failed to disclose this to [BAE-Newplan]; and

5) At paragraph 86: That each Defendant, including the directors of NLRC and the Altius companies, decided to allocate a portion of the proceeds of the sale of shares of NLRC to secure the vessel contract contrary to representations made to the public as well as [BAE-Newplan].

[51] While not encompassing all of [BAE-Newplan's] allegations against the individual directors, this is a good summary of the basis for [BAE-Newplan's] claims against them . . . .

General Principles—Personal Liability of a Director

[19] It is helpful to begin the analysis of this appeal with general principles that apply to possible personal liability of corporate directors. In *Montreal Trust Co of Canada v Scotia-McLeod Inc* (1996), 129 D.L.R. (4th) 711 (ONCA), leave to appeal refused (1996), 205 N.R. 314, Finlayson J.A., for the Court, explained limits on the scope of personal liability of directors, at pages 720 to 721:

... A corporation may be liable for contracts that its directors or officers have caused it to sign, or for representations those officers or directors have made in its name, but this is because a corporation can only operate through human agency, that is, through its so-called "directing mind." Considering that a corporation is an inanimate piece of legal machinery incapable of thought or action, the court can only determine its legal liability by assessing the conduct of those who caused the company to act in the way that it did. This does not mean, however, that if the actions of the directing minds are found wanting, that personal liability will flow through the corporation to those who caused it to act as it did. To hold the directors of Peoples personally liable, there must be some activity on their part that takes them out of the role of directing minds of the corporation. . . .

[20] The Court in *ScotiaMcLeod* also noted that assessing the personal liability of directors in the context of the relevant case law requires a "fact-specific" analysis, and that the facts giving rise to personal liability must be "specifically pleaded" (page 720). In addition, the actions of the directors "must exhibit a separate identity or interest from that of the company so as to make the act or conduct complained of their own" (page 720).

[21] The directors of the Altius companies and NLRC submit that nowhere does the statement of claim allege that the directors were acting personally or outside their role as directing minds of the companies. This submission forms the foundation of their response to BAE-Newplan's appeal.

Claims Based on a Duty of Care — Altius Directors

[22] In assessing whether the applications judge erred, it is necessary to review, in brief, principles of law relevant to the claims. Section 203(1) of the *Corporations Act*, R.S.N.L. 1990, c. C-36, addresses the fiduciary duty and duty of care required of corporate directors:

> A director and officer of a corporation in exercising his or her powers and discharging his or her duties shall
>
> (a) act honestly and in good faith with a view to the best interests of the corporation; and
>
> (b) exercise the care, diligence and skill that a reasonably prudent person would exercise in comparable circumstances.

[23] In *Peoples Department Stores Inc (Trustee of) v Wise*, 2004 SCC 68, [2004] 3 S.C.R. 461, Major and Deschamps JJ, for the Court, considered section 122(1) of the *Canada Business Corporations Act*, R.S.C. 1985, c. C-44, which is virtually the same as paragraph 203(1)(b) of this Province's *Corporations Act*. They concluded that "directors owe a duty of care to creditors, but that duty does not rise to a fiduciary duty" (paragraph 1). In the subsequent decision in *BCE Inc v 1976 Debentureholders*, 2008 SCC 69, [2008] 3 S.C.R. 560, the Court further discussed directors' duties under the *Canada Business Corporations Act*. The Court commented:

> [37] ... Often the interests of shareholders and stakeholders are co-extensive with the interests of the corporation. But if they conflict, the directors' duty is clear — it is to the corporation: *Peoples Department Stores* [supra].
>
> [66] The fact that the conduct of the directors is often at the centre of oppression actions might seem to suggest that directors are under a direct duty to individual stakeholders who may be affected by a corporate decision. Directors, acting in the best interests of the corporation, may be obliged to consider the impact of their decisions on corporate stakeholders, such as the debentureholders in these appeals. This is what we mean when we speak of a director being required to act in the best interests of the corporation viewed as a good corporate citizen. However, the directors owe a fiduciary duty to the corporation, and only to the corporation. People sometimes speak in terms of directors owing a duty to both the corporation and to stakeholders. Usually this is harmless, since the reasonable expectations of the stakeholder in a particular outcome often coincide with what is in the best interests of the corporation. However, cases (such as these appeals) may arise where these interests do not coincide. In such cases, it is important to be clear that the directors owe their duty to the corporation, not to stakeholders, and that the reasonable expectation of stakeholders is simply that the directors act in the best interests of the corporation.

(Emphasis added.)

[24] As to this appeal, the applications judge concluded that the directors of the Altius companies, other than Brian Dalton, did not owe BAE-Newplan a duty of care under section 203(1)(b):

> [60] The same can be said [that there is no possibility of a successful claim] with regard to the claims made under the **Corporations Act** in my opinion. Firstly, a breach of the duty set out in section 203(1)(a) or (b) of the **Act**, even if found as against the Altius directors, would not permit a court to order compensation pursuant to section 371(3) of the **Act**. <u>In any event, on the facts as pleaded, I am satisfied that [BAE-Newplan] cannot be a creditor of either of the Altius companies so as to ground a possible duty as regards [BAE-Newplan] for the directors personally. [BAE-Newplan] does not fall within the class of persons to whom the directors of the Altius companies owed a duty</u> ...

(Emphasis added.)

[25] In submitting that the applications judge erred in concluding that the claim against the Altius directors based on a duty of care cannot succeed, BAE-Newplan relies on four factors: first, the Altius companies established NLRC as a "non-operating, project development-stage, equity investment company of Altius Minerals to investigate the feasibility of constructing a new oil refinery"; second, Altius Minerals referred to the oil refinery project as "Altius' NLRC Project"; third, Altius Resources, a major shareholder of NLRC, was wholly owned by Altius Minerals; and, fourth, "the business decisions made by NLRC were controlled by the Altius companies in concert and acting together with the European entrepreneurs."

[26] However, these factors do not support the conclusion proposed by BAE-Newplan because no recognition or effect is given to the separate corporate entities. The applications judge determined, and BAE-Newplan concedes, that "there is no foundation set forth in the pleadings to warrant a conclusion that NLRC was set up as a sham" (paragraph 15). Further, it is clear that, while BAE-Newplan is a creditor of NLRC, it is not a creditor, or other stakeholder, of the Altius companies.

[27] Nonetheless, BAE-Newplan alleges that the directors of the Altius companies owed it a duty of care because of a relationship of proximity based on the factors set out in paragraph 25, above. Again, this submission is not persuasive. There is no basis on which to conclude that NLRC was managed other than by its directors. The fact that Altius Resources was a minority shareholder in NLRC could not impose a duty of care on the directors of the Altius company in respect of the management of NLRC. The distinction between a shareholder and a director is referenced in *Peoples Department Stores, supra*:

> [31] ... Although the shareholders are commonly said to own the corporation, in the absence of a unanimous shareholder agreement to the contrary, s. 102 of the [*Canada Business Corporations Act*] provides that it is not the shareholders, but the directors elected by the shareholders, who are responsible for managing it. This clear demarcation between the respective roles of shareholders and directors long predates the 1975 enactment of the [*Canada Business Corporations Act*] [authorities omitted].

[28] To hold the Altius directors liable for the actions of NLRC or its directors by imposing upon them a duty of care to BAE-Newplan would make the Altius directors responsible for conduct over which they had no control. It has been accepted that NLRC is not a sham corporation. With the exception of Brian Dalton and John Baker who were directors of the three companies, NLRC had a different slate of directors than either Altius company. In the absence of control over the operations of NLRC, or some

specifically pleaded activity occurring outside their role as directors of the Altius companies, the Altius directors could not be held liable for the conduct of NLRC or its directors.

[29] BAE-Newplan referred to the applications judge's statement that there "may be some foundation or 'skeleton' of a claim set out in the pleadings as against both of the Altius companies" (paragraph 57). Counsel construed this as a conclusion that the applications judge was "satisfied" that there was a potential cause of action against the Altius companies and that this could transfer responsibility to the Altius directors. This is an erroneous construction of what the applications judge wrote. The Altius companies did not make an application to be removed as defendants. Read in context, this statement was made in order to emphasize that, even if the company should be found to be liable, there remains no basis on which to extend liability to the directors.

[30] In the result, based on the pleadings, it is not possible that the directors of the Altius companies could be found to owe a duty of care to BAE-Newplan. The applications judge did not err in concluding that it is plain and obvious that a claim based on a duty of care under section 203 of the *Corporations Act* or the common law cannot succeed as against the Altius directors. Accordingly, the directors of both Altius companies are not proper parties for purposes of this claim . . . .

Summary and Disposition

. . .

[67] In the result, all the directors of NLRC and the Altius companies, including Mr. Dalton when acting in his capacity as a director of those companies, shall cease to be defendants with respect to the claims based on oppression, duty of care, negligent misrepresentation and deceit.

[68] The appeal by BAE-Newplan is dismissed. The cross-appeals by the directors of NLRC and the Altius companies are allowed . . . .

Appeal dismissed.
[Leave to appeal dismissed [2012] SCCA No 251]

In addition to attempting to expand directors' fiduciary duty, creditors have also attempted to argue, albeit to a much lesser extent, the US doctrine of "deepening insolvency." The doctrine provides an alternative theory for imposing liability on directors. It has not been accepted in Canada and the scope of the doctrine is subject to debate in the United States. Jassmine Girgis, "Deepening Insolvency in Canada?" (2008) 53 *McGill Law Journal* 167 at 169 and 175–77 summarizes the doctrine as follows:

Deepening insolvency holds directors liable for harms suffered by the corporation when its life is wrongfully prolonged. The doctrine imposes on directors a duty to the corporation, but it also indirectly benefits creditors: first, by bringing money into the debtor's estate to repay creditors if the claim against the directors is successful, and second, by restraining the actions of directors when the corporation is suffering financially, through the threat of liability. . . .

In 1983, the term "deepening insolvency" was coined when the United States Court of Appeals for the Seventh Circuit recognized the damage that can be accrued when management continues to operate an insolvent corporation . . . . "Deepening insolvency" is a nonstatutory doctrine that does not appear anywhere in the Bankruptcy Code. The absence of a statutory definition renders the doctrine uncertain in scope and, consequently, deepening insolvency has neither been universally defined nor applied, nor has it been universally accepted in the United States.

Directors, officers or other parties who exercise control over the corporation engage in deepening insolvency when they wrongfully incur further corporate debt while the corporation is insolvent and has no reasonable prospect of recovering. Deepening insolvency is premised on the acknowledgment that incurring such debt harms the corporation. Accordingly, the harm brought about by directors' failure to stop trading under the above circumstances can be avoided through the creation of personal liability under the doctrine of deepening insolvency. The objective of the liability imposed by the doctrine is to motivate directors to recognize this harm and cease trading as soon as saving the corporation is no longer a feasible prospect. . . .

Without the threat of personal liability, directors may be no worse off even if they continue to incur debt when the corporation is insolvent. Even if it is unlikely that the corporation could trade into a profitable financial state, directors have an incentive to take that chance. If they are successful, they will once again have a profitable corporation; they will keep their jobs and, if they are also shareholders, regain value in their shares. If they are unsuccessful, other than the damage done to their reputations as directors, they will suffer no additional financial loss because the limitation of their liability ensures that they are not responsible for the corporation's debts. . . .

Specifically, the injury caused to the corporation can include the decline in value of the remaining corporate assets through the incurrence of additional debt. It can cause a hastening of bankruptcy through the dissipation of corporate assets and an undermining of the relationships between the corporation and its "customers, suppliers, and employees." Due to the broad definition of deepening insolvency, while the claim is usually brought against directors and officers, it may include other defendants such as lenders or auditors.

Nevertheless, to fall within the scope of the deepening insolvency doctrine, the prolongation of the corporation's life must usually have been the result of fraud.

[Reprinted by permission of the publisher.]

Two Canadian courts have commented on the doctrine of deepening insolvency, with the appellate court concluding that it did not have to determine whether it could be recognized as a cause of action in Canada. See *Livent Inc v Deloitte & Touche LLP*, 2014 ONSC 2176 at paras 344–50 and on appeal 2016 ONCA 11 at paras 329–38 (rev'd on other grounds 2017 SCC 63).

B. The Oppression Remedy

In *Peoples Department Stores*, the Supreme Court of Canada held that directors do not owe a fiduciary duty to creditors, but it found that creditors could use the oppression remedy against directors or the corporation. While creditors may not fall within the definition of "complainant" found in section 238(a) of the *CBCA*, they can qualify as a "proper person" at the court's discretion under section 238(d), which would allow them to pursue the remedy. However, the Court in *Peoples Department Stores* did not provide further clarification on how the remedy could be used. *Peoples Department Stores* was not the first case to allow creditors to use the oppression remedy; courts had been granting creditors permission years prior to *Peoples Department Stores* (see *Sidaplex*, below, at para 12). *Peoples Department Stores* was important because it was the first Supreme Court case to specifically acknowledge creditors' standing to pursue the remedy.

In *BCE Inc v 1976 Debentureholders*, below, the second Supreme Court decision on the oppression remedy, the Court did provide that clarification. Although the case did not involve the oppression remedy in a bankruptcy and insolvency context, the Court articulated that the test complainants must meet in order to obtain an oppression remedy. Most recently, in *Wilson v Alharayeri*, 2017 SCC 39 (excerpted below), the Supreme Court laid out the test for finding directors personally liable under the oppression remedy.

In addition to creditors, a trustee in bankruptcy can also rely on the oppression remedy. In *Olympia & York Developments Ltd (Trustee of) v Olympia & York Realty Corp* (2003), 68 OR (3d) 544 (CA), the Ontario Court of Appeal (at para 45) held that "the trustee is neither automatically barred from being a complainant nor automatically entitled to that status. It is for the judge at first instance to determine in the exercise of his or her discretion whether in the circumstances of the particular case, the trustee is a proper person to be a complainant."

The oppression remedy has given rise to several challenges. Due to the breadth of the statutory language and the fact that the remedy is fact-based, articulating clear guidelines as to how exactly the test is applied has proven to be difficult, which is what Jassmine Girgis, "The Oppression Remedy: Clarifying Part II of the *BCE* Test" (2019) 96:3 *Canadian Bar Review* 484 at 486 (footnotes omitted) notes below:

> Claiming oppression is easy. Only the low bar of unfairness must be overcome. It seems to arise from any unwelcome conduct in a (usually) closely held corporation. It can be appended to any corporate misconduct claim. Broad statutory language governs the remedy, making it facially applicable to a broad range of conduct. In addition, the remedy is fact-based, being granted when a party satisfies the court that the corporation or its directors acted in a way that is oppressive or unfairly prejudicial to, or that unfairly disregards the interests of, any security holder, creditor, director or officer. In the face of these challenges, courts have struggled to maintain a clear set of applicable rules to govern when oppression has occurred. As a consequence, predicting the outcome of an oppression case is difficult.

In *Katz v Babkat Inc*, 2012 MBCA 68, the Manitoba Court of Appeal confirmed that the oppression remedy "is a discretionary order. If a judge has committed no error in either law or fact, his order should not be interfered with unless it is so clearly wrong as to amount to an injustice" (at para 3).

Even though courts have maintained that the oppression remedy is fact-based, there are several principles that can be gleaned from the case law. With regard to creditors, the main principle is that they cannot use the oppression remedy to pursue ordinary debt collection; rather, there must be something more to the case in order for them to be successful. In *Royal Trust Corp of Canada v Hordo*, [1993] OJ No 1560 (Ct J (Gen Div)), the court said (at 92):

> It does not seem to me that debt actions should be routinely turned into oppression actions ... I do not think that the court's discretion should be used to give complainant status to a creditor where the creditor's interest in the affairs of the corporation is too remote or where the complaints of the creditor have nothing to do with the circumstances giving rise to the debt or if the creditor is not proceeding in good faith. Status as a complainant should also be refused where the creditor is not in a position analogous to that of a minority shareholder and has no particular legitimate interest in the manner in which the affairs of the company are managed.

The oppression remedy is available both in and out of insolvency and with or without the presence of bad faith. Although bad faith is one of the clear indicia of oppression, it is not required, as the focus of the oppression remedy is not on the motive of the perpetrator but rather on the effect on the complainant. The most recent pronouncement on this issue was from *Wilson v Alharayeri*, below, where the court maintained, the "oppression remedy is concerned with the effects of oppressive conduct, not the intent of the oppressor" (para 42). To that end, it is clearly oppressive for the directors to convey assets out of the reach of creditors if it leaves the corporation judgement-proof (see *Builders' Floor Centre Ltd v Thiessen*, below). Oppression was also found when a creditor lost its security because the directors inadvertently failed to renew a letter of credit (see *Sidaplex*, below), and when directors failed to carry out their obligations under company law or acted in a way to prefer certain creditors (see *Danylchuk v Wolinsky*, below). For other cases involving the transfer of assets, the oppression remedy and director liability see, for example *Glasscell Isofab Inc v Thompson*, 2012 ONSC 6423; *Schreiber Foods Inc v Wepackit Inc*, 2013 ONSC 338; *Pitney Bowes of Canada Ltd v Belmonte*, 2011 ONSC 3755.

BCE Inc v 1976 Debentureholders, 2008 SCC 69, [2008] 3 SCR 560

THE COURT:

I. INTRODUCTION

[1] These appeals arise out of an offer to purchase all shares of BCE Inc. ("BCE"), a large telecommunications corporation, by a group headed by the Ontario Teachers Pension Plan Board ("Teachers"), financed in part by the assumption by Bell Canada, a wholly owned subsidiary of BCE, of a $30 billion debt. The leveraged buyout was opposed by debentureholders of Bell Canada on the ground that the increased debt contemplated by the purchase agreement would reduce the value of their bonds.... [The debentureholders] ... opposed the arrangement under s. 241 of the *CBCA* on the ground that it was oppressive to them....

II. FACTS

...

[4] At issue is a plan of arrangement valued at approximately $52 billion, for the purchase of the shares of BCE by way of a leveraged buyout. The arrangement was opposed by a group [the debentureholders], comprised mainly of financial institutions, that hold debentures issued by Bell Canada. The crux of their complaints is that the arrangement would diminish the trading value of their debentures by an average of 20 percent, while conferring a premium of approximately 40 percent on the market price of BCE shares....

[7] Bell Canada's debentures were perceived by investors to be safe investments and, up to the time of the proposed leveraged buyout, had maintained an investment grade rating. The debentureholders are some of Canada's largest and most reputable financial institutions, pension funds and insurance companies. They are major participants in the debt markets and possess an intimate and historic knowledge of the financial markets....

[14] In a press release dated April 17, 2007, BCE announced that it was reviewing its strategic alternatives with a view to further enhancing shareholder value. On the same day, a Strategic Oversight Committee ("SOC") was created. None of its members had ever been part of management at BCE. Its mandate was, notably, to set up and supervise the auction process.

[15] Following the April 17 press release, several debentureholders sent letters to the Board voicing their concerns about a potential leveraged buyout transaction. They

sought assurance that their interests would be considered by the Board. BCE replied in writing that it intended to honour the contractual terms of the trust indentures. . . .

[17] Offers were submitted by three groups. All three offers contemplated the addition of a substantial amount of new debt for which Bell Canada would be liable. All would have likely resulted in a downgrade of the debentures below investment grade. The initial offer [was] submitted by the appellant 6796508 Canada Inc. (the "Purchaser"), a corporation formed by Teachers and affiliates of Providence Equity Partners Inc. and Madison Dearborn Partners LLC. . . .

[18] The Board, after a review of the three offers and based on the recommendation of the SOC, found that the Purchaser's revised offer was in the best interests of BCE and BCE's shareholders . . . . The Board did not seek a fairness opinion in respect of the debentureholders, taking the view that their rights were not being arranged.

[19] On June 30, 2007, the Purchaser and BCE entered into a definitive agreement. On September 21, 2007, BCE's shareholders approved the arrangement by a majority of 97.93 percent. . . .

[21] As a result of the announcement of the arrangement, the credit ratings of the debentures by the time of trial had been downgraded from investment grade to below investment grade. From the perspective of the debentureholders, this downgrade was problematic for two reasons. First, it caused the debentures to decrease in value by an average of approximately 20 percent. Second, the downgrade could oblige debentureholders with credit-rating restrictions on their holdings to sell their debentures at a loss. . . .

IV. ISSUES

[30] The issues, briefly stated, are whether the Court of Appeal erred in dismissing the debentureholders' s. 241 oppression claim . . . . These questions raise the issue of what is required to establish oppression of debentureholders in a situation where a corporation is facing a change of control . . . .

V. ANALYSIS

A. Overview of Rights, Obligations, and Remedies Under the *CBCA*

. . .

[36] The directors are responsible for the governance of the corporation. In the performance of this role, the directors are subject to two duties: a fiduciary duty to the corporation under s. 122(1)(a) (the fiduciary duty); and a duty to exercise the care, diligence and skill of a reasonably prudent person in comparable circumstances under s. 122(1)(b) (the duty of care). . . . [T]his case does involve the fiduciary duty of the directors to the corporation, and particularly the "fair treatment" component of this duty, which, as will be seen, is fundamental to the reasonable expectations of stakeholders claiming an oppression remedy.

[37] The fiduciary duty of the directors to the corporation originated in the common law. It is a duty to act in the best interests of the corporation. Often the interests of shareholders and stakeholders are co-extensive with the interests of the corporation. But if they conflict, the directors' duty is clear — it is to the corporation: *Peoples Department Stores*.

[38] The fiduciary duty of the directors to the corporation is a broad, contextual concept. It is not confined to short-term profit or share value. Where the corporation is an ongoing concern, it looks to the long-term interests of the corporation. The content

of this duty varies with the situation at hand. At a minimum, it requires the directors to ensure that the corporation meets its statutory obligations. But, depending on the context, there may also be other requirements. In any event, the fiduciary duty owed by directors is mandatory; directors must look to what is in the best interests of the corporation.

[39] In *Peoples Department Stores*, this Court found that although directors *must* consider the best interests of the corporation, it may also be appropriate, although *not mandatory*, to consider the impact of corporate decisions on shareholders or particular groups of stakeholders [see para. 42 in *Peoples Department Stores*]....

[40] In considering what is in the best interests of the corporation, directors may look to the interests of, *inter alia*, shareholders, employees, creditors, consumers, governments and the environment to inform their decisions. Courts should give appropriate deference to the business judgment of directors who take into account these ancillary interests, as reflected by the business judgment rule. The "business judgment rule" accords deference to a business decision, so long as it lies within a range of reasonable alternatives: see *Maple Leaf Foods Inc v Schneider Corp* (1998), 42 O.R. (3d) 177 (C.A.); *Kerr v Danier Leather Inc*, [2007] 3 S.C.R. 331 .... It reflects the reality that directors ... are often better suited to determine what is in the best interests of the corporation. This applies to decisions on stakeholders' interests, as much as other directorial decisions.

[41] Normally only the beneficiary of a fiduciary duty can enforce the duty. In the corporate context, however, this may offer little comfort. The directors who control the corporation are unlikely to bring an action against themselves for breach of their own fiduciary duty. The shareholders cannot act in the stead of the corporation; their only power is the right to oversee the conduct of the directors by way of votes at shareholder assemblies. Other stakeholders may not even have that....

[45] ... [T]he oppression remedy focuses on harm to the legal and equitable interests of stakeholders affected by oppressive acts of a corporation or its directors. This remedy is available to a wide range of stakeholders—security holders, creditors, directors and officers....

B. The Section 241 Oppression Remedy

...

[56] In our view ... [o]ne should look first to the principles underlying the oppression remedy, and in particular the concept of reasonable expectations. If a breach of a reasonable expectation is established, one must go on to consider whether the conduct complained of amounts to "oppression," "unfair prejudice" or "unfair disregard" as set out in s. 241(2) of the *CBCA*.

[57] We preface our discussion of the twin prongs of the oppression inquiry by two preliminary observations that run throughout all the jurisprudence.

[58] First, oppression is an equitable remedy. It seeks to ensure fairness—what is "just and equitable." It gives a court broad, equitable jurisdiction to enforce not just what is legal but what is fair .... It follows that courts considering claims for oppression should look at business realities, not merely narrow legalities ....

[59] Second, like many equitable remedies, oppression is fact-specific. What is just and equitable is judged by the reasonable expectations of the stakeholders in the context and in regard to the relationships at play. Conduct that may be oppressive in one situation may not be in another.

[60] Against this background, we turn to the first prong of the inquiry, the principles underlying the remedy of oppression. In *Ebrahimi v Westbourne Galleries Ltd*, [1973] A.C. 360 (H.L.), at p. 379, Lord Wilberforce, interpreting s. 222 of the UK *Companies Act, 1948*, described the remedy of oppression in the following seminal terms:

> The words ["just and equitable"] are a recognition of the fact that a limited company is more than a mere legal entity, with a personality in law of its own: that there is room in company law for recognition of the fact that behind it, or amongst it, there are individuals, with rights, expectations and obligations *inter se* which are not necessarily submerged in the company structure.

[61] Lord Wilberforce spoke of the equitable remedy in terms of the "rights, expectations and obligations" of individuals. ... It is left for the oppression remedy to deal with the "expectations" of affected stakeholders. The reasonable expectations of these stakeholders is the cornerstone of the oppression remedy.

[62] As denoted by "reasonable," the concept of reasonable expectations is objective and contextual. The actual expectation of a particular stakeholder is not conclusive. In the context of whether it would be "just and equitable" to grant a remedy, the question is whether the expectation is reasonable having regard to the facts of the specific case, the relationships at issue, and the entire context, including the fact that there may be conflicting claims and expectations.

[63] Particular circumstances give rise to particular expectations. Stakeholders enter into relationships, with and within corporations, on the basis of understandings and expectations, upon which they are entitled to rely, provided they are reasonable in the context: see: ... *Main v Delcan Group Inc* (1999), 47 B.L.R. (2d) 200 (Ont. S.C.J.). These expectations are what the remedy of oppression seeks to uphold.

[64] Determining whether a particular expectation is reasonable is complicated by the fact that the interests and expectations of different stakeholders may conflict. The oppression remedy recognizes that a corporation is an entity that encompasses and affects various individuals and groups, some of whose interests may conflict with others. Directors or other corporate actors may make corporate decisions or seek to resolve conflicts in a way that abusively or unfairly maximizes a particular group's interest at the expense of other stakeholders. The corporation and shareholders are entitled to maximize profit and share value, to be sure, but not by treating individual stakeholders unfairly. Fair treatment—the central theme running through the oppression jurisprudence—is most fundamentally what stakeholders are entitled to "reasonably expect."

[65] Section 241(2) speaks of the "act or omission" of the corporation or any of its affiliates, the conduct of "business or affairs" of the corporation and the "powers of the directors of the corporation or any of its affiliates." Often, the conduct complained of is the conduct of the corporation or of its directors, who are responsible for the governance of the corporation. However, the conduct of other actors, such as shareholders, may also support a claim for oppression... *GATX Corp v Hawker Siddeley Canada Inc* (1996), 27 B.L.R. (2d) 251 (Ont. Ct. (Gen. Div.)). In the appeals before us, the claims for oppression are based on allegations that the directors of BCE and Bell Canada failed to comply with the reasonable expectations of the debentureholders, and it is unnecessary to go beyond this.

[66] The fact that the conduct of the directors is often at the centre of oppression actions might seem to suggest that directors are under a direct duty to individual stakeholders who may be affected by a corporate decision. Directors, acting in the best interests of the corporation, may be obliged to consider the impact of their decisions on

corporate stakeholders, such as the debentureholders in these appeals. This is what we mean when we speak of a director being required to act in the best interests of the corporation viewed as a good corporate citizen. However, the directors owe a fiduciary duty to the corporation, and only to the corporation. People sometimes speak in terms of directors owing a duty to both the corporation and to stakeholders. Usually this is harmless, since the reasonable expectations of the stakeholder in a particular outcome often coincides with what is in the best interests of the corporation. However, cases (such as these appeals) may arise where these interests do not coincide. In such cases, it is important to be clear that the directors owe their duty to the corporation, not to stakeholders, and that the reasonable expectation of stakeholders is simply that the directors act in the best interests of the corporation.

[67] Having discussed the concept of reasonable expectations that underlies the oppression remedy, we arrive at the second prong of the s. 241 oppression remedy. Even if reasonable, not every unmet expectation gives rise to claim under s. 241. The section requires that the conduct complained of amount to "oppression," "unfair prejudice" or "unfair disregard" of relevant interests. "Oppression" carries the sense of conduct that is coercive and abusive, and suggests bad faith. "Unfair prejudice" may admit of a less culpable state of mind, that nevertheless has unfair consequences. Finally, "unfair disregard" of interests extends the remedy to ignoring an interest as being of no importance, contrary to the stakeholders' reasonable expectations .... The phrases describe, in adjectival terms, ways in which corporate actors may fail to meet the reasonable expectations of stakeholders.

[68] In summary, the foregoing discussion suggests conducting two related inquiries in a claim for oppression: (1) Does the evidence support the reasonable expectation asserted by the claimant? and (2) Does the evidence establish that the reasonable expectation was violated by conduct falling within the terms "oppression," "unfair prejudice" or "unfair disregard" of a relevant interest? ...

(a) Proof of a Claimant's Reasonable Expectations

[70] At the outset, the claimant must identify the expectations that he or she claims have been violated by the conduct at issue and establish that the expectations were reasonably held. As stated above, it may be readily inferred that a stakeholder has a reasonable expectation of fair treatment. However, oppression, as discussed, generally turns on particular expectations arising in particular situations. The question becomes whether the claimant stakeholder reasonably held the particular expectation. Evidence of an expectation may take many forms depending on the facts of the case.

[71] It is impossible to catalogue exhaustively situations where a reasonable expectation may arise due to their fact-specific nature. A few generalizations, however, may be ventured. Actual unlawfulness is not required to invoke s. 241; the provision applies "where the impugned conduct is wrongful, even if it is not actually unlawful": Dickerson Committee (R.W.V. Dickerson, J.L. Howard and L. Getz), *Proposals for a New Business Corporations Law for Canada* (1971), vol. 1, at p. 163. The remedy is focused on concepts of fairness and equity rather than on legal rights. In determining whether there is a reasonable expectation or interest to be considered, the court looks beyond legality to what is fair, given all of the interests at play .... It follows that not all conduct that is harmful to a stakeholder will give rise to a remedy for oppression as against the corporation.

[72] Factors that emerge from the case law that are useful in determining whether a reasonable expectation exists include: ... [see, below, factors (i)–(vii), paras. 73–88].

(i) Commercial Practice

[73] Commercial practice plays a significant role in forming the reasonable expectations of the parties. A departure from normal business practices that has the effect of undermining or frustrating the complainant's exercise of his or her legal rights will generally (although not inevitably) give rise to a remedy. . . .

(ii) The Nature of the Corporation

[74] The size, nature and structure of the corporation are relevant factors in assessing reasonable expectations . . . . Courts may accord more latitude to the directors of a small, closely held corporation to deviate from strict formalities than to the directors of a larger public company.

(iii) Relationships

[75] Reasonable expectations may emerge from the personal relationships between the claimant and other corporate actors. Relationships between shareholders based on ties of family or friendship may be governed by different standards than relationships between arm's length shareholders in a widely held corporation. As noted in *Re Ferguson and Imax Systems Corp.*, (1983), 150 DLR (3d) 718 (Ont. CA), "when dealing with a close corporation, the court may consider the relationship between the shareholders and not simply legal rights as such" (p. 727).

(iv) Past Practice

[76] Past practice may create reasonable expectations, especially among shareholders of a closely held corporation on matters relating to participation of shareholders in the corporation's profits and governance: *Gibbons v Medical Carriers Ltd* (2001), 17 B.L.R. (3d) 280 [(Man QB)] . . . . For instance, in *Gibbons*, the court found that the shareholders had a legitimate expectation that all monies paid out of the corporation would be paid to shareholders in proportion to the percentage of shares they held. The authorization by the new directors to pay fees to themselves, for which the shareholders would not receive any comparable payments, was in breach of those expectations.

[77] It is important to note that practices and expectations can change over time. Where valid commercial reasons exist for the change and the change does not undermine the complainant's rights, there can be no reasonable expectation that directors will resist a departure from past practice: *Alberta Treasury Branches v SevenWay Capital Corp* (1999), 50 B.L.R. (2d) 294 (Alta. Q.B.), aff'd (2000), 8 B.L.R. (3d) 1 . . . .

(v) Preventive Steps

[78] In determining whether a stakeholder expectation is reasonable, the court may consider whether the claimant could have taken steps to protect itself against the prejudice it claims to have suffered. Thus it may be relevant to inquire whether a secured creditor claiming oppressive conduct could have negotiated protections against the prejudice suffered . . . .

(vi) Representations and Agreements

[79] Shareholder agreements may be viewed as reflecting the reasonable expectations of the parties . . . *Lyall v 147250 Canada Ltd* (1993), 106 D.L.R. (4th) 304 (B.C.C.A.).

[80] Reasonable expectations may also be affected by representations made to stakeholders or to the public in promotional material, prospectuses, offering circulars and other communications . . . .

(vii) Fair Resolution of Conflicting Interests

[81] As discussed, conflicts may arise between the interests of corporate stakeholders *inter se* and between stakeholders and the corporation. Where the conflict involves the interests of the corporation, it falls to the directors of the corporation to resolve them in accordance with their fiduciary duty to act in the best interests of the corporation, viewed as a good corporate citizen.

[82] The cases on oppression, taken as a whole, confirm that the duty of the directors to act in the best interests of the corporation comprehends a duty to treat individual stakeholders affected by corporate actions equitably and fairly. There are no absolute rules. In each case, the question is whether, in all the circumstances, the directors acted in the best interests of the corporation, having regard to all relevant considerations, including, but not confined to, the need to treat affected stakeholders in a fair manner, commensurate with the corporation's duties as a responsible corporate citizen.

[83] Directors may find themselves in a situation where it is impossible to please all stakeholders. The "fact that alternative transactions were rejected by the directors is irrelevant unless it can be shown that a particular alternative was definitely available and clearly more beneficial to the company than the chosen transaction": *Maple Leaf Foods*, *per* Weiler JA, at p. 192.

[84] There is no principle that one set of interests—for example the interests of shareholders—should prevail over another set of interests. Everything depends on the particular situation faced by the directors and whether, having regard to that situation, they exercised business judgment in a responsible way.

[85] On these appeals, it was suggested on behalf of the corporations that the "*Revlon* line" of cases from Delaware support the principle that where the interests of shareholders conflict with the interests of creditors, the interests of shareholders should prevail.

[86] The "*Revlon* line" refers to a series of Delaware corporate takeover cases, the two most important of which are *Revlon Inc v MacAndrews & Forbes Holdings Inc*, 506 A2d 173 (Del. 1985), and *Unocal Corp v Mesa Petroleum Co*, 493 A2d 946 (Del. 1985). In both cases, the issue was how directors should react to a hostile takeover bid. *Revlon* suggests that in such circumstances, shareholder interests should prevail over those of other stakeholders, such as creditors. *Unocal* tied this approach to situations where the corporation will not continue as a going concern, holding that although a board facing a hostile takeover "may have regard for various constituencies in discharging its responsibilities, ... such concern for non-stockholder interests is inappropriate when ... the object no longer is to protect or maintain the corporate enterprise but to sell it to the highest bidder" (p. 182).

[87] What is clear is that the *Revlon* line of cases has not displaced the fundamental rule that the duty of the directors cannot be confined to particular priority rules, but is rather a function of business judgment of what is in the best interests of the corporation, in the particular situation it faces. In a review of trends in Delaware corporate jurisprudence, former Delaware Supreme Court Chief Justice E. Norman Veasey put it this way:

> [It] is important to keep in mind the precise content of this "best interests" concept—that is, to whom this duty is owed and when. Naturally, one often thinks that directors owe this duty to both the corporation and the stockholders. That formulation is harmless in most instances because of the confluence of interests, in that what is good for the corporate entity is usually derivatively good for the stockholders. There are times, of course, when the focus is directly on the interests of the stockholders [i.e., as in *Revlon*]. But, in general,

the directors owe fiduciary duties to the *corporation*, not to the stockholders. [Emphasis in original.]

(E. Norman Veasey with Christine T. Di Guglielmo, "What Happened in Delaware Corporate Law and Governance from 1992–2004? A Retrospective on Some Key Developments" (2005), 153 *U. Pa. L. Rev.* 1399, at p. 1431)

[88] Nor does this Court's decision in *Peoples Department Stores* suggest a fixed rule that the interests of creditors must prevail. In *Peoples Department Stores*, the Court had to consider whether, in the case of a corporation under threat of bankruptcy, creditors deserved special consideration (para. 46). The Court held that the fiduciary duty to the corporation did not change in the period preceding the bankruptcy, but that if the directors breach their duty of care to a stakeholder under s. 122(1)(b) of the *CBCA*, such a stakeholder may act upon it (para. 66).

(b) Conduct Which Is Oppressive, Is Unfairly Prejudicial or Unfairly Disregards the Claimant's Relevant Interests

[89] Thus far we have discussed how a claimant establishes the first element of an action for oppression—a reasonable expectation that he or she would be treated in a certain way. However, to complete a claim for oppression, the claimant must show that the failure to meet this expectation involved unfair conduct and prejudicial consequences within s. 241 of the *CBCA*. Not every failure to meet a reasonable expectation will give rise to the equitable considerations that ground actions for oppression. The court must be satisfied that the conduct falls within the concepts of "oppression," "unfair prejudice" or "unfair disregard" of the claimant's interest, within the meaning of s. 241 of the *CBCA*. Viewed in this way, the reasonable expectations analysis that is the theoretical foundation of the oppression remedy, and the particular types of conduct described in s. 241, may be seen as complementary, rather than representing alternative approaches to the oppression remedy, as has sometimes been supposed. Together, they offer a complete picture of conduct that is unjust and inequitable, to return to the language of *Ebrahimi*.

[90] In most cases, proof of a reasonable expectation will be tied up with one or more of the concepts of oppression, unfair prejudice, or unfair disregard of interests set out in s. 241, and the two prongs will in fact merge. Nevertheless, it is worth stating that as in any action in equity, wrongful conduct, causation and compensable injury must be established in a claim for oppression.

[91] The concepts of oppression, unfair prejudice and unfairly disregarding relevant interests are adjectival. They indicate the type of wrong or conduct that the oppression remedy of s. 241 of the *CBCA* is aimed at. However, they do not represent watertight compartments, and often overlap and intermingle.

[92] The original wrong recognized in the cases was described simply as oppression, and was generally associated with conduct that has variously been described as "burdensome, harsh and wrongful," "a visible departure from standards of fair dealing," and an "abuse of power" going to the probity of how the corporation's affairs are being conducted .... It is this wrong that gave the remedy its name, which now is generally used to cover all s. 241 claims. However, the term also operates to connote a particular type of injury within the modern rubric of oppression generally—a wrong of the most serious sort.

[93] The *CBCA* has added "unfair prejudice" and "unfair disregard" of interests to the original common law concept, making it clear that wrongs falling short of the harsh and abusive conduct connoted by "oppression" may fall within s. 241. "[U]nfair

prejudice" is generally seen as involving conduct less offensive than "oppression." Examples include squeezing out a minority shareholder, failing to disclose related party transactions, changing corporate structure to drastically alter debt ratios, adopting a "poison pill" to prevent a takeover bid, paying dividends without a formal declaration, preferring some shareholders with management fees and paying directors' fees higher than the industry norm ....

[94] "[U]nfair disregard" is viewed as the least serious of the three injuries, or wrongs, mentioned in s. 241. Examples include favouring a director by failing to properly prosecute claims, improperly reducing a shareholder's dividend, or failing to deliver property belonging to the claimant ....

(2) Application to These Appeals

[95] As discussed above (at para. 68), in assessing a claim for oppression a court must answer two questions: (1) Does the evidence support the reasonable expectation the claimant asserts? and (2) Does the evidence establish that the reasonable expectation was violated by conduct falling within the terms "oppression," "unfair prejudice" or "unfair disregard" of a relevant interest?

[96] The debentureholders in this case assert two alternative expectations. Their highest position is that they had a reasonable expectation that the directors of BCE would protect their economic interests as debentureholders in Bell Canada by putting forward a plan of arrangement that would maintain the investment grade trading value of their debentures. Before this Court, however, they argued a softer alternative — a reasonable expectation that the directors would consider their economic interests in maintaining the trading value of the debentures.

[97] ... [T]he trial judge proceeded on the debentureholders' alleged expectation that the directors would act in a way that would preserve the investment grade status of their debentures. He concluded that this expectation was not made out on the evidence, since the statements by Bell Canada suggesting a commitment to retaining investment grade ratings were accompanied by warnings that explicitly precluded investors from reasonably forming such expectations, and the warnings were included in the prospectuses pursuant to which the debentures were issued.

[98] The absence of a reasonable expectation that the investment grade of the debentures would be maintained was confirmed, in the trial judge's view, by the overall context of the relationship, the nature of the corporation, its situation as the target of a bidding war, as well as by the fact that the claimants could have protected themselves against reduction in market value by negotiating appropriate contractual terms.

[99] The trial judge situated his consideration of the relevant factors in the appropriate legal context. He recognized that the directors had a fiduciary duty to act in the best interests of the corporation and that the content of this duty was affected by the various interests at stake in the context of the auction process that BCE was undergoing. He emphasized that the directors, faced with conflicting interests, might have no choice but to approve transactions that, while in the best interests of the corporation, would benefit some groups at the expense of others. He held that the fact that the shareholders stood to benefit from the transaction and that the debentureholders were prejudiced did not in itself give rise to a conclusion that the directors had breached their fiduciary duty to the corporation. All three competing bids required Bell Canada to assume additional debt, and there was no evidence that bidders were prepared to accept less leveraged debt. Under the business judgment rule,

deference should be accorded to business decisions of directors taken in good faith and in the performance of the functions they were elected to perform by the shareholders.

[100] We see no error in the principles applied by the trial judge nor in his findings of fact, which were amply supported by the evidence. We accordingly agree that the first expectation advanced in this case — that the investment grade status of the debentures would be maintained — was not established.

[101] The alternative, softer, expectation advanced is that the directors would consider the interests of the bondholders in maintaining the trading value of the debentures. . . .

[102] The evidence, objectively viewed, supports a reasonable expectation that the directors would consider the position of the debentureholders in making their decisions on the various offers under consideration. As discussed above, reasonable expectations for the purpose of a claim of oppression are not confined to legal interests. Given the potential impact on the debentureholders of the transactions under consideration, one would expect the directors, acting in the best interests of the corporation, to consider their short and long-term interests in the course of making their ultimate decision.

[103] Indeed, the evidence shows that the directors did consider the interests of the debentureholders. A number of debentureholders sent letters to the Board, expressing concern about the proposed leveraged buyout and seeking assurances that their interests would be considered. One of the directors, Mr. Pattison, met with Phillips, Hager & North, representatives of the debentureholders. The directors' response to these overtures was that the contractual terms of the debentures would be met, but no additional assurances were given.

[104] It is apparent that the directors considered the interests of the debentureholders and, having done so, concluded that while the contractual terms of the debentures would be honoured, no further commitments could be made. This fulfilled the duty of the directors to consider the debentureholders' interests. It did not amount to "unfair disregard" of the interests of the debentureholders. As discussed above, it may be impossible to satisfy all stakeholders in a given situation. In this case, the Board considered the interests of the claimant stakeholders. Having done so, and having considered its options in the difficult circumstances it faced, it made its decision, acting in what it perceived to be the best interests of the corporation.

[105] What the claimants contend for on this appeal, in reality, is not merely an expectation that their interests be considered, but an expectation that the Board would take further positive steps to restructure the purchase in a way that would provide a satisfactory purchase price to the shareholders and preserve the high market value of the debentures. At this point, the second, softer expectation asserted approaches the first alleged expectation of maintaining the investment grade rating of the debentures.

[106] The difficulty with this proposition is that there is no evidence that it was reasonable to suppose it could have been achieved. BCE, facing certain takeover, acted reasonably to create a competitive bidding process. The process attracted three bids. All of the bids were leveraged, involving a substantial increase in Bell Canada's debt. It was this factor that posed the risk to the trading value of the debentures. There is no evidence that BCE could have done anything to avoid that risk. Indeed, the evidence is to the contrary.

[107] We earlier discussed the factors to consider in determining whether an expectation is reasonable on a s. 241 oppression claim. These include commercial practice; the size, nature and structure of the corporation; the relationship between the parties; past practice; the failure to negotiate protections; agreements and representations; and the fair resolution of conflicting interests. In our view, all these factors weigh against

finding an expectation beyond honouring the contractual obligations of the debentures in this particular case.

[108] Commercial practice—indeed commercial reality—undermines the claim that a way could have been found to preserve the trading position of the debentures in the context of the leveraged buyout. This reality must have been appreciated by reasonable debentureholders. More broadly, two considerations are germane to the influence of general commercial practice on the reasonableness of the debentureholders' expectations. First, leveraged buyouts of this kind are not unusual or unforeseeable, although the transaction at issue in this case is noteworthy for its magnitude. Second, trust indentures can include change of control and credit rating covenants where those protections have been negotiated. Protections of that type would have assured debentureholders a right to vote, potentially through their trustee, on the leveraged buyout, as the trial judge pointed out. This failure to negotiate protections was significant where the debentureholders, it may be noted, generally represent some of Canada's largest and most reputable financial institutions, pension funds and insurance companies.

[109] The nature and size of the corporation also undermine the reasonableness of any expectation that the directors would reject the offers that had been presented and seek an arrangement that preserved the investment grade rating of the debentures. As discussed above (at para. 74), courts may accord greater latitude to the reasonableness of expectations formed in the context of a small, closely held corporation, rather than those relating to interests in a large, public corporation. Bell Canada had become a wholly owned subsidiary of BCE in 1983, pursuant to a plan of arrangement which saw the shareholders of Bell Canada surrender their shares in exchange for shares of BCE. Based upon the history of the relationship, it should not have been outside the contemplation of debentureholders acquiring debentures of Bell Canada under the 1996 and 1997 trust indentures, that arrangements of this type had occurred and could occur in the future.

[110] The debentureholders rely on past practice, suggesting that investment grade ratings had always been maintained. However, as noted, reasonable practices may reflect changing economic and market realities. The events that precipitated the leveraged buyout transaction were such realities. Nor did the trial judge find in this case that representations had been made to debentureholders upon which they could have reasonably relied.

[111] Finally, the claim must be considered from the perspective of the duty on the directors to resolve conflicts between the interests of corporate stakeholders in a fair manner that reflected the best interests of the corporation.

[112] The best interests of the corporation arguably favoured acceptance of the offer at the time. BCE had been put in play, and the momentum of the market made a buyout inevitable. The evidence, accepted by the trial judge, was that Bell Canada needed to undertake significant changes to continue to be successful, and that privatization would provide greater freedom to achieve its long-term goals by removing the pressure on short-term public financial reporting, and bringing in equity from sophisticated investors motivated to improve the corporation's performance. Provided that, as here, the directors' decision is found to have been within the range of reasonable choices that they could have made in weighing conflicting interests, the court will not go on to determine whether their decision was the perfect one.

[113] Considering all the relevant factors, we conclude that the debentureholders have failed to establish a reasonable expectation that could give rise to a claim for oppression. As found by the trial judge, the alleged expectation that the investment grade of the debentures would be maintained is not supported by the evidence. A reasonable expectation

that the debentureholders' interests would be considered is established, but was fulfilled. The evidence does not support a further expectation that a better arrangement could be negotiated that would meet the exigencies that the corporation was facing, while better preserving the trading value of the debentures.

[114] Given that the debentureholders have failed to establish that the expectations they assert were reasonable, or that they were not fulfilled, it is unnecessary to consider in detail whether conduct complained of was oppressive, unfairly prejudicial, or unfairly disregarded the debentureholders' interests within the terms of s. 241 of the *CBCA*. Suffice it to say that "oppression" in the sense of bad faith and abuse was not alleged, much less proved. At best, the claim was for "unfair disregard" of the interests of the debentureholders. As discussed, the evidence does not support this claim....

VI. CONCLUSION

[166] We conclude that the debentureholders have failed to establish ... oppression under s. 241 of the *CBCA* ....

Appeals allowed. Cross-appeals dismissed.

The *BCE* decision made the application of the oppression remedy more straightforward by providing a two-step test but it did not clarify how the second stage of the test would be met, which has left a gap for lower courts to fill. Jassmine Girgis writes ("The Oppression Remedy: Clarifying Part II of the *BCE* Test" (2019) 96:3 *Canadian Bar Review* 484 at 487–88 (footnotes omitted)):

In 2008, in *BCE Inc, Re*, the Supreme Court of Canada articulated a two-step framework for the oppression remedy, a remedy for protecting reasonable expectations. This framework for analysing cases built on the existing jurisprudence and attempted to inject a straightforward approach into an area of law known for its ambiguity and lack of clarity. First, it requires a court to determine whether a complainant's expectations are reasonable. Second, if the complainant's expectations are reasonable, the complainant will be entitled to a remedy if breach of those reasonable expectations is oppressive, unfairly prejudicial or unfairly disregarding of its interests. The first step of the *BCE* test and its application are unambiguous and straightforward, but the second step has done little to provide courts with guidance on how to approach these cases.

Step two of the *BCE* test frames this issue by requiring that the breach of reasonable expectations cause harm to the complainant in such a way as to meet one of the statutory components or standards of oppression, unfair prejudice or unfair disregard. The test does not, however, explain the type or amount of harm necessary to meet that requirement; the conditions necessary to satisfy the statutory components are not articulated. The analytical framework provided in the *BCE* decision is workable but it needed to be more comprehensive, as it has left lower courts with the task of identifying whether the impugned conduct rises to the level of harm required by the statute. A review of the case law shows that courts use the *BCE* test, and the outcomes are justifiable, but there is a lack of analytical clarity in the decisions, making it difficult to determine how judges reached these outcomes ...

The legislation does not define ["unfair prejudice" or "unfair disregard"] and the Supreme Court maintained that they cannot be "conclusively defined," which is correct, as they are simply descriptors of inappropriate conduct. Absent a definition, however, guidelines on how to meet these components are necessary. Although conduct will meet the standards on a case-by-case basis depending on the facts and the context of each case, rather than by ascribing legal meaning to the statutory components, one can nonetheless articulate principles to guide courts in their analysis. Specifically, identifying what effect of the conduct on the complainant is necessary to satisfy each component will clarify the courts' analysis of why certain behaviour meets the statutory standards, while other behaviour does not.

See also the following criticisms by legal scholars: J Anthony Vanduzer, "*BCE v. 1976 Debentureholders*: The Supreme Court's Hits and Misses in Its Most Incorporate Law Decision since Peoples" (2010) 43 *UBC Law Review* 205; Jeffrey G MacIntosh, "*BCE* and the Peoples' Corporate Law: Learning to Live on Quicksand" (2009) 48 *Canadian Business Law Journal* 255.

The *BCE* Court formulated a two-step test, but the principles on which it relied, principles articulating the boundaries and application of the oppression remedy, had been formed by lower courts as a result of years of oppression remedy litigation. Some of these cases are excerpted below.

Sidaplex-Plastic Suppliers Inc v Elta Group Inc (1995), 131 DLR (4th) 399, [1995] OJ No 4048 (Ct J (Gen Div)) [*Sidaplex*]

BLAIR J.: —

BACKGROUND

[1] The primary question to be addressed on this application is whether its facts give rise to one of those rare situations in which the "oppression remedy" provisions of the Ontario *Business Corporations Act* apply in the absence of bad faith or want of probity on the part of the respondents. There is also an issue under the *Bulk Sales Act*.

[2] The corporate parties are all companies engaged in the production and sale of plastics and film in the graphic arts industry. Sidaplex-Plastic Suppliers, Inc. is a judgment creditor of the defendant, the Elta Group Inc. The judgment, in the amount of $97,076.30, was obtained on consent and as part of an overall arrangement whereby a further claim by Sidaplex involving approximately $10,000 would be tried together with an outstanding action by Elta against Sidaplex claiming substantial damages for breach of fiduciary duty and breach of contract. Although the terms of the judgment itself provided that the moneys were to be paid in cash to the solicitors for Sidaplex, the parties entered into an agreement whereby the judgment would instead be secured by an irrevocable letter of credit in favour of Sidaplex, to be automatically renewed pending the disposition of the issues remaining outstanding between the parties.

[3] A letter of credit was arranged by Elta, through its bank, but instead of being renewable automatically, the letter of credit was for a fixed term. It expired on February 21, 1995. As the application for the letter of credit had sought an instrument that would be renewable automatically, the parties apparently assumed that such was the case. The letter of credit itself had been forwarded to Elta's solicitors who, in turn, forwarded it to Sidaplex's solicitors. No one apparently noticed that it was for a fixed term. Through what appears to be sheer inadvertence, the letter of credit was not renewed.

[4] Thus, Sidaplex's security for its judgment lapsed with the expiration of the letter of credit.

[5] In the meantime, Elta entered into an agreement whereby it sold the bulk of its assets to the defendant Kimoto Canada Inc., a competitor and sometimes supplier of

390 BANKRUPTCY AND INSOLVENCY LAW IN CANADA: CASES, MATERIALS, AND PROBLEMS

both Sidaplex and Elta. The proceeds of sale — something in excess of $533,000 — were utilized to eliminate Elta's indebtedness of $320,000 at the bank, and at the same time eliminate the liability of the defendant Frank Lin — Elta's sole shareholder, director and officer — to the bank on his guarantee of that indebtedness. The balance of the sale proceeds was used in one fashion or another to pay off other Elta indebtedness, including two other letters of credit totalling approximately $168,000.

[6] The sale did not comply with the provisions of the *Bulk Sales Act* RSO 1990, c. B.14. Neither Elta nor Kimoto filed particulars of the asset sale with the court, nor did they obtain an order exempting the application of the Act. Kimoto did not demand a statement of creditors pursuant to s. 4.

[7] Elta is no longer carrying on business in the graphic arts field. It has no assets.

[8] In these circumstances Sidaplex applies to the court, in its capacity as creditor, seeking to invoke the oppression remedy provisions of the *OBCA* against both Elta and Mr. Lin, in order to rescue it from its lost security position. It also relies upon the provisions of the *Bulk Sales Act*, asking that the asset transaction between Elta and Kimoto be set aside, or that Kimoto be required to pay it a sum of money in compensation for the value of the lost security.

ISSUES

[9] The following issues arise out of this:

1. Was the inadvertent failure of Elta to renew and maintain the letter of credit "oppressive conduct," as that term is employed in s. 248 of the *OBCA*, in the sense that it was unfairly prejudicial to or that it unfairly disregarded the rights of Sidaplex as creditor?
2. Was the inadvertent failure of Mr. Lin — the sole shareholder, director and officer of Elta — to cause the company to renew and maintain the letter of credit similarly "oppressive conduct," giving rise to personal liability on the part of Mr. Lin?
3. Does the failure to comply with the *Bulk Sales Act* render Kimoto liable to reimburse the applicant for the loss it has sustained as a result of the disappearance of its security?

LAW AND ANALYSIS

. . .

[10] Section 248 of the *OBCA* provides as follows:

248 (1) A complainant ... may apply to the court for an order under this section.

(2) Where, upon an application under subsection (1), the court is satisfied that in respect of a corporation or any of its affiliates,

(a) any act or omission of the corporation of any of its affiliates effects or threatens to effect a result;

(b) the business or affairs of the corporation or any of its affiliates are, have been or are threatened to be carried on or conducted in a manner; or

(c) the powers of the directors of the corporation or any of its affiliates are, have been or are threatened to be exercised in a manner,

that is oppressive or unfairly prejudicial to or that unfairly disregards the interests of any security holder, creditor, director or officer of the corporation, the court may make an order to rectify the matters complained of.

[11] A "complainant," in addition to being a current or former shareholder, director or officer of the company, is defined in s. 245 to include:

(c) any other person who, in the discretion of the court, is a proper person to make an application under this Part.

[12] It is well established now that a creditor has status to bring an application as a complainant, pursuant to s. 245(c) noted above. . . .

[13] In terms of "oppression," each of these cases turns upon its own particular facts. As Brooke JA noted, in *Ferguson v Imax Systems Corp* (1983), 43 O.R. (2d) 128, 150 D.L.R. (3d) 718 [at p.727 D.L.R.]: "[w]hat is oppressive or unfairly prejudicial in one case may not necessarily be so in the slightly different setting of another." Moreover, while some degree of bad faith or lack of probity in the impugned conduct may be the norm in such cases, neither is essential to a finding of "oppression" in the sense of conduct that is unfairly prejudicial to or which unfairly disregards the interests of the complainant, under the *OBCA*: see *Brant Investments Ltd v KeepRite Inc (1991)* 3 O.R. (3d) 289 (C.A.) at pp. 302–311, (per McKinlay JA); *First Edmonton Place Ltd v 315888 Alberta Ltd* [(1988), 40 BLR 28 (Alta QB)], at pp. 55–7.

[14] This is, in my view, one of those rare cases where the oppression remedy is applicable, notwithstanding the facts do not demonstrate any bad faith or lack of probity on the part of Elta or Mr. Lin.

[15] What the *OBCA* proscribes is "any act or omission" on the part of the corporation which "effects" a result that is "unfairly prejudicial to or that unfairly disregards the interests" of a creditor. The failure to renew the letter of credit is unquestionably an "omission" which has "effected a result" that is "prejudicial" to Sidaplex. Sidaplex has lost the security which assured payment of its judgment at a time when all other creditors, apparently, have been looked after, including unsecured trade creditors, and including Mr. Lin — the sole shareholder, officer and director of the company — who has been released from a substantial personal guarantee.

[16] Do these circumstances amount to an "unfair" prejudice, or to an "unfair" disregard of the creditor's interests, however? In my opinion, they do. In *First Edmonton Place, supra*, Mr. Justice McDonald considered the factors to be assessed in considering whether a remedy under the comparable provisions of the Alberta *Business Corporations Act* should lie. He said at p. 57:

"Assuming the absence of fraud, in what other circumstances would a remedy under s. 234 be available? In deciding what is unfair, the history and nature of the corporation, the essential nature of the relationship between the corporation and the creditor, the type of rights affected, and general commercial practice should all be material. More concretely, the test of unfair prejudice or unfair disregard should encompass the following considerations: the protection of the underlying expectation of a creditor in its arrangement with the corporation, the extent to which the acts complained of were unforeseeable or the creditor could reasonably have protected itself from such acts, and the detriment to the interests of the creditor. The elements of the formula and the list of considerations as I have stated them should not be regarded as exhaustive. Other elements and considerations may be relevant, based upon the facts of a particular case."

[17] Here, Sidaplex and Elta had an ongoing business relationship for some time, Elta being a purchaser and distributor of Sidaplex product. The continuing nature of this relationship would appear to be reflected in the consensual process that was established

to settle the outstanding differences between them: that is, the consent to the judgment for $97,076.36 and the referral of the additional $10,000 dispute for trial along with the complaints by Elta against Sidaplex. This was designed to preserve for Sidaplex, and protect, the liquidated amount which was clearly owing, while allowing the remaining, and less clear, issues to be litigated between them. It was the reasonable expectation of Sidaplex that this security would be preserved.

[18] Underlying intentions, understandings and expectations are now accepted as important underpinnings of the "oppression" remedy—using that term in its broad sense. This is as true whether the complainant is a minority shareholder or a creditor, in my opinion.

[19] Balanced against the underlying expectations of the creditor, in the set of criteria put forward in *First Edmonton Place, supra*, is the extent to which the acts complained of were unforeseeable or the creditor could reasonably have protected itself from such acts. This factor must be considered here. Counsel for Elta and Mr. Lin argues that the solicitors for Sidaplex were provided with a copy of the letter of credit and could either have refused to accept it—because it did not conform to the agreement—or, at least, have written reminding Elta that the letter of credit needed to be renewed. There is some merit in this argument, perhaps. In the end, however, it does not carry the day. Moreover, it neatly places the focus on the solicitors for Sidaplex, and sidesteps the fact that Elta's solicitors apparently never provided Elta or Mr. Lin with a copy of the letter of credit as issued either.

[20] It is Elta which had the contractual relationship with the bank vis-à-vis the letter of credit, and only Elta, through Mr. Lin, could have arranged for the letter of credit to be renewed. Sidaplex had no right or power to do so. Moreover, it was Sidaplex which was entitled to be protected, and it was Elta which had the obligation to ensure that such protection continued. In considering where the ultimate risk of the inadvertent failure to renew the letter of credit should fall, it seems to me that the proper balance is for it to fall upon the obligor, Elta and its sole directing mind, Mr. Lin.

[21] What of the liability of Mr. Lin himself?

[22] Courts have made orders against directors personally, in oppression remedy cases: see, for example, *Canadian Opera Co v Euro-American Motor Cars* [(1989) 69 OR (2d) 532 (HCJ), aff'd. (1990) 75 OR (2d) 720 (Div Ct)]; *Prime Computer of Canada Ltd v Jeffrey and Robinson & Jeffrey Ltd*, supra; *Tropxe Investments Inc v Ursus Securities Corp*, [(1991)] 6 OR (3d) 733 (Gen Div)]. These cases, in particular, have involved small, closely held corporations, where the director whose conduct was attacked has been the sole controlling owner of the corporation and its sole and directing mind; and where the conduct in question has redounded directly to the benefit of that person.

[23] Such is the case here. Mr. Lin is the sole shareholder, director and officer of Elta. He is the one who has benefitted personally from the events that have transpired because he has been relieved of his substantial exposure under his personal guarantee of Elta's indebtedness to the bank. Sidaplex, on the other hand, appears to be the only loser. All other creditors have been paid. Sidaplex has been deprived of the security for which it bargained, and on which it relied, and left with a "paper" judgment when it should not have been. That security—the letter of credit—while not directly guaranteed by Mr. Lin personally, was based upon the company's line of credit at the bank, which was in turn buttressed by Mr. Lin's guarantee. The evidence is that the bank looked primarily to that guarantee for its security, and the bank's testimony, at least, is that it would have been prepared to renew the letter of credit had Mr. Lin made the request and had he been prepared to support the renewal with his guarantee.

[24] Lawyers and judges tend to worry and fuss a great deal about whether or not a given set of circumstances permits the piercing of the "corporate veil." They do so for legitimate reasons pertaining to corporate law. While personal liability of a director in an oppression remedy situation may be founded upon such a base—as it was in the authorities referred to above—the issue, in my view, is not so much one of piercing the corporate veil as it is a question of the overall application of s. 248(2) of the *OBCA* and the interplay between its various provisions.

[25] When "oppressive" conduct (in the broad sense), has been found to have occurred under s. 248, the court has a very broad discretionary power to "make an order to rectify the matters complained of." That broad discretionary power, under s. 248(3) is to "make any interim or final order it thinks fit," including:

(j) an order compensating an aggrieved person

[26] In its targeting of the kinds of conduct encompassed by the oppression remedy provision of the *Act*, the legislature has focused specifically upon the acts or omissions of the corporation (s. 248(2)(a)), the business or affairs of the corporation (s. 248(2)(b)), and the exercise of the powers of the directors (s. 248(2)(c)). In a small, closely held corporation such as Elta, it is the director who is in the position of a Mr. Lin, who is the source of all such conduct. When the power of the director is exercised in a fashion which causes an act or omission of the corporation which effects an unfairly prejudicial result, or a result which unfairly disregards the interests of the complainant—or which causes the business or affairs of the corporation to be conducted in a manner which has the same effect—those powers themselves have been "exercised in a manner" which is caught by the section, in my opinion. Liability therefore lies directly with the director, under the section, in appropriate cases.

[27] This, in my view, is one of those cases. The proper way in which to rectify the matters complained of in this case is to make an order directing that Mr. Lin pay to Sidaplex the amount of Elta's judgment debt that should have been continually secured by the letter of credit, but which was not. That amount, as I have indicated, is $97,076.36, together with accrued interest. I so order. . . .

CONCLUSION

[34] In the summary, then, I hold that the conduct of Elta, and of Mr. Lin as its sole director, in failing to ensure that the letter of credit was renewed, in the circumstances, constitutes conduct that is unfairly prejudicial to or that unfairly disregards the interests of Sidaplex as a creditor of Elta. Elta has no assets, and there is little point in making an order against it, particularly since Sidaplex already has a judgment in its favour against Elta. Mr. Lin has been relieved from his obligations to the bank under his personal guarantee, however, in circumstances where that guarantee would in all probability have been required to be kept in place either to buttress the line of credit at the bank to support a renewed letter of credit or, more directly, to support the letter of credit itself. The appropriate disposition, in my view, in order to rectify the matter complained of, is to require Mr. Lin to compensate Sidaplex for its loss as a result of the lapsed letter of credit. That amount, as I have previously indicated, is $97,076.36, plus interest.

[35] The application against Kimoto is dismissed.

Varied on other grounds [(1998), 40 OR (3d) 563 (CA)].

Danylchuk v Wolinsky, 2007 MBCA 132, 287 DLR (4th) 646

MA Monnin JA:

[1] This is an appeal from findings of oppression under the provisions of s. 241 of the *Canada Business Corporations Act*, RSC 1985, c. C-44 (the "*CBCA*"), and an order that the appellants, Costas Ataliotis (Ataliotis) and David Wolinsky (Wolinsky), in their personal capacities, are liable, jointly and severally, to pay to the respondents an amount equal to one-half of their original investments or advancements as the case may be.

[2] The total amount of the judgment, for which the appellants are liable, is in the order of $875,000.

INTRODUCTION

[3] The appellants allege that the judge erred, firstly, in deciding the issue before her on the strength of challenged and disputed affidavit evidence instead of referring the matter for the trial of an issue and, secondly, by ordering a money award to be paid by both appellants jointly and severally.

[4] The appellants were shareholders and directors of Protos International Inc. (Protos) and Maple Leaf Distillers Inc. (Maple Leaf). Protos was a holding company which held shares in various businesses of which Maple Leaf was the most important. The respondents are either shareholders who invested in Protos or are creditors who loaned money to Protos. . . .

[8] [The trial judge] . . . proceeded to review the allegations made by the respondents and the countervailing position of the appellants and came to the following findings (at para. 64):

> I am satisfied on the affidavit evidence filed that the applicants have demonstrated oppression. The respondents have unfairly disregarded the interests of the applicants, as follows:
> 1) by using the companies which they controlled as their personal bank accounts;
> 2) by making unauthorized payments of personal expenses or expenses which had no valid corporate purpose;
> 3) by preferring the interest of some shareholders over the interest of others;
> 4) by disregarding the interests of some creditors to the advantage of others;
> 5) by not having regular shareholders' meetings to update the shareholders;
> 6) by not providing timely financial statements to the shareholders. . . .

[11] Dealing with the remedy, the appellants argue that a money judgment should not have been ordered for the simple failures of providing financial statements and calling meetings of shareholders, or for that matter for making payments as against their shareholder loans.

[12] Furthermore, the appellants also argue that there was no basis on which to make them personally and severally liable. . . .

CONCLUSIONS WITH RESPECT TO OPPRESSION

[40] I concede that the appellants presented evidence that they were entitled to proceed as they did and that there was nothing illegal in the manner in which they proceeded. That, however, does not change the fact that such conduct, as found by the judge, was oppressive as the term has been defined in the jurisprudence, namely, that the conduct of the companies' affairs by the appellants was unfairly prejudicial to, or that it unfairly disregarded

the interest of shareholders and creditors. Illegality and oppression are two entirely different concepts and oppressive actions can be, and are probably most times, legal actions.

[41] The conduct of the appellants was unfairly prejudicial to and unfairly disregarded the interest of the respondents as those terms have been defined in the decisions that I have referred to in these reasons. In arriving at her findings, the judge, according to the Act, had wide discretionary powers and she exercised them judicially and fairly.

[42] I would, therefore, dismiss the appeal with respect to the issue of finding oppression.

REMEDY

[43] This now leaves the issue of the remedy imposed by the judge. She initiates her analysis of the appropriate remedy to apply in these words (at para. 65):

> What is the appropriate remedy to be given? The applicants have asked for the return of their initial investments in Protos or the amount secured by the promissory notes in the case of the creditors. No authority has been provided by counsel for the applicants to show that this remedy has ever been granted in Canada by any court pursuant to the *CBCA*. I appreciate that the scope of the remedy section is extremely wide and allows for creative remedies to be fashioned in appropriate circumstances without the expense and time necessary to proceed to trial by statement of claim.

[44] And then she goes on to conclude (at paras. 67–69):

> The applicants invested in Protos expecting a significant return for their investment, but knowing at the same time that this was somewhat speculative. Had personal expenses not been paid and charged against the shareholders' loans by Ataliotis and Wolinsky, Protos and Maple Leaf might still have gone into receivership by virtue of the inability to finalize a lucrative contract in 2005 with Angostura Ltd. Without the oppressive actions of Wolinsky and Ataliotis the applicants may very well have still lost all of their investment. Nonetheless, the access by the respondents to funds in Protos and Maple Leaf without divulging that to the other shareholders and without allowing them to have drawn a proportionate amount of money, in my view, is unfair. And if the money accessed against the shareholders' account had been left in the company, its liquidity may have been better. That being said, it would not be equitable to force Wolinsky and Ataliotis to return the full investment as requested by the applicants.
>
> I believe an equitable remedy to be to order Wolinsky and Ataliotis jointly and severally to be liable to the applicants in the amount of one-half of their original investment or advancement, as the case may be.
>
> At first blush this might seem arbitrary. I believe it to be appropriate for a number of reasons. Section 241 of the *CBCA* allows for equitable remedies to be granted, including compensation to an aggrieved person. It would be almost impossible to quantify the exact amount that Wolinsky and Ataliotis accessed under circumstances that unfairly disregarded the interests of the shareholders and creditors in this application. Even if the matter was to proceed by way of statement of claim rather than application, oppression would be easily demonstrated by the applicants as it has been in this application but quantification would remain difficult even with a forensic accounting, and would be extremely costly to all parties. In arriving at this percentage I have attempted to balance the potential total loss of investment by the applicants with the substantial accessing of company funds by the respondents. Thus, the remedy has been fashioned as set out above. . . .

[47] The appellants argue that the remedy imposed by the judge is unprecedented and completely disproportionate to the manner in which they conducted the affairs of the company even if that conduct was found to be oppressive. They argue that the acts of oppression found to exist by the judge have no connection with the losses suffered by the shareholders or creditors and that their actions did not result in the failure of Protos. They point out that even if the respondents have lost their investments, they themselves have lost more than all of the respondents combined. They also argue that they gained no personal benefits or financial gains as a result of their conduct. . . .

[49] Finally, the appellants argue that the purpose of the legislation, and particularly the remedial portion thereof, is to rectify oppressive situations and not to reimburse investors in an enterprise that went wrong. . . .

[54] Before dealing specifically with the remedy imposed by the judge, it is useful to consider cases in which similar remedies have been imposed.

[55] *Loveridge Holdings Ltd v King-Pin Ltd* (1991), 5 B.L.R. (2d) 195 (Ont. C.J. Gen. Div.), is a decision in which a money judgment was awarded. Chapnik J stated in oral reasons (at paras. 20, 22–25):

> . . . The applicant made certain allegations of fraud and illegality against the respondent. I am not prepared to make those findings. On the evidence before me, I do not believe that the respondents acted in bad faith in that they deliberately intended to do harm to the applicant; they may well have thought that they were carrying on business for legitimate business reasons. The evidence indicates that they had carried on business in a similar fashion for several years in the past. However, in this situation, where there is a minority shareholder who has no say in the business and whose rights are being prejudiced, they cannot continue to do so.
>
> In the case of *Palmer v Carling O'Keefe Breweries of Canada Ltd* (1989), 41 B.L.R. 128, 67 OR (2d) 161, 56 D.L.R. (4th) 128, 32 O.A.C. 113 (Div. Ct.), the directors of the defendant company treated the company as though it was a private enterprise when it still had other shareholders. Thus, the court, although it found no bad faith, ordered the company to make an offer to redeem preference shares owned by some of its shareholders. At p. 172 [O.R.], Southey J stated:
>
>> Section 247 does not expressly require proof of bad faith. Whatever may be the rule in an oppression case, I do not think the statements in *Re Brant Investments Ltd and KeepRite Inc* (1987), 60 O.R. (2d) 737, 42 D.L.R. (4th) 15, 37 B.L.R. 65 (H.C.J.); *Re Pizza Pizza Ltd* (unreported, August 17, 1987), and *Bank of Montreal v Dome Petroleum Ltd* (1987), 67 C.B.R. (N.S.) 296 (Q.B.), are authority for the proposition that bad faith must be shown before an order to rectify a complaint may be made in a case of this nature. . . .

[57] Further guidance can be obtained from the Ontario Court of Appeal decision in *Budd v Gentra Inc* (1998), 111 O.A.C. 288 [CA] . . . . After a review of the principles of limited liability of directors at common law, Doherty JA goes on to distinguish the remedies available at common law with the remedies provided for under the Ontario oppression statute. He wrote (at para. 29):

> Section 241(3) vests the court with broad remedial powers. It provides that in rectifying the matter complained of "the court may make any interim or final order it thinks fit." Those words are followed by a list of 14 orders which may be made and the express indication that those specific orders do not limit the generality of the remedial power given in the opening language of s. 241(3). The specific orders referred to in s. 241(3) include the power to require "any other person to pay to a security holder any part of the monies paid by him for securities"

(s. 241(3)(g)), and the power to compensate an aggrieved person (s. 241(3)(j)). Both orders can be made against the company and/or individuals, including directors and officers.

[58] And he continues (at paras. 33–35):

If the conduct of the corporation is oppressive, unfairly prejudicial to, or unfairly disregards the interest of corporate stakeholders, the court may impose a "fit order." The nature and scope of that order is circumscribed by the requirements that the order "rectify the matter complained of" and address only the aggrieved parties' interests as corporate stakeholders: *Naneff v Con-Crete Holdings Limited et al* . . . at pp. 489–490 . . . . By providing for remedies against individuals, including directors and officers, s. 241 recognizes that the rectification of harm done to corporate stakeholders by corporate abuse may necessitate an order against individuals through whom the company acts. To the extent that the section contemplates that individuals will bear the remedial burden flowing from the oppressive exercise of corporate powers, s. 241 takes a different approach to assigning responsibility for corporate conduct than does the common law. The section permits the court to address the harm done by the conduct described in s. 241 from a broader perspective than that permitted by a simple inquiry into the true identity of the actor.

    This broader perspective is entirely consistent with the purpose of the section which is aptly described by D. Peterson in *Shareholder Remedies in Canada* (loose leaf), at p. 18.1:

> The oppression remedy may be considered the *Charter of Rights and Freedoms* of corporate law. It is a relatively new creature of statute, so it is little developed. It is broad and flexible, allowing any type of corporate activity to be the subject of judicial scrutiny. The potential protection it offers corporate stakeholders is awesome. Nevertheless, the legislative intent of the oppression remedy is to balance the interests of those claiming rights from the corporation against the ability of management to conduct business in an efficient manner. The remedy is appropriate only where as a result of corporate activity, there is some discrimination or unfair dealing amongst corporate stakeholders, a breach of a legal or equitable right, or appropriation of corporate property.

Where a plaintiff seeks a remedy against a director or officer personally under s. 241, I do not think it is accurate to suggest that the plaintiff is attempting to "circumvent the principles with respect to personal liability of directors and officers." On the contrary, the plaintiff is making a fundamentally different kind of claim than is contemplated in cases like *Peoples* [*Montreal Trust Co of Canada et al v Scotia McLeod Inc et al* (1995), 87 O.A.C. 129]. The plaintiff is not alleging that he was wronged by a director or officers acting in his or her personal capacity, but is asserting that the corporation, through the actions of the directors or officers, has acted oppressively and that in the circumstances it is appropriate (i.e., fit) to rectify that oppression by an order against the directors or officers personally.

[59] And he comes to the following conclusion (at paras. 46–47):

In my view, Farley J erred in holding that a director or officer could only be personally liable for a monetary order under s. 241 of the *C.B.C.A.* where the claim against the director or officer met the *Peoples* criteria. A director or officer may be personally liable for a monetary order under that section if that director or officer is implicated in the conduct said to constitute the oppression and if in all of the circumstances, rectification of the harm done by the oppressive conduct is appropriately made by an order requiring the director or officer to personally compensate the aggrieved parties.

In deciding whether an oppression action claiming a monetary order reveals a reasonable cause of action against directors or officers personally, the court must decide:

- Are there acts pleaded against specific directors or officers which, taken in the context of the entirety of the pleadings, could provide the basis for finding that the corporation acted oppressively within the meaning of s. 241 of the *C.B.C.A.*?
- Is there a reasonable basis in the pleadings on which a court could decide that the oppression alleged could be properly rectified by a monetary order against a director or officer personally?

[60] Finally, although stated in *obiter*, the Supreme Court of Canada in *People's Department Stores Inc (Trustee of) v Wise*, 2004 SCC 68, [2004] 3 S.C.R. 461, recognized the extraordinarily wide powers available under oppression remedy legislation ...

[62] I would conclude from the above that since the Supreme Court of Canada considers that creditors of insolvent companies can avail themselves of the remedies provided under oppression legislation and seek redress from directors of those companies, that at the very least the respondents before us are in the same if not a stronger position.

[63] At the outset, I must state that I reject out of hand the appellants' contention that a monetary remedy should not be imposed unless the finding of oppression comes following a trial of an issue. The law specifically provides that evidence of oppression may be adduced by way of affidavit evidence. Evidence is evidence whether it is presented to a judge in the form of affidavit or *viva voce* evidence and that evidence is not automatically less reliable because it happens to be in written form.

[64] A judge has a wide discretion in imposing a remedy that she or he thinks appropriate and an appellate court can only interfere with that decision if it concludes that there was an error in principle on the part of the judge or if the remedy imposed in all of the circumstances is an unjust order. I cannot come to that conclusion in this case.

[65] The appellants were both clearly implicated in the oppressive conduct of Protos as together they had total control of the company on a day-to-day basis. The respondents had advanced funds or invested in Protos because of their personal relationships and confidence with the appellants. The findings of oppression made by the judge are directly and wholly attributable to the appellants. They easily fit into the *Budd v Gentra Inc* criteria of instances where a monetary judgment can be deemed appropriate. In addition, the cases I have cited are of more than sufficient authority to justify and maintain the remedial order made by the judge.

[66] I concede that the remedy imposed is, to say the very least, significant but so are the losses incurred by the respondents. Any investor in a company such as Protos takes some element of risk with his or her investment but that investor is entitled to have that investment dealt with fairly. That was not the case with respect to Protos. There well might be no illegality in the manner the appellants dealt with the company, but their conduct prevented the shareholders and creditors from managing their investments in an informed and knowledgeable manner. They were entitled to much more than what they received from the appellants.

[67] The judge in her wisdom and discretion framed a remedy which she thought appropriate and equitable. She demonstrated no error in doing so and, therefore, I am not in a position to interfere with it even if I might consider it severe or significant.

Appeal dismissed.
[Leave to appeal dismissed [2008] SCCA No 63]

Estate of John Wood v Arius3D Corp, 2014 ONSC 3322

DM Brown J:

I. Oppression action to recover funds loaned

[1] In August, 2011, the late John Wood, having just been terminated as the Chief Executive Officer of the defendant, Arius3D Corp., indirectly lent that company $750,000 in order to finance a break fee required under an acquisition agreement Arius3D had negotiated with a company called Masterfile Corporation. Wood had made available those funds to Arius3D by advancing them to a Guernsey company, A3DL Limited, which, in turn, lent the funds to Arius3D. Wood received an August 18, 2011 promissory note from A3DL, the pre-payment term of which read, in part:

> Proceeds received from any of the companies listed on the attached schedule A (referred to as the "Irish Companies") will, at the sole discretion of the Holder, be used to repay all amounts outstanding pursuant to this Note, such payment to occur, if so determined by the Holder, the day after receipt of funds from the Irish Companies.

[2] In the result, three of the four "Irish deals" closed, with Arius3D receiving a total of $990,625 in payments in November, 2011. Arius3D did not use any of that money to repay the $750,000 loan Wood had made to finance the Masterfile break fee. Only in December, 2011 did Wood learn of the receipt of those funds. He complained to Arius3D, to no effect.

[3] In January, 2012, Wood commenced this oppression action against Arius3D, its directors and an officer, seeking damages of $950,000, consisting of the return of the $750,000 principal of his break fee loan, as well as two other amounts specified in the note from A3DL—$75,000 for a Cash Finance Fee and $125,000 on account of the Additional Finance Fee.

[4] Wood took his own life on January 23, 2013, at the age of 62. His estate, as represented by the individual plaintiff estate trustees, continued the action. Arius3D consented to the dismissal before trial of the counter-claim it initially had asserted against Wood. The trial proceeded as a hybrid trial with evidence-in-chief in part by way of affidavits. ...

C. Does the evidence establish that the reasonable expectation was violated by conduct falling within the terms "oppression," "unfair prejudice" or "unfair disregard" of a relevant interest

[124] There is no doubt, on the evidence, that Arius3D breached the undertaking it gave to Wood in Article 7 of the Break Fee Note. Not only did Arius3D not apply any of the proceeds from the three Irish deals to reduce the $750,000 loan made by Wood, Arius3D did not even tell Wood that it had received the funds until after it had spent them all. Did the failure of Arius3D to apply any of the proceeds received from the Irish companies to reduce the $750,000 break fee loan made by Wood amount to conduct which was oppressive, unfairly prejudicial or unfairly disregarded Wood's interest?

[125] Section 248(1) of the *Ontario Business Corporations Act* provides as follows:

> 248 (1) A complainant ... may apply to the court for an order under this section.
>
> (2) Where, upon an application under subsection (1), the court is satisfied that in respect of a corporation or any of its affiliates,
>
> (a) any act or omission of the corporation or any of its affiliates effects or threatens to effect a result;

(b) the business or affairs of the corporation or any of its affiliates are, have been or are threatened to be carried on or conducted in a manner; or

(c) the powers of the directors of the corporation or any of its affiliates are, have been or are threatened to be exercised in a manner,

that is oppressive or unfairly prejudicial to or that unfairly disregards the interests of any security holder, creditor, director or officer of the corporation, the court may make an order to rectify the matters complained of.

[126] Section 248 creates a sliding scale of wrongful—although not necessarily unlawful—corporate conduct running from the severe magnitude of wrongfulness captured by the term "oppression," to the lesser scale of wrongfulness of "unfair disregard." "Oppression" carries the sense of conduct that is coercive and abusive, and suggests bad faith; "unfair prejudice" may admit of a less culpable state of mind, that nevertheless has unfair consequences; and "unfair disregard" of interests extends the oppression remedy to conduct which ignores an interest as being of no importance, contrary to a stakeholder's recognized reasonable expectations [*BCE v 1976 Debentureholders*].

[127] Central to the oppression remedy is its focus on the effects of conduct, not the motivation or purpose. That is to say, oppressive conduct which causes harm to a complainant need not be undertaken with the intention of harming the complainant. If the effect of the conduct results in harm to the complainant, recovery under *OBCA* s. 248(2) may follow.

[128] I must confess that I found this part of the analysis to be the most difficult. A court's inquiry under *OBCA* s. 248(2) must be alive to the specific circumstances presented by a case. As the Supreme Court of Canada noted in *BCE Inc*, there are no absolute rules:

> The cases on oppression, taken as a whole, confirm that the duty of the directors to act in the best interests of the corporation comprehends a duty to treat individual stakeholders affected by corporate actions equitably and fairly. There are no absolute rules. In each case, the question is whether, in all the circumstances, the directors acted in the best interests of the corporation, having regard to all relevant considerations, including, but not confined to, the need to treat affected stakeholders in a fair manner, commensurate with the corporation's duties as a responsible corporate citizen [*BCE, supra*].

[129] In the present case the evidence disclosed that Arius3D, its directors and CFO were dealing with several balls in the air at the time the Irish funds began to arrive: (i) Arius3D was insolvent, certainly in terms of its inability to meet its obligations as they generally became due; (ii) its CFO and directors were trying to keep the company alive as a going-concern, hoping that by closing the Masterfile transaction Arius3D would achieve a modicum of financial stability; (iii) Wood was pressing for repayment of his $750,000 loan; and, (iv) Wood was leading a proxy fight against the incumbent Board.

[130] When a company crosses over the line into the grey-zone of pre-bankruptcy insolvency, directors and officers face an array of difficult choices and inevitably must make decisions in which there are winners and losers, all in furtherance of the best interests of the corporation. Arius3D gave strong assurances to Wood about the repayment of his loan from the proceeds of the Irish deals. It broke those promises, leaving an unsecured creditor unpaid. As enumerated by McGlone in paragraph 90 of his affidavit sworn November 5, 2013, Arius3D left many of its staff with large unpaid debts,

and its secured creditors also were left unsatisfied. Consequently, any assessment of the "fairness" or "unfairness" of conduct towards Wood must keep that larger context in mind—Arius3D broke many promises to many creditors. Put another way, at the material time Arius3D was disregarding the interests of many of its creditors, including Wood.

[131] At the same time, the evidence supports a finding that the directors of Arius3D—in particular Monych and Beutel who were the most involved—and its CFO, McGlone, were making, *in large part*, good faith efforts to keep the company afloat until the goal of closing the Masterfile transaction had been achieved. Given those circumstances, I cannot conclude that their decision to use some of the Irish deal proceeds to pay the operating expenses of $325,058 (Ex. 3, Tab 82) *unfairly* disregarded Wood's interests [Although part of the liability owed to the CRA arose after Wood had been fired, most predated his cessation as serving as a director: Ex. 3, Tab 82). By paying the CRA arrears, Arius3D reduced the personal liability of Wood as well as the other directors]. Nor could I conclude that their decision to pay the salary arrears of five employees— Arnold, Bell, Malik, Roy and Train—amounting to $66,313 *unfairly* disregarded Wood's interest.

[132] Yet, while their efforts *in large part* were good faith ones, not all were. Beutel, Monych and McGlone used some of the Irish deal funds for their own self-interest, repaying themselves unsecured loans totaling $197,000 (Beutel: $57,000; Monych: $70,000; and McGlone: $70,000) and, in the case of McGlone, salary of $30,807. Given their important roles in inducing Wood to make his $750,000 break fee loan, to then turn around, direct Arius3D to breach its undertaking to Wood and prefer their own self-interests, amounted to conduct by McGlone, Beutel and Monych which unfairly disregarded the interests of Wood. So, too, their decision to repay de Clare, his $27,500 loan which was made two months after Wood had advanced his loan and repaid within a matter of weeks. I have no doubt that McGlone, Beutel and Monych decided to do so because by that time Wood was leading a proxy fight against incumbent management. That motivation to prefer de Clare over Wood was an improper one and amounted to conduct which unfairly disregarded the interests of Wood.

[133] It is well-established that personal liability may attach to a director or officer under *OBCA* s. 248. As the Court of Appeal stated in *Budd v Gentra Inc*:

> A director or officer may be personally liable for a monetary order under [s. 241 of the *CBCA*] if that director or officer is implicated in the conduct said to constitute oppression and if in all the circumstances, rectification of the harm done by the oppressive conduct is appropriately made by an order requiring the director to personally compensate the aggrieved parties.

[134] In *Budd v Gentra Inc* the Court of Appeal continued:

> By providing for remedies against individuals, including directors and officers, s. 241 recognizes that the rectification of harm done to corporate stakeholders by corporate abuse may necessitate an order against individuals through whom the company acts. . . .
>
> To maintain an action for a monetary order against a director or officer personally, a plaintiff must plead facts which would justify that kind of order. The plaintiff must allege a basis upon which it would be "fit" to order rectification of the oppression by requiring the directors or officers to reach into their own pockets to compensate aggrieved persons. The case law provides examples of various situations in which personal orders are

appropriate. These include cases in which it is alleged that the directors or officers personally benefitted from the oppressive conduct, or furthered their control over the company
through the oppressive conduct . . .

[135] In the present case, two directors and one officer — Monych, Beutel and
McGlone — were the key decision-makers in persuading Wood to loan the $750,000 and
then in deciding not to use any of the Irish funds to reduce that loan. That latter decision
resulted in them personally benefitting by using some of the Irish funds to repay loans
which they had made to Arius3D or to pay salary arrears. I have found such conduct
unfairly disregarded the interests of Wood. In those circumstances I conclude that it is
fit to make the following orders, pursuant to *OBCA* s. 248(3)(j):

(i)   David Beutel shall pay to the plaintiffs the sum of $57,000, being the amount of his
      loan repaid by Arius3D from the Irish deal proceeds;
(ii) Perry Monych shall pay to the plaintiffs the sum of $70,000, being the amount of his
      loan repaid by Arius3D from the Irish deal proceeds; and,
(iii) James McGlone shall pay to the plaintiffs the sum of $100,807, being the amount of
      his loan and salary arrears repaid by Arius3D from the Irish deal proceeds. . . .

Order accordingly.
Affirmed [2016 ONSC 36 (Div Ct)].

Builders' Floor Centre Ltd v Thiessen, 2013 ABQB 23, 554 AR 152

KG NIELSEN J

I. Introduction

[1] The Appellants appeal the decision of the Master (2012 ABQB 86, 86 CBR (5th) 16)
setting aside the transfer of certain lands by Autumn Ridge Homes Inc. (Autumn) to
John Thiessen and Verna Thiessen.

II. Facts

[2] Autumn is an Alberta corporation. John Thiessen and Kelly Kijewski are the Directors of Autumn. J & V Holdings (1999) Inc. and 1318795 Alberta Ltd. are the shareholders in Autumn. John Thiessen and his wife, Verna Thiessen, are the shareholders in
J & V Holdings (1999) Inc. Kelly Kijewski and his wife, Donna Kijewski, are the shareholders in 1318795 Alberta Inc. John Thiessen is the President and Secretary Treasurer
of Autumn.

[3] On June 12, 2007, Autumn became the registered owner of property (the Land)
legally described as:

Plan 9322359
Block 1
Lot 2
Excepting thereout all mines and minerals

[4] Mr. and Mrs. Thiessen provided cheques totalling $100,388.77 to the solicitor act-
ing in respect of the purchase of the Land. These funds represented the purchase price
of the Land and legal fees. Mr. Thiessen deposed that Autumn then owed a shareholder
loan to J & V Holdings (1999) Inc. in respect of the funds provided.

[5] Autumn was incorporated for the purposes of constructing, *inter alia*, single family residences. Mr. Thiessen deposed that the Land was purchased for the purpose of constructing a house thereon that would be the residence for Mr. and Mrs. Thiessen (the Residence). As a result of advice received from a bank that Mr. and Mrs. Thiessen were dealing with and their accountant, the decision was made to register title to the Land in Autumn's name. This was, apparently, to promote Autumn, to establish corporate credit for Autumn and to allow Autumn to qualify for the Alberta New Home Warranty Program.

[6] On November 6, 2007, Builders' Floor Centre Ltd. (Builders') prepared a flooring installation proposal for Autumn with respect to the Residence. The proposal was accepted and on April 4, 2008, and September 16, 2008 Mr. Thiessen, on his personal credit card, provided deposits to Builders' totalling $17,500.

[7] On January 7, 2008, a mortgage between the Toronto Dominion Bank and Autumn in the sum of $457,465 was registered against title to the Land.

[8] On September 11, 2008, a mortgage between the Toronto Dominion Bank and Autumn in the amount of $682,077 was registered against title to the Land (the Corporate Mortgage). The mortgage in the amount of $457,465 was eventually discharged.

[9] In November and December 2008, Builders' supplied and installed flooring and window blinds in the Residence.

[10] On December 18, 2008, title to the Land was transferred from Autumn to Mr. and Mrs. Thiessen as joint tenants (the Transfer). The consideration shown on the Transfer of Land was $1. Mr. Thiessen swore an Affidavit of Transferee that the current value of the Land was, in his opinion, $800,000. On December 18, 2008, a mortgage between the Toronto Dominion Bank and Mr. and Mrs. Thiessen in the amount $682,077 was registered against title to the Land (the Personal Mortgage) and the Corporate Mortgage was discharged at that time.

[11] In January and February of 2009, Builders' provided an additional quote for work and materials to be provided in relation to the Residence.

[12] Builders' provided invoices to Autumn in respect of the work and materials supplied. Autumn provided a cheque to Builders' dated June 22, 2009, in the sum of $10,000 in partial payment of the invoices submitted.

[13] On November 3, 2010, Builders' commenced the within action to recover the balance of the monies outstanding in respect of the work and materials provided by Builders'.

[14] On November 30, 2010, John Thiessen made an assignment into bankruptcy.

[15] On April 4, 2011, Builders' obtained a Default Judgment against Autumn for the sum of $43,540.90 in respect of the outstanding amounts claimed, interest and costs (the Judgment). On October 26, 2011, an application by Mr. Thiessen to set aside the Judgment was denied.

[16] Autumn has made no payment to Builders' in respect of the Judgment.

[17] On September 12, 2011, Builders' received a Financial Statement of Corporate Debtor from Autumn which indicated that Autumn, at that time, had no assets beyond $10 in a Toronto Dominion Bank account.

[18] On February 3, 2012, Master Wacowich released his Reasons for Decision and directed that the Transfer be set aside and that the Registrar of Land Titles return registration of title to the Land to the name and status as it existed prior to the Transfer.

[19] An officer of Builders' has deposed that at the time Builders' began supplying work and materials to the Residence, and at all material times thereafter, Builders'

believed that Autumn was the registered owner of the Land and had no knowledge of the Transfer.

[20] Mr. Thiessen testified at questioning that Builders' had completed the supply of the work and materials at his request as an officer of Autumn. He also testified that at the time of the Transfer, the only asset owned by Autumn was the Land, and a line of credit which Autumn had with TD Canada Trust was overdrawn beyond its maximum limit of $50,000. Mr. Thiessen further testified that Autumn was never in a position to pay debts as they became due, outside of funds that were provided by Mr. and Mrs. Thiessen ....

[23] On June 29, 2012, the Appellants filed an Affidavit of Value and Valuator's Report attaching an appraisal of the Land as at December 16, 2008 (the Appraisal). The Land and the Residence were inspected by the appraiser on June 19, 2012 and the Appraisal was completed on June 22, 2012. The Appraisal valued the Land and improvements at $650,000 (qualified). The Appraisal was based on the inspection of the Land and on discussions between the appraiser and Mr. Thiessen. The appraiser commented as follows in the Appraisal:

> The subject is a detached bungalow, built in 2008. As of December 16, 2008, according to the owner, the subject were [sic] missing several interior and exterior elements including flooring on both floors, air conditioning system, a front door, landscaping/yard, deck and posts and interior painting. It was estimated that it would cost approximately $50,000 to complete the interior and there would be an additional $25,000 adjustment for negative market appeal. Since the subject property's incomplete condition and superior size/ building quality were off-setting qualities, the subject property has average market appeal.

[24] Counsel for Builders' conducted questioning of Mr. Thiessen with respect to the three mortgages registered against title to the Land at the material times, and with respect to the Appraisal.

[25] Regarding the Appraisal, Mr. Thiessen testified that: at the time of the Transfer the residence had a deck constructed on it although it was incomplete; the front door of the residence was installed sometime in December 2008; and the residence was painted, although the painting was not complete.

[26] With respect to the mortgages registered against title to the Land, Mr. Thiessen testified that: on October 23, 2008, he and Mrs. Thiessen had signed a Mortgage Application in respect of the Personal Mortgage in the sum of $682,077 and which estimated the value of the Land and the Residence at $1,065,000; the proceeds received on the Personal Mortgage were used to pay out the balance outstanding on the Corporate Mortgage in the sum of $558,768; and Mr. and Mrs. Thiessen received the sum of $138,352 (net of legal fees), being the net mortgage proceeds on the Personal Mortgage and the builders' lien holdbacks on the Corporate Mortgage ....

V. Analysis

. . .

Business Corporations Act

[81] The *Business Corporations Act*, RSA 2000, c B-9 (*BCA*) permits a "complainant" to apply for an oppression remedy. [The Alberta *Business Corporations Act* definition of complainant expressly includes a creditor.] ....

[82] In *Peoples Department Stores Inc (Trustee of) v Wise*, [2004] 3 S.C.R. 461, 2004 SCC 68, the Court commented generally on the status of creditors in Canada:

48 The Canadian legal landscape with respect to stakeholders is unique. Creditors are only one set of stakeholders, but their interests are protected in a number of ways. Some are specific, as in the case of amalgamation: s. 185 of the *CBCA*. Others cover a broad range of situations. The oppression remedy of s. 241(2)(c) of the *CBCA* and the similar provisions of provincial legislation regarding corporations grant the broadest rights to creditors of any common law jurisdiction: see D. Thomson, "Directors, Creditors and Insolvency: A Fiduciary Duty or a Duty Not to Oppress?" (2000), 58 U.T. Fac. L. Rev. 31, at p. 48. One commentator describes the oppression remedy as "the broadest, most comprehensive and most open-ended shareholder remedy in the common law world": S. M. Beck, "Minority Shareholders' Rights in the 1980s," in *Corporate Law in the 80s* (1982), 311, at p. 312. While Beck was concerned with shareholder remedies, his observation applies equally to those of creditors.

49 The fact that creditors' interests increase in relevancy as a corporation's finances deteriorate is apt to be relevant to, *inter alia*, the exercise of discretion by a court in granting standing to a party as a "complainant" under s. 238(d) of the *CBCA* as a "proper person" to bring ... an oppression remedy claim under s. 241 of the *CBCA*.

[83] It is interesting to note that although s. 241 of the *Canadian Business Corporations Act*, RSC 1985, c. C-44 (*CBCA*) is very similar to s. 242 of the *BCA*, the definition of "complainant" under the *CBCA* does not expressly include a creditor.

[84] As noted by the Court in *Remo Valente Real Estate (1990) Ltd v Portofino Riverside*, 2010 ONSC 280, 261 OAC 326 (Div Ct) at paras. 19 and 20, while there is case law to the effect that debt actions should not be routinely turned into oppression actions (see for example *First Edmonton Place Ltd v 315888 Alta Ltd* (CA), *R v Sands Motor Hotel Ltd* (1984), 28 BLR 122 (Sask QB)), creditors have been given status as complainants against a corporation where those in control of the corporation have stripped the corporation of assets or dissipated assets rendering it immune from a judgment in favour of the creditor.

[85] The Court in *A E Realisations (1985) Ltd v Time Air Inc* (1994), [1995] 3 WWR 527 (Sask QB); aff'd on other grounds (1995), [1995] 6 WWR 423 (Sask CA) held that "complainant" under s. 241 of the *CBCA* can include contingent claimants for an unliquidated demand in the category of a creditor. McDonald J contemplated this result under the *BCA* at para. 53 in *First Edmonton Place Ltd v 315888 Alta Ltd*.

[86] McDonald J also set out the general principles applicable to oppression actions under the *BCA* in *First Edmonton Place Ltd v 315888 Alta Ltd* (QB). He held that the applicant was bound to establish at least a *prima facie* case of having been subjected to oppressive or unfairly prejudicial actions or actions that unfairly disregarded its interests. McDonald J further held that the test of unfair prejudice or unfair disregard should encompass the following considerations: the protection of the underlying expectation of a creditor in its arrangement with the corporation, the extent to which the acts complained of were unforeseeable or the creditor could reasonably have protected itself from such acts, and the detriment to the interests of the creditor.

[87] The Supreme Court in *BCE Inc v 1976 Debentureholders*, 2008 SCC 69, [2008] 3 S.C.R. 560 discussed the oppression remedy under s. 241 of the *CBCA*:

45 A third remedy, grounded in the common law and endorsed by the *CBCA*, is a s. 241 action for oppression ... [which] focuses on harm to the legal and equitable interests of

stakeholders affected by oppressive acts of a corporation or its directors. This remedy is available to a wide range of stakeholders — security holders, creditors, directors and officers. . . .

68 In summary, the foregoing discussion suggests conducting two related inquiries in a claim for oppression: (1) Does the evidence support the reasonable expectation asserted by the claimant? and (2) Does the evidence establish that the reasonable expectation was violated by conduct falling within the terms "oppression," "unfair prejudice" or "unfair disregard" of a relevant interest?

[88] The Court held that in assessing the first question, useful factors in determining whether a reasonable expectation exists include: general commercial practice; the nature of the corporation; the relationship between the parties; past practice; steps the claimant could have taken to protect itself; representations and agreements; and the fair resolution of conflicts between corporate stakeholders.

[89] The learned Master cited the reasonable expectations listed in MA Springman et al, *Frauds on Creditors: Fraudulent Conveyances and Preferences* (Toronto: Thompson Reuters Canada Limited, 2009) at 24—12.1, 24-13, 24-15, 24-16:

1. A creditor reasonably expects that a corporation will not be used as a vehicle for fraud;
2. A creditor reasonably expects that the debtor will not convey away, for no consideration, exigible assets which will leave the creditor unpaid and unable to realize upon assets to satisfy the debt;
3. A creditor reasonably expects that the directors of a corporation will manage the company in accordance with their legal obligations, namely to act honestly and in good faith in the best interests of the corporation and to exercise the diligence expected of a reasonably prudent person; and
4. A creditor reasonably expects that the debtor will honour the understandings and expectations which the debtor has created and encouraged.

[90] These reasonable expectations relate to the fiduciary duties of directors. The Supreme Court in *BCE Inc v 1976 Debentureholders* stated:

82 The cases on oppression, taken as a whole, confirm that the duty of the directors to act in the best interests of the corporation comprehends a duty to treat individual stakeholders affected by corporate actions equitably and fairly . . . In each case, the question is whether, in all the circumstances, the directors acted in the best interests of the corporation, having regard to all relevant considerations, including — but not confined to — the need to treat affected stakeholders in a fair manner, commensurate with the corporation's duties as a responsible corporate citizen.

[91] I find that Builders' reasonably entertained an expectation that, assuming fair dealing, its chances of repayment would not be frustrated by the Transfer, and that it can establish a *prima facie* case of having been subjected to the type of conduct targeted by s. 242(2) of the *BCA*.

[92] While it is true that Builders' could have filed a builders' lien in this case or taken some other form of security from Autumn so as to protect itself, in my view, this alone does not disentitle Builders' from pursuing an oppression remedy. There is nothing in the evidence to suggest that such steps were necessary and in the circumstances, it was reasonable for Builders' to expect that Autumn would be operated in an appropriate manner and in a way which was not oppressive to Builders' interests. Builders' had commenced provision of work and materials to the Residence prior to the Transfer. The construction of

the Residence was a relatively simple and typical construction project. At that point in time, there was nothing to suggest that Builders' was at risk of not being paid and there was, therefore, no reason for Builders' to either file a builders' lien or seek some other form of security. Therefore, Builders' is a proper person to bring an oppression application.

[93] Further, I find that Autumn unfairly disregarded Builders' reasonable expectations as a creditor. The Transfer of Land removed, for little or no consideration, Autumn's only asset. This was conduct that was oppressive, unfairly prejudicial and that unfairly disregarded the interests of Builders' as a creditor.

[94] I conclude that the Master did not err in finding that Builders' had established entitlement to an oppression remedy.

VI. Conclusion

[95] The Master correctly determined that the Transfer was a fraudulent conveyance pursuant to the *Statute of Elizabeth* and a fraudulent preference pursuant to the *Fraudulent Preferences Act*. Further, he correctly concluded that Builders' had established entitlement to an oppression remedy pursuant to the *BCA*.

[96] Therefore, his Order stands, directing the return of the registration of title to the Land to the name and status of the registered owner as existed prior to the Transfer and directing that Builders' may seize and sell the Land and apply the proceeds to Builders' Writ of Enforcement after payment of any priority interest.

Appeal dismissed.

Wilson v Alharayeri is the Supreme Court's most recent pronouncement on directors' personal liability under the oppression remedy.

Wilson v Alharayeri, 2017 SCC 39, [2017] 1 SCR 1037

[47] To reiterate, *Budd* [*v Gentra Inc*, [1998] OJ No 3109 (CA)] provides for a two-pronged approach to personal liability. The first prong requires that the oppressive conduct be properly attributable to the director because he or she is implicated in the oppression (see *Budd*, at para. 47). In other words, the director must have exercised—or failed to have exercised—his or her powers so as to effect the oppressive . . .

[48] But this first requirement alone is an inadequate basis for holding a director personally liable. The second prong therefore requires that the imposition of personal liability be fit in all the circumstances. Fitness is necessarily an amorphous concept. But the case law has distilled at least four general principles that should guide courts in fashioning a fit order under s. 241(3). The question of director liability cannot be considered in isolation from these general principles.

[49] First, "the oppression remedy request must in itself be a fair way of dealing with the situation" (*Ballard* [*820099 Ontario Inc v Harold E Ballard Ltd*, [1991] OJ No 1082 (Ont Ct J (Gen Div))], at para. 142). The five situations identified by Koehnen relating to director liability are best understood as providing indicia of fairness. Where directors have derived a personal benefit, in the form of either an immediate financial advantage or increased control of the corporation, a personal order will tend to be a fair one. Similarly, where directors have breached a personal duty they owe as directors or misused a corporate power, it may be fair to impose personal liability. Where a remedy against the corporation would unduly prejudice other security holders, this too may militate in favour of personal liability (see Koehnen, at p. 201).

[50] To be clear, this is not a closed list of factors or a set of criteria to be slavishly applied. And as explained above, neither a personal benefit nor bad faith is a necessary condition in the personal liability equation. The appropriateness of an order under s. 241(3) turns on equitable considerations, and in the context of an oppression claim, "[i]t would be impossible, and wholly undesirable, to define the circumstances in which these considerations may arise" (*Ebrahimi v Westbourne Galleries Ltd*, [1973] A.C. 360, at p. 379 ("*Ebrahimi*")). But personal benefit and bad faith remain hallmarks of conduct properly attracting personal liability, and although the possibility of personal liability in the absence of both of these elements is not foreclosed, one of them will typically be present in cases in which it is fair and fit to hold a director personally liable for oppressive corporate conduct. With respect to these two elements, four potential scenarios can arise:

(i)   The director acted in bad faith and obtained a personal benefit;
(ii) The director acted in bad faith but did not obtain a personal benefit;
(iii) The director acted in good faith and obtained a personal benefit; and
(iv) The director acted in good faith and did not obtain a personal benefit.

[51] In general, the first and fourth scenarios will tend to be clear-cut. If the director has acted in bad faith and obtained a personal benefit, it is likely fit to hold the director personally liable for the oppression. On the other hand, where neither element is present, personal liability will generally be less fitting. The less obvious cases will tend to lie in the middle. In all cases, the trial judge must determine whether it is fair to hold the director personally liable, having regard to all the circumstances. Bad faith and personal benefit are but two factors that relate to certain circumstances within a larger factual matrix. They do not operate to the exclusion of other considerations. And they should not overwhelm the analysis.

[52] Further, even where it is appropriate to impose personal liability, this does not necessarily lead to a binary choice between the directors and the corporation. Fairness requires that, where "relief is justified to correct an oppressive type of situation, the surgery should be done with a scalpel, and not a battle axe" (*Ballard*, at para. 140). Where there is a personal benefit but no finding of bad faith, fairness may require an order to be fashioned by considering the amount of the personal benefit. In some cases, fairness may entail allocating responsibility partially to the corporation and partially to directors personally. For example, in *Wood Estate [v Arius3D Corp*, 2014 ONSC 3322], a shareholder made a short-term loan to the corporation with the reasonable expectation that it would be repaid from the proceeds of a specific transaction. Those proceeds were instead applied to corporate purposes, as well as to repayment of the loans made to the corporation by the defendant directors and officer and by another shareholder. D.M. Brown J. held the defendant directors and officer liable for the amounts used to repay their own loans and the shareholder loan, and also ordered the corporation to pay an equal amount towards the balance of the loan. As this last example shows, the fairness principle is ultimately unamenable to formulaic exposition and must be assessed on a case-by-case basis having regard to all of the circumstances.

[53] Second, as explained above, any order made under s. 241(3) should go no further than necessary to rectify the oppression . . . . This follows from s. 241's remedial purpose insofar as it aims to correct the injustice between the parties.

[54] Third, any order made under s. 241(3) may serve only to vindicate the reasonable expectations of security holders, creditors, directors or officers in their capacity

as corporate stakeholders (*Naneff* [*v Con-Crete Holdings Ltd*, 23 OR (3d) 481 (CA)], at para. 27; *Smith v Ritchie*, 2009 ABCA 373, at para. 20 (CanLII)). The oppression remedy recognizes that, behind a corporation, there are individuals with "rights, expectations and obligations inter se which are not necessarily submerged in the company structure" (*Ebrahimi*, at p. 379; see also *BCE*, at para. 60). But it protects only those expectations derived from an individual's status as a security holder, creditor, director or officer. Accordingly, remedial orders under s. 241(3) may respond only to those expectations. They may not vindicate expectations arising merely by virtue of a familial or other personal relationship. And they may not serve a purely tactical purpose. In particular, a complainant should not be permitted to jump the creditors' queue by seeking relief against a director personally. The scent of tactics may therefore be considered in determining whether or not it is appropriate to impose personal liability on a director under s. 241(3). Overall, the third principle requires that an order under s. 241(3) remain rooted in, informed by, and responsive to the reasonable expectations of the corporate stakeholder.

[55] Fourth—and finally—a court should consider the general corporate law context in exercising its remedial discretion under s. 241(3). As Farley J put it, statutory oppression "can be a help; it can't be the total law with everything else ignored or completely secondary" (*Ballard*, at para. 124). This means that director liability cannot be a surrogate for other forms of statutory or common law relief, particularly where such other relief may be more fitting in the circumstances ...

[56] Under s. 241(3), fashioning a fit remedy is a fact-dependent exercise. When it comes to the oppression remedy, Carthy JA put the matter succinctly:

> The point at which relief is justified and the extent of relief are both so dependent upon the facts of the particular case that little guidance can be obtained from comparing one case to another and I would be hesitant to enunciate any more specific principles of approach than have been set out above.
>
> (*Themadel* [*Themadel Foundation v Third Canadian Investment Trust Ltd*, 38 OR (3d) 749], at p. 754.)

[57] The four principles articulated above therefore serve as guideposts informing the flexible and discretionary approach the courts have adopted to orders under s. 241(3) of the *CBCA*. Having surveyed these principles, I turn now to their application in the instant case....

Appeal dismissed.

C. Director Disqualification

Director disqualification is a legislative scheme that seeks to protect the public from unfit directors by disqualifying them from being company directors. The concept was first mentioned as a possibility in Canada in the Tassé Report (Canada, Study Committee on Bankruptcy and Insolvency Legislation, *Report of the Study Committee on Bankruptcy and Insolvency Legislation* (Ottawa: Information Canada, 1970) (Chair: Roger Tassé), extracted in Chapter 1) and debated subsequently, but it has not taken shape. Contrast the Canadian position with the UK position, which is discussed below.

Corporate, Insolvency and Competition Policy: Statutory Review of the Bankruptcy and Insolvency Act and the Companies' Creditors Arrangement Act (Ottawa: Industry Canada, 2014)

> Given their key role in corporate governance, misconduct by directors both before and during insolvency proceedings attracts considerable attention. There are various statutory restrictions and obligations on directors to prevent, reduce and remedy misconduct (e.g. corporate, tax, environmental and employment legislation). Further, insolvency law imposes liability on directors for repayment of corporate dividends paid before bankruptcy, [*BIA* s. 101]. In corporate restructuring proceedings, their misconduct or negligence is not covered by the protective indemnification charge, [*BIA*, ss 64.1(4); *CCAA*, ss 11.51(4)] claims against them personally for wrongful conduct may survive, [*BIA*, ss 50(14) and (15); *CCAA*, ss 5.1(2) and (3)] and they can be removed from their positions if they are unreasonably impairing or acting inappropriately with respect to the proceeding, or are likely to do so [*BIA*, s 64; *CCAA*, s 11.5.]. The concern about directors using 'quick flips' to strip a company of valuable assets is addressed by mandated court scrutiny of purchases of corporate assets by directors.[*BIA*, ss 30(4), ss 30(5), ss 65.1(5), ss 65.1(6); *CCAA* ss 36(4), ss 36(5)]. Finally, if a corporation commits a bankruptcy offence—for example failing to comply with its duties as a bankrupt [*BIA* ss.198]—a director may be fined or jailed [*BIA*, s 204].
>
> However, directors are not disqualified from being a director of, or from incorporating another business, even if guilty of misconduct. Various reports, articles and proposed bills, addressed this issue but a disqualification regime has never become law in Canada. This is in contrast with the United Kingdom, where a detailed disqualification regime is in place. [*Company Directors Disqualification Act 1986* (UK), 1986, c 46.]
>
> The concept of a disqualification regime raises interesting questions regarding the need for and efficacy of such a regime. Important issues regarding the manner of implementing, the costs of implementing and maintaining, its constitutionality, and the impact on both directors' decision making and retention both before and during an insolvency proceeding must be considered.

[The issue of a Canadian director disqualification regime has been raised before. See, for example, Jassmine Girgis, "Corporate Directors' Disqualification: The New Canadian Regime?" (2009) 46:3 *Alberta Law Review* 677.]

D. Wrongful and Reckless Trading Statutes

One way to prevent the possibility of abuse of the corporate form is to impose statutory liability on the directors where the company continues to trade while insolvent. New Zealand,[1]

---

1   See *Companies Act 1993* (NZ), 1993/105, ss 135–136; and Thomas Telfer, "Risk and Insolvent Trading" in Rickett & Grantham, eds, *Corporate Personality in the 20th Century* (Oxford: Hart Publishing, 1998) 127 at 127.

England,[2] and Australia[3] have all adopted provisions that impose personal liability on directors for defined notions of wrongful, insolvent, or reckless trading.

The idea behind these statutes is to inhibit directors from continuing to operate an insolvent company at the expense of creditors. However, the imposition of statutory liability on directors may also involve costs. The legal regime must balance the need to protect creditors against the risk that a director liability regime will discourage a company's ability to innovate and take appropriate business risks. Risk taking is recognized as one of the fundamental features of company law. Professor Roy Goode ("Insolvent Trading Under English and Australian Law" (1998) 16 *Company and Securities Law Journal* 170 at 175) concludes that "risk is inherent in business activity, and if entrepreneurial activity is to be encouraged we have to accept the failure of some enterprises as the price to be paid." There is, therefore, a tension between the desirability of risk taking and the importance of deterring reckless trading. While there might be agreement on the underlying principle that directors should not continue to trade and gamble with creditors' money, the difficulty is defining precisely the point at which director liability should be imposed. Thus far, Canada has not opted to adopt a specific wrongful or reckless trading statute, but it has been debated in the past.

Industry Canada, *Efficiency and Fairness in Business Insolvencies* (Ottawa: Industry Canada, Corporate Law Policy Development, January 2001)

The issue of sanctions for conduct by directors and officers detrimental to creditors was raised as long ago as 1970, in the report of the Study Committee on Bankruptcy and Insolvency Legislation—the Tassé Committee. The report noted problems with individuals hiding under the corporate veil and commented that the inconvenience of bankruptcy to the principals of a bankrupt company often lasts no longer than the time needed to incorporate a new company. The Committee recommended imposing the status of bankrupt on a bankrupt corporation's directors and officers for up to five years, which would have made them ineligible to serve as directors under most corporations laws. It also recommended providing that no contracts with these persons should be enforceable. It further recommended exposing directors and officers to liability for the deficiency in corporate assets when transactions made were not in the corporation's interest, when a director used his company's property as his own, or when a director was responsible for defrauding creditors.

Bill C-60 of 1975, the first of a series of six omnibus bankruptcy reform bills introduced between 1975 and 1984, adopted most of the Study Committee's recommendations on directors' and officers' improper conduct. The bill contained provisions imposing liability on "agents," including directors and officers, for deficiency in the estate of a bankrupt company if the agent, in his own interest or that of a related person, caused the company, while insolvent, to carry on business or to enter into transactions contrary to the company's interest, to continue the business by ruinous borrowing or sales below

---

2   See *Insolvency Act, 1986* (UK), c 45, s 214; Andrew R Keay, *Company Directors' Responsibilities to Creditors* (New York: Cavendish-Routledge, 2007); Andrew Keay, "Wrongful Trading and the Liability of Company Directors: A Theoretical Perspective" (2005) 25 *Legal Studies* 431; and Andrew Keay "Wrongful Trading: Problems and Proposals" (2014) 65 *Northern Ireland Legal Quarterly* 63.

3   See *Corporations Act 2001* (Cth), s 558G; and Ian Ramsay, ed, *Company Directors' Liability for Insolvent Trading* (Sydney: CCH Australia and the Centre for Corporate Law and Securities Regulation, 2000). See also Jason Harris, "Director Liability for Insolvent Trading: Is the Cure Worse than the Disease?" (2009) 23 *Australian Journal of Corporate Law* 266.

cost, or to conduct the business so as to defraud, impede, obstruct or delay creditors. It also contained provisions enabling agents to be deemed bankrupt and hence ineligible to enter into enforceable credit contracts or to act as officers or directors if they were found primarily responsible for the company's insolvency. In addition, it provided that bankrupts could not act as directors or officers.

The agent liability provisions in Bill C-60 received support at the Parliamentary Committee stage. However, the provisions deeming agents to be bankrupt were criticized and the committee recommended that they be replaced by provisions prohibiting individual bankrupts or agents from carrying on the same business for two years. In fact, the deeming provisions of Bill C-60 were dropped from later bills. Bill C-17 of 1984, contained agent liability and disqualification provisions. It also proposed that liability be imposed on directors and officers of a bankrupt company for creditors' losses. The liability provision was similar to that of Bill C-60, the main difference being that it contained a good faith reliance defence. The bill also provided that, if a "caveat" was filed in respect of an agent, that person could not, while the caveat was in effect, act as a director or officer of a corporation or engage in any trade or business without disclosing the caveat. The bill also made bankrupts ineligible to act as directors or officers.

The Colter Committee reviewed Bill C-17 and recommended that directors be subject to personal liability and disqualification for wrongful conduct. Stakeholders responding to the Colter Committee's report generally supported provisions holding "responsible person(s)" to account, although the need to carefully define the terms used, such as "responsible person" or "wrongful trading," was stressed. Some concern was raised about the need to balance liability with the need to attract qualified people to take on directorships, especially during reorganizations. The Colter Committee's recommendations on "responsible persons" were not included in the 1991 bill. The issue was not discussed in the deliberations of the Bankruptcy and Insolvency Advisory Committee (BIAC), nor was it addressed in the 1997 bill.

[In 1986, the Colter Committee considered the following as a possible solution to the issue of wrongful trading: a director of a company could be personally liable for the loss suffered by creditors to the extent determined by the court if a director allowed a company to continue trading with the result that the position of existing creditors worsened or additional liabilities were incurred which were not paid and the directors knew or ought to have known that there was no reasonable prospect of avoiding that situation. This liability would arise where officers or directors of an insolvent company have authorized the company to make additional purchases of inventory in order to enhance the amount available for realization by a secured creditor whose debt they have guaranteed.[4]]

Practice Questions

Question 1
What is the distinction between debts incurred to employees for services performed during employment and amounts awarded by a court as pay in lieu of notice?

---

4   Canada, Advisory Committee on Bankruptcy and Insolvency, *Proposed Bankruptcy Act Amendments: Report of the Advisory Committee on Bankruptcy and Insolvency* (Ottawa: Minister of Supply and Services, 1986) at 113 (Colter Committee Report).

Question 2

Assume that acting on the 1986 recommendation of the Colter Committee, Parliament has adopted sections 135 and 136 of the New Zealand *Companies Act 1993*, set out below. How would you advise a director in the example that follows?

Sections 135 and 136 of the *Companies Act 1993* (1993 No. 105) (NZ) provide as follows:

135. Reckless trading—A director of a company must not—
a) Agree to the business of the company being carried on in a manner likely to create a substantial risk of serious loss to the company's creditors; or
b) Cause or allow the business of the company to be carried on in a manner likely to create a substantial risk of serious loss to the company's creditors.

136. Duty in relation to obligations—A director of a company must not agree to the company incurring an obligation unless the director believes at that time on reasonable grounds that the company will be able to perform the obligation when it is required to do so.

EXAMPLE

An engineer has an idea for a new laser switch (drug or biotech marvel) and needs funds to build an operational prototype. Whatever equity he had put into his company to fund his research is exhausted. He now seeks first-stage financing in anticipation of creating an operational prototype, generating customers, and beginning manufacturing operations. His firm's balance sheet shows negative equity and best projections show negative earnings for at least another five years. Both he and his lenders understand that only one in five high-tech companies end up turning a profit, and only one in ten end up a substantial success. But the lenders are willing to fund the company with convertible debt. The lenders calculate that they can diversify their lending over ten or more companies and ask for a rate of return on each that will leave them a profit when eight fail, one shows a profit, and one is a success (see Dale A Oesterle, "Corporate Directors' Personal Liability for 'Insolvent,' 'Reckless,' and 'Wrongful' Trading: A Recipe for Timid Directors, Hamstrung Controlling Shareholders and Skittish Lenders" (2001) 7 *New Zealand Business Law Quarterly* 20 at 26).

Question 3

In the absence of a wrongful or reckless trading provision, can directors continue to let the company trade if they know the company is insolvent? In *USF Red Star Inc v 1220103 Ontario Ltd* (2001), 13 BLR (3d) 295 (Ont Sup Ct J), Hawkins J stated:

I conclude that directors of a company may, with impunity, cause the company to order goods and services which they have no objective reason to believe the company can pay for in the absence of a preference or fraudulent activities which impair the company's ability to meet its obligations.

Is this an accurate statement of Canadian law? Would your answer differ if the director's motive for the inventory order was to reduce the director's personal guarantee to a secured creditor holding a security interest over existing and after-acquired property of the company? Which provisions in Canadian law might cover this scenario?

Question 4

Assume Geraldine and her company, Gerald Inc, entered into a contract with Philip. Under the contract, Gerald Inc supplied products to Philip, but Philip refused to pay. Gerald Inc retained a law firm to sue Philip, which the law firm did, successfully. At the time Gerald Inc retained the law firm, Geraldine knew that Gerald Inc was in a near insolvent state but nonetheless, agreed to pay the law firm's legal fees. Also, while the contract was between Gerald Inc and the law firm, the invoices for legal services were addressed to both Geraldine and Gerald Inc.

When the law firm sought compensation from Gerald Inc for its services, Gerald Inc refused to pay, and regardless, did not have enough money or assets to pay the law firm. The law firm then sued Geraldine herself. Gerald Inc maintained that the law firm did not have a contract with Geraldine; it only had one with Gerald Inc, and only Gerald Inc was liable to the law firm. How would you advise the law firm? If you advise it to pursue the oppression remedy, how would you structure your legal argument?

CHAPTER 11

Consumer Bankruptcy

"I got a job and I tried to put some money away
But I got debts no honest man can pay"

— Bruce Springsteen, *Atlantic City* (Columbia, 1982)

I. INTRODUCTION

It is a long-standing principle that the honest but unfortunate bankrupt deserves to be discharged or released from the burden of debts. But what policy basis justifies the bankruptcy discharge? In this chapter we focus on those aspects of Canada's insolvency system that are specially designed to address the problems of consumer bankruptcies. There are good reasons for the distinction between business and consumer bankruptcies. Functionally, consumer bankruptcies raise very different social, economic, and legal issues than business bankruptcies. Consumer bankrupts are eligible for a release from debts through a discharge. In contrast, as pointed out by the Supreme Court of Canada in *Orphan Well Association v Grant Thornton Ltd*, 2019 SCC 5 at para 161: "Corporations with insufficient assets to satisfy their creditors will never be discharged from bankruptcy because they cannot satisfy all their creditors' claims in full (*BIA*, s 169(4))."

Over the past thirty years there has been phenomenal growth in the number of consumer insolvencies. See the graph below and, generally, Office of the Superintendent of Bankruptcy (OSB), *Annual Statistical Reports*. More than any other chapter in the casebook, this chapter reflects the interplay of social, economic, and legal issues and the absence of an effective consumer voice in the drafting of the *Bankruptcy and Insolvency Act*, RSC 1985, c B-3 (*BIA*) consumer insolvency provisions. One could teach an entire course on consumer insolvency law.

A. Growth in Consumer Insolvencies

A variety of reasons explain the phenomenal growth in the number of consumer insolvencies since 1972. Probably the single most important factor is the commensurate growth in all forms of consumer credit during the same period and, since the mid-1970s, the impact of the availability of credit cards to most Canadian consumers. Industry Canada reports that:

> The ratio of consumer debt to personal disposable income in Canadian households has increased from approximately 110 percent in 2000 to 160 percent in 2012. The increase can be attributed to higher mortgage debt levels and an increase in home equity extraction, both associated with elevated housing prices. Higher mortgage debt levels are a

potential source of risk as Canadians may be more vulnerable to a decline in housing prices or an increase in interest rates.[1]

A number of empirical studies have been conducted in Canada over the past twenty-five years to identify the types of Canadians who go bankrupt and the reasons given by bankrupts (and, in some cases, by the trustees in bankruptcy) for their financial difficulties.

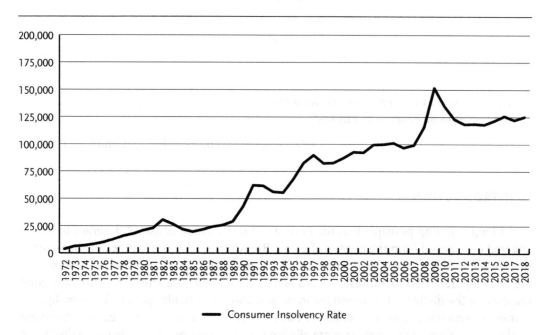

Consumer Insolvency Rate

Office of the Superintendent of Bankruptcy, *Insolvency and CCAA Statistics in Canada*, online: www.ic.gc.ca/eic/site/bsf-osb.nsf/eng/br02290.html#annual2017.

Among the most common reasons cited for bankruptcy were those related to credit card debt, adverse employment changes, and business failure (see Iain DC Ramsay, "Individual Bankruptcy: Preliminary Findings of a Socio-Legal Analysis" (1999) 37 *Osgoode Hall Law Journal* 15; Saul Schwartz, "The Empirical Dimensions of Consumer Bankruptcy: Results from a Survey of Canadian Bankrupts" (1999) 37 *Osgoode Hall Law Journal* 83).

The trustees themselves, in their reports to creditors and the court at the time of the debtor's application for discharge, often blame the bankrupt's poor money management skills. Creditors also endorse this explanation, but put much of the blame on Canada's insolvency system. Many of them believe it is too easy for debtors to go bankrupt and obtain a discharge from outstanding debts. The 1997 amendments to the *BIA* were meant to stanch the flow of bankruptcies by introducing the regime of mandatory payments of surplus income by debtors in section 68 of the *BIA* (see below, Part IV), but basic problems remain substantially the same as before.

---

1   Industry Canada, *Corporate, Insolvency and Competition Policy: Statutory Review of the Bankruptcy and Insolvency Act and the Companies' Creditors Arrangement Act* (Ottawa: Industry Canada, 2014) [footnotes omitted].

B. Bankruptcies vs Proposals

The above chart illustrating the number of consumer insolvencies represents the total of two very different proceedings. Consumer insolvencies are subdivided into consumer bankruptcy proceedings and consumer proposals. A debtor may make an assignment in *bankruptcy* (or be forced into bankruptcy by creditors) or choose to make a *proposal*. A bankruptcy will involve the debtor giving up all non-exempt property to the trustee in bankruptcy. At the end of the bankruptcy the consumer will receive a discharge (discussed below). A proposal will involve the debtor avoiding bankruptcy by entering into an agreement to pay off creditors over time. The number of consumer proposals now exceeds the number of consumer bankruptcies. In 2017, there were 57,969 consumer bankruptcies and 64,229 consumer proposals.[2] The extract below seeks to explain the increase in the number of consumer proposals.

Jason Allen & Kiana Basiri, "Impact of Bankruptcy Reform on Consumer Insolvency Choice" (2018) 44:2 *Canadian Public Policy* 100 at 100–101 and 111

> In September 2009, the Canadian government passed legislation to encourage financially distressed individuals to file for debt restructuring rather than declare bankruptcy. The amendments to the Bankruptcy and Insolvency Act included increasing the maximum debt limit (excluding debt secured by principal residence) for filing a consumer proposal (Division II), thereby allowing consumers to escape bankruptcy or the more onerous Division I proposal. It also increased the cost of filing for bankruptcy for high-income debtors. Specifically, it codified that all high-income debtors face wage garnishment for 21 months rather than 9 months....
>
> For financially distressed individuals, the decision about how to file for formal insolvency—via bankruptcy or debt restructuring—involves trade-offs. Filing for bankruptcy results in a fresh start, whereby almost all debt is forgiven, assets not protected by exemption limits are seized, and creditors must cease collection action. Filing a proposal, however, involves a formal restructuring plan with reduced debt repayment over a three- to five-year period. Debt restructuring allows individuals to keep all their assets and also maintain access to cheaper credit markets....
>
> In 2009, the Canadian government reformed the *BIA*, increasing the attractiveness of Division II proposals and increasing the cost of bankruptcy. The government policy was extremely successful in steering indebted households into the most cost-effective debt restructuring plan. Another way of seeing this is that the previous debt limit for Division II proposals was too tight. Relaxing the constraint allowed debtors to make a more cost effective choice. In addition, the *BIA* amendments led to an increase in proposals relative to bankruptcies. The main benefit of bankruptcy is debt forgiveness. The main cost is a loss of unprotected assets. The two key benefits of proposals are that filers are able to keep their assets and can maintain access to credit markets. The cost is (partial) debt repayment. Take-up of proposals increased by 11.5 percentage points after the change in legislation and has trended upward since. This would imply that individuals value the increased access to proposals, in addition to disliking the increase in wage garnishment associated with bankruptcy for those with high income.

---

2   Office of the Superintendent of Bankruptcy (OSB), *Insolvency Statistics in Canada—Annual Report 2017* (Ottawa: Innovation, Science and Economic Development Canada, 2018), online: www.ic.gc.ca/eic/site/bsf-osb.nsf/eng/h_br03876.html.

II. ROLE OF TRUSTEES

As we saw in Chapter 3, it is easy for Canadian consumer debtors to make an assignment in bankruptcy. Similarly, there is no shortage of trustees willing to offer their services and to administer the estate once the assignment has been filed with the official receiver. Trustees advertise widely—in the yellow pages of telephone directories, on radio, television, cable, and the internet—and encourage debtors to consult them about their debt problems. The difficulty debtors face at this stage is to know how to pay for the trustee's services. Most debtors cannot afford to pay even a substantial part of the trustee's fee and disbursements (now amounting to about $1,800); often, too, the debtor's estate contains only a negligible amount of non-exempt assets that could be realized to satisfy the trustee's fee and expenses. Thus, it is common for the debtor to sign an agreement with the trustee agreeing to pay the trustee's fees and disbursements by installments. If the debtor has a substantial amount of surplus income payable to the trustee under *BIA*, section 68, before the debtor's discharge, this, coupled with other income sources, may be sufficient to cover the trustee's bill before the debtor's usual discharge nine months after the bankruptcy (see ss 168 and 170).

In the article below, Stephanie Ben-Ishai and Saul Schwartz challenge the conventional wisdom that the poor are not heavy users of the insolvency system because creditors are unwilling to take risks on them and because many of the poor are judgment-proof. Consider whether you agree with the authors' recommendations. See also Jacob Ziegel, "Indigent Debtors and the Financial Accessibility of Consumer Insolvency Regimes" in Janis Sarra, ed, *Annual Review of Insolvency Law 2004* (Toronto: Thomson Carswell, 2005) 499.

Stephanie Ben-Ishai & Saul Schwartz, "New Evidence for Establishing a Debt Relief Program for Low-Income Canadians" (2019) (forthcoming) (footnotes omitted)

I. INTRODUCTION

A decade ago we asked the question: Should the bankruptcy process be more readily available to poor Canadians? At that time, several countries had recognized that it can be difficult for low-income debtors to file for bankruptcy because of the associated out-of-pocket costs. Moreover, because the financial affairs of most low-income debtors are not very complicated, bankruptcy seemed unnecessarily burdensome for both debtors and bankruptcy administrators. In our earlier article, we explored the question of whether Canadian debtors who could not afford to pay the normal fees charged by bankruptcy trustees should have low-cost access to bankruptcy through a mechanism other than the existing bankruptcy system....

One basic question is whether low-income debtors need bankruptcy. We noted in our earlier article that many are judgement-proof and, in principle, can simply refuse to respond to collection efforts. Nonetheless, that seemingly simple refusal is far more difficult than one might think and judgement-proof debtors frequently appear in trustees' offices seeking bankruptcy protection. They also seek debt relief from credit counselling agencies and we speak more about this option in later sections of this article. The second reason for believing that low-income people do not need bankruptcy is the idea that they do not accumulate very large debts and therefore have little need for bankruptcy protection.... We concluded that two principal flaws were present in the Canadian system:

i.   No national and even local uniformity exists in the treatment of poor debtors.

ii. Poor debtors face informational and financial barriers that may impede equal access to the fresh start provided by bankruptcy.

We recommended that Canada follow the lead of other jurisdictions in adopting a program that greatly lowers the out-of-pocket costs for low-income debtors seeking relief from their debts....

A decade later we can report that none of our recommendations have been adopted. We can also report that Canada now stands as an outlier among English-speaking countries in not having a low- or no-cost debt relief procedure for low income debtors. Nonetheless, our call for such a procedure is now strengthened by the empirical evidence from other jurisdictions, discussed in this volume, demonstrating that people with low income are using low-cost debt relief procedures....

Personal bankruptcy in Canada continues to be expensive and efforts by trustees to serve those who cannot afford it are scattered and not widely known. Further, while credit counselling agencies can help by providing advice (e.g., telling people they are judgement-proof) or by referring people to bankruptcy trustees, they generally focus, in terms of debt relief, on helping debtors whose income is sufficient to make payments on their debts. No systematic debt advice service exists for LILA [low income, low asset] debtors. Given that there are many Canadian LILA debtors who need relief from their debts but cannot afford it and given the experience of other countries in implementing low-cost procedures, we conclude that a low-cost procedure is needed in Canada.

II. THE INCIDENCE AND SIZE OF DEBTS ACROSS THE INCOME DISTRIBUTION

In the context of consumer bankruptcy, all those filing for bankruptcy are poor. Their debts exceed their assets and they cannot meet their financial obligations as they come due. Outside the context of consumer bankruptcy, however, poverty is usually defined in terms of income rather than wealth. Those with sufficiently low income are defined as poor regardless of the value of their debts and assets....

III. IS BANKRUPTCY CURRENTLY AN OPTION FOR LILA DEBTORS?

Many LILA debtors are judgement-proof but few know the law well enough to understand that threats from debt collectors are empty and that the calls will stop sooner rather than later. Even for those who understand that they are judgement-proof, "doing nothing" when faced with persistent and threatening collection calls is easier said than done. Because of their low income, LILA debtors will likely not qualify for the debt management plans offered by credit counselling agencies. For those who seek to resolve their debt situations, then, bankruptcy can be the best option.

The problem for the LILA debtors is that trustees may decide, rightly or wrongly, that the receipts of the estate, including any voluntary payments that the debtor can afford, are not likely to reach an acceptable level. If so, the trustee need not accept the case. Normal fees charged by trustees are a function of the receipts that the trustees earn from the debtor's estate. Section 128(1) of the *Bankruptcy and Insolvency General Rules* sets out the method by which maximum fees are to be calculated. These maximum fees are a function of the amount of funds coming into the estate with fees increasing as the amount of incoming funds increases. The fee schedule sets out the maximum fees that a trustee can collect. The trustee is to collect the first $975 of receipts, and then 35% of the receipts above $975 but less than $2000. That is to say, for the next $1,025 above $975, the trustee collects 35%. Lastly, the trustee also collects 50% of funds above $2000 to a maximum of $10,000. In practice, it seems that trustees try to realize at least $1900 on each file with little national variation, except in Quebec. The large firms in Quebec charge closer to $1350 per file and the smaller firms with more individual attention charge closer to the national rates.

At the onset of a bankruptcy, the level of receipts is generally unknown since it will depend on the amount the trustee earns for the estate by selling the debtor's assets and from the trustee's filing of the debtor's tax returns. In deciding whether or not to accept the case, trustees must determine whether they are likely to be paid for their efforts. In many cases, debtors do not have non-exempt assets and the expected amounts from the debtors' tax returns are insufficient to bring the receipts of the estate to an acceptable level. In such cases, trustees are allowed to ask the debtors to make payments to the estate over the course of the nine months of the bankruptcy. In a significant minority of bankruptcies, these voluntary payments comprise the bulk of the receipts of the estate. . . .

A. The Bankruptcy Assistance Program (BAP)

The OSB administers a little-used program called the BAP. Trustees must agree to be part of the program and those who do so are placed on a list of available trustees. The program then assigns listed trustees to administer the files of debtors who have approached at least two trustees to handle their bankruptcies, but have been turned away because of their inability to pay the standard fees. Our research in 2007–8 showed that few cases are actually filed under the BAP program.

It remains true that few BAP cases are filed. Of the 50,663 summary administration bankruptcy cases filed in the 2018 calendar year, there were only 110 BAP cases. Our 2018 interviews continue to illustrate, however, that it would be a mistake to assume that the number of LILA debtors is equal to the number of BAP cases. Perhaps a better measure of the number of low-income debtors is the number of cases in which receipts are less than $500.

There is no set fee charged by trustees for BAP cases. As in all summary administration cases, the trustee collects any tax refund arising from the pre-bankruptcy tax return. For LILA debtors, these sources might yield only a small amount of money. . . . The BAP program is clearly not a low-cost or subsidized debt relief program.

B. Summary

In Section II we demonstrated that low-income Canadian have significant debts. In this section, we demonstrate that, by and large, the currently available debt relief options — debt management plans and personal bankruptcy — are not available to LILA debtors.

We believe that the lack of uniform treatment of low-income debtors continues to be a major impediment to equal access to bankruptcy. In effect, their bankruptcies continue to be handled in a way similar to how paupers received aid before the advent of modern social assistance systems, when local charities, local churches, or municipal governments took up the task of providing for the destitute. As a result, the nature of the assistance that the poor received varied widely across Canada. Some received the assistance that they required, while others did not. Similarly, some low-income debtors have low-cost access to bankruptcy; many others do not. . . .

C. A Canadian DRO?

We propose that Canada adopt a Debt Relief Order (DRO) procedure modelled closely on those in New Zealand and the United Kingdom. A LILA debtor would be defined as a debtor with very low asset levels (with the usual exceptions) and income less than Canada's newly adopted MBM poverty line. Following Ramsay (2017), we recommend that there be no upper limit on how much debt can be discharged.

To allay creditor fears that the procedure would be a "car wash" that encourages debtors to freely and frequently avoid paying their debts, we would retain the main consequence of the New Zealand and United Kingdom procedures—the maintenance of a public record of the debtor's participation—for six years after application.

To further address creditor fears, we would adopt the DRO feature of allowing applications only through approved intermediaries. In general, these intermediaries ensure that the procedure is not being abused, checking, for example, that debtors are not hiding assets or sources of income. In the UK, these are advisors working for government-subsidized advice agencies such as Citizen's Advice or Step Change Debt Charity. No such agencies exist in Canada. Absent professional advice agencies, we recommend that the existing Canadian insolvency professionals—licensed trustees in bankruptcy and credit counselors—become the approved intermediaries, following an additional accreditation process. To fund these intermediaries, we recommend that debtors be charged a $200 application fee, payable to the intermediary.

The use of the poverty line to determine the income threshold and the use of the existing set of Canadian insolvency professionals as approved intermediaries are the two major variations that we recommend as compared to the international models.

Currently, the OSB is responsible for ensuring compliance with the *Bankruptcy and Insolvency Act* for personal bankruptcies in Canada. The Financial Consumer Agency of Canada (FCAC) is the federal agency responsible for the supervision of financial institutions with respect to consumer protection. While we are cognizant of the problem of regulatory fragmentation in Canadian financial services more generally, we are agnostic as to whether the proposed Canadian Debt Relief Order should be added to the responsibilities of the OSB or placed under the control of a different agency such as the FCAC.

VI. SUMMARY AND CONCLUSION

Many low-income Canadian families have significant debts, a fact we demonstrate in this paper by presenting information contained in the 2016 Survey of Financial Security. Managing such debts is doubtless a challenge for low-income families and there is little doubt that some could benefit from a low-cost debt relief procedure.

The current Canadian debt relief regime, however, discriminates against the low-income low-asset debtor population through filters such as trustee fees and requiring a regular source of income, effectively barring a subset of the population in dire need of access to a "fresh start". Our research demonstrates that the low-income Canadians are in a precarious position where they owe debt to their detriment, as opposed to "healthy debt" or debt tied to assets that appreciate over time. This, coupled with student loans (which are not dischargeable in bankruptcy), form a large portion of the debt that those with low-income bear.

In this article we presented four lines of evidence concerning of the number of LILA debtors who might use a Canadian low-cost debt relief procedure. First, in 2018, there were 3,499 personal bankruptcies whose estate generated less than $500, far less than the average trustee fee. This estimate is doubtless far too low because of the difficulty of finding a trustee willing to accept a low fee. Second, with the assistance of the CCS, one of Canada's largest credit counselling agencies, we analyzed a sample of debtors who seemed unlikely to have the income needed to support a debt management plan. Based on that data, we estimate that 4,500 LILA debtors approach Canadian credit counselling agencies each year. Third, social assistance recipients are certainly LILA debtors. They can fall into debt when, for whatever reason, their benefits are larger than they should be. Based on data from the Ontario ministry in charge of social assistance, there were 13,363 active social assistance recipients whose benefits began to be reduced because of benefit overpayments in 2017–2018. While this is a large number, and refers to only one of Canada's ten provinces, we do not know how many such debtors would use a low-cost procedure. The government is currently recouping the overpayment by reducing their monthly benefit by about 5%. Finally, we can calculate the number of users of the New Zealand and United Kingdome low-cost debt relief procedures on a per person basis. If we apply the resulting rates to the Canadian population, we estimate that the number of Canadian LILA debtors who would use a low-cost debt relief procedure would lie between 10,897 and 14,764.

Our best guess, based on these four lines of evidence is that between 5,000 and 10,000 LILA debtors would use a Canadian low-cost debt relief option, if one were adopted.

Canada is lagging in terms of access to debt relief for LILA debtors, however, Canadian policy makers can learn from the implementation of both the NAP and DRO, effectively adopting a regime that highlights the successes of both programs: a Canadian DRO. The Canadian DRO we propose encapsulates dimensions from both the NAP and the DRO to ensure the benefits to LILA debtors persist while containing measures to prevent abuse, like a public record and hiding assets or sources of income.

While we remain disappointed that our recommendations from a decade ago were not followed and Canada has fallen behind on access to justice issues on this front, there is a silver lining. The silver lining is witnessing what works elsewhere and the opportunity at a "fresh start" in creating our own low-cost procedure on this basis.

[Reprinted by permission of the authors.]

Anna Lund, *The Labours of Bankruptcy* (Vancouver: UBC Press, forthcoming 2020) at 60–61 (footnotes omitted)

Section 156.1 Agreements

Recognizing that some individuals require a longer period of time to pay their bankruptcy fees, the federal government amended the *Bankruptcy and Insolvency Act* in 2009 to allow debtors and trustees to enter into fee agreements that remain enforceable after a debtor's discharge. This new provision gives debtors and trustees more flexibility to reach a fee payment agreement that is acceptable to both parties. This agreement is only available to individuals who are bankrupt for their first-time. The agreement cannot provide for payments lasting more than 12 months after the debtor's discharge, and the total payments required under the agreement cannot exceed a prescribed amount, currently $1,800.

Some of the interviewees made use of the post-discharge payment agreement: their reviews were mixed. One trustee, who had only used the agreements four or five times, reported that they "seem to work pretty well" and was prepared to make greater use of them. Others were more critical. One felt that it was too much of a hassle to comply with the Office of the Superintendent's rules: "Because, there's too many conditions on it, so you think you're going to set it up to get the payment over time, and then various things might happen, some other asset comes in. Now that has to come off. And it just gets too complex." Others felt that enforcing the agreement would be prohibitively expensive or difficult. They did not want to be suing on agreements where the debt was, by definition, no more than $1,800. These trustees either opted not to use the agreement or only entered into it with a debtor who had already demonstrated a high degree of compliance. Many of the trustees who indicated that they used the agreement also indicated that they had not, and would not, attempt to enforce one.

III. EXEMPT PROPERTY

A. General Considerations and Purposes of Exemption Law

Exempt property is another troublesome area of consumer bankruptcy policy. Section 67(1)(b) of the *BIA* provides that the trustee is entitled to all of the debtor's property with the exception, *inter alia*, of property exempt from execution or seizure under any laws applicable in the province within which the property is situated and within which the bankrupt resides. From a very early date, the common law exempted a debtor's apparel, tools, and household utensils from execution, but little else. In particular, there was no exemption for the debtor's home (in some Canadian provinces there still are no such exemptions.)

What general purposes or objectives underlie exemption law? In *Saulnier v Royal Bank of Canada*, [2008] 3 SCR 166, Binnie J concluded (at para 17) that "the exemption of designated property from distribution among creditors under s. 67(1) is to allow the bankrupt to continue a living pending discharge and, when discharged, to make a fresh start."

Thomas Telfer, "The Proposed Federal Exemption Regime for the Bankruptcy and Insolvency Act" (2005) 41 *Canadian Business Law Journal* 279 at 283–85 (footnotes omitted)

> Most explanations for provincial exemption statutes begin with the fundamental premise that the statutes preserve a minimum level of subsistence and dignity for the debtor and the debtor's family. Professor Dunlop argues that "It is not acceptable that creditors, no matter how just the debt, should have the power to take from debtors the basic necessities of life." Exemption statutes permit the debtor to retain some essentials or what has been called the "basics of life while making the bulk of his or her assets available to satisfy judgment creditors." However, recent reform proposals suggest that a broader view should be taken of a necessity. In a 2001 report, *Modernization of Saskatchewan Money Judgment Enforcement Law*, professors Buckwold and Cuming recognized that beyond maintaining "a subsistence standard of living" exemption law should also permit a debtor and a debtor's family "to function as healthy, productive and contributing members of society." This broader rationale might justify a wider scope of necessities that are related to the reasonable educational, health and recreational needs of the debtor and the debtor's dependents.
>
> Existing provincial exemption statutes, however, reflect a traditional concern to protect a minimal level of existence. Under the general category of necessities many provincial exemption statutes include such items as household furniture, wearing apparel, food and fuel. Some jurisdictions recognize a motor vehicle as a basic necessity up to a fixed dollar amount. A debtor's basic necessity may also include shelter and some jurisdictions provide some form of exemption for residential property. However, there is no

consensus among the provinces and territories on the scope of the residential property exemption or whether such an exemption should exist at all.

A second major theme of exemption statutes involves preserving the means for debtors to "survive and to earn a living, thus contributing to their rehabilitation as citizens and to their capacity to repay their debts." Debtors should not be "deprived of an immediate means of livelihood." To accomplish this goal, exemption statutes protect items of personal property, such as tools of trade or agricultural implements, which assist a debtor in earning an income. Within this livelihood rationale, some provinces exempt farmland.

Preserving the economic vitality of the debtor has been justified from the broader perspective of the public interest. If creditors were permitted to "destroy debtors' economic viability, their continued maintenance would fall to society." Exemptions are said to shift the burden of support for the debtor from the "public to private credit sources." Debtors should not be "cast upon the community with nothing, penniless with the likelihood of becoming a public charge." Finally, exemption statutes minimize the judgment debtor's loss that may occur through forced execution sales. While the exempt property may be of value to the debtor, many of the debtor's personal possessions may yield little value at a sheriff's sale and in turn may impose considerable hardship on the debtor. Even where the creditor does not intend to follow through with its threat to seize and sell, "the coercive effect of a threatened seizure of necessaries often can be used to enforce direct payment from a defaulting creditor." Some provincial statutes protect items of sentimental value.

B. The Choice of Provincial Law for Federal Bankruptcy Exemptions

In the 19th century, many western US states adopted very generous homestead and farmstead exemptions in order to attract new settlers, and these provisions have survived to this day. One of the key issues in 19th century US debates about the need for national bankruptcy legislation was whether federal bankruptcy law should impose a uniform set of exemptions or whether the exemptions should continue to be governed by the law of the bankrupt's residence. The 1898 *Bankruptcy Act* adopted the latter solution. The report of the 1973 US Bankruptcy Commission recommended the adoption of a uniform federal standard. However, Congress rejected this approach and substituted a federal set of exemptions that the states are free to exclude if they wish (see US *Bankruptcy Code*, § 522). A majority of the states have made this election.

The drafter of the Canadian *Bankruptcy Act, 1919*, H.P. Grundy, chose to incorporate provincial exemption legislation to determine the types and values of property that would be exempt in a bankruptcy. As a result, bankruptcy exemptions vary widely among the provinces, though not as widely as in the United States. In particular, the western provinces are much more generous in their homestead and farmstead allowances than the other provinces. In deferring to the provinces to set exemptions, was Canada simply following the US *Bankruptcy Act* of 1898?

[Reproduced by permission of Canadian Business Law Journal Inc and Thomson Reuters Canada Limited.]

Thomas Telfer, "The Evolution of Bankruptcy Exemption Law in Canada 1867–1919: The Triumph of the Provincial Model" in Janis Sarra, ed, *Annual Review of Insolvency Law 2007* (Toronto: Thomson Carswell, 2008) 577 at 578–79 (footnotes omitted)

The Personal Insolvency Task Force (PITF) *Final Report*, published in 2002, suggests that the reliance upon provincial exemption law in the *BIA* can be traced to the influence of the US *Bankruptcy Act* of 1898. The PITF *Final Report* offers a tentative conclusion that the provincial exemption model in the *Bankruptcy Act of 1919* "was apparently copied" from the US *Bankruptcy Act* of 1898. Under the US *Bankruptcy Act*, "a bankrupt's exemptions depended on the law of the state in which the bankrupt resided at the time of bankruptcy."

Although the US *Bankruptcy Act* of 1898 may have been an influence, there are several other explanations that explain the policy choice to incorporate provincial exemptions laws into the *Bankruptcy Act* in 1919. First, the provincial model found in the 1919 Act was consistent with provisions found in the earlier Canadian bankruptcy legislation and bills which pre-dated the US *Bankruptcy Act* of 1898. Second, and perhaps more importantly, the diversity of provincial exemption laws precluded the adoption of a uniform bankruptcy exemption regime in 1919. Personal property exemption lists varied from province to province both in terms of value and types of property exempted. Additionally the existence of generous homestead exemptions in Manitoba, Saskatchewan, and Alberta and the absence of similar regimes in other provinces would have made it difficult for H.P. Grundy to draft some kind of compromise acceptable to each region. Beyond the statutory differences, a review of the case law reveals further regional differences and approaches to the interpretation of exemption statutes. Reconciliation of the provincial lists would have been nearly impossible.

If American law had any influence in Canada it was state homestead exemption statutes that provided a ready model for the Canadian western provinces of Manitoba, Saskatchewan and Alberta. The 160-acre homestead exemption could be found north and south of the border. The extensive homestead exemption, which was adopted in the Canadian west but not in other provinces, provided an important source of diversity among the provinces. However, Canadian provinces did not copy US state homestead law as a matter of convenience. The three western provinces were in a competition for immigrants with states to the south. Without such a homestead exemption north of the border there was a fear that immigrants would avoid the Canadian west in favour of the United States. The homestead exemption became a necessity in the Canadian west.

Thus when H.P. Grundy began to draft the 1919 Act, he was not starting with a clean slate, at least when it came to exemptions. The near forty-year period without a bankruptcy law had placed provincial debtor creditor law, including exemptions, at the forefront. The starting point for Parliament in 1919 was the old and diverse provincial law that had been enacted at various times and in response to various needs.

[Reproduced by permission of Thomson Reuters Canada Limited.]

C. Personal Insolvency Task Force Recommendations

The PITF felt the current disparities among the provincial exemption statutes were too great and that, at a minimum, all Canadian personal bankrupts, wherever situated, should be able to avail themselves at their option of a set of federal exemptions. The extract that follows describes the task force's position.

Personal Insolvency Task Force, *Final Report* (Ottawa: Industry Canada, Office of the Superintendent of Bankruptcy, 2002) at 24–26 (footnotes omitted)

Exemptions in the US vary enormously across the states, from the excessively generous to the very parsimonious, and this disparate result has given rise to much criticism because of the abuses to which it leads and the inherent unfairness of such a checkerboard system.

Strenuous efforts were made in the US during the passage of the *Bankruptcy Code* of 1978 to substitute a uniform federal set of exemptions for the state-determined exemptions. However, the Congress could only agree on an optional set of federal exemptions that the debtor would be free to elect if state legislation did not preclude the debtor from doing so. These optional provisions appear in Section 522 of the US *Bankruptcy Code.*

The Canadian position is similar to the position that prevailed in the US before 1978. There is a wide disparity among the provinces and territories with respect to the types of property that are exempt from seizure by the debtor's creditors, and therefore also exempt from seizure in bankruptcy, and the value of the property that is exempt. For example, some of the Canadian jurisdictions grant no exemptions in respect of the debtor's residence while others fail to include motor vehicles in the list of exempt assets. The value of the debtor's residence that is exempt from seizure in Saskatchewan, Alberta and British Columbia is substantially higher than the level of exemptions in most of the other provinces. Also, the exemption provisions in many of the provinces are badly dated and have failed to keep pace with increases in the cost of living and changes in the life styles and needs of ordinary Canadians.

These results conflict with the general theory of Canadian bankruptcy law, which proceeds from the premise that bankrupts and their creditors should be treated alike regardless of the residence or place of business of the debtor or the debtor's creditors. For example, Section 68 of the *BIA*, adopted in 1997, does not leave it up to the provinces to determine how much of the debtor's income shall be treated as surplus to the debtor's essential requirements. Instead, the Superintendent of Bankruptcy is required to determine the appropriate standards by directive, standards which are adjusted at regular intervals to reflect changes in the relevant consumer price index (CPI).

Ideally, therefore, the status of a debtor's property in bankruptcy should be treated the same way as the debtor's surplus income, and the kinds and levels of exemption should be determined by the *BIA* and not by delegation to provincial or territorial law. However, after full discussion, the Task Force concluded that a more modest approach is called for at the present time and that individual bankrupts should be able to opt for a list of federally prescribed exemptions in place of the otherwise applicable provincial or territorial exemptions. In this way the *BIA* will ensure that all bankrupts will have access to what is regarded as a reasonable set of exemptions regardless of the bankrupt's place of residence or weaknesses and gaps in the provincial or territorial legislation.

The recommendations of the Task Force are as follows:

a. There should be a federal exemptions list which the debtor, and only the debtor, can select in preference to the otherwise applicable provincial or territorial exemptions.
b. Debtors will have to make their election promptly following their assignment in bankruptcy or the making of a bankruptcy order. Where there is a joint assignment by related debtors, both parties must elect to be governed in their entirety by the federal or provincial list of exemptions; they cannot "cherry pick" among the different items in each list. If there is a deadlock between the debtors, they will be deemed to have elected the federal exemptions.
c. The specific exemptions and exemption levels recommended by the Task Force are:

   1. Apparel & household furnishings $7,500
   2. Medically prescribed aids and appliances and medication for use   No Limit
      or consumption by the debtor or the debtor's family

3. One motor vehicle whether used for personal, trade or business purposes — $3,000

4. Tools of the trade and professional books but *not* including motor vehicles used in the trade or business — $10,000

5. Debtor's residence, defined to include a house, apartment, mobile home and house boat — $5,000

d. There should be an exemption for real and personal property used by a debtor whose livelihood is derived from farming, fishing, forestry and other activities related to the natural resource sector of the economy. The amount of the exemption should be governed by applicable provincial/territorial law but is to be not less than $10,000 and not more than $20,000.

e. Registered pension plans and tax exempt life insurance annuities, but not Registered Retirement Savings Plans or RRSPs, shall continue to be governed by applicable federal or provincial law.

f. The above exemptions (other than exemptions governed by item (e)) shall extend to proceeds from the sale of, or the raising of a mortgage on, the exempt property.

g. Exemption levels are to be adjusted to the CPI as determined by regulation under the *BIA* or, preferably, by exercise of the Superintendent's Directive powers. The value of property for the purpose of the above exemptions shall be the fair market value of the property at the time of the assignment or the making of the bankruptcy order.

h. The exemptions will not apply in respect of a creditor's claim arising out of a maintenance, alimony and other family related support order governed by federal or provincial law.

i. The federal statutory exemptions, if elected by the debtor, cannot be waived by a debtor before the debtor's bankruptcy in favour of the debtor's unsecured creditors, and cannot be waived in favour of a secured creditor holding an unenforceable lien as described below in the Task Force recommendation concerning non-purchase money security interests.

* * * * *

D. Exemption Reform

The 2009 amendments to the *BIA* did not adopt the recommendations of the Personal Insolvency Task Force. However, as part of its 2014 review of the *BIA*, Industry Canada has called for submissions on a federal exemption list (see Industry Canada, *Corporate, Insolvency and Competition Policy: Statutory Review of the Bankruptcy and Insolvency Act and the Companies' Creditors Arrangement Act* (Ottawa: Industry Canada, 2014). Since the 2014 Industry Canada Report there have been no further federal exemption reforms.

There has been some reform at the provincial level. In 2004, the Uniform Law Conference of Canada (ULCC) released a *Uniform Civil Enforcement of Judgments Act*. See part 12 of the Uniform Act. The ULCC recognized that:

There is a significant degree of diversity among the provinces/territories with regard to the types of property and maximum value of items within a type of property that may be claimed as exempt from enforcement proceedings. The types of property that may be claimed as exempt are often related to the cultural and economic history of a province/territory.

The ULCC *Uniform Act* has influenced reform at the provincial level (see, for example, *Enforcement of Money Judgments Act*, SNB 2013, c 23, s 85; *Enforcement of Money Judgments Act (EMJA)* SS 2010, c E-9.22, s 93).

Tamara M Buckwold & Ronald CC Cuming, *Modernization of Saskatchewan Money Judgment Enforcement Law: Final Report* (Saskatoon: University of Saskatchewan, College of Law, 2005) at 144

> Current law dealing with exemption rights is very much in need of reform. Part X has been designed to modernize this area of the law and to provide a balanced approach to the need for protection of some of a judgment debtor's property from enforcement measures, on the one hand, and fairness to judgment creditors, on the other. The theme underlying the exemption system embodied in the EMJA is not compassion for judgment debtors. Rather, the objective is to ensure that judgment debtors are not denied the basic level of assets and income required to function as economically and socially productive individuals, and to meet the fundamental needs of their dependents. A debtor who is permitted to sustain a basic level of economic viability is likely not only to avoid becoming a civic burden through dependency on social welfare and support programs, but also to ultimately satisfy his or her creditors to a greater extent than would be possible were he or she financially prostrated. On the other hand, the tangible assets a debtor is allowed to retain in the face of unpaid creditors should amount to only what is required to meet his or her needs at a modest level. In a very few circumstances, the moral character of a creditor's claim or the conduct of the judgment debtor upon which the claim is founded justifies the limitation or even elimination of exemption entitlements in connection with the claim's satisfaction. The exemptions regimen adopted by the ULCC Draft Act largely parallels that contained in the EMJA.

E. Time for Determining the Exempt Status and Consequences of Disposition of Exempt Assets

The time for determining the exempt status of property is at the date of bankruptcy. If the debtor has sold an exempt asset prior to the bankruptcy, the debtor will not be able to claim an exemption in respect of the proceeds unless the proceeds are also given an exempt status by the applicable exemption law. In most provinces, a voluntary sale or other disposition of an exempt asset will result in the loss of the exemption (see, for example, *Armbruster v Armbruster (Trustee of)*, 2010 SKCA 125 at para 25; *Alberta (Treasury Branches) v Wilson (Trustee of)* (1996), 37 Alta LR (3d) 260 (CA)). The consequences of a disposition of an exempt asset are considered below in *Re Gruber*. If the transfer was an involuntary one, as in the case of a forced sale by a secured creditor, the proceeds were afforded an exempt status (see *Higgins Co v McNabb* (1979), 33 CBR (NS) 243 (CA)). On the meaning of forced sales see *Charles v Hernandez Becerra*, 2016 SKCA 163, below.

Re Gruber (1993), 22 CBR (3d) 262 (Alta QB)

FORSYTH J:

In this application, the Trustee seeks the advice and direction of this Honourable Court with respect to the following matter:

Do the proceeds from the bankrupt's sale of his joint interest in his home which was claimed exempt at the date of his Assignment in Bankruptcy which was sold by him prior to his discharge form an asset of the bankrupt's estate, or are these proceeds exempt?

The facts in this matter are fairly straightforward. The Bankrupt made an Assignment in Bankruptcy of February 14th, 1992, pursuant to which Deloitte & Touche Inc. was appointed as Trustee. At the time of his Assignment, the Bankrupt claimed as exempt his interest as joint tenant of certain real property which was indicated on his Statement of Affairs as having an estimated value of $138,000 subject to a mortgage in favour of Royal Trust in the amount of $90,000. At the time of the Assignment, the Bankrupt was in actual occupation of this property.

On or about May 22nd, 1992, while still an undischarged bankrupt, the Bankrupt and his wife sold their home generating a net sale of proceeds after payment of realtor's commission, legal fees, etc. of approximately $40,000. The undisputed evidence before me is that these funds have subsequently been used by the Bankrupt and his wife to support himself and his family during his bankruptcy. It should be noted that the sale of the property also was motivated in part from threats of foreclosure proceedings due to the mortgage on the property being substantially in arrears.

Complete disclosure was made by the Bankrupt to the Trustee in Bankruptcy prior to the sale of the property. The Bankrupt proceeded with the sale on the basis and understanding that the net proceeds insofar as his share was concerned would continue to be exempt to be used as he saw fit.

The concern that arises in this case appears to flow from the fact that notwithstanding that the Bankrupt was under considerable pressure to resolve the question of arrears on his mortgage he entered into what might be considered a voluntary sale rather than a forced sale and whether those circumstances change his entitlement to an exemption with respect to the net proceeds of the sale. . . .

Section 1(1)(k) of the *Exemptions Act*, RSA 1980, c. E-15, as amended, provides that:

1 (1) The following real and personal property of an execution debtor is exempt from seizure under a writ of execution: . . .

(k) the house actually occupied by the execution debtor and buildings used in connection with it, and the lot or lots on which the house and buildings are situated according to the registered plan thereof, if the value of the house, building and the lot or lots does not exceed $40000, but if the value does exceed $40000, the house, building and lot or lots may be offered for sale and if the amount bid at the sale after deducting all costs and expenses exceeds $40000 the property shall be sold and the amount received from the sale to the extent of the exemption shall be paid at once to the execution debtor and is until then exempt from seizure under any legal process, but the sale shall not be carried out or possession given to any person until the execution debtor has received $40000. . . .

It is to be noted that s. 1(1)(k) of the *Exemptions Act*, supra, requires that in order for the house for which exemption is claimed to be exempt from seizure under a writ of execution, the house must be actually occupied by the execution debtor.

There is clear case authority and it flows from the wording of the *Exemptions Act* that, absent bankruptcy, if the debtor abandons his occupation of the property or sells same, the *Exemptions Act* no longer applies to the proceeds of same and same may be subject to attachment by his execution creditors.

As previously noted, case authority is clear that the effective date for determination of the status of the exemption occurs on the date of bankruptcy. At that date the Bankrupt's property was severed into two estates: one estate that vests with the Trustee and is divisible amongst the Bankrupt's creditors, and one that remains with the Bankrupt because it is exempt under the provincial law. It should be noted that the Trustee may acquire other property of the Bankrupt if it consists of property that may be acquired by or devolve on the Bankrupt before his discharge as set forth in s. 67(c) of the *Bankruptcy Act.*

In *Re Pearson* [(1977), 14 OR (2d) 453 (Ont SC)], the trustee, as the successor to the bankrupt's estate, sought to change the designated beneficiaries of the bankrupt's RRSP so as to render it exigible under Ontario's *Insurance Act.* Henry J denied the trustee's application, stating at pp. 456–457 that:

> In my opinion, the view expressed by Houlden J is right and I respectfully adopt it. What comes into the hands of the trustee on the occurrence of the bankruptcy is the rights and interests of the insured in the insurance money and in the contract as they stood at the date of bankruptcy.... *In my opinion, so far as the creditors of the bankrupt are concerned, that situation crystallized at the time the bankruptcy occurred and that property by virtue of s. 47(b) of the Bankruptcy Act [now s. 67(1)(b) of the Act], was impressed with its character as not divisible among the creditors, for all the purposes of the bankruptcy.... [O]nce the bankruptcy occurred the provincial statute had spent its force.* There was no continuing operation of that statute in relation to creditors that could be altered by any act of the bankrupt or the trustee so as to displace the effect that s. 47(b) of the *Bankruptcy Act* had in relation to the property on the occurrence of the bankruptcy (emphasis added).

A similar view is expressed in *Pannell Kerr MacGillivray Inc v Beer* [(1988), 69 CBR (NS) 203 (Man QB)], where the facts are somewhat similar to the case at bar in that after bankruptcy, the bankrupt moved off the property and sold the property but before he was discharged from bankruptcy. The Court there held that the debtor was entitled to the proceeds from the sale of that property and Simonsen J stated at p. 206:

> I have no doubt that as of the date of bankruptcy the realty in question was exempt under s. 13(1) of the *Judgments Act.* The trustee, however, contends that the exemption was lost when the bankrupt disposed of the asset during the period when he was an undischarged bankrupt.
>
> *In my view the effective date for determination of the status of the exemption occurs on the date of bankruptcy.* Support for this conclusion is found in the decision of MacDonald J in *Re Hammill* (1984), 52 CBR (NS) 125, 32 Alta. LR (2d) 79 (QB). *If after the date of bankruptcy the bankrupt elects to convert an exempt asset into another form by selling it, the proceeds of sale do not become property which vests in the trustee for division amongst creditors.* [Emphasis added.] ...

I subscribe to the view espoused in *Re Pearson*, supra, and *Pannell Kerr MacGillivray Inc v Beer*, supra, that once an assignment in bankruptcy has been made, the determination of the property of the bankrupt which is assigned to the trustee and the property to which he can claim an exemption is made, as of the date of the assignment. As previously noted, property that may come into the hands of the bankrupt after the date of the assignment into bankruptcy may well properly flow through to the trustee in bankruptcy as property of the bankrupt estate. However, I am not satisfied that those decisions dealing with exempt assets losing their exemption have any application whatsoever in the case of a bankruptcy. If the determination of the division of property is made as of the date of bankruptcy, provisions of the *Exemptions Act* are no longer applicable after that date. In general terms, the intent of the *Bankruptcy and Insolvency Act* is, *inter alia*, to allow a bankrupt to reorganize his affairs and in due course be discharged from bankruptcy, and hopefully to maintain a solvent position thereafter. It surely could not have been intended that where a bankrupt is forced by financial constraints to sell an exempt asset in order to support his family or otherwise that he should lose that exemption even if the sale is voluntary, and thus be penalized for attempting to reduce his expenses to the benefit of his creditors. I am satisfied that an asset which is validly exempt at the date of bankruptcy remains exempt, notwithstanding the nature of any subsequent dealings with that asset.

Accordingly, turning to the facts in issue in this case, I find that the Bankrupt was entitled to the exemption of his interest in his home at the date of the bankruptcy as he was in actual occupation, and the equity was less than $40,000. The fact that he subsequently sold that property prior to his discharge, does not affect his entitlement to one-half of the net proceeds of that sale as exempt property. Therefore, the Bankrupt's interest in the net sale proceeds from his home which was claimed exempt at the date of his Assignment but subsequently sold by him is property exempt and does not comprise an asset of his bankrupt estate.

Order accordingly.

Charles v Hernandez Becerra, 2016 SKCA 163, 408 DLR (4th) 86

JACKSON and CALDWELL JJA:

[1] This is an appeal from a decision of a Queen's Bench Chambers judge declaring that the proceeds of the sale of a home belonging to Mr. Clinton Rodney Charles is exempt from seizure under s. 2(1)11 of *The Exemptions Act*, RSS 1978, c E-14 (repealed May of 2012). At this point, the actual contest is between the trustee in bankruptcy, standing in the shoes of Mr. Charles, and Ms. Maria De Lourdes Hernandez Becerra, who claims the proceeds as family property by virtue of an assignment from her former husband. ...

[4] In our respectful view, the law is settled in this jurisdiction that if the sale of exempt property is not voluntary, the debtor is entitled to claim an exemption in the proceeds. The *only* question in such circumstances is whether the sale is voluntary *within the meaning of the decided cases*. With respect to this question, the Chambers judge made no reversible error of law, mixed law and fact, or fact when he concluded that the sale was not voluntary. The Chambers judge stated the law correctly and he applied it correctly. His decision is in line with Saskatchewan jurisprudence. Thus, we would dismiss the appeal.

[5] Our decision to dismiss the appeal is best explained in relation to the following propositions:

(a) if a sale of exempt property is found not to be voluntary, the proceeds of the sale are exempt;

(b) Saskatchewan law holds that it is not necessary for a sale to be "forced" before it can be found not to be voluntary; and

(c) the Chambers judge, in the case at bar, did not commit a reversible error when he decided the sale was not voluntary.

[6] We will now proceed to explain the reasons underlying each of these propositions.

I.   If a Sale of Exempt Property Is Found Not To Be Voluntary, the Proceeds of the Sale Are Exempt

[7] Given the extensive case law with respect to this and the related issues, it is easy to forget that, at bottom, the court is dealing with a question of statutory interpretation and legislative intent.

[8] The relevant legislation is the *Bankruptcy and Insolvency Act*, RSC 1985, c B-3, s 67(1)(b)....

[9] In *Husky Oil Operations Ltd v Minister of National Revenue*, [1995] 3 SCR 453 at para 7, Gonthier J for the majority commented that the two fundamental purposes underlying the *Bankruptcy and Insolvency Act* are first, to ensure the equitable distribution of a bankrupt debtor's assets among the estate's creditors, and second, to provide for the financial rehabilitation of insolvent persons. With respect to this latter purpose, Parliament defers to the choices made by the provincial legislatures.

[10] Since the assignment in bankruptcy in this case took place in 2009, this appeal must be resolved according to *The Exemptions Act*, which was in force until May of 2012. Section 2(1)11 of that *Act* declares the exempt nature of the debtor's home:

Exemptions under executions

2 (1) The following real and personal property of an execution debtor and his family is hereby declared free from seizure by virtue of writs of execution, namely: ...

11   the house and buildings occupied by the execution debtor and also the lot or lots on which they are situated according to the registered plan thereof to the extent of $32,000 ....

[11] The historical basis of exemption law for the home pre-dates the creation of the province. Charles Dunlop describes the early history and objective of the "homesteads" exemption (C.R.B. Dunlop, *Creditor-Debtor Law in Canada*, 2d ed (Toronto: Carswell, 1995) at 470 [*Creditor-Debtor Law*]):

The homesteads exemptions, as these provisions are often called, were unknown to the common law, the earliest homestead statute having been enacted in Texas in 1839. From that date, the institution has spread to most states of the Union and to all jurisdictions in western Canada. George Haskins has described the purpose of the American homestead legislation as follows:

The principal objective of the homestead laws is generally regarded as the security of the family, which in turn benefits the community to the extent that such security prevents pauperism and provides the members of the family with some measure of stability and independence. Such laws have also been considered to be devices to encourage home ownership and to attract settlers to areas in which the home is accorded maximum protection.

As is made clear in *Creditor-Debtor Law*, the justification is expressed in similar terms today:

The obvious justification of exemptions statutes today is that they prevent judgment debtors from being stripped of all the means to support themselves and their families. It is not acceptable that creditors, no matter how just the debt, should have the power to take from debtors the basic necessities of life. Another aim often advanced to support exemptions laws is that they preserve to debtors the means to survive and to earn a living, thus contributing to their rehabilitation as citizens and to their capacity to repay their debts. It would

be possible to permit creditors to take all of their debtors' assets, thus forcing the debtors to rely on welfare, but this would appear to be a needlessly destructive and costly solution. The philosophy of the exemptions laws is to encourage debtors to survive and to carry on their lives as economic and social elements in society. Permitting creditors to seize and sell the necessary furniture and personal belongings of debtors will produce very little money on a sheriff's sale, but will cause considerable hardship to the debtors and their families as well as substantial cost to society which may have to maintain them on welfare.

(Emphasis added, footnotes omitted, at 454–455)

[12] The earliest recorded decision pertinent to this jurisdiction, which considers whether the proceeds of exempt property are in themselves exempt, is *Re Demaurez* (1901), 5 Terr LR 84 at 101 (NWT SC) [*Demaurez*]. ...

[13] Before the Territories divided into Alberta and Saskatchewan, the North-West Territories Full Court confirmed *Demaurez* in *Bocz v Spiller* (1905), 6 Terr LR 225 (WL) (NWT SC) [*Bocz*], affirming an earlier Chambers decision of Newlands J (*Bocz v Spiller* (1905), 1 WLR 366 (WL) (NWT SC) at paras 5–8).

[14] In his Chambers decision, Newlands J. wrote the following:

[5] Although a debtor has the right to do as he likes with his property which is exempt from seizure: *Temperance Insurance Co v Combe*, 28 C.L.J. 88; *Re Beatty and Finlayson*, 27 O. R. 642; *Freeman on Execution*, p. 1165; if he voluntarily converts it into other property which is not exempt from seizure that property would not be entitled to the protection given by the *Exemption Ordinance*: *Thompson on Homesteads and Exemptions*, p. 746; *Massey-Harris Co v Schram*, 5 Terr. L.R. 3[3]8. In that case Mr. Justice Scott said: "The provision exempts the homestead only so long as it remains a homestead, and where the debtor has voluntarily sold and disposed of it, the language of the provision is not wide enough to extend the exemption to the proceeds of such sale."

[6] The debtor having the right to mortgage his property, he to that extent waives his right of exemption, but it is not an unconditional waiver — it only entitles the mortgagee to subject the property to the satisfaction of his claim in like manner and to the same effect as if it were not exempt, but with respect to other creditors the property is exempt to the same extent as before the mortgage was given: *Freeman on Execution*, p. 1167.

[7] If the sale is not a voluntary one, the proceeds would, I think, be exempt from seizure, because a debtor who by a forced sale of his property loses his homestead, should not on that account be deprived of the right of acquiring another one from the surplus proceeds of the sale, if any: In *re Demaurez*, 5 Terr. L. R. 84.

[8] If his house is burned down and he has it insured, insurance money is exempt from seizure and he is entitled to receive the same to restore his home: *Osler v Winter*, 19 A.R. 94.

[9] The sale in this case was not, in my opinion, a voluntary one, but a forced sale. It is true it is under a mortgage given by him, but, as I have said, he had a right to mortgage it, and it is probable that at the time he gave the mortgage he expected to be able to pay it, and that it would not have to be sold. It is no more a voluntary sale than in In *re Demaurez*, where the land including the exemption was sold under order of the Court, the debtor having made a general assignment for the benefit of creditors. No sale which is ordered by the Court can be considered voluntary, as the debtor has no choice in the matter; he must either pay the amount due or the land will be sold.

(Emphasis added)

...

[16] Since *Bocz* and *Purdy*, the courts have continued to hold that the right to claim an exemption in sale proceeds is lost in the case of a voluntary sale *only*: *National Trust Co v Stancul* (1915), 7 WWR 1389 (Sask SC); *Royal Trust Company v Dekker*, [1976] 6 WWR 577 (Sask QB); and *Tripp v Gray*, [1978] 4 WWR 543 (Sask QB).

[17] The converse is also true: if the sale of exempt property is not voluntary, the right to claim an exemption extends to the proceeds. The only real issue is what is meant by a "voluntary" sale....

II. Saskatchewan Law Holds That It Is Not Necessary For a Sale To Be "Forced" Before It Can Be Found Not To Be Voluntary

. . .

[39] Thus, the law in this jurisdiction—as it has been interpreted by the Court of Queen's Bench and the Registrars in Bankruptcy since 1979 when *McNabb* issued—is that whether a sale is not voluntary depends on a purposeful interpretation of *The Exemptions Act* as applied to all of the relevant circumstances. The courts and bankruptcy registrar have found a sale not to be voluntary in the absence of a court order or the commencement of foreclosure proceedings.

[40] Having regard for these cases, the law is best expressed in these terms: if a bankrupt sells property that is exempt under s. 2(1)11 of *The Exemptions Act*, the judge considers whether the choice to sell the home, having regard for the whole of the evidence, is voluntary or is not voluntary. No one criterion is controlling, but in each case the judge considers the degree of compulsion caused by all financial circumstances that the bankrupt faced before deciding to sell....

III. The Chambers Judge, in the Case at Bar, Did Not Commit a Reversible Error When He Decided the Sale Was Not Voluntary

[42] The house was sold on March 27, 2009. Mr. Charles made his assignment in bankruptcy on May 14, 2009. The sale price paid out the value of the mortgage, which was approximately $200,000 (exclusive of taxes and legal fees), leaving approximately $29,000—which has been held in trust since then, pending resolution of this matter....

[44] Under the heading "Information Relating to the Affairs of the bankrupt," Mr. Charles indicated the following:

9(a) April, 2009 sold personal residence for net proceeds of $243,000.00. Proceeds after mortgage payout, realtor commission and legal fees of approximately $29,000.00 held in solicitor's trust account pending matrimonial property settlement.

2008–February, 2009 redeemed RRSP's and Canada Savings Bonds for net proceeds of approximately $45,000.00. Proceeds used for child and spousal support, home renovations, living expenses and debt servicing costs.

14. **Give Reasons for financial difficulty:**
Marital breakdown/assisting children and former spouse financially/large income tax obligation as a result of RRSP redemptions/unable to maintain payments.

(at AF157)

[45] That was the evidence before the Chambers judge when he first heard this matter....

[51] [T]here is no basis upon which to interfere with the following finding of the Chambers judge:

> [13] As to the second issue, I am also satisfied that the sale of the family home was not voluntary. The petitioner was doing everything he could to maintain the home for his family. It got to the point where he could no longer manage the payments and the petitioner and respondent concluded they had no choice but to sell the family home. . . .

[53] . . . At the time of the sale of the home, Mr. Charles had debt in excess of assets of over $350,000. Mr. Charles was behind in his mortgage payments. He owed significant debts. His creditors included Revenue Canada. He owed support to his wife and children. Waiting for the bank to commence mortgage proceedings in these circumstances would not only have delayed the inevitable, it would have reduced the amount of the proceeds of the sale of the home due to interest and legal costs. In our view, the Chambers judge's conclusion that the petitioner and respondent "had no choice but to sell the family home" is a finding of fact that was entirely open to the Chambers judge and unassailable by this Court.

[54] Thus, for these reasons, we would dismiss the appeal. . . .

Appeal dismissed.

F. Exempt Property and Valuation Issues

Provincial exemption legislation may exempt certain types of property regardless of value or the legislation may specify that some types of property will be exempt up to a maximum dollar value. Generally, property exceeding that capped amount is available to creditors. Where an exemption is subject to a value cap, when should a valuation of that exemption take place? Should the valuation take place as of the date of bankruptcy? Alternatively, should the trustee in bankruptcy or a creditor be entitled to ask for a valuation post-discharge where the exempt property has significantly appreciated in value? *Re McKay* examines valuation issues in relation to a value-capped exemption.

Re McKay, 2002 ABQB 598, 35 CBR (4th) 275

REGISTRAR FUNDUK:

[1] This is an application by Canadian Imperial Bank of Commerce ("CIBC") for an order that the bankrupt pay $21,375 to it, which is what the bankrupt netted above his $20,000 exemption when the co-owned principal residence was voluntarily sold some time after the date of bankruptcy. . . .

Facts

[5] In 1996 the bankrupt made a proposal, which was approved by the Court in March, 1997. The bankrupt carried on with the proposal for some time but eventually found it impossible to continue. On June 18, 1999 he assigned himself into bankruptcy. On that date he and his wife were the joint owners of the house and it was their principal residence.

[6] The *Bankruptcy and Insolvency Act* ("*BIA*") requires a bankrupt to provide a sworn statement giving certain information: s. 49(2). It is called a statement of affairs.

[7] In the statement of affairs which accompanied the assignment the bankrupt shows the house to have an "estimated dollar value" of $300,000 and that it is encumbered with a mortgage for $274,000.

[8] The bankrupt is a second time bankrupt so he was not entitled to an automatic discharge. He had to come to Court to get a discharge.

[9] The bankrupt's application for discharge was heard . . . on August 23, 2000.

[10] The bankrupt gave affidavit evidence in support of his discharge. He does testify about the house but the evidence is about the money that he had spent to repair and upgrade it. The house is over 65 years old and is in the Old Glenora area in Edmonton. The bankrupt, who is a lawyer, is not qualified to give opinion evidence about the value of the house. He does not do so.

[11] The bankrupt was cross-examined by CIBC's lawyer in March 2000. The cross-examination does touch on the house, but of course does not deal with its value. All that is in evidence is that the house was bought in July, 1995 for $275,000. . . . The exhibits to the cross-examination and the answers to undertakings are not relevant to the value of the house at the date of bankruptcy.

[12] The trustee's s. 170 report, which is required for every application for discharge, says that the house is "exempt" and that its value "as per Statement of Affairs" is $300,000.

[13] On August 23, 2000 Registrar Alberstat gave a conditional order for discharge. The operative part of the order, for today, is that the bankrupt pay 45 monthly payments of $1,500. The formal order says nothing about the house. It does not show that what the bankrupt was ordered to pay includes a "component" for the bankrupt's equity in the house, whatever it might be.

[14] CIBC was present at the application for discharge. It was an objecting creditor.

[15] The underlying facts which bring the parties before me are these. In February 2001 the bankrupt and his wife sold the house. At that date the bankrupt was still in bankruptcy, although there is the conditional order of discharge. The sale netted the bankruptcy $21,375 *above* the $20,000 exemption that s. 88(g) *Civil Enforcement Act* ("CEA") combined with s. 37(1)(e) Alta. Reg. 276/95 gives a debtor who is a joint tenant of the principal residence.

[16] The trustee demanded that the bankrupt pay him the $21,375. The bankrupt refused. Mr. McCabe, for the bankrupt, replied to the trustee on September 6, 2001. That part of his reply relevant to the issue before me is as follows:

> The real cause of the exceptional sale price received by the MacKay's appears to be that houses, generally, and more particularly, houses in Old Glenora have gone up in value, dramatically, since the summer of 1999.
>
> Our position is that the value of property, and the calculation of any equity, is to be done as of the date of bankruptcy. That was done, here, and as you correctly concluded, the available exemption was less than the reasonable costs to sell the property. As far as we are concerned, that is the end of the matter.

[17] The trustee declined to challenge the bankrupt's position and invited CIBC to get a s. 38 *BIA* order. CIBC got an order on March 12, 2002. The operative paragraph says:

> 1. [CIBC] may and is hereby authorized to commence proceedings in his own name and at his own risk and expense, for entitlement to $21,355.00, which represents the Bankrupt's equity in the Bankrupt's residence which is over and above the Bankrupt's exemption. . . .

[49] In Alberta exemptions are a matter of legislation, either by the Legislature acting within its constitutional jurisdiction or by Parliament acting within its constitutional jurisdiction. The most common Alberta legislation relevant to exemptions is the *Civil Enforcement Act*, although it is not the only Alberta exemptions legislation.

[50] In a bankruptcy the bankrupt's property passing to the trustee falls into three general classes:

(1) property which is not exempt;
(2) property which is wholly exempt regardless of its value;
(3) property which the bankrupt has a limited exemption for.

[51] The first class needs no explanation, and it is not relevant to the issue before me.

[52] The second class of property is where the legislation gives an exemption without a quantitative limit. One example is a life insurance policy which fits within s. 580(2) *Insurance Act*: see *Re McCallum* (2001), 283 AR 282 (Alta. QB). That insurance contract is exempt regardless of its value. Another example is an insurance policy which fits within s. 688(2) *Insurance Act*. That insurance contract is exempt regardless of its value. An example of that is *Re Pearson* referred to in *Ramgotra*. In that case the bankrupt was the owner of the insurance contract and the insured and his wife the designated beneficiary. The relevant Ontario legislation is set out in the decision and is identical to Alberta's s. 688(2) *Insurance Act*.

[53] If property is wholly exempt regardless of its value there is no need to debate at which point in time it should be valued for exemption purposes. That which is wholly exempt regardless of value remains wholly exempt. The value of wholly exempt property is simply not relevant for realization purposes because the trustee is prohibited from realizing on it. . . .

[55] The third class of property is that for which the bankrupt has a limited exemption. Those most commonly run across in both bankruptcy and non-bankruptcy cases is property identified in s. 88 *Civil Enforcement Act*. Some is limited by a dollar amount set by Alta. Reg. 276/95: clauses (b), (c), (d), (g) and (h). Some has a non-money limit: clauses (a), (e), and (f) and (i). Where any equity in the property exceeds the limited exemption the property is subject to realization by creditors, s. 89(1), subject to the protection given to the debtor by s.-s. (2).

[56] In the application before me the house was the bankrupt's principal residence [s. 88(g)] at the date of bankruptcy so he has as a matter of law whatever exemption the law gives him at that time. . . .

[61] I do not accept that the relevant value of limited exemption property for realization purposes should be its value at the date of bankruptcy to give bankrupts immediate certainty. A bankruptcy is not a one day circus with the finale being at the end of the day. An assignment is a start of a legal process which will continue for some time. Only time will spell the finale. The only certainties for a bankrupt at the date of bankruptcy are:

(1) he has assigned all his property to the trustee;
(2) his unsecured creditors cannot proceed against him without leave of the Court;
(3) when he exits the bankruptcy he can keep that which the law says is exempt. . . .

[63] At the "estate-administration stage" of the bankruptcy the trustee cannot exercise his distribution powers to use that which is exempt for the benefit of the creditors: *Ramgotra*, para. 48. But that which is exempt is the "maximum exemption" set out in the Regulation. The trustee is not required to transfer back to the bankrupt more than that and the bankrupt is not entitled to get back more than that. . . .

[80] I turn now to Mr. McCabe's third position.

[81] Nobody says that there need not be a cut-off date for dealing with the issue posed before me. I agree that the bankrupt should not be left to twist in the wind indefinitely. *Re Zemlak* 42 DLR (4th) 395 (Sask. CA) recognizes that. It indicates that the issue should be at least dealt with at the bankrupt's application for discharge, pp. 403–04:

In the factual context of this case we conclude that a non-exempt equity did not exist at the time of the application for discharge. On that ground alone the caveat should be vacated if it were not for the trustee's position that any increase in the equity will accrue to the benefit of the creditors. In argument before this court the appellant's counsel used the following example in his factum to illustrate the ultimate result—a result which was not disputed by the respondent:

The following is submitted as a specific example of the ultimate result if the Learned Chambers Judge is correct:

i. At the date of discharge of the Trustee a Bankrupt's home is valued at $50,000.00;

ii. The $50,000.00 is apportioned by way of an $18,000.00 real property mortgage and $32,000.00 exempt equity.

iii. At the time of discharge, the Trustee does not specifically return the home to the Bankrupt pursuant to s. 22(1);

iv. Some 30 or 40 years later the discharged bankrupt has paid off the mortgage and the home, through inflation, is then valued at $82,000.00;

v. When the discharge bankrupt moves to a retirement home, he would be entitled to his $32,000.00 exemption and the Trustee would distribute the $50,000.00 non-exempt equity to the creditors without any obligation to maintain or administer the home in the intervening years.

If this result were permitted, property acquired by the debtor after an absolute discharge in bankruptcy would be appropriated to payment of the discharged debtor's debts. The equity built up in the property after issue of an absolute order would form a realizable fund for creditors at some future date, notwithstanding the final discharge. Such a result does not comport with the philosophy of the Act.

We have no doubt that the Registrar in Bankruptcy would have recognized the importance of this issue if the material had alerted him to it. Since the registrar is familiar with the established practice of title clearing in the Land titles Office upon filing of the certificate of the bankrupt's discharge, he would undoubtedly have suggested that the bankrupt obtain counsel to deal with the matter at that stage. Accordingly, the respondent should not now be heard to say that it is entitled to maintain the caveat.

[82] I agree with that approach.

[83] A trustee can realize for the surplus equity in limited exemptions property before the bankrupt's application for discharge. *ICI Paints [v Gazette* 2001 ABQB 233] does not prohibit that. The trustee can also decide to deal with that on the bankrupt's application for discharge if he considers that to be the best time and best method for realizing on the surplus. Again, this is a practical decision by the trustee: *Re Rassell* [1999 ABCA 232].

[84] It is not uncommon for a trustee to wait until the bankrupt's application for discharge to deal with the surplus equity. An example is *Re Sawatsky* [2001 ABQB 504]. Conditional orders of discharge are sometimes a practical and effective means to deal with a surplus equity in property, be it land or chattels. I have given such orders over the years and I am confident others have also done so.

[85] There are advantages to surplus equity being realized that way. First, the trustee must do a s. 170 report and he makes recommendations about what order is appropriate. If he recommends a conditional order of discharge for the surplus equity proved creditors (who are given a copy of the report) might not be as opposed to the bankrupt's discharge. Second, a conditional order is a cost effective method of realizing on the surplus equity. Third, a bankrupt who wants to keep the property and pay a reasonable price for

the surplus equity may not presently have the money to do it. Instead of adjourning the application for discharge until the bankrupt is able to pay and has paid the conditional order gives a present finality, which is necessary at some point. In effect, the bankrupt buys now on time. The conditional order can even be ordered to be a charge against the property and be registered as such.

[86] The trustee is not the only person who can ask for a conditional order of discharge as a way to realize on the surplus equity in property. Proved creditors have a status to ask for that. If a trustee declines to realize on surplus equity prior to the application for discharge or declines to ask for a conditional order of discharge creditors have a right to pursue surplus equity in a timely manner. It is not uncommon for creditors to appear on applications for discharge and submit that the bankrupt should not be unconditionally discharged.

[87] If a surplus equity has not been realized on by the trustee, creditors who want realization have two options. First, they can appear at the application for discharge and ask for a conditional order for payment of the surplus equity. If that is given the surplus equity is shared between all proved creditors. Alternatively, a creditor can get a s. 38 order in a timely manner to let it realize for the surplus equity and if it gets the order and does realize on the surplus equity it does not have to share with other creditors. . . .

[98] *Ramgotra* speaks of a two-stage analysis, the second stage being the estate-administration stage. At the estate-administration stage the trustee deals with limited exemption property. He cannot use that which is exempt for the benefit of creditors; para. 48.

[99] If the trustee has not dealt with limited exemption property prior to the bankrupt's discharge the discharge is to be considered as an estate-administration stage for that property. That brings finality for all. Viewing the discharge as part of the estate-administration stage for dealing with wholly exempt or limited exemption property fits within the second stage of the *Ramgotra* analysis.

[100] Regardless whether a bankrupt has gotten an absolute, suspended or conditional discharge nobody can *later* raise an issue about surplus equity in a house. The discharge is the latest time that that issue is to be dealt with, if anyone wants to make that an issue.

[101] If a conditional order is given requiring the bankrupt to pay for the surplus equity nobody can later ride the market, up or down, to revisit that. If the house value later goes up the trustee and creditors cannot ask that the bankrupt now pay more. If the house value later goes down the bankrupt cannot ask that he now pay less.

[102] I have in my recitation of the facts outlined the sequence of events. There is nothing in the Court record showing that the bankrupt's equity in the house was an issue at any time prior to the discharge or at his application for discharge.

[103] CIBC did not raise an issue about the bankrupt's equity in the house until some months after the conditional order of discharge and only after the house was sold some months after the conditional order of discharge.

[104] It is too late. . . .

[110] The message to trustees and creditors is—advance claims for surplus equity in limited exemptions property by no later than the bankrupt's application for discharge, or forget it.

Application dismissed.

G. Non-purchase Money Security Interests in Exempt Personal Property

If the debtor has given a creditor a pre-bankruptcy security interest in exempt property, in general, provincial law does not prevent the secured party from enforcing its security interest. This is true where the secured party holds a purchase money security interest in the chattel. For example, provincial exemption law will not prevent a dealer or bank that has financed the purchase of a motor vehicle from repossessing the vehicle after the debtor's bankruptcy. This is generally (though not uniformly) regarded as a fair result. However, the position may be viewed very differently if the secured party holds a non-purchase money security interest in exempt property.

For example, in *Re Vanhove* (1994), 20 OR (3d) 653 (Ont Ct J (Gen Div)) the debtor granted a security interest by way of a chattel mortgage over household furniture and the secured party perfected its interest. Under section 2 of the Ontario *Execution Act*, RSO 1990, c E.24, household furniture is an exempt category of personal property. The debtor defaulted under the terms of the security agreement. The court held that the secured party was not precluded from enforcing its security interest against the household furniture because the *Execution Act* only applied to execution proceedings such as the enforcement of a judgment and not to secured creditors enforcing a security interest. The court held that the secured creditor was entitled to an order requiring delivery of the household furniture.

Many of the provinces now make non-purchase money security interests in exempt property unenforceable. See for example section 62(2) of the Ontario *Personal Property Security Act*, RSO 1990, c P.10 (*PPSA*). The PITF recommended the inclusion of a provision to deal with non-purchase money security agreements in the *BIA* to ensure uniform treatment of bankrupts across Canada (see PITF, *Final Report* (2002) at 27–28).

H. RRSP Exemptions in Bankruptcy

Section 67(1)(b.3) of the *BIA*, enacted as part of the 2009 amendments, now expressly provides an exemption for RRSPs. The provision confirms that property in an RRSP is not property that is divisible among the bankrupt's creditors (*Fiorito v Wiggins*, 2017 ONCA 765 at para 24; *Thibodeau v Thibodeau*, 2011 ONCA 110 at para 62). The provision creates uniform treatment of RRSPs in a bankruptcy (*Mullen (Re)*, 2016 NSSC 203 at para 40). The protection extended to bankrupts in section 67(1)(b.3) does not cover property contributed to such a plan in the twelve months, or any longer period that the court may specify, before the date of the bankruptcy. What is the rationale for this exception?

Should RRSPs be considered in the same context as other categories of exempt property such as household furniture, tools of trade, motor vehicles, or, in the case of some provinces, residential homes or farmland? In other words, do the same policy justifications that have been offered for the traditional categories of exempt property apply to RRSPs?

There is an interplay between provincial law and section 67(1)(b.3). The federal exemption specifies that it does not limit the existing provincial exemptions. Many provinces have enacted provisions creating an exemption for RRSPs (see, for example, Saskatchewan's *The Registered Plan (Retirement Income) Exemption Act*, SS 2010, c 10, Manitoba's *The Registered Retirement Savings Protection Act*, CCSM c R116, and Newfoundland's *Judgment Enforcement Act*, SNL 1996, c J-1.1, s 131.1). In these provinces, the RRSP will be fully exempt, including the contributions made immediately before the bankruptcy.

IV. DEBTOR'S OBLIGATION TO CONTRIBUTE SURPLUS INCOME TO THE ESTATE

A. Surplus Income

Before 1966, the *BIA* contained no explicit provisions dealing with the disposition of the debtor's income during bankruptcy. The only relevant provision was section 67(1)(c), entitling the trustee to claim the debtor's non-exempt property. In *Industrial Acceptance Corp v Lalonde*, [1952] 2 SCR 109, the Supreme Court held this included the debtor's income. However, that decision left it unclear what part of the debtor's income remained exempt. To clarify the position, section 68 was added to the *BIA* in 1966 (SC 1966–67, c 32, s 10), authorizing the trustee, and requiring them to do so if required by the inspectors, to make an application to the court for an income payment order. Initially, the amendment applied only to the debtor's earnings from employment, but it was subsequently enlarged to include other forms of remuneration. The court was given complete discretion in responding to the application "having regard to the family responsibilities and personal situation of the debtor." In a later decision, the Supreme Court of Canada held that section 68 constituted a complete code with respect to the trustee's power to attach a debtor's earnings (*Marzetti v Marzetti*, [1994] 2 SCR 765). For background to section 68, see Jacob Ziegel, *Comparative Consumer Insolvency Regimes—A Canadian Perspective* (Oxford: Hart Publishing, 2003) at 27–28.

Creditors were unhappy with the way trustees applied section 68 in practice and thought it left too much to the trustee's discretion. As a result, section 68 was completely revised in 1997, making it *mandatory* for the bankrupt to pay over to the trustee the surplus portion of their income as determined by policy directives issued by the Office of the Superintendent of Bankruptcy. Surplus income was again an issue in the 2009 reforms. In its 2003 report, the Standing Senate Committee on Banking, Trade and Commerce, estimated that 15–20 percent of bankrupts have surplus income.[3] "The Committee, in the interests of fairness and responsibility, believes that bankrupts with surplus income should be required to make contributions to their estate that would increase the moneys available for distribution to creditors" (61–62). The 2009 amendments clarify what constitutes "total income" as well as setting out a new statutory standard of "surplus income." If a debtor has surplus income it will have an impact on the time period a debtor will have to wait for their discharge. This is discussed below under Part V, "Discharge."

Note that Parliament excludes from the definition of "total income" amounts received by the bankrupt between the date of the bankruptcy and the date of the discharge as a gift, a legacy, or an inheritance or as any other windfall (s 68(2)(b)).

The following materials address the impact of the surplus income requirements. For a general discussion of surplus income see Stephanie Ben-Ishai, "Means-Testing" in Stephanie Ben-Ishai and Anthony Duggan, eds, *Canadian Bankruptcy and Insolvency Law: Bill C-55, Statute c. 47 and Beyond* (Markham: LexisNexis, 2007) at 344.

In *Kallenberger v Beck (Trustee of)*, 2005 ABQB 895 at para 15, the court concluded that "[s]ection 68 recognizes a reality of life, namely, even a bankrupt needs something to live on while their affairs are being controlled by their Trustee." However, the courts suggest that a balance must be struck between the interests of the bankrupt and creditors. "The Act holds that the bankrupt must be entitled to a fair and reasonable amount for the maintenance of himself or herself and the family. On the other hand, certain sacrifices have to be made for

---

3   Standing Senate Committee on Banking, Trade and Commerce, *Debtors and Creditors Sharing the Burden: A Review of the* Bankruptcy and Insolvency Act *and the* Companies' Creditors Arrangement Act (Ottawa: Senate, November 2003) (Chair: Hon Richard H Kroft) at 60.

the benefit of the creditors." (*Re Jakola* (2005), 13 CBR (5th) 198 (Ont Sup Ct J) at para 30; see also *Re Wilson*, 2016 NBQB 59.)

At issue is how to determine the appropriate standard of surplus income such that a bankrupt is able to maintain a reasonable standard of living. Under section 68(1) of the *BIA*, the "Superintendent shall, by directive, establish ... the standards for determining surplus income." See also *Directive No. 11R2-2018*, "Surplus Income." According to *BIA*, section 68(3), the "trustee *shall*, having regard to the applicable standards and to the personal and family situation of the bankrupt, determine whether the bankrupt has surplus income" [emphasis added]. Appendix A of *Directive No. 11R2-2018* which establishes the Superintendent's Standards, relies on low income cut-offs (LICO) compiled by Statistics Canada.

The LICO standards were developed by Statistics Canada for quite different purposes. If the Surplus Income Directive does not accurately reflect the financial position of debtors and their dependents, it will have an impact on whether the bankrupt will be able to make surplus income payments. The implications of not being able to make surplus income payments are significant because those bankrupts will not be able to secure a nine-month discharge. Does *Directive No. 11R2-2018* give the trustee any discretion to take into account the debtor's family situation or the debtor's social, economic, or geographic situation?

Does the new definition of total income in section 68(2) alter the result in *Re Landry*? What strategic behaviour on the part of bankrupts is the definition of total income trying to avoid?

Re Landry (2000), 50 OR (3d) 1 (CA) (footnotes omitted)

CHARRON JA (for the Court):

[1] The respondent, Nycole Landry, declared bankruptcy on June 4, 1997 and the appellant, Deloitte & Touche, was appointed trustee of the bankrupt's estate. Landry has been discharged from bankruptcy on October 15, 1998. The trustee has not yet been discharged and is still attempting to realize upon the assets of the bankrupt's estate for the benefit of the creditors. This proceeding concerns one potential asset.

A. THE FACTS

...

[3] In 1993, Landry was dismissed from her employment as a pilot with First Air. That same year, she brought a claim for unjust dismissal against First Air under the *Canada Labour Code*, RSC 1985, c. L-2. At the end of a first hearing, the arbitrator found that Landry had been unjustly dismissed.

[4] The employer successfully appealed the arbitrator's finding and a new hearing was ordered. Shortly before the second hearing, Landry changed solicitors. In May 1997, the first solicitor's costs were assessed in the amount of $77,500. Landry declared bankruptcy on June 4, 1997. The first solicitor is the main, if not the only, creditor in the bankruptcy.

[5] Landry obtained an absolute discharge from her bankruptcy on October 15, 1998 which effectively discharged her from her debt to the first solicitor. The trustee did not oppose the discharge but made it clear to Landry that the trustee maintained the right to claim any part of an eventual award of damages for unjust dismissal.

[6] In December 1998, at the conclusion of a second hearing under the *Canada Labour Code*, a different arbitrator also found that Landry was unjustly dismissed. When the trustee became aware of the arbitrator's decision, the trustee unsuccessfully attempted to intervene in the proceedings to claim the first solicitor's costs.

[7] The arbitrator's decision on the award has not yet been delivered and apparently awaits the outcome of this appeal. Although the exact amount is uncertain, the parties agree that Landry can expect to receive, as part of the award, some moneys for lost wages.

B. THE TRUSTEE'S MOTION

[8] In the spring of 1999, the trustee moved before Chadwick J under ss. 67, 68 and 71 of the *Bankruptcy and Insolvency Act*, RSC 1985, c. B-3 (the "*BIA*") for various forms of relief with respect to the expected arbitrator's award. The trustee sought a declaration that any amount awarded in relation to lost wages constituted property of the bankrupt that vested in the trustee for the benefit of the creditors, either through the automatic operation of ss. 67 and 71(2) or pursuant to an order that the court should make under section 68. (Simply put, s. 67 defines the property of the bankrupt that is divisible among the creditors, s. 71(2) is a general vesting provision and s. 68 makes specific provisions with respect to either the "total income" of the bankrupt, if the current provision applies, or the bankrupt's "salary, wages, or other remuneration" from employment, if the former version applies.) The trustee also sought a declaration that Landry's claim against First Air vested in the trustee on the date of bankruptcy and that the trustee was therefore entitled to intervene in the proceedings before the arbitrator to seek an order for costs in relation to the first solicitor's account. Finally, the trustee sought an order for a lien under s. 34 of the *Solicitors Act*, RSO 1990, c. S.15.

C. THE DECISION UNDER APPEAL

[9] Chadwick J held that, even if that part of the settlement related to wages in lieu of notice could arguably form part of the bankrupt estate under s. 67, 80 per cent of this amount would be exempt pursuant to the provisions of the *Wages Act*, RSO 1990, c. W.1 incorporated under s. 67(1)(b) of the *BIA*. In view of the small amount of money that could be apportioned, the motions judge stated that he was not prepared to make any order under s. 67. The motions judge held further that the current s. 68 applied but that the trustee was precluded from resorting to its provisions because the section applied only to undischarged bankrupts and because the trustee had not followed the procedure set out under s. 68. On the question of costs, the motions judge held that neither the trustee nor the former solicitors had any status in seeking an order for costs before the arbitrator as the costs are those of the client Landry and that she had waived her claim for costs as a result of her bankruptcy. Finally the motions judge refused to make an order for a lien under the *Solicitors Act* and dismissed the trustee's motion. The trustee appeals from this decision on all questions except that the trustee does not pursue the request for a lien under the *Solicitors Act*.

D. THE ISSUES ON THE APPEAL

[10] This appeal therefore raises the following questions:
1. Does Landry's claim against First Air or any part of the resulting award constitute property of the bankrupt that vests in the trustee under ss. 67 and 71(2) of the *BIA*?
2. If so, does any exemption apply pursuant to s. 67(1)(b) so as to except any part of the property from the estate of the bankrupt?
3. Is s. 67 superseded by the provisions of s. 68 in relation to a bankrupt's wages?

4. If so, which provision applies, the former s. 68, which was in force at the time Landry declared bankruptcy, or the present s. 68, which was in force at the time the trustee brought its motion?
5, Is the trustee precluded from resorting to s. 68 after the discharge of the bankrupt?
6. Is the trustee precluded from resorting to the current s. 68 because the procedure set out thereunder has not been followed?
7. Does the trustee have standing to intervene in the proceeding under the Canada Labour Code to claim Landry's costs incurred at the first arbitration hearing?

E. ANALYSIS

1. Does Landry's claim against First Air or any part of the resulting award constitute property of the bankrupt that vests in the trustee under ss. 67 and 71(2) of the *BIA*?

[11] As stated earlier, s. 71(2) is a general vesting provision. It reads as follows: ...

  [12] "Property" is defined under s. 2 of the *BIA* as including: ...

  [13] "Things in action" encompass a claim for damages for breach of contract, including an action for wrongful dismissal: *Wallace v United Grain Growers Ltd,* [1997] 3 SCR 701. The parties do not dispute that Landry's claim against her former employer under the Canada Labour Code is a "thing in action" and therefore constitutes "property" for the purpose of the *BIA*. Hence, pursuant to s. 71(2), Landry's claim against her former employer would vest in the trustee on the date she declared bankruptcy and she would cease to have any capacity to deal with it. However, s. 71(2) is subject to the other provisions of the *BIA*.

  [14] Section 67 of the *BIA* defines what property of a bankrupt is divisible among her creditors and can serve to restrict the ambit of s. 71(2). . . .

  [15] It is clear that s. 67(1)(c) is wide enough to encompass Landry's claim against her former employer and, consequently, any award of damages (other than those relating to personal claims, see fn. 1, supra) would form part of the property divisible among her creditors under that provision. A question then arises whether any part of the property falls within the exception made for exempt property under s. 67(1)(b).

2. Does any exemption apply pursuant to s. 67(1)(b) so as to except any part of the property from the estate of the bankrupt?

[16] As provided under s. 67(1)(b), the property of the bankrupt divisible among her creditors shall not comprise any property that as against Landry is exempt from execution or seizure under the laws of Ontario. Landry relies on s. 7(2) of the Ontario *Wages Act* which provides that "80 per cent of a person's wages are exempt from seizure or garnishment." Therefore, if any part of the arbitrator's award constitutes "wages" within the meaning of s. 7(2), 80 per cent of that amount would not constitute property divisible among Landry's creditors and, hence, would not vest in the trustee.

  [17] At the hearing, counsel did not seriously dispute that the case of *Wallace, supra,* provides support for the contention that the arbitrator's award of damages for unjust dismissal, in so far as it relates to lost wages, can be equated to actual wages.

  [18] Wallace made a voluntary assignment into personal bankruptcy and remained an undischarged bankrupt when he commenced an action for wrongful dismissal against his former employer. A question arose whether Wallace could bring this action in his own name given the vesting provisions under s. 71(2) of the [then] *Bankruptcy Act* which, as s. 71(2) of the present *BIA*, provided that a bankrupt ceases to have any capacity to deal with his property.

[19] Iacobucci J, in the majority judgment (all justices were in agreement on this issue), stated (para. 58) that the wording of the Act is clear and that an undischarged bankrupt has no capacity to deal with his or her property, including an action for breach of contract, outside the circumstances described in s. 99(1) (which circumstances are of no relevance to this appeal). The court held further that the Act made no distinction whether that property was acquired before or after the assignment in bankruptcy. However, the court went on to consider the provisions of s. 68(1) of the *Bankruptcy Act* as it then read (this is the provision which was in force at the time Landry declared bankruptcy) and concluded that it carved out an additional exception to this general rule. Section 68(1), in this earlier version, provided as follows:

68 (1) Notwithstanding subsection 67(1), where a bankrupt

(a) is in receipt of, or is entitled to receive, any money as salary, wages or other remuneration from a person employing the bankrupt ...

the trustee may, on the trustee's own initiative or, if directed by the inspectors or the creditors, shall, make an application to the court for an order directing the payment to the trustee of such part of the money as the court may determine, having regard to the family responsibilities and personal situation of the bankrupt.

[20] More will be said about the effect of s. 68 later in these reasons. What is of relevance to the question presently under consideration is the finding by the court that Wallace, an undischarged bankrupt, could maintain his action against his former employer for damages for wrongful dismissal not because of the timing of the acquisition of the property "but rather, because of the nature of the property in question" (para. 59) which the court equated to "wages." Iacobucci J wrote as follows (paras. 65–66):

As I see the matter, the underlying nature of the damages awarded in a wrongful dismissal action is clearly akin to the "wages" referred to in s. 68(1). In the absence of just cause, an employer remains free to dismiss an employee at any time provided that reasonable notice of the termination is given. In providing the employee with reasonable notice, the employer has two options: either to require the employee to continue working for the duration of that period or to give the employee pay in lieu of notice: D. Harris, *Wrongful Dismissal* (1989 (loose-leaf)), at p. 3-10. There can be no doubt that if the employer opted to require the employee to continue working during the notice period, his or her earnings during this time would constitute wages or salary under s. 68(1) of the Act. The only difference between these earnings and pay in lieu of notice is that the employee receives a lump sum payment instead of having that sum spread out over the course of the notice period. The nature of those funds remains the same and thus s. 68(1) will also apply in these circumstances.

In the event that an employee is wrongfully dismissed, the measure of damages for wrongful dismissal is the salary that the employee would have earned had the employee worked during the period of notice to which he or she was entitled: *Sylvester v British Columbia*, [1997] 2 SCR 315. The fact that this sum is awarded as damages at trial in no way alters the fundamental character of the money. An award of damages in a wrongful dismissal action is in reality the wages that the employer ought to have paid the employee either over the course of the period of reasonable notice or as pay in lieu of notice. Therefore, in accordance with the exception which is carved out in s. 68(1) for "salary, wages or other remuneration," this money is not divisible among a bankrupt's creditors and does not vest in the trustee. The right of action is the means of attaining these damages and is similarly exempt.

[21] On the authority of *Wallace*, I conclude that, to the extent that the arbitrator's award relates to the pay Landry should have received in lieu of notice, the moneys would constitute "wages" for the purpose of the s. 67(1)(b) exception. However, what is also clear from *Wallace* is that s. 67 must be considered in conjunction with s. 68. This brings us to the next question.

3. Is s. 67 superseded by the provisions of s. 68 in relation to a bankrupt's wages?
[22] Two versions of s. 68 must be taken into account: the former version under the *Bankruptcy Act* that was considered in Wallace and the current version under the *BIA* which will be discussed shortly. There are two reasons why both versions must be examined. The first is that the former version and its interconnection with s. 67 was considered by the Supreme Court of Canada in *Wallace* and in *Marzetti v Marzetti*, [1994] 2 SCR 765 and the question arises whether the reasoning in those cases applies to the new version. The second reason is that the trustee contends that the former version is applicable to this case since it was in force at the time Landry declared bankruptcy rather than the current version which was in force at the time the motion was brought. This latter argument forms the subject-matter of the next question on this appeal and will be dealt with later. I will now deal with the interpretation of s. 68 and its interconnection with s. 67.

a) The Former s. 68
[23] Section 68 under the Bankruptcy Act provided the trustee with the means to obtain part of a bankrupt's salary, wages or other remuneration from employment notwithstanding the provisions contained in s. 67(1). For our purposes, it is only necessary to consider s. 68(1) and I reproduce it again for convenience: ...

[24] This provision was considered at length by the Supreme Court of Canada in Marzetti. The particular facts and a number of other issues in Marzetti are not relevant to our discussion. What is relevant to this case is the Court's consideration of the interconnection between s. 67 and s. 68. Iacobucci J, in writing for the court, set out the issue as follows (at 178):

> ... I must determine whether s. 68 always controls the disposition of a bankrupt's wages. Is s. 68 a substantive provision, that is, one which always removes wages from the scope of s. 67, or does it simply create a procedural device for trustees?

[25] Following his analysis, he concluded as follows (at 185):

> To summarize briefly, it is my opinion that the language of s. 68, the inferred purpose of that provision, and the decision of this Court in *Vachon [v Canada Employment and Immigration Commission*, [1985] 2 SCR 417] all support the conclusion that s. 68 is a substantive provision, one which is intended to operate as a complete code in respect of a bankrupt's salary, wages, or other remuneration. These forms of property cannot fall within s. 67(c) of the *Bankruptcy Act* as a bankrupt's after-acquired "property," and they cannot be considered "property of a bankrupt divisible among his creditors" for the purposes of s. 67. They do not vest in the trustee through the simple operation of law.

[26] Hence, the Supreme Court in *Marzetti*, and later in *Wallace*, has authoritatively determined that s. 68 supersedes the provisions of s. 67 in so far as "salary, wages or other remuneration" from employment are concerned. It follows that, if this provision is applicable to this case, the Ontario *Wages Act* does not apply and neither does any other part of s. 67. There is no automatic vesting of Landry's claim against First Air or of any part of the arbitrator's award. The trustee, and the court, must look exclusively to s. 68

to determine what part, if any, of the award will form part of the bankrupt's estate for distribution to the creditors. The question becomes, does the same interpretation apply to the current s. 68 under the *BIA*?

b) s. 68 Under the BIA

[27] The current s. 68 in the *BIA* differs from the former version in a number of respects. The full text is appended to these reasons for ease of reference. First, the section does not refer to "salary, wages or other remuneration" but to "total income." "[T]otal income" is defined for the purpose of s. 68 as including, "*notwithstanding s. 67(1)(b)* and (b.1), all revenues of a bankrupt of whatever nature or source." The section still allows the trustee to apply to the court for a determination of the amount that a bankrupt is required to pay to the estate of the bankrupt out of her total income but an elaborate procedure must be followed before such an application is made. For our purposes, this procedure can be summarized as follows.

[28] First, the superintendent is directed to establish standards for determining the portion of the total income of an individual bankrupt that exceeds that which is necessary to enable the bankrupt to maintain a reasonable standard of living. Second, the trustee, having regard to these standards and to the personal and family situation of the bankrupt, must fix the amount that the bankrupt is required to pay, inform the official receiver of his decision and take reasonable measures to ensure that the bankrupt complies with the requirement to pay. Third, where the official receiver determines that the fixed amount is not in accordance with the applicable standards, the official receiver must recommend an appropriate amount. Fourth, where the trustee and the bankrupt disagree on the amount to be paid, the trustee must send to the official receiver a request that the matter be determined by mediation. A creditor can also make a request for mediation. Fifth, the mediation takes place in accordance with prescribed procedures.

[29] In addition to this procedure, an application may be made to the court under s. 68(10): . . .

[30] In my view, the reasoning in *Marzetti* and *Wallace* that led to the conclusion that s. 68 was a complete code with respect to wages applies equally to this new section. The current provision applies to the "total income" of the bankrupt and, as such, is even wider than the earlier reference to "salary, wages and other remuneration"; the provision expressly excludes the application of s. 67(1)(b); its purpose is no different than that described in *Marzetti* (except that applications to the court now appear to be limited to those cases where the issue cannot be otherwise resolved); and the jurisprudential principles reviewed by the Supreme Court in *Marzetti* are equally relevant.

[31] I therefore conclude that s. 67 is superseded by the provisions of the current s. 68 in so far as the "total income" of the bankrupt is concerned. It follows that, as in *Wallace*, Landry's claim against her former employer and any consequent award relating to lost wages do not automatically vest in the trustee under ss. 67 and 71. Resort can only be had to s. 68 for payment of any portion thereof to the estate of the bankrupt. . . .

5. Is the trustee precluded from resorting to s. 68 after the discharge of the bankrupt?

[35] The motions judge held that s. 68 was no longer available to a trustee after the discharge of a bankrupt. First, the motions judge noted that s. 68 refers to "a bankrupt" and that s. 2 defined "bankrupt" as "a person who has made an assignment or against whom a receiving order has been made or the legal status of that person." Second, the motions judge held that the section was intended to apply in the period from the assignment in

bankruptcy or the receivership order until the discharge of the bankrupt. He therefore concluded that s. 68 applied to a bankrupt and not to a discharged bankrupt.

[36] In my view, this interpretation cannot be supported.

[37] First, it disregards the fact that the definition of "bankrupt" does not only refer to "the legal status of [the] person"—since Landry has been discharged, it is correct to say that she is no longer in the state of bankruptcy, but also to "a person who has made an assignment"—a description that clearly applies to Landry.

[38] Second, the motions judge erred in his interpretation of the scope of the section. Although, from a practical standpoint, s. 68 may apply more commonly to periodic wages received during the period of time between the assignment and the discharge, I see nothing in the language of the provision that restricts its application to this time frame. It is clear from *Wallace* and *Marzetti* that s. 68 applies because of the nature of the property in question, regardless of the timing of the acquisition of the property or of the fact that the payment is made in a lump sum.

[39] Third, I do not see any policy reason why, in situations such as in this case where the income is only to be received after the discharge, resort to s. 68 would nonetheless have to be made before the discharge. Indeed, given the procedure set out under s. 68, it may be impossible to resort to its provisions before payment is made or at least its quantum ascertained. Further, if resort to s. 68 were to be limited to the pre-discharge period, the trustee or the creditors would likely oppose any discharge if any payment of income was still pending at the time the bankrupt applied for a discharge. I am therefore concerned that such an interpretation would have the effect of unnecessarily postponing discharges until the full administration of the estate is completed. In cases where there is pending litigation over the payment of such income, the delay in obtaining a discharge could prove quite substantial. This result, in my view would militate against the prompt rehabilitation of the bankrupt. Finally, such an interpretation runs contrary to the established principle and practice that the trustee's obligation to realize and distribute the estate of the bankrupt continues until the trustee is discharged regardless of the prior discharge of the bankrupt: see *Re Salloum* (1990), 1 CBR (3d) 204 (BCCA).

[40] I therefore conclude that the trustee is not precluded from resorting to s. 68 by the fact that Landry has been discharged.

Appeal allowed.

Conforti (Re), 2015 ONCA 268, 24 CBR (6th) 286

PEPALL JA:

Introduction

[1] This appeal involves the impact of bankruptcy on a victim of a motor vehicle accident.

[2] The appellant, Vincenzo Francesco Conforti, was permanently disabled as a result of a motor vehicle accident and is unable to continue to work in his previous employment as a truck driver. He claimed statutory accident benefits ("SABs") and also commenced an action for damages. Two and a half years after the accident, he filed an assignment in bankruptcy. While bankrupt, he received financial assistance from the Ontario Ministry of Community and Social Services (the "Government"). He also received proceeds from the settlements of his SABs claim and his action. The appellant failed to disclose either of the settlements to his Trustee in Bankruptcy.

[3] As part of the bankruptcy proceedings, the Trustee was required to calculate the appellant's total and surplus income under s. 68 of the *Bankruptcy and Insolvency Act*, R.S.C. 1985, c. B-3 ("*BIA*") to ascertain if any amount was available for distribution to the appellant's creditors. The Trustee sought directions from the court on the appropriate treatment to be accorded the financial assistance and the settlement payments received by the appellant. At the same time, the appellant asked the court for a discharge from bankruptcy.

[4] The motion judge provided directions and included all of the financial assistance, all of the SABs settlement, and a pro-rated portion of the settlement of the action proceeds in the appellant's total income calculation. This resulted in surplus income of $27,986.28 available for creditors. He also imposed a $15,000 penalty on the appellant due to his non-disclosure. The appellant was granted a discharge upon payment of these two sums.

[5] The appellant appeals certain parts of the motion judge's order. He submits that the motion judge erred in his treatment of the financial assistance and settlement payments and in his pro-rating methodology. He argues that no surplus income was owed to the Trustee for distribution to creditors. He accepts that he should be admonished for his conduct, but submits that a penalty of $15,000 was only appropriate if no surplus income was payable.

[6] For the reasons that follow, I would allow the appeal....

[10] On November 16, 2009, the appellant settled his SABs claim for a payment of approximately $21,000 after deduction of legal fees and disbursements. The appellant did not disclose the receipt of the SABs settlement payment to the Trustee. He paid this amount to an old friend, Gino Crupi. Mr. Crupi had allegedly lent him money in 1976 although this debt obligation was not disclosed on the appellant's sworn statement of affairs. No documentation existed regarding the alleged loan.

[11] On February 10, 2010, the appellant settled his personal injury action for the sum of $275,000 inclusive of costs and disbursements. Pursuant to executed minutes of settlement, the appellant was to deliver a release from the Trustee to the defendant in the action....

(d) Discharge Application
[15] The appellant applied to court for a discharge from bankruptcy. The appellant's unsecured claims amounted to approximately $105,000 and the appellant's debt to the Government was approximately $38,000. Both the Trustee and the appellant's principal creditor, Central Mortgage and Housing Corporation, opposed the request for a discharge. At the same time, the Trustee also sought directions from the court on the issues of property and income inclusions.

[16] The Trustee took the position that both the SABs and the personal injury settlement proceeds constituted capital assets, not income, and accordingly, they should be paid to the Trustee for distribution to the appellant's creditors pursuant to s. 67 of the *BIA*. In the alternative, the Trustee argued that the settlement proceeds, along with the financial assistance payments, formed part of the appellant's total income in the years of receipt, pursuant to s. 68. If so, this would result in surplus income available for the benefit of his creditors. The Trustee also sought a penalty as a condition of the appellant's discharge from bankruptcy.

[17] The appellant differed. He argued that the settlement proceeds were not capital assets and that while some elements of the settlement proceeds constituted income, they should be pro-rated over time. As a result, he argued that there was no surplus income available for distribution to his creditors. He acknowledged that some penalty was justified.

Applicable Legal Principles

[18] To understand the parties' dispute, it is helpful to describe the scheme reflected in ss. 67 and 68 of the *BIA*. As a general proposition, s. 67 of the *BIA* deals with property of the bankrupt and s. 68 deals with the bankrupt's income.

[19] One of the purposes of the *BIA* is to ensure that all property owned by a bankrupt at the date of bankruptcy will, with certain exceptions, vest in the trustee for realization and distribution to the bankrupt's creditors: *Husky Oil Operations Ltd v Minister of National Revenue*, [1995] 3 S.C.R. 453, at pp. 470–471.

[20] Section 67(1)(c) states that subject to certain exceptions, the property of a bankrupt divisible among his creditors shall comprise: "all property wherever situated of the bankrupt at the date of the bankruptcy or that may be acquired by or devolve on the bankrupt before their discharge."

[21] Historically, subject to any amount exempted from seizure by provincial law, the salary of a bankrupt vested in the trustee: see e.g. *Industrial Acceptance Corp v Lalonde*, [1952] 2 S.C.R. 109. This changed in 1966, when the predecessor to s. 68 was added to the legislation, creating a bifurcated regime under which property and income were treated separately. Section 68 creates a scheme designed to determine which portion of a bankrupt's "total income" is "surplus income" available in part for distribution to creditors. In *Marzetti v Marzetti*, [1994] 2 S.C.R. 765, at p. 794, the Supreme Court described s. 68 as a complete code governing the income of a bankrupt, and held that any proceedings to claim a share of the earnings of a bankrupt had to be brought under s. 68. A trustee therefore looks to s. 68 to determine what portion, if any, of the bankrupt's revenues forms part of the bankrupt's estate available for distribution to creditors: *Landry, Re* (2000), 50 O.R. (3d) 1 (C.A.), at para. 26, and *Watt v Beallor Beallor Burns Inc* (2004), 1 C.B.R. (5th) 141, aff'd (2004), 1 C.B.R. (5th) 149 (Ont. C.A.).

[22] Total income is defined in s. 68(2) of the *BIA* . . . .

[23] *Re Millin* (2005), 13 C.B.R. (5th) 91 (B.C.S.C.), at para. 34, held that the revenues described in s. 68(2)(a) should be "a substitution for income, akin to income, in the nature of income or to have retained its (previous) character of income." Examples of payments that have been held to be encompassed by the s. 68(2)(a) definition of total income include lost wages, disability payments, severance payments, and income tax refunds. . . .

[24] Surplus income is defined in s. 68(2) as "the portion of a bankrupt individual's total income that exceeds that which is necessary to enable the bankrupt individual to maintain a reasonable standard of living, having regard to the applicable standards". Under s. 68(1), the Superintendent must establish, by Directive, the standards for determining the surplus income of an individual bankrupt, and the amount that a bankrupt who has surplus income is required to pay to the estate of the bankrupt. As stated in Directive 11R-2014, the Directive is intended to assist the trustee in "determining equitably and consistently the portion of the bankrupt's income that should be paid into the bankrupt's estate": Industry Canada, Office of the Superintendent of Bankruptcy Canada, "Directive No. 11R2-2014" (March 18, 2014), at p. 2. The Directive is updated annually so as to reflect current standards based on information produced by Statistics Canada. Superintendent's Directive No. 11R2-2012 was applicable to the matters in issue in this appeal.

[25] Under ss. 68(3) and (4) of the *BIA*, the Trustee is required to determine whether the bankrupt has surplus income and, if so, fix the amount the bankrupt is required to pay to the estate. In making that determination, the trustee is to have regard to the applicable standards and to the personal and family situation of the bankrupt. Under

the statutory scheme, the trustee obtains proof of income and expense information for the bankrupt's family unit (which includes the bankrupt), determines the total monthly income of the bankrupt's family unit, deducts certain non-discretionary expenses such as spousal and child support payments and "expenses associated with a medical condition," and then uses the standards in the applicable Superintendent's Directive to ascertain whether there is any surplus income. Subject to certain adjustments, if the bankrupt has monthly surplus income equal to or greater than $200, the bankrupt is required to pay 50 per cent to the estate for the benefit of creditors. Other provisions in the Superintendent's Directive address the duration of the payments of surplus income.

[26] Broadly speaking therefore, s. 68 reflects a balance between the interests of a bankrupt's unsecured creditors to share in the bankrupt's estate and a bankrupt's ability to maintain a reasonable standard of living. The Supreme Court has held that s. 68 is to be interpreted broadly having regard "to the family responsibilities and personal situation of the bankrupt": *Wallace*, at paras. 67–68. As stated in *Marzetti*, this approach reflects an "overriding concern for the support of families". Moreover, s. 68(2)(a) is to be interpreted in a manner that is consistent with the fresh start principle that underlies the bankruptcy regime.

[27] As is evident from the language of the *BIA*, revenue earned or received after a bankrupt's discharge does not fall within s. 68. . . .

[39] The bankrupt was therefore ordered to pay $27,986.28 [by the motions judge] on account of surplus income plus the penalty of $15,000 for a total of $42,986.28. On payment of the sum of $42,986.28, the appellant would be discharged from bankruptcy.

Analysis

(a) Financial Assistance
[40] As mentioned, the appellant submits that the motion judge erred in including the financial assistance payments in the appellant's total income calculation. I agree. . . .

[43] . . . The motion judge's decision left the appellant exposed to an obligation to repay 100 per cent of the debt to the Government, while the inclusion of this amount in the appellant's total income calculation effectively imposed an additional payment obligation on him.

[44] In my view, the motion judge erred in including approximately $38,000 on account of the financial assistance payments in the appellant's total income calculation. I would allow the appeal in this regard.

(b) Future Care, Housekeeping and Costs
[45] The appellant also submits that the motion judge erred in including the settlement allocations totalling $55,000 for future care ($7,000), housekeeping ($15,000) and costs, disbursements and HST ($33,000) less an additional amount in legal fees for a net inclusion of $39,000 in the total income calculation.

[46] I agree.

[47] All $33,000 of the $55,000 was paid in legal costs, disbursements and HST. The motion judge erred in treating any part of this amount as income received by the appellant.

[48] The appellant submits that the remaining $22,000 allocated to future care and housekeeping constituted "expenses associated with a medical condition" under s. 5(3)(d) of the Superintendent's Directive. As such, he argues that these sums ought to have been deducted from the income of the appellant's family unit and ought not to have

formed part of the total income calculation. Alternatively, he argues that the payments are akin to damages for pain and suffering and ought not to be included in income.

[49] Section 5(3) deductions from income are non-discretionary in nature. Indeed, s. 5(3) expressly refers to them as such. As mentioned, the deductions include such things as child and spousal support payments. The damages allocated for the cost of care and housekeeping services cannot be so characterized. They are amounts paid to the appellant to be used as he chooses and hence are discretionary. As such, they do not constitute deductions from total income under s. 5(3) of the Superintendent's Directive.

[50] They are, however, damages that are personal to the appellant and bear a close relationship to damages on account of pain and suffering. There is extensive support for the proposition that damages for pain and suffering do not fall under s. 67 or s. 68 of the BIA: *Re Holley* (1986), 54 O.R. (2d) 225 (C.A.) and *Re Hollister* [1926] 3 D.L.R. 707 (Ont. H.C.J.). As stated by Goodman J.A. in *Re Holley*: "it is not the policy of the law to convert into money for the creditors the mental or physical anguish of the debtor." The damages allocated to future care and housekeeping are intended to alleviate the appellant's injured state. It is therefore appropriate to treat them in the same manner as damages for pain and suffering.

[51] I would therefore allow the appeal so as to exclude the amount of $39,000 (representing the $55,000 less $16,000 in additional costs) from the total income calculation.

(c) SABs Settlement Proceeds

[52] The appellant argues that the motion judge erred in including all of the SABs settlement proceeds of approximately $21,000 in the appellant's total income calculation in 2009.

[53] I disagree.

[54] The appellant paid all of the proceeds to Mr. Crupi. He did not disclose any debt owed to Mr. Crupi in his statement of affairs; he did not disclose the debt to his Trustee; and he did not disclose to the Trustee that he had paid the full sum of $21,892.59 to Mr. Crupi. In these circumstances and based on the record before him, it was open to the motion judge to treat this lump sum payment as income in the year of receipt. I would not give effect to this ground of appeal....

[58] As a result of this and the other adjustments relating to the financial assistance payments and the settlement payments on account of future care, housekeeping and costs, there is no surplus income to be paid by the appellant. Accordingly, the appeal relating to surplus income is allowed ...

(e) Penalty

[59] This leaves the issue of the penalty. In the event that the appeal on surplus income were allowed, the appellant had no objection to the penalty of $15,000. Indeed, before this court, the appellant's counsel properly acknowledged that the appellant deserved to be sanctioned for his conduct. I agree. The penalty of $15,000 is therefore affirmed.

Disposition

[60] For these reasons, I would allow the appeal in part. I would vary the order under appeal by removing the requirement to pay surplus income and by reducing the payment of $42,986.28 payable by the appellant to $15,000.

Appeal allowed in part.

B. Secured Creditors and Surplus Income

In *Cargill Ltd v Meyers Norris Penny Ltd*, 2008 MBCA 104 (*Cargill*), the Manitoba Court of Appeal considered the rights of secured creditors and section 68. In *Cargill*, a farmer executed security agreements in favour of two secured creditors. The security agreements contained after-acquired property clauses. Both secured parties perfected their security interests. The farmer subsequently made an assignment in bankruptcy. After the bankruptcy, the Canadian Agricultural Income Stabilization Program (CAIS), a federal government assistance program designed to help farmers, made a payment of $159,000 to the trustee. The Court of Appeal considered whether the secured creditors were entitled to the whole amount of the fund or whether section 68 of the *BIA* applied to allow an amount for the bankrupt to maintain a reasonable standard of living. As you read the extract below, consider whether bankrupts will be at the mercy of whatever provincial legislation there may be restricting or invalidating assignment of wages and other earnings. Is this consistent with the policy of *BIA*, section 68? Should *BIA*, section 67, be amended to impose restrictions on the validity of security interests affecting an individual debtor's income without waiting for provincial initiatives? The provincial *PPSA*s have a provision outlawing after-acquired property clauses in consumer contexts. See, for example, Ontario *PPSA*, section 12(2)(b). Does the *PPSA* provision go far enough in this context?

Cargill Ltd v Meyers Norris Penny Ltd, 2008 MBCA 104, 47 CBR (5th) 214

FREEDMAN JA:

[40] "[I]t is only after the requirements of s. 68 of [the Act] have been met that the equitable assignment of Cargill and CIBC can attach the CAIS proceeds" (at para 54). This meant that the CAIS Money was only available to creditors of the bankrupt to the extent that the CAIS Money exceeded what was necessary for the bankrupt to maintain a reasonable standard of living.

[41] In making this finding, it is my view, with respect, that the judge erred. It is important to keep in mind that, as argued here by the Creditors, "the rights of secured creditors are dealt with outside the confines" of the Act, except if there is specific statutory language to the contrary. This is effectively explained in The Honourable L.W. Houlden, The Honourable Geoffrey B. Morawetz & Dr. Janis P. Sarra, *The 2008 Annotated Bankruptcy and Insolvency Act* (Toronto: Carswell, 2007) at 630: "Where a debtor has made an assignment ... the policy of the Act is not to interfere with secured creditors except insofar as may be necessary to protect the estate as to any surplus in the assets covered by the security ...." Once the CAIS Money was in the hands of the Trustee, it was presumptively captured by the security agreements, unless some statutory or other governing provision clearly negated that result.

[42] Section 68 is intended to assist the trustee in accessing the bankrupt's wages for the benefit of the estate's creditors; ... there is no indication in the legislation that s. 68 was intended to alter the position of secured creditors *vis-à-vis* the bankrupt. Section 69.3(2) states that the position of secured creditors is not altered by the bankruptcy of the debtor and ss. 71 and 136(1) confirm the priority granted to secured creditors by the bankruptcy regime....

[43] *Marzetti* did not involve the rights of a secured creditor. None of the other cases cited in relation to this issue involved the rights of secured creditors. Section 68 of the Act does not limit or restrict a secured creditor's interest in a bankrupt's assets which, by

that section, are characterized as "total income." The Trustee is, of course, limited and restricted by the provisions of s. 68, and it must apply distributable funds in accordance with that section, but funds in the Trustee's hands to which a secured creditor has a supervening right cannot fall within that category.

[44] In my opinion, the law is clear that, unless otherwise expressly provided in the Act or another governing provision, to quote again from Houlden, Morawetz & Sarra, "secured creditors may ignore the bankruptcy and deal with their security in the usual manner" (at p. 630) (*Federal Business Development Bank v Quebec (Commission de la santé et de la sécurité du travail)*, [1988] 1 SCR 1061). This is so even though the monies in question have been realized through the efforts of the Trustee.

[45] The general scheme of distribution under the Act (s. 136(1)) is stated to be "[s]ubject to the rights of secured creditors." Moreover, while there are a few sections in the Act which provide that particular provisions apply to secured creditors (see, e.g., s. 69.3(2), among others), none have been identified here that could defeat the present claims of the Creditors.

[46] I will add that, in my opinion, Menzies J went a little too far in *Lintott v Bank of Montreal*, 2004 MBQB 214, 188 Man. R (2d) 228, when he said that "[s]ection 68 is a complete code for determining what if any portion of a bankrupt's total income will be made available for distribution among creditors whether secured or not" (at para. 25). As indicated, the rights of secured creditors are not impaired by bankruptcy unless expressly so provided in legislation, and s. 68 does not so provide.

[47] To summarize, nothing has been pointed out, in the Act or elsewhere, that could adversely affect and limit the rights of the Creditors to claim the CAIS Money under their admittedly valid and perfected security agreements. Absent explicit legislative provisions ... the interests of secured creditors prevail over those of a bankruptcy trustee, even with respect to the income of the bankrupt.... [I]t follows that the Creditors prevail over the Trustee, as s. 68 has no application to them. This is not to say that payments from CAIS may not form part of a bankrupt's "total income" for the purposes of s. 68, but that question does not arise in this case, as s. 68 has no application to the Creditors here.

[48] Accordingly, I would hold that the rights and interests of the Creditors by virtue of their security agreements apply to the CAIS Money without reduction as a result of the application of s. 68 of the Act, and in this respect I would allow the cross-appeal.

Appeal dismissed; cross-appeal allowed.

V. DISCHARGE

A. The Discharge Regime

The question of whether individual bankrupts should be entitled to a discharge from their debts after they have gone into bankruptcy and surrendered their non-exempt property was a heated topic for debate throughout much of the nineteenth century in the United States, England, and Canada. In England and Canada, the debate only affected traders and merchants because, for the most part, the legislation only applied to them. In the United States, the critical turning point came with the adoption of the 1898 *Bankruptcy Act*, which provided for an unconditional discharge for all individual debtors with the exception of non-dischargeable debts. The British *Bankruptcy Act 1883* also applied to all types of individuals but creditors were entitled to oppose the discharge and the judge was given a broad discretion to grant or refuse the application or to grant it conditionally and on terms.

It was the British model that was adopted in the Canadian *Bankruptcy Act* of 1919. The essential features of the *Bankruptcy Act* were the following: the debtor could apply for a discharge at any time. When the debtor applied, the court had complete discretion in dealing with the application unless the debtor had committed an offence or had otherwise misconducted themselves, or if the realizable assets were worth less than 50 cents on the dollar. If these restrictions did not apply, the court could grant or refuse the discharge, suspend the discharge, or make a conditional discharge order linked to the debtor's future earnings or the debtor's income or after-acquired property. The court had to refuse the application or suspend it for two years if the debtor had committed a bankruptcy offence.

The 1949 *Bankruptcy Act* introduced an important procedural change in deeming the bankrupt to have made a discharge application no earlier than three months after the bankruptcy order and no later than twelve months. In the case of a first-time individual bankrupt, the 1992 amendments simplified the procedure still further by deeming the application to be made nine months from the date of the bankruptcy order unless the debtor had waived this entitlement.

From the beginning, a discharge application was accompanied by a report from the trustee about the debtor's conduct and the factors leading to the debtor's bankruptcy. The 1997 amendments retained this requirement and tightened it substantially. The trustee is now also required to report on (1) whether the debtor had made the required surplus income payments and (2) whether the debtor could have made a viable proposal, as well as to provide the court with the trustee's own recommendations. In setting up this seemingly complex discharge structure, the federal Parliament was obviously striving to strike a balance between enabling a "poor and unfortunate" Canadian debtor to make a fresh start and sending a strong signal to debtors that debts could not be sloughed off easily regardless of the debtor's financial circumstances, past conduct, and capacity to make future payments. Nevertheless, on paper at least, the provisions are heavily creditor-oriented and retain a nineteenth-century anti-discharge bias.

After the repeal of the *Insolvent Act of 1875* in 1880, Canada was left without a national bankruptcy law and more importantly debtors could not obtain a statutory discharge for a period of nearly forty years. The following extract considers how debtors and creditors responded to the absence of a discharge and provides an explanation for why a discharge regime was eventually enacted in 1919.

Thomas GW Telfer, *Ruin and Redemption: The Struggle for a Canadian Bankruptcy Act, 1867–1919* (Toronto: University of Toronto Press & Osgoode Society for Canadian Legal History, 2014) at 145–147, 162–166, and 168 (footnotes omitted)

> The *Bankruptcy Act of 1919* re-established a national bankruptcy law after a nearly forty-year period. It created the framework for much of twentieth and twenty-first century Canadian bankruptcy law.... [I]mportantly, the new federal legislation allowed debtors to apply for a discharge and obtain a release of their debts. Provincial law did not offer a statutory discharge.... Parliament's achievement can in part be explained by the influence of new national interest groups that pressed for reform. The Canadian Bar Association (CBA) and the [Canadian Credit Men's Trust Association] (CCMTA) lobbied for a new federal bankruptcy act. Although passed as a government measure, the origins of the Act can be traced to the drafting efforts of [H.P.] Grundy on behalf of the CCMTA....

While important, the above factors do not provide a complete explanation for the emergence of the legislation in 1919. It is unlikely that reform would have occurred unless there was transformation of attitudes towards the discharge. The discharge was no longer perceived as an evil, as in the nineteenth century, but it was proclaimed as a necessary form of business regulation. . . .

The acceptability of the discharge at the federal level in 1919. . . did not entirely represent the triumph of forgiveness or concerns for the rehabilitation of the debtor. Simply put, the discharge became acceptable in 1919 because it satisfied the interests of creditors. The 1919 Act should not be viewed as a triumph for debtors' rights. . . .

The reasons in favour of the discharge in 1919 bear a striking resemblance to the origins of the discharge in England. While the original English bankruptcy statute of 1543 established many of the principal elements of bankruptcy legislation, no discharge was available by statute in England until 1705. The bankruptcy discharge is often viewed as one of the essential elements of modern bankruptcy law as it allows debtors to obtain a release of their debts. However, when one examines the historical context of 1705, it is clear that debtor rehabilitation was not the prime motivating factor behind the legislation. The discharge was aimed at "the recovery of the most assets for the benefit of the creditors." Therefore the English Parliament was not motivated by generosity to debtors. Creditor interests lay at the heart of the English reform and the change had only a limited beneficial effect on most debtors. As Emily Kadens has demonstrated, eighteenth century English creditors were struggling to see that if all promises to pay were fully enforced then debtors would lose their incentive to earn in the face of debt. Indeed, such a regime led debtors to cheat. Conversely, if the discharge provided an incentive for debtors to disclose, in theory, debtors should be less inclined to cheat. Between 1867 and 1919 Canadian creditors faced a similar challenge in recognizing these truths. . . .

[In late nineteenth and early twentieth century Canada,] [w]ithout a discharge the debtor became "absolutely cornered" and then proceeded to cheat general creditors for the benefit of "his friends and family." Without a formal statutory release of debts, "the question of discharge rest[ed] wholly [as] a matter of bargain between a debtor and his creditors." . . . Debtors attempted to deal with the lack of a discharge by seeking the signatures of all of their creditors to a composition agreement. Any special treatment given to holdout creditors adversely affected the level of dividend paid to the other creditors. Creditors privately decided to release a debtor on self-interested motives rather than on larger public policy goals such as the reduction of fraud. Inevitably creditors granted dishonest debtors a release:

> It seems to me, in considering the matter of discharge, that one of the chief faults of the present law, and of some of the previous Acts, is that too often, through the selfishness of creditors looking only to their own immediate interests, or what they think to be their immediate interest, men are discharged, or allowed to make composition and settlements, who, speaking commercially, at any rate, if not legally, would be much better sent to jail. . . .

The discharge therefore came to be viewed not as an interference of a debtor's moral obligation to pay all debts, but rather as a new regulatory feature that would come to benefit creditors. . . . Some saw regulating the conduct of the debtor as a broader matter of public policy:

> [I]t must be the duty of the court to decide the extent to which the debtor has been responsible for his own misfortune, and where it is shown that the disordered state of his business is brought about through no dishonesty or wilful negligence, the law ought

to consider it a matter of public policy to see that after a certain length of time the debtor is once more permitted to engage in business on his own account. . . .

The honest but unfortunate debtor came to replace the evil and untrustworthy character of the nineteenth century. . . . A properly drawn discharge provision could filter out the difference between the two types of debtors. This made a discharge broadly acceptable. . . .

By way of contrast, the discharge had been challenged in the nineteenth century on the basis that debtors had a moral obligation to repay debts. But in 1918 and 1919 Parliament did not debate the specific discharge provisions of the new bankruptcy bills. Instead, Parliament focused on a clause-by-clause analysis of other more technical matters and constitutional issues. The discharge had therefore been transformed from a nineteenth century evil to an essential form of business regulation. . . .

[© Osgoode Society for Canadian Legal History 2014.
Reprinted with permission of the publisher.]

B. Applications for Discharge and Rehabilitation

Anna Lund, *The Labours of Bankruptcy* (Vancouver: UBC Press, forthcoming, 2020) at 1 and 16–19 (footnotes omitted)

Narrative Account of a Discharge Hearing for a High Income Tax Debtor

[The facts of Greg's story are drawn from an application heard by the registrar of bankruptcy in Edmonton, Alberta on 15 September 2016.]

Greg owned a couple of companies that provided services to big oilfield operations. When his father died, he inherited a valuable piece of land, sold it for $3 million, and invested the proceeds. The price of oil fell and Greg's companies started to struggle financially. Greg withdrew the invested funds to pay corporate debts. He also spent some of the money on himself—he bought a vacation property and a boat. After the money ran out, he had to sell the boat and the vacation property at a significant loss. Then the tax man came calling. The Canada Revenue Agency realized that Greg had not paid taxes for years. Greg's tax bill, with the penalties and interest, added up to $1.9 million. Greg could not repay these amounts and made an assignment into bankruptcy.

Greg filed for bankruptcy in Edmonton, Alberta. His discharge hearing is held at the Law Courts, located in the city centre. The structure, built in the early 1970's, looks like an upside down concrete pyramid. Bankruptcy hearings are held in the afternoon, starting at 2:00 pm. On the day of the hearing, Greg shows up early. Likely, his trustee warned him to be early so he would have enough time to get through security. An individual entering the Law Courts must pass through a metal detector. Security guards use a baggage screener to ensure that no weapons are being brought into the building. Once he is through security, Greg takes an elevator to the second floor.

Greg arrives in a narrow hallway outside of the courtroom. The hallway is lined with chairs and couches, all of which face the wood paneled door of the courtroom. Half a dozen other individuals are seated, waiting for court to start. The individuals range in age from a woman in her 40s, sitting with a bankers box next to her feet, to an elderly, white-haired couple. One woman is wearing a green denim blazer, black pants, and dress shoes. Everyone else's attire is significantly less formal. A few sport sneakers. One has on a pair of hiking boots. The woman with the bankers box is wearing strappy sandals that reveal a small ankle tattoo.

One individual jokes, "I wonder if this is going to be like Judge Judy." A few of the people sitting near him guffaw nervously. He is referring to an American television show where individuals have their legal disputes resolved by an aggressive female judge who is known for berating litigants. The show's tagline is "justice with an attitude."

Other than that one joke, the people assembled on the benches sit quietly, waiting to be ushered into the courtroom. At one end of the hall, a television hangs from the ceiling. It plays a looping video explaining the basics of foreclosure proceedings to non-lawyers. In the morning, the courtroom is filled with lawyers for banks, applying to sell the homes of individuals who have fallen behind on their mortgage payments. The video is intended to help those individual homeowners understand the foreclosure process.

About ten minutes before 2:00 pm, men in suits start to arrive, the insolvency trustees. They file past the seated individuals and into the courtroom. Some pop back out again. An insolvency trustee greets the elderly couple. He is administering the gentleman's bankruptcy and explains to the couple how he expects the afternoon hearing will go. The man's bankruptcy was precipitated by bad luck. He bought an apartment unit in a condominium complex that was under construction. The builder never finished the job and the building was eventually condemned. The elderly man owed debts for buying a condominium that he never got to live in. He filed for bankruptcy and a creditor objected to his discharge. The elderly man is involved in litigation against the builder and if he recovers any money, the creditor wants a share of it. The elderly man's trustee explains that he has negotiated with the creditor's lawyer about how to structure the discharge order to ensure the creditor shares in any proceeds if the lawsuit against the builder succeeds.

At 1:55 pm, Greg and the other individuals sitting in the hallway start to file into court. On the other side of the substantial wooden doors, the individuals find themselves facing the Registrar's bench. The judicial officer, who presides in bankruptcy court, is called the Registrar. The structure of the position differs from province to province. In Newfoundland, senior court administrators sit as Registrars. In Nova Scotia and Saskatchewan, there are full-time Registrars. In Alberta, there is a class of judicial officers called Masters, who hear a mixed bag of applications, including foreclosures and procedural disputes in civil lawsuits. The Masters do double-duty, sitting as Registrars in bankruptcy court a few afternoons a week.

The Registrar's bench has two levels. The uppermost level is where the Registrar sits, immediately in front of and underneath a bronze Provincial court of arms. The Registrar has not entered the courtroom yet, so his seat is empty. On the lower level, to the right of the Registrar, sits the Clerk, a middle-aged woman with curly blonde hair. The Clerk is taking attendance. The men in suits approach her and identify which matter they will be speaking to and which party they are representing. She confirms the spelling of their names for the court's records. A trustee, the one helping the elderly man, seems to know her well and they joke with each other. He asks if anyone else has checked in on his matter, and the Clerk points to a gentleman in a suit, the creditor's lawyer. The trustee and the creditor's lawyer have never met in person before; all their business has been conducted by telephone. The trustee introduces himself and they have a quick chat in the courtroom.

Three rows of pews face the Registrar's bench. As the individuals file in, they try to find space to sit. The attendees leave a respectful distance between themselves and the next person in the pew, giving the courtroom the impression of being much fuller than it is.

At 2:00 pm sharp the Clerk addresses everyone in attendance, "I've started the digital recording, all phones should be on silent." She gets up from her desk and leaves through a door in the back-right corner of the room. A minute later she comes back in through the same door, followed by the Registrar. She announces, "All rise. This court is now in session." The courtroom attendees stand up in unison. Those familiar with courtroom procedure bow to the Registrar. The Registrar takes his seat; the courtroom attendees follow the Registrar's lead and sit down.

The first matter is the discharge of the elderly man who bought into the defunct condominium. His trustee and the creditor's lawyer have already agreed to the terms of the discharge order, and the application only takes a couple of minutes. During the application, both the trustee and the lawyer stand at a large desk facing the Registrar. The elderly man gets his discharge with a direction that any proceeds recovered from the lawsuit with the builder will be paid to the creditor. Afterwards, he shuffles slowly out of the courtroom with his wife, who leans heavily on a cane.

The second matter poses more of a challenge for the Registrar. The trustee is applying for a discharge for his client, Jeff. Jeff has his own lawyer, who stands to the right of the trustee during the application. Jeff remains seated on one of the benches for the entire application. He is a stocky man, and looks like he has not shaved for a couple of days. He wears dark cargo pants, a gray, rumpled polo shirt, and hiking boots. Two creditors have opposed his discharge: Jessica, his ex-common-law spouse—the woman with the bankers box—and her mother, the lady in the green blazer. The mother, Belinda, alleges that she lent Jeff significant funds, almost $200,000, and that he misused them. She alleges that Jeff has repeatedly lied to the court. If Belinda can show that Jeff's conduct amounted to fraud, then he is not entitled to an absolute discharge, and the debt owed to Belinda may survive bankruptcy. The *Bankruptcy and Insolvency Act* identifies some types of debts that survive bankruptcy, meaning they are not released by the discharge. A creditor can compel the debtor to pay such a debt, even after the debtor completes the bankruptcy process and receives a discharge.

The bankers box is filled with documents, which are intended to prove Jeff's fraud. Some of the documents are from the bankruptcy proceedings and some are from related family law litigation. Jessica tries to walk the Registrar through the voluminous submissions. She is visibly upset, talks very quickly and provides an overwhelming level of detail. Belinda gestures a couple of times with her hand, indicating to Jessica that she needs to slow down. The Registrar struggles to make sense of the documents and the oral submissions. Belinda stands up and tries to summarize the key issues in the case: she has been taken advantage of, Jeff is a liar and a cheat. Jeff's lawyer stands up and offers a different characterization of the facts: Jeff and Jessica both mismanaged money, Jeff needs relief from his debts, and Belinda is just one of many creditors who is being forced to forgo collecting a debt.

The Registrar decides that he is not in a position to make a decision about the alleged fraud. A trial may be required. In a trial, the presiding judge will have the benefit of hearing from each witness and can make findings about their credibility. The Registrar grants the discharge, but leaves it open for Jessica and Belinda to take the allegation of fraud to trial. If successful, Belinda will be able to enforce her debt against Jeff, notwithstanding his discharge.

The third matter is adjourned to a future date. The bankrupt was provided with some documents minutes before the hearing and asked for some time to review them.

Greg's matter is the last one on the list. Recall that he spent some of a $3 million inheritance trying to save his business, and the balance went towards items of a more discretionary and personal nature: a boat and a vacation property. At the time he started bankruptcy proceedings, he owed almost $2 million in unpaid taxes, penalties, and interest. Since the collapse of his business, he has been living in reduced circumstances, working a low-paying farm job. The Canada Revenue Agency's lawyer is in attendance at the hearing. The lawyer acknowledges that Greg will never be able to repay a substantial portion of his debt. The Revenue Agency and the trustee have worked out a compromise, a conditional discharge order. They are proposing that Greg pay $200 per month for three years, and during that same period of time provide his trustee with monthly income and expense statements, as well as proof that he is filing and paying all his taxes. After three years, if all the conditions are fulfilled, then Greg will receive a discharge. The Registrar describes the compromise as very generous, and grants the order with the proposed conditions.

Greg leaves the courtroom. Back out in the hallway, some of the men in suits are milling about and talking. Bankruptcy court is over for the day, and Greg is on his way home.

[Reprinted with permission of the Publisher from *The Labours of Bankruptcy* by Anna Lund © University of British Columbia Press 2020. All rights reserved by the Publisher.]

For a critical analysis of the 2009 reforms and the argument that they have the potential to entrench the "deviant-debtor" construct in Canada's consumer bankruptcy system, thus positioning bankruptcy law as a response to deviant behaviour, see Stephanie Ben-Ishai, "Discharge," in Ben-Ishai and Duggan, above, at 357. Anna Lund also considers the role of rehabilitation in an application for a debtor's discharge.

Anna Lund, "407 ETR, Moloney and the Contested Meaning of Rehabilitation in Canada's Personal Bankruptcy System" (2016) 79 *Saskatchewan Law Review* 265 at 273–78 (footnotes omitted)

Courts grapple with what it means to rehabilitate a debtor at application for discharge hearings. In my prior research, I reviewed a decade's worth of written decisions from application for discharge hearings, and tracked the different ways in which judicial officers authoring the decisions characterize rehabilitation. Divergent views on rehabilitation emerge from this review. In this section, I provide some background on when application for discharge hearings are held, and then marshal evidence to show how the reasons of judicial officers reflect two views of rehabilitation: one focused on the discharge as a tool for effecting rehabilitation and another focused on rehabilitation as a prerequisite to getting a discharge.

Application for discharge hearings occur in a small number of bankruptcy files—roughly 10 per cent. Recall that the effect of the discharge is to release an individual from most pre-bankruptcy debts. Most individuals who make an assignment into bankruptcy will be automatically discharged after a set amount of time has elapsed, without being required to appear at an application for discharge hearing. For example, a first time bankrupt with no surplus income will be automatically discharged after nine months. An individual may be denied an automatic discharge if someone lodges an opposition to the individual's discharge. A licensed insolvency trustee, a creditor or the federal Office of the Superintendent of Bankruptcy may lodge an opposition, and when such an opposition is lodged it triggers a court hearing at which the presiding judicial officer must decide whether the individual should be discharged. Discharge hearings also occur in some files where the individual bankrupt has no entitlement to an automatic discharge: individuals who are bankrupt for the third (or fourth or fifth) time and individuals who make assignments into bankruptcy with large tax debts do not receive an automatic discharge. In such cases, the trustee is tasked with bringing an application for the bankrupt's discharge.

When judicial officers hear applications for discharge, they have a number of options for disposing with the applications. They can grant an absolute discharge, which takes effect immediately. They can delay the discharge to a future date, or stipulate that it will only take effect once the debtor has fulfilled one or more conditions. They can refuse a bankrupt's discharge, with the result that the individual will remain in bankruptcy until he or she can convince a judicial officer that he or she deserves to be discharged. The judicial officers may also adjourn an application *sine die* (i.e., indefinitely), leaving it to the bankrupt to bring the matter back before a court. Judicial officers often explain their decisions on applications for discharge as being motivated by a desire to ensure that the individual is rehabilitated.

A common characterization of rehabilitation offered by judicial officers is narrowly financial: "It allows an insolvent debtor who is overburdened by debt to employ a process by which he or she can shed those debts and obtain a 'fresh start.'" According to this characterization, the very act of discharging an individual's debts rehabilitates them. As newly unencumbered individuals, they are expected to engage as productive members of the workforce, consumers, and risk-taking entrepreneurs.

Judicial officers voice concern that impeding the debtor's access to a discharge undermines the debtor's rehabilitation. In one case, a student had borrowed money from a bank to finance an engineering degree, but subsequently developed health issues with both mental and physical components, left school, and was unemployed and living at home with his mother. The judicial officer granted the debtor an absolute discharge, reasoning that a refusal or a suspension would only be "another impediment to [the debtor] in dealing with his substantial personal problems." In another case, the judicial officer rejected the creditor's suggestion that a debtor's discharge be conditioned on a large payment, because it would take the debtor eight years to satisfy the payment. The judicial officer reasoned that such a delay would overly retard the debtor's financial rehabilitation. Instead, the judicial officer suspended the debtor's discharge for fourteen months, during which time the debtor was required to continue to make surplus income payments. These decisions reflect a narrow conception of the fresh start, where debtors are rehabilitated through the release of their debts.

In a similar vein, the courts recognize that denying a debtor a discharge may result in a debtor experiencing additional burdens or disadvantages. Remaining undischarged can impact a debtor's ability to earn income from an occupation. For instance, the debtor may require a professional licence to carry out work, but be disentitled from holding that licence while bankrupt. In one case, where evidence of such a conundrum was before the court, the judicial officer granted the debtor a discharge, suspended for only one day. The judicial officer recognized that a longer discharge could impact the debtor's ability to work, and reasoned that "[h]e must be able to work, if he is to re-establish himself." Cases like this reflect a broader fresh start approach that goes beyond providing the debtor with a financial blank slate, but continues to promote rehabilitation by granting a discharge.

Contrary to this approach, in a number of decisions, judicial officers conceive of rehabilitation as a prerequisite that must be achieved before a debtor will be discharged. Judicial officers may equate rehabilitation with education, reflecting a belief that many individuals are driven to bankruptcy because they lack an adequate level of financial literacy. Sometimes, a judicial officer may be of the opinion that the mere fact of making an assignment into bankruptcy is enough to jolt debtors into better financial choices—that the debtors "[learn] from what has happened to them." Many judicial officers require more evidence of rehabilitation before they will grant a debtor a discharge.

A debtor completing duties during bankruptcy may be some evidence that the debtor has been rehabilitated. A bankrupt's duties include attending counselling, which allows a debtor "to learn from his or her financial mistakes with a view to not repeating them." Other duties include providing monthly income and expense reports to one's trustee, as well as the information the trustee needs to complete tax returns. Judicial officers regularly enforce debtor compliance by denying discharges to debtors who fail to complete their duties. As one noted, "Parliament did not impose duties on bankrupts for their convenience, but to foster rehabilitation, and as part of the price, if you will, of society's absolution of debt."

A debtor's post-assignment conduct may lead a judicial officer to conclude that a debtor has not yet undergone sufficient rehabilitation and consequently should not be granted a discharge. For instance, a tax protestor who makes an assignment into bankruptcy to escape a large tax debt to Canada Revenue Agency ("CRA") demonstrates a lack of rehabilitation when he continues to maintain that he has no obligation to pay tax. A second time bankrupt, whose bankruptcies were both caused by gambling, demonstrates a lack of rehabilitation by continuing to "yield to the sweet temptations of Lady Luck, and her siren song of easy fortunes and riches." The extravagant spender evidences a lack of rehabilitation when his post assignment choices include a six month stay at a Belizean resort, and maintaining a membership at an elite private club.

Judicial officers may also draw inferences about the extent to which a debtor has been rehabilitated from the attitude the debtor displays toward the court—and the trustee. The debtor need not "approach the court as a penitent might approach the confessional" but "[s]ome personal acknowledgement of blame and acceptance of individual responsibility for the consequences that the bankruptcy has wrought, however, are essential." Courts infer a lack of rehabilitation when a debtor displays a lack of remorse or contrition, or appears too willing to heap blame on another party. These attitudes are inconsistent with the acknowledgement of blame and acceptance of personal responsibility that are perceived to be a key part of the rehabilitation process.

Where the debtor's conduct and attitude has "demonstrated that rehabilitation was of little or no concern to him," judicial officers may attempt to craft discharge orders that "ensure the process results in a meaningful education and learning experience to avoid repeat bankruptcies." When crafting rehabilitative discharge orders, judicial officers may favour a large conditional payment on the premise that it has a "salutary and rehabilitative effect." In one case, the judicial officer opted to condition the debtor's discharge on a repayment obligation of an amount equal to 40 per cent of the proven liabilities, rather than refusing the discharge. The judicial officer reasoned that a refusal would only be punitive, whereas a conditional order could be rehabilitative, because the debtor could still obtain a discharge through "hard work and financial discipline." Similarly, in another case the judicial officer conditioned the debtor's discharge on a modest repayment obligation of $8,100, reasoning that it was in the debtor's "best interests to create and maintain a payment plan for the monies due to the trustee." And in a third case, the judicial officer found that the debtor had lived extravagantly at the expense of his creditors and conditioned the debtor's discharge on making forty-eight monthly payments of $1,000. The judicial officer reasoned that the payments would force the debtor to "'curtail his expenses ... and live within his means.'"

In addition to payments, judicial officers craft creative conditions to remedy debtors' behaviours. An individual whose bankruptcy was precipitated by unpaid taxes may be required to show that post-assignment tax obligations have been dealt with to CRA's satisfaction. In cases where gambling is a contributing factor to the debtor's financial difficulties, the judicial officer may order the debtor to attend counselling or to undertake not to gamble for a set period of time. Where the debtor has lived with undue extravagance, the Court may condition the debtor's discharge on attending further financial counselling sessions to help the debtor learn "to avoid consumer temptation ... so as to live within her means."

This second group of decisions characterizes rehabilitation as something a debtor must do prior to receiving a discharge. People rehabilitate themselves by completing the duties assigned to them during bankruptcy, and fulfilling conditions imposed on them in discharge orders. Often, the conditions include mandatory payments.

[Reprinted by permission of the publisher.]

C. The Theory of the Bankruptcy Discharge

1) Why should there be a right of discharge?
The traditional argument in favour of the discharge is that it causes debtors to work more after bankruptcy: if debtors had to pay all or part of their future earnings to creditors, they would have less incentive to work (*Local Loan Co v Hunt*, 202 US 234 (1934)). An additional compelling argument, supported by Thomas Jackson, is that the discharge encourages debtors to take risks and fuel market activity (see Thomas Jackson, *The Logic and Limits of Bankruptcy Law* (Washington, DC: Beard Books, 2001)). It does so by offering a form of consumption insurance—if a debtor has a financial reversal, they lose their non-exempt assets and income but the rest of their personal wealth, including their human capital, is protected. The discharge shifts the risk of bad spending decisions from the debtor to their creditors. This shift is justified by the fact that creditors are more likely to be repeat players in the market for credit and, accordingly, in a better position to assess the debtor's risk. Further, creditors are better able to limit their risk by diversifying—that is, by lending to numerous debtors.

2) Why is the discharge non-waivable?
Why can't individual debtors and creditors agree that the discharge will not apply to their agreement and reduce the cost of credit to the debtor accordingly? The primary answer comes from behavioural economics:

- A waiver may make the debtor's family worse off because its members bear most of the cost, but the debtor may not take their family's welfare sufficiently into account when they decide to give a waiver.
- Debtors may underestimate the probability of a financial reversal and thus give a waiver even when it is against their self-interest (incomplete heuristics argument).
- In addition, various externalities may be created by allowing individual debtors and creditors to waive the discharge:
- If the debtor cannot discharge their debts, they have less incentive to work; thus, if waivers were allowed, there might be social costs in the form of reduced productivity.

- Prohibiting waivers benefits the government itself. The discharge is a partial substitute for social welfare programs; if waivers were allowed, the government might have to spend more on social welfare.

3) Why isn't the discharge free?

The discharge is not free. In return for the discharge, the debtor has to give up their non-exempt assets and also a portion of their future earnings (to the extent *BIA*, section 68, requires). There is also a second-order cost: by using bankruptcy to obtain a discharge, the debtor sends out a negative signal about their creditworthiness and this may affect their access to credit in future. Given the benefits of the discharge, why not make it free—in other words, give the debtor a discharge without requiring them to surrender assets or income? According to Jackson (at 250), the answer is that "the availability of the discharge presents a cost as well as a benefit to the individual debtor: the more readily available the benefit, the higher the cost of credit."

4) Competing ideas about the bankruptcy discharge

Iain Ramsay, *Personal Insolvency in the 21st Century: A Comparative Analysis of the US and Europe* (Oxford: Hart Publishing, 2017) at 16–17

> Narratives provide a framework of ideas about the goals of a policy, the nature of the problem addressed, and the most appropriate instruments to achieve these goals. . . . Personal insolvency narratives are constructed from contrasting and conflicting ideas. These include the concepts of a fresh start, a second chance, the prevention of social exclusion, and the promotion of entrepreneurialism (responsible risk taking). Counter narratives include the influential *pacta sunt seranda*—the 'common sense' idea that 'one pays back one's debts' associated with the maintenance of 'good payment culture' –the control of moral hazard, and the importance of personal responsibility reflected in the slogan 'can pay should pay'. These ideas represent the toolkit for political argument, and policymakers often claim that they have drawn a balance between these values. . . . No unequivocal answers exist as to the scope of the fresh start, how much of an individual's human capital should be devoted to repaying creditors in an insolvency, what specific assets should be exempt from seizure, and which debts should be excluded from the fresh start.

Insolvency Debtor/Creditor Regimes Task Force, *Report on the Treatment of the Insolvency of Natural Persons* (Working Group on the Treatment of the Insolvency of Natural Persons, World Bank, 2013) at 115

> One of the principal purposes of an insolvency system for natural persons is to re-establish the debtor's economic capability, in other words, economic rehabilitation. Rehabilitation can be said to include three elements. First, the debtor has to be freed from excessive debt. . . . Second, the debtor should be treated on an equal basis with non-debtors after receiving relief (the principle of non-discrimination). Third, the debtor should be able to avoid becoming excessively indebted again in the future, which may require some attempt to change debtors' attitudes concerning proper credit use. . . . The most effective form of relief from debt is a fresh start, which in historical usage refers to a straight discharge; that is, to the possibility to be freed from debt without a payment plan.

Re McAfee (1988), 67 CBR (NS) 209 (BCCA)

LOCKE JA (for the Court):

This appeal concerns the principles to be applied on an application to discharge a bankrupt, and considers some of the factors to be taken into account in setting a condition.

The chambers judge imposed as a condition of discharge that the bankrupt consent to a judgment for $40,000. Westmore, a principal creditor, opposed the discharge, and now appeals, arguing that this is inequitable under the circumstances and is not enough. Broadly, the grounds for appeal are that the chambers judge erred in law and misconstrued relevant facts when he held that the bankrupt was blameless in relation to his financial problems, and conducted himself properly during bankruptcy; and in particular failed to give due weight to the bankrupt's present and future large income.

FACTS:

The respondent, John A. McAfee, practised law in Kelowna, BC but has always engaged in business. From the mid-1970s up until the spring of 1982, he controlled and operated a company called Old MacDonald's Farms Ltd. ("MacDonalds") in the Okanagan which operated a children's amusement park. In the spring of 1982 the facility was sold to third parties for $1,500,000.

In 1978 he and others promoted a large amusement park development in Calgary known as "Calaway Park." The land was purchased, approvals were obtained and construction started in the spring of 1981 and opened in the summer of 1982. It was a financial disaster and all investors lost their equity. The Bank of America, the Northland Bank and the Royal Bank of Canada were all involved in financing this venture; with the collapse of the real estate market the loans were called and in November of 1982 McAfee was on a guarantee for $17.5 million. He entered into negotiations to attempt to resolve his liability and managed to restructure the liability and settled it by liquidating some major assets but lost something more than half of his net worth, which in 1980 he estimated at near $4 million.

The appellant, Hilton H. Westmore, through his company Enchant Resources Ltd. ("Enchant"), on January 15, 1978, bought 20 shares of the capital stock of MacDonald's and advanced $144,000 to it by way of a shareholder loan. On April 30, 1980, the parties entered into two agreements, which in substance provided for the repurchase by McAfee of Westmore's shares by paying out the shareholders' loan, together with an immediate cash payment. The first payment under these agreements was to be made on September 30, 1983. On April 1, 1982, the company sold its assets for $1.5 million. Because McAfee believed that Westmore, by virtue of the agreements, had ceased to be a shareholder of the company and that Enchant was otherwise adequately secured, he caused his company to engage in certain corporate manoeuvres which had the effect of seeing that large cash payments were made by way of dividend to himself and used by him to pay off guarantees to various banks. In giving judgment in the action, *Westmore v McAfee* (1986), 70 BCLR 332, in an action brought by Westmore to enforce payment of the money due under the agreements of 1980, Macdonald J concluded two things: first, the transactions involved had been unfairly prejudicial and oppressive to Westmore, but second, that McAfee was under the mistaken but honest belief that Westmore had ceased to be a shareholder of the company. In the result, a claim for breach of fiduciary duties was dismissed but judgment to complete the sale in the sum of $300,000 was given against McAfee, his wife Brenda McAfee and his private company, McAfee Enterprises Inc.

When MacDonald's was sold, McAfee took back as part of the purchase price, a debenture of $550,000 payable to him and the purchasers defaulted. He repurchased the enterprise in 1983 as described, but it continued to lose money and, on November 28, 1985, the Northland Bank who had assisted in the purchase demanded payment in full of the debt of MacDonald's in the sum of $897,132.72, guaranteed personally by McAfee. On January 14, 1986, just prior to the Westmore action hearing, McAfee negotiated a settlement with the bank whereby he was released from this guarantee in return for the grant of a second mortgage in favour of the bank in the sum of $85,000 over his residence in Kelowna.

After the judgment was obtained and up until July, 1986, McAfee negotiated with Westmore with regard to his large liability to Westmore but Westmore was furious and would not entertain any of the comparatively small settlement proposals and demanded payment of the full amount. At the same time, Revenue Canada advanced a claim of nearly a quarter of a million dollars, some of the liability arising from non-payment of tax on the MacDonald's dividends.

In the meantime, McAfee had gone back to practising law in earnest in Kelowna. Westmore had threatened to levy execution and McAfee went to the Law Society and disclosed his financial position, received some assurances that he would be able to continue practice, and ultimately on July 31st, executed an assignment for the general benefit of creditors. On November 5, 1986, a proposal in bankruptcy made by Brenda McAfee was rejected by her creditor (Westmore) and, pursuant to s. 39 of the *Bankruptcy Act*, RSC 1970, c. B-3, she was thereupon deemed to have made an assignment on that same day.

Nine months later, on March 27, 1987, McAfee petitioned the court for an order of discharge....

McAfee filed his business records which disclosed his violent irregularities in income but he estimated his net income for the year ending October, 1987, at about $100,000. The chambers judge had the advantage of hearing the respondent examined and cross-examined in open court. Westmore's counsel submitted the offer of $12,000 was wholly inadequate and suggested $200,000 as more appropriate. Following this, the chambers judge reserved and when he gave his judgment next day he made two important findings:

1. For the most part McAfee had conducted himself properly and should not be criticized because bad economic times and poor judgment brought about his financial collapse.
2. The fact that no moneys were paid to the trustee since the declaration of bankruptcy in August, 1986, was a proper matter to take into account in settling any terms or conditions for discharge in view of the fact that he was able to earn a substantial income at the present time and into the future.

He then ordered the respondent to enter into a consent judgment for $40,000 as a condition of discharge....

The trustee is to give his opinion in the statutory report and s. 140(5) states that the report is evidence of the statements therein contained. It is to be noticed that there is a difference in the burden of proof as to s. 143(1)(a) and the remaining 12 subsections. As to this, an important point was settled by the Quebec Court of Appeal in *Re Samson v L'Alliance Nationale* (1935), 17 CBR 304, under slightly different wording, where Mr. Justice Barclay said:

> Under section 141(8), for the purposes of this section 143a, the report of the trustees shall be prima facie evidence of the statements therein contained ... This report of the trustees cannot be disregarded. As was said in *Re Gorman* (1922), 2 CBR 454, the trade creditors

who oppose the application must show conclusively some misconduct or impropriety on the part of the bankrupt other than what is to be inferred from the small dividend paid, before they are in a position to contend effectively against his discharge. There is, therefore, *prima facie* evidence contained in the trustees' report which shifts the onus of proof to the opposing creditor....

Most of the principles of law governing the discharge of a bankrupt are found in *Links v Robinson* 1971 5 WWR 531. These were adopted by this court in *Patterson v Royal Bank* (1984), 49 BCLR 234, and in *Re Markel* [(1986), 63 CBR (NS) 7 (BCCA)]. Underlying principles were also put succinctly by Hutcheon JA in *Re Marshall* [(1986), 62 CBR (NS) 118 (BCCA)], where he said:

> "On that point it would seem to me that the judge in bankruptcy must consider two principles: the first is that of the rehabilitation of the bankrupt, and the second is that of the integrity of the bankruptcy system ..."

I would wish to adopt, without referring to the authorities other than *Re Posner* (1960), 3 CBR (NS) 49, a statement of Anderson J in *Re Raftis* (1984), 53 CBR (NS) 19, where he gave a compendious expression of the sometimes conflicting principles of discharge extracted from the cases:

1. In considering the question of discharge, the Court must have regard not only to the interests of the bankrupt and his creditors, but also to the interests of the public ...
2. The Legislature has always recognized the interest that the State has in a debtor being released from the overwhelming pressure of his debts, and that it is undesirable that a citizen should be so weighed down by his debts as to be incapable of performing the ordinary duties of citizenship ...
3. One of the objects of the *Bankruptcy Act* was to enable an honest debtor, who had been unfortunate in business, to secure a discharge so he might make a new start ...
4. The bankruptcy courts should not be converted into a sort of clearing-house for the liquidation of debts irrespective of the circumstances under which they were created ...
5. The success or failure of any bankruptcy system depends upon the administration of the discharge provisions of the Act ...
6. The Court is not to be regarded as a sort of charitable institution ...
7. It is incumbent upon the Court to guard against laxity in granting discharges so as not to offend against commercial morality. It is nevertheless the duty of the Court to administer the *Bankruptcy Act* in such a way as to assist honest debtors who have been unfortunate ...
8. The discharge is not a matter of right ...

These principles impose upon a judge the obligation of considering and balancing the interests of the bankrupt, of the creditors and of the public.

When Westmore opposed the discharge he took the following grounds as I appreciate them:

1. that the primary reason the bankrupt made an assignment was to avoid the consequences of the Westmore judgment;
2. that the respondent's conduct before and after bankruptcy should have been subject to censure;
3. that the court in making its order failed to consider the respondent's extravagant style of living during bankruptcy, but, of more importance, the fact that he was

continuing his practice as a lawyer with some substantial assurance of future income.

The first ground was that the order for discharge should have been refused because the financial situation of the respondent did not arise from circumstances for which he could not justly be held responsible, i.e., he was culpably responsible for his own condition.

The trustee stated that he:

" ... does not believe that the bankrupt can be held responsible for his insolvency, which appears to have arisen from guarantees of corporate debts ... Mr. McAfee executed a settlement agreement with the Northland Bank reducing this debt from $897,000 to $85,000 based on the assumption that this debt was the last of his onerous financial problems. Subsequently the court found him liable as guarantor of loans by Enchant Resources Ltd. to Old Macdonald's Farms of some $335,000. He could not meet this obligation and was forced to consider bankruptcy. For these reasons, the trustee does not believe the bankrupt can be held responsible for his insolvency ..."

This is a pretty sketchy and not wholly accurate account of the causes of the bankruptcy, as it was conceded by the respondent that the debts to the appellant and to Revenue Canada—his principal liabilities—did not arise from guarantees at all.

The argument rests upon *Kozack v Richter*, [1974] SCR 832, where Pigeon J for the court, where the debt had arisen from a judgment for damages arising out of grossly negligent driving, said [at 615]:

"... In the present case, the respondent's bankruptcy was precipitated by his condemnation to pay damages to the appellant. This being due to a finding of 'wilful and wanton misconduct' on his part, certainly his financial predicament cannot be said to have arisen "from circumstances for which he cannot justly be held responsible ..."

and in those circumstances the court declined to make an order of discharge....

I cannot find here anything other than a superficial resemblance between the case at bar and *Kozack*. McAfee swore he arranged to satisfy his outstanding liabilities as far as he could so that he could in the end avoid bankruptcy. The trial judge accepted this, and from my independent review of the facts I see no ground for disturbing his conclusion. However, this is not to say that the facts are to be forgotten in the exercise of a discretion....

The authorities above are all examples of the court examining widely varying patterns and endeavouring to balance the three interested parties of bankrupt, creditor and public. In the circumstances displayed in *Markel* the discharge was originally granted on a $40,000 condition. In *Raftis* the balance was struck at $60,000; In *Harley*, BCCA February 11, 1986 (unreported), $100,000 was ordered; and in *Atkin* [*Re* (1987), 65 CBR (NS) 296 (Ont Sup Ct J)] $150,000 was deemed to be fair. No one formula will do.

Here the bankrupt discharged the onus he has of establishing that his assets had not diminished through his own culpability. However, McAfee did not, as did Markel, make any substantial effort after the assignment to make any payments to anybody out of his income; all of his efforts were devoted to preserve his own assets and himself. This is not a bankruptcy offence, but is a factor. A monthly income in excess of the Superintendent's guidelines by $50,000 a year must surely be considered, and the style of living which he continues is appropriate to a wealthy man, but the appearance of wealth is not essential to enable one to successfully practise law. I think on principle that appropriate appearances ought to be maintainable. But in view of the past and the future, I think that more than a modest living standard is inappropriate. The fact that children go to university or to private school is desirable and acknowledged by every parent, but life sometimes does not permit it. There are other schools, and there are student loans.

I would not venture to alter the chamber judge's assessment of all the factors did I not deem it a matter of degree. I have had the advantage of considering a long argument and many authorities not quoted to him. When I look at this application for discharge I see a man who has met many misfortunes but at the same time he is now rid of half a million dollars of liability. It appears to me he has a future. In view of the authorities and the facts in this case, I would set as an appropriate condition, a consent to judgment in the sum of $80,000 plus the taxed costs of this appeal. I would further wish to adopt a procedure mentioned in some of the Ontario cases to which I have referred: rather than set a time-table and an amount per month or per year, I would leave it to the discretion of the trustee to set an appropriate schedule of payments, with an acceleration clause on default, and I would direct that as this will lengthen the term of his engagement the trustee should be appropriately remunerated by McAfee, and that there be liberty to apply to this court if the details cannot be satisfactorily arranged. McAfee therefore stands absolutely discharged subject to consenting to an appropriate form of judgment....

Appeal allowed in part.

Alberta (Attorney General) v Moloney, 2015 SCC 51, [2015] 3 SCR 327

GASCON J (ABELLA, ROTHSTEIN, CROMWELL, MOLDAVER, KARAKATSANIS and WAGNER JJ concurring):

I. OVERVIEW

[1] In Canada, the federal and provincial levels of government must enact laws within the limits of their respective spheres of jurisdiction. The *Constitution Act, 1867* defines which matters fall within the exclusive legislative authority of each level. Still, even when acting within its own sphere, one level of government will sometimes affect matters within the other's sphere of jurisdiction. The resulting legislative overlap may, on occasion, lead to a conflict between otherwise valid federal and provincial laws. In this appeal, the Court must decide whether such a conflict exists, and if so, resolve it.

[2] The alleged conflict in this case concerns, on the one hand, the federal *Bankruptcy and Insolvency Act*, R.S.C. 1985, c. B-3 ("*BIA*"), and on the other hand, Alberta's *Traffic Safety Act*, R.S.A. 2000, c. T-6 ("*TSA*"). It stems from a car accident caused by the respondent while he was uninsured, contrary to s. 54 of the *TSA*. The province of Alberta compensated the individual injured in the accident and sought to recover the amount of the compensation from the respondent. The latter, however, made an assignment in bankruptcy and was eventually discharged. The *BIA* governs bankruptcy and provides that, upon discharge, the respondent is released from all debts that are claims provable in bankruptcy. The *TSA* governs the activity of driving, including vehicle permits and driver's licences, and allows the province to suspend the respondent's licence and permits until he pays the amount of the compensation.

[3] As a result of his bankruptcy and subsequent discharge, the respondent did not pay the amount of the compensation in full; because of this failure to pay, Alberta suspended his vehicle permits and driver's licence. The respondent contested this suspension, arguing that the *TSA* conflicted with the *BIA*, in that it frustrated the purposes of

bankruptcy. The province replied that there was no conflict since the *TSA* was regulatory in nature and did not purport to enforce a discharged debt. The Court of Queen's Bench and the Court of Appeal found that there was a conflict between the federal and provincial laws. Relying on the doctrine of federal paramountcy, they declared the impugned provision of the *TSA* to be inoperative to the extent of the conflict. I agree with the outcome reached by the lower courts, and I would dismiss the appeal.

II. FACTS

[4] The car accident caused by the respondent occurred in 1989. In 1996, the individual injured in the accident obtained judgment against the respondent in the amount of $194,875. The Administrator appointed under the *Motor Vehicle Accident Claims Act*, R.S.A. 2000, c. M-22 ("*MVACA*"), indemnified the injured party for the amount of the judgment debt and was assigned the debt in accordance with the *MVACA*. Initially, the respondent made arrangements with the Administrator to pay the debt in instalments. Some years later, however, in January 2008, he made an assignment in bankruptcy. He listed the Administrator's claim in his Statement of Affairs. It is not disputed that the judgment debt assigned to the Administrator was a claim provable in bankruptcy. It was, by far, the respondent's most substantial debt and, in fact, the reason for his financial difficulties. At the time of the assignment, the outstanding amount due to the Administrator stood at $195,823.

[5] In June 2011, the respondent obtained an absolute discharge, which no one opposed. In October of the same year, he received a letter from the Director, Driver Fitness and Monitoring, notifying him that, by application of s. 102(1) of the *TSA*, his operator's licence and vehicle registration privileges would be suspended until payment of the outstanding amount of the judgment debt. Later, in November, his lawyer received another letter, this time from Motor Vehicle Accident Recoveries, advising the respondent that he "remains indebted for the judgment debt obtained against him ... 'until the judgment is satisfied or discharged, otherwise than by a discharge in bankruptcy'" (A.R., at p. 49). The letter proposed that new payment arrangements be made, failing which the suspension of his driving privileges would continue.

[6] Given this situation, in March 2012, the respondent sought an order from the Court of Queen's Bench to stay the suspension of his driving privileges. He claimed that he had been discharged in bankruptcy and that s. 178 of the *BIA* precluded the Administrator from enforcing the judgment debt. . . .

IV. ISSUE

[12] The Chief Justice formulated the following constitutional question:

> Is s. 102(2) of Alberta *Traffic Safety Act*, R.S.A. 2000, c. T-6, constitutionally inoperative by reason of the doctrine of federal paramountcy?

Although the constitutional question, as formulated, refers only to s. 102(2), the proceedings below and the parties' submissions concern the section in its entirety. Accordingly, I will examine all of the relevant aspects of s. 102.

V. ANALYSIS

[13] Various government actors have been involved in this dispute. Unless otherwise specified, I will refer to the province of Alberta as encompassing these different actors.

I will first review the principles applicable to the doctrine of federal paramountcy and then apply them to the facts of this appeal.

A. The Doctrine of Federal Paramountcy

[14] Each level of government—Parliament, on the one hand, and the provincial legislatures, on the other—has exclusive authority to enact legislation with respect to certain subject matters. Sections 91 and 92 of the *Constitution Act, 1867* assign each power to the level of government best suited to exercise it: *Reference re Secession of Quebec,* [1998] 2 S.C.R. 217 (*"Secession Reference"*), at para. 58. Broad powers were given to the provincial legislatures with respect to local matters, in recognition of regional diversity, while powers relating to matters of national importance were given to Parliament, to ensure unity: *Canadian Western Bank v Alberta,* 2007 SCC 22, [2007] 2 S.C.R. 3, at para. 22.

[15] Legislative powers are exclusive, and one government is not subordinate to the other: *Secession Reference,* at para. 58, citing *Reference re Initiative & Referendum Act,* [1919] A.C. 935 (PC), at p. 942. However, the legislative matrix is not as clearly defined as ss. 91 and 92 might suggest. It is often impossible for one level of government to legislate effectively within its jurisdiction without affecting matters that are within the other level's jurisdiction.... Furthermore, it is often impossible to make a statute fall squarely within a single head of power.... This leads to overlap in the exercise of provincial and federal powers. The tendency has been to allow these overlaps to occur as long as each level of government properly pursues objectives that fall within its jurisdiction.... This tendency reflects the theory of co-operative federalism....

[16] That said, there comes a point where legislative overlap jeopardizes the balance between unity and diversity. In certain circumstances, the powers of one level of government must be protected against intrusions, even incidental ones, by the other level: *Western Bank,* at para. 32. To protect against such intrusions, the Court has developed various constitutional doctrines. For the purposes of this appeal, I need only refer to one: the doctrine of federal paramountcy. This doctrine "recognizes that where laws of the federal and provincial levels come into conflict, there must be a rule to resolve the impasse": *Western Bank,* at para. 32. When there is a genuine "inconsistency" between federal and provincial legislation, that is, when "the operational effects of provincial legislation are incompatible with federal legislation", the federal law prevails.... The question thus becomes how to determine whether such a conflict exists....

[18] A conflict is said to arise in one of two situations, which form the two branches of the paramountcy test: (1) there is an operational conflict because it is impossible to comply with both laws, or (2) although it is possible to comply with both laws, the operation of the provincial law frustrates the purpose of the federal enactment.

[19] What is considered to be the first branch of the test was described as follows in *Multiple Access,* the seminal decision of the Court on this issue:

> In principle, there would seem to be no good reasons to speak of paramountcy and preclusion except where there is <u>actual conflict in operation</u> as where one enactment says "yes" and the other says "no"; "the same citizens are being told to do inconsistent things"; compliance with one is defiance of the other. [Emphasis added; p. 191.] ...

[25] If there is no conflict under the first branch of the test, one may still be found under the second branch. In *Bank of Montreal v Hall,* [1990] 1 S.C.R. 121, the Court formulated what is now considered to be the second branch of the test. It framed the

question as being "whether operation of the provincial Act is compatible with the federal legislative purpose" (p. 155). In other words, the effect of the provincial law may frustrate the purpose of the federal law, even though it does "not entail a direct violation of the federal law's provisions": *Western Bank*, at para. 73. . . .

[29] In sum, if the operation of the provincial law has the effect of making it impossible to comply with the federal law, or if it is technically possible to comply with both laws, but the operation of the provincial law still has the effect of frustrating Parliament's purpose, there is a conflict. Such a conflict results in the provincial law being inoperative, but only to the extent of the conflict with the federal law: *Western Bank*, at para. 69; *Rothmans*, at para. 11; *Mangat*, at para. 74. In practice, this means that the provincial law remains valid, but will be read down so as to not conflict with the federal law, though only for as long as the conflict exists. . . .

[30] I now turn to the application of the doctrine to the facts of this appeal.

B. Application

(1) The Legislative Schemes at Issue

[31] The first step of the analysis is to ensure that the impugned federal and provincial provisions are independently valid. Early in the proceedings, the parties recognized the validity of the relevant provisions of the *BIA* and the *TSA*. Before this Court, they again conceded the validity of both laws. The only question is whether their concurrent operation results in a conflict. This requires analyzing the legislative schemes at issue at the outset so as to reach a proper understanding of the provisions that are allegedly in conflict.

(a) The Bankruptcy and Insolvency Act

[32] Parliament enacted the *BIA* pursuant to its jurisdiction over matters of bankruptcy and insolvency under s. 91(21) of the *Constitution Act, 1867*. The *BIA*, notably through the specific provisions discussed below, furthers two purposes: the equitable distribution of the bankrupt's assets among his or her creditors and the bankrupt's financial rehabilitation (*Husky Oil*, at para. 7).

[33] The first purpose of bankruptcy, the equitable distribution of assets, is achieved through a single proceeding model. Under this model, creditors of the bankrupt wishing to enforce a claim provable in bankruptcy must participate in one collective proceeding. This ensures that the assets of the bankrupt are distributed fairly amongst the creditors. As a general rule, all creditors rank equally and share rateably in the bankrupt's assets. . . .

[36] The second purpose of the *BIA*, the financial rehabilitation of the debtor, is achieved through the discharge of the debtor's outstanding debts at the end of the bankruptcy: *Husky Oil*, at para. 7. Section 178(2) of the *BIA* provides:

> (2) Subject to subsection (1), an order of discharge releases the bankrupt from all claims provable in bankruptcy.

From the perspective of the creditors, the discharge means they are unable to enforce their provable claims: *Schreyer v Schreyer*, 2011 SCC 35, [2011] 2 S.C.R. 605, at para. 21. This, in effect, gives the insolvent person a "fresh start", in that he or she is "freed from the burdens of pre-existing indebtedness": Wood, at p. 273; see also *Industrial Acceptance Corp v Lalonde*, [1952] 2 S.C.R. 109, at p. 120. This fresh start is not only designed for the well-being of the bankrupt debtor and his or her family; rehabilitation helps the discharged bankrupt to reintegrate into economic life so he or she can become a productive member of society: Wood, at pp. 274–75; L.W. Houlden, G.B. Morawetz and J. Sarra, *Bankruptcy and Insolvency Law of Canada* (4th ed. (loose-leaf), at p. 6-283. In many cases of consumer bankruptcy, the debtor has very few or no assets to distribute to his or her creditors. In those cases, rehabilitation becomes the primary objective of bankruptcy: Wood, at p. 37.

[37] Although it is an important purpose of the *BIA*, financial rehabilitation also has its limits. Section 178(1) of the *BIA* lists debts that are not released by discharge and that survive bankruptcy. Furthermore, s. 172 provides that an order of discharge may be denied, suspended, or granted subject to conditions. These provisions demonstrate Parliament's attempt to balance financial rehabilitation with other policy objectives, such as confidence in the credit system, that require certain debts to survive bankruptcy: Wood, at pp. 273 and 289.

[38] Discharge is the main rehabilitative tool contained in the *BIA*, but it is not the only one. As Professor Wood, at p. 273, observes:

> The bankruptcy discharge is one of the primary mechanisms through which bankruptcy law attempts to provide for the economic rehabilitation of the debtor. However, it is not the only means by which bankruptcy law seeks to meet this objective. The exclusion of exempt property from distribution to creditors, the surplus income provisions, and mandatory credit counselling also are directed towards this goal.

[39] Another means of rehabilitation is the automatic stay of proceedings contained in s. 69.3 of the *BIA*. The stay not only ensures that creditors are redirected into the collective proceeding described above, it also ensures that creditors are precluded from seizing property that is exempt from distribution to creditors. This is an important part of the bankrupt's financial rehabilitation:

> The rehabilitation of the bankrupt is not the result only of his discharge. It begins when he is put into bankruptcy with measures designed to give him the minimum needed for subsistence.
>
> (*Vachon v Canada (Employment & Immigration Commission)*, [1985] 2 S.C.R. 417, at p. 430.)

. . .

[41] In the context of this appeal, we are specifically concerned with an alleged conflict between, on the one hand, one provision of the *BIA*, namely s. 178, the purpose of which is to ensure the financial rehabilitation of the debtor, and, on the other hand, one provision (s. 102) of the provincial scheme, to which I will now turn.

(b) The Alberta Traffic Safety Act

[42] The *TSA* is the provincial scheme with which the *BIA* is alleged to conflict. Pursuant to s. 92(13) of the *Constitution Act, 1867*, provincial legislatures have the power to legislate with regard to property and civil rights. The Court has long recognized that this power includes traffic regulation and the authority to set conditions for driver's licences and vehicle permits. . . . The *TSA* is a comprehensive legislative scheme for traffic regulation, "covering virtually all aspects of the regulation of highways and motor vehicles in Alberta", with the aim of ensuring road safety. . . .

[43] Under s. 54(1) of the *TSA*, no one is allowed to drive or have a motor vehicle on a public road unless the vehicle is insured. Under s. 54(4), a person who contravenes s. 54(1) is liable to a fine or imprisonment. The Registrar of Motor Vehicle Services may also disqualify a person from driving and cancel his or her vehicle registration until that person shows proof of insurance: s. 54(5) and (7).

[44] In the event that an uninsured driver causes an accident, Alberta has implemented a compensation program governed by the *MVACA*. A victim injured in the accident may sue the uninsured driver for damages. If the victim is successful but the uninsured driver does not pay, the victim may then apply to the Administrator under the *MVACA* for compensation in the amount of the unsatisfied judgment: s. 5(1). If authorized, the payment is drawn from the General Revenue Fund of the province: s. 5(2). The judgment is then assigned to the Administrator, who can take steps to enforce it against the judgment debtor. The Administrator is thus deemed to be the judgment creditor: s. 5(7).

[45] Section 102 of the *TSA*, the provision at issue in this appeal, complements the *MVACA* program. It allows the Registrar to suspend the debtor's driver's licence and vehicle permits until the judgment debt is paid, up to a maximum amount of $200,000. . . .

[47] The purpose and effect of s. 102 are obvious when it is read in its context: it is meant to deprive the judgment debtor of driving privileges until the judgment arising from a motor vehicle accident is paid in full, or periodic payments in satisfaction of the judgment are being made under s. 103. It is, in substance, a debt collection mechanism. Since the parties conceded that the judgment debt in this appeal is a claim provable in bankruptcy, I would add that the purpose and effect of s. 102, in the context of this appeal, are to suspend a debtor's driving privileges until payment of a provable claim. . . .

[54] . . . A regulatory charge remains a debt owed to the province, which s. 102 is meant to collect. Not only is it a debt, but it is, like the underlying judgment debt, a provable claim.

[55] According to s. 121(1) of the *BIA*, a provable claim must meet three criteria: (1) there must be a debt, liability or obligation owed to a creditor, (2) which was incurred before the debtor became bankrupt, and (3) it must be possible to attach a monetary value to the debt, liability or obligation (*Newfoundland and Labrador v AbitibiBowater Inc*, 2012 SCC 67, [2012] 3 S.C.R. 443, at para. 26). Even if the judgment debt were characterized as a regulatory charge, it would meet these criteria. The regulatory charge would arise from a payment made to the victim of an accident caused by the respondent. The respondent's liability to the province arose prior to his assignment in bankruptcy, and it is clearly monetary in nature. As a result, the province's claim for the regulatory charge would be provable in bankruptcy and must be treated as part of the bankruptcy process: *AbitibiBowater*, at para. 40; *Vachon*, at p. 426; *Ontario (Minister of Finance) v Clarke*, 2013 ONSC 1920, 115 O.R. (3d) 33, at para. 52.

[56] Therefore, whether one considers the province's claim as a judgment debt or as the resulting regulatory charge, it is still provable in bankruptcy. It follows that the effect of s. 102 is to allow a judgment creditor to deprive the debtor of his or her driving privileges until the debt is paid. In the end, the provision thus compels the payment of a provable claim. Driving is unlike other activities. For many, it is necessary to function meaningfully in society. As such, driving often cannot be seen as a genuine "choice": *R v White*, [1999] 2 S.C.R. 417 (S.C.C.), at para. 55. The effect of the provincial scheme undoubtedly amounts to coercion in that regard. . . .

[58] As stated previously, neither the parties nor the courts below disputed that s. 102, as a whole, is *intra vires* the province. The dominant purpose and effect of s. 102 are to suspend driving privileges until payment of a judgment debt. This enforcement scheme is part of the provincial regulation of driving privileges in Alberta. There is no doubt that assuring the financial responsibility of drivers and regulating driving privileges fall within the province's jurisdiction regarding property and civil rights under s. 92(13) of the *Constitution Act, 1867*. Given this and the way the case has been argued

and decided, this appeal is, in my view, properly disposed of by applying the doctrine of paramountcy and ascertaining whether a conflict exists between the *BIA* and the *TSA*.

[59] Whether the provincial scheme has the effect of rendering a discharge in bankruptcy "ineffective as against a provincial debt" or negating the operability of a federal law as the Superintendent of Bankruptcy argues (factum, at paras. 11–12) is better resolved as a question of paramountcy. I would add that the words "otherwise than by a discharge in bankruptcy" are necessary only because the province lists the discharge in general, in addition to the satisfaction of the debt, as an event ending the suspension of the privilege. Had the legislation defined the satisfaction of the debt as the sole event capable of ending the suspension, the dominant feature of the provision would remain the same, although the issue of conflict with a discharge in bankruptcy would still arise.…

(2) The Conflict Between the *BIA* and the *TSA*

(a) Operational Conflict

[60] … In a case like this one, the test for operational conflict cannot be limited to asking whether the respondent can comply with both laws by renouncing the protection afforded to him or her under the federal law or the privilege he or she is otherwise entitled to under the provincial law. In that regard, the debtor's response to the suspension of his or her driving privileges is not determinative. In analyzing the operational conflict at issue in this case, we cannot disregard the fact that whether the debtor pays or not, the province, as a creditor, is still compelling payment of a provable claim that has been released, which is in direct contradiction with s. 178(2) of the *BIA*:

> If [the respondent] pays the debt, then the provincial law will have required him to pay a debt that has been released by the federal law. If [he] does not pay the debt, then the provincial law will have punished him — by withholding his driver's licence — for failing to pay a debt that has been released by the federal law.
>
> (*Gorguis v Saskatchewan Government Insurance*, 2011 SKQB 132, 372 Sask. R. 152, at para. 25; sent back for rehearing by the Saskatchewan Court of Appeal, which did not address the court's comments on this point (2013 SKCA 32, 414 Sask. R. 5).)

Thus, the laws at issue give inconsistent answers to the question whether there is an enforceable obligation: one law says yes and the other says no.

[61] On the one hand, s. 178(2) of the *BIA* provides that "an order of discharge releases the bankrupt from all claims provable in bankruptcy"….

[62] On the other hand, s. 102(2) of the *TSA* empowers the province to continue to pressure a debtor by withholding his or her driving privileges "until the judgment is satisfied or discharged, otherwise than by a discharge in bankruptcy". As I mentioned above in my analysis of the legislative schemes, the language of this provision is clear: it provides for the satisfaction of the judgment debt by excluding the impact of a discharge in bankruptcy.

[63] One law consequently provides for the release of all claims provable in bankruptcy and prohibits creditors from enforcing them, while the other disregards this release and allows for the use of a debt enforcement mechanism on such a claim by precisely excluding a discharge in bankruptcy. This is a true incompatibility. Both laws cannot operate concurrently (*Sun Indalex*, at para. 60; *Lafarge*, at para. 82; *M & D Farm*, at para. 41; *Multiple Access*, at p. 191), "apply concurrently" (*Western Bank*, at para. 72) or "operate side by side without conflict" (*Marine Services*, at para. 76). The facts of this appeal indeed show an actual conflict in operation of the two provisions. This is a case

where the provincial law says "yes" ("Alberta can enforce this provable claim"), while the federal law says "no" ("Alberta cannot enforce this provable claim"). The provincial law gives the province a right that the federal law denies, and maintains a liability from which the debtor has been released under the federal law....

[75] I therefore conclude that s. 102 of the *TSA* allows the province, or a third party creditor, to enforce a provable claim that has been released. To that extent, it conflicts with s. 178(2) of the *BIA*. It is impossible for the province to apply s. 102 without contravening s. 178(2) and, as a result, for the respondent to simultaneously be liable to pay the judgment debt under the provincial scheme and be released from that same claim pursuant to s. 178(2): *Lafarge*, at para. 82; *M & D Farm*, at para. 41. Section 178 is a complete code in that it sets out which debts are released on discharge and which debts survive bankruptcy. In effect, s. 102 creates a new class of exempt debts that is not listed in s. 178(1). Hence, in the words used by my colleague in her reasons (paras. 95, 110 and 128), "the provincial law allows the very same thing"—the enforcement of a debt released under s. 178(2) of the *BIA*—that "the federal law prohibits". The result is an operational conflict between the provincial and federal provisions.

[76] Although this conclusion makes it unnecessary to discuss the second branch of the test, I will nonetheless address it in order to respond to the province's arguments.

(b) Frustration of Federal Purpose

(i) Financial Rehabilitation

[77] Like the lower courts, I find that the province's use of its administrative powers relating to driving privileges to burden the respondent until he repays a discharged debt frustrates the financial rehabilitation of the bankrupt. The effect of s. 102 directly contradicts and defeats the purpose of the discharge provided for in s. 178(2):

> The *BIA* permits an honest but unfortunate debtor to obtain a discharge from debts subject to reasonable conditions. The *Act* is designed to permit a bankrupt to receive, after a specified period a complete discharge of all his or her debts in order that he or she may be able to integrate into the business of life of the country as a useful citizen free from the crushing burden of debts....

> [Emphasis added.]

> (Houlden, Morawetz and Sarra, at p. 1–2.1)

As explained already, the language of s. 178(2) makes it clear that the purpose of this provision is to give effect to one of the goals underlying the *BIA* regime—the financial rehabilitation of the debtor—by releasing "the bankrupt from all claims provable in bankruptcy". In other words, s. 178(2) is aimed precisely at providing the bankrupt with a fresh start. The facts of this case establish that the province's use of s. 102 despite the respondent's discharge undermines this purpose.

[78] The respondent was a truck driver. In 1996, after the accident, the province was assigned the judgment rendered against him in the amount of $194,875. In 2008, after attempting to pay the debt in instalments for about 12 years, he made an assignment in bankruptcy. At that time, the outstanding amount of the debt had increased to $195,823; it was, by far, the largest of the respondent's financial liabilities. In 12 years, the respondent had not been able to keep up with his interest payments. The crushing burden of the province's claim against him was the main reason for his bankruptcy. In 2012, at the time his application for discharge was heard, the respondent had only

managed to pay the judgment debt down to $192,103.79. By the effect of s. 102, he was exiting bankruptcy while carrying the same financial burden that had caused his bankruptcy four years earlier. If s. 102 is allowed to operate despite the respondent's discharge, the respondent is not offered the opportunity to rehabilitate that Parliament intended to give him. This is particularly compelling in the respondent's case. As a truck driver, his ability to gain a livelihood is tied to his ability to drive. But more generally, inability to drive can constitute a significant impediment to any person's capacity to earn income: see *Lucar, Re* (2001), 32 C.B.R. (4th) 270 (Ont. S.C.J.), at paras. 22–23.

[79] In furthering financial rehabilitation, Parliament expressly selected which debts survive bankruptcy and which are discharged: s. 178(1) and (2). It did so having regard to competing policy objectives. This is a delicate exercise, because the more claims that survive bankruptcy, the more difficult it becomes for a debtor to rehabilitate: *AbitibiBowater*, at para. 35; *Schreyer*, at para. 19. In 1970, the Study Committee on Bankruptcy and Insolvency Legislation emphasized this concern:

> ... much of the rehabilitative effect of his discharge and release from debts is lost, when a bankrupt is left with substantial debts after his discharge. Indeed, in some cases, it may almost be regarded as a mockery of the bankruptcy system to take all of the sizable property of a debtor, distribute it among the creditors and then leave the debtor to cope with some of his largest creditors from whose debts he has not been released.
>
> (*Bankruptcy and Insolvency: Report of the Study Committee on Bankruptcy and Insolvency Legislation* (1970), at para. 3.2.085)

When operating in the context of bankruptcy, s. 102 undermines this balancing exercise and imperils the bankrupt's ability to rehabilitate. In effect, s. 102 creates a new class of debts that survive bankruptcy. As such, it leaves the debtor with a substantial financial liability that was not contemplated by Parliament. Had Parliament intended judgment debts arising from motor vehicle accidents, or the resulting regulatory charges, to survive bankruptcy, it would have stated so expressly in s. 178(1) of the *BIA*. It did not. Together, s. 178(1) and (2) are comprehensive. It is beyond the province's constitutional authority to interfere with Parliament's discretion in that regard.

[80] Notwithstanding this, Alberta asserts that, like any creditor, the province is allowed to form a new binding contract with the discharged bankrupt for the repayment of the debt. In its view, the respondent's driving privileges can serve as fresh consideration for such a contract. I disagree. Like the Court of Appeal, I conclude that this alleged fresh consideration is neither genuine nor consistent with the purpose of s. 178(2).

[81] As a general rule, a creditor cannot cause a debtor to revive an obligation from which the debtor was released, unless the creditor offers fresh consideration: Wood, at p. 301. Between private parties, it is arguable that a debtor may freely agree to revive a discharged debt in exchange for the creditor's provision of goods or services. The province, however, is unlike any private creditor. While a private creditor is under no obligation to provide goods or services, the province cannot withhold the respondent's driving privileges arbitrarily. Suspension of privileges by administrative bodies must be based on a legal rule.... In the case at bar, the effect and purpose of s. 102 are to compel payment of a discharged debt, which conflicts with s. 178(2). As a result, s. 102 is, to that extent, inoperative and cannot ground the province's authority to withhold the respondent's privileges. If those privileges are being suspended on the sole basis that the respondent refuses to satisfy a judgment debt that was released in bankruptcy, the

province is acting without authority. The province's promise to refrain from doing what it has no authority to do cannot constitute fresh consideration capable of supporting any contract. This includes a contract for the repayment of a discharged debt. More importantly, the respondent need not enter into such a contract in order to recover his driving privileges, because the province has no authority to withhold them.

[82] Finally, Alberta's other assertion, to the effect that Parliament's power over bankruptcy and insolvency matters does not extend to the regulation of driving privileges, does not entail that the province can withhold those privileges on the basis of an unpaid released debt. In my view, the province is conflating the scope of Parliament's authority and the consequences of the conflict between the *BIA* and the *TSA*. The financial responsibility of drivers is a valid matter of provincial concern and jurisdiction, and the province can set the conditions for driving privileges with this consideration in mind. Nonetheless, when the province denies a person's driving privileges on the sole basis that he or she refuses to pay a debt that was discharged in bankruptcy, the province's condition conflicts with s. 178(2) of the *BIA* and is, to that extent, inoperative. To so conclude does not transfer the power to regulate driving privileges to Parliament. The obligation to grant those privileges flows from the provisions of the provincial law that remain operative.

[83] The rehabilitative purpose of s. 178(2) is not meant to give debtors a fresh start in all aspects of their lives. Bankruptcy does not purport to erase all the consequences of a bankrupt's past conduct. However, by ensuring that all provable claims are treated as part of the bankruptcy regime, the *BIA* gives debtors an opportunity to rehabilitate themselves financially. While this does not amount to erasing all regulatory consequences of their past conduct, it is certainly meant to free them from the financial burden of past indebtedness. . . .

VI. DISPOSITION

[90] In my view, the doctrine of paramountcy dictates that s. 102 of the *TSA* is inoperative to the extent that it conflicts with the *BIA*, and in particular s. 178(2). Therefore, the province cannot withhold the respondent's driving privileges on the basis of an unsatisfied but discharged judgment debt. I would dismiss the appeal with costs and answer the constitutional question as follows:

Is s. 102(2) of Alberta *Traffic Safety Act*, R.S.A. 2000, c. T-6, constitutionally inoperative by reason of the doctrine of federal paramountcy?

Answer: Yes, s. 102 of the Alberta *Traffic Safety Act* is inoperative to the extent that it is used to enforce a debt discharged in bankruptcy.

Appeal dismissed.

407 ETR Concession Co v Canada (Superintendent of Bankruptcy), 2015 SCC 52, [2015] 3 SCR 397 (*407 ETR*)

[In a companion case, the Supreme Court had to consider the impact of provincial legislation upon the discharge in *407 ETR*. The reasons are set out in Chapter 2. Ontario legislation entitled the province to suspend a vehicle permit for non-payment of tolls. Section 22(4) of the *407 Act* had the purported effect of enabling toll debt to be enforced against a discharged bankrupt through the suspension of their vehicle permit by Ontario's Registrar of Motor Vehicles. The Court had to assess the following issue:]

The question at issue is whether Ontario's *Highway 407 Act, 1998*, S.O. 1998, c. 28 ("*407 Act*"), which sets out a debt enforcement mechanism in favour of the private owner and operator of an open-access toll highway, conflicts with the federal *Bankruptcy and Insolvency Act*, R.S.C. 1985, c. B-3 ("*BIA*"), which provides that a discharged bankrupt is released from all provable claims.

The Supreme Court found an operational conflict between provincial and federal law. The Court also found that the provincial provision "frustrate[d] the financial rehabilitation purpose pursuant to s. 178(2)" (at para 31).

D. The 2009 Amendments

The 2009 amendments impact three components of the bankruptcy discharge: (1) automatic discharge; (2) creditors' participation and pay-out; and (3) bankrupts with high income tax debt.

1) Automatic Discharge

Building on the recommendations in the PITF *Final Report* and the 2003 Senate Report (see footnote 3), the 2009 reforms increase the availability of the automatic discharge while, at the same time, increasing for some debtors the period before eligibility for an automatic discharge. Bankrupts with surplus income are no longer eligible for the automatic discharge after nine months. Rather, they must wait for the expiration of a twenty-one–month period while continuing to make surplus income payments to the trustee. See *BIA*, section 168.1(1)(a)(ii).

2) Repeat Bankruptcies

In addition, there is now an automatic discharge for second-time bankrupts who do not have surplus income following the expiration of a twenty-four–month period. See *BIA*, section 168.1(1)(b)(i). Where a second-time bankrupt has surplus income, the automatic discharge is available following the expiration of a thirty-six–month period, during which the bankrupt must make surplus income payments to the trustee: see *BIA* section 168.1(1)(b)(ii). What is the justification for the different treatment of repeat bankrupts? Where there is a third-, fourth-, or fifth-time bankruptcy the court may not make an order of an absolute discharge. The court must either refuse the discharge, suspend the discharge, or grant a conditional discharge. See *BIA* sections 173(1)(j) and 172(2).

The following table shows the percentage of total bankruptcies filed by consumers with one or more previous bankruptcies; see Office of Superintendent of Bankruptcy Report BKH-QRA-3444, 21 January 2019, on file with the author. What explains the rising numbers of repeat bankruptcies?

Year	% of Total Consumer Bankruptcies
2010	14.99
2011	15.57
2012	16.11
2013	17.26
2014	18.7
2015	19.48
2016	19.9
2017	20.77
2018	20.98

Thomas GW Telfer, "Repeat Bankruptcies and the Integrity of the Canadian Bankruptcy Process"
(2014) 55 *Canadian Business Law Journal* 231 at 239–41

One of the often-cited purposes of bankruptcy law is to permit the rehabilitation of the debtor "as a citizen, unfettered by past debts." [*Industrial Acceptance Corp v Lalonde*, [1952] 2 SCR 109, at para. 34] The bankruptcy regime thus allows an honest but unfortunate debtor to "reintegrate into the business life of the country as a useful citizen free from the crushing burden of his or her debts." The Ontario Court of Appeal in *Bank of Montreal v Giannotti* [(2000), 51 OR (3d) 544 (CA)] cited the following passage from Houlden and Morawetz's *Bankruptcy Law of Canada*: "The Act permits an honest debtor, who has been unfortunate in business, to secure a discharge so that he or she can make a fresh start and resume his or her place in the business community."

The underlying assumption of rehabilitation is that the debtor will be able to make a "new start" without the need to resort to bankruptcy again. The United States Supreme Court in *Local Loan Co v Hunt* [292 US 234 (1934), at p. 244.] emphasized the nature of the fresh start:

> One of the primary purposes of the Bankruptcy Act is to "relieve the honest debtor from the weight of oppressive indebtedness, and permit him to start afresh free from the obligations and responsibilities consequent upon business misfortunes." . . . This purpose of the act has been again and again emphasized by the courts as being of public as well as private interest, in that it gives to the honest but unfortunate debtor who surrenders for distribution the property which he owns at the time of bankruptcy, a new opportunity in life and a clear field for future effort, unhampered by the pressure and discouragement of pre-existing debt.

The "clear field for future effort" assumes that the debtor will be reintegrated into the economic life of society or will resume his or her place in the community without the need for another bankruptcy.

Rehabilitation often gives way when there is a repeat filing. The specific provisions in the *BIA* that deal with repeat bankruptcies suggest that other considerations beyond rehabilitation become relevant. In the case of multiple bankruptcies, "the Court's focus shifts from a rehabilitative one to one of concern for the integrity of the system, protection of creditors and as a brake against future assignment." The British Columbia Supreme Court in *Re Willier* [2005 BCSC 1138] recognized the change in policy objectives:

> By the time an individual has entered a third bankruptcy, the purpose and intent of the *Act* shifts from its remedial purpose of assisting well-intentioned but unfortunate debtors to one of protecting society, and in particular unsuspecting potential creditors. The best intentions and hopes of such bankrupts become subordinated to the need to protect others from the bankrupt's demonstrated financial incompetence, negligence, and carelessness.

The competing objectives of rehabilitation and the protection of the integrity of the bankruptcy regime are difficult to reconcile. If one is to preserve the public interest or the integrity of the bankruptcy regime by refusing the discharge or by imposing a suspension or conditional order, it will be at the expense of the debtor's rehabilitation. Indeed "continued access to the bankruptcy process suggests that rehabilitation has not worked." The new automatic discharge for second time bankrupts after 24 or 36 months has however, provided a compromise in balancing the two objectives; rehabilitation and the integrity of the system. The automatic administrative discharge fulfills a rehabilitative function while the waiting period sends a signal that there is a consequence to using the bankruptcy regime for a second time. The shift from rehabilitation to the integrity of the bankruptcy regime represents a concern over the control of the moral hazard problem.

[Reproduced by permission of Canadian Business Law Journal Inc
and Thomson Reuters Canada Limited.]

Ongo (Re), 2018 NSSC 326, 2018 CarswellNS 999

BALMANOUKIAN, REGISTRAR:

[1] First and second-time summary bankrupts who comply with all of their duties are eligible to receive automatic absolute discharges, pursuant to section 168.1 of the *Bankruptcy and Insolvency Act*, RSC 1985, c. B-3, as amended (the "*BIA*"). A third and subsequent bankruptcy, regardless of circumstances, must come before the Court for disposition.

[2] In *Kusch, Re*, 2007 BCSC 618, Master Young referred to a fourth bankruptcy as "a highly unusual situation indeed."

[3] As of 2014, there appears only to have been only one reported case of a fifth-time bankruptcy: Thomas G.W. Telfer, "Repeat Bankruptcies and the Integrity of the Canadian Bankruptcy Process," 2014 Canadian Business Law Journal 231.

[4] This is presumably the second.

[5] Mr. Ongo's prior bankruptcies, in 1998, 2000, 2005, and 2011 (when Mr. Ongo was approximately 34, 36, 41, and 47 years old) were described by the Trustee as "due to business failures." Indeed, in reviewing the public Court files from the third and fourth insolvencies, I found a combination of tax and other debt that appears to be mostly business related.

[6] Mr. Ongo has remained in the food industry, but is now an employee. The current bankruptcy consists entirely of consumer debt—credit cards, a payday lender, and a car loan—totalling $37,750. He does not have, nor has a meaningful prospect of having, surplus income within the meaning of Section 68 and Directive 11R2.

[7] The Trustee recommends submission of income and expenses by the bankrupt until February 2020 and a suspension until February 2023, being some five years after the assignment. In its submission, Mr. Ongo's current situation is distinguishable from his prior bankruptcies due to the changed nature of the debt from commercial to consumer.

[8] So what is to be done?

[9] In *Boivin, Re*, 2008 BCSC 221, Registrar Blok, while recognizing as do I that "each case ... turns on its own facts," summarized the caselaw as follows:

> A fourth bankruptcy is a very serious matter. Indeed, even for applications involving third-time bankrupts the courts have expressed reluctance in ordering a bankrupt's discharge, at least not without a lengthy suspension or similarly onerous terms. The reasons for this are aptly captured in *Re Willier* (2005), 14 C.B.R. (5th) 130, 2005 BCSC 1138 (CanLII), at paras. 12 and 13:
>
>> By the time an individual has entered a third bankruptcy, the purpose and intent of the *Act* shifts from its remedial purpose of assisting well-intentioned but unfortunate debtors to one of protecting society, and in particular unsuspecting potential

creditors. <u>The best intentions and hopes of such bankrupts become subordinated to the need to protect others from the bankrupt's demonstrated financial incompetence, negligence, and carelessness.</u> If there can be a concept of debtors' recidivism, it is demonstrated in stark relief by a third-time bankrupt.

To even consider a discharge for a third time bankrupt the court must be satisfied that the bankrupt has gained sufficient insight and made sufficient changes in his or her life that it is not reasonably possible that further bankruptcy will occur.

To similar effect is the following, found in *Re Hardy* (1979), 30 C.B.R. (N.S.) 95 (Ont. S.C.) at para. 3:

In my view, a third bankruptcy is one too many. The well-recognized principle underlying bankruptcy law is that a debtor may, in proper circumstances, be relieved of his obligations and enabled to re-establish himself financially. <u>I do not consider that he should be enabled to do so on a recurring basis. The process of the Act and of the court should not be considered to bestow a licence to incur debts and be purged of them at periodic intervals.</u>

I am aware of only two other recent cases in this province involving fourth-time bankrupts, both decided by Master Young. In *Re Kusch* (2007), 33 C.B.R. (5th) 208, 2007 BCSC 618 (CanLII), the bankrupt was refused a discharge and was denied leave to reapply for a discharge for a period of two years. The learned master commented that on a reapplication she expected that there would still not be an unconditional discharge granted. In *Re Mulligan*, 2007 BCSC 1784 (CanLII), the bankrupt's discharge was suspended for 15 years, the master emphasizing that society needed to be protected from the bankrupt's incompetent use of credit.

[emphasis added]

[10] In bankruptcy freemasonry, this is usually called the "clearing house for debt."

[11] Rephrased for modernity, in *Re Legault*, 1994 CanLII 2996 (BCCA) at para. 31 Madam Justice Southin referred to this as the need to avoid using the insolvency process as a "fiscal carwash". While she was in dissent, the majority agreed with this sentiment at para. 51.

[12] So what of Mr. Ongo? There is no indication, despite the meaningful tax and public debts of his prior bankruptcies, to suggest he is a rogue or dishonest, characteristics which appear in many of the bankruptcy cases in which discharges are refused or subject to stringent conditions. I do note in passing, however, that his 2005 assignment was only discharged in 2011, presumably to pave the way for his fourth assignment the same year.

[13] I interpret the Trustee's assertion that "the other bankruptcies were commercial and this one is not" in a somewhat different fashion than does the Trustee. I interpret it to mean that not only is Mr. Ongo unable to operate within his business' means, but is also unable to operate within his own. The current bankruptcy, as I have said, consists entirely of consumer credit—credit cards, a payday lender, and a (secured) car loan.

[14] In this regard, I have considered the decision of Master Young in *Re Mulligan*, 2007 BCSC 1784, a decision which in turn applied *Willier*. The Court was dealing with Ms. Mulligan's fourth bankruptcy, all of which were for comparatively modest amounts. She had health issues and at least some of her financial woes came from providing assistance to family members. Despite this lack of moral default, the Court, after quoting the same passage in *Willier, Re* I have repeated above, stated:

Society does need to be protected from Mrs. Mulligan's incompetent use of credit. I believe her bankruptcies have been for small amounts because it was all that was available to her. I know she does use the credit for family reasons and because of illnesses. I know that she has not lived an exotic lifestyle at all. She said in court before me that she had not had a vacation in recent memory. She has not been cavalier about her credit but still, in all likelihood, her expenses will exceed her meagre income.

She has repeatedly shown that she cannot budget within her means, and so I am accepting the recommendation of the Superintendent, and I am suspending the discharge for 15 years. This bankruptcy is unavailable to her now, and she will be forced to live within her financial means.

[15] I accept this reasoning as authority for the proposition that moral taint may be an aggravating factor in determining the circumstances of one's discharge, but the lack of such taint does not preclude the Court from its role in balancing creditor interests with those of the debtor.

[16] *Re Hiebert*, 2008 SKQB 153 involved four bankruptcies over 31 years with a 67 year old "kind, generous, and well-intentioned man." Registrar Schwann said:

As noted above, the test to be applied on a third or fourth bankruptcy shifts from rehabilitating a well-intentioned but unfortunate debtor to one of protecting society generally and unsuspecting creditors in particular. Can society be protected from this bankrupt? Has he gained any insight or committed to change sufficient to forestall a subsequent bankruptcy? Unfortunately, although a seemingly kind, generous and well intentioned man, Hiebert's attitude displayed no remorse, and more to the point, shed no light or insight gained concerning appropriate use of credit and financial management.

Quite the contrary, I sense a measure of justification borne of necessity and desperation, that is, credit cards could and should be used to augment income regardless of ability to re-pay.

Having regard to the facts, I am not satisfied that Hiebert has gained sufficient insight into proper financial management, budgeting and use of credit, nor am I persuaded that he has made appropriate changes in his life to prevent another bankruptcy from occurring. Regrettably, I conclude that the protection of society and unsuspecting creditors can only be achieved by refusing his discharge application.

[17] Professor Telfer's article, *supra*, reports that in 2012 there were 12 fifth-time bankruptcies nationwide. Most of the cases I have cited of fourth-time bankruptcies involve assignments over a period of many years and, by the time of the fourth discharge application, often involve persons of advanced years.

[18] Here, we have five bankruptcies over 20 years.

[19] Mr. Ongo is 54. All of his assignments have been after the very useful tool of debtor counselling became mandatory in 1992. This has apparently borne little fruit.

[20] From all of this I must conclude, as I commented at the hearing, that enabling — I use the word deliberately — Mr. Ongo to have access to credit would be akin to providing a firearm to a child.

[21] I have given careful consideration to the appropriate remedy. I do not believe an order for payment into the estate would be appropriate here, given Mr. Ongo's current and expected level of income. What is more important, I think, is that the disposition of this case provide meaningful protection against "unsuspecting creditors."

[22] I have, in reviewing the above and in exercise of my discretion, decided to refuse the application for discharge. Having done so, the question is then whether I should provide leave to re-apply and if so, at what point in time.

[23] When an application is simply refused, the only way the bankrupt can attain a discharge in the future is to apply to vary the order under s. 187(5): Houlden, Morawetz & Sarra, *Annotated Bankruptcy and Insolvency Act* at section H37(2). I do not believe that, either, would be appropriate in this case.

[24] Neither is a suspension for three years as suggested by the Trustee. I believe all that does is provide a period of purgatory in which the bankrupt will spend his time earning indulgences. I am not convinced that at the end of such a process he would, fiscally, sin no more.

[25] I am refusing the application for discharge with leave to re-apply in 10 years from the date of this decision. That will interrupt the two-to-seven year pattern Mr. Ongo has had for the last 20 years, and bring him to the edge of his senior years. Hopefully, that will do what the prior procedures and counselling have not done, namely instill the necessary habits to live within his cash flow. I remind him that it is an offence under s. 199 of the *BIA* to engage in trade, or obtain credit from any person of $1000 or more without disclosing that he is an undischarged bankrupt.

[26] I am, as recommended by the Trustee, ordering the Bankrupt to submit income and expense statements, and any surplus income pursuant to Directive 11R2, on a monthly basis to and including February 29, 2020.

[27] Lastly, am also ordering the Bankrupt to pay the balance of $1,750 remaining under his voluntary payment agreement. This was described in the Trustee's affidavit as being the balance payable under a fee agreement, for a total of $2,400. Although I am ordering the balance under the agreement to be paid, for certainty, the Trustee's fees in this summary administration shall be governed by Rule 128.

Application dismissed.

3) Bankrupts with High Income Tax Debt

The 2009 reforms provide that bankrupts with more than $200,000 (including principal, interest, and penalties) in personal income tax debt (federal and/or provincial) representing 75 percent or more of their total unsecured debts will not be eligible for an automatic discharge and an application for discharge will be required. For a first- or second-time bankrupt, the timing of the automatic discharge (including the new timing for surplus income payers) dictates the first time that an application for discharge may be made. Where a bankrupt has been bankrupt on more than two other occasions, the hearing may not be held until thirty-six months have expired.

On an application for discharge, the court cannot grant an absolute discharge for bankrupts that fall under the section (see *BIA*, section 172.1(1)). A court may refuse the discharge, suspend the discharge, or provide a conditional discharge. The onus is on the bankrupt to justify the relief that is requested. The statute directs the court to consider the following factors: (1) the bankrupt's circumstances at the time the personal income tax debt was incurred; (2) the efforts made by the bankrupt to pay the personal income tax; (3) whether the bankrupt paid other debts while failing to make reasonable efforts to pay the personal income tax debt; and (4) the bankrupt's financial prospects for the future. The court may modify the discharge order after one year (see *BIA*, section 172.1).

Canada (Attorney General) v Koch, 2012 QCCA 2207

[21] Parliament enacted the restrictive regime in section 172.1 for discharge from bankruptcy for persons with high levels of personal income tax debt as a means of recognizing the socially important character of that kind of debt. Prior to that time, in the exercise of their discretion to grant discharges, courts had long frowned upon debtors who treated the money they owed to the taxation authorities as a sort of second-class debt, to be paid only after the debtor made good liabilities for matters he or she felt more pressing. In *Joli-Coeur*, [*Québec (sous ministre du Revenu) v Joli-Coeur (syndic)*, [1996] JQ No 3922 (CA)] Gendreau, JA of this Court observed that liabilities for unpaid taxes should enjoy what he elegantly called a "social priority" given that the well-being of society as a whole depended on the timely payment of income taxes. . . .

[22] The restrictive legislative regime for discharging of bankrupts in section 172.1, including the prohibition against granting absolute discharges, reflects this same sentiment. This is plain when one considers the rationale for the proposed new rules in a text prepared for the public by Industry Canada in 2005, which text remains a useful account of legislative policy notwithstanding certain later amendments brought to section 172.1:

> **Rationale**
>
> This new section introduces a new procedure for discharging bankrupts with high personal income tax debt. It is aimed at those individuals who have an outstanding personal income tax debt (federal and/or provincial) in excess of $200,000 (including principal, interest and penalties) where the amount owing represents 75% or more of the bankrupt's total unsecured proven claims. This new section is designed to ensure that bankrupts with significant personal income tax debt do not abuse the insolvency system by paying their other creditors to the exclusion of the government. These bankrupts will not be eligible for an automatic discharge and an application for discharge will be required. The onus will be on the debtor to justify any relief to be granted by the court. . . .
>
> [Emphasis added.]

E. Non-dischargeable Debts and Liabilities

A general principle behind consumer bankruptcy in Canada is that, following discharge from bankruptcy, an individual is free from their debts and, at the same time, they retain their experiences, knowledge, and values, which can contribute to their becoming a productive member of society again and provide them with a fresh start. In recognition that not all individuals who attempt to make use of the bankruptcy process are honest but unfortunate debtors with the types of debts for which it is intended, a number of exceptions to the fresh start are provided for under existing legislation (see *BIA*, s 178). These exceptions are in addition to *BIA*, section 173, which confers broad discretion on courts to attach conditions to discharge and to deny it entirely if objection is raised to the discharge. It is important to note that the exceptions from discharge cover much more than dishonest or criminal conduct by the bankrupt. Canada is not alone in making various types of debts and liabilities non-dischargeable, and the list varies from jurisdiction to jurisdiction. In recent history, a common form of debt found in the list is student loans. A consideration of this exception to the discharge provides a good vehicle for better understanding the theory behind the discharge and is also a significant issue in bankruptcy policy. The following excerpt highlights a number of the key issues.

Stephanie Ben-Ishai, "Student Loans in Bankruptcy: Report to the Canadian Association of Insolvency and Restructuring Professionals" (Produced for CAIRP; unpublished, 2013)

In Canada, government-funded student loans are not automatically discharged in the bankruptcy process. A debtor may only have their government-funded student loans discharged after seven years have passed since the debtor completed their studies. However, a student debtor can apply for the discharge of her government-funded student loans after five years on hardship grounds if she can satisfy the court that she has acted in good faith in connection with the student loans and that, without discharge of the student loans, she will continue to experience financial difficulty to such an extent that she will be unable to pay the debt. On the other hand, there is no such special treatment for private student loans and, provided that they meet the usual requirements, private student loans are provable debts that are discharged in bankruptcy.

Section 178 of the *Bankruptcy and Insolvency Act* (*BIA*) [is the governing provision]. Section 178 applies specifically to student loans made under the Canada Student Loans Act, the *Canada Student Financial Assistance Act*, or any enactment of a province that provides for loans or guarantees of loans to students; in essence, the provision applies to government-funded student loans and not to private loans between students and financial institutions or other lenders. The following section outlines the amendment history of section 178. It also outlines the major arguments in favour of and against the special treatment of government-funded student loans. Finally, this section details the Office of the Superintendent of Bankruptcy's (OSB) stated rationales for the most recent amendments to section 178.

Legislative Amendment History

Prior to September 1997, student loans were treated the same way in bankruptcy as any other consumer debt; student loans were discharged along with most other consumer debts when the debtor was discharged from bankruptcy. However, if a trustee or creditor suspected that a debtor was abusing the system, they could oppose their discharge from bankruptcy or refuse to accept their consumer proposal. In September 1997, amendments were made to the *BIA* which served to make government-funded student loans non-dischargeable in bankruptcy if the debtor filed for bankruptcy before ceasing full-time or part-time studies or within two years after completing their studies. According to section 178 of the *BIA*, the discharge of government-funded student loans could only occur as a result of a special hearing held after two years had passed since the completion of studies and only if the result of the hearing was a finding that the debtor had made a good faith effort to repay the debt and that repayment would result in significant financial hardship. However, a debtor who filed for bankruptcy after the completion of the two-year term could discharge their government-funded student loans in the same manner that all other consumer debts were discharged. . . .

In September 2009, the most recent amendments to section 178 of the *BIA* came into force. The provision was changed to reduce the time period required before government-funded student loans could be discharged from ten years to seven years. In addition, the provision now allows debtors to apply for discharge of their government-funded student loans on hardship grounds after five years, rather than the ten years previously required, provided that the debtor can demonstrate her good faith attempts to repay the debt and that she has and will continue to experience financial difficulty to such an extent as she will be unable to pay the debt. This change also means that the time period for regular discharge of student loans and the time period for discharge on hardship grounds are no longer the same, as they were in the previous versions of the provision.

Arguments In Favour of the Non-Dischargeability of Student Loans

The Personal Insolvency Task Force (PITF), in their analysis of student loans and bankruptcy, noted arguments in favour of the non-dischargeability of student loans. These arguments were later echoed by the Standing Senate Committee on Banking, Trade, and Commerce (the Senate Committee) in their subsequent Report. In the PITF's opinion, the most compelling argument in favour of making student loans non-dischargeable was that former students have the ability to repay their loans because they will presumably have higher-than-average future incomes. This argument rests on the presumption that some former student debtors are only temporarily insolvent. It also rests on the presumption that these debtors have borrowed to increase their future income and are retaining the increased future income while using bankruptcy to avoid repaying their debts. The PITF noted that examples cited in support of this argument often concern professionals, such as doctors and lawyers, who use bankruptcy to rid themselves of six-figure student loans before commencing lucrative jobs.

The PITF also phrased this same argument in terms of the acquisition of human capital. Students take on student loans to finance the acquisition of human capital. However, unlike physical capital, human capital cannot be used as security for a loan. Since students have no fear that the asset financed by the loan can be repossessed, they can safely file for bankruptcy.

The second major argument in favour of the non-dischargeability of student loans enunciated by the PITF was that because the Canadian Student Loans Program (CSLP) and provincial loan programs increased their volume of lending in the 1990s, allowing the discharge of student loans would increase government loan losses. The increase in volume of lending could be attributed to both an increase in tuition fees and the elimination of several provincial student grant programs, both increasing the need for students to borrow. However, this increase could also be attributed to government decisions to increase the amounts that could be borrowed from their programs. This increase in student borrowing was presumed to create an increase in the loan losses experienced by governments because they had guaranteed the loans. The thrust of the argument is that by making student loans non-dischargeable, the loan losses might be reduced if former students, denied a discharge of student loans, make loan payments that they would not otherwise have made.

The final major argument outlined by the PITF was that other forms of debt relief are available to former students. The PITF report outlined two types of relief. First, the CSLP had a program called Interest Relief, which at the time allowed eligible debtors to defer repayment on their student loans for specified periods (up to 54 months), during which time the CSLP paid the interest on the loans. Some of the provincial loan programs also had similar Interest Relief systems. To be eligible for Interest Relief, the debtor could not be delinquent on their student loans and had to meet low-income eligibility criteria. Second, where a debtor borrowed quite heavily, some provinces had loan remission programs that forgave part of the value of the student loans. In their report, the PITF noted that a similar program was being developed by the CSLP; since the publication of the PITF's report, the CSLP has implemented a similar program detailed in the next section of this Report. In summary, this argument against discharge asserts that the relief provided by these alternative programs is enough to render relief through bankruptcy unnecessary. The PITF pointed out, however, that although these are alternative debt relief options that are not available to other debtors, they are no substitute for the "fresh start" provided through bankruptcy.

Arguments Against the Non-Dischargeability of Student Loans

The PITF also noted several arguments in favour of allowing the discharge of student loans, arguments which were once again reiterated in the Senate Committee Report. The first argument outlined by the PITF was that student loans are no different from other dischargeable personal debts that can be discharged and those seeking to discharge student loans are no different than other bankrupts. The PITF suggested that debtors seeking bankruptcy protection with student loans among their liabilities are no different than other potential bankrupts and that "they are not typically young professionals but are rather a cross-section of all those engaged in post-secondary education, including many who never graduated from the program for which they borrowed." The argument states that if this is the case, there is no reason to make student loans non-dischargeable. In support of this argument, the PITF pointed to an empirical study by Schwartz and Anderson which indicated that those seeking to discharge student loans in bankruptcy were generally not young professionals looking to go on to lucrative careers; these debtors had lower median incomes, were more likely to have received social assistance, and had jobs that were similar to those of other bankrupts.

The second argument put forth by the PITF was that the prohibition on the discharge of student loans constitutes age discrimination because most student loan borrowers are young people. At the time, this argument was the basis for an ongoing Charter challenge of the law prohibiting the discharge of student loans.

The final argument outlined by the PITF was that discharge of student loans should be allowed because some debtors experience special hardship that makes it virtually impossible to repay their student loans. In support of this argument, the PITF provided the real-life example of a medical student who had amassed over $100,000 in student loans only to suffer a nervous breakdown. As a result of the breakdown, the student could not practice medicine but was still left with the student loan debt. Although the PITF recognized that this story and others only represent anecdotal evidence, it noted that the possibility for special hardship in student loan debtors is evident.

Provincial and Federal Student Loan Relief Measures in Canada

In Ontario, Saskatchewan, New Brunswick, Newfoundland and Labrador, and British Columbia, federal and provincial student loans are integrated and students who qualify for assistance receive an integrated federal-provincial student loan. As a result of the Integrated Student Loans, borrowers are only required to complete one application, one need assessment, one loan certificate and loan agreement form, and receive common repayment assistance measures. Consequently, student debtors in these provinces have only one student loan and make a single payment when repaying their student loans. All integrated student loans are administered by the National Student Loans Service Centre (NSLSC).

All of the other provinces, Alberta, Manitoba, Nova Scotia, and Prince Edward Island, provide their own government-funded student loans that are not fully integrated with federal student loans.

Notwithstanding the loan integration process, in all of the provinces other than Quebec, students experience a six-month grace period after they finish their studies or stop being a full-time student, during which time students are not required to make loan payments and interest is not charged on their provincial loan, but does accumulate on the federal portion of their student loan.

In addition, every province, other than Quebec, provides a Repayment Assistance Plan (RAP) to student debtors. In Ontario, Saskatchewan, New Brunswick, Newfoundland and Labrador, British Columbia, Alberta, and Nova Scotia, the provincial RAP is administered in conjunction with the federal RAP and Applicants apply for both the federal and provincial RAPs in one application through the National Student Loans Service Centre (NSLSC). The remaining provinces, Manitoba and Prince Edward Island, administer their RAPs outside of the realm of the federal RAP and with their own provincial applications. However, the federal RAP and the RAPs of these nine programs are substantially the same in terms of eligibility requirements and the relief granted. To be eligible for the RAP, a student debtor must be unable to afford the standard monthly payment. Under the RAP, borrowers make an affordable student loan payment based on their gross family income and family size. Loan payments do not exceed 20 percent of a borrower's gross family income. Some borrowers may not have to make any payments at all until their income increases. Borrowers will have a maximum repayment period of 15 years under the RAP (10 years for borrowers with permanent disabilities). Enrolment in the RAP is not automatic and student debtors must re-apply every six months.

The RAP works in two stages. During stage 1, the federal or provincial government covers the interest amount owing that is not covered by the student debtor's newly adjusted affordable payment. This may last for up to five years during the ten-year period after the student debtor leaves school. Stage 2 is for student debtors for which financial difficulty continues to persist. It commences once the student debtor completes stage 1 or has been in repayment for ten years after she has left school. During stage 2, the federal or provincial government continues to cover the interest covered in stage 1, but also begins to cover a portion of the principal on the student loan. The balance of the loan is gradually paid off such that no student loan debt remains after 15 years of leaving school (or 10 years for student debtors with a permanent disability).

[Reprinted by permission of the publisher.]

Canada (Attorney General) v Collins, 2013 NLCA 17, 334 Nfld & PEIR 318

WELSH JA:

[1] This appeal engages the question of when a student loan may be dischargeable under the terms of the *Bankruptcy and Insolvency Act*, RSC 1985, c. B-3.

BACKGROUND

[2] Leslie Collins attended post-secondary studies in two blocks of time. From September 1998 to December 2001, she attended Memorial University of Newfoundland as a full-time student. For these studies she received a student loan under the *Canada Student Financial Assistance Act*, SC 1994, c. 28 (the "*Financial Assistance Act*").

[3] From September 2003 to August 2006, Ms. Collins attended the College of the North Atlantic completing a diploma in Geomatics Engineering Technology. She did not apply for additional financial assistance during this course of study. However, she obtained a deferral of payment of her loan under the *Financial Assistance Act* together with forgiveness of the accruing interest for this period of time. For this purpose Ms.

Collins provided the necessary documentation, a Confirmation of Enrolment as provided for under the *Canada Student Financial Assistance Regulations*, SOR/95-329, and a Continuation or Reinstatement of Interest-Free Status as provided for under the *Student Financial Assistance Regulations*, NLR 105/03.

[4] Ms. Collins made an assignment in bankruptcy on December 9, 2010 and obtained an absolute discharge on September 10, 2011. However, in January 2012 she was advised by the Royal Bank of Canada that her student loan had not been discharged. She received a similar notification from Canada Student Loans in February 2012. The position of the Bank and Canada Student Loans that the loan had not been discharged was based on an interpretation of section 178(1)(g) of the *Bankruptcy and Insolvency Act* (the "Act") which provides that a student loan is not dischargeable until "seven years after the date on which the bankrupt ceased to be a full- or part-time student".

[5] In an oral decision, the applications judge determined that the proper date from which to calculate the seven years for purposes of section 178(1)(g)(ii) of the Act was December 2001, the date when Ms. Collins completed the course of studies for which she had obtained a student loan. Since the assignment in bankruptcy occurred more than seven years after that date, he concluded that the loan was dischargeable under the Act.

[6] The appellant, the Minister of National Revenue (the "Minister"), submits that the applications judge erred by calculating the seven-year period from December 2001 rather than August 2006 when Ms. Collins completed her second post-secondary course of studies.

ISSUE

[7] At issue is whether the applications judge erred in determining that the seven-year delay in discharge of a student loan under the Act runs from when the bankrupt ceases to be a student in relation to that loan or whether the commencement date is re-set where the bankrupt has returned to being a student prior to the assignment in bankruptcy.

ANALYSIS

[8] Section 178(1)(g) of the *Bankruptcy and Insolvency Act* provides for a delay in the discharge of a student loan debt where an assignment in bankruptcy is made....

[9] Because Ms. Collins had ceased to be a student when she filed an assignment in bankruptcy, subparagraph (ii) applies. That provision must be given a purposive interpretation based on the language used. Unfortunately, there are two ways in which the language may be interpreted. The question is whether the date refers to the date when the bankrupt "finally" ceased to be a student prior to the bankruptcy or when the bankrupt ceased to be a student "in relation to the particular loan". In assessing this question, although Ms. Collins did not obtain a student loan for her second block of studies, the analysis necessarily requires some consideration of the situation where, in fact, a second loan has been obtained.

[10] Counsel for the Minister submits that the words "full- or part-time student" must be interpreted using the definitions found in the legislation that is specified in paragraph (g). To support this submission he relies on the phrase "under the applicable Act or enactment" which appears in subparagraph (i). However, that phrase does not appear in subparagraph (ii). The inclusion of the phrase in the one and its exclusion in the other leads to the assumption that the phrase was not meant to apply to

subparagraph (ii) where it is not mentioned. This is a long-standing principle of statutory interpretation. It follows that the interpretation of subparagraph (ii) is not dependent on the definitions of "full- or part-time student" in other legislation.

[11] Looking, then, at the language of section 178(1), subparagraph (ii) is governed by paragraph (g) which refers to "any debt or obligation in respect of a loan". The reference to "a loan" in the context of this phrase supports an interpretation that the provision applies to a particular loan, rather than cumulative loans. When read with subparagraph (ii), this language supports the conclusion that the seven-year period runs from the date on which the bankrupt ceased to be a student in relation to that particular loan. I agree with the position expressed in *Re Hildebrand*, 2010 SKQB 321, 360 Sask. R. 128, which would apply equally where the individual, upon returning to school, did not obtain a further student loan:

> [31] There is nothing in this provision to suggest or even imply that the date the bankrupt ceased to be a full- or part-time student must somehow relate or connect to the totality of his or her government student loans. In my view, this language supports the opposite conclusion, that is, whether a student loan debt survives depends on when the bankrupt ceased to be a full- or part-time student *in relation to that debt*. . . .

> (Italics in original.)

[12] However, counsel for the Minister submits that the deferral of payment and forgiveness of interest during Ms. Collins' second block of post-secondary studies has the effect of re-setting the date for purposes of the seven-year calculation to August 2006. For the following reasons, this submission is not persuasive.

[13] During an additional course of studies, the debt from a prior loan is not extinguished, but merely deferred. Had Parliament intended to calculate the seven-year period taking the deferred time into account, by either re-setting the start date or exempting the deferral time from calculation of the seven years, section 178 could have been drafted to achieve that objective. However, the provision is silent as to events that occur after the debtor ceased to be a student with respect to the loan at issue. There is nothing in section 178 to indicate that Parliament was concerned with the nature of activities the student was undertaking during the referenced seven years, including additional studies.

[14] To interpret section 178(1)(g)(ii) without regard to events occurring after the bankrupt ceased to be a student in relation to the particular loan is consistent with the purpose as well as the language of the Act. A helpful summary of the purpose of the Act, in the context of a student loan, is found in *Minto, Re* (1999), 14 C.B.R. (4th) 235 (Sask. Q.B.), at paragraph 16:

> . . .

> 5. The broad purpose of the *Act* is to permit honest but unfortunate debtors to obtain a discharge from their obligations in order to facilitate a return to stable participation in social and economic life, while balancing this objective against the interests of creditors. Section 178(1)(g) reflects a policy decision which accords with this objective and recognizes that student loans involve a situation where funds are advanced when there is no existing capacity of the debtor to repay the debt, but education obtained will hopefully enable the debtor to begin active and fruitful participation in the economy at some later date. Realization of earning potential associated with education can take some period of time after leaving school, so Parliament saw fit to disallow the immediate discharge of student loans, in this case for two years [now seven years] after ceasing to be a student. This

measure addressed the perceived abuse of students using the *Act* to obtain a discharge of student loans prior to making reasonable efforts to realize upon their earning potential achieved through education.

[15] I would add that, consistent with the above principles, the language of section 178(1) of the Act is properly construed narrowly because it operates "as an exception to the fresh start principle" which underlies the *Bankruptcy and Insolvency Act* (*Hildebrand, Re, supra*, at paragraph 34).

[16] The above analysis of the language and purpose of the Act leads to the conclusion that the seven-year delay in discharging a student loan debt begins to run from the date when the debtor ceased to be a student in relation to that loan. However, the Minister submits that this Court should follow the decision in *Québec (Attorney General) v NP*, 2011 QCCA 726, 83 C.B.R. (5th) 1, which reaches a contrary conclusion. In *NP*, Leger JA, for the Court, summarized:

> [51] In summary, I believe that paragraph 178(1)(g) of the [*Bankruptcy and Insolvency Act*] refers to one single date when studies end. The clock is turned back to zero when a student goes back to school. In my opinion, this is the only interpretation that respects the legislator's intention to avoid opportunistic bankruptcies, to give the Minister the opportunity to recover loans granted under more than advantageous conditions, and finally, to ensure that the right to bankruptcy is reasonably exercised, after a period that gives the student time to build on his assets so acquired.

[17] In support of this conclusion, the Court in *P (N)* was of the view that "a restrictive approach is not required here just because section 178 lists exceptions to the general principle of discharging the bankrupt" (paragraph 42). Leger JA opined that it was unnecessary to resort to the principle of statutory interpretation regarding an exception of this type, as referenced in *Hildebrand* (paragraph 15, above), because any ambiguity in section 178(1)(g) could be resolved using a purposive interpretation of the language. On this point, I prefer the approach adopted in *Hildebrand* which employs all the relevant statutory interpretation principles that may be of assistance in interpreting section 178(1)(g)(ii).

[18] Further, I cannot agree with the conclusion in *P (N)* that section 178(1)(g) applies only when the debtor "finally" ceases to be a student:

> [46] I must therefore conclude that, with respect to the application of the exception in paragraph 178(1)(g), there is only one date when studies end, and it is calculated from the time the student finally ceases to be a full- or part-time student. In my opinion, the fact that ten years passed between the two periods of study changes absolutely nothing in this case because, according to the proposed interpretation, the respondent simply did not stop being a student in 1986....

[19] In my view, the circumstances in *NP* where there was a ten-year gap in the debtor's pursuit of studies provide an example of why the appropriate interpretation of section 178(1)(g) is that the seven-year period begins to run when the debtor ceases to be a student in relation to the particular loan. The approach adopted in *NP*, in fact, may encourage those wishing to return to studies to make an assignment in bankruptcy before proceeding with a plan to pursue a new educational goal. By contrast, to attach the seven-year delay from bankruptcy discharge to the particular loan may encourage a return to studies which, if successful in leading to future economic viability, would

preclude the need for an assignment in bankruptcy and result in repayment of all loans. I do not accept the proposition adopted in *NP*, which is, to an extent, speculative:

> [49] Finally, it is equally important that an individual who resumes studying without hav-ing repaid a loan for which he or she is in default under section 29 of the AFAEE is not eligible for financial assistance "unless the person has made an agreement with the Min-ister with respect to repayment terms and conditions". The respondent in this case had to sign an acknowledgement of debts in order to receive new student loans in 1997. If he had declared bankruptcy prior to resuming his studies, there is every reason to believe he would have been asked to repay the loan from which he would have been discharged before granting him a new loan.
>
> [50] Indeed, an Alberta statute expressly provides that bankrupts may not obtain stu-dent loans unless they have repaid those for which they were exempted....
>
> (Emphasis added.)

[20] If the intention was to preclude a bankrupt, who has not repaid a student loan debt, from obtaining a student loan in order to pursue a new course of studies, an express provision to that effect could be expected. This possibility is not a basis on which to conclude that section 178(1)(g)(ii) should be interpreted such that a return to status as a student has the effect of re-setting the date from which to calculate the seven-year period. This is particularly clear in the circumstances now before this Court where the return to studies did not involve obtaining a further student loan.

[21] I note, finally, on this point that the objective associated with undertaking addi-tional studies would seem to be consistent with, rather than contrary to, the purpose of the *Bankruptcy and Insolvency Act*, that is, to facilitate the individual's future participa-tion in the economy. In balancing the interests advanced by the Act with the objective of discouraging individuals from taking improper advantage of the student loan program, the seven-year delay in discharge of a student loan debt provided for under the Act, and attached to the particular loan, is a significant period of time which should dissuade opportunistic bankruptcies.

[22] The conclusion follows that the seven-year delay in discharge of a student loan debt pursuant to section 178(1)(g)(ii) begins to run from the date when the individual ceases to be a student in relation to the particular loan. A return to studies does not re-set the clock for calculation of the delay period.

SUMMARY AND DISPOSITION

[23] The trial judge did not err in concluding that the seven-year delay applicable to the discharge of a student loan debt runs from the date when the bankrupt ceased to be a student in relation to the particular loan. In this case, that date is December 2001. The assignment in bankruptcy having been made more than seven years after that date, the student loan debt is dischargeable under the Act.

[24] Accordingly, I would dismiss the appeal.

Appeal dismissed.

There is a division on the proper approach to be taken on the interpretation of the student loan provision. *St Dennis v Ontario (Ministry of Training, Colleges & Universities)*, 2017 ONSC 2417, followed the approach of the NLCA. However, in *Mallory (Re)*, 2015 BCSC 5, the British Columbia Supreme Court stated at para 84 that the *Collins* interpretation of section 178(1)(g) "resulted in an error in law." The Court in *Mallory* preferred to follow the Quebec Court of Appeal decision in *Québec (Procureur général) c NP*, 2011 QCCA 726.

VI. REAFFIRMATION OF DISCHARGED LIABILITIES

Stephanie Ben-Ishai, "Reaffirmation of Debt in Consumer Bankruptcy in Canada" (2015) 56 *Canadian Business Law Journal* **238 at 238–50 (endnotes omitted)**

I. INTRODUCTION

A cornerstone of the consumer bankruptcy system in Canada is the individual's right to a "fresh start" provided by the bankruptcy discharge. Under Section 178(2) of the Bankruptcy and Insolvency Act (the "*BIA*") a discharged bankrupt is released from all liabilities, with the exception of those outlined under Section 178(1) of the *BIA*. However, creditors' interests are also a significant counterweight to the fresh start that bankruptcy offers as consumer lending is integral to the Canadian economy . . .

A major issue regarding reaffirmation in the consumer context is that statistics about the prevalence of these types of arrangements are not available in Canada. Anecdotal evidence suggests that bankrupts enter into reaffirmation agreements as a condition of obtaining new credit following a bankruptcy. At present, reaffirmation agreements are not regulated under the *BIA*. Critics argue that reaffirmation agreements undermine the fresh start principle by reactivating pre-bankruptcy debts. On the other hand, following a bankruptcy a debtor may have difficulty obtaining credit and reaffirmation of an agreement may be the sole means by which a bankrupt can obtain credit. Further, a debtor may have a strong need or desire to retain a particular asset following bankruptcy due to the transaction and psychological costs associated with replacing an asset. Creditors too may value an asset, especially used household goods, less than an outstanding loan. . . .

II. REAFFIRMATION IN CANADA

1. Definition of Reaffirmation

A debt reaffirmation occurs when a bankrupt revives or reaffirms personal responsibility for liabilities which have been or will be released upon discharge of the bankrupt. Reaffirmation can occur through conduct or through express agreement. Reaffirmation by conduct occurs where the bankrupt continues to make payments to creditors even though the relevant debts have been discharged. Reaffirmation by express agreement occurs when bankrupts enter into written agreements with creditors to repay debts even if the debts were released upon the bankruptcy discharge. Written agreements will likely be enforceable where sufficient or new consideration is offered, such as the granting of new credit.

With respect to secured creditors, if a debtor's default entitles the secured creditor to seize collateral that the debtor does not want to lose, the debtor may be prepared to agree to repay a debt that would otherwise be discharged in return for the creditor's agreement to refrain from exercising her rights of realization. The creditor's forbearance to exercise an existing legal right is consideration for the debtor's agreement to pay a sum of money. The amount of the debt and the terms may be different from the original agreement.

2. Treatment of Reaffirmation in Canadian Case Law

The leading reaffirmation case in Canada is *Seaboard Acceptance Corp v Moen*. In this case, Seaboard Acceptance Corporation Ltd. ("Seaboard") entered into a standard form written contract with the defendant, Moen. Under the terms of the contract Moen agreed to lease a motor vehicle for three years. The contract required the defendant to pay Seaboard a rental fee for the use of the vehicle each month. There was also a clause in the contract which provided that if the defendant became insolvent Seaboard would repossess the vehicle. Moen took possession of the vehicle and subsequently made a voluntary assignment into bankruptcy but did not inform the trustee of the lease contract with Seaboard. Moen was awarded an absolute discharge from bankruptcy. Moen made the required monthly payments to Seaboard throughout the bankruptcy but then, after discharge, defaulted on the lease contract. Following the default, the vehicle was returned. Seaboard calculated the amount outstanding under the contract and made a demand for the balance owing.

The Court had to determine whether Seaboard was capable of collecting the amount owing or whether the amount was discharged in the bankruptcy. The British Columbia Court of Appeal upheld the trial judgment in favour of Seaboard. Justice Lambert, writing for the Court, determined that the lease contract continued throughout bankruptcy and continued after the discharge from the bankruptcy; in essence the lease was never terminated. The fact that there might have been a claim provable in bankruptcy or that a claim provable in bankruptcy might have been made does not affect the fact that the contract itself continued. The Court of Appeal maintained that this was not a novation, but a continuation of the contract. In effect, the contract was endorsed by the defendant's conduct after the discharge.

A more recent pronouncement on reaffirmation in the Canadian context can be found in the British Columbia Supreme Court case *Bridgewater Bank v Simms*. In this case, the defendants filed assignments into bankruptcy and, unlike the creditor in *Moen*, Bridgewater Bank filed proofs of claim as a secured creditor in the bankruptcy proceeding. Throughout the bankruptcy, the Simms continued to maintain the mortgage with full payments. As a result of these payments the court held that where the debtor files an assignment in bankruptcy but thereafter maintains possession of the property and continues to fulfill the obligations due under the contract following the assignment in bankruptcy, the contract is affirmed, including the covenant to pay ...

3. Personal Insolvency Task Force Final Report

The Personal Insolvency Task Force (the "PITF") was established by the Office of the Superintendent of Bankruptcy (the "OSB") in October 2000 and included 23 consumer insolvency stakeholders such as creditors, trustees, debt counsellors, lawyers and judges. It was asked to review the consumer bankruptcy provisions of the BIA, explore alternative models of the consumer insolvency process and develop recommendations for improvements to the process.

The PITF does not recommend a blanket ban on reaffirmations. Instead, it recommends that the BIA is amended to limit the availability of reaffirmation according to whether the debt is unsecured or secured ...

4. Report of the Standing Senate Committee on Banking, Trade and Commerce

After reviewing findings from the PITF and evidence from other witnesses both for and against reaffirmation agreements, the 2003 report issued by the Standing Senate Committee on Banking, Trade and Commerce (the " Senate Committee") recommended amending the to prohibit reaffirmation by conduct or by express agreement. The Senate Committee relied heavily on the notion that reaffirmation agreements are inconsistent with the fresh start principle; referred to as "a hallmark of insolvency law in Canada." The Senate Committee determined that banning reaffirmations is a solution that is consistent with the fresh start principle and a solution that supports the objectives of fairness and predictability by eliminating the opportunity for a debtor to selectively pay one or more, but not all, of their creditors.

5.   Industry Canada Report on the Operation and Administration of the *Bankruptcy and Insolvency Act* and the *Companies' Creditors Arrangement Act*

The consumer insolvency portion of the Industry Canada Report was the result of consultations with over 250 stakeholders, responses to discussion papers and a review of a draft copy of the PITF Final Report. Stakeholders included small and large businesses, academics, lawyers, judges, financial institutions, the credit industry, labour, and various federal and provincial government agencies.

According to the Industry Canada Report, stakeholder consultations support the view that, except in a few specific circumstances, there should not be any legislative intervention to control reaffirmation agreements. In fact, many stakeholders noted that efforts to pay debts that have been discharged should be encouraged. Despite evidence of reaffirmation being fairly frequent in the United States, without any empirical evidence for Canadian markets, stakeholders questioned the frequency of reaffirmation in the consumer insolvency context. The lack of evidence of a substantial problem of debtor abuse combined with the fact that many consider voluntary repayment to be a positive gesture, led to minimal interest among the stakeholder group for intrusive action by the legislature. The PITF recommendations received partial support from in the Industry Canada Report but the stakeholders did not see the justification in distinguishing between secured and unsecured debt. The Industry Canada Report also revealed there was a very strong opposition to the PITF recommendation to criminalize inappropriate payments. Finally, the stakeholders maintained that any intervention in this area should be focused on coercion by creditors and reaffirmation by conduct.

III. PROVINCIAL "SEIZE OR SUE" LEGISLATION

1. Overview

Provincial "seize or sue" legislation provides, with some variation, a safeguard on reaffirmation agreements involving secured debt. In such provinces, where a debtor reaffirms a secured debt and the debtor later commits an act of default after emerging from bankruptcy, the creditor may repossess the asset but may not assert a claim against the debtor for the deficiency. The fresh start problems associated with reaffirmation are eliminated in such a context. In addition, reaffirming such a debt allows the creditor to continue to collect the outstanding loan amount in most instances.

Provincial "seize or sue" legislation applies to certain types of secured creditors inside and outside of bankruptcy and operates to give creditors the right to repossesses secured consumer collateral and retain the proceeds on sale. The secured creditor is not allowed to also collect a portion of the deficiency or its unsecured claim in addition to the asset value. In contrast, in provinces without "seize or sue" legislation, a secured creditor can allow a bankrupt to keep the collateral in a bankruptcy, reaffirm the debt and not lose the right to sue on the deficiency (on the basis that it was discharged in the bankruptcy) at a later point in time post-bankruptcy if the debtor defaults on the new agreement.

Specifically, in some Canadian provinces the relevant legislation requires that creditors choose whether to seize or sue the collateral used to secure consumer loans. In other provinces, such as Ontario, there is no restriction on deficiency claims. Under a "seize or sue" regime the creditor must elect whether to pursue the amount owed through ordinary debt recovery proceedings or to repossess the secured property and sell it to satisfy the outstanding debt. If the creditor elects to repossess the collateral, the whole debt is subsequently discharged and the creditor has no additional recourse for any other money owing on the debt after the collateral is sold. In British Columbia, Yukon and Northwest Territories the "seize or sue" provision applies to security interests over consumer goods. In Alberta and Manitoba, the relevant "seize or sue" legislation applies only in the context of a conditional sale or time sale agreement. In Saskatchewan, the relevant legislation imposes a seize-only regime.

Commentators have noted that "seize or sue" legislation provides an incentive for the creditor to engage in responsible lending by forcing creditors to consider the adequacy of security at the time of entering the loan agreement. From a debtor's perspective, "seize or sue" legislation provides stronger consumer protection because it prevents against a situation where the debtor no longer has access to the collateral (because it has been repossessed) and yet still owes money on the collateral.

Servus Credit Union v Sulyok, 2018 ABQB 860, 64 CBR (6th) 10

JE TOPOLNISKI J:

Introduction

[1] Servus Credit Union Ltd ("Servus") appeals a Master in Chamber's decision refusing a deficiency judgement in a high-ratio mortgage foreclosure.

[2] Arguing that a secured creditor with a provable claim in the mortgagor's bankruptcy can enforce a personal promise to pay after the bankrupt's discharge, Servus' focus is on the interplay of sections 178(2) and 84.2 of the *Bankruptcy and Insolvency Act*, RSC 1985, c B-3 (*BIA*). Section 178(2) concerns the release of certain debts on discharge from bankruptcy (such that the creditor is unable to enforce). Section 84.2 precludes a creditor from terminating or amending a contract with a bankrupt if the contract is in good standing.

[3] For the reasons that follow, I grant Servus' appeal.

[4] I conclude that s 84.2 is not relevant as there was a default, albeit a relatively minor one, in the mortgage during the currency of the bankruptcy. Servus chose (perhaps understandably) not to rely upon the default to ground foreclosure proceedings, but that forbearance enabled Mr. Sulyok to retain the property until after his discharge from bankruptcy, and the only live issue is whether, despite not having enforced earlier, Servus could still enforce on the personal promise to pay any deficiency.

[5] I conclude that the discharge from bankruptcy did not release Servus' claim for the deficiency; rather the parties' conduct indicated that the contract itself was continued, and that it continued to regulate the parties' relationship post-discharge. While there is case law and academic commentary recommending that the notion of implied reaffirmation of a contract be ended, Parliament was aware of this concern when the *BIA* was last amended and elected not to do so. As a result, the parties effectively reaffirmed the promise to pay any deficiency sustained by Servus in the event of enforcement proceedings, and Mr. Sulyok is liable for it. This approach balances the rehabilitative goals of giving honest, but unfortunate debtors a fresh start and promoting fiscal responsibility. It further balances the interests of all stakeholders.

[6] Amending the *BIA* to address express reaffirmation is a task for Parliament, which it has chosen not to do. I have recommended that the Superintendent of Bankruptcy consider requiring licensed insolvency trustees to include counselling on the topic of reaffirmation and continuing liability on a personal promise to pay as part of their general counselling responsibilities under the *BIA* and pursuant to her directives. . . .

Facts

[8] The essential facts, set out in chronological order below, are few.

[9] In 2007, the respondent, Mr. Sulyok and his then spouse, Ms. Tomlinson, granted a high ratio mortgage to Servus, which provided that the debtors would be liable for any deficiency under the provisions of the *Law of Property Act*, RSA 2000, c L-7 and solicitor-client costs in the event of enforcement.

[10] When Mr. Sulyok and Ms. Tomlinson separated in the spring of 2015, Ms. Tomlinson remained in the property until the late summer of 2015, and then rented it to tenants. She made all of the monthly payments from April 2015 until January 2017.

[11] In February 2016, Mr. Sulyok made an assignment in bankruptcy. Servus filed a proof of claim as a secured creditor only. The circumstances prompting the filing are unknown.

[12] Mr. Sulyok was discharged from bankruptcy on November 30, 2016.

[13] The mortgage was in default in late January 2017. Then, Mr. Sulyok informed Servus that he planned to move into the property, which he did by March 20, 2017. Also by this date, Mr. Sulyok had cured an earlier default arising from non-payment of condominium arrears, and made a part payment on outstanding mortgage arrears.

[14] Servus commenced foreclosure proceedings in May, 2017 after Mr. Sulyok advised it that he would make no further payments to cure outstanding defaults and was abandoning the property.

[15] Servus obtained an Order for Sale to Plaintiff, also commonly called a Rice Order, with a $73,199.92 deficiency (the Deficiency), and later sought judgement against both Mr. Sulyok and Ms. Tomlinson for the Deficiency.

[16] The Master refused to grant judgement against Mr. Sulyok for the Deficiency and ordered costs against Servus: *Servus Credit Union Ltd v Sulyok*, 2017 ABQB 611. . . .

Grounds of Appeal

[20] The grounds of appeal are that the Master erred by 1) concluding that the Deficiency was "released" or "extinguished" on Mr. Sulyok's discharge from bankruptcy. . . .

Analysis

1.   The Legislative Framework

a. Purpose and Interpretation of the BIA

[22] The *BIA* is designed to give debtors and creditors certainty in their dealings with one another. It serves two distinct goals—the equitable distribution of a bankrupt's assets among the estate's creditors and the financial rehabilitation of insolvent individuals: *Husky Oil Operations Ltd v Minister of National Revenue*, [1995] 3 S.C.R. 453 at para 7. It is a commercial statute that is to be broadly interpreted in its entire context and harmoniously with its object and scheme. . . .

c. Section 178

[29] Section 178(2) provides that, subject to specific types of provable claims deemed by Parliament to warrant the continuation of a creditor's right to enforce claims described in s 178(1), none of which apply in this case, an order of discharge releases the bankrupt from all claims provable in bankruptcy. Put simply, this means that creditors are unable to enforce on any claims unless they fit within s 178(1): *Schreyer v Schreyer*, [2011] 2 SCR 605, 2011 SCC 35 at para 21; *Alberta (Attorney General) v Moloney*, [2015] 3 SCR 327, at para 66. Stated another way, while the claim is not "extinguished", it cannot be acted on.

[30] The purpose of this is explained in *Moloney* at para 77:

> . . . [T]he language of s. 178(2) makes it clear that the purpose of this provision is to give effect to one of the goals underlying the *BIA* regime—the financial rehabilitation of the debtor—by releasing "the bankrupt from all claims provable in bankruptcy". In other words, s. 178(2) is aimed precisely at providing the bankrupt with a fresh start.

d. Provable claims

[31] Section 121 of the *BIA* provides. . . .

[32] To be a provable claim, a debt or liability must be due either at law or in equity by the bankrupt to the person seeking to prove a claim: *Re Excelsior Electric Dairy Machinery Ltd* (1922), 2 CBR 599, [1923] 3 DLR 1176 (Ont SC) at para 8. Applying ss 121 and 135 of the *BIA*, the Supreme Court of Canada in *Schreyer* (at para 26) held that the claim will be deemed to be provable if: 1) the debt exists and can be liquidated; 2) the underlying obligation exists as of the date of bankruptcy; and 3) no exemption applies: at para 26.

[33] A secured creditor need not file a proof of security unless required to do so under demand of a trustee to prove its security under s 128(1). Here, Servus filed a proof of claim as a secured creditor holding assets of the debtor valued $227,678.26 and attaching a copy of the mortgage. It did not claim a deficiency as an unsecured creditor. Whether it did so at the behest of the trustee pursuant to s 81(4) or otherwise is unknown. . . .

4. Reaffirmation

a. Reaffirmation by continued payment (the Seaboard Approach)

[50] *Seaboard Acceptance Corporation v Moen* (1986), 62 CBR (NS) 143, [1986] BCJ No 87 (BCCA) is the first reported case concluding that the test for post-discharge survival of a personal promise to pay is whether the bankrupt continued to make payments on the debt. The bankrupt entered into a long-term lease for a vehicle. She did not inform the lessor that she was in bankruptcy, but kept the payments in good standing throughout the bankruptcy and for a period after her discharge. The lessor successfully sued for a

deficiency on her personal promise to pay when she later defaulted. In dismissing the appeal, Lambert JA said this at paras 17–18:

> ... Under what basis was that possession retained and on what basis were those payments made? In my opinion, the proper view is that the contract continued throughout the bankruptcy and continued after the discharge from bankruptcy; it was never terminated in accordance with its provisions for termination, and the fact that there might have been a claim provable in bankruptcy, or that a claim provable in bankruptcy might have been made, does not affect the fact that the contract itself continued and continued to regulate the relationship of the parties after the discharge from bankruptcy.
>
> In my opinion, what occurred in this case was not, strictly speaking, a novation, as that term is properly understood, but was merely a continuation of the contract, and a continued abiding by the terms of the contract that had been made between the parties. In effect, the contract was endorsed by the defendant after the discharge.

[51] A series of mortgage foreclosure cases follow the *Seaboard* Approach....

b. Cases Requiring Novation and More

[62] The cases disagreeing with or distinguishing the *Seaboard* Approach include *Scotia Mortgage Corp v Winchester* (1997), 205 AR 147, 46 CBR (3d) 314 (QB); in *Day c Banque Laurentienne du Canada*, 2014 QCCA 449, and *Scotia Mortgage Corporation v Berkers*, 2016 NSSC 12. These cases hold that mere possession and continued payment is insufficient to warrant liability on a personal promise to pay. Rather, there must be a clear acknowledgment of the continuing obligation. As the Master did in this case, some Courts impose the additional requirement of fresh consideration....

c. Reaffirmation does not require fresh consideration

[81] While the Supreme Court has not expressly addressed the issue of whether a personal promise can survive bankruptcy discharge, it made a revealing *obiter* comment in *Moloney* at para 81 (citations omitted):

> As a general rule, a creditor cannot cause a debtor to revive an obligation **from which the debtor was released**, unless the creditor offers fresh consideration. Between private parties, it is arguable that a debtor may freely agree to revive a discharged debt in exchange for the creditor's provision of goods or services. (Emphasis added)

[82] It remains a question whether this general rule applies when the debtor has continued to make payments during and after the bankruptcy and discharge.

[83] In a recent decision, *Rosas v Toca*, 2018 BCCA 191, the British Columbia Court of Appeal ruled that absent duress, unconscionability, or other public policy concerns, there is no need for fresh consideration to vary contractual terms. The Court gave this helpful summary at para 4:

> The time has come to reform the doctrine of consideration as it applies in this context, and modify the pre-existing duty rule, as so many commentators and several courts have suggested. When parties to a contract agree to vary its terms, the variation should be enforceable without fresh consideration, absent duress, unconscionability, or other public policy concerns, which would render an otherwise valid term unenforceable. A variation supported by valid consideration may continue to be enforceable for that reason, but a lack of fresh consideration will no longer be determinative. In this way the legitimate

expectations of the parties can be protected. To do otherwise would be to let the doctrine of consideration work an injustice.

[84] I agree with this approach, which in my view is consistent with that taken in *Seaboard*.

Conclusion on the Correct Approach

[91] In my view, it is entirely relevant that Parliament had the *2003 Senate Report* recommendations when the *BIA* was last amended, but chose not to follow them.

[93] In my view, requiring something more, be it fresh consideration or an express reaffirmation, fails to adequately balance the rights of all stakeholders — be they creditors, debtors or co-signors. Accepting that the fresh start principle is a sound policy underlying the *BIA* and that financial haircuts are an expected aspect of bankruptcy, there is also a need to consider and weigh all interests. There are clear examples where simply favouring rehabilitation of the bankrupt could result in significant injustice, i.e. where long periods of time elapse post-discharge, or where the mortgaged property is a revenue property, as was the case for the entirety of the bankruptcy period here.

[94] In this regard, I note that in *Moloney*, at para 83, the Court noted:

> The rehabilitative purpose of s. 178(2) is not meant to give debtors a fresh start in all aspects of their lives. Bankruptcy does not purport to erase all the consequences of a bankrupt's past conduct.

[95] As evidenced by the provisions of the *BIA* addressing financial counselling (ss 66.13, 157.1, 168) and the treatment of surplus income (s 68), the rehabilitative purpose of the *BIA* requires more than just invoking the fresh start principle. Parliament not only expects bankrupts to learn from their financial mistakes, it mandates that they be counselled to learn and take responsibility for their financial affairs.

[96] Appreciative of the benefit of requiring express reaffirmation on bankruptcy, that is a task for Parliament. However, the Superintendent of Bankruptcy can address the issue by requiring trustees to include the topic as part of their counselling responsibilities under the *BIA* and the Superintendent's Directive No. 1R4, *Counselling in Insolvency Matters*, issued January 29, 2018. I recommend that the Superintendent take whatever actions that she deems appropriate in this regard.

[97] I conclude that when the debtor files an assignment in bankruptcy, but maintains possession of the property and continues to make the payments due under the contract, the debtor has affirmed the contract, including the covenant to pay.

[98] I therefore grant Servus' appeal of the Master's decision.

Appeal allowed.

Practice Questions

Question 1
What is the meaning of *pacta sunt seranda* and how is it relevant to the debate over the discharge?

Question 2
With respect to exempt property, what is the effect of a voluntary sale of an exempt asset? In contrast, what is the impact if the transfer of exempt property is an involuntary sale, such as

a forced sale by a secured creditor? If a debtor sells a mortgaged property due to financial difficulty before the secured creditor takes action, is that an involuntary sale meaning that the proceeds are exempt? What policy underpins the answer to this question?

Question 3

Compare the exemptions in the Saskatchewan *EMJA*, section 91, and the Ontario *Execution Act*, RSO 1990, c E.24, s 2. What explains the different approaches in the two regimes?

Question 4

Alice commenced studies at Concordia University in September 2005. She completed her BA in December 2008. Her Concordia studies were financed by a Canada Student Loan under the *Canada Student Financial Assistance Act*, SC 1994, c 28. Alice worked part time for the period January 2012 to August 2013. In September 2013, she enrolled in a finance program at Fanshawe College in London, Ontario. She was able to self-finance her second course of studies and did not take out any loans. Alice completed her Fanshawe program in June 2016. She was unable to find work after graduating and in September 2017, Alice made an assignment in bankruptcy. Her biggest liability is her $60,000 Concordia student loan. You have been asked to advise the trustee in bankruptcy who wants to know whether the student loan is discharged.

Question 5

Should student loans be non-dischargeable? What are the arguments in favour of a making student loans non-dischargeable? Are there any arguments that would support treating student loans like any other debt that can be discharged? What view do you adopt?

PART III

The *Companies' Creditors Arrangement Act*

CHAPTER 12

CCAA Overview

I. INTRODUCTION

Writing in 1970, Roger Tassé described the history of bankruptcy and insolvency law as that of an "expanding concept"[1] (see chapters 1 and 2). Subsequent developments in restructuring law in particular have given his words the aura of prophecy. The recessions of the 1980s and 1990s precipitated the rapid growth and expansion of restructuring law as an area of bankruptcy and insolvency practice. This phenomenon was, and continues to be, driven in large part by high-profile reorganizations of big companies, including major retailers (e.g., Eaton's, Target Canada, Sears), airlines (e.g., Canadian Airlines, Air Canada), and manufacturers (e.g. Algoma Steel, Stelco), among others. These restructurings represented real-time responses to avert corporate bankruptcies, and lent corporate restructuring practice its solutions-oriented approach to the problem of financial distress and insolvency. The *Companies' Creditors Arrangement Act*, RSC 1985, c C-36 (*CCAA*) was at the center of these developments, and it remains the centerpiece of Canadian corporate restructuring law today.

Although corporate restructuring is often associated with bankruptcy and insolvency law, it is broader and more informal than this association implies. It is important to realize that much restructuring occurs before the point of insolvency and out of the public spotlight, through private negotiations between corporations and their largest creditors. The terms "restructuring" and "reorganization" are informal and interchangeable, and do not have a specific legal definition. A company may also have a choice between several legislative regimes to deal with its financial distress, including a commercial proposal under the *Bankruptcy and Insolvency Act*, RSC 1985 c B-3 (*BIA*), part III, division I, the *CCAA*, and the arrangement provision of the *Canada Business Corporations Act*, RSC 1985, c C-44 for federal companies. Therefore, a decision to file under the *CCAA* is the election of one option among several options.

This chapter, along with chapters 13–15, deals with proceedings under the *CCAA*. Part II, below, identifies the essential features of restructuring law; explains the relationship between the *CCAA* and the *BIA* proposals regime; and chronicles the shift from *CCAA* restructuring proceedings to *CCAA* liquidation proceedings. Part III addresses the scope of the *CCAA*. Part IV deals with the initial filing in *CCAA* proceedings and Part V is concerned with the stay of creditors' remedies in *CCAA* proceedings.

Chapter 13 deals with various issues relating to the carrying on of the debtor's business during the course of *CCAA* proceedings. Chapter 14 relates to creditors' claims in *CCAA*

---

1 Canada, Study Committee on Bankruptcy and Insolvency Legislation, *Report of the Study Committee on Bankruptcy and Insolvency Legislation* (Ottawa: Information Canada, 1970) (Chair: Roger Tassé) at 5 [Tassé Report].

proceedings and Chapter 15 deals with creditor and court approval of *CCAA* plans in restructuring proceedings.

II. THE ESSENTIALS OF RESTRUCTURING LAW

[handwritten margin note: debtors assets vest in the trustee + debtor loses control]

A. Restructuring vs Bankruptcy

In *BIA* bankruptcy proceedings, the debtor's assets vest in the trustee. If the debtor is in business, the business also vests in the trustee and the debtor loses control. The trustee may keep the business going, but this will usually just be temporary so that the trustee can negotiate a going concern sale to a willing buyer. Sooner or later, the trustee will sell the business, either on a going concern basis or piecemeal, and they will distribute the proceeds among creditors in the order the *BIA* requires. If the debtor is a company, dissolution is the usual sequel to bankruptcy. Dissolution puts the company out of existence.

[handwritten margin note: current mgmt remains in place]
[handwritten margin note: rescue rather than murder]
[handwritten margin note: purpose is to create a plan]

  CCAA restructuring proceedings are different in a number of ways. First, when a company goes into *CCAA* protection, its assets do not vest in a trustee. Instead, current management usually stays in place and continues to run the company during the proceedings. Secondly, in restructuring proceedings, the objective is to rescue the company, not kill it off. A company files for protection under the *CCAA* by applying to the court for an initial order which, among other things, imposes a stay on creditors' proceedings against the company (see Part IV, below). The purpose of the stay is to buy time for the debtor to put together a plan its creditors will accept and also which will allow the company to continue in business after it has met its obligations under the plan. Thirdly, and related to the last point, the company's obligations under the plan substitute for the obligations it originally owed creditors. For example, if the plan provides for creditors to receive 25 cents on the dollar and the debtor meets this obligation, it is released from paying the balance of the debt.

  In *Century Services Inc v Canada (Attorney General)*, 2010 SCC 60 (*Century Services*), the Supreme Court of Canada explained the rescue function of *CCAA* restructuring proceedings as follows (at paras 14, 15, and 18):

[handwritten margin note: Outcome 1: breathing space for solvency]

[14] ... There are three ways of exiting *CCAA* proceedings. The best outcome is achieved when the stay of proceedings provides the debtor with some breathing space during which solvency is restored and the *CCAA* process terminates without reorganization being needed. The second most desirable outcome occurs when the debtor's compromise

[handwritten margin note: Outcome 2: compromise is accepted by creditors]

or arrangement is accepted by its creditors and the reorganized company emerges from the *CCAA* proceedings as a going concern. Lastly, if the compromise or arrangement fails, either the company or its creditors usually seek to have the debtor's assets liquidated under the applicable provisions of the *BIA* or to place the debtor into receivership ...

[15] ... [T]he purpose of the *CCAA*—Canada's first reorganization statute—is to permit the debtor to continue to carry on business and, where possible, avoid the social and economic costs of liquidating its assets...

[18] ... Reorganization serves the public interest by facilitating the survival of companies supplying goods or services crucial to the health of the economy or saving large numbers of jobs... Insolvency could be so widely felt as to impact stakeholders other than creditors and employees... [Reorganization may be] justified in terms of rehabilitating companies that are key elements in a complex web of interdependent economic relationships in order to avoid the negative consequences of liquidation.

The *CCAA* regime is one of debtor-in-possession. In other words, when *CCAA* proceedings are commenced, the company's current management will typically stay in place and continue to manage the enterprise throughout the proceedings. In this respect, the *CCAA* is comparable to Chapter 11 of the United States *Bankruptcy Code*. By contrast, in England corporate reorganizations are provided for under the *Enterprise Act 2002*, which requires the appointment by the court of an administrator to take over the business of the company while the plan is being worked out. Most other Commonwealth countries, including Australia, follow the English model. The thinking behind the debtor-in-possession model is that current management is likely to know the business best and replacing them with an outside administrator may be disruptive. The thinking behind the English approach is that it was under current management's watch that the debtor became insolvent and so leaving them in place could be described as akin to putting the fox in charge of the hen-house. In Canada, the *CCAA* addresses this concern by requiring the appointment of a monitor whose function, broadly speaking, is to keep a watch on management throughout the proceedings: see further, Chapter 13, Part II.

A typical *CCAA* plan might provide for creditors who have provable claims to receive X cents on the dollar in full satisfaction of their claims. The plan may also provide for creditors to take shares in the debtor in full or partial satisfaction of their claims. Apart from addressing creditors' claims, the plan may include measures aimed at increasing the debtor's profitability going forward (for example, organizational changes or a new business model). The plan binds creditors who agree to it as a matter of contract law. It also binds minority creditors by virtue of the statute (*CCAA*, s 6). This last feature may seem oppressive, but the palliatives are that creditors have the right to vote on the plan under court supervision and also that the court itself must approve the plan.

Restructuring proceedings (also referred to as corporate rescue) have three main policy objectives: (1) the maximization of returns to creditors; (2) the protection of wider stakeholder interests; and (3) debtor rehabilitation.

1) Maximizing Creditor Returns

Creditors may recover more in restructuring proceedings than they would in bankruptcy. The reasons for this are hinted at in the passage from the *Century Services* case quoted above. In some cases, restructuring proceedings may allow the debtor to trade out of its financial difficulties altogether, in which case, of course, creditors may end up being paid in full. In other cases, the restructuring proceedings may allow the debtor to make key changes to its operations, for example, by shedding unprofitable divisions or improving management and workplace efficiencies. In this scenario, creditors may recover, if not 100 cents on the dollar, at least more than they would in liquidation proceedings, simply by virtue of the fact that the debtor continues as a going concern with the prospect of generating sufficient revenue to partially satisfy creditors' claims. It is implicit in *CCAA* restructuring proceedings that creditors will recover more than they would in bankruptcy proceedings because otherwise they will vote against the plan. This means that when the debtor is putting the plan together, it must at least ensure sure that the plan makes the majority of creditors better off than they would be in bankruptcy. But the debtor also has to remember that the plan needs court approval and so it cannot disregard the minority either: a court would disapprove a plan that gave majority creditors more than they would get in bankruptcy but minority creditors less.

2) Protection of Wider Stakeholder Interests

According to one school of thought, the maximization of creditor returns is the only legitimate goal of bankruptcy law in general and restructuring law in particular (see the Jackson and Baird extracts in Chapter 1, Part IV). According to another school of thought, there are other relevant considerations, such as saving jobs or keeping the company town alive (see the Warren extract in Chapter 1, Part IV). In other words, restructuring an insolvent company may be preferable to putting it into bankruptcy, having regard to the interests of stakeholders whose livelihood depends on the company staying in business. This consideration is front and center in the Supreme Court of Canada's observations in *Century Services*, quoted above. But while the protection of non-creditor stakeholder interests may be a desirable consequence of restructuring proceedings, it cannot be the paramount consideration. Otherwise, creditors might be forced into restructuring proceedings even in cases where they would do better by putting the debtor into bankruptcy, while inefficient businesses would be kept running simply to serve the interests of the debtor's workers, suppliers, customers, and the like. Lower returns to creditors in insolvency proceedings are likely to be reflected in the price and availability of credit. Furthermore, if the protection of wider stakeholder interests really were the main policy objective, the insolvency laws would be too limited a solution. Stakeholder interests may be affected whenever a company closes down, down-sizes, or relocates, but none of these events necessarily implicates the insolvency laws.

3) Debtor Rehabilitation

In *Century Services*, the Supreme Court also mentions debtor rehabilitation as a goal of *CCAA* restructuring proceedings. In the context of individual bankruptcies, the rehabilitation goal is reflected in the *BIA* discharge provisions. The discharge frees the debtor from liability for payment of pre-bankruptcy debts. In other words, it wipes the slate clean and gives the debtor a fresh start. One function of the fresh start policy is to encourage entrepreneurial risk-taking; the discharge means that an individual can go into business knowing that if the enterprise does not work out, at least their human capital will be protected, along with whatever cushion of assets the bankruptcy laws say the debtor can keep. In this respect, the bankruptcy laws are similar to the concept of limited shareholder liability in the corporations laws.

Generally speaking, the *BIA* discharge is only available to individual debtors: a corporation may not obtain a discharge unless all creditors' claims are satisfied in full: see *BIA*, section 169(4). For corporations, elements of the fresh start policy can be seen in the restructuring laws. Once the debtor has complied with the requirements of a restructuring plan, it is no longer liable in respect of debts that have been compromised by the plan. In other words, compliance with the plan wipes the sale clean, much like the bankruptcy discharge.

In *Century Services*, the Supreme Court linked the rehabilitation objective with the importance of protecting wider stakeholder interests: rehabilitating a company is important not for the sake of the company itself, but to preserve the "complex web of economic relationships" (para 18) to which the company is party and to avoid harm to the other parties to those relationships. However, the rehabilitation objective can also be viewed from the perspective of the debtor company's shareholders. If the company is liquidated, the shareholders will typically lose their investments, but if it can be rescued and the business becomes prosperous again, the shareholders' interests may be at least partially salvaged: see David Bish, "The Plight of Receiverships in a *CCAA* World," commenting on the position of shareholders in *CCAA* liquidation proceedings relative to restructuring proceedings.[2] The partial protection shareholders receive in restructuring proceedings provides an incentive to investment in much the same way that the *BIA* discharge provides an incentive for individuals to engage in entrepreneurial activity.

---

2   David Bish, "The Plight of Receiverships in a *CCAA* World" (2013) 2 *Journal of the Insolvency Institute of Canada* 221 at 233.

B. *CCAA* Plans vs *BIA* Proposals

The two main insolvency restructuring regimes in Canada are the *CCAA* and the *BIA* commercial proposals regime. The bifurcation in the main corporate restructuring regimes came about largely by historical accident, but proposals to merge the two regimes have consistently met with resistance for reasons which will be explained below. While the *CCAA* and *BIA* commercial proposal provisions are the most commonly used regimes, it is important to note that there are also industry-specific restructuring statutes for insolvent companies: one for farms (*Farm Debt Mediation Act*, SC 1997, c 21), another for railways (*Canada Transportation Act*, SC 1996, c 10, ss 140–46), and a third for financial institutions (*Winding-Up and Restructuring Act*, RSC 1985, c W-11). In the case of large farms, the debtor company may have three restructuring regimes to choose from, each with unique advantages and disadvantages (see Stephanie Ben-Ishai and Virginia Torrie, "Farm Insolvency in Canada" (2013) 2 *Journal of the Insolvency Institute of Canada* 33). As discussed below (Part III, "Scope of the *CCAA*"), the way that courts have recently interpreted the *CCAA* as it relates to railway companies appears to indicate a state of flux in terms of its potential applicability and the potential applicability of the *Canada Transportation Act*, SC 1996, c 10, provisions. The state of the *Winding-Up and Restructuring Act* is probably the least clear of all. This Act only applies in the case of a financially distressed financial institution—a phenomenon which, fortunately, has been a relatively rare event in Canada. As a result, the *Winding-Up and Restructuring Act* has been seldom used (see Bruce Welling and Thomas Telfer, "The Winding-Up and Restructuring Act: Realigning Insolvency's Orphan to the Modern Law Reform Process" (2008) 24 *Banking and Finance Law Review* 233; Stephanie Ben-Ishai, "Bank Bankruptcy in Canada: A Comparative Perspective" (2009) 25 *Banking and Finance Law Review* 59). Although industry-specific restructuring regimes are not the focus of this chapter, it is important to be aware of them because they significantly alter the legal rules pertaining to restructuring in cases where they apply.

The terms "reorganization" and "restructuring" are used interchangeably in Canada and the United States to describe the restructuring of the debts of an insolvent business, but neither term is used in the Canadian legislation. The *CCAA* speaks of an arrangement, but without defining the term. Part III, division I, of the *BIA* uses the term "proposal." "Proposal" is defined in *BIA*, section 2, as "including" a proposal for a composition, for an extension of time, or for a scheme of arrangement. "Composition" and "arrangement" are not defined, but, given the non-exhaustive definition of "proposal," it probably does not matter. Composition is usually understood to mean an arrangement whereby creditors agree to accept less than full repayment of what is owing to them as contrasted with a proposal for an extension of time, which simply gives the debtor more time to pay the debts. A scheme of arrangement usually implies a more elaborate proposal, possibly involving a restructuring of the classes of creditors and equity holders in the debtor corporation coupled with a reduction in the amount that is repayable and the period in which it must be paid: see *ATB Financial v Metcalfe & Mansfield Alternative Investments II Corp*, 2008 ONCA 587 at paras 60 and 61. In this casebook, "reorganization" and "restructuring" are used in a non-technical sense to denote any and all of these methods of rescuing an insolvent business.

The *CCAA* was enacted in 1933, at the height of the Great Depression. It was based on provisions in the English *Companies Act 1929*. The objective was to provide a workable method for companies to reorganize and avoid bankruptcy. Amendments in 1953 restricted the application of the statute to companies that had an outstanding issue of bonds or debentures and a trustee to protect the interests of the bond- or debenture-holders. Thereafter, the *CCAA* largely fell into disuse. In 1970, the Tassé Committee published a major report recommending substantial changes to the bankruptcy laws, including the repeal of the *CCAA* and the integration of the *CCAA* reorganization procedures into a new and comprehensive Bankruptcy Act. But this recommendation was never adopted.

In 1984, the Mulroney government established the Colter Committee to recommend reform of the bankruptcy laws in areas where it was most needed. The Colter Committee's 1986 report paid particular attention to the need for modern and efficient alternatives to commercial and consumer bankruptcies. These recommendations were adopted in the 1992 amendments to the *BIA*, which enacted a new part III, division I, dealing with business proposals, and division II, dealing with consumer proposals. The Committee did not indicate what should be done with the *CCAA* and the assumption appears to have been that it would simply die from disuse or that it would eventually be repealed. But, as it happens, between 1986 and 1992, the *CCAA* had come into use again, partly because practitioners managed to find a way around the restrictions introduced by the 1953 amendments and partly also because the courts proved to be remarkably creative in adapting the skeletal provisions of the *CCAA* to modern restructuring needs. Insolvency practitioners found that they preferred the court-driven and, as judicially construed, flexible provisions of the *CCAA* to the more rule-driven new *BIA*, part III.I, provisions. This philosophy was also shared by the members of the *BIA* Advisory Committee established by the federal government in 1994 to make recommendations for the next round of insolvency amendments. The Committee recommended retention of the *CCAA*, but with significant changes, which were enacted as part of the 1997 *CCAA* amendments. One of the amendments repealed the restriction on the statute's application, introduced in 1953, and replaced it with a provision stating that the Act applies to any company or affiliated debtor companies where the total claims against the company or its affiliates exceeds $5 million (*CCAA*, s 3(1)). Subject to this exception, corporate debtors in Canada now have a choice of two very differently inspired regimes to reorganize their affairs.

Briefly stated, the difference between the two regimes is that the debtor initiates the *BIA* reorganization procedure by filing either a proposal or a notice of intention to make a proposal. The procedure is an administrative one and there is no need for a court application. Creditors meet and vote on the proposal subject to rules that are spelled out in the statute itself. The court's main function is to approve the proposal once creditors have voted on it. (The court's other functions include hearing applications for extensions of time to file a proposal and applications by creditors opposing the proposal to terminate the proceedings.) In contrast, the debtor initiates the *CCAA* reorganization procedure by making an application to the court. The debtor puts together a plan for submission to creditors subject to timelines that the court imposes on a case-by-case basis. Creditors meet and vote on the plan subject to the court's direction, and, at the end of the process, the court decides whether or not to approve the plan. In short, the *BIA* business proposals regime is a statute-driven one, while the *CCAA* regime is a court-driven one. Proponents of the bifurcated system argue that the two regimes serve different interests: large firms prefer the greater flexibility that the *CCAA* offers, while smaller firms prefer the *BIA* regime because it is cheaper and, given its greater reliance on bright-line statutory rules, more predictable. Largely on the basis of these views, the Standing Senate Committee on Banking, Trade and Commerce in its 2003 Report recommended that "the *Bankruptcy and Insolvency Act* and the *Companies' Creditors Arrangement Act* continue to exist as separate statutes."[3] However, the 2009 amendments

---

3 Standing Senate Committee on Banking, Trade and Commerce, *Debtors and Creditors Sharing the Burden: A Review of the* Bankruptcy and Insolvency Act *and the* Companies' Creditors Arrangement Act (Ottawa: Senate, November 2003) (Chair: Hon Richard H Kroft) at 170–73.

have made a number of changes to the *CCAA*, most of which are aimed at reducing the court's discretion by substituting statutory rules (examples include the new provisions governing debtor-in-possession financing, executory contracts and asset sales); of course, the more rule-oriented the *CCAA* becomes, the weaker the argument for maintaining the separate regimes: see, further, Jacob Ziegel, "The *BIA* and *CCAA* Interface" in Stephanie Ben-Ishai and Anthony Duggan, eds, *Canadian Bankruptcy and Insolvency Law: Bill C-55, Statute c. 47 and Beyond* (Toronto: LexisNexis, 2007) at 307.

In *PricewaterhouseCoopers Inc v Ramdath*, 2018 MBCA 71, the Manitoba Court of Appeal considered whether to grant leave to appeal a decision of the bankruptcy court related to *BIA* proceedings. In determining the criteria for leave to appeal a decision made pursuant to the *BIA*, the court noted, "to the extent possible, it is preferable that these statutes [the *BIA* and the *CCAA*] be interpreted in a similar manner" and "the criteria for leave to appeal a decision in a *BIA* proceeding should be similar to the criteria for leave to appeal a decision in a *CCAA* proceeding" (para 19). The court relied on the principle from *Century Services* that the statutes be read harmoniously.

C. *CCAA* Restructurings vs *CCAA* Liquidations

The Supreme Court's account of the *CCAA* regime in *Century Services* focuses solely on restructuring proceedings. But there has been a marked shift over the past decade or so from use of the *CCAA* as a restructuring mechanism to its use as a vehicle for liquidating insolvent companies. The difference between the two types of proceedings has been summarized as follows:

> *Reorganization.* Traditionally, the debtor would prepare a plan of arrangement designed to rehabilitate the debtor corporation so that it could continue in business and avoid bankruptcy. The debtor would present this plan at a meeting of its creditors for their approval. If a majority of each class of creditors representing two-thirds of the value of the debt held vote in favour of the plan, the court may sanction the plan and the debtor may proceed to implement it. . . .

> *Liquidating CCAA.* [The debtor's] assets are sold either piecemeal or on a going concern basis under the *CCAA* court's supervision. The sales may occur pursuant to a plan that has been approved by the creditors, or they may occur in the absence of a plan. Notably, many recent *CCAA* proceedings have been liquidating *CCAAs* from the outset. That is, the debtor never intended to present a reorganization plan to its creditors, and merely applied for *CCAA* protection so that it could begin a marketing process to sell substantially all of its assets. In such cases, the debtor might present a post-sale plan to its creditors that is essentially a plan of distribution of the sale proceeds, or the debtor may simply enter bankruptcy proceedings.[4]

CCAA liquidating proceedings are often commenced or instigated by a secured creditor as an alternative to putting the debtor into receivership (see further below).

Bish, above, summarizes the main features of liquidating *CCAA* proceedings as follows:

- realization focus (though often called a "restructuring")

---

4   Alfonso Nocilla, "Is 'Corporate Rescue' Working in Canada?" (2013) 53 *Canadian Business Law Journal* 382 at 384–85 (Nocilla, "Is 'Corporate Rescue' Working in Canada?").

- debtor is in control, though this may be notional in some cases; secured creditor has considerable influence over the debtor especially where also the DIP (debtor-in-possession) lender
- principal secured creditors are often not stayed
- virtually unheard of for proceedings to be commenced without the knowledge of the principal secured creditors
- proceedings most often centered on sale of debtor's assets and distribution of proceeds; true restructuring proceedings are uncommon. There may be little direct negotiation (other than between debtor and principal secured creditor). Unsecured creditors have little impact or substantive participation
- court officer often focused on participation in sale process and realization objectives. Often secured creditors have the only real economic interest — unsecured creditors are commonly "out of the money"
- secured creditors may have significant input in selection of Court officer
- unsecured creditors frequently do not recover any value — unsecured creditors often have no significant role and may be seen as a nuisance more than a party having an economic interest at stake (i.e., impairing efforts to maximize recovery for secured creditors, and adding cost and delay to the process when asserting rights or interests)
- secured creditors generally will not accept value distributed to unsecured creditors unless they are first paid out in full
- there is no automatic consequence to an unsuccessful sale process or plan. With most proceedings ending with a sale transaction and no plan or active creditor negotiations, there is no bankruptcy threat
- the debtor usually does not continue in operation (i.e., due to sale of assets); where it does, its equity is usually transferred to creditors
- existing shareholders rarely maintain control over a company that continues to carry on business
- the status of directors, officers and senior management with the debtor and any go-forward role is … in the hands of the secured creditors and/or the subsequent purchaser of the business[5]

In a recent study, Nocilla examined the outcomes of *CCAA* proceedings in the years 2002–2012. He identified a total of 250 proceedings in those years, of which approximately one-third were liquidating *CCAA*s. Most of these liquidating *CCAA*s were carried out before the debtor had presented a plan (Nocilla, at 387–92).

This trend is hard to square with either the history or the language of the statute which, as the Supreme Court remarks in *Century Services*, clearly has a restructuring focus. Nevertheless, the Ontario courts began approving *CCAA* liquidating proceedings in 1998 (*Canadian Red Cross Society, Re* (1998), 5 CBR (4th) 299 (Ont Ct J (Gen Div)) and the courts in other provinces, while initially disapproving, have started to follow suit. Nocilla reports that between 2002 and 2012, there were seventy-five liquidating *CCAA*s across Canada, broken down as follows: Alberta (7); British Columbia (8); Manitoba (3); New Brunswick (2); Newfoundland and Labrador (0); Nova Scotia (0); Ontario (43); Prince Edward Island (0); Quebec (11); and Saskatchewan (1).

The enactment of *CCAA*, section 36, as part of the 2009 amendments was an important development in this connection. Section 36 is headed "Restriction on disposal of business assets"; it provides that a debtor company may not dispose of assets outside the ordinary

---

5   Bish, above note 2 at 226–29.

course of business without court approval and it sets out the factors a court must take into account before authorizing a sale. On one view, this provision appears to give the legislature's approval to liquidating *CCAA* proceedings. On the other hand, section 36 could be read as meaning that assets sales are permissible, but only in the context of a plan of arrangement. Needless to say, proponents of liquidating *CCAA*s prefer the wider reading.

In policy terms, the main arguments in support of liquidating *CCAA*s are that they produce higher returns for creditors than restructuring proceedings and that they are not inconsistent with the rescue culture which underpins the *CCAA*. In successful restructuring proceedings, the debtor company and its business are both saved and so the twin objectives of protecting wider stakeholder interests and debtor rehabilitation are both met. In successful liquidation proceedings, while the debtor company is typically killed off, the business itself survives in the hands of the new owner and so wider stakeholder interests are as effectively protected as they would be in a restructuring. However, these arguments are controversial. Opponents of liquidating *CCAA*s point to the lack of empirical evidence to support claims that creditors' returns from liquidating *CCAA* proceedings are higher than they are from restructurings. They also argue that the main beneficiaries in liquidating *CCAA*s are secured creditors and that secured creditors' interests are opposed to the interests of the unsecured creditors. A fully secured creditor will typically prefer a liquidation to a restructuring provided the expected sale proceeds are sufficient to pay out its claim and regardless of whether the sale maximizes the returns to the creditors generally. Furthermore, the debtor company's shareholders typically recover nothing in a liquidation and so liquidating *CCAA*s are inconsistent with at least one version of the rehabilitation objective described above. For a fuller account of these and related arguments see, for example, Nocilla, "Is 'Corporate Rescue' Working in Canada?" above; Roderick J Wood, "Rescue and Liquidation in Restructuring Law" (2013) 53 *Canadian Business Law Journal* 407; and Bish, above footnote 2. See also Alfonso Nocilla, "The History of the Companies' Creditors Arrangement Act and the Future of Restructuring Law in Canada" (2014) 56:1 *Canadian Business Law Journal* 73, an extract from which appears below. The extract provides a good overview of the competing legal and policy arguments, not just in Canada, but in the United States and the United Kingdom as well.

Alfonso Nocilla, "The History of the Companies' Creditors Arrangement Act and the Future of Restructuring Law in Canada" (2014) 56:1 *Canadian Business Law Journal* 73 (footnotes omitted)

David Bish argues that Canadian restructuring law has undergone a paradigm shift in recent decades. Specifically, he argues that the CCAA's traditional rehabilitation focus has given way to a new realization focus:

Ironically, we appear to have come full circle. After a century of having increasingly embraced restructuring, expanded notions of rehabilitation and voluntary, debtor-in-possession (DIP) insolvency proceedings, we have increasingly reverted to giving creditors greater control of insolvency processes, proceedings and outcomes at the expense of the debtors' opportunity to restructure. The current climate is extraordinarily receptive to realization over restructuring.

Bish further notes that "there has been an intentional confusing of realization and restructuring: it has become routine to refer to realization proceedings as a form of restructuring, obfuscating the distinction." In other words, the CCAA is increasingly being used as a liquidation tool, but the language of the CCAA—and, indeed, the whole framework of the Act—are still geared toward reorganization.

This shift in focus from reorganization to liquidation has important implications. Bish observes that the CCAA's historical purposes "had nothing to do with creditor realizations, and a purposive approach to statutory interpretation does not support the idea that the CCAA was intended to be a creditor's tool of choice for realizing on security." In my view, there are two key principles that have driven Canadian restructuring law historically which are relevant to this recent shift in the CCAA's focus: the preservation of going-concern value, and the public interest.

(a) Preserving Going-Concern Value

According to this principle, insolvency law aims to solve a common pool problem. Specifically, when a firm becomes insolvent, a collective action problem arises as the distressed firm's creditors race to enforce their individual security interests against the firm's assets, thereby dismantling the firm piecemeal when it was worth more as a going concern. Insolvency law prevents this race by imposing a compulsory collective process on all creditors. It is implicit in this process that the creditors as a whole would favour preserving an insolvent firm's business where doing so would result in greater returns for all of them.

In the United States, bankruptcy law scholars have been engaged in a long debate over the merits of rehabilitating insolvent firms. For example, Douglas Baird has argued that the reorganization provisions of Chapter 11 of the U.S. Bankruptcy Code merely delay the inevitable for many insolvent firms. According to Baird, most firms that enter Chapter 11 cannot survive in the marketplace because their business models are fundamentally flawed:

> ... [M]ost of the firms in Chapter 11 are relatively small enterprises that cannot survive in the marketplace. For them, Chapter 11 only postpones the inevitable. The firm is a retail establishment that has picked the wrong product or the wrong location or both. Some firms, like some horses, should be taken out to the back pasture and shot.

More recently, Baird and Robert Rasmussen have argued that financial innovations and changes in the capital structure of firms may have rendered traditional reorganizations obsolete:

> In the past, the bargains that parties reached among themselves followed a few familiar patterns. While there were many possible deals, the players naturally gravitated toward only a few. In the new environment, with different players holding different stakes, the old patterns no longer apply and new ones have yet to take shape. There are no longer organized groups... The types of institutions vary—from banks and broker-dealers to hedge funds and private equity firms. The current environment is one in which there are no natural leaders (or followers) among the creditors to perform the shuttle diplomacy required to build a consensus. Without familiar benchmarks, there is no shared understanding of what form a plan should take. Coalition formation is harder. Worse yet, in some cases there may be no stable equilibrium at all. To use the language of cooperative game theory, the core may be empty.

On the other hand, Elizabeth Warren and Jay Westbrook have argued that Chapter 11 success rates are reasonably high for firms that survive the initial filing and go on to propose a reorganization plan. In addition, the Chapter 11 process eliminates the truly hopeless firms fairly quickly:

> The data reveal that the cases—both those that exit the system and those that confirm plans of reorganization—moved at a lively pace. They also suggest that, at least between 1994 and 2002, the system showed signs of improvement. While the data cannot answer

the normative question about whether the movement is as substantial as it should have been, they are adequate to dispel the notion that great numbers of debtors were hiding out in Chapter 11 for years, just mowing the lawn and waiting for the market to turn.

Moreover, Lynn LoPucki and Joseph Doherty have presented research suggesting that on average, Chapter 11 sales yield dramatically lower returns for creditors than reorganizations. Accordingly, market efficiency cannot explain the shift toward sales, and more sinister factors must be at play:

> Possible explanations for this market failure are not in short supply. The managers who decided to sell these companies rather than reorganize them frequently had conflicts of interest. So did the investment bankers who advised the managers and solicited bids. The stalking-horse bidders received protections in the form of breakup fees and substantial minimum bid increments that discouraged other bidders. The costs of participating in the bidding were high because the companies' situations were complex and changed rapidly. Bidders other than the stalking horse had little chance of winning. As a result, only a single bidder appeared at most bankruptcy auctions.

As for the "empty core" problem, Baird and Rasmussen are clearly correct that financial innovations have made modern restructurings more complicated than they were in the past. Nor is this development unique to restructurings in the United States. For instance, Vanessa Finch has raised similar concerns in the United Kingdom:

> A particular worry relating to insolvency risks is the possibility that the popularity of derivatives may impede recoveries in times of corporate trouble because the hedge funds or other holders of credit will enforce debts rapidly against defaulters. In the world of the "new capital" the troubled company may have no friendly ear at the bank to turn to and creditors who have purchased derivatives may possess few motivations to explore turnaround possibilities.

But Finch suggests that the problem is manageable and could be addressed by maximising transparency with respect to the interests held in companies, "whether these be structured debt packages or retentions of title." Moreover, it is worth noting that reorganizations have always been complex matters. For example, David Skeel has pointed out that the traditional characterization of reorganization as a straightforward negotiation among several groups of like-minded creditors merely "provided a template for a messy and complicated process." There were challenges to achieving consensus in reorganizations in the past, just as there are today, and "there were corporate raiders in the early twentieth century, just as there are now."

Although the Chapter 11 debate in the United States is currently at a standstill, the debate in Canada over the relative merits of reorganization and liquidation is only beginning. This debate focuses on the question of whether and under what circumstances liquidating CCAAs should be permitted. Clearly, section 36 authorizes courts to approve asset sales under the CCAA, but it says little about how courts should exercise this power. So far as the creditor value-maximization theory is concerned, the wholesale liquidation of an insolvent firm's assets under the CCAA would be justified if the sale yielded greater returns for creditors than a sale through receivership or bankruptcy. However, proponents of liquidating CCAAs have produced no evidence to support the assertion that liquidating CCAAs are more efficient or more likely to maximize returns for creditors generally than bankruptcy or receivership sales.

(b) The Public Interest

The second key principle underlying Canadian restructuring law is the "public interest." In *Century Services*, the Supreme Court of Canada stated that courts supervising insolvency reorganizations should consider the impact of the reorganization process on the broader community:

> [T]he court must often be cognizant of the various interests at stake in the reorganization, which can extend beyond those of the debtor and creditors to include employees, directors, shareholders, and even other parties doing business with the insolvent company... In addition, courts must recognize that on occasion the broader public interest will be engaged by aspects of the reorganization and may be a factor against which the decision of whether to allow a particular action will be weighed (emphasis added).

Although the Supreme Court provided little guidance as to what the "public interest" means in the context of the CCAA, it pointed to earlier decisions and commentaries that do provide some guidance. For example, the Court cited *Red Cross* and *Air Canada* as examples of restructurings where the outcomes clearly had implications for the broader community. The Court also recognized the historical importance of the CCAA's public interest goal, as early commentators such as Stanley Edwards expressed:

> Another reason which is usually operative in favour of reorganization is the interest of the public in the continuation of the enterprise, particularly if the company supplies commodities or services that are necessary or desirable to large numbers of consumers, or if it employs large numbers of workers who would be thrown out of employment by its liquidation. This public interest may be reflected in the decisions of the creditors and shareholders of the company and is undoubtedly a factor which a court would wish to consider in deciding whether to sanction an arrangement under the CCAA.

The above statements reflect the widely accepted principle that corporate insolvency law should do more than simply maximize returns for a narrow group of creditors, but should also look to the needs of the broader community of insolvency stakeholders. Roy Goode has expressed this concept as follows:

> But there are values to be protected that go beyond the interests of those with accrued rights at the commencement of the insolvency process. One of these is the investigation of the directors' conduct with a view to sanctions for improper trading and disqualification so as to protect the public against future misconduct, a course of action available in England through the winding up process even where the company has no assets at all. Another is the interest of the workforce in preserving its investment of labour, expertise and loyalty to the enterprise, and a third is that of the community at large, for example, in the continuance of the business or the payment of clean-up costs of pollution. To focus so exclusively on maximizing returns to creditors is to ignore the fact that there may be different ways of protecting creditors, some of which will also benefit other interests, such as those of employees, shareholders and the local community, and in so doing may even advance creditors' interests.

It is beyond the scope of this paper to fully explore the concept of the public interest and its role in CCAA proceedings. Suffice it to say that the CCAA was not intended merely to serve the interests of creditors—it also has a broader goal of minimizing the negative consequences of insolvency for employees, suppliers, customers and the wider community. At the same time, we should recognize that the concept of the public interest is closely tied to the CCAA's traditional rescue purpose, and both its meaning and application are blurred in liquidating CCAAs.

(c) Conclusion

The CCAA was designed to facilitate reorganization plans, and the structure of the Act reflects this purpose:

> The whole CCAA process is geared towards the development of a plan of arrangement that will be presented before the creditors for their acceptance or rejection... Indeed, the very title of the Act anticipates the negotiation of a consensual arrangement amongst the creditors and the debtor.

Despite this clear purpose, courts now regularly approve liquidating CCAAs in cases where the debtor has no intention of presenting a plan to its creditors. As they did with instant trust deeds, a number of courts have suggested that the requirement of a plan is now outdated and unnecessary. The salient difference between trust deeds and plans of arrangement, however, is that the CCAA is fundamentally an Act to facilitate plans of arrangement. This clear mismatch between the CCAA's traditional purposes and its modern use as a liquidation mechanism has led to predictable problems. There is controversy in the courts and the academy over the purposes of the legislation, and this has made judicial outcomes less predictable. Beyond these concerns, however, there are additional reasons why liquidating CCAAs that are carried out in the absence of plans of arrangement are problematic. Put simply, the risk is that the sale process will be used to alter the distributional entitlements that creditors would enjoy in a traditional restructuring or liquidation. Stephanie Ben-Ishai and Stephen Lubben have expressed this problem as follows:

> It is not a harm to creditors, voluntary or involuntary, when a sale results in little or no recovery for unsecured creditors or shareholders. Rather, the key issue is whether the sale results in the realization of less value by junior claimants than a traditional reorganization or liquidation... A sale thus could result in the realization of equal value, but see that value diverted to senior creditors. This is a problem of redistribution... Thus, there is a real concern that the sale process might facilitate collusion between management and senior creditors to squeeze out junior creditors and shareholders.

Similarly, Ralph Brubaker and Charles Tabb have argued that new approaches to Chapter 11 reorganizations may be undermining creditors' rights:

> The heart of the matter is this: whether reorganization value is captured by "sale" or by "plan" is not the critical question, as long as the method chosen preserves and upholds chapter 11's distributional norms. Given that any particular "plan" can be structured as a "sale," and any "sale" can be effectuated through a "plan" structure, it may simply be impossible to meaningfully distinguish between the two through some sort of "true sale" versus "true reorganization" construct in a manner that can preserve those distributional norms. We submit, therefore, that courts confronting these issues must keep their primary focus on the core need to protect the normative distributional entitlements of stakeholders, whether the reorganization proceeds by sale or plan. If the mechanism used impairs or obstructs the court's ability to fulfill that central protective role, then and only then should the court reject the reorganization vehicle.

In the U.K., John Armour, Audrey Hsu and Adrian Walters recently compared realizations from sales in receiverships with those carried out under the *Enterprise Act 2002.*

The *Enterprise Act* marked an important shift in British insolvency law because it introduced an "administration" procedure that favoured rescue over liquidation. Ostensibly, the *Enterprise Act* shifted power away from secured to unsecured creditors in order to promote value-maximization in insolvency sales. However, the results of Armour, Hsu and Walters' study show that although administration sales increased recoveries compared to receivership sales, the direct costs of administration were also significantly higher. In other words, unsecured creditors may be no better off under administration than receivership, despite the clear purpose of the *Enterprise Act* to improve unsecured creditors' positions. One possible explanation for these results is that administration costs were higher because insolvency practitioners were still familiarizing themselves with the new regime. Whatever the reasons may be, however, it is clear that secured creditors have enjoyed higher recoveries in administration sales on average.

[Reproduced by permission of Canadian Business Law Journal Inc and Thomson Reuters Canada Limited.]

D. Notes

1) Liquidating *CCAA* proceedings are functionally equivalent to receiverships. It therefore needs to be asked how secured creditors came to favour *CCAA* liquidations over receiverships. Undoubtedly, the Supreme Court of Canada's decision in *GMAC Commercial Credit Corp—Canada v TCT Logistics Inc*, 2006 SCC 35 (*TCT*), was a major factor in the shift. In the *TCT* case, the court held that provincial labour boards have the exclusive jurisdiction to determine whether a receiver is a successor employer, and that a court could not shield a receiver from prospective liabilities by declaring that a receiver is not a successor employer. "In one fell swoop, receivership became anathema" and so "insolvency practitioners set to work doing what they do best: they aggressively and creatively fashioned a new realization paradigm by looking to the *CCAA* as a means to leave a debtor in possession of its assets, yet ensuring that the principal secured creditors wielded significant control over the process."[6] The 2009 *BIA* amendments have reduced receivers' exposure to successor liability, but the protection is not comprehensive and so the new provisions have proved insufficient to halt the trend.

    Bish identifies various other advantages to secured creditors of *CCAA* liquidating proceedings, such as:

    - principal secured creditors have significant influence on the *CCAA* process and outcome, especially if also a DIP lender
    - principal secured creditors receive favourable treatment not available to other creditors, typically justified on the basis of their providing DIP financing and/or having the principal or only economic interest
    - debtor is often expressly precluded from compromising or challenging the claims of such secured creditors
    - there are numerous ways to structure affairs to ensure that nothing is done that is not in accordance with the principal secured creditors' wishes
    - often the principal secured creditors have an informational advantage over other creditors (including access to sale process and bid information not given to others, and having special access to the monitor)

---

6   Bish, above note 2 at 235–36.

- there is an enhanced ability for secured creditors to end up owning the assets of the debtor, including through credit-bidding[7]

2) The prevailing view that the *CCAA* was intended to facilitate going-concern restructuring to advance the public interest finds little support in the historical record. In the first full-length study of the *CCAA*, Professor Virginia Torrie draws on previously untapped historical documents to show that the Act was actually intended to be a remedy for large secured creditors, and represented the extension of receivership proceedings into federal insolvency law. The "public interest" value of the *CCAA* in the 1930s (to the extent that there was one) was to help avoid the insolvencies of financial institutions (for example, life insurance companies) by allowing them to restructure debtors to which they had extended large secured loans (usually in the form of bonds). Early 1930s *CCAAs* displayed little or no regard for stakeholders, such as workers, that are often at the centre of press coverage of modern *CCAAs*. As an extension of receivership proceedings, early *CCAAs* were typically conducted through liquidations and sales, leaving weaker creditors with claims against an empty estate. Torrie argues that the modern view of the *CCAA's* remedial objectives and the transition to a DIP restructuring regime is the product of ad hoc, case law developments in the 1980s and 1990s, which have assumed a path-dependent quality based on the chronic reproduction of case law precedents. She posits that the authoritativeness of the prevailing view of *CCAA* history stems from how often it has been—and continues to be—repeated; by academics, counsel, and judges. In this sense it is a social and political construct, rather than an accurate representation of history. In this line, the "recent trend" toward liquidating *CCAAs* represents the unconscious repetition of the Act's early history, showcasing the driving role of powerful creditors in *CCAA* proceedings, rather than a genuinely "new" direction in *CCAA* law. (See Virginia Torrie, *Reinventing Bankruptcy Law: A History of the Companies' Creditors Arrangement Act* (Toronto: University of Toronto Press, forthcoming).)

III. SCOPE OF THE CCAA

The application of the *CCAA* is subject to the following limitations (*CCAA*, ss 2(1), 3(1)):

1. the Act applies only if the debtor is a company or an income trust, but not if the debtor is a bank, telegraph company, an insurance company, or a company to which the *Trust and Loan Companies Act* applies;
2. total claims against the debtor or its affiliated companies must exceed $5 million; and
3. the debtor must be bankrupt or insolvent, or have committed an act of bankruptcy or be subject to winding-up proceedings under the *Winding-up and Restructuring Act*.

Although these provisions set out "limitations" on the *CCAA's* scope, courts have tended to adopt a purposive approach to interpreting the statute's provisions, and a fluid approach to interpreting restrictions in particular (see *Re Essar Steel Algoma Inc*, 2016 ONCA 138). It is important to realize that the caselaw includes many instances of judges exercising discretion to circumvent statutory restrictions, often in furtherance of the *CCAA's* remedial objectives. A recent example of this occurred in the Montréal, Maine and Atlantic Railway insolvency. This insolvency arose due to claims stemming from a train derailment in Lac-Mégantic, Quebec in

---

7   *Ibid* at 238–40.

2013. As the company in question operated a railway, it would seem to have been a situation where the *Canada Transportation Act* insolvency provisions clearly applied, as at the time the CCAA expressly excluded railway companies from its scope, a restriction that had been contained in the Act since it was first enacted (s 2(1)). Nevertheless, the debtor applied under the *CCAA*. In its initial application, the debtor submitted that despite operating a railway, it was not actually a "railway company," and therefore was not prevented from restructuring under the *CCAA* (see *Re Montréal, Maine & Atlantic Canada Co*, 2013 QCCS 4039). No party objected to this submission and the court allowed the company to apply under the Act, as the *CCAA* facilitated greater options for restructuring than the *Canada Transportation Act*. (See, further, Bernard Jolin and Serge Gaudet, "When a Railway Company is not really a 'Railway Company'" (2002) 19 *National Insolvency Review* 47). The result of such judicial interpretations is that the limitation against railway companies does not function as a limitation at all. Interestingly, in 2018, Parliament amended the *CCAA* to remove the limitation against railway companies filing under the Act.[8] Railway companies now appear to have a choice of whether to use the *Canada Transportation Act* or the *CCAA* to restructure their affairs. (See, further, Virginia Torrie, *Reinventing Bankruptcy Law: A History of the Companies' Creditors Arrangement Act* (Toronto: University of Toronto Press, forthcoming), ch 8, "Judicial Sanction of 'Tactical Devices.'")

A common theme in the fluid interpretation of *CCAA* provisions is that of expanding the Act's scope to instances in which a plain reading of the statute would suggest it should not apply. Notwithstanding the potential benefits of flexibility in corporate restructuring, this approach to interpreting *CCAA* provisions seems to depart from established methods of statutory interpretation. Purposive interpretation is meant to give effect to statutory provisions, not circumvent them. This principle, in turn, is based on the idea that the role of the legislature is to make changes to legislation, whereas the role of the courts is to interpret and apply legislation (not change it). In the context of the *CCAA* law, Parliament and the courts appear to have switched roles. Situating the locus of change in the courts and using statutory interpretation to effect changes in legislation poses challenges for democratic principles such as representative government, the rule of law, and the idea that statutes should convey clear expectations. The most striking example of this phenomenon is the absence of section 8 (titled "Scope of Act") from discussions about the scope of the *CCAA*. This is discussed by Professor Virginia Torrie in the following extract:

Virginia Torrie, *Reinventing Bankruptcy Law: A History of the Companies' Creditors Arrangement Act* (Toronto: University of Toronto Press, forthcoming) (footnotes omitted)

7

Purposive Interpretation and Pro-Active Judging: 1980s–1990s

. . . Although the CCAA makes no mention of the public interest, it does expressly address the interests of creditors:

> *Scope of Act*
> 8. <u>This Act is in extension and not in limitation of the provisions of any instrument now</u>
> <u>or hereafter existing governing the rights of creditors or any class of them</u> and has full

---

8   *Transportation Modernization Act*, SC 2018 c 10, s 89, amending *Companies' Creditors Arrangement Act*, RSC 1985, c C-36, s 2(1) "debtor company."

force and effect notwithstanding anything to the contrary contained in any such instrument. [Emphasis added.]

I have not found any reported decisions that substantively address the underlined portion of this provision, despite the fact that it dates back to the CCAA's original enactment, remains in the current version of the Act, and has been little changed since 1933.... Inexplicably the provision titled "Scope of Act" is missing from discussions about the scope of the CCAA.

A number of cases consider the latter part of section 8 in terms of the court's power to restrain the exercise of creditors' rights under "other instruments" in the course of CCAA proceedings. Courts have relied on this section almost exclusively to justify the staying of creditor-initiated proceedings, such as creditor remedies under the *Bank Act* or those specified in contract.

On its face this appears to serve as the type of limitation that this section prohibits. Yet reported cases do not reconcile this inconsistency. Judicial reasoning in cases such as *Chef Ready* (1990) fell back on "the broad public policy objectives of the C.C.A.A." instead as a sort of counter-balance to a limitation (in the form of the stay) of creditor remedies such as seizure and receivership. This seems to imply that insolvency law must curtail the rights of creditors (usually secured creditors) to some extent (if only through a delay on realization) in order to preserve the possibility that a "greater good" might be achieved through reorganization. In other words, it is the debtor, or a broad constituency of stakeholders, whose interests are extended, and not limited, by the Act.

On the other hand, viewing the CCAA as a bondholder remedy reconciles the two statements contained in section 8 of the Act. The CCAA *extended*, and *did not limit*, the provisions of an instrument governing the rights of bondholders by providing a statutory restructuring mechanism for their benefit that built on existing practices under majority provisions. Nevertheless, this section did not compel bondholders to use the Act if instead they preferred to use the majority provisions in their trust deed only, which many did. The portion of the provision that reads "any instrument now or hereafter existing" also speaks to the fact that the CCAA was enacted to address two specific problems: cover drafting defects in existing trust deeds and providing for the possibility of compliance with New York Stock Exchange listing requirements on a going-forward basis.

According to a bondholder-remedy understanding of the CCAA, the latter half of section 8 prohibited "contracting out" of the Act's ambit, and arguably also prohibited contracting around the "purpose" of the statute as expressed in the first part of the provision. Historically, the CCAA probably had to contain a provision against "contracting out" of its scope in order to satisfy US listing requirements....

Section 8 was the most appropriate starting point for determining the purposes of the CCAA [in the 1980s and 1990s]. When this provision is read in light of the trust deed provision, and the definitions of "company" and "debtor company," it established that the policy behind the Act was to facilitate reorganizations of companies for the benefit of their bondholders, and could only be applied when used as such.

[Reprinted by permission of the author and publisher.]

The following cases address the insolvency requirement.

Enterprise Capital Management Inc v Semi-Tech Corp (1999), 10 CBR (4th) 133 (Ont Sup Ct J) [*Semi-Tech*]

GROUND J:

[1] This application is brought by Enterprise Capital Management Inc. ("Enterprise"), on its own behalf and on behalf of funds managed by it, and with the support of other holders of Senior Secured Discount Notes (the "Notes") of Semi-Tech Corporation ("Semi-Tech") for, inter alia, an order declaring that Semi-Tech is a corporation to which the *Companies' Creditors Arrangement Act*, RSC 1985, Chapter C-36 (the "CCAA") and the *Business Corporations Act*, RSO 1990, Chapter B.16 (the "OBCA") apply, for an order authorizing the applicant to file a plan or plans of compromise or arrangement in respect of Semi-Tech under the CCAA and the OBCA, an order appointing KPMG Inc. ("KPMG") as monitor of Semi-Tech to assist Enterprise in developing the plan and to monitor the property of Semi-Tech and conduct the business and affairs of Semi-Tech until discharged by this Court. The application also seeks orders restricting the management and control of Semi-Tech and its operations by prohibiting Semi-Tech from making any payments to certain senior officers and directors, from voting any of the shares of Semi-Tech (Global) Company Limited ("Global") or the Singer Company NV ("Singer"), altering any material contracts between controlling parties and corporations in which Semi-Tech has a substantial equity interest, prohibiting Semi-Tech and its officers and directors from dealing with its assets or making payments to creditors except in the ordinary course of business and removing the current directors of Semi-Tech and appointing directors to be specified in the plan.

Background

[2] Semi-Tech is a holding company. Its common shares trade on the Toronto Stock Exchange. Its primary direct holdings are control blocks of two public companies, Singer and Global. Singer trades on the New York Stock Exchange and Global trades on the Hong Kong Stock Exchange. Both Singer and Global hold controlling interests in other public companies. For example, Singer holds approximately 80% of the common shares of G.M. Pfaff AG ("Pfaff") which shares are traded on the Frankfurt Stock Exchange. Global holds direct and indirect controlling interests in Akai Electric Co. Ltd. ("Akai") and Sansui Electric Co. Limited ("Sansui") whose shares are traded on the Tokyo, Osaka and Nagoya Stock Exchanges as well as Tomei International Holding Limited ("Tomei"), whose shares are traded on the Hong Kong Stock Exchange.

[3] As the financial statements of the companies are based on United States dollars, the dollar references herein are to United States dollars.

[4] Semi-Tech acquired its interest in Singer from Global in 1993. The acquisition price of $848 million was funded by a public issue of common shares raising $548 million and the issuance of the Notes, raising $300 million. In the 1993 Prospectus filed in connection with the issuance of its common shares and Notes, Semi-Tech described the purpose of its acquisition of Singer and described Global's plans for continued investment in turnaround opportunities in the developing word, particularly Asia. The terms of the Notes were negotiated with the original holders. The Notes provide that no payments of principal are due until 2003 and no interest is payable until 2001.

[5] The Notes are secured by a pledge of 25,300,000 shares of Singer, representing approximately 50% of the outstanding shares of Singer. The trust indenture dated

August 18, 1993 (the "Trust Indenture"), under which the Notes are secured, provides that, if an Event of Default were to occur, the Noteholders, acting through their trustee and in accordance with the terms set out in the Trust Indenture, could accelerate the maturity date of the Notes and enforce their security in the Singer shares.

[6] I am satisfied that the Applicant would be able to establish that Semi-Tech has breached certain of the covenants contained in the Trust Indenture. However, in that the appropriate notices of covenant defaults have not been given and the time periods allowed to remedy defaults following such notices have not elapsed, it is conceded that at this date there is no "Event of Default" as defined in the Trust Indenture.

[7] The most recent audited and unaudited financial statements for Semi-Tech, Singer and Global indicate substantial shareholders' equity in each company although the audited financial statements for the companies as at the end of their January, 1999 fiscal years are not yet issued and are not before this Court. The market prices of the shares of Singer and Global are depressed and the total market value of the shares of Singer and Global held by Semi-Tech as of the date of the application was approximately $120,000,000. The total principal amount of the Notes outstanding as of September 30, 1998 was approximately $531,000,000 and it is alleged by Enterprise that this amount has been increasing by approximately $5,000,000 per month since September, 1998 as the redemption price of the Notes gradually increases toward their ultimate maturity date. There are no other significant liabilities of Semi-Tech.

Submissions

[8] It is conceded that there is no evidence before this Court of Semi-Tech being unable to meet its obligations as they generally became due. It appears to be the position of Enterprise that Semi-Tech is insolvent under the test set out in clause (c) of the definition of "insolvent person" in subsection 2(1) of the *Bankruptcy and Insolvency Act*, RSC 1985, c. B-3 as amended (the "BIA"), which definition is applicable to defining a "debtor company" as being "insolvent" under section 2 of the CCAA. It is the position of Enterprise that, having regard to the market value of the shares of Singer and Global, which are effectively the only assets of Semi-Tech, they are not, in the aggregate, at a fair valuation or if disposed of at a fairly conducted sale under legal process, sufficient to enable payment of Semi-Tech's obligations due and accruing due.

[9] Enterprise submits that in determining obligations "due and accruing due" for purposes of the insolvency test in clause (c) of the definition of "insolvent person" in subsection 2(1) of the BIA, the Court should not limit its consideration to debts which have matured and that accordingly a debtor is insolvent if its present assets are insufficient to meet its liabilities at maturity. Enterprise relies on certain American authorities to support this proposition.

[10] Enterprise further takes the position that the principal amount of Notes outstanding are obligations due and accruing due because of the occurrence of defaults under certain covenants in the Trust Indenture which defaults have not been waived. Enterprise relies on an Abstract of issues discussed by the Emerging Issues Committee of the Canadian Institute of Chartered Accountants as contained in the CIAC Handbook which recommends that, if there has been a default under certain types of covenants in an instrument under which debt securities are outstanding and such default has not been waived or arrangements in place to cure the default, the principal amount of such debt securities should be included in current liabilities in a financial statement.

[11] Semi-Tech submits that the determination of whether the value of its property is sufficient to enable payment of its obligations due and accruing due is a "present exercise" and that the Court should not speculate as to whether the company will eventually be unable to meet its liabilities as they fall due. Semi-Tech states that its audited financial statements are appropriate evidence of solvency sufficient to rebut any allegations of insolvency, that such financial statements indicate substantial shareholders equity in Semi-Tech, that no reduction has been made by its auditors in the market value of the securities it holds and that the Notes have not been recorded as current liabilities as would be recommended by the CICA Handbook provision referred to above.

[12] It is the further submission of Semi-Tech that the market value of the shares of Singer and Global is not determinative of the value of the assets of Semi-Tech which are controlling interests in Singer and Global and which would attract a control block premium and that, to determine the value of such assets, would require expert evidence from underwriters or others at a trial. In addition, Semi-Tech submits that, to value such assets, one must have regard to the financial statements of Singer and Global. The financial statements of Singer and Global before this Court indicate a substantial shareholders' equity in each of Singer and Global which would indicate the value of the controlling interests in each of those companies. Semi-Tech also submits that the CICA Handbook is not definitive of the question of whether the Notes are obligations "due or accruing due" for purposes of the insolvency test and that the Notes are not now due or accruing due in that no payments of interest or principal are due until the years 2001 and 2003 respectively and no Event of Default has occurred under the Trust Indenture accelerating the maturity date of the Notes.

Reasons

[13] I accept the submission of Semi-Tech that to determine the fair valuation of Semi-Tech's assets, being principally the control blocks of shares of Singer and Global, one cannot simply multiply the number of shares by their current market prices. The Court must recognize that the control blocks, if disposed of by Semi-Tech, would attract control block premiums and that accordingly a determination of fair valuation would require expert evidence from underwriters or others as to the market value of such control blocks. It does seem to me however that, if the Notes represent obligations "due and accruing due" in an amount in excess of $531,000,000, it is highly unlikely that control block premiums would increase the fair valuation of such control blocks from the value of $120,000,000 based on current share prices to anything approaching $531,000,000.

[14] I am not satisfied that one can rely upon the fact that the financial statements of Semi-Tech indicate a shareholders equity to rebut a finding of insolvency based on a comparison of fair valuation of assets to the amount of obligations due and accruing due. Financial statements are based upon historic figures and on a going concern assumption and do not necessarily reflect what would result if the company as of this date sold all its assets at a fair valuation and was required to pay all of its obligations due and accruing due. In *Lin v Lee* (June 27, 1996), Doc. Vancouver C944487 (BCSC), Coultas J referred to this assumption as stated in the CICA Handbook.

> An assumption underlying the preparation of financial statements in accordance with generally accepted accounting principles is that the enterprise will be able to realize assets and discharge liabilities in the normal course of business for the foreseeable future. This is commonly referred to as the going concern assumption.

[15] It therefore becomes necessary to determine whether the principal amount of the Notes constitutes an obligation "due or accruing due" as of date of this application.

[16] There is a paucity of helpful authority on the meaning of "accruing due" for purposes of a definition of insolvency. Historically in 1933, in *P Lyall & Sons Construction Co v Baker*, [1933] OR 286 (Ont. CA), the Ontario Court of Appeal, in determining a question of set-off under the Dominion *Winding Up Act* had to determine whether the amount claimed as a set-off was a debt due or accruing due to the company in liquidation for purposes of that Act. Marsten JA at pages 292–293 quoted from Moss JA in *Mail Printing Co v Clarkson* (1898), 25 OAR 1 (Ont. CA) at page 8:

> A debt is defined to be a sum of money which is certainly, and at all event, payable without regard to the fact whether it be payable now or at a future time. And an accruing debt is a debt not yet actually payable, but a debt which is represented by an existing obligation; per Lindley LJ in *Webb v Stenton* (1883) 11 QBD at p. 529.

[17] Whatever relevance such definition may have had for purposes of dealing with claims by and against companies in liquidation under the old winding up legislation, it is apparent to me that it should not be applied to definitions of insolvency. To include every debt payable at some future date in "accruing due" for the purposes of insolvency tests would render numerous corporations, with long term debt due over a period of years in the future and anticipated to be paid out of future income, "insolvent" for purposes of the BIA and therefore the CCAA. For the same reason, I do not accept the statement quoted in the Enterprise factum from the decision of the Bankruptcy Court for the Southern District of New York in *Centennial Textiles Inc, Re*, 220 BR 165 (USNYDC 1998) that "if the present saleable value of assets are less than the amount required to pay existing debt as they mature, the debtor is insolvent." In my view the obligations, which are to be measured against the fair valuation of a company's property as being obligations due and accruing due, must be limited to obligations currently payable or properly chargeable to the accounting period during which the test is being applied as, for example, a sinking fund payment due within the current year. Black's Law Dictionary defines "accrued liability" as "an obligation or debt which is properly chargeable in a given accounting period but which is not yet paid or payable." The principal amount of the Notes is neither due nor accruing due in this sense.

[18] In addition, even if the reference in the CICA Handbook is applicable to the covenant defaults alleged by Enterprise, this simply means that it is recommended that, in applicable situations for purposes of preparing a financial statement, the accountants should show long term debt as a current liability. As stated above, I do not think reference should be made to financial statements for the purpose of determining whether a company is "insolvent" as that term is defined in the BIA and applicable to the CCAA. In the case at bar, where the Notes do not mature until 2003, there has been no Event of Default and no acceleration of the maturity of the Notes, the fact that accountants may, in certain circumstances of a covenant default, determine to show long term debt as a current liability in the financial statements, presumably with some explanatory note, is not in my view determinative of such debt being an obligation "accruing due" for purposes of the insolvency test.

[19] Accordingly, on the basis of the evidence now before this Court, I am unable to conclude that Semi-Tech is insolvent within the meaning of clause (c) of the definition of "insolvent person" in subsection 2(1) of the BIA which definition is applicable to the CCAA.

[20] Although it is moot in view of my finding that Semi-Tech is not insolvent within the meaning of clause (c) of subsection 2(1) of the BIA, I wish to comment on certain

other aspects of this application. Even where the Court has found a company to be insolvent, the Court must in exercising its discretion under the CCAA, determine whether in all the circumstances it is appropriate that an order be made pursuant to the CCAA. In making such determination, the Court must have regard to the interests of all the stakeholders, not only those represented before the Court on the application, and must take into account any public interest involved.

[21] I adopt the statement of Blair J in his November 27, 1998 endorsement in the application of *Skydome Corp, Re* [(November 27, 1998), Blair J (Ont. Gen. Div.)] under the CCAA:

> Thus there is a broader public dimension which must be considered and weighed in the balance on this Application as well as the interests of those most directly affected: see *Anvil Range Mining Corporation*, unreported decision of the Ontario Court of Justice, General Division, August 20, 1998. As was stated in that case:
>
> > The court in its supervisory capacity has a broader mandate. In a receivership such as this one which works well into the social and economic fabric of a territory, that mandate must encompass having an eye for the social consequences of the receivership too. These interests cannot override the lawful interests of secured creditors ultimately but they can and must be weighed in the balance as the process works its way through.

The *Anvil Range* case concerned a CCAA proceeding which had been turned into a receivership but the same principles apply in my view to a case such as this.

[22] In addition the Court must be conscious of the purpose and intent of the CCAA. The statute was originally enacted in 1933 to provide for an alternative to bankruptcy or liquidation of companies in financial difficulties during the depression years and for court sanction of plans of compromise and arrangement between companies and their creditors which would permit a restructuring and the continued operation of the companies' businesses and continued production and employment by the companies. In the Houlden and Morawetz annotated Bankruptcy and Insolvency Act at page 10A-2, the authors describe the purpose and intent of the CCAA as follows:

> The CCAA has a broad remedial purpose giving a debtor an opportunity to find a way out of financial difficulties short of bankruptcy, foreclosure or the seizure of assets through receivership proceedings. It allows the debtor to find a plan that will enable him to meet the demands of his creditors through refinancing with new lending, equity financing or the sale of the business as a going concern. This alternative may well give the creditors of all classes a larger return and protect the jobs of the company's employees: *Diemaster Tool Inc v Skvortsoff (Trustee of)* (1991), 3 CBR (3d) 133 (Ont. Gen. Div.).

[23] It is usual on initial applications under the CCAA for the applicant to submit to the Court at least a general outline of the type of plan of compromise and arrangement between the company and its creditors proposed by the applicant. The application now before this Court is somewhat of a rarity in that the application is brought by an applicant representing a group of creditors and not by the company itself as is the usual case. Enterprise has submitted that it is not in a position to submit an outline of a plan to the Court in that it lacks sufficient information and has been unable to obtain such information from Semi-Tech. Enterprise points out that, in the usual case, the application is brought by the company, the company has all the necessary information at hand and

has usually had the assistance of a firm which is the proposed monitor and which has worked with the company in preparing an outline of a plan.

[24] I have some difficulty with the submission of Enterprise that it does not have sufficient information available to submit an outline of a plan. Semi-Tech is a public company, as are Singer and Global and a number of the subsidiaries of Singer and Global, and I would have thought that sufficient information is easily accessible by Enterprise to prepare a general outline of what compromises or arrangements are proposed as between Semi-Tech and its creditors and in particular what is proposed as to either a disposition of the shares of Singer and/or Global or a restructuring of either of those companies. There is no such information before the Court and no indication that Semi-Tech will be involved in the preparation of a draft plan to be put before the Court other than as a source of information.

[25] In the absence of any indication that Enterprise proposes a plan which would consist of some compromise or arrangement between Semi-Tech and its creditors and permit the continued operation of Semi-Tech and its subsidiaries in some restructured form, it appears to me that it would be inappropriate to make any order pursuant to the CCAA. If the Noteholders intend simply to liquidate the assets of Semi-Tech and distribute the proceeds, it would appear that they could do so by proceeding under the Trust Indenture on the basis of the alleged covenant defaults, accelerating the maturity date of the Notes, realizing on their security in the shares of Singer and recovering any balance due on the Notes by the appointment of a receiver or otherwise.

[26] If any such steps were taken by the Noteholders, Semi-Tech could at that time bring its own application pursuant to the CCAA outlining a restructuring plan which would permit the continued operation of the company and its subsidiaries and be in conformity with the purpose and intent of the legislation. I am conscious however that, although the evidence before this Court on this point was somewhat inconclusive, the application is alleged to be brought with the consent of an informal committee of Noteholders representing 52.3% in principal amount of the outstanding Notes and that the holder of a further 20% in principal amount of outstanding Notes is alleged to support the application. In view of this, it would appear unlikely that any plan brought forward by Semi-Tech would receive the approval of creditors required by the CCAA....

Application dismissed.

Re Stelco Inc (2004), 48 CBR (4th) 299 (Ont Sup Ct J) [*Stelco*]

FARLEY J:

[1] As argued this motion by Locals 1005, 5328 and 8782 United Steel Workers of America (collectively "Union") to rescind the initial order and dismiss the application of Stelco Inc. ("Stelco") and various of its subsidiaries (collectively "Sub Applicants") for access to the protection and process of the *Companies' Creditors Arrangement Act* ("CCAA") was that this access should be denied on the basis that Stelco was not a "debtor company" as defined in s. 2 of the CCAA because it was not insolvent....

[11] The Union, supported by the International United Steel Workers of America ("International"), indicated that if certain of the obligations of Stelco were taken into account in the determination of insolvency, then a very good number of large Canadian corporations would be able to make an application under the CCAA. I am of the view that this concern can be addressed as follows. The test of insolvency is to be determined on its

own merits, not on the basis that an otherwise technically insolvent corporation should not be allowed to apply. However, if a technically insolvent corporation were to apply and there was no material advantage to the corporation and its stakeholders (in other words, a pressing need to restructure), then one would expect that the court's discretion would be judicially exercised against granting CCAA protection and ancillary relief. In the case of Stelco, it is recognized, as discussed above, that it is in crisis and in need of restructuring—which restructuring, if it is insolvent, would be best accomplished within a CCAA proceeding. Further, I am of the view that the track record of CCAA proceedings in this country demonstrates a healthy respect for the fundamental concerns of interested parties and stakeholders. I have consistently observed that much more can be achieved by negotiations outside the courtroom where there is a reasonable exchange of information, views and the exploration of possible solutions and negotiations held on a without prejudice basis than likely can be achieved by resorting to the legal combative atmosphere of the courtroom. A mutual problem requires a mutual solution. The basic interest of the CCAA is to rehabilitate insolvent corporations for the benefit of all stakeholders. To do this, the cause(s) of the insolvency must be fixed on a long term viable basis so that the corporation may be turned around. It is not achieved by positional bargaining in a tug of war between two parties, each trying for a larger slice of a defined size pie; it may be achieved by taking steps involving shorter term equitable sacrifices and implementing sensible approaches to improve productivity to ensure that the pie grows sufficiently for the long term to accommodate the reasonable needs of the parties....

[13] ... On a practical basis, I would note that all too often corporations will wait too long before applying, at least this was a significant problem in the early 1990s. In *Re Inducon Development Corp* (1991), 8 CBR (3d) 306 (Ont. Gen. Div.), I observed:

> Secondly, CCAA is designed to be remedial; it is not, however, designed to be preventative. CCAA should not be the last gasp of a dying company; it should be implemented, if it is to be implemented, at a stage prior to the death throe.

[14] It seems to me that the phrase "death throe" could be reasonably replaced with "death spiral." In *Re Cumberland Trading Inc* (1994), 23 CBR (3d) 225 (Ont. Gen. Div.), I went on to expand on this at p. 228:

> I would also observe that all too frequently debtors wait until virtually the last moment, the last moment, or in some cases, beyond the last moment before even beginning to think about reorganizational (and the attendant support that any successful reorganization requires from the creditors). I noted the lamentable tendency of debtors to deal with these situations as "last gasp" desperation moves in *Re Inducon Development Corp* (1992), 8 CBR (3d) 308 (Ont. Gen. Div.). To deal with matters on this basis minimizes the chances of success, even if "success" may have been available with earlier spade work.

[15] I have not been able to find in the CCAA reported cases any instance where there has been an objection to a corporation availing itself of the facilities of the CCAA on the basis of whether the corporation was insolvent. Indeed, as indicated above, the major concern here has been that an applicant leaves it so late that the timetable of necessary steps may get impossibly compressed. That is not to say that there have not been objections by parties opposing the application on various other grounds. Prior to the 1992 amendments, there had to be debentures (plural) issued pursuant to a trust deed; I recall that in *Nova Metal Products Inc v Comiskey (Trustee of)*, (1990), 1 CBR (3d) 101; 1 OR (3d) 280 (CA), the initial application was rejected in the morning because there

had only been one debenture issued but another one was issued prior to the return to court that afternoon. This case stands for the general proposition that the CCAA should be given a large and liberal interpretation. I should note that there was in *Enterprise Capital Management Inc v Semi-Tech Corp* (1999), 10 CBR (4th) 133 (Ont. SCJ) a determination that in a creditor application, the corporation was found not to be insolvent, but see below as to BIA test (c) my views as to the correctness of this decision....

[24] I note in particular that the (b), (c) and (d) aspects of the definition of "debtor company" all refer to other statutes, including the BIA; (a) does not. Section 12 of the CCAA defines "claims" with reference over to the BIA (and otherwise refers to the BIA and the *Winding-Up and Restructuring Act*). It seems to me that there is merit in considering that the test for insolvency under the CCAA may differ somewhat from that under the BIA, so as to meet the special circumstances of the CCAA and those corporations which would apply under it. In that respect, I am mindful of the above discussion regarding the time that is usually and necessarily (in the circumstances) taken in a CCAA reorganization restructuring which is engaged in coming up with a plan of compromise and arrangement. The BIA definition would appear to have been historically focussed on the question of bankruptcy—and not reorganization of a corporation under a proposal since before 1992, secured creditors could not be forced to compromise their claims, so that in practice there were no reorganizations under the former *Bankruptcy Act* unless all secured creditors voluntarily agreed to have their secured claims compromised. The BIA definition then was essentially useful for being a pre-condition to the "end" situation of a bankruptcy petition or voluntary receiving order where the upshot would be a realization on the bankrupt's assets (not likely involving the business carried on—and certainly not by the bankrupt). Insolvency under the BIA is also important as to the Paulian action events (eg., fraudulent preferences, settlements) as to the conduct of the debtor *prior* to the bankruptcy; similarly as to the question of provincial preference legislation. Reorganization under a plan or proposal, on the contrary, is with a general objective of the applicant continuing to exist, albeit that the CCAA may also be used to have an orderly disposition of the assets and undertaking in whole or in part.

[25] It seems to me that given the time and steps involved in a reorganization, and the condition of insolvency perforce requires an expanded meaning under the CCAA. Query whether the definition under the BIA is now sufficient in that light for the allowance of sufficient time to carry through with a realistically viable proposal within the maximum of six months allowed under the BIA? I think it sufficient to note that there would not be much sense in providing for a rehabilitation program of restructuring/ reorganization under either statute if the entry test was that the applicant could not apply until a rather late stage of its financial difficulties with the rather automatic result that in situations of complexity of any material degree, the applicant would not have the financial resources sufficient to carry through to hopefully a successful end. This would indeed be contrary to the renewed emphasis of Parliament on "rescues" as exhibited by the 1992 and 1997 amendments to the CCAA and the BIA.

[26] Allow me now to examine whether Stelco has been successful in meeting the onus of demonstrating with credible evidence on a common sense basis that it is insolvent within the meaning required by the CCAA in regard to the interpretation of "debtor company" in the context and within the purpose of that legislation.... It seems to me that the CCAA test of insolvency advocated by Stelco and which I have determined is a proper interpretation is that the BIA definition of (a), (b) or (c) of insolvent

person is acceptable with the caveat that as to (a), a financially troubled corporation is insolvent if it is reasonably expected to run out of liquidity within reasonable proximity of time as compared with the time reasonably required to implement a restructuring. That is, there should be a reasonable cushion, which cushion may be adjusted and indeed become in effect an encroachment depending upon reasonable access to DIP between financing. In the present case, Stelco accepts the view of the Union's affiant, Michael Mackey of Deloitte and Touche that it will otherwise run out of funding by November 2004. . . .

[29] In my view, the Union's position that Stelco is not insolvent under BIA (a) because it has not entirely used up its cash and cash facilities (including its credit line), that is, it [has] not yet as of January 29, 2004 run out of liquidity conflates inappropriately the (a) test with the (b) test. The Union's view would render the (a) test necessarily as being redundant. . . .

[40] It seems to me that if the BIA (a) test is restrictively dealt with (as per my question to Union counsel as to how far in the future should one look on a prospective basis being answered "24 hours") then Stelco would not be insolvent under that test. However, I am of the view that that would be unduly restrictive and a proper contextual and purposive interpretation to be given when it is being used for a restructuring purpose even under BIA would be to see whether there is a reasonably foreseeable (at the time of filing) expectation that there is a looming liquidity condition or crisis which will result in the applicant running out of "cash" to pay its debts as they generally become due in the future without the benefit of the stay and ancillary protection and procedure by court authorization pursuant to an order. I think this is the more appropriate interpretation of BIA (a) test in the context of a reorganization or "rescue" as opposed to a threshold to bankruptcy consideration or a fraudulent preferences proceeding. On that basis, I would find Stelco insolvent from the date of filing. Even if one were not to give the latter interpretation to the BIA (a) test, clearly for the above reasons and analysis, if one looks at the meaning of "insolvent" within the context of a CCAA reorganization or rescue solely, then of necessity, the time horizon must be such that the liquidity crisis would occur in the sense of running out of "cash" but for the grant of the CCAA order. On that basis Stelco is certainly insolvent given its limited cash resources unused, its need for a cushion, its rate of cash burn recently experienced and anticipated.

[41] What about the BIA (c) test which may be roughly referred to as an assets compared with obligations test. See *New Quebec Reglan Mines Ltd v Blok-Andersen*, [1993] OJ No. 727 (Gen. Div.) as to fair value and fair market valuation. The Union observed that there was no intention by Stelco to wind itself up or proceed with a sale of some or all of its assets and undertaking and therefore some of the liabilities which Stelco and Stephen took into account would not crystallize. However, as I discussed at the time of the hearing, the (c) test is what one might reasonably call or describe as an "artificial" or notional/hypothetical test. It presumes certain things which are in fact not necessarily contemplated to take place or to be involved. . . .

[50] To my view the preferable interpretation to be given to "sufficient to enable payment of all his obligations, due and accruing due" is to be determined in the context of this test as a whole. What is being put up to satisfy those obligations is the debtor's assets and undertaking *in total*; in other words, the debtor in essence is taken as having sold everything. There would be no residual assets and undertaking to pay off any obligations which would not be encompassed by the phrase "all of his obligations, due and accruing due." Surely, there cannot be "orphan" obligations which are left hanging

unsatisfied. It seems to me that the intention of "due and accruing due" was to cover off all obligations of whatever nature or kind and leave nothing in limbo. . . .

[69] In the end result, I have concluded on the balance of probabilities that Stelco is insolvent and therefore it is a "debtor company" as at the date of filing and entitled to apply for the CCAA initial order. My conclusion is that (i) BIA test (c) strongly shows Stelco is insolvent; (ii) BIA test (a) demonstrates, to a less certain but sufficient basis, an insolvency; and (iii) the "new" CCAA test again strongly supports the conclusion of insolvency. I am further of the opinion that I properly exercised my discretion in granting Stelco and the Sub Applicants the initial order on January 29, 2004 and I would confirm that as of the present date with effect on the date of filing. The Union's motion is therefore dismissed.

Motion dismissed.

Leave to appeal in the *Stelco* case was refused both by the Ontario Court of Appeal (*Re Stelco*, [2004] OJ No 1903) and the Supreme Court of Canada (*Re Stelco*, [2004] SCCA No 336).

The decisions in *Semi-Tech* and *Stelco* appear to be contradictory. Note, however, that in *Semi-Tech*, the CCAA proceedings were initiated by a creditor. In *Stelco*, the proceedings were initiated by the debtor itself. The parties who initiated the proceedings may provide a basis for distinguishing the two cases. *Stelco* was followed in *Re Priszm Income Fund*, 2011 ONSC 2061 and *Re Lemare Holdings Ltd*, 2012 BCSC 1591.

IV. THE INITIAL FILING

CCAA proceedings are initiated by means of an application to the court by the debtor, a creditor, or the debtor's trustee in bankruptcy or liquidator: *CCAA*, sections 4 and 5 ("the initial application"). The application may be made to a court in the province within which the company has its head office or chief place of business. If the company has neither, then the application may be made in the province within which any of the assets of the company are situated.

An application for an initial order under the *CCAA* can be made on an *ex parte* basis. This may be useful if there is a real prospect that creditors will attempt to exercise their enforcement remedies against the debtor's assets before the court hears the matter. Sometimes the initial application is made only with notice to the major creditors if it is impracticable to identify and notify all the creditors. A projected cash-flow statement and copies of financial statements prepared in the prior year must be submitted with an application for an initial order.

The initial application usually requests an order containing the following components:

- abridging service of notice of the application;
- declaring the debtor company to be one to which the *CCAA* applies;
- authorizing the debtor company to continue its business operations and continue in possession of its property;
- staying proceedings against the debtor company;
- appointing a monitor;
- authorizing the debtor company to obtain interim financing (DIP financing);
- indemnifying the debtor company's directors and officers for liability that they incur following the date of the initial order;
- creating charges against the property that secure the administrative expenses, the interim financing, and the indemnification of directors and officers and that give priority over all other security interests and encumbrances;

- authorizing the debtor company to file a plan of arrangement; and
- permitting interested parties to apply to the court for variation or amendment of the order (a "comeback" clause).

CCAA, section 11.02, governs the court's power to order a stay of proceedings. The stay of proceedings provided for in the initial order cannot exceed thirty days. The applicant will therefore need to bring a subsequent application before the court for a stay of proceedings of a longer duration. This permits parties affected by the initial order to have an opportunity to express their views concerning the eligibility of the debtor or the appropriateness of the order. Under *CCAA*, section 23, the monitor must notify every known creditor who has a claim of more than $1,000 against the company and advise them of the order.

In a number of provinces, insolvency practitioners, working in conjunction with the courts, have developed an initial-order template. The aim is to both expedite the commencement of proceedings and minimize the risk of prejudice to interested parties who may not have had an opportunity to read the proposed order or make submissions on it. Parties are free to vary the template to suit their circumstances, but all variations must be blacklined for easy identification by other parties and the court. The Ontario initial-order template was developed by the Commercial List User's Committee. The Commercial List is a specialized commercial court within the Ontario Superior Court of Justice in Toronto, which deals exclusively with commercial and insolvency matters. The Commercial List Users' Committee comprises judges, practitioners, and court administrators. There are similar initial-order templates in Alberta, British Columbia, Quebec, and Saskatchewan. The current version of the Ontario initial-order template can be viewed at www.ontariocourts.ca/scj/files/forms/com/intitial-order-CCAA-EN.doc. In *Sproule v Nortel Networks Corporation*, 2009 ONCA 833, the Ontario Court of Appeal confirmed that the *CCAA* stay provisions apply in liquidation proceedings, as well as in restructuring proceedings. The court said (at para 46):

> It appears that the company will not be restructured, but instead its assets will be sold. It is necessary to continue operations in order to maintain maximum value for this process to achieve the highest prices and therefore the best outcome for all stakeholders. It is true that the basis for the very broad stay power has traditionally been expressed as a necessary aspect of the restructuring process, leading to a plan of arrangement for the newly restructured entity. However, we see no reason in the present circumstances why the same analysis cannot apply during a sale process that requires the business to be carried on as a going concern.

CCAA, section 11.02(3), provides that, to qualify for a stay order, the applicant must satisfy the court that the order is "appropriate" and, in the case of an application other than an initial application, that "the applicant has acted, and is acting, in good faith and with due diligence." The court may rule against the applicant on the appropriateness ground if there is evidence suggesting that the restructuring has no reasonable chance of success: see *Bargain Harold's Discount*, extracted below. *San Francisco Gifts*, also extracted below, addresses the meaning of "good faith."

Bargain Harold's Discount Ltd v Paribas Bank of Canada (1992), 7 OR (3d) 362 (Ont Ct J (Gen Div))

> AUSTIN J: This is an application by Bargain Harold's Discount Limited for an order under s. 11 of the *Companies' Creditors Arrangement Act*, RSC 1985, c. C-36 [the CCAA or the Act]. It is opposed by a number of secured creditors. Paribas is the first secured creditor

in terms of priority. It has either commenced an action or intends to do so and in that action has brought a motion for the appointment of a receiver and manager....

The jurisprudence is clear that if it is obvious that no plan will be found acceptable to the required percentages of creditors, then the application should be refused. The fact that Paribas, the Royal Bank and K Mart now say there is no plan that they would approve, does not put an end to the inquiry. All affected constituencies must be considered, including secured, preferred and unsecured creditors, employees, landlords, shareholders, and the public generally....

As to the degree of persuasion required, Doherty JA in *Elan [Corp v Comiskey (Trustee of)* (1990), 1 OR (3d) 289 (CA)] said at p. 316 OR:

> I agree that the feasibility of the plan is a relevant and significant factor to be considered in determining whether to order a meeting of creditors: Edwards, "Re-organizations under the Companies' Creditors Arrangement Act," supra, at pp. 594–95. I would not, however, impose a heavy burden on the debtor company to establish the likelihood of ultimate success from the outset. As the Act will often be the last refuge for failing companies, it is to be expected that many of the proposed plans of re-organization will involve variables and contingencies which will make the plan's ultimate acceptability to the creditors and the court very uncertain at the time the initial application is made.

In *Ultracare Management Inc et al v Gammon et al* (1990), 1 OR (3d) 321, (Ont Ct J (Gen Div)), Hoilett J, at p. 330f, suggests that the test is whether the plan, or in the present case, any plan, "has a probable chance of acceptance."

These two standards are in conflict, *Ultracare* requiring the probability of success, and *Elan* requiring something less. Having regard to the nature of the legislation, I prefer the test enunciated by Doherty JA in *Elan.* In *First Treasury Financial Inc v Cango Petroleums Inc* (1991), 3 CBR (3d) 232 (Ont Ct J (Gen Div)), at p. 238, I expressed the view that the statute required "a reasonable chance" that a plan would be accepted.

A court must be concerned with the nature of the evidence presented in cases such as this. The applicant's main affidavit was sworn on February 25, Paribas' affidavit on the 26th, and the applicant's in response on the 26th. There has been no opportunity for cross-examination. As a consequence, there is a very heavy responsibility on counsel and the court must be mindful of the frailties of the evidence.

Section 6 of the CCAA requires approval of the plan or arrangement by a majority in number representing three-fourths in value of the creditors. Where there are different classes of creditors, the section requires a majority in number representing three-fourths in value of the creditors in each class. Having regard to the evidence presented and its shortcomings, I am unable to conclude that there is any reasonable prospect of the applicant being able to devise a plan or arrangement which would meet the approval requirements of s. 6 of the Act. Amongst the most important elements in reaching this decision is the fact that the applicant still does not know the precise nature of the problem which brought about its present financial circumstances. According to its own auditors, the cause or causes may never be known. There is also the fact, probably related to this first element, that the applicant has no specific idea how its operation can be salvaged, other than to suggest "downsizing." There is no reason to believe that that downsizing can be done any more efficiently by the applicant than by a receiver.

Next is the need to borrow still more money from the Royal Bank in order to continue in business at all. The fact that the Royal Bank may be paid out on March 6 is irrelevant. In order to carry on during the proposed stay period, the applicant requires funds.

No source other than the Royal Bank, or in its shoes, K Mart, has been suggested. More to the point, perhaps, no offer has been made by QECC or by CCFL, both of whom are substantial shareholders and both of whom, it was argued, are in a position to assist in refinancing.

Another factor is the failed or abandoned attempt to raise $15 million in October 1992. Yet another is the complete loss of confidence in the management of the company. To this is added the failure of the applicant to suggest who the new management might be.

The only proposal suggested by way of an alternative to a CCAA order was the appointment of a receiver and manager. As in *Cango*, there is no reason to believe that if a receiver were appointed, any more unemployment would result than if the present applicant were left in charge.

At the conclusion of the hearing of this matter on February 26, I indicated my intention to reserve my decision. Counsel for the applicant indicated that as its financial difficulties were now a matter of public knowledge, some order should be made to protect the company pending my decision. As counsel were unable to agree on anything, I made an interim order under s. 11 of the CCAA and appointed Price Waterhouse monitor for the interim period. That order and monitorship is now terminated.

An order will go dismissing the CCAA application. An order will also go appointing Price Waterhouse as receiver and manager of the applicant, effective immediately. If there is any difficulty in settling the form of order, I may be spoken to. Although the question was not raised during the course of argument, the order should confer upon the receiver the power to make an assignment in bankruptcy should it be so advised. A major asset of Bargain Harold's consists of leases. A trustee in bankruptcy has much wider powers to deal with leases than does a receiver.

Application dismissed.

Re San Francisco Gifts Ltd, 2005 ABQB 91, 10 CBR (5th) 275

TOPOLINSKI J:

INTRODUCTION

[1] The San Francisco group of companies (San Francisco) obtained *Companies' Creditors Arrangement Act* (CCAA) protection on January 7, 2000 (Initial Order). Key to that protection was the requisite stay of proceedings that gives a debtor company breathing room to formulate a plan of arrangement. The stay was extended three times thereafter with the expectation that the entire CCAA process would be completed by February 7th, 2005. That date was not met. Accordingly, San Francisco now applies to have the stay extended to June 30, 2005.

[2] A small group of landlords opposes the motion on the basis of San Francisco's recent guilty plea to *Copyright Act* offenses and the sentencing judge's description of San Francisco's conduct as: "... a despicable fraud on the public. Not only not insignificant but bordering on a massive scale ...." The landlords suggest that this precludes any possibility of the company having acted in "good faith" and therefore having met the statutory prerequisite to an extension. Further, they contend that extending the stay would bring the administration of justice into disrepute.

[3] San Francisco acknowledges that its conduct was stupid, offensive and dangerous. That said, it contends that it already has been sanctioned and that it has "paid its

debt to society." It argues that subjecting it to another consequence in this proceeding would be akin to double jeopardy. Apart from the obvious consequential harm to the company itself, San Francisco expresses concern that its creditors might be disadvantaged if it is forced into bankruptcy.

[4] While there has been some delay in moving this matter forward towards the creditor vote, this delay is primarily attributable to the time it took San Francisco to deal with leave to appeal my classification decision of September 28, 2004. Despite the opposing landlords' mild protestations to the contrary, it is evident that the company has acted with due diligence. The real focus of this application is on the meaning and scope of the term "good faith" as that term is used in s. 11(6) of the CCAA, and on whether San Francisco's conduct renders it unworthy of the protective umbrella of the Act in its restructuring efforts. It also raises questions about the role of a supervising court in CCAA proceedings.

BACKGROUND

[5] San Francisco operates a national chain of novelty goods stores from its head office in Edmonton, Alberta. It currently has 62 locations and approximately 400 employees.

[6] The group of companies is comprised of the operating company, San Francisco Gifts Ltd., and a number of hollow nominee companies. The operating company holds all of the group's assets. It is 100 percent owned by Laurier Investments Corp., which in turn is 100 percent owned by Barry Slawsky (Slawsky), the driving force behind the companies.

[7] Apart from typical priority challenges in insolvency matters, this proceeding has been punctuated by a series of challenges to the process and its continuation, led primarily by a group of landlords that includes the opposing landlords.

[8] On December 30, 2004, San Francisco pleaded guilty to nine charges under s. 42 of the *Copyright Act*, which creates offences for a variety of conduct constituting wilful copyright infringement. The evidence in that proceeding established that:

(a) An investigation by the St. John's, Newfoundland, Fire Marshall, arising from a complaint about a faulty lamp sold by San Francisco, led to the discovery that the lamp bore a counterfeit safety certification label commonly called a "UL" label. The RCMP conducted searches of San Francisco stores across the country, its head office, and a warehouse, which turned up other counterfeit electrical UL labels as well as counterfeit products bearing the symbols of trademark holders of Playboy, Marvel Comics and others.

(b) Counterfeit UL labels were found in the offices of Slawsky and San Francisco's Head of Sales. There was also a fax from "a Chinese location" found in Slawsky's office that threatened that a report to Canadian authorities about the counterfeit safety labels would be made if payment was not forthcoming.

(c) *Copyright Act* charges against Slawsky were withdrawn when San Francisco entered a plea of guilty to the charges.

(d) The sentencing judge accepted counsels' joint submission that a $150,000.00 fine would be appropriate. In passing sentence, he condemned the company's conduct, particularly as it related to the counterfeit labels, expressing grave concern for the safety of unknowing consumers.

(e) San Francisco was co-operative during the RCMP investigation and the Crown's prosecution of the case.

(f) San Francisco had been convicted of similar offences in 1998.

[9] Judge Stevens-Guille's condemnation of San Francisco's conduct was the subject of local and national newspaper coverage.

[10] The company paid the $150,000.00 fine from last year's profits.

ANALYSIS

. . .

[11] The well established remedial purpose of the CCAA is to facilitate the making of a compromise or arrangement by an insolvent company with its creditors to the end that the company is able to stay in business. The premise is that this will result in a benefit to the company, its creditors and employees. The Act is to be given a large and liberal interpretation.

[12] The court's jurisdiction under s. 11(6) [now section 11.02(3)] to extend a stay of proceedings (beyond the initial 30 days of a CCAA order) is preconditioned on the applicant satisfying it that:
(a) circumstances exist that make such an order appropriate; and
(b) the applicant has acted, and is acting, in good faith and with due diligence.

[13] Whether it is "appropriate" to make the order is not dependant on finding "due diligence" and "good faith." Indeed, refusal on that basis can be the result of an independent or interconnected finding. Stays of proceedings have been refused where the company is hopelessly insolvent; has acted in bad faith; or where the plan of arrangement is unworkable, impractical or essentially doomed to failure. . . .

[28] The court's role during the stay period has been described as a supervisory one, meant to: ". . . preserve the *status quo* and to move the process along to the point where an arrangement or compromise is approved or it is evident that the attempt is doomed to failure." That is not to say that the supervising judge is limited to a myopic view of balance sheets, scheduling of creditors' meetings and the like. On the contrary, this role requires attention to changing circumstances and vigilance in ensuring that a delicate balance of interests is maintained.

[29] Although the supervising judge's main concern centres on actions affecting stakeholders in the proceeding, she is also responsible for protecting the institutional integrity of the CCAA courts, preserving their public esteem, and doing equity. She cannot turn a blind eye to corporate conduct that could affect the public's confidence in the CCAA process but must be alive to concerns of offensive business practices that are of such gravity that the interests of stakeholders in the proceeding must yield to those of the public at large.

CONCLUSIONS

[30] While "good faith" in the context of stay applications is generally focused on the debtor's dealings with stakeholders, concern for the broader public interest mandates that a stay not be granted if the result will be to condone wrongdoing.

[31] Although there is a possibility that a debtor company's business practices will be so offensive as to warrant refusal of a stay extension on public policy grounds, this is not such a case. Clearly, San Francisco's sale of knockoff goods was illegal and offensive. Most troubling was its sale to an unwitting public of goods bearing counterfeit safety labels. Allowing the stay to continue in this case is not to minimize the repugnant nature of San Francisco's conduct. However, the company has been condemned for its illegal conduct in the appropriate forum and punishment levied. Denying the stay

extension application would be an additional form of punishment. Of greater concern is the effect that it would have on San Francisco's creditors, particularly the unsecured creditors, who would be denied their right to vote on the plan and whatever chance they might have for a small financial recovery, one which they, for the most part, patiently await.

[32] San Francisco has met the prerequisites that it has acted and is acting with due diligence and in good faith in working towards presenting a plan of arrangement to its creditors. Appreciating that the CCAA is to be given a broad and liberal interpretation to give effect to its remedial purpose, I am satisfied that, in the circumstances, extending the stay of proceedings is appropriate. The stay is extended to July 19, 2005. The revised time frame for next steps in the proceedings is set out on the attached Schedule.

[33] Although San Francisco has paid the $150,000.00 fine, the Monitor is satisfied that the company's current cash flow statements indicate that it is financially viable. Whether San Francisco can weather any loss of public confidence arising from its actions and resulting conviction is yet to be seen. Its creditors may look more critically at the plan of arrangement, and its customers and business associates may reconsider the value of their continued relationship with the company. However, that is sheer speculation.

* * * * *

A. Consolidation of CCAA Proceedings

A question of growing importance, domestically and internationally, is whether a court can make a single bankruptcy order for a group of companies, or permit them to make a consolidated application under the *CCAA* or a consolidated proposal under part III of the *BIA*. The effect of such an order is to create a single corpus of assets and liabilities; as a result, some creditors will recover more and others less than if there were no consolidation. Such "substantive consolidations" must be distinguished from "procedural consolidations," which are merely mechanisms for the more efficient administration of related insolvent debtors and involve no commingling of assets and liabilities of members of the group.

Substantive consolidation orders are usually sought where the debtor and its creditors have themselves treated the related corporations as a single enterprise (in some cases, the creditors may not even have been aware of the multiple legal personalities) or where assets and liabilities of members of the group have been so completely commingled that it would be expensive to try to disentangle them. The latter scenario applied to the group affairs of the Bank of Credit and Commerce International (BCCI), which went bankrupt in the early 1990s with unmet liabilities to depositors of about $10 billion. The British courts approved a recommendation from the liquidators that the assets and liabilities of the group be consolidated for greater efficiency.

US courts have long accepted the doctrine of substantive as well as procedural consolidation, but they have been divided about the tests to be applied in determining when a consolidation order should be made. There are no provisions in Canadian insolvency legislation authorizing consolidation orders. Nevertheless, according to one count, at least sixteen plans of arrangement were attempted under the *CCAA* in the 1980s and early 1990s and several well-known ones were approved by the courts. The best known of these is the consolidation order made in the *Northland Properties Ltd* (73 CBR (NS) 195) *CCAA* proceedings.

Michael McNaughton & Mary Arzoumanidis, "Substantive Consolidation in the Insolvency of Corporate Groups: A Comparative Analysis" in Janis P Sarra, ed, *Annual Review of Insolvency Law 2006* (Toronto: Thomson Reuters, 2007) at 525–29, 540, and 543–45 (footnotes omitted)

Large corporations are increasingly structured as corporate groups to accommodate the complexities of operating in the modern business environment. In fact, the corporate group is the most typical corporate structure of a large enterprise. Although each member of the corporate group retains a separate legal personality, the affairs of the corporate group are often conducted as if it were a single commercial entity. This may be evidenced through the use of extensive inter-company loans, commingling of assets, overlap in personnel, and a failure to keep proper financial records for each individual member of the group.

In the context of insolvency, the complex structure of corporate groups creates unique problems. Corporate groups test the limits of the separate legal personality principle since the insolvency no longer concerns a single debtor, but rather a bundle of related companies. The insolvency of a group of companies also raises the fundamental problem of ascertaining which assets within the corporate group belong to which company, and which creditor claims exist against each related company. Consequently, these difficulties necessitate a closer look into the interrelationship of the component parent, subsidiary and related companies in order to determine the extent of integration between the separate legal entities constituting the group. This considerably increases the complexity of the insolvency proceedings and poses new demands on the legal system to yield novel doctrines that address the inherently difficult problems associated with the insolvency of a corporate group.

In a liquidation or reorganization of a corporate group, the doctrine of substantive consolidation has emerged in order to provide a mechanism whereby the court may treat the separate legal entities belonging to the corporate group as one. In particular, substantive consolidation allows for the combination of the assets and liabilities of two or more members of the group, extinguishes inter-company debt and creates a single fund from which all claims against the consolidated debtors are satisfied. In effect, under substantive consolidation, claims of creditors against separate debtors instantly become claims against a single entity. . . .

At the outset, substantive consolidation should be distinguished from procedural consolidation; the latter is a distinct device permitting the joint administration of the estates of related companies. In Canada, as in the United States, an order for procedural consolidation is almost *de rigueur* in insolvency proceedings under the CCAA and the BIA. Procedural consolidation merely promotes administrative convenience and cost efficiency since a single court has jurisdiction over multiple related debtors. Unlike substantive consolidation however, procedural consolidation does not have substantive consequences. It does not alter the substantive rights and liabilities of creditors and debtors, nor does it affect the allocation of assets or the *pro rata* satisfaction of claims. Further, since procedural consolidation does not eliminate inter-company claims, the possibility to attack inter-company transfers as fraudulent or preferential transactions still exists. Accordingly, procedural consolidation results in each debtor remaining separate and distinct, with the substantive rights of all concerned intact. . . .

The primary aim of substantive consolidation is to ensure the equitable treatment of all creditors. Even though substantive consolidation should not effectively benefit one group of creditors to the detriment of another group, its effects can be quite dramatic on creditor recoveries. Substantive consolidation effectively redistributes wealth among creditors of the related entities and individual creditors will invariably realize asymmetric losses or gains. Separate debtors forming part of a corporate group will have differing ratios of assets-to-liabilities, varying levels of solvency or disparities in encumbered assets. In substantive consolidation, creditors of entities with lower ratios of assets-to-liabilities will benefit from the higher asset-to-liability ratio of the consolidated group. Creditors of entities with higher asset-to-liability ratios will receive a proportionately smaller satisfaction of their claims as a result of consolidation.

The effects of substantive consolidation on creditor recoveries may be illustrated by the following example. Assume Company A has $6 million in liabilities and $1 million in assets. Assume further that Company B is a related company and has $4 million in liabilities and $2 million in assets. Outside substantive consolidation, creditors of Company A would receive 17 cents on the dollar for their claims, while creditors of Company B would receive 50 cents on the dollar. In substantive collaboration, all creditors will receive 30 cents on the dollar for their claims. . . .

The few reported decisions do provide a set of factors that a Court [in Canada] may consider in determining whether to grant substantive consolidation. These factors include:

- the degree of difficulty in identifying each company's individual assets and liabilities;
- the extent of intermingling of assets and operational functions between each individual company;
- the extent to which costs associated with administering each estate separately would reduce or diminish the potential recoveries of creditors; and
- the degree of prejudice that each creditor might suffer upon consolidation.

What emerges from the few decided cases under the CCAA is that where substantive consolidation has been approved, the courts have emphasized that no injury was being done to any particular creditor or creditors or that no objection was made. . . .

The CCAA does not contain any provisions that specifically authorize a court to consolidate the assets and liabilities of two separate entities. As a result, where the courts have authorized consolidation order, they have relied on their equitable jurisdiction and discretionary powers under the CCAA to consolidate the estates of related debtors.

In the context of CCAA proceedings, one of the first and only reported decisions to consider and analyze the issue of substantive consolidation was the decision of the British Columbia Superior Court in *Northland Properties Ltd, Re.* In that case, the debtor companies sought, inter alia, a prospective order approving the preparation of a single reorganization plan for all the companies. The Court however determined that consolidation was not appropriate at that stage of the proceedings and refused to make the order. . . .

In considering whether substantive consolidation was appropriate in this case, Justice Trainor noted the paucity of Canadian jurisprudence and thus relied upon various US decisions which set out the tests to he considered on an application for substantive consolidation. He began his analysis by adopting the balancing test articulated in *Baker & Getty Financial Services Inc, Re,* which stated as follows:

> The propriety of ordering substantive consolidation is determined by a balancing of interests. The relevant enquiry asks whether the "creditors will suffer greater prejudice in the absence of consolidation than the debtors (and any objecting creditors) will suffer from its imposition.

After adopting this test, Trainor J listed the factors identified in *Vecco,* commonly referred to as the "elements of consolidation," which were developed by the courts to assist in the balancing of interests and then considered the test set out in *Re Snider Brothers Inc*, where the Court stated in making an application for substantive consolidation, "it must be clearly shown that not only are the 'elements of consolidation' present . . . but that the court's action is necessary to prevent harm or prejudice, or to effect a benefit generally." Ultimately it was found inappropriate in this case to make a consolidating order without first obtaining creditor approval since the effect of the order would be to approve an amalgamation of the companies. However, Justice Trainor stated that the debtor companies could return for court sanction of a consolidated plan once they obtained the approval of their creditors. Hence, it was implicit in Justice Trainor's decision that the court had authority to approve a consolidation plan under the appropriate circumstances. . . .

On appeal, the British Columbia Court of Appeal affirmed Justice Trainor's decision and thereby confirmed that a CCAA court has the jurisdiction to entertain a consolidated plan. The Court of Appeal accepted that the correct test for substantive consolidation was that set out in *Re Snider Bros* and interestingly also found statutory authority to make a consolidation order in s. 20 of the CCAA. . . .

Although the decisions stemming from the Northland proceedings confirm that substantive consolidation is part of Canadian law, the courts failed to provide significant analysis of the principles to be applied in making a consolidation order. Since those decisions, few cases have addressed the issue of substantive consolidation in any meaningful way, and even fewer have offered any guidance as to how courts should attack the consolidation inquiry. More significantly, none of the subsequent cases have explicitly considered the decision in Northland Properties and have instead focused on facts of each particular case.

[Reprinted by permission of the publisher.]

V. SCOPE OF THE STAY

Re Doman Industries Ltd (Trustee of), 2003 BCSC 376, 41 CBR (4th) 29

TYSOE J:

[15] The law is clear that the court has the jurisdiction under the CCAA to impose a stay during the restructuring period to prevent a creditor relying on an event of default to accelerate the payment of indebtedness owed by the debtor company or to prevent a non-creditor relying on a breach of a contract with the debtor company to terminate the contract. It is also my view that the court has similar jurisdiction to grant a permanent stay surviving the restructuring of the debtor company in respect of events of default or breaches occurring prior to the restructuring. In this regard, I agree with the following reasoning of Spence J at para. 32 of the supplementary reasons in *Playdium* [(2001) 31 CBR (4th) 302]:

> In interpreting s. 11(4) [now s. 11.02(2)], including the "such terms" clause, the remedial nature of the CCAA must be taken into account. If no permanent order could be made under s. 11(4) it would not be possible to order, for example, that the insolvency defaults which occasioned the CCAA order could not be asserted by the Famous Players after the stay period. If such an order could not be made, the CCAA regime would prospectively be of little or no value because even though a compromise of creditor claims might be worked out in the stay period, Famous Players (or for that matter, any similar third party)

could then assert the insolvency default and terminate, so that the stay would not provide any protection for the continuing prospects of the business. In view of the remedial nature of the CCAA, the Court should not take such a restrictive view of the s. 11(4) jurisdiction.

[16] Spence J made the above comments in the context of a third party which had a contract with the debtor company. In my opinion, the reasoning applies equally to a creditor of the debtor company in circumstances where the debtor company has chosen not to compromise the indebtedness owed to it. The decision in *Luscar Ltd v Smoky River Coal Ltd*, 1999 ABCA 179 is an example of a permanent stay being granted in respect of a creditor of the restructuring company.

[17] Accordingly, it is my view that the court does have the jurisdiction to grant a permanent stay preventing the Senior Secured Noteholders and the Trustee under the Trust Indenture from relying on events of default existing prior to or during the restructuring period to accelerate the repayment of the indebtedness owing under the Notes. It may be that the court would decline to exercise its jurisdiction in respect of monetary defaults but this point is academic in the present case because the Doman Group does intend to pay the overdue interest on the Notes upon implementation of the Reorganization Plan. . . .

[20] The third issue is whether the court has the jurisdiction to effectively stay the operation of Section 4.16 of the Trust Indenture. Although I understand that there is an issue as to whether the giving of 85% of the equity in the Doman Group to the Unsecured Noteholders as part of the reorganization would constitute a change of control for the purposes of the current version of the provincial forestry legislation, counsel for the Doman Group conceded that it would constitute a Change of Control within the meaning of Section 4.16.

[21] The language of s. [11.02] of the CCAA, on a literal interpretation, is very broad and the case authorities have held that it should receive a liberal interpretation in view of the remedial nature of the CCAA. However, in my opinion, a liberal interpretation of s. [11.02] does not permit the court to excuse the debtor company from fulfilling its contractual obligations arising after the implementation of a plan of compromise or arrangement.

[22] In my view, there are numerous purposes of stays under s. [11.02] of the CCAA. One of the purposes is to maintain the status quo among creditors while a debtor company endeavours to reorganize or restructure its financial affairs. Another purpose is to prevent creditors and other parties from acting on the insolvency of the debtor company or other contractual breaches caused by the insolvency to terminate contracts or accelerate the repayment of the indebtedness owing by the debtor company when it would interfere with the ability of the debtor company to reorganize or restructure its financial affairs. An additional purpose is to relieve the debtor company of the burden of dealing with litigation against it so that it may focus on restructuring its financial affairs. As I have observed above, a further purpose is to prevent the frustration of a reorganization or restructuring plan after its implementation on the basis of events of default or breaches which existed prior to or during the restructuring period. All of these purposes are to facilitate a debtor company in restructuring its financial affairs. On the other hand, it is my opinion that Parliament did not intend s. [11.02] to authorize courts to stay proceedings in respect of defaults or breaches which occur after the implementation of the reorganization or restructuring plan, even if they arise as a result of the implementation of the plan.

Order accordingly.

More recently in *8640025 Canada Inc, Re*, 2017 BCSC 303, creditors of the insolvent company sought to add three companies to the proceedings as petitioners, as the companies were "closely intertwined." The applicants argued that the interpretation of s. 11 of the CCAA in *Century Services* allowed the Court to "exercise its discretion" and apply the CCAA to a company that the CCAA would otherwise not apply to. The Court rejected this argument, stating, "Despite the urgings of the applicants, I cannot read the reasons of Madam Justice Deschamps, in *Re Ted Leroy Trucking Ltd* [*Century Services*] as instructing judges when, at the outset of a CCAA proceeding they are considering the application of the Act to a company, to exercise an expansive or inherent jurisdiction thereby making it applicable to a company that does not meet the test found in s. 3."

Terrace Bay Pulp (Re), 2013 ONSC 5111

Morawetz J

[1] Terrace Bay Pulp Inc. ("Terrace Bay" or the "Applicant") brought this motion for an order declaring that the proceeding known as *R v Terrace Bay Pulp Inc and Gino LeBlanc*, brought by the Ministry of Labour (the "Ministry") against the Applicant, (the "First OHSA Proceeding"), and the proceeding known as *R v Terrace Bay Pulp Inc, Venschore Mechanical Ltd, Joseph Mykietyn, Arthur Szczepaniak and Alain Zborowski*, brought by the Ministry against the Applicant, (the "Second OHSA Proceeding," and together with the First OHSA Proceeding, the "OHSA Proceedings"), in connection with alleged violations under the *Occupational Health and Safety Act (Ontario)* (the "OHSA"), are stayed.

[2] Terrace Bay obtained protection from its creditors under the *Companies' Creditors Arrangement Act* ("CCAA") on January 25, 2012. On that date, an order (the "Initial Order") was granted and Ernst & Young Inc. was appointed as Monitor.

[3] These CCAA proceedings are hereinafter referred to as the "Current CCAA Proceeding."

[4] Previously, by order granted March 11, 2009, Terrace Bay filed for and obtained protection under the CCAA, (the "First CCAA Proceeding").

[5] On September 15, 2010, Terrace Bay implemented a Plan of Compromise in the First CCAA Proceeding (the "Plan"). The Plan contemplated the issuance of a promissory note (the "Plan Note") for the benefit of holders of proven unsecured claims in the First CCAA Proceeding (collectively, the "Plan Note Beneficiaries").

[6] The Plan Note Beneficiaries shared *pari passu* in the Plan Note, which is secured against all assets and property of Terrace Bay (the "Property").

[7] On January 10, 2012, the First OHSA Proceeding was commenced, in connection with alleged violations under the OHSA. The First OHSA Proceeding has been discontinued as against all defendants other than Terrace Bay and Gino LeBlanc.

[8] On October 15, 2012, the Second OHSA Proceeding was commenced, in connection with further alleged violations of the OHSA.

[9] Terrace Bay is insolvent. It commenced the Current CCAA Proceeding in order to conduct a marketing and sales process for its business and non-business assets. In July 2012, Terrace Bay sold its operating assets relating to its pulp mill (the "Mill") to a third party. As a result of the sale, Terrace Bay no longer operates the Mill or any other business and all of its former employees to the extent not assumed by the purchaser, have been terminated.

[10] Terrace Bay is currently evaluating Letters of Intent received with respect to its non-business assets. It has obtained a stay of proceedings in the Current CCAA Proceeding until October 31, 2013.

[11] The incidents giving rise to the OHSA Proceedings occurred prior to the commencement of the Current CCAA Proceeding.

[12] The First OHSA Proceeding was commenced in response to an incident which occurred on January 13, 2011. A Terrace Bay employee was injured while working in the wood-handling department of the Mill. Terrace Bay was charged with various offences under the OHSA, including the offence of failing, as an employer, to ensure that the prescribed measures and procedures were carried out in the Mill.

[13] The Second OHSA Proceeding was commenced in response to a blow-tank explosion which blew part of the roof off the Mill on October 31, 2011 (the "October 31 Incident"). The October 31 Incident resulted in the death of a Mill employee. Two other individuals employed by a contractor sustained injuries. Charges were laid against Terrace Bay, Venschore Mechanical Ltd. (a contractor engaged by Terrace Bay) and three supervisors employed by Terrace Bay. Terrace Bay was charged with, among other things, failure to provide adequate instructions to employees.

[14] Terrace Bay's limited operating expenses are funded from cash on hand in connection with cash flow projections which have been approved by the court (the "Approved Expenses").

[15] Expenses related to the defence of OHSA Proceedings are not included in the Approved Expenses. The balance of Terrace Bay's assets after payment of operating expenses, is held for the benefit of Terrace Bay's creditors and are subject to distribution only upon further order of the court.

[16] The issues on this motion are as follows:

(a) Are the OHSA Proceedings stayed by the Initial Order?

(b) In light of the position of the Ministry that the OHSA Proceedings are not stayed pursuant to the Initial Order, should the OHSA Proceedings be stayed pursuant to section 11.1(4) of the CCAA?

(c) Is there a conflict between the CCAA and the statutory requirements to which Terrace Bay is subject pursuant to the OHSA.

[17] Pursuant to section 11.02(2) of the CCAA, a broad stay of proceedings was granted, which is reflected at paragraphs 10 and 11 of the Initial Order.

[18] Section 11.1(1) of the CCAA defines a "regulatory body." It is acknowledged that the Ministry, in this case, is a "regulatory body" for the purposes of section 11.1, as it is responsible for administering the OHSA. . . .

[20] The Applicant takes the position that the only remedy available to the Ministry in the event of a conviction of Terrace Bay in both of the OHSA Proceedings is monetary. Section 66(2) of the OHSA provides that the maximum fine that may be imposed upon a corporation is $500,000 (plus any applicable victim fine surcharge). Terrace Bay takes the position that any fine ordered upon a conviction of Terrace Bay in either of the OHSA Proceedings would be a financial obligation of Terrace Bay and the Ministry would be an unsecured creditor in respect of such amounts, and its claim would be subject to the payment of prior claims.

[21] Further, the costs and expenses, including legal expenses, that would be incurred by Terrace Bay in defending the OHSA Proceedings would be significant and would be borne wholly by Terrace Bay's creditors, in the form of diminished proceeds available for distribution by Terrace Bay. Terrace Bay takes the position that in light of its insolvency in the Current CCAA Proceeding, it must consider the interests of these stakeholders in determining whether to defend the OHSA Proceedings.

[22] Terrace Bay further submits that the Ministry has exercised its enforcement power by commencing the OHSA Proceedings, requiring Terrace Bay to incur a financial obligation in order to defend itself in the OHSA Proceedings. The only remedy, counsel submits, available to the Ministry against Terrace Bay, should it be successful in prosecuting Terrace Bay, is a monetary fine. As such, the Ministry is enforcing its right [as a creditor of Terrace Bay]. Counsel submits that such a claim falls to be administered as a claim against Terrace Bay in the Current CCAA Proceeding and should be stayed.

[23] Terrace Bay submits that the stay of proceedings provided for in paragraphs 10 and 11 of the Initial Order should be effective to impose such stay. Alternatively, Terrace Bay seeks a declaration pursuant to section 11.1(4) of the CCAA that the Ministry is seeking to enforce its rights as a creditor and that the enforcement of such right be stayed.

[24] In response, the Ministry submits that Terrace Bay has fundamentally misunderstood the purpose of a regulatory prosecution in that prosecutions are not brought to collect money; they are commenced where there is sufficient evidence of a contravention and where it is in the public interest to proceed.

[25] Further, the Ministry points out that Terrace Bay has not moved for an order under section 11.1(3) of the CCAA, submitting that Terrace Bay could not meet the test. Section 11.1(3) permits a regulatory proceeding to be stayed where the debtor company can prove that a viable compromise or arrangement could not be made and is not contrary to the public interest.

[26] Instead, counsel to the Ministry submits that Terrace Bay purports to rely on section 111(4) of the CCAA which allows a court to stay regulatory proceedings only where the regulatory body is found to be seeking to enforce its rights as a creditor. In doing so, the Ministry submits that Terrace Bay has improperly applied the Supreme Court's recent decision in *Newfoundland and Labrador v Abitibi Bowater Inc*, 2012 SCC 67 ("*Abitibi*").

[27] The Ministry takes the position that the OHSA Proceedings do not involve the enforcement of creditor rights, stating that in this case the Ministry is not acting as a creditor with a claim to enforce. Rather, it is acting solely in its capacity as regulator.

[28] The Ministry takes the position that the OHSA Proceedings fall directly within the scope of 11.1(2).

[29] In *Abitibi*, the Province of Newfoundland and Labrador (the "Province") issued various orders against a CCAA debtor pursuant to a provincial environmental legislation. The Province then brought a motion for an order that it was not barred from enforcing its orders against the debtor.

[30] The Supreme Court of Canada set out the following three requirements for determining when an order of a regulator should be seen as a "claim" within the meaning of the CCAA:

(a) there must be a debt, liability or obligation to a creditor;

(b) the debt, liability or obligation must be incurred before the debtor becomes bankrupt; and

(c) it must be possible to attach a monetary value to the debt, liability or obligation.

[31] The Applicant takes the position that the three requirements set out in *Abitibi* are satisfied. With respect to the first requirement, counsel to the Applicant submits that the Supreme Court of Canada in *Abitibi* held that the only relevant determination is whether the regulatory body has exercised its enforcement power against the debtor.

[32] In this case, counsel submits that the Ministry has exercised its enforcement power against Terrace Bay by commencing the OHSA Proceedings, requiring Terrace Bay to incur a financial obligation in order to defend itself in the OHSA Proceedings.

[33] In response, the Ministry takes the position that a monetary liability or obligation would arise only if, and when, a court makes a finding of guilt, and enters a conviction and imposes a fine as a sentence in the OHSA Proceeding. Further, counsel submits that it is not possible to attach a monetary value to Terrace Bay's liability. In order to crystalize the obligation, a number of steps must be taken. A court must make a finding of guilt, enter a conviction and impose a fine. Further, in a regulatory prosecution, under the *Provincial Offences Act*, it is open to a court to impose a non-monetary penalty i.e., the court may suspend the passing of sentence and require the defendant to comply with terms of a probation order. Counsel submits that on the record, it is not sufficiently certain that a monetary penalty will ultimately be imposed against Terrace Bay.

[34] In support of its position, the Applicant relies upon *Nortel Networks Corporation (Re)*, 2012 ONSC 1213 and *Northstar Aerospace (Re)*, 2012 ONSC 4423. Appeals of both decisions were argued concurrently at the Court of Appeal for Ontario and the decision is currently under reserve.

[35] In *Nortel*, one of the points considered was whether the actions of the Ministry of the Environment ("MOE") required Nortel to respond in a way that caused Nortel to incur a financial obligation. A similar issue arose in *Northstar*. I held in both cases, that the actions of the MOE would require the debtor to incur a financial obligation.

[36] In my view, the issue in this case is different. It seems to me that, the OHSA Proceedings do not, at this stage, require Terrace Bay to respond in a way that causes it to incur a financial obligation.

[37] There are two potential financial obligations that have to be considered. The first is whether OHSA Proceedings could result in a financial penalty being imposed as against Terrace Bay. This has not yet been determined. This situation is to be contrasted with *Nortel* and *Northstar*, where, in response to actions taken by the MOE, the debtors, both Nortel and Northstar, would be required to expend resources in response to the actions taken by the MOE. In this case, there is another step to be taken, i.e., there would have to be a finding of guilt before any penalty could be imposed.

[38] The second type of financial obligation is the expenditure of resources to defend its actions. I do not doubt that if Terrace Bay makes a decision to defend the action, it will incur a financial obligation. However, it does, in this case, have a choice. It can choose to either defend or not to defend the OHSA Proceedings. That is not to suggest that the choice is an enviable one. Clearly it is not. However, the fact remains that Terrace Bay can either choose to incur a financial obligation, by defending, or not to incur a financial obligation, by not defending. In this respect, the *Nortel* and *Northstar* decisions are distinguishable.

[39] At this stage, the OHSA Proceedings do not force or require Terrace Bay to expend any funds or resources. Terrace Bay is not being asked to respond to any orders issued by the Ministry. Further, any time and resources that Terrace Bay expends in relation to the OHSA Proceedings, are at its sole discretion.

[40] At this stage, it seems to me that the Ministry cannot be considered to be acting as a creditor with respect to the OHSA Proceedings. Its activities, at this stage, are regulatory or prosecutorial in nature.

[41] As a result, I have concluded that the first part of the *Abitibi* test has not been met.

[42] Having reached this conclusion, it is unnecessary to address the second and third part of the *Abitibi* test.

[43] Terrace Bay also served a notice of constitutional question, in which it argues that the OHSA Proceedings are barred by virtue of the doctrine of federal paramouncy.

[44] The doctrine of paramouncy arises only where there is a conflict between valid federal and provincial legislation, either because compliance of both laws is impossible (impossibility of dual compliance) or because compliance with the provincial law would frustrate the purposes of the federal law.

[45] I have concluded that the Crown is not, at this stage, seeking to enforce its rights as a creditor, through the OHSA Proceedings. Thus, it seems to me that there is no conflict between 11.1(4) of the CCAA and the OHSA Proceeding and there is no merit to the submissions put forth by Terrace Bay on this issue.

[46] In the result, the motion of Terrace Bay for an order declaring that the OHSA Proceedings are stayed is dismissed.

Practice Questions

Question 1

Cool Games Inc is a video game development company in Vancouver, BC. Cool Games Inc recently released a new game that took two years to develop. The company will not have another game ready for release for several months. The newly released game did not sell as well as Cool Games Inc had hoped. The directors of Cool Games Inc worry that creditors will start to demand repayment of their debts and decide to reorganize. They apply under the *CCAA*. Who are the stakeholders affected by the reorganization of Cool Games Inc? How would those stakeholders be affected if the company were to liquidate and dissolve instead of reorganizing?

Question 2

The *CCAA* provides for a debtor-in-possession model for restructuring proceedings, meaning that current management stays in place once restructuring proceedings are commenced. What are the advantages and disadvantages of a debtor-in-possession insolvency regime?

Question 3

Companies can choose whether to commence *CCAA* proceedings or *BIA* bankruptcy proceedings. What are the potential advantages of undergoing *CCAA* proceedings as opposed to a *BIA* bankruptcy?

Question 4

The *CCAA* and *BIA* Commercial Proposals are the two main insolvency restructuring regimes in Canada. Do you think these two regimes should remain separate? Or should the federal government amalgamate the two into a single restructuring regime?

Question 5

Why might a company choose to use the *CCAA* for liquidation proceedings as opposed to for reorganizing proceedings? Should liquidations be allowed under the *CCAA*?

Question 6

Do you generally agree that judges should exercise their discretion to circumvent statutory restrictions in furtherance of the *CCAA*'s remedial objectives? Why or why not?

Question 7

In the United States, a petitioning creditor does not have to allege or prove insolvency under chapter 11. Under the *CCAA*, in order for a company to qualify as a "debtor company," the company must be insolvent. However, in *Stelco*, the judge noted that the threshold to prove insolvency under the *CCAA* is much lower than the threshold for proving insolvency under the *BIA*. Would there be any advantage in abolishing the insolvency requirement under the *CCAA* for voluntary proceedings? See J Ziegel, "Should Proof of the Debtor's Insolvency Be Dispensed with in Voluntary Insolvency Proceedings?" in Janis P Sarra, ed, *Annual Review of Insolvency Law 2006* (Toronto: Thomson Reuters, 2007) at 21.

Question 8

Comfy Cushions Ltd was recently sent an invoice from its fabric supplier for $3.5 million. The directors of Comfy Cushions Ltd realized that, while they could pay this debt, it would result in serious cash flow issues for the company. The directors want to know if they can apply for *CCAA* protection. What are the prerequisites for the application of the *CCAA*?

Question 9

In order to have the *CCAA* stay of proceedings extended to cover the *OHSA* proceedings, Terrace Bay would need to bring an application under section 11.1(3). Section 11.1(2) states, "Subject to subsection (3), no order made under section 11.02 affects a regulatory body's investigation in respect of the debtor company or an action, suit or proceeding that is taken in respect of the company by or before the regulatory body, other than the enforcement of a payment ordered by the regulatory body or the court. Section 11.1(3) provides:

> On application by the company and on notice to the regulatory body and to the persons who are likely to be affected by the order, the court may order that subsection (2) not apply in respect of one or more of the actions, suits or proceedings taken by or before the regulatory body if in the court's opinion
>
> (a) a viable compromise or arrangement could not be made in respect of the company if that subsection were to apply; and
> (b) it is not contrary to the public interest that the regulatory body be affected by the order made under section 11.02.

What evidence would Terrace Bay need to adduce to demonstrate that without such an order extending the stay to the regulatory body, "a viable compromise or arrangement could not be made"? Does this language suggest that the subsection is not applicable where a liquidating *CCAA* is involved?

Question 10

Consider the interests of each of the following stakeholders. For each stakeholder, consider which form of debt resolution (*BIA* bankruptcy or *CCAA* restructuring) you would prefer that the debtor use and why:

a) a secured creditor;
b) an unsecured creditor;
c) a minority shareholder;
d) an employee; and
e) a supplier.

Business Operations in a *CCAA* Proceeding

I. INTRODUCTION

This chapter deals with various aspects of carrying on business while subject to *Companies' Creditors Arrangement Act*, RSC 1985, c C-36 (*CCAA*) proceedings. Section II contains a discussion about the monitor's role in the proceedings. The *CCAA* provides for the appointment of a monitor to perform a watchdog function due to the concerns about how the debtor's existing management should operate upon the commencement of restructuring proceedings. The *CCAA* establishes a debtor-in-possession regime, on the rationale that, as a general rule, the debtor's existing management is likely to do a better job of running the debtor's business during the proceedings than an administrator or the like appointed from outside, who may not know the ins and outs of the business as well. On the other hand, leaving the current management in charge carries with it certain obvious concerns, not the least of which is that the debtor became insolvent on the current management's watch and this may reflect on its competence. Section III deals with the duty of the debtor company's directors to avoid conflicts of interest in the course of *CCAA* proceedings, with particular reference to the Supreme Court of Canada's decision in *Sun Indalex Finance, LLC v United Steelworkers*. Section IV deals with the debtor's right to disclaim, affirm, and assign executory contracts in *CCAA* proceedings. Section V discusses the special provisions in the *CCAA* relating to derivatives or "eligible financial contracts." Section VI addresses the question of debtor-in-possession, or interim, financing. If the debtor is to carry on business during the restructuring process, it will typically need a fresh injection of funds. On the other hand, potential new lenders may not be ready to come to the table unless the debtor can assure them of priority over existing creditors. This creates a conflict between the interest of the stakeholders at large in the debtor being able to continue in business and the interest of the subset of creditors whose priority position will be affected if the debtor accedes to the new lender's demands. Section VIII deals with aspects of the sale process in liquidating *CCAA*s. Court approval of a sale is typically the last formal stage of a liquidating *CCAA* (assuming the absence of a plan). The last formal stage of *CCAA* restructuring proceedings is typically court approval of the plan. Approval of *CCAA* plans is dealt with in Chapter 15.

II. THE MONITOR

Under *CCAA* proceedings, the monitor is an officer of the court. The monitor must ensure that the court and the creditors receive accurate and timely information about the proceedings by monitoring the business and financial affairs of the company (*CCAA*, s 11.7(1)). The specific statutory functions and duties are set out in *CCAA*, section 23. The Office of the Superintendent of Bankruptcy provides for supervision of monitors (*CCAA*, ss 27–32).

The monitor's obligations have been the focus of increased scrutiny over the last two decades. Until 1997, judges appointed monitors under their inherent or equitable jurisdiction but in 1997, it became mandatory to appoint a monitor in *CCAA* restructurings. *CCAA*, section 11.7, provides that the monitor must be a licensed trustee, and, as a general rule, a trustee may not be appointed as monitor if the trustee has served as a director or is connected with the debtor in various other specified ways.

The role of the monitor as a possible counterweight to the *CCAA* "debtor-in-possession" regime has faced increased scrutiny over the last decade. Once appointed, the monitor, as an officer of the court, can only be relieved of their duties by the court. The monitor is not a representative or advocate of any of the stakeholders, including the debtor company. To that end, any report or assessment made by the monitor must be independent. Conflicts of interest can arise, however, because in addition to these duties, the monitor must also help the debtor through the restructuring process. The following excerpts from *8640025 Canada Inc, (Re)* and *Re Winalta Inc* address the role of the monitor and potential conflicts of interest.

8640025 Canada Inc (Re), 2018 BCCA 93, 58 CBR (6th) 257

The Role of the Monitor

[47] The use of court-appointed monitors has also been an innovation in the courts' treatment of *CCAA* cases. Prior to 1997, monitors were appointed pursuant to the inherent jurisdiction of the superior courts. They reviewed the financial and business affairs of the debtor, provided independent information to the court on the progress of the proceedings, and assisted in administrative matters such as notifying creditors and organizing and managing meetings of creditors: see Sarra, *Rescue* at 257.

[48] The professionalism and impartiality of the monitor's role were codified in 1997 following the recommendations of a task force that reported in 1994: see Sarra at 258. Section 11.7(1) now requires that a monitor be appointed by a court on the initial application and that the person so appointed be a trustee within the meaning of s. 2(1) of the *BIA*. Section 11.7(2) disqualifies certain persons who would have an interest in the debtor or would not be seen to be impartial. As officers of the court, monitors must remain impartial and "objectively look out for be concerned for the interests of all stakeholders": see *Re Laidlaw Inc* (2002) 34 C.B.R. (4th) 72 (Ont. S.C.J.), *per* Farley J.

[49] Section 23 sets out the various duties of monitors, which apply unless the court orders otherwise. Generally, these are duties of monitoring the company's business affairs and reporting to the court thereon, carrying out appraisals or investigations considered necessary by the monitor, assisting the company's creditors in certain respects, advising the court on the "reasonableness and fairness" of any proposed compromise or arrangement, making certain documents publicly available and carrying out "any other functions in relation to the company that the court may direct." Courts have used s. 23(1)(k) liberally to assign additional functions to monitors that go beyond investigating and reporting to the court. As noted by Yaad Rotem in "Contemplating a Corporate Governance Model for Bankruptcy Reorganizations: Lessons from Canada", (2008) 3 *Va. L.& Bus. Rev.* 125, monitors have been authorized to act as financial advisors to the parties or the court, to facilitate or mediate between management and creditors, and to fulfill certain functions of directors or managers. (At 148.) The monitor may even effectively replace the board of directors and senior management of a corporation: see *Re Royal Oak Mines Inc* (1999) 11 C.B.R. (4th) 122 (Ont. Gen. Div.) Thus Professor Sarra writes:

Long gone are the days when the monitor acted as a passive observer, reporting to the court. Monitors now play a range of roles, including mediator or facilitator in the negotiations, debtor advisor, creditor assuager and officer of the court. The recent amendments bolster this authority, requiring in a number of instances, such as DIP Financing and the sale of assets to related parties, that the court consider the views of the monitor. However, the court has observed that while the support or approval of the monitor is an important factor, it is not decisive in and of itself. The courts continue to stress the need for independence and impartiality of the monitor. In approving a series of agreements that provided the debtors with certainty with respect to ongoing funding, the resolution of inter-company issues, and a settlement with taxing authorities, the court held it was appropriate to place reliance on the views of the monitor who had the benefit of intensive involvement for over a year and was active in the negotiations leading up to the proposed settlement. [*Evolution, supra* at 234–5; emphasis added.]

In this case, it will be recalled, the April order 'enhanced' the Monitor's powers: it contemplated that the Monitor would carry out the day-to-day management of the petitioners' operations.

[50] In recent years, Canadian courts have also adopted the practice of appointing claims officers to assist in determining the "amount represented by a claim of any secured or unsecured creditor" under s. 20 of the *CCAA*. Various provinces have developed model claims process orders, but these vary widely across Canada. Where the order provides for the appointment of a claims officer, that officer may be given the authority to determine the procedure for adjudicating such claims and may reach a determination of the value that is often stated to be final and binding on the company or creditor, subject to any further order of the court.

Appeal allowed.

Re *Winalta Inc*, 2011 ABQB 399, 84 CBR (5th) 157

Topolniski J: . . .

[8] The Winalta Group's operations and assets are located in Alberta, except for a small holding in Saskatchewan. Its head office is in Edmonton.

[9] In November 2009, HSBC entered into a forbearance agreement with the Winalta Group, which owed it in excess of $47 million (the "Forbearance Agreement"). The Winalta Group agreed to Deloitte & Touche Inc. being retained as HSBC's private monitor, commonly called a "look see" consultant. The Winalta group also agreed to give HSBC a consent receivership order that could be filed with no strings attached.

[10] The Winalta Group was not a party to the private monitor agreement between HSBC and Deloitte & Touche Inc., although it was responsible for payment of the private monitor's fees pursuant to the security held by HSBC. It was aware that the private monitor agreement provided for a six percent flat "administration fee" that would be charged by Deloitte & Touche Inc. in lieu of "customary disbursements such as postage, telephone, faxes, and routine photocopying." Charges for "reasonable out of pocket expenses" for travel expenses were not included in the "administration fee."

[11] Clearly, HSBC was in the position of power. It agreed to support the Winalta Group's restructuring and to fund its operations throughout the *CCAA* process on the following conditions:

(i)   the monitor would be Deloitte & Touche Inc. (the Monitor) and a Vancouver partner of that firm, Jervis Rodriquez, would be the "partner in charge" of the file;

(ii) HSBC would be unaffected by the *CCAA* proceedings;

(iii) the initial order presented to the court for consideration would authorize the Monitor to report to HSBC; and

(iv) the Winalta's Group's indebtedness to HSBC would be retired by October 30, 2010.

[12] On April 26, 2010, the initial order was granted as the Winalta Group and HSBC had planned (Initial Order).

[13] HSBC continued to provide operating and overdraft facilities to the Winalta Group during the *CCAA* process, as outlined in the Initial Order, which also provided that the Monitor could report to HSBC on certain matters, the details of which are discussed in the context of the Winalta Group's allegation that the Monitor breached its fiduciary duties.

[14] The Winalta Group did not seek DIP financing. Its quest for takeout financing to meet the October 30, 2010 cutoff imposed by HSBC was frustrated when HSBC refused to fund the costs associated with obtaining replacement financing without a three million dollar guarantee. A stakeholder came to the rescue. The Winalta Group is of the view that HSBC's refusal to pay the costs is directly attributable to the Monitor's actions in connection with the September NVR.

[15] There is nothing in the evidence or the submissions made at the hearing of this application that hints at a strained relationship between the Winalta Group and the Monitor before the Winalta Group learned when it examined a Deloitte & Touche Inc. partner in the context of this application that the Monitor had provided HSBC with the September NVR.

[16] The Monitor's interim accounts were sent at regular intervals. They described activities typical of a monitor in a *CCAA* restructuring, including intense activity in the early phases tapering off as the process unfolded, with a spike around the time of the claims bar date and creditors' meeting. There is no suggestion that the Winalta Group voiced concern about the Monitor's interim accounts. Up until the present application, it seems to have been squarely focused on the goal of obtaining a positive creditor vote and paying its debt to HSBC by the cutoff date....

B. Breach of Fiduciary Duty/Conflict of Interest

[67] A monitor appointed under the *CCAA* is an officer of the court who is required to perform the obligations mandated by the court and under the common law. A monitor owes a fiduciary duty to the stakeholders; is required to account to the court; is to act independently; and must treat all parties reasonably and fairly, including creditors, the debtor and its shareholders.

[68] Kevin P. McElcheran describes the monitor's role in the following terms in Commercial Insolvency in Canada (Markham, Ont.: LexisNexis Butterworths, 2005) at p. 236:

> The monitor is an officer of the court. It is the court's eyes and ears with a mandate to assist the court in its supervisory role. The monitor is not an advocate for the debtor company or any party in the *CCAA* process. It has a duty to evaluate the activities of the debtor company and comment independently on such actions in any report to the court and the creditors.

[69] The Winalta Group contends that the Monitor breached its fiduciary duty (and implicitly placed itself in a conflict of interest position) by providing HSBC with the September NVR without its knowledge or consent. The onus of establishing the allegation of breach of fiduciary duty lies with the Winalta Group.

[70] The September NVR was sent to HSBC via e-mail. It included a summary of the Monitor's analysis and backup spreadsheets for the following two scenarios:
(1) the bank appoints a receiver for all companies on September 7, 2010;
(2) the bank supports the company through the *CCAA* and is paid out on October 31, 2010 through a refinancing of the assets of Oilfield and Carriers.

The author of the e-mail asked the recipient to confirm his availability to discuss the scenarios with Messrs. Rodriquez and Keeble the next day.

[71] Mr. Keeble's responses to questioning, filed March 18, 2011, reference three other reports from the Monitor to HSBC dated June 7, August 12, and August 18, 2010, all of which discussed the estimated value of HSBC's security in various scenarios (Other NVRs). The Winalta Group neither complained of nor referred to the Other NVRs in its evidence or submissions. In the absence of any complaint and evidence, the sole focus of this inquiry is on the September NVR.

[72] The Winalta Group's complaints concerning the September NVR are that it was prepared and issued without its knowledge and it lead to HSBC's refusal to fund its takeout financing costs. Articulated in the language used to describe a *CCAA* monitor's duties, the Winalta Group is saying that the Monitor favoured HSBC (placing it in an advantageous position over other creditors) and failed to avoid an actual or perceived conflict of interest.

[73] Accusations of bias and breach of fiduciary duty can harm the public's confidence in the insolvency system and, if unfounded, the insolvency practitioner's good name. A careful investigation into allegations of misconduct is, therefore, essential. The process should entail the following steps:
1. A review of the monitor's duties and powers as defined by the *CCAA* and court orders relevant to the allegation.
2. An assessment of the monitor's actions in the contextual framework of the relevant provisions of the *CCAA* and court orders.
3. If the monitor failed to discharge its duties or exceeded its powers, the court should then:
   (a) determine if damage is attributable to the monitor's conduct, including damage to the integrity of the insolvency system; and
   (b) ascertain the appropriate fee reduction (bearing in mind that other bodies are charged with the responsibility of ethical concerns arising from a *CCAA* monitor's conduct).

Step 1: Reviewing the monitor's duties and powers as defined by the *CCAA* and court orders relevant to the allegation

(a) The monitor's fiduciary and ethical duties
[74] Section 25 of the *CCAA* provides that:

> 25. In exercising any of his or her powers in performing any of his or her duties and functions, the monitor must act honestly and in good faith and comply with the *Code of Ethics* referred to in section 13.5 of the *Bankruptcy and Insolvency Act*.

[75] Section 13.5 of the *Bankruptcy and Insolvency Act*, 1985 R.S.C. 1985, c. B-3 ("*BIA*") provides that a trustee shall comply with the prescribed *Code of Ethics*. The *Code of Ethics* is found in Rules 34 to 53 of the *Bankruptcy and Insolvency General Rules*, C.R.C., c. 368 under the *BIA*. These Rules provide in part that:

(a) Every trustee shall maintain the high standards of ethics that are central to the maintenance of public trust and confidence in administration of the Act (Rule 34).

(b) Trustees shall be honest and impartial and shall provide interested parties with full and accurate information as required by the Act with respect to the professional engagements of the trustees (Rule 39).

(c) Trustees who are acting with respect to any professional engagement shall avoid any influence, interest or relationship that impairs, or appears in the opinion of an informed person to impair, their professional judgment (Rule 44).

[76] In addition, *CCAA* monitors are subject to the ethical standards imposed on them by their governing professional bodies.

[77] A recurring theme found in the case law is that the monitor's duty is to ensure that no creditor has an advantage over another (A recurring theme found in the case law is that the monitor's duty is to ensure that no creditor has an advantage over another (see *Siscoe & Savoie v Royal Bank of Canada* (1994), 29 C.B.R. (3d) 1 at 8 (N.B.C.A.); *Re Laidlaw Inc* (2002), 34 C.B.R. (4th) 72 at para. 2 (Ont. S.C.J.); *Re United Used Auto & Truck Parts Ltd* (1999), 12 C.B.R. (4th) 144 at para. 20 (B.C.S.C.); and *Re 843504 Alberta Ltd*, 2003 ABQB 1015 at para. 19, 351 A.R. 223). The following observations made by Farley J in *Re Confederation Treasury Services Ltd* (1995), 37 C.B.R. (3d) 237 at 247 (Ont. Ct. (Gen. Div.)) about a bankruptcy trustee's duty of impartiality resonate:

> The appointment is not a franchise to make money (although a trustee should be rewarded for its efforts on behalf of the estate) nor to favour one party or one side. The trustee is an impartial officer of the Court; woe be to it if it does not act impartially towards the creditors of the estate.

[78] In his article, *Conflicts of Interest and the Insolvency Practitioner: Keeping up Appearances* (1996), 40 C.B.R. (3d) 56, Eric O. Peterson tackles the issue of conflict of interest in circumstances where an insolvency practitioner wears two hats. At p. 74, he states:

> ... The duties of a *CCAA* monitor are defined by standard terms in the court order, and are typically owed to the court, the creditors and the debtor company. Therefore, a private monitor or receiver would have a potential conflict of interest in accepting an engagement as *CCAA* monitor of the same debtor. The engagements are at cross purposes.

[79] Mr. Peterson cautions (at p. 75) that even if an experienced business person consents to the insolvency practitioner wearing two hats, the insolvency practitioner should bear in mind Mr. Justice Benjamin Cardozo's statement that a fiduciary must be held to something stricter than the morals of the marketplace.

[80] Not surprisingly, there may be heightened sensitivity about the work of a *CCAA* monitor who has chosen to wear two hats. Unfounded accusations may be made due to an honestly held suspicion about where the monitor's loyalties lie rather than out of spite or malice.

[81] Common sense dictates that *CCAA* monitors should conduct their affairs in an open and transparent fashion in all of their dealings with the debtor and the creditors alike. The reason is simple. Transparency promotes public confidence and mitigates against unfounded allegations of bias. Secrecy breeds suspicion.

[82] Public confidence in the insolvency system is dependent on it being fair, just and accessible. Bias, whether perceived or actual, undermines the public's faith in the system. In order to safeguard against that risk, a *CCAA* monitor must act with professional

neutrality, and scrupulously avoid placing itself in a position of potential or actual conflict of interest.

(b) The Monitor's legislated and court ordered duties

[83] One of a monitor's functions is to serve as a conduit of information for the creditors. This did not, however, give the Monitor here *carte blanche* to conduct the analysis in the September NVR and issue it to HSBC. Such authority must be found in the *CCAA* or the court orders made in the proceeding.

[84] Subsections 23(h) and (i) of the *CCAA* deal with the monitor's duty to report to the court. Subsection 23(h) requires the monitor to promptly advise the court if it is of the opinion that it would be more beneficial to the creditors if *BIA* proceedings were taken. Section 23(i) requires the monitor to advise the court on the reasonableness and fairness of any compromise or arrangement that is proposed between the debtor and its creditors. Typically, this report is shared with the creditors just before or at the creditors' meeting to vote on the proposed compromise or arrangement.

[85] The provisions in the Initial Order describing the Monitor's reporting functions are central to this inquiry. They must be read contextually.

[86] HSBC was an unaffected creditor that continued to provide financing to the Winalta Group by an operating line of credit and overdraft facility. There was no DIP financing as HSBC was, in effect, the interim financier. Clause 22 of the Initial Order speaks to HSBC's role as a financier during the *CCAA* process.

[87] Clause 28(d) of the Initial Order reads, in part, as follows:

> 28. The Monitor, in addition to its prescribed rights and obligations under the *CCAA*, is hereby directed and empowered to:
> (d) advise the Applicants in their preparation of the Applicant's cash flow statements and reporting required by HSBC or any DIP lender, which information shall be reviewed with the Monitor and delivered to HSBC or any DIP lender and its counsel on a periodic basis, but not less than weekly, or as otherwise agreed to by HSBC and any DIP lender. [Emphasis added.]

[88] Clause 30 of the Initial Order states:

> The Monitor shall provide HSBC and any other creditor of the Applicants' and any DIP Lender with information provided by the Applicants in response to reasonable requests for information made in writing by such creditor addressed to the Monitor. The Monitor shall not have any responsibility or liability with respect to the information disseminated by it pursuant to this paragraph. In the case of information that the Monitor has been advised by the Applicants is confidential, the Monitor shall not provide such information to creditors unless otherwise directed by the Court or on such terms as the Monitor and the Applicants may agree. [Emphasis added.]

[89] The Monitor's capacity to report to HSBC was limited to the parameters of these provisions.

Step 2: Assessing the Monitor's actions

. . .

(b) Interpreting the relevant provisions of the Initial Order and the CCAA

[98] The object of the *CCAA* is to enable insolvent companies to carry on business in the ordinary course or to otherwise deal with their assets so that a plan of arrangement

or compromise can be prepared, filed and considered by their creditors and the court. While this object does not play as significant a role in interpreting clauses 28(d) and 30 of the Initial Order as it might in other cases, nevertheless it is relevant.

[99] Section 23 of the *CCAA* sets out certain reporting requirements for a court-appointed monitor. None of these authorized the Monitor in this case to provide HSBC with the analysis contained in the September NVR, without the knowledge and consent of the Winalta Group or the court.

[100] Clause 28(d) of the Initial Order empowers and obliges the Monitor to give advice to the Winalta Group about its preparation of cash flow statements and reports required of it by HSBC or any DIP lender. It is clear from the plain and ordinary language of the provision that it applies to instances where the Winalta Group reports to HSBC. It is the Winalta Group's job to do the reporting. The Monitor's job is to assist the Winalta Group and to review the reports before they are delivered to the relevant lender. A contrary finding would render the words "and reviewed with the Monitor" nonsensical.

[101] If there is any ambiguity in clause 28(d), it is about who is to deliver the reports. The use of the word "and" after the words "shall be reviewed with the Monitor" is open to the interpretation that the Monitor is to deliver the reports. As nothing turns on that point, I need not decide it.

[102] I am entitled to and do assume that the parties' affected by clause 28(d) carefully crafted that provision and agreed to its terms. Had they intended the Monitor to undertake the analysis contained in the September NVR and to provide it to HSBC, they would have said so. Whether such a provision would have been granted is another question altogether.

[103] This interpretation is supported by contrasting clause 28(d) with the unambiguous language of clause 30, which refers to the Monitor providing information to HSBC (given to the Monitor by the Winalta Group and declared by it to be non-confidential). Unlike clause 28(d), clause 30 absolves the Monitor of responsibility and liability for its acts. Presumably, the parties would have included similar protection in clause 28(d) if it was intended that the Monitor have the authority it claims.

[104] Interpreting clause 28(d) as referring to reports by the Winalta Group rather than the Monitor also is supported by reading the Initial Order as a whole. Clause 22 speaks to HSBC continuing to provide operating and overdraft facilities to the Winalta Group. As HSBS, in effect, is an interim lender, it is logical that the Winalta Group is obliged under the Initial Order to provide it (and any DIP lender) with cash flow statements and any other required reports on a weekly basis (after having the information reviewed by the Monitor, presumably for accuracy).

[105] Finally, this interpretation is supported by reference to the object of the *CCAA*, which is to have debtors remain in and control their business operations throughout the term of the restructuring. The debtor is the party that reports to its interim lenders.

[106] The Monitor's interpretation of clause 28(d) as authorizing it to prepare and deliver the September NVR to HSBC does not withstand scrutiny. That clause neither expressly nor implicitly authorized the Monitor's conduct in that regard. If the Monitor had any hesitation about the scope of its authority under this clause (which I am of the clear view it ought to have had), its obligation was to seek clarification from the court before proceeding as it did.

[107] Clause 30 is unambiguous. To a degree, it supports the Monitor's action as its plain and ordinary language permits the Monitor to release to HSBC (or any DIP lender) information provided by the Winalta Group which it did not declare to be confidential.

The Monitor's notes to the September NVR refer to estimated asset realizations, closing dates for certain transactions, and accounts receivable. Presumably, the Monitor obtained that information from the Winalta Group.

[108] However, the Monitor's estimate of receivership fees, its various calculations, and its analysis stand on a completely different footing. By definition, that is not "information provided by the Winalta Group." Clause 30 does not authorize the Monitor to take information legitimately obtained from the Winalta Group and to use it as the basis for preparing and issuing the type of analysis contained in the September NVR report. Presumably, this provision (which was granted as presented) reflects a negotiated agreement and was carefully crafted.

[109] The Monitor says that it would have prepared and given any creditor the type of analysis contained in the September NVR on demand, irrespective of the creditor's stake. That may be so (or not), but it does not mean that it is authorized or appropriate for it to do so, particularly without the knowledge and consent of the Winalta Group.

[110] The Monitor's interpretation of clause 30 as authorizing it to prepare and deliver the September NVR to HSBC fails to withstand full scrutiny. Clause 30 did not authorize the Monitor to provide anything over and above the information provided by the Winalta Group. Again, if the Monitor had any hesitation about the scope of its authority under this clause (which I am of the clear view it ought to have had), its obligation was to seek clarification from the court before proceeding as it did.

[111] Read contextually, neither the express language nor the spirit of clauses 28(d) and 30 of the Initial Order authorized the Monitor to issue certain of the information contained in the September NVR. Its authority was limited to relaying non-confidential raw data obtained from the Winalta Group. HSBC could then have interpreted the data (alone or with the assistance of another insolvency practitioner).

[112] The Monitor was not transparent in its dealings with HSBC surrounding the September NVR.

[113] Regrettably, and despite any well intentioned motivation that might be imputed to the Monitor, I find that the Monitor lost sight of the bright line separating its duties as an impartial court officer and a private consultant to HSBC when it provided HSBC with the analysis in the September NVR, thereby creating a perception of bias.

[114] In circumstances where the Monitor ought to have been keenly attuned to heightened sensitivity about perceptions of bias, it should have sought clarification of the reporting provisions in the Initial Order before conducting the analysis in the September NVR and issuing it to HSBC. The Monitor failed to recognize the need to do so. Instead, it elected to rely on an unsustainable interpretation of clauses 28(d) and 30 of the Initial Order.

Step 3

(a) Determining if damage is attributable to the Monitor's conduct, including damage to the integrity of the insolvency system

[115] HSBC's refusal to fund the Winalta Group's costs for procuring takeout financing appears to have fallen on the heels of it receiving the September NVR. Whether that was a mere coincidence or not has not been established by the Winalta Group.

[116] No authority was cited for the proposition that the court is entitled to reduce a court-appointed monitor's fees on a basis "akin to punitive damages." However, *Murphy v Sally Creek Environs Corp (Trustee of)*, 2010 ONCA 312, 67 C.B.R. (5th) 161 is informative, although distinguishable on its facts.

[117] *Murphy* concerned the reduction of a trustee in bankruptcy's fees for misconduct where the relationship between the trustee and largest unsecured creditor had spoiled. The trustee rationalized acting without the approval of two inspectors he considered to be the "handmaidens" of the largest unsecured creditor. At times, the trustee acted contrary to the inspectors' express wishes. Concluding that the trustee had sided against it, the creditor complained to various regulatory bodies, alleging serious wrongdoing and mismanagement by the trustee.

[118] On taxation, the registrar found the trustee guilty of 15 acts of misconduct ranging from multiple breaches of statutory duties to lying to regulatory bodies about the conduct of the estate. The registrar reduced the trustee's fees from $240,000.00 to $1.00 and disallowed or reduced many disbursements. The registrar's decision was appealed to Ontario's Superior Court of Justice and, in turn, to the Ontario Court of Appeal, which directed (at para. 125) that in preventing unjustifiable payments, the court should begin by considering discrete deductions for misconduct that cost the estate quantifiable amounts. The court also directed (at para. 126) that the court should consider the degree and extent of the misconduct, and its effect on the estate, the affected creditors, and the integrity of the bankruptcy process in general.

[119] These directives apply equally to a court-appointed *CCAA* monitor.

[120] In the present case, there is no quantifiable loss, nor is there evidence of damage to the estate. However, the Monitor's failure to scrupulously avoid a conflict of interest negatively impacts the integrity of the insolvency system.

(b) Ascertaining the appropriate fee reduction

[121] There is very little guidance on how the court is to assess an appropriate fee reduction where there is no quantifiable loss (*Re Nelson* (2006), 24 C.B.R. (5th) 40 at para. 31 (Ont. S.C.J.)).

[122] Reducing a court-appointed officer's fee is not intended to be punitive, but rather is an expression of the court's refusal to endorse the misconduct (*Murphy* at para. 112; *Re Nelson* at para. 31).

[123] Placing a value on the erosion of the public's confidence is an extremely difficult task, particularly given that the object of the exercise is not to punish the offending party. Arbitrarily choosing a figure as a means of refusing to endorse the misconduct is unfair. In the circumstances of this case, I am of the view that the fairer approach is to deprive the Monitor of any charges associated with its misconduct.

[124] Accordingly, the Monitor is to provide affidavit evidence within 60 days particularizing all charges associated with its analysis in the September NVR, following which I will determine the appropriate fee reduction. Should the Monitor fail to provide this information, I will have no alternative but to reduce the Fee otherwise.

IV. CONCLUSIONS

[125] The onus on this application rested with the Monitor to establish that its Fee was fair and reasonable. It has fallen short of doing so in a number of respects.

[126] The Monitor exceeded its statutory and court ordered authority by conducting the analysis in the September NVR and providing it to HSBC. The Monitor failed to act with transparency in its dealings with its former client and blurred the bright line dividing its duties as a court-appointed *CCAA* monitor and a private monitor.

Order accordingly.

III. GOVERNANCE

Problems can arise for company directors in several different ways. One way is through the execution of their duties, both the fiduciary duty and their statutory duty of care. In carrying out their fiduciary duty, company directors must "act honestly and in good faith with a view to the best interests of the corporation" (*Canada Business Corporations Act*, RSC 1985, c C-44, s 122(1)(a) [*CBCA*]). In *Peoples Department Stores Inc (Trustee of) v Wise*, 2004 SCC 68 (*Peoples*), the Supreme Court had to decide whether "the best interests of the corporation" encompasses creditors' interests when a company is nearing insolvency. It found that the "vicinity of insolvency" has no legal meaning (para 46), and that "the interests of the corporation are not to be confused with the interests of the creditors or those of any other stakeholder" (para 43). It concluded by maintaining that "at all times, directors and officers owe their fiduciary duty to the corporation" (para 43).

The statutory duty of care is different; it requires directors to "exercise the care, diligence and skill that a reasonably prudent person would exercise in comparable circumstances" (see *CBCA*, s 122(1)(b)). In *Peoples*, the Court held, "in determining whether they are acting with a view to the best interests of the corporation it may be legitimate, given all the circumstances of a given case, for the board of directors to consider, *inter alia*, the interests of shareholders, employees, suppliers, creditors, consumers, governments and the environment" (para 42). See also *BCE Inc v 1976 Debentureholders*, 2008 SCC 69 (*BCE*) (excerpted in Chapter 10) . The problem with the decision is that it assumes that these various interests are invariably aligned, which is not always the case. For example, assume a corporation is close to insolvency. The directors are presented with a risky business opportunity which will return substantial value to the corporation if it pays off, but will result in significant losses if it fails. Taking up the opportunity may be in the shareholders' interests because they have nothing to lose if the venture fails, but everything to gain if it succeeds. But this course of action may not be in the creditors' interests because they will bear the loss in the likely event that the venture fails. In this type of case, clearly the interests of the shareholders and creditors are not aligned, and the *Peoples* and *BCE* cases give directors little guidance on how they should decide (see Andrew Kent et al, "Canadian Business Restructuring Law: When Should A Court Say 'No'?" (2008) 24 *Business & Finance Law Review* 1 at 6–13).

Company directors also face conflicts of interest. *Peoples*, *BCE*, and *Sun Indalex Finance, LLC v United Steelworkers*, 2013 SCC 6 (*Indalex*) (excerpted below) were all concerned with the director's duty to avoid conflicts of interest. But there is an important difference between the cases. In *Peoples* and *BCE*, the directors owed duties only in their capacity as directors, but there was a potential conflict between the interests of different stakeholders in relation to how the duty was exercised. By contrast, in *Indalex*, the directors were wearing two hats, which gave rise to conflict. They owed one set of duties to the corporation in their capacity as directors and they owed another set of duties to the plan beneficiaries in their capacity as the plan administrators. In *Peoples* and *BCE*, the court's response was to deny the potential conflict of interest. In *Indalex*, the Court responded by limiting the nature and scope of the plan administrator's duties so as to minimize the potential for conflict with directors' duties.

Due to issues arising out of governance and conflicts of interest, directors may be compelled to leave a corporation during a *CCAA* restructuring, either at the behest of an interested party, or on their own volition. *CCAA*, section 11.5, allows the court, on the application of an interested party, to make an order removing one or more of the debtor company's directors from office if the court is satisfied that "the director is unreasonably impairing or is likely to unreasonably impair the possibility of a viable [restructuring] or is acting or is likely to act inappropriately as a director in the circumstances." The provision reverses the Ontario Court of Appeal's decision in *Re Stelco Inc* (2005), 75 OR (3d) 5 (CA). Section 11.5 is relevant to the case where creditors have lost faith in one or more directors, but the directors are reluctant to resign, and it provides a possible remedy for creditors who are concerned that the debtor company's directors may act contrary to the creditors' interests. For a critical analysis of section 11.5, see Marie Bruchet, "Director Removal Under the *CCAA*" (2008) 24 *Business & Finance Law Review* 269.

The reverse scenario is also a concern—namely, where directors are reluctant to stay, even though creditors want the current management to remain in place. Directors may want to resign in order to avoid personal liability, both for the company's existing debts and for any further debts the company may incur going forward (provincial legislation makes directors personally responsible for the company's debts in certain circumstances). On the other hand, creditors may want the directors to stay—for example, because the directors have a close knowledge of the debtor's business that would be hard to replicate. The statute contains a number of provisions addressing this problem. *CCAA*, section 11.03, authorizes the inclusion in the stay order of provisions staying proceedings against directors. Section 5.1 provides for the inclusion of directors in the debtor's plan. Section 11.51 authorizes the court to impose a charge on the debtor's assets for the purpose of indemnifying a director against liabilities incurred after the commencement of the *CCAA* proceedings.

Sun Indalex Finance, LLC v United Steelworkers, 2013 SCC 6, [2013] 1 SCR 271

[The following summary of the facts is taken from the judgment of Cromwell J at paras 90–97]:

[90] Indalex Limited is the parent company of three non-operating Canadian companies. I will refer to both Indalex Limited individually and to the group of companies collectively as "Indalex", unless the context requires further clarity. Indalex Limited is the wholly owned subsidiary of its U.S. parent, Indalex Holding Corp. which owned and conducted related operations in the U.S. through its U.S. subsidiaries which I will refer to as the "U.S. debtors".

[91] In late March and early April of 2009, Indalex and the U.S. debtors were insolvent and sought protection from their creditors, the former under the Canadian *CCAA*, and the latter under the United States Bankruptcy Code, 11 U.S.C., Chapter 11. The dispute giving rise to these appeals concern the priority granted to lenders in the *CCAA* process for funds advanced to Indalex and whether that priority overrides the claims of two of Indalex's pension plans for funds owed to them.

[92] Indalex was the sponsor and administrator of two registered pension plans relevant to these proceedings, one for salaried employees and the other for executive employees. At the time of seeking *CCAA* protection, the salaried plan was being wound up (with a wind-up date of December 31, 2006) and was estimated to have a wind-up deficiency (as of the end of 2007) of roughly $2.252 million. The executive plan, while it was not being wound up, had been closed to new members since 2005. It was estimated to have a deficiency of roughly $2.996 million on wind up. At the time the *CCAA* proceedings were started, all regular current service contributions had been made to both plans.

[93] Shortly after Indalex received *CCAA* protection, the *CCAA* judge authorized the company to enter into debtor in possession ("DIP") financing in order to allow it to continue to operate. The court granted the DIP lenders, a syndicate of banks, a "super priority" over "all other security interests, trusts, liens, charges and encumbrances, statutory

or otherwise": initial order, at para. 35 (Joint A.R., vol. I, at pp. 123–24). Repayment of these amounts was guaranteed by the U.S. debtors.

[94] Ultimately, with the approval of the *CCAA* court, Indalex sold its business; the purchaser did not assume pension liabilities. A reserve fund was established by the *CCAA* Monitor to answer any outstanding claims. The proceeds of the sale were not sufficient to pay back the DIP lenders and so the U.S. debtors, as guarantors, paid the shortfall and stepped into the shoes of the DIP lenders in terms of priority.

[95] The appellant Sun Indalex is a pre-*CCAA* secured creditor of both Indalex and the U.S. debtors. It claims the reserve fund on the basis that the US$10.75 million paid by the guarantors would otherwise have been available to Sun Indalex as a secured creditor of the U.S. debtors in the U.S. bankruptcy proceedings. The respondent plan beneficiaries claim the reserve fund on the basis that they have a wind-up deficiency which is covered by a deemed trust created by s. 57(4) of the *PBA*. This deemed trust includes "an amount of money equal to employer contributions *accrued to the date of the wind up but not yet due* under the plan or regulations" (s. 57(4)). They also claim the reserve fund on the basis of a constructive trust arising from Indalex's failure to live up to its fiduciary duties as plan administrator.

[96] The reserve fund is not sufficient to pay back both Sun Indalex and the pension plans and so the main question on the main appeals is which of the creditors is entitled to priority for their respective claims.

[97] The judge at first instance rejected the plan beneficiaries' deemed trust arguments and held that, with respect to the wind-up deficiency, the plan beneficiaries were unsecured creditors, ranking behind those benefitting from the "super priority" and secured creditors (2010 ONSC 1114, 79 C.C.P.B. 301). The Court of Appeal reversed this ruling and held that pension plan deficiencies were subject to deemed and constructive trusts which had priority over the DIP financing and over other secured creditors (2011 ONCA 265, 104 O.R. (3d) 641). Sun Indalex, the trustee in bankruptcy and the Monitor appeal.

[On appeal to the Supreme Court, four issues were raised]:

[25] ...
1. Does the deemed trust provided for in s.57(4) of the PBA apply to wind-up deficiencies?
2. If so, does the deemed trust supersede the DIP charge?
3. Did Indalex have any fiduciary obligations to the Plan Members when making decisions in the context of the insolvency proceedings?
4. Did the Court of Appeal properly exercise its discretion in imposing a constructive trust to remedy the breaches of fiduciary duties?

[The following extracts relate to the third and fourth of these issues. Further extracts from the case, relating to the first and second issues, appear in Chapter 14, below.]

DESCHAMPS J (Moldaver J concurring): ...

C. Did Indalex Have a Fiduciary Obligation to the Plan Members?

...

[62] The first stage of a fiduciary duty analysis is to determine whether and when fiduciary obligations arise. The Court has recognized that there are circumstances in which a pension plan administrator has fiduciary obligations to plan members both at

common law and under statute (*Burke v Hudson's Bay Co*, 2010 SCC 34, [2010] 2 S.C.R. 273, at para. 41). It is clear that the indicia of a fiduciary relationship attach in this case between the Plan Members and Indalex as plan administrator. Sun Indalex and the Monitor do not dispute this proposition.

[63] However, Sun Indalex and the Monitor argue that the employer has a fiduciary duty only when it acts as plan administrator—when it is wearing its administrator's "hat". They contend that, outside the plan administration context, when directors make decisions in the best interests of the corporation, the employer is wearing solely its "corporate hat". On this view, decisions made by the employer in its corporate capacity are not burdened by the corporation's fiduciary obligations to its pension plan members and, consequently, cannot be found to conflict with plan members' interests. This is not the correct approach to take in determining the scope of the fiduciary obligations of an employer acting as plan administrator.

[64] Only persons or entities authorized by the *PBA* can act as plan administrators (ss. 1(1) and 8(1)(a)). The employer is one of them. A corporate employer that chooses to act as plan administrator accepts the fiduciary obligations attached to that function. Since the directors of a corporation also have a fiduciary duty to the corporation, the fact that the corporate employer can act as administrator of a pension plan means that s. 8(1)(a) of the *PBA* is based on the assumption that not all decisions taken by directors in managing a corporation will result in conflict with the corporation's duties to the plan's members. However, the corporate employer must be prepared to resolve conflicts where they arise. Reorganization proceedings place considerable burdens on any debtor, but these burdens do not release an employer that acts as plan administrator from its fiduciary obligations.

[65] Section 22(4) of the *PBA* explicitly provides that a plan administrator must not permit its own interest to conflict with its duties in respect of the pension fund. Thus, where an employer's own interests do not converge with those of the plan's members, it must ask itself whether there is a potential conflict and, if so, what can be done to resolve the conflict. Where interests do conflict, I do not find the two hats metaphor helpful. The solution is not to determine whether a given decision can be classified as being related to either the management of the corporation or the administration of the pension plan. The employer may well take a sound management decision, and yet do something that harms the interests of the plan's members. An employer acting as a plan administrator is not permitted to disregard its fiduciary obligations to plan members and favour the competing interests of the corporation on the basis that it is wearing a "corporate hat". What is important is to consider the consequences of the decision, not its nature.

[66] When the interests the employer seeks to advance on behalf of the corporation conflict with interests the employer has a duty to preserve as plan administrator, a solution must be found to ensure that the plan members' interests are taken care of. This may mean that the corporation puts the members on notice, or that it finds a replacement administrator, appoints representative counsel or finds some other means to resolve the conflict. The solution has to fit the problem, and the same solution may not be appropriate in every case.

[67] In the instant case, Indalex's fiduciary obligations as plan administrator did in fact conflict with management decisions that needed to be taken in the best interests of the corporation. Indalex had a number of responsibilities as plan administrator. For example, s. 56(1) of the *PBA* required it to ensure that contributions were paid when due. Section 56(2) required that it notify the Superintendent if contributions were not paid when due. It was also up to Indalex under s. 59 to commence proceedings to obtain

payment of contributions that were due but not paid. Indalex, as an employer, paid all the contributions that were due. However, its insolvency put contributions that had accrued to the date of the wind up at risk. In an insolvency context, the administrator's claim for contributions that have accrued is a provable claim.

[68] In the context of this case, the fact that Indalex, as plan administrator, might have to claim accrued contributions from itself means that it would have to simultaneously adopt conflicting positions on whether contributions had accrued as of the date of liquidation and whether a deemed trust had arisen in respect of wind-up deficiencies. This is indicative of a clear conflict between Indalex's interests and those of the Plan Members. As soon as it saw, or ought to have seen, a potential for conflict, Indalex should have taken steps to ensure that the interests of the Plan Members were protected. It did not do so. On the contrary, it contested the position the Plan Members advanced. At the very least, Indalex breached its duty to avoid conflicts of interest (s. 22(4) *PBA*).

[69] Since the Plan Members seek an equitable remedy, it is important to identify the point at which Indalex should have moved to ensure that their interests were safeguarded. Before doing so, I would stress that factual contexts are needed to analyse conflicts between interests, and that it is neither necessary nor useful to attempt to map out all the situations in which conflicts may arise.

[70] As I mentioned above, insolvency puts the employer's contributions at risk. This does not mean that the decision to commence insolvency proceedings entails on its own a breach of a fiduciary obligation. The commencement of insolvency proceedings in this case on April 3, 2009 in an emergency situation was explained by Timothy R. J. Stubbs, the then-president of Indalex. The company was in default to its lender, it faced legal proceedings for unpaid bills, it had received a termination notice effective April 6 from its insurers, and suppliers had stopped supplying on credit. These circumstances called for urgent action by Indalex lest a creditor start bankruptcy proceedings and in so doing jeopardize ongoing operations and jobs. Several facts lead me to conclude that the stay sought in this case did not, in and of itself, put Indalex in a conflict of interest.

[71] First, a stay operates only to freeze the parties' rights. In most cases, stays are obtained *ex parte*. One of the reasons for refraining from giving notice of the initial stay motion is to avert a situation in which creditors race to court to secure benefits that they would not enjoy in insolvency. Subjecting as many creditors as possible to a single process is seen as a way to treat all of them more equitably. In this context, plan members are placed on the same footing as the other creditors and have no special entitlement to notice. Second, one of the conclusions of the order Indalex sought was that it was to be served on all creditors, with a few exceptions, within 10 days. The notice allowed any interested party to apply to vary the order. Third, Indalex was permitted to pay all pension benefits. Although the order excluded special solvency payments, no ruling was made at that point on the merits of the creditors' competing claims, and a stay gave the Plan Members the possibility of presenting their arguments on the deemed trust rather than losing it altogether as a result of a bankruptcy proceeding, which was the alternative.

[72] Whereas the stay itself did not put Indalex in a conflict of interest, the proceedings that followed had adverse consequences. On April 8, 2009, Indalex brought a motion to amend and restate the initial order in order to apply for DIP financing. This motion had been foreseen. Mr. Stubbs had mentioned in the affidavit he signed in support of the initial order that the lenders had agreed to extend their financing, but that Indalex would be in need of authorization in order to secure financing to continue its

operations. However, the initial order had not yet been served on the Plan Members as of April 8. Short notice of the motion was given to the USW rather than to all the individual Plan Members, but the USW did not appear. The Plan Members were quite simply not represented on the motion to amend the initial stay order requesting authorization to grant the DIP charge.

[73] In seeking to have a court approve a form of financing by which one creditor was granted priority over all other creditors, Indalex was asking the *CCAA* court to override the Plan Members' priority. This was a case in which Indalex's directors permitted the corporation's best interests to be put ahead of those of the Plan Members. The directors may have fulfilled their fiduciary duty to Indalex, but they placed Indalex in the position of failing to fulfil its obligations as plan administrator. The corporation's interest was to seek the best possible avenue to survive in an insolvency context. The pursuit of this interest was not compatible with the plan administrator's duty to the Plan Members to ensure that all contributions were paid into the funds. In the context of this case, the plan administrator's duty to the Plan Members meant, in particular, that it should at least have given them the opportunity to present their arguments. This duty meant, at the very least, that they were entitled to reasonable notice of the DIP financing motion. The terms of that motion, presented without appropriate notice, conflicted with the interests of the Plan Members. Because Indalex supported the motion asking that a priority be granted to its lender, it could not at the same time argue for a priority based on the deemed trust.

[74] The Court of Appeal found a number of other breaches. I agree with Cromwell J that none of the subsequent proceedings had a negative impact on the Plan Members' rights. The events that occurred, in particular the second DIP financing motion and the sale process, were predictable and, in a way, typical of reorganizations. Notice was given in all cases. The Plan Members were represented by able counsel. More importantly, the court ordered that funds be reserved and that a full hearing be held to argue the issues.

[75] The Monitor and George L. Miller, Indalex U.S.'s trustee in bankruptcy, argue that the Plan Members should have appealed the Amended Initial Order authorizing the DIP charge, and were precluded from subsequently arguing that their claim ranked in priority to that of the DIP lenders. They take the position that the collateral attack doctrine bars the Plan Members from challenging the DIP financing order. This argument is not convincing. The Plan Members did not receive notice of the motion to approve the DIP financing. Counsel for the Executive Plan's members presented the argument of that plan's members at the first opportunity and repeated it each time he had an occasion to do so. The only time he withdrew their opposition was at the hearing of the motion for authorization to increase the DIP loan amount after being told that the only purpose of the motion was to increase the amount of the authorized loan. The *CCAA* judge set a hearing date for the very purpose of presenting the arguments that Indalex, as plan administrator, could have presented when it requested the amendment to the initial order. It cannot now be argued, therefore, that the Plan Members are barred from defending their interests by the collateral attack doctrine.

D. Would an Equitable Remedy Be Appropriate in the Circumstances?

[76] The definition of "secured creditor" in s. 2 of the *CCAA* includes a trust in respect of the debtor's property. The Amended Initial Order (at para. 45) provided that the DIP lenders' claims ranked in priority to all trusts, "statutory or otherwise". Indalex U.S. was

subrogated to the DIP lenders' claim by operation of the guarantee in the DIP lending agreement.

[77] Counsel for the Executive Plan's members argues that the doctrine of equitable subordination should apply to subordinate Indalex U.S.'s subrogated claim to those of the Plan Members. This Court discussed the doctrine of equitable subordination in *Canada Deposit Insurance Corp v Canadian Commercial Bank*, [1992] 3 S.C.R. 558, but did not endorse it, leaving it for future determination (p. 609). I do not need to endorse it here either. Suffice to say that there is no evidence that the lenders committed a wrong or that they engaged in inequitable conduct, and no party has contested the validity of Indalex U.S.'s payment of the US$10 million shortfall.

[78] This leaves the constructive trust remedy ordered by the Court of Appeal. It is settled law that proprietary remedies are generally awarded only with respect to property that is directly related to a wrong or that can be traced to such property. I agree with my colleague Cromwell J that this condition is not met in the case at bar. I adopt his reasoning on this issue.

[79] Moreover, I am of the view that it was unreasonable for the Court of Appeal to reorder the priorities in this case. The breach of fiduciary duty identified in this case is, in substance, the lack of notice. Since the Plan Members were allowed to fully argue their case at a hearing specifically held to adjudicate their rights, the *CCAA* court was in a position to fully appreciate the parties' positions.

[80] It is difficult to see what gains the Plan Members would have secured had they received notice of the motion that resulted in the Amended Initial Order. The *CCAA* judge made it clear, and his finding is supported by logic, that there was no alternative to the DIP loan that would allow for the sale of the assets on a going-concern basis. The Plan Members presented no evidence to the contrary. They rely on conjecture alone. The Plan Members invoke other cases in which notice was given to plan members and in which the members were able to fully argue their positions. However, in none of those cases were plan members able to secure any additional benefits. Furthermore, the Plan Members were allowed to fully argue their case. As a result, even though Indalex breached its fiduciary duty to notify the Plan Members of the motion that resulted in the Amended Initial Order, their claim remains subordinate to that of Indalex U.S....

CROMWELL J (McLachlin CJ and Rothstein J concurring): . . .

[180] The Court of Appeal found that during the *CCAA* proceedings Indalex breached its fiduciary obligations as administrator of the pension plans: para. 116. As a remedy, it imposed a remedial constructive trust over the reserve fund, effectively giving the plan beneficiaries recovery of 100 cents on the dollar in priority to all other creditors, including creditors entitled to the super priority ordered by the *CCAA* court.

[181] The breaches identified by the Court of Appeal fall into three categories. First, Indalex breached the prohibition against a fiduciary being in a position of conflict of interest because its interests in dealing with its insolvency conflicted with its duties as plan administrator to act in the best interests of the plans' members and beneficiaries: para. 142. According to the Court of Appeal, the simple fact that Indalex found itself in this position of conflict of interest was, of itself, a breach of its fiduciary duty as plan administrator. Second, Indalex breached its fiduciary duty by applying, without notice to the plans' beneficiaries, for *CCAA* protection: para. 139. Third, Indalex breached its fiduciary duty by seeking and/or obtaining various relief in the *CCAA* proceedings including the "super priority" in favour of the DIP lenders, approval of the sale of the business

knowing that no payment would be made to the underfunded plans over the statutory deemed trusts and seeking to be put into bankruptcy with the intention of defeating the deemed trust claims: para. 139. As a remedy for these breaches of fiduciary duty the court imposed a constructive trust.

[182] In my view, the Court of Appeal took much too expansive a view of the fiduciary duties owed by Indalex as plan administrator and found breaches where there were none. As I see it, the only breach of fiduciary duty committed by Indalex occurred when, upon insolvency, Indalex's corporate interests were in obvious conflict with its fiduciary duty as plan administrator to ensure that all contributions were made to the plans when due. The breach was not in failing to avoid this conflict—the conflict itself was unavoidable. Its breach was in failing to address the conflict to ensure that the plan beneficiaries had the opportunity to have representation in the *CCAA* proceedings as if there were independent plan administrators. I also conclude that a remedial constructive trust is not available as a remedy for this breach....

[185] [T]he conclusion that Indalex as plan administrator had fiduciary duties to the plan beneficiaries is the beginning, not the end of the inquiry. This is because fiduciary duties do not exist at large, but arise from and relate to the specific legal interests at stake....

[186] The nature and scope of the fiduciary duty must, therefore, be assessed in the legal framework governing the relationship out of which the fiduciary duty arises.... So, for example, as a general rule, a fiduciary has a duty of loyalty including the duty to avoid conflicts of interest.... However, this general rule may have to be modified in light of the legal framework within which a particular fiduciary duty must be exercised. In my respectful view, this is such a case....

[193] [An] important aspect of the legal context for Indalex's fiduciary duties as a plan administrator is that it was acting in the dual role of an employer-administrator. This dual role is expressly permitted under s. 8(1)(a) of the *PBA*, but this provision creates a situation where a single entity potentially owes two sets of fiduciary duties (one to the corporation and the other to the plan members).

[194] This was the case for Indalex. As an employer-administrator, Indalex acted through its board of directors and so it was that body which owed fiduciary duties to the plan members. The board of directors also owed a fiduciary duty to the company to act in its best interests: *Canada Business Corporations Act*, R.S.C. 1985, c. C-44, s. 122(1)(a); *BCE Inc v 1976 Debentureholders*, 2008 SCC 69, [2008] 3 S.C.R. 560, at para. 36. In deciding what is in the best interests of the corporation, a board may look to the interests of shareholders, employees, creditors and others. But where those interests are not aligned or may conflict, it is for the directors, acting lawfully and through the exercise of business judgment, to decide what is in the overall best interests of the corporation. Thus, the board of Indalex, as an employer-administrator, could not always act exclusively in the interests of the plan beneficiaries; it also owed duties to Indalex as a corporation.

[195] Against the background of these legal principles, I turn to consider the Court of Appeal's findings in relation to Indalex's breach of its fiduciary duties as administrator of the plans. As noted, they fall into three categories: being in a conflict of interest position; taking steps to reduce pension obligations in the *CCAA* proceedings; and seeking bankruptcy status....

[197] The Court of Appeal in effect concluded that a conflict of interest arises whenever Indalex makes business decisions that have "the potential to affect the Plans beneficiaries' rights" (para. 132) and that whenever such a conflict of interest arose, the

employer-administrator was immediately in breach of its fiduciary duties to the plan members. Respectfully, this position puts the matter far too broadly. It cannot be the case that a conflict arises simply because the employer, exercising its management powers in the best interests of the corporation, does something that has the potential to affect the plan beneficiaries.

[198] This conclusion flows inevitably from the statutory context. The existence of apparent conflicts that are inherent in the two roles being performed by the same party cannot be a breach of fiduciary duty because those conflicts are specifically authorized by the statute which permits one party to play both roles. As noted earlier, the *PBA* specifically permits employers to act as plan administrators (s. 8(1)(a)). Moreover, the broader business interests of the employer corporation and the interests of pension beneficiaries in getting the promised benefits are almost always at least potentially in conflict. Every important business decision has the potential to put at risk the solvency of the corporation and therefore its ability to live up to its pension obligations. The employer, within the limits set out in the plan documents and the legislation generally, has the authority to amend the plan unilaterally and even to terminate it. These steps may well not serve the best interests of plan beneficiaries.

[199] Similarly, the simple existence of the sort of conflicts of interest identified by the Court of Appeal—those inherent in the employer's exercise of business judgment—cannot of themselves be a breach of the administrator's fiduciary duty. Once again, that conclusion is inconsistent with the statutory scheme that expressly permits an employer to act as plan administrator.

[200] How, then, should we identify conflicts of interest in this context?

[201] In *R v Neil*, 2002 SCC 70, [2002] 3 S.C.R. 631, Binnie J referred to the *Restatement Third, The Law Governing Lawyers* (2000), at § 121, to explain when a conflict of interest occurs in the context of the lawyer-client relationship: para. 31. In my view, the same general principle, adapted to the circumstances, applies with respect to employer-administrators. Thus, a situation of conflict of interest occurs when there is a substantial risk that the employer-administrator's representation of the plan beneficiaries would be materially and adversely affected by the employer-administrator's duties to the corporation. I would recall here, however, that the employer-administrator's obligation to represent the plan beneficiaries extends only to those tasks and duties that I have described above.

[202] In light of the foregoing, I am of the view that the Court of Appeal erred when it found, in effect, that a conflict of interest arose whenever Indalex was making decisions that "had the potential to affect the Plans beneficiaries' rights": para. 132. The Court of Appeal expressed both the potential for conflict of interest or duty and the fiduciary duty of the plan administrator much too broadly.

[Justice Cromwell, agreeing with Deschamps J, went on to hold that: (1) the Court of Appeal was wrong in finding that Indalex breached its fiduciary duty simply by commencing *CCAA* proceedings while knowing that the plans were under-funded and by failing to give the plan beneficiaries notice of the proceedings; (2) the Court of Appeal was correct in finding that Indalex breached its fiduciary duty by failing to ensure that the plan beneficiaries had the opportunity to be as fully represented in the *CCAA* proceedings as if there had been an independent plan administrator; and (3) the plan beneficiaries suffered no loss as a result of the breach and it was not appropriate to grant them constructive trust relief.]

IV. EXECUTORY CONTRACTS

A. Introduction

Chapter 6 deals with the disclaimer, affirmation, and assignment of executory contracts in *Bankruptcy and Insolvency Act*, RSC 1985, c B-3 (*BIA*) bankruptcy proceedings. The following commentary and materials relate to the disclaimer, affirmation, and assignment of executory contracts in *CCAA* proceedings. They should be read in conjunction with Chapter 6.

Contracts govern every aspect of carrying on business. Businesses commence and continue operating by entering into contracts, and these contracts do not cease to operate simply because a business runs into financial difficulties. Once a debtor has commenced *CCAA* proceedings, these contracts must be reviewed to determine whether it is profitable for the debtor to continue performing, or whether it is in the debtor's interests to cease performing. These determinations are part of the restructuring process; unloading arduous contracts is one way to revive the business. For that reason, the legislation gives the debtor the ability to pick and choose between the contracts it wishes to continue performing.

Executory contracts are contracts where there are outstanding obligations on both sides; these are contracts that have not been fully performed by either side, and performance of them requires the continued participation of both parties. Importantly, these are not contracts where one party has fully performed and the other party has yet to perform; in these circumstances, the other party has reaped the benefits and if it refuses to perform, the party that has performed can sue for breach of contract. Rather, executory contracts are contracts that one party wants to perform in order to obtain the performance of the other party, but the other party has a right of termination. In the restructuring context, the debtor may not wish to perform on an executory contract, that is, it may wish to disclaim the contract. It is allowed to do so under restructuring law. It may also wish to affirm the contract or assign it to a third party. The sections below discuss how the debtor can accomplish any of these options in restructuring proceedings.

B. Disclaimer

Disclaimer is, in effect, an election not to perform the contract. It is governed by *CCAA*, section 32. In short, the debtor has the right to disclaim agreements if it meets the statutory requirements. Disclaimer gives the counterparty a claim for damages. *CCAA*, section 19(1)(b), provides that those claims "that may be dealt with by a compromise or arrangement in respect of a debtor company are claims that relate to debts or liabilities, present or future, to which the [debtor] may become subject before the compromise or arrangement is sanctioned by reason of any obligation incurred by the company" before the commencement of the proceedings. This provision tracks *BIA*, section 121(1), and the effect is that the claim of a contract counterparty following the debtor's disclaimer may be compromised as part of a *CCAA* plan. In other words, the counterparty's claim is a provable one (see Chapter 6, Part II(A), above).

The statutory right of disclaimer was added with the 2009 amendments. Prior to these amendments, the right of a debtor in *CCAA* proceedings to disclaim agreements depended on the general law of contract, supplemented by the provisions of the initial order. This was justified on the basis that, outside *CCAA* proceedings, a party may disclaim a contract if it chooses, but in the absence of a lawful excuse, it would be liable in damages to the counterparty. The debtor in *CCAA* proceedings is the same legal entity as it was before (see *Re Air Canada*, (2003)

45 CBR (4th) 13 (Ont Sup Ct J)) and, therefore, at least as far as the common law is concerned, it has the same right of disclaimer. In summary, as a general rule at common law, a debtor in CCAA proceedings is bound by its pre-filing contracts, unless it elects to disclaim them.

The main features of CCAA, section 32, are as follows:

- the monitor must first approve the proposed disclaimer;
- following this, the debtor must notify the counterparty, and the counterparty has fifteen days to apply to the court for disallowance of the disclaimer;
- if the monitor does not approve the proposed disclaimer, the debtor may apply to the court for an order allowing the disclaimer;
- in hearing an application by either the counterparty or the debtor, the court must consider whether the disclaimer "would enhance the prospects of a viable compromise or arrangement being made in respect of the company" and whether the disclaimer "would likely cause significant financial hardship [to the counterparty]";
- if a contract is disclaimed, the counterparty has a provable claim in the CCAA proceedings for any loss; and
- there are certain contracts to which the section does not apply, including eligible financial contracts, collective agreements and a lease of real property where the debtor is the lessor.

CCAA, section 32, loosely corresponds with the provisions governing the rejection of executory contracts in §365 of the US Bankruptcy Code, 11 USC §101. A notable difference is that the latter relates to "executory contracts," whereas the CCAA provision applies to "agreements." Although the Bankruptcy Code does not define "executory contract," the term is generally accepted to mean "a contract under which the obligations of both the bankrupt and the other party to the contract are so far unperformed that the failure of either to complete performance would constitute a material breach excusing the performance of the other" (Vern Countryman, "Executory Contracts in Bankruptcy" (1973) 57 Minnesota Law Review 439 at 460; the "Countryman definition"). The key feature of the Countryman definition is that, to qualify as an executory contract, an agreement must remain at least partially unperformed on both sides. Does the different wording in CCAA, section 32, mean that the provision applies even to contracts that are fully performed on one or both sides? No, and the answer is implicit in the word "disclaimer." Disclaimer is the debtor's election not to perform the contract and it is the corollary of affirmation (see Chapter 6, Part II(A), above). Therefore, the statutory right of disclaimer necessarily presupposes that there are outstanding obligations on the debtor's side. By implication there must also be outstanding obligations on the counterparty's side because otherwise the need for the debtor to elect between affirming and disclaiming the contract does not arise: the debtor already has the benefit of the contract and the counterparty already has a provable claim in respect of the debtor's non-performance. See Anthony Duggan and Norman Siebrasse, "The Disclaimer, Affirmation and Assignment of Intellectual Property Licenses in Insolvency" (2014) 3 Journal of the Insolvency Institute of Canada 163 at 165–69.

Don Greenfield et al, "When Insolvency and Restructuring Law Supercedes Contract" (2017) 55 Alberta Law Review 349 at 359–60 (footnotes omitted)

Another mechanism by which Canadian insolvency legislation can alter the contractual obligations of a debtor company to its creditors and non-creditors is through the disclaimer provisions of the CCAA and the BIA. Section 32(1) of the CCAA states:

[A] debtor company may—on notice given in the prescribed form and manner to the other parties to the agreement and the monitor—disclaim or resiliate any agreement to which the company is a party on the day on which proceedings commence under this Act. The company may not give notice unless the monitor approves the proposed disclaimer or resiliation.

These provisions were enacted by Parliament in 2009 to codify the debtor's ability to disclaim contracts. They allow the debtor to terminate, or "disclaim" in insolvency parlance, contracts if such termination enhances value or facilitates the restructuring of the debtor company, despite some harm to the counterparties to the contract. If a disclaimer is approved, either by the monitor or by the court, the counterparty can make a claim in the insolvency proceeding for damages resulting from the disclaimer as an unsecured creditor. ...

In deciding to approve a disclaimer, a court must consider the following factors: (a) whether the monitor approved the proposed disclaimer; (b) whether a disclaimer will enhance the prospects of a viable compromise or arrangement; and (c) whether a disclaimer will likely cause significant financial hardship to a counterparty to the agreement. It is fair to say that these factors are strongly in favour of the ability to disclaim contracts. It will be rare that a disclaimer is not allowed, subject to certain cases where it is not permitted for policy or other reasons.

In the recent, unreported decision of *Credit Suisse AG v Southern Pacific Resource Corp* the applicant, Altex Energy Ltd. (Altex) was a trade creditor of Southern Pacific Resource Corp. (Southern Pacific). After Southern Pacific applied for a stay of proceedings under the *CCAA*, it issued a notice to disclaim a terminal construction and rail services agreement. The disclaimer was not opposed by any counterparty and Southern Pacific ceased using Altex's services at the date of the disclaimer. Altex argued in its application that it was entitled to payment for the 30 day period from the date of the notice of disclaimer. Southern Pacific said the disclaimer took immediate effect. Justice Romaine held that the counterparty to the disclaimed contract was not entitled to payment after the date of the disclaimer notice, arguably contrary to the plain wording of the section.

[Permission granted by Ken Lenz Q.C., Partner and Co-Head, Litigation, Bennett Jones LLP.]

If the debtor's workplace is unionized, the employment relationship between the debtor and its employees will be governed by a collective agreement. Collective agreements are ongoing contracts that, absent other statutory provisions, would be governed by the executory contract provisions in *CCAA*, section 32, leaving the debtor with the ability to disclaim these contracts. In fact, collective agreements are governed by *CCAA*, section 33, and *CCAA*, section 32, does not apply to them. Section 33 provides, in part, that if a debtor in *CCAA* proceedings wants to alter a collective agreement against the wishes of the union, it must apply to the court for an order authorizing it serve a notice to bargain on the union. The court may only issue an order if it is satisfied that (a) a viable compromise or arrangement could not be made without taking into account the terms of the collective agreement; (b) the debtor has made good faith efforts to negotiate with the union; and (c) a failure to issue the order would be likely to cause irreparable damage to the company. Consider what the potentially adverse consequences are of a debtor not being able to disclaim a collective agreement. For a discussion, see David Baird and Ronald Davis, "Labour Issues" in Stephanie Ben-Ishai and Anthony Duggan, eds, *Canadian Bankruptcy and Insolvency Law: Bill C-55, Statute c.47 and Beyond* (Markham: LexisNexis, 2007) 68.

The following extract considers the meaning and purpose of section 33 and its relationship with the applicable law immediately prior to the 2009 amendments.

White Birch Paper Holding Company (Arrangement relatif à), 2010 QCCS 2590, [2010] RJQ 1518 (footnotes omitted)

MONGEON JSC:

Introduction

[1] The debtors have been under CCAA protection since February 24, 2010. The various companies in White Birch Group have continued to operate since that date and, where the Group employs unionized employees, the working conditions of these workers have been governed by the various collective agreements in force when the Initial Order was issued.

[2] These collective agreements contain various provisions creating obligations for the various employers in the Group (including Stadacona Limited Partnership ("Stadacona")) toward workers who are not currently working or former workers who are now retired. More specifically, certain former workers who have benefited from a special early retirement or voluntary separation program are entitled, under the terms of such programs, to life insurance, health insurance, and dental insurance at Stadacona's expense until the age of 65.

Factual background

[3] On April 26, 2010, Stadacona announced to its early retirees and its former employees who had opted for voluntary separation under the terms of the aforementioned programs, that it intended, effective June 1, 2010, to stop paying the insurance premiums in question and announced to them that, effective June 1, they would no longer be covered by the various insurance policies in question.

[4] The application from the Communications, Energy and Paperworkers Union of Canada (CEP), Locals 137, 200 and 250 (the "Union"), is therefore submitted to this Court in order to obtain the following declarations: . . .

The intended scope of section 33 CCAA

[30] Section 33 was passed during the last revision of the CCAA in September 2009.

[31] The Union sees it as a new provision that, in its view, would make any collective agreement completely immutable unless an amendment was negotiated and approved by the Court. Furthermore, if the Union were right, all employer obligations and all unionized employee rights arising from the collective agreement (including, where applicable, all pension plans incorporated therein) would be enforceable notwithstanding any initial order unless an agreement was made after notice was given under section 33 CCAA. In the undersigned's opinion, this would mean excluding the entire collective labour relations process from the application of the CCAA, except to the extent the Court can intervene, following notice and after bargaining has failed. According to a reading of, inter alia, section 33(8) of the CCAA, the Court would not have any manoeuvring room and the employer would, in particular, be required to fulfill all of its monetary obligations toward former employees who had retired and no longer work and to whom no consideration for work is therefore provided.

[32] For its part, Stadacona claims that the terms and conditions of the collective agreement apply only to the unionized employees the company keeps and needs to

ensure operational productivity. In other words, the employer may reduce its workforce, but if it has some of its employees performing work, they are then entitled to complete coverage of the working conditions negotiated and recorded in the collective agreement. In addition, the employer is not required to indemnify anyone who does not perform work in exchange for consideration (s. 11.01 CCAA).

[33] The parties submitted no jurisprudential example interpreting section 33 CCAA or defining its intended scope.

[34] The Union relies on the work of the House of Commons during the discussions concerning the passage of Bill C-55. Even if such a reference may be useful, however, it applies only if the legislation in question entails difficulties in interpretation.

[35] More specifically, the Union relies on the various testimonies provided before the Parliamentary Committee to suggest that collective agreements are now raised to the rank of absolute contracts which are completely outside the restructuring process and the CCAA unless the Union and the employer agree otherwise. That, however, would be tantamount to paralyzing the employer with respect to reducing its costs by any means at all, and to providing the Union with a veto with regard to the restructuring process.

[36] That does not mean that section 33 CCAA has no effect; far from it. In the Court's opinion, however, section 33 CCAA in fact codifies what Quebec and Canadian case law has established as applicable principles when a debtor company, bound to its employees under a collective agreement, obtains CCAA protection.

[37] Furthermore, if the Union's position were accepted, Stadacona would be required to continue to pay large amounts of money to former employees who do not perform any work in exchange (in this case, $52,000 a month or $624,000 a year). These third-party creditors would then be in a privileged position vis-à-vis all other creditors of the company for whom collection of claims has been stayed.

[38] There is no doubt that Stadacona's obligation to pay life, health and dental insurance premiums for its retirees originated prior to February 24, 2010. It is therefore an obligation stayed by the initial order unless it qualifies as any of the exceptions under section 11.01 CCAA (formerly section 11.3 CCAA).

[39] Below is the Union's statement (notes and authorities filed at the hearing).

[TRANSLATION]

6. The applicant Union respectfully submits that by adding section 33 to the CCAA, Parliament wanted to add more protection for collective agreements. The purpose of the amendment, which came into force on September 18, 2009, is to allow collective agreements to be maintained integrally and to provide for a revision process, which was not followed by Stadacona in the present case.

7. The principle stated in section 33 CCAA goes beyond the concept of valuable consideration stipulated in section 11.01(a) CCAA (formerly s.11.3 CCAA)....

9. As a result of the amendments made to the CCAA, the applicant Union respectfully submits that the employer cannot unilaterally alter the terms of the collective agreement or breach it by eliminating benefits without having first complied with the procedure set out in section 33 CCAA and obtained the agreement of the Union following bargaining. In the interim, compliance with the collective agreement is required and *the applicant Union's only remedy is to apply to this Court because all proceedings have been stayed in accordance with Section 9 of the initial order as well as the extension order dated March 26, 2010.* (Emphasis added.)

10. During the consideration of Bill C-55, which led to the enactment of the CCAA amendments that came into force on September 18, 2009, the Honourable Joe Fontana, Minister of Labour and Housing, declared as follows:

> If leave were granted to both parties, the union and the insolvent employer would be subject to a requirement to bargain in good faith over possible amendments to any existing collective agreement. Should the parties be unable—and I want to repeat, unable—to reach an agreement on such amendments, then the existing collective agreement would remain in place and could not be changed by the courts. Should the parties reach an agreement on concessions, then the bargaining agent would become an unsecured creditor for an amount equal to the value of those concessions.
>
> Mr. Chairman, these amendments to the Bankruptcy and Insolvency Act and the Companies' Creditors Arrangement Act have been developed with the intention of creating a fair and balanced regime for the conduct of labour-management relations in an insolvency situation *and to ensure appropriate protection for all employees.*
>
> So if one is accessing the CCAA or bankruptcy, we're trying to make sure we don't go to the American model—if I can put it that way—and throw out the collective agreement that essentially respects, as part 1 of the Labour Code does, that the two parties, employers and employees, have come to an agreement on how they will deal with certain issues. We want to maintain that standard. *To ensure that the collective agreements are respected, even under receivership or bankruptcy, they can't just be holus-bolus thrown out by a particular judge, and so on.* That's why I think we've put in place some greater clarity as to what the responsibilities would be.
>
> As we've said, *notice must be given to reopen the collective agreement,* and it's only with the agreement of both parties, especially the employees, that such a thing could happen. If they don't agree with the notice or want to fight the notice, they can. If they can't come to an agreement, if the collective agreement is open, the employees can essentially say no.
>
> *So for all intents and purposes, they have a veto on whether or not a collective agreement should be reopened.* I think this is a fundamental value that we want to maintain in our system. This bill essentially does that and clarifies what has been very unclear in terms of what courts have been able to do with collective agreements.

[40] There is nothing in the foregoing that empowers the Court to protect the claims of former employees who are now retirees and could be deprived of employee benefits of the nature discussed in the present case. The remarks above must be read in a context where Stadacona continues to employ unionized employees. Then the salary and benefits (including group insurance) that the employer must pay them are the ones which prevail in the collective agreements in force. That is the true intended scope of section 33 CCAA, and this interpretation does not conflict in any way with the statement of Minister Fontana, *supra.*

[41] Though section 33 CCAA came into force only in 2009, it was enacted in 2005 shortly after *Mine Jeffrey Inc* [[2003] RJQ 420].

[42] The Court is of the view that section 33 CCAA codifies the principles that Dalphond JA established in finding that, where there is a collective agreement in force between unionized employees and a debtor company subject to the CCAA, the

employees called to render services or perform work for the debtor company after an Initial Order has been issued must be compensated in accordance with the terms of the collective agreement and not at the monitor's discretion.

[43] In Section V of his judgment on the working conditions of employees continued or recalled (versus former employees who have retired), Dalphond JA wrote:

[TRANSLATION]

[47] Section 11.3 of the CCAA does not allow a court to order suppliers of goods and services, including employees, *to provide goods or services without being paid immediately by the monitor. In my opinion, the consideration payable cannot be unilaterally imposed by the monitor or the court.* . . .

[50] In short, nothing in the CCAA authorizes the monitor or the court to *unilaterally stop payment of the consideration payable to the person providing a good or service to the debtor company.* Furthermore, such consideration *must have been agreed upon with the supplier before the goods or services were provided, or must have been agreed upon before the initial* order, as for example in a contract of successive performance, or be the consideration applicable under the Act, a regulation, a rate or market rules. The situation is once again similar to that of a debtor governed by the BIA.

[51] In the present case, *since the certifications are not affected by the orders made,* since the layoff of all unionized employees does not terminate the certifications, and since people were recalled on the following day or later to fill positions covered by the certifications, *it follows that the consideration to be paid to such persons must be that stipulated in the collective agreements or in any amendment thereto negotiated with the appropriate union. Such consideration includes the salary and other benefits associated with such persons rendering services since the initial order.* Furthermore, any other suppliers *may further require payment of any amounts due at the date of the initial order (s. 11.3(a) in fine); within the meaning of the CCAA, they will be creditors with regard to such amounts and will possibly be offered an arrangement by the debtor.*

[52] The respondent points out that the impugned order stays the enforcement of the collective agreements only temporarily and that it is possible under the court's powers to issue stays. *I am of the opinion that such a stay is unlawful when it unilaterally overrides the provisions of collective agreements concerning consideration payable to recalled employees covered by the certifications.* Besides the fact that section 11.3 of the CCAA prohibits any stay with regard to the immediate enforcement of their right to consideration, it is clear that the debtor did not undertake to later pay them the difference between what they received and what they were entitled to receive under the collective agreements. *This is not a stay, but an amendment to working conditions decreed unilaterally by the monitor,* which infringes the appellants' rights arising from the certifications.

[53] I would add that the monitor's power to terminate a contract, with or without the leave of the court, seems to me to be hardly applicable to a collective agreement because of the federal or provincial statutory framework applicable thereto, as the case may be, which makes it more than just a simple bilateral contract, but a truly original instrument. In any case, what would be the point of disclaiming or resiliating collective agreements if the certifications remain, resulting in the obligation for the employer to negotiate the applicable conditions with the appropriate union in the event of a new provision of services by the employees covered by the said certifications? This is the equivalent of negotiating a new agreement or agreeing on amendments to the existing agreement.

(Emphasis added.)

[44] Then, in Section VI regarding the staying of payments required to remedy the pension fund shortfall and to maintain insurance for the benefit of retirees, Dalphond JA added:

[TRANSLATION]

[54] Under collective agreements, Jeffrey Mine Inc. must make up any unfunded liabilities through appropriate monthly payments. Unfunded liabilities were between $30,000,000 and $35,000,000 in November 2002 and would require monthly payments of $400,000 to $500,000 for the next five years.

[55] In his testimony before the trial judge, the monitor explained that *the debtor's current financial position made such payments impossible* since the profits from the contract with the U.S. purchaser were supposed to be used for more immediate purposes for the debtor's survival. *I am of the opinion that the Superior Court had the power to allow the stay of such monthly payments* and that, under the circumstances, its decision cannot be varied in appeal.

(Emphasis added.)

[45] After citing Royal Oak Mines Inc. [2001] O.J., No. 562 (Ont. C.A.) paras. [11] to [16], Dalphond JA added:

[TRANSLATION]

[57] In this case, the collective agreements were not altered when the Superior Court *authorized the monitor to stay the payment of pension plan contributions,* [TRANSLATION] *"except, ... for the employees whose services were retained by the monitor".* Indeed, the obligations of Jeffrey Mine Inc. with regard to the amounts payable to the pension fund under the collective agreements continue to exist, but they are not honoured because there are insufficient funds. Under the reorganization plan, arrangements may be made regarding payment of the amounts then due.

[58] *The same applies to the loss of some employee benefits for the persons who have not rendered any services to the debtor since the initial order.* These persons become creditors of the debtor company up to the monetary value of the benefits lost because payment of the premiums was stopped by Jeffrey Mine Inc.; the fact that these benefits were provided for in the collective agreements does not change anything.

[59] Lastly, the days of accumulated leave at the time of the initial order and any remuneration then not paid by Jeffrey Mine Inc. remain claims against the debtor that the monitor is not required to pay (s. 11.8 CCAA) and may be ineligible claims under the reorganization plan.

[46] He concludes as follows:

[60] Collective agreements continue to apply like any contract of successive performance not varied by agreement after the initial order or not terminated (assuming that this is possible for collective agreements). The monitor or the court cannot vary them unilaterally. That being said, distinctions should be made regarding payment of the resulting claims.

[61] *Accordingly, unionized employees kept or recalled are entitled to be paid immediately by the monitor for any service rendered after the order date (s. 11.3), in accordance with the terms of the collective agreement applicable in its original version or altered with the consent of the union concerned. For prior services, however, the obligations not discharged by Jeffrey Mine Inc. result*

from the claims against Jeffrey Mine Inc., for which the monitor cannot be held liable (s. 11.8 CCAA) and the employees cannot require immediate payment (s. 11.3 CCAA).

(Emphasis added.)

[47] That is exactly what section 33 CCAA contemplates. Collective agreements continue to apply provided that they refer only to the employees who continue to work.

[48] By codifying the principles of *Mine Jeffrey*, Parliament did not intend for collective agreements to be applied beyond these principles. If it had, it would have given unions complete power over the success or failure of any restructuring under the CCAA.

[49] When faced with a similar issue in Nortel Networks Corporation (Re), Geoffrey Morawetz J writes:

[53] There is no doubt that the views of the Union and the Former Employees differ from that of the Applicants. The Union insists that the Applicants honour the Collective Agreement. The Former Employees want treatment that is consistent with that being provided to the Union. The record also establishes that the financial predicament faced by retirees and Former Employees is, in many cases, serious. The record references examples where individuals are largely dependent upon the employee benefits that, until recently, they were receiving.

[54] However, the Applicants contend that since all of the employee obligations are unsecured it is improper to prefer retirees and the former Employees over the other unsecured creditors of the Applicants and furthermore, the financial pressure facing the Applicants precludes them from paying all of these outstanding obligations.

[55] Counsel to the Union contends that the *Applicants must pay for the full measure of its bargain with the Union while the Collective Agreement remains in force and further that the court does not have the jurisdiction to authorize a party, in this case the Applicants, to unilaterally determine which provisions of the collective Agreement they will abide by while the contract is in operation.* Counsel further contends that Section 11.3 of the CCAA precludes the court from authorizing the Applicants to make selective determinations as to which parts of the Collective Agreement they will abide by and that by failing to abide by the terms of the Collective Agreement, the Applicants acted as if the Collective Agreement between themselves and the Union has been amended to the extent that the Applicants are no longer bound by all of its terms and need merely address any loss through the plan of arrangement.

(Emphasis added.)

to then conclude:

[66] *I am unable to agree with the Union's argument. In my view, section 11.3 is an exception to the general stay provision authorized by section 11 provided for in the Initial Order.* As such, it seems to me that section 11.3 should be narrowly construed. (See *Ruth Sullivan, Sullivan on the Construction of Statues, 5th ed.* (Markham, Ont.: LexisNexis Canada Inc., 2008) at 483–485.) *Section 11.3 applies to services provided after the date of the Initial Order.* The ordinary meaning of "services" must be considered in the context of the phrase "services, ... provided after the order is made". *On a plain reading, it contemplates, in my view, some activity on behalf of the service provider which is performed after the date of the Initial Order.* The CCAA contemplates that during the reorganization process, pre-filing debts are not paid, absent exceptional circumstances and services provided after the date of the Initial Order will be paid for the purpose of ensuring the continued supply of services.

[67] *The flaw in the argument of the Union is that it equates the crystallization of a payment obligation under the Collective Agreement to a provision of a service within the meaning*

of section 11.3. The triggering of the payment obligation may have arisen after the Initial Order but it does not follow that a service has been provided after the Initial Order. Section 11.3 contemplates, in my view, *some current activity by a service provider post-filing that gives rise to a payment obligation post-filing.* The distinction being that the claims of the Union for termination and severance pay are based, for the most part, on services that were provided pre-filing. Likewise, obligations for benefits arising from RAP and VRO are again based, for the most part, on services provided pre-filing. The exact time of when the payment obligation crystallized is not, in my view, the determining factor under section 11.3. Rather, the key factor is whether the employee performed services after the date of the Initial Order. If so, he or she is entitled to compensation benefits for such current service.

(Emphasis added.)

[50] In conclusion, the Court is of the opinion that the coming into force of section 33 CCAA as part of the December 18, 2009, amendments has not changed the reasoning in *Mine Jeffrey* and *Nortel* in any way.

[51] The Union is wrong in thinking that the collective agreement is outside the scope of the CCAA and that only an agreement may alter its terms and conditions. When Parliament passed section 33 CCAA, it clearly wanted to give it the scope under *Mine Jeffrey*, and when the provision came into force (shortly after the decision of the Ontario Superior Court of Justice in *Nortel*), it kept this same vision.

[52] The CCAA has to be taken as a whole, and its provisions must be construed within the general context of the purpose of this Act. Its purpose is, in fact, to enable distressed companies to avoid the pressure of their contractual obligations, to have a period of respite during which they will be able to propose a restructuring plan, shielded from their creditors, and hope to start again on a new footing. If the debtor company is nevertheless required to fulfill all its obligations, it is tantamount to saying that the CCAA does nothing. Choices—sometimes difficult ones—must therefore be made, and all stakeholders interested in having the company survive and not be forced to close down must then compromise their rights.

[53] First of all, section 11 CCAA confirms the quasi-total rule of intervention of the court to make "any order that it considers appropriate" but "subject to the restrictions set out in this Act".

[54] The stay order that the court may then make under section 11.02 is therefore quite broad: the debtor company is literally shielded from legal proceedings for the time period that the court may prescribe.

[55] The CCAA includes certain exceptions to this general principle. These exceptions, however, must be construed as such. They are indeed exceptions.

[56] Section 33 CCAA is under the "Agreements" section of the CCAA. It is preceded by section 32 CCAA that states, as a general principle, that the debtor may "disclaim or resiliate any agreement to which the company is a party" by following the procedure provided in that section.

[57] Section 33 CCAA limits the application of section 32 by stipulating that the debtor cannot unilaterally set aside a collective agreement or alter it except as provided in the said section.

[58] The same applies to section 34 CCAA, which also constitutes an exception to the general principle of setting aside contractual agreements binding on the debtor company.

[59] The interpretation of 33 CCAA and the definition of its scope must not distort the general principles of the CCAA. A collective agreement cannot be made so inflexible

that the Union would be, for all practical purposes, in a near absolute position of control over the restructuring process. That is why *Mines Jeffrey* and *Nortel* restricted the application of collective agreements to unionized employees called to perform work so that the others (employees not working or retired) became the debtor's unsecured creditors.

[60] The undersigned considers that construing section 33 CCAA otherwise or assigning it any other intended scope would rob the CCAA overall of much of its flexibility and efficiency.

[61] In conclusion, the undersigned is of the opinion that section 33 CCAA should be applied only in situations where member employees of a bargaining unit continue to perform work after an initial order has been issued. Otherwise, the spirit of the entire corporate reorganization process under the CCAA would suffer as a result.

Application dismissed.

C. Affirmation and Assignment

The *CCAA* says nothing explicitly about the right to affirm contracts in *CCAA* proceedings. However, a right of affirmation derives by implication from the statutory right of disclaimer in s 32. The effect of this provision seems to be that if the debtor does not take the prescribed steps to disclaim a contract then, subject to what is said below, the contract remains on foot.

The matter becomes more complicated if the contract contains an *ipso facto* clause and the counterparty elects to terminate the contract upon commencement of the *CCAA* proceedings. This is prevented under *CCAA*, section 34, which prohibits any person from terminating or amending an agreement with the debtor company by reason only that restructuring proceedings have been commenced. *CCAA*, section 34, parallels *BIA*, section 84.2, discussed above in Chapter 6, Part III(C). Note that the provision gives the court power, on application by the counterparty, to waive the application of the section on the ground of "significant financial hardship" (*CCAA*, section 34(6)).

CCAA, section 11.4 (critical suppliers), is another provision relevant to the debtor's right to insist on the continued performance of contracts. There is some overlap between sections 11.4 and 34. For discussion, see Anthony Duggan, "Partly Performed Contracts" in Stephanie Ben-Ishai and Anthony Duggan, eds, *Canadian Bankruptcy and Insolvency Law: Bill C-55, Statute c.47 and Beyond* (Markham: LexisNexis, 2007) 15 at 39–40.

CCAA, section 11.3, codifies the rules governing assignments. *CCAA*, section 11.3, parallels *BIA*, 84.1, discussed above in Chapter 6, Part IV. The provision requires court approval for an assignment and it directs the court to take account of whether (a) the monitor approved the proposed assignment; (b) the proposed assignee "would be able to perform the obligations [under the contract]"; and (c) it would be "appropriate" to assign the contract to the proposed assignee.

V. DERIVATIVES

Derivatives are financial contracts that derive their value from the value of another asset, such as a commodity, currency, market index, interest rate, stock, or bond. The value of the derivative depends on the value of the underlying asset. Derivatives are a type of executory contract, meaning that without a statutory exemption, the *CCAA* provisions on executory contracts will apply to derivatives. This would be problematic because parties want to be able to terminate these contracts in the event of a restructuring. See the passages from the article below outlining the arguments of the Canadian Bankers Association to exempt EFCs from *CCAA* restructurings. This issue has been addressed in the *CCAA* through the creation of types of contracts called "eligible financial contracts." *CCAA*, sections 32 and 34, do not apply to eligible financial contracts.

"Eligible financial contract" was previously defined in *CCAA*, section 11.1(1), by reference to a long but incomplete shopping list of specific transactions. The courts had considerable difficulty with the definition (*Re Blue Range Resource Corp*, 2000 ABCA 239; *Re Androscoggin Energy LLC* (2005), 75 OR (3d) 552 (CA); *Re Calpine Canada Energy Ltd*, 2006 ABQB 153). In response to concerns voiced both by commentators and the courts themselves, the old definition was repealed and the definition is now prescribed by the regulations (*CCAA*, section 11.05(2)). The aims are to facilitate changes to the definition in response to rapidly occurring developments in the marketplace and to achieve greater consistency with the United States and the European Union. The operative part of the new definition, as prescribed by the *Eligible Financial Contract General Rules (Companies' Creditor Arrangement Act)*, SOR/2007-257 reads as follows:

1. The following definitions apply in these Regulations.

"derivatives agreement" means a financial agreement whose obligations are derived from, referenced to, or based on, one or more underlying reference items such as interest rates, indices, currencies, commodities, securities or other ownership interests, credit or guarantee obligations, debt securities, climatic variables, bandwidth, freight rates, emission rights, real property indices and inflation or other macroeconomic data and includes
   (a) a contract for differences or a swap, including a total return swap, price return swap, default swap or basis swap;
   (b) a futures agreement;
   (c) a cap, collar, floor or spread;
   (d) an option; and
   (e) a spot or forward.

"financial intermediary" means
   (a) a clearing agency; or
   (b) a person, including a broker, bank or trust company, that in the ordinary course of business maintains securities accounts or futures accounts for others.

2. The following kinds of financial agreements are prescribed for the purpose of the definition "eligible financial contract" in subsection 2(1) of the *Companies' Creditors Arrangement Act*:
   (a) a derivatives agreement, whether settled by payment or delivery, that
      (i) trades on a futures or options exchange or board, or other regulated market, or
      (ii) is the subject of recurrent dealings in the derivatives markets or in the over-the-counter securities or commodities markets;
   (b) an agreement to
      (i) borrow or lend securities or commodities, including an agreement to transfer securities or commodities under which the borrower may repay the loan with other securities or commodities, cash or cash equivalents,
      (ii) clear or settle securities, futures, options or derivatives transactions, or
      (iii) act as a depository for securities;

(c) a repurchase, reverse repurchase or buy-sellback agreement with respect to securities or commodities;

(d) a margin loan in so far as it is in respect of a securities account or futures account maintained by a financial intermediary;

(e) any combination of agreements referred to in any of paragraphs (a) to (d);

(f) a master agreement in so far as it is in respect of an agreement referred to in any of paragraphs (a) to (e);

(g) a master agreement in so far as it is in respect of a master agreement referred to in paragraph (f);

(h) a guarantee of, or an indemnity or reimbursement obligation with respect to, the liabilities under an agreement referred to in any of paragraphs (a) to (g); and

(i) an agreement relating to financial collateral, including any form of security or security interest in collateral and a title transfer credit support agreement, with respect to an agreement referred to in any of paragraphs (a) to (h).

These concepts are explained in greater detail below.

Stephanie Ben-Ishai & Peter Kolla, "Derivatives and the CCAA" in Stephanie Ben-Ishai & Anthony Duggan, eds, *Canadian Bankruptcy and Insolvency Law: Bill C-55, Statute c. 47 and Beyond* (Markham: LexisNexis, 2007) 46, at 49–51, and 55–57 (footnotes omitted)

Overview of Derivatives

Derivatives are financial instruments whose price is derived from the underlying value of an asset such as a currency, a commodity, a stock, or an index. The respective rights of the parties to these derivatives are embodied in a derivatives contract, which has obligations that extend into the future concerning performance of the contract. As such, derivatives contracts are a category of executory contract. Businesses use derivatives contracts to manage the risks of changes in the price of an asset, because derivatives can act like a form of insurance to protect against unknown variables that can affect this future price. There are many types of derivatives, including forward contracts, options, and swaps.

The example of forward contracts in the commodities industry illustrates well the risk-managing purpose of derivatives. A forward contract is a contract where at a specified time in the future, the buyer agrees to purchase and the seller agrees to deliver a specified amount of a commodity at a specified price. For those using commodities as inputs, these contracts ensure a fixed supply of a commodity without the risk that its cost will increase. The forward contract also guarantees to those supplying the commodity a fixed market without the risk that the price will decrease. Of course, both parties eliminate the possibility of beneficial movements of prices. However, given the volatility of commodity prices, the large capital investments of extracting commodities or building facilities to utilize the commodities, and the length of time before such investments become profitable, it can be optimal to sacrifice the potential for a large windfall in exchange for increased certainty.

There are two principal types of derivatives. Over-the-counter (OTC) derivatives consist of customizable and privately negotiated contracts, while futures are derivatives that are standardized and traded on exchanges. Futures, traded on exchanges and guaranteed by a clearing organization, raise few concerns about the possibility of future contracts not being honoured. In contrast, since OTC derivatives are negotiated between two parties, the ongoing creditworthiness of the parties to the contract is an important issue.

This is especially true when the purpose of entering a derivatives contract is to reduce risk, and since derivatives contracts involve the performance of future obligations.

The importance of risk management in OTC derivatives contracts is illustrated by the fact that most OTC contracts provide that security be demanded when one party is "out of the money" on its contractual obligations. This term refers to the situation where the price at which one party has agreed to buy, sell, or provide some other sort of protection has become negative when compared with the prevailing market price. Comparisons between the price of a derivative and the prevailing market price are known as "marking to market." After marking to market, the "in the money" counterparty to the derivatives contract faces the risk that the "out of the money" counterparty will not be able to fulfill the contractual obligation when it becomes due. The provision of security by the "out of the money" counterparty reduces that risk. In the event that the security cannot be provided, the "in the money" counterparty can terminate the derivatives contract, usually according to explicit provisions in the contract itself, and enter into another contract with a different counterparty.

Thus far, the discussion has centred upon single derivatives transactions. However, the standard form of derivatives transactions, developed by the International Swaps and Derivatives Association, Inc. (ISDA) and called the ISDA "master agreement," provides for derivatives contracts that are more complex than a single transaction. Master agreements can govern a series of discrete transactions, allowing for a net payment to be made on all the transactions occurring during a specified period between the counterparties instead of numerous payments back and forth. This represents the basis for another important characteristic of derivatives contracts that reduces risk, which is known as "close-out netting." Close-out netting is a process that, according to the contractual terms of the derivatives contract, occurs in the event of a default on the derivatives contract before the contractual maturity date. It allows the netting of all the "in the money" transactions against all "out of the money" transactions that are governed by a single master derivatives agreement. The close-out netting process provides that the outstanding financial value of the entire master agreement can be determined and paid out. Berl Nadler observes the following risk-reducing properties of the close-out netting process:

> Close-out netting is a critical risk reduction tool and has been estimated to reduce the value of exposures under derivatives transactions by as much as 70 percent. It does so by enabling parties to offset amounts owing under different transactions under a master agreement against each other upon termination of the master agreement, thereby reducing the financial exposure and credit risk of each of the parties to the master agreement.

What follows from this analysis of derivatives is that the primary objective of OTC derivatives contracts is to reduce risks that are inherent to business and finance. Whether by the very structure of the derivatives contract itself, a swap or a forward contract for example, or by the specific provisions within the contract, such as close-out netting, risk reduction is fundamental to derivatives contracts. Accordingly, Canadian bankruptcy and insolvency legislation affords special treatment for derivatives contracts. The mechanics of and reasons for this special treatment are the topics of the following sections.

Legislative History and Justifications for EFC Treatment

In 1992, the BIA was amended to exempt [derivatives] from the stay in bankruptcy proceedings, but a similar provision was not introduced into the CCAA. During its ultimately successful lobbying efforts to have EFCs exempted in CCAA restructurings, the Canadian Bankers Association provided the following justifications for its position:

> A recent amendment to Chapter 11 of the US *Bankruptcy Code* does permit counter-parties
> to terminate or close out hedging contracts during a stay period if one of these becomes
> insolvent. Similar legislation we feel is needed in Canada to ensure the continued com-
> petitiveness of Canadian financial markets and their ability to be part of these contracts
> when the other party is in fact a US entity or a US citizen. The contracts being discussed,
> which we have called eligible financial contracts ["EFCs"], are, however, important in their
> limited sphere. They help Canadian and other corporations world wide to manage risks
> such as changes in interest rates and in currency exchange rates.

This passage highlights two main arguments in support of exempting EFCs in CCAA
restructurings. The first is that EFCs help manage risks, and therefore the bankruptcy
system should further this goal to promote stability. As Biery *et al.* have summarized,

> Given that the objective of most eligible financial contracts is to manage risk, there is logic
> to the view that a party who is essentially seeking insurance against risk should not be
> held in a contract with a debtor who may choose to terminate the contract if it becomes
> a money-losing proposition. Instead, the counter-party ought to be able to terminate its
> contract with the debtor and be entitled to move quickly to obtain the sort of protection it
> wants elsewhere, from a party who has the ability to provide it.

The second justification outlined by the Canadian Bankers Association is solely concerned with regulatory competition between the United States and Canada: in order for
Canadian financial companies to remain competitive with their American counterparts,
the argument goes, Canadian bankruptcy legislation must imitate American law. This,
the second justification suggests, will level the playing field between the two countries.
Additionally, even though this line of argument will not be pursued in this chapter, a
public choice theory analysis reveals another motivation of the Canadian Bankers Association. Exemptions for EFCs in Canadian restructuring legislation can be assumed to
benefit Canadian banks during restructurings, at the expense of debtors who are their
counterparties in derivatives contracts.

The restructuring of affiliates of the Confederation Life Insurance Company in
1994 brought to light the consequences of the absence of EFC exemptions in the CCAA.
Nadler has commented that Justice Houlden's order to stay proceedings, which prevented the termination of derivatives contracts, "effectively allowed the Applicants to
'cherry pick' Derivatives Contracts by choosing to terminate certain agreements in which
the Applicants were in the money while continuing others." The pre-1997 CCAA structure clearly favoured the policy goal of restructuring companies, over that of reducing
the risk of counterparties to derivatives contracts.

The Government of Canada released a white paper in 1995, entitled *Enhancing the
Safety and Soundness of the Canadian Financial System*, which argued for excluding EFCs
from the CCAA stay. The justification for this position was to reduce the exposure of
financial institutions and their counterparties in derivatives contracts to unnecessary
risk, due to an inability to terminate derivatives contracts in the event of insolvency. The
claim followed from the fact that restructurings under the CCAA generally take between
six and 12 months to complete, and that such a period of time without the risk reduction
provided by EFCs was unacceptable. Justice Farley has emphasized the importance of
derivatives contracts generally:

> It would seem as a matter of public policy that such a valuable tool which has become a
> key fundamental for the interlocking financial activities of virtually every major financial

and many major non-financial corporations in Canada (and having international links) should not be dealt with in such a manner as to seriously affect its efficiency.

As an expression of precisely this public policy, and after "intense lobbying by the financial industry," the CCAA was amended in September 1997 to include the section 11.1 exemptions for EFCs from a stay of proceedings.

[Reprinted by permission of the publisher.]

The treatment of derivatives and other eligible financial contracts under Canadian insolvency law continues to be under heightened international scrutiny following the 2008 financial crisis. The following excerpt is from the Insolvency Institute of Canada's Report of the Task Force on Derivatives and highlights a number of ongoing issues and reform proposals.

"Report of the Task Force on Derivatives" (14 November 2013) *Insolvency Institute of Canada* at 1–5, online: www.insolvency.ca/en/iicresources/iicreportsandpublications.asp (footnotes omitted)

OVERVIEW

Canadian commercial insolvency law is part of the national framework legislation which is designed to minimize the impact of an insolvency event upon the Canadian economy and to promote a successful restructuring of business enterprises undergoing financial difficulties. A successful restructuring (whether under the same corporate structure, a new legal entity or through a sale of business operations as a going concern) optimizes value for stakeholders, saves jobs, supports communities that rely on local industries, protects the public from losing vital services and encourages the survival of more competitive industries. In the case of financial institutions, the restructuring is also effected to protect special stakeholders such as depositors or policyholders and minimize potential "runs on the bank" which would create instability in financial markets, impair overall liquidity in the financial world and increase systemic risk.

Insolvency law promotes a going concern restructuring of a viable business entity's affairs. When a business entity is brought under insolvency protection, the BIA and CCAA provide a broad stay of rights and remedies against the insolvent entity to encourage a going-concern restructuring of the business where possible. This broad stay is a fundamental tool of Canadian restructuring insolvency laws. The stay in part prevents a forced liquidation of a struggling business by staying (a) secured and unsecured creditors from realizing on the assets of the insolvent entity and (b) solvent counterparties from terminating contracts with the insolvent entity. Similarly, the *Canada Deposit Insurance Corporation Act* ("CDIC Act") provides a broad stay of proceedings and a process to allow the *Canada Deposit Insurance Corporation* ("CDIC") to attempt to restructure a deposit-taking financial institution.

The legislative reforms regarding EFCs under Canadian insolvency law have been piecemeal. EFC protection was introduced into the BIA beginning in 1992, followed by more extensive amendments to the Canadian insolvency laws which generally came into force in 1997 and 2009. Amendments were also made to the CDIC Act and the *Payment Clearing and Settlement Act* ("PCSA") to deal with EFCs entered into by certain financial institutions.

The insolvency regime for EFCs consists of a series of exemptions from the law that ordinarily applies to contracts upon the commencement of insolvency proceedings. The

EFC "safe harbours" primarily provide an exemption from the stay of proceedings to permit the termination of EFCs by the solvent counterparty, the determination of the net amount owing under the terminated EFCs, the realization upon financial collateral posted in respect of EFCs and protect the priority thereof.

At the outset, the exemptions under insolvency law for the termination and netting of EFCs were in part promulgated on the basis of concerns for certainty in financial markets and competitiveness vis-à-vis the United States and other global markets. After the safe harbor provisions were added to the United States Bankruptcy Code, similar protections were added in Canada to ensure that the Canadian market kept pace with global markets. In addition, it was felt that an exemption from stays against termination of EFCs would provide solvent parties with certainty in their dealings, with the antici-pated result of encouraging the availability of risk hedging derivatives for all Canadian enterprises, including those in financial distress.

EFC protection is a significant exception to the stay of proceedings under the CCAA and BIA. There are two main purposes of the EFC safe harbours: (i) to protect non-de-faulting counterparties from the risk of increasing exposure to the insolvent counter-party under the EFC and (ii) to reduce systemic risk in Canadian and global financial markets. Non-defaulting counterparties may be at risk because, in certain instances, the amounts under the EFCs are very substantial and the value of the underlying products subject to EFCs are volatile in nature and can change dramatically during an insolvency proceeding. If the solvent counterparty to an EFC is subject to a stay of proceedings and therefore unable to terminate its EFCs with the insolvent counterparty, there is a risk that the value of such EFCs could deteriorate sufficiently (from the insolvent counter-party's perspective) to put the solvent counterparty at risk. Systemic risk may arise where the solvent counterparty is a systemically important institution or where the solvent counterparty has entered into EFCs with one or more other counterparties. In extreme cases, the failure of one counterparty could have a domino effect, where the failure of one counterparty, particularly a derivatives dealer, triggers the failure of a second counterparty who is also a derivatives dealer and the failure of the second counterparty could trigger the failure of others. Multiple insolvencies may cause a lack of liquidity in the financial sector and unavailability of credit to solvent enterprises and, ultimately, systemic risk. The systemic risk could spread to global markets and lead to world-wide financial instability and, in extreme cases, recession.

The 2008 global financial and liquidity crisis precipitated recognition by governments and regulators of the need for a better understanding and more comprehensive regulation of derivatives. At the Pittsburgh Summit in 2009, the G20, including Canada, committed to strengthening the regulation, supervision and infrastructure of the global financial system (the "G20 Commitments"). The G20 Commitments include a commitment to attempt to mitigate systemic risk, particularly in the area of over-the-counter ("OTC") derivatives, by increasing the transparency of the OTC derivatives market and ensur-ing more consistent treatment of derivatives in different jurisdictions. To limit systemic risk, the G20 committed in part to the development of an internationally coordinated and comprehensive regulatory framework to facilitate the central clearing of most OTC derivatives according to internationally accepted standards, including insolvency rules.

Recent Canadian federal legislative amendments have focused on meeting the G20 Commitments. Amendments to the PCSA and the CDIC Act were enacted in 2012 pri-marily to facilitate the clearing and settlement of OTC derivatives by central counterpar-ties and to further facilitate the restructuring of insolvent financial institutions by CDIC.

At the provincial level, the Canadian Securities Administrators are introducing rules to regulate more closely the OTC derivatives market and to provide for the central clearing of OTC derivatives.

Combating systemic risk is an important goal. However, the goal of reducing systemic risk has to be balanced against important Canadian insolvency principles which encourage restructuring. The Task Force has considered the treatment of derivatives in Canadian insolvency law in this light. The Task Force is of the view that the current treatment of EFCs in the Canadian insolvency regime does not always strike the right balance between protecting against systemic risk and allowing insolvent commercial enterprises to restructure. The current regime may in some cases impede the restructuring of insolvent enterprises by placing too much emphasis on attempting to reduce systemic risk.

In other cases, the protections against systemic risk may be improved and the Task Force supports strengthening some of the EFC safe harbours. In particular, additional protections should be provided to ensure that EFC counterparties have better priority to financial collateral. This protection against systemic risk can be granted without impeding a restructuring.

As currently drafted, the EFC safe harbours may in some cases deprive the insolvent estate of value to which the estate and its creditors should be entitled. Further, the EFC safe harbours may delay or prevent certain liabilities of the insolvent entity from being crystallized. The Task Force has made certain recommendations aimed at maximizing the value of the estate and enhancing the prospects of a restructuring of an insolvent enterprise without unduly increasing the potential for systemic risk.

In making its recommendations, the Task Force is cognizant of the fact that the global and Canadian regulators have reached a broad consensus that the EFCs entered into by most commercial enterprises pose little or no risk to major financial institutions and therefore do not give rise to systemic risk on a global scale. Global and Canadian regulators have accordingly determined that EFC transactions with commercial enterprise "end-users" of EFCs should be exempt from the mandatory central clearing regime that is being developed primarily for financial institutions. The Task Force recognizes that there is still a potential for systemic risk arising as a result of the failure of a commercial enterprise. However, the Task Force is of the view that the emphasis solely on the potential for systemic risk, however remote, may in some instances be disproportionate given the impact that the EFC safe harbours may have on the ability of a commercial enterprise to restructure and on the recoveries of other creditors of the insolvent counterparty.

As noted above, EFCs receive special protection because (i) liabilities under EFCs are often based upon large notional amounts and (ii) the values of the underlying reference items and the financial collateral securing EFC obligations are highly volatile and significant fluctuation of these values can occur during an insolvency proceeding.

In addition, the EFC exemptions were introduced to make Canadian institutions competitive in the global derivatives market and to ensure Canadian enterprises have access to the global derivatives markets.

For these reasons, the Task Force does not recommend a repeal of the fundamental EFC safe harbour provisions under the BIA, the CCAA and, to the extent they are available in respect of a trading company, the WURA, but rather recommends a series of modifications to alleviate the EFC safe harbour provisions with a view to achieving a better balance between the objectives of insolvency legislation and financial risk.

The Task Force is making recommendations regarding the following broad categories:

A. Allow the termination of EFCs by the insolvent entity or its court appointed officer.

B. Allow the assignment of EFCs by the insolvent entity or its court appointed officer.

C. Prohibit walk-away clauses in EFC contracts.

D. Increase the priority of EFC financial collateral.

E. Protect the central clearing of OTC derivatives.

F. Protect EFCs in receiverships.

[First published with the Insolvency Institute of Canada and reproduced here with their kind permission.]

VI. INTERIM (DIP) FINANCING

Once restructuring proceedings are commenced, creditors are stayed from pursuing the debtor, which gives the debtor some breathing space in which it can operate its business. To do that, though, it needs financing. This is known as "interim financing," though it is still frequently referred to as "debtor-in-possession (DIP) financing". "DIP financing" is an American term to refer to the debtor that remains in possession of its business after filing for restructuring proceedings. It refers to interim financing, and the two terms are often used interchangeably.

At this point, it is important to distinguish between pre-filing and post-filing creditors. Pre-filing creditors have existing claims against the debtor and are subject to the plan of reorganization while post-filing creditors extend financing after the debtor has commenced restructuring proceedings and are not subject to the plan. Given the nature of the debtor's financial position in restructuring, post-filing creditors will typically deal with the debtor on less risky terms, such as requiring enhanced priority for their loans, which requires the subordination of existing loans.

CCAA, section 11.2, provides a statutory scheme to govern interim financing. Before the enactment of section 11.2, the decision to grant interim financing fell under the courts' inherent or equitable jurisdiction, which created much debate over the scope of the court's jurisdiction and discretion to issue interim financing orders. Now that these orders are governed by statute, there is much more predictability and certainty as to when they can be granted and to their scope. The Alberta Court of Appeal in *Canada (Deputy Attorney General) v Temple City Housing Inc*, 2008 ABCA 1, at para 13, referring to the amendments, noted, "[t]he amendments to the *CCAA* include specific authority to grant super-priority to DIP financing such as the loan in this case .... However, once it has been proclaimed in force, the issue of the *CCAA* judge's inherent jurisdiction to order such priorities will not be an issue in future *CCAA* proceedings." That said, questions have been raised about whether problems with uncertainty and lack of predictability existed prior to the amendments, and whether the amendments were required. Janis Sarra, in "Debtor in Possession (DIP) Financing: The Jurisdiction of Canadian Courts to Grant Super-Priority Financing in *CCAA* Applications" (2000) 23 *Dalhousie Law Journal* 337 at 381 writes:

> While this codification might create greater certainty, it reflects precisely what the courts are doing now, using the flexibility of the process to ensure a proper balancing of creditor and other stakeholder interests. It is worth noting that in the current debate about whether interim financing should be the subject of statutory amendment, there are no cases cited in which the courts have failed to exercise their discretion reasonably and in a restrained manner. Thus, it is unclear why statutory amendment is required.

There are two notable points about section 11.2. First, the legislation gives the court the express power to grant security for interim financing in priority to existing charges or secured claims. Thus, secured creditor X, who may have been first in time and in priority, may well find itself second in priority to secured creditor Y, who has provided interim financing. Second, section 11.2 provides guidelines that the courts are to consider on an interim financing application.

Interim financing may be provided by a new lender or it may be provided by an existing senior operating lender. An existing lender may wish to provide such financing because the terms of the loan gives the interim lender considerable control in respect of the direction of the restructuring. The court order authorizing the interim financing will typically provide that it is not subject to the *CCAA* stay of proceedings, and the terms of the loan may impose stringent covenants and conditions that will give the interim lender the power to enforce in the event of default.

The main features of section 11.2 follow:

- On application by a debtor company, a court may make an order declaring that all or part of the company's property is subject to a charge in favour of a person who agrees to lend to the company an amount approved by the court as required by the company.
- The application by the debtor company must be on notice to secured creditors who are likely to be affected by the security or charge.
- The security or charge may not secure an obligation that exists before the order is made.
- The new provisions enable the court to deal with the priority of existing secured creditors in relation to the new charge. The court may order that the security or charge rank in priority over the claim of any secured creditor of the company.
- The legislation also contemplates the possibility of more than one order for interim financing being made. Assume that the court made an order for interim financing in favour of A on July 15. If a subsequent application is made and an order is granted in favour of B, the court may only order that B has priority over A with A's consent.
- In deciding whether to make an order, the court is to consider among other things:
  » the period during which the company is expected to be subject to proceedings under the *CCAA*;
  » how the company's business and financial affairs are to be managed during the proceedings;
  » whether the company's management has the confidence of its major creditors;
  » whether the loan would enhance the proposal of a viable compromise or arrangement being made in respect of the company;
  » the nature and value of the company's property;
  » whether any creditor would be materially prejudiced as a result of the security or charge; and
  » the monitor's report, if any.

Although *CCAA*, section 11.2(1), provides that the interim financing charge "may not secure an obligation that exists before the order is made," Canadian courts have authorized the use of roll-ups. In the case of a simple roll-up, the funds provided by the interim lender are used to pay down some or all of the interim lender's pre-filing debt. In the case of a creeping roll-up, the court authorizes the pre-filing debt of the DIP lender to be repaid from the operating revenues of the business (see Ray Rutman et al, "Creeping Roll-Up DIP" (2012) 1 *Journal of the Insolvency Institute of Canada* 161). It is argued that this does not amount to cross-collateralization in violation of *CCAA*, section 11.2(1), since the pre-filing debt is paid out and is not secured by the interim financing charge. Under what circumstances should a court permit a roll-up given that its effect is to give the lender a preference over the other creditors in respect of pre-filing debts? Below are two excerpts that summarize the concept of interim financing and provide an overview of the landscape since the codification of interim financing.

Michael B Rotsztain & Alexandra Dostal, "Debtor-in-Possession Financing" in Stephanie Ben-Ishai & Anthony Duggan, eds, *Canadian Bankruptcy and Insolvency Law: Bill C-55, Statute c. 47 and Beyond* (Markham: LexisNexis, 2007) 227 at 227–29

Although debtor-in-possession (DIP) or interim financing is a relatively new concept in Canadian insolvency proceedings, it has become an essential element of many Canadian corporate restructurings. The term "debtor-in-possession" is borrowed from American legislation, in which DIP financing is codified. . . .

As a result of their precarious financial position, insolvent companies are often unable to access existing credit facilities or obtain new conventional credit facilities after they have commenced BIA or CCAA restructuring proceedings. A restructuring company needs a source of credit to finance continuing operations while it attempts to formulate and negotiate a plan of arrangement or considers other options. The funds borrowed in DIP financings can be used for a number of restructuring-related purposes, such as paying operating costs of the business during the restructuring proceedings and paying advisors. DIP financing may be sourced from either existing creditors or from parties with no interest in the restructuring; however, such financing is most often obtained from existing secured creditors who already have a large stake in the proceedings.

DIP financing is usually accompanied by charges over the debtor's assets, granted by the court to secure the repayment of the funds advanced by the DIP lender and related obligations of the debtor. These charges may rank subordinate to, equal to, or in priority to existing charges. The ranking of court-ordered DIP financing charges has been the most controversial aspect of DIP financing. Secured creditors' rights in collateral have historically been well protected in Canada. The security position of secured creditors whose charges are subordinated to DIP financing charges may, however, be eroded without their consent. As a result, some have argued that granting a priority DIP financing charge (or "priming" existing secured creditors) is tantamount to expropriation of the property of secured creditors, and that this should not be permitted without specific legislative authority.

Janis Sarra, "The Evolution of the Companies' Creditors Arrangement Act in Light of Recent Developments" (2011) 50 *Canadian Business Law Journal* 211 at 216–19 (footnotes omitted)

Previous case law on financing after the commencement of CCAA proceedings, called debtor-in-possession (DIP) financing, focused on the authority of the court to authorize such financing; and apportionment of the costs of the financing. While DIP financing was initially hotly contested on jurisdictional grounds, it became widely endorsed by the courts as a measure to "keep the lights on" in terms of operational financing during the period of negotiations for a restructuring plan.

Effective September 2009, the court's authority to authorize such financing was codified. The amendments also articulate criteria for assessing requests for financing that will be given priority of payment over other creditors' claims. The factors that the court is to consider include, but are not limited to: the period during which the company is expected to be subject to CCAA proceedings; how the business is to be managed; whether management has the confidence of the debtor's major creditors; whether the loan will enhance the prospects of a viable compromise or arrangement with the company's creditors; the nature and value of the company's property; whether any creditor will be materially prejudiced as a result of the charge; and the monitor's views on the application.

The criteria essentially codify the tests previously used by the courts, but offer greater transparency for creditors and other stakeholders that are not repeat players in CCAA proceedings. The first case law under the new provisions suggests that the court is not restricted to the factors enumerated in the statute, nor is it required to give equal weight and consideration to all the factors. The court has approved DIP financing with a priority charge where it was necessary to ensure continued operation of the debtor as a business enterprise while it undergoes restructuring; having regard to the potential material prejudice to creditors, the preservation of employment, and the prospects for a successful workout.

There is an issue regarding the propriety of the DIP financier determining, through the terms of its facility, other aspects of the CCAA proceeding. For example, in *Re Abi-tibiBowater Inc*, the interim financing was provided on condition that the funds could not be used to make special contributions to pension plans; and as a result, the court concluded that it was necessary to suspend the required contributions to the pension plan. While a DIP lender should be able to negotiate some control terms in a DIP facility, the court needs to be cognizant of the degree to which such conditions will constrain its authority in future decisions.

Significantly, in some instances, the courts have been careful to consider the implications of proposed financing. The Quebec Superior Court dismissed a motion to approve a funding agreement proposed by the DIP lenders under which the lenders would acquire all the shares of the Canadian debtor company. The court held that the CCAA is aimed at enabling a debtor company to weather its financial difficulties and continue to operate in the interests of creditors and society in general. A plan must be achieved at the best cost and under the best possible conditions, with the requisite support of creditors. Here, in the court's view, the cumulative effect of the absence of any legitimate process to canvass funding proposals; the narrow definition of what constituted a superior proposal under the plan funding agreement; the lack of flexibility given to the board of directors to qualify a superior proposal as superior; the chilling effect of the high break fee; and the lack of evidence of a value maximizing process were all factors that worked against the objective of a sufficiently transparent and open process....

There is also an issue whether DIP financing should be granted where the circumstances indicate that the financing will consume considerable resources without any assurance that the debtor will be able to negotiate a successful plan. It is important that the court be prepared to decline DIP financing where the debtor seeks only to prolong the period before an inevitable liquidation; and/or where there is no possibility for a plan. The challenge is to ensure that such a decision is not premature in circumstances where creditors are initially unwilling to come to the negotiation table. The cases that have declined to grant DIP financing have relied in part on the fact that there were not ongoing operations, employees and trade supply relations to protect during the interim period.

Another recent issue is the approval of DIP financing charges that encumber assets of Canadian debtor entities to meet financing needs of related entities in the United States.

The genesis of this change is the increasingly interrelated nature of global business enterprises and consequent increase in cross-border proceedings; and the lack of financing that was available during the worst of the financial crisis in 2008–2009. The downside risk is that Canadian creditors that may have had access to the value of those assets may lose the ability to realize on their claims. The potential upside is the preservation of the business, jobs and trade relationships of the parent and subsidiary companies, which overall may be more valuable. Canadian courts have held that where the successful restructuring of the CCAA entities appeared to be inextricably intertwined with the restructuring of the enterprise in the Chapter 11 U.S. Bankruptcy Code proceedings and the financing was needed to continue day-to-day operations, crossborder charges should be authorized.

[Reproduced by permission of Canadian Business Law Journal Inc
and Thomson Reuters Canada Limited.]

* * * * *

In addition to interim financing, courts have authorized the creation of a post-filing trade creditors' charge. Instead of paying cash for supplies acquired after the commencement of *CCAA* proceedings, the debtor sought to induce suppliers to continue to supply goods and services through a court-ordered charge on the assets that secured payment of these obligations (see *Re Westar Mining Ltd* (1992), 70 BCLR (2d) 6 (SC); *Re Smoky River Coal Ltd*, 2001 ABCA 209). The charge was usually afforded priority over existing secured creditors, but ranked below the other court-ordered charges. The 2009 amendments to the *CCAA* make no mention of this type of order. Can a court make this type of order following the amendment?

VII. CRITICAL SUPPLIERS

The debtor business' ongoing operation during restructuring and approval of a plan may require the guarantee that certain goods or services will continue to be supplied. *CCAA*, s 11.01, provides that the court-ordered stay of proceedings does not have the effect of prohibiting a person from requiring immediate payment for goods, services, use of leased or licensed property, or other valuable consideration provided after the order is made. Suppliers will generally supply goods and services to the company only on the basis of cash on delivery. This is one of the reasons many debtors in restructuring proceedings require interim financing. Some suppliers may not be content to be paid for post-filing orders. They may refuse to supply any new orders unless their pre-filing obligations are paid. This poses a problem for the company if the goods or services cannot be obtained from other suppliers.

Canadian courts have made critical supplier orders that have authorized the company to pay pre-filing obligations of critical suppliers (see *Re Air Canada* (2003), 47 CBR (4th) 163 (Ont Sup Ct J)). *CCAA*, section 11.4, permits a court to make an order requiring a critical supplier to supply any goods or services specified by the court to the company on any terms and conditions that are consistent with the supply relationship or that the court considers appropriate. There is some debate over the jurisdictional basis for a critical supplier order that permits the payment of pre-filing obligations. Some commentators argue that a court does so pursuant to *CCAA*, section 11.4(2), which allows a court to set the terms and conditions of the supply contract (see Philippe Belanger, "Critical Suppliers: What Does Section

11.4 CCRA Mean?" (2010) 26 *Business & Finance Law Review* 1). Is this view consistent with the approach taken in *Northstar Aerospace Inc (Re)*, excerpted below?

A critical supplier order is not needed if the company has a long-term supply contract in place. The supplier cannot lawfully refuse to deliver because the CCAA stay of proceedings prevents the supplier from terminating the contract so long as it is paid for current orders. Justice Easterbrook, in *In re Kmart Corp*, 359 F (3d) 866 (7th Cir 2004) at 873, thought that the critical suppliers threat is a hollow one, even where the supplier is not under a contractual obligation to supply any new orders:

> Some supposedly critical vendors will continue to do business with the debtor because they must. They may, for example, have long term contracts, and the automatic stay prevents these vendors from walking away as long as the debtor pays for new deliveries.... Fleming Companies, which received the largest critical-vendors payment because it sold Kmart between $70 million and $100 million of groceries and related goods weekly, was one of these. No matter how much Fleming would have liked to dump Kmart, it had no right to do so. It was unnecessary to compensate Fleming for continuing to make deliveries that it was legally required to make. Nor was Fleming likely to walk away even if it had a legal right to do so. Each new delivery produced a profit; as long as Kmart continued to pay for new product, why would any vendor drop the account? That would be a self-inflicted wound. To abjure new profits because of old debts would be to commit the sunk-cost fallacy; well-managed businesses are unlikely to do this. Firms that disdain current profits because of old losses are unlikely to stay in business. They might as well burn money or drop it into the ocean. Again Fleming illustrates the point. When Kmart stopped buying its products after the contract expired, Fleming collapsed (Kmart had accounted for more than 50% of its business) and filed its own bankruptcy petition. Fleming was hardly likely to have quit selling of its own volition, only to expire the sooner.

Northstar Aerospace Inc (Re), 2012 ONSC 4546, 2012 CarswellOnt 9721

DM BROWN J:

[1] Northstar Aerospace, Inc. ("Northstar Inc."), Northstar Aerospace (Canada) Inc. ("Northstar Canada"), 2007775 Ontario Inc. and 3024308 Nova Scotia Company (collectively, the "CCAA Entities") applied for and were granted protection under the Companies' Creditors Arrangement Act (the "CCAA") pursuant to an Initial Order of this court dated June 14, 2012 (the "Initial Order"). Ernst & Young Inc. was appointed as Monitor (the "Monitor") of the CCAA Entities and FTI Consulting Canada Inc. ("FTI Consulting") was appointed Chief Restructuring Officer ("CRO") of the CCAA Entities.

[2] Certain of Northstar Canada's direct and indirect U.S. subsidiaries (the "Chapter 11 Entities") commenced insolvency proceedings (the "Chapter 11 Proceedings") pursuant to Chapter 11 of the United States Bankruptcy Code on June 14, 2012 in the United States Bankruptcy Court for the District of Delaware (the "U.S. Court"). The CCAA Entities and the Chapter 11 Entities are sometimes collectively referred to herein as "Northstar".

[3] Northstar supplies components and assemblies for the commercial and military aerospace markets, and provides related services. Northstar provides goods and services to customers all over the world, including military defence suppliers, as well as the U.S. army. Northstar's products are used in the Boeing CH-47 Chinook helicopters, Boeing AH-64 Apache helicopters, Sikorsky UH-60 Blackhawk helicopters, AgustaWestland

Links/Wildcat helicopters, the Boeing F-22 Raptor Fighter aircraft and various other helicopters and aircraft.

[4] The history of this proceeding is set out in previous endorsements of Morawetz J, most recently his Reasons dated July 30, 2012, (2012 ONSC 4423) approving the Heligear Transaction, vesting all of the Canadian Purchased Assets in the Canadian Purchaser free and clear of all restrictions, and authorizing and directing the Monitor, on the closing of the Heligear Transaction, to make distributions to the DIP Agent for the DIP Lenders and to the Lenders in accordance with their legal priorities.

[5] The Heligear Transaction has not yet closed.

[6] Changsha Zhongchuan Transmission Machinery Co., Ltd., a manufacturer of gears located in Hunan, The People's Republic of China, is the exclusive supplier to Northstar Canada of the gears that make up the components in gearboxes sold by Northstar to General Electric Company on an on-going basis. According to Nigel Meakin, a senior managing director of the CRO, the gears provided by Changsha are essential to Northstar's continued supply of gearboxes to GE on a timely basis in accordance with the Revenue Sharing Agreement between Northstar Canada and GE.

[7] Changsha rendered two invoices to Northstar Canada totaling US$ 135,226.06 prior to the Initial Order. Those invoices remain unpaid. Notwithstanding that paragraph 17 of the Initial Order requires Changsha to continue supplying goods to Northstar Canada, Changsha has informed the CCAA Entities that until the two invoices are paid, it will not supply further materials to Northstar Canada. The evidence discloses that re-sourcing the gears would take approximately 12 months, and the inability of Northstar to deliver gearboxes "may imminently impact GE production lines".

[8] Under the Heligear Transaction the amounts owing under the Changsha invoices might be treated as Cure Costs, making them payable by the CCAA Entities on closing. The CRO deposed, however, that given the urgency of obtaining supply from Changsha, it is necessary for payment of the invoices to be made whether or not the amounts are Cure Costs and, in any event, payment is required earlier than the closing date.

[9] The CCAA Entities therefore move for an order authorizing them to make a payment of US$ 135,223.06 to Changsha in respect of those amounts owing for supplies delivered prior to the commencement of these CCAA proceedings.

II. Positions of the parties

[10] The Monitor supports the relief requested. Fifth Third Bank does not oppose the relief sought; Boeing Capital supports the motion. All wish to see the Heligear Transaction close quickly. No interested person appeared to oppose the motion or communicated its opposition to the CCAA Entities or the Monitor.

III. Analysis

[11] In *Cinram International Inc. (Re)* [2012 ONSC 3767] Morawetz J accepted, as an accurate summary of the applicable law on this issue, the following portions of the applicant's factum in that case:

> *Entitlement to Make Pre-Filing Payments*
>
> 67. There is ample authority supporting the Court's general jurisdiction to permit payment of pre-filing obligations to persons whose services are critical to the ongoing operations of the debtor companies. This jurisdiction of the Court is not ousted by Section 11.4 of the

CCAA, which became effective as part of the 2009 amendments to the CCAA and codified the Court's practice of declaring a person to be a critical supplier and granting a charge on the debtor's property in favour of such critical supplier. As noted by Pepall J in *Re Canwest Global*, the recent amendments, including Section 11.4, do not detract from the inherently flexible nature of the CCAA or the Court's broad and inherent jurisdiction to make such orders that will facilitate the debtor's restructuring of its business as a going concern.

Canwest Global supra, at paras. 41 and 43; Book of Authorities, Tab 1.

68. There are many cases since the 2009 amendments where the Courts have authorized the applicants to pay certain pre-filing amounts where the applicants were not seeking a charge in respect of critical suppliers. In granting this authority, the Courts considered a number of factors, including:

a. whether the goods and services were integral to the business of the applicants;

b. the applicants' dependency on the uninterrupted supply of the goods or services;

c. the fact that no payments would be made without the consent of the Monitor;

d. the Monitor's support and willingness to work with the applicants to ensure that payments to suppliers in respect of pre-filing liabilities are minimized;

e. whether the applicants had sufficient inventory of the goods on hand to meet their needs; and

f. the effect on the debtors' ongoing operations and ability to restructure if they were unable to make pre-filing payments to their critical suppliers.

Canwest Global supra, at para. 43; Book of Authorities, Tab 1.

Re Brainhunter Inc, [2009] O.J. No. 5207 (Sup. Ct. J. [Commercial List]) at para. 21 [Brainhunter]; Book of Authorities, Tab 13.

Re Priszm Income Fund (2012), 75 C.B.R. (5th) 213 (Ont. Sup. Ct. J.) at paras. 29–34; Book of Authorities, Tab 14.

[12] In the present case the evidence disclosed that the materials supplied by Changsha are integral to the business of the CCAA Entities, they depend on the uninterrupted supply of those goods, and they lack a sufficient inventory of the goods on hand to meet their needs, with the potential of imminently affecting the production lines of GE, one of their customers.

[13] The Monitor supports the order sought; no party opposes the motion.

[14] Although Changsha is subject to the critical supplier provisions of the Initial Order, the simple reality of the situation is that Changsha is located outside the jurisdiction of this court and the courts in the parallel U.S. Chapter 11 proceedings. Enforcement of the Initial Order against Changsha could not occur in a timely fashion. In my view, this practical reality weighs heavily in favour of granting the order sought, although granting the order, in a sense, rewards improper conduct by a critical supplier who has ignored an order of this court and has the effect of countenancing a form of hard-ball queue-jumping.

[15] That said, in light of the support by interested parties for the order sought, business realities must prevail in order to ensure the continued operation of Northstar Canada pending closing of the Heligear Transaction. Accordingly, I grant the order requested by the CCAA Entities and authorize them to pay Changsha the amount of US$ 135,223.06 in satisfaction of the two invoices.

Motion granted.

VIII. ASPECTS OF THE SALE PROCESS IN LIQUIDATING *CCAAS*

Debtors often sell assets in order to downsize operations during restructuring proceedings. If debtors wish to sell their assets outside the ordinary course of business, however, as part of "asset sales that extend well beyond a sale of redundant assets as part of a downsizing of operations" (Shelley C Fitzpatrick, "Liquidating *CCAAs*—Are We Praying to False Gods" in Janis P Sarra, ed, *Annual Review of Insolvency Law 2008* (Canada: Thomson Carswell, 2009) at 41), they need court approval. These types of sales are sometimes referred to as "preplan sales" or as "liquidating *CCAAs*" and are governed by *CCAA*, section 36. Section 36 is seen by some as the statutory sanction of liquidating *CCAAs*. Liquidating *CCAAs* typically involve a sale of all or substantially all the debtor's assets, which is broader than what is codified in section 36, but there are those who nonetheless maintain that these sales fall within the spirit of section 36. This view is not unanimously held. See Alfonso Nocilla, "Asset Sales Under the Companies' Creditors Arrangement Act and the Failure of Section 36" (2012) 52:2 *Canadian Business Law Journal* 226 at 227, where he concludes that "s 36 has done nothing to resolve the ongoing disagreement among judges and academics over liquidating *CCAAs*."

Some see liquidating *CCAAs* as being contrary to the policy goal of the legislation, which is to keep companies together to avoid the disastrous consequences to stakeholders. However, the shift from traditional restructuring to liquidating *CCAAs* has been occurring for the last three decades. These sales can occur on a piecemeal or a going-concern basis. A going-concern sale involves selling the assets together, and possibly selling the firm as a going concern, which preserves the value of the assets and fulfills the public interest goals of the legislation, whereas a piecemeal sale of the assets neither preserves value nor fulfills these goals.

Section 36 provides that a debtor company must obtain court approval before selling all or any of its assets outside the ordinary course of business and it sets out a list of factors the court must take into account in deciding whether to authorize the sale. These include the reasonableness of the proposed sale process and the reasonableness of the proposed outcome (whether the consideration to be received for the assets is reasonable and fair, taking into account their market value). The factors listed in section 36 largely replicate the principles articulated by the Ontario Court of Appeal in *Royal Bank of Canada v Soundair Corp* (1991) 4 OR (3d) 1 (CA) (*Soundair*). *Soundair* was a receivership case, but the courts imported the principles into the *CCAA* context prior to the enactment of section 36 (see, for example, *Canadian Red Cross Society, Re* (1998), 5 CBR (4th) 299 (Ont Ct J (GenDiv))).

The debtor company must obtain court approval for both the sale process and the sale itself. Section 36 applies only to court approval of the actual sale. This is clear by inference from the wording of the provision: "in deciding whether to grant the authorization, the court is to consider ... whether the process leading to the proposed sale ... was reasonable in the circumstances" (see *Re Brainhunter Inc* (2009), 62 CBR (5th) 41 (Ont Sup Ct J) (*Brainhunter*)). In *Brainhunter*, the court held that in applications to approve a proposed sale process, the criteria identified in *Re Nortel Networks Corp* (2009), 55 CBR (5th) 229 (Ont Sup Ct J) at para 49 apply, viz.:

(a) Is a sale transaction warranted at this time?
(b) Will the sale benefit the whole "economic community"?
(c) Do any of the debtor's creditors have a bona fide reason to object to a sale of the business?
(d) Is there a better viable alternative?

It is still unsettled how, if at all, these criteria differ from the section 36 criteria for approving the sale itself. It is also open to question whether a court, having previously approved the sale process, would be likely to disapprove the sale itself in the exercise of its discretion under section 36. For a fuller discussion of these and other difficulties with section 36, see Alfonso Nocilla, "Asset Sales Under the Companies' Creditors Arrangement Act and the Failure of Section 36" (2012) 52 *Canadian Business Law Journal* 226.

The following two extracts discuss the sale process. The first discusses the stalking horse process, which is a sale process now widely used in *CCAA* proceedings as a means of ensuring compliance with the requirements for court approval at both the pre- and post-sale stages. The second discusses the principles and criteria courts use to assess preplan sales.

Ashley Taylor & Yannick Katirai, "An Analysis of Stalking Horse Processes in Canadian Insolvency Proceedings" (2013) 2 *Journal of the Insolvency Institute of Canada* 95 at 95–102 (footnotes omitted)

a) What is a Stalking Horse Process?

Stalking horse processes are a relatively recent phenomenon in Canada — one of the earliest uses of a stalking horse process in a Canadian insolvency proceeding was in *Stelco*, discussed below. Since then, as liquidating CCAA proceedings have grown in popularity, so too have stalking horse processes, aided in part by the interaction between Canadian CCAA proceedings and U.S. Chapter 11 proceedings.

Historically, sales of an insolvent debtor's assets were conducted by way of tender. A tender process typically begins with the debtor obtaining court approval of the proposed sale process. With the approval in hand, the debtor and its financial advisors attempt to solicit interest in the company as a going concern or for some or all of its assets. Frequently, a "teaser" package containing high-level information about the business and assets is prepared and circulated to logical potential purchasers. Interested parties who execute a non-disclosure agreement are granted access to detailed information in order to conduct due diligence.

After a period of time for interested parties to complete their diligence, the debtor will establish a deadline for the submission of offers. The debtor, in conjunction with its financial advisors, will review the tendered bids and select the "best" bid. Following negotiation of an agreement of purchase and sale, the debtor will seek court approval of the agreement. In such a process, there is generally an obligation on the bidders to "put their best foot forward" as the process does not provide for subsequent rounds of bidding.

In contrast, in a stalking horse process, the debtor's marketing efforts are divided into two distinct phases. First, the debtor will conduct a preliminary marketing effort in order to find a "stalking horse." This preliminary marketing can be conducted inside or outside of a formal insolvency process and will ideally involve competition between many potential purchasers. The preliminary process culminates in the negotiation of an agreement of purchase and sale (commonly called the stalking horse agreement) in respect of some or all of the debtor's assets. Although it is contemplated (and hoped) that the stalking horse agreement will not constitute the final agreement of purchase and sale, the agreement must be one that the debtor can and is willing to close. If no superior bid is elicited during the second stage, the stalking horse agreement will become the definitive agreement.

Many stalking horse agreements (and the bid processes that accompany those agreements), include features intended to compensate the stalking horse bidder for the risk and expense it incurs and the time and effort it expends to participate in a process that is designed to benefit the debtor and its stakeholders. As described in our review of market practices below, certain features have become commonplace in stalking horse processes and have been regularly approved by courts, including a break fee and expense reimbursements payable to the stalking horse bidder if it is not ultimately successful in closing the proposed transaction. In some cases, the stalking horse bidder may attempt to negotiate additional protections for itself that could potentially stifle an open, competitive and value-maximizing auction.

Once the stalking horse agreement has been negotiated and finalized, the debtor typically seeks court approval of the agreement and a set of bid procedures that establish the rules for marketing the assets covered by the stalking horse agreement and for any resulting auction. This initial scrutiny provides the court, the debtor's stakeholders, and prospective bidders, the opportunity to review and potentially challenge both provisions in the stalking horse agreement, as well as any bid procedures that they believe are unduly onerous or will stifle a fair auction.

Once the stalking horse agreement has been approved by the court, the debtor and its advisors will broadly market the assets. Potentially interested bidders who execute the appropriate non-disclosure agreement, will be given access to detailed financial and other information (often through the use of an electronic data room, meetings with management and site visits) in order to conduct their due diligence. As discussed above, the stalking horse agreement acts as a starting point from which other bidders will draft their offers by adding, removing, or revising terms.

If a superior offer is received for the assets covered by the stalking horse agreement, the debtor will conduct an auction of the assets involving the stalking horse bidder and any other party who submitted a superior bid. Following one or more rounds of bidding, the debtor will select the "highest and/or best" bid and take that offer to court for approval. If no other bidder submits a superior offer then no auction will be conducted and the debtor will seek final approval of the stalking horse agreement.

b) Advantages and Disadvantages of Stalking Horse Processes

(i) A Brief Aside on Court Approval of Sales Generally
Sales in formal insolvency proceedings are by their nature subject to judicial oversight. As described below, court approval of a sale process engages different considerations than approval of the sale itself. Even so, because the process is a means to an end, the factors that a court will consider in approving the sale should guide and inform the choices made by the debtor in structuring the sale process. It follows that when evaluating a proposed stalking horse process, a court should also consider the factors relating to approval of the final sale.

The principles governing the approval of a court-supervised sale process are well-established. Before the 2009 amendments to the CCAA, courts in Ontario and elsewhere in Canada have focused on the four principles set out in the Ontario Court of Appeal's decision in *Soundair* as incorporated into the CCAA by *Canadian Red Cross Society (Re)*. These factors, which generally overlap with the factors set out at section 36(3) of the CCAA, are as follows:

1. It should consider whether the receiver has made a sufficient effort to get the best price and has not acted improvidently.
2. It should consider the interests of all parties.

3. It should consider the efficacy and integrity of the process by which offers are obtained.
4. It should consider whether there has been unfairness in the working out of the process.

The factors set out in section 36(3) of the CCAA are as follows:

36 (3) In deciding whether to grant the authorization, the court is to consider, among other things,

(a) whether the process leading to the proposed sale or disposition was reasonable in the circumstances;

(b) whether the monitor approved the process leading to the proposed sale or disposition;

(c) whether the monitor filed with the court a report stating that in their opinion the sale or disposition would be more beneficial to the creditors than a sale or disposition under a bankruptcy;

(d) the extent to which the creditors were consulted;

(e) the effects of the proposed sale or disposition on the creditors and other interested parties; and

(f) whether the consideration to be received for the assets is reasonable and fair, taking into account their market value.

Significantly, these factors emphasize the integrity of the sale process rather than whether the process resulted in the highest possible purchase price being obtained for the assets. Indeed, the first factor in each set of factors directly calls for an evaluation of the process that resulted in the ultimate sale.

(ii) Stalking Horse Processes and Court Approval of Sales
One of the primary arguments in support of stalking horse processes is that they maximize the value obtained for the assets being sold, thereby improving recoveries by stakeholders. These processes maximize value in a number of ways. Among other things, they provide a "price floor" for the assets being sold, which not only requires higher bids from other bidders but also provides an "endorsement" of the value of the assets being sold. In this way, they increased the likelihood that other potential bidders will submit a superior bid and possibly reduce the amount of time required for due diligence. In addition, the process can create a competitive environment within which interested bidders can engage in an open auction.

Similarly, the greater transparency and certainty offered by a court-approved procedure and the fact that bids may be compared on an "apples-to-apples" basis may further encourage prospective bidders to participate. Unlike tender processes, where any tender that complies with the call for tender may be considered, prospective bidders in stalking horse processes are required to submit bids that can be compared with the form of the stalking horse agreement which encourages the submission of bids that are similar in form to the stalking horse agreement. Due to this, differences in economic terms and changes in the conditionality of the agreement are more easily assessed by the debtor and its advisors than in a tender, and all participants know what target they are aiming at (even it that target may move during the auction).

Arguments that stalking horse processes maximize value—though persuasive and relevant to the approval of the sale process and the resultant sale—are arguably secondary to whether a stalking horse process protects the integrity of the sale process and promotes its fairness and reasonableness.

Some of the other advantages of negotiating a stalking horse agreement include: (a) its existence can provide comfort to stakeholders by demonstrating to the debtor's stakeholders, including customers, suppliers, and employees, that the business will be continuing in the longer term; (b) it establishes the broad structure and parameters of an agreement that will be followed by other bidders; and (c) it justifies the granting of additional time to conduct a full marketing of its assets by demonstrating to stakeholders and the Court that the debtor is acting with due diligence to implement the sale process.

The bid procedures set out the parameters of the second stage of the sale process, including the timelines for the conduct of the sale, the requirements for eligibility to participate, and the necessary features of a valid bid. Pre-approval of the bid procedures prior to the secondary marketing fosters transparency and openness, and should establish a level playing field where no contestant has an unfair advantage and neither the debtor nor the prospective purchasers are unduly privileged. . . .

Stalking horse processes promote these goals through public disclosure of the economic terms of the baseline bid, the use of established bid procedures, the opportunity to submit a superior bid, and an open auction.

c) Bid Protections and Other Issues

Typically, the stalking horse agreement and the bidding procedures contain a package of protections and incentives intended to compensate stalking horse bidders for participating in the sale process and creating a competitive market. Bid procedures will set out the amount by which another bid must exceed the stalking horse bid (often called the overbid) and the amount each subsequent bid must exceed the prior bid (the bid increment). These packages are justified on pragmatic grounds: few commercially minded bidders will act as a stalking horse without being compensated for the time, money, and effort they expend, and for the risk they incur as a result of their participation in a process that could ultimately benefit someone else (the debtor, its stakeholders, or another bidder).

A stalking horse bidder may attempt to exert pressure on the debtor to tailor the bid protections in order to decrease the likelihood of a superior bid being submitted or to give the stalking horse bidder an unfair edge in the ensuing auction. Some commentators have argued that stalking horse processes are more susceptible to manipulation than traditional tender processes because of the role played by the stalking horse bidder in establishing the parameters of the sale process.

A stalking horse bidder may attempt to tilt the playing field in its favour by negotiating terms in the stalking horse agreement and the accompanying bid procedures that raise hurdles that deter participation by prospective bidders or that make such participation prohibitively expensive. For example, a stalking horse bidder may restrict its competition by insisting on a more restrictive definition of a "qualified bidder." In addition to imposing restrictions on what constitutes a valid bid, a stalking horse bidder can potentially restrict flexibility and make superior offers uneconomical by including terms in the stalking horse agreement that are inconsistent with market norms or are unworkable for some or most competing bidders.

Furthermore, stalking horse bidders may attempt to influence the timelines for completion of the sale process. Stalking horse bidders are understandably eager to conclude the sale process as quickly as possible so as to minimize risk and uncertainty for themselves. However, some stalking horse bidders may seek abbreviated timelines in order to achieve a competitive advantage over prospective bidders. By reducing the amount of time available for such bidders to conduct due diligence and to consider whether and how much to bid in the auction, stalking horse bidders may hope to leverage their head start in conducting due diligence. If the debtor-in-possession (DIP) lender is selected to serve as stalking horse bidder—as in the *PCAS* case, discussed below—the potential for such interference is enhanced because the DIP lender can separately influence the supply and timing of funding.

While the debtor, in consultation with its advisors, nominally determines these aspects of the sale process, a stalking horse bidder may try to stifle competition through these factors. While it is natural that stalking horse bidders will act in their own self-interest in negotiating the stalking horse agreement and the bid procedures, courts have been wary of allowing such self-interest to adversely affect the integrity of the sale process. While courts now accept that protections and incentives for the stalking horse bidder are necessary, they will scrutinize the type and extent of such features to ensure that there is no unreasonably detrimental effect on stakeholders. Therefore, debtors and proposed stalking horse bidders should be alert to these considerations when structuring stalking horse agreements and bid procedures.

In contrast, other potential bidders and the debtors' stakeholders will attempt to minimize the amount and type of such protections as it is in their interest to have the most active auction possible. After all, at the end of the day, they will bear the cost of such protections. A review of market practices provides a range of reasonable options. Nevertheless, terms that are more favourable to a stalking horse bidder may be justifiable if they are the result of a thorough canvassing of the market or a competitive stalking horse selection process.

[First published with the Insolvency Institute of Canada in 2013 and reproduced here with their kind permission.]

Jason Dolman & Gabriel Faure, "Preplan Sales Under Section 65.13 BIA and Section 36 CCAA" (2017) 59 *Canadian Business Law Journal* 332 at 342–57 (footnotes omitted)

III. SOLICITATION OF POTENTIALLY INTERESTED PURCHASERS

The sale process seeks to ensure maximum realization by obtaining as many advantageous offers as possible. This is commonly accomplished by identifying a range of potential purchasers, who are provided with initial solicitation documentation and, if they express interest, are then granted confidential access to further information for purposes of due diligence.

Identifying and soliciting potentially interested purchasers is a key factor in the effectiveness of the sale process. Hence, in *Mecachrome*, Gascon J refused to approve a sale to the debtors' interim lenders, holding that "there has to be some demonstration by the [debtors] that reasonable attempts have been made to properly canvass the market".

1.   Selection of Potentially Interested Purchasers

There are a number of ways to identify potentially interested purchasers for solicitation. By way of example, research at Industry Canada and discussions with the debtors have been considered reasonable means of identifying possible purchasers.

The selection of potentially interested purchasers need not extend beyond the parties susceptible of having a commercial interest, even if they are few in number. For example, the Ontario Court of Appeal decided in *Soundair* that, for the sale of a regional airline, it was reasonable to solicit only the two major airlines operating a hub in the airport from which the regional airline was based. Similarly, Gascon J ruled in *AbitibiBowater (2009)* that it was reasonable to market a hydroelectric facility only to Quebec's electric utility monopoly: . . .

The omission of potentially interested purchasers is not in itself fatal to court approval, as long as the process was reasonable.

2. Sale to a Related Party

The identification and solicitation of potentially interested purchasers has a heightened importance if a sale to a person related to the debtor is envisaged, given that, in such circumstances, the debtor has an interest in selling its assets for a price below fair market value. Justice Morawetz ruled that, when courts are asked to authorize sales to related parties, they "subject the proposed sale to greater scrutiny to ensure a transparency and integrity in the marketing and sales process". Hence, ss. 65.13 of the BIA and 36 of the CCAA require a demonstration that "good faith efforts were made to sell or otherwise dispose of the assets to persons who are not related to the insolvent person". Industry Canada indicates that the purpose of this statutory requirement is to prevent possible abuse by business owners "who engage in serial bankruptcies" by buying assets from the estate and continuing "their original business basically unaffected while creditors are left unpaid".

A court is not likely to approve a preplan sale where parties related to the debtor have intentionally restricted the market of potential purchasers. In *Hypnotic*, the debtor sought to sell its assets to a related party, asserting that no arms-length purchaser could operate its nightclub business without the consent of its sublessor (also a related party) and that no such consent would be given. Justice Cumming refused to authorize the sale. By contrast, a sale to a related party was approved in *Plafolift*, where the debtors' industrial specialization limited the number of potential purchasers.

3. Absence of Solicitation

Although the solicitation of potential interested purchasers generally maximizes the consideration received for the assets, it may not be the best course of action in all circumstances. In exceptional circumstances, courts have authorized preplan sales where no significant solicitation process was conducted.

In *Re Fairmont Resort Properties Ltd*, Romaine J deferred to the opinion of the court officer that going through a sale process would not improve the return to creditors, given that such process would take from nine to 12 months, be costly and require ongoing interim financing. Preplan sales without solicitation were also approved in cases where the debtor had insufficient working capital to finance the process or to finance itself during the process, where the solicitation process would have seriously jeopardized the debtor's relationship with its customers or where only one party was in a position to make an offer. In certain cases, publicity surrounding the sale process may have a prejudicial or even fatal impact on the debtor's business, such that a sale as a going concern would no longer be a viable option.

IV. THE BIDDING PROCESS

The solicitation of potentially interested purchasers is usually followed by a bidding process. As Blair J once commented, "there is a certain general wisdom that an open bidding process usually produces a better price".

1. Deadline to Submit Bids

The delay between the beginning of the solicitation and the deadline to submit bids "must allow a sufficient opportunity for potential purchasers to come forward with offers", while minimizing further financial deterioration of the debtor. A short delay benefits bidders which already have knowledge of the assets, such as secured creditors or a possible purchaser which has already undertaken some due diligence. However, as authors have noted, "a timetable for the sale of a business in distress is a fast track ride that requires interested parties to move quickly or miss the opportunity". Thus, it was held by Gascon J in *Boutique Euphoria*, that a delay of 20 days to submit offers for the business of a clothing retailer was reasonable, given the significant expenses that would be incurred by the debtor in the short term. Similarly, in *Sanjel*, a delay of 12 to 25 days to provide non-binding indications of interest and 16 days for final offers was recognized as reasonable, given the high cash burn situation of the debtors and the deteriorating market. Even shorter delays have been permitted where, prior to the insolvency proceedings, the debtor had already solicited potential purchasers.

2. Stalking Horse Bids

The baseline for a bidding process may be established by a stalking horse bid: a sale agreement between the debtor and a purchaser, conditional upon the absence of any superior bid during the subsequent auction. Other potentially interested parties are encouraged to compete with the bid of the stalking horse, which may, in turn, increase its bid. As Professor Sarra explains, the rationale behind this mechanism "is that the stalking horse has undertaken considerable due diligence in determining the value of the debtor corporation, and other potential bidders can rely, to an extent, on the value attached by that bidder based on that due diligence". The certainty of a stalking horse bid also provides stability to the employees, suppliers and customers of the debtor.

As well, it "establishes the broad structure and parameters of an agreement that will be followed by other bidders". Hence, stalking horse bidding processes have "been recognized by Canadian courts as a reasonable and useful element of a sales process."

Care should be taken to ensure that the stalking horse agreement does not stifle competition during the subsequent auction by unduly favouring the stalking horse bidder. In *Mecachrome*, Gascon J refused to endorse a stalking horse process because the agreement narrowly defined what could constitute a superior bid, such that "the possibility of even seeing other bidders" was seriously limited. The process should be flexible and favour improvement upon the terms of the stalking horse agreement.

Another element of stalking horse agreements susceptible of inhibiting offers is the break-up fee payable to the stalking horse bidder in the event that the debtor accepts a different offer. As Gascon J stated in Boutique Euphoria, "excessive economic incentives in terms of a break up fee or other fee may chill the market and deter other potential bidders." There must be some evidence as to how the break-up fee was calculated and how it compares to the expenses incurred by the stalking horse, although a premium over expenses may be expected as a price for stability. In an empirical review of 17 stalking horse processes conducted under the CCAA between 2004 and 2012, authors Ashley Taylor and Yannick Katirai reported an average break-up fee of 3.2% of the price of the stalking horse bid.

3. Credit Bids

The consideration received by the debtor for its assets need not be paid in cash. A secured creditor may offer to set off the price with all or part of the debt it is owed, a practice known as credit bidding and described by Morawetz J as "well-established in Canada insolvency law." As Professor Sarra notes, "credit bidding may be used as an alternative path to foreclosure unless a third party is willing to pay more than the secured creditor." When considering such a bid, the court officer should obtain a legal opinion as to the validity and enforceability of the security of the creditor.

The amount of a credit bid "should not exceed, but should be allowed to go as ... high as the face value amount of the credit instrument upon which the credit bidder is allowed to rely" and "should not be limited to the fair market value of the corresponding encumbered assets", as stated by Mongeon J in *White Birch (CS)*. On this point, Canadian law is therefore aligned with authorities from the United States, where credit bidding is prevalent.

A credit bid by a secured creditor is not prejudicial to other creditors if the security in question extends to all of the assets sold and the credit bidder pays "any outstanding obligations to prior ranking creditors or obligations secured by priority court-ordered charges." However, safeguards should be put in place to preclude an under-secured creditor from acquiring unencumbered assets with the under-secured portion of its debt. By way of example, in *White Birch (CS)*, the credit bidder was required to allocate a minimum amount of cash to the unencumbered assets equivalent to their estimated realization value, although other methods could have been used.

V. BID SELECTION AND APPROVAL OF THE SALE

1. Choosing the Winning Bid

Choosing the winning bid is not necessarily a mechanical exercise of identifying the highest dollar amount. It is a complex exercise regarding which the court should not "second-guess the commercial and business judgment" of the debtor and the court officer, especially when the chosen offer is supported by creditors. Where it is too difficult to compare offers, the debtor may elect to seek clarifications and/or request amended bids. The price is obviously an important factor in the choice of the winning bid. However, the goal of a preplan sale "is not to obtain the best possible price at any cost, but to do everything reasonably possible with a view to obtaining the best price." The solicitation documentation should thus indicate that a number of factors will influence the choice of the winning bid. By way of example, these factors may include transaction risk, implementation costs, and the continuity of the business.

Here, transaction risk refers to the risk that a transaction may not ultimately be consummated. In *AbitibiBowater (2010)*, the debtor chose an unconditional offer over a higher-priced offer from a bidder that had not sufficiently demonstrated its ability to pay the price or to fund future environmental obligations. Justice Gascon approved the sale, noting that the debtor and the court officer:

> ... were "entitled to prefer a bird in the hand to two in the bush" and were reasonable in preferring a lower-priced unconditional offer over a higher priced offer that was subject to ambiguous caveats and unsatisfactory funding commitments.

Similarly, the chosen bid in *Rail Power* was unconditional and 2.9% lower in price than a competing offer that was conditional upon satisfactory due diligence. Considering the importance of transaction risk, the sale process may provide that only firm and fully-financed bids are acceptable.

The continuity of the business may offer advantages to certain suppliers, employees, customers and other stakeholders, such as future commercial transactions and employment opportunities. However, it is unclear to what extent the debtor and the court officer may consider the interests of non-creditor stakeholders, such as employees, when choosing the winning bid. . . .

2. Sufficiency and Reasonableness of the Consideration

The consideration received by the debtor for its assets is central to the approval of a pre-plan sale; it is thus addressed under three criteria in ss. 65.13(4) of the BIA and 36(3) of the CCAA.

(a) Sufficiency in Comparison to Bankruptcy

Paragraph (c) of both provisions states that the court is to consider whether the court officer "filed with the court a report stating that in their opinion the sale or disposition would be more beneficial to the creditors than a sale or disposition under a bankruptcy." The court is thus invited to compare the consideration with the proceeds that could be expected from a piecemeal liquidation, where the value of some assets—such as goodwill, tax refunds and work in progress—is greatly diminished, if not lost entirely.

When the court officer opines on the liquidation value, it should account for the costs of conservation and realization of the assets. Furthermore, the opinion of the court officer should be based on its own analysis of relevant and verified information and not solely on representations made by the debtor. In *CPVC*, the court held that the court officer's recommendation was based on unverified and insufficient information and was not sufficiently reliable to establish that the preplan sale would be more beneficial to the creditors than a liquidation.

(b) Sufficiency in Context of Sale to Related Party

If the sale is to be made to a person related to the debtor, paras. 65.13(5)(b) of the BIA and 36(4)(b) of the CCAA require that "the consideration to be received is superior to the consideration that would be received under any other offer made in accordance with the process leading to the proposed sale or disposition". As indicated in Part V(1), above, the legislator did not require that the consideration be "higher" than other offers, but rather "superior", suggesting that the chosen bid may be more advantageous, even if the dollar amount is lower. The statutes require that the consideration to be received from a related party be compared only to offers actually made pursuant to the solicitation process.

(c) Reasonableness in Comparison to Market Value

The consideration to be received by the debtor for its assets is also scrutinized under para. (f) of ss. 65.13(4) of the BIA and 36(3) of the CCAA, which require the court to consider whether the consideration "is reasonable and fair, taking into account their market value."

Other offers, received either prior or subsequent to the sale process, have been seen as indicative of the "market value" and hence of the reasonableness of the consideration. . .

The reasonableness of consideration can also be determined by financial analysis. In *AbitibiBowater* (2009), the court relied on the court officer's compilation of comparable trading and transaction multiples, discounted cash flow analyses and sensitivity analysis to conclude that the consideration was reasonable. When the value of the transaction is too low to warrant such an analysis, a comparison of the consideration to the book value of the assets sold might be sufficient. Finally, the approval of the sale by affected creditors may indicate that the consideration is reasonable.

Although the reasonableness of consideration forms a distinct statutory criterion, it does not always receive a distinct analysis. Instead, courts often assess this factor by referring to the superiority of the consideration over the liquidation or by considering that any winning bid resulting from an approved sale process must necessarily yield reasonable consideration. For example, Kane J considered the expected liquidation value in *Komtech* when stating that, "[g]iven the realization value estimate, it appears that the consideration to be paid under the [asset purchase agreement] is reasonable and fair." In *Nelson Education*, Newbould J accepted that the results of the sale process indicated that the consideration was reasonable and should be relied on for that determination. Similarly, in *Veris Gold*, Fitzpatrick J noted that, "[w]hile no appraisals of the assets have been obtained, that fair market value is reflected in the market response to the extensive sales efforts undertaken."

3. The Effects of the Sale on the Creditors and Other Interested parties

In *Re Nortel Networks Corp*, Newbould J noted that "[i]t is a fundamental tenet of insolvency law that all debts shall be paid pari passu and all unsecured creditors receive equal treatment". However, in considering the myriad interests at play under the CCAA, courts have aimed for fair, reasonable and equitable treatment, which is not necessarily equal treatment.

Therefore, in the context of s. 36(3)(e) of the CCAA, courts will assess the effect of a preplan sale on the creditors and other interested parties as a whole...

Does the BIA provide courts the same discretion to approve a preplan sale that provides equitable but not equal treatment of creditors? The CCAA does not contain a provision similar to s. 141 of the BIA, which provides that "[s]ubject to this Act, all claims proved in a bankruptcy shall be paid rateably."...

VI. CONTESTATION OF THE SALE

1. Opportunity for Secured Creditors to Contest

While creditors have ample opportunity to inexpensively vote against a proposal or a plan of compromise or arrangement that involves a sale of assets, they do not have the option of voting against a preplan sale. Also, creditors that would be entitled to contest an application for court approval of a proposal or plan of compromise or arrangement will not necessarily have the opportunity to contest a preplan sale. Secured creditors may oppose the debtor's motion for approval of a preplan sale, but unsecured creditors typically have no opportunity to contest it, as they often do not receive notice of the sale until after it has been approved. Preplan sales have thus been criticized in the United States for marginalizing creditors.

2. Standing of Unsuccessful Bidders to Contest

There is controversy as to who has standing to contest the approval of a preplan sale. A leading authority on this point is *Skyepharma PLC v Hyal Pharmaceutical Corp*, in which the Ontario Court of Appeal held that unsuccessful bidders have no standing to challenge the motion to authorize the preplan sale because they have no legal or proprietary right in the property being sold. Justice O'Connor explained that the "fundamental purpose of the sale approval motion was to consider the best interests of the parties with a direct interest in the proceeds of the sale, primarily the creditors" and that the involvement of unsuccessful bidders would unduly delay the approval.

However, O'Connor J also observed that, "[i]n limited circumstances, a prospective purchaser may become entitled to participate in a sale approval motion." Indeed, unsuccessful bidders in a number of cases were held to have standing to oppose a preplan sale on the grounds that they were also creditors or that the court officer erred in the sale process. In other cases, unsuccessful bidders were nevertheless allowed to make representations, even though their standing was challenged.

Where standing is an issue, one solution may be for the unsuccessful bidder to address its complaint to the court officer, who would then report to the court. This avenue was suggested in the recent ruling of *Bloom Lake*, in which Hamilton J questioned the approach adopted in *Skyepharma*. He noted that the unsuccessful bidder may be the only party with an interest in raising issues of unfairness and lack of integrity....
[Reproduced by permission of Canadian Business Law Journal Inc and Thomson Reuters Canada Limited.]

* * * * *

Most *CCAA* liquidations are carried out in the absence of a formal plan and so creditors are not given an opportunity to vote on the proposed sale. It follows that the court's role in overseeing the sale is critical to the protection of creditors' interests. Some commentators are reasonably sanguine about the courts' capacity to perform this function. For example, Taylor and Katirai, in the article from which the above extract is taken, express confidence that the potential for abuse "will be tempered by a watchful judiciary concerned with preserving the fairness and integrity of the sale processes, and with upholding the over-arching goals of the *CCAA*" (at 112). But others worry that courts lack the resources to act effectively as gate-keepers and that "instead, the court decides what is best for the creditors based on the statements of the Monitor and, often, incumbent management of the debtor company" (Nocilla, "Asset Sales" at 243). See, more generally, David Bish, "The Plight of Receiverships in a CCAA World" (2013) *Journal of the Insolvency Institute of Canada* 221; Roderick J Wood, "Rescue and Liquidation in Restructuring Law" (2013) 53 *Canadian Business Law Journal* 407.

The more frequent use of the stalking horse process in Canada has in turn given rise to another issue—the use of credit bidding. This occurs when a secured party bids the face value of its secured debt in an asset sale in order to acquire the business. In *White Birch Paper Holding Company (Arrangement relatif à)*, 2010 QCCS 4915, Mongeon J stated:

[34] Furthermore, many comments were made today with respect to the dollar value of a credit bid versus the dollar value of a cash bid. I think that it is appropriate to conclude that if credit bidding is to take place, it goes without saying that the amount of the credit bid should not exceed, but should be allowed to go as, high as the face value amount of the credit instrument upon which the credit bidder is allowed to rely. The credit bid should not be limited to the fair market value of the corresponding encumbered assets. It would then be just impossible to function otherwise because it would require an evaluation of such encumbered assets, a difficult, complex and costly exercise.

Credit-bidding provides a means by which the secured creditor can ensure that the assets are not sold for an unacceptably low price. If the other bids are too low, the secured creditor can step in and acquire the assets through a credit bid. A credit bid can only be made in respect of property that is collateral for the secured debt. If there are other unencumbered assets that are being sold as well, the secured creditor must pay cash for these other assets. One concern with credit bidding is that the secured creditor may attempt to influence the sale process, for instance by setting short timeframes, to prevent competitive bids from being made. Although a secured creditor will ordinarily be strongly motivated to obtain the best possible price on an asset sale in order to reduce its secured debt, a secured creditor who bids at the sale will also wish to acquire the assets at the lowest possible price. This would be to the detriment of junior creditors who might otherwise have a claim to the surplus value in the event that the sale process provided sufficient funds to fully satisfy the secured debt of the senior creditor. For this reason, the monitor and the court play an important role in ensuring the transparency and integrity of the sale process.

Practice Questions

Question 1
On 1 August 2015, Company Inc (Company) obtained an initial order under the *CCAA*. Monitor Inc (Monitor) was appointed as the monitor for Company. Company has several shareholders who loaned it money on an unsecured basis (Shareholders). As a result, they are unsecured creditors.

Prior to the Company filing under the *CCAA*, the Monitor had provided consulting services to it, which included an independent evaluation of the potential options relating to the one of Company's developments, an evaluation of the debt structure of one of its related companies, and general consulting regarding the formal or informal restructuring of the Company. The Monitor disclosed these activities in its pre-filing report. Additionally, in the Monitor's fourth report, it disclosed that it had recently determined that an accounting firm related to the Monitor had acted as an auditor for the Company fifteen years prior.

On 1 September 2016, the Shareholders commenced an action to have the Monitor removed and replaced. They allege that the Monitor has a conflict of interest due to having provided consulting services for the Company, and due to the fact that a related company had acted as auditor for the Company.

Do you see any issues arising from the above scenario?

Question 2
Dragons Inc (Dragons) is an oil and gas company. It brought an application seeking approval of a sale of all its assets. This application was supported by the Monitor. Dragons' assets consist primarily of petroleum and natural gas leases, along with the required equipment. Several of the assets are leased and some are subject to contract between Dragons and the owners of the land being affected. What this means is that the sale transaction must contain an assignment of the underlying contracts.

The purchaser of the assets is a shell company. It will purchase the business, and it will debt finance substantially all the purchase price. The purchaser has no equity, and it is leveraging the purchase from cash flow of the insolvent company's operations. However, the cash flow for the insolvent company's business is strong; its insolvency did not arise from losses resulting from its operations.

One particular concern, given this is an oil and gas company, is the environmental risk that these operations create.

The Monitor has approved the proposed assignments.

What are some of the issues that should be flagged in this purchase? What are some of the considerations to determine whether the court should approve the requested approval and vesting order that would compel the assignment of these executory contracts pursuant to section 11.3 of the *CCAA*?

CHAPTER 14
Claims in a *CCAA* Proceeding

I. INTRODUCTION

A creditor must prove it has a valid claim in order to be part of a restructuring. Section 2(1) of the *Companies' Creditors Arrangement Act*, RSC 1985, c C-36 (*CCAA*) defines a "claim" as any indebtedness, liability, or obligation that would be a debt provable in a bankruptcy under the *Bankruptcy and Insolvency Act*, RSC 1985, c B-3 (*BIA*). Section 19(1) of the *CCAA* provides that the only claims that may be dealt with by a compromise or arrangement are (1) claims that relate to debts or liabilities, present or future, to which the company is subject on the day that restructuring proceedings are commenced; and (2) claims that relate to debts or liabilities, present or future, to which the company may become subject before the compromise or arrangement is sanctioned by reason of any obligation incurred by the company before restructuring proceedings are commenced. This language confirms that liabilities arising from the disclaimer of executory contracts that had been entered into before the commencement of restructuring proceedings are properly dealt with in a plan of compromise or arrangement. The relevant date for determining the existence of a claim is the date of the initial *CCAA* application; if the proceeding was initiated under the *BIA* but later switched to the *CCAA*, the relevant date is the date of the initial bankruptcy event.

Section 19(1) of the *CCAA* thus differentiates between pre-filing obligations and post-filing obligations. Pre-filing obligations (those that relate to debts or liabilities that were incurred before the commencement of the insolvency proceedings or that arise out of the disclaimer of contracts that had been entered into before the commencement of restructuring proceedings) may be compromised or otherwise affected by a plan of compromise or arrangement. Creditors that hold pre-filing claims can vote for or against the plan. Claims that arise after this date are not affected by the plan. This does not mean that post-filing creditors are free of risk of loss; if the restructuring fails and the debtor goes into bankruptcy, post-filing creditors will be adversely affected. For this reason, a company that is in restructuring proceedings often must take steps to ensure that the post-filing creditors either are paid in cash or that a post-filing trade creditors' charge is created in order to induce them to extend credit to a financially distressed firm.

Unlike the *BIA*, the *CCAA* does not provide a statutory procedure for the proof and valuation of claims held by creditors. Instead, the claims process is established by a claims procedure order from the court. The claims procedure order sets out how creditors are notified of the process and establishes the procedure that the creditors must employ to prove their claims. In some *CCAA* proceedings, a reverse claims procedure is used. The notice discloses the amounts owing to the various creditors based on the debtor's records, and the creditors are required to act only if they disagree with the amount disclosed in the notice.

The claims procedure order may provide that the monitor will determine the validity and amount of the claims. Alternatively, the order may provide for the appointment of a claims officer who is responsible for the validation and assessment of claims. The claims procedure order will also provide a claims bar date. Section 12 of the *CCAA* provides that the court may fix deadlines for the purposes of voting and for the purposes of distributions under a plan. Proofs of claims must be filed before the expiration of the claims bar date. It has been held that "a claims bar order and its schedule should not purport to 'forever bar' a claim without a saving provision" and a saving provision could make it clear that a claimant may bring a claim after the claims bar date with leave of the court.[1]

The failure to notify a known creditor of the *CCAA* proceedings as required by the claims procedure order will generally mean that the creditor is not bound by the plan of arrangement (see *Ivorylane Corp v Country Style Realty Ltd*, 2004 CarswellOnt 2567 (Sup Ct J), aff'd (2005), 11 CBR (5th) 230 (CA)). Even if a creditor has not been properly notified, the creditor may nevertheless be bound if the creditor knows of the *CCAA* proceedings but chooses not to participate in the hopes of obtaining the full value of its claim following the restructuring (see *Lindsay v Transtec Canada Ltd* (1994), 28 CBR (3d) 110 (BCSC)).

II. DISPUTED AND LATE CLAIMS

The claims procedure order establishes how disputed claims will be resolved. These orders can deal with disputed claims in many ways. The order can specify that the monitor will resolve the dispute and if the parties disagree with the monitor's assessment, they can have the matter heard by a claims officer or a court. If the monitor's decision is referred to the court, it will be determined by a trial *de novo*. If the claims officer's decision is referred to the court, the standard of review is the same as in any appellate proceedings, thereby affording considerable deference to the claims officer.

Pacer Construction Holdings Corporation v Pacer Promec Energy Corporation, 2018 ABCA 113, 67 Alta LR (6th) 281

The Court:

[1] The appellant FTI Consulting Canada Inc (hereafter "the Receiver") is the court-appointed receiver of both Pacer Promec Energy Corporation and Pacer Promec Energy Construction Corporation.

[2] FDS Prime Energy Services Ltd (hereafter "Prime") subcontracted with Pacer Promec Energy Construction Corporation for work to be completed on the site of Canadian Natural Resources Limited's (hereafter "CNRL") Alberta Horizon plant. Prime eventually filed liens on property owned by Pacer Promec Energy Corporation.

[3] Since the Receiver of Pacer Promec Energy Corporation and Pacer Promec Energy Construction Corporation is the same, and there are no substantive distinctions between the two for the purposes of this appeal, as did the chambers judge below we will continue to refer to the corporations in receivership as "PPEC".

[4] Prime submitted to the Receiver a secured proof of claim in the amount of $2,996,050 ("Lien 1") relating to work that Prime claimed to have done pursuant to four contracts and three purchase orders.

1 *Re Blue Range Resource Corp*, 2000 ABCA 285 at para 10.

[5] The Receiver disallowed Lien 1, and the disputed claim was then dealt with pursuant to the Claims Procedure Order granted in the PPEC receiverships, a procedure presided over by an appointed Claims Officer.

[6] Lengthy affidavits and extensive written submissions were tendered before the Claims Officer, and the primary deponents representing Prime and the Receiver were both cross-examined. In addition, the Claims Officer requested and received affidavits from former employees of PPEC, who also underwent cross-examination. An oral hearing took place before the Claims Officer, following which supplemental written submissions were sought and received.

[7] The Claims Officer partially allowed Prime's Lien 1 claim, but only to the extent of $87,377.42. The chambers judge upheld the Claims Officer's determination that monies claimed under various contracts and purchase orders for work done more than 45 days before the registration of Lien 1, were not secured by Lien 1. No appeal has been taken in respect of these contracts and purchase orders.

[8] The primary point of disagreement between Prime and the Receiver in respect of the balance of Lien 1 was whether subcontract N5000 was terminated or abandoned. The Receiver took the position that subcontract N5000 was terminated or abandoned in December of 2014, after which time Prime merely rented scaffolding to the Receiver pursuant to a new contract. Prime took the contrary position, asserting that subcontract N5000 subsisted, there was never a new contract, and that the underlying claim was filed within time.

[9] The Claims Officer agreed with the Receiver.

[10] Prime took the matter to the Court of Queen's Bench. In reviewing the Claims Officer's determinations in respect of Lien 1, the chambers judge decided that subcontract N5000 was not terminated in November or December of 2014, but instead continued until at least May 5, 2015. Since the Receiver took no steps to terminate Prime's subcontract prior to May 5, 2015, Lien 1 filed on July 2, 2015 was valid: *Pacer Construction Holdings Corp v Pacer Promec Energy Corp*, 2016 ABQB 697 ("Decision").

[11] The chambers judge made no comment about the value of Lien 1.

[12] Subsequent to registering Lien 1, Prime registered a second lien for $1,309,761.46 ("Lien 2").

[13] The Receiver applied before the chambers judge to have Lien 2 discharged and the related claim dismissed because Prime had not submitted a Proof of Claim notwithstanding the Claims Procedure Order, and despite being reminded to do so on May 3, 2016 and June 3, 2016 by the Receiver's legal counsel.

[14] The chambers judge declined to dismiss the claim or order discharge of Lien 2, finding that there was "nothing improper in Prime not making a claim under the Claims Procedure Order by June 19, 2015 [the stipulated deadline to make claims]": Decision at para 221. Further, he was of the view that if a filed claim was required under the Claims Procedure Order, then this would be the appropriate case to extend the time within which Prime could make such a claim until "after CNRL has provided the information it is gathering on the subject". The chambers judge declined to make a determination as to whether the claim was actually caught by the Claims Procedure Order.

[15] On appeal, the Receiver contends that the chambers judge's decisions in respect of both Lien 1 and Lien 2 warrant intervention. Specifically, the Receiver asks this Court to restore the decision of the Claims Officer dismissing Lien 1 (with the exception of the secured amount of $87,377.42 admitted by the Receiver to be owing), and dismiss Lien 2, direct the underlying lien be discharged, and award the Receiver its costs.

[16] For the reasons that follow, the appeal is dismissed....

[43] The Receiver raised three grounds of appeal, contending that the chambers judge erred by

(a) conducting a hearing *de novo*, as opposed to a true appeal;

(b) determining that subcontract N5000 continued past December 2014, and therefore the amounts owing under it were secured by Lien 1; and

(c) failing to discharge Lien 2 and dismiss Prime's claim based on its failure to comply with the Claims Procedure Order.

[44] The parties seemed to be substantially in agreement that grounds (a) and (c) are questions of law reviewable by this Court on a correctness standard, and ground (b) is a question of mixed fact and law reviewable by this Court on a standard of palpable and overriding error.

Analysis

Ground 1: Did the Chambers Judge Err by Conducting a De Novo Hearing, As Opposed to a True Appeal?

[45] The essential question is this: what is the correct standard of review that ought to have been selected and applied by the chambers judge in reviewing the dispositions of the Claims Officer?

[46] The selection by the chambers judge of the appropriate standard of review when assessing the Claims Officer's determinations is a question of law, reviewable by this Court for correctness: *Housen v Nikolaisen*, 2002 SCC 33 at para 8, [2002] 2 S.C.R. 235. About this, there is no dispute.

[47] The claims process was governed by the Claims Procedure Order issued by the Court of Queen's Bench of Alberta on May 7, 2015, which provided:

> **44** The Claims Officer will review all materials and evidence in respect of the Claim referred to the Claims Officer and, unless the Claim can be consensually resolved, shall render a disposition of the Claim, and any recommendations the Claims Officer has in respect of the Claim
>
> **45** The disposition and recommendations of the Claims Officer in respect of any Claim *are subject to final determination by this Honourable Court*, unless agreed to by the Receiver and the Claimant, in which case the disposition and recommendations of the Claims Officer will be binding upon the Receiver and the Claimant.[Emphasis added]

[48] In paragraphs 14 and 15 of the Decision, the chambers judge summarized the position of the Receiver and Prime in the following terms:

> **14** One of the key issues on Prime's application is to determine how the Court should approach the Claims Officer's adjudication. Prime says the Court is to approach the issues afresh, to make its own determination on a review of the evidence and not to restrict itself to looking at alleged errors of the Claims Officer. Essentially, Prime characterizes the process before the Court as a hearing *de novo*.
>
> **15** FTI, on the other hand, characterizes the process as an appeal on the record, and argues that the standard of review is reasonableness, having regard to the expertise of the Claims Officer.

[49] The chambers judge concluded that unless the terms of the Claims Procedure Order had specified otherwise, and it did not, then the "final determination by this Honourable

Court" wording set out in paragraph 45 of the Claims Procedure Order was akin to the language relating to an appeal from a master in chambers; thus, mandating a hearing *de novo*: Decision at paras 32–33.

[50] On appeal, the Receiver contended that the chambers judge erred in law in finding that a *de novo* hearing was appropriate and by conducting such a hearing. It argued that instead, the chambers judge ought to have heard the matter as a "true appeal" and accorded the Claims Officer's determinations the highest degree of deference, except on questions of law. The Receiver submitted that the standard of review ought to be the same under common law claims processes and in respect of the decisions of Claims Officers, as the review mechanism in place for appeals under the *Companies' Creditors Arrangement Act*, RSC 1985, c C-36 [*CCAA*] or the *Bankruptcy and Insolvency Act*, RSC 1985 c B-3 [*BIA*]. Or, to put it another way, the Receiver contended that "[o]n an appeal from a disallowance of a claim, the court should only intervene in the case of an error of law or a palpable and overriding error of fact", citing *DBDC Spadina Ltd v Walton*, 2015 ONSC 5608 at para 3.

[51] In contrast, Prime submitted that the chambers judge utilized the correct approach by conducting a hearing *de novo*. It further contended that, in any event, except where the Claims Officer erred in law, the chambers judge actually did defer to the determinations of the Claims Officer on the palpable and overriding standard, despite what was said in the Decision about the correct standard of review.

[52] In our view, to properly analyze this ground of appeal it is necessary to consider in some detail the relevant portions of the Claims Procedure Order, and the process itself.

i. The Claims Process and the Claims Procedure Order

[53] As provided in para 45 of the Claims Procedure Order:

> **45** The disposition and recommendations of the Claims Officer in respect of any Claim *are subject to final determination by this Honourable Court*, unless agreed to by the Receiver and the Claimant, in which case the disposition and recommendations of the Claims Officer will be binding upon the Receiver and the Claimant. [Emphasis added]

[54] This Court must determine the correct interpretation of the phrase "subject to final determination of this Honorable Court". The Claims Procedure Order does not expressly stipulate what this phrase means in the context of the standard of review to be used by a reviewing court when asked to make a "final determination" on the "disposition and recommendations of the Claims Officer".

[55] The starting point for our analysis is to situate these words in the context of the actual claims process followed by the Claims Officer in reviewing Prime's claims, as described in the Claims Officer's disposition at para 12:

> **12** For purposes of this disposition the Claims Officer had the benefit of reading the Claims Officer Package prepared by the Receiver's Counsel containing all documents associated with the Claim, including the Proof of Claim, the Notice of Revision or Disallowance, the Dispute Notice, and other documentation or information relevant to the Claim. In addition the Claims Officer has had the benefit of reading the Brief of the Court-Appointed Receiver along with the Affidavit of ... and the benefit of reviewing supplementary Briefs subsequently submitted by Counsel to address one issue that surfaced following the Hearing. All such materials were carefully reviewed.

[56] The claims process thus described, including all of the evidence before the Claims Officer was, for all intents and purposes, a process closely analogous to that which normally precedes a decision in special chambers. That is, evidence was given by the

participants, there was an opportunity to test the tendered evidence through cross-examination, the transcripts from cross-examination formed part of the evidence that went before the Claims Officer, there was an oral hearing with full argument made by counsel for the participants, and supplementary briefs were provided following the hearing.

[57] In our view, at such a hearing, the participants would reasonably have been expected to bring forward their best evidence, make their best arguments, and would have done all that they considered necessary for the Claims Officer to reach an efficient, expeditious and complete disposition of all disputed claims on their merits.

ii. Did the Chambers Judge Select and Apply the Correct Standard of Review?

[58] The short answer to this question is: we cannot be sure. This is because, in our view, the chambers judge incorporated disparate, but ultimately irreconcilable, statements about the applicable standard of review, but then went on to apply the correct standard of review in his analysis. This requires further explanation.

[59] First, the chambers judge decided that the integrity of the claims process followed by PPEC's creditors would best be preserved if certain specified factors were considered by the reviewing court, on a case by case basis, in relation to each of the impugned determinations.

[60] The chambers judge explained this viewpoint by referring to *Coast Capital Savings Credit Union v Symphony Development Corp*, 2011 BCSC 333 at para 24, 199 ACWS (3d) 447 [*Symphony*], cited at paragraph 30 of the Decision:

> **24** The integrity of the claims process followed by the receiver and the creditors to date is both maintained and promoted if the review process to be undertaken by the Court in respect of each of the receiver's impugned decisions is carefully determined on a case-by-case basis, having regard to the following factors:
> (a) the dollar amount involved;
> (b) relevance of the further evidence proposed to be adduced;
> (c) historical context including laches; and
> (d) the sources of new evidence sought to be adduced.

. . .

[62] The chambers judge nevertheless concluded as follows at paras 32–35:

> **32** Ultimately, despite authority to the contrary, I am unwilling to give a claims officer appointed by the Court the same level of deference the judge appointing him has, absent clear directions to that effect in the Claims Procedure Order. I do not believe that an appointee or delegee should automatically be given greater deference than a Master in Chambers. I prefer the approach taken by Walker J in [*Symphony*] which mandates a flexible approach. In BC, appeals from masters in chambers are treated as true appeals, other than appeals involving the exercise of a discretion. A reviewing judge may exercise his or her own discretion without deferring to the Master. See *Abermin Corp v Granges Exploration Ltd*, 1990 CanLII 1352 (BC SC).
>
> **33** It appears that cases under the CCAA have consistently treated reviews or appeals from a claims officer appointed by order under that legislation as "true appeals" and not as *de novo* hearings.
>
> **34** In Alberta, I am of the view that in proceedings not governed by the CCAA or the BIA, appeals or reviews of claims officers' decisions should follow the same approach as appeals from Masters in Chambers. Here, that means that decisions of claims review officers are generally to be treated as hearings *de novo* [as per the decision in *Bahcheli v Yorkton Securities Inc*, 2012 ABCA 166 [*Bahcheli*]].

35 The exception to that would be where the claims review order specifies a different standard of review to be applied on appeal. It seems to me that this would be easy to incorporate in a claims review order, and would have the relevant parties address their minds to appeals and reviews at the outset . . .

[63] The first and most fundamental difficulty stemming from the chambers judge's finding that appeal of determinations made by claims officers are reviewed by way of "hearings *de novo*", is that the phrase "*de novo*" itself creates significant confusion.

[64] The particular difficulty in ascribing a consistent, and precise, meaning to the phrase "*de novo*" is highlighted in *Transglobal Communications Group Inc (Re)*, 2009 ABQB 195 at para 37, (2009), 473 AR 167:

37 It is important, at the outset, for this Court to provide a guidepost in its use of the phrase appeal "*de novo*." Courts have described appeals *de novo* in many different ways, including:

(a) new evidence or cross-examination is possible, *Ross v McRoberts*, (1999), 237 A.R. 244 (C.A.); *Taylor v Alberta (Workers' Compensation Board)*, [2005] A.J. No. 968 (Q.B.); *Dickey v Pep Homes Ltd*, 2006 ABCA 402

(b) new grounds may be raised, *678667 Alta Ltd v Allendale Bingo Corporation*, [2001] A.J. No. 1303 (Q.B.)

(c) consideration by the reviewing judge afresh in which the court may substitute its opinion, judicially reasoned, for that of the lower court, *Primrose Drilling Ventures Ltd v Carter*, 2008 ABQB 605 at para. 14

(d) an entirely new case is presented, independent of the original case, *Minister of Human Resources Development v Landry* (2005), 31 Admin. L.R. (4th) 13 at para. 10 (F.C.A.)

(e) an appeal heard on the basis of the case originally presented to the tribunal, with the addition of new facts that the tribunal accepted when it revised its decision, *Landry* at para. 10

[65] It appears, then, that some courts treat a "hearing *de novo*" as "an entirely new case . . . independent of the original case", while other courts use the terminology of "hearing *de novo*" to denote a hearing where "new evidence" or "new grounds" may be considered, while still other courts use the term "*de novo*" to describe that a reviewing court may substitute its own opinion for that of the original decision-maker.

[66] There is a critical distinction between a hearing *de novo*, and an appeal on the quite different standard of what has been called "concurrence", or correctness. The distinction is ably explained by The Honourable Roger P Kerans & Kim M Willey in *Standard of Review Employed by Appellate Courts*, 2nd ed (Edmonton: Juriliber, 2006) at 43–44:

43 In a true *de novo* hearing, the reviewing tribunal makes its own decision on the issues with no regard to the proceeding before the first tribunal. This is the complete absence of deference. Like absolute deference, it is, strictly speaking, not a standard of review because there is no review.

44 When it views a matter afresh, a reviewing court asks, "What is the right decision?" That is not quite the question implied by the concurrence (correctness) standard, which is: "Was the decision of the first court right?" The second question raises a presumption of fitness, or correctness, about the first decision and allows a reviewer to let a decision stand unless persuaded of a better one. The first requires the reviewer to decide the case.

[67] According to Kerans and Willey, simply put, the *de novo* approach the chambers judge purported to select would obviate any need to discuss the Claims Officer's decision at all, because the content of the earlier decision would be immaterial.

[68] Yet despite declaring an unwillingness "to give a claims officer appointed by the Court the same level of deference the judge appointing him has, absent clear directions to that effect in the Claims Procedure Order", the chambers judge did not seem to apply a purely non-deferential *de novo* approach. Indeed, he noted that the Claims Officer conducted a "fair and transparent process and gave well thought out and logical reasons for his decision", to which he would not have hesitated to defer had the Claims Procedure Order so provided.

[69] It is not entirely clear, then, what standard of review was selected or applied. At the end of his comments on the standard of review, the chambers judge determined that he need not decide "the matter on the basis as to whether deference is owed or not ... [as] the result is the same using either approach". The chambers judge went on to extensively review the decision of the Claims Officer, ultimately concluding, first, that the Claims Officer had erred on the correctness standard in determining that the subcontract had been terminated or abandoned. In the alternative, the chambers judge also found that on the reasonableness standard, the Claims Officer's decision demonstrated palpable and overriding error and his acceptance of certain evidence was "flawed and tainted": Decision at paras 38, 124, 143, 159–162.

[70] Still later in the Decision, the chambers judge seemed to adopt or endorse the Claims Officer's fact findings, and legal analysis. For example, the question of whether there was a prevenient arrangement was primarily a fact-driven analysis undertaken by the Claims Officer, with which the chambers judge agreed at para 190 of his Decision. Rather than undertaking fresh fact-findings and legal analyses, the chambers judge made no independent findings but instead concluded that the Claims Officer's decisions were lawful or reasonable. In the process, the chambers judge summoned in aid the very essence of the legal effect of deference: he ratified an outcome of findings below rather than generating the decision between the parties afresh.

[71] Still elsewhere in his reasons, the chambers judge said that new evidence could be presented without leave, appearing to accept that the Court's review may go well beyond merely having the ability to substitute its own opinion for that of the Claims Officer, and putting it squarely in the realm of hearing a "new case" even though it has always been permissible for an appeal judge to admit a wide range of evidence. While additional evidence on appeal may change the underpinning upon which earlier findings of fact and mixed fact and law were based, that consequence does not necessarily convert the mandated review process into a hearing *de novo*.

[72] In sum, at the outset the chambers judge faced the problem of determining whether under the Claims Procedure Order, the role of the Claims Officer should be treated as tantamount to that of a first instance decision maker or that of a type of advisory referee.

[73] The answer to the question of whether deference was owed principally turned on the wording of the Claims Procedure Order, which, having been made by a judge of co-ordinate jurisdiction, was not subject to collateral adjustment by the chambers judge. The chambers judge started instead by resorting to an analogy, masters in chambers, in the interpretive exercise here, but having done so set him on an incorrect course.

[74] On its face, the Claims Procedure Order provided for a conclusive determination of rights by the Claims Officer if the parties agreed. That could only mean that the order intended that the decision of the Claims Officer had a conclusive legal effect with the blessing of the Court under those circumstances. The order also provided that the Claims Officer would make a "disposition" in all instances, agreed or not. That the court

could later make a "final determination" connotes nothing about the court's standard of review of the Claims Officer's "disposition". Plainly it means that the court would have the power to change the "disposition" but it says nothing else about standard of review. Unfortunately, having started with an analogy here, the chambers judge ended up with a blended result that is neither clear nor manageable.

[75] Once it is taken that the Claims Officer is a first instance decision maker, the only question is the extent and topics of deference contemplated in the original Claims Procedure Order. While the wording of the order is silent in this respect, it does not contemplate a "final determination" by the court that is entirely divorced from assessing the reasons of the Claims Officer. It reads: "The disposition and recommendations of the Claims Officer in respect of any Claim *are subject to final determination by this Honourable Court*"; that is, the disposition made by the Claims Officer is subject to being confirmed or reversed by the court, not that the record or the lower decision is to be ignored.

[76] Similarly, it might be recalled that the *Supreme Court Act*, RSC 1985 c S-26, enacted pursuant to the *Constitution Act*, 1867 provides in section 52 that "... the judgment of the Court is, in all cases, final and conclusive." The word "final" there does not instruct as to the review standard that Court necessarily applies to all courts and tribunals below it, and there is more than one such standard.

[77] Although the respondent Prime seems to support the view that the Claims Officer's decision was not inherently binding and therefore logically could not be the subject-matter of an appeal on the record, we reject this notion.

[78] In sum, we are not persuaded that the chambers judge stated, selected or consistently applied the correct standard of review. We must therefore consider the issue of standard of review afresh, and then measure the chambers judge's decisions against the appropriate review standard.

[79] First, though, we briefly set out the position of the Receiver and Prime as their submissions on this point were helpful. . . .

iv. What is the Correct Standard of Review?

[83] For the reasons previously given, we are of the view that the Claims Officer made a disposition which is subject to a true appeal, or "final determination by [the chambers judge]".

[84] The wording of the Claims Procedure Order is as follows:

43 In fulfilling its duties under the Order, the Claims Officer is empowered, but not required (and subject always to the further Order by this Court), to:

(a) communicate with and convene meetings with the Receiver and Affected Creditor as is necessary in the circumstances;

(b) request additional documentation or information from the Receiver, the Affected Creditor, or any other person;

(c) request written submissions, including legal submissions, from the Receiver and the Affected Creditor;

(d) establish such rules and procedures as are necessary for:

  (i) the discovery of information relating to the Claim, and

  (ii) the taking of evidence from the parties at the hearing of the Claim, whether by way of Affidavit or *vive voce* evidence;

(e) conduct a hearing of the Claim in person, by written materials only, or in any other manner determined by the Claims Officer;

(f) engage legal counsel or other experts or advisors;

(g) issue written reasons in support of the Claims Officer's disposition of the Claim;

(h) make written recommendations to the Court with respect to the disposition of the claim; and

(i) seek advice and direction from the Court in connection with this Order or the processing of the Claim.

44 The Claims Officer will review all materials and evidence in respect of the Claim referred to the Claims Officer and, unless the Claim can be consensually resolved, shall render a disposition of the Claim, and any recommendations the Claims Officer has in respect of the Claim.

45 The disposition and recommendations of the Claims Officer in respect of any Claim are subject to final determination by this Honourable Court, unless agreed to by the Receiver and the Claimant, in which case the disposition and recommendations of the Claims Officer will be binding upon the Receiver and the Claimant. [Emphasis added]

[85] Regrettably, the Claims Procedure Order did not use express language to identify the applicable standard of review to be applied by the chambers judge in reviewing the Claims Officer's disposition. . . .

[87] Rather, in our view, the meaning of the words set out in the Claims Procedure Order must be read in the context of the relevant factual matrix, and their interpretation must have regard to the intentions of the parties, in the circumstances of a receivership. Here, the Claims Officer was "empowered" under the Claims Procedure Order to conduct a full hearing with evidence being tendered, legal submissions made, and a detailed written decision being issued. He did exactly that.

[88] In contrast to the comprehensive claims process before this Claims Officer, in other cases such as *Scott* the claims process had "none of the indicia identified by Gabrielson J. at para 10 of *Big Sky Farms Inc* [2010 SKQB 255] to create an appeal on the record. There [was] no adversarial proceeding before a claims officer where evidence may be tendered and where the parties are subject to cross-examination. Obviously, there is no decision of a trier of fact . . ."

[89] The essential point made in *Scott* at para 18 is this: "not all claims process orders are the same. One must consider the nature and extent of the order to determine whether the application before the court is actually an appeal on the record." In our view, one must also consider the nature of the claims process itself, in the context of the particular case under review, and decide whether the wording of the Claims Procedure Order was intended to create an appeal on the record. In *Scott*, there was no decision made by a claims officer. Rather, the claims process order allowed for the reviewing court to determine the validity of the claim which had been disallowed by a receiver. Such an appeal would undoubtedly and necessarily involve the admission and consideration of evidence before the reviewing court that had not earlier been considered by a decision-maker.

[90] In contrast, here, the Claims Procedure Order allowed the reviewing court to make a final determination about the "disposition" made by the Claims Officer. That disposition was made on exactly the same evidence and argument as was before the reviewing court, including documentary evidence, written and oral argument, and that the Claims Officer had "the benefit of speaking directly with" some of the witnesses. While no explicit standard of review is set out in the Claims Procedure Order, in our view the claims process here, and the record it created, militated against requiring an entirely new hearing, and certainly not when no fresh evidence was tendered on review.

[91] Although Prime contended that the Claims Officer did not conduct a "'trial-like proceeding'" because he "did not hear oral evidence or cross-examination of the

numerous deponents, and there were no expert reports tendered", in our view this is not dispositive. Indeed, the vast majority of proceedings decided in the Court of Queen's Bench engage adversarial processes that fall short of the ultimate rigour of a trial, and do not include *viva voce* evidence, oral cross-examination, or expert opinions. The fact that a first instance decision maker might in whole or in part rely upon written evidence, does not mean that all deference is ousted. As recently noted by both the majority and dissent in *IFP Technologies (Canada) Inc v EnCana Midstream and Marketing*, 2017 ABCA 157 [*IFP Technologies*] under motion [2017] SCCA No 303 (QL) (SCC No 37712), a trial on a paper record is reviewed in the same manner as a trial with live witnesses. As Watson JA in dissent wrote at paras 289–292: . . .

[92] Fraser CJA for the majority in *IFP Technologies*, did not materially differ on the question of whether the nature of the evidence changed the basis for deference. She wrote at paras 72–73: . . .

[93] Unless there is clear and express wording to the contrary, receivers and claimants participating in a receivership situation rightly ought to expect to engage in a process by which claims are fairly and efficiently adjudicated, with a meaningful court review process in place where disagreements about the Claims Officer's decision can be resolved. The claims process must serve the best interests of the commercial parties, including that it is *generally* the intention of the parties to limit the number, length and costs of hearings and appeals, and to recognize the expertise of those who engage in the claims process and that in a receivership, resources are finite.

[94] As noted by the Receiver, "[h]ere the Claims Officer implemented a procedure which was virtually indistinguishable from a Queen's Bench special chambers application, with all the usual procedural and evidentiary safeguards in place. As a result the review of his decision should have proceeded as a true appeal, not a rehearing." We agree. The claims process here allowed for a fair, transparent and comprehensive adversarial process. The wording of the Claims Procedure Order must be interpreted to reflect the intention of the participants to limit any review of the Claims Officer's decision to a true appeal on the record.

[95] Moreover, such an approach is consistent with a considerable body of relatively recent, persuasive case law, albeit in the context of *CCAA* proceedings. For example, in *General Motors Corp v Tiercon Industries Inc*, 2009 CanLII 72341 at paras 11–12 (Ont SC) [*Tiercon*], confirmed at 2010 ONCA 666, Morawetz J summarized the applicable standards of review in an analogous situation:

11 The Claims Procedure Order provides that a party may appeal a final determination of the Claims Officer.

12 The appropriate standard of review for the appeal of the decision of the Claims Officer is as follows:

(a) With respect to pure questions of law, the standard of review is correctness.

(b) With respect to questions of fact, the standard of review is that such findings are not to be reversed unless it can be established that the decision maker made a palpable and overriding error.

(c) With respect to questions of mixed fact and law, the standard of review, is that, in the absence of an "extricable" legal error or a palpable and overriding error, a finding of the decision maker should not be interfered with.

(d) With respect to the assessment of damages, a damage assessment should not be overturned unless it is based upon a wrong principle of law or the damage is so inordinately high or low that it must be an erroneous estimate of damages. . . .

[96] In that case, the "role of the court on ... appeal is to review the decision of the Claims Officer. It is not to conduct a trial de novo": *Tiercon* at para 69. In our view, this is the preferred judicial approach when a claims process order is silent as to the applicable standard of review on appeal, and the claims process itself has allowed for a full hearing before a decision maker. Bearing this in mind, drafters of such orders would be well-advised to turn their minds to standard of review if the intention is to allow for any kind of less deferential appeal....

[101] In our view, there is no principled basis to depart from the appellate standard of review widely endorsed for *CCAA* proceedings, by reason only that the Claims Officer is court-appointed and not subject to the *BIA* or the *CCAA*. Indeed, the Receiver makes the valid point that under those statutes the functions of a claims officer are not legislatively prescribed either. Therefore, whether by appointment under statute or by common law, the function of the Claims Officer in a receivership ought to be assessed in the same manner—by asking and answering this question: what purposes and objectives are served by the claims process, the Claims Procedure Order, and the Claims Officer's function?

[102] In Alberta, these purposes and objectives are functionally the same: to achieve cost-effective, timely decisions, and procedural and systemic fairness and efficiency. These same purposes and objectives also recognize the reality of limited judicial resources and inherent systemic delays that disrupt timely reviews by the court.

[103] All of this calls for a stricter deferential standard than a "*de novo*" review or "no deference". Rather, the standard of review ought to be that which is set out in *Tiercon* above concerning decisions made by claims officers, and in a different context in *Housen v Nikolaisen*, 2002 SCC 33, [2002] 2 SCR 235.

[104] The standard of review set in both of these cases is correctness on questions of law, and palpable and overriding error on questions of fact or mixed fact and law. Nothing precludes the reviewing judge, in the appropriate case, from admitting additional evidence provided the judge is satisfied with the explanation as to why it was not adduced during the initial claims process where the parties ought to have put their best case forward. Automatically accepting additional evidence on appeal, without any gatekeeping scrutiny, would encourage a careless approach to the claims process and have the effect of transferring the obligations imposed upon Claims Officers to the court.

[105] We conclude that neither the original Claims Procedure Order and claims process, nor the parties, would be well served by the judicial approach promoted by the chambers judge of a *de novo* hearing. Such an approach is devoid of the adjudicative pragmatism expected in commercial matters and, thus, is basically unfit for the urgent realities of participants caught up in a dynamic receivership situation. Such an approach ignores the undoubted expertise of the participants and the Claims Officer, which would undercut presumptions of fitness with regard to both the process, and the Claims Officer. Finally, such a judicial approach would render a claims process—that was intended to operate with expediency—ineffectual, costly, time-consuming and uncertain.

[106] For the foregoing reasons, we are of the view that the chambers judge was wrong in determining that the Claims Officer was not entitled to the "same level of deference [as] the judge appointing him ... ", and that a *de novo* approach to review was required. To the contrary, the Claims Officer's decision is to be assessed on a standard of review as follows: (1) on questions of law, correctness; (2) on questions of fact or questions of mixed fact and law, palpable and overriding error.

[107] Having determined the correct standard of review, we must now consider whether the chambers judge, despite his statements to the contrary, actually applied the

appropriate standard of review when he reviewed the Claims Officer's disposition. This brings us to the second ground of appeal . . .

Appeal dismissed.

8640025 Canada Inc (Re), 2018 BCCA 93, 58 CBR (6th) 257

NEWBURY JA:

[1] This is the second time this court has been asked to intervene in connection with a proposed sale on behalf of the petitioning companies 8640025 Canada Inc. ("864") and a subsidiary thereof, Teliphone Data Centres Inc., of certain business assets to a purchaser ("Distributel") pursuant to s. 36 of the *Companies' Creditors Arrangement Act* ("*CCAA*"). It is also the second time that the proposed sale has foundered on the issue of whether the petitioners in fact own the assets in question such that the assets can be sold in the *CCAA* proceeding. Uncertainty on that point arises because the purchaser wishes to acquire all the assets pertaining to a complex and highly integrated telecommunications business (the "Business") carried on by several corporations comprising the "TNW Group of Companies". The petitioners are part of that Group and are insolvent. They have sought the protection of the *CCAA*. Other members of the Group, appellants in this court, are *not* insolvent and are therefore not part of the *CCAA* proceeding. (We were not told what exactly membership in the 'Group' entails.) . . .

[12] In this court's analysis, the evidence suggesting that some of the assets to be sold belonged to Teliphone Corp. or "other entities not before the Court", together with the Monitor's inability to confirm that the assets were assets of the petitioners, had precluded the court below from approving the Asset Purchase Agreement. In the words of Hunter JA, "The *CCAA* Court had *no jurisdiction* to authorize the sale of assets other than the assets of the petitioners and TNW Networks Corp." (My emphasis.) The appeal was allowed and the order of July 18, 2017 approving the Asset Purchase Agreement was set aside. The stay of proceedings was extended to give interested parties an opportunity to consider the implications of the judgment . . . .

[61] What then is the standard of review applicable to the determinations made by the Monitor in this instance as to the saleability (i.e., ownership) of the Disputed Assets in the course of determining the appellants' proofs of claims? As Teliphone Corp. observed in its factum, the *CCAA* does not expressly contemplate property ownership disputes. There appears to be no decision of an appellate court that establishes an appropriate process to determine *ownership* issues, or determines the applicable standard of review. Nevertheless, since the *CCAA* and *BIA* are to be regarded as parts of a larger scheme of insolvency legislation it is useful to consider comparable decision-makers under the *BIA*. *Galaxy* [2004 BCCA 284] determined the decision of a trustee concerning compliance with a "mandatory" provision under the *BIA*—an issue of law—was reviewable on a correctness standard. Subsequent lower court decisions have adopted similar reasoning with respect to decisions of trustees allowing or rejecting proofs of claim under s. 81(2) . . .

[62] The process followed by the Monitor in the case at bar was not the creature of any statute but of the Supreme Court's order of September 2017. As the Monitor states in its factum:

> The Disputed Property Claims Process was customized for the purpose of these *CCAA* proceedings. The Monitor was authorized to fulfill the function of the arbiter, as it had developed considerable knowledge of this factually complex *CCAA* matter, was less costly

than involving an outside party, and was unable to do so to meet the urgency of the circumstances. An extremely compressed timeline was involved, and no outside party could realistically fulfill the role in the circumstances. [At para. 53.]

As mentioned earlier, the order specified that any Claiming Party dissatisfied with the Monitor's decision could appeal to the court; as well, s. 13 of the *CCAA* provided an appeal with leave.

[63] The Process followed by the Monitor did not entail a formal hearing of witnesses' testimony, but clearly involved the examination of many documents, public and private, and lengthy affidavits of representatives of interested persons. The Monitor asserts that by making it the "arbiter" of the parties' disputes regarding assets, those parties could be taken to have understood that the Monitor would consider the information, documents and evidence it had amassed over the previous nine months, as well as any further evidence that the Claiming Persons were invited to file if they wished. Thus, the Monitor says, there was never any expectation of a "record" in the sense of a formal body of evidence to be considered by it. The Monitor analogizes the process it followed to the "reasonable investigations" normally conducted by trustees in bankruptcy in reviewing claims, citing paras. 39 and 42 of *Re Sran* [2010 BCSC 937]. It goes on to assert that without a "record", it was "frankly impossible for the *CCAA* judge to consider the Monitor's *factual* determination on the basis of correctness." (My emphasis.)

[64] I agree that *factual* determinations and those of *mixed fact and law* are not subject to a correctness standard, but should now be subject to a standard of palpable and overriding error. However, in this case, the fact a sale of assets was being proposed made it necessary for the Monitor to determine exactly what assets were property of the petitioners or TNW Networks—a decision likely to involve issues of law not usually made by monitors under the *CCAA*. This court's decision of August 17, 2017 leaves no doubt, for example, that the Monitor here did not have the authority, as a matter of law, to approve the sale of assets belonging to entities other than the Petitioners and TNW Networks. Obviously, this court regarded this principle as one of law, and indeed of jurisdiction.

[65] In my view, these considerations all support the conclusion that the appeal contemplated by the September order was correctly regarded as a "true appeal" (at least in the absence of any determination that a *de novo* hearing was required to avoid a miscarriage of justice); and that the standard of review, on *extricable* questions of *law*, was correctness. To the extent that questions of law—for example the question of whether the assets of a company that is not in *CCAA* [emphasis added] proceedings may be sold by reason of the fact that its *parent company* is in *CCAA* proceedings—can be "extricated", the correctness standard applies. But obviously, not all issues entailed in determining a proof of claim will be extricable issues of law. Indeed, *most* such issues (including the valuation of creditors' claims) will be ones of fact or mixed fact and law, to which the applicable standard will be that of palpable and overriding error.

[66] This result recognizes that although a formal adversarial process did not take place before the Monitor, the Monitor considered a great deal of evidence and *viva voce* testimony as well as taking advantage of his pre-existing familiarity with the factual background of the matters before him. Indeed, this is one of the reasons the Monitor was chosen to conduct the disputed claims process. Given that the Monitor is an officer of the Court, that it is expected to be "above the fray" and that it is qualified to act as a trustee under the *BIA* and thus has some special expertise, it seems to me that its decisions of fact or mixed fact and law made in the course of ruling on proofs of claim are

appropriately assessed on the deferential standard of "palpable and overriding error". This conclusion is also consistent with the objectives of efficiency, certainty and cost-saving that underlie *CCAA* proceedings.

Disposition

[67] I would therefore allow the appeal, set aside the chambers judge's order and answer the question posed on this appeal as indicated in these reasons. I would also remit the matter of the Monitor's rejection of the proof of claim to the Supreme Court of British Columbia to be dealt with in accordance with these reasons.

Appeal allowed.

UBG Builders Inc (Re), 2016 ABQB 472, 39 CBR (6th) 256

CM JONES J:

I. Introduction

[1] This case deals with the position taken by a Monitor in proceedings under the *Companies Creditors Arrangement Act*, RSC 1985, c C-36 ("*CCAA*") in respect of claims advanced by, and payments made to, an unsecured creditor.

II. Background

[2] Valmont at Aspen Stone Limited Partnership ("Valmont LP") was one of many limited partnerships comprising what has been described as the "UBG Group of Companies" ("UBG"). Valmont at Aspen Stone Inc. ("Valmont Inc.") was the general partner of the Valmont LP. UBG was engaged in residential construction in Alberta and in the United States. Economic circumstances led UBG to obtain protection under the *CCAA* ("*CCAA* Proceedings") resulting in an Order of this Court ("*CCAA* Initial Order") on May 9, 2012.

[3] Valmont LP undertook a multiphase residential condominium project located in Calgary, known as Valmont at Aspen Stone ("Project"). Square Foot Real Estate Corporation ("Square Foot") entered into a Sales Management Agreement effective September 28, 2011 ("Agreement"), with an entity referred to as Valmont at Aspen Stone Ltd. I assume for purposes of this judgment that reference in the Agreement to Valmont at Aspen Stone Ltd. was intended to mean Valmont Inc. as general partner. Pursuant to the Agreement, Square Foot was appointed the exclusive agent to promote and sell units in the second and third phases of the Project.

[4] In furtherance of its duties under the Agreement, Square Foot arranged purchase and sale agreements ("Contracts") with 79 prospective purchasers ("Purchasers") of condominium units ("Units"). As a result of Square Foot's efforts, 73 Offers to Purchase ("OTP") were signed prior to the *CCAA* Initial Order and 6 were signed thereafter.

[5] As discussed in detail below, Square Foot was to receive the total commission payable under the Agreement in two tranches. Those two tranches are referred to in this judgment as front end commissions ("FEC") and back end commissions ("BEC").

[6] The entire amount of FEC payable to Square Foot under the Agreement was either paid by Valmont LP to Square Foot prior to May 9, 2012 or accepted for payment by Ernst & Young Inc. ("Monitor") and paid by it subsequent to May 9, 2012.

[7] Pursuant to an Order of this Court granted on August 30, 2013 ("Sale Approval and Vesting Order"), the Project was sold to 771280 Alberta Ltd. ("771"). I understand 771 to be a subsidiary of the entity referred to as "RDL" in submissions before me. This was not a sale of individual, completed Units. Rather, it was a sale was of the unfinished Project *en bloc.*

[8] After 771 purchased the Project, of the 79 OTPs signed up by Square Foot, approximately one-third, in respect of which Square Foot claims BEC in the amount of $175,166, were cancelled. Deposits received by Valmont LP in respect of these OTPs were not paid to 771, so 771 refunded deposits to these Purchasers from its own funds. The remaining OTPs, in respect of which Square Foot claims BEC in the amount of $269,326.40, were amended by 771 and the Purchasers. The Court was advised that the Purchasers either paid a higher purchase price or bought a different Unit.

[9] Square Foot asserts that it is entitled to BEC in respect of all 79 OTPs in the aggregate amount of $444,492.39 plus GST. It seeks recognition as an unsecured creditor of Valmont LP in respect of these BEC. In the alternative, Square Foot seeks $269,326.40 plus GST, which it claims is attributable to Units ultimately sold by 771 and which it refers to as "sales achieved by Square Foot". The Monitor denies Square Foot's claim to BEC in its entirety.

[10] Square Foot's claims relate to buildings "C" and "D" of the Project. Closings occurred in respect of Units in Building "B" of the Project prior to *CCAA* Proceedings. Buildings "C" and "D" were only partially completed when *CCAA* Proceedings commenced. No closings in respect of Units in these two buildings had taken place.

[11] Square Foot received FEC in respect of 79 OTPs in the amount of $399,601.19. None of those OTPs resulted in sales that closed, the original Contracts being either cancelled or renegotiated. As discussed below, the terms of the Agreement entitled Square Foot to FEC as soon as the "subject to" period ended and a deal became "firm".

[12] Square Foot, it appears, had advice from legal counsel throughout *CCAA* Proceedings. It replaced its counsel with current counsel sometime in early December 2013.

[13] This Court granted a Claims Procedure Order on June 15, 2012. A Claims Bar Date of July 31, 2012 was established by that Order. Notice to Creditors, attached to the Claims Procedure Order as Schedule "A" provided, *inter alia*, that:

> Any creditor having a claim against an entity forming UBG arising before May 9, 2012, of any nature whatsoever, including unsecured, secured, contingent or Unliquidated Claim is required to file, in the manner set out in this Notice to Creditors, a Proof of Claim in the prescribed form.

[14] The Proof of Claim form attached as Schedule "B" to the Claim Procedure Order provided that:

> *Claims should not include the value of goods and/or services supplied after May 9, 2012.* [Emphasis added.]

The *CCAA* Debtor [Valmont LP] was, as at May 9, 2012, and still is indebted to the creditor in the sum of $_____ as shown by the statement of account attached hereto and marked "Schedule A".

[15] This excerpt is important because Square Foot takes the position that liability for BEC arose prior to *CCAA* Proceedings and only payment thereof was deferred.

[16] Square Foot did not file a Proof of Claim in respect of BEC prior to the Claims Bar Date. It apparently was advised by its former counsel that it could not submit a

claim in respect of amounts it had not yet invoiced. Further, it appears to have been advised that it could not submit an invoice for BEC until a sale closed. Square Foot's former counsel appears to have taken the position that closing occurred when a Purchaser remitted the balance of the purchase price and title was transferred.

[17] Square Foot filed the following Proofs of Claim after the Claims Bar Date:

a) Supplemental Proof of Claim with respect to additional FEC – November 18, 2013. This claim, though filed after the Claims Bar Date, was allowed by the Monitor;

b) Amended Proof of Claim adding a new secured claim in the amount of $143,710.03 with respect to the "Sales Centre" – October 7, 2013. This amended a filing on July 30, 2012 in respect of FEC. This claim initially was disallowed by the Monitor, but an amount ultimately was negotiated and paid pursuant to a Consent Order dated June 9, 2014;

c) Proof of Claim in respect of BEC - April 11, 2014; and

d) "Supplemental" Proof of Claim with respect to BEC - July 21, 2014.

[18] When Square Foot's Proof of Claim filed April 11, 2014 was disallowed by the Monitor, it filed a Notice of Dispute and the Supplemental Proof of Claim, seeking to amend its Proof of Claim filed on July 30, 2012. If Square Foot's entire claim for BEC of $444,492.39 plus GST set out in its Proof of Claim is not allowed, it seeks, in the alternative by way of the Supplemental Proof of Claim, $269,326.40 plus GST, representing BEC "on the sales of units achieved by Square Foot, where the sale of the unit ultimately closed".

III. Issues

[19] Three issues arise in this matter. First, given the Claims Bar Date of July 31, 2012, I must first consider if Square Foot's Proof of Claim for BEC filed April 11, 2014 should be accepted.

[20] Second, if I direct that this Proof of Claim be accepted notwithstanding late filing, I must interpret the Agreement to determine if Square Foot is entitled to the claimed BEC.

[21] These two issues are, of course, related and there may be some overlap between them. Nevertheless, they are analytically distinct and must be considered separately.

[22] Third, the Monitor asserts that Valmont LP made improper payments to Square Foot on March 16, 2012 and April 5, 2012 ("Payments"). The Payments, the Monitor asserts, were made to Square Foot as a creditor of Valmont LP, gave rise to a preference over Valmont LP's other creditors and are therefore void. It seeks an Order requiring Square Foot, on account of Valmont LP, to pay to the Monitor the sum of $111,991.28.

IV. Analysis

A. Late Filing

[23] Square Foot argues that its Proof of Claim filed April 11, 2014 in respect of BEC should be accepted as properly filed and dealt with on its merits. It argues that it kept the Monitor and UBG fully informed of its claims to BEC throughout *CCAA* Proceedings.

[24] The Monitor denies Square Foot's claim for BEC and asserts that it never gave any assurance of payment to Square Foot. The Monitor also argues that Square Foot has no entitlement to BEC under the Agreement and that it is futile to allow late filing of a Proof of Claim that would yield nothing.

[25] The test on an application for late filing of a claim under the *CCAA* was set out by the Court of Appeal in *Re Blue Range Resource Corp*, 2000 ABCA 285, 271 AR 138 at para 26:

Therefore, the appropriate criteria to apply to the late claimants is as follows:

1. Was the delay caused by inadvertence and if so, did the claimant act in good faith?
2. What is the effect of permitting the claim in terms of the existence and impact of any relevant prejudice caused by the delay?
3. If relevant prejudice is found, can it be alleviated by attaching appropriate conditions to an order permitting late filing?
4. If relevant prejudice is found which cannot be alleviated, are there any other considerations which may nonetheless warrant an order permitting late filing?

1. Inadvertence

[26] Turning to the first criterion, I note that the Court of Appeal stated in *Blue Range* at para 27 that "In the context of the criteria, 'inadvertent' includes carelessness, negligence, accident, and is unintentional." In subsequent cases, this Court has expressed concern about creditors "lying in the weeds" and seeking to secure some advantage by late filing; see, for example, *Re BA Energy Inc,* 2010 ABQB 507, 70 CBR (5th) 24 and *Royal Bank of Canada v Cow Harbour Construction Ltd,* 2011 ABQB 223, 516 A.R. 125.

[27] Square Foot argues that there is no evidence that it was attempting to circumvent the *CCAA* process or that it was in some way "lying in the weeds". It argues that it had good reasons not to file formal Proofs of Claim for BEC. The Monitor had advised at the First Meeting of Creditors on May 15, 2012 that creditors were to file Proofs of Claim only on currently-owed invoices as of May 9, 2012 and that if Proofs of Claim submitted included items not invoiced prior to *CCAA* Proceedings, not only would they be discarded but the position of legitimate pre-*CCAA* invoice claims would be jeopardized. Square Foot decided not to file Proofs of Claim for BEC because the Project was not then complete and BEC was not payable until closing, which had not yet occurred. Moreover, Square Foot asserts that it relied on the advice of its then-counsel to not include BEC in its Proof of Claim for FEC filed November 18, 2013 because they were not yet "invoiced" sales.

[28] Square Foot seems to suggest that it was caught between a rock and a hard place. It was told by the Monitor that the claims procedure dictated that it should not file Proofs of Claim except in respect of invoiced amounts. It acknowledges that, as of the date of the Claims Procedure Order of June 15, 2012, the Project was not complete and no closings had taken place. It acknowledges that BEC were not payable until closing had occurred. Invoices could be submitted only after closing.

[29] Square Foot claims to have informally reminded the Monitor of its claim for BEC in February 2014 at a meeting with counsel for the Monitor. Square Foot's counsel followed up with a letter on April 1, 2014, received no reply to that letter and promptly filed Proofs of Claim.

[30] At the same time, Square Foot continued to contribute to post-*CCAA* efforts to effect sales, made periodic inquiries through Larry Scammell and Don Poirier (representatives of UBG) regarding the Monitor's awareness of its BEC claim, sought clarification of who (Valmont LP or 771) would be responsible for its BEC and attempted to make a deal with 771. When no deal with 771 was forthcoming, Square Foot formally submitted a Proof of Claim for its BEC.

[31] The Monitor takes the position that Square Foot's failure to file its BEC by the Claims Bar Date was not inadvertent and instead represents a "calculated risk". The Monitor notes that Square Foot had filed some claims by the Claims Bar Date of July 31, 2012 and so was fully aware of it. Its BEC claim was filed in April of 2014, many months thereafter. The Monitor suggests that Square Foot voluntarily and knowingly assumed that Valmont LP would finish the Project and close the sales to the Purchasers under

the OTPs. When it became apparent that the Project would be sold *en bloc* and that its entitlement to BEC could be effectively eliminated, Square Foot chose to try to establish a relationship with 771 that might lead to payment of the BEC once Units were sold by 771. The evidence suggests that Square Foot indeed made inquiries of UBG, the Monitor and 771 in that regard. Apparently, 771 never responded to Square Foot's inquiry.

[32] The Monitor suggests that Square Foot made a conscious decision to attempt to have 771 engage it to assist in selling Units in the Project, rather than attempting to collect BEC from the fund standing in place of the Project as a result of the Sale Approval and Vesting Order. When that proved unsuccessful, Square Foot filed its Proof of Claim.

[33] The Monitor bases its argument, in part, on its position that Square Foot had no entitlement to BEC under the Agreement. The Monitor takes the position that any BEC claim Square Foot filed prior to the Claims Bar Date would have had to await a determination by the Monitor that sales of the 79 Units under the OTPs were completed, that Valmont LP had received the purchase price for the Units and that Square Foot had invoiced Valmont LP for BEC. The Monitor refers to Scammell's Questioning, in which he affirmed his understanding that BEC was payable when a "unit was turned over to the purchaser". It would be "perverse" the Monitor argues, to now accept a claim for BEC after it had been conclusively established that the contingencies entitling Square Foot to BEC never occurred.

[34] This argument ignores the importance of assessing Square Foot's entitlement to late file a Proof of Claim for BEC separately from its potential entitlement to BEC under the Agreement. As noted above, the late filing and Agreement interpretation issues must be analyzed separately.

[35] In my view, Square Foot was not simply waiting in the weeds. It participated in the claims process, was alert to its potential entitlement to BEC and engaged counsel to assist it.

[36] Counsel for the Monitor asserted that Square Foot could have filed its claim for BEC as a contingent claim by the Claims Bar Date. There is unchallenged evidence that the Monitor advised creditors at the First Creditors Meeting that Proofs of Claim should not be submitted in respect of claims not yet invoiced. That should, in my view, have alerted Square Foot to the need to file a contingent claim for BEC on or before the Claims Bar Date.

[37] The somewhat ambiguous nature of the Proof of Claims form utilized in these *CCAA* Proceedings may have contributed to Square Foot's decision. As noted above, it provided that "Claims should not include the value of good and/or services supplied after May 9, 2012". Nevertheless, I find that Square Foot could have protected its claim to BEC without breaching that provision by filing a contingent claim. Alternatively, if, as discussed *infra*, Square Foot believed liability for BEC had already crystalized, subject to deferred payment, it could have issued an invoice for BEC prior to the Claims Bar Date on the premise that BEC was owing but not yet "due". Presumably, Square Foot could have waived any right it had asserted to a contingent BEC as of the Claims Bar Date, had 771 engaged it on the condition that it do so.

[38] I accept the argument that Square Foot believed its best option was to seek an arrangement with 771, rather than to press for payment of BEC. I believe that decision reflected what should have been its anxiety about its entitlement under the Agreement to BEC, in light of the circumstances, discussed at length above, which arose in respect of *CCAA* Proceedings and the Sale Approval and Vesting Order.

[39] In *Re SemCanada Crude Co*, 2012 ABQB 489, 546 AR 203, a case involving a somewhat similar "judgment call" by a creditor, Romaine J stated at paras 52 and 53:

Celtic's failure to make a timely claim was not unintentional. It submits that it "simply" did not perceive it had a right to damages because it did not believe that the IGPA had been suspended. Celtic was aware of the *CCAA* proceedings from the time of the Initial Order and retained counsel with respect to the proceedings throughout. It filed a Proof of Claim for a different kind of claim. It cannot argue that its failure to file a claim was careless, negligent or accidental; it was Celtic's deliberate choice, acting with the advice of counsel, to maintain its position that the IGPA had not been suspended, but amended, without providing for the possibility that this position would be found to be incorrect and that it may have a claim for damages arising from a suspension. . . .

Celtic submits that the possibility of suspension damages must also have been apparent to SemCAMS and the BA before the Plan was negotiated and presented to creditors. That is beside the point; the Claims Process in *CCAA* proceedings requires creditors to identify and to file their claims or be barred from pursuing them. It is not up to the debtor company to guess at potential claims, or whether creditors will decide to pursue them.

[40] Square Foot was not a casualty of a claims procedure that did not adequately address the type of potential claim its interpretation of the Agreement gave rise to. It knew it could file a contingent claim. Its failure to submit a contingent claim for BEC by the Claims Bar Date or to obtain written confirmation that the Monitor agreed with its decision not to actually issue an invoice for BEC prior to the Claims Bar Date may have been careless or negligent. However, I do not find it to be inadvertent or unintentional.

[41] Square Foot also argues that its claim for BEC was well known to the Monitor and that its failure to file a formal Proof of Claim by the Claims Bar Date was inadvertent in the sense that it arose from Square Foot's understanding that the Monitor would recognize its claim. Square Foot argues that, while the Monitor never gave *direct* assurances that BEC would be paid, the Monitor had known since the commencement of *CCAA* Proceedings about the basis for and quantum of Square Foot's BEC claims. Square Foot does not formally advance an estoppel argument in response to the Monitor's denial, nor does it formally advance the argument that Square Foot relied to its detriment on representations made by the Monitor. Rather, it argues that it would be unfair to deny Square Foot the ability to advance its BEC claims as an unsecured creditor. Square Foot points out that the Monitor did accept certain late filed claims for FEC.

[42] The Monitor does not deny that it had some knowledge of Square Foot's potential BEC claims, but distinguishes between the provision of information regarding potential BEC and the formal submission of a Proof of Claim. The Monitor argues that it must rely strictly on the Proof of Claim process, approved by this Court, to ensure equal treatment of all creditors.

[43] Scammell's and Poirier's evidence, the Monitor argues, establishes that BEC become payable only out of Unit sale proceeds and only when a Unit sale to a Purchaser closed. It also establishes that any assurances by Scammell and Poirier regarding payment of BEC were given in the context of a sale of Units by Valmont LP and that Square Foot was warned that a sale of the Project *en bloc* would mean that Square Foot would need to look to 771, not Valmont LP, for payment of BEC. However, 771 did not respond to Square Foot's overtures.

[44] While this matter is discussed in more detail in respect of the fourth *Blue Range* criterion, it is relevant here because it informs the analysis of Square Foot's intentions. If it knew or ought to have known that it could not look to 771 for its BEC, yet it still did not file a Proof of Claim, can its decision to not do so be said to have arisen unintentionally, through inadvertence?

[45] There is sufficient evidence regarding communications with the Monitor through Scammell and Poirier to suggest to me that the Monitor was aware that Square Foot might assert a claim to BEC. That, however, is different from the assertion of a formal claim, with ensuing consequences, as part of a claims procedure. The Monitor's awareness of Square Foot's BEC claim does not amount to a waiver of the requirement for that claim to be submitted in accordance with proper claims procedure.

[46] In this respect, I take guidance from the following comments by Romaine J. in *Re BA Energy* at para 41:

> The objective of a claims procedure order is to attempt to ensure that all legitimate creditors come forward on a timely basis. A claims procedure order provides the debtor and the Monitor with the information necessary to fashion a plan that may prove acceptable to the requisite majority of creditors given the financial circumstances of the debtor and that may be sanctioned by the court. The fact that accurate information relating to the amount and nature of claims is essential for the formulation of a successful plan requires that the specifics of a claims procedure order should generally be observed and enforced, and that the acceptance of a late claim should not be an automatic outcome. The applicant for such an order must provide some explanation for the late filing and the reviewing court must consider any prejudice caused by the delay.

[47] Though it appears the Monitor was less proactive than it might have been in attempting to clarify if and how Square Foot would advance a claim for BEC, the responsibility for advancing a claim lies with the creditor, not the Monitor and I am not satisfied that the Monitor was responsible for doing more. The Monitor's awareness of Square Foot's BEC claim does not obviate Square Foot's responsibility for pursuing that claim in the appropriate manner and it cannot be said that Square Foot was unaware of the claims process. Therefore, I find that Square Foot's failure to file a Proof of Claim for BEC prior to the Claims Bar Date was not the result of inadvertence.

2. Prejudice

[48] The second *Blue Range* criterion requires consideration of any prejudice resulting from the delay in filing the claim. The Court of Appeal held at para 40 of *Blue Range* that "In a *CCAA* context, as in a *BIA* context, the fact that Enron and the other Creditors will receive less money if late and late amended claims are allowed is not prejudice relevant to this criterion."

[49] Square Foot argues that assurances were given that the contracts it had assisted in negotiating with Purchasers before *CCAA* Proceedings commenced would somehow be transferred as part of the *en bloc* sale of the Project, that their value would be recouped in the sale price by the Monitor and that BEC would be paid to Square Foot. Square Foot was advised by Scammell that if 771 did not contract with Square Foot, BEC would be "covered off by the Monitor" in the receipt of the purchase price to be negotiated with 771.

[50] Indeed, the evidence satisfies me that, once it became clear the Project would be sold *en bloc*, Scammell advised Square Foot to contact 771 and attempt to negotiate a deal directly with it. By then, however, the Claims Bar Date had come and gone. The Sale Approval and Vesting Order, which presumably reflected the deal negotiated between the Monitor and 771, specifically relieved 771 from any liability Valmont LP may have had to Square Foot. It appears that Square Foot did not object to the terms of the Sale Approval and Vesting Order. Should this operate to deny it the ability to late file a Proof of Claim for BEC?

[51] In my view, it should not. The terms of the Sale Approval and Vesting Order should operate only to limit what might otherwise be Square Foot's claim for BEC to sale proceeds of the Project which the Monitor holds in place of individual Units and the Project itself. The only prejudice that would result from this would be a diminution in the amount received by other creditors; the Court of Appeal has held that this does not constitute prejudice for this purpose....

4. Other Considerations

[53] As alluded to above, Square Foot's primary argument in favour of its application for late filing is that it reasonably relied on representations that its claim for BEC would be recognized notwithstanding the absence of a formal Proof of Claim. Though it does not plead estoppel, misrepresentation or breach of duty, the inference Square Foot would have this Court draw is that it would unfair to deny it the ability to have its BEC considered along with other unsecured creditors in dividing up the Claims Reserve. In this respect, the comments of Romaine J in *Re BA Energy* at para 34 are apposite: "It is clear from the nature of the [*Blue Range*] criteria that the question of whether a late claim should be accepted is an equitable consideration, taking into account the specific circumstances of each case."

[54] Square Foot seeks to establish that the Monitor, through Scammell and Poirier, had full and timely information regarding its BEC. Tim Taylor, a representative of Square Foot, stated as follows in an Affidavit:

> In the post-*CCAA* period, it was confirmed by Larry Scammell that all 'back-end' commissions would be paid at the time of Closing on any deals that were directly written by Square Foot. Mr. Scammell also confirmed that this information was passed along to the Monitor and to the Purchaser.

[55] Square Foot asserts that both Scammell and Poirier confirmed the accuracy of this statement during questioning and that it is reasonable to conclude that the Monitor knew that Scammell and Poirier had assured Square Foot that it would be paid BEC.

[56] Square Foot referred to various events as "evidence" of a commitment by the Monitor to honour BEC, including: (1) Scammell's confirmation that he received a spreadsheet depicting both FEC and BEC and forwarded it to the Monitor; (2) a telephone conversation among Simon Kowalkow (a representative of Square Foot), Scammell and Poirier on November 30, 2012 suggesting that Scammell and Poirier knew what had been paid and what was outstanding; (3) Poirier's confirmation that Square Foot would be paid at the time of closing; (4) Scammell's confirmation that he would pass to the Monitor information received on December 21, 2012 from Kowalkow and Taylor regarding BEC; (5) Scammell's alleged discussions with the Monitor regarding a 50/50 split of commission between FEC and BEC; and (6) Taylor's understanding that BEC would be paid once construction was completed and Unit sales closed, together with Poirier's confirmation that if the Project was built, Square Foot would receive its BEC.

[57] The reasonableness of Square Foot's reliance on this "evidence" is premised on the assertion that Scammell and Poirier were acting as agents or representatives of the Monitor and were able to bind the Monitor. The Monitor expressly denies this assertion; its position is that Scammell and Poirier were employees of UBG, not agents or representatives of the Monitor.

[58] The evidence satisfies me that Scammell and Poirier were in frequent contact with Taylor during *CCAA* Proceedings, that the Monitor was aware of the circumstances

in which Square Foot could become entitled under the Agreement to receive FEC and BEC and that the Monitor knew the quantum of Square Foot's potential BEC claim.

[59] However, the evidence does not satisfy me that Scammell and Poirier were imbued with authority to commit the Monitor to anything. They were employed by UBG, not by Ernst & Young. If representations were made, they do not constitute representations or assurances by the Monitor that it would recognize BEC. If Square Foot chose to rely on advice from Scammell and Poirier, it did so at its peril. There is a significant difference between relying on representatives of UBG as conduits for information to and from the Monitor and relying on those representatives for conclusions regarding legal rights. Square Foot could have instructed its then counsel to obtain confirmation from the Monitor or its counsel that no further actions were required for the Monitor to recognize its claim for BEC. There is no evidence before me that it did so.

[60] Further, the evidence suggests that once it became apparent that the Project would be sold *en bloc*, Square Foot was being told to make arrangements directly with 771. The Monitor argues that if Scammell gave any assurances to Square Foot, he did so only in the context of sales closed by Valmont LP, not by 771. It asserts that Valmont LP never become liable to pay BEC and that 771 was relieved by the Sale Approval and Vesting Order from any liability under the Agreement for BEC that might be owed to Square Foot.

[61] Square Foot argues that it was entitled to expect the Monitor to treat it reasonably and honourably by having its BEC recognized in the sale price to 771.

[62] Ultimately, one-third of the Contracts negotiated by Square Foot were cancelled. The Court was advised that 771 refunded deposits advanced by these Purchasers, notwithstanding that it had not received those deposits from Valmont LP. New/amended contracts were put in place with the other two-thirds of the Purchasers. There is no evidence before the Court as to whether the purchase price for the Project reflected an understanding between the Monitor and 771 respecting Square Foot's claims to BEC. What is clear is that Square Foot neither objected to the Sale Approval and Vesting Order nor sought assurances from the Monitor that its BEC formed part of the deal with 771. That being the case, it simply is not evident to me that the Monitor's actions can be characterized as dishonourable or unreasonable.

[63] Square Foot notes that, once *CCAA* Proceedings commenced, it was asked to stay on by UBG and it continued to staff the Valmont LP sales centre. To quote counsel for Square Foot "It's a member of the family". Square Foot notes that Scammell confirmed that Square Foot's efforts added value by keeping many buyers in place and finding new buyers, which promoted the sale of the project to 771. Square Foot argued that it was an integral part of UBG's marketing efforts and that it added considerable value to completion of the Project, even after Valmont LP entered *CCAA* Proceedings. At Questioning, Poirier confirmed the accuracy of the following comment in Taylor's Affidavit:

> Square Foot believes that it was largely through its efforts that the ultimate buyer of the project was presented with a nearly-completed project (from a design and marketing perspective), where all it had to do was "turn the lights back on". No re-branding, marketing, tweaking, or re-designing had to be done and no money had to be put into these line items for the new owner to have a very viable, marketable project.

[64] No evidence was provided to support these assertions. In my view, the Monitor's acquiescence to Square Foot's continued sales efforts is not evidence that the Monitor considered Square Foot's contribution significant or somehow worthy of recognition of its BEC claim without compliance with the established claims procedure. There was

no evidence from 771 to support the assertion that Square Foot's efforts lightened its burden. It makes sense that Square Foot would, in its own interests, continue its function during this pre-*en bloc* sale phase in order to maximize retention of Purchasers.

[65] I must consider if, under the circumstances, it would be inequitable to deny Square Foot the ability to late file a Proof of Claim for BEC. I conclude that a denial would not be inequitable. It is clear that Square Foot acted in reliance on its dealings with Scammell and Poirier, but the evidence does not satisfy me that those gentlemen were able to bind the Monitor to any undertakings or understandings. They were merely a conduit through which Square Foot found it convenient to communicate with the Monitor. Square Foot was not justified in basing its claims submission strategy on Scammell's and Poirier's understandings of industry practice or contract interpretation. Square Foot could, and should, have protected its BEC claim by filing a contingent Proof of Claim or by seeking assurances directly from the Monitor or its counsel.

[66] In the result, Square Foot's application to late file a Proof of Claim for BEC is denied....

Application dismissed.

III. MASS TORT CLAIMS

American courts have on several occasions had to wrestle with the meaning of "creditor" and "claim" under the US *Bankruptcy Code*, 11 USC §101, when corporations sought protection under chapter 11 against current and prospective mass tort claims brought, or liable to be brought, against them by alleged victims of asbestosis (*Johns-Manville Corp*) or wearers of the Dalkon Shield (*AH Robins Co*). In the article extracted below, Professor McKenzie provides a current account of the treatment of mass tort claims in bankruptcy, the limitations of bankruptcy, and the political economy of law reform in this area.

In contrast to the *Bankruptcy Code* Chapter 11 situation, the vast majority of *CCAA* cases do not involve situations where tort claims caused the insolvency of the company (in the sense that, had the tort debt not existed, the *CCAA* proceedings would not have been commenced) or are a major claim in the insolvency proceeding. The following chart summarizes examples of Canadian *CCAA* cases dealing with mass tort claims:

	Case	Nature of the Litigation
1)	*Canadian Red Cross Society, Re* (2000), 19 CBR (4th) 158 (Ont Sup Ct J)	Transfusion-related claims
2)	*Babcock & Wilcox Canada Ltd* (2000), 18 CBR (4th) 157 (Ont Sup Ct J)	Application granted under former section 18.6 of the *CCAA* for stay of actions and enforcements against corporation in respect of asbestos tort claims
3)	*Les Oblats de Marie Immaculee du Manitoba (Re)*, 2004 MBQB 71	Sexual abuse claims against Catholic priests
4)	*United Properties Ltd (Re)*, 2005 BCSC 1858	Developer was involved in construction of two condominiums that developed leaks—"leaky condo" litigation initiated against the developer; developer sought protection under the *CCAA*

	Case	Nature of the Litigation
5)	*Muscletech Research & Development Inc (Re)* (2007), 30 CBR (5th) 59 (Ont Sup Ct J)	Product liability claims related to health supplements
6)	*ATB Financial v Metcalfe & Mansfield Alternative Investments II Corp* (2008), 43 CBR (5th) 269 (Ont Sup Ct J)	Litigation related to the sale of Asset Backed Commercial Paper
7)	*Grace Canada Inc (Re)* (2008), 50 CBR (5th) 25 (Ont Sup Ct J)	Product liability claims against parent—ancillary proceedings commenced under *CCAA* to facilitate and coordinate US proceedings and deal with Canadian class actions
8)	*Labourers' Pension Fund of Central and Eastern Canada (Trustees of) v Sino-Forest Corp*, 2012 ONSC 7050, 2013 ONSC 1078, leave to appeal to CA refused 2013 ONCA 456, notice of appeal filed 2014 CarswellOnt 3023	Securities class action settlement
9)	*The Cash Store Financial Services Incl (Re)*, 2015 ONSC 7538	Securities class action against 1511419 Ontario Inc, formerly known as The Cash Store Financial Services Inc, for making false and misleading statements regarding Cash Store's financial results, assets, business structure and transactions, causing Cash Store's securities to trade at artificially inflated prices
10)	*Poseidon Concepts Corp, Re*, 2018 CarswellAlta 951 (QB)	Securities class action settlement to shareholders involving allegations of misrepresentations in financial statements and corporate disclosure documents
11)	*Montreal, Maine & Atlantic City Canada Co/ Montreal, Maine & Atlantique Canada Cie, Re*, 2015 QCCS 3235, 29 CBR (6th) 287 (court approved plan of arrangement)	Cross-border insolvency case arising from Lac-Mégantic train derailment which killed forty-seven people and destroyed more than forty buildings
12)	*Cline Mining Corp, Re*, 2015 ONSC 622	Class action alleging violation of the U.S. federal *Worker Adjustment and Retraining Notification Act (WARN Act)*
13)	*Arctic Glacier Income Fund, Re*, 2013 CarswellMan 797 (QB)	Class action settlement involving allegations of unlawful conspiracy to fix price of packaged ice
14)	*JTI-Macdonald Corp, Re*, 2019 ONSC 1625 *Imperial Tobacco Limited, et al, Re*, 2019 ONSC 1684 *Re Rothmans, Benson & Hedges*, CV-19-616779-00CL	Class action against a trio of tobacco companies for health complications experienced by smokers

As discussed below, one way that American debtors have dealt with so-called future claimants is by setting up trusts and appointing representatives, resulting in significant cost, business disruption, litigation, and additional months or years added to the bankruptcy case. In *In re Chemtura Corp*, Case No 13 Civ 2023 (JMF) (SDNY 10 February 2014), aff'g Case No 09-11233 (REG) (Bankr SDNY 7 February 2013) (ECF No 5817), the Southern District of New York affirmed a bankruptcy court ruling confirming that there is an alternate path to discharge mass tort claims by relying on a tailored and comprehensive program for giving notice to claimants whose injuries are discovered after the commencement of restructuring proceedings without the need for the appointment of future claims representatives or the establishing of trusts for claims.

Troy A McKenzie, "Toward a Bankruptcy Model for Non-Class Aggregate Litigation" (2012) 87 *New York University Law Review* 960 at 1005–8 and 1010–12 (footnotes omitted)

The bankruptcy process also facilitates final peace in mass tort cases through the treatment of claims against a debtor's estate. The Code provides a broad definition of a "claim," including debts that have already been liquidated as well as unmatured, contingent, and unliquidated obligations. Along with the broad definition of a claim, the Code provides procedures for dealing with claims that are not yet fixed in their amount.

A bankruptcy court must estimate contingent or unliquidated claims as necessary to avoid undue delay in the administration of the case. Typically, estimation occurs when the contingency on which the asserted liability rests has not occurred (and may not occur until much later in time) or when liquidation will similarly lead to delay. For purposes of the bankruptcy process, claims estimation makes it feasible to allow a claim—that is, to permit the holder of the claim to participate in the distribution of the debtor's assets—so that the claimant may vote on a debtor's plan of reorganization, even if it is not possible to resolve fully the value of the claim. In mass tort cases, estimation of personal injury claims permits a court to allow claimants, including future claimants, to participate in the bankruptcy proceedings, even if they have not yet reduced their claims against the debtor-defendant to judgment. By doing so, the bankruptcy court can craft a plan that will reflect the interests of those claimants and effectively bind them.

The Code also permits a court to discharge debts. In a Chapter 11 case, all property of the debtor's bankruptcy estate returns to the debtor when a plan of reorganization is confirmed at the close of the bankruptcy case. More importantly, upon vesting with the debtor, the property dealt with by the plan is free and clear of all liens, claims, or interests, and confirmation of a plan of reorganization serves to discharge any debt that arose before the commencement of the case. In effect, the debtor's plan of reorganization becomes the governing document setting forth the treatment of the rights and obligations of interested parties after confirmation of the plan.

Crucially for absent claimants, the bankruptcy discharge reaches beyond those who participated in the proceedings through plan confirmation. The discharge is binding even against a claimant who did not submit a proof of claim in the bankruptcy or who submitted a proof of claim and objected to the plan. Confirmation of the debtor's plan of reorganization therefore precludes any further litigation of all questions that could have been raised pertaining to the plan. The res judicata effect of a bankruptcy plan is enhanced by the doctrine of equitable mootness, which bars appellate review if it would disturb transactions that have been consummated during or after a bankruptcy case in connection with the plan. Thus, bankruptcy holds out the possibility of achieving binding resolution of all liabilities of the debtor-defendant, even when future claimants may appear to seek compensation years later.

In addition to the binding effect of a plan of reorganization, bankruptcy courts may enjoin future proceedings against the debtor that seek to collect on debts resolved by the plan. The bankruptcy court in the Johns-Manville case expanded on this power by issuing a "channeling injunction" under the general equitable powers of the court. The injunction directed future asbestos claims to a trust created for the benefit of asbestos claimants. The trust, funded in large part by insurance proceeds and shares in the reorganized firm, provided a continuing source of compensation for future claimants while protecting the reorganized firm's value as a going concern. In essence, the trust and channeling injunction system created an administrative structure for reconciling and compensating asbestos injuries that would manifest themselves far into the future. The chief difficulty of asbestos litigation—the long tail of liability that threatened to stretch far into the future after manufacturers had ceased producing the product—could be addressed in this way. . . .

The approval of a debtor's bankruptcy plan requires democratic input from various constituencies. The Code imposes a series of steps before plan confirmation that canvass eligible holders of claims against, and interests in, the debtor with respect to the proposed plan. The process, although elaborate, aims to generate broad consensus among interested parties with respect to the debtor's fate.

The plan voting process begins with disclosure. The Code requires as a first step that proponents of a plan must draft and circulate a disclosure statement for holders of claims and interests. In essence, the disclosure statement functions like a prospectus in a securities offering. It must lay out the classification of various claims against the debtor, the intended disposition of the debtor's assets, and a description of the debtor's path out of bankruptcy. Crucially, no solicitation of votes in favor of or against the plan may occur until the bankruptcy court approves the disclosure statement as containing adequate information.

The voting process also takes into account differences among creditors. A plan must sort claims that are "substantially similar" into various classes for voting purposes. Substantial similarity means more than similar priority—that is, two claims that are general unsecured claims of the same priority may not necessarily be considered substantially similar. But this test is flexible and pragmatic. Claims do not need to be identical in all respects to be placed in the same class for plan voting purposes, and claims that may share similar features do not always need to be put in the same class.

The plan voting process requires the effective consent of claimants before a plan is confirmed. That consent, however, balances the voice of individual claimants with group-based voting rules. First, each class is treated separately for voting purposes, and a class is deemed to accept the plan if those who hold two-thirds in amount and a majority by number of claims duly voted approve it. . . .

Despite its ability to achieve coordination and finality, the bankruptcy process raises a number of concerns that have hampered its use beyond a limited number of mass tort cases. Those concerns fall roughly into three categories: delay, expense, and uncertainty. Mass tort bankruptcy cases may take years to emerge from the bankruptcy courts. The progenitor of the modern mass tort bankruptcy case, the Johns-Manville asbestos bankruptcy, lingered in court for six years. Bankruptcy cases—and the required submission to the oversight of courts, committees of interested parties, and the U.S. Trustee—can be expensive and can greatly limit the degrees of freedom of debtor-defendants. More worryingly, innovation in mass tort bankruptcy cases is often slow to receive judicial approval, leaving uncertainty about the legitimacy of some uses of bankruptcy as a mass tort resolution device. A related cause for uncertainty is the imperfect track record in bankruptcy cases of providing adequate funds to compensate future claimants. For example, the Johns-Manville future claimants trust proved insufficient and was restructured twice.

Some of these concerns are not specific to the mass tort context, such as the delay and expense in closing bankruptcy cases (a longstanding criticism of Chapter 11 generally). Others are more closely attuned to the mass tort context, such as the low recoveries for claimants that may result (generally from poor estimation of the number and value of future claims). Still others touch more specifically on the architecture of the Bankruptcy Code — chiefly, the disagreement about whether future claimants have "claims" that may be adjudicated under the Code.

One lingering problem is that only a claim, a right to payment that arises before a plan of reorganization is confirmed, may be discharged in bankruptcy. The ability to participate in the bankruptcy case and vote on the plan of reorganization as a creditor is generally reserved to those who hold claims. Courts have not been consistent in their treatment of tort victims whose injuries arise from pre-confirmation conduct but do not manifest until after confirmation. Some courts have adopted the rule that if a tort plaintiff did not have some relationship with the debtor before plan confirmation, then there is no "claim" for bankruptcy purposes. As a result, even in mass tort litigation best suited to treatment in bankruptcy — that is, when "long tail" tort liability threatens the enterprise value of the firm — litigants have been reluctant to resort to bankruptcy.

Another lingering concern is that bankruptcy can be an expensive process. Although the direct costs of a bankruptcy case are subject to debate, the bankruptcy process is commonly perceived to be complicated and potentially costly. That view is shared by defendants in mass tort cases and by the plaintiffs who would become creditors in a bankruptcy case. Beyond the immediate costs of a bankruptcy filing, firms fear the reputational costs of pursuing bankruptcy relief. Merck, for example, strenuously avoided pursuing a bankruptcy filing when the initial wave of Vioxx litigation began to mount.

The resistance to bankruptcy is not irrational. A bankruptcy filing alters the relationship among various constituencies in a firm. The management of the firm no longer has a fiduciary responsibility solely to its shareholders but owes duties as "debtor in possession" to the entire bankruptcy estate, which includes creditors. Bankruptcy requires managers of a firm to act under the supervision of the bankruptcy court. Major undertakings — and some not-so-major undertakings — require the approval of the bankruptcy court, typically after notice and a hearing. In other words, bankruptcy brings with it the prospect of second-guessing and public exposure for a multitude of corporate decisions.

[Reprinted by permission of the publisher.]

IV. PRIORITIES

The *BIA* establishes a statutory scheme of distribution for bankruptcy proceedings (see Chapter 9), but there are no corresponding provisions in the *CCAA*. Instead, the plan of compromise or arrangement determines the amounts that will be recovered by the various classes of claimants. This does not mean that priorities are irrelevant in a restructuring. The bargaining over the terms of the agreement occurs in the shadow of the law. A claim that is entitled to priority will usually be afforded more favourable treatment in the plan. A plan of arrangement will typically divide the creditor into a number of different classes — for example, the plan may create a class of unsecured creditors and a class of secured creditors. The class of secured creditors will not be inclined to vote in favour of the plan if their priority status is not recognized. Furthermore, a court will usually be unwilling to approve the plan if it gives a creditor less than what it would receive on a bankruptcy liquidation.

When determining priorities, one begins with the priority status of the claim under non-insolvency law principles. For example, the priority status of a consensual security interest in personal property is determined by provincial personal property security legislation. The priority of other kinds of proprietary claims may be governed by legislation. In the absence of any legislative priority rule, the priority status of the claim will be determined by the priority principles of property law. The *CCAA* contains a number of priority provisions that provide for an express priority rule for certain types of claims. In these instances, the non-insolvency priority rules are displaced and the express priority rule set out in the *CCAA* will govern.

A. Secured Creditors

Section 2(1) of the *CCAA* defines a "secured creditor." Like the definition of a secured creditor in the *BIA*, it covers security interests in real and personal property that arise consensually or by operation of law. Personal property security legislation does not subordinate an unperfected security interest on the commencement of restructuring proceedings (but it does subordinate it on the commencement of bankruptcy proceedings, see *TRG Services Inc (Re)* (2006), 26 CBR (5th) 203 (Ont Sup Ct J); *PSINet Ltd (Re)* (2002), 30 CBR (4th) 226 (Ont Sup Ct J); also see Anthony Duggan, "The Status of Unperfected Security Interests in Insolvency Proceedings" (2008) 24 *Business & Finance Law Review* 103). Although registration is not needed in order to give the security interest priority over the unsecured creditors who have not taken the appropriate steps to enforce their judgments, a secured creditor may wish to ensure that it is properly perfected, for two reasons. First, it will want to maintain priority if the restructuring is unsuccessful and the debtor goes into bankruptcy. Second, it will want to preserve its priority against other parties who acquire an interest in the debtor's assets. Secured parties may, however, encounter difficulties when attempting to register a financing statement after restructuring proceedings are commenced, because the stay of proceedings may prevent creditors from taking such action. If the stay of proceedings prevents registration, a secured creditor can apply to court to have the stay lifted in order to permit registration. In many instances, the drafting of the stay provision permits post-filing registration of security interests. If this is the case, a court application is not needed.

B. Unsecured Creditors

Unsecured creditors have no proprietary right in the debtor's assets, and therefore have no basis to claim priority over other claimants. The situation becomes more complicated if the unsecured creditor has obtained judgment and has registered or filed a writ or judgment against land. Many provinces also provide for registration of writs or judgments in the personal property security registry. If registration or filing has been effected, the unsecured creditor, now a judgment enforcement creditor, obtains priority over prior unperfected security interests and subsequently created interests in the asset. Unlike the case in bankruptcy proceedings, the commencement of restructuring proceedings does not extinguish the writ or judgment. Therefore, the priority of such interests over other subordinated claims to the same asset must be recognized in the restructuring proceedings.

C. Subordinated Claims

Creditors may agree, through subordination or postponement agreements, to postpone their claims until other claims or all claims in a class have been paid out. The courts will generally give effect to a contractual subordination. The only creditors who have the benefit of the subordination agreements are those that are subject to the agreement. See the discussion in Chapter 9. As is the case in bankruptcy proceedings, the subordination provision is given effect by requiring the subordinated creditor to turn over any dividends or other amounts received in the insolvency proceedings to the benefiting creditors.

D. Crown Claims

Sections 38 and 39 of the *CCAA* are similar in operation to sections 86 and 87 of the *BIA*. A Crown claim is afforded the status of an unsecured claim unless (1) it is of a kind that is ordinarily available to other creditors; (2) the Crown claim is registered under the real or personal property provincial registry systems before the commencement of *CCAA* proceedings; or (3) the Crown claim is covered by the statutory garnishment device that is used to recover source deductions of income tax, Canada Pension Plan, and employment insurance. See the discussion of Crown claims in Chapter 8.

E. Deemed Trusts

Section 37 of the *CCAA* is similar to sections 67(2) and (3) of the *BIA*. A statutory deemed trust in favour of the Crown is not effective unless a trust would have been recognized in the absence of the statutory provision. An exception is made for the statutory deemed trust that secures unpaid source deductions of income tax, employment insurance, and Canada Pension Plan contributions. See the discussion of Deemed Trusts in Chapter 8.

Section 222 of the *Excise Tax Act*, RSC 1985, c E-15 (*ETA*), creates a statutory deemed trust in respect of GST that has been collected. The provision indicates that the deemed trust is effective despite any other legislation, other than the *BIA*. Section 67(2) of the *BIA* provides that a deemed trust is ineffective "notwithstanding any provision in federal or provincial legislation." This has been most recently confirmed in *Callidus Capital Corp v Canada*, 2018 SCC 47, where the Supreme Court upheld the dissenting judgment of the Federal Court of Appeal. It confirmed that the bankruptcy of a tax debtor and section 222.1 of the *ETA* "render[ed] the deemed trust under section 222 of the *ETA* ineffective as against a secured creditor who received, prior to the bankruptcy, proceeds from the assets of the tax debtor that were deemed to be held in trust for the Plaintiff."

Section 37 of the *CCAA* provides that a deemed trust is ineffective "despite any provision in federal or provincial legislation." Both the *ETA* and the *CCAA* therefore purport to prevail over any other provincial or federal legislation to the contrary. In the case of restructurings pursuant to the commercial proposal provisions of the *BIA*, the *ETA* deemed trust is clearly ineffective because the provisions of the *ETA* indicate that contrary provisions in the *BIA* are to prevail. But in the case of restructurings under the *CCAA*, both sets of federal provisions purport to prevail over any other federal or provincial statute. The Supreme Court of Canada in *Century Services Inc v Canada (Attorney General)*, [2010] 3 SCR 379 held that the provisions in the *CCAA* are to prevail over the provisions in the *ETA*. This decision was in part based on the undesirable consequences that would result if the *ETA* deemed trust was ineffective in a restructuring under part III, division I, of the *BIA*, but effective in a restructuring under the *CCAA*. Justice Deschamps stated:

> [47] Moreover, a strange asymmetry would arise if the interpretation giving the ETA priority over the CCAA urged by the Crown is adopted here: the Crown would retain

priority over GST claims during CCAA proceedings but not in bankruptcy. As courts have reflected, this can only encourage statute shopping by secured creditors in cases such as this one where the debtor's assets cannot satisfy both the secured creditors' and the Crown's claims.... If creditors' claims were better protected by liquidation under the BIA, creditors' incentives would lie overwhelmingly with avoiding proceedings under the CCAA and not risking a failed reorganization. Giving a key player in any insolvency such skewed incentives against reorganizing under the CCAA can only undermine that statute's remedial objectives and risk inviting the very social ills that it was enacted to avert.

Section 37 only covers deemed trusts in favour of the Crown. Legislation that creates statutory deemed trusts in favour of persons other than the Crown are not affected by this provision. Legislation that creates a deemed trust in favour of employees for unpaid wages or in respect of pension benefits therefore are not rendered ineffective by the commencement of CCAA proceedings. This situation set the stage in *Sun Indalex Finance, LLC v United Steelworkers*, 2013 SCC 6, for a priority dispute between employees and retirees who were claiming pursuant to a provincial deemed trust under pension benefits legislation and an interim lender who provided DIP financing pursuant to an order that authorized it and that granted the lender priority over any other interest. In the excerpt below, the Supreme Court of Canada deals with two issues: (1) which obligations are subject to the provincial statutory deemed trust; and (2) do the priority provisions of the provincial statutes prevail over the court order that gave the DIP charge priority over any other interest?

Sun Indalex Finance, LLC v United Steelworkers, 2013 SCC 6, [2013] 1 SCR 271

[The facts are reproduced in the extract of this decision in Chapter 13, Part III, above.]

DESCHAMPS J:

III. Analysis

A. Does the Deemed Trust Provided for in Section 57(4) of the *PBA* Apply to Wind-up Deficiencies?

[26] The first issue is whether the statutory deemed trust provided for in s. 57(4) of the *PBA* extends to wind-up deficiencies. This question is one of statutory interpretation, which requires examination of both the wording and context of the relevant provisions of the *PBA*. Section 57(4) of the *PBA* affords protection to members of a pension plan with respect to their employer's contributions upon wind up of the plan. The provision reads:

57. ...

(4) Where a pension plan is wound up in whole or in part, an employer who is required to pay contributions to the pension fund shall be deemed to hold in trust for the beneficiaries of the pension plan an amount of money equal to employer contributions accrued to the date of the wind up but not yet due under the plan or regulations.

[27] The most obvious interpretation is that where a plan is wound up, this provision protects all contributions that have accrued but are not yet due. The words used appear to include the contribution the employer is to make where a plan being wound up is in a deficit position. This quite straightforward interpretation, which is consistent with both the historical broadening of the protection and the remedial purpose of the provision, is being challenged on the basis of a narrow definition of the word "accrued".

I do not find that this argument justifies limiting the protection afforded to plan members by the Ontario legislature.

[28] The *PBA* sets out the rules for the operation of funded contributory defined benefit pension plans in Ontario. In an ongoing plan, an employer must pay into a fund all contributions it withholds from its employees' salaries. In addition, while the plan is ongoing, the employer must make two kinds of payments. One relates to current service contributions—the employer's own regular contributions to the pension fund as required by the plan. The other ensures that the fund is sufficient to meet the plan's liabilities. The employees' interest in having the contributions made while the plan is ongoing is protected by a deemed trust provided for in s. 57(3) of the *PBA*.

[29] The *PBA* also establishes a comprehensive scheme for winding up a pension plan. Section 75(1)(a) imposes on the employer the obligation to "pay" an amount equal to the total of all "payments" that are due or that have accrued and have not been paid into the fund. In addition, s. 75(1)(b) sets out a formula for calculating the amount that must be paid to ensure that the fund is sufficient to cover all liabilities upon wind up. Within six months after the effective date of the wind up, the plan administrator must file a wind-up report that lists the plan's assets and liabilities as of the date of the wind up. If the wind-up report shows an actuarial deficit, the employer must make wind-up deficiency payments. Consequently, s. 75(1)(a) and (b) jointly determine the amount of the contributions owed when a plan is wound up.

[30] It is common ground that the contributions provided for in s. 75(1)(a) are covered by the wind-up deemed trust. The only question is whether it also applies to the deficiency payments required by s. 75(1)(b). I would answer this question in the affirmative in view of the provision's wording, context and purpose....

[35] In *Hydro-Electric Power Commission of Ontario v Albright* (1922), 64 S.C.R. 306, Duff J considered the meaning of the word "accrued" in interpreting the scope of a covenant. He found that

> the word "<u>accrued</u>" according to well recognized usage has, as applied to rights or liabilities the <u>meaning simply of completely constituted</u>—and it may have this meaning although it appears from the context that the right completely constituted or the liability completely constituted is one which is only exercisable or enforceable *in futuro*—a debt for example which is *debitum in praesenti solvendum in futuro*. [Emphasis added; pp. 312–13.]

[36] Thus, a contribution has "accrued" when the liabilities are completely constituted, even if the payment itself will not fall due until a later date. If this principle is applied to the facts of this case, the liabilities related to contributions to the fund allocated for payment of the pension benefits contemplated in s. 75(1)(b) are completely constituted at the time of the wind up, because no pension entitlements arise after that date. In other words, no new liabilities accrue at the time of or after the wind up. Even the portion of the contributions that is related to the elections plan members may make upon wind up has "accrued to the date of the wind up", because it is based on rights employees earned before the wind-up date.

[37] The fact that the precise amount of the contribution is not determined as of the time of the wind up does not make it a contingent contribution that cannot have accrued for accounting purposes (*Canadian Pacific Ltd v MNR* (1998), 41 O.R. (3d) 606 (C.A.), at p. 621). The use of the word "accrued" does not limit liabilities to amounts that can be determined with precision. As a result, the words "contributions accrued" can encompass the contributions mandated by s. 75(1)(b) of the *PBA*.

[38] The legislative history supports my conclusion that wind-up deficiency contributions are protected by the deemed trust provision. The Ontario legislature has consistently expanded the protection afforded in respect of pension plan contributions. . . .

[43] Therefore, in my view, the legislative history leads to the conclusion that adopting a narrow interpretation that would dissociate the employer's payment provided for in s. 75(1)(b) of the *PBA* from the one provided for in s. 75(1)(a) would be contrary to the Ontario legislature's trend toward broadening the protection. Since the provision respecting wind-up payments sets out the amounts that are owed upon wind up, I see no historical, legal or logical reason to conclude that the wind-up deemed trust provision does not encompass all of them.

[44] Thus, I am of the view that the words and context of s. 57(4) lend themselves easily to an interpretation that includes the wind-up deficiency payments, and I find additional support for this in the purpose of the provision. The deemed trust provision is a remedial one. Its purpose is to protect the interests of plan members. This purpose militates against adopting the limited scope proposed by Indalex and some of the interveners. In the case of competing priorities between creditors, the remedial purpose favours an approach that includes all wind-up payments in the value of the deemed trust in order to achieve a broad protection.

[45] In sum, the relevant provisions, the legislative history and the purpose are all consistent with inclusion of the wind-up deficiency in the protection afforded to members with respect to employer contributions upon the wind up of their pension plan. I therefore find that the Court of Appeal correctly held with respect to the Salaried Plan, which had been wound up as of December 31, 2006, that Indalex was deemed to hold in trust the amount necessary to satisfy the wind-up deficiency.

[46] The situation is different with respect to the Executive Plan. Unlike s. 57(3), which provides that the deemed trust protecting employer contributions exists while a plan is ongoing, s. 57(4) provides that the wind-up deemed trust comes into existence only when the plan is wound up. This is a choice made by the Ontario legislature. I would not interfere with it. Thus, the deemed trust entitlement arises only once the condition precedent of the plan being wound up has been fulfilled. This is true even if it is certain that the plan will be wound up in the future. At the time of the sale, the Executive Plan was in the process of being, but had not yet been, wound up. Consequently, the deemed trust provision does not apply to the employer's wind-up deficiency payments in respect of that plan.

[47] The Court of Appeal declined to decide whether a deemed trust arose in relation to the Executive Plan, stating that it was unnecessary to decide this issue. However, the court expressed concern that a reasoning that deprived the Executive Plan's members of the benefit of a deemed trust would mean that a company under *CCAA* protection could avoid the priority of the *PBA* deemed trust simply by not winding up an underfunded pension plan. The fear was that Indalex could have relied on its own inaction to avoid the consequences that flow from a wind up. I am not convinced that the Court of Appeal's concern has any impact on the question whether a deemed trust exists, and I doubt that an employer could avoid the consequences of such a security interest simply by refusing to wind up a pension plan. The Superintendent may take a number of steps, including ordering the wind up of a pension plan under s. 69(1) of the *PBA* in a variety of circumstances (see s. 69(1)(d) *PBA*). The Superintendent did not choose to order that the plan be wound up in this case.

B. Does the Deemed Trust Supersede the DIP Charge?

[48] The finding that the interests of the Salaried Plan's members in all the employer's wind-up contributions to the Salaried Plan are protected by a deemed trust does not mean that part of the money reserved by the Monitor from the sale proceeds must be remitted to the Salaried Plan's fund. This will be the case only if the provincial priorities provided for in s. 30(7) of the *PPSA* ensure that the claim of the Salaried Plan's members has priority over the DIP charge. Section 30(7) reads as follows:

> (7) A security interest in an account or inventory and its proceeds is subordinate to the interest of a person who is the beneficiary of a deemed trust arising under the *Employment Standards Act* or under the *Pension Benefits Act*.

The effect of s. 30(7) is to enable the Salaried Plan's members to recover from the reserve fund, insofar as it relates to an account or inventory and its proceeds in Ontario, ahead of all other secured creditors.

[49] The Appellants argue that any provincial deemed trust is subordinate to the DIP charge authorized by the *CCAA* order. They put forward two central arguments to support their contention. First, they submit that the *PBA* deemed trust does not apply in *CCAA* proceedings because the relevant priorities are those of the federal insolvency scheme, which do not include provincial deemed trusts. Second, they argue that by virtue of the doctrine of federal paramountcy the DIP charge supersedes the *PBA* deemed trust.

[50] The Appellants' first argument would expand the holding of *Century Services Inc v Canada (Attorney General)*, 2010 SCC 60, [2010] 3 S.C.R. 379, so as to apply federal bankruptcy priorities to *CCAA* proceedings, with the effect that claims would be treated similarly under the *CCAA* and the *BIA*. In *Century Services*, the Court noted that there are points at which the two schemes converge:

> Another point of convergence of the *CCAA* and the *BIA* relates to priorities. Because the *CCAA* is silent about what happens if reorganization fails, the *BIA* scheme of liquidation and distribution necessarily supplies the backdrop for what will happen if a *CCAA* reorganization is ultimately unsuccessful. [para. 23]

[51] In order to avoid a race to liquidation under the *BIA*, courts will favour an interpretation of the *CCAA* that affords creditors analogous entitlements. Yet this does not mean that courts may read bankruptcy priorities into the *CCAA* at will. Provincial legislation defines the priorities to which creditors are entitled until that legislation is ousted by Parliament. Parliament did not expressly apply all bankruptcy priorities either to *CCAA* proceedings or to proposals under the *BIA*. Although the creditors of a corporation that is attempting to reorganize may bargain in the shadow of their bankruptcy entitlements, those entitlements remain only shadows until bankruptcy occurs. At the outset of the insolvency proceedings, Indalex opted for a process governed by the *CCAA*, leaving no doubt that although it wanted to protect its employees' jobs, it would not survive as their employer. This was not a case in which a failed arrangement forced a company into liquidation under the *BIA*. Indalex achieved the goal it was pursuing. It chose to sell its assets under the *CCAA*, not the *BIA*.

[52] The provincial deemed trust under the *PBA* continues to apply in *CCAA* proceedings, subject to the doctrine of federal paramountcy (*Crystalline Investments Ltd v Domgroup Ltd*, 2004 SCC 3, [2004] 1 S.C.R. 60, at para. 43). The Court of Appeal therefore did not err in finding that at the end of a *CCAA* liquidation proceeding, priorities may be determined by the *PPSA*'s scheme rather than the federal scheme set out in the *BIA*.

[53] The Appellants' second argument is that an order granting priority to the plan's members on the basis of the deemed trust provided for by the Ontario legislature would be unconstitutional in that it would conflict with the order granting priority to the DIP lenders that was made under the *CCAA*. They argue that the doctrine of paramountcy resolves this conflict, as it would render the provincial law inoperative to the extent that it is incompatible with the federal law.

[54] There is a preliminary question that must be addressed before determining whether the doctrine of paramountcy applies in this context. This question arises because the Court of Appeal found that although the *CCAA* court had the power to authorize a DIP charge that would supersede the deemed trust, the order in this case did not have such an effect because paramountcy had not been invoked. As a result, the priority of the deemed trust over secured creditors by virtue of s. 30(7) of the *PPSA* remained in effect, and the Plan Members' claim ranked in priority to the claim of the DIP lenders established in the *CCAA* order.

[55] With respect, I cannot accept this approach to the doctrine of federal paramountcy. This doctrine resolves conflicts in the application of overlapping valid provincial and federal legislation (*Canadian Western Bank v Alberta*, 2007 SCC 22, [2007] 2 S.C.R. 3, at paras. 32 and 69). Paramountcy is a question of law. As a result, subject to the application of the rules on the admissibility of new evidence, it can be raised even if it was not invoked in an initial proceeding.

[56] A party relying on paramountcy must "demonstrate that the federal and provincial laws are in fact incompatible by establishing either that it is impossible to comply with both laws or that to apply the provincial law would frustrate the purpose of the federal law" (*Canadian Western Bank*, at para. 75). This Court has in fact applied the doctrine of paramountcy in the area of bankruptcy and insolvency to come to the conclusion that a provincial legislature cannot, through measures such as a deemed trust, affect priorities granted under federal legislation (*Husky Oil*).

[57] None of the parties question the validity of either the federal provision that enables a *CCAA* court to make an order authorizing a DIP charge or the provincial provision that establishes the priority of the deemed trust. However, in considering whether the *CCAA* court has, in exercising its discretion to assess a claim, validly affected a provincial priority, the reviewing court should remind itself of the rule of interpretation stated in *Attorney General of Canada v Law Society of British Columbia*, [1982] 2 S.C.R. 307 (at p. 356), and reproduced in *Canadian Western Bank* (at para. 75):

> When a federal statute can be properly interpreted so as not to interfere with a provincial statute, such an interpretation is to be applied in preference to another applicable construction which would bring about a conflict between the two statutes.

[58] In the instant case, the *CCAA* judge, in authorizing the DIP charge, did not consider the fact that the Salaried Plan's members had a claim that was protected by a deemed trust, nor did he explicitly note that ordinary creditors, such as the Executive Plan's members, had not received notice of the DIP loan motion. However, he did consider factors that were relevant to the remedial objective of the *CCAA* and found that Indalex had in fact demonstrated that the *CCAA*'s purpose would be frustrated without the DIP charge. It will be helpful to quote the reasons he gave on April 17, 2009 in authorizing the DIP charge ((2009), 52 C.B.R. (5th) 61):

(a) the Applicants are in need of the additional financing in order to support operations during the period of a going concern restructuring;

(b) there is a benefit to the breathing space that would be afforded by the DIP Financing that will permit the Applicants to identify a going concern solution;

(c) there is no other alternative available to the Applicants for a going concern solution;

(d) a stand-alone solution is impractical given the integrated nature of the business of Indalex Canada and Indalex U.S.;

(e) given the collateral base of Indalex U.S., the Monitor is satisfied that it is unlikely that the Post-Filing Guarantee with respect to the U.S. Additional Advances will ever be called and the Monitor is also satisfied that the benefits to stakeholders far out-weighs the risk associated with this aspect of the Post-Filing Guarantee;

(f) the benefit to stakeholders and creditors of the DIP Financing outweighs any poten-tial prejudice to unsecured creditors that may arise as a result of the granting of super-priority secured financing against the assets of the Applicants;

(g) the Pre-Filing Security has been reviewed by counsel to the Monitor and it appears that the unsecured creditors of the Canadian debtors will be in no worse position as a result of the Post-Filing Guarantee than they were otherwise, prior to the *CCAA* filing, as a result of the limitation of the Canadian guarantee set forth in the draft Amended and Restated Initial Order ... ; and

(h) the balancing of the prejudice weighs in favour of the approval of the DIP Financing. [para. 9]

[59] Given that there was no alternative for a going-concern solution, it is difficult to accept the Court of Appeal's sweeping intimation that the DIP lenders would have accepted that their claim ranked below claims resulting from the deemed trust. There is no evidence in the record that gives credence to this suggestion. Not only is it contra-dicted by the *CCAA* judge's findings of fact, but case after case has shown that "the prim-ing of the DIP facility is a key aspect of the debtor's ability to attempt a workout" (J. P. Sarra, *Rescue! The Companies' Creditors Arrangement Act* (2007), at p. 97). The harsh reality is that lending is governed by the commercial imperatives of the lenders, not by the inter-ests of the plan members or the policy considerations that lead provincial governments to legislate in favour of pension fund beneficiaries. The reasons given by Morawetz J in response to the first attempt of the Executive Plan's members to reserve their rights on June 12, 2009 are instructive. He indicated that any uncertainty as to whether the lenders would withhold advances or whether they would have priority if advances were made did "not represent a positive development". He found that, in the absence of any alternative, the relief sought was "necessary and appropriate" (2009 CanLII 37906, at paras. 7–8).

[60] In this case, compliance with the provincial law necessarily entails defiance of the order made under federal law. On the one hand, s. 30(7) of the *PPSA* required a part of the proceeds from the sale related to assets described in the provincial statute to be paid to the plan's administrator before other secured creditors were paid. On the other hand, the Amended Initial Order provided that the DIP charge ranked in priority to "all other security interests, trusts, liens, charges and encumbrances, statutory or otherwise" (para. 45). Granting priority to the DIP lenders subordinates the claims of other stakeholders, including the Plan Members. This court-ordered priority based on the *CCAA* has the same effect as a statutory priority. The federal and provincial laws are inconsistent, as they give rise to different, and conflicting, orders of priority. As a result of the application of the doctrine of federal paramountcy, the DIP charge supersedes the deemed trust.

* * * * *

Another kind of controversy arises where the *CCAA* proceedings involve a liquidation of the business. The stay of proceedings granted by the court under the *CCAA* prevents creditors from bringing an application for a bankruptcy order under the *BIA*. Following the sale of the business, creditors may apply to the court seeking to lift the *CCAA* stay of proceedings. Often their motive for doing so is to invoke the bankruptcy scheme of distribution. Although a statutory deemed trust in favour of a person other than the Crown is fully effective under the *CCAA*, in bankruptcy it is rendered ineffective unless the court finds a trust independently of the statutory provision (see *British Columbia v Henfrey Samson Belair Ltd*, [1989] 2 SCR 24 in Chapter 8). The commencement of bankruptcy proceedings therefore has the effect of destroying the statutory deemed trust.

Some of the priority rules in the *CCAA* are substantially similar to those that apply in a bankruptcy — for example, the rules concerning both Crown and environmental claims are the same; however, in other instances, the rules are different. A lessor's right of distress is ineffective in bankruptcy, but fully effective in a restructuring. A supplier may repossess thirty-day goods in bankruptcy, but not in restructuring proceedings. This produces the possibility of statute-shopping. Parties will attempt to invoke the insolvency statute that gives them the most favourable priority status. The problem is compounded because *CCAA* restructuring proceedings are now frequently used to liquidate the business through a going-concern sale to a third party (see Tamara M Buckwold and Roderick J Wood, "Priorities" in Stephanie Ben-Ishai and Anthony Duggan, eds, *Canadian Bankruptcy and Insolvency Law: Bill C-55, Statute c. 47 and Beyond* (Markham: LexisNexis, 2007) 101).

The employment standards legislation in some provinces creates a statutory charge or deemed trust in favour of unpaid employees. For example, section 109 of the Alberta *Employment Standards Code*, RSA 2000, c E-9, provides that unpaid wages to a maximum of $7,500 per employee are secured by a statutory security interest. It is given priority over any other claim other than a purchase-money security interest. This statutory security is ineffective in bankruptcy proceedings, because it conflicts with the bankruptcy scheme of distribution that gives employees a preferred claim in respect of unpaid wages to the extent of $2,000. Because there is no similar scheme of distribution set out in the *CCAA*, the statutory security interest in favour of employees will be effective in restructuring proceedings. However, the statutory security interest is lost if the restructuring involves a liquidating plan and the court permits the commencement of bankruptcy proceedings following the sale.

Another issue concerns the priority of a DIP charge in competition with a statutory deemed trust in respect of source deductions under section 227(4.1) of the *Income Tax Act*, RSC 1985, c 1 (5th Supp) (*ITA*). Section 11.2(2) of the *CCAA* authorizes the court to order that the security or charge ranks in priority over the claim of any secured creditor of the company. Section 11 of the *CCAA* authorizes a court to make any other order that it considers appropriate in the circumstances subject to the restrictions in the *CCAA*. However, section 227(4.1) of the *ITA* provides that the deemed trust has priority over any secured creditor. Moreover, the *ITA* provides that its provisions govern over "any other enactment of Canada, any enactment of a province or any other law" (s 227(4.1)). Justice Romaine in *Temple City Housing Inc (Re)*, 2007 ABQB 786, held that the deemed trust was similar to a floating charge over all the assets of the tax debtor. It did not attach specifically to particular assets, and the debtor was therefore able to alienate property in the ordinary course of business. It remains to be seen whether this decision will find favour outside of Alberta. The difficulty is that it ignores the express wording of the statute, which gives the deemed trust priority over any other secured creditor. In *Rosedale Farms Ltd (Re)*, 2017 NSSC 160, a case that involved similar provisions in the *BIA*, Moir J of the Nova Scotia Supreme Court disagreed with Romaine J's *Temple City* ruling. Then, in *Canada North Group Inc (Companies' Creditors Arrangement Act)*, 2017 ABQB 550 (*Canada North*), Topolniski

J of the Alberta QB distinguished the case from the Nova Scotia ruling (on the basis that the Nova Scotia case involved the *BIA*, not the *CCAA*) and stated that even if not distinguishable she agrees with Romaine J. *Canada North* is now before the Alberta Court of Appeal (leave granted in *Canada v Canada North Group Inc*, 2017 ABCA 363).

F. Thirty-Day Goods

Unlike the case in either bankruptcy or receivership proceedings, in *CCAA* proceedings, a supplier of goods is not given a special right to repossess thirty-day goods — that is, goods delivered within thirty days before the bankruptcy or receivership. See *BIA*, section 81.1, and the discussion of unpaid suppliers in Chapter 9. It was thought that the right would interfere with attempts to rescue financially distressed debtors, and should be limited to insolvency proceedings that result in the liquidation of a commercial debtor. One may question whether this rationale holds true given the subsequent widespread use of the *CCAA* to liquidate companies. In the case of failed restructuring proceedings, courts have ordered that the restructuring period — that is, the time between the application for the initial order and the subsequent bankruptcy or receivership — should not be counted for the purposes of calculating the thirty-day period. In many cases, this is a hollow right, as the goods will have been sold or transformed during this period. The statutory security in favour of agricultural suppliers created by section 81.2 of the *BIA* is also limited to bankruptcy and receivership proceedings and does not arise in respect of restructuring proceedings.

G. Environmental Claims

The *CCAA* adopts the same approach as the *BIA* to environmental claims. See the discussion of environmental claims in Chapter 9. Section 11.8(8) of the *CCAA* creates a charge against the land affected by the environmental condition as well as on any contiguous real property. The charge has priority over any other claim, right, charge, or security against the property. Section 11.8(3) protects the monitor from liability for pre-appointment damage, and the monitor is liable for post-appointment damages only if they occur as a result of gross negligence or wilful misconduct. Section 11.8(5) provides that a monitor may choose to comply with the remediation order or may abandon the interest in the property.

H. Wage and Pension Claims

The *Wage Earner Protection Program Act*, SC 2005, c 47, s1, does not cover employees who have claims for unpaid wages in *CCAA* proceedings. See the discussion of these claims in Chapter 9. Nor does the statutory security for unpaid wages created by sections 81.3 and 81.4 of the *BIA* apply in respect of restructuring proceedings. Instead, a limitation is imposed on a court's ability to sanction a plan under the *CCAA*. Section 6(5) of the *CCAA* permits a court to sanction a plan only if the employees and former employees receive no less than the amount secured by their statutory security for unpaid wages together with all wages and salary earned after the commencement of restructuring proceedings.

A similar approach is taken in respect of unpaid pension contributions. The statutory security created by sections 81.5 and 81.6 of the *BIA* do not come into operation in restructuring proceedings. Section 6(6) of the *CCAA* permits a court to sanction a plan only if the employee pension contributions have been paid in full, or if the parties have entered into an agreement approved by the relevant pension regulator.

I. Equity Claims

As with bankruptcy proceedings, equity claims are effectively subordinated in restructuring proceedings. See Chapter 9. Section 22.1 of the *CCAA* provides that equity claimants must be placed in their own separate class and cannot vote on the plan unless a court orders otherwise. Section 6(8) of the *CCAA* prevents a court from sanctioning any plan that provides any distribution to equity claimants unless all non-equity claims are paid in full. See Chapter 15, Part V.

V. AVOIDABLE TRANSACTIONS

The *BIA* contains provisions that give a trustee in bankruptcy the power to impugn certain types of pre-bankruptcy transactions as preferences or transfers at undervalue. See the discussion in Chapter 5. Under the *BIA*, a transaction can be impugned if it occurs within a fixed period prior to the date of the initial bankruptcy event.

The *CCAA*, section 36.1, provides for the integration of these provisions. Section 36.1(2) of the *CCAA* provides that a reference to the "date of bankruptcy" is to be read as the day on which proceedings commence under the *CCAA*. Section 36.1(1) gives the monitor the power to avoid or otherwise impeach transfers that occur before the commencement of restructuring proceedings. Thus, the monitor may seek to avoid a preferential transfer or payment made by the insolvent debtor company to an arm's-length party in the three-month period prior to the commencement of *CCAA* proceedings or to a non-arm's-length party in the one-year period prior to the commencement of *CCAA* proceedings. Section 36.1(1) also incorporates section 38 of the *BIA*. This gives creditors the option of instituting proceedings to impugn a transfer if the monitor decides not to do so.

The plan of compromise or arrangement may contain a provision by which the creditors agree not to invoke the avoidance powers. Section 23(1)(d.1) of the *CCAA* places a duty on the monitor to provide an opinion of the reasonableness of the term in its report on the state of the debtor's business.

VI. SET-OFF

The *CCAA*, section 21, provides that the law of set-off applies to all claims made against the debtor company and to all actions instituted by it for recovery of debts due to the company. This means that a creditor owing an obligation to a debtor is able to set off that obligation with obligations the debtor owes to that creditor. This can improve the position of a creditor holding the right of set-off. Several Canadian courts have considered the issue of set-off in the context of the *CCAA*. Often the issue is whether on the facts of the particular case there is a sufficiently close connection between the contracts so as to permit equitable set-off (see, for example, *SemCanada Crude Company (Re)*, 2009 ABQB 397).

The issue of set-off was examined earlier in connection with bankruptcy proceedings. See Chapter 4. Issues of set-off arise in restructuring proceedings as well. As the next case illustrates, it may be easier for a party to assert a right of set-off in restructuring proceedings because the commencement of the proceedings does not result in a loss of mutuality of dealings between the parties.

North American Tungsten Corporation Ltd (Re), 2015 BCSC 1382, 28 CBR (6th) 147

BUTLER J (orally):

[1] I am ruling on the applications I have heard on July 27 and today...

[2] There are two competing applications before me dealing with a claimed right of set-off in favour of Global Tungsten and Powders Corp. ("GTP"). The applications are brought in the context of the orders I have made in this proceeding under the *Companies' Creditors Arrangement Act*, R.S.C. 1985, c. C-36, dealing with the company, North American Tungsten Corporation ("NATC"). In particular, the applications concern the terms contained in the amended and restated initial order.

[3] The relevant facts are well-known to the parties, but I will summarize them briefly. NATC produces tungsten from its Cantung Mine and sells the product to two purchasers, one of which is GTP. Pursuant to a supply agreement, NATC annually supplies a specified quantity of tungsten concentrate to GTP. At the same time the parties entered into the supply agreement, they entered into a loan agreement. The indebtedness under the loan agreement is secured by a security agreement on all property connected with the Mactung Mine. As of filing, the indebtedness under the loan agreement was well in excess of $4 million. It is approximately $4.4 million.

[4] Since the filing, NATC has continued to supply GTP with tungsten pursuant to the supply agreement. The payment terms require payment within 30 days. For a period after filing, GTP continued to make payments when due. On July 22, it gave notice to NATC that it would set off amounts owing under the loan agreement against payments due as a result of post-filing deliveries of tungsten. NATC then brought this application for a declaration that GTP was in breach of the stay provisions of the amended initial order, and for an order that GTP pay amounts due. It also sought an injunction to permanently restrain GTP from exercising rights of set-off.

[5] GTP opposes that application and brought an application in response seeking a declaration that it does have a valid right of set-off with respect to amounts it owes NATC under the supply agreement against amounts owed by NATC to GTP under the loan agreement.

[6] On July 27, 2015, I heard part of the application by telephone. I made an order declaring that GTP was in breach of the stay provisions of the amended initial order and required it to pay for tungsten delivered to it after June 9, 2015. I found that GTP was not in contempt of the amended original order as asserted by NATC, and I indicated that I would hear more fulsome argument on both applications today. I have done that, and have also considered the application brought by GTP today asking that I reconsider the order of July 27, 2015.

Ruling

[7] GTP has delivered a detailed written argument today, and I will follow the issues raised in that argument as it provides a convenient way to consider the issues that are before the Court.

Issue 1: Is there a debt due and owing by NATC to GTP?

[The court found that NATC failed to pay the 30 June 2015 loan payment, putting it in default.]

Issue 2: In any event, is it immaterial that the debt has not yet fallen due for payment?

[10] I also agree with the submissions of GTP on this issue. Even if it could be said that the time for payment of the NATC debt had not arrived, that would not defeat GTP's right of set-off.

[11] As noted in Palmer, *The Law of Set-off in Canada*, (Aurora, Ontario, Canada Law Book Inc., 1993) p. 34, a debt, for the purpose of set-off, "is a sum of money which is certainly, and at all events, payable without regard to the fact whether it be payable now or at a future time." The monies owing by NATC under the loan agreement are "certainly, and at all events", payable to GTP.

Issue 3: Is legal set-off available for pre-filing and post-filing obligations?

[12] GTP relies on the provisions of s. 21 of the *CCAA* and on the decision in *Air Canada (Re)*, [2003] O.J. No. 6058 (Ont. S.C.J.).

[13] Section 21 reads as follows:

> 21. The law of set-off or compensation applies to all claims made against a debtor company and to all actions instituted by it for the recovery of debts due to the company in the same manner and to the same extent as if the company were plaintiff or defendant, as the case may be.

[14] The circumstances in *Air Canada* were different from those before this Court. The issue raised was whether the second sentence in a term in the initial order should be struck out. The term in that order read as follows:

> THIS COURT ORDERS that persons may exercise only such rights of set off as are permitted under Section 18.1 of the *CCAA* as of the date of this order. For greater certainty, no person may set off any obligations of an Applicant to such person which arose prior to such date.

[15] Air Canada took the position that there is no right to a legal set-off as between pre-filing and post-filing obligations, and that the term of the order should not be varied. Farley J disagreed and struck the second sentence from the term of the order. Academics have accepted that the ruling stands for the proposition that mutuality is not severed by the granting of an initial order on a *CCAA* proceeding, such that set-off is available between pre-filing and post-filing obligations.

[16] For example, in his article "Air Canada and Stelco: Legal Developments and Practical Lessons" in *the Annual Review of Insolvency Law* (Toronto: Carswell, 2006), Robert Thornton summarized the decision as follows at page 14:

> ... Farley, J held that there was no loss of mutuality upon the commencement of a *CCAA* proceeding. Accordingly, legal set-off is available both in respect of debts existing as of the date of an initial order, and in respect of debts that arose after the date of the initial order.

[17] NATC says that *Air Canada* is wrongly decided and points to decisions dealing with proposals under the *Bankruptcy and Insolvency Act*. There is some merit to the policy arguments that are advanced by NATC. It says that it would make sense, from a policy perspective, to arrive at such a conclusion because: a stay of proceedings assists in preserving the status quo as of the filing date; after a filing, a company ceases to act solely in its own corporate interests and begins to operate under the mandatory scrutiny of a monitor; and, the debtor's objective ceases to be focused solely on maximizing profits.

[18] While I find there are some merits to the policy arguments, in order to arrive at the decision sought by NATC, I would have to find that *Air Canada* was wrongly decided. I am simply not prepared to do so on the basis of the material and the argument before me.

[19] In addition, given the decision I have arrived at with regard to the grant of a temporal stay, I need not wrestle with this issue, as my conclusion does not rest on this finding.

Issue 4: Does the Court have jurisdiction to stay set-off rights once those have been determined?

[20] I am using that terminology for the issue because that is how it is phrased by Mr. Siddall in his submissions today. GTP gives three reasons for its position that the Court does not have the right to stay set-off rights. It says, first of all, that the case law does not support or anticipate such a stay once the creditor's set-off rights have been determined; secondly, it says that a temporal stay in the case at bar would effectively extinguish GTP's set-off rights under s. 21 causing significant prejudice to GTP; and, third, that the scope of the Court's discretion under the *CCAA* does not extend to extinguishing rights which have been specifically conferred by that statute.

[21] Starting with the first of these submissions, NATC relies on *Air Canada* and on *Tucker v Aero Inventory (UK) Limited*, 2009 CanLII 63138 (Ont. S.C.), for the argument that the court does have the power to grant a temporal stay of set-off rights. GTP says both are distinguishable. It notes that *Air Canada* was by consent and in *Tucker* and in *Air Canada*, the stay was only being put in place until a determination of the set-off rights.

[22] Here GTP says it is asking the Court to determine its set-off rights today such that any extension of the stay cannot be granted beyond an order determining that right. GTP says this would be contrary to s. 21.

[23] I disagree. This is a very narrow reading of *Tucker* and *Air Canada*. This argument places far too much emphasis on the term "determination". In fact, those cases refer to "determination and enforcement' of set-off rights.

[24] For example, at para. 25 of *Air Canada*, Farley J said:

> With respect to the question of what I have described as a temporal stay, there does not appear to be any opposition by the Moving Creditors to the proposition that whatever their rights of set-off in substance are determined to be, that such determination and enforcement of such determined rights should await until a convenient time when AC has stabilized (or I suppose, alternatively cratered). It would seem to me that the likely time for this would be in conjunction with the formation of a reorganization plan of arrangement and compromise.

[25] It is significant that the reference in *Air Canada* was to determination *and enforcement* so that set-off rights would be considered when the company has stabilized or cratered. In other words, it is the enforcement that is key, not determination, and that should await the outcome of the restructuring process. In other words, a temporal stay of rights can be granted to further the purpose of the initial order and the purposes of the *Act*. Such a stay can apply to enforcement of set-off rights even where it is acknowledged those rights exist.

[26] I turn to GTP's argument that it would suffer significant prejudice. It says it will suffer prejudice because a temporal stay in this case would effectively extinguish its set-off rights. In other words, it may never be able to set off its debts for new tungsten purchases against NATC's pre-filing debt to GTP.

[27] In my view, that is an illusory prejudice. GTP's position post-filing has not been prejudiced in any way. It is able to purchase tungsten for which it must pay the going rate. Its financial situation, by having to pay for purchases, is exactly what it would be if it had to go to another source for tungsten. In other words, if NATC had ceased production, rather than the initial order being made, GTP's situation would be no different than it is under the temporal stay. This is not a prejudice which, in my view, has any significance.

[28] GTP also argues that I cannot grant a temporal stay now that the set-off claims have been determined in the sense that I have concluded that mutuality is not affected by the initial order. I see no reason in principle on a reading of s. 21 of the *Act* as to why there cannot be such a stay. All creditors' claims are stayed, subject to the exceptions set out in s. 11.02. Section 21, as I read it, does not exempt set-off claims from stays, determined or not. It merely confirms the rights of set-off. Exempting set-off claims would not accord with the policy of the *Act*. Sections 11 and 11.02 of the *Act* give the Court a very broad discretion which must be exercised in furtherance of *CCAA* purposes. Quite simply, it would be illogical if the Court had the discretion to broadly stay claims and proceedings and make relevant ancillary orders necessary to further the purpose of the *Act* and the purpose of the initial order, but could not do so with regard to set-off claims.

[29] Of course, the application here is made in the context of the amended initial order. That order must be considered in relation to all of the facts and circumstances. I ruled, on July 27, 2015, that the purported set-off was in breach of that order. As I indicated, the terms of para. 16 of the amended initial order are broad enough to include a stay of the remedy of set-off.

[30] GTP relies in part on para. 10(d) of the amended initial order and that reads as follows:

> 9. Except as specifically permitted herein the petitioner is directed until further Order of this Court
>
> (d) to not grant credit except in the ordinary course of the Business only to its customers for goods and services actually supplied to those customers, provided such customers agree that there is no right of set-off in respect of amounts owing for such goods and services against any debt owing by the Petitioner to such customers as of the Order Date.

[31] I do not read that term as supportive of GTP's position. NATC could not grant credit to GTP without its agreement. GTP says that it was up to NATC to either come to it and get agreement or go to the court and get agreement, but I take a different view. Given the stay provision of para. 16 of the initial order, the remedy of set-off was stayed. If there was any ambiguity in light of the provisions of para. 10(d), there was an obligation on the part of GTP to get the approval or consent of the petitioner and the monitor to apply the set-off or, alternatively, to come to court. Of course, this is precisely what para. 16 of the initial order requires GTP to do.

[32] Finally, I have concluded that I will exercise my discretion to continue the stay with respect to the set-off claims. I am doing so because:

1. In order to preserve the status quo to effect a restructuring, a stay of the set-off is, and was, absolutely essential.
2. The amended initial order and the extension order were based on a detailed program. I need not highlight all of the aspects of it, but these included a reduction in the underground mining, cost cutting, disposal of equipment, and an orderly closure and maintenance of the Cantung Mine, all of which was predicated on cash

flow. The cash flow was based on the continuation of the two supply agreements. Obviously, that would be thrown into disarray if the stay was not continued.

3. GTP had notice of all steps which had been taken along the way and was indeed actively consulted. It never raised any issue about set-off for 45 days following the initial order. Indeed, its only position was that assets should be put up for sale. It said nothing about exercising its right of set-off with respect to pre-filing debt.

4. Great prejudice to the other stakeholders would flow if GTP was now permitted to exercise its set-off. The status quo would be significantly altered and the restructuring would effectively be at an end. I accept that Callidus would very likely not extend any further credit at this point.

[33] When I consider all of those factors, as well as my view that there is no prejudice to GTP, it is appropriate to continue the temporal stay of GTP's set-off rights for so long as the stay granted by the amended initial order continues, which is to October 31, 2015.

[34] That is the conclusion of my ruling. . . .

Company's application granted in part; creditor's application dismissed.

Practice Questions

Question 1

Assume a *CCAA* proceeding in which the fees and disbursements of counsel, including those of its experts and advisors, and the applicable taxes, are disputed. The total disputed amount is $1.9 million. This is a claim in which the court appointed counsel for a group of franchisees, under the Appointment and Fee Order, which also provided that individual members of the group could opt-out, in which case counsel would not act for them. After eleven members opted out, counsel went on to represent the remaining franchisees. Those who settled earlier paid proportionately less than those who settled later. Two of the franchisees are now in court, objecting that the fees are too high. Discuss factors the court will consider in determining whether to interfere with the fees.

Question 2

The failure to perfect a security interest will result in its subordination to the trustee in bankruptcy upon a bankruptcy. What effect will failure to perfect have in a restructuring proceeding? In other words, what effect does the *CCAA* have on a creditor holding an unperfected/unregistered security interest? Keep in mind that the monitor, unlike the trustee in bankruptcy, is not the representative of unsecured creditors. While coming up with your answer, consider the following scenario: Assume two secured creditors have security in the same asset, which is worth $500,000. Secured Party 1 entered into a security agreement with the debtor on 1 September 2013, but it failed to perfect its interest, which is $50,000. Secured Party 2 entered into a security agreement with the debtor on 1 September 2015, and it perfected its interest, which is $550,000. How might a monitor resolve this conflict? How might a court resolve it? What are the competing considerations in this scenario?

CHAPTER 15

CCAA Plans and Approval

I. INTRODUCTION

The goal in a commercial restructuring is to come up with a plan of which the creditors will approve. This is different than a private workout, which is a compromise or arrangement between debtor and creditors concluded outside a formal insolvency restructuring regime, and which is governed by ordinary principles of contract law. In order for a *CCAA* plan to become binding on creditors, the creditors must approve it. Creditors are separated into different classes and the creditors in each class must vote on the plan. It is not necessary that this consent be unanimous; rather, only a majority of creditors who hold at least two thirds of the value of claims in the same class must approve it for it to be binding on all creditors of that class, even the dissenting ones. If the plan is approved by creditors, it is then put before the court to be sanctioned. This permits the court to consider the plan's fairness — an important check on the actions and conduct of the debtor company and the other creditors.

II. VOTING AND CLASSIFICATION OF CLAIMS

Sections 4 and 5 of the *CCAA* permit a court to order a meeting of creditors. The court will issue a meeting and approval order that sets out the rules and procedure for the meeting. Section 6 of the *CCAA* provides that the plan must be approved by a majority in number representing two-thirds of the value of the creditors (where there is only one class of creditors) or two-thirds of the value of each class of creditors (where there is more than one class of creditors). The percentage requirements are calculated on the basis of the creditors who actually vote on the plan, rather than on the basis of all the creditors who are affected by it. For example, where there are seventy creditors, and fifty of them vote on the plan — whether for or against — the vote must be carried by at least twenty-six of the creditors (a majority in number) who hold two-thirds of the value of the claims.

A creditor may be related to the debtor company — for example, a wholly or partially owned subsidiary corporation may have made an inter-corporate loan to the parent corporation. Section 22(3) of the *CCAA* provides that a creditor who is related to the debtor company may vote against but not for the plan.

The classification of claims is of fundamental importance under the *CCAA*. It is governed by *CCAA*, section 22, which is largely a codification of the principles that have been developed in caselaw. Not surprisingly, the debtor company and the various creditors will attempt to attain a classification scheme that gives them a superior bargaining position. A creditor would ideally wish to be placed in its own separate class, because this would give it the power to veto any plan. Failing this, a creditor would wish to be placed in a class in which it could block approval of the plan by the other creditors. For example, a creditor who holds 35 percent of the value of the claims of a class of creditors can prevent approval of the plan by the class. The debtor, in developing the plan, will attempt to structure the plan in such a way as to swamp any dissenting creditors within a class of creditors who are inclined to approve it.

Creditors are typically grouped together based on a "commonality of interest" or a "non-fragmentation" test, both discussed in the *Norcen Energy Resources Ltd v Oakwood Petroleums Ltd* (1988), 64 Alta LR (2d) 139 (QB) excerpt below. Justice Paperny, in *Re Canadian Airlines Corp* (2000), 19 CBR (4th) 12 (Alta QB), sets out the following principles for assessing commonality of interest (at para 31):

1. Commonality of interest should be viewed based on the non-fragmentation test, not on an identity-of-interest test;
2. The interests to be considered are the legal interests that a creditor holds qua creditor in relationship to the debtor company prior to and under the plan as well as on liquidation;
3. The commonality of interests are to be viewed purposively, bearing in mind the object of the CCCA—namely to facilitate reorganizations if at all possible;
4. In placing a broad and purposive interpretation on the CCCA, the court should be careful to resist classification approaches that would potentially jeopardize viable plans;
5. Absent bad faith, the motivations of creditors to approve or disapprove are irrelevant;
6. The requirement of creditors being able to consult together means being able to assess their legal entitlement *as creditors* before or after the plan in a similar manner.

In *Re Woodward's Ltd* (1993), 20 CBR (3d) 74 (BCSC), Tysoe J applied a non-fragmentation test to determine which of the holders of different types of unsecured claims (terminated employees, a debenture holder, equipment financiers, creditors holding a guarantee from one debtor's parent company, and lessors whose lease had been repudiated) could be joined in a single class for voting on a plan of arrangement. The employees wished to be placed in their own separate class for the purposes of voting on the plan. Justice Tysoe refused this request on the ground that the employees and the other unsecured creditors had identical legal interests. He stated (at paras 18–19):

The legal rights of the terminated employees are the same as the legal rights of the trade suppliers. They are both creditors with unsecured claims against the Operating Company (the secured and preferred amounts payable to employees under provincial legislation and the *Bankruptcy and Insolvency Act* have already been paid to the terminated employees). In a bankruptcy or other liquidation they would both receive the same pro rata amount of their claims. They are to receive the same pro rata amount of their claims under the Reorganization Plan.

The fact that there is a recognized difference between contracts of employment and ordinary commercial contracts is not relevant because the contracts of employment of the terminated employees have come to an end. The terminated employees have claims for damages against Woodward's for wrongful dismissal. Once the amount of damages for an employee has been agreed upon or determined by the Court, the difference between the two types of contracts becomes historical and the employee has the same rights as any other unsecured creditor. The differences between the two types of contracts may result in the employees receiving higher amounts of damages but the differences do not warrant the terminated employees being entitled to a higher distribution than the other unsecured creditors.

Even if the legal rights of the creditors differ, they may be placed in the same class of creditors if the difference in legal rights does not prevent the creditors from sharing a sufficient commonality of interest. Justice Tysoe held that this commonality of interest is lacking when the plan denies some of the creditors a valuable right to which they would otherwise be entitled. The plan proposed that the same payment (37 percent of the value of their claim) would be made to creditors who held claims solely against the debtor company as well as to creditors who in addition had been given an unsecured guarantee by an affiliated company. Justice Tysoe held that the classification scheme was unfair to the extent that both kinds of creditors were placed in the same class. He stated (at paras 35–36):

> The Reorganization Plan ignores the fact that the holders of guarantees are unsecured creditors of both companies. It proposes that they receive the same 37% proportion of their indebtedness as the other General Creditors and their status as creditors of the Holding Company is not reflected.
>
> In view of the fact that the holders of guarantees do have different legal rights from the other members of the class of General Creditors, it is necessary to decide whether the rights are so dissimilar that they cannot vote on the Reorganization Plan with a common interest. It was submitted by counsel for Woodward's that there is a common interest because the holders of guarantees will still receive more under the Reorganization Plan than they will be paid upon a liquidation of the two companies. I do not think that this is sufficient to create a commonality of interest with the other members in the class of General Creditors who have lesser legal rights. To the contrary, I believe that this is an example of what Bowen LJ had in mind in the *Sovereign Life* case [[1892] 2 QB 573 (CA)], when he used the term "confiscation." By being a minority in the class of General Creditors, the holders of guarantees can have their guarantees confiscated by a vote of the requisite majority of the class who do not have the same rights. The holders of guarantees could be forced to accept the same proportionate amount as the other members of the class and to receive no value in respect of legal rights that they uniquely enjoy and that would have value in a liquidation of the two companies.

Sometimes a class of creditor is not brought within the plan. These creditors are typically referred to as unaffected creditors. They do not vote on the plan because their rights are not compromised or impaired, which consequently means they are not being asked to agree to a compromise or other alteration of their rights against the debtor company. Once the stay of proceedings is lifted, they are entitled to exercise and enjoy their full legal rights against the debtor company.

The ability to bind dissenting creditors applies only within a class of creditors. A court cannot impose a plan on a class of creditors that does not approve the plan by a dual majority. Consider the following example: A plan of compromise and arrangement creates three classes of creditors: (1) secured creditors, (2) unsecured creditors, and (3) lessors. The secured creditors and unsecured creditors approve the plan by a dual majority, but the lessors do not. The class of lessors did not vote in favour of the plan and are not bound by it. An unresolved issue is whether the plan will nevertheless be binding on the two classes who voted in favour of it, or if the underlying assumption is that all classes must vote in favour of the plan for it to bind any class of creditor. A plan may contain a "drop-out" clause providing that a class that does not approve a plan is to be treated as unaffected creditors. Courts have given effect to such provisions (see *Olympia & York Developments Ltd v Royal Trust Co* (1993), 12 OR (3d) 500 (Ct J (Gen Div)). If the plan is silent, a court must decide the question. If the plan is not viable without the inclusion of the non-approving class of creditors, a court will be unlikely to sanction it so as to bind the classes of creditors who approved it.

The US *Bankruptcy Code*, 11 USC §101, gives a court the power to "cram down" a Chapter 11 plan on a dissenting class of creditors. However, a court may only exercise the power if it is fair and equitable to do so. This has been interpreted to mean that the plan must provide for a distribution strictly in accordance with the priority entitlements of the claimants (this is referred to as the "absolute priority rule"). In other words, the class that is subject to the cram-down must be paid in full before any class of claimants that are lower in priority ranking receive anything. Although US restructuring law adopts an identity of interest test that leads to a greater number of classes of creditors, this is mitigated by the power of the court to cram down the plan on a dissenting class. In contrast, the non-fragmentation approach leads to fewer classes of creditors and, therefore, results in a lesser need for a cram-down power.

Section 22(1) of the *CCAA* provides that the debtor must apply to court for approval of a classification scheme for voting at a meeting. The next case examines the principles that will be applied by a court in determining whether a classification scheme is fair and reasonable.

Norcen Energy Resources Ltd v Oakwood Petroleums Ltd (1988), 64 Alta LR (2d) 139 (QB)

FORSYTH J:

On 12th December 1988 Oakwood Petroleums Limited ("Oakwood") filed with the court a plan of arrangement ("the plan") made pursuant to the *Companies' Creditors Arrangement Act* (Canada), RSC 1970, c. C-25 [now RSC 1985, c. C-36] ("CCAA"), as amended, ss. 185 and 185.1 [now ss. 191 and 192] of the Canada *Business Corporations Act*, SC 1974-75-76 [now RSC 1985, c. C-44] as amended, and s. 186 of the *Business Corporations Act* (Alberta), SA 1981, c. B-15, as amended.

On 16th December 1988 Oakwood brought an application before me for an order which would, *inter alia*, approve the classification of creditors and shareholders proposed in the plan. I would note that the classifications requested are made pursuant to ss. 4, 5 and 6 of the CCAA for the purpose of holding a vote within each class to approve the plan.

Since my concern primarily is with the secured creditors of Oakwood, I shall set out, in part, the sections of the CCAA relevant to the court's authority with respect to compromises with secured creditors:

> 5. Where a compromise or arrangement is proposed between a debtor company and its secured creditors or any class of them, the court may ... order a meeting of such creditors or class of creditors....
>
> 6. Where a majority in numbers representing three-fourths in value of the creditors, or class of creditors, as the case may be, present and voting either in person or by proxy at the meeting or meetings ... held pursuant to sections 4 and 5 ... agree to any compromise or arrangement ... [it] may be sanctioned by the court, and if so sanctioned is binding on all the creditors....

The plan filed with the court envisions five separate classes of creditors and shareholders. They are as follows:

(i)   The secured creditors;

(ii) The unsecured creditors;

(iii) The preferred shareholders of Oakwood;

(iv) The common shareholders and holders of class A non-voting shares of Oakwood;

(v) The shareholders of New York Oils Ltd.

With the exception of the proposed class comprising the secured creditors of Oakwood, there has been for the moment no objection to the proposed groupings. I add here that shareholders of course have not yet had notice of the proposal with respect to voting percentages and classes with respect to their particular interests. With that caveat, and leaving aside the proposed single class of secured creditors, I am satisfied that the other classes suggested are appropriate and they are approved.

I turn now to the proposed one class of secured creditors. The membership of and proposed scheme of voting within the secured creditors class is dependent upon the value of each creditor's security as determined by Sceptre Resources Ltd. ("Sceptre"), the purchaser under the plan.

As a result of those valuations, the membership of that class was determined to include: the Bank of Montreal, the ABC noteholders, the Royal Bank of Canada, the National Bank of Canada and the HongKong Bank of Canada and the Bank of America Canada. Within the class, each secured creditor will receive one vote for each dollar of "security value." The valuations made by Sceptre represent what it considers to be a fair value for the securities.

Any dispute over the amount of money each creditor is to receive for its security will be determined at a subsequent fairness hearing where approval of the plan will be sought. Further, it should be noted that all counsel have agreed that, on the facts of this case, any errors made in the valuations would not result in any significant shift of voting power within the proposed class so as to alter the outcome of any vote. Therefore, the valuations made by Sceptre do not appear to be a major issue before me at this time insofar as voting is concerned.

The issue with which I am concerned arises from the objection raised by two of Oakwood's secured creditors, namely, HongKong Bank and Bank of America Canada, that they are grouped together with the other secured creditors. They have brought applications before me seeking leave to realize upon their security or, in the alternative, to be constituted a separate and exclusive class of creditors and to be entitled to vote as such at any meeting convened pursuant to the plan.

The very narrow issue which I must address concerns the propriety of classifying all the secured creditors of the company into one group. Counsel for Oakwood and Sceptre have attempted to justify their classifications by reference to the "commonality of interests test" described in *Sovereign Life Assur Co v Dodd*, [1892] 2 QB 573 (CA). That test received the approval of the Alberta Court of Appeal in *Savage v Amoco Acquisition Co.* (1988), 59 Alta. LR (2d) 260, 68 CBR (NS) 154, 87 AR 321, where Kerans JA, on behalf of the court, stated [pp. 264–65]:

> "We agree that the basic rule for the creation of groups for the consideration of fundamental corporate changes was expressed by Lord Esher in *Sovereign Life Assur. Co. v. Dodd,* [*supra*] when he said, speaking about creditors:
>
>> "... if we find a different state of facts existing among different creditors which may differently affect their minds and their judgments, they must be divided into different classes."

In the case of *Sovereign Life Assur Co,* Bowen LJ went on to state at p. 583 that the class:

"... must be confined to those persons whose rights are not so dissimilar as to make it impossible for them to consult together with a view to their common interest."

Counsel also made reference to two other "tests" which they argued must be complied with — the "minority veto test" and the "bona fide lack of oppression test." The former, it is argued, holds that the classes must not be so numerous as to give a veto power to an otherwise insignificant minority. In support of this test, they cite my judgment in *Amoco Can Petroleum Co v Dome Petroleum Ltd,* Calgary No. 8701-20108, 28th January 1988 (not yet reported).

I would restrict my comments on the applicability of this test to the fact that, in the *Amoco* case, I was dealing with "a very small minority group of [shareholders] near the bottom of the chain of priorities." Such is not the case here.

In support of the "bona fide lack of oppression test," counsel cite *Re Alabama, New Orleans, Texas & Pac Junction Ry Co,* [1891] 1 Ch. 213 (CA), where Lindley LJ stated at p. 239:

"The Court must look at the scheme, and see whether the Act has been complied with, whether the majority are acting *bona fide,* and whether they are coercing the minority in order to promote interests adverse to those of the class whom they purport to represent...."

Whether this test is properly considered at this stage, that is, whether the issue is the constitution of a membership of a class, is not necessary for me to decide as there have been no allegations by the HongKong Bank or Bank of America as to a lack of bona fides.

What I am left with, then, is the application to the facts of this case of the "commonality of interests test" while keeping in mind that the proposed plan of arrangement arises under the CCAA.

Sceptre and Oakwood have argued that the secured creditors' interests are sufficiently common that they can be grouped together as one class. That class is comprised of six institutional lenders (I would note that the ABC noteholders are actually a group of ten lenders) who have each taken first charges as security on assets upon which they have the right to realize in order to recover their claims. The same method of valuation was applied to each secured claim in order to determine the security value under the plan.

On the other hand, HongKong Bank and Bank of America have argued that their interests are distinguishable from the secured creditors class as a whole and from other secured creditors on an individual basis. While they have identified a number of individually distinguishing features of their interests vis-à-vis those of other secured parties (which I will address later), they have put forth the proposition that since each creditor has taken separate security on different assets, the necessary commonality of interests is not present. The rationale offered is that the different assets may give rise to a different state of facts which could alter the creditors' view as to the propriety of participating in the plan. For example, it was suggested that the relative ease of marketability of a distinct asset as opposed to the other assets granted as security could lead that secured creditor to choose to disapprove of the proposed plan. Similarly, the realization potential of assets may also lead to distinctions in the interests of the secured creditors and consequently bear upon their desire to participate in the plan.

In support of this proposition, the HongKong Bank and Bank of America draw from comments made by Ronald N. Robertson, QC, in a publication entitled "Legal Problems on Reorganization of Major Financial and Commercial Debtors," Canadian Bar Association — Ontario Continuing Legal Education, 5th April 1983, at p. 15, and by Stanley E. Edwards in an earlier article, "Reorganizations Under the *Companies' Creditors Arrangement Act*" (1947), 25 *Can. Bar Rev.* 587, at p. 603. Both authors gave credence to this "identity of interest" proposition that secured creditors should not be members of the same class "unless their security is on the same or substantially the same property and in equal priority." They also made reference to a case decided under c. 11 of the *Bankruptcy Code* of the United States of America which, while not applying that proposition in that given set of facts, accepted it as a "general rule." That authority is *Re Palisades-on-the-Desplaines; Seidel v Palisades-on-the-Desplaines*, 89 F2d 214 at 217–18 (1937, Ill.).

Basically, in putting forth that proposition, the HongKong Bank and Bank of America are asserting that they have made advances to Oakwood on the strength of certain security which they identified as sufficient and desirable security and which they alone have the right to realize upon. Of course, the logical extension of that argument is that in the facts of this case each secured creditor must itself comprise a class of creditors. While counsel for the HongKong Bank and Bank of America suggested it was not necessary to do so in this case, as they are the only secured creditors opposed to the classification put forth, in principle such would have to be the case if I were to accept their proposition.

To put the issue in another light, what I must decide is whether the holding of distinct security by each creditor necessitates a separate class of creditor for each, or whether notwithstanding this factor that they each share, nevertheless this factor does not override the grouping into one class of creditors. In my opinion, this decision cannot be made without considering the underlying purpose of the CCAA....

In this regard, I would make extensive reference to the article by Mr. Robertson, QC, where, in discussing the classification of creditors under the CCAA and after stating the proposition referred to by counsel for the HongKong Bank and Bank of America, he states at p. 16 in his article:

An initial, almost instinctive, response that differences in claims and property subject to security automatically means segregation into different classes does not necessarily make economic or legal sense in the context of an act such as the CCAA.

And later at pp. 19 and 20, in commenting on the article by Mr. Edwards, he states:

However, if the trend of Edwards' suggestions that secured creditors can only be classed together when they held [sic] security of the same priority, that perhaps classes should be sub-divided into further groups according to whether or not a member of the class also holds some other security or form of interest in the debtor company, *the multiplicity of discrete classes or sub-classes might be so compounded as to defeat the object of the act.* As Edwards himself says, the subdivision of voting groups and the counting of angels on the heads of pins must stop somewhere and some forms of differences must surely be disregarded.

In summarizing his discussion, he states on pp. 20–21:

From the foregoing one can perceive at least two potentially conflicting approaches to the issue of classification. On the one hand there is the concept that members of a class ought to have the same "interest" in the company, ought to be only creditors entitled to look to the same "source" or "fund" for payment, and ought to encompass all of the creditors who do have such an identity of legal rights. *On the other hand, there is recognition that the legislative intent is to facilitate reorganization, that excessive fragmentation of classes may be counter-productive and that some degree of difference between claims should not preclude creditors being put in the same class.*

It is fundamental to any imposed plan or reorganization that strict legal rights are going to be altered and that such alteration may be imposed against the will of at least some creditors. When one considers the complexity and magnitude of contemporary large business organizations, and the potential consequences of their failure it may be that the courts will be compelled to focus less on whether there is any identity of legal rights and rather focus on whether or not those constituting the class are persons, to use Lord Esher's phrase, "whose rights are not so dissimilar as to make it impossible for them to consult together with a view to their common interest. . . . "

If the plan of reorganization is such that the creditors' particular priorities and securities are preserved, especially in the event of ultimate failure, *it may be that the courts will, for example in an apt case decide that creditors who have basically made the same kinds of loans against the same kind of security, even though on different terms and against different particular secured assets, do have a sufficient similarity of interest to warrant being put into one class and being made subject to the will of the required majority of that class.* [emphasis added]

These comments may be reduced to two cogent points. First, it is clear that the CCAA grants a court the authority to alter the legal rights of parties other than the debtor company without their consent. Second, the primary purpose of the Act is to facilitate reorganizations and this factor must be given due consideration at every stage of the process, including the classification of creditors made under a proposed plan. To accept the "identity of interest" proposition as a starting point in the classification of creditors necessarily results in a "multiplicity of discrete classes" which would make any reorganization difficult, if not impossible, to achieve.

In the result, given that this planned reorganization arises under the CCAA, I must reject the arguments put forth by the HongKong Bank and the Bank of America, that since they hold separate security over different assets, they must therefore be classified as a separate class of creditors.

I turn now to the other factors which the HongKong Bank and Bank of America submit distinguishes them on individual bases from other creditors of Oakwood. The HongKong Bank and Bank of America argue that the values used by Sceptre are significantly understated. With respect to the Bank of Montreal, it is alleged that that bank actually holds security valued close to, if not in excess of, the outstanding amount of its loans when compared to the HongKong Bank and Bank of America whose security, those banks allege, is approximately equal to the amount of its loans. It is submitted that a plan which understates the value of assets results in the oversecured party being more inclined to support a plan under which they will receive, without the difficulties of realization, close to full payments of their loans.

The problem with this argument is that it is a throwback to the "identity of interest" proposition. Differing security positions and changing security values are a fact of life in the world of secured financing. To accept this argument would again result in a different class of creditor for each secured lender, with the possible exception of the ABC noteholders who could be lumped with the HongKong Bank or Bank of America, as their percentage realization under the proposed plan is approximately equal to that of the HongKong Bank and Bank of America.

Further, the HongKong Bank and Bank of America also submit that since the Royal Bank and National Bank of Canada are so much more undersecured on their loans, they too have a distinct interest in participating in the plan which is not shared by themselves. The sum total of their submissions would seem to be that, since oversecured and undersecured lenders have a greater incentive to participate, it is only those lenders, such as themselves with just the right amount of security, that do not share that common interest. Frankly, it appears to me that these arguments are drawn from the fact that they are the only secured creditors of Oakwood who would prefer to retain their right to realize upon their security, as opposed to participating in the plan. I do not wish to suggest that they should be chided for taking such a position, but surely expressed approval or disapproval of the plan is not a valid reason to create different classes of creditors. Further, as I have already clearly stated, the CCAA can validly be used to alter or remove the rights of creditors.

Finally, I wish to address the argument that, since Sceptre has made arrangements with the Royal Bank of Canada relating to the purchase of Oakwood, it has an interest not shared by the other secured creditors. The Royal Bank's position as a principal lender in the reorganization is separate from its status as a secured creditor of Oakwood and arises from a separate business decision. In the absence of any allegation that the Royal Bank will not act bona fide in considering the benefit of the plan of the secured creditors as a class, the HongKong Bank and Bank of America cannot be heard to criticize the Royal Bank's presence in the same class.

In light of my conclusions, the result is that I approve the proposed classification of secured creditors into one class.

Application granted.

III. ACQUISITION OF CLAIMS

Investors may seek to acquire claims from creditors, a practice known as "claims trading." Smaller creditors can sell their claims, which allows them to exit the restructuring process and leaves investors to take their place at the bargaining table. Investors can buy enough claims to gain leverage in the bargaining. There is much debate about the effect of these funds in the restructuring process. Investors may be motivated to own the business and replace management, or they could push for emergence from restructuring proceedings as fast as possible in order to monetarize the claims, whether or not the debtor has been rehabilitated, thereby potentially affecting the debtor's inclination for recidivism.

A person who acquires a claim of another creditor is counted as a single creditor for the purposes of voting on the plan. In other words, the acquisition of the claim only affects the money value of the claim that can be voted by the creditor who acquired the claim—it does not give the creditor the right to be counted as two creditors for the purposes of the vote (see *Re Canadian Airlines Corp* (2000), 19 CBR (4th) 12 (Alta QB)). The investor obtains the same rights to vote on the plan as the original creditor.

Under the US *Bankruptcy Code*, the bankruptcy court is permitted to disqualify votes where the creditor is not acting in good faith. A distinction is drawn between efforts to obtain a veto or blocking position in order to enhance its position as a creditor and actions and efforts to do so for an ulterior motive, such as eliminating a competitor, seeking preferential treatment by threatening to block a fair plan, or promoting a competing plan in which it is the chief beneficiary (see *In re Allegheny International, Inc*, 118 BR 282 (Bktcy WD Pa 1990); *In re Marin Town Center*, 142 BR 374 (ND Cal 18 February 1992).

In the excerpt below from *Blackburn Developments (Re)*, the Court considered an argument to disallow voting by a creditor with regard to sanctioning the plan of arrangement under the *CCAA*. The Court decided to allow the creditor to vote "as long as their actions are not unlawful or do not result in a substantial injustice" (para 44). Following that is an excerpt from *Callidus Capital Corporation v 9354-9186 Québec Inc (Bluberi Gaming Technologies Inc)*, 2019 QCCA 171, in which the court held that voting rights should not be excluded on equitable grounds. It maintained that a creditor's voting rights should not be excluded even if the debtor is suing that creditor for behaviour that is alleged to have caused the debtor's financial demise, as doing so starts to look like equitable subordination, a doctrine that has not been formally adopted in Canadian insolvency law.

Blackburn Developments Ltd (Re), 2011 BCSC 1671, 27 BCLR (5th) 199

SEWELL J:

[1] The petitioner, Blackburn Developments Ltd. ("Blackburn"), is a real estate development company that undertook a very large residential real estate development project near Chilliwack, British Columbia. The development went on for many years. Blackburn sold some lots. In order to meet its financial obligations over the years it granted a large number of mortgages over its development lands and a golf course that was an important part of the development.

[2] By 2010 and probably before, Blackburn was insolvent. It had incurred many millions of dollars of losses and owed its creditors, both secured and unsecured, in excess of $80,000,000. While many creditors had mortgage security over the Blackburn real estate portfolio, the value of the properties charged was not sufficient to satisfy the amounts secured by the mortgages and most mortgage creditors were in fact unsecured or faced large deficiencies. Despite Blackburn's difficulties, its management was still hopeful of restructuring its affairs. It was recognized that it had potentially valuable losses that could be monetized through a corporate reorganization. However, it was far behind in preparing its financial statements and filing its required income tax returns, and it was therefore impossible to value its tax attributes.

[3] In February 2011 Blackburn sought protection pursuant to the *Companies' Creditors Arrangement Act*, R.S.C. 1985, c. C-36 [*CCAA*]. On February 23, 2011 it obtained an order (the "Initial Order") granting a stay of proceedings against it to permit it to prepare a plan of arrangement (the "Plan") to present to its creditors.

[4] From the outset of these proceedings it was apparent that Blackburn had two potential sources of funds to finance the Plan. The first was the development potential of its real estate holdings. The second was its tax attributes. It was also apparent that Blackburn faced formidable obstacles to completing a Plan. These included the chaotic state of its financial records, its lack of liquidity, the complicated state of the title to its real estate holdings, and the scepticism of some of its secured creditors about its ability to bring forward an acceptable plan. . . .

[12] In the period up to August 30, 2011 management of Blackburn pursued a restructuring, as contemplated in the Initial Order. The only entity that showed a serious interest in pursuing a restructuring with Blackburn was Streetwise, a company that specialized in realizing value from financially distressed enterprises. Streetwise is a self-described "vulture fund". By August 30, 2011, discussions between management of Blackburn and

Streetwise had advanced to the point that the directors of Blackburn had concluded that Streetwise's restructuring proposal offered the best recovery for creditors. . . .

[16] The Monitor did not pursue Streetwise's proposal for the reasons set out in paragraph 3.10 of the Monitor's 11th Report. Among those reasons was the fact that the Landus Group ("Landus") did not support the proposed transaction and in the Monitor's view no restructuring proposal could succeed without the support of Landus because Landus held sufficient unsecured claims to defeat any plan. On September 23, the Monitor informed Streetwise that it was moving forward with a preferred bidder.

[17] On September 30, I approved The Pinnacle RTS on the recommendation of the Monitor. As part of that order I directed Blackburn to execute the Pinnacle RTS. I did so despite the fact that Streetwise sought to have the Monitor or the Court consider a revised offer from it. While I have already given my reasons for approving the Pinnacle RTS I repeat that I was concerned that the *CCAA* proceedings had already become prolonged, that restructuring costs were mounting alarmingly and that the Streetwise proposal did not have the support of Landus, without whose support no Plan could be approved.

[18] However, Blackburn was unable to execute the Pinnacle RTS because both its directors, Messrs. Wellsby and Wilson, resigned. On October 5, I made a further order authorizing the Monitor to execute the Pinnacle RTS on behalf of Blackburn and to take the steps necessary to bring the a plan of arrangement implementing the Pinnacle RTS (the "Pinnacle Plan") to a meeting of creditors for approval. At the same time I ordered that Blackburn and its principals, including its former directors, cease restructuring activities.

[19] In my brief oral reasons I tried to make it clear that I was in no way restricting any creditor from exercising its rights to oppose the Pinnacle Plan or to persuade other creditors to vote against it.

[20] Streetwise did not appeal the September 30 order. However it did proceed to acquire the claims of those creditors who had signed letters of intent prior to September 30 and to purchase other claims. As a result Streetwise had by the end of October acquired claims in the amount of approximately $38,000,000, including approximately $7,500,000 in related party claims. The related party claims are subject to a challenge. However, even excluding those claims, Streetwise was the assignee of $30,500,000 in claims, more than sufficient to defeat the implementing of the Pinnacle Plan.

[21] At the meeting of creditors held on November 21 Streetwise voted all its claims against approval of the Pinnacle Plan and it was defeated. However, the Monitor, supported by Landus and Pinnacle, seeks an order disallowing Streetwise's votes. If those votes are disallowed the result will be that the Pinnacle Plan will be approved by a sufficient number of creditors to be approved in accordance with s. 6 of the *CCAA*. . . .

[27] In this case Streetwise undoubtedly became involved in the Blackburn *CCAA* proceedings because it wished to acquire the tax attributes of Blackburn for itself. This is obvious from the terms of its September 16th offer to the Monitor. However the critical question is not why Streetwise first became interested in Blackburn but whether it voted against the Plan for an improper purpose. In deciding this matter I must proceed on the basis that Streetwise is a creditor pursuant to legally valid assignments. It is of course implicit in the position taken by the Monitor that Streetwise is entitled to share in the distribution to creditors that this is so.

[28] I do not find it necessary to decide whether a judge supervising a *CCAA* proceeding has the jurisdiction to disallow the votes of a creditor while at the same time recognizing that the creditor has a valid claim for purposes of distribution. As is often the case in *CCAA* matters, the parties urgently require a decision. I will therefore proceed

on the assumption that I have that jurisdiction. In so doing, I will attempt to adopt the analysis and apply the principles set out in *Laserworks*.

[29] *Laserworks* was a case decided in the context of a proposal under the *Bankruptcy and Insolvency Act* [*BIA*]. In that case *Laserworks* made a proposal to its creditors. A competitor purchased sufficient claims to allow it to defeat the proposal. Under the *BIA* this had the effect of putting *Laserworks* into bankruptcy, thereby eliminating it as a competitor, the very purpose for which the competitor had purchased the claims. The remaining creditors favoured approval of the proposal. The Nova Scotia Court of Appeal found that the creditor had voted its claims for an improper purpose and that the Registrar had the discretion to disallow the votes of that creditor.

[30] In *Laserworks*, the court set out the basis on which it thought it appropriate to intervene to disallow votes at paras. 50–56 as follows:

> [50] Motive or purpose is not relevant to objections to proofs of claim based on statutory exceptions under the BIA. These are established in several sections, including s. 109(1), persons who had not duly proved and lodged a claim; s. 54(3), a relative of the debtor (who may vote against but not for a proposal); 109(4), the debtor as proxy for a creditor; s.109(6), a creditor who did not deal with the debtor at arm's length (with exceptions); s. 110(1), a person with a claim acquired after the bankruptcy unless the entire claim is acquired; s. 111, a creditor with a claim on or secured by a current bill of exchange (subject to conditions); s. 112, a creditor holding security (subject to conditions); and s. 113(2), a trustee as proxy (subject to restrictions). See also s. 109, the trustee as creditor.
>
> [51] (It will be noted that many of these exceptions arise from circumstances that could give rise to conflict of interest. This will be considered further under the fourth ground of appeal.)
>
> [52] However the statutory exceptions are not a code exhausting the forms in which substantial injustice may manifest itself. Objections will be sustained under s. 108(3) if they result from a crime or a tort against the debtor or a creditor. In the present appeal, and in the authorities cited by the Registrar, the substantial injustice assumes the guise of tortious behavior, to which motive is relevant. In the s. 108(3) context the commonest torts, or instances of substantial injustice arising from tortious behavior, relate to abuse of process and fraud. However conspiracy to harm was also found in *Dimples Diapers*.
>
> [53] Tortious or tort-like behavior falling short of a fully developed tort susceptible of formal proof or definition can nevertheless result in substantial injustice, particularly for persons at a point so vulnerable they must resort to insolvency protection. (See *Shepard*.) In my view that is why Parliament chose the language it did in s. 187(9): to create a discretionary jurisdiction in courts that is not fettered, for example, by the high standards required for establishing such torts as abuse of process in other contexts. What remains to be considered is the threshold level of the substantial injustice which will result in remedial action by the court.

(ii) The Authorities

[54] The four cases cited by the Registrar establish that the threshold is crossed when the BIA is used for an improper purpose. An improper purpose is any purpose collateral to the purpose for which the bankruptcy and insolvency legislation was enacted by Parliament.

[55] Farley J held in *Dimples Diapers* that:

> ... the *Bankruptcy Act*, R.S.C. 1985, c. B-3 has as its purpose the provision of "the orderly and fair distribution of the property of a bankrupt among its creditors on

a pari passu basis". (L.W.Houlden and C.H.Morawetz, Bankruptcy Law of Canada, 3rd ed. (looseleaf) (Toronto: Carswell, 1989) at p. 1–3 [A&4]. . . .

[56] In the cases cited the improper purpose takes the form of abuse of process or tortious behavior closely analogous to abuse of process. In each case the court reacted to what could be seen as substantial injustice. The remedy of choice arising under s. 43(7) is refusal of the petition. The appropriate remedy in the present case is rejection of the tainted votes.

[31] The court elaborated on the concept of substantial injustice at paras. 72–74, in a portion of the judgment dealing with class voting, as follows:

[72] Hardie Boys J cited the same passage quoted above by Justice Stewart from Vicount Haldane's judgment. It concludes that there is a restriction on powers conferred on a majority of a special class in order to enable that majority to bind a minority:

... They must be exercised subject to a general principle, which is applicable to all authorities conferred on majorities of classes enabling them to bind minorities; namely, that the power given must be exercised for the purpose of benefiting the class as a whole, and not merely individual members only.

[73] Hardie Boys J considered *Re Farmers' Co-operative*, which was also cited by Justice Stewart, in which votes of several creditors who were competitors of the debtor were disallowed.

... In a later development of the same matter, but not now involving the Court's sanction under s. 205, Gallen J accepted that the Court has an overriding control, not limited to the approval stage under s. 205, and may restrict a right to vote where the equities of a particular situation require it: see [1992] 1 NZLR 348. It is unnecessary for present purposes to decide whether these cases were correctly decided, for even if they were, the principle is not of unlimited application, and does not apply to the exercise of voting rights generally. This is clear from what Viscount Haldane said in the *British America Nickel* case. Immediately after the passage already quoted, his Lordship said

Subject to this, the power may be unrestricted. It may be free from the general principle in question when the power arises not in connection with a class, but only under a general title which confers the vote as a right of property attaching to a share.

Thus in *Pender v Lushington* (1877) 6 Ch. D. Jessel MR said there is:

... no obligation on a shareholder of a company to give his vote merely with a view to what other persons may consider the interests of the company at large. He has a right, if he thinks fit, to give his vote from motives or promptings of what he considers his own individual interest.

While the voting rights conferred by Part XV of the *Insolvency Act* are not akin to a "right of property attaching to a share", they are rights conferred without reservation. There is no requirement for class voting; there is instead a general right conferred equally on all creditors. The rationale of the principle does not apply. It is well settled that the motive (short of fraud) of a petitioning creditor, no matter how reprehensible, is irrelevant to his right to obtain an order of adjudication:

King v Henderson [1898] AC 720, *Re King, ex parte Commercial Bank of Australia Ltd (No 2)*, [1920] VLR 490. The motive of a creditor voting on a proposal, really the other side of the coin to a petition for adjudication, can be no different. That is not to say that there may be no remedy in an extreme case, such as fraud or mistake. But certainly where, as here, there are perfectly legitimate reasons for opposing the proposal, a creditor is not to be denied that right because he may have some other motive as well...

[74] If the exception made for fraud is broadened to "substantial injustice" I would take Hardie Boys J.'s conclusions to be a fair statement of the law in Canada as well, as applied by Canadian courts in the cases cited by the Registrar. The New Zealand court included mistake as well as fraud as an exception. A creditor is not to be deprived of the right to vote for wrongful motives alone; motive must be coupled with a tortious act to support a finding of improper purpose.

[32] The reference to "substantial injustice" in paragraph 74 of *Laserworks* finds its origin in s. 187(9) of the *BIA*. No such express provision is found in the *CCAA*. However, assuming without deciding that the same jurisdiction can be found in s. 11 of the *CCAA*, the test promulgated in *Laserworks* is difficult to meet. As I understand that test I must be satisfied that there has been conduct amounting to an abuse of process or other tortious or near tortious character and that that conduct has resulted in a substantial injustice before I can exercise my discretion to disallow a vote of a creditor.

[33] In its submissions to me the Monitor placed particular emphasis on the fact that Streetwise was actively seeking to acquire the tax attributes of Blackburn. It points out that after I had approved the Pinnacle RTS, Streetwise continued to acquire claims. It submits that the inescapable inference to be drawn from these facts is that Streetwise acquired the claims and voted to block approval of the Pinnacle Plan not for the purpose of achieving the purposes of the *CCAA*, but for the improper purpose of forcing a situation in which it would acquire the tax attributes for itself....

[40] It seems to me that this case raises squarely the appropriateness of permitting "vulture funds" to participate in insolvency restructurings. In my view there is no compelling argument that the activities of vulture funds are undesirable. Even if there were, I think it is the role of Parliament and not the courts to address what limits, if any, should be placed on the activities of such funds. I also note that in this case the terms of the Pinnacle RTS were significantly improved after it became apparent that Streetwise had a substantial position in the claims. There is no doubt that the Pinnacle Plan put to the creditors on November 21 was significantly superior to that recommended by the Monitor on September 30. The inference that I draw from that is that the enhancements to the offer were motivated by a desire to enlist creditor support in the face of the Streetwise opposition to the Plan.

[41] I think that the cases cited to me by the Monitor in which bad faith was found are distinguishable from this case. Firstly, the courts in those cases found that the creditor who acquired claims had no *bona fide* intention of profiting from realizing on those claims. In the American cases the courts relied on the fact that the claims were acquired at par or close to par as evidence that the acquiring party did not regard the investment in the claims as a legitimate profit making venture. In all three cases the acquiring creditor did not put forward any plausibly credible evidence that it acquired the claims to make a profit on them or that there was any reasonable prospect of a greater recovery for creditors if the plan or proposal was defeated. In addition, as far as I am able to discern,

none of the cases involved an assignee that had become involved in the process with the support of management of the insolvent company. Finally I can see no indication that the plans or proposals under consideration in those cases were in effect liquidation proposals, as is the case in this proceeding.

[42] In *DBSB* [*In re DBSB North America Inc*, 421 BR 133 (Bankr SDNY 2009)] the Court found that the acquiring creditor had no *bona fide* interest in profiting from an investment in the debt as the debt was purchased at par. In *Allegheny* [*In re Allegheny International Inc*, 118 BR 282 (Bankr WD Pa 1990)] the Court also found as a fact that the acquiring creditor, Japonica, had no *bona fide* intention to profit from its investment in the debt. In addition it acquired *de facto* blocking positions in two separate classes whose interests were in direct conflict. These actions were in the Court's view inconsistent with Japonica's actions being carried out for economic reasons.

[43] I also question whether the US decisions are consistent with the law in Canada. Firstly, the US decisions concern the exercise of an express statutory power to disallow votes. It appears from the cases cited that US courts have been prepared to exercise that power in situations in which they conclude that the votes have been exercised in aid of a plan to acquire control of the debtor company. I must frankly say that I find the distinction made in those cases between pursuing economic interests as a creditor and as a potential owner difficult to grasp. In both cases the creditor is pursuing its economic interests. Both American decisions acknowledge that acquiring debt with a view to making a profit is not bad faith behaviour. Thus the activities of a vulture fund are permissible under US law.

[44] As I have already stated, I think that the policy approach taken in *Laserworks* is preferable to that of the US authorities. As the above quoted passages make clear, the Court in *Laserworks* recognized that creditors are entitled to vote their claims in what they as creditors perceived to be their own economic interests as long as their actions are not unlawful or do not result in a substantial injustice.

[45] I think this approach is preferable because it recognizes that the effect of such an order is to deprive the assignee of a statutory right and to subject it to having its contractual rights compromised against its will. In my view such a result would only be appropriate in the clearest of cases. . . .

[50] After hearing the submissions of all parties and considering the extensive evidence before me I have concluded that in this case there was a genuine difference of opinion about the best course to follow to maximize recovery for the unsecured creditors of Blackburn. The Monitor was clearly of the view that it was futile to proceed with a restructuring without the support of Landus, which effectively had a blocking position given the extent of unsecured debt that it held. I accept that Streetwise and the directors of Blackburn held the genuine belief that the Pinnacle Plan unfairly favoured Landus and did not provide a fair dividend to unsecured creditors.

[51] In this case I cannot find that the predominate purpose of Streetwise's negative vote was to acquire control of Blackburn and hence its tax attributes. Mr. Sethi has denied that that was the predominate purpose and the surrounding circumstances do not lead to that conclusion. In addition, the liquidation analysis prepared by the Monitor does not lead to the conclusion that creditors will be worse off under liquidation.

[52] Accordingly, the application to disallow Streetwise's votes is dismissed. With that dismissal there is no approved Plan to be sanctioned and it follows that that application is also dismissed.

Order accordingly.

Callidus Capital Corporation v 9354-9186 Québec Inc (Bluberi Gaming Technologies Inc), 2019 QCCA 171, leave to appeal to SCC filed

Schrager JCA:

I. Introduction

[19] A debtor company, subject to an order under the *Companies' Creditors Arrangement Act*, has no assets except a litigious claim against its secured creditor. Who should decide whether to pursue the claim or accept a settlement — the debtor or the creditors? This is the bare bones issue in this case.

[20] We are tasked to decide the appeal launched by Callidus Capital Corporation ("Callidus"), the secured creditor, as well as a group of creditors ("Creditors' Group") from the judgment of March 16, 2018, issued by the Superior Court, District of Montreal (the Honourable Jean-François Michaud), dismissing the Appellant's *Motion for an order for the convening, holding and conduct of a creditors' meeting and extension of the stay period* and granting the Debtors' *Amended Application for litigation funding and a litigation financing charge* in order to file a $200 million lawsuit against Callidus.

[21] The judge authorized financing to allow the debtors (the Respondents) to proceed with their lawsuit. I propose that this Court intervene, as I believe that the judgment is tainted with errors in the appreciation of the facts, but more significantly, errors of law in the application of the *CCAA*, particularly the notion of that which constitutes a plan of arrangement.

II. Facts

[22] The "facts" are the product of a progressive filing of detailed proceedings supported by affidavits, documents and observations of the Monitor. While not unusual in *CCAA* practice, the lack of any trial or other contradictory fact-finding process leads, in the instant case, to certain questions about the judge's conclusions concerning the proposed lawsuit which influenced the outcome of the proceedings before him in an erroneous fashion. I will explain below as required. However, the basic facts as stated by the judge are not the subject of contestation.

[23] In 1994, Mr. Gérard Duhamel founded Bluberi Gaming Technologies inc., now the Respondent 9354-9186 Québec inc. ("Bluberi Gaming"). The company developed and sold casino games and gaming machines.

[24] Bluberi Group inc. (now the Respondent 9354-9178 Québec inc., "Bluberi Group") is a holding company and the sole shareholder of Bluberi Gaming; it also held the shares of Bluberi USA, which shares have now been sold. Through a family trust, Mr. Duhamel controls Bluberi Group and thus, Bluberi Gaming. At all relevant times, he appears as the sole director of Bluberi Gaming (even after a board of directors was established at the behest of Appellant Callidus).

[25] In 2012, the Respondents sought financing from the Appellant Callidus known in the industry as an asset-based lender. In August of 2012, it made available credit and advanced approximately $24 million to Bluberi. The credit facilities were amended over time such that by 2015, approximately $86 million was outstanding. The loan agreement and related documents do not form part of the appeal record, though much of their content and application are integral to resolving the issues here.

[26] Things did not go well. Sales and profits forecasted by Mr. Duhamel did not materialize. Bluberi Gaming was losing money. Callidus advanced still more funds and became more proactive. Having lost faith in Mr. Duhamel's management abilities, it insisted in 2015 that a chief operating officer be hired and that a board of independent directors be formed. It appears that these directors, though active, never became *de jure* directors of Bluberi Gaming.

[27] On November 11, 2015, the Respondents filed a *Petition for the issuance of an initial order* under the *CCAA*. In the petition, they complained about Callidus' *de facto* governance and the fact that ill-advised decisions made by the Appellant Callidus had brought about a liquidity crisis, making it impossible for Bluberi Gaming to respect its obligations, including paying its employees. The Respondents and the Monitor believed that Bluberi could sustain its operations through its cash flow, without the further advance of funds by Callidus.

[28] Callidus contested the motion on several grounds. As appears from its written contestation and supporting affidavit, its version of the governance and contractual issues paints a different picture as will be set forth in more detail below. Suffice it to say, that on November 12, 2015, the Respondents' originating motion was granted and Michaud, J.S.C., issued an initial stay order under the *CCAA*. The impleaded party herein, Ernst & Young, was named *CCAA* monitor.

[29] On January 28, 2016, a sale solicitation process ("SSP") was sought by the Respondents and authorized by the *CCAA* Court to permit Bluberi Gaming to divest itself of all of its assets.

[30] Four offers were received; the best was submitted by Callidus. In June 2016, after months of negotiations the parties finalized an Asset Purchase Agreement ("APA"), on terms approved by the Monitor. By this transaction, Callidus and two companies under its control purchased all the Respondents' assets through a credit bid. Consequently, except for an undischarged claim of $3 million, Callidus' secured claim against Bluberi ($135.7 million) was extinguished.

[31] According to sections 1.1 and 3.3 g) of the APA, the Respondents excluded the "Bluberi Retained Claims" from the sale. This is their only remaining asset and they expressed their intention to file a lawsuit for damages against Callidus (and others) for a substantial amount.

[32] On September 11, 2017, Bluberi Gaming filed an *Application for the issuance of an order extending the stay of proceedings and authorizing an interim financing*, seeking approval for a $20 million interim lender priority charge to finance its litigation against Callidus. The lender was identified as a joint venture company (9364-9739 Québec inc.) in which Mr. Duhamel was involved. It would make available $2 million to finance the litigation against Callidus. Evidently, the $20 million charge was required to secure repayment of the loan and the success fee which according to Respondents' plan would be half the net proceeds of the litigation.

[33] On September 18, 2017, in addition to contesting the interim financing application, the Appellant Callidus proposed a plan of arrangement. Supported by Deloitte, one of Bluberi Gaming's creditors, it filed a *Motion for an order for the convening, holding and conduct of a creditors' meeting and extension of the stay period*. This plan, as amended, provided that accepted claims of Bluberi's former employees would be paid in full and that on average, creditors having claims above $3,000 would recover approximately one third of amounts owing. The Monitor concluded that such plan was fair and reasonable and recommended its approval by the creditors.

[34] On October 4, 2017, in response to Callidus' plan, the Respondents filed their own *Plan of arrangement,* which foresaw that half the proceeds of the litigation after payment of expenses would be distributed to creditors, if the net proceeds exceeded $20 million.

[35] On October 5, 2017, Justice Michaud ordered both parties to share the Monitor's fees and expenses related to the presentation of the plans of arrangement. He considered it to the creditors' advantage that two competing plans of arrangement be presented to them for a vote at one and the same meeting. The conduct of a claims process (to identify, verify and establish the provable claims) would be required, followed by the convocation of a creditors' meeting. He provided that the failure to deposit funds with the Monitor in order to share such costs would be deemed a bar to the Respondents presenting their plan of arrangement.

[36] The Respondents withdrew their plan and did not comply with the funding requirements that the judge ordered.

[37] On December 15, 2017, Cailidus' plan, as amended, was submitted to a vote. Even though 92 out of the 100 creditors casting votes were in favour of the plan, the majority of two thirds in value was not reached because SMT Hautes Technologies ("SMT"), holding 36.7% of total debt, voted against. Callidus did not seek to vote on this plan since its $3 million remaining debt was secured and no valuation of that security was submitted by it with a view to voting the ordinary portion of the claim.

[38] On February 6, 2018, the Respondents filed an *Application* seeking the authorization of a litigation funding agreement ("LFA") with IMF Bentham Limited and the constitution of a $20 million super-priority charge on the claim against Callidus. On February 12, 2018, the Creditors' Group filed a contestation.

[39] In addition to this contestation, Callidus sponsored a new plan of arrangement and filed a *motion to convene a creditors' meeting* to hold a vote on the plan. Callidus increased its contribution to $2,880,000. Bluberi's former employees would be paid in full while other creditors would recover from 35% to 100% of their accepted claims.

[40] The Appellant Creditors' Group requested the *CCAA* Court to "declare that Callidus shall be entitled to exercise its voting rights at the Creditors' Meeting for the unsecured portion of its amended proof of claim (...)". If Callidus voted, the required two thirds of value majority would likely be achieved so that Callidus would obtain a release from the Respondents of their litigious claim.

[41] Justice Michaud issued his judgment on March 16, 2018 and leave to appeal was granted on April 20, 2018 to Callidus and the Creditors' Group. The latter is comprised of former employees, a trade supplier and a professional firm. Both Bentham and the Monitor have filed memoranda in support of the Respondents' position and were heard through counsel at the hearing before this Court. ...

IV. Issues in Dispute

[47] The resolution of this appeal requires the examination of three questions:
1) Did the judge err in denying the Appellant Callidus the right to vote on the plan of arrangement proposed by it?
2) Did the judge err in authorizing the LFA without submitting it and the proposal to sue Callidus by way of a plan of arrangement to a vote of the creditors?
3) Did the judge err in approving the terms of the LFA while authorizing significant portions to be kept confidential? ...

VI. Callidus' right to vote

[49] On December 15, 2017, the creditors voted on the amended plan of arrangement proposed by Callidus, whereby it would fund a $2.5 million distribution to the creditors of Bluberi, excluding itself. It did not value its security to allow it to vote its claim as ordinary. The plan provided that it would receive a release from the Respondents' claim in damages against it. As previously stated, the Monitor opined that the plan was fair and reasonable. 92 creditors representing $3,450,882 of debt voted in favour while 8 creditors representing $2,375,913 voted against. Thus, while there was a majority in number of creditors, the vote of 59.27% of total value of claims in favour did not achieve the 2/3 majority in value required under the *CCAA*. In fact, it was one creditor, SMT, with a claim of $2,313,085 representing 36.7% of the value which voted against and which was apparently and remains the impediment to the acceptance of such arrangement.

[50] The new Callidus plan is essentially the same as the old one except that its contribution is increased to $2,880,000 and it is proposed that Callidus vote with the ordinary creditors though it does renounce to receiving any dividend. The plan provides that employees and the first $3,000 of other claims be paid in full. The balance of claims will be paid on a *pro rata* basis.

[51] The Monitor tabulated the resulting outcome for the creditors, reported by the judge, as follows:

Creditors Description	Number	Claim Amount	Proposed Dividend	Recovery
Creditors above $200K (excl. Employees)	5	$4,944,742	$1,726,987	35%
Creditors between $3,001 and $200K (excl. Employees)	20	$384,500	$172,691	Between 39% and 99%
Creditors below $3K (excl. Employees)	22	$29,798	$29,798	100%
Former employees, active in New Bluberi	11	$107,891	$107,891	100%
Former employees, inactive in New Bluberi	80	$842,632	$842,632	100%
Total	138	$6,309,563	$2,880,000	46%

[52] While supporting the judge's conclusion that Callidus should be excluded from voting because it intended to vote for an improper purpose, the Respondents and Bentham proffered in their memoranda that Callidus is related to the debtors and is thus, precluded from voting in favour of the arrangement in virtue of Section 22(3) *CCAA*. The Respondents plead that the *de facto* control exercised by Callidus over the affairs of Bluberi Gaming makes it a "related person".

[53] There is no validity to such argument as the judge correctly decided. "Related person" is defined in Section 4 *BIA* to which Section 2(2) *CCAA* refers. Voting control is required. Callidus holds no shares nor the voting rights over any shares of either the Respondents.

[54] If Callidus had acquired voting rights attached to the shares of the Respondents then it could be maintained that Callidus was a "related person" within the meaning of Section 2(2) *CCAA* and Section 4 *BIA* so that it could vote against but not for the plan of arrangement in virtue of Section 22(3) *CCAA*.

[55] Indeed, in the spring of 2015, Callidus presented Mr. Duhamel with a voting trust agreement, which purportedly (the draft is not filed in the record) would have transferred

the voting rights in the shares of the Respondents, though Mr. Duhamel or entities controlled by him would retain ownership of the shares. However, Mr. Duhamel refused to sign. Callidus later contended that voting control was nevertheless wrested from Mr. Duhamel or his family trust by the effect of the charging provisions in the deeds of hypothec and the defaults of the Respondents, However, that contention was dismissed, without appeal, by Justice Michaud in a judgment of November 8, 2015, Indeed, throughout the process up to the instant application before the Superior Court, Mr. Duhamel continued to act as the Respondents' director. He resigned from the US entity pursuant to the request of Callidus to accommodate the sale transaction. However, there is no indication that the voting control of Mr. Duhamel (or his family trust) was altered, let alone transferred to the Appellant Callidus.

[56] Accordingly, it cannot be asserted that Callidus had voting control over the shares of the Respondents so that it would be a related person within the statutory definition of the *CCAA*.

[57] There is no impediment to a creditor proposing a plan of arrangement as the judge himself acknowledged in ordering the first creditors' meeting. That a creditor sponsors a plan and stands to gain by it is not an indication of bad faith and does not preclude the sponsoring creditor from voting on the plan. Moreover, there is nothing improper in voting as ordinary for the deficiency in security as long as such deficiency is reasonably calculated. Here, the amount of $3 million is the balance remaining due to Callidus after its purchase of the Respondents' assets by way of the credit bid. The amount was approved by the judge at the time of the APA and found to be in order in the *a quo* judgment. Valuing the security for the remaining debt of $3 million at nil is on its face, reasonable given that the litigious claim is the sole remaining asset. It was not considered otherwise by the judge.

[58] However and as indicated above, the judge essentially decided that the behaviour of Callidus and the purpose it sought to achieve by filing the plan and voting thereon was improper and thus, he precluded it from voting.

[59] Improper purpose developed as a reason for a court to exercise its jurisdiction to dismiss or stay a petition for a bankruptcy order under what is now Sections 43(7) and 43(11) *BIA*, even though the basic prerequisites (debt and act of bankruptcy) for the making of such an order are present. The discretion arises from the statute. Improper purpose in filing the petition is a reason to exercise the discretion; it is not the source of the existence of the discretion in law. The exercise of discretion, which is not legally available, is an error in principle to which deference is not due by an appellate court.

[60] The judge relied primarily on the *Laserworks* judgment of the Nova Scotia Court of Appeal where it was found, based on evidence before the court of first instance that the purchase of debt with a view to exercising votes against the approval of a proposal under the *BIA* was done in order to bankrupt the debtor company and eliminate a competitor from the marketplace. The court decided that this was improper and justified precluding that creditor from voting its claims. It underlined that the party was not originally a creditor and set out deliberately to cause injury to the debtor by bankrupting it.

[61] It must also be underlined that the result of a vote defeating a proposal is a deemed assignment in bankruptcy. As such, the reliance on the notion of improper purpose to deny the creditor a vote in *Laserworks* exhibits some harmony with the general scheme of bankruptcy law where improper purpose can justify the exercise of judicial discretion to dismiss or stay a petition. Indeed, case law relied on by the Nova Scotia Court of Appeal provide examples of bankruptcy petitions being denied or stayed under Sections 43(7) and 43(11) *BIA* because they were filed for an improper purpose. The

dynamic of a vote on an arrangement under the *CCAA* is different in that failure to achieve the statutory majority for approval does not automatically result in bankruptcy.

[62] Even if *Laserworks* is correctly decided as a matter of law and the discretion to preclude a creditor from voting exists despite the absence of statutory language, its application should be reserved for the clearest of cases. The facts here are entirely different from those in *Laserworks* as they were in *Blackburn Developments* where the British Columbia Supreme Court refused to preclude the "vulture fund" who had purchased a controlling block of claims from voting to defeat a plan of arrangement with a view to the debtor's liquidation. The vulture fund intended to acquire the debtor's tax credits in such liquidation. The monitor contended that this was an improper purpose which should preclude the fund from voting. After a trial on the issue before the *CCAA* supervising judge, it was held that it remained unclear that the fund's negative vote was intended solely to acquire tax credits. Moreover, the monitor's analysis of the liquidation scenario did not indicate that creditors would be worse off than under the proposed plan of arrangement. In the case at bar, it is far from clear that creditors will not ultimately be better off with the Callidus settlement than the financed litigation option.

[63] The clear and transparent purpose of Callidus in proposing the plan is to obtain a release from the Respondents' claim against it, or, in other words, to settle the threatened lawsuit. I cannot fathom that seeking a settlement of litigation for valuable consideration constitutes an improper purpose. I underline that the proposed settlement yields full payment to employees and creditors of small amounts while providing payment of 35–39% of larger claims. A more modest payout (under the initial plan as amended) was, in the opinion of the Monitor, fair and reasonable.

[64] Obtaining a release through a plan of arrangement even for third parties and plan sponsors is not improper and has been recognized as an integral part of the *CCAA* arrangement landscape.

[65] The Callidus offer to settle was only proposed once the Respondents appeared to have secured financing to institute the lawsuit. The Monitor who took an active role in this appeal finds something sinister in this timing but it strikes me merely as business pragmatics, which is not an improper purpose.

[66] As for the judge's finding of heavy-handed behaviour and strenuous contestation of proceedings by Callidus, I fail to see how this justifies the exclusion of the Appellant's voting rights. Firstly, a perusal of the contestation filed by Callidus to the initial *CCAA* filing paints a very different factual picture of the relationship between it and the Respondents, which I will discuss in more detail below in looking at the proposed lawsuit. Moreover, there was no sanction issued by the judge against Callidus over the life of the matter for any abuse in its conduct before the court or of any proceedings or contestation filed by it. I underline as I indicated at the outset of these reasons that there was no fact-finding inquiry by the judge. He relied on affidavits and evidently, his impressions formed during the course of the *CCAA* process, which he supervised.

[67] SMT voted against the Callidus' plan which, given the quantum of its claim, was sufficient to defeat it. There is an allegation by Callidus in its contestation to the approval of the LFA that SMT offered to sell its debt to Callidus for more than the Callidus sponsored arrangement would yield. Should SMT's voting rights be annulled because of the promotion of such self-interest? Obviously not, but I mention this as an illustration of the unstable legal (if not evidentiary) terrain upon which such process rests.

[68] This Court long ago decided that voting rights should not be excluded on supposed "equitable grounds". Each creditor is entitled to vote unless the law specifically

precludes such right. Even when the debtor is suing the creditor, such fact is not justification to exclude such creditor from a vote. The *BIA* provides that such creditor could be disqualified from acting as an inspector but no part of the *BIA* precludes the voting rights in such circumstances. I am well aware that operating under the *CCAA* regime may open the door to the exercise of greater judicial discretion, but there is no reasonable basis in law for the judge's exercise of discretion to exclude the Callidus vote because it is seeking a release from the debtors' proposed lawsuit for alleged damages arising from the parties' commercial dealings. The "courts should not use equity to do what they wish Parliament had done through legislation". While the discretionary nature of much of a supervising judge's jurisdiction should make an appeal court reticent to interfere, errors in principle and unreasonable exercise of discretion, justify appellate intervention. Such is the case here.

[69] Cancelling voting rights for behaviour which allegedly caused the debtors' financial demise based on allegations and a proposed lawsuit, is a slippery slope. It is perilous to embark on this type of inquiry in a superficial manner based on allegations (even if supported by affidavits). Voting rights are basic to the scheme of creditor democracy under the *BIA* and *CCAA*. Creditors have two basic rights: to participate in the distribution of the debtor's assets and to participate in the decision-making process of the insolvency through the exercise of their voting rights. Here the judge relied on allegations of a yet to be instituted lawsuit against the creditor to deny the latter's voting rights. This is not an appropriate exercise of discretion. Denial of a fundamental right should not depend on unproven allegations.

[70] Moreover, the judge's enquiry begins to resemble the application of equitable subordination. This doctrine, where a creditor guilty of inequitable conduct towards the debtor has its claim subordinated in the debtor's insolvency is part of American bankruptcy law. It has not been recognized by the Ontario Court of Appeal as forming part of the insolvency law of Canada.

[71] Our Court has also made it clear that a creditor has a right to vote its own self-interest even if that interest appears contrary to that of the mass of creditors or to the debtor. In *Cantrex*, the debtor had sued its secured creditor for improvident and negligent realization. The only asset remaining when the debtor put its proposal to a vote was the lawsuit against such secured creditor. The latter sought to vote the unsecured portion of its claim in order to defeat the proposal. Our Court allowed it to vote. Equally, it is not open to disallow a vote in similar circumstances by arguing a conflict of interest. I see no reason not to respect the precedent established in *Cantrex*.

[72] It was urged by the Respondents and the Monitor that if Callidus is permitted to vote, it should do so in a separate class since it alone amongst ordinary creditors receives a release of a claim of $200 million. This argument appears not to have been raised before the supervising judge as he does not treat it in his reasons. Nevertheless, in response to this submission, I would state the following.

[73] It is not unknown to the practice that a plan sponsor votes on a plan (if it is also a creditor) and that the plan includes a provision for a release in favour of the sponsor. After all, the obtaining of a release is the reason that Callidus is sponsoring the plan. It is also not unknown that a plan sponsor votes in the same class as ordinary creditors.

[74] In this case, Callidus is both a creditor and a plan sponsor. Upon valuation of its security, it should vote with the ordinary creditors. The plan is a settlement of proposed litigation targeting it. In such capacity, it is only natural that it receives a release. The crossover between the two capacities is that it has renounced to participation in the

dividend. I see nothing in this state of affairs to justify an order that Callidus exercise its voting rights in a separate and distinct class of ordinary creditors.

[75] As for the quantum of the benefit received from the plan by Callidus (i.e. $200 million) the amount of the proposed claim is not supported by the slightest substantiation in the record before us.

[76] In summary, Callidus seeks to vote its own claim, the quantum of which was previously approved by the judge. The self-interest it promotes is the release from the debtor's proposed litigation. In consideration of the release, Callidus will fund payment to the mass of creditors on terms that the vast majority of such creditors wish to accept. This is not an improper purpose either legally or on any interpretation of the facts of this case so that in precluding Callidus from voting, the judge committed a reviewable error.

VII. Submission of the LFA to the creditors' vote as part of a plan of arrangement

[77] The rationale behind interim or DIP (debtor-in-possession) financing is to allow the debtor subject to the *CCAA* to continue operations or "keep the lights on". This rationale applies pre and post the codifying amendments of 2009 to the *CCAA*:

> The premise underlying interim financing is that it is a benefit to all stakeholders as it allows the debtor to protect going concern value while it attempts to devise a plan of compromise or arrangement acceptable to creditors.

[78] While the original premise of maintaining operations may have been expanded in the applications and manifestation of such financing in recent years, characterizing the LFA as interim financing in the circumstances of this case transcended the nature of such financing. There is no connection between the financing and the debtors' commercial operations. The financing is an accessory to and part of the plan of arrangement previously proposed by the Respondents as a means to making some payment to unsecured creditors through the lawsuit. As such, it should be submitted to the creditors for their vote. The judge's failure to so construe the LFA constituted reviewable error as he misconstrued in law the notion of interim financing and misapplied that notion to the factual circumstances of the case. Moreover, given the circumstances and sequence of events, I think that the judge's approval of the LFA as interim financing after he had previously ordered a similar scheme to be submitted to the creditors as part of a plan, constitutes a manifest error of fact and a non-judicious exercise of his discretion. It will be remembered that the judge initially ordered that both the initial Callidus plan and the debtors' plan be submitted to the creditors subject to the condition that each party support the meeting costs which the debtors failed to do. Following the failure of the Callidus plan to receive a vote of the statutory majority, the judge approved the LFA exercising his powers under Section 11.2 *CCAA*. This juridical "about face" appears, if nothing more, to be an inappropriate exercise of discretion constituting palpable error.

[79] "Compromise" or "arrangement" are not defined terms in the *CCAA*. The Respondents, like the judge, rely heavily on the reasons of the Court of Appeal for Ontario ("ONCA") in *Crystallex* for guidance to determine whether the LFA should be submitted to a creditors' vote. . . .

[82] In my view, the judgment of the Court of Appeal does not have any precedential value for the present case. The factual matrix of this case is completely different. We are faced with two possible and competing sources of creditor recovery—i.e. litigation or the offer of settlement of that litigation by Callidus, the secured creditor and potential

defendant in the litigation. The only competing interests in *Crystallex* were as between the debtor (together with the DIP lender) and the noteholders as to who would finance the litigation.

[83] The Respondents contend that by rejecting the initial Callidus plan as amended, the creditors in effect approved the litigation scenario. I strongly disagree. Firstly, the LFA, which greatly effects the creditors' share in any eventual litigation proceeds, has never been submitted to creditors for approval. Secondly, the vote against the Callidus plan was carried by one creditor. Nothing indicates that the 92 votes in favour of the Callidus plan, in any way, favour the Respondents' scheme. This is all aside from Callidus' vote in the matter. . . .

[85] I do not subscribe to a restrictive definition of what constitutes an arrangement. There is no justification in the statute, nor consistent support in the practice or case law for such a view. The term should be given a broad interpretation appropriate to the remedial purpose of the *CCAA*. An arrangement or proposal can encompass both a compromise of creditors' claims as well as the process undertaken to satisfy them. The tool of the "liquidating proposal" under the *BIA* is an example where creditors are asked to approve the debtor liquidating its assets to then pay creditors *pro rata* from the proceeds. The "holding proposal" simply called for a vote by creditors to "wait and see". Such schemes seek to arrange the terms of payment or manner of satisfying claims; they are also "arrangements".

[86] The Court of Appeal for Ontario itself in *Metcalfe* adhered to a broad meaning of arrangement which requires examination of the content of the scheme overall as well as the context in which it is proposed. An arrangement includes any scheme to reorganize the affairs of the debtor and virtually any content is permissible subject to the creditors' agreement. The Court of Appeal cited with approval case law from the United Kingdom for the proposition that it is not a necessary element of an arrangement that it should alter the rights existing between the debtor and its creditors. This is where the focus should be with a view to determining whether the scheme put forward by Respondents is an arrangement.

[87] Bluberi Gaming is not operating and there is no indication that it will recommence any business operations. The Respondents' only "raison d'être" is the pursuit of the proposed litigation which is the only potential source of recovery for the creditors (other than the Callidus plan). As such, focusing on whether the LFA viewed in isolation altered creditors' rights is overly restrictive as an analysis to determine whether the scheme constitutes an arrangement. However, if I were to apply such criteria as a test, the scheme proposed by the Respondents with the LFA would qualify as an arrangement, since it allows the Respondents to decide with Bentham whether to accept any settlement of the litigation. The scheme sets the stage for "alteration of creditors' rights" as the reasons of the Court of Appeal in *Crystallex* would have it. They could very well receive nothing in a settlement where the funds generated were only sufficient to pay the lawyers and Bentham.

[88] Sophistry aside, rather than being paid on normal contractual or commercial terms, the creditors are told to await the outcome of the prosecution of a litigious claim for the debtors to obtain cash to perhaps pay something at some future date. I think their legal rights are "taken away" or "compromised".

[89] It is fundamental that creditors approve the Respondents' scheme as a whole, including the LFA which is accessory to the major thrust of the proposal—i.e. sue the secured creditor and distribute the proceeds net of lawyers' fees and lender advances

and success fee. As such, as part of their approval of the financing of such litigation, they should be able to exercise control at the approval stage by introducing measures to have input in managing the litigation on an ongoing basis, if they so desire. For example, the LFA, as currently written, allows Bentham to discontinue at any time, which could conceivably mean no recovery for creditors without any say in the process. Moreover, as it stands, any eventual offer of settlement is decided by the Respondents upon consultation with Bentham (which as stated always has the option to withdraw). No committee of creditors has any say in this or any other decision going forward in the proposed litigation. The decision on risk acceptance should be the dominion of the creditors and not the judiciary. The scheme (litigation and LFA) should be submitted as a plan to the creditors for their approval.

[90] I refrain from further comment on the LFA so has not to prejudice any eventual negotiation and to be consistent with myself that in the present circumstances the LFA should be approved by the creditors and not the judiciary. However, I do add my agreement with the creditors that the LFA is akin to an equity investment. The contingent nature of the repayment is such that Bentham is investing in the Respondents because of the litigation asset and it will benefit by preference over the existing creditors upon any successful judgment or settlement. Seen in this manner, the LFA does alter the creditors' rights by means of subordination and is a further justification for characterizing the scheme as an arrangement. In this regard, it must be pointed out that in *Crystallex* it was only the advances and interest due to the litigation lender that benefitted from a priority. The success fee ranked subsequent to the ordinary claims. That is not the case under the LFA, which provides for priority payment of Bentham for advances and success fee.

[91] In the present case, there was a choice of recovery for the creditors—i.e. the Callidus plan as amended and now the second Callidus plan or, alternatively the scheme put forward by the Respondents. This distinguishes this case from the facts in *Crystallex*. In my mind, the only manner of proceeding that made and makes sense for the creditors is to put both options before them for a vote. This was the initial reaction of the supervising judge. However, as indicated above, he imposed a condition that in order for either parties' plan to be submitted to the creditors, they had to deposit funds with the Monitor to support the costs of the claims' process and the meeting, which the Respondents failed to do. They withdrew their plan from the creditors. I think the judge's initial approach was the correct one—i.e. that both plans be presented to the creditors for a vote. Events may have taken on a momentum of their own but it became a mistake in the exercise of discretion after these events to approve the LFA under Section 11.2 *CCAA*, when a previous funding agreement should have but was not presented to the creditors because of the Respondents' inability or unwillingness to contribute to the funding of the decision-making process, the whole as the judge originally ordered.

[92] Incidentally, the Respondents' initial plan provided for a scheme of distribution of litigation proceeds where after payment of half of the proceeds to the litigation financier and professional fees, the creditors could receive up to 100% of their claims. With the LFA, there is no undertaking of any payment to the creditors. Rather, after payment of Bentham and fees, the Respondents will be left to decide whether to file a plan and what to offer in such plan.

[93] I find it incongruous that the Respondents can now bypass the judge's rationale of the original order, that their funding arrangements for the proposed litigation be submitted as part of a plan to the creditors and that the LFA should be approved as interim financing under Section 11.2 *CCAA*. It appears that the creditors have been dragged into

a process by default given the debtors' failure to comply with the judge's order to deposit funds with the Monitor coupled with the vote of one creditor against the Callidus' plan.

[94] The judge states that a prime motivation for him to authorize the LFA was the absence of any other avenue of creditor recovery. However, as the Respondents point out, in the absence of any plan, bankruptcy is an option. The Respondents' recourse against the Appellant would accrue to a trustee who, with the advice of elected inspectors, would have the option to sue the Appellant and seek such financing and other assistance required to support the litigation initiative. In this regard, the Respondents' objection to submitting their litigation scheme including the LFA hints of an attempt to protect the interest of the shareholder, Mr. Duhamel. We know that he had an interest in the first litigation financier proposed (9364-9739 Québec inc.); we are not aware of any interest he could have in the LFA, although, I note that he is, together with the Respondents and Bentham, a party to that agreement. Moreover, the "waterfall" or scheme of distribution of litigation proceeds provides that after the lawyer and Bentham, the Respondents, which Mr. Duhamel controls, receive the funds. There is no protection of the creditors.

[95] The Respondents seek to justify the LFA and its approval by the judge without a creditors' vote as fundamental to their access to justice. This is perhaps so but the issue in this insolvency case is whether the scheme of which the LFA forms part should be submitted to the creditors for their approval. This is particularly fitting given that the competing plan seeks the settlement of the litigation, which the LFA would finance.

[96] As part of his analysis, the judge reproduced some of the allegations from the proceedings that underpinned the proposed lawsuit and found that they are serious or at least not frivolous. He remarked that the allegations are in substance also found in the motion he granted for an initial *CCAA* order. These allegations, not proven, nor subject to any serious contradictory debate let alone a trial were contested by Callidus in writing in the court record which contestation was supported by an affidavit. The content of this contestation is nowhere mentioned by the judge. I find some of the Respondents' accusations, which the judge considered serious, to be vague at least without the backdrop of the loan documents that would disclose default clauses and available remedies. Moreover, not mentioning the Callidus version of events is erroneous. A brief summary of such contestation indicates that after Callidus commenced financing the Respondents in 2012, the hard facts on the ground led it to take a more stringent attitude towards its debtors. In such regard, rather than selling 3,300 machines in 2013 as Mr. Duhamel had apparently forecasted, he sold 324. Forecasted gross revenue of $46,355,000 in 2013 became $17,442,000 generating a loss of $9,661,000, which continued with losses of approximately $3,800,000 in 2014 and $ 17,500,000 in the first 9 months of 2015. This appears to predate, at least in part, the alleged heavy-handed behaviour of Callidus leading to the *CCAA* filing. Moreover, the proposed litigation does not attempt an explanation of how a company that had generated considerable financial losses by the end of 2013 could subsequently have suffered $200 million of damage at the hands of Callidus. As well, the proceedings and positions of Callidus before the lower court nowhere appear to have been sanctioned by the judge as abusive as permitted by the provisions of Articles 51 and following of the Quebec *Code of Civil Procedure*. The presence of competing facts, which the judge does not mention, underlines the perilous nature of the exercise he embarked upon. Appropriate disclosure of the apparent merit of the lawsuit is one element for the creditors to consider in deciding whether to pursue the litigation proposed by the Respondents.

[97] Since I propose to quash and substitute an order that the Respondents' scheme be the object of a plan of arrangement subject to creditor approval, it would make sense, as the

judge originally ordered, that the plan of arrangement (including the LFA) of the debtors be submitted to a meeting of creditors at one and the same time as the new plan of Callidus.

[98] There remains the outstanding issue of what access to the LFA the creditors should have....

IX. Conclusion

[101] For all of the above reasons, I propose to allow the appeal and set aside the *a quo* judgment. The appropriate orders should issue so that a meeting of creditors be ordered where the new Callidus plan is submitted for a vote. The actual orders can be determined by the judge. His meeting order of October 12, 2017 can serve as a guide with the appropriate modifications.

[102] The meeting expenses will be for the account of Callidus as it has offered accordingly to the Monitor, It will have the right to vote its claim of $3 million as an ordinary creditor (upon the filing of the appropriate claim valuing its security), at such and any other meeting and including particularly the right to vote on the plan sponsored by it.

[103] At one and the same meeting, if the Respondents with the support of Bentham so desire, they may also submit a plan of arrangement, which will include the pursuit of the proposed litigation and the LFA by reference or incorporation. The complete unredacted terms of the LFA should be presented to members of the Appellant Creditors' Group and their professionals upon signature of a non-disclosure agreement, which the Monitor's counsel should prepare. Similarly, other creditors and their professionals should have an opportunity to consult a non-redacted LFA through the Monitor upon execution of the non-disclosure agreement. Callidus will not have access to an unredacted version of the LFA.

Appeal allowed.

IV. TREATMENT OF SHAREHOLDERS

The *CCAA* does not indicate how existing shareholders of the debtor company are to be dealt with in a plan of arrangement. Rather, section 42 of the *CCAA* provides that the Act may be applied together with the provision of any other federal or provincial Act that authorizes or makes provision for the sanction of compromises or arrangements between a company and its shareholders. Many of the Canadian incorporation statutes provide that a court may make an order amending the corporation's constating documents without the need for shareholder approval (see, for example, *Canada Business Corporations Act*, RSC 1985, c C-44, s 91). However, some incorporations statutes may not contain this type of provision, and shareholders might attempt to exploit the absence of such a provision and demand some value in the restructuring in order to obtain their consent. In *Re Loewen Group Inc* (2001), 32 CBR (4th) 54 (*Loewen*), Farley J makes it clear that, for insolvency purposes, the court can authorize the vesting of property under a plan free of shareholder claims even if the law governing the debtor's incorporation requires shareholder approval of any change in the company's structure.

Subsequent amendments to the *CCAA* added subsection 6(2), which provides that "[i]f a court sanctions a compromise or arrangement, it may order that the debtor's constating instrument be amended in accordance with the compromise or arrangement to reflect any change that may lawfully be made under federal or provincial law." Although this language may not be as clear as one might desire (the reference to a change that may lawfully be made could conceivably be interpreted as including any legal requirement for shareholder consent), the background documents indicate that the intention was to prevent shareholders from attempting to block implementation of a plan by withholding their consent. It is likely that courts will view this provision as codifying the position taken by Farley J in *Loewen*.

Sometimes a plan may throw the existing shareholders a small bone (for example, 1 to 2 percent of the equity in the company's restructured capitalization) so as to enlist their support for approval of the new share structure before the court hearing the application under the relevant business corporations statute. Douglas Baird and Donald Bernstein, in "Absolute Priority, Valuation Uncertainty, and the Reorganization Bargain" (2006) 115 *Yale Law Journal* 1930, argue that reorganizations which confer value on junior claimants despite the fact that the claims of senior creditors are not fully satisfied may be attributable to uncertainty over the value of the firm. This difficulty is not encountered in a liquidating *CCAA*, since the value of the firm is established through the sale of the assets. In a traditional reorganization, there may be considerable uncertainty concerning cash flows and appropriate discounts rates. In order to avoid costly litigation and delay in obtaining a judicial valuation based on expert testimony, the parties can strike a deal by which the junior party obtains some recovery. But if, as in the case of *Re Stelco Inc* (2006), 17 CBR (5th) 78 (Ont Sup Ct J), the corporation is clearly underwater, the creditors will be less inclined to agree to a plan that gives value to shareholders.

Re Stelco Inc (2006), 17 CBR (5th) 78 (Ont Sup Ct J)

FARLEY J:

[1] The Applicants (collectively "Stelco") moved for:

(a) a declaration that Stelco has complied with the provisions of the *Companies' Creditors Arrangement Act* ("CCAA") and the orders of this court made in this CCAA proceeding;

(b) a declaration that the Stelco plan of arrangement pursuant to the CCAA and the reorganization of Stelco Inc. ("S") under the *Canada Business Corporations Act* ("CBCA") (collectively the "Plan") as voted on by the affected creditors of Stelco is fair and reasonable;

(c) an order sanctioning and approving the Plan; and

(d) an order extending the Stay Period and Stay Date in the Initial Order until March 31, 2006.

[2] This relief was unopposed by any of the stakeholders except for various existing shareholders of S (who may also be employees or retirees of Stelco). In particular there was organized objection to the Plan, especially as in essence the Plan would eliminate the existing shareholders, by a group of shareholders (AGF Management Ltd., Stephen Stow, Pollitt & Co., Levi Giesbrecht, Joe Falco and Phil Dawson) who have styled themselves as "The Equity Holders" ("EH")....

[13] Is the Plan fair, reasonable and equitable for the existing shareholders of S? They will be wiped out under the Plan and their shares eliminated. New equity will be created in which the existing shareholders will not participate. They have not been allowed to vote on the Plan.

[14] It is well established that a reorganization pursuant to s. 191 of the CBCA may be made in conjunction with a sanction order under the CCAA and that such a reorganization may result in the cancellation of existing shares of the reorganized corporation based on those shares/equity having no present value (in the sense of both value "now" and the likelihood of same having value in the reasonably foreseeable future, absent the

reorganization including new debt and equity injections and permitted indulgences or other considerations and adjustments). See *Re Beatrice Foods Inc*, (1996), 43 C.B.R. (4th) 10 (Ont. Gen. Div.) at para. 10–15; *Re Laidlaw Inc* (2003), 39 C.B.R. (4th) 230 (Ont. S.J.C.); *Algoma* at para. 7; *Cable Satisfaction International Inc v Richter & Associés Inc* (2004), 48 C.B.R. (4th) 205 (Que. S.C.) at p. 217. The Dickenson Report, which articulated the basis for the reform of corporate law that resulted in the enactment of the CBCA, described the object of s. 191 as being:

> to enable the court to effect any necessary amendment to the articles of the corporation in order to achieve the objective of the reorganization without having to comply with all the formalities of the Draft Act, <u>particularly shareholder approval of the proposed amendment</u> (emphasis added): R.W.V. Dickenson, J.L. Howard, L. Getz, *Proposals for a New Business Corporations Law for Canada*, vol. 1 (Ottawa: Information Canada. 1971) at p. 124.

[15] The fairness, reasonableness and equitable aspects of a plan must be assessed in the context of the hierarchy of interests recognized by insolvency legislation and jurisprudence. See *Canadian Airlines* at pp. 36–7 where Paperny J stated:

> Where a company is insolvent, only the creditors maintain a meaningful stake in its assets. Through the mechanism of liquidation or insolvency legislation, the interests of shareholders are pushed to the bottom rung of the priority ladder. The expectations of creditors and shareholders must be viewed and measured against an altered financial and legal landscape. Shareholders cannot reasonably expect to maintain a financial interest in an insolvent company where creditors' claims are not being paid in full. It is through the lens of insolvency that the court must consider whether the acts of the company are in fact oppressive, unfairly prejudicial or unfairly disregarded. CCAA proceedings have recognized that shareholders may not have "a true interest to be protected" because there is no reasonable prospect of economic value to be realized by the shareholders given the existing financial misfortunes of the company: *Royal Oak Mines Ltd*, supra, para. 4., *Re Cadillac Fairview Inc* (March 7, 1995), Doc. B28/95 (Ont. Gen. Div. [Commercial List]), and *T Eaton Company*, supra.
>
> To avail itself of the protection of the CCAA, a company must be insolvent. The CCAA considers the hierarchy of interests and assesses fairness and reasonableness in that context. The court's mandate not to sanction a plan in the absence of fairness necessitates the determination as to whether the complaints of dissenting creditors and shareholders are legitimate, bearing in mind the company's financial state. The articulated purpose of the Act and the jurisprudence interpreting it, "widens the lens" to balance a broader range of interests that includes creditors and shareholders and beyond to the company, the employees and the public, and tests the fairness of the plan with reference to its impact on all of the constituents.
>
> It is through the lens of insolvency legislation that the rights and interests of both shareholders and creditors must be considered. The reduction or elimination of rights of both groups is a function of the insolvency and not of oppressive conduct in the operation of the CCAA. The antithesis of oppression is fairness, the guiding test for judicial sanction. If a plan unfairly disregards or is unfairly prejudicial it will not be approved. However, the court retains the power to compromise or prejudice rights to effect a broader purpose, the restructuring of an insolvent company, provided that the plan does so in a fair manner."

[16] The question then is does the equity presently existing in S have true value at the present time independent of the Plan and what the Plan brings to the table? If it does then the interests of the EH and the other existing shareholders must be considered

appropriately in the Plan. This is fairly put in K.P. McElcheran, *Commercial Insolvency in Canada* (Toronto, Lexis Nexis Canada Inc.: 2005) at p. 290 as:

> If, at the time of the sanction hearing, the business and assets of the debtor have a value greater than the claims of the creditors, a plan of arrangement would not be fair and reasonable if it did not offer fair consideration to the shareholders.

[17] However if the shareholders truly have no economic interest to protect (keeping in mind that insolvency and the depth of that insolvency may vary according to which particular test of insolvency is applied in respect of a CCAA proceeding: as to which, see *Re Stelco Inc*, [2004] O.J. No. 1257 (S.C.J. [Commercial List]), leave to appeal dismissed [2004] O.J. No. 1903 (C.A.), leave to appeal dismissed (S.C.C.) No. 30447). In *Cable Satisfaction*, Chaput J at p. 218 observed that when shareholders have no economic interest to protect, then they have no claim to a right under the proposed arrangement and the "[m]ore so when, as in the present case, the shareholders are not contributing to any of the funding required by the Plan." I do note in the case of the Stelco Plan and the events leading up to it, including the capital raising and sale processes, that despite talk of an equity financing by certain shareholders, including the EH, no concrete offer ever surfaced.

[18] If the existing equity has no true value at present, then what is to be gained by putting off to tomorrow (the ever present and continuous problem in these proceedings of manāna—which never comes) what should be done today. The EH speculate, with no concrete basis for foundation as demonstrably illustrated by the eve of hearing Taylor affidavit discussed above, that something good may happen. I am of the view that that approach was accurately described in court by one counsel as a desperation Hail Mary pass and the willingness of someone, without any of his own chips, in the poker game willing to bet the farm of someone else who does have an economic interest in Stelco.

[19] I also think it fair to observe that in the determination of whether someone has an economic value, that analysis should be conducted on a reasonable and probable basis. In a somewhat different but applicable context, I observed in *New Quebec Raglan Mines Ltd v Blok-Andersen*, [1993] O.J. No. 727 at p. 3:

> The "highest price" is not the price which could be derived on the basis of the most optimistic and risky assumptions without any regard as to their likelihood of being realized. It also seems to me that prudence would involve a consideration that there be certain fall back positions. Even in betting on horses, the most savvy and luckiest punter will not continue to stake all his winnings of the previous race on the next (and so on). If he does, he will go home wearing the barrel before the last race is run.

Alternatively there is a saying: "If wishes were horses, then beggars would ride." ...

[22] Allow me to return to the pivotal point concerning the question of whether the Plan is fair, reasonable and equitable, vis-à-vis the existing equity. The EH retained Navigant Consulting which relied upon the views of Metal Bulletin Research ("MBR") which, *inter alia*, predicted a selling spot price of hot roll steel at $525 U.S. per ton. Navigant's conclusion in its December 8, 2005 report was that the value of residual shareholder equity was between $1.1 to $1.3 billion or a per share value of between $10.76 and $12.71. However, when Stelco pointed out certain deficiencies in this analysis, Navigant took some of these into account and reduced its assessment of value to between $745 million to $945 million for residual shareholder value on per share value of $7.29 to $9.24, using a discounted cash flow ("DCF") approach. Navigant tested the DCF approach against the EBITDA approach. It is interesting to note that on the EBITDA

analysis approach Navigant only comes up to a conclusion that the equity is valued at $8 million to $83 million or $0.09 to $0.81 per share. If the Court were to accept that as an accurate valuation, or something at least of positive value even if not in that neighbourhood, then I would have to take into account existing shareholder interests in determining whether the Plan was fair, reasonable and equitable — and not only vis-à-vis the affected creditors but also vis-à-vis the interests of the existing shareholders given that at least some of their equity would be above water. I understand the pain and disappointment of the existing shareholders, particularly those who have worked hard and long with perhaps their life savings tied up in S shares, but regretfully for them I am not able to come to a conclusion that the existing equity has a true positive value.

[23] The fight in the Stelco CCAA proceedings has been long and hard. No holds have been barred as major affected creditors have scrapped to maximize their recovery. There were direct protracted negotiations between a number of major affected creditors and the new equity sponsors under the Plan, all of whom had access to the confidential information of Stelco pursuant to Non Disclosure Agreements. These negotiations established a value of $5.50 per share for the *new* common shares of a *restructured* Stelco. That translates into an enterprise value (not an equity value since debt/liabilities must be taken into consideration) of $816.6 million for Stelco, or a recovery of approximately 65% for affected creditors. The parties engaged in these negotiations are sophisticated experienced enterprises. There would be no particular reason to believe that in the competition involved here that realistic values were ignored. Further, the affected creditors generally were rather resoundingly of the view by their vote that an anticipated 65% recovery was as good as they could reasonably expect. . . .

[29] I would note that Farley Cohen, the principal author of the Navigant report, does not have experience in dealing with integrated steel companies. I find it unusual that he would have customized his approach in calculating equity value by not deducting the Asset Based Lenders loan. Brad Fraser of BMO Nesbitt Burns stated that such customization was contrary to the practice at his firms both present and past and that the Navigant's approach was internally inconsistent with respect thereto as to 2005 to 2009 cash flows as contrasted with terminal value. The Navigant report appears to have forecasted a high selling price for steel combined with low costs for imports such as coal and scrap, which would be contrary to historical complementary movements between steel prices and these inputs. . . .

[The court then engaged in a detailed analysis of the valuation methodology of Navigant Consulting in which the court highlighted a number of difficulties associated with its assumptions.]

[37] The end result is that given the above analysis, I have no hesitation in concluding that it would be preferable to rely upon the analysis of UBS, BMO Nesbitt Burns and Ernst & Young Orenda, both as to their direct views as to the enterprise value of existing Stelco and as to their criticism of the Navigant and MBR reports concerning Stelco. Therefore, I conclude that the existing shareholders cannot lay claim to there being any existing equity value. Given that conclusion, it would be inappropriate to justify cutting in these existing shareholders for any piece of the emergent restructured Stelco. If that were to happen, especially given the relative values and the depth of submersion of existing equity, then it would be unfair, unreasonable and inequitable for the affected creditors.

[Order sanctioning and approving plan granted.]

Motion dismissed.

V. TREATMENT OF EQUITY CLAIMS

Shareholders will usually receive little or nothing in a restructuring, as they are among the last creditors to be paid. This has led to attempts to improve their status by asserting a cause of action against the debtor company. The shareholders may assert a claim to be a creditor, on the ground that the company is obliged to pay them a dividend or some other form of corporate distribution. They may also attempt to sue the debtor company for damages for misrepresentation or seek to rescind the contract and recover the consideration that they paid in respect of the issuance of the shares. The courts generally disallowed such claims, and used a variety of legal techniques, such as equitable subordination, or refusing to allow them on the basis that they do not fall under the definition of a claim, to reach this result (see *Re Central Capital Corp* (1996), 27 OR (3d) 494 (CA); *Re Blue Range Resource Corp*, 2000 ABQB 4; see also the discussion in Chapter 9 and Chapter 14.

Provisions in the *CCAA* ensure that these types of claims will be subordinate to the claims of ordinary unsecured creditors. The definition of "equity claim" includes a claim for a dividend, return of capital, a redemption or retraction obligation, and a monetary loss resulting from the ownership sale or purchase of an equity interest or rescission of a purchase or sale of an equity interest (s 2(1)). Section 22.1 of the *CCAA* provides that holders of equity interests must be placed in their own separate class and do not have a right to vote on a plan unless a court orders otherwise. Section 6(8) of the *CCAA* provides that a court may not sanction a plan that provides any distribution to equity claimants unless all non-equity claims are paid in full. In *Bul River Mineral Corporation (Re)*, 2014 BCSC 1732, the court maintained that these provisions are seen as both codifying previous case law, and also providing "a more concrete definition of 'equity claims' and by such definition a broadening and more expensive definition of such claims" (para 82). The court further stated that "Parliament has now clearly cast the net widely in terms of the broad definition of equity claims such that claims that might have previously escaped such characterization will now be caught by the *CCAA*" (para 82). The court concluded that these provisions must be read in light of the original purpose of the *CCAA*, which has, at its core, "a fair and efficient resolution of competing claims in a situation (insolvency) where all obligations or expectations cannot be fulfilled" (para 101). Ultimately, that means "equity will take a back seat in terms of any recovery where there are outstanding debt claims" (para 101). It was such before the amendments, and arguably more so after, given the enhanced definition of "equity claims."

One commentator has argued that this approach goes too far and that claims arising pursuant to provincial securities regulation statutes that seek to protect investors from fraud or misrepresentation should not be postponed to the claims of other creditors (see J Sarra, "From Subordination to Parity: An International Comparison of Equity Securities Claims in Insolvency Proceedings" (2007) 16 *International Insolvency Review* 181).

VI. COURT APPROVAL

The *CCAA* provides for certain mandatory features in a plan of compromise or arrangement. If the plan does not contain these features, a court cannot approve it and it therefore will not bind the creditors. There are three mandatory requirements. First, section 6(3) of the *CCAA* provides that unremitted source deductions of income tax, Canada Pension Plan, and employment insurance that have been deducted from the pay of employees must be paid within six months after court approval of the plan unless the Crown agrees otherwise.

Second, section 6(5) provides that the plan must give employees at least as much as the preferred amount that they would have been qualified to receive in a bankruptcy and all amounts earned after the commencement of the restructuring. Finally, section 6(6) provides that the plan must provide for the payment of unremitted pension contributions, but this requirement can be omitted from the plan if the parties have reached an agreement concerning those amounts that has been approved by the relevant pension regulator.

As stated in *Re Canadian Airlines Corp*, 2000 ABQB 442 at para 60, before approving the plan the court must ensure:

(1) there must be strict compliance with all statutory requirements and adherence to the previous orders of the court;

(2) all materials filed and procedures carried out must be examined to determine if anything has been done or purported to be done which is not authorized by the *CCAA*; and

(3) the Plan must be fair and reasonable.

The following matters must be considered in deciding whether a plan was fair and reasonable (*Re Canadian Airlines Corp* at para 96):

a. the composition of the unsecured vote;
b. what creditors would receive on liquidation or bankruptcy as compared to the Plan;
c. alternatives available to the Plan and bankruptcy;
d. oppression;
e. unfairness to shareholders; and
f. the public interest.

If a plan is not approved by the creditors or is not sanctioned by the court, this does not result in an automatic bankruptcy, as is the case under the commercial proposal provisions of the *BIA*. Instead, the creditors are able to assert their enforcement rights and remedies as soon as the stay of proceedings granted by the court comes to an end. The usual result is that the debtor or the creditors will institute bankruptcy or receivership proceedings.

The following three cases discuss the test courts use in determining whether to sanction a plan and the criteria that it will use to determine if a plan is fair and reasonable. The plan in *Sammi Atlas, Re* (1998), 3 CBR (4th) 171 (Ont Ct J (Gen Div)), referred to in *Lutheran Church*, included a sliding-scale formula intended to "protecting (or helping out) the little guy" (para 8) and in *Metcalfe & Mansfield Alternative Investments II Corp (Re)*, 2008 ONCA 587, the plan included provisions releasing third parties from claims that were not fraudulent.

Lutheran Church Canada (Re), 2016 ABQB 419, 38 CBR (6th) 36 [*Lutheran Church*]

BE ROMAINE J:

I. Introduction

[1] This *CCAA* proceeding has been complicated by some unusual features. There are approximately 2,592 creditors of the Church extension fund with proven claims of approximately $95.7 million, plus 12 trade creditors with claims of approximately $957,000. There are 896 investors in the Church investment corporation with outstanding claims of $22.4 million. Many of these creditors and investors invested their funds at least in part because of their connection to the Lutheran Church. Many of them are elderly. Some of them are angry that what they thought were safe vehicles for investment,

given the involvement of their Church, have proven not to be immune to insolvency. Some of them invested their life savings at a time of life when such funds are their only security during retirement. Inevitably, there is bitterness, a lack of trust and a variety of different opinions about the outcome of this insolvency restructuring.

[2] A group of creditors have applied to replace the Monitor at a time when the last two plans of arrangement and compromise in these proceedings had been approved by the requisite double majority of creditors. I dismiss the application to replace the Monitor on the basis that there is no reason arising from conflict or breach of duty to do so. I find that the proposed plans are within my jurisdiction to sanction are fair and reasonable in the circumstances and should be sanctioned. These are my reasons. . . .

6. Are the Plans Fair and Reasonable?

a. Overview

[142] Farley, J in *Re: Sammi Atlas Inc*, [1998] O.J. No. 1089 at para 4 provided a useful description of the Court's duty in determining whether a proposed plan is fair and reasonable:

> . . . is the Plan fair and reasonable? A Plan under the *CCAA* is a compromise; it cannot be expected to be perfect. It should be approved if it is fair, reasonable and equitable. Equitable treatment is not necessarily equal treatment. Equal treatment may be contrary to equitable treatment. One must look at the creditors as a whole (i.e. generally) and to the objecting creditors (specifically) and see if rights are compromised in an attempt to balance interests (and have the pain of the compromise equitably shared) as opposed to a confiscation of rights. It is recognized that the *CCAA* contemplates that a minority of creditors is bound by the Plan which a majority have approved—subject only to the court determining that the Plan is fair and reasonable: see *Northland Properties Ltd* at p.201; *Olympia & York Developments Ltd* at p.509.

In an earlier case, he commented:

> In the give and take of a *CCAA* plan negotiation, it is clear that equitable treatment need not necessarily involve equal treatment. There is some give and some get in trying to come up with an overall plan which Blair J in *Olympia & York* likened to a sharing of the pain. Simply put, any *CCAA* arrangement will involve pain—if for nothing else than the realization that one has made a bad investment/loan: *Re: Central Guarantee Trust Ltd*, [1993] O.J. No. 1479.

[143] The objection of the opposing Depositors to these plans focus mainly on whether the different treatment of some creditors results in inequitable treatment, whether the plans are flawed is any respect and how much weight I should accord to the approval of the majority.

b. Deference to the Majority

[144] Dealing with the important factor of the approval of the plans by the requisite double majority of creditors, the Court in *Re Muscletech Research & Development Inc*, [2007] O.J. No. 695 at para 18 commented:

> It has been held that in determining whether to sanction a plan, the court must exercise its equitable jurisdiction and consider the prejudice to the various parties that would flow from granting or refusing to grant approval of the plan and must consider alternatives available to the Applicants if the plan is not approved. An important factor to be

considered by the court in determining whether the plan is fair and reasonable is the degree of approval given to the plan by the creditors. It has also been held that, in determining whether to approve the plan, a court should not second-guess the business aspects of the plan or substitute its views for that of the stakeholders who have approved the plan.

[145] The opposing Depositors, however, invite me to do just that. They refer to a remark by McLachlen, J (as she then was), in *Re Gold Texas Resources* [1989] B.C.J. No. 167 at page 4, to the effect that the court should determine whether "there is not within an apparent majority some undisclosed or unwarranted coercion of the minority. . . . (i)t must be satisfied that the majority is acting *bona fide* and in good faith".

[146] The opposing Depositors submit that, in considering the voting results, I should keep in mind that the many of the Depositors "are not businessmen" and that 60% of them are senior citizens over 60 years of age. I note that some of the opposing creditors are also "not businessmen" and are over 60, but the Court is not asked to discount their opposing votes for that reason.

[147] I have read the considerable disclosure about the plans prepared and distributed by the Monitor, and note the extraordinary efforts of the Monitor and the District Group to ensure that Depositors had the opportunity to ask questions at the information meetings. The Depositors have had months to inform themselves of the plans. Even if the disputed development disclosure had been necessary, there were roughly 1 1/2 months from the Monitor's disclosure of the documents to the vote on the District Plan. It would be patronizing for the Court to assume anything other than the Depositors were capable of reading the materials, asking relevant questions and exercising judgment in their own best interest. Business sophistication is not a necessity in making an informed choice.

[148] The opposing Depositors also submit that there is evidence of efforts by Church officials to influence the outcome of the vote in favour of the plans. This evidence consists of affidavits from the opposing Depositors or their supporters that accuse various Church pastors of efforts to intimidate or silence those who oppose the plans. These allegations have been made against individuals who are not direct parties in these proceedings, at such a time and in such circumstances that it was not possible for them to respond.

[149] As seen from the allegations against the Monitor, to which the Monitor had an opportunity to respond, there may be very different perceptions about what actually occurred during the incidents described in the allegations. I appreciate that it must be uncomfortable to be at odds with your religious community on an important issue. However, these allegations would bear greater weight if the terms of the plans were prejudicial to the Depositors as a whole, or the allegations were supported by the Creditor's Committees but they are not. It is not unreasonable or irrational for Depositors to have voted in favour of the plans.

[150] I am unable to accept on the evidence before me that the Depositors who voted in favour of the plans did so because they were coerced by church officials. This does a disservice to those who exercised their right to vote and to have an opinion on the plans, no matter what their level of sophistication, their age or their religious persuasion. . . .

7. Conclusion

[172] As noted at para 18 of *Metcalfe*:

Effective insolvency restructurings would not be possible without a statutory mechanism to bind an unwilling minority of creditors. Unanimity is frequently impossible in such situations. But the minority must be protected too. Parliament's solution to this quandary was to permit a wide range of proposals to be negotiated and put forward (the compromise or arrangement) and to bind all creditors by class to the terms of the plan, but to do so only where the proposal can gain the support of the requisite "double majority" of votes and obtain the sanction of the court on the basis that it is fair and reasonable. In this way, the scheme of the *CCAA* supports the intention of Parliament to encourage a wide variety of solutions to corporate insolvencies without unjustifiably overriding the rights of dissenting creditors.

[173] In this case, the requisite double majority, after significant disclosure and opportunities to review and question the plans, have voted in favour of the plans. The Creditors' Committees of DIL and the District, who have the duty to act in the best interests of the body of creditors, support the plans.

[174] The Monitor supports the plans, and there is no reason in this case to give the Monitor's opinion less than the usual deference and weight.

[175] Measuring the plans against available commercial alternatives leads me to the conclusion that they provide greater benefits to Depositors and other creditors than a forced liquidation in a depressed real estate market.

[176] The plans preserve the District's core operations. I accept that the Representative Action provisions are appropriate and reasonable in the circumstances of this restructuring, that, in addition to the benefits identified by the Monitor of stream-lined proceedings, the avoidance of multiple communications and the potential of increased recovery, Depositors will benefit from the oversight of the Subcommittees and the Representative Action process will be able to incorporate cause of action, such as derivative actions, that are normally outside the scope of class actions.

[177] The insolvency of the District Group has caused heartbreak and hardship for many people, as is the case in any insolvency. In the end, the majority of affected creditors have accepted plans that resolve their collective problems to the extent possible in difficult circumstances. As noted in *Metcalfe* "in insolvency restructuring proceedings almost everyone loses something": para 117. That is certainly the case here, and the best that can be done is to try to ensure that the plans are a reasonable "balancing of prejudices". It is not possible to please all stakeholders.

[178] The balance of interests clearly favours approval. I am satisfied that the DIL and District plans are fair and reasonable and should be sanctioned.

Application dismissed.

League Assets Corp (Re), 2015 BCSC 619

FITZPATRICK J:

INTRODUCTION

[1] These are restructuring proceedings brought by the petitioners, known as the "League Assets Group", pursuant to the *Companies' Creditors Arrangement Act*, R.S.C. 1985, c. C-36 (the "*CCAA*"). Since the fall of 2013, the focus of the proceedings has been the sale or realization of the various real estate investments held by the League Assets

Group with a view to liquidating the assets and providing recovery to the substantial secured, unsecured and equity stakeholders.

[2] Much of the background of the League Assets Group and these proceedings have already been discussed in my earlier reasons for judgment: *League Assets Corp (Re)*, 2013 BCSC 2043; 2015 BCSC 42.

[3] One of the investments that was held by certain members of the League Assets Group petitioners (which, for ease of reference, I will simply refer to as "League"), comprised an approximate 13-acre development site, with some existing retail buildings, known as the Colwood City Center project (the "Colwood Lands") located in Colwood, British Columbia. Millions of dollars were spent on the development of the Colwood Lands, which included monies raised through secured and unsecured loans and from investors.

[4] One of the secured creditors holding a mortgage against the Colwood Lands was Epix Colwood Limited Partnership, as represented by its general partner, Epix Colwood GP Inc. and the bare trustee holding the debt and security, being 0995115 B.C. Ltd. (who I will collectively refer to as "Epix" or the "Epix Entities").

[5] In mid-2014, League had essentially determined that the Colwood Lands would yield no equity beyond amounts owing to the first, and possibly second, mortgagees, which included Epix. However, League subsequently realized that substantial value from the development could be raised through a tax-driven restructuring transaction that saw most of the secured debt paid and some recovery obtained for the other stakeholders. Through that transaction, the secured debt owing to Epix was to be fully repaid.

[6] Before this Court approved the Colwood Lands restructuring transaction in these proceedings, issues arose as to the amount owing to Epix under its security. It is well-taken that League and PricewaterhouseCoopers Inc., as monitor (the "Monitor"), agreed to a certain payout figure with Epix, although such agreement was under certain exigent circumstances. That agreement was not accepted or approved by the court for reasons discussed below and this Court gave subsequent directions and orders toward determining the proper payout figure owing to Epix. All monies claimed by Epix were paid to it upon the completion of the transaction in October 2014, save for $200,000 which was withheld and remained in a trust account. Subsequently, this sum was paid to the Monitor.

[7] After disclosure by Epix, and further investigations by the Monitor, it has since been determined that amounts claimed by Epix in its earlier payout statement, which were the subject of the agreement, were not properly chargeable to League under its security documentation. The Monitor now seeks an order setting the payout balance as of October 10, 2014 and an order that Epix repay the excess amount it was paid. The amount claimed is $129,393.35 less whatever amount may be claimed by way of Epix's taxable costs.

[8] Epix opposes the relief sought by the Monitor and brings a counter-application for specific performance of the settlement agreement between it, League, and the Monitor as to the amount to be paid to it. If such relief were granted, Epix claims the sum of $200,000 plus interest from the funds that were withheld and are now held by the Monitor, as proposal trustee, for distribution to the Colwood unsecured creditors and investors. . . .

(a) The "Settlement Agreement"

[79] Epix's application to enforce the agreement is premised on two bases; namely, that it had a valid settlement agreement with League and the Monitor, and that the agreement was or should be approved by the court.

[80] The *CCAA* is a business statute and I agree that it is usually highly desirable that compromises and settlements be achieved to smooth the waters for a successful restructuring. Where court approval of such settlements is required, the relevant statutory authority is found in s. 11, which provides that the court may grant any orders that are "appropriate in the circumstances."

[81] Deschamps J in *Century Services Inc v Canada (Attorney General)*, 2010 SCC 60 [hereinafter *Century Services Inc.*], described the general parameters that drive the court's consideration as to whether the relief sought is appropriate:

> [70] The general language of the *CCAA* should not be read as being restricted by the availability of more specific orders. However, the requirements of appropriateness, good faith, and due diligence are baseline considerations that a court should always bear in mind when exercising *CCAA* authority. Appropriateness under the *CCAA* is assessed by inquiring whether the order sought advances the policy objectives underlying the *CCAA*. The question is whether the order will usefully further efforts to achieve the remedial purpose of the *CCAA*—avoiding the social and economic losses resulting from liquidation of an insolvent company. I would add that appropriateness extends not only to the purpose of the order, but also to the means it employs. Courts should be mindful that chances for successful reorganizations are enhanced where participants achieve common ground and all stakeholders are treated as advantageously and fairly as the circumstances permit.

[82] Epix relies on a number of cases that involve the court considering whether a plan of arrangement should be sanctioned as "fair and reasonable" pursuant to the *CCAA*.

[83] In *Northland Properties Ltd (Re)* [1989] 73 C.B.R. (N.S.) 175 (B.C.S.C.), aff'd *Northland Properties Ltd v Excelsior Life Insurance Co of Canada*, [1989] 34 B.C.L.R. (2d) 122 (C.A.), an agreement was reached with a creditor that led to a positive vote on the plan, although that agreement was criticized as providing an "excessive payment" to that creditor beyond what others received. In the Court of Appeal, McEachern C.J.B.C. stated at 132:

> ... it remains to be considered whether the plan is fair and reasonable. I wish to refer to three matters.
>
> First, the authorities warn us against second-guessing businessmen (see *Re Alabama*, supra, at p. 244). In this case, the companies and their advisors, the bank and its advisors, and all the creditors except the two appellants, voted for the plan. As the authorities say, we should not be astute in finding technical arguments to overcome the decision of such a majority.
>
> Secondly, I wish to mention Mr. Czepil's argument that the plan was unfair, perhaps not conceptually, but operationally by authorizing negotiations. He says this put the parties in a difficult position when it came to vote because they risked retribution if they failed to reach agreement and then voted against the plan. He complains that some benefits offered in negotiations are no longer available to his clients.
>
> With respect, negotiations between businessmen are much to be desired and I would not wish to say anything that would impede that salutory process. If negotiations lead to unfairness, then other considerations, of course, arise. But that, in my view, is not this case.
>
> Thirdly, the plan assures all the priority mortgagees the full market value of their security without liquidation expenses. That is more than they could expect to receive if there had been no plan.

[84] I agree that many of the considerations of the court addressed by the Court of Appeal in *Northland Properties* equally apply in circumstances other than where a plan is approved. Most importantly, for the purposes of this matter, the underpinning of the court approval of the plan was disclosure of this particular creditor's treatment to the creditors and other stakeholders and to the court. In *Northland Properties* at 131, the Court of Appeal noted that the agreement with the creditor was "fully disclosed in the plan". It was in that sense that deference was granted to the decision of the business people in terms of whether a creditor would vote in favour of or against the plan.

[85] The comments of Farley J in *PSINet Ltd (Re)*, [2002] 33 C.B.R. (4th) 284 at 287 (Ont. S.C.J.), were to similar effect in approving a plan where the "creditors have had sufficient time and information to make a reasoned decision". See also *Sammi Atlas Inc (Re)*, [1998], 3 C.B.R. (4th) 171 at 174 (Ont. Gen. Div.); *VicWest Corp (Re)*, [2003] O.J. No. 3772 (S.C.J.), at paras. 19–21.

[86] Epix argues that its negotiations with League and the Monitor were "open" and that agreement was achieved by a process that was "fair". Epix further argues that with League and the Monitor having entered into the agreement, it is not appropriate to now "second guess" that agreement.

[87] I confess to having some difficulty with Epix's submissions. In particular, I fail to see how these negotiations would have been "open" or "fair" when neither League nor the Monitor had the underlying information and documentation in order to truly assess what Epix was owed under its security in relation to what was being claimed. Only very sparse payout details were provided. By October 9, 2014, Epix had specifically refused to provide the necessary backup for the principal balance claimed.

[88] It is, of course, the case that no one forced League and the Monitor to enter into this agreement. At the time, as the Monitor described in its report quoted above, Epix's consent was considered to be "critical" in terms of obtaining court approval of the Onni Group transaction. It is debatable whether the agreement was provident. However, any criticism of the Monitor and League must be tempered by the reality of the circumstances where there was extreme pressure to obtain court approval by the deadline so as to obtain the significant financial benefits for the other creditors. It was plain to see that League and the Monitor had many other issues to address in addition to those relating to Epix.

[89] The other difficulty with Epix's argument is that, even if an agreement was reached and disclosed to the court, there was no application for court approval of it. Indeed, Epix's counsel made sure he had the agreement of League's counsel that he would say nothing to the court beyond that an agreement had been reached.

[90] There is no dispute, in that League and the Monitor were never authorized under the ARIO, or any other court order, to agree to a settlement without court approval. The ARIO authorized League to carry on its business "in the ordinary course". The ARIO, at para. 11, directed League:

(a) to make no payments of principal, interest thereon or otherwise on account of amounts owing by [League] to any of their creditors as of the Order Date except as authorized by this Order[.]

[91] I fail to see how Epix can now argue the fairness of this agreement, and why the court should respect that agreement, when Epix took particular pains to ensure that the true consideration to be received by Epix for its "consent" was never disclosed to League, the Monitor and, also, the court.

[92] Mr. DiMartile certainly knew what that consideration was. He states that Epix agreed to the transaction, and by doing so, "lost the opportunity to develop the property". His rationale for the agreement was premised on Epix being "made whole as to the costs and expenses incurred by it to put it in a position where that development potential was real."

[93] The difficulty is that Mr. DiMartile made sure that League and the Monitor did not know the rationale for Epix's agreement, not the true nature of it, save for the $200,000 which was disclosed in Epix's affidavit distributed only on the morning of the hearing. Even that figure wasn't accurate in light of the later disclosure. When the court later specifically asked about the true consideration, Epix's counsel refused to respond. Specifically, Epix refused to disclose to the court that it was, indeed, claiming monies over and above what League was contractually obliged to pay under the Quest/Epix loan and security documentation.

[94] This could hardly be described as Epix acting in good faith and, as per the authorities on which it relies, fully disclosing the extent of the benefit that it was to receive for all to consider and exercise their business judgment in terms of accessing whether the agreement was fair and reasonable.

[95] It remains the case that there is still no application being brought by anyone to approve the "settlement" agreement.

[96] It was more than evident, at the time of the hearing, that there had been a lack of disclosure by Epix and that, at least the $200,000 penalty referred to, was a significant issue that required some review. It remained the case that League and the Monitor, and certainly the court, were not in a position to assess the reasonableness of the terms proposed. This was entirely the aggressive and ill-conceived strategy of Epix that sought to gain an improper advantage by reason of the circumstances.

[97] In its notice of application dated March 27, 2015, Epix argues that the court proceeded to deprive it of the consideration that it granted. It states:

> Nor was it open to the court to proceed on the basis of the consent provided by Epix as part of the agreement, and then deprive Epix of the consideration pursuant to which its consent was given. Such as result is not only not in accordance with the authorities as to the role of the court in assessing compromised, it is totally unfair to Epix who achieved an agreement as to the price of providing their consent, to then have the court take that negotiated consideration away.

[98] This argument is entirely without merit. The first, and obvious response, is that the agreement provided that Epix would take no position on the application. No consent was offered or taken, although I acknowledge that the Monitor continues to refer to Epix having agreed to consent to the Onni Group transaction.

[99] Further, having been advised of the fact of the agreement (but not the rationale for it), and having enquired about the circumstances surrounding that agreement, I rejected approval of any such settlement in terms of what League would be allowed to pay Epix. In the face of the court's rejection of the agreement, Epix withdrew its "non-opposition" and argued against court approval of the Onni Group transaction. Epix's counsel's later statement of account to Epix confirmed that the legal services provided on October 9 included "argue opposition" to the application to approve the Onni Group transaction. Accordingly, the basis upon which League and the Monitor agreed to the payout balance was withdrawn.

[100] Having decided to oppose the application, Epix's former counsel made two main submissions on October 9. Both arguments were re-argued on this application.

[101] Firstly, Epix argues that the Colwood Development Order and the order absolute had to be set aside, stayed, or varied in some way to permit the Onni Group transaction to proceed, absent Epix's consent. Epix says that only with its consent were League and the Monitor able to deliver the Onni Group transaction to the stakeholders which "bestowed a benefit on the other creditors which would not otherwise have been available to them."

[102] But Epix's then and present submission fails to recognize that the conditions that Epix negotiated with League's counsel on the day of the hearing were, despite the withdrawal of Epix's consent or non-opposition, specifically designed to ensure that Epix's rights and security were not affected, save for the purpose of paying out the loan and obtaining a discharge of the mortgage. The conditions, set out above, required that, until that time, the Colwood Development Order was unaffected, as were the orders in the foreclosure proceeding, including the order absolute.

[103] Secondly, Epix agrees that the Colwood Development Order did not prevent League from redeeming the mortgage but that League did not redeem its mortgage.

[104] On this issue, Epix refers to the well-known rule that a mortgagor must "redeem up", in that it precludes a mortgagor from redeeming a mortgage without redeeming all mortgages between that mortgagee and himself. The reason is that by granting a second (or subsequent) mortgage(s), the mortgagor has assigned its right to redeem such that it only has the right to redeem the last of the charges. As such, a mortgagor cannot redeem a first mortgage by paying it off and claiming a conveyance of the debt and property which would put the mortgagor in a position to obtain an order absolute so as to vest off subsequent mortgages: *Giroday Sawmills Ltd v Grun*, 2002 BCSC 1694, at paras. 15–21; *Bank of Montreal v Oldroyd*, 2005 BCSC 1070, at paras. 9–10.

[105] Epix argues that League's payment did not constitute redemption of the mortgage debt by which League could require a conveyance of the Epix debt and property. The above authorities support that conclusion.

[106] However, there is no dispute that up to the time of the registration of the order absolute, League was entitled to deliver sufficient funds to Epix to repay the amounts owing under the mortgage and require delivery of a mortgage discharge: *Oldroyd* at paras, 14, 16. This is exactly what happened in that both Epix and Meckelborg (and other priority secured claims) were paid and discharges were then required. In response, Epix argues that this only resulted in the other secured creditors moving up in priority. That may have been the case, but the effect of the Colwood Restructuring Order was to set the value of the Colwood Lands at the amount of the interim financing such that all of the subsequent secured debt became unsecured debt, which was later addressed in the bankruptcy proposal proceedings as such.

[107] Even if these other secured creditors were affected by the Colwood Restructuring Order, Epix was not and has no basis upon which to complain.

[108] Epix's arguments against the approval of the Onni Group transaction were as unpersuasive on this application as they were on October 9, although they were not articulated then to the same degree as they are now. Even in the face of the agreement, these arguments were rejected by the court on October 9. In the calmness of the aftermath of court approval of the Onni Group transaction, and having further time to consider these issues for the purposes of this application, both League and the Monitor support this view. Only the extreme exigencies of the situation on October 9 prevented such assessment of the basis of Epix's potential opposition to the application.

[109] Given the re-emergence of these arguments, issues arise as to *res judicata* and issue estoppel. Issue estoppel, as a form of *res judicata*, precludes "relitigation of

the constituent issues or material facts necessarily embraced" within a cause of action: *Danyluk v Ainsworth Technologies Inc*, 2001 SCC 44, at para. 20.

[110] The well-known three-part test for successfully invoking issue estoppel is: (1) the issue must be the same as the one decided in the prior decision; (2) the prior judicial decision must have been final; and (3) the parties to both proceedings must be the same, or their privies: *Toronto (City) v CUPE, Local 79*, 2003 SCC 63, at para. 23.

[111] As noted in *Danyluk*, the requirement that the same issue be determined was discussed by Middleton JA in *McIntosh v Parent*, [1924] 4 D.L.R. 420 at 422 (Ont. C.A.):

> ... When a question is litigated, the judgment of the Court is a final determination as between the parties and their privies. <u>Any right, question, or fact distinctly put in issue and directly determined</u> by a court of competent jurisdiction as a ground of recovery, or as an answer to a claim set up, cannot be re-tried in a subsequent suit between the same parties or their privies, though for a different cause of action. The right, question, or fact, <u>once determined</u>, must, as between them, be taken to be conclusively established so long as the judgment remains.
>
> [Emphasis added].

[112] In *Danyluk*, Mr. Justice Binnie for the Court stated, "estoppel extends to the material facts and the conclusions of law or of mixed fact and law ("the questions") that were necessarily (even if not explicitly) determined in the earlier proceedings" or such issues as are "necessarily bound up with the determination of that "issue" in the prior proceeding"; paras. 24, 54.

[113] I am satisfied that the issue as to the appropriateness of the agreement, and the later arguments advanced by Epix in opposition to the application were before the court, albeit the former in an unsatisfactory manner, were subsequently determined and were rejected. As such, Epix is not in a position to re-litigate those same issues at this time as against the same persons involved, being League and the Monitor. Epix did not seek to appeal the orders granted on October 9.

[114] If there was any doubt about what had been decided, ordered and directed on October 9, Epix would have been disabused of that notion when it received the Monitor's application in November 2014 to obtain recovery of the $200,000 held by Epix's former counsel. As stated above, Epix did not even attend on the application. Epix's present application to enforce the agreement and compel the Monitor to repay the $200,000 plus interest, is nothing more than a collateral attack on the November 19, 2014 order which directed that the monies be paid to the proposal trustee and to "vest" in the proposal trustee and form part of the bankruptcy estates.

[115] Further, on November 19, 2014, the court ordered that Epix provide further details about the payout amounts, all in aid of assisting the Monitor in the task assigned to it toward discerning exactly what was owing to Epix under its security. If, as Epix now argues, that process was irrelevant by reason of any agreement, then there was no need for any such process. That order also makes it clear that the Monitor was tasked with reviewing all of the Epix payout balance, not just that relating to the $200,000 issue. As such, the entirety of the appropriateness of the Epix payout balance remained to be determined.

[116] Only at the January 8, 2015 hearing did Epix's new counsel allude to an application to enforce what it called a "settlement agreement", although that application would not be brought until five months after October 2014, and only in response to the Monitor's application to recover what it considered to have been an overpayment of monies to Epix.

[117] I cannot leave this issue without drawing a parallel between Epix's past and current position and the position of certain secured creditors addressed by this Court in *Agro Pacific Industries Ltd (Re)*, 2000 BCSC 879.

[118] In *Agro Pacific*, the debtor, Agro Pacific, had filed for protection under the *CCAA* and an application was brought before Thackray J (as he then was) for an extension of the stay. Various secured creditors, being Bank of Montreal and Cathedral Ventures, proposed that they receive a "success fee" in consideration of them agreeing not to oppose the stay extension. Agro Pacific agreed to pay such fees to buy peace with these secured creditors. In addition, despite the monitor noting that these fees would be a "special benefit" to these creditors, the monitor concluded that the fees were "not unreasonable".

[119] Various unsecured creditors (in the interests of full disclosure, my former clients), opposed, pointing out that the fees would be borne by them and were therefore unfair. These submissions were accepted by the court, noting that payment of the fees would upset the *status quo* and "move the goals posts":

> [16] The term "success fee" does not get this application off to a savoury start. Why should anyone be credited with the success of these proceedings? All parties in this matter face risks but the legislative scheme of the *Companies' Creditors Arrangement Act*, R.S.C. 1985, c. C-36 is designed ... to allow a company to continue its business activities "in as normal a manner as possible while reorganizing." The legislation must be taken "as giving hope that reorganization, rather than bankruptcy, will eventually benefit all interested parties."
>
> [17] In *Re Woodward's Ltd* (1993), 77 B.C.L.R. (2d) 332 (S.C.), Tysoe J traced the purpose of the stay under the CCAA. He noted that it was first summarized by Wachowich J *in Meridian Developments Inc v Toronto Dominion Bank*, [1984] 5 W.W.R. 215 (Alta. Q.B.). Tysoe J continued his review of the legislative intent with reference to *Quintette Coal Ltd v Nippon Steel Corp* (1990), 80 C.B.R. (N.S.) 98 (B.C.S.C.) and *Alberta-Pacific Terminals* (1991), 8 C.B.R. (3d) 99 (B.C.S.C.). He then authored what he saw to be the three objectives of maintaining the status quo, the first of which is:
>
> > To suspend or freeze the rights of all creditors as they existed as at the date of the stay order (which, in British Columbia, is normally the day on which the CCAA proceedings are commenced). This objective is intended to allow the insolvent company an opportunity to reorganize itself without any creditor having an advantage over the company or <u>any other creditor</u>.

[18] Ms. Fitzpatrick used the term "level playing field" and said that Bank of Montreal and Cathedral are trying to manoeuvre. That is a way of referencing the *status quo* and of the call of Wachowich J. in *Meridian* "to prevent any manoeuvres" among creditors. He said that s. 11 was designed "to prevent any manoeuvres for positioning among creditors during the interim period which would give the aggressive creditor an advantage to the prejudice of others who were less aggressive."

[19] I would extend that thought to say that the Courts must guard against allowing secured creditors to run the process. This is not in any way suggesting that the secured creditors must not have their position recognized. As I said in my earlier reasons, the secured creditors are the ones "who make the financial means available so that companies such as Agro can operate."

[20] However, it must be remembered that the relationships were made by the parties when they entered into commercial contracts, contracts that contemplated insolvency and

litigation. *Consequently, when that contemplation becomes reality, caution should be exercised in bettering the deal for specific creditors or classes of creditors. To do so alters commercial reality and might frustrate the legislative intent of maintaining the status quo.*

[21] Counsel for the Monitor, Cathedral and Bank of Montreal focused on the size of the success fee rather than on the principle. They categorized the amount as "not unreasonable." That definition arises from a comparison of concessions relative to the size of the success fee. While I hesitate to rule in a manner adverse to that recommended by the Monitor, I came away with the feeling that the Monitor was less than enthusiastic about the whole concept of a success fee. Rather, it simply concluded that it was to become a reality.

[22] As for Bank of Montreal and Cathedral, my opinion is that they don't want to be treated substantially differently than NBC. I did not hear anything from any of the secured creditors that bore upon principles. Indeed, I must reflect that the Court was not favoured with <u>any</u> material from the secured creditors.

[23] I hearken to what is often submitted in criminal sentence hearings. That is, that the *major factor must be one of general deterrence. Regardless of the merit in the secured creditors' position, it is more important to let future contenders for favoured positions know that the Court is going to be most reluctant to move the goal posts.*

[Underlining in the original. Italics added.]

[120] Epix sought to manoeuver and move the goal posts here and did so in a decidedly unfair and unreasonable manner. In *Agro Pacific*, the secured creditors had at least bothered to tell the other creditors and the court of the price of their cooperation.

[121] Epix argued that no one complained about its payout amount that it had negotiated, and that the secured creditors who obtained no recovery from the interim financing and who then became unsecured creditors, supported the Onni Group transaction as being "better than nothing".

[122] With respect, this submission is fundamentally at odds with the court's role in considering whether to grant orders sought in a restructuring proceeding. As the comments of the Court in *Century Services* make plain, fairness is the touchstone upon which the court acts as a referee of sorts during these types of proceedings. Fairness must be considered in relation to all stakeholders and not just those stakeholders who have sufficient monies or time to attend applications either with or without counsel. In *Agro Pacific*, some unsecured creditors were represented but many others were not.

[123] In this case, the unsecured creditors and investors in League, in relation to the Colwood Lands, included many individuals and many of those have essentially lost their life savings. They stood to gain nothing if Epix obtained the Colwood Lands through the foreclosure and, even by reason of the Onni Group restructuring, estimated recoveries are anticipated to be only a very small percentage of their claims. The excess amounts claimed by Epix, and paid to it, only exacerbate their losses. The court would be remiss to abdicate its role in these proceedings by disregarding their interests simply because the cost of retaining counsel to appear would only increase their losses.

[124] Epix's manoeuvering in this proceeding, in relation to the October 9 hearing, represented nothing more than a naked attempt to gain a significant financial advantage to the detriment of these other stakeholders.

Application granted; cross-application dismissed.

Metcalfe & Mansfield Alternative Investments II Corp (Re), 2008 ONCA 587, 92 OR (3d) 513

BLAIR JA:

A. INTRODUCTION

[1] In August 2007 a liquidity crisis suddenly threatened the Canadian market in Asset Backed Commercial Paper ("ABCP"). The crisis was triggered by a loss of confidence amongst investors stemming from the news of widespread defaults on US sub-prime mortgages. The loss of confidence placed the Canadian financial market at risk generally and was reflective of an economic volatility worldwide.

[2] By agreement amongst the major Canadian participants, the $32 billion Canadian market in third-party ABCP was frozen on August 13, 2007 pending an attempt to resolve the crisis through a restructuring of that market. The Pan-Canadian Investors Committee, chaired by Purdy Crawford, C.C., Q.C., was formed and ultimately put forward the creditor-initiated Plan of Compromise and Arrangement that forms the subject-matter of these proceedings. The Plan was sanctioned by Colin L. Campbell J. on June 5, 2008.

[3] Certain creditors who opposed the Plan seek leave to appeal and, if leave is granted, appeal from that decision. They raise an important point regarding the permissible scope of a restructuring under the *Companies' Creditors Arrangement Act*, R.S.C. 1985, c. C-36 as amended ("CCAA"): can the court sanction a Plan that calls for creditors to provide releases to third parties who are themselves solvent and not creditors of the debtor company? They also argue that, if the answer to this question is yes, the application judge erred in holding that this Plan, with its particular releases (which bar some claims even in fraud), was fair and reasonable and therefore [erred] in sanctioning it under the CCAA....

B. FACTS

The Parties

[7] The appellants are holders of ABCP Notes who oppose the Plan. They do so principally on the basis that it requires them to grant releases to third party financial institutions against whom they say they have claims for relief arising out of their purchase of ABCP Notes. Amongst them are an airline, a tour operator, a mining company, a wireless provider, a pharmaceuticals retailer, and several holding companies and energy companies.

[8] Each of the appellants has large sums invested in ABCP—in some cases, hundreds of millions of dollars. Nonetheless, the collective holdings of the appellants—slightly over $1 billion—represent only a small fraction of the more than $32 billion of ABCP involved in the restructuring.

[9] The lead respondent is the Pan-Canadian Investors Committee which was responsible for the creation and negotiation of the Plan on behalf of the creditors. Other respondents include various major international financial institutions, the five largest Canadian banks, several trust companies, and some smaller holders of ABCP product. They participated in the market in a number of different ways.

The ABCP Market

[10] Asset Backed Commercial Paper is a sophisticated and hitherto well-accepted financial instrument. It is primarily a form of short-term investment—usually 30 to 90 days—typically with a low interest yield only slightly better than that available through

other short-term paper from a government or bank. It is said to be "asset backed" because the cash that is used to purchase an ABCP Note is converted into a portfolio of financial assets or other asset interests that in turn provide security for the repayment of the notes.

[11] ABCP was often presented by those selling it as a safe investment, somewhat like a guaranteed investment certificate.

[12] The Canadian market for ABCP is significant and administratively complex. As of August 2007, investors had placed over $116 billion in Canadian ABCP. Investors range from individual pensioners to large institutional bodies. On the selling and distribution end, numerous players are involved, including chartered banks, investment houses and other financial institutions. Some of these players participated in multiple ways. The Plan in this proceeding relates to approximately $32 billion of non-bank sponsored ABCP the restructuring of which is considered essential to the preservation of the Canadian ABCP market....

The Liquidity Crisis

[17] The types of assets and asset interests acquired to "back" the ABCP Notes are varied and complex. They were generally long-term assets such as residential mortgages, credit card receivables, auto loans, cash collateralized debt obligations and derivative investments such as credit default swaps. Their particular characteristics do not matter for the purpose of this appeal, but they shared a common feature that proved to be the Achilles heel of the ABCP market: because of their long-term nature there was an inherent timing mismatch between the cash they generated and the cash needed to repay maturing ABCP Notes.

[18] When uncertainty began to spread through the ABCP marketplace in the summer of 2007, investors stopped buying the ABCP product and existing Noteholders ceased to roll over their maturing notes. There was no cash to redeem those notes. Although calls were made on the Liquidity Providers for payment, most of the Liquidity Providers declined to fund the redemption of the notes, arguing that the conditions for liquidity funding had not been met in the circumstances. Hence the "liquidity crisis" in the ABCP market.

[19] The crisis was fuelled largely by a lack of transparency in the ABCP scheme. Investors could not tell what assets were backing their notes—partly because the ABCP Notes were often sold before or at the same time as the assets backing them were acquired; partly because of the sheer complexity of certain of the underlying assets; and partly because of assertions of confidentiality by those involved with the assets. As fears arising from the spreading U.S. sub-prime mortgage crisis mushroomed, investors became increasingly concerned that their ABCP Notes may be supported by those crumbling assets. For the reasons outlined above, however, they were unable to redeem their maturing ABCP Notes....

The Plan

a) *Plan Overview*

[24] Although the ABCP market involves many different players and kinds of assets, each with their own challenges, the committee opted for a single plan. In Mr. Crawford's words, "all of the ABCP suffers from common problems that are best addressed by a common solution." The Plan the Committee developed is highly complex and involves many parties. In its essence, the Plan would convert the Noteholders' paper—which has been frozen and therefore effectively worthless for many months—into new, long-term

notes that would trade freely, but with a discounted face value. The hope is that a strong secondary market for the notes will emerge in the long run.

[25] The Plan aims to improve transparency by providing investors with detailed information about the assets supporting their ABCP Notes. It also addresses the timing mismatch between the notes and the assets by adjusting the maturity provisions and interest rates on the new notes. Further, the Plan adjusts some of the underlying credit default swap contracts by increasing the thresholds for default triggering events; in this way, the likelihood of a forced liquidation flowing from the credit default swap holder's prior security is reduced and, in turn, the risk for ABCP investors is decreased.

[26] Under the Plan, the vast majority of the assets underlying ABCP would be pooled into two master asset vehicles (MAV1 and MAV2). The pooling is designed to increase the collateral available and thus make the notes more secure.

[27] The Plan does not apply to investors holding less than $1 million of notes. However, certain Dealers have agreed to buy the ABCP of those of their customers holding less than the $1-million threshold, and to extend financial assistance to these customers. Principal among these Dealers are National Bank and Canaccord, two of the respondent financial institutions the appellants most object to releasing. The application judge found that these developments appeared to be designed to secure votes in favour of the Plan by various Noteholders, and were apparently successful in doing so. If the Plan is approved, they also provide considerable relief to the many small investors who find themselves unwittingly caught in the ABDP collapse.

b) The Releases

[28] This appeal focuses on one specific aspect of the Plan: the comprehensive series of releases of third parties provided for in Article 10.

[29] The Plan calls for the release of Canadian banks, Dealers, Noteholders, Asset Providers, Issuer Trustees, Liquidity Providers, and other market participants — in Mr. Crawford's words, "virtually all participants in the Canadian ABCP market" — from any liability associated with ABCP, with the exception of certain narrow claims relating to fraud. For instance, under the Plan as approved, creditors will have to give up their claims against the Dealers who sold them their ABCP Notes, including challenges to the way the Dealers characterized the ABCP and provided (or did not provide) information about the ABCP. The claims against the proposed defendants are mainly in tort: negligence, misrepresentation, negligent misrepresentation, failure to act prudently as a dealer/advisor, acting in conflict of interest, and in a few cases fraud or potential fraud. There are also allegations of breach of fiduciary duty and claims for other equitable relief.

[30] The application judge found that, in general, the claims for damages include the face value of the Notes, plus interest and additional penalties and damages.

[31] The releases, in effect, are part of a *quid pro quo*. Generally speaking, they are designed to compensate various participants in the market for the contributions they would make to the restructuring. Those contributions under the Plan include the requirements that:

a) Asset Providers assume an increased risk in their credit default swap contracts, disclose certain proprietary information in relation to the assets, and provide below-cost financing for margin funding facilities that are designed to make the notes more secure;

b) Sponsors — who in addition have cooperated with the Investors' Committee throughout the process, including by sharing certain proprietary information — give up their existing contracts;

c) The Canadian banks provide below-cost financing for the margin funding facility and,

d) Other parties make other contributions under the Plan.

[32] According to Mr. Crawford's affidavit, the releases are part of the Plan "because certain key participants, whose participation is vital to the restructuring, have made comprehensive releases a condition for their participation."

The CCAA Proceedings to Date

[33] On March 17, 2008 the applicants sought and obtained an Initial Order under the CCAA staying any proceedings relating to the ABCP crisis and providing for a meeting of the Noteholders to vote on the proposed Plan. The meeting was held on April 25th. The vote was overwhelmingly in support of the Plan — 96% of the Noteholders voted in favour. At the instance of certain Noteholders, and as requested by the application judge (who has supervised the proceedings from the outset), the Monitor broke down the voting results according to those Noteholders who had worked on or with the Investors' Committee to develop the Plan and those Noteholders who had not. Re-calculated on this basis the results remained firmly in favour of the proposed Plan — 99% of those connected with the development of the Plan voted positively, as did 80% of those Noteholders who had not been involved in its formulation.

[34] The vote thus provided the Plan with the "double majority" approval — a majority of creditors representing two-thirds in value of the claims — required under s. 6 of the CCAA.

[35] Following the successful vote, the applicants sought court approval of the Plan under s. 6. Hearings were held on May 12 and 13. On May 16, the application judge issued a brief endorsement in which he concluded that he did not have sufficient facts to decide whether all the releases proposed in the Plan were authorized by the CCAA. While the application judge was prepared to approve the releases of negligence claims, he was not prepared at that point to sanction the release of fraud claims. Noting the urgency of the situation and the serious consequences that would result from the Plan's failure, the application judge nevertheless directed the parties back to the bargaining table to try to work out a claims process for addressing legitimate claims of fraud.

[36] The result of this renegotiation was a "fraud carve-out" — an amendment to the Plan excluding certain fraud claims from the Plan's releases. The carve-out did not encompass all possible claims of fraud, however. It was limited in three key respects. First, it applied only to claims against ABCP Dealers. Secondly, it applied only to cases involving an express fraudulent misrepresentation made with the intention to induce purchase and in circumstances where the person making the representation knew it to be false. Thirdly, the carve-out limited available damages to the value of the notes, minus any funds distributed as part of the Plan. The appellants argue vigorously that such a limited release respecting fraud claims is unacceptable and should not have been sanctioned by the application judge.

[37] A second sanction hearing — this time involving the amended Plan (with the fraud carve-out) — was held on June 3, 2008. Two days later, Campbell J released his reasons for decision, approving and sanctioning the Plan on the basis both that he had jurisdiction to sanction a Plan calling for third-party releases and that the Plan including the third-party releases in question here was fair and reasonable.

[38] The appellants attack both of these determinations.

C. LAW AND ANALYSIS

[39] There are two principal questions for determination on this appeal:

1) As a matter of law, may a CCAA plan contain a release of claims against anyone other than the debtor company or its directors?
2) If the answer to that question is yes, did the application judge err in the exercise of his discretion to sanction the Plan as fair and reasonable given the nature of the releases called for under it?

(1) Legal Authority for the Releases

[40] The standard of review on this first issue—whether, as a matter of law, a CCAA plan may contain third-party releases—is correctness.

[41] The appellants submit that a court has no jurisdiction or legal authority under the CCAA to sanction a plan that imposes an obligation on creditors to give releases to third parties other than the directors of the debtor company. The requirement that objecting creditors release claims against third parties is illegal, they contend, because:

a) on a proper interpretation, the CCAA does not permit such releases;
b) the court is not entitled to "fill in the gaps" in the CCAA or rely upon its inherent jurisdiction to create such authority because to do so would be contrary to the principle that Parliament did not intend to interfere with private property rights or rights of action in the absence of clear statutory language to that effect;
c) the releases constitute an unconstitutional confiscation of private property that is within the exclusive domain of the provinces under s. 92 of the *Constitution Act, 1867*;
d) the releases are invalid under Quebec rules of public order; and because
e) the prevailing jurisprudence supports these conclusions.

[42] I would not give effect to any of these submissions....

[43] On a proper interpretation, in my view, the CCAA permits the inclusion of third party releases in a plan of compromise or arrangement to be sanctioned by the court where those releases are reasonably connected to the proposed restructuring. I am led to this conclusion by a combination of (a) the open-ended, flexible character of the CCAA itself, (b) the broad nature of the term "compromise or arrangement" as used in the Act, and (c) the express statutory effect of the "double-majority" vote and court sanction which render the plan binding on all creditors, including those unwilling to accept certain portions of it. The first of these signals a flexible approach to the application of the Act in new and evolving situations, an active judicial role in its application and interpretation, and a liberal approach to that interpretation. The second provides the entrée to negotiations between the parties affected in the restructuring and furnishes them with the ability to apply the broad scope of their ingenuity in fashioning the proposal. The latter afford necessary protection to unwilling creditors who may be deprived of certain of their civil and property rights as a result of the process.

[44] The CCAA is skeletal in nature. It does not contain a comprehensive code that lays out all that is permitted or barred. Judges must therefore play a role in fleshing out the details of the statutory scheme. The scope of the Act and the powers of the court under it are not limitless. It is beyond controversy, however, that the CCAA is remedial legislation to be liberally construed in accordance with the modern purposive approach to statutory interpretation. It is designed to be a flexible instrument and it is that very flexibility which gives the Act its efficacy: *Canadian Red Cross Society (Re)* (1998), 5 C.B.R. (4th) 299 (Ont. Gen. Div.). As Farley J noted in *Re Dylex Ltd* (1995), 31 C.B.R. (3d) 106

at 111 (Ont. Gen. Div.), "[t]he history of CCAA law has been an evolution of judicial inter-pretation." . . .

[53] An interpretation of the CCAA that recognizes its broader socio-economic pur-poses and objects is apt in this case. As the application judge pointed out, the restructur-ing underpins the financial viability of the Canadian ABCP market itself.

[54] The appellants argue that the application judge erred in taking this approach and in treating the Plan and the proceedings as an attempt to restructure a financial market (the ABCP market) rather than simply the affairs between the debtor corpora-tions who caused the ABCP Notes to be issued and their creditors. The Act is designed, they say, only to effect reorganizations between a corporate debtor and its creditors and not to attempt to restructure entire marketplaces.

[55] This perspective is flawed in at least two respects, however, in my opinion. First, it reflects a view of the purpose and objects of the CCAA that is too narrow. Secondly, it overlooks the reality of the ABCP marketplace and the context of the restructuring in question here. It may be true that, in their capacity as ABCP *Dealers*, the releasee financial institutions are "third-parties" to the restructuring in the sense that they are not creditors of the debtor corporations. However, in their capacities as *Asset Providers* and *Liquidity Providers*, they are not only creditors but they are prior secured creditors to the Notehold-ers. Furthermore—as the application judge found—in these latter capacities they are making significant contributions to the restructuring by "foregoing immediate rights to assets and . . . providing real and tangible input for the preservation and enhancement of the Notes" (para. 76). In this context, therefore, the application judge's remark at para. 50 that the restructuring "involves the commitment and participation of all parties" in the ABCP market makes sense, as do his earlier comments at paras. 48–49:

> Given the nature of the ABCP market and all of its participants, it is more appropriate to consider all Noteholders as claimants and the object of the Plan to restore liquidity to the assets being the Notes themselves. The restoration of the liquidity of the market necessi-tates the participation (including more tangible contribution by many) of all Noteholders.
>
> In these circumstances, *it is unduly technical to classify the Issuer Trustees as debtors and the claims of the Noteholders as between themselves and others as being those of third party creditors,* although I recognize that the restructuring structure of the CCAA requires the corporations as the vehicles for restructuring. [Emphasis added.]

. . .

[60] While there may be little practical distinction between "compromise" and "arrange-ment" in many respects, the two are not necessarily the same. "Arrangement" is broader than "compromise" and would appear to include any scheme for reorganizing the affairs of the debtor: Houlden & Morawetz, *Bankruptcy and Insolvency Law of Canada,* loose-leaf, 3rd ed., vol. 4 (Toronto: Thomson Carswell) at 10A-12.2, N§10. It has been said to be "a very wide and indefinite [word]": *Re Refund of Dues under Timber Regulations,* [1935] A.C. 184 at 197 (P.C.), affirming S.C.C. [1933] S.C.R. 616. See also, *Re Guardian Assur Co,* [1917] 1 Ch. 431 at 448, 450; *Re T&N Ltd and Others (No. 3),* [2007] 1 All E.R. 851 (Ch.).

[61] The CCAA is a sketch, an outline, a supporting framework for the resolution of corporate insolvencies in the public interest. Parliament wisely avoided attempting to anticipate the myriad of business deals that could evolve from the fertile and creative minds of negotiators restructuring their financial affairs. It left the shape and details of those deals to be worked out within the framework of the comprehensive and flexible concepts of a "compromise" and "arrangement." I see no reason why a release in favour

of a third party, negotiated as part of a package between a debtor and creditor and reasonably relating to the proposed restructuring cannot fall within that framework.

[62] A proposal under the *Bankruptcy and Insolvency Act*, RS, 1985, c. B-3 (the "BIA") is a contract: *Employers' Liability Assurance Corp Ltd v Ideal Petroleum (1959) Ltd.* [1978] 1 S.C.R. 230 at 239; *Society of Composers, Authors & Music Publishers of Canada v Armitage* (2000), 50 O.R. (3d) 688 at para. 11 (C.A.). In my view, a compromise or arrangement under the CCAA is directly analogous to a proposal for these purposes, and therefore is to be treated as a contract between the debtor and its creditors. Consequently, parties are entitled to put anything into such a plan that could lawfully be incorporated into any contract. See *Re Air Canada* (2004), 2 C.B.R. (5th) 4 at para. 6 (Ont. S.C.J.); *Olympia & York Developments Ltd v Royal Trust Co* (1993), 12 O.R. (3d) 500 at 518 (Gen. Div.).

[63] There is nothing to prevent a debtor and a creditor from including in a contract between them a term providing that the creditor release a third party. The term is binding as between the debtor and creditor. In the CCAA context, therefore, a plan of compromise or arrangement may propose that creditors agree to compromise claims against the debtor and to release third parties, just as any debtor and creditor might agree to such a term in a contract between them. Once the statutory mechanism regarding voter approval and court sanctioning has been complied with, the plan—including the provision for releases—becomes binding on all creditors (including the dissenting minority)....

[68] Parliament's reliance on the expansive terms "compromise" or "arrangement" does not stand alone, however. Effective insolvency restructurings would not be possible without a statutory mechanism to bind an unwilling minority of creditors. Unanimity is frequently impossible in such situations. But the minority must be protected too. Parliament's solution to this quandary was to permit a wide range of proposals to be negotiated and put forward (the compromise or arrangement) and to bind *all* creditors by class to the terms of the plan, but to do so only where the proposal can gain the support of the requisite "double majority" of votes ["A majority is two-thirds of the value of the creditors (s 6)"] *and* obtain the sanction of the court on the basis that it is fair and reasonable. In this way, the scheme of the CCAA supports the intention of Parliament to encourage a wide variety of solutions to corporate insolvencies without unjustifiably overriding the rights of dissenting creditors....

[69] In keeping with this scheme and purpose, I do not suggest that any and all releases between creditors of the debtor company seeking to restructure and third parties may be made the subject of a compromise or arrangement between the debtor and its creditors. Nor do I think the fact that the releases may be "necessary" in the sense that the third parties or the debtor may refuse to proceed without them, of itself, advances the argument in favour of finding jurisdiction (although it may well be relevant in terms of the fairness and reasonableness analysis).

[70] The release of the claim in question must be justified as part of the compromise or arrangement between the debtor and its creditors. In short, there must be a reasonable connection between the third party claim being compromised in the plan and the restructuring achieved by the plan to warrant inclusion of the third party release in the plan. This nexus exists here, in my view.

[71] In the course of his reasons, the application judge made the following findings, all of which are amply supported on the record:

a) The parties to be released are necessary and essential to the restructuring of the debtor;

b) *The claims to be released are rationally related to the purpose of the Plan and necessary for it;*

c) The Plan cannot succeed without the releases;

d) *The parties who are to have claims against them released are contributing in a tangible and realistic way to the Plan;* and

e) The Plan will benefit not only the debtor companies but creditor Noteholders generally.

[72] Here, then ... there is a close connection between the claims being released and the restructuring proposal. The tort claims arise out of the sale and distribution of the ABCP Notes and their collapse in value, just as do the contractual claims of the creditors against the debtor companies. The purpose of the restructuring is to stabilize and shore up the value of those notes in the long run. The third parties being released are making separate contributions to enable those results to materialize. Those contributions are identified earlier, at para. 31 of these reasons. The application judge found that the claims being released are not independent of or unrelated to the claims that the Noteholders have against the debtor companies; they are closely connected to the value of the ABCP Notes and are required for the Plan to succeed. At paras. 76–77 he said:

> [76] I do not consider that the Plan in this case involves a change in relationship among creditors "that does not directly involve the Company." Those who support the Plan and are to be released are "directly involved in the Company" in the sense that many are foregoing immediate rights to assets and are providing real and tangible input for the preservation and enhancement of the Notes. It would be unduly restrictive to suggest that the moving parties' claims against released parties do not involve the Company, since the claims are directly related to the value of the Notes. The value of the Notes is in this case the value of the Company.
>
> [77] This Plan, as it deals with releases, doesn't change the relationship of the creditors apart from involving the Company and its Notes.

[73] I am satisfied that the wording of the CCAA—construed in light of the purpose, objects and scheme of the Act and in accordance with the modern principles of statutory interpretation—supports the court's jurisdiction and authority to sanction the Plan. ...

(2) The Plan Is "Fair and Reasonable"

[106] The second major attack on the application judge's decision is that he erred in finding that the Plan is "fair and reasonable" and in sanctioning it on that basis. This attack is centred on the nature of the third-party releases contemplated and, in particular, on the fact that they will permit the release of some claims based in fraud.

[107] Whether a plan of compromise or arrangement is fair and reasonable is a matter of mixed fact and law, and one on which the application judge exercises a large measure of discretion. The standard of review on this issue is therefore one of deference. In the absence of a demonstrable error an appellate court will not interfere: see *Re Ravelston Corp Ltd* (2007), 31 C.B.R. (5th) 233 (Ont. C.A.).

[108] I would not interfere with the application judge's decision in this regard. While the notion of releases in favour of third parties—including leading Canadian financial institutions—that extend to claims of fraud is distasteful, there is no legal impediment to the inclusion of a release for claims based in fraud in a plan of compromise or arrangement. The application judge had been living with and supervising the ABCP restructuring from its outset. He was intimately attuned to its dynamics. In the end he concluded that the benefits of the Plan to the creditors as a whole, and to the debtor

companies, outweighed the negative aspects of compelling the unwilling appellants to execute the releases as finally put forward.

[109] The application judge was concerned about the inclusion of fraud in the contemplated releases and at the May hearing adjourned the final disposition of the sanctioning hearing in an effort to encourage the parties to negotiate a resolution. The result was the "fraud carve-out" referred to earlier in these reasons.

[110] The appellants argue that the fraud carve-out is inadequate because of its narrow scope. It (i) applies only to ABCP Dealers, (ii) limits the type of damages that may be claimed (no punitive damages, for example), (iii) defines "fraud" narrowly, excluding many rights that would be protected by common law, equity and the Quebec concept of public order, and (iv) limits claims to representations made directly to Noteholders. The appellants submit it is contrary to public policy to sanction a plan containing such a limited restriction on the type of fraud claims that may be pursued against the third parties.

[111] The law does not condone fraud. It is the most serious kind of civil claim. There is therefore some force to the appellants' submission. On the other hand, as noted, there is no legal impediment to granting the release of an antecedent claim in fraud, provided the claim is in the contemplation of the parties to the release at the time it is given: *Fotinis Restaurant Corp v White Spot Ltd* (1998), 38 B.L.R. (2d) 251 at paras. 9 and 18 (B.C.S.C.). There may be disputes about the scope or extent of what is released, but parties are entitled to settle allegations of fraud in civil proceedings — the claims here all being untested allegations of fraud — and to include releases of such claims as part of that settlement.

[112] The application judge was alive to the merits of the appellants' submissions. He was satisfied in the end, however, that the need "to avoid the potential cascade of litigation that . . . would result if a broader 'carve out' were to be allowed" (para. 113) outweighed the negative aspects of approving releases with the narrower carve-out provision. Implementation of the Plan, in his view, would work to the overall greater benefit of the Noteholders as a whole. I can find no error in principle in the exercise of his discretion in arriving at this decision. It was his call to make. . . .

[115] The appellants all contend that the obligation to release the third parties from claims in fraud, tort, breach of fiduciary duty, etc. is confiscatory and amounts to a requirement that they — as individual creditors — make the equivalent of a greater financial contribution to the Plan. In his usual lively fashion, Mr. Sternberg asked us the same rhetorical question he posed to the application judge. As he put it, how could the court countenance the compromise of what in the future might turn out to be fraud perpetrated at the highest levels of Canadian and foreign banks? Several appellants complain that the proposed Plan is unfair to them because they will make very little additional recovery if the Plan goes forward, but will be required to forfeit a cause of action against third-party financial institutions that may yield them significant recovery. Others protest that they are being treated unequally because they are ineligible for relief programs that Liquidity Providers such as Canaccord have made available to other smaller investors.

[116] All of these arguments are persuasive to varying degrees when considered in isolation. The application judge did not have that luxury, however. He was required to consider the circumstances of the restructuring as a whole, including the reality that many of the financial institutions were not only acting as Dealers or brokers of the ABCP Notes (with the impugned releases relating to the financial institutions in these capacities, for the most part) but also as Asset and Liquidity Providers (with the financial institutions making significant contributions to the restructuring in these capacities).

[117] In insolvency restructuring proceedings almost everyone loses something. To the extent that creditors are required to compromise their claims, it can always be proclaimed that their rights are being unfairly confiscated and that they are being called upon to make the equivalent of a further financial contribution to the compromise or arrangement. Judges have observed on a number of occasions that CCAA proceedings involve "a balancing of prejudices," inasmuch as everyone is adversely affected in some fashion.

[118] Here, the debtor corporations being restructured represent the issuers of the more than $32 billion in non-bank sponsored ABCP Notes. The proposed compromise and arrangement affects that entire segment of the ABCP market and the financial markets as a whole. In that respect, the application judge was correct in adverting to the importance of the restructuring to the resolution of the ABCP liquidity crisis and to the need to restore confidence in the financial system in Canada. He was required to consider and balance the interests of all Noteholders, not just the interests of the appellants, whose notes represent only about 3% of that total. That is what he did.

[119] The application judge noted at para. 126 that the Plan represented "a reasonable balance between benefit to all Noteholders and enhanced recovery for those who can make out specific claims in fraud" within the fraud carve-out provisions of the releases. He also recognized at para. 134 that:

> No Plan of this size and complexity could be expected to satisfy all affected by it. The size of the majority who have approved it is testament to its overall fairness. No plan to address a crisis of this magnitude can work perfect equity among all stakeholders.

[120] In my view we ought not to interfere with his decision that the Plan is fair and reasonable in all the circumstances.

Appeal dismissed.

Practice Questions

Question 1

Assume a restructuring with the following groups of creditors: secured creditors, lessors, tort claimants, banks holding unsecured credit card debt, trade creditors, and customers entitled to a refund. How would you classify these creditors? What factor(s) would you consider in your classification scheme?

Question 2

The plan below applies to the unsecured creditors class. How might a court deal with the following proposal for a plan? What are the important considerations?

a) Creditors holding debt of $10,000 or less to receive cash of 90 percent of the proven claim;
b) Creditors holding debt of $10,001 to $75,000 to receive cash of 80 percent of the first $10,000 and 60 percent of balance; and
c) Creditors holding debt of in excess of $75,000 to receive shares on a formula basis (subject to creditor agreeing to limit claims to $75,000 so as to obtain cash as per the previous formula).

Question 3

Daddy Shark Enterprises (Daddy Shark) purchased shares of TDL Ltd (TDL) on the Toronto Stock Exchange. Five days later, Daddy Shark undertook a hostile takeover bid of TDL, through which it sought to acquire all issued and outstanding shares. Daddy Shark paid the TDL shareholders by way of a share exchange: it exchanged TDL shares for Daddy Shark shares. It also acquired shares by exchanging Daddy Shark treasury shares for TDL shares. Daddy Shark acquired control of TDL, and it is now the sole shareholder.

After the takeover, Daddy Shark caused TDL to apply for protection under the *CCAA*. In making its decision to embark on a takeover, Daddy Shark maintains that it relied on publicly disclosed information provided by TDL. Once the takeover was complete, Daddy Shark says that it discovered that the information was misleading, and that TDL shares were essentially without value. Daddy Shark has claimed as an unsecured creditor in the restructuring, for $175 million. The claim consists of the price of shares Daddy Shark acquired for cash, the share exchange loss, and the transaction costs of the takeover.

Is Daddy Shark claiming as an unsecured creditor, thereby ranking equally with the other unsecured creditors, or is it claiming as a shareholder, thereby ranking after the unsecured creditors of TDL?

PART IV

Insolvency Proposals

CHAPTER 16

Proposals Under the *BIA*

I. INTRODUCTION

This chapter examines the two restructuring processes contained in the *Bankruptcy and Insolvency Act*, RSC 1985, c B-3 (*BIA*). These are Division I, or commercial proposals, and Division II, or consumer proposals. This chapter will describe the history of restructuring proceedings in the *BIA* and explain the key features of the two types of proposals. Commercial proposals can be used by corporations, other business entities, or individuals. Part III of this chapter describes key features of the commercial proposal provisions by highlighting the similarities and differences between commercial proposals and *Companies' Creditors Arrangement Act*, RSC 1985, c C-36 (*CCAA*) proceedings. This approach builds on the material covered in chapters 12–15 and helps explain why a business may choose to restructure using a commercial proposal rather than the *CCAA* or vice versa. A consumer proposal can only be made by an individual with a limited amount of debt (see Part IV(B) on eligibility below). Part IV of this chapter describes key features of the consumer proposal process by contrasting them with the commercial proposal process, thereby helping to explain why an individual may prefer one to the other.

Commercial and consumer proposals are both restructuring regimes, as contrasted with the bankruptcy liquidation regime. Recall that in bankruptcy, all of the debtor's non-exempt property is transferred to the trustee, in exchange for which the debtor may be able to discharge its debts. In a proposal process, the debtor makes an offer to its creditors with respect to the debts the debtor owes. The offer can take many different forms. Often the debtor offers to repay a portion of their debts. The debtor might offer to repay all of the debt, but over a longer period of time than was originally agreed to. Alternatively, where the debtor is a corporation, it may offer the creditors shares in the corporation in lieu of paying its debts. If the proposal becomes binding and the debtor fulfills the terms, it will have some or all of its debts forgiven as contemplated in the proposal. For example, imagine the debtor offers to repay 60 percent of the debt owed to each creditor; once it makes those payments, the remaining 40 percent of the debt is released.

Commercial and consumer proposals are built on a model similar to *CCAA* proceedings: a debtor makes a proposal to its creditors, the creditors vote on the proposal, and a court evaluates the proposal. If a sufficient number of creditors vote in favour of the proposal and a court approves it, it becomes binding on all the creditors to whom the proposal was made. In other words, creditors can be bound by a proposal even if they did not vote for it.

II. HISTORY OF THE PROPOSAL PROVISIONS

The *Bankruptcy Act, 1919*[1] contained skeletal provisions, copied from the British *Bankruptcy Act*,[2] enabling insolvent debtors, not restricted to particular types of debtors, to make a proposal to their creditors for the payment of their debts and thereby avoid bankruptcy. However, the 1919 Act's commitment to a rescue philosophy was weak for the following reasons: (1) a proposal could only be made to unsecured creditors; (2) no interim period was allowed between initiating the proceedings and filing the proposal; and (3) filing the proposal did not entitle the debtor to repudiate executory contracts or preclude creditors from terminating their contracts with the debtor. Not surprisingly, therefore, proposals did not play an important role in Canada's bankruptcy regime in the interwar period, as the law did not enable a workout unless most of the major creditors of a debtor were willing to cooperate in devising a going-forward financial arrangement with the debtor.

In the post-World War II period, there was a strong revival of interest in strengthening the restructuring options available to insolvent debtors. The Tassé Report,[3] discussed in chapters 1 and 2, contained ambitious recommendations for recasting the proposal provisions and replacing the *CCAA*. These recommendations were incorporated in varying forms in successive bills introduced in Parliament between 1975 and 1984. However, none of the bills was enacted—for reasons that had less to do with the merits of the bills than with lack of political will by successive governments to secure the bills' adoption. To resolve the deadlock, the 1984 Colter Committee (see Chapter 1) was given the mandate to recommend changes to the bankruptcy regime that they deemed to be most urgent.

The Colter Committee's 1986 Report[4] singled out commercial and consumer proposals as two of the areas deserving prompt remedial action. As far as commercial proposals were concerned, the report recommended the following changes: (1) the debtor should be allowed an interim period to give notice of intention to file a proposal before having to file the proposal itself; (2) proposals should be allowed to target secured as well as unsecured creditors, thereby also giving the debtor the protection of a stay of proceedings against secured as well as unsecured creditors; and (3) the debtor should be allowed to disclaim executory contracts and realty leases, and third parties should be restrained from terminating contracts that were important for the debtor's economic survival. The report also recommended that consumer debtors should be provided with an expedited restructuring process. The Colter Committee recommendations involving proposals were adopted in the *BIA* 1992 amendments.

Commercial proposals have proved popular with debtors from the beginning of the new regime. Their number increased steadily between 1993 and 2002, from 1,005 to 1,911 respectively, and from 7.9 percent of the number of business filings in 1993 to 18.3 percent in 2002. Their use decreased over the following years as the Canadian economy boomed and the number of distressed businesses declined. Another rise occurred during the height of the 2008–10 global financial crisis, leveling off in recent years. From 2007 to 2012, business proposals as a percentage of all business insolvency filings increased from 17.3 percent to

---

1   *Bankruptcy Act*, SC 1919, c 36.

2   *Bankruptcy Act, 1914*, 4 & 5 Geo 5, c 59.

3   Canada, Study Committee on Bankruptcy and Insolvency Legislation, *Report of the Study Committee on Bankruptcy and Insolvency Legislation* (Ottawa: Information Canada, 1970) (Chair: Roger Tassé) [Tassé Report].

4   Advisory Committee on Bankruptcy and Insolvency, *Proposed Bankruptcy Act Amendments: Report of the Advisory Committee on Bankruptcy and Insolvency* (Ottawa: Supply and Services Canada, 1986).

25.7 percent.[5] In 2018 there were 903 business proposals, compared with 2,677 business bankruptcies, together involving $7.6 billion in debt.[6] Yet it is important to note that a number of proposals are not successfully completed and the business is ultimately liquidated either through bankruptcy or receivership.

Consumer debtors' initial response to the new consumer proposal option was modest. In 1995, only 2,491 filed consumer proposals, but by 2007 this number had grown to 19,486. The increase over this period is partly attributable to the 1997 amendments to the *BIA*, requiring individual bankrupts to make mandatory surplus income payments, and thereby making bankruptcy less attractive for debtors with moderate to good earnings.[7] Another plausible reason is that in 1998 the fee structure in the bankruptcy rules was substantially changed to give trustees a stronger incentive than they had before to recommend consumer proposals to their clients.[8] The 2009 amendments substantially increased the amount of debt a person could have and still qualify as a "consumer debtor," meaning many more individuals could file consumer proposals. By 2017, consumers were more likely to file a proposal (64,229) versus a bankruptcy (57,969) (OSB Annual Statistics, 2018).

Note that the Office of the Superintendent of Bankruptcy uses a different definition than the *BIA* when classifying a proposal as being either a business or consumer proposal. The Office of the Superintendent of Bankruptcy classifies an individual as a consumer if "more than 50% of [their] total liabilities [relate] to consumer goods and services"; a business is "any commercial entity or organization other than an individual, or an individual who has incurred 50% or more of total liabilities as a result of operating a business."[9]

III. COMMERCIAL PROPOSALS

A. Introduction

Any person, including a corporation or a natural (i.e., "flesh and blood") person can be the subject of a commercial proposal, as long as they are either insolvent or bankrupt (*BIA*, s 50(1)). Businesses that do not have sufficient debt to qualify for restructuring under the *CCAA* can restructure using a commercial proposal (see Chapter 12). A business that qualifies to restructure under the *CCAA* may still opt to restructure using a commercial proposal, because it views the process as being more rule driven, and consequently less uncertain and less expensive (see the discussion in Chapter 12 comparing the *CCAA* and commercial proposals).

---

5 Industry Canada, "Statutory Review of the *Bankruptcy and Insolvency Act* and *Companies' Creditors Arrangement Act*" (2014), online: www.ic.gc.ca/eic/site/cilp-pdci.nsf/eng/h_cl00870.html.

6 Office of the Superintendent of Bankruptcy (OSB), *Insolvency Statistics in Canada—2018* (Ottawa: Office of the Superintendent of Bankruptcy, 2019), online: www.ic.gc.ca/eic/site/bsf-osb.nsf/eng/br04047.html [OSB, Annual Statistics, 2018].

7 Thomas Telfer, "Access to Discharge in Canadian Bankruptcy Law and the New Role of Surplus Income: A Historical Perspective" in Charles Rickett & Thomas Teller, eds, *International Perspectives on Consumer Access to Justice* (Cambridge, UK: Cambridge University Press, 2003) 231.

8 Iain Ramsay, "Market Imperatives, Professional Discretion and the Role of Intermediaries in Consumer Bankruptcy: A Comparative Study of the Canadian Trustee in Bankruptcy" (2000) 74 *American Bankruptcy Law Journal* 399.

9 OSB, Annual Statistics, 2018, above note 6.

The amendments in 2009 sought to harmonize the *CCAA* and commercial proposal regimes. Consequently, many of the provisions that relate to commercial proposals have equivalents in the *CCAA* and have already been discussed earlier in this text. See the table below:

Topic	*BIA* Commercial Proposals	*CCAA*	Textbook Reference
Interim financing	s 50.6	s 11.2	Chapter 13, Part VI
Requirements regarding pension funds	s 60(1.5)	s 6(6)	Chapter 14, Part IV
Removal and replacement of directors	s 64	s 11.5	Chapter 13, Part III
Director's charge	s 64.1	s 11.51	Chapter 13, Part III
Administrative charge	s 64.2	s 11.52	
Ipso facto, acceleration and forfeiture clauses	s 65.1	s 34	Chapter 13, Part IV
Resiliation or disclaimer of agreements	s 65.11	s 32	Chapter 13, Part IV
Eligible financial contract definition	s 2, Eligible Financial Contract General Rules (*BIA*)	s 2, Eligible Financial Contract General Rules (*CCAA*)	Chapter 13, Part V
Assignment of contracts	s 66, 84.1	s 11.3	Chapter 13, Part IV
Collective agreement and notice of bargaining	s 65.12	s 33	Chapter 13, Part IV
Disposition of assets outside of ordinary course of business	s 65.13	s 36	Chapter 13, Part VIII
Subordination of equity claims	s 54.1	s 22.1	Chapter 15, Part V
Compromise of "non-dischargeable" debts	s 62(2.1)	s 19(2)	

The statutory provisions added to the commercial proposal provisions of the *BIA* in 2009 differ from those added to the *CCAA* in 2009 in two major respects. First, the critical supplier provisions that are found in section 11.4 of the *CCAA*, discussed in Chapter 13, Part VII, have no counterpart in the *BIA*. Second, the *BIA* commercial proposal provisions have no equivalent to section 11 of the *CCAA*, which permits a court to make any order that it considers appropriate in the circumstances subject to the restrictions set out in the *CCAA*.

There are other differences between the commercial proposals and *CCAA* proceedings, including:

- The process for commencing proceedings,
- The requirement for performance security,
- The rules around disclaiming or resiliating a commercial lease, and
- The effect of the proposal failing or being annulled.

B. Commencing a Commercial Proposal

Recall that to commence proceedings under the *CCAA*, a party must apply to the court for an Initial Order. The Initial Order will set out the scope of the stay. A court application is not required to commence proceedings under the commercial proposal provisions.

Jacob S Ziegel & Rajvinder S Sahni, "An Empirical Investigation of Corporate Division 1 Proposals in the Toronto Bankruptcy Region" (2003) 41 *Osgoode Hall Law Journal* 665 at 673–75 (footnotes omitted)

A reorganization can be initiated under the BIA either by the filing of a proposal [*BIA*, s 50(1)] or the filing of a notice of intention (NOI) to file a proposal [*BIA* s 50.4(1)]. Only an insolvent debtor can file a NOI, while a proposal can also be filed by a liquidator, a bankrupt person, the trustee of a bankrupt estate, or a receiver on behalf of secured creditors. In both cases, a stay of proceedings takes effect immediately on the filing of the document and is binding on all secured and unsecured creditors, including [with some exceptions] the Crown. [*BIA* ss 69, 69.1]. [The stay does not operate against a secured creditor who: (1) takes possession of the collateral before the filing of the NOI or proposal; or (2) serves a s 244 enforcement notice more than 10 days before the NOI is filed]. There are no court proceedings at this stage and no creditor's consent is required. Equally important, the debtor company remains in possession and, so far as its resources permit, continues to carry on business as before.

In practice, most corporate debtors prefer to follow the NOI route. However, the Colter Committee was alert to the abuses to which a similar procedure has led under Chapter 11 of the US *Bankruptcy Code*. As a result, the Canadian regime contains the following safeguards to keep debtors on a short leash.

First, the debtor must appoint a trustee who is willing to act as monitor for the creditors' benefit and with whom the debtor must file a projected cash flow statement relating to the business within ten days of the NOI. The trustee in turn must sign a report on the reasonableness of the cash flow statement, which must be filed by the debtor with the official receiver together with the other documents. [*BIA*, s 50.4(2)(b)]. The debtor must also give the trustee full access to its books for the purpose of monitoring the debtor's business and financial affairs. The trustee in turn is obliged to notify creditors of any adverse change in the debtor's financial condition subsequent to the initial filing [*BIA*, s 50.4(7)].

Second, the debtor must file its proposal within thirty days of the NOI [*BIA*, s 50.4(8)]; failure to do so results in an automatic deemed assignment in bankruptcy. The debtor can apply for an extension of time to file the proposal but no extension can run for more than forty-five days at a time. There is no restriction on the number of extensions for which the debtor can apply but they cannot exceed five months in duration from the end of the thirty days following the NOI [*BIA*, s 50.4(9)]. The debtor must also meet some demanding tests before the Court can grant an extension. The Court must be satisfied that (a) the debtor is acting in good faith and with due diligence; (b) if given an extension, the debtor "would likely be able to make a viable proposal"; and, (c) "no creditor would be materially prejudiced if the extension being applied for were granted" [ibid.].

Third, any creditor is free at any time to apply for termination of the proceedings on the ground that the debtor "will not likely be able to make a proposal ... that will be accepted by the creditors" [*BIA*, s 50.4(11)]. In practice, hostile creditors do not avail themselves of this ground as often as might be expected but seemingly prefer to wait until the creditors' meeting to cast their vote against the proposal.

[Reprint permission requested.]

In the case of *Kocken Energy Systems Inc (Re)*, below, the debtor company applied for an extension of the time for making a proposal, but its main secured creditor opposed the application.

Kocken Energy Systems Inc (Re), 2017 NSSC 80, 50 CBR (6th) 168

MOIR J (orally):

Introduction

[1] Kocken Energy Systems Incorporated filed a notice of intention to make a proposal on December 7, 2016. It moves to extend the deadline for filing the proposal by the maximum allowed under the Bankruptcy and Insolvency Act, forty five days. Its major secured creditor, the Bank of Montreal, opposes the extension. It says that the stay should end and Kocken should be bankrupt. Alternatively, the extension should be no more than thirty days.

Facts

[2] Kocken manufacturers specialized process equipment for the oil and gas industry. The company's predecessor did business in Alberta since about 2005. By 2007, it had just two shareholders, William Famulak and Arthur Sager. In 2011, they decided to move manufacturing to Eastern Canada. In 2015, Kocken acquired a plant at St. Antoine, New Brunswick.

[3] The Bank of Montreal provided financing to purchase the plant as well as current financing. Kocken also had a relationship with the Royal Bank of Canada.

[4] On Tuesday, November 8, 2016 the Bank of Montreal stopped extending current credit. Kocken reverted to the Royal Bank. The Bank of Montreal invited Pricewaterhouse-Coopers to review Kocken's performance and make recommendations. Pricewaterhouse-Coopers prepared, and Bank of Montreal and Kocken endorsed, an engagement letter dated November 14. Mr. David Boyd took charge of the assignment. (I have an affidavit from him.)

[5] PricewaterhouseCoopers studied the St. Antoine plant, read accounting records, and interviewed Kocken operatives until about November 21, 2015. After that, it reported to the Bank of Montreal. The bank issued a notice of intention to enforce security on November 25.

Kocken and Bank of Montreal Breakdown

[6] I have the affidavit of Ms. Anna Graham for the bank. She swears to a debt well over $3 million dollars and security in the St. Antoine plant, personal property, accounts receivable, and inventory. She also swears to these defaults at para 9 of her affidavit:

> Based on the information available to BMO, the Borrower has breached its obligations to BMO including the following: insufficient working capital to meet financial covenants, inability to fund current operations, entering into the Reorganization, as defined in the Boyd Affidavit, failing to provide financial statements and information, ceasing to conduct its banking with BMO and disposing of assets subject to the Security.

[7] In para. 10, Ms. Graham swears that these defaults continue. She adds that Kocken failed to respond to requests for basic information. She offers her opinion that Kocken is deliberately hiding information.

[8] At the heart of Ms. Graham's concerns is the belief that Kocken underwent some kind of reorganization and Kocken assets are being transferred to a related company recently incorporated in Barbados. That company is Kocken Energy Systems International Incorporated.

[9] That this is the fundamental concern underlying the bank's decisions to suspend current financing, to enforce security, and to oppose the proposal is apparent from para 16 of Mr. Boyd's affidavit as well as Ms. Graham's affidavit as a whole.

[10] According to Mr. Sager, Kocken was simply a manufacturer. Most contracts for the sale of manufactured equipment and the intellectual property behind the equipment were with Mr. Famulak independently. Mr. Sager retained Mr. Rick Ormston, an accountant and consultant of Halifax about establishing a company that would be the design and engineering base for Mr. Famulak. That consultation lead to the Barbados company I mentioned, which I shall refer to as Kocken Barbados.

[11] Mr. Ormston developed a plan, the details of which were unknown to the Bank of Montreal or PricewaterhouseCoopers. There are numerous contradictions between Mr. Boyd's affidavit and Mr. Sager's second affidavit, which responded to Mr. Boyd's. The contradictions concern what one said to the other, what Mr. Sager informed Mr. Boyd, and the subjects on which information was withheld or unavailable.

[12] No one was cross-examined and I am in no position to resolve the evidentiary contradictions. The conflicting evidence is therefore unhelpful for making findings. Similarly, Ms. Graham's affidavit contains many generalized opinions without the raw facts required for findings on her subjects. I am, however, satisfied on three points.

[13] Firstly, neither the Bank of Montreal nor PricewaterhouseCoopers knew the details of the Ormston plan. The absence of information left the bank and the insolvency practitioners with serious questions, itemized at para 18 of Mr. Boyd's affidavit. Secondly, these questions were relevant to the bank's interest in Kocken inventory and receivables. Thirdly, the bank and the insolvency practitioners had a rationally founded suspicion that equipment may be transferred to Kocken Barbados without payment, compromising the bank's interest in inventory and receivables.

Recent Developments

[14] In the last three working days, Kocken made some disclosure to the bank and PricewaterhouseCoopers. Most importantly, Kocken delivered a copy of the Ormston plan. It referred to draft documents that had not been disclosed yet, but the bank and the trustee must now know what the plan was really about.

Disposition

[15] Subsection 50.4(9) provides three thresholds that the insolvent must prove before the Court has any discretion to grant an extension:
(a) the insolvent person has acted, and is acting, in good faith and with due diligence;
(b) the insolvent person would likely be able to make a viable proposal if the extension being applied for were granted; and,
(c) no creditor would be materially prejudiced if the extension being applied for were granted.

[16] I am not prepared to embrace the generalized allegations made in Ms. Graham's affidavit because this Court makes findings on evidence of raw fact. Nor can I resolve the evidentiary contradictions between Mr. Sager and Mr. Boyd. What is left suggests good faith and due diligence.

[17] I reject the submission that Kocken's initial evidence failed to disclose material facts. This submission is premised on the PricewaterhouseCoopers characterization of the relationship between Kocken and Kocken Barbados. As I said, the contradictions between the evidence of Mr. Boyd and Mr. Sager are irresolvable at present. The rest of the evidence supports good faith and due diligence.

[18] I am satisfied on the first threshold.

[19] Next is the requirement that a viable proposal is likely to be made.

[20] Ms. Graham swears that the Bank of Montreal "has lost all confidence and trust in current management and ownership". "BMO will not engage in negotiations." She is of the view "that any proposal is doomed to fail". The Bank of Montreal is the primary secured creditor and its support will be necessary when the time comes for a vote.

[21] Such statements by a secured creditor with a veto are not determinative. They are forecasts rather than evidence of present fact. We must not assume intransigence in a world in which misunderstandings occur, they are sometimes corrected, and trust is sometimes restored in whole or in part. Nor may we, in this case, assume that the proposed terms will require a restoration of confidence or trust or a continuing relationship with the Bank of Montreal.

[22] I have some difficulty with the decision of Justice Penny in *NS United Kaiun Kaisha Ltd V Cogent Fibre Inc* 2015 ONSC 5139, which suggests that s 50.4(9)(b) requires at least a hint of what the insolvent will offer to the secured creditor and what the proposal will contain. It is in the nature of proposals that they are developed and, if an extension is needed, the proposal is developing.

[23] The requirement is "would likely be able to make a viable proposal", not "has settled on terms likely to be accepted". I think that is the point made by Justice Goodfellow in *H & H Fisheries Ltd (Re)* 2005 NSSC 346, when he says that s 50.4(9)(b) means "that a reasonable level of effort dictated by the circumstances must have been made that gives some indication of the likelihood a viable proposal will be advanced within the time frame of the extension applied for."

[24] The affidavits prove the cash flow projections, the preparation of other documents or reports, arrangements for appraisals, the trustee's investigation of accounts receivable, and the trustee's opinion that time is required for analysis of revenue and expense. Further, terms for a proposal are being discussed and need more development. In the meantime, Kocken has remained in operation. I am told that one appraisal has been delivered and another is close. All of this has been done over the holiday season. This evidence satisfies me that there is a better than even chance of a viable proposal being developed.

[25] Finally, I have only one reservation about "no creditor would be materially prejudiced". The reservation stems from very strange purchase orders from Kocken Barbados to Kocken with very large prices. They purport to be conditional on resolving issues between Kocken and the Bank of Montreal.

[26] By virtue of its s. 178 security, the bank owns the inventory. The extension would prejudice the bank if it was used to deliver inventory off shore without getting paid first.

[27] I can diminish my concern by exercising my inherent jurisdiction to control this proceeding and the parties to it. I will order that Kocken give four business days' notice to the bank before it ships anything out of Canada and, along with the notice, advise the bank of the amount to be paid and the arrangements for payment. In view of my willingness to make such an order, I find that no creditor will be prejudiced by the order extending time.

[28] I am prepared to extend the period for filing a proposal by the full 45 days, counting from last Thursday.

Motion granted with conditions.

Kocken's creditors, including the Bank of Montreal, eventually voted in favour of the proposal. The court issued written reasons approving the proposal (see *Kocken Energy Systems*

Inc (Re), 2017 NSSC 215). Kocken requested the written reasons because the court's earlier decision (excerpted above) led to unfavourable new reports that injured Kocken's business reputation. With respect to the Bank of Montreal's change of position, the court noted:

> [5] Also, we have here an example of something seldom written about but relevant in early challenges to a reorganization effort. A secured creditor who is able to veto a pro-posal, or a plan of arrangement, vehemently opposes the effort from the beginning and says it is doomed because the creditor will exercise its veto when the time comes. That forecast does not always come true.

C. Performance Security

Recall that in a bankruptcy, there are limits on a debtor's ability to access a discharge. Some debts, set out in *BIA*, section 178, are non-dischargeable. Additionally, if a discharge hearing is triggered, and the court is satisfied that a *BIA*, section 173, fact is present, the court cannot grant an absolute discharge—it must suspend the discharge, attach conditions to it, or refuse it altogether (*BIA*, s 172). These provisions are relevant in the commercial proposal process, too.

A debtor can use the commercial proposal process to discharge a section 178 debt, but only if two criteria are met. The proposal must explicitly contemplate that the debt will be dis-charged and the creditor to whom the debt is owed must vote for the proposal (*BIA*, s 62(2.1)). There is a comparable provision in *CCAA*, section 19(2).

If one of the *BIA*, section 173, facts applies to a debtor making a commercial proposal, the debtor must provide financial security as part of its proposal (*BIA*, s 59(3)). For example, the debtor may grant the trustee a security interest in its assets that the trustee can enforce if the debtor defaults on the proposal. There is no comparable provision in the *CCAA* or the rules governing consumer proposals.

The normal rule is that a debtor must provide financial security equal in value to at least 50 percent of its unsecured claims; however, a court can reduce the value of the financial security required. In the case of *Re Wandler*, 2007 ABQB 153, Topolniski J held that the debtor must provide evidence of why a reduction from 50 percent is warranted, and even if a reduc-tion is warranted, the court does not have the discretion to reduce the performance security to 0 percent. Justice Topolniski also explained why the performance security provision is incorporated into the legislation:

> [26] The s. 59(3) requirement for performance security is designed to further the inter-ests of creditors and the public ... the requirement under s. 59(3) for performance secur-ity applies only in a specified circumstance; where the debtor's situation or past conduct is blameworthy, falling within s. 173.
>
> [27] While s. 173 facts might well lead to a measure of skepticism that the debtor will satisfy his or her obligations under the proposal, they serve primarily as a reflection of public policy. Section 59(3) and s 172(2) both refer to the facts set out in s. 173.
>
> [28] Section 172(2) stipulates that, on proof of any of those facts, the Court shall refuse to discharge the bankrupt, shall suspend the discharge for a period that the Court thinks proper, or shall grant the discharge on condition that the bankrupt perform such acts, pay such moneys, consent to such judgments or comply with such other terms as the Court may direct.
>
> [29] In *Ex parte Reed; In Re Reed, Bowen & Co* [(1886) 17 QBD 244 at 250], Lord Esher M.R. commented on the reason why the English *Bankruptcy Act* of 1883 had been passed, stating:

It was because of the known and proved behaviour of creditors with regard to their insolvent debtors that this Act was passed, taking away from the majority of creditors that power which they had so recklessly and carelessly used, and putting a controlling power into the hands of the Court for the purpose of protecting the creditors against their own recklessness; for the purpose of preventing a majority of creditors from dealing thus recklessly, not only with their own property, but with that of the minority, <u>and of enforcing, so far as the legislature could, a more careful and moral conduct on the part of debtors.</u> [Emphasis added]

[30] In moving in Canada for leave to introduce Bill No 25 in respect of bankruptcy on March 27, 1918, Mr. S.W. Jacobs stated:

At present no distinction whatever is made as between the honest and the dishonest debtor in the matter of obtaining a discharge; they are all thrown into the discard. By this measure it is proposed that the courts shall carefully scrutinize the business dealings and the business relations of traders, and shall make a distinction—shall separate the sheep from the goats. When the Court is of the opinion that a debtor has been obliged to assign through misfortune, he shall be given the necessary relief. *If, on the other hand, it should be found, in scrutinizing his affairs, that he wrecked his own business wilfully, then, of course, he should receive no relief whatever.* That is the crux of every bankruptcy law ... [*Official Debates of the House of Commons of the Dominion of Canada*, 13th Parliament, 1st Session, 8-9 George V, 1918, vol.1, p.206] [Emphasis added.]

[31] That Bill was not passed, but the one which was during the next session of Parliament, and which was the forerunner of the current *BIA*, reflected the same public policy of fostering moral conduct on the part of debtors.

[32] Like the s. 172(2) requirement, the prohibition against approving a proposal where any of the s. 173 facts have been proved against the debtor unless the debtor provides reasonable security for the payment serves to protect not only the interests of creditors but also the public's interest in commercial morality [*Re Gardner* (1921), 1 CBR 421 at para 8 (Ont SC); *Re Stone* (1976), 22 CBR (NS) 152 at para 2 (Ont SC); *Re Silbernagel* (2006), 20 CBR (5th) 155 (Ont Sup Ct J)].

D. Executory Contracts: Commercial Leases

The part of the *BIA* governing commercial proposals contains provisions similar to the *CCAA*, which empowers the debtor to disclaim or resiliate agreements: compare *BIA*, section 65.11, and *CCAA*, section 32, and see Chapter 13. However, the legislation governing commercial proposals contains additional provisions, stipulating a debtor-tenant's powers vis-à-vis a commercial lease. There are no comparable provisions in the *CCAA* governing the disclaimer by debtor-tenants of commercial leases; they would be dealt with under the general provision regarding the disclaimer of executory contracts.

Sections 65.2–65.22 of the *BIA* govern the disclaimer of commercial leases in a commercial proposal, when the debtor is the tenant. The debtor can disclaim or resiliate any lease on thirty days' notice, given between when an NOI is filed and when the proposal is filed or upon filing the proposal. The debtor's proposal must set out how the lessor's claim will be calculated—the proposal can specify either that the lessor can claim the actual losses resulting from the disclaimer of the lease, or an amount equal to the lesser of:

- a full year's worth of rent following the disclaimer AND 15 percent of the rent for the remainder of the lease's term, or
- three years' worth of rent.

The lessor can apply to court to challenge the disclaimer. Such an application must be made within fifteen days of the debtor giving the notice of the disclaimer. A court must set aside a disclaimer unless the debtor can show that its ability to make a viable proposal is contingent on disclaiming the challenged lease and all other leases it has purported to disclaim (*BIA*, s 66.2(2)–(3)).

E. The Effect of the Proposal Failing or Being Annulled

A debtor who restructures under the commercial proposal provisions faces greater jeopardy than a debtor who opts to restructure under the *CCAA* or the consumer proposal provisions. A debtor is deemed to have made an assignment into bankruptcy if any of the following occur during the commercial proposal proceedings:

- The debtor files a notice of intention, but then fails to file the requisite supporting documents (for example, the cash flow statement) (*BIA*, s 50.4(8)).
- The debtor files a notice of intention, and then fails to file a proposal during the thirty-day period or any court-ordered extension (*BIA*, s 50.4(8)).
- A court terminates the proceedings between when the notice of intention and the proposal are filed (*BIA*, s 50.4(11)).
- Prior to the meeting of the creditors, a court deems that the creditors have refused the proposal (*BIA*, ss 50(12)–(12.1)).
- At their meeting, the creditors refuse the proposal (*BIA*, s 57).
- A court refuses to approve the proposal (*BIA*, s 61(2)).
- A court annuls the proposal (*BIA*, s 63(4)). A court can annul a proposal in a number of different situations including if the initial court approval of the proposal was obtained by fraud, the debtor defaults on the terms of the proposal, the proposal cannot continue without injustice or undue delay, or the debtor has committed an offence under the *BIA* (s 63(1), (3)). The case of *North Shore Manor Limited (Re)*, 2013 NLTD(G) 83, 14 CBR (6th) 280 (SC), considers when a court will annul a proposal.

North Shore Manor Limited (Re), 2013 NLTD(G) 83, 14 CBR (6th) 280 (SC)

[The debtor company had filed a notice of intention, and after a number of extensions, made a proposal to its creditors. The proposal contemplated that the debtor would find financing to pay out the existing secured and unsecured creditors by 15 April 2012, or liquidate its assets under the supervision of a trustee. The proposal was accepted by the creditors and approved by the court, but then the debtor defaulted on the terms of the proposal (i.e., was unable to arrange for the necessary financing and did not list its assets for sale). The inspectors granted a number of extensions to allow the debtor to comply with the proposal, but the debtor remained in default. The trustee issued a notice of default and applied under section 63 of the *BIA* to annul the proposal.]

HURLEY J:

[27] According to the wording of section 63.(1), the power to annul a Proposal is discretionary. (*Gavex (Re)* (1989), 77 C.B.R. (N.S.) 102, 18 A.C.W.S. (3d) 387 (B.C.S.C.)). The onus

is on the person applying to annul the Proposal to establish one of the pre-conditions described in section 63.(1) of the BIA (*544553 BC Ltd v Sunshine Coast Mechanical Contractors Inc*, 2000 BCCA 356, 18 C.B.R. (4th) 153).

[28] It is clear from the evidence reviewed at the hearing that the provisions dealing with time limits in carrying out the Proposal have been breached. The Debtor did not comply with the direction to list its assets for sale notwithstanding the generous extensions granted by the Inspectors.

[29] The Trustee submits that the Proposal should also be annulled on the basis of undue delay in carrying out the provisions. This pre-condition set out in section 63.(1) of the *Act* may be of lesser significance in the present case as the Proposal set specific time limits which were extended by the Inspectors. However, the power to annul is discretionary and the presence or absence of delay may be considered even in face of a breach of such time limits. There may be a case where the delay is insignificant or where the delay is not prejudicial to the creditors. Also, in this case the Debtor is requesting an extension to present an amended Proposal to obtaining financing. Therefore, the existence of past delay and the passage of time are considerations in assessing the merits of this request.

[30] The issue of failure to list the Debtor's assets within the time limits aside, the Court is of the opinion the attempt to refinance the Debtor's property has been exhaustively pursued and further delays are not warranted. However, it would seem that the failure to obtain financing cannot be attributed to a lack of effort on the part of the Debtor.

[31] Also, the Court must also consider the issue of prejudice to the creditors in extending the time for the Debtor to present an amended Proposal. As an example of potential prejudice to the creditors, the Court refers to an affidavit on behalf of BDC sworn to on November 17, 2011, opposing extending the time to file the Proposal wherein the following is stated:

> 10. BDC has obtained an appraisal of North Shore Manor, 38 - 60 Main Street, Irish Town, indicating a stressed sale value of $2,500,000.00 — an amounted which would not satisfy the current North Shore debt to BDC. The shortfall increases daily through accruing interest and costs.

Some 17 months later, the potential shortfall has significantly increased.

[32] In review the affidavits before me, in addition to the costs of the Trustee and its counsel, one must consider the value of the time expended by senior persons with the secured creditors and with other creditors. The various creditors are now in favour of annulling the Proposal. They are entitled to an order as requested by the Trustee.

[33] Accordingly, it is hereby ordered that effective today's date April 23, 2013:

1. That the Proposal approved by Order of this Honourable Court made on 1 May, 2012, is hereby annulled.
2. It is further ordered that the Debtor is deemed, pursuant to subsection 63(4) of the *BIA*, to have hereby made an assignment of its property and that the property is vested in PricewaterhouseCoopers Inc., the Trustee.

Application granted.

When a proposal is annulled, a debtor is deemed to have made an assignment into bankruptcy. In cases such as *Re No 289 Taurus Ventures Ltd*, 2000 BCSC 490 and *544553 BC Ltd v Sunshine Coast Mechanical Contractors Inc*, 2000 BCCA 356 (*544553 BC Ltd*), courts have considered whether they can annul the proposal even if there is no evidence that the creditors will fare better in a bankruptcy than in the commercial proposal process. Courts have answered this question in the affirmative. Writing for the British Columbia Court of Appeal in *544553 BC Ltd*, Southin JA reasoned:

> [8] In my view there is no principle of law that a judge may not annul a proposal if there is no prospect of benefit to the creditors. That may be something for him to take into account, but there is no principle of law that if he exercises his discretion under s. 63 to annul the proposal in the absence of evidence of benefit to the creditors that he has committed an error in the exercise of his discretion. The onus lies upon him who applies to annul the proposal to establish one of the pre-conditions of an annulment: a default, or it appears that the proposal cannot continue without injustice or undue delay, or that the approval of the Court was obtained by fraud. But once that pre-condition is established, the Court's discretion is not bound by any principle such as that put forward by the appellants here.

IV. CONSUMER PROPOSALS

A. Introduction

Consumer proposals provide individuals with a restructuring option that may be preferable to either bankruptcy or making a commercial proposal. An insolvent consumer may prefer to make a consumer proposal rather than making an assignment into bankruptcy:

- To avoid the stigma of bankruptcy;
- To protect non-exempt assets that would become part of the estate in a bankruptcy;
- In response to the stricter rules governing discharge from bankruptcy. Debtors with surplus income must wait twenty-one months (first-time bankrupts) or thirty-six months (second-time bankrupts) before being eligible for discharge (*BIA*, s 168.1). During the period between the assignment and the discharge, debtors with surplus income must pay a portion of that income to their trustees (*BIA*, s 68). A debtor with more than $200,000 in personal income tax debt representing 75 percent or more of the debtor's total unsecured debts is not eligible for automatic discharge, and an application for discharge is required (*BIA*, s 172.1);
- Because it is a section 173 fact (i.e., precluding an absolute discharge) for a debtor to make an assignment into bankruptcy if they could have made a viable proposal instead (*BIA*, s 173(1)(n)).

Creditors have their own reasons for supporting alternatives to bankruptcy, such as consumer proposals. To them, bankruptcy sends the wrong message—that it is easy to slough off debts and walk away from one's obligations—whereas the various alternatives to straight bankruptcy involve the debtor making at least partial payments on the debts for a longer period.

In practice, the difference between a bankruptcy and a consumer proposal is more a question of degree and perception than of substance. The reason for this is that, generally, only debtors with surplus income are able to opt for a consumer proposal, and these are the same debtors that would be required to make income contributions in a bankruptcy.

As compared to commercial proposals, consumer proposals are intended to provide an expedited restructuring process for individuals with a limited amount of debt. Consumer proposals differ from commercial proposals in a number of important respects, including:

- the eligibility criteria to commence a consumer proposal,
- the acceptance and approval process,
- the applicability to secured creditors,
- the mandatory counselling requirement, and
- the annulment provisions.

B. Eligibility to Commence a Consumer Proposal

The class of debtors who can make a consumer proposal is more limited as compared to those who can make a commercial proposal. The consumer proposal is intended to provide an expedited restructuring process to individuals with relatively uncomplicated finances. Only a natural (i.e., "flesh and blood") person with less than $250,000 in debt can make a consumer proposal (*BIA*, s 66.11). When calculating whether a person exceeds this threshold amount of debt, one excludes any debt secured against the debtor's principal residence. For example, if a debtor had purchased a home using a mortgage, the mortgage would not count towards the debt threshold. Note that prior to 2009, the debt ceiling for making a consumer proposal was $75,000, and cases decided prior to the 2009 amendments reference this lower amount.

A person called an administrator oversees a consumer proposal. An administrator should not file a consumer proposal for a person whom they know is ineligible (e.g., who has debt in excess of the threshold amount); however, it sometimes does not become evident that a person is ineligible until after the proposal has already been filed. For example, the debtor may have estimated their relevant debt (debt other than a mortgage on the principal residence) as being worth $245,000 but then their creditors may file proofs of claim that total $255,000. Upon becoming aware that the individual was ineligible to file a consumer proposal, an administrator must inform the creditors and the official receiver, but the proposal is not automatically invalidated (*BIA*, s 66.13(4)). If court approval (or deemed approval) has not yet been obtained, the administrator should arrange for an approval hearing and advise the court of the eligibility issue (*Re H and K Ter Mors* (1998), 128 Man R (2d) 23 (QB)). If the proposal has already been approved (or deemed approved) by the court, the administrator does not need to apply to have it re-approved; however a creditor or the official receiver could apply to have it annulled (*Re Jalal*, (2003) 42 CBR (4th) 260 (Ont Sup Ct J) (*Re Jalal*)). In either instance, the court has the discretion to approve or refuse to annul a proposal, even if the debtor was not eligible. In deciding to exercise its discretion, the court will consider if the terms of the proposal are reasonable, if they are fair to the debtor and the creditors, and if the proposal complies with the statutory requirements (which include that the proposal does not exceed five years in length, prioritizes payment of claims that would be accorded priority in bankruptcy, and provides for payment of administrator's fees and distributions to creditors; *Re Jalal*, *ibid* at para 8; *BIA*, s 66.12(5)–(6)).

C. The Acceptance and Approval Process

The consumer proposal process is intended to provide consumer debtors with an expedited acceptance and approval process as compared to the commercial proposal.

Recall that a commercial proposal is overseen by a proposal trustee, who plays a role similar to that of a monitor in a *CCAA* proceeding. The proposal trustee must call a meeting of the creditors, at which the creditors vote on whether or not to accept the proposal. The proposal is accepted if a majority in number and two-thirds in value of the creditors vote in favour of the proposal. If there are multiple classes of creditors, the proposal is only accepted if a majority in number and two-thirds in value of the creditors in each class vote in favour of the proposal (*BIA*, s 54(2)). The proposal trustee must then apply to court to have the proposal approved (*BIA*, s 58).

In a consumer proposal, the administrator is not required to hold a creditors' meeting unless requested to do so, either by the official receiver or by one or more creditors holding at least 25 percent of the debtor's proven claims (*BIA*, s 66.15(2)). If forty-five days pass from the time the proposal is filed and no such request has been made, the creditors are deemed to have accepted the proposal (*BIA*, s 66.18(2)). Even if a meeting is required, the threshold of creditor support required for a consumer proposal to be accepted is lower as compared to a commercial proposal: creditors holding a majority in value of the unsecured claims must vote in favour of a consumer proposal for it to be adopted (*BIA*, ss 66.19, 115). Unlike a commercial proposal, creditors are not divided into different classes in a consumer proposal; instead they vote as one class.

After the creditors have accepted or been deemed to have accepted a proposal, a court must approve a consumer proposal, but this may occur without a hearing. An administrator must arrange for an approval hearing if requested to do so by the official receiver or any interested person within fifteen days following the proposal's acceptance or deemed acceptance. If the requirement to hold a hearing is not triggered, a court is deemed to have approved the proposal (*BIA*, s 66.22).

Unlike a commercial proposal, if the creditors reject the consumer proposal, a court refuses to approve it, or the proposal is later annulled, the debtor does not automatically become bankrupt. In these situations, the stay is lifted and the creditors can enforce their claims against the debtor.

D. Secured Creditors

When a debtor files a Notice of Intention or a commercial proposal, the resulting automatic stay will prevent most secured creditors from enforcing their security (*BIA*, ss 69, 69.1). Additionally, a commercial proposal can be made to the debtor's secured creditors. A secured creditor is bound by the proposal if a majority in number and two-thirds in value of the creditors in a class of secured creditors vote in favour of the proposal (*BIA*, s 62(2)). A proposal can be adopted even if a class of secured creditors vote against it—the proposal would then only be binding on any other classes of secured creditors who accepted the proposal and all the unsecured creditors.

When a debtor files a consumer proposal, the resulting automatic stay does not prevent secured creditors from enforcing their security, unless a court orders otherwise (*BIA*, s 69.2). A consumer proposal must be made to creditors, generally, but is only binding on secured creditors who opt to file a proof of claim in the proceedings (*BIA*, ss 66.28(2), 124–134).

E. Mandatory Counselling

Like individuals who file for bankruptcy, individuals who file a consumer proposal must attend two sessions of financial counselling or they will not be eligible to receive a certificate confirming completion of the proposal (*BIA*, s 66.38). Individuals who file a commercial proposal are not subject to the same requirement.

The concept of credit counselling—teaching consumers how to use credit wisely and how to manage household budgets—has strong roots in Canada, as it has in many Western countries with growing debt problems. In 2005, the United States followed the Canadian model and made credit counselling a *mandatory* part of the consumer bankruptcy process. The following extracts describe the Canadian requirements and provide a preliminary assessment of the effectiveness of the requirement.

Jacob S Ziegel, *Comparative Consumer Insolvency Regimes* (Oxford: Hart Publishing, 2003) at 50–51 (footnotes omitted)

Canada was the first common law jurisdiction to introduce mandatory credit counselling as part of the consumer bankruptcy process. The requirement was first introduced as part of the 1992 amendments to the BIA and was extended in the 1997 amendments to consumer proposals. Failure to comply with the requirement deprives the debtor of the right to an automatic discharge. In addition to the counselling, which only takes place after the assignment or filing of a proposal, the trustee or administrator of a proposal must also complete an assessment of the debtor *before* the assignment or proposal. The assessment requirement arises from an OSB directive and not from the Act. Nevertheless, it is an essential component of the counselling process since the trustee or administrator is obliged to review the debtor's income, assets and liabilities and to advise the debtor of the various options open to him to address his financial problems. The debtor must also be told about the surplus income payment requirements under s 68 if a straight bankruptcy is his choice and, if a proposal is under consideration, the trustee/administrator must satisfy herself that the debtor is in a position to make a viable proposal. A difficulty about the assessment requirement is that the trustee/administrator may not be perceived to be wholly disinterested since the size of their fees will depend on the nature of the debtor's choice.

So far as the statutory counselling is concerned, it has two stages. The first stage must be conducted 10–60 days after the assignment or filing of the proposal; the second stage cannot occur before 30 days following the end of the first session and cannot be later than 120 days after the effective date of the bankruptcy or filing of the consumer proposal. The first counselling session is quite benign and is designed to instruct the debtor in proper money management, spending and shopping habits, and obtaining and using credit. The second counselling session is much more controversial and apparently envisages the counsellor playing the combined role of social worker and psychologist to determine whether there are non-budgetary reasons for the debtor's financial problems. Not surprisingly, many trustees feel uncomfortable filling this role.

Credit counselling has very much become the flavour of the month in all jurisdictions grappling with the problems. of overcommitted debtors. Nevertheless, the lasting value of counselling provided after the damage has been done still has to be proven. There is broad consensus that ideally budgetary management courses should be included in high school curricula but the prospects of this happening on a widespread basis appear slim. Educational authorities in Canada complain that the high school calendar is already too crowded.

[© Jacob Ziegel, 2003, Comparative Consumer Insolvency Regimes, Hart Publishing; used by permission of Bloomsbury Publishing Plc]

Saul Schwartz, "Counselling the Overindebted: A Comparative Perspective" (Ottawa: Office of the Superintendent of Bankruptcy, 2005), online: www.ic.gc.ca/app/oca/crd/dcmnt.do?id= 1860&lang=eng (footnotes omitted)

Based on the observation of a number of first and second counselling sessions and on interviews with several experienced counsellors, it is clear that the sessions are often used primarily to maintain contact with the debtors, to provide rudimentary budget advice and to address questions and issues related to the bankruptcy process that the debtor is experiencing. For example, in one interview, the bankrupt had suffered a nervous breakdown, an event that led, at least indirectly, to his insolvency. In the interview I observed, the bankrupt was clearly having trouble understanding any questions beyond the most simple and straightforward. He knew that his wife was dealing with all the financial affairs of the family and was clearly focused on making sure that he remembered to give the trustee the cheques representing the trustee's fee. The trustee asked several questions about "how things were going" and could draw out only perfunctory answers. Since it was evident that any efforts at financial education would be futile, the trustee quickly ended the session.

Another session with another trustee involved a woman who, while working full-time, had established a small gift shop with financial support of her family. For a time, business was good and the woman and her family prospered. Then two simultaneous events destroyed that prosperity. First, the woman lost her voice, for reasons that have eluded her doctors. She could not work any longer, either on her full-time job or in the gift shop. Second, the SARS crisis hit Toronto and the gift shop failed. When I observed her second counselling session, she could speak only with evident discomfort and in a voice that was barely audible. And even that level of function was an improvement, the result of non-traditional treatment in her native Lebanon. The woman was accompanied by her brother, a Toronto-area financial planner who had been supporting her since her misfortunes had begun some years earlier. In this case, the counsellor first went through the events of the past months to make sure that there had been no material change in the woman's circumstances. The woman had run up substantial credit card debts, before the loss of her voice and the collapse of her business, and the counsellor thought it necessary to remind the bankrupt that it would have been more prudent to have limited the size of her credit card balances, even when times were good, in anticipation of the possibility that times would turn bad. That advice, plus some suggestions that the woman should explore job possibilities that did not require speech, comprised the financial education component of the session.

At the suggestion of the OSB, I interviewed two counsellors—one a trustee and one a counselling specialist—who strongly believe in the efficacy of Canadian bankruptcy counselling.

The trustee supports mandatory counselling despite believing, as do most trustees, that bankruptcy is not often an avoidable consequence of personal irresponsibility or ignorance. Counselling is therefore not necessarily about teaching all bankrupts about prudent financial management. Instead, he believes that counselling provides the opportunity to provide advice that is tailored to individual situations and that can help the debtors with the rehabilitation process, understood as "getting back on their feet" after the bankruptcy. He gave the example of a bankrupt who had been a vice-president in a major bank before losing his job. The trustee said that it was clear that the sort of financial counselling envisioned under the BIA would not be of benefit to this particular bankrupt. Instead, the trustee focused on assuring the bankrupt that even though he had lost his job, he was still a competent individual and would be able to find new work that would be both remunerative and satisfying. In other words, the counselling was not about financial matters but about building the confidence of the bankrupt and helping him rehabilitate himself.

This trustee thought that every bankrupt could benefit from the counselling, as long as the counsellor was sensitive to the needs of the bankrupt. Nonetheless, this trustee was clear that beneficial counselling was the exception rather than the norm under the current system. Nonetheless, he felt that even if only 1 in 10 bankrupts benefited from counselling, the counselling was worthwhile and should be continued. He gave the example of an immigrant who was bankrupt because he really did not understand how the Canadian financial system worked. In that case, the trustee provided the sort of fast-paced course in financial management mentioned above. As a result, the bankrupt was able to re-establish his life and, when the trustee later met him in other contexts, always credited the trustee's advice for his later success. Even if this kind of success is unusual, the trustee believed that it is "worth it."

I asked if trustees should try to identify those who could benefit from counselling and counsel only those who needed it. He was reluctant to move toward such a system, however, because he saw such choices as "too much responsibility" for the trustees.

The second person to whom I was referred by the OSB has been involved in mandatory bankruptcy counselling in Canada since its inception in 1992. In the early days of the system, she toured Canada with Dave Stewart talking to trustees about how the new system would work. She believes passionately in the efficacy of counselling as an educational process and believes that its apparent ineffectiveness could be overcome through a more intense commitment on the part of the insolvency community and by providing better training for counsellors.

Many trustees believe that their clients' bankruptcies are unavoidable because they are caused by events such as unemployment, illness or family disruption. This counsellor believes, however, that prudent financial management would prevent most bankruptcies even when unemployment, illness or family disruption are involved. Her rationale is that prudent financial management demands that individuals and families protect themselves from insolvency either by saving enough to carry them through unemployment, illness or family disruption or by not borrowing when those events are possible. She therefore believes that 90 per cent of bankruptcies would not be necessary if the bankrupts had been financially prudent. Driven by that belief, she provides all bankrupts with extensive information on prudent financial behaviour and believes that many are able to use that information to better manage their personal finances. The information she provides differs in both volume and depth from the information provided by most other trustees.

She also differs from most trustees in how hard she works to discover the cause of bankruptcy. While some trustees might simply scribble "bad management" or "unemployment" in the relevant part of Form xxx, this counsellor tries to confront bankrupts with what she believes to be the true cause. Given her view that most bankruptcies are the responsibility of the bankrupt, she tries to force the debtor to accept that responsibility. She does not shy away from asking whether the debtor has drug problems or a gambling addiction or a predilection toward compulsive shopping. Because she believes so strongly in the therapeutic effects of accepting responsibility, she is ready for the debtor to be upset by these investigations and prepared to support [the debtor] in the aftermath with referrals to appropriate sources of help.

In summary, I believe that Canadian bankruptcy counselling does not fulfill the promise of financial education. Even if the system helps the rare bankrupt, it seems wasteful to have a system in which the vast majority of counselling is either unnecessary or ineffective. And, since I do not believe that most bankruptcies are the result of financial imprudence, I do not think it advisable to train all counsellors to follow the example the counsellor discussed in the last paragraph.

Nonetheless, the counselling still plays a valuable role in the bankruptcy process by facilitating and informing that process. Whether this role implies mandatory sessions or face-to-face contact, however, is arguable.

F. Annulling a Consumer Proposal

The *BIA* allows for a consumer proposal to be annulled in two ways:

- Automatic annulment when the debtor has missed a set number of payments. Where payments under the consumer proposal are to be made monthly or more frequently, the proposal is automatically annulled if the debtor is in default for an amount that is equal to or more than the amount of three payments. Where payments are due less frequently than monthly, the proposal is automatically annulled if the debtor is in default for more than three months on any payment (*BIA*, s 66.31); and
- Court-approved annulment, which is necessary or available in other cases where, *inter alia*, the debtor is in default of performance of any other provision of the consumer proposal, a court is satisfied that the consumer proposal cannot continue without injustice or undue delay, or court approval was obtained by fraud (*BIA*, s 66.3).

If a debtor is having difficulty complying with a proposal, rather than allowing for it to be deemed annulled, the administrator may apply to amend the proposal. The administrator files the amendment and the amendment must then be accepted (or deemed accepted) by the creditors and approved (or deemed approved) by the court (*BIA*, s 66.37). The creditors and consumer debtor may also agree to a different process for amending the consumer proposal by including an amendment provision in the proposal. For example, in the case of *Dondale (Re)*, 2009 BCCA 10 (*Re Dondale*), the British Columbia Court of Appeal held that the debtors and creditors could include the following term in a consumer proposal:

7 (a) the creditors may appoint up to three inspectors responsible for the Consumer Proposal of the consumer debtor. The inspectors may have, in addition to any powers of inspectors under the Act, the power to

 (i) receive any notice of default in the performance of a provision of the Consumer Proposal and waive any such default, and

 (ii) approve any amendment to the Consumer Proposal without calling a meeting of creditors, if the amendment would alter the schedule for and the amount of the payments to be made by the consumer debtor, but would not change the total amount to be paid; and

 (b) in the absence of appointed Inspectors the Administrator of this Consumer Proposal shall have the power to extend the time for the making of any payment required to be made pursuant to this Proposal provided that no such extension shall extend beyond the five years following the approval of this Proposal by the court.

The court in *Re Dondale*, held that the provision did not allow the administrator to waive a default, but rather to avoid one (at para 24):

The purpose and effect of clause 7(b) is not to override the annulment provision in the *Act*. Rather, it is to avoid it before it becomes operative. If the [debtors] have legitimate difficulty in meeting the payment schedule at any time during the five-year period because their income flow is erratic, the administrator can rearrange the payment schedule from time to time to make the monthly payments correspond more closely to the flow of their income. However, if they miss three payments in a row before the schedule can be adjusted by the administrator, or if they miss three payments in a row under the adjusted schedule (or if the adjusted payment schedule provides for payments less frequently than monthly and one payment falls in arrears for more than three months), s. 66.31 will become operative and there will be a deemed annulment.

In a case regarding a Division I proposal, a similar provision was disallowed on the basis that it was inconsistent with the provisions governing Division I proposals. The court described the rules relating to Division I proposal as being "distinct and more stringent" compared with those relating to Division II proposals (*Schultz (Re)*, 2014 ABQB 432 at para 15).

If a proposal has been deemed annulled, an administrator may be able to automatically revive it, but the administrator must take action within thirty days of the deemed annulment. The administrator sends a notice of its intention to revive the proposal to all the creditors. The creditors have sixty days to object. If no creditors file an objection during the sixty-day period, the proposal is automatically revived. Additionally, at any time the administrator can apply to court to revive a consumer proposal. The revival provisions are not available to an individual who filed a consumer proposal while bankrupt (*BIA*, s 66.31).

The case of *Automotive Finance Corp v Davies* considers when it is appropriate to annul a consumer proposal.

Automotive Finance Corp v Davies, 2002 BCSC 509, 33 CBR (4th) 22

[The consumer debtors John Geraint Davies (GD) and April Davies (AD) provided a personal guarantee of corporate debt owed to Automotive Finance Corporation (AFC). When it became evident that GD and AD would be called on to satisfy the guarantee, they consulted an insolvency trustee, John Todd ("Todd") of Todd McMahon Inc. The trustee recommended that they file a consumer proposal. GD and AD only fell under the threshold amount for filing a consumer proposal (which was $75,000 per person at the time) if their liability on the corporate guarantee was not included in the proposal. Based on the trustee's advice, GD and AD filed consumer proposals and did not include the corporate guarantee in their list of liabilities. They did not notify AFC of the proposal. The proposal was accepted by the other creditors and approved by the court, and GD and AD completed all the terms of the proposal. When AFC learned of the proposal, it applied to have it annulled pursuant to section 66.3 of the *BIA*.]

Issue

[20] Ought the Court to exercise its discretion to grant an annulment of the Consumer Proposal in issue?

Discussion

[21] It is agreed the Court retains the discretion to determine whether an annulment of a Consumer Proposal ought to be allowed. Section 66.3(1) provides:

> Where default is made in the performance of any provision in the Consumer Proposal, or where it appears to the Court:

(a) that the debtor was not eligible to make a Consumer Proposal when the Consumer Proposal was filed,

(b) that the Consumer Proposal cannot continue without injustice or undue delay, or

(c) that the approval of a court was obtained by fraud,

the Court may, on application with such notice as the Court may direct to the consumer debtor, and, if applicable, to the administrator and to the creditors, annul the Consumer Proposal.

[22] The real issues are the factors to be considered by the Court in exercising the discretionary power provided in s 66.13. Ms. Ferris submits that considering the terms of s. 66.13(4), it is clear that a consumer debtor's simple ineligibility to file a Consumer Proposal will not automatically result in annulment. Section 66.13(4) provides:

> Where the administrator determines, after filing a Consumer Proposal under paragraph 2(d), that it should not have been filed because the debtor was not eligible to make a Consumer Proposal, the administrator shall forthwith so inform the creditors and Official Receiver, but the Consumer Proposal is not invalid by reason only that the debtor was not eligible to make the consumer proposal.

[23] Both counsel point to the decision of the Court in *Minister of National Revenue v Engdahl* (1994), 27 C.B.R. (3d) 114 (Sask. Q.B. in Bankruptcy); affirmed on appeal 29 C.B.R. (3d) 111 (Sask. C.A.) as setting out the factors to be taken into account in the exercise of the Court's discretion.

[24] In *Engdahl*, the debtor filed a Consumer Proposal disclosing his debts and liabilities, including a liability to Revenue Canada. At that point, the outstanding liability was $13,200 for the 1990 and 1991 tax years and an estimated liability of $12,600 for the 1992 tax year. The proposal was approved. The debtor's 1992 tax return was later reassessed disclosing an indebtedness to Revenue Canada of $39,756.03. Then, upon the 1990 and 1991 returns being reassessed, a further indebtedness of $92,819.89 was disclosed.

[25] After the Certificate of Full Performance of the Consumer Proposal was issued by the debtor's administrator, Revenue Canada applied for an order under s 66.3(1) of the Act to annul the proposal. As in the case at bar, the application was based on the proposition that the debtor had not been eligible to make a Consumer Proposal since his unsecured debts exceeded $75,000 at the time he filed the proposal.

[26] At page 124 of the trial judgment, Gunn J noted as follows:

> The function of a court sitting in bankruptcy and insolvency matters is to take into account the interests of a debtor and his creditors and balance their interests while maintaining the integrity and confidence of the public.

[27] Considering that statement of principle, he concluded at page 125:

> ... In the circumstances of this case I do not feel it is an appropriate case in which to annul the Consumer Proposal given the actions of Revenue Canada Taxation. I accept that the debtor did not know he was ineligible at the time of making the proposal. He has completed all his requirements pursuant to the proposal and has received the Certificate of Compliance from the administrator. I am not satisfied any benefit will accrue to the unsecured creditors if the proposal were to be annulled, based on the debtor's belief he will be forced to make an assignment in bankruptcy if the proposal were to be annulled.

[28] Likewise in this case, Ms. Ferris submits that at the time they filed their Consumer Proposal, neither GD nor AD had any idea they were ineligible to make such a proposal, and that they relied innocently on Todd's advice that their guarantees of Alda's debt were not matters which required disclosure in the Consumer Proposal forms. GD and AD have completed all requirements pursuant to their proposals and they have

likewise received Certificates of Compliance from their Administrator. It is unclear that any benefit will necessarily accrue to the unsecured creditors if their proposals were to be annulled.

[29] Finally, Ms. Ferris submits that the Court must balance the interest of the debtors and the creditors while maintaining the integrity and confidence of the public, as Gunn J noted in *Engdahl*. She submits that the public's confidence in the *Act* and the process of consumer proposals would be lost, were innocent debtors like GD and AD to find their Consumer Proposals annulled in circumstances such as those in the case at bar.

[30] I am not persuaded that the decision in *Engdahl* is of any particular assistance to the respondent. In *Engdahl*, there was no evidence of anything more than a small debt owed to Revenue Canada as at the time the Consumer Proposals were filed. The much larger debt to Revenue Canada, as revealed by the assessments, did not accrue until after the proposals were filed. In the case at bar, GD's exposure under the guarantees was well understood by him, and indeed it was that exposure which led him to seek out the advice of Todd. As I understand the evidence, excluding AFC, GD's and AD's total debt was in the sum of approximately $192,280. Neither Mr. Schwartz nor Ms. Ferris were able to say what portion of that debt constituted the mortgage on the personal residence which was to be excluded from the calculation.

[31] In any case, by any measure, the largest single creditor which loomed on the debtors' horizon was AFC, which held a guarantee worth in excess of $277,000. This debt was not included in the <u>Statement of Affairs</u> completed by GD and AD. Nor was AFC provided with any notice of the Consumer Proposal.

[32] Ms. Ferris has submitted that Gunn J's reasons in *Engdahl*, were aimed at ensuring the exercise of judicial discretion such as to maintain the public's confidence in the "integrity" of the bankruptcy process. She submitted that the granting of the annulment of the Consumer Proposal in the case at bar would undermine the debtor's, as well as the other creditors' reliance upon the process, and the certificates granted.

[33] It strikes me that if the Consumer Proposal process is to have any "integrity," it must rest firmly on the foundation that all proper debts and liabilities will be disclosed by debtors seeking the protection of the *Act*; that the administrators will properly investigate the debtor's financial affairs; and that all creditors will be provided with proper notice of a Consumer Proposal so as to be able to elect to participate in the process if they choose. Assuming the *Act* is complied with, the debtors, creditors and the public generally, can expect that the purpose of the *Act* will be fulfilled — that is there will be an orderly and equitable distribution of the debtors' assets.

[34] If a clear error, such as that which was committed in the case at bar, is allowed to stand without ramification, leaving the creditor (who received no notice of the Consumer Proposal) to absorb the loss, then the integrity of the process has surely been undermined. The creditor would be left with no remedy either against the debtor or for that matter the Administrator, whose error caused the loss. . . .

Consumer proposal annulled.

G. Other Restructuring Options for Canadian Consumer Debtors

In addition to bankruptcy and Division I or II proposals, Canadian consumers have other options for debt relief available to them. If they live in Alberta and Nova Scotia, they can apply for a Part X Order. Canadian consumers may also set up a debt-management plan with a private credit counselling company.

1) Part X Orders

Part X Orders are another option for consumer debtors who wish to set up a payment plan to repay their debts. There are several key differences between Part X Orders and consumer proposals. Roderick Wood, in *Bankruptcy and Insolvency Law*, 2d ed (Toronto: Irwin Law, 2015) at 574–75 writes:

> A consolidation [aka Part X] order is not voted upon by the creditors or approved by the Court. It is a mechanism under which the various debts are consolidated into a single amount that is paid to the clerk of a court and then distributed to the creditors by way of dividend. A consolidation order does not permit a compromise of the claims. A debtor must pay the debts in full, except that the interest on the debt that accrues after the consolidation order is fixed at 5 percent.

Part X Orders started as a provincial initiative, intended to address a gap in the federal insolvency regime. The 1919 *Bankruptcy Act* contained provisions enabling any debtor, not just consumer debtors, to make a proposal to the debtor's creditors instead of filing for bankruptcy. However, the provisions were not consumer-friendly, and, in any event, a 1923 amendment permitted the presentation of a proposal only after bankruptcy. In 1932, Manitoba enacted an *Orderly Payment of Debts Act*, which introduced a simple procedure that enabled a debtor to apply to the clerk of the county court for an order staying creditors' collection efforts while the debtor made installment payments that the clerk determined to be reasonable, based on the debtor's aggregate debts. However, the debtor was still obliged to pay off all the debts. Alberta adopted similar legislation in 1959, but it was struck down by the Supreme Court of Canada as unconstitutional in *Validity of Orderly Payment of Debts Act, 1959 (Alta)*, [1960] SCR 571, excerpted in Chapter 2.

To fill the gap created by the decision, in 1965, the federal government added a new Part X to the *BIA*, essentially replicating the Manitoba and Alberta provisions. Part X applies only in Alberta and Nova Scotia. Before 1992, Part X enjoyed considerable popularity among low-income consumers. Since then, support has dropped off significantly. By 1998, the total number of Part X orders amounted to only 1,539. The reasons for this decline were: (1) Part X does not provide for release of any part of the debts and, therefore, does not help those consumers with heavy debt burdens and negligible surplus income; (2) consumer bankruptcies have become much more accessible and affordable even for low-income consumers; and (3) consumer proposals, added in 1992, provide more effective relief than does Part X.

2) Debt Management Plans

Private credit counselling companies may assist a debtor in negotiating a repayment plan with their creditors. These plans require the debtor to make payments to the credit counselling company, which then keeps a portion of each payment and distributes the balance to the creditors. Unlike a proposal under the *BIA*, there is no way to bind creditors to the plan unless they agree to be bound by it.

Stephanie Ben-Ishai noted in 2013 that there were at least three types of credit counselling companies:

> [F]or-profit companies that specialize in creating debt management plans or repairing damaged credit ratings.... not-for-profit organizations that claim to provide credit counselling along with debt management plans and credit repair....
>
> [As well as] small community-based not-for-profit organizations that have other more charitable goals and outcomes.[10]

She reported these organizations are largely self-regulated through different industry associations, but concluded that this model of regulation was insufficient. The standards to which credit counsellors are held are not easily discoverable, compliance is inconsistent across the industry, and to the extent any government regulations exist (for example, the *Competition Act* prohibits fraudulent behaviour and misleading marketing to the public), it is not being effectively enforced. Ben-Ishai recommended government regulation building on the standards currently used by the industry associations. She suggested that the American *Uniform Debt Management Services Act* might be a worthy model to emulate:

> The Uniform Debt Management Services Act (UDMSA) was finalized in 2005 and immediately adopted in a number of states. Under the UDMSA, providers of debt management services must be registered within their state and follow standards for the specific agreement reached with a consumer. The UDMSA requires providers: to act in good faith; to maintain toll-free communications that permit clients to speak with a counsellor during business hours; and to determine that the DMP is suitable for the consumer. The National Conference of Commissioners on Uniform State Laws recently approved a number of amendments to the Act. The Act can be divided into three main sections: registration, agreements, and enforcement. The UDMSA's critical changes are:
>
> 1. Registration: requirements for agencies wishing to register under the Act and with their state; such registration is required before the agency can act as a debt management provider;
> 2. Prerequisites and Disclosures: agencies must provide certain documents and information to debtors prior to entering into an agreement;
> 3. Fee Structure: limits are set as to the type and amount of fees allowed;
> 4. Enforcement and Remedies: both administratively and individually; the administrator of the Act can investigate complaints and seek remedies under the Act, and individuals may bring civil actions for noncompliance.
>
> The UDMSA left it up to each state to decide whether the statute applies to for-profit entities in addition to not-for-profit agencies, and so far, all states that have adopted the UDMSA have included for-profit agencies. The Act is limited to companies that act as intermediaries between debtors and creditors. This limit partially addresses the issue of blurry industry partitions in that it does not cover any counselling that does not include an organized payment plan like a DMP, but it often treats debt management and debt settlement services as the same.
>
> Another potential concern regarding the UDMSA is that only lawyers can assist in filing a petition for bankruptcy and, according to the Department of Justice, counsellors

---

10 Stephanie Ben-Ishai, "Report on a Consultation on the Regulation of the Credit Counselling Industry in Ontario" in Janis P Sarra, ed, *Annual Review of Insolvency Law 2013* (Toronto: Thomson Carswell, 2014) 639 at 641. Reprinted by permission of the publisher.

cannot give debtors advice as to whether or not they should file. With funding for not-for-profits coming primarily from "fair share" donations, agencies might be tempted to discourage debtors from filing for bankruptcy. The UDMSA now requires counsellors to inform debtors that they are encouraged to inquire about all of their debt relief options, including bankruptcy. The Act does not, however, provide guidance as to how much advice counsellors can give with respect to filing for bankruptcy.[11]

Practice Questions
Your client, Gilda, ran an automotive shop. She set up a company, Auto Shop Ltd, to operate the shop. Auto Shop Ltd got an operating line of credit from Main Street Bank. The business is losing money and Gilda wants to either wind it up or sell it to someone else to operate. Additionally, the business has caused Gilda financial difficulties and she needs to reduce the amount of debt she is required to pay. She has never sought debt relief before and finds the process overwhelming. She has provided you the following information about the finances of Auto Shop Ltd and her personal finances.

Auto Shop Ltd

▶ Assets
  • Auto Shop Ltd has equipment worth $200,000
  • Auto Shop Ltd has accounts receivable worth $50,000

▶ Liabilities
  • Auto Shop Ltd owes $300,000 to the Main Street Bank. This amount is secured against all of Auto Shop Ltd's present and after-acquired personal property.
  • Auto Shop Ltd owes $30,000 to its lessor, in unpaid back rent. This amount is unsecured.
  • Auto Shop Ltd owes $175,000 to four trade creditors. These amounts are unsecured.

Gilda

▶ Assets
  • Her condominium apartment is worth $500,000 (she has $100,000 of equity in it). She lives in the condominium apartment and, if possible, would like to keep it.
  • She has RRSPs in the amount of $40,000. The last deposit was made three years ago, when she received an income tax refund.
  • She has some clothes and personal effects that would either be exempt or of negligible value.

▶ Liabilities
  • She owes $400,000 on a mortgage, secured against her condominium apartment.
  • She owes $45,000 on her credit card. She explains to you that she started charging business expenses to her credit card when she was trying to keep the automotive shop afloat.
  • She owes $135,000 to the Canada Revenue Agency in unpaid personal income tax, interest, and late penalties.

Gilda has found a job working as a mechanic. Her income is sufficiently large that she would be required to pay surplus income if she filed for bankruptcy.

---

11 Ben-Ishai, *ibid* at 649–51.

Question 1
What advice would you give to Gilda about Auto Shop Ltd's debt relief options?

Question 2
Auto Shop Ltd files a Notice of Intention to Make a Proposal on 1 March.

a) Assuming there are no further applications to court, by what date must Auto Shop Ltd file its proposal if it wishes to avoid an automatic bankruptcy?

b) On 9 March of the same year, the lessor becomes concerned that Auto Shop Ltd is not being honest about its financial situation. It decides it would prefer for Auto Shop Ltd to be liquidated by a trustee in bankruptcy proceedings. What advice should a lawyer give the lessor?

c) While putting together a proposal, Gilda determines that Auto Shop Ltd could continue operating in its current premises, but would be more profitable if it moved to a different location, with lower monthly lease payments. She asks you if Auto Shop Ltd can disclaim its current lease. What advice do you give her?

d) Can Auto Shop Ltd file a proposal *for the first time* on 1 October of the same year in which it filed the Notice of Intention?

e) Auto Shop Ltd's proposal has two classes of creditors — one for secured creditors and one for unsecured creditors. Can the proposal be accepted and approved if Main Street Bank and the lessor both vote against it?

Question 3
What advice would you give to Gilda about her *personal* debt relief options?

Question 4
How would your advice to Gilda about her personal debt relief options change in the following situations?

a) She tells you that she personally guaranteed Auto Shop Ltd's operating line of credit from Main Street Bank. Pursuant to the terms of the guarantee, she is jointly and severally liable for any amounts borrowed by Auto Shop Ltd.

b) She tells you her new job is a nine-month contract, and she is not certain whether she will be able to find work in her field after the contract expires.

c) She is reassessed by the Canada Revenue Agency, and her personal income tax debt, plus interest, and penalties total $201,000.

PART V

Receiverships and Cross-Border Insolvencies

Receiverships

Trigger: SPs want a SAs have all encompassing SIs will appoint a receiver manager

RM can take control of business.

I. INTRODUCTION

Secured creditors who have been granted an all-encompassing security interest in the debtor's assets will usually also be given the power to appoint a receiver-manager in the event of a default under the security agreement. If this power is exercised, the receiver-manager will take possession and control of the business from the debtor. The receiver-manager will operate the business in the hope of selling it to a buyer as a going concern.

The law relating to receiverships is complicated by the fact that there are two different sources of receivership law. A receiver-manager may be appointed pursuant to the contractual power contained in the security agreement. Alternatively, a court exercising its equitable jurisdiction may appoint a receiver-manager. The rules and principles governing these two types of receiverships differ in many important respects, although these differences have been reduced somewhat by legislation. The law relating to receiverships is also complicated by the fact that there are several different federal and provincial statutes that regulate receiverships, and there is considerable overlap in their provisions.

II. THE POSITION AT COMMON LAW

For several centuries, equity has employed the remedial device of a court-appointed receiver and manager to administer assets while a dispute is being resolved or to assist in the enforcement of a judgment where the legal enforcement mechanisms were inadequate. The privately appointed receivership has a much shorter history and traces its genesis to, approximately, the middle of the nineteenth century. Historically, in the case of realty mortgages, mortgagees were reluctant to take possession of the land because the courts held the mortgagees strictly to account for maladministration. Mortgagees were reluctant to apply for court-appointed receivers because the device is expensive and can require many court hearings. Ingenious counsel thereupon hit on the device of a contractual clause allowing the secured creditor, on the debtor's default, to appoint a private receiver-manager to take possession of the collateral and manage the business until it was disposed of. To make sure that the secured creditor could not be held responsible for the receiver's actions, and that the receiver would have plenary powers to manage the business, the clause also provided (and continues to provide) that the receiver shall be deemed to be the debtor's agent.

Strictly speaking, a distinction is drawn between a person who is appointed to collect income and rent from a property and a person who also has the power to manage the business of the debtor. The former is referred to as a receiver, while the latter is referred to as a receiver and manager (or receiver-manager). The appointee is virtually always given a power of management over the business, and it has therefore become usual to refer to the latter simply as a receiver. This usage will be adopted here, but it should be kept in mind that the receiver must be given a power of management either by the security agreement (in the case of a privately appointed receiver) or by the court order (in the case of a court-appointed receiver).

The powers of a court-appointed receiver were derived from the order appointing the receiver. The powers of a privately appointed receiver were derived from the terms of the security agreement. A secured creditor who had the power to appoint a privately appointed receiver pursuant to its security agreement was not compelled to do so and could instead seek to have a receiver appointed by a court. A secured creditor could also seek to have a privately appointed receiver converted into a court-appointed receiver. The next case discusses the difference between these two kinds of receiverships.

Ostrander v Niagara Helicopters Ltd (1973), 1 OR (2d) 281 (Ont H Ct J)

STARK J:

In spite of the lengthy evidence that was taken in these proceedings continuing over many days, I am satisfied that the real questions involved have become quite narrowed and confined. This result was mainly achieved by the very careful and thorough arguments of all counsel and by their careful review of the evidence. Summarily stated the facts are briefly these. The company known as Niagara Helicopters Limited (hereinafter referred to for convenience as "Niagara"), was founded by the plaintiff Paul S. Ostrander who was the owner of 90% of the stock of the company. This company operated out of the City of Niagara Falls providing charter commercial air services, a flight school, tourist operations and various other services using helicopters. While Ostrander was an experienced helicopter pilot he proved to be an inept financial manager and when the company experienced serious financial difficulties the defendant Roynat was approached for a substantial loan by way of bond mortgage. A debenture dated October 1, 1969, (ex. 1) was entered into between Niagara Helicopters Limited and the Canada Trust Company as trustee, as a result of which Roynat became the single debenture holder. An initial advance of $125,000 was made on November 4, 1969. Two or three months later Niagara defaulted on the loan and the insurance on its aircraft was cancelled. On January 16, 1970, the defendant, C.R. Bawden, was appointed as receiver-manager by virtue of the default provisions contained in the deed of trust. It was admitted by counsel for the plaintiff and was placed on the record that all powers of the trustee were properly delegated to Roynat pursuant to s. 9.2 of the debenture and, in effect, Bawden was appointed receiver and manager as the agent of Roynat for the purpose of protecting and enforcing its security. The defendant Bawden was considered by Roynat to be an experienced receiver-manager, having acted in that capacity on many previous occasions. Bawden took immediate steps to reinstate the insurance, came to the conclusion that the company was a viable operation, although it lacked working capital, and a further $15,000 was advanced under the debenture. Bawden's duties as receiver-manager were then terminated but Roynat insisted that the company retain a financial adviser; and with the consent of Ostrander, indeed it appears with the urging of Ostrander, Bawden acted in this capacity. However, during this period the financial position of Niagara deteriorated mainly because of Ostrander's inability to operate the company efficiently and due also to his frequent absences from the company for various reasons and Roynat became increasingly concerned as to the safety of its security. Thus, ex. 50 indicated that during the year ending December 31, 1970, a loss of $84,000 had been incurred as opposed to a net loss the previous year of $65,000. By February 24, 1971, it was necessary to again call in the loan and once again Bawden was appointed receiver-manager in accordance with the terms of the debenture and was instructed by Roynat to find a buyer for the shares as being the best possibility for all concerned. Bawden had had some previous satisfactory dealings with principals in the defendant company New Unisphere and this company displayed interest in Niagara. Negotiations were opened between New Unisphere and Ostrander, both parties being represented by independent counsel, and an agreement was formalized. The agreement was finally negotiated and signed and appears herein as ex. 20. No evidence was presented to indicate undue influence by Bawden or anyone else with respect to the negotiations and execution of this agreement. Indeed, from Ostrander's standpoint it was a highly desirable agreement in which Ostrander would have received a substantial payment for his shares. It appears from the evidence that Bawden did all he could reasonably do to assist in the completion of this deal and in postponing public sale of the assets as long as this could be done. However, delays occurred, probably caused by both parties in meeting the terms of the agreement, and as the fall of 1971 approached Roynat became increasingly concerned about the position of its security and urged and instructed Bawden to proceed with preparations for the sale of the assets by public tender. Conditions for sale were prepared, advertisements were duly inserted in the newspapers and a closing date fixed for the receipt of bids. The final date for the receipt of bids was September 24, 1971. . . .

Only two tenders for the working assets of the company as listed in the conditions of sale were received. One of these tenders was a hastily written offer which turned out to be ambiguous in meaning, made by White and prepared in the few moments that preceded the opening. The other tender was the Toprow tender, the benefits of which were later assigned to Baltraco. It was admitted by all parties that since the defendant New Unisphere is the sole owner of its subsidiaries Baltraco Limited and Toprow Investments Limited, that the Toprow bid may fairly be regarded as in fact the bid of New Unisphere Limited. After two or three days' consideration, the Toprow tender was accepted, the decision being made by Roynat's representatives acting on its own views and acting as well on the advice of Bawden. . . .

Commencing in June, 1971, and continuing until November of the same year, Bawden began purchasing for his own personal account through his broker shares in New Unisphere. The total of his purchases amounted to 42,000 shares for a total purchase price of approximately $20,000. These shares represented a 2% interest in the total issued shares of New Unisphere. The shares of that company are listed on the public exchanges. Bawden admitted quite frankly in his evidence that under the circumstances this was a "stupid" thing to do. His own counsel admitted to the Court that, "of all the matters brought before this Court by the plaintiff, this was the only one which has any appearance of substance. There is no question, whatever, that Mr. Bawden should not in the circumstances have been purchasing shares in New Unisphere." Bawden in his evidence contended that his decision to purchase New Unisphere shares had no connection whatever with Niagara, that he does speculate in the market to a considerable extent and that he was interested in this company because of its holdings in certain well known oil producing companies. In placing great stress upon these dealings, the plaintiff submits that Bawden, acting as receiver-manager was in a fiduciary position, that even if there was no actual fraud involved there was constructive fraud, that Bawden had created a conflict between his interests and his duty and that these dealings must vitiate the ultimate deal with Toprow. He argues also that Roynat must be responsible for the misdeeds of its agents. I should hasten to point out that there is not one shred of evidence to indicate that Roynat, Canada Trust or New Unisphere or its subsidiaries had any knowledge of these purchases by Bawden. However, because of the suspicious nature of these circumstances it appeared to me that there was an onus thrown upon the defendants to uphold the validity of the Toprow sale and to satisfy the Court that the decision to make that sale was not in any way affected or influenced by Bawden's foolish purchase of these shares.

My decision might well be otherwise if I had come to the conclusion that Bawden as receiver-manager was acting in a fiduciary capacity. I am satisfied that he was not. His role was that of agent for a mortgagee in possession. The purpose of his employment was to protect the security of the bondholder. Subsequently his duty was to sell the assets and realize the proceeds for the benefit of the mortgagee. Of course he owed a duty to account in due course to the mortgagor for any surplus; and in order to be sure there would be a surplus he was duty bound to comply with the full terms of the conditions of sale set out in the debenture, to advertise the property and to take reasonable steps to obtain the best offer possible. Certainly he owed a duty to everybody to act in good faith and without fraud. But this is not to say that his relations to Ostrander or to Niagara or to both were fiduciary in nature. A very clear distinction must be drawn between the duties and obligations of a receiver-manager, such as Bawden, appointed by virtue of the contractual clauses of a mortgage deed and the duties and obligations of a receiver-manager who is appointed by the Court and whose sole authority is derived from that Court appointment and from the directions given him by the Court. In the latter case he is an officer of the Court; is very definitely in a fiduciary capacity to all parties involved in the contest. The borrower, in consideration of the receipt by him of the proceeds of the loan agrees in advance to the terms of the trust deed and to the provisions by which the security may be enforced. In this document he accepts in advance the conditions upon which a sale is to be made, the nature of the advertising that is to be done, the fixing of the amount of the reserve bid and all the other provisions contained therein relating to the conduct of the sale. In carrying on the business of the company pending the sale, he acts as agent for the lender and he makes the decisions formerly made by the proprietors of the company. Indeed, in the case at hand, Mr. Bawden found it necessary to require that Ostrander absent himself completely from the operations of the business and this Ostrander consented to do. As long as the receiver-manager acts reasonably in the conduct of the business and of course without any ulterior interest, and as long as he ensures that a fair sale is conducted and that he ultimately makes a proper accounting to the mortgagor, he has fulfilled his role which is chiefly of course to protect the security for the benefit of the bondholder. I can see no evidence of any fiduciary relationship existing between Ostrander and Bawden. Mr. Papazian in his able argument put it very forcibly to the Court that the duties and obligations of a receiver-manager appointed by the Court and a receiver-manager appointed under the terms of a bond mortgage without a Court order, were in precisely the same position, each being under fiduciary obligations to the mortgagor. I do not accept that view and I am satisfied that the cases clearly distinguish between them. A good example of the obligation placed upon the Court-appointed receiver-manager is provided by *Re Newdigate Colliery, Ltd,* [1912] 1 Ch. 468. That case was authority for the proposition that it is the duty of the receiver and manager of the property and undertaking of a company to preserve the goodwill as well as the assets of the business, and it would be inconsistent with that duty for him to disregard contracts entered into by the company before his appointment. At p. 477 Buckley LJ, described the duties of the Court-appointed receiver and manager in this way:

The receiver and manager is a person who under an order of the Court has been put in a position of duty and responsibility as regards the management and carrying on of this business, and has standing behind him—I do not know what word to use that will not create a misapprehension, but I will call them "constituents"—the persons to whom he is responsible in the matter, namely, the mortgagees and the mortgagor, being the persons entitled respectively to the mortgage and the equity of redemption. If we were to accede to the application which is made to us, and to allow the receiver and manager to sell the coal at an enhanced price, the result would be that the enhanced price would fall within the security of the mortgagees and they would have the benefit of it; but, on the other hand, there would be created in favour of the persons who had originally contracted to purchase the coal a right to damages against the mortgagor, the company, with the result that there would be large sums of damages owing.

Lord Justice Buckley then continued with language which further accentuates the difference between the two classes of receiver-managers:

It has been truly said that in the case of a legal mortgage the legal mortgagee can take possession if he choose of the mortgaged property, and being in possession can say "I have nothing to do with the mortgagor's contracts. I shall deal with this property as seems to me most to my advantage." No doubt that would be so, but he would be a legal mortgagee in possession, with both the advantages and the disadvantages of that position. This appellant is not in that position. He is an equitable mortgagee who has obtained an order of the Court under which its officer takes possession of assets in which the mortgagee and mortgagor are both interested, with the duty and responsibility of dealing with them fairly in the interest of both parties.

It appears to me unfortunate that the same terms "receiver-manager" are customarily applied to both types of offices, when in fact they are quite different. The difference is well pointed out in the case of *Re B Johnson & Co (Builders) Ltd*, [1955] 1 Ch. 634, where it was held that a receiver and manager of a company's property appointed by a debenture holder was not an officer of the company within the meaning of the *Companies Act*. The language of Evershed M.R., at p. 644 is in point:

The situation of someone appointed by a mortgagee or a debenture holder to be a receiver and manager—as it is said, "out of court"—is familiar. It has long been recognized and established that receivers and managers so appointed are, by the effect of the statute law, or of the terms of the debenture, or both, treated, while in possession of the company's assets and exercising the various powers conferred upon them, as agents of the company, in order that they may be able to deal effectively with third parties. But, in such a case as the present at any rate, it is quite plain that a person appointed as receiver and manager is concerned, not for the benefit of the company but for the benefit of the mortgagee bank, to realize the security; that is the whole purpose of his appointment. . .

Again, at p. 662, Lord Justice Jenkins stated:

The company is entitled to any surplus of assets remaining after the debenture debt has been discharged, and is entitled to proper accounts. But the whole purpose of the receiver and manager's appointment would obviously be stultified if the company could claim that a receiver and manager owes it any duty comparable to the duty owed to a company by its own directors or managers. . . .

The duties of a receiver and manager for debenture holders are widely different from those of a manager of the company. He is under no obligation to carry on the company's business at the expense of the debenture holders. Therefore he commits no breach of duty to the company by refusing to do so, even though his discontinuance of the business may be detrimental from the company's point of view. Again, his power of sale is, in effect, that of a mortgagee, and he therefore commits no breach of duty to the company by a bona fide sale, even though he might have obtained a higher price and even though, from the point of view of the company, as distinct from the debenture holders, the terms might be regarded as disadvantageous.

In a word, in the absence of fraud or mala fides (of which there is not the faintest suggestion here), the company cannot complain of any act or omission of the receiver and manager, provided that he does nothing that he is not empowered to do, and omits nothing that he is enjoined to do by the terms of his appointment. If the company conceives that it has any claim against the receiver and manager for breach of some duty owed by him to the company, the issue is not whether the receiver and manager has done or omitted to do anything which it would be wrongful in a manager of a company to do or omit, but whether he has exceeded or abused or wrongfully omitted to use the special powers and discretions vested in him pursuant to the contract of loan constituted by the debenture for the special purpose of enabling the assets comprised in the debenture holders' security to be preserved and realized.

... While I find that the purchase by Mr. Bawden of the shares in New Unisphere, in the amounts and at the times when he did, were purchases which he should better not have made, I cannot find anything in these transactions to impugn the validity of the final sale by tender. I am satisfied that Mr. Bawden and his principal Roynat did the very best they could to protect their own security but at the same time went out of their way to assist Ostrander in so far as his private negotiations had any hopes of success. Other than the tactless purchase of these shares and the minor misjudgment with respect to certain payments with which I have already dealt, I can find nothing censurable in Mr. Bawden's conduct. I am satisfied that the power of sale was exercised in a fair and proper manner and that in the opinion of Roynat and its advisers the better offer was obtained. I do not consider it necessary to analyse in detail the nature of the offers that were being considered because no evidence has been placed before the Court to show that the Toprow offer was a disadvantageous one or that the White offer was a better one. Certainly as far as New Unisphere and its subsidiaries are concerned there is no evidence to indicate that they had the slightest knowledge of the purchases by Bawden and they are in the position of purchasers in good faith without notice of any such wrongdoing, if such it were, and accordingly the sale must stand. No legal or moral stigma of any kind should be attached to any defendant in this action and the most that can be said against Mr. Bawden is that he was guilty of misjudgment in certain respects. There was an aura of suspicion which had to be dispelled by the defendants and which they have succeeded in doing. I do not think the plaintiff should be further penalized than by dismissing his action against the defendants with costs, except that in the case of the proceedings against Bawden who was separately represented, the action should be dismissed without costs. As already indicated, there should be a reference to pass accounts and to fix the receiver-manager's costs. If any questions arise as to the drawing up of the judgment, I may of course be spoken to.

Action dismissed.

A security agreement that provides for the appointment of a receiver will virtually always also contain a deemed agency clause that provides that the receiver is deemed to act as agent of the debtor. The unusual feature of a deemed agency clause is that although the receiver's power to manage the business is derived from the debtor (the debtor is the principal and the receiver is the agent), the principal is not permitted to revoke the agency, and the agent's primary obligation is owed to the secured creditor rather than to the principal. This gives the receiver the power to carry on the debtor's business. It also has the effect of insulating the secured creditor from liability arising out of wrongful acts of the receiver. However, a privately appointed receiver will not be considered an agent of the debtor for all purposes.

A deemed agency provision is a contractual provision between the debtor and the secured creditor. Upon a bankruptcy of the debtor, the deemed agency clause ceases to operate because the debtor's title to the assets and the debtor's power to deal with the assets is automatically transferred to the debtor's trustee in bankruptcy (see *Gosling v Gaskell*, [1897] AC 575 (HL)).

A court-appointed receiver has independent status and acts as neither agent of the secured creditor nor the debtor. As a consequence, a court-appointed receiver is personally liable for any post-receivership contracts that are entered into, but has a right of indemnity from the assets under receivership. A privately appointed receiver is not personally liable on such contracts, because the receiver acts as agent of the debtor in incurring the obligation. However, a receiver may expressly or impliedly consent to personal liability on such obligations.

Peat Marwick Ltd v Consumers' Gas Co (1980), 29 OR (2d) 336 (CA)

HOULDEN JA:

Peat Marwick Limited, the receiver and manager of the undertaking and assets of Rigidflex Canada Limited, brought this action for (a) recovery of the sum of $2,823.33 paid to the Consumers' Gas Company under protest, (b) a declaration that it was entitled to a supply of gas pursuant to s. 55 of the *Public Utilities Act*, R.S.O. 1970, c. 390, to the premises at 55 Denison Rd. E., in the Boroughs of North York and York, and (c) a declaration that Consumers' Gas was not entitled to discontinue gas services to the said premises. Galligan J dismissed the action with costs: see (1979), 23 O.R. (2d) 659. In this appeal, Peat Marwick asks that it be awarded judgment against Consumers' Gas for the amount paid under protest together with interest from the date of payment to the date of judgment.

Canadian Imperial Bank of Commerce was the banker of Rigidflex Canada Limited, a manufacturer of garden hose and plastic pipe. As security for advances made to Rigidflex, the bank held the following security:

(1) Security by way of assignment under s. 88 of the *Bank Act*, R.S.C. 1970, c. B-1, on all the inventory of Rigidflex;
(2) A floating charge debenture dated 6th December 1976, in the amount of $2,300,000. The debenture was properly registered in accordance with the *Corporation Securities Registration Act*, R.S.O. 1970, c. 88.
(3) A general security agreement dated 20th December 1976. The agreement was properly registered in accordance with the *Personal Property Security Act*, R.S.O. 1970, c. 344.

... The floating charge debenture, like the general security agreement, charged all the property of Rigidflex in favour of the bank as security for a loan of $2,300,000. If default occurred in payment of principal or interest, the bank had the power by instrument in writing to appoint a receiver (which term included a receiver and manager). The deben-ture conferred wide powers on the receiver, including the right to take possession of the premises of Rigidflex and to carry on the business. The clause listing the powers of the receiver contained the following provision:

> The receiver shall for all purposes be deemed to be the agent of the Company and not of the Bank, and the Company shall be solely responsible for his acts or defaults and for his remuneration.

Default having occurred in the payments to the bank, the bank, by letter dated 31st August 1977, appointed Peat Marwick as receiver and manager pursuant to the floating charge debenture and to the general security agreement, and as agent pursuant to the bank's s. 88 security. The bank instructed the receiver and manager to enter into posses-sion of the property of Rigidflex and to carry on the business. Rigidflex was the tenant of the premises at 55 Denison Rd. E., in the Boroughs of North York and York. Acting on the bank's instructions, Peat Marwick took possession of the said premises and pro-ceeded to liquidate the assets covered by the bank's security. It took its instructions regarding the realization of the assets from the bank, not from Rigidflex.

By letter of 2nd September 1977 Peat Marwick advised Consumers' Gas of its appoint-ment as receiver and manager. The letter read in part as follows:

> You are hereby advised that our firm has been appointed Receiver and Manager for the above Three Companies [one of which was Rigidflex] pursuant to debenture security held by the Canadian Imperial Bank of Commerce as of August 31, 1977.
>
> In this connection we request that you contact a Representative of Peat Marwick Lim-ited at 248-5544 and arrange forthwith to have particular Meter Readings taken in order to determine the status of your account with the above Three Companies as of the above date.
>
> In our capacity as Receiver and Manager of the above Three companies, we hereby undertake to be responsible for consumption subsequent to the meter reading as referred to above.

At this time, there was $2,823.33 owing to Consumers' Gas for gas supplied to 55 Deni-son Rd. E. prior to the appointment of the receiver.

The arrangements suggested by Peat Marwick in its letter of 2nd September 1977 were not satisfactory to Consumers' Gas, and on 12th September 1977 it terminated the supply of gas to 55 Denison Rd. E. An application was then made by Peat Marwick to Osler J for a mandatory injunction requiring Consumers' Gas to open a new account in the name of Peat Marwick and to provide an adequate supply of gas to the said premises. On 4th October 1977 Osler J delivered written reasons dismissing the application: see 18 O.R. (2d) 631, 83 D.L.R (3d) 450, 26 C.B.R. (N.S.) 195. Peat Marwick then arranged with Consumers' Gas to pay the arrears of $2,823.33 under protest without prejudice to its rights to seek recovery of the said sum in this action.

Sections 55 and 59 of the *Public Utilities Act* are relevant for this appeal. They provide:

> 55. Where there is a sufficient supply of the public utility the corporation shall supply all buildings within the municipality situate upon land lying along the line of any supply pipe, wire or rod, upon the request in writing of the owner, occupant or other person in charge of any such building.

> 59. If any person supplied with any public utility neglects to pay the rent, rate or charge due to the company at any of the times fixed for the payment thereof, the company, or any

person acting under its authority, on giving forty-eight hours previous notice, may stop the supply from entering the premises of the person by cutting off the service pipes or by such other means as the company or its officers consider proper, and the company may recover the rent or charge due up to that time, together with the expenses of cutting off the supply, notwithstanding any contract to furnish it for a longer time.

Consumers' Gas is a supplier of a public utility. Section 55 requires it to supply gas to the owner, occupant or other person in charge of a building. Section 59, however, is designed to protect Consumers' Gas and other suppliers of public utilities from being required to continue the supply of a utility if their accounts are not being paid. Mr. Thomson conceded that, if Peat Marwick when it took possession of the premises of Rigidflex was, in fact, acting as the agent of Rigidflex, then Consumers' Gas was entitled under s. 59 to terminate the supply of gas; however, he contended that, notwithstanding the wording of the floating charge debenture, Peat Marwick was acting not as the agent of Rigidflex but as the agent of the bank.

... It seems to me that the receiver and manager in a situation like the present is wearing two hats. When wearing one hat, he is the agent of the debtor company; when wearing the other, the agent of the debenture holder. In occupying the premises of the debtor and in carrying on the business, the receiver and manager acts as the agent of the debtor company. In realizing the security of the debenture holder, notwithstanding the language of the debenture, he acts as the agent of the debenture holder and thus is able to confer title on a purchaser free of encumbrances.

There are substantial benefits which accrue to a debenture holder from providing in a debenture that a receiver and manager, when appointed, shall be deemed to be the agent of the debtor company. L.C.B. Gower, *The Principles of Modern Company Law*, 3rd ed., at p. 436 summarizes the effect of such a provision in these words:

> A receiver appointed out of court, on the other hand, might be expected to be an agent of the party appointing him, namely, the debentureholder or trustee, but in practice, the debenture will invariably provide, expressly or impliedly, that the receiver shall be deemed to be the agent of the company. Prior to the 1948 Act [s. 369(2) of the *Companies Act*, 1948 (U.K.), c. 38], this distinction had important consequences, for the former type of receiver would be personally liable on contracts into which he entered, whereas the latter would not, unless he pledged his personal credit.

There is no legislation in Ontario equivalent to s. 369(2) of the English *Companies Act* of 1948 so that the distinction mentioned by Gower still has important consequences in this province: see also *Kerr on Receivers*, 15th ed., pp. 325–26.

The Canadian law as to the effect of appointing a receiver as agent for the debtor company is well summed up in Fraser & Stewart, *Company Law of Canada*, 5th ed., p. 448:

> Unless the trust deed states, as it ought, that the receiver is to be deemed the agent of the company, he will be deemed to be the agent of the bondholders or the trustee, who will be liable for any default on his part: *Re Vimbos, Ltd,* [1900] 1 Ch. 470; *Robinson Printing Co v Chic Ltd,* [1905] 2 Ch. 123 (debenture holders held to be personally liable for debts incurred by the receiver). If the receiver is the agent of the bondholders he can claim remuneration from them: *Deyes v Wood,* [1911] 1 K.B. 806 (C.A.). It is now the practice to use apt words making the receiver the agent of the company and expressly excluding any liability of the bondholders not only to the receiver for his remuneration and expenses, but also to anyone having any dealings with the receiver: *Cully v Parsons,* (1924) 93 L.J. Ch. 42. See *Central*

London Electricity Ltd v Berners [1945] W.N. 51 (undertaking given by receiver on behalf of bondholders without authority).

The decision of *Re Smith, Ex p. Mason*, [1893] 1 Q.B. 323, while it did not involve a receiver and manager, is, I believe, of assistance. In that case, a receiving order in bankruptcy was made against the debtor, and the official receiver took possession of the debtor's premises. The gas company cut off the supply of gas to the premises and refused to reconnect it until its account was paid. The official receiver paid the amount of the arrears under protest. Subsequently the debtor was adjudged bankrupt, and the trustee in bankruptcy applied for an order that the amount paid to the gas company should be refunded to the bankrupt estate. Vaughan Williams J dismissed the application on the ground that, when the official receiver took possession of the debtor's premises, the debtor's occupation of the premises had not come to an end and, therefore, the gas company was entitled under statutory powers similar to s. 59 of the *Public Utilities Act* to refuse to supply gas to the official receiver. Similarly, in this case, it seems to me that, by virtue of the wording of the debenture, Rigidflex's possession did not come to an end when Peat Marwick, as receiver and manager, took possession of its premises. Consequently, the gas company was entitled to exercise the powers conferred by s. 59 of the *Public Utilities Act* and to refuse to supply gas unless the arrears were paid.

If the court were to hold, as Mr. Thomson has submitted, that the receiver and manager was the agent of the bank and hence not liable for the amount owing for gas supplied prior to the appointment of the receiver and manager, then it would, as I see it, give the bank the best of both worlds. If the receiver and manager became involved in some difficulty, the bank, to avoid liability, could claim that the receiver and manager was the agent of the debtor company: see Fraser & Stewart, p. 448. If, however, there were amounts owing for public utilities supplied prior to the appointment of the receiver and manager, the bank, to avoid liability, could claim that the receiver and manager was its agent.

If the bank chooses to provide in its debenture that the receiver and manager shall be deemed to be the agent of the debtor company, then it must not only take the benefits, but it must also accept the detriments which flow from such a provision. The gas was supplied to Rigidflex. The bank took possession of the premises as the agent of Rigidflex and did not pay the arrears owing for gas supplied to Rigidflex. Consumers' Gas was, therefore, entitled to exercise the powers given to it by s. 59 of the *Public Utilities Act* and to terminate the supply of gas.

For the foregoing reasons, I would dismiss the appeal with costs.

Appeal dismissed.

III. THE STATUTORY REGULATION OF RECEIVERSHIPS

During the 1970s and 1980s, secured creditors typically chose to appoint a privately appointed receiver, rather than apply for the appointment of a court-appointed receiver. There were two reasons for this preference. First, a private appointment was usually less expensive than a court-appointed one. Second, the privately appointed receiver owed their primary obligation to the secured creditor and was not required to consider the interests of other parties. At common law, a privately appointed receiver is under no obligation to tell the debtor's unsecured creditors what is happening and owes no general duty of care to them or to the debtor with respect to the assets under the receiver's control.

The widespread use of receiverships by secured creditors gave rise to a number of concerns. Secured creditors would often appoint a private receiver immediately upon a default by the debtor. Within hours, the receiver would take over control of the business. The privately appointed receiver owed its primary obligation to the secured creditor, leaving the other interested parties in the dark concerning the conduct of the receivership, because they had no right to information or an accounting. As long as the sale of the assets was fairly conducted, the receiver was under no obligation to consider the interests of any other party.

Legislation was subsequently introduced to address these problems. Unfortunately, these provisions are scattered across a number of different federal and provincial statutes, and there is a considerable degree of overlap. The *Canada Business Corporations Act*, RSC 1985, c C-44 (*CBCA*) contains receivership provisions, as do some, but not all, provincial business corporations statutes. The provincial *Personal Property Security Acts* also contain provisions respecting receiverships.

In 1992, Part XI (ss 243–52) was added to the *BIA*. Its provisions impose a number of different accounting and reporting obligations on receivers, which ensures that interested third parties will have access to relevant information. The statutes significantly modify the obligation owed by a privately appointed receiver, who is required to act in good faith and in a commercially reasonable manner: see *BIA*, section 247. Many of the statutes also give the court broad supervisory powers over privately appointed receivers. For example, section 100 of the *CBCA* gives the court the power to make the following orders:

(a) an order appointing, replacing or discharging a receiver or receiver-manager and approving their accounts;

(b) an order determining the notice to be given to any person or dispensing with notice to any person;

(c) an order fixing the remuneration of the receiver or receiver-manager;

(d) an order requiring the receiver or receiver-manager, or a person by or on behalf of whom the receiver or receiver-manager is appointed, to make good any default in connection with the receiver's or receiver-manager's custody or management of the property and business of the corporation, or to relieve any such person from any default on such terms as the court thinks fit, and to confirm any act of the receiver or receiver-manager; and

(e) an order giving directions on any matter relating to the duties of the receiver or receiver-manager.

Note that section 100(d) permits a court to make a secured creditor liable for the wrongful conduct of a receiver. This gives the court the power to override a deemed agency clause, which would otherwise be effective in insulating a secured creditor from liability. Under what circumstances would a court be justified in invoking this provision?

The *BIA* also imposes a number of restrictions on the persons who may act as receiver. Section 13.4 provides that a trustee may not act for a secured creditor or realize collateral unless the trustee has a written opinion from independent legal counsel that the security is valid and enforceable against the estate. The trustee must also notify the superintendent and the estate's creditors and inspectors that he is also acting for the secured creditor. The 2009 amendments to the *BIA* added a new qualification requirement. Only a licensed trustee may act as receiver (see s 243(4)).

Section 244 of the *BIA* requires that a secured creditor give notice of its intention to appoint a receiver or otherwise enforce a security interest in substantially all the assets of the debtor. The statutory notice period is ten days. At common law, the courts had developed the common law reasonable notice doctrine. A secured creditor was not permitted to immediately enforce a security interest upon default, but was required to give the debtor a reasonable time to satisfy the obligation. One of the difficulties with the common law doctrine was that the amount of time required to be given depended on all the facts and circumstances of the case, and this uncertainty gave rise to much litigation. Some cases have found that, in addition to the statutory notice period, the common law notice requirement still applies.

John Deere Credit Inc v Doyle Salewski Lemieux Inc (1997), 36 OR (3d) 259 (CA)

GOUDGE JA (for the court):

The appellant is a secured creditor of Ready Rental and Supply Limited ("RRSL"). The respondent is the trustee of RRSL pursuant to a notice of intention to make a proposal under the *Bankruptcy and Insolvency Act*, R.S.C. 1985, c. B-3, as am. by S.C. 1992, c. 27.

The order under appeal allowed the respondent's motion. It restrained the appellant from realizing on its security and further required the appellant to return any security interest of which it had already taken possession. The order also dismissed the appellant's cross-motion for an order that it be permitted to realize on its security unimpeded by the stay provided by s. 69(1) of the *Bankruptcy and Insolvency Act* or, alternatively, that it be released from the operation of that stay on equitable grounds.

The facts relevant to this appeal are straightforward. On May 29, 1997 the appellant delivered by hand to RRSL, pursuant to s. 244(1) of the *Bankruptcy and Insolvency Act*, a notice of intention to enforce security for each conditional sales agreement it had with RRSL. On Sunday, June 8, 1997, RRSL transmitted a notice of intention to make a proposal to the office of the Official Receiver in Toronto. The next day, June 9, when the office reopened, this notice was filed with the Official Receiver. Thereafter, when the appellant attended at RRSL to repossess the equipment, the debtor company asserted the protection of the stay provided in the legislation and the motions referred to above were brought.

The central issue on this appeal is whether the appellant's rights as a secured creditor are stayed by the filing by RRSL of the notice of intention to make a proposal. The germane sections of the *Bankruptcy and Insolvency Act* are as follows: ... [See *BIA* ss 50.4(1), 69(1), 244.]

Also of relevance is Rule 112 of the Bankruptcy and Insolvency Rules, C.R.C. 1978, c. 368:

> 112. Where the time for doing any act or taking any proceeding expires on a Sunday or other day on which the offices of the court are closed, and by reason thereof the act or proceeding cannot be done or taken on that day, the act or proceeding shall, for the purpose of determining the time when the act was done or the proceeding taken, be deemed to be done or taken on the next day on which such offices are open.

Finally, regard must be had to s. 26 of the *Interpretation Act*, R.S.C. 1985, c. I-21:

> 26. Where the time limited for the doing of a thing expires or falls on a holiday, the thing may be done on the day next following that is not a holiday.

Section 244 requires a secured creditor to send the prescribed notice and then wait ten days before enforcing the security.

Section 69 entitles the insolvent person to file a proposal and thereby prevent a secured creditor from enforcing the security unless that creditor had sent the prescribed notice more than ten days earlier.

While these are separate legislative provisions, in my view they cover the same time period. Until a secured creditor, having sent the prescribed notice, has waited the time necessary before being able to enforce the security, the insolvent person can file a proposal staying that creditor's right to proceed to enforce the security.

Hence, for the purposes of the issue on appeal, the effect of ss 244 and 69 taken together is that a secured creditor must send a notice of intention to enforce his security and then wait for the expiry of ten days. Only thereafter can the security interest be enforced without the consent of the insolvent person. The latter has the same ten days following the day on which the notice was sent to file a notice of intention to make a proposal and gain the protection of the stay provisions. In effect, the two sections are designed so that the insolvent person has these ten days to determine whether to give up the security provided or to continue with the proposal proceedings.

Where the ten-day period available to the insolvent person to file and thereby gain the protection of a stay expires on a Sunday, it is my view that the insolvent person may file a notice of intention to make a proposal on Monday, the next day, so as to trigger the stay provided by s. 69. While Rule 112 is not felicitously worded, when s. 26 of the *Interpretation Act* is used to inform its meaning, this result is clearly prescribed. In *Ohayon Jewelry Inc v Libarian Jewels & Settings Ltd (Trustee of)* (1987), 63 O.R. (2d) 157, 66 C.B.R. (N.S.) 302 (S.C.), the court adopted this interpretation of the statutory scheme. Indeed, without this interpretation the insolvent person would have to file his notice on the preceding Friday (since filing is impossible on either Saturday or Sunday) and would therefore have only eight days to decide which way to proceed rather than the ten days prescribed by s. 69(2)(b).

I therefore conclude that on the central issue the appellant fails. Its notice of intention to enforce security was sent on May 29, 1997. The ten-day period that followed ended on Sunday, June 8. This permitted RRSL to file its notice of intention to make a proposal on Monday, June 9, so as to raise the stay provided for in s. 69(2)(b).

The appellant also argued that it ought to be relieved from the effect of the stay for equitable reasons, as is permitted by s. 69.4 of the *Bankruptcy and Insolvency Act*. Given that the material filed by the appellant on this issue was no more than a bare assertion of the possibility of the value of its security declining over time if it could not repossess that security, I am unprepared to allow the appeal on this basis. . . .

Appeal dismissed.

Beresford Building Supplies (1984) Ltd v Caisse Populaire de Petit-Rocher Ltée, [1996] 175 NBR (2d) 321 (QB (TD))

McINTYRE J:

[1] On February 21, 1994 the defendant Caisse Populaire de Petit-Rocher (La Caisse) crystallized a debenture dated March 2, 1990. It appointed the second defendant Belliveau, Pellerin as receiver and closed down the plaintiffs' business. The plaintiffs take action claiming that no notice was given, as required, both at common law and under subsection 244(1) of the *Bankruptcy and Insolvency Act*, R.S.C. 1985, ch. B-3 as amended. The plaintiffs' action is also founded on trespass, conversion and breach of fiduciary duty. . . .

[3] Clifford and Martin Comeau purchased Beresford Building Supplies (B.B.S.) in 1984. They incorporated the business under the corporate name Beresford Building Supplies (1984) Ltd. and became owners at 50% each. From 1984 until 1990 B.B.S.

conducted its banking business with the National Bank in Petit-Rocher with an operating line of credit of $650,000.

[4] In 1990 B.B.S. approached La Caisse with a view of obtaining a loan for a new business venture. The then manager, after reviewing the financial statements, offered to become B.B.S.'s banker. B.B.S. accepted. La Caisse gave B.B.S. a line of credit of $875,000 plus an additional $260,000 loan secured by a demand note. La Caisse further secured its loans by a debenture, an assignment of accounts receivable, promissory notes and the personal guarantees of Clifford and Martin Comeau. The land and building as well as the chattels of B.B.S. had previously been mortgaged in favour of the Federal Business Development Bank.

[5] Between 1987 and 1992 the financial statements of B.B.S. showed a reasonable profit. In 1988 the net income was $75,007, in 1989 it was $118,984 and $57,475 in 1990. The financial picture changed in 1991 with a net loss of $7,334 followed by net losses of $95,961 in 1992 and $533,740 in 1993.

[6] In June 1992 Gilles Poirier, former manager at the National Bank in Petit-Rocher, became the new manager at La Caisse. It took him little time to become aware of B.B.S.'s financial difficulties. Indeed, by October 30, 1992, B.B.S. had exceeded its allowable credit by almost $400,000. . . .

[8] With the financial situation of B.B.S. deteriorating from day to day La Caisse, on July 19, 1993, served on B.B.S. and Clifford and Martin Comeau a notice of intention to enforce security pursuant to subsection 244(1) of the *Bankruptcy and Insolvency Act*, as well as a letter of demand for payment of $1,070,905.59. B.B.S. was given 30 days or until August 19th to pay. Clifford and Martin Comeau were also served with a demand under their personal guarantees.

[9] Following service of the demand the parties met in an attempt to prevent the closure of the business. La Caisse manager, Mr. Poirier, had heard that Clifford and Martin had a brother who may have been able to provide financial assistance and he discussed that possibility with Clifford Comeau. He was told that Henry Comeau would not be interested unless there was something in it for him. Poirier says he had given the lengthy 30 days' notice precisely because he wanted to give B.B.S. every opportunity to find a solution to its financial problems. At the last hour, on August 19, 1993, a conditional agreement was reached between B.B.S. and La Caisse. Basically the agreement provided for the payment of $300,000 by November 30, 1993 and subsequent payments of $100,000 and $200,000 on the 30th of November in each subsequent year until 1998. The agreement, which was confirmed and approved by the Board of Directors of La Caisse on August 20th, contains the proviso, however, that the demand of July 19, 1993 is to remain effective until the payment is made of $300,000 due by November 30, 1993. The July 19th demand notice was to become null and void upon receipt of $300,000 by the stipulated date. On the same date, August 19th, B.B.S. made a deposit of $88,000. $18,000 of the amount was to remain in the account as working capital and $70,000 was assessed against the debt. It was the last amount which La Caisse was to receive. La Caisse did not receive the additional $230,000 by November 30, 1993. No additional payments were made on the debt after August 19, 1993. Any amount deposited after that date was to cover cheques in circulation.

[Justice McIntyre refers to evidence that Comeau had told Poirier in December 1993 or early January 1994 that Comeau would soon receive $50,000 from Mario Jean, and that Poirier had said that if the $50,000 was paid in reduction of the debt he would recommend to the Caisse Populaire's board of directors that Beresford should be given more time to pay the balance of the debt. Comeau never paid the $50,000. The judgment continued:]

[13] … When Poirier found out that La Caisse was not going to receive any money from the Mario Jean receivable, he did not present the draft letter of February 1st to his Board. When the Board met in mid-February the decision was made to call in the receiver. A declaration of crystallization and a notice of appointment of a receiver were served on B.B.S. and on Clifford and Martin Comeau. The inventory was sold "en bloc" on May 5th and, as earlier indicated, there is no dispute as to the amount recovered. B.B.S. filed for bankruptcy shortly thereafter. It is agreed that the trustee has consented to the continuance of the present action. …

[14] Considering the events that transpired following the agreement of August 20, 1993, B.B.S. contends that La Caisse had, in effect, nullified its notice of July 19, 1993, thereby requiring new notice. To put it in the words of counsel for the plaintiffs in his pre-trial brief, "La Caisse had in effect misrepresented its position throughout to B.B.S. and its principals, obtaining as much security as they possibly could, and then without notice, precipitously closed down the family business. This completely prevented the Comeau's from obtaining other funds (which could have been hundreds of thousands of dollars) from their brother Henry, which would have alleviated entirely the situation with La Caisse and even allowed B.B.S. to seek alternative financing with other bankers with whom the Comeau's had a relationship."

[15] That a debtor is entitled to reasonable notice from a creditor making a demand for payment is now settled law. See *Lister v Dunlop Canada Ltd*, [1982] 1 S.C.R. 726, *Royal Bank of Canada v Estabrooks Pontiac Buick Ltd* (1985), 60 N.B.R. (2d) 160 (N.B.C.A.), *Canadian Imperial Bank of Commerce v Prosser* (1982), 41 N.B.R. (2d) 656. Although the length of the notice will vary depending on the particular circumstances in each case, the authorities agree that it will generally be of short duration. To put it in the words of McLachlin J (as she then was) in *CIBC v Quesnel Machinery Ltd*, 62 C.B.R. (N.S.) 91 at 93:

> What constitutes reasonable notice depends on the facts of the particular case; thus depending on the circumstances, reasonable notice may range from a few days, as in Lister, to no time at all.

See also *Jeannette BBQ Ltée and Haché v Caisse Populaire de Tracadie Ltée* (1991), 117 N.B.R. (2d) 129 (N.B.C.A.) and *Kavcar Investments Ltd et al v Aetna Financial Services Ltd and Coopers and Lybrand* (1989), 35 O.A.C. 305; 62 D.L.R. (4th) 277 (Ont. C.A.).

[16] The common law requirement of notice to the debtor before calling in the receiver became statutory in certain cases by the enactment of the *Bankruptcy and Insolvency Act*, R.S.C. 1985, ch. B-3. Subsection 244(1) and (2) provides as follows: …

[17] It is argued by counsel for the plaintiffs that the common law requirement of reasonable notice continues to exist despite the statutory notice in section 244 of the *Bankruptcy and Insolvency Act*. I agree that there may indeed be circumstances calling for notice to be given outside the context of the *Bankruptcy and Insolvency Act*. The plaintiffs argue that before calling in the receiver on February 21, 1994 the defendant should have served another section 244 notice and at the very least it had an obligation to give the plaintiffs reasonable notice (the common law notice) of its decision to bring in the receiver.

[18] The situation in this case is not much different than that in *Delron Computers Inc v Peat Marwick Thorne Inc* (1995), 31 C.B.R. (3d) 75 (Sask. Q.B.). *Delron* was cited by

both parties to these proceedings but to advance two different positions. Delron had given security interest in its personal property to ITT in exchange for two lines of credit. As a result of a breach of the covenants in the agreement, ITT delivered a notice of intention to enforce security, a letter demanding repayment, and a letter of proposal suggesting a plan to maintain the credit for two months which Delron accepted but then failed to respect the terms thereof. ITT appointed a receiver who took possession of the premises and of the assets. Delron brought an application for a stay pursuant to paragraph 248(1)(b) of the *Bankruptcy and Insolvency Act* on grounds that ITT had failed to give notice under subsection 244(1) of its intention to enforce the security. In dismissing the application, Gerein, J. concluded that a second statutory notice was not required as the parties had not entered into a "new" or "replacement" security agreement. The purpose of the proposal being strictly to "better safeguard the position of ITT in return for it (Delron) maintaining their existing lines of credit." The proposal pertained to the operation of Delron's business and not to the original agreements. In the circumstances, the provisions contained in the proposal did not constitute a new agreement.

[19] In the present case I conclude that the acceptance by La Caisse on August 20, 1993 (Exhibit No. 2, Tab 127) of B.B.S.'s refinancing proposal was intended as a means of securing La Caisse's position whilst allowing B.B.S. to continue operating. It was not, in any manner, meant to replace the existing security agreements. In fact, it is so stated clearly at the last line on page one, "Toutes les garanties déjà existantes demeurent en vigueur." That being so, it was not necessary to give a second section 244 notice.

[20] The plaintiffs submit, however, that the Court must be satisfied not only that the statutory requirements of notice have been complied with but also the common law requirements as well. Like Gerein J in *Delron*, I adopt the position taken by Farley J in *Prudential Assurance Co v 90 Eglinton Ltd Partnership* (1994), 25 C.B.R. (3d) 139 (Ont. Gen. Div.) at pp 152–3, that it is unnecessary to give both a statutory notice and a common law notice. One notice is sufficient. Whenever the provisions of the *Bankruptcy and Insolvency Act* apply a minimum 10-day notice is required in order to enforce a demand loan. Where no minimum notice is required whether by statute or otherwise the common law principle of reasonable notice applies.

[21] In the present case I am satisfied on a balance that La Caisse never revoked the notice of July 19th to call in its loan. An arrangement was worked out on August 20, 1993 to keep B.B.S. in operation but B.B.S.'s failure to pay $300,000 by November 30, 1993 amounted to a breach of the repayment arrangement. It was explicit in the offer of August 20th that the notice to call in the loan remained in effect until the amount of $300,000 was paid. The November 30th deadline passed and no amount was paid. In my view La Caisse was then in a position to call in the receiver at anytime without further notice. The fact that it waited until February 21st, 1994 indicates only that it gave B.B.S. every opportunity to find a solution to its financial problem. The argument that they expected to receive a second or final notice before making a final effort at looking for financing from another source is not realistic and is unacceptable. As for the draft letter of February 1st, 1994, I am satisfied, on a balance, that Clifford Comeau knew that Poirier could not make such a commitment on his own. Mr. Comeau is an experienced businessman who knew that Poirier required the approval of his Board before the draft of February 1st could become a formal proposal. In any event, the $50,000 promised from the Mario Jean receivable was never paid. I conclude that on February 21st La Caisse had every right to call in the receiver without further notice to B.B.S. I agree with the statement of Gerein J in *Delron* at pp. 84–85:

To my way of thinking, it is not inconsistent for a creditor to intend to realize on its security; give notice to that effect; and still be willing to resolve or attempt to resolve the difficulty. The creditor is simply communicating the fact that its intended course is capable of change. If one were to adopt the applicant's position, a creditor would always be at risk if an arrangement was entered into; for it may be construed as establishing a lack of the intent required by the section. This certainly would be contrary to business efficacy....

Action dismissed.

IV. PRIORITIES

As a general rule, the invocation of a receivership does not affect the priority ranking of the persons who hold interests in the debtor's assets. The priority will therefore be governed by the ordinary rules regulating such interests. This means that a lessor who has exercised a right of distress will be entitled to priority over a secured creditor. Similarly, a statutory deemed trust will generally be entitled to priority over a secured creditor if the deemed trust was the first to attach or if the statute creating it contains a priority provision that subordinates a prior secured creditor. However, there are a number of provisions in the *BIA* that alter the ranking of certain types of claims in respect of receiverships. These are summarized below:

- *Thirty-day goods*: The right of a supplier to repossess thirty-day goods under section 81.1 also applies to a receivership.
- *Agricultural supplier charge*: The statutory charge on inventory in favour of a farmer, fisherman, or aquaculturalist created by section 81.2 applies to a receivership.
- *Employee charge*: A statutory charge that secures the unpaid wages of employees up to a maximum of $2,000 per employee is created by section 81.4 and is applicable to receiverships.
- *Pensions charge*: A statutory charge that secures unpaid pension contributions is created by section 81.6 and is applicable to receiverships.
- *Environmental charge*: The statutory charge that secures environmental remediation costs created by section 14.06(7) also applies to a receivership.

However, *BIA*, sections 86 and 87 or sections 67(2) and (3), do not apply to receiverships. As a consequence, statutory deemed trusts and statutory liens or charges in favour of the Crown are fully effective in a receivership. Although a lessor's right to distress is extinguished by the commencement of bankruptcy proceedings, the same does not hold true in a receivership. The statutory scheme of distribution that classifies certain types of claims as preferred claims applies only in bankruptcy proceedings. There is therefore no conflict between the federal and provincial statutes. By way of contrast, the conflict between the federal bankruptcy scheme of distribution and provincial statutes that purported to give the claim a higher priority led the Supreme Court of Canada to conclude that provincial statutes were inoperative in bankruptcy proceedings (see *Husky Oil Operations Ltd v Minister of National Revenue*, excerpted in Chapter 8.)

Secured creditors who have caused a receiver to be appointed often attempt to invoke bankruptcy proceedings in order to improve their priority ranking. The courts have not interceded to prevent them from doing so (see *Bank of Montreal v Scott Road Enterprises Ltd*, excerpted in Chapter 3). Tamara Buckwold and Roderick Wood, in "Priorities," in Stephanie

Ben-Ishai and Anthony Duggan, eds, *Canadian Bankruptcy and Insolvency Law: Bill C-55, Statute c. 47 and Beyond* (Toronto: LexisNexis, 2007) at 101, have observed that the existence of different priority rankings in bankruptcy, restructuring, and receivership proceedings results in regime shopping by creditors. They argue that this creates greater uncertainty for creditors in assessing insolvency risk, and that, insofar as possible, the same priority ranking should govern. They conclude (at 143):

> Fierce debates inevitably arise in insolvency law reform over the relative merits of certain claimants, and whether a particular class of claimants, such as unpaid employees, should be ranked higher than others. These are matters of central importance in insolvency law reform. However, these debates tend to overshadow an equally important matter. The priority rules differ within the major insolvency regimes, and these differences provide a strong incentive for parties to engage in strategic behaviour that seeks to procure the insolvency regime under which their claim is afforded the highest ranking. The recent legislative trend has been to create priority rules that operate with substantially similar effect within each of the insolvency regimes. This is an encouraging development. However, comprehensive insolvency law reform must go further than this. It must not be content with ensuring this only in respect of new priority rules that are enacted. It must attempt, as far as possible, to create a consistent set of priority rules that operate across all insolvency regimes.

V. THE CURRENT APPROACH TO RECEIVERSHIPS

In order to alleviate the risk that the debtor might dispose of or dissipate the assets during this period, the secured creditor is given the ability to apply to court for the appointment of an interim receiver. *BIA*, section 47(1), provides that the appointment of an interim receiver is effective for thirty days unless the court orders a longer period. It also comes to an end if a receiver or trustee takes possession of the property. The powers of an interim receiver are limited to those of a conservatory nature. Section 47(2) provides that a court may direct that an interim receiver take possession of the property, exercise control over the debtor's business, take conservatory measures, and summarily dispose of assets that are perishable or likely to depreciate rapidly in value.

Interim receivership is to be used where a secured creditor has a legitimate concern that the assets will be dissipated or disposed of before the secured creditor is able to enforce its security. Interim receivers cannot be used to liquidate the debtor's business. The court is not given the power to direct a sale of the assets or the business, or to direct the interim receiver to take such other action as the court considers advisable.

Although an interim receiver can no longer be used to liquidate the debtor's business, new provisions have been added that give the bankruptcy court the power to appoint a receiver, including a national receiver. Section 243(1) allows the bankruptcy court to appoint a receiver with power to take possession of the debtor's assets, exercise control over the debtor's business, and take any other action that the court considers advisable. This allows the court to confer the same kinds of powers that were formerly afforded to interim receivers, as was recognized by Moir J in *Re Railside Developments Ltd*, 2010 NSSC 13 at para 62:

> Having made interim receivership clearly interim, Parliament overhauled Part IX - Secured Creditors and Receivers to bring in a national receivership regime. Subsection 243(1) now gives the bankruptcy courts power to appoint receivers where the former

subsections applied to the superior courts as provincially constituted and exercising their ordinary jurisdiction.

Section 243(1.1) provides that a court may not appoint a receiver before the expiration of the ten-day notice period under section 244 unless the debtor consents to earlier enforcement or if the court considers it appropriate to do so. Section 243(5) provides that the application is to be made to the bankruptcy court having jurisdiction in the judicial district of the locality of the debtor.

The provisions of the *BIA* that impose obligations on receivers or create special priority rules in respect of receivers apply to a receiver appointed by a bankruptcy court pursuant to section 243(1). These provisions continue to apply to receivers appointed by a provincial superior court under business corporations legislation, personal property security legislation, or pursuant to the court's equitable jurisdiction to appoint receivers (recognized in the provincial judicature statutes, such as section 101(1) of the Ontario *Courts of Justice Act*, RSO 1990, c C.43), as well as to privately appointed receivers.

Labour relations legislation provides that a subsequent employer is bound by the employment obligations found in the collective agreements of its predecessor. The statutes give exclusive jurisdiction to labour relation boards to decide successor employer issues. Given the nature of their appointment, these statutes would expose receivers to liability. To that end, the *BIA* specifically addresses the question of successor liability. Section 14.06(1.2) provides that a trustee or receiver is not by reason of that fact personally liable in respect of a liability, including one as a successor employer, that exists before the trustee or receiver is appointed or that is calculated by reference to a period before the appointment.

Saskatchewan (Attorney General) v Lemare Lake Logging Ltd, 2015 SCC 53, [2015] 3 SCR 419

Judgment of Abella, Cromwell, Moldaver, Karakatsanis, Wagner and Gascon JJ delivered by ABELLA and GASCON JJ:

[1] Prior to 2005, receivership proceedings involving assets in more than one province were complicated by the simultaneous appointment of different receivers in different jurisdictions. Because of the inefficiency resulting from this multiplicity of proceedings, the federal government amended its bankruptcy legislation to permit their consolidation through the appointment of a national receiver. This appeal involves a constitutional challenge to provincial farm legislation on the grounds that it conflicts with this national receivership regime. For the reasons that follow, we see no such conflict.

Background

[2] Lemare Lake Logging Ltd., a secured creditor, brought an application pursuant to s. 243(1) of the *Bankruptcy and Insolvency Act*, R.S.C. 1985, c. B-3 (*BIA*), for the appointment of a receiver over substantially all of the assets except livestock of its debtor, 3L Cattle Company Ltd., a "farmer" within the meaning of *The Saskatchewan Farm Security Act*, S.S. 1988–89, c. S-17.1 (*SFSA*). 3L Cattle contested the appointment and argued that Lemare Lake had to comply with Part II of the *SFSA* before seeking the appointment of a receiver under s. 243(1).

[3] Part II of the *SFSA* provides that, before starting an action with respect to farm land, a creditor must serve a "notice of intention", engage in mandatory mediation, and prove that the debtor has no reasonable possibility of meeting its obligations or is not making a sincere and reasonable effort to meet its obligations. This includes an action for a receivership order pursuant to s. 243(1) of the *BIA*.

[4] Lemare Lake argued that the doctrine of paramountcy rendered certain provisions of the *SFSA* constitutionally inoperative where an application is made to appoint a receiver pursuant to s. 243(1) of the *BIA*. . . .

[14] Before this Court, the submissions were focussed on whether ss. 9 to 22 in Part II of the *SFSA* are constitutionally inoperative when an application is made to appoint a national receiver under s. 243(1) of the *BIA* by reason of the doctrine of paramountcy. For the following reasons, we agree with the chambers judge that there is no conflict, and therefore that ss. 9 to 22 of the *SFSA* are not constitutionally inoperable.

Analysis

[15] The guiding mantra of the paramountcy analysis is that "where there is an inconsistency between validly enacted but overlapping provincial and federal legislation, the provincial legislation is inoperative to the extent of the inconsistency". . .

[16] The first step in the analysis is to determine whether the federal and provincial laws are validly enacted. This requires looking at the pith and substance of the legislation to determine whether the matter comes within the jurisdiction of the enacting legislature. Assuming both laws are validly enacted, the second step requires consideration of whether any overlap between the two laws constitutes a conflict sufficient to render the provincial law inoperative. A provincial law will be deemed to be inoperative to the extent that it conflicts with or is inconsistent with the federal law . . .

[17] Two kinds of conflict are at play: (1) an *operational conflict*, where compliance with both the federal and provincial law is impossible; and (2) *frustration of purpose*, where the provincial law thwarts the purpose of the federal law . . .

[18] The operational conflict branch of the paramountcy doctrine requires that there be "actual conflict" between the federal and provincial legislation, that is, "the same citizens are being told to do inconsistent things": *Multiple Access Ltd v McCutcheon*, [1982] 2 S.C.R. 161, at p. 191. Stated otherwise, operational conflict arises "where one enactment says 'yes' and the other says 'no', such that 'compliance with one is defiance of the other'" . . . In *M & D Farm Ltd v Manitoba Agricultural Credit Corp.*, [1999] 2 S.C.R. 961, for example, an order granting leave to commence foreclosure proceedings under provincial legislation in circumstances where a stay had been granted under a federal statute, was found to be operationally inconsistent because the order made under the provincial statute purported to authorize the very litigation that the federal stay prohibited: paras. 39–42.

[19] Under the second branch of the paramountcy analysis, provincial legislation will be found to be inoperative when it frustrates the purpose of a federal law: *Canadian Western Bank*, at para. 73. In *Law Society of British Columbia v Mangat*, [2001] 3 S.C.R. 113, for example, this Court held that provincial legislation prohibiting non-lawyers from practising law for a fee before a tribunal, conflicted with federal legislation providing that a non-lawyer could represent a party before the Immigration and Refugee Board, even for a fee. Acknowledging that dual compliance was not strictly impossible because a person could either join the Law Society or not charge a fee, the Court nonetheless found the provincial law to be "contrary to Parliament's purpose": para. 72.

[20] Significantly, against the background of the two paramountcy paradigms of operational conflict and frustration of purpose, this Court cautioned in *Canadian Western Bank* that "[t]he fact that Parliament has legislated in respect of a matter does not lead to the presumption that in so doing it intended to rule out any possible provincial action in respect of that subject": para. 74. The fundamental rule of constitutional interpretation

is, instead, that "[w]hen a federal statute can be properly interpreted so as not to interfere with a provincial statute, such an interpretation is to be applied in preference to another applicable construction which would bring about a conflict between the two statutes"...

[21] Given the guiding principle of cooperative federalism, paramountcy must be narrowly construed. Whether under the operational conflict or the frustration of federal purpose branches of the paramountcy analysis, courts must take a "restrained approach", and harmonious interpretations of federal and provincial legislation should be favoured over interpretations that result in incompatibility...

[22] Constitutional doctrine should give due weight to the principle of cooperative federalism: *Canadian Western Bank*, at para. 24. This principle allows for some interplay, and indeed overlap, between both federal and provincial legislation ... Cooperative federalism accordingly "normally favours — except where there is an actual conflict — the application of valid rules adopted by governments at both levels as opposed to favouring a principle of relative inapplicability designed to protect powers assigned exclusively to the federal government or to the provinces"...

[23] While the principle of cooperative federalism cannot be seen as imposing limits on the otherwise valid exercise of legislative competence, it may be invoked to "facilitate interlocking federal and provincial legislative schemes and to avoid unnecessary constraints on provincial legislative action": *Quebec (Attorney General) v Canada (Attorney General)*, [2015] 1 S.C.R. 693, at paras. 17–19. In line with this principle, absent clear evidence that Parliament intended a broader statutory purpose, courts should avoid an expansive interpretation of the purpose of federal legislation which will bring it into conflict with provincial legislation. As this Court said in *Marcotte*, "care must be taken not to give too broad a scope to paramountcy on the basis of frustration of federal purpose": para. 72; see also *Canadian Western Bank*, at para. 74. This means that the purpose of federal legislation should not be artificially broadened beyond its intended scope. To improperly broaden the intended purpose of a federal enactment is inconsistent with the principle of cooperative federalism. At some point in the future, it may be argued that the two branches of the paramountcy test are no longer analytically necessary or useful, but that is a question for another day.

[24] The litigation in this case proceeded on the assumption that s. 243 of the *BIA* and Part II of the *SFSA* were validly enacted. Section 243 of the *BIA* falls within Parliament's exclusive power to enact laws in relation to bankruptcy and insolvency, while Part II of the *SFSA* falls within Saskatchewan's power to enact laws in relation to property and civil rights: *Constitution Act, 1867*, ss. 91(21) and 92(13).

[25] The parties essentially accepted the conclusion of the chambers judge and the Court of Appeal about the absence of operational conflict because it is possible to comply with both statutes by obtaining an order under the *SFSA* before seeking the appointment of a receiver under s. 243 of the *BIA*. The creditor can comply with both laws by observing the longer periods required by provincial law. In that regard, the federal law is permissive and the provincial law, more restrictive. This has been regularly considered not to constitute an operational conflict .... The issue before this Court therefore centres on whether the Court of Appeal was right to conclude that the provincial legislation frustrates the purpose of the federal legislation.

[26] To prove that provincial legislation frustrates the purpose of a federal enactment, the party relying on the doctrine "must first establish the purpose of the relevant federal statute, and then prove that the provincial legislation is incompatible with this purpose".... Clear proof of purpose is required: *COPA*, at para. 68. The burden a party

faces in successfully invoking paramountcy is accordingly a high one; provincial legislation restricting the scope of permissive federal legislation is insufficient on its own: *COPA*, at para. 66; see also *Ryan Estate*, at para. 69.

[27] And, as previously noted, paramountcy must be applied with restraint. In the absence of "very clear" statutory language to the contrary, courts should not presume that Parliament intended to "occupy the field" and render inoperative provincial legislation in relation to the subject: ...

[28] It is in light of the above principles that we turn to the federal and provincial provisions at issue.

[29] Section 243(1) is found in Part XI of the *BIA*, dealing with secured creditors and receivers. It authorizes a court, upon the application of a secured creditor, to appoint a receiver where such appointment is "just or convenient": ...

[30] In s. 243, courts are given the authority to appoint a receiver with the power to act nationally, thereby eliminating the need to apply to courts in multiple jurisdictions for the appointment of a receiver.

[31] Under s. 244(1), a secured creditor who intends to enforce a security on all or substantially all of the inventory, accounts receivable or other property of an insolvent debtor that was acquired for, or used in relation to, a business carried on by the insolvent person, is generally required to send a notice of that intention to the insolvent person. Section 243(1.1) states that, where notice is to be sent under s. 244(1), the appointment of a national receiver cannot be made before the expiry of 10 days after the day on which the secured creditor sends the notice: ...

[32] The national receivership regime does not oust a secured creditor's power to have a receiver appointed privately, or by court order under provincial law or any other federal law. Where, however, that receiver takes possession or control of all or substantially all of the inventory, accounts receivable or other property of the insolvent debtor or bankrupt, he or she is a "receiver" for purposes of Part XI of the *BIA* and must comply with the provisions in that part: see s. 243(2).

[33] The provincial scheme at issue, the *SFSA*, was enacted in 1988, with roots in legislation governing Saskatchewan farm land dating back several decades ...

[34] Part II of the *SFSA* is entitled "Farm Land Security". Its purpose is "to afford protection to farmers against loss of their farm land": s. 4.

[35] Subject to ss. 11 to 21, s. 9(1)(d) of the *SFSA* prohibits commencement of any "action" with respect to farm land. "[A]ction" is defined in s. 3 to include an action in court by a mortgagee with respect to farm land for the sale or possession of mortgaged farm land: s. 3(a)(ii). It includes an application for the appointment of a receiver under s. 243(1) of the *BIA*. Section 11(1)(a) states that, where a mortgagee makes an application with respect to a mortgage on farm land, the court may, on any terms and conditions that it considers just and equitable, order that s. 9(1)(d) does not apply. Where such an order is made, the mortgagee may then commence or continue an action with respect to that mortgage: s. 11(2). Failure to seek an order pursuant to s. 11 renders any action commenced without an order a nullity: s. 11(3). ...

[46] Section 243(1.1) states that, in the case of an insolvent person in respect of whose property a notice is to be sent under s. 244(1), the court may not appoint a receiver under s. 243(1) before the expiry of 10 days after the day on which the secured creditor sends the notice, unless the insolvent person consents or the court considers it appropriate to appoint a receiver sooner. The effect of the provision is to set a minimum waiting period. This does not preclude *longer* waiting periods under provincial law. There is nothing

in the words of the provision suggesting that this waiting period should be treated as a ceiling, rather than a floor, nor is there any authority that supports treating the waiting period as a maximum.

[47] In fact, the discretionary nature of the s. 243 remedy—as evidenced by the fact that the provision provides that a court "may" appoint a receiver if it is "just or convenient" to do so—lends further support to a narrower reading of the provision's purpose. A secured creditor is not entitled to appointment of a receiver. Rather, s. 243 is permissive, allowing a court to appoint a receiver where it is just or convenient. Provincial interference with a discretion granted under federal law is not, by itself, sufficient to establish frustration of federal purpose: *COPA*, at para. 66; see also *114957 Canada Ltée.*

[48] This case is thus easily distinguishable from *Bank of Montreal v Hall*, [1990] 1 S.C.R. 121, where the Court held that a security interest created pursuant to federal law could not, constitutionally, be subjected to the procedures for enforcement of security interests prescribed by provincial legislation. Unlike the self-executing remedy at issue in that case, where the bank could seize the chattel upon default without the need to go to court, the appointment of a s. 243 receiver is not mandatory. More importantly, in contrast with *Hall*, the s. 243 receivership remedy cannot be said to create a "complete code": p. 155. Nothing in the text of the provision or the *BIA* more generally suggests that s. 243 is meant to be a comprehensive remedy, exclusive of provincial law. The provision itself recognizes that a receiver may still be appointed under a security agreement or other provincial or federal laws, and creates no right to the appointment of a national receiver: s. 243(2)(*b*). As this Court observed in *COPA*, at para. 66, "permissive federal legislation, without more, will not establish that a federal purpose is frustrated when provincial legislation restricts the scope of the federal permission".

[49] Any uncertainty about whether s. 243 was meant to displace provincial legislation like the *SFSA* is further mitigated by s. 72(1) of the *BIA*, which states:

> 72.(1) The provisions of this Act shall not be deemed to abrogate or supersede the substantive provisions of any other law or statute relating to property and civil rights that are not in conflict with this Act, and the trustee is entitled to avail himself of all rights and remedies provided by that law or statute as supplementary to and in addition to the rights and remedies provided by this Act.

This too demonstrates that Parliament has explicitly recognized the continued operation of provincial law in the bankruptcy and insolvency context, except to the extent that it is inconsistent with the *BIA*: see *GMAC Commercial Credit Corp—Canada v TCT Logistics Inc*, [2006] 2 S.C.R. 123, at paras. 46–47.

[50] Other provisions of the *BIA* further support a more narrow reading of s. 243's purpose. Notably, s. 47 of the *BIA* empowers a court to appoint an interim receiver where a notice of intention to enforce a security was sent or is about to be sent under s. 244(1). Where there is an urgent need for the appointment of a receiver, the *BIA* thus provides a mechanism for the appointment of an interim receiver .... While s. 48 of the *BIA* provides that ss. 43 to 46 do not apply to individuals whose principal occupation is farming, the provision does not exempt farmers from the operation of s. 47. This shows that Parliament thinks farmers generally warrant special consideration, but not in cases where an interim receiver under s. 47 is found to be warranted. Promptness and timeliness is a concern that Parliament appears to have addressed precisely through the interim receivership regime. The potential conflict, if any, between s. 47 of the *BIA* and Part II of the *SFSA* is not, however, at issue in this appeal.

[51] The legislative history of s. 243 of the *BIA* further supports a narrow construction of the provision's purpose focussed on the establishment of a national receivership regime. The purpose of a court-appointed receiver, generally, "is to preserve and protect the property in question pending resolution of the issues between the parties" .... While historically receivership law was primarily a remedy for secured creditors, the legislative regulation of receiverships has resulted in many significant rights also being given to the debtor and other interested parties as well: Wood, at p. 459.

[Paras 52–66, which provide a detailed summary of the legislative changes, are omitted from this excerpt.]

[67] The preceding review confirms that s. 243's purpose is simply the establishment of a regime allowing for the appointment of a national receiver, thereby eliminating the need to apply for the appointment of a receiver in multiple jurisdictions: see Wood, at pp. 466–67. The 2005 and 2007 amendments to the *BIA* made clear that interim receivers were to be temporary in nature and have more limited powers, as originally intended, but gave courts the power to appoint a receiver with authority to act nationally, thereby increasing efficiency and removing the need to seek the appointment of a receiver in each jurisdiction where the debtor has assets...

[68] Section 243 was thus aimed at the establishment of a national receivership regime. Its purpose was to avoid a multiplicity of proceedings and the inefficiency resulting from them. There is no evidentiary basis for concluding that it was meant to circumvent the procedural and substantive requirements of the provincial laws where the appointment is sought. General considerations of promptness and timeliness, no doubt a valid concern in any bankruptcy or receivership process, cannot be used to trump the specific purpose of s. 243 and to artificially extend the provision's purpose to create a conflict with provincial legislation. Construing s. 243's purpose more broadly in the absence of clear evidence that Parliament intended a broader statutory purpose, is inconsistent with the requisite restrained approach to paramountcy and with the fundamental rule of constitutional interpretation referred to earlier in our reasons: paras. 20–21. Vague and imprecise notions like timeliness or effectiveness cannot amount to an overarching federal purpose that would prevent coexistence with provincial laws like the *SFSA*...

[69] Our conclusion is further bolstered by the operation of the federal *Farm Debt Mediation Act*, S.C. 1997, c. 21 (*FDMA*), legislation which allows an insolvent farmer to bring an application to stay proceedings by the farmer's creditors in order to engage in mediation and a review of the farmer's financial affairs: ss. 5 to 14. Under the *FDMA*, a security holder must give a farmer at least 15 business days' notice before seeking either to enforce any remedy against the property of a farmer or to commence any proceedings or any action, execution or other proceedings for the recovery of a debt, the realization of any security or the taking of any property of a farmer: s. 21. Before or after receiving such notice, the farmer may apply for a 30-day stay of proceedings against all creditors, a review of the farmer's financial affairs, and mediation between the farmer and all the farmer's creditors for the purpose of assisting them to reach a mutually acceptable arrangement: ss. 5(1)(*a*) and 7(1)(*b*); see also Bennett at p. 135. Where extension of the 30-day period is essential to the formulation of an arrangement between the farmer and the farmer's creditors, the stay can be extended for up to an additional 90 days: s. 13(1). When the stay is in effect, no creditor can enforce any remedy against the property of a farmer or commence or continue any proceedings or any action, execution or other

proceedings for the recovery of a debt, the realization of any security or the taking of any property of a farmer, notwithstanding any other law: s. 12.

[70] In describing the *FDMA*'s predecessor legislation in *M & D Farm*, this Court explained that the legislation was "intended to create a standstill period or moratorium of short duration" to give a farmer "a breathing space in which to attempt to reorganize his or her financial affairs" with "the assistance of a neutral panel to mediate with creditors": para. 18.

[71] While the federal *FDMA* and the provincial *SFSA* have different substantive and procedural requirements, they have similar purposes, and are aimed at the protection of farmer debtors. It is notable that Parliament has recognized that the receivership provision under s. 243 can be subordinated to similar delays in other legislation (including a 120-day stay under the *FDMA*, in comparison with 150 days under the *SFSA*), to allow for mediation and review of a farmer's financial situation. Given the presumption that Parliament does not enact related statutes that are inconsistent with one another, courts should avoid an interpretation of a federal statute which does not accommodate similar limitations imposed under a provincial statute: *Ryan Estate*, at paras. 80–81. In light of the *FDMA*, it follows that Parliament intended neither to preclude all notice periods longer than the 10-day notice period provided in the *BIA* nor to oust legislation which is intended to favour mediation between creditors and farmers regarding the enforcement of a security.

[72] Given these considerations and this analysis, we do not agree with the Court of Appeal's finding that the purpose of s. 243 was to afford a timely remedy to secured creditors. What seemed "self-evident" to the Court of Appeal (paras. 51–52), and led to its conclusion that the 10-day waiting period under s. 243(1.1) was a ceiling, is, with respect, neither supported by the evidence, nor compatible with a restrained approach to paramountcy. Furthermore, on this record, there is simply no evidence to support *amicus*'s argument that the 150-day delay or the other conditions in the *SFSA* frustrate any effectiveness or timeliness concerns. It is the burden of *amicus* to not only establish that these are, in fact, the purposes of s. 243, but also that the evidence supports a finding that the provincial law frustrates them in some way. The record is silent in that regard. That a recourse may take longer, or may have additional requirements, does not render it automatically ineffective or untimely, particularly when the assets at stake are farm lands.

Conclusion

[73] *Amicus* has, with respect, been unable to satisfy his burden to prove that ss. 9 to 22 of the *SFSA* conflict with the purpose of s. 243 of the *BIA*. Parliament's purpose of providing bankruptcy courts with the power to appoint a national receiver is not frustrated by the procedural and substantive conditions set out in the provincial legislation. While these conditions require a secured creditor to seek leave before bringing an application for the appointment of a receiver under s. 243 — a process which takes at least 150 days and imposes other procedural and substantive requirements — they do not hinder the purpose of allowing for the appointment of a national receiver. The purpose of permissive federal legislation is not frustrated simply because provincial legislation restricts the scope of that permission: *COPA*, at para. 66; *Ryan Estate*, at para. 69; see also *Rothmans, Benson & Hedges Inc.* The "high standard" for applying the paramountcy doctrine on the basis of frustration of federal purpose has accordingly not been met: *Ryan Estate*, at para. 84.

[74] The Court of Appeal's conclusion that Part II of the *SFSA* is constitutionally inoperative where an application is made to appoint a receiver pursuant to s. 243(1) of the *BIA*, is accordingly set aside. In view of the agreement of the parties, there will be no further order with respect to costs.

[The dissenting judgment focused on the importance of timeliness and efficiency in receivership proceedings.]

[75] CÔTÉ J. (dissenting)—It may be an old cliché, but in Canadian bankruptcy and insolvency law, its wisdom is unavoidable: time is of the essence. In the past, this Court has acknowledged that restructuring proceedings are a "hothouse of real-time litigation".... Timeliness is no less important for the appointment of a receiver—whether interim or full—as the receiver at once preserves and manages property while enforcing a secured creditor's rights.

[76] In light of this, I am of the view that a balance has been struck by Parliament in s. 243 of the *Bankruptcy and Insolvency Act*, R.S.C. 1985, c. B-3 ("*BIA*"), between the competing interests of secured creditors and insolvent debtors in the often dramatic circumstances surrounding a debtor's insolvency. While I agree with the majority's conclusion that Parliament's intention in enacting s. 243 *BIA* was to enable a secured creditor to apply for the appointment of an effective *national* receiver, I must dissent, because I do not believe that a full purposive account of s. 243 can end there. I am of the mind that Parliament also intended to establish a process for appointing national receivers that is timely, sensitive to the totality of circumstances and capable of responding to the emergencies that are known to occur in practice. In my view, these purposes are clearly on display in s. 243 *BIA*. To the extent that the operation of Part II of *The Saskatchewan Farm Security Act*, S.S. 1988–89, c. S-17.1 ("*SFSA*"), is incompatible with these purposes and with the federally calibrated balance that s. 243 represents, I see a frustration of purpose....

B. Narrow Construction of the Federal Purpose Endorsed by the Majority

[91] The majority sees in s. 243 only one purpose: to enable secured creditors to apply for the appointment of a national receiver, thereby eliminating the need to undertake the lengthy and cumbersome process of applying for a receiver in multiple jurisdictions. Respectfully, I cannot subscribe to so narrow a reading.

[92] I agree with my colleagues' assessment of the problem that *prompted* Parliament to introduce the national receivership scheme in what is now s. 243 *BIA*. Before that section was introduced, many had expressed concerns that the absence of a national receivership regime required secured creditors to undertake the cumbersome process of applying for a receiver in each province. In addition, a practice had emerged in some provinces of appointing interim receivers under s. 47 *BIA* and conferring broad nation-wide powers on them for indefinite periods, often lasting through to the final liquidation of a debtor's assets and displacing the intended role of a receiver appointed under the auspices of provincial law... Indeed, in 2006 this Court waded into the controversy. Abella J, for a majority of the Court, cautioned against an "open-ended" reading of s. 47 based on "jurisdictional largesse" in regard to unilateral declarations regarding third party rights: *GMAC Commercial Credit Corp—Canada v TCT Logistics Inc*, 2006 SCC 35, [2006] 2 S.C.R. 123, at paras. 45–46.

[93] The amendments passed in 2005 (c. 47) and 2007 (c. 36), both brought into force in 2009, aimed to bring clarity and consistency to the system of receivership under the

BIA. First, the amendments limited the powers of interim receivers appointed under s. 47 *BIA* as well as the duration of their appointments, which clearly became "interim" in nature. Second, Parliament reworked Part XI of the *BIA* so that s. 243 provided for the appointment of a national receiver over all or substantially all of an insolvent debtor's assets. This receivership regime is not exclusive; s. 243(2) *BIA* makes it clear that a national receiver may also be appointed by private agreement or under another Act, whether provincial or federal.

[94] I do not dispute that s. 243 *BIA*'s introduction was *prompted* by a need for a national full receiver, which would ensure that a secured creditor did not have to undertake the process of applying for a receiver in every province and would limit the need to have recourse to an interim receiver over indefinite periods. I also agree that receivers appointed under Part XI are subject to a uniform set of standards and duties.

[95] However, my colleagues have, in construing the federal purpose, focused principally on the specific mischief that prompted Parliament to amend Part XI of the *BIA* in 2005 and 2007, while largely overlooking the federal purposes related to receivership law that were given effect when Part XI was introduced in 1992 and that have carried through to modern day s. 243. It must be remembered that s. 243 is the product of an incremental evolution. The prescribed 10-day notice period for secured creditors seeking to enforce a security on all or substantially all of the inventory, accounts receivable or other property of a business debtor was among the first rules codified in Part XI of the *BIA* in 1992. It was designed to apply to receivers governed by the common law or by provincial legislation. In my view, it was then that Parliament struck a balance between the interest of secured creditors in a timely remedy and that of insolvent debtors in being afforded enough time to arrange their financial affairs. The 2005 and 2007 amendments — the latest steps in this legislative evolution — were specifically intended to provide secured creditors with access to a national receivership. However, I am convinced that the foundational purposes that have animated federal receivership law since 1992 must form part of any credible account of the federal purpose underlying today's s. 243. I fear that if this Court disregards these foundational purposes in its frustration of purpose analysis, the provinces will be left free to mangle the receivership scheme such that it no longer functions as Parliament intended it to.

[96] I will now attempt to address more specifically a number of arguments raised by my colleagues. In short, they argue that a narrow construction of s. 243's purpose is supported by the text of the *BIA*, by extrinsic evidence regarding its legislative history and by the purpose and operation of the *Farm Debt Mediation Act*, S.C. 1997, c. 21 ("*FDMA*"). Respectfully, I do not agree. ...

[128] I stress that in my view none of these factors is, on its own, determinative of the issue. Taking the operation of Part II of the *SFSA* as a whole, however, it is clear to me that the provincial legislation cannot operate in real time, and is in fact intended to hinder the timely appointment of a receiver over mortgaged farmland. It is therefore clear that Part II of the *SFSA* frustrates the purpose of s. 243 *BIA*, thereby triggering the application of the doctrine of federal paramountcy.

Appeal allowed.

* * * * *

The *Lemare Lake Logging* case raises questions about its applicability to real-time litigation. Roderick Wood, in "The Incremental Evolution of National Receivership Law and the Elusive Search for Federal Purpose" (2017) 26 *Constitutional Forum* 1 at 5 (footnotes omitted), argues:

> It is in the practices of the courts in hearing receivership proceedings that ideas of urgency and timeliness are most strongly encountered. And it is here that the majority decision of the Supreme Court of Canada is most out of step with the day-to-day activities of insolvency lawyers and judges. The majority suggests that timeliness and real-time responsiveness to changing dynamics are aspects of restructuring law, but are not animating features of receivership law. The idea of real-time litigation refers to the sensitivity to time that is necessary when delays can rapidly erode asset value. Real-time litigation is operationalized in two ways: through the special supervisory role of the judge who will hear several applications from the commencement of the proceedings to their conclusion; and, through the unique role of the insolvency practitioner who serves as a court officer (the monitor, trustee, or receiver) and provides the court and the creditors with critical information. Although the idea of real-time litigation was first developed in connection with restructuring proceedings, insolvency lawyers and professionals now recognize that these are more generalized insolvency law norms that guide the commercial list judges in all insolvency proceedings. Indeed, with the advent of the liquidating *CCAA*, there has been a blurring of the differences between restructuring and receiverships that further supports the application of the norms to both receivership and restructuring proceedings without differentiation.

For more commentary on this decision, see Virginia Torrie "Should Paramountcy Protect Secured Creditor Rights: *Saskatchewan v Lemare Lake Logging* in Historical Context" (2017) 22 *Review of Constitutional Studies* 405 and Jonathan Milani "Frustrating the Purpose of the Receivership Remedy: Federal Paramountcy in *Saskatchewan (Attorney General) v Lemare Lake Logging Ltd*" (2017) 80 *Saskatchewan Law Review* 253.

Discussion

The just and convenient test in *BIA*, section 243(1), is the same test that has been traditionally applied for the court appointment of a receiver. The pre-amendment case law on when such an appointment is appropriate continues to be relevant. There is some disagreement about the weight that should be given to the fact that the secured creditor has the right to privately appoint a receiver pursuant to the terms of the security agreement. Justice Burnyeat in *United Savings Credit Union v F & R Brokers Inc*, 2003 BCSC 640 at para 15 stated that "unless the mortgagor or charge holder can show that extraordinary circumstances are present, the appointment of a Receiver or Receiver Manager at the instigation of a foreclosing mortgagee should be made as a matter of course if the mortgagee can show default under the mortgage." See also *Potentia Renewables Inc v Deltro Electric Ltd*, 2018 ONSC 3437 at para 47, where the court determined that it should not lightly interfere with a contractual provision reached by the parties on the appointment of a receiver. However, other courts have departed from this view. Justice Willcock, in *Textron Financial Canada Limited v Chetwynd Motels Ltd*, 2010 BCSC 477 at para 55 stated:

> In light of these authorities, I conclude that the statutory requirement that the appointment of a receiver be just and convenient does not permit or require me to begin my assessment of the material with the presumption that the plaintiff is entitled to a

court-appointed receiver unless the defendant can demonstrate a compelling commercial or other reason why the order should not be made.

The fact that the secured creditor has the right to make a private appointment of a receiver is a strong factor that a court can consider, but the court must also consider other matters as well and should not grant the order if there are other remedies, The Alberta Court of Appeal in *BG International Limited v Canadian Superior Energy Inc*, 2009 ABCA 127 at paras 16–17 stated that:

> We agree that the appointment of a receiver is a remedy that should not be lightly granted. The chambers judge on such an application should carefully explore whether there are other remedies, short of a receivership, that could serve to protect the interests of the applicant.… Justice and convenience can only be established by considering and balancing the position of both parties. The onus is on the applicant. The respondent does not have to prove any special hardship, much less "undue hardship" to resist such an application. The effect of the mere granting of the receivership order must always be considered, and if possible a remedy short of receivership should be used.

The latter view, that a receivership is "extraordinary relief which should be granted cautiously and sparingly" has been upheld by more recent cases (see *Cascade Divide Enterprises Inc v Laliberte*, 2013 BCSC 263 at para 81 and *Schmidt v Balcom*, 2016 BCSC 2438 at para 75).

The sale process involved in a court appointed receivership is very similar to the sale process in a liquidating *CCAA* except that the statutory requirements for approval in *CCAA*, section 36, are not applicable. See the discussion in Chapter 13, Part VII. The sale process most often takes the form of a sale by tender, but in appropriate cases a stalking horse sales process may be used (see *Callidus Capital Corporation v Xchange Technology Group LLC*, 2013 ONSC 6783). *Royal Bank of Canada v Soundair Corporation* (1991), 4 OR (3d) 1 (CA) (*Soundair*) established the following criteria to be applied when considering the approval of a sale by a receiver:

(1) whether the receiver has made a sufficient effort to get the best price and has not acted improvidently;

(2) whether the interests of all parties have been considered;

(3) the efficacy and integrity of the process by which offers are obtained; and

(4) whether there has been unfairness in the working out of the process.

When the sales process is not transparent, the court cannot determine whether the *Soundair* principles have been met. In *Jaycap Financial Ltd v Snowdon Block Inc*, 2019 ABCA 47, Romaine J determined that without transparency, and the "significant questions left unanswered by the Receiver," there were "serious concerns about the efficacy, fairness and integrity of the process the receiver followed … to approve the second asset purchase agreement" (para 33).

VI. TEMPLATE RECEIVERSHIP ORDERS

Uncertainty over the appropriateness of terms in a receivership order led to the development of template receivership orders. In Ontario, a subcommittee of the Commercial List Users' Committee developed a standard form receivership order together with an explanatory note. Similar template receivership orders have been developed in British Columbia, Alberta, and Saskatchewan. The template receivership order provided for the concurrent appointment of a receiver under *BIA*, section 243(1), and provincial statutes that regulated receiverships were brought into play. The template receivership orders were drafted to avoid the excesses of earlier orders in that they did not attempt to immunize the receiver from liability beyond that provided by statute. Variation in a template order was possible, but the changes had to be blacklined or struck out so as to specifically bring them to the attention of the court.

The template receivership orders include the following features:

1) Concurrent appointment of the receiver as an interim receiver under the *BIA* and as a receiver-manager pursuant to provincial legislation.

2) Conferral of a wide range of powers on the receiver, including the power to:

   - take possession and control of the property and protect and preserve it;
   - manage, operate, and carry on the business;
   - cease carrying on all or part of the business and performing any contract;
   - engage consultants and experts;
   - commence, continue, or defend a legal action and settle or compromise legal proceedings;
   - market the property for sale; and
   - report to, meet, and discuss matters concerning the property with interested stakeholders.

3) Provisions that prevent commencement or continuation of any proceedings against the debtor or the debtor's property and that stay all rights and remedies against the debtor or the receiver or those affecting the property except with the consent of the receiver or the leave of the court.

4) Provisions that prevent any person from terminating, repudiating, or failing to perform any right, renewal right, contract, or licence or from discontinuing the supply of goods or services pursuant to an agreement or a statutory or regulatory mandate without the consent of the receiver or the leave of the court.

5) Provision for the creation of a superpriority charge on the assets under receivership that secure the receiver's fee and a charge that secures any borrowings by the receiver that has priority over any prior secured creditor.

6) A comeback clause under which any interested party can apply to the court to vary or amend the order.

The template receivership orders in Ontario and British Columbia provide that a receiver incurs no liability or obligation as a result of its appointment or carrying out of the provisions of the order, except for any gross negligence or wilful misconduct on its part. Although section 243(1) of the *BIA* does away with the need to appoint a receiver under several different statutes, it appears that concurrent appointments are still being asked for and granted. Justice Yamauchi in *Canadian Western Bank v 702348 Alberta Ltd*, 2009 ABQB 271 at para 25, aff'd 2010 ABCA 227, commented:

> The court purportedly appointed the Receiver pursuant to a number of different provisions of various statutes. This is unfortunate, because without guidance on the statute from which the Receiver purports to derive its powers or under which the Receiver must fulfill its duties, this Court must try to match the various provisions of the Receivership Order with the statute under which the Receiver is purporting to act. A better approach would be to outline the statute under which the Receiver seeks to derive its power. Otherwise, unanticipated consequences could result, if the court were to grant the Receiver a particular power under a statute for which the court has no authority.

Practice Questions

Equity Capital Inc (Equity) made two demand credit facilities available to Sensory Corporation (Sensory). The first facility is a revolving operating loan facility with a credit limit up to $4.5 million; the second facility is a non-revolving reducing loan facility with a credit limit up to $3.5 million. The security for all amounts owing from Sensory to Equity is detailed in a general security agreement (GSA) dated 1 September 2019, which grants Equity a security over all Sensory's present and after-acquired personal property, and all present and after-acquired real, immoveable, and leasehold property. Equity registered its security in the Alberta Personal Property Registry (PPR). Equity has also entered into subordination agreements with one other registrant in the PPR.

Sensory began to experience cash flow problems in 2018 and it sought Equity's approval to defer monthly interest payments on both facilities while it carried out a sale process. Unfortunately, Sensory only received one bid in the sale process, and that bid was insufficient to pay Sensory's outstanding indebtedness.

The relationship between Equity and Sensory has deteriorated. Sensory has failed to pay to Equity all amounts due when owing. It has also failed to maintain a replacement reserve of cash, which it is required to do under the GSA. The Debt Service Coverage ratio is less than required under the GSA. In addition, Sensory has failed to provide unconsolidated financial statements to Equity within ninety days after the end of each fiscal year, as well as further information regarding its assets, operations, and financial condition, upon request. Essentially, Sensory has failed to respond to Equity's demand letters, and it has ceased responding to any attempts at communication by Equity.

Equity has now removed Sensory's access to credit under the two demand credit facilities. You are the Senior Vice President and Chief Risk Officer at Equity. Draft an argument specifying the facts and events that would support the appointment of a receiver over Sensory. Remember that, at this point, you do not have very much information about Sensory's financial situation.

CHAPTER 18

Cross-Border Insolvencies

I. INTRODUCTION

This chapter deals with a branch of the conflict of laws commonly referred to as "cross-border insolvency law" or "international insolvency or bankruptcy law." In a globalized world, it is common for businesses to operate in many different countries, and this creates an additional layer of complexity when those businesses become insolvent. A business may have assets and creditors spread across multiple countries, and those countries may have insolvency laws that vary—both with respect to procedures and substantive outcomes. The following example illustrates some of the issues that may arise.

American Oil Co is a corporation incorporated under Delaware law. Its head office is in Los Angeles, United States, and it has branch offices across Canada. American Oil Co also has a subsidiary operating in Canada that was incorporated under provincial law, Canadian Oil Co. American Oil Co has become financially distressed as a result of depressed world energy prices.

1) Can either or both American Oil Co and Canadian Oil Co start insolvency proceedings in Canada? The question of when Canadian courts will take jurisdiction over a debtor is addressed below in Part II.

2) If American Oil Co and Canadian Oil Co start insolvency proceedings in the United States, will Canadian courts enforce orders granted by the American bankruptcy court (for example, a stay of proceedings)? The question of when Canadian courts will cooperate with foreign courts and enforce their insolvency orders is addressed below in Part III.

3) If Canadian Oil Co discharges its debts through American insolvency proceedings, will that discharge be enforceable in Canada? The question of when a foreign discharge of debt will be enforceable is addressed below in Part IV.

4) When exercising its powers in cross-border insolvency proceedings, will a Canadian court ensure that Canadian secured creditors are accorded privileged treatment, comparable to the privileged treatment they receive under Canadian insolvency law? Will a Canadian court provide comparable protection to foreign secured creditors? The position of Canadian courts towards secured creditors is addressed below in Part V.

5) Will American Oil Co and Canadian Oil Co be treated as separate entities, requiring separate insolvency proceedings? Can the two companies' insolvency proceedings be consolidated for the purpose of administrative efficiency? Can the two companies' assets and liabilities be treated as the assets and liabilities of one company, if doing so results in a fairer distribution to the companies' creditors? The issues applicable to the cross-border insolvencies of corporate groups are addressed below in Part VI.

6) If Canadian Oil Co made a number of preferential payments to a non-arm's length creditor prior to commencing insolvency proceedings, should those payments be impeached using American or Canadian law? The question of which jurisdiction's avoidance power should be used is addressed below in Part VII.

II. JURISDICTION OF CANADIAN COURTS

Creditors may have various reasons for wanting to initiate insolvency proceedings in Canada, such as to prevent Canadian assets from being removed to the foreign jurisdiction without the creditors' consent, or to ensure that the Canadian-based assets are distributed in accordance with the *Bankruptcy and Insolvency Act*, RSC 1985 c B-3 (*BIA*) distributional rules. The jurisdiction of Canadian courts over insolvent individuals and companies has long been determined by Canadian bankruptcy legislation.

An assignment can be made by an "insolvent person," which is defined in section 2(1) as "a person who is not bankrupt and who resides, carries on business or has property in Canada, whose liabilities to creditors provable as claims under this Act amount to one thousand dollars" and who meets one of the three insolvency tests, discussed above in Chapter 3. The "property" jurisdictional base was added to the *BIA* in 1997 and greatly increases the jurisdiction of Canadian courts, particularly because there is no requirement that the bulk of the debtor's property must be located in Canada.

In the case of involuntary proceedings, the *BIA* provides that the bankruptcy application may be brought in Canada against a "debtor," which is defined in section 2(1) to include "an insolvent person and any person who, at the time an act of bankruptcy was committed by him, resided or carried on business in Canada and, where the context requires, includes a bankrupt."

Despite the broad definition of debtor, it is not clear whether the location of property is alone sufficient to give a court jurisdiction in involuntary proceedings. The point can be argued both ways, for example see *Re Dalsto* (2002), 38 CBR (4th) 181 (Ont Sup Ct J), and *Re Chauvco Resources International*, 1999 ABQB 56.

Note that the definition of "insolvent person" uses the present tense, that is, resides, carries on business, or has property, whereas the definition of debtor uses the past tense. This difference in verb tenses proved important in the case of *Pocklington (Re)*, 2017 ABQB 621. In *Pocklington*, the court was asked whether an individual could file a Division I proposal in Canada. To do so, the individual had to fit within the definition of "insolvent person."

Pocklington (Re), 2017 ABQB 621, 417 DLR (4th) 566 (footnotes omitted)

[Peter Pocklington may be best known as the former owner of the Edmonton Oilers, who made the decision to trade Wayne Gretzky to the Los Angeles Kings. He was also an energetic entrepreneur, who operated many businesses in Alberta. In the 1980s, his businesses received a $67-million bailout from the Alberta government. Pocklington defaulted on the contract governing the bailout, and the Alberta government acquired a judgment against Pocklington as a result of the default. By 2017, the Alberta government's judgment was valued at $13.5 million. Pocklington relocated to California in the 1990s and became subject to additional claims there because of his American business ventures. He filed for Chapter 7 bankruptcy in the United States in 2008, plead guilty to bankruptcy fraud in 2010, and a court permanently denied his application for an American discharge in 2010.

Pocklington then filed a commercial proposal in Canada, proposing to pay his creditors $2 million (from an undisclosed source) on $21.6 million in claims.

Pocklington claimed that he met the definition of insolvent person by "point[ing] to a longstanding line of cases that stand for the proposition that the mere existence of trade debts in Alberta constitutes a constructive, or deemed, carrying on of business and therefore qualifies him as an 'insolvent person'" (at para 29). The Alberta government countered that a person with a trade debt could be subject to an involuntary bankruptcy order, but could not make a voluntary assignment into bankruptcy nor a proposal. The court agreed with the Alberta government and declared Pocklington's proposal to be a nullity.]

[52] The well-established twin fundamental purposes of the *BIA* are to ensure the equitable distribution of a bankrupt's assets among the estate's creditors and to provide for the financial rehabilitation of insolvent persons. Professor Roderick J Wood suggests a third objective: "the prevention of fraud and abuse of the bankruptcy system, the promotion of commercial morality, and the protection of the credit system."

[53] *BIA* s 50(1) provides that an *insolvent person* can make a proposal. While the primary objective of this provision is financial rehabilitation, the second objective of the *BIA* is also in play because there must also be a mechanism for orderly distribution of the insolvent person's assets in the event the proposal fails.

[54] While not in issue in this case, the impact of *Donaldson* warrants discussion of the voluntary assignment provision. *BIA* s 49(1) provides that an insolvent person can make a voluntary assignment in bankruptcy. As noted by the *Donaldson* Court, both objects of the *BIA* are in play in that scenario.

[55] Section 2 defines insolvent person as:

> *insolvent person* means a person who is not bankrupt and who resides, <u>carries on business</u> or has property in Canada . . .

> *personne insolvable* Personne qui n'est pas en faillite et qui réside au Canada ou y exerce ses activités ou qui a des biens au Canada . . .

[56] Both French and English definitions use the present tense of the verb "to carry [on]".

[57] In contrast, *BIA* s 43 provides that a bankruptcy order can be sought against a <u>debtor</u>, which is defined as:

> *debtor* includes an insolvent person and any person who, at the time an act of bankruptcy was committed by him, resided or <u>carried on business</u> in Canada. . .

> *débiteur* Sont assimilées à un débiteur toute personne insolvable et toute personne qui, à l'époque où elle a commis un acte de faillite, résidait au Canada ou y <u>exerçait des activités</u>. . .

[58] Both the French and English definitions use the past tense of the verb "to carry [on]".

[59] Unlike the UK's bankruptcy laws of 1914 and 1986 that do not employ the term "insolvent person", the *BIA* has done so since 1927. This definition was expanded in 1952 to include ". . . a person who is not bankrupt and who resides or *carries on business* in Canada, whose liabilities to creditors provable as claims under this Act amount to one thousand dollars . . ."

[60] A plain reading of these definitions using their grammatical and ordinary [*sic*] is indicative of Parliament deliberately choosing different thresholds for different scenarios. For a creditor-driven bankruptcy, there must be a link with a person having *carried*

on business at the time of the alleged act of bankruptcy. For a debtor-driven proposal or voluntary bankruptcy, the link must be to a business that the person *carries* on.

[61] The distinction between the requirement for past activity for a creditor-driven proceeding and present activity for a debtor-driven one results in more favourable treatment of creditors over debtors. In Pocklington's view, this produces an absurd result by defeating the purpose of the *BIA*. In contrast, the Province contends that allowing an individual in Pocklington's circumstance to access *BIA* relief creates an absurdity, since it is abusive of the process and cannot possibly be what Parliament intended.

[62] In my view, the existence of the twin objects of the *BIA* does not equate to automatic equal treatment under it. Indeed, Parliament is fully capable of creating different entry thresholds to address different goals and mischiefs.

[63] As to the mischief addressed, it is not unheard of for businesspersons to abscond from a jurisdiction leaving their business debts behind. The long-arm approach addresses this. Excepting *Granatstein* and *Donaldson*, every relevant case applying the long-arm approach concerns creditor recourse in respect to an absconding business debtor. Here, I note that like the *BIA*'s definition of "debtor", the governing statute at issue in Theophile and Bird employs the past tense (*"has carried on business* in England") to link the act of bankruptcy to the ability to petition a person into bankruptcy. I also note that unlike the *BIA*, the UK's *Insolvency Act 1986* and *Bankruptcy Act, 1914* do not employ the term "insolvent person".

[64] Pocklington points to this obiter phrase in *North v Skipton Building Society* to support the notion that the specific language used by Parliament is not in and of itself an answer:

> It is common ground that the phrase "has carried on a business" is not defined for the purposes of the *Insolvency Act 1986*. The phrase "carrying on a business" is a chameleon phrase which takes its meaning from context.

[65] While the term "chameleon phrase" is an interesting one that may have application elsewhere, it has no place for interpreting the presumed careful and consistent wording used by Parliament to set out what the terms "debtor" and "insolvent person" mean in the context of creditor-driven and debtor-driven *BIA* proceedings.

[66] Relevant only to the extent of involving statutory interpretation of past and present tense use in insolvency legislation is *Williams v Simpson*. The issue was recognition of an English bankruptcy proceeding under New Zealand's *Insolvency (Cross-border) Act 2006*, which provides for such recognition if the debtor had an "establishment", meaning a place of operations in England, where debtor carried out a non-transitory economic activity with human means or good or services.

[67] The Court refused to follow *Theophile* and *Bird* noting that the local law uses the present tense (*"carries* on a non-transitory economic activity") which is different to the past tense used in the English law.

[68] In the result, I find that Parliament's choice of language is intended to permit only those insolvent persons who reside or have property in Canada or who have current business interests in Canada to access the *BIA* proposal provisions. The mere existence of dated trade debts does not suffice.

[69] Pocklington's NOI and proposal are a nullity from the date of their filing.

Application granted.

* * * * *

The *Companies' Creditors Arrangement Act*, RSC 1985, c C-36 (*CCAA*) can be used by a company incorporated in Canada or a company incorporated elsewhere if it has assets or does business in Canada (*CCAA*, s 2, "company").

The Canadian trustee in bankruptcy is entitled to claim the debtor's property wherever it is located—in Canada or elsewhere (*BIA*, s 2(1), "property," and s 67(1)). Likewise, the debtor's foreign, as well as Canadian, creditors will be subject to the Canadian court's jurisdiction and will be entitled to file proofs of claim (*BIA*, s 2(1), "creditor"). Absent special *BIA* rules, the question whether the estate has a valid claim to particular property and whether a creditor has a valid secured or unsecured claim will be governed by general conflict of laws principles (American Law Institute, Transnational Insolvency Project, *International Statement of Canadian Bankruptcy Law*, Part II.D (Huntington, NY: Juris Publishing, 2003)).

Difficulties also arise in determining the ranking of foreign creditors under the *BIA*'s superpriority and preferred claim provisions. It seems clear that non-preferred creditors, Canadian and foreign, will be treated alike. Other cases are more complex. Consider three:

- *Foreign revenue claims.* Normally, Canadian courts will not recognize and enforce foreign revenue claims. Yet, on the particular facts in *Re Sefel Geophysical Ltd* (1988), 54 DLR (4th) 117 (Alta QB), Forsyth J recognized a US tax claim.

- *Foreign employee claims.* Amendments to the *Wage Earners Protection Program Act*, SC 2005, c-46, clarify that payments under that program are available to employees, whose employers have sought recognition in Canada of a foreign insolvency proceeding, but the program will only reimburse employees for eligible wages earned in Canada: *A second Act to implement certain provisions of the budget tabled in Parliament on February 27, 2018 and other measures*, SC 2018, c 27, s 629(2).

- *Foreign farmer claims.* The superpriority security interest available to "farmers" under *BIA*, section 81.2, is only available to people carrying out farming activities in Canada, because "farm" is defined as "land in Canada used for the purpose of farming." The territorial restriction of this superpriority has created tensions with the United States (Anna Lund, "Engaging Canadians in Commercial Law Reform: Insights and Lessons from the 2014 Industry Canada Consultation on Insolvency Legislation" (2016) 58 *Canadian Business Law Journal* 123).

III. RECOGNITION AND ENFORCEMENT OF FOREIGN INSOLVENCIES

A. Theoretical Approaches

When a debtor has connections with multiple jurisdictions, there are, theoretically, different ways of managing the debtor's insolvency. Two key theoretical binaries that may apply are: (1) territorialism versus universalism, and (2) unified proceedings versus plural proceedings.

The Supreme Court of Canada adopted the following definition of territorialism and universalism in the case of *Holt Cargo Systems Inc v ABC Containerline NV (Trustees of)*, 2001 SCC 90 at para 23, citing *Re Treco*, 240 F3d 148 (US CA 2nd Cir 2001) at 153:

Under the "territoriality" approach, or the "Grab Rule," the court in each jurisdiction where the debtor has assets distributes the assets located in that jurisdiction pursuant to local rules. Under the "universality" approach, a primary insolvency is instituted in the debtor's domiciliary country, and ancillary courts in other jurisdictions—typically in jurisdictions where the debtor has assets—defer to the foreign proceeding and in effect collaborate to facilitate the centralized liquidation of the debtor's estate according to the rules of the debtor's home country.

In a unified proceeding, all of a debtor's assets and liabilities will be dealt with in one proceeding, whereas in plural proceedings, a debtor's assets and liabilities will be dealt with in multiple proceedings, taking place in the various jurisdictions where the debtor resided, operated, or held property. For example, imagine that a company, North American Pickle Co, carried on business in both Canada and the United States, but was headquartered in Toronto. Its insolvency proceedings could take many different forms:

- Unified, universal approach—all assets and liabilities are dealt with through insolvency proceedings in Canada applying Canadian law. Note that when a universal approach is adopted, there must be a method for determining which jurisdiction's insolvency laws should apply. See the discussion below of the "centre of main interest" (COMI) test used in the United Nations Commission on International Trade Law (UNCITRAL) Model Law on Cross-Border Insolvency (1997),[1] as enacted in the *BIA* and the *CCAA*.
- Pluralist, territorial approach—the Canadian assets and liabilities are dealt with in Canadian proceedings using Canadian law and the American assets and liabilities are dealt with in American proceedings using American law. A key question when a territorial approach is adopted is how to determine the location of an asset. With tangible assets, this can be a straightforward exercise, but the question of location can become more complex when assets are intangible: for example, see the *Nortel Networks* decision, excerpted below in Part VI.
- Unified, territorial approach—all assets and liabilities are dealt with through insolvency proceedings in Canada, but the Canadian court applies Canadian insolvency law to the Canadian assets and liabilities and American law to the American assets and liabilities.
- Pluralist, universal approach—the Canadian assets and liabilities are dealt with in Canadian proceedings using Canadian law and the American assets and liabilities are dealt with in American proceedings, but the American court applies Canadian legal principles—often by enforcing orders granted in the Canadian proceedings.

Jay Westbrook, a leading American international insolvency scholar, is a strong advocate of the universalist theory. He has argued in many articles that the universalist approach makes most sense, is more efficient than the other theories, and provides greater predictability of results in a world dominated by large multinational corporations, where the most important assets of a debtor are often held in intangible form and their location can be switched to another jurisdiction with the click of a computer button.

Canadian courts have generally adopted some variation of "modified universalism," which involves recognizing and giving effect to foreign insolvency orders, but with a number of exceptions and qualifications. In particular, Anglo-Canadian courts have consistently held that the existence of insolvency proceedings in a foreign jurisdiction does not preclude initiation of proceedings in Canada or the United Kingdom, although, as a matter of practice, the bankruptcy order is usually confined to assets of the debtor located within the jurisdiction.

---

1   See United Nations Commission on International Trade Law, UNCITRAL Model Law on Cross-Border Insolvency (1997), online: www.uncitral.org/uncitral/en/uncitral_texts/insolvency/1997Model.html.

B. Evolution of Canadian Law

The common law rule applied by Canadian courts for a number of years was that recognition would be given to a foreign bankruptcy order if it had been granted by a court or agency of competent jurisdiction in the jurisdiction of the debtor's domicile. "Domicile" here meant, as elsewhere in the conflict of laws, the jurisdiction with which the debtor was deemed to have the closest connection. In the case of a corporation, this approach meant the corporation's place of incorporation. See, for example, *Williams v Rice*, [1926] 3 DLR 225 (Man KB) and *Re IIT* (1975), 8 OR (2d) 359 (High Ct J).

Registrar Funduk's lively judgment in *Singer Sewing Machine Co of Canada Ltd (Re) (Trustee of)*, 2000 ABQB 116 reflects the narrow approach that Canadian courts historically took to recognizing and enforcing foreign bankruptcy judgments. In that case, the Canadian bankruptcy registrar refused to recognize and enforce an American Chapter 11 order, which purported to apply to both an American parent company and its Canadian subsidiary. Registrar Funduk reasoned (at para 26):

> Comity does not require me to recognize a chapter 11 order over a Canadian company carrying on business only in Canada and whose assets are all in Canada. Who the shareholders are is irrelevant and who the creditors are is irrelevant. Under Alberta law neither gives an American bankruptcy court jurisdiction over Singer Canada.

Comity, mentioned above by Registrar Funduk, is an important principle in private international law. The Supreme Court of Canada endorsed the following definition of comity in the case of *Morguard Investments Ltd v De Savoye*, [1990] 3 SCR 1077 at 1096, citing *Hilton v Guyot*, 159 US 113 (1895) at 163–64:

> "Comity" in the legal sense, is neither a matter of absolute obligation, on the one hand, nor of mere courtesy and good will, upon the other. But it is the recognition which one nation allows within its territory to the legislative, executive or judicial acts of another nation, having due regard both to international duty and convenience, and to the rights of its own citizens or of other persons who are under the protection of its laws.

In *Morguard*, a judgment creditor sought to have an Alberta judgment recognized in British Columbia. The judgment arose in foreclosure proceedings against land that was owned by the defendant and located in Alberta. The Supreme Court of Canada held that it was appropriate for the British Columbia Court to recognize the Alberta judgment because there was a substantial connection between Alberta (the jurisdiction granting the initial judgment) and the damages suffered by the judgment creditor. The SCC noted, at 1098:

> The business community operates in a world economy, and we correctly speak of a "world community" even in the face of decentralized political and legal power. Accommodating the flow of wealth, skills and people across state lines has now become imperative.

Many subsequent lower courts interpreted the Supreme Court's judgment in *Morguard* as meaning that, absent special circumstances, a foreign judgment will be enforced in Canada if there is a "substantial connection" between the foreign jurisdiction and the defendant. The Supreme Court confirmed the correctness of this interpretation in *Beals v Saldanha*, 2003 SCC 72.

In the Canadian cross-border insolvency case of *Babcock & Wilcox Canada Ltd* (2000), 18 CBR (4th) 157 (Ont Sup Ct J), Farley J cited the doctrine of comity, *Morguard*, above, and section 18.6 of the *CCAA* (discussed below) when adopting an expansive view of when foreign insolvency orders should be recognized in Canada. *Babcock & Wilcox* was factually similar to *Singer Sewing Machine Co*, above: the Canadian subsidiary was seeking to enforce a stay order granted in American Chapter 11 proceedings. Unlike Registrar Funduk in *Singer Sewing Machine Co*, Farley J allowed the application:

[9] In the context of cross-border insolvencies, Canadian and US Courts have made efforts to complement, coordinate and where appropriate accommodate the proceedings of the other. Examples of this would include *Olympia & York Developments Ltd, Ever fresh Beverages Inc* and *Loewen Group Inc v Continental Insurance Co of Canada* [(1997), 48 CCLI (2d) 119 (BC SC)]. Other examples involve the situation where a multi-jurisdictional proceeding is specifically connected to one jurisdiction with that jurisdiction's court being allowed to exercise principal control over the insolvency process: see *Roberts v Picture Butte Municipal Hospital* (1998), [1998] AJ No 817 (QB), at pp 5-7. . . .

[10] In *Roberts*, Forsythe J at pp 5-7 noted that steps within the proceedings themselves are also subject to the dictates of comity in recognizing and enforcing a US Bankruptcy Court stay in the Dow Corning litigation [*Taylor v Dow Corning Australia Pty Ltd* (December 19, 1997), Doc 8438/95 (Australia Vic Sup Ct)] as to a debtor in Canada so as to promote greater efficiency, certainty and consistency in connection with the debtor's restructuring efforts. Foreign claimants were provided for in the US corporation's plan. Forsyth J stated:

> Comity and cooperation are increasingly important in the bankruptcy context. *As internationalization increases, more parties have assets and carry on activities in several jurisdictions. Without some coordination there would be multiple proceedings, inconsistent judgments and general uncertainty.*
>
> . . . *I find that common sense dictates that these matters would be best dealt with by one court, and in the interest of promoting international comity it seems the forum for this case is in the US Bankruptcy Court.* Thus, in either case, whether there has been an attornment or not, I conclude it is appropriate for me to exercise my discretion and apply the principles of comity and grant the Defendant's stay application. I reach this conclusion based on all the circumstances, including the clear wording of the US Bankruptcy Code provision, the similar philosophies and procedures in Canada and the US, the Plaintiff's attornment to the jurisdiction of the US Bankruptcy Court, and the incredible number of claims outstanding . . .
>
> (emphasis added)

[11] The *CCAA* as remedial legislation should be given a liberal interpretation to facilitate its objectives. . . .

[12] . . . The philosophy of the practice in international matters relating to the *CCAA* is set forth in *Olympia & York Developments Ltd v Royal Trust Co* (1993), 20 CBR (3d) 165 (Ont Gen Div), at p 167 where Blair J stated:

> The Olympia & York re-organization involves proceedings in three different jurisdictions: Canada, the United States and the United Kingdom. Insolvency disputes with international overtones and involving property and assets in a multiplicity of jurisdictions are becoming increasingly frequent. Often there are differences in legal concepts - sometimes substantive, sometimes procedural—between the jurisdictions. The Courts of the various jurisdictions should seek to cooperate amongst themselves, in my view, in facilitating the trans-border resolution of such disputes as a whole, where that can be done in a fashion consistent with their own fundamental principles of jurisprudence. The interests of international cooperation and comity, and the interests of developing at least some degree of certitude in international business and commerce, call for nothing less.

C. The 1997 Amendments

In *Babcock & Wilcox,* Farley J made reference to section 18.6 of the *CCAA.* Along with comparable provisions in the *BIA,* this provision governed cross-border insolvency proceedings from its introduction in 1997 to 2009, when Canada adopted a version of the UNCITRAL Model Law.

Canadian attempts to legislate with respect to cross border insolvencies pre-date 1997. The 1970 Tassé Report[2] recommended legislation to facilitate the recognition of foreign bankruptcy orders in Canada. Bill C-17, introduced in Parliament in 1984, gave effect to this recommendation and contained four substantial sections (ss 313–17) devoted to this topic. Bill C-17 was never enacted into law.

Work was resumed in the 1990s on a new set of cross-border insolvency provisions. Some Canadian practitioners felt that the 1984 proposals were too liberal. There was particular concern by banking representatives that the proposals would permit foreign representatives to move Canadian assets, or the proceeds from their disposition, out of Canada. There was also a strong bias in favour of concurrent proceedings for the administration of Canadian-situated assets and for close cooperation between Canadian and foreign judges in the administration of the debtor's Canadian and foreign assets. These perspectives were reflected in Part XIII of the *BIA,* adopted in the 1997 amendments, and the substantially identical provisions in section 18.6 of the *CCAA.* Boiled down to their essentials, the 1997 amendments supported cooperation with, and assistance to, foreign insolvency representatives as long as the cooperation did not prejudice the interests of Canadian creditors.

Justice Farley relied on section 18.6 of the *CCAA* in *Babcock & Wilcox* to justify imposing the American stay against the Canadian subsidiary. Subsection 18.6(4) provided:

> Nothing in this section prevents the court, on the application of a foreign representative or any other interested person, from applying such legal or equitable rules governing the recognition of foreign insolvency orders and assistance to foreign representatives as are not inconsistent with the provisions of this Act.

Justice Farley determined that the Canadian subsidiary qualified as an "interested person" and was thus entitled to bring the application for recognition of the American order pursuant to the principles of comity and cooperation.

D. The UNCITRAL Model Law and Its Canadian Enactment

The UNCITRAL Model Law on Cross-Border Insolvencies (Model Law) is intended to facilitate cross-border insolvencies. It respects the differences among national procedural laws and focuses on authorizing and encouraging cooperation and coordination between jurisdictions rather than attempting the unification of substantive insolvency law. It sets out rules that govern:

- access by foreign insolvency representatives and foreign creditors to courts in the enacting jurisdictions;
- recognition by courts in the enacting jurisdictions of foreign insolvency proceedings;
- relief, including staying actions against the debtor in the enacting jurisdiction and the enforcement of foreign insolvency orders by the courts of the enacting jurisdictions; and
- cooperation and coordination between courts.

---

2 Canada, Study Committee on Bankruptcy and Insolvency Legislation, *Report of the Study Committee on Bankruptcy and Insolvency Legislation* (Ottawa: Information Canada, 1970) (Chair: Roger Tassé) [Tassé Report].

Because it is a model law, it was promulgated in one form by UNCITRAL and countries can either adopt it without changes or in an amended form. The UN approved the Model Law in 1997.[3] As of the writing of this textbook, some version of the Model Law has been enacted in forty-six jurisdictions, including Canada, the United States (Chapter 15 of the *Bankruptcy Code*, adopted in 2005), and the United Kingdom. It has not been enacted in a majority of the world's countries, and notably not by Brazil, China, or Russia—all three of whom are significant economic players on the world stage. The European Union has adopted the European Insolvency Regulation, which shares many similarities with the Model Law.

The Model Law establishes a system for the recognition of foreign insolvency proceedings based on a model of modified universalism. When courts receive a request to recognize a foreign insolvency proceeding, they determine whether the proceeding is taking place in the debtor's home jurisdiction. Courts grant a greater degree of deference to insolvency proceedings in the debtor's home jurisdiction, though they retain the discretion to make orders that are inconsistent with the proceedings in the home jurisdiction. Courts grant less deference to proceedings taking place in jurisdictions other than the debtor's home jurisdiction, though they still strive to cooperate and coordinate proceedings. This model is deployed using the following concepts:

- A debtor's home jurisdiction is the jurisdiction where its COMI is located. There is a rebuttable presumption that the debtor's COMI is located where an individual debtor is resident or where a corporate debtor has its registered office (see Model Law, article 16; *BIA*, s 268(2); *CCAA*, s 45(2)). A party wishing to rebut this presumption should elicit evidence showing that the debtor is more closely connected with a different jurisdiction. Key factors a court will look at include: "(a) where the central administration of the debtor takes place, and (b) which is readily ascertainable by creditors" (UNCITRAL Model Law on Cross-Border Insolvency Guide to Enactment and Interpretation (2013) at 71). Canadian courts have added a third factor that should be considered when assessing a debtor's COMI: the location of the debtor's principal assets or operations (*Lightsquared LP (Re)*, 2012 ONSC 2994 at para 25).
- Proceedings in the debtor's home jurisdiction are called foreign main proceedings.
- Proceedings in a jurisdiction other than the debtor's home jurisdiction are called foreign non-main proceedings. Under the Model Law, to qualify as a foreign non-main proceeding it must be demonstrated that the debtor has an "establishment" in the foreign jurisdiction. An establishment is defined as "any place of operations where the debtor carries out a non-transitory economic activity with human means and goods or services," Model Law, article 2. As discussed below, this requirement was not incorporated into the Canadian version of the Model Law.
- Foreign main proceedings and foreign non-main proceedings are collectively referred to as foreign proceedings.

A person involved in the foreign proceeding applies in an enacting jurisdiction to have the foreign proceedings recognized. This person is called a foreign representative (definition Model Law, article 2; *BIA*, s 268(1); *CCAA*, s 45(1)). The person who acts as foreign representative will vary, depending on the domestic insolvency rules in the foreign jurisdiction.

---

3   UNCITRAL, Commission on International Trade Law, UNCITRAL Model Law on Cross-Border Insolvency with Guide to Enactment and Interpretation, General Assembly Resolution 52/158, passed on 15 December 1997, online: www.uncitral.org/uncitral/en/uncitral_texts/insolvency/1997Model.html.

For example, if recognition was being sought for Canadian *CCAA* proceedings in the United States, the monitor may act as the foreign representative (see Ontario Superior Court of Justice, Commercial List (Toronto Region), *Companies' Creditors Arrangement Act Initial Order Form*[4] at para 49). If recognition was being sought for American Chapter 11 proceedings in Canada, the debtor corporation may act as the foreign representative (see *Re Digital Domain Media Group Inc*, 2012 BCSC 1565).

The effect of a court in an enacting jurisdiction granting recognition to the foreign proceedings will depend on whether it decides that the proceedings are foreign main proceedings or foreign non-main proceedings. One key difference relates to the stay. When a foreign main proceeding is recognized, enforcement actions against the debtor in the enacting jurisdiction are automatically stayed. Conversely, when a foreign non-main proceeding is recognized, a court has the option of staying enforcement actions against the debtor, but the stay is not automatic (Model Law, articles 20–21; *BIA*, ss 271–72; *CCAA*, ss 48–49). A court in the enacting jurisdiction is empowered to recognize and enforce additional orders made by the foreign court, regardless of whether it is a foreign main or non-main proceeding (Model Law, article 21; *BIA*, s 272; *CCAA*, s 48).

Another key difference that flows from whether foreign proceedings are characterized as foreign main or foreign non-main proceedings relates to the effect of domestic insolvency proceedings commenced in the enacting jurisdiction after the recognition of the foreign proceeding. Once a foreign main proceeding is recognized, domestic insolvency proceedings should be limited to assets located in the enacting jurisdiction (Model Law, article 28).

While the Model Law admonishes courts to cooperate with one another "to the maximum extent possible," it recognizes that in some situations a court in an enacting jurisdiction may be justified in declining a request for recognition or relief from a foreign representative (Model Law, article 25). A court in an enacting jurisdiction is always entitled to "refuse to take an action" under the Model Law, if doing so would be "manifestly contrary to the public policy of the state" (Model Law, article 6). Additionally, courts in the enacting jurisdiction are instructed to ensure that the interests of the debtor, creditors and other interested persons are "adequately protected" whenever they are granting or denying relief as part of an application for recognition of foreign insolvency proceedings (Model Law, article 22). To ensure that this adequate level of protection is obtained, courts can attach conditions to any orders they grant (Model Law, article 22).

Other provisions in the Model Law deal with:

- *Access*: The Model Law gives foreign representatives and foreign creditors access to the courts in the enacting jurisdiction. For example, if the debtor is already undergoing domestic insolvency proceedings in the enacting jurisdiction, the foreign representative and foreign creditors have rights to participate in the domestic proceedings (Model Law, articles 12 & 13).
- *Cooperation and coordination*: The Model Law facilitates cooperation between courts. For example, the Model Law sanctions direct court-to-court communication (Model Law, article 25).
- *Coordinating multiple foreign or foreign and domestic proceedings*: The Model Law sets out rules to guide courts faced with requests to recognize multiple foreign proceedings or to recognize foreign proceedings when domestic proceedings are underway. It

---

4   Available online: www.ontariocourts.ca/scj/practice/practice-directions/toronto/#Commercial_List_ Forms_including_Model_Orders.

provides rules stipulating which orders should receive precedence (Model Law, articles 29–30).

- *The hotchpot rule* (Model Law, article 32): The hotchpot rule is intended to "to avoid situations in which a creditor might make claims and be paid in multiple insolvency proceedings in different jurisdictions, thereby potentially obtaining more favourable treatment than other creditors."[5]

The hotchpot rule is best illustrated with an example. Imagine that a debtor company is undergoing concurrent insolvency proceedings in Country A and Country B, and both proceedings result in distributions to the creditors. Creditor 1 and Creditor 2 are both general unsecured creditors, and both are owed $100,000. However, Creditor 1 files proofs of claim in both Country A's and Country B's insolvency proceedings, whereas Creditor 2 only files a proof of claim in Country B's insolvency proceedings. Creditor 1 receives a distribution of $20,000 in Country A's insolvency proceedings. If Country B has enacted the hotchpot rule, Creditor 1 will not be entitled to any distribution until Creditor 2 has received at least $20,000. So if Country B had $30,000 to distribute to the general unsecured creditors, it would be divided as follows (for the sake of this illustration, assume Creditor 1 and Creditor 2 are the only two general, unsecured creditors):

	Country A $20,000 to distribute	Country B $30,000 to distribute	Total Received by Each Creditor
Creditor 1 (owed $100,000)	$20,000	$5,000	$25,000
Creditor 2 (owed $100,000)	Does not file proof of claim, does not receive a distribution	$25,000	$25,000

Part XIII of the *BIA* and the *CCAA* were amended in 2009 to largely adopt the UNCITRAL Model Law. The *BIA* and *CCAA* cross-border provisions essentially mirror one another; however, the Canadian legislation differs from the Model Law provisions. These differences are outlined below.

Jacob Ziegel, "Cross-Border Insolvencies" in Stephanie Ben-Ishai and Anthony Duggan, eds, *Canadian Bankruptcy and Insolvency Law: Bill C-55, Statute c. 47 and Beyond* **(Markham: Lexis-Nexis, 2007) 290 at 297–301 (footnotes omitted)**

(a) [*BIA*] Section 268(1) [or *CCAA*, s 45] The definition of FNMP [foreign non-main proceeding] ... differs substantially from the definition in the Model Law. Article 2(c) of the Model Law requires the debtor to have an "establishment" in the place of the foreign proceedings. "Establishment" is defined in art. 2(f) as any place of operations where the debtor carries out a non-transitory economic activity with human means and involving goods or services. [Section] 268(1) does not require the debtor to have an "establishment" in the foreign jurisdiction. Instead, it defines FNMP as "a foreign proceeding *other than* a foreign main proceeding" [emphasis added]. This suggests that a Canadian court will or may be obliged to cooperate with or recognize a foreign proceeding even if the debtor has no place of business in the foreign jurisdiction.

---

5   Above note 3 at 32.

This open-ended provision is at odds with the standard *Morguard* test adopted by Canadian courts in many recent cross-border proceedings that there must be a substantial connection between the debtor and the foreign jurisdiction before the Canadian court will extend its assistance to the foreign order....

(c) [*BIA*] Section 271 [or *CCAA*, s 48] deals with the effect of recognition of an FMP [foreign main proceeding]. Section 271(2) has no counterpart in art. 20 of the Model Law. It excludes subsection (1) [the mandatory stay that occurs when a Canadian court recognizes a foreign main proceeding] entirely if *BIA* proceedings are in progress in Canada at the time of the foreign representative's application. Subsection (3) also has no Model Law counterpart. It makes the recognition of an FMP subject to exceptions that would apply if the foreign proceedings had taken place in Canada under the *BIA*. It is not clear what types of exclusions the Bill C-55 drafters had in mind. Section 271(4) also has no Model Law counterpart and may conflict with art. 28 of the Model Law, which deals with proceedings in the enacting state after recognition of an FMP. Section 271(4) retains the right of parties to commence or continue proceedings under the *BIA*, the *CCAA* or the WURA. Section 271(4) conflicts with the Model Law philosophy that the locus of the debtor's main interests should govern all proceedings against the debtor and that proceedings against the foreign debtor in the enacting state should be confined to proceedings involving locally situated assets. Section 271(4) may need to be amended to reflect the same policy.

(d) [*BIA*] Section 272 [or *CCAA*, s 49] deals with the orders a Canadian court can make on recognition of the foreign proceedings. Section 272 has no counterpart to article 21(2) of the Model Law, [which authorizes] the forum court to [entrust] "distribution" of all or part of local assets to the foreign representative if the court is satisfied that the interests of local creditors are adequately protected. Presumably the Canadian drafters were concerned that the Model Law power might be abused, but this could be said of all discretionary powers under the Model Law or the *BIA*. There appears to be no good reason to exclude article 21(2) of the Model Law....

(h) Section 284(1) [or *CCAA*, s 61(1)] is another troubling provision in Bill C-55 which has no counterpart in the Model Law. [Subsection] 1 provides that nothing in Part XIII prevents the court on the application of a foreign representative or other interested person from applying any legal or equitable rules governing the recognition of foreign insolvency orders and assistance to foreign representatives "that are not inconsistent with the provisions of this Act." [Section] 284(1) is a reincarnation of existing *BIA* s 268(5), which was invoked by Farley J in *Babcock & Wilcox Canada, supra,* to recognize the ch 11 order in Canada without requiring the US debtor to initiate new insolvency proceedings under the *BIA*.

[Reprinted by permission of the publisher.]

In addition to the differences cited by Ziegel, the Canadian legislators made two additional changes to the Model Law that are worthy of note:

1) The Model Law provides that courts in the enacting jurisdiction can refuse to take any action that would be *manifestly* contrary to public policy. The Canadian provisions delete the adverb "manifestly," suggesting that Canadian courts may have greater leeway to refuse to take action on the basis of public policy (*BIA*, s 284(2); *CCAA*, 61(2)).

2) The Canadian hotchpot rule directs that a distribution to a creditor in Canadian insolvency proceedings should ensure that similarly situated creditors receive a *pro rata* distribution,

taking account of (a) property a creditor has received by way of a distribution in foreign insolvency proceedings, and also (b) property the creditor has received as a result of a transaction, if that transaction would be impeachable as a preference or transfer at undervalue in Canada (*BIA*, s 283; *CCAA*, s 60).

IV. DISCHARGE OF DEBTS UNDER FOREIGN INSOLVENCY LAW

Another issue posing difficulties in the past is the discharge of debts under foreign insolvency law. The general Anglo-Canadian conflict of laws rule is that the discharge of a debt is governed by the proper law of the debt, which may be that of Canada or any other country deemed to have a close connection with the debt. However, the rule does not apply to the discharge of debts under the *BIA* because the discharge provisions (ss 168.1–182) have always been understood to apply to *all* debts, whatever the governing law of the debt, unless otherwise provided in the *BIA*. Section 178 enumerates non-dischargeable debts, but these provisions also do not turn on the proper law of the debt.

Nevertheless, in an 1890 decision, the English Court of Appeal decided in *Gibbs & Sons v Société Industrielle et Commerciale*, [1890] 6 WLUK 82 (Eng), that a foreign insolvency law or order discharging or modifying a debt or other contractual obligation, or a claim for damages for breach of such an obligation, will not be recognized unless the discharge or variation is also recognized under the proper law of the debt or obligation. *Gibbs & Sons* involved the liquidation of a French incorporated company. Prior to the French company's liquidation, it contracted to purchase copper from an English business. The contract was made, and was to be performed in England. The French company breached the contract, but French liquidation law barred the English business from claiming for damages for breach of contract. The English business sued the French company in England for damages, and the French company argued that they were barred from bringing the claim by French liquidation rules. The English Court of Appeal held that the French law, even if it was akin to a discharge, would not bar a suit in England because the contract was governed by English law. The *Gibbs* rule was approved by the Privy Council in an 1898 decision, *New Zealand Loan and Mercantile Agency Co v Morrison*, [1898] AC 349. For a powerful criticism of this aspect of the decision, as well as other aspects, see John Honsberger, "Canadian Recognition of Foreign Judicially Supervised Arrangements" (1990) 76 *Canadian Bankruptcy Reports* 204.

The *Gibbs* rule has not been much discussed in Canadian cases, but has been recognized or enforced in the context of personal insolvencies (see, for example, *International Harvester Co v Zarbok*, [1918] 3 WWR 38 (Sask QB); *Re Taylor* (1988), 68 CBR (NS) 93 (PEISC); *Re Bialek* (1994), 18 OR (3d) 462 (Ct J (Gen Div)), extracted below). The rule has been much criticized by commentators as seriously at odds with the principles underlying the recognition of foreign insolvencies, and because the English and Canadian bankruptcy acts themselves provide for discharges from personal insolvencies regardless of the proper law of the debts being discharged. In addition to the criticisms by Honsberger, see Ian F Fletcher, *The Law of Insolvency*, 4th ed (London: Sweet & Maxwell, 2009), which criticizes Lord Esher's judgment as "insular and xenophobic in the extreme" and Philip Smart, *Cross-Border Insolvency* (London: Butterworths, 1991) ch 8. It seems reasonable to conclude, therefore, that the *Gibbs* rule is ripe for reconsideration by the Supreme Court of Canada and will probably not be followed.

Re Bialek (1994), 18 OR (3d) 462 (Ct J (Gen Div))

[The bankrupt was practicing medicine in Canada, but had been trained in the United States and owed over $200,000 in unpaid student loans to various American government lenders. The American student loan creditors opposed his discharge, but also took the position that a Canadian discharge would not be enforceable in the United States.]

LANE J:

Counsel for the US student lenders took the position that those loans would not be discharged by any order of this court. They would no longer be enforceable in this country, but would be in the US. Counsel for the bankrupt argued that I should not hear counsel for the US opponent because the opponent was refusing to submit to the jurisdiction of the court. He relied on the decision of McQuaid J in *Re Taylor* (1988), 68 CBR (NS) 93 (PEISC), where US student lender agencies took the same position as is taken before me. He also relied on *Paul Magder Furs Ltd v Ontario (Attorney General)* (1991), 85 DLR (4th) 694 (CA), where the court refused an audience to an appellant who had repeatedly disobeyed an order of the court and would not undertake to obey it pending his appeal. In *Magder*, the appellant was in contempt already and was refusing to obey in Ontario an order of an Ontario court. These opponents are admitting that the order of discharge from bankruptcy would be effective and would be obeyed by them in this country. They assert that the court's jurisdiction does not extend to discharging a debt incurred under a contract governed by the law of the United States. I do not think that the *Magder* principle applies to the case before me. ...

Counsel for the opponent submits that a discharge under the bankruptcy laws of this country of a contractual debt governed by the law of the US, while fully effective here, cannot, under recognized rules of private international law, prevent enforcement of the debt in the US. If this position is correct according to our concepts of private international law, then there can be no objection to his stating that position before me. It would not be a question of refusing to submit to the jurisdiction of the Ontario court, but rather one of drawing to this court's attention a recognized limit on its jurisdiction.

In the 12th edition of *Dicey and Morris on the Conflict of Laws* (1993), at p. 1181:

> "... a discharge of a contractual debt under the bankruptcy law of the country whose law governs the contract is a valid discharge in England. Conversely, a discharge of a contractual debt under the bankruptcy law of any other foreign country ... is not a valid discharge in England." ...

The contracts under which the debt in question arose were a series of promissory notes in favour of US banks, guaranteed by the US government under the US Health Education Assistance Loan Program authorized by legislation. Each note was accompanied by an application form filled out by Barry Bialek, giving his US citizenship, a US address and stating an intent to enrol in a US educational institution. Each note specifies that it is to be construed according to the US legislation authorizing the program. The proper law of these contracts can only be US law, being that law with which the contracts have their closest and most real connection.

Thus, according to our own notions of private international law, a bankruptcy discharge would not affect the debt arising from these contracts unless it is a discharge of the courts of the US as the proper law of the contracts. The position of the United States' government before me is thus not a refusal to accept the jurisdiction of the court, but merely a statement of the limits of that jurisdiction according to our own law.

For these reasons, and with great respect, I cannot follow *Re Taylor*. My normal reluctance to differ from a judge in a sister province is reduced by the fact that, as is noted by the learned judge, the point was one on which no jurisprudence had been brought to his attention.

Conditional discharge granted.

V. SECURED CREDITOR PROBLEMS

It is a well-established rule in the conflict of laws that the validity, effect, and priority of security interests in personal property is governed by the *lex situs* of the property at the time of creation of the security interest. These rules are now enshrined in sections 5 to 8 of the Ontario *Personal Property Security Act* (PPSA) and the similar provisions in the PPSAs of the other provinces. The same rules apply even more strongly to security interests in real property. The rule applies equally in Canadian bankruptcies because BIA, section 71(1), provides that title to the debtor's property vests in the trustee, subject to the right of secured creditors; and because BIA, section 72(1), preserves the substantive provisions of any other law or statute relating to property and civil rights that is not in conflict with the BIA. Prior to the Supreme Court's decision in *Holt Cargo Systems Inc v ABC Containerline NV (Trustees of)*, 2001 SCC 90, extracted below, it was generally assumed that a Canadian court would not allow a trustee to remove Canadian-situated assets out of Canada without the secured party's consent or without the court being satisfied that the security interest would be recognized and given the same priority in the foreign jurisdiction as it enjoyed under Canadian law. However, it was unclear whether Canadian courts would show the same solicitude for security interests against property situated *outside* Canada in favour of foreign secured parties where the property was subsequently brought into Canada. In *Holt Cargo*, in an unusual factual setting, the Supreme Court answered "yes" to the question and Binnie J's comprehensive judgment for the Court reaffirmed Canada's support for a modified form of universalism.

Holt Cargo Systems Inc v ABC Containerline NV (Trustees of), 2001 SCC 90, [2001] 3 SCR 907 [*Holt Cargo*]

[In *Holt Cargo*, a Belgian shipping company started insolvency proceedings in Belgium. One of its ships had previously been detained in Canada as a result of maritime law proceedings started by an American company, Holt Cargo Systems, which were litigated in Canada's Federal Court. Holt had a lien on the ship for services provided to the ship in the United States, and thus Holt was treated as a secured creditor under Canadian insolvency law. The Belgian insolvency trustee requested that the Federal Court proceedings be stayed so that the Belgian trustee could take possession of the ship or of the proceeds from its sale. The Federal Court refused the trustee's request. The Supreme Court of Canada held that the Federal Court was entitled to do so, noting that under Canadian insolvency law, a trustee takes a debtor's property subject to the rights of any secured creditors.]

[53] ... The fact remains, however, that Canadian public policy, expressed through the Act, strongly supports the rights of claimants whom we would regard as secured creditors. Our law considers it in the interests of commercial activity generally that

secured rights be protected. It seems to me that MacKay J correctly regarded Holt as a "secured creditor" in bankruptcy terms, and in the exercise of his discretion under [the stay provision of] the *Federal Court Act,* he was entirely justified in putting considerable weight on that factor.

[The Supreme Court of Canada rejected the Belgian trustee's argument that the Federal Court ought to have deferred to the Belgian bankruptcy court on the basis of comity. It noted that the Federal Court retained discretion not to enforce the foreign court order depending on the facts of a particular case.]

[86] Where a stay is sought of Canadian proceedings in deference to a foreign bankruptcy court, the Canadian court before which the stay application is made (in this case the Federal Court) ought to be mindful of the difficulties confronting the bankruptcy trustees in the fulfilment of their public mandate to bring order out of financial disorder and the desirability of maximizing the size of the bankrupt estate. These objectives are furthered by minimizing the multiplicity of proceedings, and the attendant costs, and the possibility of inconsistent decisions in relation to the same claims or assets.

[87] Nevertheless, courts must have regard to the need to do justice to the particular litigants who come before them as well as to the public interest in the efficient administration of bankrupt estates. It would be inappropriate to elevate any one consideration to a controlling position in the exercise of a bankruptcy court's discretion to dismiss a petition under s 43(7) or to stay proceedings under Part XIII of the Act or in the Federal Court's decision to stay proceedings under s 50 of the *Federal Court Act.* Discretion should not be thus predetermined. The desirability of international coordination is an important consideration. In some cases, it may be the controlling consideration. The courts nevertheless have to exercise their discretion to stay or not to stay domestic proceedings according to all of the relevant facts of a particular case.

Appeal dismissed.

VI. TREATMENT OF CORPORATE GROUPS

Businesses operating in multiple jurisdictions may carry out all their activities through one corporation, however, it is very common for such businesses to carry out their activities through multiple related corporations (and other legal entities, such as partnerships). These multiple-entity concerns are called "corporate groups" or "enterprise groups." In Canadian law, the doctrine of separate corporate personality dictates that each corporation should be treated as a distinct person, unless there is a compelling reason to disregard the corporate form. For example, usually the debts of one corporation cannot be satisfied using the assets of an affiliated corporation and court orders made against one corporation do not bind an affiliated corporation.

When corporate groups undergo insolvency proceedings, interested parties may ask courts to disregard the separateness of the corporations for reasons of efficiency or fairness. In *Singer Sewing Machine Co,* discussed above, the American parent company commenced insolvency proceedings under Chapter 11 and sought to restructure a Canadian affiliate as part of those proceedings. While the American bankruptcy judge was prepared to take jurisdiction over the Canadian affiliate, Registrar Funduk of the Alberta Court of Queen's Bench, refused to recognize the Chapter 11 proceedings as far as they purported to apply to the

Canadian affiliate. He provided two reasons for refusing to do so: first, the Canadian company was not insolvent, and second, the US bankruptcy court lacked jurisdiction over the Alberta incorporated company. In his reasons, he provided a succinct summary of the doctrine of separate corporate personality:

> [11] Canadian law says that a corporation is a person in law. Canadian law says that a corporation has an existence separate from its shareholders. Canadian law says that a shareholder is not liable for the corporation's debts. Canadian law says that a shareholder does not own the corporation's assets. Canadian law says that a corporation's business activities are not the shareholder's business activities.

Registrar Funduk's decision stands in contrast to Farley J's Ontario Superior Court decision in *Babcock & Wilcox*, discussed above, where the latter extended recognition in Canada to a stay of proceedings order issued by Brown J in Louisiana against asbestos tort claimants seeking to sue Babcock & Wilcox's Canadian subsidiary in Canada. Justice Farley granted Brown J's request for assistance even though Babcock & Wilcox Canada was not a party to the US proceedings and was not itself insolvent. The two decisions are difficult to reconcile and clearly took a different view of what comity involves in the corporate group area.

Several judgments have recognized corporate groups under the *BIA* and *CCAA* cross-border provisions and allowed for various degrees of procedural consolidation, meaning that the separate entities in the corporate group undergo insolvency proceedings together. For example, the Caesars Entertainment enterprise group, which comprised 173 entities, was able to restructure using American proceedings because the Ontario Superior Court was willing to recognize and enforce orders from the American proceedings as against a lone Canadian subsidiary (*Caesers Entertainment Operating Company Inc (Re)*, 2015 ONSC 712). However, recognition for the purposes of procedural consolidation is not a rubber stamp; a court makes an independent assessment of the merits of an application for recognition. While the cross-border provisions are aimed at fostering cooperation between jurisdictions, this objective cannot set aside the discretion vested in a court under the cross-border insolvency provisions, such as *BIA*, section 272, which specifies that a court can make "appropriate orders" in recognition proceedings, if necessary to protect the debtor's property or the interests of creditors, and *BIA*, section 284(2), which specifies that nothing in Part XIII requires a court to make an order that is contrary to public policy.

When enterprise groups adopt some form of procedural consolidation while undergoing cross-border insolvency proceedings, an important question can be whether the COMI of one of the component entities should be determined having regard for where the enterprise group (or the parent company in the enterprise group) is administered from, or if a separate determination should be made for each entity having regard to its specific organization. Jeremy Opolsky, in his article "COMI's Fifth Year in Canada: Centre of Main Interest and the Inescapable Corporate Group" in Janis P Sarra, ed, *Annual Review of Insolvency Law 2013* (Toronto: Thomson Carswell, 2014) at 233, describes the Canadian approach (at 267):

> It is blackletter law that a debtor's COMI is to be determined without regard to its affiliation with a corporate group. However, it is difficult to overlook the fact that in the Canadian COMI cases to date, all the debtors were members of integrated corporate enterprise groups. Each case noted the level of integration between the Canadian-registered debtor and the corporate group, and the relevant facts undergirding the COMI finding all tied directly to the debtor's position within the group. Thus, it is likely that the level of integration of the group was an important factor ... in determining the COMI.

A more controversial issue relates to imposing substantive consolidation on an insolvent corporate group. Roderick Wood defines substantive consolidation as "a pooling of assets and a pooling of claims. Instead of recognizing the separate assets and separate liabilities of each business entity the assets and the claims are treated as if they were all held by or against a single entity" in *Bankruptcy and Insolvency Law*, 2d ed (Toronto: Irwin Law, 2015) at 358. For example, imagine that a corporate group comprises two entities, each with different levels of indebtedness and different asset holdings.

Corporate Group Entities	Total Value of Assets	Total Value of Liabilities	Distribution to Creditor Owed $1,000
Entity A	$8,000	$100,000	$80
Entity B	$50,000	$100,000	$500
Consolidated Totals	$58,000	$200,000	$290

For the sake of this table, assume that all of the entities' creditors are general, unsecured creditors. If the assets are distributed while respecting the separate corporate personalities of Entity A and Entity B, Entity A's creditors will receive 8 cents/dollar, whereas Entity B's creditors will receive 50 cents/dollar. If the assets of Entity A and Entity B are consolidated, all of the creditors will receive 29 cents/dollar. Entity A's creditors will benefit significantly from substantive consolidation, whereas Entity B's creditors have a strong incentive to resist it.

The question of substantive consolidation was litigated in the insolvency proceedings of the Nortel Networks enterprise group.

Nortel Networks Corporation (Re), 2015 ONSC 2987, 27 CBR (6th) 175, leave to appeal to CA refused 2016 ONCA 332, appeal to SCC discontinued 8 May 2017 (footnotes omitted)

[Nortel Networks Corporation was a Canadian telecommunications company that operated a global business through over 140 affiliated entities operating in over sixty countries. It commenced insolvency proceedings in Canada under the *CCAA* and affiliated entities commenced proceedings in the United States under Chapter 11 of the *Bankruptcy Code* and in the United Kingdom under the *UK Insolvency Act, 1986*. The interested parties agreed to sell off Nortel's assets and then litigate over how to allocate the sales proceeds among the Canadian, American, and English proceedings.

Given the multiple, concurrent insolvency proceedings, an initial difficulty facing the interested parties was which court should decide how to allocate the sales proceeds. The allocation decision was made jointly by the Canadian and American bankruptcy courts, as described by Newbould J in his judgment:]

[8] A joint hearing was held for this allocation dispute. The courtrooms in Toronto and Wilmington were set up electronically so that lawyers and witnesses could and did appear in either courtroom and communicate with a lawyer, witness or the judge in the other courtroom through state of the art telecommunications services.

[9] After the evidence was heard, written closing and reply briefs were filed by the parties and oral argument was made. It was agreed that at the conclusion of the case that each Court would release its decision at the same time. This judgment is being released at the same time as the opinion of Judge Gross in Wilmington.

[10] Judge Gross in Wilmington and I have communicated with each other in accordance with the Protocol with a view to determining whether consistent rulings can be

made by both Courts. We have come to the conclusion that a consistent ruling can and should be made by both Courts. We have come to this conclusion in the exercise of our independent and exclusive jurisdiction in each of our jurisdictions. These insolvency proceedings have now lasted over six years at unimaginable expense and they should if at all possible come to a final resolution. It is in all of the parties' interests for that to occur. Consistent decisions that we both agree with will facilitate such a resolution.

[A second, trickier question was how the sales proceeds should be allocated. The sales proceeds were being held in escrow pending resolution of this question, and Newbould J refers to the sales proceeds as "the lockbox funds." The sales proceeds were primarily derived from the sale of the enterprise group's intellectual property (patents), and this intellectual property had been developed with contributions from many different entities in the corporate group. Justice Newbould described the organization of Nortel as a "matrix structure": see the excerpt below.

The Canadian parties argued that the sales proceeds should be primarily allocated to the Canadian proceedings because the patents were held by a Canadian entity. The American parties argued that the sales proceeds should be allocated according to where the patents had generated revenue, which would result in significant value being allocated to the American proceedings. The parties involved in the English proceedings, who were drawn from Europe, the Middle East, and Africa (EMEA), took the position that the proceeds should be allocated having regard for each entity's contribution to the corporate group's research and development activities. Note that Newbould J refers to the Nortel entities involved in research and development as the RPEs, short for Residual Profit Entities.

The courts rejected all three proposals, and decided instead to allocate the sales proceeds *pro rata* among the three proceedings, depending on the value of claims filed in each proceeding. Justice Newbould offered the following explanation for reaching this allocation decision]:

[202] This is an unprecedented case involving insolvencies of many corporations and bankrupt estates in different jurisdictions. The intangible assets that were sold, being by far the largest type of asset sold, were not separately located in any one jurisdiction or owned separately in different jurisdictions. They were created by all of the RPEs located in different jurisdictions. Nortel was organized along global product lines and global R&D projects pursuant to a horizontally integrated matrix structure and no one entity or region was able to provide the full line of Nortel products and services. R&D took place in various labs around the world in a collaborative fashion. R&D was organized around a particular project, not particular geographical locations or legal entities, and was managed on a global basis. The fact that Nortel ensured that legal entities were properly created and advised in the various countries in which it operated in order to meet local legal requirements does not mean that Nortel operated a separate business in each country. It did not.

[203] Nortel's matrix structure also allowed Nortel to draw on employees from different functional disciplines worldwide (*e.g.* sales, R&D, operations, finance, general and administrative, etc), regardless of region or country according to need. Individuals could be part of a team with horizontal responsibility without removing them from their respective position vertically (or departmentally) within the Nortel group.

[204] In these circumstances, what principles should be applied to determine the allocation of the proceeds of the asset sales? In my view, doing what is just in the unique circumstances of this case should govern the allocation.

[205] A court has wide powers in a proceeding to do what is just in the circumstances. Section 11(1) provides that a court may make any order it considers appropriate in the circumstances. Although this section was provided by an amendment that came into force after Nortel filed under the *CCAA*, and therefore by the amendment the new section does not apply to Nortel, it has been held that the provision merely reflects past jurisdiction. In *Century Services*, Deschamps J stated:

> 65 I agree with Justice Georgina R Jackson and Professor Janis Sarra that the most appropriate approach is a hierarchical one in which courts rely first on an interpretation of the provisions of the *CCAA* text before turning to inherent or equitable jurisdiction to anchor measures taken in a *CCAA* proceeding (see G R Jackson and J Sarra, "Selecting the Judicial Tool to get the Job Done: An Examination of Statutory Interpretation, Discretionary Power and Inherent Jurisdiction in Insolvency Matters", in J P Sarra, ed, *Annual Review of Insolvency Law 2007* (2008), 41, at p 42). The authors conclude that when given an appropriately purposive and liberal interpretation, the *CCAA* will be sufficient in most instances to ground measures necessary to achieve its objectives (p 94).
>
> 67 The initial grant of authority under the *CCAA* empowered a court "where an application is made under this Act in respect of a company ... on the application of any person interested in the matter ..., subject to this Act, [to] make an order under this section" (*CCAA* s. 11(1)). The plain language of the statute was very broad.
>
> 68 In this regard, though not strictly applicable to the case at bar, I note that Parliament has in recent amendments changed the wording contained in s 11(1), making explicit the discretionary authority of the court under the *CCAA*. Thus in s 11 of the *CCAA* as currently enacted, a court may, "subject to the restrictions set out in this Act, ... make any order that it considers appropriate in the circumstances" (SC 2005, c 47, s 128). <u>Parliament appears to have endorsed the broad reading of CCAA authority developed by the jurisprudence.</u> (underlining added)

[206] This Court has a broad inherent jurisdiction to make orders as required to fill in gaps or lacunae not covered by specific provisions in the *CCAA*. As a superior court of general jurisdiction, the Superior Court of Justice has all of the powers that are necessary to do justice between the parties. Except where provided specifically to the contrary, the Court's jurisdiction is unlimited and unrestricted in substantive law in civil matters. [Citations omitted]

[207] In *Century Services Inc v Canada (Attorney General)*, 2010 SCC 60 at paras 57-61, it was recognized by the Supreme Court and stated by Justice Deschamps that the *CCAA* is skeletal in nature and does not contain a comprehensive code that lays out all that is permitted, that the incremental exercise of judicial discretion with respect to the *CCAA* has been adapted and has evolved to meet contemporary business and social needs and that when large companies encounter difficulty and reorganizations become increasingly complex, *CCAA* courts have been called upon to innovate accordingly.

[208] In this case, insolvency practitioners, academics, international bodies, and others have watched as Nortel's early success in maximizing the value of its global assets through cooperation has disintegrated into value-erosive adversarial and territorial litigation described by many as scorched earth litigation. The costs have well exceeded $1 billion. A global solution in this unprecedented situation is required and perforce, as this situation has not been faced before, it will by its nature involve innovation. Our courts have such jurisdiction.

[209] It is a fundamental tenet of insolvency law that all debts shall be paid *pari passu* and all unsecured creditors receive equal treatment. [Citations omitted] A pro rata allocation in this case goes partway towards such a result.

[210] According to the various protocols, the task in this proceeding is to determine the amount that is to be allocated to each of the Canadian, US and EMEA Debtors' Estates. I do not read the protocols or the IFSA as precluding a pro rata allocation. While payment to the Selling Debtors is to be made from the $7.3 billion in the lockbox funds, neither the protocols nor the IFSA determine how the allocation is to be made.

[211] Directing a pro rata allocation will constitute an allocation as required. Once the lockbox funds have been allocated, it will be up to each Nortel Estate acting under the supervision of its presiding court to administer claims in accordance with its applicable law. A pro rata allocation can be achieved by directing an allocation of the lockbox funds to each Debtor Estate based on the percentage that the claims against that Estate bear to the total claims against all of the Debtor Estates.

[212] It is argued that a pro rata allocation would constitute an impermissible substantive consolidation of the Estates, or as put by the US Debtors, an impermissible "global substantive consolidation". I do not agree. A pro rata allocation in this case would not constitute a substantive consolidation and, even if it did, it would in my view be permissible within established case law.

[213] In a liquidation or reorganization of a corporate group, the doctrine of substantive consolidation has emerged in order to provide a mechanism whereby the court may treat the separate legal entities belonging to the corporate group as one. In particular, substantive consolidation allows for the combination of the assets and liabilities of two or more members of the group, extinguishes inter-company debt and creates a single fund from which all claims against the consolidated debtors are satisfied. In effect, under substantive consolidation, claims of creditors against separate debtors instantly become claims against a single entity.

[214] A pro rata allocation in this case would not constitute a substantive consolidation, either actual or deemed, for a number of reasons. First, and most importantly, the lockbox funds are largely due to the sale of IP and no one Debtor Estate has any right to these funds. It cannot be said that these funds in whole or in part belonged to any one Estate or that they constituted separate assets of two or more Estates that would be combined. Put another way, there would be no "wealth transfer" as advocated by the bondholders. The IFSA, made on behalf of 38 Nortel debtor entities in Canada, the US and EMEA, recognized that the funds would be put into a single fund undifferentiated as to the Debtor Estates and then allocated to them on some basis to be agreed or determined in this litigation. Second, the various entities in the various Estates are not being treated as one entity and the creditors of each entity will not become creditors of a single entity. Each entity remains separate and with its own creditors and its own cash on hand and will be administered separately. The inter-company claims are not eliminated.

[215] Even if it could be said that a pro rata allocation involved substantive consolidation, which it cannot, I do not see case law precluding it in the unique circumstances of this case international case [*sic*]. Even in domestic cases, *CCAA* plans involving substantive consolidation are not unknown.

[216] In Canada, neither the *CCAA* nor the *BIA* contains express provisions authorizing substantive consolidation. Similarly, the US Bankruptcy Code does not explicitly permit substantive consolidation. However, courts in both jurisdictions have rendered consolidating orders on the basis of their equitable jurisdiction. See M MacNaughton

and M Azoumanidis, *Substantive Consolidation in the Insolvency of Corporate Groups: A Comparative Analysis, Annual Review of Insolvency Law, 2007,* J Sarra, ed (Carswell: 2008).

[217] In *Rescue! The Companies' Creditors Arrangement Act* by Dr Janis Sarra, Carswell 2007, the grounds for permitting substantive consolidation were described as follows at page 242:

> The court will allow a consolidated plan of arrangement or compromise to be filed for two or more related companies in appropriate circumstances. For example, in *PSINet Ltd* the Court allowed consolidation of proceedings for four companies that were intertwined and essentially operated as one business. The Court found the filing of a consolidated plan avoided complex issues regarding the allocation of the proceeds realized from the sale of the assets, and that although consolidation by its nature would benefit some creditors and prejudice others, the prejudice had been ameliorated by concessions made by the parent corporation, which was also the major creditor. Other cases of consolidated proceedings such as Philip Services Canadian Airlines, Air Canada and Stelco, all proceeded without issues in respect of consolidation.
>
> Generally, the courts will determine whether to consolidate proceedings by assessing whether the benefits will outweigh the prejudice to particular creditors if the proceedings are consolidated. In particular, the court will examine whether the assets and liabilities are so intertwined that it is difficult to separate them for purposes of dealing with different entities. The court will also consider whether consolidation is fair and reasonable in the circumstances of the case.

[218] In *Re Lehndorff General Partner Ltd* (1993), 17 CBR 3d 24, Justice Farley held that a consolidated plan was appropriate, noting that there was significant intertwining of the debtor companies, including multiple instances of inter-company debt, cross-default provisions and guarantees and the existence and operation of a centralized cash-management system. All of these features were present in Nortel.

[219] In *Re PSINet Ltd* (2002), 33 CBR (4th) 284, Justice Farley noted that a plan of arrangement based on substantive consolidation avoided the "complex and likely litigious issues" that could result from the allocation of the proceeds of the sale of substantially all of the debtor companies' assets. He also noted that the consolidated plan reflected the intertwined nature of the debtors and their operation. In that case, Farley J stated that the overall effect of a consolidation was required:

> In the circumstances of this case, the filing of a consolidated plan is appropriate given the intertwining elements discussed above. See *Northland Properties Ltd, Re,* 69 CBR (NS) 266 (BCSC), affirmed (BCCA), *supra,* at p 202; *Lehndorff General Partner Ltd, Re,* 17 CBR (3d) 24 (Ont Gen Div [Commercial List]) at p 31. While consolidation by its very nature will benefit some creditors and prejudice others, it is appropriate to look at the overall general effect.

[220] In *Northland Properties*, a case involving a proposed plan for several companies that operated as a single entity, Justice Trainor considered the tests for permitting a substantive consolidation. He looked to US law for guidance and began his analysis by adopting the balancing test articulated in *Re Baker and Getty Fin Services In.*, US Bankruptcy Court, ND Ohio (1987) 78 BR 139:

> The propriety of ordering substantive consolidation is determined by a balancing of interests. The relevant enquiry asks whether "the creditors will suffer greater prejudice in the absence of consolidation than the debtors (and any objecting creditors) will suffer from its imposition".

[221] Trainor J then went on to list seven factors which had been developed to assist in the balancing of interests. Those factors were:

1. difficulty in segregating assets;
2. presence of consolidated financial statements;
3. profitability of consolidation at a single location;
4. commingling of assets and business functions;
5. unity of interests in ownership;
6. existence of intercorporate loan guarantees; and
7. transfer of assets without observance of corporate formalities.

[222] In considering these factors, it is clear beyond peradventure that Nortel has had significant difficulty in determining the ownership of its principle assets, namely the $7.3 billion representing the proceeds of the sales of the lines of business and the residual patent portfolio. This amount constitutes over 80% of the total assets of all of the Nortel entities. This issue has taken several years of litigation and untoward costs in the parties attempting to establish an entitlement to it. As the MRDA does not govern how the sales proceeds are to be allocated, there is no one right way to separate them. It cannot be said that there is no question which entity is entitled to the sale proceeds or in what amount. It is clear that these assets are in the language of Dr Janis Serra "so intertwined that it is difficult to separate them for purposes of dealing with different entities".

[223] Moreover, the evidence in this case is clear and uncontested that Nortel (a) had fully integrated and interdependent operations; (b) had intercompany guarantees for its primary indebtedness; (c) operated a consolidated treasury system in which generated cash was used throughout the Nortel Group as required; (d) disseminated consolidated financial information throughout its entire history, save for the year before its bankruptcy; and (e) created IP through integrated R&D activates that were global in scope.

[224] When consolidation occurs, some creditors may be prejudiced if they would have had a greater recovery of so many cents on the dollar against their debtor if there had been no consolidation. Conversely, other creditors may be benefitted by consolidation if they would have had a lesser recovery against their debtor if there had been no consolidation. In this case, even if a pro rata allocation amounted to a consolidation, the issue would be moot because it cannot be said that without consolidation one class of creditors, including the bondholders, would necessarily have had a greater recovery than with consolidation. The reason for this is that there has been no recognized measurable right in any one of the selling Debtor Estates to all or a fixed portion of the proceeds of sale.

Order accordingly.

VII. IMPEACHING TRANSACTIONS

An unresolved issue in Canadian proceedings is whether Canadian laws dealing with preferences, transfers at undervalue and fraudulent conveyances can be used to impeach transactions that took place in a foreign country. Conversely, can Canadian transactions be impeached using foreign impeachment legislation?

In the leading US decision of *In re Maxwell Communication Corporation plc*, 93 F (3d) 1036 (2d Cir 1996), the American bankruptcy court addressed this question in a British-US context. The debtor sought to recover payments it had made to three banks (Barclays Bank plc, National Westminster Bank plc and Société Générale) prior to starting parallel insolvency proceedings in the United States and England. It sought to impeach the transactions in the American Chapter 11 proceedings using provisions from the US *Bankruptcy Code*. The American bankruptcy court dismissed the debtor's application to impeach the transactions, ruling that there was a stronger connection between the transactions and England, and therefore English law should be applied. The debtor appealed to the United State Court of Appeals for the Second Circuit.

In re Maxwell Communication Corporation plc, 93 F (3d) 1036 (2d Cir 1996)

CARDAMONE Circuit Judge:

B. Primacy of English Law

England has a much closer connection to these disputes than does the United States. The debtor and most of its creditors — not only the beneficiaries of the pre-petition transfers — are British. Maxwell was incorporated under the laws of England, largely controlled by British nationals, governed by a British board of directors, and managed in London by British executives. These connecting factors indicated what the bankruptcy judge called the "Englishness" of the debtor. . . . These same factors, particularly the fact that most of Maxwell's debt was incurred in England, show that England has the strongest connection to the present litigation.

Although an avoidance action concededly affects creditors other than the transferee, because scrutiny of the transfer is at the heart of such a suit it is assuredly most relevant that the transfers in this case related primarily to England. The $30 million received by Barclays came from an account at National Westminster in London and, while it was routed through Barclays' New York branch like all payments received in US dollars, it was immediately credited to an overdraft account maintained in England. Plaintiffs claim no particular United States connection to the other alleged transfers to Barclays, all of which were denominated in the amended complaint in pounds sterling. Similarly, the transfers to National Westminster and Société Générale were made to and from accounts maintained in Great Britain.

Further, the overdraft facilities and other credit transactions between the transferee banks and the debtor resulted from negotiations that took place in England and were administered primarily there. English law applied to the resolution of disputes arising under such agreements. We recognize that some of the money transferred to the banks came from the proceeds of the sale of Maxwell subsidiaries in the United States, which is a subject we discuss in a moment. In almost all other respects, however, the credit transactions were centered in London and the fund transfers occurred there.

C. Relative Interests of Forum and Foreign States

Given the considerably lesser American connection to the dispute, the bankruptcy court believed its forum's interests were "not very compelling." *Maxwell I*, 170 BR at 818. Virtually the only factor linking the transfers to the United States — that the sale of certain Maxwell subsidiaries in the United States provided the source of some of the funds — is not particularly weighty because those companies were sold as going concerns. Hence, the potential effect that such sales might have had on local economies is not here implicated.

The examiner warns that dire consequences would result from a failure to enforce the Code's avoidance provision. The first one he mentions is that such a course ignores §103(a) of the Code. This contention is one we have already addressed and rejected. The examiner next urges that the purposes underlying §547 and §502(d) would be thwarted unless both of these provisions were applied in all Chapter 11 proceedings. Although the non-application of these or other *Bankruptcy Code* provisions certainly might detract from the Code's policies in other cases, here the negative effects are insubstantial. The principal policies underlying the Code's avoidance provisions are equal distribution to creditors and preserving the value of the estate through the discouragement of aggressive pre-petition tactics causing dismemberment of the debtor. *Wolas,* 502 US at 161, 112 S Ct at 533. These policies are effectuated, although in a somewhat different way, by the provisions' British counterpart. *See Maxwell I,* 170 BR at 818.

In the present case, in which there is a parallel insolvency proceeding taking place in another country, failure to apply §547 and §502(d) does not free creditors from the constraints of avoidance law, nor does it severely undercut the policy of equal distribution. All avoidance laws are necessarily limited in scope because time limits and other conditions are imposed on the voidability of transactions. Although a different result might be warranted were there no parallel proceeding in England—and, hence, no alternative mechanism for voiding preferences—we cannot say the United States has a significant interest in applying its avoidance law. Moreover, as noted, international comity is a policy that Congress expressly made part of the *Bankruptcy Code,* and a decision consistent with comity therefore furthers the Code's policy.

Because of the strong British connection to the present dispute, it follows that England has a stronger interest than the United States in applying its own avoidance law to these actions. Its law implicates that country's interest in promoting what Parliament apparently viewed as the appropriate compromise between equality of distribution and other important commercial interests, for instance, ensuring potentially insolvent debtors' ability to secure essential ongoing financing. In addition, although complexity in the conduct of transnational insolvencies makes choice-of-law prognostication imprecise, we agree with the lower courts that English law could have been expected to apply.

Appeal dismissed.

The American scholar Jay Westbrook was retained as *amicus curiae* by the district court. He favoured adoption of the "home jurisdiction" rule specifically in the case of a corporate debtor (the law of incorporation of the debtor corporation) on the grounds of its simplicity and predictability of outcome, and the advantage it confers in enabling contracting parties to plan their affairs with greater certainty (see Ian F Fletcher, *Private International Law* (Oxford: Clarendon Press, 1999) at 77, n 169). As the above judgment shows, the US circuit court rejected this approach and, probably, rightly so. The place of incorporation may be quite arbitrary and, if used as a touchstone, would enable the parties to incorporate in an offshore haven, or to reincorporate there, in order to take advantage of lax avoidance rules.

Parties engaged in seemingly normal and legitimate pre-bankruptcy transactions may not consider what the law of the debtor's incorporation says about the transaction. Consider the following example: X, a Canadian bank located in Toronto, makes a loan to Y, a US company incorporated under Delaware law. Y is delinquent in repaying the loan and X threatens to sue if Y does not make prompt payment. Y makes the payment. It is unlikely that the parties will consult Delaware law, or even the US *Bankruptcy Code,* to determine whether the repayment can be impeached as a preference.

An effectiveness or interest test, such as the test adopted in *Maxwell,* strikes a better balance between a home jurisdiction test (as favoured by Westbrook) and a territorial test, turning on the law of the jurisdiction in which the bankruptcy proceedings are initiated.

The question of avoiding actions arose in the case of Pope and Talbot, where an American parent company and Canadian operating company filed parallel insolvency proceedings in the United States and Canada. An initial attempt in 2007 to restructure the companies failed, resulting in concurrent liquidation proceedings in 2008: Chapter 7 in the United States and bankruptcy in Canada. The trustee in the Chapter 7 proceedings sought to impeach trans-actions made by the debtor in the ninety days prior to when it commenced American insol-vency proceedings—it brought its application in the American bankruptcy court pursuant to the impeachment provisions of the US *Bankruptcy Code*. Many Canadian creditors took the position that the impeachment of any transactions should be governed by Canadian insolvency law. The American and Canadian bankruptcy judges convened a joint hearing via video link to decide on the procedure for determining which substantive law would apply to the transactions. They delivered a joint ruling (Kieran E Siddall, "The Cross-Border Pursuit of Preference Claims in Pope & Talbot" in Janis P Sarra, ed, *Annual Review of Insolvency Law 2010* (Toronto: Thomson Carswell, 2011) 327 at 335):

> [W]hereby the courts directed that the BC court would hear and make an initial ruling on the proper or substantive law applicable to the transactions. In oral reasons for judg-ment, [the American] Judge Sontchi commented that the vast bulk of the parties were located in British Columbia and that it would be easier and more efficient for the Chap-ter 7 trustee to have to fly to British Columbia or have British Columbia counsel partici-pate in that decision in front of [the Canadian] Mr Justice Walker than it would be for 250 Canadian entities, in Judge Sontchi's estimate, to travel to Delaware to be heard. The courts further resolved that the BC court's ruling would be sent to the Delaware court for its consideration on a *de novo* basis.

The avoidance actions were settled before the Canadian or American courts ruled on which substantive rule would apply. Siddall, *ibid*, suggests that if the British Columbia Court had been required to resolve the question of whether the transactions were impeachable under Canadian law, it should have proceeded as follows (at 350–52):

1. Does the Canadian impeachment provision apply extraterritorially.
   a. If yes, proceed to question 3
   b. If no, proceed to question 2
2. Did the transaction take place in Canada?
   a. If yes, proceed to question 3
   b. If no, do not apply the Canadian impeachment provision.
3. Would it offend comity to apply the Canadian impeachment provision to this trans-action?
   a. If yes, do not apply the Canadian impeachment provision.
   b. If no, apply the Canadian impeachment provision.

Practice Questions

The Wheel Baron (US) Ltd (WBU) is an American car parts company, incorporated in Dela-ware. The Wheel Baron (Canada) Ltd (WBC) is a wholly owned subsidiary, incorporated in Ontario with a registered office in Toronto. The companies operate retail outlets where discerning automobile enthusiasts can purchase fancy wheels for their cars. WBU carries out all the enterprise group's American operations and WBC carries out all the enterprise group's Canadian operations. Both companies mistakenly sold a brand of wheels that had been recalled by the manufacturer. As a result of the companies' failure to comply with the recall, a number of car enthusiasts suffered serious injuries and started lawsuits in Canada and the United States against WBU and WBC.

WBU and WBC file Chapter 11 petitions in the United States court and are consequently protected by an automatic stay under the *Bankruptcy Code*.

Question 1

After WBU and WBC file their Chapter 11 petitions, but before any further steps are taken, you are approached by Valerie Bourgeron, a Canadian car enthusiast. She was seriously injured after purchasing wheels from WBC. She wishes to file a statement of claim against WBC in Ontario Superior Court. What advice do you give her?

Question 2

WBC applies, as a foreign representative, to have WBC's Chapter 11 proceedings recognized in Canada as foreign main proceedings.

a) How will Valerie's claim against WBC be affected if the court grants WBC's application?
b) Valerie instructs you to appear at WBC's application and take the position that WBC's Chapter 11 proceedings should be recognized as foreign non-main proceedings. What arguments will you advance to support your claim?

Question 3

The Canadian court grants the application to recognize the Chapter 11 proceedings as foreign main proceedings. Valerie wishes to start involuntary bankruptcy proceedings under Canada's *BIA* against WBU and WBC. She has evidence that both companies have failed to meet their liabilities as they fall due. The Canadian court has previously determined that WBC's shares (which are owned by WBU) are located in Canada. What advice do you give her?

Question 4

In the process of doing research for Valerie's case, you learn of a small island nation, whose bankruptcy laws are very favourable to creditors with personal injury claims, like Valerie. The distribution rules give personal injury claimants priority over voluntary secured creditors. Even though WBC has no connection to this island, the island's courts have been willing to take jurisdiction over the insolvency proceedings of foreign companies. If she starts insolvency proceedings against WBC on this island (assume she can), Valerie wants to know if the Canadian court is likely to recognize the proceedings and enforce any distribution orders granted by the island's courts as against WBC's Canadian assets. What advice do you give her?

Table of Cases

This table of cases contains only those cases discussed or mentioned in the authors' commentary, or those cases from which excerpts have been included. Excerpts are marked in bold.